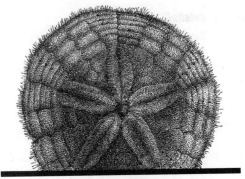

JAVA™
ENTERPRISE
IN A NUTSHELL

A Desktop Quick Reference

Second Edition

*Jim Farley, William Crawford &
David Flanagan*

O'REILLY®

Beijing • Cambridge • Farnham • Köln • Paris • Sebastopol • Taipei • Tokyo

Java™ Enterprise in a Nutshell, Second Edition

by Jim Farley, William Crawford, and David Flanagan

Published by O'Reilly & Associates, Inc., 1005 Gravenstein Highway North,
Sebastopol, CA 95472.

O'Reilly & Associates books may be purchased for educational, business, or sales
promotional use. Online editions are also available for most titles
(*safari.oreilly.com*). For more information, contact our corporate/institutional sales
department: (800) 998-9938 or *corporate@oreilly.com*.

Editors: Paula Ferguson and Robert Eckstein

Production Editor: Mary Anne Weeks Mayo

Cover Designer: Edie Freedman

Printing History:

September 1999: First Edition.

April 2002: Second Edition.

ISBN: 0-596-00152-5
[M]

Table of Contents

Preface

This book is a desktop quick reference for Java™ programmers who are writing enterprise applications. The first part of the book provides a fast-paced introduction to the key Java Enterprise APIs: JDBC™, RMI, Java IDL (CORBA), servlets, JSP, JNDI, JavaMail, XML, and Enterprise JavaBeans™. These chapters are followed by a quick-reference section that succinctly details most classes of those APIs, as well as a few other Enterprise APIs.

This book complements the best-selling *Java in a Nutshell* and *Java Foundation Classes in a Nutshell*, and parallels O'Reilly's *J2ME in a Nutshell. Java in a Nutshell* introduces the Java programming language itself and provides an API quick reference for the core packages and classes of the Java platform, while *Java Foundation in a Nutshell* offers a fast-paced tutorial on the Java APIs that comprise the Java Foundation Classes (JFC) and provides corresponding quick-reference material. Finally, *J2ME in a Nutshell* introduces the Java 2 Micro Edition, and covers programming strategies for working with the Mobile Information Device Profile (MIDP) and Connected, Limited Device Configuration (CLDC) APIs.

Contents of This Book

This book is divided into three parts:

Part I, *Introducing the Java Enterprise APIs*
The chapters in this part introduce the key Enterprise APIs and provide enough information so that you can start using them right away.

Part II, *Enterprise Reference*
This part contains reference chapters that help you work with technologies key to the Enterprise APIs, such as SQL and IDL. It also contains chapters that cover the tools provided with Sun's Java Development Kit for RMI and Java IDL.

Part III, *API Quick Reference*

> This part is a quick reference for the Java Enterprise APIs; it forms the bulk of the book. Please be sure to read the *How To Use This Quick Reference* section, which appears at the beginning of this part. It explains how to get the most out of this book.

Related Books

O'Reilly & Associates publishes an entire series of books on Java programming. These books include *Java in a Nutshell, Java Foundation Classes in a Nutshell,* and *J2ME in a Nutshell*. You can find a complete list of O'Reilly's Java books at *http://java.oreilly.com.*:

Java Servlet Programming, by Jason Hunter with William Crawford
> A guide to writing servlets that covers dynamic web content, maintaining state information, session tracking, database connectivity using JDBC, and applet-servlet communication.

JavaServer Pages, by Hans Bergsten
> A guide to writing JavaServer Pages (JSP), which use Java servlets to create effective, reusable web applications

Java Distributed Computing, by Jim Farley
> A programmer's guide to writing distributed applications with Java

Database Programming with JDBC and Java, by George Reese
> An advanced tutorial on JDBC that presents a robust model for developing Java database programs

Java Message Service, by Richard Monson-Haefel and David A. Chappell
> A thorough introduction to the Java Message Service (JMS), a standardized API for enterprise-based message-oriented middleware (MOM)

Enterprise JavaBeans, by Richard Monson-Haefel
> A thorough introduction to EJB for the enterprise software developer

Java and XML, by Brett McLaughlin
> A programmer's guide to writing Java applications that use the Extensible Markup Language (XML)

Java and XSLT, by Eric M. Burke
> An advanced tutorial on embedding XML processing and transformations into Java applications

Java Programming Resources Online

This book is designed for speedy access to frequently needed information. It does not, and cannot, tell you everything you need to know about the Java Enterprise APIs. In addition to the books listed in the previous section, there are several valuable (and free) electronic sources of information about Java programming.

Sun's web site for all things related to Java is *http://java.sun.com*. The web site specifically for Java developers is *http://developer.java.sun.com*. Much of the content on this developer site is password-protected, and access to it requires (free) registration.

Some of the Enterprise APIs covered in this book are part of the core Java 2 platform, so if you have downloaded the JDK, you have the classes for APIs such as JDBC, RMI, parts of XML, and Java IDL. Other APIs are standard extensions, however, so if you want to use, say, JNDI or servlets, you have to download the classes separately. The best way to get the latest APIs is to start on Sun's Products and APIs page at *http://java.sun.com/products/* and find the appropriate API.

Sun distributes electronic documentation for all Java classes and methods in its *javadoc* HTML format. Although this documentation is rough or outdated in places, it is still an excellent starting point when you need to know more about a particular Java package, class, method, or field. If you don't already have the *javadoc* files with your Java distribution, see *http://java.sun.com/docs/* for a link to the latest available version.

Finally, don't forget O'Reilly's Java web site. *http://java.oreilly.com* contains Java news and commentary. In addition, the O'Reilly network offers OnJava.com at *http://www.onjava.com/*, which contains insightful tips and tricks for every level of Java programmer.

Examples Online

The examples in this book are available online and can be downloaded from the home page for the book at *http://www.oreilly.com/catalog/jentnut2/*. You may also want to visit this site for important notes or errata about the book.

Conventions Used in This Book

The following formatting conventions are used in this book:

Italic
> Used for emphasis and to signify the first use of a term. Italic is also used for commands, email addresses, web sites, FTP sites, file and directory names, and newsgroups.

Bold
> Occasionally used to refer to particular keys on a computer keyboard or to portions of a user interface, such as the **Back** button or the **Options** menu.

`Constant width`
> Used in all Java code and generally for anything that you would type literally when programming, including options, keywords, data types, constants, method names, variables, class names, and interface names.

`Constant width italic`
> Used for the names of function arguments, and generally as a placeholder to indicate an item that should be replaced with an actual value in your program.

Franklin Gothic Book Condensed
> Used for the Java class synopses in Part III. This very narrow font allows us to fit a lot of information on the page without a lot of distracting line breaks. This font is also used for code entities in the descriptions in Part III.

Franklin Gothic Demi Condensed

Used for highlighting class, method, field, property, and constructor names in Part III, which makes it easier to scan the class synopses.

Franklin Gothic Book Compressed Italic

Used for method parameter names and comments in Part III.

Comments and Questions

Please address comments and questions concerning this book to the publisher:

O'Reilly & Associates, Inc.
1005 Gravenstein Highway North
Sebastopol, CA 95472
(800) 998-9938 (in the United States or Canada)
(707) 829-0515 (international or local)
(707) 829-0104 (fax)

There's a web page for this book that lists errata, examples, and additional information::

http://www.oreilly.com/catalog/jentnut2/

To comment or ask technical questions about this book, send email to:

bookquestions@oreilly.com

For more information about ORA books, conferences, Resource Centers, and the O'Reilly Network:

http://www.oreilly.com

For more information about this book and others:

http://www.oreilly.com

Acknowledgments

This book is an outgrowth of the best-selling *Java in a Nutshell*. We'd like to thank all the readers who made that book a success and who wrote in with comments, suggestions, and praise. The authors would like to say a big thank you to the book's technical reviewers, whose constructive criticism has done much to improve this work: Andy Deitsch, Jason Hunter, William Smith, Gary Letourneau., Jonathan Kaplan, and Eric Friedman We would also like to thank Kris Magnusson for his help with the JNDI chapter in the first edition of this book. Although Kris was unable to help with the second edition, his insight and experience was invaluable to the rest of us while creating the second edition.

Jim Farley

A writing project of any kind requires a much larger cast of characters than those listed on the cover. The editors (Paula Ferguson for the first edition, Bob Eckstein for the second) deserve mention above all, not only for doing their usual excellent editing job, but also for roping in three disobedient authors, as opposed to the usual one disobedient author. I'd like to thank David Flanagan for putting together the API listings and the introductory chapter, as well as providing great technical review comments, all of which helped integrate this into the "Java Nutshell" set. Technical reviewers are the unsung heroes of writing projects such as this one, so many thanks to Brian Ploetz and Gail Bowman for reviewing the second edition, and to Andy Deitsch, Bill Smith, Jason Hunter, and Gary Letourneau for the first.

To my wife Sandy Mallalieu, who has somehow not only accepted the fact that her husband enjoys spending much of his free time on writing projects like this, but is also supportive and inspiring through it all—well, what else is there to say? My extended family, and my colleagues at Harvard, were supportive as always, and getting through efforts such as this makes me appreciate them both all the more. And for the late-night inspiration, my undying gratitude to Madeline and to Declan MacManus.

William Crawford

Writing projects would be impossible without the support of everyone at Invantage, which this time around means Martin Streeter, Nicholas Riley, Tarin McTague and Ed Marcus. Bob Eckstein gets the patient editor award for this edition, and Jonathan Kaplan and Eric Friedman (plus others mentioned elsewhere) were willing to take time out to do a technical review on the whole package. Eric also pushed me to include more on XML messaging, which didn't make it into this book, but will be available soon under separate cover. All remaining errors are solely our responsibility.

Sam Carner, Vanessa Wolf, Elizabeth Evans, Curtis Weiss, and Rebecca Goetz tolerated the flurries of writing and research and provided support in times of trouble (and an excuse to get out of the house occasionally) as did Bill, Francine, and Faith Crawford.

While I can't get away with dedicating all of the book, I'd like to dedicate the Java and XML chapter to the memory of William F. Crawford, valve industry impresario and business technology enthusiast.

David Flanagan

Java Enterprise in a Nutshell is a book I've wished I could write for some time now. Time constraints and my own lack of expertise in enterprise computing have kept me from doing it myself, and so I am deeply grateful to Jim Farley, William Crawford, and Kris Magnusson, who are experts and who did all the hard work to make this book a reality. I owe an extra thanks to Jim Farley for taking the time to help me understand Enterprise JavaBeans and the JTA and JTS transaction APIs. Paula Ferguson and Robert Eckstein also earn my sincere thanks: both had the unenviable task of editing material from multiple authors and fitting it seamlessly together into a single book.

PART I

Introducing the Java Enterprise APIs

Part I is an introduction to the key Enterprise APIs. These chapters provide enough information for you to get started using these APIs right away.

CHAPTER 1

Introduction

This book is an introduction to, and quick reference for, the Java Enterprise APIs. Some of these APIs are a core part of the Java platform, while others are standard extensions to the platform. Together, however, they enable Java programs to use and interact with a suite of distributed network services that are commonly used in enterprise computing.

These APIs can be used individually to integrate specific enterprise functionality into your applications. Or, you can use them within the Java 2 Platform, Enterprise Edition (J2EE), which integrates all of the APIs discussed in this book into a well-defined application framework. What's the difference? Well, besides guaranteeing a certain level of support for the various enterprise-related Java APIs, a compliant J2EE server also provides certain application services that are critical for developing, deploying, and managing applications in an enterprise environment. These include application assembly and deployment facilities that let you configure runtime application properties and resources at deploy time, in a standard format, as well as a unified security model that applies to various types of components that can be defined within J2EE.

Enterprise Computing Defined

Before we go any further, let's be clear. The term *enterprise computing* is simply a synonym for distributed computing: computation done by groups of programs interacting over a network.

Anyone can write distributed applications: you don't have to work for a major corporation, university, government agency, or any other kind of large-scale "enterprise" to program with the Java Enterprise APIs. Small businesses may not have the same enterprise-scale distributed computing needs large organizations have, but most still engage in plenty of distributed computing. With the explosive growth of the Internet and of network services, just about anyone can find a reason to write distributed applications. One such reason is that it is fun. When distributed computing is used to leverage the power of the network, the results can be amazingly cool!

So, if the Java Enterprise APIs aren't used exclusively by enterprises, why aren't they called the Java Distributed Computing APIs? The reasons are simple. First, enterprise is a hot buzzword these days—everyone in the networking industry wants to be working on enterprise something. Second, large enterprises have lots of money to spend on costly hardware for running their expensive network server software. Since the enterprise is where the money is, we get the word "enterprise" in the APIs.

Enterprise Computing Demystified

Enterprise computing has a reputation for complexity and, for the uninitiated, is often surrounded by a shroud of mystery. Here are some reasons enterprise computing can seem intimidating:

- Enterprise computing usually takes place in a heterogeneous network: one in which the computers range from large mainframes and supercomputers down to PCs (including both top-of-the-line 64-bit processors and outdated 386's). The computers were purchased at different times from a variety of different vendors and run two or three or more different operating systems. The only common denominator is that all the computers in the network speak the same fundamental network protocol (usually TCP/IP).

- A variety of server applications run on top of the heterogeneous network hardware. An enterprise might have database software from three different companies, each of which defines different, incompatible extensions.

- Enterprise computing involves the use of many different network protocols and standards. Some standards overlap in small or significant ways. Many have been extended in various vendor-specific, nonstandard ways. Some are quite old and use a vocabulary and terminology that dates back to an earlier era of computing. This creates a confusing alphabet soup of acronyms.

- Enterprise computing has only recently emerged as an integrated discipline of its own. Although today enterprise development models are becoming more cohesive and encompassing, many enterprises are still left with lots of "legacy systems" that are aggregated in an ad hoc way.

- Enterprise programmers, like many of us in the high-tech world, tend to make their work seem more complicated than it actually is. This is a natural human tendency—to be part of the "in" group and keep outsiders out—but this seems somehow magnified within the computer industry.

Java helps to alleviate these intimidating aspects of enterprise computing. First, since Java is platform-independent, the heterogeneous nature of the network ceases to be an issue. Second, the Java Enterprise APIs form a single, standard layer on top of various proprietary or vendor-enhanced APIs. For example, the JDBC API provides a single, standard, consistent way to interact with a relational database server, regardless of the database vendor and of the underlying network protocol the database server uses to communicate with clients. Finally, recall that many enterprise protocols and standards were developed before the days of object-oriented programming. The object-oriented power and elegance of the Java language allow the Java Enterprise APIs to be simpler, easier to use, and easier to understand than the non-Java APIs upon which they are layered.

The messages you should take away from this discussion are:

- Enterprise computing is for everyone.
- Any programmer can write distributed applications using the Java Enterprise APIs.

With that said, it is important to understand that distributed computing actually is somewhat more complicated than nondistributed computing. Just as using threads in a program introduces complexities that don't exist in single-threaded programs, using network services in a program introduces complexities that don't exist in programs that run entirely on one computer. While multithreaded programs have to deal with the issues of thread synchronization and deadlock, distributed applications have to deal with the possibilities of network failure and the complexities of distributed transaction processing. Do not fear, however: the complexities of distributed computing aren't overwhelming, and, with a little study, any programmer can master them.

The Java Enterprise APIs

The Java Enterprise APIs provide support for a number of the most commonly used distributed computing technologies and network services. These APIs are described in the sections that follow. The APIs are building blocks for distributed applications. At the end of the chapter, there are descriptions of some enterprise computing scenarios that illustrate how these separate APIs can be used together to produce an enterprise application.

JDBC: Working with Databases

JDBC (Java Database Connectivity) is the Java Enterprise API for working with relational database systems. JDBC allows a Java program to send SQL query and update statements to a database server and to retrieve and iterate through query results returned by the server. JDBC also allows you to get metainformation about the database and its tables from the database server.

The JDBC API is independent of vendor-specific APIs defined by particular database systems. The JDBC architecture relies upon a Driver class that hides the details of communicating with a database server. Each database server product requires a custom Driver implementation to allow Java programs to communicate with it. Major database vendors have made JDBC drivers available for their products. In addition, a "bridge" driver exists to enable Java programs to communicate with databases through existing ODBC drivers.

The JDBC API is found in the java.sql package, which was introduced in Java 1.1. Java 2 (including the 1.2, 1.3, and 1.4 versions) updated the core APIs to use JDBC 2.0, which adds a number of new classes to this package to support advanced database features. JDBC 2.0 also provides additional features in the javax.sql standard extension package. javax.sql includes classes for treating database query results as JavaBeans, for pooling database connections, and for obtaining database connection information from a name service. The extension package also supports scrollable result sets, batch updates, and the storage of Java objects in databases. AS of this printing, the JDBC 3.0 specifications have been finalized and should be available in mid-2002.

The JDBC API is simple and well-designed. Programmers who are familiar with SQL and database programming in general should find it very easy to work with databases in Java. See Chapter 2 for details on JDBC and Chapter 12 for a quick reference to SQL.

RMI: Remote Method Invocation

Remote method invocation is a programming model that provides a high-level, generic approach to distributed computing. This model extends the object-oriented programming paradigm to distributed client-server programming: it allows a client to communicate with a server by invoking methods on remote objects that reside on the server. RMI is implemented in the java.rmi package and its subpackages, which were introduced in Java 1.1 and were enhanced in Versions 1.2, 1.3, and 1.4 of the Java 2 platform.

The Java RMI implementation is full-featured, but still simple and easy to use. It gains much of its simplicity by being built on top of a network-centric and dynamically extensible platform, of course. But it also gains simplicity by requiring both client and server to be implemented in Java. This requirement ensures that both client and server share a common set of data types and have access to the object serialization and deserialization features of the java.io package, for example. On the other hand, this means that it is more difficult to use RMI with distributed objects written in languages other than Java, such as objects that exist on legacy servers. The default remote-method communication protocol used by RMI will only allow Java code to interact with RMI objects. So one option for interfacing with non-Java legacy code over RMI is to use the Java Native Interface (JNI). Another is to use RMI/IIOP, which was made a standard part of the core Java APIs in Version 1.3 of the Java 2 platform. RMI/IIOP is an optional communication protocol that allows RMI objects to interact with CORBA-based remote objects. Since CORBA objects can be implemented in many languages, this also bridges the language gap. We discuss both of these options in this book, but in practice, RMI is an excellent distributed object solution for situations in which it is clear that clients and servers will be written in Java. Fortunately, there are many such situations.

The java.rmi package makes it easy to create networked, object-oriented programs. Programmers who have spent time writing networked applications using lower-level protocols are usually amazed by the power of RMI. By making RMI so easy, java.rmi points the way to future applications and systems that consist of loose groups of objects interacting with each other over a network. These objects may act both as clients, by calling methods of other objects, and as servers, by exposing their own methods to other objects. See Chapter 3 for a tutorial on using RMI.

Java IDL: CORBA Distributed Objects

As we've just discussed, RMI is a distributed object solution that works especially well when both client and server are written in Java. It is more work, and therefore less attractive, in heterogeneous environments in which clients and servers may be written in arbitrary languages. For environments like these, the Java 2 platform includes a CORBA-based solution for remote method invocation on distributed objects.

CORBA (Common Object Request Broker Architecture) is a widely used standard defined by the Object Management Group (OMG). The Java binding of this standard is implemented as a core part of the Java 2 platform in the org.omg.CORBA package and its subpackages. The implementation includes a simple Object Request Broker (ORB) that a Java application can use to communicate (as both a client and a server) with other ORBs, and thus with other CORBA objects.

The interfaces to remote CORBA objects are described in a platform- and language-independent way with the Interface Definition Language (IDL). Sun provides an IDL compiler that translates an IDL declaration of a remote interface into the Java stub classes needed for implementing the IDL interface in Java, or for connecting to a remote implementation of the interface from your Java code.

A number of Java implementations of the CORBA standard are available from various vendors. This book documents Sun's implementation, known as Java IDL. It is covered in detail in Chapter 4. The syntax of the IDL language itself is summarized in Chapter 14.

JAXP: XML Parsing and Messaging

The eXtensible Markup Language (XML) is a nearly ubiquitous presence in enterprise development. Data and content storage was just the start for XML; it's rapidly spread to become a powerful tool in messaging, RPC, web interfaces, enterprise system integration, and other areas. J2EE 1.3–compliant application servers include the Java API for XML Parsing (JAXP), which is a pluggable API that supports both SAX and DOM parsing of XML content, as well as XSLT-based transformations of XML. JAXP 1.1, the version noted in the J2EE 1.3 specification, supports the SAX 2 and DOM 2 parsing APIs, as well as the XSLT 1.0 transform API. JAXP offers both a standard API for performing parsing and transformations of XML, and a pluggability API for using various XML parsing engines (such as Xerces and Xalan) to perform the underlying processing. JAXP is covered briefly in Chapter 9. The JAXP APIs are covered in *Java in a Nutshell, Fourth Edition,* by David Flanagan (O'Reilly & Associates, Inc.).

JNDI: Accessing Naming and Directory Services

JNDI (Java Naming and Directory Interface) is the Java Enterprise API for working with networked naming and directory services. It allows Java programs to use name servers and directory servers to look up objects or data by name and search for objects or data according to a set of specified attribute values. JNDI is implemented in the javax.naming package and its subpackages as a standard extension to the Java 2 platform.

The JNDI API is not specific to any particular name or directory server protocol. Instead, it is a generic API that is general enough to work with any name or directory server. To support a particular protocol, plug a service provider for that protocol into a JNDI installation. Service providers have been implemented for the most common protocols, such as NIS, LDAP, and Novell's NDS. Service providers have also been written to interact with the RMI and CORBA object registries. JNDI is covered in detail in Chapter 7.

JMS: Enterprise Messaging

JMS (Java Message Service) is the Java Enterprise API for working with networked messaging services and for writing message-oriented middleware (fondly referred to as MOM).

The word "message" means different things in different contexts. In the context of JMS, a message is a chunk of data that is sent from one system to another in an asynchronous manner. The data serves as a kind of event notification and is almost always intended to be read by a computer program, not by a human. In a nondistributed system that uses the standard Java event model, an Event object notifies the program that some important event (such as the user clicking a mouse button) has occurred. In a distributed system, a message serves a similar purpose: it notifies some part of the system that an interesting event has occurred. So you can think of a networked message service as a distributed event notification system.

JMS is also a good complement to the synchronous communication provided by RMI and CORBA. When an RMI client, for example, makes a remote method call on a server object, the client will block until the remote method returns. JMS provides a way for you to communicate asynchronously with a remote process: you can send your message and carry on with useful work while the message is delivered and processed at the receiving end. If there's a response from the receiver(s), a callback can be invoked on your end, and you can deal with it then.

Like JNDI and JDBC, JMS is an API layered on top of existing, vendor-specific messaging services. In order to use JMS in your application, you need to obtain a JMS provider implementation that supports your particular message server. Some J2EE application servers bundle their own JMS providers that you can use as message servers; some of them provide easy ways to bridge their application servers to other message services like IBM MQSeries or SonicMQ; others provide neither, and leave it to you to obtain and install a JMS provider.

Chapter 10 provides a short tutorial on using JMS.

JavaMail: Email-Based Messaging

Email is another critical communication protocol for enterprise systems. Email is a widespread tool used for interpersonal messaging in a wide variety of contexts, from corporate communications to family-reunion planning, as anyone reading this book is surely aware. In an enterprise application context, email can also be an important tool for end-user event notifications (e.g., a notice that a lower-priced flight has matched your travel profile), for content delivery (e.g., a weekly "e-zine" delivered automatically from a content-management system), and for system monitoring (e.g., a notice to a system administrator that connectivity to a critical information system has been lost).

J2EE's tool for composing, sending and receiving email is the JavaMail API, contained in the `javax.mail` package. For dealing with various types of content in MIME-based email messages, a companion API called the JavaBeans Activation Framework and provided in the `javax.activation` package is used in conjunction with JavaMail (the "Activation" in the name refers to activating a content handler to deal with a particular type of content). Chapter 11 is a tutorial on the use of these APIs.

Enterprise JavaBeans: Distributed Components

Enterprise JavaBeans do for server-side enterprise programs what JavaBeans do for client-side GUIs. Enterprise JavaBeans (EJB) is a component model for units of business logic and business data. Thin client programming models that take business logic out of the client and put it on a server or in a middle tier have many advantages in enterprise applications. However, the task of writing this middleware has always been complicated by the fact that business logic must be mixed in with code for handling transactions, security, networking, and so on.

The EJB model attempts to separate high-level business logic from low-level housekeeping chores. A bean in the EJB model is an RMI remote object that implements business logic or represents business data. The difference between an enterprise bean and a run-of-the-mill RMI remote object is that EJB components run within an EJB container, which in turn runs within an EJB server. The container and server may provide features such as transaction management, resource pooling, lifecycle management, security, name services, distribution services, and so on. With all these services provided by the container and server, enterprise beans (and enterprise bean programmers) are free to focus purely on business logic. EJB servers are expected to provide a core set of component services, such as lifecycle management, instance pooling, distributed transaction management, and security.

The EJB specification is a document that specifies the contracts to be maintained and conventions to be followed by EJB servers, containers, and beans. Writing EJB components is easy: simply write code to implement your business logic, taking care to follow the rules and conventions imposed by the EJB model.

EJB components can also run within the larger J2EE framework. In addition to the stand-alone EJB component services, EJBs running within a J2EE server can be composed with other components into J2EE applications.

Unlike the other Java Enterprise APIs, EJB is not really an API; it is a framework for component-based enterprise computing. The key to understanding Enterprise JavaBeans lies in the interactions among beans, containers, and the EJB server. These interactions are described in detail in Chapter 8. There is, of course, an API associated with the EJB application framework, in the form of the `javax.ejb` and `javax.ejb.deployment` packages. You'll find complete API quick-reference information for these packages in Part III.

Servlets and JavaServer Pages (JSPs): Web-Based Components/UIs

A *servlet* is a piece of Java code that runs within a server to provide a service to a client. The name "servlet" is a takeoff on applet—a servlet is a server-side applet. The Java Servlet API provides a generic mechanism for extending the functionality of any kind of server that uses a protocol based on requests and responses.

For the most part, servlets are used behind web servers for dynamic generation of HTML content. On the growing number of web/application servers that support them, servlets are a Java-based replacement for CGI scripts. They can also replace competing technologies, such as Microsoft's Active Server Pages (ASP) or Netscape's Server-Side JavaScript. The advantage of servlets over these other technologies is that servlets are portable among operating systems and among servers. Servlets are also compiled objects that are persistent between invocations, which gives them major performance benefits over parsed CGI programs. Servlets also have full access to the rest of the Java platform, so features such as database access are automatically supported.

The Servlet API differs from many other Java Enterprise APIs in that it is not a Java layer on top of an existing network service or protocol. Instead, servlets are a Java-specific enhancement to the world of enterprise computing. With the advent of the Internet and the World Wide Web, many enterprises are interested in taking advantage of web browsers—universally available thin-clients that can run on any desktop. Under this model, the web server becomes enterprise middleware and is responsible for running applications for clients. Servlets are a perfect fit here. The user makes a request to the web server, the web server invokes the appropriate servlet, and the servlet uses JNDI, JDBC, and other Java Enterprise APIs to fulfill the request, returning the result to the user, usually in the form of HTML-formatted text.

The Servlet API is a standard extension to the Java 2 platform, implemented in the `javax.servlet` and `javax.servlet.http` packages. The `javax.servlet` package defines classes that represent generic client requests and server responses, while the `javax.servlet.http` package provides specific support for the HTTP protocol, including classes for tracking multiple client requests that are all part of a single client session. See Chapter 5 for details on servlet programming.

JavaServer Pages (JSPs) are closely related to Java servlets. You can think of JSPs as an alternative approach to creating servlets, in one sense. JSPs are similar to alternative technologies such as PHP and Microsoft Active Server Pages—they all provide a way to insert dynamic elements directly into HTML pages. In the case of JSPs, dynamic elements invoke Java code through references and calls to JavaBeans, custom tags that act as dynamic macros that are implemented by JavaBeans, or raw Java code snippets. The tie-in with servlets comes when a JSP server receives a request for a JSP. The JSP is converted automatically to a Java servlet, and your Java code snippets and JavaBean references are mapped into the generated servlet. Chapter 6 provides details on writing JSPs.

Both servlets and JSPs can be deployed as "web components" within the J2EE framework, where they depend on all the standard services guaranteed by the servlet and JSP specifications, as well as the ability to reference EJB components, participate in the broader security services of J2EE, etc.

JTA: Managing Distributed Transactions

The JTA, or Java Transaction API, is a Java Enterprise API for managing distributed transactions. Distributed transactions are one of the things that make distributed systems more complicated than nondistributed programs. To understand distributed transactions, you must first understand simple, nondistributed transactions.

A *transaction* is a group of several operations that must behave *atomically*: as if they constituted a single, indivisible operation. Consider a banking application that allows a user to transfer money from a checking account to a savings account. If the two account balances are stored in a database, the application must perform two database updates to handle a transfer—it must subtract money from the checking account and add money to the savings account. These two operations must behave atomically. To see why, imagine what would happen if the database server crashed after money had been subtracted from the checking account but before it had been added to the savings account. The customer would lose money!

To make multiple operations atomic, we use transactions. In our banking example, we first begin a transaction, then perform the two database updates. While these updates are in progress, no other threads can see the updated account balances. If both updates complete successfully, we end the transaction by *committing* it. This makes the updated account balances available to any other clients of the database. On the other hand, if either of the database updates fails, we *rollback* the transaction, reverting the accounts to their original balances. Other clients are again given access to the database, and they see no changes in the account balances. The JDBC API supports transactions on databases. The database server is required to do some complex work to support transactions, but for the application programmer, the API is easy: simply begin a transaction, perform the desired operations, and then either commit or rollback the transaction.

Distributed transactions are, unfortunately, quite a bit more complex than the simple transactions just described. Imagine, for example, a program that transfers money from an account stored in one database to another account stored in a different database running on a different server. In this case, there are two different servers involved in the transaction, so the process of committing or rolling back the transaction must be externally coordinated. Distributed transactions are performed using a complex procedure known as the *two-phase commit protocol* (the details of this protocol aren't important here). What is important is that we could write our account transfer code so that it implements the two-phase commit protocol itself, coordinating the entire distributed transaction with the two database servers. This would be tedious and error-prone, however. In practice, distributed transactions are coordinated by a specialized distributed transaction service.

This brings us, finally, to the JTA. The JTA is a Java API for working with transaction services. It defines a Java binding for the standard XA API for distributed transactions (XA is a standard defined by the Open Group). Using the JTA, we can write a program that communicates with a distributed transaction service and uses that service to coordinate a distributed transaction that involves a transfer of money between database records in two different databases.

Unfortunately, however, using the JTA in this way is still complex and error-prone. Modern enterprise applications are typically designed to run within some kind of application server, such as an Enterprise JavaBeans server or a full J2EE server. The server uses JTA to handle distributed transactions transparently for the application. Under this model, JTA becomes a low-level API used by server implementors, not by typical enterprise programmers. Therefore, this book doesn't include a tutorial chapter on JTA. It does, however, contain a complete API quick reference for the javax.transaction and javax.transactions.xa packages (see Part III). Chapter 8 also has a brief section on JTA, since it is one of the supporting APIs that provides EJB with its distributed transaction support.

Enterprise Computing Scenarios

The previous sections have been rapid-fire introductions to the Java Enterprise APIs that are part of the J2EE framework. Don't worry if you didn't understand all the information presented there: the rest of the chapters in this Part cover the APIs in more detail. The important message you should take from this chapter is that the Java Enterprise APIs are building blocks that work together to enable you to write distributed Java applications for enterprise computing. The network infrastructure of every enterprise is unique, and the Java Enterprise APIs can be combined in any number of ways to meet the specific needs and goals of a particular enterprise.

Figure 1-1 shows a network schematic for a hypothetical enterprise. It illustrates some of the many possible interconnections among network services and shows the Java Enterprise APIs that facilitate those interconnections. The figure is followed by example scenarios that demonstrate how the Java Enterprise APIs might be used to solve typical enterprise computing problems. You may find it useful to refer to Figure 1-1 while reading through the scenarios, but note that the figure doesn't illustrate the specific scenarios presented here.

Enabling E-Commerce for a Mail-Order Enterprise

CornCo Inc. runs a successful catalog-based mail-order business selling fresh flavored popcorn. They want to expand into the exciting world of electronic commerce over the Internet. Here's how they might do it:[*]

- A customer visits the company's web site, *www.cornco.com*, and uses a web browser to interact with the company's web server. This allows the customer to view the company's products and make selections to purchase.

- The web server uses a shopping-cart servlet to keep track of the products the customer has chosen to buy. The HTTP protocol is itself stateless, but servlets

---

[*] This example is intended to illustrate only how the Java Enterprise APIs can be used together. We have ignored efficiency considerations, so the resulting design might not actually be practical for a large-scale e-commerce web site.

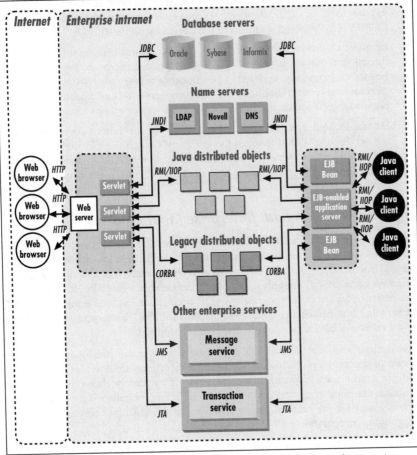

Figure 1-1: The distributed computing architecture of a hypothetical enterprise

can persist between client requests, so this shopping-cart servlet can remember the customer's selections even while the customer continues to browse the web site.

- When the customer is done browsing and is ready to purchase the selected products, the web server invokes a different checkout servlet. This servlet performs a number of important tasks, using several Enterprise APIs.

- The checkout servlet uses JDBC to retrieve the list of products to be purchased (stored in a database by the shopping-cart servlet).

- Next, the servlet queries the customer for a shipping address, a billing address, and other required information, and then uses JDBC again to store this information in a customer database. This database can be used, for example, by the CornCo marketing department for direct mail purposes.

- The servlet then sends the customer's billing address and total purchase price to the billing server. This server is a legacy application, specific to CornCo, that has a nonstandard interface. Fortunately, however, the billing server exports itself as a CORBA object, so the servlet can treat the entire server as a CORBA remote object and invoke the necessary methods on it.

- In order to ensure the very freshest product, CornCo maintains warehouses throughout the world. CornCo is a growing company, so the list of warehouses is frequently updated. The checkout servlet uses JNDI to contact a directory server and then uses the directory server to find a warehouse that is close to the customer and has the customer's requested products in stock.

- Having located a warehouse that can fulfill the customer's order, the checkout servlet uses JMS to contact the company's enterprise messaging service. It uses this service to send the customer's order to the selected warehouse in the form of a message. This message is delivered to and queued up on the local computer at the warehouse.

Updating CornCo with Enterprise JavaBeans

You may have noticed a flaw in the previous scenario. The checkout servlet sends billing information to one server, and then sends fulfillment information to another server. But it performs these two actions independently, without any attempt to maintain transactional integrity and make them behave atomically. In other words, if a network failure or server crash were to occur after the billing information had been sent, but before the fulfillment information had been sent, the customer might receive a bill for popcorn that was never shipped.

The designers of the e-commerce system described in the previous section were aware of this problem, but since distributed transactions are complex, and CornCo did not own a transaction management server, they simply chose to ignore it. In practice, the number of customers who would have problems would be small, and it was easier for the original programmers to let the customer service department sort out any irregularities.

But now, CornCo has hired a new Vice President of Information Systems. She's tough as nails, and likes all her i's dotted and her t's crossed. She won't stand for this sloppy state of affairs. As her first official act as VP, she buys a high-end J2EE application server and gives her e-commerce team the job of revamping the online ordering system to use it. The modified design might work like this:

- The customer interacts with the web server and the shopping-cart servlet in the same way as before.

- The checkout servlet is totally rewritten. Now it is merely a front-end for an Enterprise JavaBeans component that handles the interactions with the ordering and fulfillment servers and with the marketing database. The servlet uses JNDI to look up the enterprise bean, and then uses RMI to invoke methods on the bean (recall that all enterprise beans are RMI remote objects).

- The major functionality of the checkout servlet is moved to a new checkout bean. The bean stores customer data in the marketing database using JDBC, sends billing information to the billing server using CORBA, looks up a warehouse using JNDI, and sends shipping information to the warehouse using JMS. The bean doesn't explicitly coordinate all these activities into a distributed transaction, however. Instead, when the bean is deployed within the EJB container provided with the J2EE server, the system administrator configures the EJB component so that the server automatically wraps a distributed transaction around all of its actions. That is, when the checkout() method of the bean is called, it always behaves as an atomic operation.

- In order for this automatic distributed transaction management to work, another change is required in the conversion from checkout servlet to checkout bean. The checkout servlet managed all its own connections to other enterprise services, but enterprise beans don't typically do this. Instead, they rely on their server for connection management. Thus, when the checkout bean wants to connect to the marketing database or the enterprise messaging system, for example, it asks the EJB server to establish that connection for it. The server doesn't need to know what the bean does with the connection, but it does need to manage the connection, if it is to perform transaction management on the connection.

Other Enterprise APIs

There are a number of initiatives and APIs brewing in the Java community that could be classified as "enterprise APIs" but have not been included in this Nutshell book. We mention a few of them here, for the interested reader.

The area of XML-based "web services" (services that can be discovered and invoked using XML-based protocols delivered over HTTP) is a hotbed of activity at the time of this writing. The combination of XML, a portable data/content framework, and HTTP, a ubiquitous communications protocol, is a natural and powerful one. APIs and frameworks are being proposed and developed around a number of XML-based protocols such as SOAP, WSDL, UDDI, ebXML, etc. Sun has initiated a series of its own APIs around XML (*http://java.sun.com/xml*). We discuss JAXP in some detail in the book (see Chapter 9). There are others not covered in this book, such as the Java API for XML Messaging (JAXM), the Java API for XML Registries (JAXR), which supports ebXML. and the Java API for XML Binding (JAXB), which provides a means for marshalling and unmarshalling Java Objects to and from XML representations.

There are also a number of other third-party efforts to support web services in Java, being driven by IBM, BEA, and other players in the Java community, as well as the open source efforts of Apache (*http://www.apache.org*), OASIS (*http://www.oasis-open.org*) and others. At the time of this writing, the subject of XML-based web services is somewhat unfocused in the market, and more complete coverage requires much more material than we could provide in this Nutshell book. However, the Java XML APIs will receive more coverage in their own volume once they mature.

Jini (*http://www.sun.com/jini*) is a next-generation networking system designed to enable instantaneous networking between unrelated devices, without external communication. Jini is a system for distributed computing; it includes a name service, a distributed transaction service, and a distributed event service. Although these services overlap with JNDI, JTS, and JMS, Jini is fundamentally different from these J2EE APIs. The Enterprise APIs are designed to bring Java into existing enterprises and to interoperate with existing protocols and services. Jini, on the other hand, is a next-generation networking system that was designed from scratch, with no concern for compatibility with today's distributed systems.

Project JXTA (*http://www.jxta.org*) is a framework for developing peer-to-peer systems that involve processes on traditional servers, agents on PDAs and other mobile devices, embedded systems on automobiles and consumer devices, etc. There is a large overlap between the functionality provided by JXTA and Jini, so it is hard to judge what the final form (if any) of these two frameworks will be in the standard Java environment, or whether they will continue as independent APIs.

CHAPTER 2

JDBC

The JDBC* API provides Java applications with mid-level access to most database systems, via the Structured Query Language (SQL). JDBC is a key enterprise API, as it's hard to imagine an enterprise application that doesn't use a database in some way.

In the first edition of this book, we focused on the original JDBC 1.0 API, and touched briefly on the new features provided by the JDBC 2.0 API. JDBC 2.1 is now a standard component of the J2SE platform, and drivers supporting the upgraded specification are widely available. In this edition, we discuss the JDBC 2. 1 API and the JDBC 2.0 Optional Packages (previously known as the JDBC 2.0 Standard Extension) and take a look at the upcoming JDBC 3.0 API.

A word of caution: while the java.sql package is not tremendously complex, it does require grounding in general database concepts and the SQL language itself. This book includes a brief SQL reference (see Chapter 12), but if you have never worked with a relational database system before, this chapter is not the place to start. For a more complete treatment of JDBC and general database concepts, we recommend *Database Programming with JDBC and Java* by George Reese (O'Reilly).

JDBC Architecture

Different database systems have surprisingly little in common: just a similar purpose and a mostly compatible query language. Beyond that, every database has its own API that you must learn to write programs that interact with the database. This has meant that writing code capable of interfacing with databases from more than one vendor has been a daunting challenge. Cross-database APIs exist, most

---

* According to Sun, JDBC is not an acronym for Java Database Connectivity.

notably Microsoft's ODBC API, but these tend to find themselves, at best, limited to a particular platform.

JDBC is Sun's attempt to create a platform-neutral interface between databases and Java. With JDBC, you can count on a standard set of database access features and (usually) a particular subset of SQL, SQL-92. The JDBC API defines a set of interfaces that encapsulate major database functionality, including running queries, processing results, and determining configuration information. A database vendor or third-party developer writes a JDBC *driver*, which is a set of classes that implements these interfaces for a particular database system. An application can use a number of drivers interchangeably. Figure 2-1 shows how an application uses JDBC to interact with one or more databases without knowing about the underlying driver implementations.

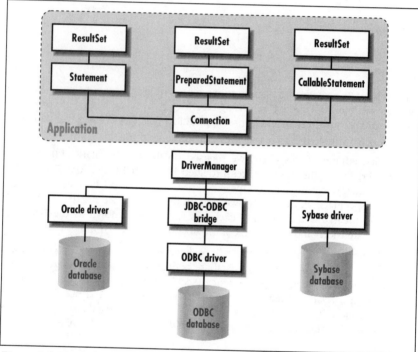

Figure 2-1: JDBC-database interaction

JDBC Basics

Before we discuss all of the individual components of JDBC, let's look at a simple example that incorporates most of the major pieces of JDBC functionality. Example 2-1 loads a driver, connects to the database, executes some SQL, and retrieves the results. It also keeps an eye out for any database-related errors.

Example 2-1: A Simple JDBC Example

```java
import java.sql.*;

public class JDBCSample {

  public static void main(java.lang.String[] args) {
    try {
      // This is where we load the driver
      Class.forName("sun.jdbc.odbc.JdbcOdbcDriver");
    }
    catch (ClassNotFoundException e) {
      System.out.println("Unable to load Driver Class");
      return;
    }

    try {
      // All database access is within a try/catch block. Connect to database,
      // specifying particular database, username, and password
      Connection con = DriverManager.getConnection("jdbc:odbc:companydb",
                  "", "");

      // Create and execute an SQL Statement
      Statement stmt = con.createStatement();
      ResultSet rs = stmt.executeQuery("SELECT FIRST_NAME FROM EMPLOYEES");

      // Display the SQL Results
      while(rs.next()) {
        System.out.println(rs.getString("FIRST_NAME"));
      }

      // Make sure our database resources are released
      rs.close();
      stmt.close();
      con.close();

    }
    catch (SQLException se) {
      // Inform user of any SQL errors
      System.out.println("SQL Exception: " + se.getMessage());
      se.printStackTrace(System.out);
    }
  }
}
```

Example 2-1 starts out by loading a JDBC driver class (in this case, Sun's JDBC-ODBC Bridge). Then it creates a database connection, represented by a `Connection` object, using that driver. With the database connection, we can create a `Statement` object to represent an SQL statement. Executing an SQL statement produces a `ResultSet` that contains the results of a query. The program displays the results and then cleans up the resources it has used. If an error occurs, a `SQLException` is thrown, so our program traps that exception and displays some of the information it encapsulates.

Clearly, there is a lot going on in this simple program. Every Java application that uses JDBC follows these basic steps, so the following sections discuss each step in much more detail.

JDBC Drivers

Before you can use a driver, it must be registered with the JDBC DriverManager. This is typically done by loading the driver class using the Class.forName() method:

```
try {
 Class.forName("sun.jdbc.odbc.JdbcOdbcDriver");
 Class.forName("com.oracle.jdbc.OracleDriver");
}
catch (ClassNotFoundException e) {
 /* Handle Exception */
}
```

One reason most programs call Class.forName() is that this method accepts a String argument, meaning that the program can store driver selection information dynamically (e.g., in a properties file).

Another way to register drivers is to add the driver classes to the jdbc.drivers property. To use this technique, add a line like the following to ~/.hotjava/ properties (on Windows systems this file can be found in your Java SDK installation directory):

```
jdbc.drivers=com.oracle.jdbc.OracleDriver:foo.driver.dbDriver:
    com.al.AlDriver;
```

Separate the names of individual drivers with colons and be sure the line ends with a semicolon. (Programs rarely use this approach, as it requires additional configuration work on the part of end users.) Every user needs to have the appropriate JDBC driver classes specified in his properties file.

Finally, drivers can be loaded by a J2EE server and provided to the application via JNDI. We'll see more about that the end of this chapter.

JDBC drivers are available for most database platforms, from a number of vendors and in a number of different flavors. There are four categories of drivers:

Type 1 JDBC-ODBC bridge drivers

Type 1 drivers use a bridge technology to connect a Java client to an ODBC database system. The JDBC-ODBC Bridge from Sun and InterSolv is the only existing example of a Type 1 driver. Type 1 drivers require some sort of non-Java software to be installed on the machine running your code, and they are implemented using native code.

Type 2 Native-API partly Java drivers

Type 2 drivers use a native code library to access a database, wrapping a thin layer of Java around the native library. For example, with Oracle databases, the native access might be through the Oracle Call Interface (OCI) libraries that were originally designed for C/C++ programmers. Type 2 drivers are implemented with native code, so they may perform better than all-Java drivers, but they also add an element of risk, as a defect in the native code can crash the Java Virtual Machine.

Type 3 Net-protocol All-Java drivers

Type 3 drivers define a generic network protocol that interfaces with a piece of custom middleware. The middleware component might use any other type of driver to provide the actual database access. BEA's WebLogic product line (formerly known as WebLogic Tengah and before that as jdbcKona/T3) is an example. These drivers are especially useful for applet deployment, since the actual JDBC classes can be written entirely in Java and downloaded by the client on the fly.

Type 4 Native-protocol All-Java drivers

Type 4 drivers are written entirely in Java. They understand database-specific networking protocols and can access the database directly without any additional software. These drivers are also well suited for applet programming, provided that the Java security manager allows TCP/IP connections to the database server.

When you are selecting a driver, you need to balance speed, reliability, and portability. Different applications have different needs. A standalone, GUI-intensive program that always runs on a Windows NT system will benefit from the additional speed of a Type 2, native-code driver. An applet might need to use a Type 3 driver to get around a firewall. A servlet that is deployed across multiple platforms might require the flexibility of a Type 4 driver.

A list of currently available JDBC drivers is available at *http://java.sun.com/products/jdbc/jdbc.drivers.html*.

JDBC URLs

A JDBC driver uses a JDBC URL to identify and connect to a particular database. These URLs are generally of the form:

```
jdbc:driver:databasename
```

The actual standard is quite fluid, however, as different databases require different information to connect successfully. For example, the Oracle JDBC-Thin driver uses a URL of the form:

```
jdbc:oracle:thin:@site:port:database
```

while the JDBC-ODBC Bridge uses:

```
jdbc:odbc:datasource;odbcoptions
```

The only requirement is that a driver be able to recognize its own URLs.

The JDBC-ODBC Bridge

The JDBC-ODBC Bridge ships with JDK 1.1 and the Java 2 SDK for Windows and Solaris systems. The bridge provides an interface between JDBC and database drivers written using Microsoft's Open DataBase Connectivity (ODBC) API. The bridge was originally written to allow the developer community to get up and running quickly with JDBC. Since the bridge makes extensive use of native method calls, it is not recommended for long-term or high-volume deployment.

The bridge is not a required component of the Java SDK, so it is not supported by most web browsers or other runtime environments. Using the bridge in an applet requires a browser with a JVM that supports the JDBC-ODBC Bridge, as well as a properly configured ODBC driver and data source on the client side. Finally, due to different implementations of the native methods interface, the bridge doesn't work with some development environments, most notably Microsoft Visual J++.

The JDBC URL subprotocol *odbc* has been reserved for the bridge. Like most JDBC URLs, it allows programs to encode extra information about the connection. ODBC URLs are of the form:

```
jdbc:odbc:datasourcename[;attribute-name=attribute-value]*
```

For instance, a JDBC URL pointing to an ODBC data source named companydb with the CacheSize attribute set to 10 looks like this:

```
jdbc:odbc:companydb;CacheSize=10
```

Connecting to the Database

The java.sql.Connection object, which encapsulates a single connection to a particular database, forms the basis of all JDBC data-handling code. An application can maintain multiple connections, up to the limits imposed by the database system itself. A standard small office or web server Oracle installation can support 50 or so connections, while a major corporate database could host several thousand. The DriverManager.getConnection() method creates a connection:

```
Connection con = DriverManager.getConnection("url", "user", "password");
```

You pass three arguments to getConnection(): a JDBC URL, a database username, and a password. For databases that don't require explicit logins, the user and password strings should be left blank. When the method is called, the DriverManager queries each registered driver, asking if it understands the URL. If a driver recognizes the URL, it returns a Connection object. Because the getConnection() method checks each driver in turn, you should avoid loading more drivers than are necessary for your application.

The getConnection() method has two other variants that are less frequently used. One variant takes a single String argument and tries to create a connection to that JDBC URL without a username or password, or with a username and password embedded in the URL itself. The other version takes a JDBC URL and a java.util. Properties object that contains a set of name/value pairs. You generally need to provide at least username=value and password=value pairs.

When a Connection has outlived its usefulness, you should be sure to explicitly close it by calling its close() method. This frees up any memory being used by the object, and, more importantly, it releases any other database resources the connection may be holding on to. These resources (cursors, handles, and so on) can be much more valuable than a few bytes of memory, as they are often quite limited. This is particularly important in applications such as servlets that might need to create and destroy thousands of JDBC connections between restarts.

Because of the way some JDBC drivers are designed, it is not safe to rely on Java's garbage collection to remove unneeded JDBC connections.

The JDBC 2.0 standard extension, discussed later in this chapter, provides a facility for *connection pooling*, whereby an application can maintain several open database connections and spread the load among them. This is often necessary for enterprise-level applications, such as servlets, that may be called upon to perform tens of thousands of database transactions a day.

Statements

Once you have created a Connection, you can begin using it to execute SQL statements. This is usually done via Statement objects. There are actually three kinds of statements in JDBC:

Statement
> Represents a basic SQL statement

PreparedStatement
> Represents a precompiled SQL statement, which can offer improved performance

CallableStatement
> Allows JDBC programs complete access to stored procedures within the database itself

We're just going to discuss the Statement object for now; PreparedStatement and CallableStatement are covered in detail later in this chapter.

To get a Statement object, call the createStatement() method of a Connection:

```
Statement stmt = con.createStatement();
```

Once you have created a Statement, use it to execute SQL statements. A statement can either be a query that returns results or an operation that manipulates the database in some way. If you are performing a query, use the executeQuery() method of the Statement object:

```
ResultSet rs = stmt.executeQuery("SELECT * FROM CUSTOMERS");
```

Here we've used executeQuery() to run a SELECT statement. This call returns a ResultSet object that contains the results of the query (we'll take a closer look at ResultSet in the next section).

Statement also provides an executeUpdate() method, for running SQL statements that don't return results, such as the UPDATE and DELETE statements. executeUpdate() returns an integer that indicates the number of rows in the database that were altered.

If you don't know whether a SQL statement is going to return results (such as when the user is entering the statement in a form field), you can use the execute() method of Statement. This method returns true if there is a result associated with the statement. In this case, the ResultSet can be retrieved using the getResultSet() method and the number of updated rows can be retrieved using getUpdateCount():

```
Statement unknownSQL = con.createStatement();
if(unknownSQL.execute(sqlString)) {
  ResultSet rs = unknownSQL.getResultSet();
  // display the results
  }
else {
  System.out.println("Rows updated: " + unknownSQL.getUpdateCount());
  }
```

It is important to remember that a `Statement` object represents a single SQL statement. A call to `executeQuery()`, `executeUpdate()`, or `execute()` implicitly closes
any active `ResultSet` associated with the `Statement`. In other words, you need to
be sure you are done with the results from a query before you execute another
query with the same `Statement` object. If your application needs to execute more
than one simultaneous query, you need to use multiple `Statement` objects. As a
general rule, calling the `close()` method of any JDBC object also closes any
dependent objects, such as a `Statement` generated by a `Connection` or a `ResultSet`
generated by a `Statement`, but well-written JDBC code closes everything explicitly.

Multiple Result Sets

It is possible to write a SQL statement that returns more than one `ResultSet` or
update count (exact methods of doing so vary depending on the database). The
`Statement` object supports this functionality via the `getMoreResults()` method.
Calling this method implicitly closes any existing `ResultSet` and moves to the next
set of results for the statement. `getMoreResults()` returns `true` if there is another
`ResultSet` available to be retrieved by `getResultSet()`. However, the method
returns `false` if the next statement is an update, even if there is another set of
results waiting farther down the line. To be sure you've processed all the results
for a `Statement`, you need to check that `getMoreResults()` returns `false` and that
`getUpdateCount()` returns -1.

We can modify the previous `execute()` example to handle multiple results:

```
Statement unknownSQL = con.createStatement();
unknownSQL.execute(sqlString);
while (true) {
  rs = unknownSQL.getResultSet();
  if(rs != null)
  // display the results
  else
  // process the update data

  // Advance and quit if done
  if((unknownSQL.getMoreResults() == false) &&
  (unknownSQL.getUpdateCount() == -1))
  break;
  }
```

Statements that return multiple results are actually quite rare. They generally arise
from stored procedures or SQL implementations that allow multiple statements to
be executed in a batch. Under SyBase, for instance, multiple `SELECT` statements
may be separated by newline (\n) characters.

Results

When an SQL query executes, the results form a pseudo-table that contains all rows that fit the query criteria. For instance, here's a textual representation of the results of the query string "SELECT NAME, CUSTOMER_ID, PHONE FROM CUSTOMERS":

```
NAME                                CUSTOMER_ID  PHONE
--------------------------------    -----------  --------------------
Jane Markham                            1        617 555-1212
Louis Smith                             2        617 555-1213
Woodrow Lang                            3        508 555-7171
Dr. John Smith                          4        (011) 42 323-1239
```

This kind of textual representation is not very useful for Java programs. Instead, JDBC uses the java.sql.ResultSet interface to encapsulate the query results as Java primitive types and objects. You can think of a ResultSet as an object that represents an underlying table of query results, where you use method calls to navigate between rows and retrieve particular column values.

A Java program might handle the previous query as follows:

```
Statement stmt = con.createStatement();
ResultSet rs = stmt.executeQuery(
  "SELECT NAME, CUSTOMER_ID, PHONE FROM CUSTOMERS");

while(rs.next()) {
  System.out.print("Customer #" + rs.getString("CUSTOMER_ID"));
  System.out.print(", " + rs.getString("NAME"));
  System.out.println(", is at " + rs.getString("PHONE"));
}
rs.close();
stmt.close();
```

Here's the resulting output:

```
Customer #1, Jane Markham, is at 617 555-1212
Customer #2, Louis Smith, is at 617 555-1213
Customer #3, Woodrow Lang, is at 508 555-7171
Customer #4, Dr. John Smith, is at (011) 42 323-1239
```

The code loops through each row of the ResultSet using the next() method. When you start working with a ResultSet, you are positioned before the first row of results. That means you have to call next() once just to access the first row. Each time you call next(), you move to the next row. If there are no more rows to read, next() returns false. Note that with the JDBC 1.0 ResultSet, you can only move forward through the results and, since there is no way to go back to the beginning, you can read them only once. The JDBC 2.0 ResultSet, which we discuss later, overcomes these limitations.

Individual column values are read using the getString() method. getString() is one of a family of getXXX() methods, each of which returns data of a particular type. There are two versions of each getXXX() method: one that takes the case-insensitive String name of the column to be read (e.g., "PHONE", "CUSTOMER_ID") and one that takes a SQL-style column index. Note that column indexes run from 1 to *n*, unlike Java array indexes, which run from 0 to *n*-1, where *n* is the number of columns.

The most important getXXX() method is getObject(), which can return any kind of data packaged in an object wrapper. For example, calling getObject() on an integer field returns an Integer object, while calling it on a date field yields a java.sql.Date object. Table 2-1 lists the different getXXX() methods, along with the corresponding SQL data type and Java data type. Where the return type for a getXXX() method is different from the Java type, the return type is shown in parentheses. Note that thejava.sql.Types class defines integer constants that represent the standard SQL data types.

Table 2-1: SQL Data Types, Java Types, and Default getXXX() Methods

SQL Data Type	Java Type	getXXX() Method
CHAR	String	getString()
VARCHAR	String	getString()
LONGVARCHAR	String	getString()
NUMERIC	java.math.BigDecimal	getBigDecimal()
DECIMAL	java.math.BigDecimal	getBigDecimal()
BIT	Boolean (boolean)	getBoolean()
TINYINT	Integer (byte)	getByte()
SMALLINT	Integer (short)	getShort()
INTEGER	Integer (int)	getInt()
BIGINT	Long (long)	getLong()
REAL	Float (float)	getFloat()
FLOAT	Double (double)	getDouble()
DOUBLE	Double (double)	getDouble()
BINARY	byte[]	getBytes()
VARBINARY	byte[]	getBytes()
LONGVARBINARY	byte[]	getBytes()
DATE	java.sql.Date	getDate()
TIME	java.sql.Time	getTime()
TIMESTAMP	java.sql.Timestamp	getTimestamp()
BLOB	java.sql.Blob	getBlob()
CLOB	java.sql.Clob	getClob()

Note that this table merely lists the default mappings according to the JDBC specification, and some drivers don't follow these mappings exactly. Also, a certain amount of casting is permitted. For instance, the getString() method returns a String representation of just about any data type.

Handling Nulls

Sometimes database columns contain null, or empty, values. However, because of the way certain database APIs are written, it is impossible for JDBC to provide a method to determine before the fact whether or not a column is null.* Methods that don't return an object of some sort are especially vulnerable. getInt(), for instance, resorts to returning a value of -1. JDBC deals with this problem via the wasNull() method, which indicates whether or not the last column read was null:

```
int numberInStock = rs.getInt("STOCK");
if(rs.wasNull())
  System.out.println("Result was null");
else
  System.out.println("In Stock: " + numberInStock);
```

Alternately, you can call getObject() and test to see if the result is null:†

```
Object numberInStock = rs.getObject("STOCK");
if(numberInStock == null)
  System.out.println("Result was null");
```

Large Data Types

You can retrieve large chunks of data from a ResultSet as a stream. This can be useful when reading images from a database or loading large documents from a data store, for example. The relevant ResultSet methods are getAsciiStream(), getBinaryStream(), and getUnicodeStream(), where each method has column name and column index variants, just like the other getXXX() methods. Each of these methods returns an InputStream. Here's a code sample that retrieves an image from a PICTURES table and writes the image to an OutputStream of some kind (this might be a ServletOutputStream for a Java servlet that produces a GIF from a database):

```
ResultSet rs =
  stmt.executeQuery("SELECT IMAGE FROM PICTURES WHERE PID = " +
  req.getParameter("PID"));

if (rs.next()) {
  BufferedInputStream gifData =
  new BufferedInputStream(rs.getBinaryStream("IMAGE"));
  byte[] buf = new byte[4 * 1024]; // 4K buffer
  int len;
  while ((len = gifData.read(buf, 0, buf.length)) != -1) {
  out.write(buf, 0, len);
  }
}
```

The JDBC 2.0 API includes Blob and Clob objects to handle large data types; we discuss these objects later in this chapter.

---

* The driver can figure this out after reading the object, but since some driver implementations and database connection protocols allow you to reliably read a value from a column only once, implementing an isNull() method requires the ResultSet to cache the entire row in memory. While many programs do exactly this, it is not appropriate behavior for the lowest-level result handler.

† Some drivers, including early versions of Oracle's JDBC drivers, don't properly support this behavior.

Dates and Times

JDBC defines three classes devoted to storing date and time information: `java.sql.Date`, `java.sql.Time`, and `java.sql.Timestamp`. These correspond to the SQL DATE, TIME, and TIMESTAMP types. The `java.util.Date` class is not suitable for any of them, so JDBC defines a new set of wrapper classes that extend (or limit) the standard `Date` class to fit the JDBC mold.

The SQL DATE type contains only a date, so the `java.sql.Date` class contains only a day, month, and year. SQL TIME (`java.sql.Time`) includes only a time of day, without date information. SQL TIMESTAMP (`java.sql.Timestamp`) includes both, but at nanosecond precision (the standard `Date` class is incapable of handling more than milliseconds).

Since different DBMS packages have different methods of encoding date and time information, JDBC supports the ISO date escape sequences, and individual drivers must translate these sequences into whatever form the underlying DBMS requires. The syntax for dates, times, and timestamps is:

```
{d 'yyyy-mm-dd'}
{t 'hh:mm:ss'}
{ts 'yyyy-mm-dd hh:mm:ss.ms.microseconds.ns'}
```

A TIMESTAMP needs only to be specified up to seconds; the remaining values are optional. Here is an example that uses a date escape sequence (where dateSQL is a `Statement` of some sort):

```
dateSQL.execute("INSERT INTO FRIENDS(BIRTHDAY) VALUES ({d '1978-12-
14'})");
```

Advanced Results Handling

With JDBC 1.0, the functionality provided by the `ResultSet` interface is rather limited. There is no support for updates of any kind, and access to rows is limited to a single, sequential read (i.e., first row, second row, third row, etc., and no going back). JDBC 2.0 supports scrollable and updateable result sets, which allows for advanced record navigation and in-place data manipulation.

With scrolling, you can move forward and backward through the results of a query, rather than just using the `next()` method to move to the next row. In terms of scrolling, there are now three distinct types of `ResultSet` objects: forward-only (as in JDBC 1.0), scroll-insensitive, and scroll-sensitive. A scroll-insensitive result set generally doesn't reflect changes to the underlying data, while scroll-sensitive ones do. In fact, the number of rows in a sensitive result set doesn't even need to be fixed.

As of JDBC 2.0, result sets are also updateable. From this perspective, there are two different kinds of result sets: read-only result sets that don't allow changes to the underlying data and updateable result sets that allow such changes, subject to transaction limitations and so on.

To create an updateable, scroll-sensitive result set, we pass two extra arguments to the `createStatement()` method.

```
Statement stmt = con.createStatement(ResultSet.TYPE_SCROLL_SENSITIVE,
  ResultSet.CONCUR_UPDATEABLE);
```

If you don't pass any arguments to createStatement(), you get a forward-only, read-only result set, just as you would using JDBC 1.0. Note that if you specify a scrollable result set (either sensitive or insensitive), you must also specify whether or not the result set is updateable. After you have created a scrollable ResultSet, use the methods listed in Table 2-2 to navigate through it. As with JDBC 1.0, when you start working with a ResultSet, you are positioned before the first row of results.

Table 2-2: JDBC 2.0 Record Scrolling Functions

Method	Function
first()	Move to the first record.
last()	Move to the last record.
next()	Move to the next record.
previous()	Move to the previous record.
beforeFirst()	Move to immediately before the first record.
afterLast()	Move to immediately after the last record.
absolute(*int*)	Move to an absolute row number. Takes a positive or negative argument.
relative(*int*)	Move backward or forward a specified number of rows. Takes a positive or negative argument.

The JDBC 2.0 API also includes a number of methods that tell you where you are in a ResultSet. You can think of your position in a ResultSet as the location of a cursor in the results. The isFirst() and isLast() methods return true if the cursor is located on the first or last record, respectively. isAfterLast() returns true if the cursor is after the last row in the result set, while isBeforeFirst() returns true if the cursor is before the first row.

With an updateable ResultSet, you can change data in an existing row, insert an entirely new row, or delete an existing row. To change data in an existing row, use the newupdateXXX() methods of ResultSet. Let's assume we want to update the CUSTOMER_ID field of the first row we retrieve (okay, it's a contrived example, but bear with us):

```
Statement stmt = con.createStatement(ResultSet.TYPE_SCROLL_SENSITIVE,
  ResultSet.CONCUR_UPDATEABLE);
ResultSet rs = stmt.executeQuery("SELECT NAME, CUSTOMER_ID FROM
CUSTOMERS");

rs.first();
rs.updateInt(2, 35243);
rs.updateRow();
```

Here we use first() to navigate to the first row of the result set and then call updateInt() to change the value of the customer ID column in the result set. After making the change, call updateRow() to actually make the change in the database. If you forget to call updateRow() before moving to another row in the result set, any changes you made are lost. If you need to make a number of changes in a single row, do so with multiple calls to updateXXX() methods and then a single call to updateRow(). Just be sure you call updateRow() before moving on to another row.

The technique for inserting a row is similar to updating data in an existing row, with a few important differences. The first step is to move to what is called the insert row, using the moveToInsertRow() method. The *insert row* is a blank row associated with the ResultSet that contains all the fields, but no data; you can think of it as a pseudo-row in which you can compose a new row. After you have moved to the insert row, use updateXXX() methods to load new data into the insert row and then call insertRow() to append the new row to the ResultSet and the underlying database. Here's an example that adds a new customer to the database:

```
ResultSet rs = stmt.executeQuery(
    "SELECT NAME, CUSTOMER_ID FROM CUSTOMERS");
rs.moveToInsertRow();
rs.updateString(1, "Tom Flynn");
rs.updateInt(2, 35244);
rs.insertRow();
```

Note that you don't have to supply a value for every column, as long as the columns you omit can accept null values. If you don't specify a value for a column that can't be null, you'll get a SQLException. After you call insertRow(), you can create another new row, or you can move back to the ResultSet using the various navigation methods shown in Table 2-2. One final navigation method that isn't listed in the table is moveToCurrentRow(). This method takes you back to where you were before you called moveToInsertRow(); it can only be called while you are in the insert row.

Deleting a row from an updateable result set is easy. Simply move to the row you want to delete and call the deleteRow() method. Here's how to delete the last record in a ResultSet:

```
rs.last();
rs.deleteRow();
```

Calling deleteRow() also deletes the row from the underlying database.

Note that not all ResultSet objects are updateable. In general, the query must reference only a single table without any joins. Due to differences in database implementations, there is no single set of requirements for what makes an updateable ResultSet.

As useful as scrollable and updateable result sets are, the JDBC 2.0 specification doesn't require driver vendors to support them. If you are building middleware or some other kind of system that requires interaction with a wide range of database drivers, you should avoid this functionality for the time being. The extended JDBC 2.0 DatabaseMetaData object can provide information about scrolling and concurrency support.

Java-Aware Databases

Java is object-oriented; relational databases aren't. As a result, it's decidedly diffi-cult to shoehorn a Java object into a stubbornly primitive-oriented database table. Luckily, the wind is changing, and newer database systems, including object-oriented database management systems (OODBMS) and Java-relational database management systems,* provide direct support for storing and manipulating objects. While a regular relational database can store only a limited number of primitive types, a JDBMS system can store entire, arbitrary Java objects.

Say we want to store a customized Java Account object in the ACCOUNTS table in a database. With a standard DBMS and JDBC 1.0, we have to pull each piece of data (account number, account holder, balance, etc.) out of the Account object and write it to a complicated database table. To get data out, we reverse the process. Short of serializing the Account object and writing it to a binary field (a rather complex operation), we're stuck with this clumsy approach.†

With JDBC 2.0, the getObject() method has been extended to support these new Java-aware databases. Provided that the database supports a Java-object type, we can read the Account object just like any primitive type:

```
ResultSet rs = stmt.executeQuery("SELECT ACCOUNT FROM ACCOUNTS");
rs.next();
Account a = (Account)rs.getObject(1);
```

To store an object, we use a PreparedStatement and the setObject() method:

```
Account a = new Account();
// Fill in appropriate fields in Account object

PreparedStatement stmt = con.prepareStatement(
  "INSERT INTO ACCOUNTS (ACCOUNT) VALUE (?)");
stmt.setObject(1, a);
stmt.executeUpdate();
```

A column that stores a Java object has a type of Types.JAVA_OBJECT. The JDBC API doesn't take any special steps to locate the bytecodes associated with any particular class, so you should make sure that any necessary objects can be instan-tiated with a call to Class.forName().

Handling Errors

Any JDBC object that encounters an error serious enough to halt execution throws a SQLException. For example, database connection errors, malformed SQL state-ments, and insufficient database privileges all throw SQLException objects.

---

* This is Sun's term. We have yet to see any packages actually marketed as Java-relational da-tabases, but many newer packages, including Oracle 8i, are capable of storing Java classes. A number of these products also use Java as a trigger language, generally in a JDBC structure.

† Various commercial products, such as Sun's Forte developer tool, automatically handle map-ping objects to database records and vice versa. Check the site *http://www.javasoft.com/products/java-blend/index.html* for more information.

The SQLException class extends the normal java.lang.Exception class and defines an additional method called getNextException(). This allows JDBC classes to chain a series of SQLException objects together. SQLException also defines the getSQLState() and getErrorCode() methods to provide additional information about an error. The value returned by getSQLState() is one of the ANSI-92 SQL state codes; these codes are listed in Chapter 12. getErrorCode() returns a vendor-specific error code.

An extremely conscientious application might have a catch block that looks something like this:

```
try {
    // Actual database code
}
catch (SQLException e) {
    while(e != null) {
    System.out.println("\nSQL Exception:");
    System.out.println(e.getMessage());
    System.out.println("ANSI-92 SQL State: " + e.getSQLState());
    System.out.println("Vendor Error Code: " + e.getErrorCode());
    e = e.getNextException();
    }
}
```

SQL Warnings

JDBC classes also have the option of generating (but not throwing) a SQLWarning exception when something is not quite right, but at the same time, not sufficiently serious to warrant halting the entire program. For example, attempting to set a transaction isolation mode that is not supported by the underlying database might generate a warning rather than an exception. Remember, exactly what qualifies as a warning condition varies by database.

SQLWarning encapsulates the same information as SQLException and is used in a similar fashion. However, unlike SQLException objects, which are caught in try/catch blocks, warnings are retrieved using the getWarnings() methods of the Connection, Statement, ResultSet, CallableStatement, and PreparedStatement interfaces. SQLWarning implements the getMessage(), getSQLState(), and getErrorCode() methods in the same manner as SQLException.

If you are debugging an application, and you want to be aware of every little thing that goes wrong within the database, you might use a printWarnings() method like this one:

```
void printWarnings(SQLWarning warn) {
    while (warn != null) {
    System.out.println("\nSQL Warning:");
    System.out.println(warn.getMessage());
    System.out.println("ANSI-92 SQL State: " + warn.getSQLState());
    System.out.println("Vendor Error Code: " + warn.getErrorCode());
    warn = warn.getNextWarning();
    }
}
```

You can then use the `printWarnings()` method as follows:

```
// Database initialization code here
ResultSet rs = stmt.executeQuery("SELECT * FROM CUSTOMERS");
printWarnings(stmt.getWarnings());
printWarnings(rs.getWarnings());
// Rest of database code
```

Prepared Statements

The PreparedStatement object is a close relative of the Statement object. Both accomplish roughly the same thing: running SQL statements. PreparedStatement, however, allows you to precompile your SQL and run it repeatedly, adjusting specific parameters as necessary. Since processing SQL strings is a large part of a database's overhead, getting compilation out of the way at the start can significantly improve performance. With proper use, it can also simplify otherwise tedious database tasks.

As with Statement, you create a PreparedStatement object from a Connection object. In this case, though, the SQL is specified at creation instead of execution, using the prepareStatement() method of Connection:

```
PreparedStatement pstmt = con.prepareStatement(
  "INSERT INTO EMPLOYEES (NAME, PHONE) VALUES (?, ?)");
```

This SQL statement inserts a new row into the EMPLOYEES table, setting the NAME and PHONE columns to certain values. Since the whole point of a PreparedStatement is to be able to execute the statement repeatedly, we don't specify values in the call to prepareStatement(), but instead use question marks (?) to indicate parameters for the statement. To actually run the statement, we specify values for the parameters and then execute the statement:

```
pstmt.clearParameters();
pstmt.setString(1, "Jimmy Adelphi");
pstmt.setString(2, "201 555-7823");
pstmt.executeUpdate();
```

Before setting parameters, we clear out any previously specified parameters with the clearParameters() method. Then we can set the value for each parameter (indexed from 1 to the number of question marks) using the setString() method. PreparedStatement defines numerous setXXX() methods for specifying different types of parameters; see the java.sql reference material later in this book for a complete list. Finally, we use the executeUpdate() method to run the SQL.

The setObject() method can insert Java object types into the database, provided that those objects can be converted to standard SQL types. setObject() comes in three flavors:

```
setObject(int parameterIndex, Object x, int targetSqlType, int scale)
setObject(int parameterIndex, Object x, int targetSqlType)
setObject(int parameterIndex, Object x)
```

Calling setObject() with only a parameter index and an Object causes the method to try and automatically map the Object to a standard SQL type (see Table 2-1). Calling setObject() with a type specified allows you to control the mapping. The setXXX() methods work a little differently, in that they attempt to map Java primitive types to JDBC types.

You can use PreparedStatement to insert null values into a database, either by calling the setNull() method or by passing a null value to one of the setXXX() methods that take an Object. In either case, you must specify the target SQL type.

Let's clarify with an example. We want to set the first parameter of a prepared statement to the value of an Integer object, while the second parameter, which is a VARCHAR, should be null. Here's some code that does that:

```
Integer i = new Integer(32);
pstmt.setObject(1, i, Types.INTEGER);
pstmt.setObject(2, null, Types.VARCHAR);
// or pstmt.setNull(2, Types.VARCHAR);
```

Batch Updates

The original JDBC standard was not very efficient for loading large amounts of information into a database. Even if you use a PreparedStatement, your program still executes a separate query for each piece of data inserted. If your software inserts 10,000 rows into the database, it can introduce a substantial performance bottleneck.

The new addBatch() method of Statement allows you to lump multiple update statements as a unit and execute them at once. Call addBatch() after you create the statement, and before execution:

```
con.setAutoCommit(false); // If some fail, we want to rollback the rest
Statement stmt = con.createStatement();

stmt.addBatch(
"INSERT INTO CUSTOMERS VALUES (1, "J Smith", "617 555-1323");
stmt.addBatch(
"INSERT INTO CUSTOMERS VALUES (2, "A Smith", "617 555-1132");
stmt.addBatch(
"INSERT INTO CUSTOMERS VALUES (3, "C Smith", "617 555-1238");
stmt.addBatch(
"INSERT INTO CUSTOMERS VALUES (4, "K Smith", "617 555-7823");

int[] upCounts = stmt.executeBatch();
con.commit();
```

Notice that we turn transaction auto-commit off before creating the batch. This is because we want to roll back all the SQL statements if one or more of them fail to execute properly (a more detailed discussion of transaction handling may be found later in this chapter, in the section "Transactions"). After calling addBatch() multiple times to create our batch, we call executeBatch() to send the SQL statements off to the database to be executed as a batch. Batch statements are executed in the order they are added to the batch. executeBatch() returns an array of update counts, in which each value in the array represents the number of rows affected by the corresponding batch statement. If you need to remove the statements from a pending batch job, you can call clearBatch(), as long as you call it before calling executeBatch().

Note that you can use only SQL statements that return an update count (e.g., CREATE, DROP, INSERT, UPDATE, DELETE) as part of a batch. If you include a statement that returns a result set, such as SELECT, you get a SQLException when you execute the batch. If one of the statements in a batch can't be executed for some reason, executeBatch() throws a BatchUpdateException. This exception, derived from SQLException, contains an array of update counts for the batch statements that executed successfully before the exception was thrown. If we then call rollback(), the components of the batch transaction that did execute successfully will be rolled back.

The addBatch() method works slightly differently for PreparedStatement and CallableStatement objects. To use batch updating with a PreparedStatement, create the statement normally, set the input parameters, and then call the addBatch() method with no arguments. Repeat as necessary and then call executeBatch() when you're finished:

```
con.setAutoCommit(false); // If some fail, we want to rollback the rest
PreparedStatement stmt = con.prepareStatement(
  "INSERT INTO CUSTOMERS VALUES (?,?,?)");

stmt.setInt(1,1);
stmt.setString(2, "J Smith");
stmt.setString(3, "617 555-1323");
stmt.addBatch();

stmt.setInt(1,2);
stmt.setString(2, "A Smith");
stmt.setString(3, "617 555-1132");
stmt.addBatch();

int[] upCounts = stmt.executeBatch();
con.commit();
```

This batch functionality also works with CallableStatement objects for stored procedures. The catch is that each stored procedure must return an update count and may not take any OUT or INOUT parameters.

BLOBs and CLOBs

As users began to increase the volume of data stored in databases, vendors introduced support for Large Objects (LOBs). The two varieties of LOBs, binary large objects (BLOBs) and character large objects (CLOBs), store large amounts of binary or character data, respectively.

Support for LOB types across databases varies. Some don't support them at all, and most have unique type names (BINARY, LONG RAW, and so forth). JDBC 1.0 makes programs retrieve BLOB and CLOB data using the getBinaryStream() or getAsciiStream() methods. (A third method, getUnicodeStream(), has been deprecated in favor of the new getCharacterStream() method, which returns a Reader.)

In JDBC 2.0, the ResultSet interface includes getBlob() and getClob() methods, which return Blob and Clob objects, respectively. The Blob and Clob objects themselves allow access to their data via streams (the getBinaryStream() method of Blob and the getCharacterStream() method of Clob) or via direct-read methods (the getBytes() method of Blob and the getSubString() method of Clob).

To retrieve the data from a CLOB, simply retrieve the Clob object and call the getCharacterStream() method:

```
String s;
Clob clob = blobResultSet.getBlob("CLOBFIELD");
BufferedReader clobData = new BufferedReader(clob.getCharacterStream());
while((s = clobData.readLine()) != null)
  System.out.println(s);
```

In addition, you can set Blob and Clob objects when you are working with a PreparedStatement, using the setBlob() and setClob() methods. While the API provides update methods for streams, there are no updateBlob() or updateClob() methods, and the Blob interface provides no mechanism for altering the contents of a Blob already stored in the database (although some drivers support updating of BLOB and CLOB types via the setBinaryStream() and setCharacterStream() methods of PreparedStatement). Note that the lifespan of a Blob or Clob object is limited to the transaction that created it.

JDBC driver support for BLOB and CLOB types varies wildly. Some vendors don't support any LOB functionality at all, and others (including Oracle) have added extensions to allow manipulation of LOB data. Check your driver documentation for more details.

Metadata

Most JDBC programs are designed to work with a specific database and particular tables in that database; the program knows exactly what kind of data it is dealing with. Some applications, however, need to dynamically discover information about result set structures or underlying database configurations. This information is called *metadata*, and JDBC provides two classes for dealing with it: DatabaseMetaData and ResultSetMetaData. If you are developing a JDBC application that will be deployed outside a known environment, you need to be familiar with these interfaces.

DatabaseMetaData

You can retrieve general information about the structure of a database with the java.sql.DatabaseMetaData interface. By making thorough use of this class, a program can tailor its SQL and use of JDBC on the fly, to accommodate different levels of database and JDBC driver support.

Database metadata is associated with a particular connection, so DatabaseMetaData objects are created with the getMetaData() method of Connection:

```
DatabaseMetaData dbmeta = con.getMetaData();
```

DatabaseMetaData provides an overwhelming number of methods you can call to get actual configuration information about the database. Some of these return String objects (getURL()), some return boolean values (nullsAreSortedHigh()), and still others return integers (getMaxConnections()).

A number of other methods return ResultSet objects. These methods, such as getColumns(), getTableTypes(), and getPrivileges(), generally encapsulate complex or variable-length information. The getTables() method, for instance, returns a ResultSet that contains the name of every table in the database as well as a good deal of extra information.

Many of the DatabaseMetaData methods take string patterns as arguments, allowing for simple wildcard searching. A percent sign (%) substitutes for any number of characters, and an underscore (_) calls for a single character match. Thus, %CUSTOMER% matches NEW_CUSTOMERS, CUSTOMER, and CUSTOMERS, while CUSTOMER% matches only CUSTOMER and CUSTOMERS. All of these patterns are case-sensitive.

Example 2-2 shows a simple program that displays some basic database character-istics, a list of tables, and a list of indexes on each table. The program assumes a JDBC driver with full support for all the DatabaseMetaData commands.

Example 2-2: DBViewer Program

```java
import java.sql.*;
import java.util.StringTokenizer;

public class DBViewer {

  final static String jdbcURL = "jdbc:odbc:customerdsn";
  final static String jdbcDriver = "sun.jdbc.odbc.JdbcOdbcDriver";

  public static void main(java.lang.String[] args) {

    System.out.println("--- Database Viewer ---");

    try {
      Class.forName(jdbcDriver);
      Connection con = DriverManager.getConnection(jdbcURL, "", "");

      DatabaseMetaData dbmd = con.getMetaData();

      System.out.println("Driver Name: " + dbmd.getDriverName());
      System.out.println("Database Product:
          " + dbmd.getDatabaseProductName());
      System.out.println("SQL Keywords Supported:");
      StringTokenizer st = new StringTokenizer(dbmd.getSQLKeywords(), ",");
      while(st.hasMoreTokens())
        System.out.println(" " + st.nextToken());

      // Get a ResultSet that contains all of the tables in this database
      // We specify a table_type of "TABLE" to prevent seeing system tables,
      // views and so forth
      String[] tableTypes = { "TABLE" };
      ResultSet allTables = dbmd.getTables(null,null,null,tableTypes);
      while(allTables.next()) {
        String table_name = allTables.getString("TABLE_NAME");
        System.out.println("Table Name: " + table_name);
        System.out.println("Table Type:
```

Example 2-2: DBViewer Program (continued)

```
              " + allTables.getString("TABLE_TYPE"));
          System.out.println("Indexes: ");

          // Get a list of all the indexes for this table
          ResultSet indexList =
                       dbmd.getIndexInfo(null,null,table_name,false,false);
          while(indexList.next()) {
            System.out.println(" Index Name:
                       "+indexList.getString("INDEX_NAME"));
            System.out.println(" Column Name:
                       "+indexList.getString("COLUMN_NAME"));
          }
          indexList.close();
        }

      allTables.close();
      con.close();
    }
    catch (ClassNotFoundException e) {
      System.out.println("Unable to load database driver class");
    }
    catch (SQLException e) {
      System.out.println("SQL Exception: " + e.getMessage());
    }
  }
}
```

Here's some sample output when this program is run against a Microsoft Access database via the JDBC-ODBC bridge (snipped slightly to prevent several pages of uninteresting text):

```
--- Database Viewer ---
Driver Name: JDBC-ODBC Bridge (odbcjt32.dll)
Database Product: ACCESS
SQL Keywords Supported:
 ALPHANUMERIC
 AUTOINCREMENT
 BINARY
 BYTE
 FLOAT8
 ...
Table Name: Customers
Table Type: TABLE
Indexes:
 Index Name: PrimaryKey
 Column Name:CustNo
 Index Name: AddressIndex
 Column Name:Address
 ...
```

ResultSetMetaData

The ResultSetMetaData interface provides information about the structure of a
particular ResultSet. Data provided by ResultSetMetaData includes the number of
available columns, the names of those columns, and the kind of data available in
each. Example 2-3 shows a short program that displays the contents of a table and
shows the data type for each column.

Example 2-3: TableViewer Program

```
import java.sql.*;
import java.util.StringTokenizer;

public class TableViewer {

    final static String jdbcURL = "jdbc:oracle:customerdb";
    final static String jdbcDriver = "oracle.jdbc.driver.OracleDriver";
    final static String table = "CUSTOMERS";

    public static void main(java.lang.String[] args) {

        System.out.println("--- Table Viewer ---");

        try {
            Class.forName(jdbcDriver);
            Connection con = DriverManager.getConnection(jdbcURL, "", "");
            Statement stmt = con.createStatement();
            ResultSet rs = stmt.executeQuery("SELECT * FROM "+ table);

            ResultSetMetaData rsmd = rs.getMetaData();
            int columnCount = rsmd.getColumnCount();
            for(int col = 1; col <= columnCount; col++) {
                System.out.print(rsmd.getColumnLabel(col));
                System.out.print(" (" + rsmd.getColumnTypeName(col)+")");
                if(col < columnCount)
                    System.out.print(", ");
            }
            System.out.println();

            while(rs.next()) {
                for(int col = 1; col <= columnCount; col++) {
                    System.out.print(rs.getString(col));
                    if(col < columnCount)
                        System.out.print(", ");
                }
                System.out.println();
            }

            rs.close();
            stmt.close();
            con.close();
        }
```

Example 2-3: TableViewer Program (continued)

```
    catch (ClassNotFoundException e) {
      System.out.println("Unable to load database driver class");
    }
    catch (SQLException e) {
      System.out.println("SQL Exception: " + e.getMessage());
    }
  }
}
```

The key methods used here are getColumnCount( ), getColumnLabel( ), and getColumnTypeName( ). Note that type names returned by getColumnTypeName( ) are database-specific (e.g., Oracle refers to a string value as a VARCHAR; Microsoft Access calls it TEXT). Here's some sample output for TableViewer:

```
--- Table Viewer ---
CustNo (SHORT), CustName (VARCHAR), CustAddress (VARCHAR)
1, Jane Markham, 12 Stevens St
2, Louis Smith, 45 Morrison Lane
3, Woodrow Lang, 4 Times Square
```

Transactions

A *transaction* is a group of several operations that must behave atomically, i.e., as if they are a single, indivisible operation. With regards to databases, transactions allow you to combine one or more database actions into a single atomic unit. If you have an application that needs to execute multiple SQL statements to fulfill one goal (say, an inventory management system that needs to move items from an INVENTORY table to a SHIPPING table), you probably want to use JDBC's transaction services to accomplish the goal.

Working with a transaction involves the following steps: start the transaction, perform its component operations, and then either commit the transaction if all the component operations succeed or roll it back if one of the operations fails. The ability to roll back a transaction is the key feature. This means that if any one SQL statement fails, the entire operation fails, and it is as though none of the component operations took place. Therefore it is impossible to end up with a situation where, for example, the INVENTORY table has been debited, but the SHIPPING table has not been credited.

Another issue with transactions and databases concerns changes to the database becoming visible to the rest of the system. Transactions can operate at varying levels of isolation from the rest of the database. At the most isolated level, the results of all the component SQL statements become visible to the rest of the system only when the transaction is committed. In other words, nobody sees the reduced inventory before the shipping data is updated.

The Connection object in JDBC is responsible for transaction management. With JDBC, you are always using transactions in some form. By default, a new connection starts out in transaction auto-commit mode, which means that every SQL statement is executed as an individual transaction that is immediately committed to the database.

To perform a transaction that uses multiple statements, you have to call the setAutoCommit() method with a false argument. (You can check the status of auto-commit with the getAutoCommit() method.) Now you can execute the SQL statements that comprise your transaction. When you are done, call the commit() method to commit the transaction or the rollback() method to undo it. Here's an example:

```
try {
  con.setAutoCommit(false);
  // run some SQL
  stmt.executeUpdate("UPDATE INVENTORY SET ONHAND = 10 WHERE ID = 5");
  stmt.executeUpdate("INSERT INTO SHIPPING (QTY) VALUES (5)");
  con.commit();
}
catch (SQLException e) {
  con.rollback(); //undo the results of the transaction
}
```

When auto-commit is set to false, you must remember to call commit() (or rollback()) at the end of each transaction, or your changes will be lost.

JDBC supports a number of transaction isolation modes that allow you to control how the database deals with transaction conflicts—in other words, who sees what when. JDBC defines five modes, some of which may not be supported by all databases. The default mode varies depending on the underlying database and driver. Higher isolation levels yield poorer performance. Here are the five standard options, which are defined as integer constants in the Connection interface:

TRANSACTION_NONE
    Transactions are either disabled or not supported.

TRANSACTION_READ_UNCOMMITTED
    Minimal transaction support that allows dirty reads. In other words, other transactions can see the results of a transaction's SQL statements before the transaction commits itself. If you roll back your transaction, other transactions may be left with invalid data.

TRANSACTION_READ_COMMITTED
    Transactions are prevented from reading rows with uncommitted changes; in other words, dirty reads aren't allowed.

TRANSACTION_REPEATABLE_READ
    Protects against repeatable reads as well as dirty reads. Say one transaction reads a row that is subsequently altered (and committed) by another transaction. If the first transaction reads the row again, the first transaction doesn't get a different value the second time around. The new data is visible to the first transaction only after it calls commit() and performs another read.

TRANSACTION_SERIALIZABLE
    Provides all the support of TRANSACTION_REAPEATABLE_READ and guards against row insertions as well. Say one transaction reads a set of rows, and then another transaction adds a row to the set. If the first transaction reads the set again, it doesn't see the newly added row. Put another way, this level of isolation forces the database to treat transactions as if they occurred one at a time.

Transaction isolation modes are set by the setTransactionIsolation() method. For example:

```
con.setTransactionIsolation(TRANSACTION_READ_COMMITTED);
```

You can use the DatabaseMetaData class to determine the transaction support of the underlying database. The most useful methods are getDefaultTransaction-Isolation(), supportsTransactions(), supportsTransactionIsolationLevel(), and supportsDataDefinitionAndDataManipulationTransactions() (which may well be the longest method name in the Java API).

An application that uses transactions is a prime candidate for also using a connection pool (available in JDBC 2.0). Since each database transaction requires its own Connection object, an application that performs multiple simultaneous transactions (for instance, spawning threads that perform database updates) needs multiple connections available. Maintaining a pool of connections is much more efficient than creating a new one whenever you need a new transaction.

Stored Procedures

Most RDBMS systems include some sort of internal programming language (e.g., Oracle's PL/SQL). These languages allow database developers to embed procedural application code directly within the database and then call that code from other applications. The advantage of this approach is that the code can be written just once and then used in multiple different applications (even with different platforms and languages). It also allows application code to be divorced from the underlying table structure. If stored procedures handle all of the SQL, and applications just call the procedures, only the stored procedures need to be modified if the table structure is changed later on.

Here is an Oracle PL/SQL stored procedure:*

```
CREATE OR REPLACE PROCEDURE sp_interest
(id IN INTEGER
bal IN OUT FLOAT) IS
BEGIN
SELECT balance
INTO bal
FROM accounts
WHERE account_id = id;

bal := bal + bal * 0.03;

UPDATE accounts
SET balance = bal
WHERE account_id = id;

END;
```

---

* If it looks familiar, that's because it is from George Reese's *Database Programming with JDBC* (O'Reilly).

This PL/SQL procedure takes two input values, an account ID and a balance, and returns an updated balance.

The `CallableStatement` interface is the JDBC object that supports stored procedures. The `Connection` class has a `prepareCall()` method that is very similar to the `prepareStatement()` method we used to create a `PreparedStatement`. Because each database has its own syntax for accessing stored procedures, JDBC defines a standardized escape syntax for accessing stored procedures with `CallableStatement`. The syntax for a stored procedure that doesn't return a result set is:

```
{call procedure_name[(?[,?...])]}
```

The syntax for a stored procedure that returns a result is:

```
{? = call procedure_name[(?[,?...])]}
```

In this syntax, each question mark (?) represents a placeholder for a procedure parameter or a return value. Note that the parameters are optional. The JDBC driver is responsible for translating the escape syntax into the database's own stored procedure syntax.

Here's a code fragment that uses `CallableStatement` to run the `sp_interest` stored procedure:

```
CallableStatment cstmt = con.prepareCall("{call sp_interest(?,?)}");
cstmt.registerOutParameter(2, Types.FLOAT);
cstmt.setInt(1, accountID);
cstmt.setFloat(2, 2343.23);
cstmt.execute();
out.println("New Balance:" + cstmt.getFloat(2));
```

In this example, we first create a `CallableStatement` using the `prepareCall()` method and passing in the appropriate escape syntax for the stored procedure. Since this stored procedure has an output parameter (actually, in this case, an IN OUT parameter, which means it also serves as an input parameter), we use the `registerOutParameter()` method to identify that parameter as an output of type FLOAT. Note that just as with prepared statements, substituted parameters are numbered from 1 to n, left to right. Any time you have an output parameter in a stored procedure, you need to register its type using `registerOutParameter()` before you execute the stored procedure.

Next we set the two input parameters, the account ID and the balance, using the appropriate `setXXX()` methods. Finally, we execute the stored procedure and then use the `getFloat()` method to display the new balance. The `getXXX()` methods of `CallableStatement` are similar to those of the `ResultSet`.

You need to use `CallableStatement` only with stored procedures that have output values, such as the one we just saw. You can use either of the other statement objects to execute stored procedures that take parameters but don't return anything.

Escape Sequences

Escape sequences allow JDBC programs to package certain database commands in a database-independent manner. Since different databases implement different features (especially scalar SQL functions) in different ways, in order to be truly portable, JDBC needs to provide a standard way to access at least a subset of that functionality. We've already seen escape sequences twice: with the various SQL date and time functions, and with the CallableStatement object.

A JDBC escape sequence consists of a pair of curly braces, a keyword, and a set of parameters. Thus, call is the keyword for stored procedures, while d, t, and ts are keywords for dates and times. One keyword we haven't seen yet is escape. This keyword specifies the character that is used to escape wildcard characters in a LIKE statement:

```
stmt.executeQuery(
    "SELECT * FROM ApiDocs WHERE Field_Name like 'TRANS\_%' {escape '\'}");
```

Normally, the underscore (_) character is treated as a single-character wildcard, while the percent sign (%) is the multiple-character wildcard. By specifying the backslash (\) as the escape character, we can match on the underscore character itself. Note that the escape keyword can also be used outside wildcard searches. For example, SQL string termination characters (such as the single quote) need to be escaped when appearing within strings.

The fn keyword allows the use of internal scalar database functions. Scalar functions are a fairly standard component of most database architectures, even though the actual implementations vary. For instance, many databases support the SOUNDEX(string) function, which translates a character string into a numerical representation of its sound. Another function, DIFFERENCE(string1, string2), computes the difference between the soundex values for two strings. If the values are close enough, you can assume the two words sound the same ("Beacon" and "Bacon"). If your database supports DIFFERENCE, you can use it by executing a SQL statement that looks like this:

```
{fn DIFFERENCE("Beacon", "Bacon")}
```

Available scalar functions differ depending on the database being used. Also, some drivers, such as Oracle's, don't support the {fn} escape mechanism at all.

The last escape keyword is oj, which is used for outer joins. The syntax is simply:

```
{oj outer-join}
```

Outer joins aren't supported by some databases and are sufficiently complex (and unrelated to the JDBC API per se) as to be beyond the scope of this chapter. For more information, consult the SQL documentation for your database.

Note that when performance is an issue, you can use the setEscapeProcessing() method of Statement to turn off escape-sequence processing.

The JDBC Optional Package

The javax.sql package is an optional extension of the JDBC 2.1 API. It includes support for a variety of enterprise-development activities. It's a standard component of the J2EE platform, and the supporting classes can also be downloaded separately for use with any Java 2 system.

DataSource Objects

The DataSource interface provides an alternative to the DriverManager class and conventional JDBC URLs. Instead, information about a database is stored within a naming service and retrieved via the JNDI API. Connection information (drivers, server locations, and so forth) are stored within the DataSource object, which uses them to create the actual Connection object used to execute JDBC commands. DataSource objects are also used to provide native driver-level support for connection pooling and distributed transactions.

Each DataSource is assigned a logical name, by convention beginning with "jdbc/". The logical name and associated connection metadata are configured in the J2EE setup process. This makes code more portable and allows for easy changes in drivers and connection information. Accessing a DataSource via JNDI is very simple:

```
Context ctx = new InitialContext();
DataSource ds = (DataSource)ctx.lookup("jdbc/CamelDB");
Connection con = ds.getConnection("lawrence", "arabia");
```

The first two lines obtain the DataSource object from the naming service. The getConnection() method of DataSource then logs into the database and returns a Connection object. Unlike DriverManager, the only information required is a username and password.

Connection pooling

The ConnectionPoolDataSource provides a transparent interface to a "pool" of available Connection objects. When using a connection pool, the JVM creates a set of connections and distributes them to programs as needed (often on a per-thread basis). Once a connection has been used, it is returned to the pool to be reused later. This eliminates the substantial overhead of creating a new Connection for each request (a delay that can often be measured in seconds). For applications that make intensive use of database connections over extended periods, such as Java servlets (see Chapter 5), this added efficiency can be vital.

Like regular DataSources, connection pools are configured by the J2EE server administrator, and must be supported by the database driver itself. Developers need only to remember to explicitly close all Connection objects after use, which is good programming practice anyway. The best way to handle this is via a try... catch...finally block:

```
Connection con = null;
try {
 ds = (DataSource)cvs.lookup("jdbc/oasisDB");
 con = ds.getConnection("larry1", "camel");
 // ... some worthwhile action
} catch (Exception e) {
} finally {
```

```
        if(con != null)
            con.close();
    }
```

It is also possible to perform connection pooling without the JDBC Optional Packages. An excellent open source connection pool, in use since 1998, is available from JavaExchange at *http://www.javaexchange.com*. It allows failure-tolerant pooling of connections using any JDBC driver.

Distributed transactions

With appropriate driver support, the XADataSource interface can also be used to create connections supporting distributed transactions. Like pooled connections, the DataSource must be configured by the administrator of the J2EE environment.

While connections supporting distributed transactions are nearly indistinguishable from regular connections, there is a functional difference: auto-commit mode defaults to off, and when a connection is used within a distributed transaction, the rollback(), commit(), and setAutoCommit() methods should not be called.

Connections received from an XADataSource may be used for nondistributed transactions as well. All of the usual transaction management commands may be used in a nondistributed transaction.

RowSets

The JDBC 2.0 optional package also includes a new RowSet interface. A RowSet, as the name implies, encapsulates a set of rows produced by a query. Since a RowSet is a JavaBean, it can be used easily in a graphical development environment.

The J2EE environment doesn't ship with any RowSet implementations, but Sun has made a number available at *http://developer.java.sun.com/developer/earlyAccess/ crs/index.html*. Here's how to use the simplest of these, JdbcRowSet, which simply encapsulates a ResultSet:

```
sun.jdbc.rowset.JdbcRowSet jdbcRowSet
    = new sun.jdbc.rowset.JdbcRowSet();
jdbcRowSet.setCommand("SELECT * FROM CUSTOMERS WHERE CUSTNO = ?");
jdbcRowSet.setUrl("jdbc:oracle:thin:@dbhost.co.com:1521:ORCL");
jdbcRowSet.setUsername("SAMSON");
jdbcRowSet.setPassword("DELILAH");
jdbcRowSet.setType(ResultSet.TYPE_SCROLL_INSENSITIVE);
jdbcRowSet.setConcurrency(ResultSet.CONCUR_UPDATABLE);
jdbcRowSet.setInt(1, 10);
jdbcRowSet.execute();

jdbcRowSet.first();
System.out.println(jdbcRowSet.getString(1));
jdbcRowSet.last();
System.out.println(jdbcRowSet.getString(1));

jdbcRowSet.close();
```

The getXXX and setXXX methods are the same as in the ResultSet interface. Support for scrollable and updateable row sets depends on the underlying driver and database implementation.

The addRowSetListener() method of RowSet can be used to register other components as listeners. They must implement the RowSetListener interface to be implemented.

The sun.jdbc.rowset package also contains a CachedRowSet object that will hold a ResultSet independently of the originating JDBC connection.

```
Connection con = DriverManager.getConnection(dbURL, dbUser, dbPassword);
Statement stmt = con.createStatement();
ResultSet rs = stmt.executeQuery("SELECT * FROM CUSTOMERS");
CachedRowSet crs = new CachedRowSet();
crs.populate(rs);
rs.close();
stmt.close();
crs.next();
System.out.println(crs.getString("CUSTNAME"));
```

In order to update a CachedRowSet, you must set the JDBC connection information and specify the underlying SQL via the setCommand() method. Now, let's continue our code sample:

```
crs.setUrl(dbURL);
crs.setUsername(dbUser);
crs.setPassword(dbPassword);
crs.setCommand("SELECT * FROM CUSTOMERS");
//...
crs.setString("CUSTNAME", "John Smith");
crs.updateRow();
crs.moveToCurrentRow();
crs.acceptChanges();
```

Note that we call the acceptChanges() method after performing our update. This is necessary to propagate the changes back to the original datasource.

The final RowSet available from Sun is the WebRowSet, which is identical to the CachedRowSet but has a persistence engine based on XML.

While a RowSet object would generally be used with JDBC, there is no actual requirement that this be so. RowSet implementations could be written to act against tabular data, text files, and more esoteric storage mechanisms.

JDBC 3.0

At the time of this writing, Version 3.0 of the JDBC API was in its fourth proposed final draft, and was on target for inclusion in J2SE and J2EE Version 1.4. JDBC 3.0 adds increased support for SQL99 features, increasingly capable transaction support, full read/write handling of BLOB and CLOB fields, URL datatypes, and various minor enhancements to the rest of the API. JDBC 3.0 adds a number of methods to the DatabaseMetaData interface, allowing programmers to determine which new features are supported.

JDBC 3.0 is also intended to integrate well with the J2EE Connector standard, allowing drivers and configuration information to be packaged into a Resource adapter ARchive, or RAR file. This allows easier deployment of JDBC connections into a J2EE server, but doesn't change the way programmers interact with the API.

Savepoints

Savepoints allow transactions to be partially rolled back. If the underlying database and driver support the functionality, the new setSavepoint(String name) method of Connection creates a named savepoint in the current transaction, and returns an object implementing the Savepoint interface. The object can be passed to the rollback() method of Connection to roll back all components of the current transaction that took place after the setSavepoint() method was called:

```
Statement stmt = con.createStatement();
stmt.executeUpdate("delete from clients");
stmt.executeUpdate("insert into clients (NAME, ID) values ('Charles
Babbage', 1)");
Savepoint save = con.setSavepoint("INSERT_POINT");
stmt.executeUpdate("update clients set NAME = 'Ada Lovelace' where ID =
1");
con.rollback(save);
con.commit();
```

This example will leave the "clients" table with a single row, with a value of 1 in the ID column and "Charles Babbage" in the NAME column.

Savepoints can't be used in distributed transactions.

SQL99 Types

SQL99 added a number of new datatypes to the SQL92 standard that guided earlier versions of the JDBC specification. Out of these, JDBC 3.0 introduces the DATALINK type, which maps to a java.net.URL object. DATALINK fields can be retrieved from queries using the new getURL() method of ResultSet.

The SQL99 specification also defines BLOB and CLOB datatypes for Binary and Character Large Objects (LOBs). Initial support for BLOB and CLOB types was added in JDBC 2.0, but they were read-only. The java.sql.Blob interface now includes a setBytes() method to alter the BLOB's content, and the java.sql.Clob class includes a setString() method.

It's up to the driver whether to update a local copy of the LOB or to directly update the copy in the database. The locatorsUpdateCopy() method of DatabaseMetaData will tell you which approach is used by your driver. If the method returns true, you'll need to issue a separate update statement to commit the changes to the LOB back to the database. To insert data in a new BLOB or CLOB field, first create a row with an empty LOB, select the row, retrieve the LOB, edit its contents, and write it back if necessary.

Modified Blob and Clob objects can be passed to the setBlob() and setClob() methods of PreparedStatement, and to the new updateBlob() and updateClob() methods of ResultSet (for updateable result sets).

CHAPTER 3

Remote Method Invocation

This chapter examines the Java Remote Method Invocation (RMI) API—Java's native scheme for creating and using remote objects. Java RMI provides the following elements:

- Remote object implementations

- Client interfaces, or stubs, to remote objects

- A remote object registry for finding objects on the network

- A facility for automatically creating (activating) remote objects on-demand

- A network protocol for communication between remote objects and their client

Each of these elements (except the last one) has a Java interface defined for it within the java.rmi package and its subpackages, which comprise the RMI API. Using these interfaces, you can develop remote objects and the clients that use them to create a distributed application that resides on hosts across the network.

Introduction to RMI

RMI is the distributed object system that is built into the core Java environment. You can think of RMI as a built-in facility for Java that allows you to interact with objects that are actually running in Java virtual machines on remote hosts on the network. With RMI (and other distributed object APIs we discuss in this book), you can get a reference to an object that "lives" in a remote process and invokes methods on it as if it were a local object running within the same virtual machine as your code (hence the name, "Remote Method Invocation API").

Another way to characterize RMI (and other remote object schemes) is in terms of the granularity of the distribution that it enables. The Java servlet and JavaServer Page (JSP) APIs, described in Chapters 5 and 6, allow you to distribute applications at the view level. Putting a servlet or JSP front-end on your server-side object model serves to export a web-based (typically HTML) interface to your application, which any remote web browser can access. The Java networking APIs, embodied in the java.net and java.io packages, allow you to open up very narrow, low-level data connections to your Java process, for simple data exchanges or "heartbeat" purposes (make a successful connection and transmit a few bytes to confirm that a process is alive). RMI and other remote object systems fall somewhere in-between the two. They allow you to export functionality at the object level, allowing remote clients to interact directly with individual objects, in the same way they do with local objects: using (remote) method calls.

RMI was added to the core Java API in Version 1.1 of the JDK (and enhanced for Version 1.2 of the Java 2 platform), in recognition of the critical need for support for distributed objects in distributed-application development. Prior to RMI and other remote object schemes, writing a distributed application involved basic socket programming, in which a "raw" communication channel was used to pass messages and data between two remote processes. Now, with RMI and distributed objects, you can "export" an object as a remote object, so that other remote processes/agents can access it directly as a Java object. So, instead of defining a low-level message protocol and data transmission format between processes in your distributed application, use Java interfaces as the "protocol" and the exported method arguments become the data transmission format. The distributed object system (RMI in this case) handles all the underlying networking needed to make your remote method calls work.

Java RMI is normally a Java-only distributed object scheme; if you are using the default RMI communication protocol (Java Remote Method Protocol, or JRMP), objects in an RMI-based distributed application have to be implemented in Java. Some other distributed object schemes, most notably CORBA, are language-independent, which means that the objects can be implemented in any language that has a defined binding. With CORBA, for example, bindings exist for C, C++, Java, Smalltalk, and Ada, among other languages.

The advantages of RMI primarily revolve around the fact that it is "Java-native." Since RMI is part of the core Java API and is built to work directly with Java objects within the Java VM, the integration of its remote object facilities into a Java application is almost seamless. You really can use RMI-enabled objects as if they live in the local Java environment. And since Java RMI is built on the assumption that both the client and server are Java objects, RMI can extend the internal garbage-collection mechanisms of the standard Java VM to provide distributed garbage collection of remotely exported objects.

If you have a distributed application with heterogeneous components, some of which are written in Java and some which aren't, you have a few choices. You can use RMI, wrapping the non-Java code with RMI-enabled Java objects using the Java Native Interface (JNI). At the end of this chapter, we discuss this first option in some detail, to give you a feeling for where it could be useful and where it wouldn't. Another option is to use another object distribution scheme, such as CORBA, that supports language-independent object interfaces. Chapter 4 covers the Java interface to CORBA that is included in the Java 2 SDK. A third option involves using RMI/IIOP, which allows RMI objects to communicate directly with remote CORBA objects (implemented in any language supported by CORBA) over IIOP. We discuss this option in some detail at the end of this chapter.

RMI in Action

Before we start examining the details of using RMI, let's look at a simple RMI remote object at work. We can create an Account object that represents some kind of bank account and then use RMI to export it as a remote object so that remote clients (e.g., ATMs, personal finance software running on a PC, etc.) can access it and carry out transactions.

The first step is to define the interface for our remote object. Example 3-1 shows the Account interface. You can tell that it's an RMI object because it extends the java.rmi.Remote interface. Another signal that this is meant for remote access is that each method can throw a java.rmi.RemoteException. The Account interface includes methods to get the account name and balance, and to make deposits, withdrawals, and transfers.

Example 3-1: A Remote Account Interface

```
import java.rmi.Remote;
import java.rmi.RemoteException;
import java.util.List;

public interface Account extends java.rmi.Remote {
    // Get the name on the account
    public String getName() throws RemoteException;
    // Get current balance
    public float getBalance() throws RemoteException;
    // Take some money away
    public void withdraw(float amt) throws RemoteException;
    // Put some money in
    public void deposit(float amt) throws RemoteException;
    // Move some money from one account into this one
    public void transfer(float amt, Account src)
        throws RemoteException, InsufficientFundsException;
    // Make a number of transfers from other accounts into this one
    public void transfer(List amts, List srcs)
        throws RemoteException, InsufficientFundsException;
}
```

The next step is to create an implementation of this interface, which leads to the AccountImpl class shown in Example 3-2. This class implements all the methods listed in the Account interface and adds a constructor that takes the name of the new account to be created. Notice that the AccountImpl class implements the Account interface, but it also extends the java.rmi.UnicastRemoteObject class. The UnicastRemoteObject class provides some of the basic remote functionality for server objects.

Example 3-2: Implementation of the Remote Account Interface

```java
import java.rmi.server.UnicastRemoteObject;
import java.rmi.RemoteException;
import java.util.List;
import java.util.ListIterator;

public class AccountImpl extends UnicastRemoteObject implements Account {
  // Our current balance
  private float mBalance = 0;
  // Name on account
  private String mName = "";
  // Create a new account with the given name
  }

  public String getName() throws RemoteException {
    return mName;
  }
  public float getBalance() throws RemoteException {
    return mBalance;
  }
  // Withdraw some funds
  public void withdraw(float amt) throws RemoteException {
    mBalance -= amt;
    // Make sure balance never drops below zero
    mBalance = Math.max(mBalance, 0);

    // Log transaction...
    System.out.println("--> Withdrew " + amt + " from account " + getName());
    System.out.println("    New balance: " + getBalance());
  }
  // Deposit some funds
  public void deposit(float amt) throws RemoteException {
    mBalance += amt;
    // Log transaction...
    System.out.println("--> Deposited " + amt +
                                        " into account " + getName());
    System.out.println("    New balance: " + getBalance());
  }
  // Move some funds from another (remote) account into this one
  public void transfer(float amt, Account src)
    throws RemoteException, InsufficientFundsException {
    if (checkTransfer(src, this, amt)) {
      src.withdraw(amt);
      this.deposit(amt);
      // Log transaction...
      System.out.println(
              "--> Transferred " + amt + " from account " + getName());
      System.out.println("    New balance: " + getBalance());
    }
    else {
```

Example 3-2: Implementation of the Remote Account Interface (continued)

```
      throw new InsufficientFundsException(
        "Source account balance is less " + "than the requested transfer.");
    }
  }
  // Make several transfers from other (remote) accounts into this one
  public void transfer(List amts, List srcs)
    throws RemoteException, InsufficientFundsException {
    ListIterator amtCurs = amts.listIterator();
    ListIterator srcCurs = srcs.listIterator();
    // Iterate through the accounts and the amounts to be
    // transferred from each (assumes amounts are given as Float
    // objects)
    while (amtCurs.hasNext() && srcCurs.hasNext()) {
      Float amt = (Float)amtCurs.next();
      Account src = (Account)srcCurs.next();
      // Make the transaction
      this.transfer(amt.floatValue(), src);
    }
  }
  // Check to see if transfer is possible, given the two accounts involved
  private boolean checkTransfer(Account src, Account dest, float amt) {
    boolean approved = false;
    try {
      if (src.getBalance() >= amt) {
        approved = true;
      }
    }
    catch (RemoteException re) {
      // If some remote exception occurred, then the transfer is still
      // compromised, so return false
      approved = false;
    }
    return approved;
  }
}
```

Once the remote interface and an implementation of it are complete, you need to compile both Java files with your favorite Java compiler. After this is done, use the RMI stub/skeleton compiler to generate a client stub and a server skeleton for the AccountImpl object. The stub and skeleton compiler handle the communication between the client application and the server object. With Sun's Java SDK, the RMI compiler is called *rmic*, and you can invoke it for this example like so:

```
% rmic -d /home/classes AccountImpl
```

The stub and skeleton classes are generated and stored in the directory given by the -d option (*/home/classes*, in this case). This examples assume that the AccountImpl class and the */home/classes* directory are already in your CLASSPATH before you run the RMI compiler.

There's just one more thing we need to do before we can actually use our remote object: register it with an RMI registry, so that remote clients can find it on the network. The utility class that follows, AccountReg, does this by creating an

`AccountImpl` object and then binding it to a name in the local registry using the `java.rmi.Naming` interface. After it's done registering the object, the class goes into a `wait()`, which allows remote clients to connect to the remote object:

```java
import java.rmi.Naming;

public class AccountReg {
  public static void main(String argv[]) {
    try {
      // Make an Account with a given name
      AccountImpl acct = new AccountImpl("Jim.Farley");

      // Register it with the local naming registry
      Naming.rebind("JimF", acct);
      System.out.println("Registered account.");
    }
    catch (Exception e) {
      e.printStackTrace();

    }
  }
}
```

After you compile the `AccountReg` class, you can run its `main()` method to register an `Account` with the local RMI registry. First, however, you need to start the registry. With Sun's Java SDK, the registry can be started using the *rmiregistry* utility. On a Unix machine, this can be done like so:

```
objhost% rmiregistry &
```

Once the registry is started, you can invoke the `main()` method on the `AccountReg` class simply by running it:

```
objhost% java AccountReg
Registered account.
```

Now we have a remote `Account` object that is ready and waiting for a client to access it and call its methods. The following client code does just this, by first looking up the remote `Account` object using the `java.rmi.Naming` interface (and assuming that the `Account` object was registered on a machine named *objhost.org*), and then calling the deposit method on the `Account` object:

```java
import java.rmi.Naming;

public class AccountClient {
  public static void main(String argv[]) {
    try {
      // Lookup account object
      Account jimAcct = (Account)Naming.lookup("rmi://objhost.org/JimF");

      // Make deposit
      jimAcct.deposit(12000);

      // Report results and balance.
      System.out.println("Deposited 12,000 into account owned by " +
                          jimAcct.getName());
```

```
      System.out.println("Balance now totals: " + jimAcct.getBalance());
    }
    catch (Exception e) {
      System.out.println("Error while looking up account:");
      e.printStackTrace();
    }
  }
}
```

The first time you run this client, here's what you'd do:

```
% java AccountClient
Deposited 12,000 into account owned by Jim.Farley
Balance now totals: 12000.0
```

For the sake of this example, we assume that the client process is running on a machine with all the necessary classes available locally (the Account interface and the stub classes generated from the AccountImpl implementation). This makes running the example much simpler, and is the way we suggest you try the examples initially. Later in the chapter, we'll see how to deal with loading these classes remotely and dynamically, when the client doesn't necessarily have them locally.

RMI Architecture

Now that we've seen a complete example of an RMI object in action, let's look at what makes remote objects work, starting with an overview of the underlying RMI architecture. There are three layers that comprise the basic remote-object communication facilities in RMI:

Stub/skeleton layer
> Provides the interface that client and server application objects use to interact with each other.

Remote reference layer
> The middleware between the stub/skeleton layer and the underlying transport protocol. This layer handles the creation and management of remote object references.

Transport protocol layer
> The binary data protocol that sends remote object requests over the wire.

These layers interact with each other as shown in Figure 3-1. In this figure, the server is the application that provides remotely accessible objects, while the client is any remote application that communicates with these server objects.

In a distributed object system, the distinctions between clients and servers can get pretty blurry at times. Consider the case where one process registers a remote-enabled object with the RMI naming service, and a number of remote processes are accessing it. We might be tempted to call the first process the server and the other processes the clients. But what if one of the clients calls a method on the remote object, passing a reference to an RMI object that's local to the client. Now the server has a reference to and is using an object exported from the client, which turns the tables somewhat. The "server" is really the server for one object and the client of another object, and the "client" is a client and a server, too. For the sake of discussion, we refer to a process in a distributed application as a server or client if its role in the overall system is generally limited to one or the other. In peer-to-peer systems, where there is no clear client or server, we refer to elements of the system in terms of application-specific roles (e.g., chat participant, chat facilitator).

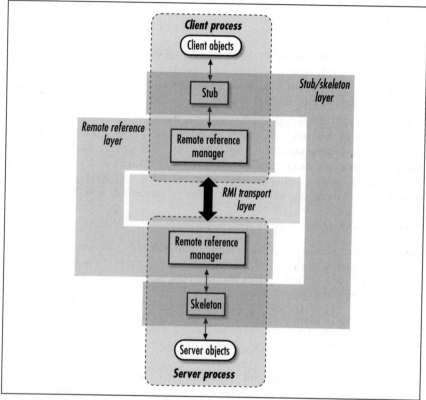

Figure 3-1: The RMI runtime architecture

As you can see in Figure 3-1, a client makes a request of a remote object using a client-side stub; the server object receives this request from a server-side object skeleton. A client initiates a remote method invocation by calling a method on a stub object. The stub maintains an internal reference to the remote object it represents and forwards the method invocation request through the remote reference layer by *marshalling* the method arguments into serialized form and asking the remote reference layer to forward the method request and arguments to the appropriate remote object. Marshalling involves converting local objects into portable form so that they can be transmitted to a remote process. Each object is checked as it is marshaled, to determine whether it implements the java.rmi.Remote interface. If it does, its remote reference is used as its marshaled data. If it isn't a Remote object, the argument is serialized into bytes that are sent to the remote host and reconstituted into a copy of the local object. If the argument is neither Remote nor Serializable, the stub throws a java.rmi.MarshalException back to the client.

If the marshalling of method arguments succeeds, the client-side remote reference layer receives the remote reference and marshaled arguments from the stub. This layer converts the client request into low-level RMI transport requests according to the type of remote object communication being used. In RMI, remote objects can (potentially) run under several different communication styles, such as point-to-point object references, replicated objects, or multicast objects. The remote reference layer is responsible for knowing which communication style is in effect for a given remote object and generating the corresponding transport-level requests. In the current released version of RMI (bundled with Version 1.4 of Java 2), the only communication style provided out of the box is point-to-point object references, so this is the only style we'll discuss in this chapter. For a point-to-point communication, the remote reference layer constructs a single network-level request and sends it over the wire to the sole remote object that corresponds to the remote reference passed along with the request.

On the server, the server-side remote reference layer receives the transport-level request and converts it into a request for the server skeleton that matches the referenced object. The skeleton converts the remote request into the appropriate method call on the actual server object, which involves *unmarshalling* the method arguments into the server 'environment and passing them to the server object. As you might expect, unmarshalling is the inverse procedure to the marshalling process on the client. Arguments sent as remote references are converted into local stubs on the server, and arguments sent as serialized objects are converted into local copies of the originals.

If the method call generates a return value or an exception, the skeleton marshals the object for transport back to the client and forwards it through the server reference layer. This result is sent back using the appropriate transport protocol, where it passes through the client reference layer and stub, is unmarshaled by the stub, and is finally handed back to the client thread that invoked the remote method.

RMI Object Services

On top of its remote object architecture, RMI provides some basic object services you can use in your distributed application. These include an object naming/registry service, a remote object activation service, and distributed garbage collection.

Naming/registry service

When a server process wants to export some RMI-based service to clients, it does so by registering one or more RMI-enabled objects with its local RMI registry (represented by the Registry interface). Each object is registered with a name clients can use to reference it. A client can obtain a stub reference to the remote object by asking for the object by name through the Naming interface. The Naming. lookup() method takes the fully qualified name of a remote object and locates the object on the network. The object's fully qualified name is in a URL-like syntax that includes the name of the object's host and the object's registered name.

It's important to note that, although the Naming interface is a default naming service provided with RMI, the RMI registry can be tied into other naming services by vendors. Sun has provided a binding to the RMI registry through the Java Naming and Directory Interface (JNDI), for example. See Chapter 7 for more details on how JNDI can be used to look up objects (remote or otherwise).

Once the lookup() method locates the object's host, it consults the RMI registry on that host and asks for the object by name. If the registry finds the object, it generates a remote reference to the object and delivers it to the client process, where it is converted into a stub reference that is returned to the caller. Once the client has a remote reference to the server object, communication between the client and the server commences as described earlier. We'll talk in more detail about the Naming and Registry interfaces later in this chapter.

Object activation service

The remote object activation service was introduced to RMI in Version 1.2 of the Java 2 platform. It provides a way for server objects to be started on an as-needed basis. Without remote activation, a server object has to be registered with the RMI registry service from within a running Java virtual machine. A remote object registered this way is only available during the lifetime of the Java VM that registered it. If the server VM halts or crashes for some reason, the server object becomes unavailable and any existing client references to the object become invalid. Any further attempts by clients to call methods through these now-invalid references result in RMI exceptions being thrown back to the client.

The RMI activation service provides a way for a server object to be activated automatically when a client requests it. The activation service creates the server object dynamically within a new or existing virtual machine, and obtains a reference to this newly created object for the client that caused the activation. A server object that wants to be activated automatically needs to register an activation method with the RMI activation daemon running on its host. We'll discuss the RMI activation service in more detail later in the chapter.

Distributed garbage collection

The last of the remote object services, distributed garbage collection, is a fairly automatic process that you as an application developer should never have to worry about. Every server that contains RMI-exported objects automatically maintains a list of remote references to the objects it serves. Each client that requests and receives a reference to a remote object, either explicitly through the registry/naming service or implicitly as the result of a remote method call, is issued this remote object reference through the remote reference layer of the object's host process. The reference layer automatically keeps a record of this reference in the form of an expirable "lease" on the object. When the client is done with the reference and allows the remote stub to go out of scope, or when the lease on the object expires, the reference layer on the host automatically deletes the record of the remote reference and notifies the client's reference layer that this remote reference has expired. The concept of expirable leases, as opposed to strict on/off references, is used to deal with situations where a client-side failure or a network failure keeps the client from notifying the server that it is done with its reference to an object.

When an RMI object has no further remote references recorded in the remote reference layer, then its eligibility for garbage collection is based solely on its local references, like any other Java object. If there are also no local references to the object (this reference list is kept by the Java VM itself as part of its normal garbage-collection algorithm), the object is marked as garbage and picked up by the next run of the system garbage collector.

Defining Remote Objects

Now that you have a basic idea of how Java RMI works, we can explore the details of creating and using distributed objects with RMI in more detail. As mentioned earlier, defining a remote RMI object involves specifying a remote interface for the object, then providing a class that implements this interface. The remote interface and implementation class are then used by RMI to generate a client stub and server skeleton for your remote object. The communication between local objects and remote objects is handled using these client stubs and server skeletons. The relationships among stubs, skeletons, and the objects that use them are shown in Figure 3-2.

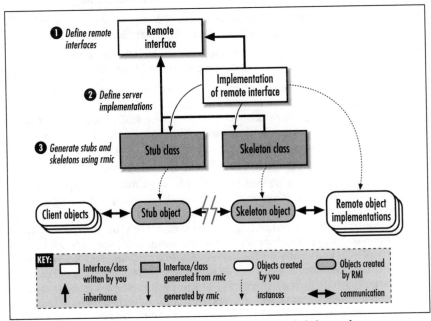

Figure 3-2: Relationships among remote object, stub, and skeleton classes

When a client gets a reference to a remote object (details on how this reference is obtained come later) and then calls methods on this object reference, there needs to be a way for the method request to get transmitted back to the actual object on the remote server and for the results of the method call to get transmitted back to the client. This is what the generated stub and skeleton classes are for. They act as the communication link between the client and your exported remote object, making it seem to the client that the object actually exists within its Java VM.

The RMI compiler (*rmic*) automatically generates these stub and skeleton classes for you. Based on the remote interface and implementation class you provide, *rmic* generates stub and skeleton classes that implement the remote interface and act as go-betweens for the client application and the actual server object. For the client stub class, the compiler generates an implementation of each remote method that simply packages up (marshals) the method arguments and transmits them to the server. For the server skeleton class, the RMI compiler generates another set of implementations of the remote methods, but these are designed to receive the method arguments from the remote method call, unpackage them, and make the corresponding method call on the object implementation. Whatever the method call generates (return data or an exception), the results are packaged and transmitted back to the remote client. The client stub method (which is still executing at this point) unpackages the results and delivers them to the client as the result of its remote method call.

So as we saw earlier in the chapter, the first step in creating your remote objects is to define the remote interfaces for the types of objects you need to use in a distributed object context. This isn't much different from defining the public interfaces in a nondistributed application, with the following exceptions:

- Every object you want to distribute using RMI has to directly or indirectly extend an interface that extends the java.rmi.Remote interface.

- Every method in the remote interface has to declare that it throws a java.rmi.RemoteException or one of the parent classes of RemoteException.*

RMI imposes the first requirement to allow it to differentiate quickly between objects that are enabled for remote distribution and those that aren't. As we've already seen, during a remote method invocation, the RMI runtime system needs to be able to determine whether each argument to the remote method is a Remote object or not. The Remote interface, which is simply a tag interface that marks remote objects, makes it easy to perform this check.

The second requirement is needed to deal with errors that can happen during a remote session. When a client makes a method call on a remote object, any number of errors can occur, preventing the remote method call from completing. These include client-side errors (e.g., an argument can't be marshaled), errors during the transport of data between client and server (e.g., the network connection is dropped), and errors on the server side (e.g., the method throws a local exception that needs to be sent back to the remote caller). The RemoteException class is used by RMI as a base exception class for any of the different types of problems that might occur during a remote method call. Any method you declare in a Remote interface is assumed to be remotely callable, so every method has to declare that it might throw a RemoteException, or one of its parent interfaces.

In Example 3-1 we saw the Account interface, a remote interface that declares six remote methods: getName(), getBalance(), withdraw(), deposit() and two forms

---

* Note that prior to Java 1.2, the RMI specification required that every method on a remote interface had to throw RemoteException specifically. As of Java 1.2, this was loosened to allow any superclass of RemoteException. One reason for this change is to make it easier to define generic interfaces that support both local and remote objects.

of transfer(). Since we want to use this interface in an RMI setting, we've declared that the interface extends the Remote interface. In addition, each method has arguments and return values that are either Remote or Serializable, and each method is declared as throwing a RemoteException.

With the remote interface defined, the next thing we need to do is write a class that implements the interface. We saw the implementation of the Account interface, the AccountImpl class, in Example 3-2. This class has implementations of the six remote methods defined in the Account interface; it also has a nonremote method, checkTransfer(), verify that a funds transfer between two accounts can be made. Notice that the checkTransfer() method doesn't have to be declared as throwing a RemoteException, since it isn't a remotely callable method. Only the methods that participate in the remote method protocol of the RMI runtime need to declare that they can throw RemoteExceptions or one of its parent exceptions. The methods in your implementation class that participate in the RMI runtime include implementations of any methods declared in the remote interface (withdraw(), transfer(), etc. in our example), and, if you're extending UnicastRemoteObject, any constructors on your implementation class. Any other methods you define in your implementation class (like checkTransfer()) are considered non-remote (i.e., they are only callable from within the local Java virtual machine where the object exists).

Constructors are required to have RemoteException in their throws clause because an RMI implementation class that extends UnicastRemoteObject is "exported" and made accessible to remote method invocations when it is constructed. The RemoteException in the throws clause of the constructor is required to cover any problems that may occur during the RMI export process. All of the constructors on UnicastRemoteObject throw RemoteException because they all call the static UnicastRemoteObject.exportObject() methods internally, so the Java compiler will force you to include RemoteException in the throws clause of your implementation class.

Key RMI Classes for Remote Object Implementations

You probably noticed that our AccountImpl class also extends the UnicastRemoteObject class. This is a class in the java.rmi.server package that extends java.rmi.server.RemoteServer, which itself extends java.rmi.server. RemoteObject, the base class for all RMI remote objects. There are four key classes related to writing server object implementations:

RemoteObject
> RemoteObject implements both the Remote and Serializable interfaces. Although the RemoteObject class is in the java.rmi.server package, it is used by both the client and server portions of a remote object reference. Both client stubs and server implementations are subclassed (directly or indirectly) from RemoteObject. A RemoteObject contains the remote reference for a particular remote object.
>
> RemoteObject is an abstract class that reimplements the equals(), hashCode(), and toString() methods inherited from Object in a way that makes sense and is practical for remote objects. The equals() method, for example, is

implemented to return `true` if the internal remote references of the two
`RemoteObject` objects are equal, (i.e., if they both point to the same server
object).

RemoteServer

RemoteServer is an abstract class that extends `RemoteObject`. It defines a set of
static methods that are useful for implementing server objects in RMI, and it
acts as a base class for classes that define various semantics for remote
objects. In principle, a remote object can behave according to a simple point-
to-point reference scheme; it can have replicated copies of itself scattered
across the network that need to be kept synchronized, or any number of
other scenarios. JDK 1.1 supported only point-to-point, nonpersistent remote
references with the `UnicastRemoteObject` class. The Java 2 SDK 1.2 introduced the RMI activation system, so current versions of the core Java API
include another subclass of `RemoteServer`: `Activatable`.

UnicastRemoteObject

This is a concrete subclass of `RemoteServer` that implements point-to-point
remote references over TCP/IP networks. These references are nonpersistent:
remote references to a server object are only valid during the lifetime of the
server object. Before the server object is created (inside a virtual machine
running on the host) or after the object has been destroyed, a client can't
obtain remote references to the object. In addition, if the virtual machine
containing the object exits (intentionally or otherwise), any existing remote
references on clients become invalid and generate `RemoteException` objects if
used.

Activatable

This concrete subclass of `RemoteServer` is part of the RMI object activation
facility and can be found in the `java.rmi.activation` package. It implements
a server object that supports persistent remote references. If a remote method
request is received on the server host for an `Activatable` object and the target
object is not executing at the time, the object can be started automatically by
the RMI activation daemon.

Creating the Stubs and Skeletons

After you define the remote Java interface and implementation class, compile them
into Java bytecodes using a standard Java compiler. Then you use the RMI stub/
skeleton compiler, *rmic*, to generate the stub and skeleton interfaces that are used
at either end of the RMI communication link, as was shown in Figure 3-1. In its
simplest form, you can run *rmic* with the fully qualified classname of your implementation class as the only argument. For example, once we've compiled the
Account and AccountImpl classes, we can generate the stubs and skeletons for the
remote Account object with the following command (Unix version):

```
% rmic AccountImpl
```

If the RMI compiler is successful, this command generates the stub and skeleton
classes, AccountImpl_Stub and AccountImpl_Skel, in the current directory. The
rmic compiler has additional arguments that let you specify where the generated
classes should be stored, whether to print warnings, etc. For example, if you want

the stub and skeleton classes to reside in the directory */usr/local/classes*, you can run the command using the -d option:

```
% rmic -d /usr/local/classes AccountImpl
```

This command generates the stub and skeleton classes in the specified directory. A full description of the *rmic* utility and its options is given in Chapter 13.

Accessing Remote Objects as a Client

Now that we've defined a remote object interface and its server implementation, and generated the stub and skeleton classes that RMI uses to establish the link between the server object and the remote client, it's time to look at how you make your remote objects available to remote clients.

The Registry and Naming Services

The first remote object reference in an RMI distributed application is typically obtained through the RMI registry facility and the Naming interface. Every host that wants to export remote references to local Java objects must be running an RMI registry daemon of some kind. A registry daemon listens (on a particular port) for requests from remote clients for references to objects served on that host. The standard Sun Java SDK distribution provides an RMI registry daemon, *rmiregistry*. This utility simply creates a Registry object that listens to a specified port and then goes into a wait loop, waiting for local processes to register objects with it or for clients to connect and look up RMI objects in its registry. You start the registry daemon by running the *rmiregistry* command, with an optional argument that specifies a port to listen to:

```
objhost% rmiregistry 5000 &
```

Without the port argument, the RMI registry daemon listens on port 1099. Typically, you run the registry daemon in the background (i.e., put an & at the end of the command on a Unix system or run start rmiregistry [*port*] in a DOS window on a Windows system), or run it as a service at startup.

Once the RMI registry is running on a host, you can register remote objects with it using one of these classes: the java.rmi.registry.Registry interface, the java.rmi.registry.LocateRegistry class, or the java.rmi.Naming class.

A Registry object represents an interface to a local or remote RMI object registry. The bind() and rebind() methods can register an object with a name in the local registry, where the name for an object can be any unique string. If you try to bind() an object to a name that has already been used, the registry throws an AlreadyBoundException. If you think that an object may already be bound to the name you want to register, use the rebind() method instead. You can remove an object binding using the unbind() method. Note that these three methods (bind(), rebind(), and unbind()) can be called only by clients running on the same host as the registry. If a remote client attempts to call these methods, the client receives a java.rmi.AccessException. You can locate a particular object in the registry using the lookup() method, while list() returns the names of all the objects registered with the local registry. Note that only Remote objects can be bound to names in the Registry. Remote objects are capable of supporting remote references. Standard Java classes aren't, so they can't be exported to remote clients through the Registry.

The LocateRegistry class provides a set of static methods a client can use to get references to local and remote registries, in the form of Registry objects. There are four versions of the static getRegistry() method, so that you can get a reference to either a local registry or a remote registry running on a particular host, listening to either the default port (1099) or a specified port. There's also a static createRegistry() method that takes a port number as an argument. This method starts a registry running within the current Java VM on the given local port and returns the Registry object it creates.

Using the LocateRegistry and Registry interfaces, we can register one of our AccountImpl remote objects on the local host with the following code:

```
AccountImpl server = new AccountImpl("Jim.Farley");
Registry localRegistry = LocateRegistry.getRegistry();
try {
  localRegistry.bind("JimF", server);
}
catch (RemoteException re) { // Handle failed remote operation }
catch (AlreadyBoundException abe) { // Already one there }
catch (AccessException ae) { // Shouldn't happen, but... }
```

If this operation is successful (i.e., it doesn't raise any exceptions), the local registry has an AccountImpl remote object registered under the name "JimF." Remote clients can now look up the object using a combination of the LocateRegistry and Registry interfaces, or take the simpler approach and use the Naming class.

The Naming class lets a client look up local and remote objects using a URL-like naming syntax. The URL of a registered RMI remote object is typically in the format shown in Figure 3-3. Notice that the only required element of the URL is the actual object name. The protocol defaults to *rmi:*, the hostname defaults to the local host, and the port number defaults to 1099. Note that the default Naming class provided with Sun's Java SDK accepts only the *rmi:* protocol on object URLs. If you attempt to use any other protocol, a java.net.MalformedURLException is thrown by the lookup() method.

Figure 3-3: Anatomy of an RMI object URL

If we have a client running on a remote host that wants to look up the AccountImpl we registered, and the AccountImpl object is running on a host named *rmiremote.farley.org*, the client can get a remote reference to the object with one line of code:

```
Account jimsAccount =
    (Account)Naming.lookup("rmi://rmiremote.farley.org/JimF");
```

If we have a client running on the same host as the `AccountImpl` object, the remote reference can be retrieved using the degenerate URL:

```
Account jimsAccount = (Account)Naming.lookup("JimF");
```

Alternately, you can use the `LocateRegistry` and `Registry` interfaces to look up the same object, using an extra line of code to find the remote `Registry` through the `LocateRegistry` interface:

```
Registry rmtRegistry = LocateRegistry.getRegistry("rmiremote.farley.
org");
Account jimsAccount =
    (Account)rmtRegistry.lookup("JimF");
```

When you look up objects through an actual `Registry` object, you don't have the option of using the URL syntax for the name, because you don't need it. The hostname and port of the remote host are specified when you locate the `Registry` through the `LocateRegistry` interface, and the RMI protocol is implied, so all you need is the registered name of the object. With the `Naming` class, you can reduce a remote object lookup to a single method call, but the name must now include the host, port number, and registered object name, bundled into a URL. Internally, the `Naming` object parses the host and port number from the URL for you, finds the remote `Registry` using the `LocateRegistry` interface, and asks the `Registry` for the remote object using the object name in the URL.

The principal use for the `Registry` and `Naming` classes in an RMI application is as a means to bootstrap your distributed application. A server process typically exports just a few key objects through its local RMI registry daemon. Clients look up these objects through the `Naming` facility to get remote references to them. Any other remote objects that need to be shared between the two processes can be exported through remote method calls.

Remote Method Arguments and Return Values

As already mentioned, a critical element of executing a remote method call is the marshalling and unmarshalling of the method arguments and, once the method has executed, the reverse marshalling and unmarshalling of the method's return value. RMI handles this process for you automatically, but you need to understand how different types of objects are transmitted from the method caller to the server object and back again. More importantly, you need to know which types of objects can't be used in remote method calls at all.

When you call a method on a remote object, the arguments to the method have to be serializable. That is, they need to be primitive Java data types (like `int`, `float`, etc.) or Java objects that implement `java.io.Serializable`. The same restriction applies to the return value of the remote method. This restriction is enforced at runtime, when you actually make the remote method call, rather than at compile time, when you generate the stubs and skeletons using the *rmic* compiler.

The RMI stub and skeleton layer decides how to send method arguments and return values over the network, based on whether a particular object is `Remote`, `Serializable`, or neither.

- If the object is a `Remote` object, a remote reference for the object is generated, and the reference is marshaled and sent to the remote process. The remote reference is received on the other end and converted into a stub for the original object. This process applies to both method arguments and return values.

- If the object is `Serializable` but not `Remote`, the object is serialized and streamed to the remote process in byte form. The receiver converts the bytes into a copy of the original object.

- If the method argument or return value is not serializable (i.e., it's not a primitive data type or an object that implements `Serializable`), the object can't be sent to the remote client, and a `java.rmi.MarshalException` is thrown.

The principal difference between remote and nonremote objects is that remote objects are sent *by reference*, while nonremote, serializable objects are sent *by copy*. In other words, a remote reference maintains a link to the original object it references, so changes can be made to the original object through the remote stub. If the server object calls update methods on an argument to a remote method, and you want the updates to be made on the original object on the client side, the argument needs to be a `Remote` object that automatically exports a stub to the server object. Similarly, if the return value of a remote method call is intended to be a reference to an object living on the server, the server implementation needs to ensure that the object returned is a `Remote` object.

It's important to consider, whenever you pass either a remote reference or a serializable object from one VM to another in a remote method argument, whether the classes needed to unmarshal the method argument are available on the other side of the method call. If the receiver of the remote method argument has the necessary class definitions (the remote interface and stub class for remote references or the actual class definition for serializable objects) in its local `CLASSPATH` or some other local `ClassLoader` context, then you're fine. If it doesn't, you need to configure things so that the receiver of the method call can dynamically load the needed classes from the caller. We discuss how this happens in the section "Dynamically Loaded Classes."

Factory Classes

When a reference to a remote object is obtained through the RMI registry and then used to request additional remote references, the registered remote object is often referred to as a *factory class*.

Factory classes are useful in distributed applications that use remote objects because in most cases you can't predict beforehand the kind and number of remote objects that will need to be shared between two processes. To make a remote object visible to clients through the RMI registry service, you need to explicitly create the object inside a Java VM on the server and then register that object using the `bind()` or `rebind()` method on the `Registry`. Using remote references obtained through method calls on factory objects, however, the client application can dynamically request the creation of new remote objects, without the objects being registered individually with the server registry.

As an example, suppose we're building a remote banking system, using the Account object we've been working with throughout this chapter. We want to set up a centralized server that provides account services to remote clients running on PCs, embedded in ATMs, etc. On the server, we could run an RMI registry, create an Account object for every account we have on record, and register each one with the RMI registry service using the account name. In this scheme, registering accounts with the RMI registry goes something like this:

```
Registry local = LocateRegistry.getRegistry();
local.bind("Abrams, John", new AccountImpl("John Abrams"));
local.bind("Barts, Homer", new AccountImpl("Homer Barts"));
    .
    .
    .
```

As you can imagine, this is quite unwieldy in practice. Starting the server can take a long time, as thousands of accounts need to be registered, many of them unnecessarily, since many accounts may not see any activity before the next downtime. More importantly, accounts that are created or closed during the server's lifetime somehow need to be added or removed from the RMI registry, as well as from the bank's database of accounts. A much more sensible approach is to define a factory class for Account objects, along the lines of the following interface:

```
import java.rmi.Remote;
import java.rmi.RemoteException;

public interface AccountManager extends Remote {
  public Account getAccount(String name) throws RemoteException;
  public boolean newAccount(Account s) throws RemoteException;
}
```

The AccountManager lets a client ask for an account by name, using the getAccount() remote method. The method returns a reference to an Account object that corresponds to the account. Once the client has the Account reference, transactions against the account can be done through method calls on the Account object. The AccountManager also has a newAccount() method that allows clients to add new accounts to the manager's underlying database.

The server implementation of the getAccount() method simply needs to look up the named account in the account database, create an AccountImpl object to represent the account, and return the object to the remote client as a remote reference. Since Account objects are Remote objects, the RMI remote reference layer automatically creates a remote reference for the Account object, and the client that called the getAccount() method receives a stub for the Account object on the server.

Using the factory object to find accounts is more manageable than using the RMI registry. The bank maintains a database of accounts and their status, so the server implementation of the AccountManager can access that database directly to find accounts and create corresponding Account remote objects. Trying to keep the RMI registry in sync with the bank database makes the registry an unnecessary shadow of the main database of accounts, giving the bank two databases to maintain.

Dynamically Loaded Classes

The RMI runtime system has a dynamic class-loading facility that loads the classes it needs while executing remote method calls. In some situations, you don't need to worry much about how your application classes are obtained by the various agents in an RMI application. This is especially true if you have direct access to all hosts involved in the distributed system (i.e., if you can install your application classes in the local CLASSPATH for each machine participating in the application). For instance, when discussing the earlier Account example, we assumed all the relevant classes (Account, AccountImpl, stub, and skeleton classes) were installed on both the client and the server. However, if your distributed application involves remote agents running on hosts that aren't directly under your control, you need to understand how RMI loads classes at runtime, so you can ensure that each remote agent can find the classes it needs in order to run.

As with any Java application, the Java runtime system is responsible for loading the classes needed to initiate an RMI session. Starting an interaction with a remote object means loading the RMI API classes themselves, as well as the base interface for the remote object and the stub class for the remote interface. On the server side, the skeleton class for the remote object and the actual implementation class need to be loaded in order to run the server object that is being remotely exported.

The classes that are referenced directly by a given Java class are normally loaded by the same class loader that loaded the class itself. So, in an RMI client that does a Naming lookup to find a remote object, the stub interface for the remote object is loaded using the class loader for the class doing the lookup. If the RMI client is a Java application (started using the *java* command to invoke the main() method on an object), the default (local) class loader tries to find the remote interface locally, from the local CLASSPATH. If the RMI client is an applet loaded in a web page, the AppletClassLoader tries to look for the remote interface on the applet's host, in the codebase of the applet.

The RMI runtime system provides its own class loader, the RMIClassLoader, to augment the default class loading process just described. The RMIClassLoader loads stubs and skeleton classes for remote interfaces, as well as the classes for objects used as remote method arguments or return values. These classes usually aren't explicitly referenced by your RMI application itself, but they are needed by the RMI runtime system for generating remote references and marshalling/unmarshalling method arguments and return values.

When it's loading the bytecodes for class definitions, the RMI runtime system first attempts to use the default class loader for the local context (i.e., an AppletClassLoader for an applet or the system class loader for a Java application). If the referenced class isn't found using the default local class loader, the RMIClassLoader tries to load the class bytecodes remotely according to the procedures explained next.

Configuring Clients and Servers for Remote Class Loading

When the RMI runtime system marshals a remote object stub, method argument, or return value, it encodes a URL in the marshaled bytestream to tell the process on the receiving end of the stream where to look for the class file for the marshaled object. If the class for the object being marshaled was loaded by a nondefault class loader (e.g., the `AppletClassLoader` or the `RMIClassLoader`), the codebase of that class loader is encoded in the marshaled stream. If the class was loaded by the default class loader from the local `CLASSPATH`, the value of the `java.rmi.server.codebase` property for the Java VM marshalling the object is sent in the stream. This property is not set by default in the Java VM, so you need to make sure that it's set to a URL that points to the location of the necessary class files. One way to do this is to include a command-line argument when starting the Java VM, as in:

```
% java -Djava.rmi.server.codebase=http://objhost.org/classes/ RMIProcess
```

Here we start a Java process with its codebase set to *http://objhost.org/classes/*. This means that any remote process that needs to load classes for objects received from this process during an RMI session should use this HTTP URL in order to find them (if the classes can't be found on the local `CLASSPATH`, that is). This applies either if `RMIProcess` is serving remote objects itself through an RMI registry or if `RMIProcess` is passing objects into methods it is calling on other remote objects. In the first case, a remote client that needs to load the stub classes for the objects exported by `RMIProcess` uses the codebase to find these classes. In the second case, a remote process uses the codebase to load the classes for method arguments that `RMIProcess` is passing into remote method calls it makes.

If an RMI runtime system is trying to unmarshal an object stub, method argument, or return value and it doesn't find the class using the default class loader (e.g., the system class loader, which looks on the local `CLASSPATH` first), the `RMIClassLoader` can use the URL in the marshal stream to look for the class bytecodes remotely. The `RMIClassLoader` takes the URL from the marshaled bytestream and opens a URL connection to the specified host to load the needed classes. If both the local class search and this remote URL search fail to find the required classes, the unmarshal operation generates an exception, and the remote method call fails.

Note that in order for a Java runtime system to even attempt to load classes remotely, it has to have a security manager installed that allows remote class loading. The `java.rmi.RMISecurityManager` can be used for this. In both your RMI object server and clients, include the following line before any RMI calls:

```
System.setSecurityManager(new RMISecurityManager());
```

If you don't set the security manager, the Java VM is allowed to look for classes locally, and your RMI calls will work only if all of the required classes can be found on the local `CLASSPATH`.

Another issue with dynamically loading remote classes is that the default Java security policy doesn't allow all the networking operations required to resolve a class from a remote host. So, if you have an RMI client or server that needs to resolve classes remotely, you need to use a policy file that opens up network permissions to allow this. We don't go into all the details of network policies or the syntax of the security policy file,* but at minimum, you need to add the following line to the policy file on the RMI client:

```
permission java.net.SocketPermission "objhost.org", "accept,connect";
```

This line allows the client to connect to any port on *objhost.org* and to accept connections from *objhost.org* on any of those ports. If you want to make this a bit more restrictive, since we're using HTTP as the protocol for downloading classes, you really just need port 80 access to/from *objhost.org*, so use this line in the policy file instead:

```
permission java.net.SocketPermission "objhost.org:80", "accept,connect";
```

The policy file change is needed in order to bypass the stricter rules imposed by the RMISecurityManager, and allow the RMI runtime to create the network connections it needs. You can either add this permission to the default policy file used by your Java runtime (if you are using Sun's JRE, this is in *JAVA_HOME/lib/security/java.policy*, where *JAVA_HOME* is the root of your Java runtime installation), or you can create a custom policy file (perhaps by copying and editing the default one) and use it specifically for this application. If you've made a modified policy file, you can specify it on the command line when you start your RMI process, in a similar way to setting the codebase property in our earlier example:

```
% java -Djava.security.policy=mypolicy.txt RMIProcess
```

As a simple example, suppose we want to use our earlier Account example to export an Account object on one host and access that Account on another host, where the only class available locally is the Account interface class itself. On the server, we start an RMI registry† and run the AccountReg class as before, but since we want remote clients to be able to load the stub classes remotely, we need to set the codebase property to where the clients can find these classes:

```
% java -Djava.rmi.server.codebase=http://objhost.org/classes/ AccountReg
Registered account.
```

We've set the codebase to *http://objhost.org/classes/*, so we have to make sure that an HTTP server is running on the *objhost.org* machine and that the necessary class files (e.g., the AccountImpl stub class) are in the *classes* directory of that HTTP server's document root.

Now, it may seem strange that we need to provide an HTTP server in order to download classes between two RMI processes. The RMI registry can provide remote objects to remote callers, why can't it provide class definitions as well? The reason that the designers of the RMI specification did not tie dynamic class loading to the RMI registry is because they did not want the RMI registry to be a strictly required element of the RMI architecture. In order to leave open the possibility of using other naming services to register RMI remote objects (CORBA, LDAP, custom

---

* For details on Java security policies and files, see *Java Security*, by Scott Oaks (O'Reilly).

† Note that in order for the RMI registry to recognize and pass along the codebase property you specify, it has to be started in such a way that it can't find any of the remotely loaded classes on its CLASSPATH. So start your RMI registry with a CLASSPATH that doesn't include the stub and skeleton classes, etc., then run your RMI server with a CLASSPATH that includes all required classes.

systems), they needed to keep the RMI registry an optional component. There-fore, dynamic class loading had to be a separate, but portable, process, hence the HTTP process that exists in the specification. Luckily, in JDK 1.4, the ability to customize the behavior of the RMIClassLoader was added to RMI, which opens up the possibility of implementing other dynamic class loading schemes (if the HTTP scheme doesn't fit your needs). See the RMI API listing for RMIClassLoader and RMIClassLoaderSpi (both in the java.rmi.server package) for details.

Now we can run the AccountClient class on the remote client as before, but the client's host machine doesn't have the stub class for the AccountImpl remote object available locally. When the AccountClient tries to look up the remote Account object, we want the stub class to be loaded remotely. Two simple changes to our Account example make this possible. First, add a line to the AccountClient main() method that sets the RMISecurityManager, in order to allow for remote class loading:

```
import java.rmi.Naming;
import java.rmi.RMISecurityManager;

public class AccountClient {
  public static void main(String argv[]) {
  try {
  // Set the RMI security manager,
  // in case we need to load remote classes
  System.setSecurityManager(new RMISecurityManager());

  // Lookup account object
  Account jimAcct = (Account)Naming.lookup("rmi://objhost.org/JimF");
  .
  .
  .
```

The other change is to use a more lenient policy file when running AccountClient so the necessary network operations can be performed. Again, we don't discuss the syntax of the policy file here, but assuming you've put the required policy settings into a file named *rmipolicy.txt*, you can start the client like so:

```
% java -Djava.security.policy=rmipolicy.txt AccountClient
Deposited 12,000 into account owned by JimF
Balance now totals: 12000.0
```

You'll notice that the -Djava.rmi.server.codebase= option isn't needed here, because the client isn't providing class definitions to the Account server. If we were passing arguments into remote methods called on the Account server, and the classes for these arguments weren't available, then we would have to set up the AccountClient in a similar way to what we just described for the Account server (i.e., set up an HTTP-accessible codebase and export it to the server by setting the java.rmi.server.codebase property of the client's VM).

Loading Classes from Applets

Virtually all the steps we've outlined for running an RMI client to allow it to remotely load classes apply to applets as well. The only difference is that the classes for applets are loaded using an `AppletClassLoader`, which checks the applet's codebase for any classes required to run the applet. The default security policy for applets already allows for remote loading of classes, since this is how an applet works in the first place, so there's no need to change the security policy when using RMI within an applet. All you need to do to ensure that the applet finds the remote interface and stub class for the RMI object is to put them in the server directory that corresponds to the applet's codebase.

Remote Object Activation

Automatic activation of remote objects was added to RMI as of Java 1.2. The activation subsystem in RMI provides you with two basic features: the ability to have remote objects instantiated (activated) on-demand by client requests, and the ability for remote object references to remain valid across server crashes, making the references persistent. These features can be quite useful in certain types of distributed applications.

For example, think back to the `AccountManager` class we discussed when we talked about factory objects. We might not want to keep the `AccountManager` running on our server 24 hours a day; perhaps it consumes lots of server resources (memory, database connections, etc.), so we don't want it running unless it is being used. Using the RMI activation service, we can set up the `AccountManager` so that it doesn't start running until the first client requests an `Account`. In addition, after some period of inactivity, we can have the `AccountManager` shut down to conserve server resources and then reactivated the next time a client asks for an `Account`.

If a remote object is made activatable, it can be registered with the RMI registry without actually being instantiated. Normally, RMI remote objects (based on the `UnicastRemoteObject` interface) provide only nonpersistent references to themselves. Such a reference can be created for a client only if the referenced object already exists in a remote Java VM. In addition, the remote reference is valid only during the lifetime of the remote object. The remote object activation service adds support for persistent remote references that can be created even if the remote object is not running at the time of the request. This can persist beyond the lifetime of an individual server object.

The key features provided by the RMI activation service include:

- The ability to automatically create remote objects, triggered by requests for references to these objects.

- Support for activation groups, in which groups of activatable remote objects are executed in the same Java VM, which is automatically started by the activation service if needed.

- The ability to restart remote objects if they exit or are destroyed due to a system failure of some kind. This can add a certain degree of fault tolerance to RMI applications.

In the RMI activation system, activatable objects belong to activation groups, and each activation group runs within its own Java VM. If you don't group your activatable objects, instead simply assigning a new activation group to each activatable object you create, each object then runs inside a separate Java VM.

You typically define an activatable remote object by:

- Subclassing your remote object implementation from the `Activatable` class provided in the `java.rmi.activation` package
- Providing activation constructors in the server implementation
- Registering the object and its activation method with the activation service

If you want remote clients to directly access your activatable object, you also need to register the object with the RMI registry, so that it can be found by name on the network. You can register an activatable class with the registry without actually creating an instance of the remote object, as we'll see shortly.

You can also create an activatable object without subclassing the `Activatable` class. This might be necessary if you need to extend another class and the Java single-inheritance limit keeps you from also extending `Activatable`. For most of this section, we'll just discuss the case in which you're subclassing `Activatable`; we'll only mention this other approach when needed.

Persistent Remote References

The primary difference between an activatable remote object and a nonactivatable one is that a remote reference to an activatable object doesn't need to have a "live" object behind it. If an activatable object is not running (e.g., it hasn't been constructed yet, or it has been garbage-collected by its Java VM, or its VM has exited), a remote reference to the object can still be exported to a client. The client receives a stub, as usual, and can make remote method invocations through the stub. When the first method is invoked, the activation service running on the server sees that the object is not active and goes about activating the object for the client. If the object doesn't have a VM to run in, the activation system starts one. The object is then activated using information that has been registered with the activation system. This information includes the object's class name, a URL that can load the class bytecodes if they're not found in the local `CLASSPATH`, and data to pass into the object's activation constructor. Once the object has been activated, the method invocation takes place, and the results are marshaled and sent back to the client.

As long as the object stays running, future method requests are handled as usual. If the object stops running for some reason (e.g, it is garbage-collected, or its VM dies), the next method request by a client triggers the activation service again, and the object is reactivated. This is what is meant by persistent remote references: remote references to activatable objects can persist across multiple lifetimes of the actual server object.

Defining an Activatable Remote Object

Naturally, before you can register and use an activatable object with the RMI activation system, you need to define the remote interface and the server implementation for the object. The `java.rmi.activation` package provides the classes you need to define an activatable remote object. You usually define a remote object as activatable by subclassing it from `Activatable` and defining a special constructor that activates the object. You also have to register the object with the activation service on the server host.

Other than that, the implementation of an activatable remote object is similar to that of a nonactivatable one. Start with a remote interface that contains the methods you want to export from your object. The interface should extend `Remote`, and each method should throw a `RemoteException` (or, as of Java 1.2, any parent of `RemoteException`). The server implementation implements this interface and extends a concrete implementation of the `java.rmi.server.RemoteServer` class. Since you're defining an activatable remote object, you typically extend `java.rmi.activation.Activatable` directly and use its constructors to initialize, register, and activate your remote object. If you choose not to extend `Activatable` directly, you have to use the static `exportObject()` methods on the `Activatable` class to register your object with the activation runtime system.

The Activatable class

The `Activatable` class has four constructors. Here are signatures for two of them:

```
protected Activatable(String src, MarshalledObject data,
  boolean restart, int port) throws RemoteException
protected Activatable(String src, MarshalledObject data,
  boolean restart, int port, RMIClientSocketFactory csfactory,
  RMIServerSocketFactory ssfactory) throws RemoteException
```

These two constructors are *initialization* constructors. Use them when you decide to proactively create one of your remote objects and register it with the RMI activation service. In this case, the object already exists when a client first makes a method request on it, but if the object is destroyed, the next client request causes the object to be reactivated. These constructors register an object with the local activation service and export the object so that it can receive remote method requests. Both constructors have the following arguments in common:

- The `String` parameter is a URL that indicates where class bytecodes required by this object can be located. This information is exported to a remote client so it can dynamically load classes required to unmarshal method return values, for example. If a null value is passed in for this argument, remote clients of the activatable object can't dynamically load classes, and therefore needs the required classes available locally.

- The `MarshalledObject` parameter provides initialization data for the object; this parameter is necessary because data is typically sent from the activation daemon's VM to the VM designated to run the activatable object and the two might not be the same (more on this later).

- The `boolean` flag indicates whether the object should be automatically recreated when its home VM or its activation group is restarted (e.g., after a server restart).

- The `int` parameter specifies the port on which the object is exported. A port of zero tells the RMI runtime system to export the object on a random open port.

The second initialization constructor takes custom client and server socket factories that create socket communications between the server and the clients of the object. Customized socket factories were added to RMI as of the Java 2 SDK 1.2. They aren't discussed in this chapter, but you can consult Part III for more details.

The other two `Activatable` constructors have the following signatures:

```
protected Activatable(ActivationID id, int port) throws RemoteException
protected Activatable(ActivationID id, int port,
  RMIClientSocketFactory csfactory, RMIServerSocketFactory ssfactory)
  throws RemoteException
```

These constructors are *(re)activation* constructors. The activation system uses them to activate a remote object that has received a remote method request, but isn't currently active. The `ActivationID` is a persistent ID issued by the activation system for the remote object, and the port number is the port that exports the remote object. The second constructor again takes custom server and client socket factories.

The `Activatable` class also has a set of `exportObject()` methods that correspond to the constructors just described. You can use these methods when an activatable object doesn't directly extend the `Activatable` class. You call the appropriate `exportObject()` methods from within the constructors of the class, so they serve the same function as calling the `Activatable` constructors during initialization of an `Activatable` subclass.

Implementing an activatable object

You can implement an activatable remote object in two ways: derive the remote object from the `Activatable` class directly and make the required calls to the `Activatable` constructors in its constructors, or have the class implement a `Remote` interface and make the required calls to the static `exportObject()` methods in its constructors.

In either case, when the activation system activates a remote object, it looks for a constructor on the class that takes two arguments: an `ActivationID` and a `MarshalledObject`. The activation system calls this constructor, passing in an `ActivationID` it generates for the object and the `MarshalledObject` registered for the activatable object by the first constructor we just discussed.

This means you have to provide a constructor with this signature in your implementation of an activatable object. In this constructor, you should call either one of the (re)activation constructors on the `Activatable` parent class (if your class extends `Activatable`), or the corresponding `Activatable.exportObject()` method (if you didn't extend `Activatable`). In this call, you pass on the `ActivationID` issued by the activation system and specify the port for the exported remote object (a port number of 0 causes the object to be exported on a random open port).

In addition to this required constructor, you can define other constructors for your remote object implementation as needed. If you want your object to be reactivatable, any additional constructors should call one of the initialization constructors on `Activatable` (using `super()`) or the corresponding `exportObject()` method, passing in a valid source URL and a `MarshalledObject` to be used as an argument if the object is reactivated. If the object is destroyed at some point, and a subsequent remote method request is received for it, the activation system reactivates the object by calling the required (re)activation constructor on the object's class, passing in this MarshalledObject argument.

Example 3-3 shows a partial listing of an activatable implementation of the Account interface from Example 3-1. The primary differences between this implementation and the nonactivatable one in Example 3-2 are that this new implementation extends the java.rmi.activation.Activatable class instead of UnicastRemoteObject, and its constructors support the activation system. We've also defined a helper class, AccountState, that is used to wrap the account's state information (e.g., its name and balance) so that it can be held within a MarshalledObject for initialization data. (This is described later in this section.)

Example 3-3: An Activatable Version of the This or That Server

```java
import java.rmi.server.UnicastRemoteObject;
import java.rmi.activation.*;
import java.rmi.MarshalledObject;
import java.rmi.RemoteException;
import java.util.List;
import java.util.ListIterator;
import java.io.IOException;

/**
 * ActivatableAccountImpl: Activatable implementation of the Account remote
 * interface.
 */

public class ActivatableAccountImpl extends Activatable implements Account {
  // Our current balance
  private float mBalance = 0;
  // Name on account
  private String mName = "";

  // "Regular" constructor used to create a "pre-activated" server
  public ActivatableAccountImpl(String name)
    throws RemoteException, ActivationException, IOException {
    // Register and export object (on random open port)
    // Note that we're
    super(null, new MarshalledObject(new AccountState(name, 0f)), false, 0);
    mName = name;
  }
  // Constructor called by the activation runtime to (re)activate
  // and export the server
  protected ActivatableAccountImpl(ActivationID id, MarshalledObject arg)
      throws RemoteException, ActivationException {
    // Export this object with the given activation id, on random port
    super(id, 0);
    System.out.println("Activating an account");
    // Check incoming data (account state) passed in with activation request
    try {
      Object oarg = arg.get();
```

```
    if (oarg instanceof AccountState) {
      AccountState s = (AccountState)oarg;
      // Set our name and balance based on incoming state
      mName = s.name;
      mBalance = s.balance;
    }
    else {
      System.out.println("Unknown argument type received on activation: " +
                    oarg.getClass().getName());

    }
  }
  catch(Exception e) {
    System.out.println("Error retrieving argument to activation");
  }
}
// Remainder of implementation is identical to AccountImpl
//  .
//  .
//  .
}


// Define a structure to hold our state information in a single marshalled
// object, so that we can register it with the activation system
class AccountState {
  public float balance = 0f;
  public String name = null;
  public AccountState(String n, float b) {
    name = n;
    balance = b;
  }
}
```

The first constructor for `ActivatableAccountImpl` is a public one, used to construct an account for a user with the given name. The constructor registers the new object with the activation system by calling the constructor of its parent, `Activatable`. As we discussed earlier, the first argument to the `Activatable` constructor is the URL for the codebase (which is null, in this case, to indicate that we don't support dynamic class loading). The second argument, the (re)initialization data for the activatable object, is created by wrapping the state of the account (the name and balance, held in an `AccountState` object, a utility class defined at the end of the code listing) in a `MarshalledObject`. If the Account needs to be reactivated later, the activation daemon will use this `MarshalledObject` to initialize the reactivated Account, as explained below. The third and fourth arguments indicate that we only want the object activated on-demand, and that it can be exported on any random available port on the local machine.

The second constructor is used by the activation system, and must be found on your implementation class when the activation system looks for it during a reactivation attempt. If an object of this type needs to be activated (or reactivated after a crash of some sort), this constructor is called to create the remote object. The constructor takes an `ActivationID` argument, issued by the activation system, and the MarshalledObject that was previously registered for the object with the activation system. Our ActivatableAccountImpl constructor exports the object by calling the second constructor on the Activatable class, then initializes itself with the data from the MarshalledObject.

Registering Activatable Objects

There are several ways to register an activatable object with its local activation system. In each case, the activation system needs to be told how to create (or recreate) the object. The information the activation system needs to activate an object is encapsulated in the ActivationDesc class. An ActivationDesc object contains the name of the class for the remote object, a URL with the network location of the bytecodes for the class, a MarshalledObject to be used as the initialization data for the object, and the group assignment for the object.

The simplest way to register an Activatable object is to create an instance of the object. In our example, we've derived our server implementation from the Activatable class, so the public constructor on the ActivatableAccountImpl class registers the object by calling the necessary constructor on Activatable. Thus, we can create and register one of these as follows:

```
// Make an activation group for the object
ActivationGroupDesc gdesc = new ActivationGroupDesc(null, null);
ActivationGroupID gid = ActivationGroup.getSystem().registerGroup(gdesc);
ActivationGroup.createGroup(gid, gdesc, 0);

// Make an Account object, which registers itself with activation system
Account account = new ActivatableAccountImpl(accountName);

// Register with naming service
LocateRegistry.getRegistry().rebind(accountName, account);
```

The first four lines are required to create an activation group for our activatable object. We'll talk more about activation groups shortly. For now, all you need to know is that this code creates the default activation group for the current VM. Any remote object that isn't specifically assigned to a group is placed in this default group.

The activatable object itself is created by simply calling the public ActivatableAccountImpl constructor. This constructor registers the object with the activation system by calling the appropriate Activatable constructor, as we've already discussed. Since we haven't specified an activation group for the object, it is placed in the default group we just created. If we hadn't created that default group, the activation system would throw an exception here, when the object is registered.

Aside from the creation of the activation group, this example looks a lot like our other examples of registering RMI objects. The difference here is that if the process dies off at some point, the activation system can reactivate the activatable object in a new Java VM using the information provided in the ActivationDesc for the object. In this case, we're relying on the Activatable constructor (which is called by our ActivatableAccountImpl constructor) to create and register an

`ActivationDesc` for our object using the information we passed into it when we called it from our constructor.

When an object needs to be activated, the activation system first looks up the `ActivationDesc` for the object and then looks for the class referenced in the `ActivationDesc`, using the codebase URL specified in the `ActivationDesc` to load the class bytecodes, if necessary. Once the class has been loaded, the activation system creates an instance of the class by calling the activation constructor, which takes an `ActivationID` and a `MarshalledObject` as arguments. The `ActivationID` is issued by the activation system, and the `MarshalledObject` contains the data previously registered with the `ActivationDesc`. In our activatable `Account` in Example 3-3, the activation system calls the second constructor on our `ActivatableAccountImpl` class. The new object passes the `ActivationID` up to the `Activatable` constructor so that it can be recorded, and the account state (name and balance) is pulled from the `MarshalledObject`. The `Activatable` constructor takes care of creating and registering an `ActivationDesc` for the object and exporting the object with the activation system.

Registering an activatable object without instantiating

A more complicated, but often more useful way to register a remote object is to create an `ActivationDesc` for it and then register this information directly with the activation system, *without* creating an instance of the object. The static `Activatable.register()` method accepts an `ActivationDesc` object and registers it with the activation system directly. Here's how we can do that:

```
// Make a codebase and activation argument for the object
String src = "http://objhost.org/classes";
MarshalledObject actArg = new MarshalledObject("MyAccount");

// Create the ActivationDesc and get a stub for the object
ActivationDesc desc =
    new ActivationDesc("oreilly.jent.rmi.ActivatableAccountImpl",
    src, actArg);
Account accountStub =
    (Account)Activatable.register(desc);
```

When we create the `ActivationDesc` for the object, we specify the name of the class to use for creating the object, a codebase for finding the class, and a `MarshalledObject` that is passed to the object when it's activated. The `ActivationDesc` is used in the call to the `Activatable.register()` method, which returns a `RemoteStub` for the activatable object. Since we know this stub is for an object that implements the `Account` interface, we can safely cast it to an `Account`. We can also use this reference to register the remote object with the local RMI naming registry:

```
LocateRegistry.getRegistry().bind("Account", accountStub);
```

Although not shown here, note that you also have to create an activation group for the object, just like we did in our earlier example, before you can register it with the activation service.

So, to recap, we've registered a remote object with the activation system and the RMI naming registry without actually creating the object itself. When a client tries to look up the object, it gets back a remote stub, with no active object behind it on the server. When the client calls a method on the stub, however, the activation system on the server creates the object, using the information in the ActivationDesc we provided.

Passing data with the MarshalledObject

The sole option for passing arguments to activatable objects before they are activated is through the MarshalledObject contained within the ActivationDesc for the object. However, once the ActivationDesc is registered with the activation system, you can't dynamically update the contents of the MarshalledObject. This is a serious problem in our example, if you've been following it closely. We wrap the account state (the account owner's name and the account balance) and register it with the activation system just once, when we create and/or register the object. As clients interact with the Account, the balance is going to change, but our registered MarshalledObject is not going to change along with it. If the VM of the Account crashes, and the Account is reactivated using the MarshalledObject registered for it, the balance will be set back to the value it was when the object was first registered with the activation system.

There are a number of ways to get around this problem and make the initialization arguments more dynamic. One is to bundle a filename or URL into the MarshalledObject, rather than the data itself. We could then keep the data behind the file or URL updated with the current state of the Account. At the point that the object is activated, it can read data from the file or URL and use the up-to-date data during activation. Alternatively, if this was a real-world example and our account information was stored persistently in a database, we would just need to pass the account ID in the initialization parameters, and the Account object could then read the current state of the Account from the database.

Activation Groups

Every activatable RMI object belongs to an activation group. Each group of activatable objects runs within the same Java VM on the server host. In essence, activation groups are a way of defining collections of activatable remote objects that should share the same physical address space. We've already seen how to set up an activation group, since we had to do this before registering our activatable object with the activation system. In this section, we'll take a look at creating activation groups in a bit more detail and discuss what the activation group is actually doing for you.

Activation groups in RMI are more than just a way of organizing remote objects. Each activation group is responsible for monitoring, activating, and reactivating the objects it contains. The objects involved in maintaining an activation group are shown in Figure 3-4. Note that you don't normally need to interact with the underlying objects themselves. Simply set up your ActivationGroup objects and assign activatable objects to them; the activation system does the rest for you.

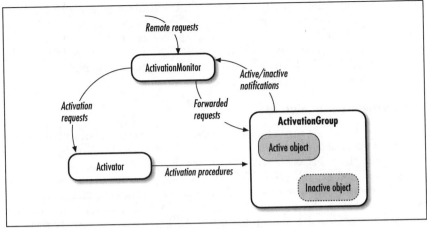

Figure 3-4: The components of the activation system

An `ActivationGroup` is created when the first object in the group needs to be activated. The `Activator` is responsible for creating a VM for the `ActivationGroup` to run in, and for starting the `ActivationGroup` using the information in the registered object's `ActivationGroupDesc`, if it has one. If the remote object doesn't have a specified group, a default one is created. The new `ActivationGroup` object is then told to activate the requested remote object by calling its `newInstance()` method. The arguments the `Activator` passes into this method are the `ActivationID` for the new object and the `ActivationDesc` that the `Activator` has registered for the object.

The `ActivationDesc` gives an `ActivationGroup` everything it needs to activate the remote object. The `ActivationGroup` takes the class name for the object and looks for the class bytecodes. First it checks the local CLASSPATH, and if that pulls up nothing, it uses the URL in the `ActivationDesc` to load the class from the given URL. Once the class is loaded, an instance of the class is created by calling the activation constructor on the class (e.g., the constructor that has an `ActivationID` argument and a `MarshalledObject` argument). The `ActivationID` and `MarshalledObject` come from the call to the `newInstance()` method. The new, active remote object is returned to the `Activator` as a serialized `MarshalledObject`. This is done for two reasons. First, the `Activator` runs in a separate Java VM, so the active object reference needs to be transferred from one VM to another, and the easiest way to do this is to serialize it and transmit it in that form. Second, since the object has been bundled into a `MarshalledObject`, the `Activator` doesn't need to load the object's bytecodes unless absolutely necessary. In most cases, the `Activator` doesn't need to interact directly with the object itself, so it doesn't need to waste time loading unnecessary bytecodes.

Each `ActivationGroup` has an `ActivationMonitor` associated with it. The `ActivationGroup` has to tell the `ActivationMonitor` whenever an object becomes active or inactive. An activatable object is responsible for informing its `ActivationGroup` when it becomes active and inactive, by calling the group's `activeObject()` and `inactiveObject()` methods, respectively. The `ActivationGroup`, in turn, passes the information on to the `ActivationMonitor` by calling identical methods on the monitor object. When the object becomes inactive, the `ActivationMonitor` makes note of it and arranges for the object to be reactivated the next time a method request comes in for it. If an entire `ActivationGroup` becomes inactive, the `ActivationMonitor` is informed through its `inactiveGroup()` method. The next request for an object in that group causes the `Activator` to recreate the group.

Registering activation groups

An `ActivationGroup` is registered with the activation system in roughly the same way as an activatable object. You have to create an `ActivationGroupDesc` object that contains the name of the class for the group, the URL where the class byte-codes can be loaded, and a `MarshalledObject` that is given to the `ActivationGroup` as initialization data. Unlike activatable objects, though, the class of a group has to be a concrete subclass of `ActivationGroup`. Register the `ActivationGroupDesc` by calling the static `ActivationSystem.registerGroup()` method, passing in the `ActivationGroupDesc`. The `ActivationSystem` returns an `ActivationGroupID` that can assign specific objects to the group.

Assigning activatable objects to groups

Assign an activatable object to a group by specifying the group ID in the `ActivationDesc` registered with the activation system. The `ActivationGroupID` returned by the `ActivationSystem.registerGroup()` method can be passed into the `ActivationDesc` constructor.

Before you can register a remote object with the activation system, you need to create a group for it. For our activatable Account example, we can run Java code along the following lines on the object server (note that we've left out the exception handling):

```
// Make an activation group for the object
ActivationGroupDesc gdesc = new ActivationGroupDesc(null, null);
ActivationGroupID gid =
 ActivationGroup.getSystem().registerGroup(gdesc);
ActivationGroup.createGroup(gid, gdesc, 0);

// Set up ActivationDesc for object
String codebaseURL = "http://objhost.org/classes";
String accountName = "Fred";
MarshalledObject activationArg = new MarshalledObject(accountName);
ActivationDesc desc =
 new ActivationDesc(gid, "oreilly.jent.rmi.ActivatableAccountImpl",
 codebaseURL, activationArg);
Account accountRef = (Account)Activatable.register(desc);
LocateRegistry.getRegistry().rebind(accountName, accountRef);
```

Here we're using the `ActivatableAccountImpl` class and registering a remote object with the activation system without actually instantiating it. Before we register our remote object, we create an `ActivationGroupDesc`, then use it to register and create a new activation group with the activation system. After we create the activation group (using the `ActivationGroup.createGroup()` method), we use the `ActivationGroupID` for our new group to make an `ActivationDesc` for our remote object. We use that to register the object with the activation system. The activation system generates a remote stub for our object, and we register that with the RMI naming registry.

Since each ActivationGroup is started within its own VM if it's initially activated by the activation system, grouping objects is a convenient way to partition your remote objects into shared address spaces on your server.

The Activation Daemon

The heart of the RMI activation system is the activation daemon, which runs on the host for an activatable object. The activation daemon is responsible for intercepting remote method requests on activatable objects and orchestrating the activation of the object, if needed.

The activation daemon provided with the Java SDK, *rmid*, runs a Java VM that includes a java.rmi.activation.Activator object. The Activator is responsible for keeping a registry of activatable objects, along with the information needed to activate them. This information is in two parts: an ActivationDesc object and an optional ActivationGroupDesc. The ActivationGroupDesc identifies the group of activatable objects to which the object should be added and describes how to start the group if it doesn't exist. The ActivationDesc includes all information needed to activate the object itself. An activatable object has to be registered with the activation system in one of the ways described earlier to be started automatically by the Activator.

If a remote method request is received by the RMI runtime system on a host, and the target object hasn't been created yet, the Activator is asked to activate it. The Activator looks up the ActivationDesc (and ActivationGroupDesc, if present) for the object. If the object has an ActivationGroup assigned to it, and the ActivationGroup doesn't exist yet, a Java VM is started for the group, and the ActivationGroupDesc data is used to start an ActivationGroup object within the new VM. If the object has no ActivationGroup associated with it, it's given its own ActivationGroup running in its own VM. The group is then asked to start the requested object, using the ActivationDesc object registered for the object. Once the ActivationGroup activates the object within its VM, the Activator is notified, and the now-active remote reference is returned to the RMI runtime system. The RMI runtime system forwards the remote method request through the reference to the object, and the return value is exported back to the client as usual.

The daemon's dual personality

When you start the *rmid* daemon, it creates an Activator and then listens on the default port of 1098 for activation requests. There is also a -port command-line option that lets you specify a different port for the VM to use. In addition to running the Activator, the *rmid* daemon also runs its own RMI Registry. If needed, you can register local objects with the daemon's internal Registry by specifying the daemon's port when you call the `bind()` or `rebind()` method of the Registry. For example, if *rmid* is running on its default port of 1098:

```
RemoteObject server = ...
Registry local = LocateRegistry.getRegistry(1098);
local.bind(server, "Server");
```

This way, you can consolidate your activation system and your naming service into one VM on your server.

RMI and Native Method Calls

RMI is a Java-only remote object scheme, so it doesn't provide a direct connection between objects implemented in different languages, like CORBA does. But, using Java's Native Interface API, it is possible to wrap existing C or C++ code with a Java interface and then export this interface remotely through RMI.

To demonstrate, let's suppose we have some (legacy) native code that implements a service we want to export through RMI to remote clients. We can create an implementation of our Account interface that uses this native code to implement the doSomething() method on our remote interface. The implementation for a NativeAccountImpl is shown in Example 3-4. The only significant difference between this implementation and our original AccountImpl is that the doSomething() method is declared native, so the method body is left empty.

Example 3-4: Remote Object Using a Native Method Implementation

```
import java.rmi.server.UnicastRemoteObject;
import java.rmi.RemoteException;
import java.util.List;
import java.util.ListIterator;

/**
 * NativeAccountImpl: Implementation of the Account remote interface using
 * JNI native methods for the account transactions.
 */

public class NativeAccountImpl extends
                             UnicastRemoteObject implements Account {
  // Our current balance
  private float mBalance = 0;
  // Name on account
  private String mName = "";
  // Create a new account with the given name
  public NativeAccountImpl(String name) throws RemoteException {
    mName = name;
  }

  public String getName() throws RemoteException {
    return mName;
  }
  public float getBalance() throws RemoteException {
    return mBalance;
  }
```

```
// Withdraw some funds
native public void withdraw(float amt)
throws RemoteException, InsufficientFundsException;
// Deposit some funds
native public void deposit(float amt) throws RemoteException;
// Move some funds from another (remote) account into this one
native public void transfer(float amt, Account src)
throws RemoteException, InsufficientFundsException;

// Remainder of implementation is identical to AccountImpl...
```

We can compile this RMI class and generate the stubs and skeletons for it using the RMI compiler, just like with our other RMI examples. But once this is done, we need to provide native implementations for the withdraw( ), deposit( ), and transfer( ) methods. To start, we can generate a C/C++ header file for the native methods using the *javah* tool:

```
% javah -jni -d . NativeAccountImpl
```

The -jni option tells the *javah* tool to generate JNI-compliant header files (as opposed to header files based on the earlier native method interface that shipped with Java 1.0). Invoking this command generates a JNI C/C++ header file that looks something like the following:

```
/* DO NOT EDIT THIS FILE - it is machine generated */
#include <jni.h>
/* Header for class oreilly_jent_rmi_NativeAccountImpl */

#ifndef _Included_oreilly_jent_rmi_NativeAccountImpl
#define _Included_oreilly_jent_rmi_NativeAccountImpl
#ifdef __cplusplus
extern "C" {
#endif
// NOTE: Some pre-processor directives deleted for clarity...
/*
 * Class: oreilly_jent_rmi_NativeAccountImpl
 * Method: withdraw
 * Signature: (F)V
 */
JNIEXPORT void JNICALL Java_oreilly_jent_rmi_NativeAccountImpl_withdraw
  (JNIEnv *, jobject, jfloat);

/*
 * Class: oreilly_jent_rmi_NativeAccountImpl
 * Method: deposit
 * Signature: (F)V
 */
JNIEXPORT void JNICALL Java_oreilly_jent_rmi_NativeAccountImpl_deposit
  (JNIEnv *, jobject, jfloat);

/*
 * Class: oreilly_jent_rmi_NativeAccountImpl
 * Method: transfer
```

```
* Signature: (FLoreilly/jent/rmi/Account;)V
*/
JNIEXPORT void JNICALL Java_oreilly_jent_rmi_NativeAccountImpl_transfer
  (JNIEnv *, jobject, jfloat, jobject);

#ifdef __cplusplus
}
#endif
#endif
```

The only details worth noting in this header file are the inclusion of the *jni.h* header file (which is provided with the Java SDK) and the actual method declarations. The *jni.h* header file provides declarations and definitions for all of the data structures and utility methods provided by the JNI API. The method declarations have a signature that corresponds to the native methods declared on our Java class. When you invoke the withdraw() method on the NativeAccountImpl, for example, the Java VM looks for a native method that matches the signature (shown here) for the Java_oreilly_jent_rmi_NativeAccountImpl_withdraw function.

Now all we need to do is implement the C/C++ functions declared in our JNI-generated header file. This is where we tie our Java methods to some legacy native code. In this case, suppose the native code is wrapped up in a single C/C++ function called dbInvoke(). This function is available in a native library on the server platform (e.g., a DLL file on Windows or a shared library on Unix). We want to use our Java method to invoke this native function to perform various operations on the database holding our account information, so we can implement the Java_NativeAccountImpl_withdraw() function along these lines:

```
#include <jni.h>
#include "oreilly_jent_rmi_NativeAccountImpl.h"

JNIEXPORT void JNICALL Java_oreilly_jent_rmi_NativeAccountImpl_withdraw
  (JNIEnv * env, jobject me, jfloat amt) {
  // Call the native method that will withdraw the money from the account

  // First, get the name of the account holder from the account object
  jclass acctCls =
    (*env)->FindClass(env, "oreilly/jent/rmi/NativeAccountImpl");
  jmethodID nameMID = env.GetMethodID(env, acctCls,
                          "getName", "()Ljava/lang/String;");
  jobject nObj = (*env)->CallObjectMethod(env, me, nameMID);
  const char* name = (*env)->GetStringUTFChars(env, (jstring)nObj, 0);

  // Now call the native function to withdraw money from the account
  // stored in the non-JDBC database...
  int err = dbInvoke("update ACCOUNT ...");
  if (err > 0) {
  // IF an error occurs, assume its a balance problem and throw an
  // InsufficientFundsException
  jclass excCls =
```

```
(*env)->FindClass(env, "oreilly/jent/rmi/InsufficientFundsException");
(*env)->ThrowNew(env, excCls, "Error during withdrawal.");
  }
}
```

The first part of the function gets the name of the Account that is the target of the withdrawal. From native code, this simple method call is rather convoluted—first, we locate the Java class definition through the JNI environment, then we get a handle on the method we want to call, and finally we call the method on the reference to the NativeAccountImpl object passed in as a function argument. The Java String return value of the getName() method is returned to us in the native environment as a jobject structure, which we convert to a C/C++ char array. When this is complete, we can then invoke the native dbInvoke() function to pass SQL commands to the account database. If some kind of error occurs during the database call, then we throw an exception back to the Java environment.

Once we compile this C/C++ code (linking with the native library that contains the dbInvoke() function), we can export remote NativeAccountImpl objects. Then remote clients can call the withdraw(), deposit(), or transfer() methods. These remote method calls in turn cause the invocation of native code on the server, when the object implementation calls its native methods.

Note that in order for the server object to find its native method, the native library containing the dbInvoke() function has to be loaded into the server object's VM using the System.loadLibrary() method. You can do this either in the application code that uses the native method or by adding a static initializer to the class. You can have the library loaded automatically when the NativeAccountImpl class is referenced:

```
static { System.loadLibrary("nativeDB"); }
```

The System.loadLibrary() method automatically converts the library name that you provide to a platform-specific filename. So if the previous example is run on a Solaris machine, the Java VM looks for a library file named *libnativeDB.so*. On a Windows machine, it looks for *nativeDB.dll*.

RMI with JNI Versus CORBA

There are pros and cons to using RMI and JNI to export legacy native code using Java remote objects, as opposed to using CORBA. With CORBA, a CORBA object implemented in the same language as the native code (C/C++ for our example) is created and exported on the server. Remote Java clients can get a Java stub to this CORBA object using JavaIDL, or any third-party Java CORBA implementation (see Chapter 4 for details).

One obvious advantage of the CORBA approach is that you don't need to have Java on the server. Since this is presumably a legacy server, perhaps a mainframe of some sort, finding a stable Java VM and development kit for the platform may be a problem. If a Java implementation isn't available or if installing additional software on the legacy server isn't desirable, CORBA is your only option.

An advantage of the RMI/JNI approach is that you're running Java at both ends of the remote communication and avoiding the use of CORBA entirely. CORBA is a rich distributed object API, but it may be overkill for your application. Using the simpler RMI API and keeping your code development strictly in Java (with some minimal C/C++ to interface to the legacy code) might be an advantage to you in this case.

RMI Over IIOP

Another approach for connecting RMI objects to non-Java objects is the ability for RMI objects to communicate directly with remote CORBA objects using IIOP, the CORBA network interface protocol.* The standard RMI implementation provided with Java uses an RMI-specific protocol, JRMP, to communicate over the network. RMI/IIOP allows RMI objects to use the CORBA network protocol, IIOP, to communicate with other objects. This means that an RMI object using RMI/IIOP can communicate with a remote CORBA object, regardless of the implementation language of the CORBA object. Likewise, a CORBA object can interact with your Java RMI objects directly. This really gives you the best of both worlds, since you can then implement your remote clients using RMI and use either CORBA or RMI/JNI on the server to interface to any native legacy code.

In order to convert your RMI objects to use IIOP, there are some changes you need to make:

- Any implementation classes should extend the `javax.rmi.Portable-RemoteObject` class, rather than `java.rmi.server.UnicastRemoteObject`.

- All your stub and skeleton classes need to be regenerated using the updated *rmic* compiler provided with the RMI/IIOP installation. This updated compiler has an -iiop option that produces stubs and ties (*ties* refers to skeletons in the CORBA vernacular). These stubs and ties handle the link between client and server objects, but use IIOP rather than JRMP.

- All use of the RMI `Naming` registry has to be converted to use JNDI to talk to a CORBA Naming Service. Objects that you export are bound to names in the CORBA Naming Service through the JNDI context, and remote objects you look up are accessed from the Naming Service through the JNDI context.

- Instead of using the standard Java casting operator on remote objects you look up, use the `javax.rmi.PortableRemoteObject.narrow()` method.

To give you a taste for how to use RMI/IIOP with your RMI classes, let's convert our first `Account` example to use RMI/IIOP. First, we need to update the `AccountImpl` class to extend `PortableRemoteObject`. The following fragment of the `IIOPAccountImpl` class does that:

```
import javax.rmi.PortableRemoteObject;
import java.rmi.RemoteException;
import java.util.List;
import java.util.ListIterator;
```

---

* The RMI-IIOP tools and classes became a standard part of the Java core environment as of JDK 1.3. If you are using an earlier version of Java 2, you need to download the RMI-IIOP tools and libraries from *http://java.sun.com/products/rmi-iiop/*.

```
public class IIOPAccountImpl extends PortableRemoteObject implements
Account {
  // Remainder of implementation is identical
```

We can compile the updated IIOPAccountImpl using the regular Java compiler, then use the extended *rmic* compiler included with RMI/IIOP to generate IIOP stubs and ties:

```
% rmic -iiop -d /home/myclasses IIOPAccountImpl
```

This generates an *IIOPAccountImpl_Stub* class and an *IIOPAccountImpl_Tie* class, which act as the IIOP stub and tie for the remote object.

In the CORBA world, remote objects are looked up using the CORBA Naming Service, so we need to update the AccountReg class to use JNDI to register an Account object with a CORBA Naming Service, rather than the RMI registry. The updated IIOPAccountReg class looks like this:

```
import javax.naming.*;
import java.rmi.*;

public class IIOPAccountReg {
  public static void main(String argv[]) {
    try {
      // Make an Account with a given name
      IIOPAccountImpl acct = new IIOPAccountImpl("Jim.Farley");

      // Get a reference to CORBA naming service using JNDI
      Hashtable props = new Hashtable();
      props.put("java.naming.factory.initial",
          "com.sun.jndi.cosnaming.CNCtxFactory");
      props.put("java.naming.provider.url", "iiop://objhost.org:900");
      Context ctx = new InitialContext(props);

      // Register our Account with the CORBA naming service
      ctx.rebind("JimF", acct);
      System.out.println("Registered account.");
    }
    catch (Exception e) {
      e.printStackTrace();
    }
  }
}
```

Refer to Chapter 7 for details on the properties used to create the JNDI context and what they mean. All you need to glean from this is that we're trying to connect to a naming service running on *objhost.org*, listening to port 900. Once we are connected, we register the new IIOPAccountImpl object with the naming service using the Context.rebind() method.

Finally, we need to update our client so that it works with RMI/IIOP. Instead of using an RMI registry to look up the remote Account object, the client needs to use JNDI to connect to the same CORBA Naming Service that now hosts our Account object and ask for the Account by name. The updated IIOPAccountClient is shown here. Notice that we've also changed the client to use the PortableRemoteObject.narrow() method, instead of just casting the object returned from the lookup:

```
import javax.naming.*;
import java.rmi.RMISecurityManager;

public class IIOPAccountClient {
  public static void main(String argv[]) {
    try {
    // Lookup account object
    Hashtable props = new Hashtable();
    props.put("java.naming.factory.initial",
        "com.sun.jndi.cosnaming.CNCtxFactory");
    props.put("java.naming.provider.url", "iiop://objhost.org:900");
    Context ctx = new InitialContext(props);
    Account jimAcct =
      (Account)PortableRemoteObject.narrow(ctx.lookup("JimF"),
                                            Account.class);

    // Make deposit
    jimAcct.deposit(12000);

    // Report results and balance.
    System.out.println("Deposited 12,000 into account owned by " +
                                            jimAcct.getName());
      System.out.println("Balance now totals: " + jimAcct.getBalance());
    }
    catch (Exception e) {
      System.out.println("Error while looking up account:");
      e.printStackTrace();
    }
  }
}
```

In order to register the server object, we need a CORBA Naming Service running, just like we need an RMI registry with standard RMI. The RMI/IIOP package includes a special naming service that is started using the *tnameserv* utility. This tool is similar to the naming service provided with Java IDL (and discussed in Chapter 4), but this version is a CORBA Naming Service that also provides JNDI access. On *objhost.org*, we need to start the naming service like so:

```
objhost% tnameserv -ORBInitialPort 900
```

Now we can run IIOPAccountReg to register the Account object with the naming service, then run our IIOPAccountClient to access the Account and make a deposit. All network communications are now taking place using IIOP rather than the RMI protocol.

Accessing RMI Objects from CORBA

Since our Account object is now speaking IIOP, we can also access it from other, non-Java CORBA clients. First, we need to get an IDL interface for the Account interface, which can be done using the *rmic* compiler provided with RMI/IIOP. The -idl option generates an IDL mapping of a Java RMI interface using the Java-to-IDL mapping defined by the CORBA standard. With this IDL mapping, we can generate language-specific stubs that allow any CORBA client talk to our Java remote object. See Chapter 4 for more details on using IDL and generating language-specific interfaces from it.

CHAPTER 4

Java IDL (CORBA)

The Java IDL API, introduced in Version 1.2 of the Java 2 platform, provides an interface between Java programs and distributed objects and services built using the Common Object Request Broker Architecture (CORBA). CORBA is a standard defined by the Object Management Group (OMG). It describes an architecture, interfaces, and protocols that distributed objects can use to interact with each other. Part of the CORBA standard is the Interface Definition Language (IDL), which is an implementation-independent language for describing the interfaces of remote-capable objects. There are standard mappings defined by the OMG for converting IDL interfaces into C++ classes, C code, and Java classes, among others (a complete list is provided later in the chapter). These generated classes use the underlying CORBA framework to communicate with remote clients and give you the basis for implementing and exporting your own distributed objects. Java IDL is Sun's implementation of the standard IDL-to-Java mapping and is provided by Sun with the standard Java SDK in the `org.omg.CORBA` package, the `org.omg.CosNaming` package, and other `org.omg.*` packages.

Like RMI, Java IDL gives you a way to access remote objects over the network. It also provides the tools you need to make your objects accessible to other CORBA clients. If you export a Java class using Java IDL, it's possible to create an instance of that class and publish it through a naming/directory service. A remote client can find this object, call methods on it, and receive data from it, just as if it were running on the client's local machine. Unlike RMI, however, objects that are exported using CORBA can be accessed by clients implemented in any language with an IDL binding (not just Java).

The CORBA standard is extensive, to say the least. In addition to the basic remote object architecture and the syntax of IDL, it also includes specifications for several distributed object services, like an object naming service, a security policy service, and persistent object services. It would be foolhardy to attempt to cover all these topics completely in one chapter, so we won't. Instead, we'll just cover the basic features of the CORBA architecture and the IDL syntax. We'll also look at the

Naming Service, which is key to almost every CORBA application because it provides a standard way to find remote CORBA objects on the network. After that, we'll take a look at the Java IDL API and the *idlj* compiler and how they work together to give you an interface from your Java code to CORBA objects and services. They also provide the tools you need to create your own CORBA objects, implemented in Java.

The rest of this chapter is broken down roughly into three parts. In the first part, we'll look at an overview of the CORBA architecture and how it allows you to create, export, access, and manage remote objects. In the second part, we'll explore the details of creating your own CORBA objects. Finally, we'll look how clients can remotely access your CORBA objects.

A Note on Evolving Standards

At the time CORBA support was first made part of the core Java API (with the introduction of Java 2 Version 1.2), the CORBA specification and the IDL-to-Java binding for CORBA were in a bit of flux. The server-side object adaptor interface (the interface between remote object implementations and the core CORBA object services) had been altered significantly by the OMG in Version 2.3 of the CORBA specification. The Basic Object Adaptor (BOA) interface had been replaced by the Portable Object Adaptor (POA), which, as the name suggests, provides a portable implementation interface for CORBA server-side objects. This filled a gap in the specification left by the BOA that led to vendor-specific extensions and, therefore, CORBA server objects that were dependent on particular vendor ORB implementations. The standard IDL-to-Java mapping, however, took some time to be updated to support the new POA; and JDK 1.2 was released before the new version of the Java mapping. As a stopgap measure, the first version of Java IDL in JDK 1.2 used a server-side object adaptor interface based on an ImplBase scheme (described in detail later in this chapter). By the time JDK 1.4 was introduced in beta in 2001, the POA-compatible version of the IDL-to-Java mapping had been released, and the Java IDL packages, as well as the IDL-to-Java compiler in JDK 1.4, were based on this mapping.

Another recent addition to the CORBA specifications is the Interoperable Naming Service (INS) interface, which adds new utilities and functionality on top of the standard CORBA Naming Service. INS was incorporated into the CORBA 2.3 specification, and support for it in Java IDL was introduced in JDK 1.4.

In this chapter, we will discuss both the POA and "pre-POA" versions of Java IDL. If you are using JDK 1.4 or later, you are using a POA-compatible mapping of the CORBA interfaces. If you are using JDK 1.3 or JDK 1.2, you are using the "pre-POA" version of the IDL-to-Java mapping that Sun used prior to adding the POA support. Most of the examples in the chapter will be shown in both their POA and pre-POA versions—examples labeled as POA-compatible is usable in JDK 1.4 or later, while examples labeled pre-POA can be used in JDK 1.3 or 1.2 environments. We will also discuss both the original Naming Service interface and the new Interoperable Naming Service (INS) interface. Again, if you are using JDK 1.4 or later, you have access to the INS interface and the Naming Service provided with the Java IDL. The Object Request Broker (ORB) supports these extended features. If you are using a prior version of the JDK, you have to use the original Naming Service interface.

The CORBA Architecture

At its core, the CORBA architecture for distributed objects shares many features with the architecture used by Java RMI. A description of a remote object is used to generate a client stub interface and a server skeleton interface for the object. A client application invokes methods on a remote object using the client stub. The method request is transmitted through the underlying infrastructure to the remote host, where the server skeleton for the object is asked to invoke the method on the object itself. Any data resulting from the method call (return values, exceptions) is transmitted back to the client by the communication infrastructure.

But that's where the similarities between CORBA and RMI end. CORBA was designed from the start to be a language-independent distributed object standard, so it is much more extensive and detailed in its specification than RMI is (or needs to be). For the most part, these extra details are required in CORBA because it needs to support languages that have different built-in features. Some languages, like C++, directly support objects, while others, like C, don't. The CORBA standard needs to include a detailed specification of an object model so that nonobject-oriented languages can take advantage of CORBA. Java includes built-in support for communicating object interfaces and examining them abstractly (using Java bytecodes and the Java Reflection API). Many other languages don't. So the CORBA specification includes details about a Dynamic Invocation Interface and a Dynamic Skeleton Interface, which can be implemented in languages that don't have their own facilities for these operations. In languages that do have these capabilities, like Java, there needs to be a mapping between the built-in features and the features as defined by the CORBA specification.

The rest of this section provides an overview of the major components that make up the CORBA architecture: the Interface Definition Language, which is how CORBA interfaces are defined; the Object Request Broker (ORB) and Object Adaptor, which are responsible for handling all interactions between remote objects and the applications that use them; the Naming Service, which is a standard service in CORBA that lets remote clients find remote objects on the network; and the inter-ORB communication protocol, which handles the low-level communication between processes in a CORBA context.

Interface Definition Language

The Interface Definition Language provides the primary way of describing data types in CORBA. IDL is independent of any particular programming language. Mappings, or bindings, from IDL to specific programming languages are defined and standardized as part of the CORBA specification. At the time of this writing, standard bindings for C, C++, Smalltalk, Ada, COBOL, Lisp, Python and Java have been approved by the OMG. Chapter 14 contains a complete description of IDL syntax.

The central CORBA functions, services, and facilities, such as the ORB and the Naming Service, are also specified in IDL. This means that a particular language binding also specifies the bindings for the core CORBA functions to that language. Sun's Java IDL API follows the Java IDL mapping defined by the OMG standards. This allows you to run your CORBA-based Java code in any compliant Java implementation of the CORBA standard, provided you stick to standard elements of the Java binding. Note, however, that Sun's implementation includes some nonstandard elements; they are highlighted in this chapter where appropriate.

The Object Request Broker and the Object Adaptor

The core of the CORBA architecture is the Object Request Broker, as shown in Figure 4-1. Each machine involved in a CORBA application must have an ORB running in order for processes on that machine to interact with CORBA objects running in remote processes. Object clients and servers make requests through their ORBs; the ORB is responsible for making the requests happen or indicating why they can't. The client ORB provides a stub for a remote object. Requests made on the stub are transferred from the client's ORB to the ORB servicing the implementation of the target object. The request is passed on to the implementation through an object adaptor and the object's skeleton interface.

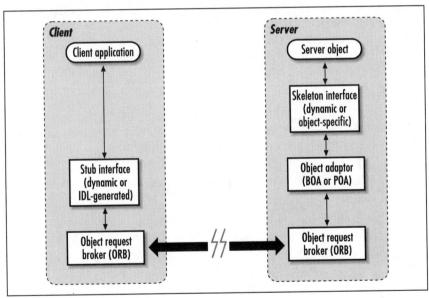

Figure 4-1: Basic CORBA architecture

The skeleton interface is specific to the type of object that is exported remotely through CORBA. Among other things, it provides a wrapper interface that the ORB and object adaptor can use to invoke methods on behalf of the client or as part of the lifecycle management of the object. The object adaptor provides a general facility that "plugs" a server object into a particular CORBA runtime environment. Older versions of the CORBA specification and Java IDL supported a Basic Object Adaptor (BOA) interface, while newer versions (CORBA 2.3 and later, JDK 1.4 and later) support a Portable Object Adaptor interface (we'll discuss the difference later in the chapter). All server objects can use the object adaptor to interact with the core functionality of the ORB, and the ORB in turn can use the object adaptor to pass along client requests and lifecycle notifications to the server object. Typically, an IDL compiler is used to generate the skeleton interface for a particular IDL interface; this generated skeleton interface will include calls to the object adaptor that are supported by the CORBA environment in use.

The Naming Service

The CORBA Naming Service (sometimes abbreviated to *COSNaming*, from "CORBA Object Services, Naming") provides a directory naming structure for remote objects. The CORBA Naming Service is one of the naming and directory services supported by JNDI, so the concepts used in its API are similar to the general model of Contexts and DirContexts used in JNDI.

The naming tree always starts with a root node, and subnodes of the object tree can be created by an application. Actual objects are stored by name at the leaves of the tree. Figure 4-2 depicts an example set of objects[*] registered within a Naming Service directory. The fully qualified name of an object in the directory is the ordered list of all of its parent nodes, starting from the root node and including the leaf name of the object itself. So, the full name of the object labeled "Fred" is "Living thing," "Animal," "Man," "Fred," in that order.

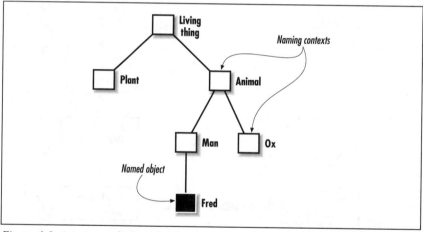

Figure 4-2: A naming directory

Each branch in the directory tree is called a *naming context*, and leaf objects have *bindings* to specific names. Each node in the naming directory is represented by an org.omg.CosNaming.NamingContext object. Each NamingContext can be asked to find an object within its branch of the tree by asking for the object by name, relative to that particular naming context. You can get a reference to the root context of the naming directory from an ORB using the resolve_initial_references()

---

[*] Example adapted from *Categories*, by Aristotle. Please pardon the categorization "man," as opposed to "human." This is the typical translation of Aristotle's original Greek, perhaps because political correctness wasn't in fashion in 350 B.C.

method. Once you have a reference to the root of the naming directory, you can perform lookups of CORBA objects, as well as register your own CORBA objects with the Naming Service. We'll see more concrete details of utilizing the CORBA Naming Service later in this chapter in the section "Putting It in the Public Eye."

Inter-ORB Communication

Version 2.0 (and later) of the CORBA standard includes specifications for inter-ORB communication protocols that can transmit object requests between various ORBs running on the network. The protocols are independent of the particular ORB implementations running at either end of the communication link. An ORB implemented in Java can talk to another ORB implemented in C, as long as they're both compliant with the CORBA standard and use the same CORBA communication protocol. The inter-ORB protocol is responsible for delivering messages between two cooperating ORBs. These messages might be method requests, return types, error messages, etc. The inter-ORB protocol also deals with differences between the two ORB implementations, like machine-level byte ordering and alignment. As a CORBA application developer, you shouldn't have to deal directly with the low-level communication protocol between ORBs. If you want two ORBs to talk to each other, you need to ensure that they are compatible in terms of CORBA compliance levels (do they support similar levels of the CORBA specification?) and that they both speak a common, standard inter-ORB protocol.

The Internet Inter-ORB Protocol (IIOP) is an inter-ORB protocol based on TCP/IP. TCP/IP is by far the most commonly used network protocol on the Internet, so IIOP is the most commonly used CORBA communication protocol. There are other standard CORBA protocols defined for other network environments, however. The DCE Common Inter-ORB Protocol (DCE-CIOP), for example, allows ORBs to communicate on top of DCE-RPC.

Creating CORBA Objects

Now that we have a better understanding of the various components of the CORBA architecture, let's walk through the creation of CORBA objects using Java IDL. In order to distribute a Java object over the network using CORBA, you have to define your own CORBA-enabled interface and its implementation. This involves doing the following:

- Writing an interface in the CORBA Interface Definition Language

- Generating a Java base interface, plus a Java stub and skeleton class, using an IDL-to-Java compiler

- Writing a server-side implementation of the Java base interface

We'll walk through these steps one by one, starting with a quick primer on CORBA IDL, followed by the requirements for creating a Java implementation of an IDL-defined remote object.

An IDL Primer

The syntax of both Java and IDL were modeled to some extent on C++, so there are a lot of similarities between the two in terms of syntax. Interfaces in IDL are declared much like classes in C++ and, thus, classes or interfaces in Java. The major differences between IDL and Java are:

- IDL is a declaration language. In IDL, you declare only the names and types for interfaces, data members, methods, method parameters, etc. Method implementations are created in the implementation language you choose (in this case Java), after you've used an IDL compiler to convert your IDL interface to your target language.

- IDL, like C++, includes nonclass data structure definitions, like structs, unions, and enumerations.

- Method parameters in IDL include modifiers that specify whether they are input, output, or input/output variables. In Java, all primitive data types are passed by value, and all object data types are passed by reference.

- An IDL file can include multiple public interfaces. Only a single public class can be defined in a given Java file (although Java does allow for multiple inner classes within a single public class definition, and multiple nonpublic classes per file).

- Modules, which are similar to Java packages, can be nested within other modules in the same IDL file, and interfaces in multiple distinct modules can be defined in the same IDL file. In Java, you can define a class only within a single package in a single Java file.

Modules

Modules are declared in IDL using the `module` keyword, followed by a name for the module and an opening brace that starts the module scope. Everything defined within the scope of this module (interfaces, constants, other modules) falls within the module and is referenced in other IDL modules using the syntax `modulename::x`. Suppose that you want all your classes to be contained in a module called `corba`, which is part of a larger module called `jent` (an abbreviation of the title of this book). In IDL this is declared as follows:

```
// IDL
module jent {
  module corba {
    interface NeatExample ...
  };
};
```

If you want to reference the `NeatExample` interface in other IDL files, you use the syntax `jent::corba::NeatExample`, which may look familiar to readers who have done C++ programming. Java programmers should note the semicolons following the closing braces on the module definitions, which are required in IDL but not in Java. A semicolon is also required after the close of an interface definition.

Interfaces

Interfaces declared in IDL are mapped into classes or interfaces in Java. As mentioned earlier, IDL is used only to declare modules, interfaces, and their methods. Methods on IDL interfaces are always left abstract, to be defined in the programming language you use to implement the interfaces.

The declaration of an interface includes an interface header and an interface body. The header specifies the name of the interface and the interfaces it inherits from (if any). Here is an IDL interface header:

```
interface PrintServer : Server { ...
```

This header starts the declaration of an interface called `PrintServer` that inherits all the methods and data members defined in the `Server` interface. An IDL interface can inherit from multiple interfaces; simply separate the interface names with commas in the inheritance part of the header.

Data members and methods

The interface body declares all the data members (or attributes) and methods of an interface. Data members are declared using the `attribute` keyword. At a minimum, the declaration includes a name and a type (see Chapter 14 for a complete list of the basic data types available in IDL and the mapping to Java types). The declaration can optionally specify whether the attribute is read-only or not, using the `readonly` keyword. By default, every attribute you declare is readable and writable (for Java, this means that the IDL compiler generates public read and write methods for it). Here is an example declaration for a read-only `string` attribute:

```
readonly attribute string myString;
```

You declare a method by specifying its name, return type, and parameters, at a minimum. You can also optionally declare exceptions the method might raise, the invocation semantics of the method, and the context for the method call (see Chapter 14 for more details). Here is the declaration for a simple method that returns a `string`:

```
string parseString(in string buffer);
```

This declares a method called `parseString()` that accepts a single `string` argument and returns a `string` value.

A complete IDL example

Now let's tie all these basic elements together. Here's a complete IDL example that declares a module within another module, which itself contains several interfaces:

```
module OS {
  module services {
    interface Server {
      readonly attribute string serverName;
      boolean init(in string sName);
    };
```

```
interface Printable {
  boolean print(in string header);
};

interface PrintServer : Server {
  boolean printThis(in Printable p);
};
};
};
```

The first interface, Server, has a single read-only string attribute and an init()
method that accepts a string and returns a boolean. The Printable interface has a
single print() method that accepts a string header. Finally, the PrintServer interface extends the Server interface (hence inheriting all its methods and attributes)
and adds a printThis() method that accepts a Printable object and returns a
boolean. In all cases, we've declared our method arguments as input-only (i.e.,
pass-by-value), using the in keyword.

Turning IDL into Java

Once you've described your remote interfaces in IDL, you need to generate Java
classes that act as a starting point for implementing those remote interfaces in Java
using an IDL-to-Java compiler. Every standard IDL-to-Java compiler (whether it's a
POA-compliant or pre-POA version) can generate the following Java classes from
an IDL interface:

- A *Java interface* with the same name as the IDL interface (e.g., Server). This
  interface includes Java method declarations that are a mapping of the operations declared in the IDL interface. In later versions of Sun's IDL-to-Java mapping (JDK 1.3 and later), an *interfaceNameOperations* interface (e.g.,
  ServerOperations) is generated that contains these method declarations. The
  object's mapped Java interface extends this interface. This "operations" interface was added to the standard CORBA IDL-to-Java mapping, and the IDL-to-
  Java compiler in JDK 1.3 was updated to reflect this. This same operations
  interface is extended by the server-side skeleton interfaces. In earlier versions
  of Java IDL (JDK 1.2), the object's Java interface contains the method declarations directly, and there is no operations interface created.

- A *helper* class whose name is the name of the IDL interface with "Helper"
  appended to it (e.g., ServerHelper). The primary purpose of this class is to
  provide a static narrow() method that can safely cast CORBA Object references to the Java interface type. The helper class also provides other useful
  static methods, such as read() and write() methods that allow you to read
  and write an object of the corresponding type using I/O streams.

- A *holder* class whose name is the name of the IDL interface with "Holder"
  appended to it (e.g., ServerHolder). This class is used when objects with this
  interface are used as out or inout arguments in remote CORBA methods.
  Instead of being passed directly into the remote method, the object is
  wrapped with its holder before being passed. When a remote method has
  parameters that are declared as out or inout, the server-side method has to be
  able to update the argument it is passed and return the updated value. The

only way to guarantee this, even for primitive Java data types, is to force out and inout arguments to be wrapped in Java holder classes, which are filled with the output value of the argument when the method returns. Also, inout arguments are initialized with the desired input value before the remote method is called in Java.

- A *client stub* class, called _*interface-name*Stub, that acts as a client-side implementation of the interface. This stub class implements the generated Java interface for the object, but simply knows how to convert client method calls into ORB requests that are forwarded to the actual remote object. The stub class for an interface named Server is called _ServerStub.

These classes comprise the "outward-facing" mapping of the CORBA object's interface (the interfaces that clients of the object use directly). The IDL-to-Java compiler can also generate server-side skeleton classes you can use to implement the server-side implementation of the remote CORBA interface. In pre-POA versions of Java IDL, the IDL-to-Java compiler (*idltojava* in JDK 1.2,[*] *idlj* in JDK 1.3) is based on the ImplBase inheritance approach to creating server implementations. The pre-POA Java IDL compilers generate the server-side code in the form:

- A *server skeleton* class called _*interface-name*ImplBase, which is a base class for a server-side implementation of the interface. The base class can accept requests for the object from the ORB and channel return values back through the ORB to the remote client. The skeleton class for an interface named Server is called _ServerImplBase.

In POA-compliant versions of Sun's *idlj* compiler, a similar _*interfaceName*Stub client-side interface is generated, but instead of the server-side ImplBase inheritance scheme used in earlier versions, the compiler generates:

- A server skeleton class named interfaceNamePOA (e.g, ServerPOA), which implements a generated *interfaceName*Operations interface and extends the POA-related server-side interfaces. The interfaceNameOperations interface contains Java mappings of all the methods declared in the IDL definition. This class serves the same basic role as the ImplBase class generated in earlier versions of Java IDL, but it utilizes the standard POA interfaces to interact with the server-side ORB functions.

So, in addition to generating a client-side Java mapping of the IDL interface and some helper classes for the Java interface, the IDL-to-Java compiler also creates subclasses that act as an interface between a CORBA client and the ORB, between the server-side implementation and the ORB. Chapter 16 provides a complete reference for the JDK 1.3 and 1.4 versions of Sun's *idlj* compiler. We will use this IDL-to-Java tool in the examples in this chapter. Remember, though, that any Java mapping of the CORBA standard should include its own IDL-to-Java compiler to generate these Java classes from the IDL interfaces you write. In addition, the Java that these tools generate should be compliant with the standard IDL mapping for Java, published by the OMG in the CORBA standard. Tools developed before the

---

[*] Although Java IDL was a standard part of Java 1.2, Sun only offered the early-access version of its *idltojava* compiler, which you have to download separately from *http://developer.java. sun.com/developer/earlyAccess/jdk12/idltojava.html.*

POA-compliant IDL-to-Java mapping will tend to use some non-standard server-side object adaptor styles, while those developed after the POA was introduced should generate POA-compliant server skeleton classes. So when using third-party Java-based CORBA tools and ORBs, it's important to understand which version of the core CORBA spec, the IDL-to-Java mapping they support.

The delegation server-side model

The scheme described above (and demonstrated in Example 4-1) for the generated server-side code for a CORBA object is called an *inheritance-based model*. It depends on the server-side implementation directly extending a generated class (interfaceNamePOA for POA-compliant environments and _interfaceNameImplBase for pre-POA environments). There is another option, called the *delegation model*, available to you in terms of how you "plug" your server code into the CORBA environment.

The delegation model is based on a scheme in which an server-side delegate is generated by the IDL compiler. This delegate extends the generated skeleton class, and implements each of the mapped remote methods by delegating the incoming method request to a delegate object. This delegate object needs to implement the interfaceNameOperations interface generated by the IDL compiler, but it doesn't have to extend a concrete or abstract base class. This can prove to be useful in cases where you have a preexisting Java class with its own inheritance scheme and want to "export" this class through CORBA for remote access. Because Java prohibits multiple inheritance, you don't have the option of extending both the existing class and the generated skeleton class. With the delegation model, you can define a simple delegate class that extends the preexisting Java class, and implements the interfaceNameOperations interface generated by the compiler. You can then "publish" an instance of the original class by creating an instance of the new delegate class and an instance of the generated delegation-based server object, and associating the server object with your delegate.

We won't provide full details of the delegation model here, but it's important to realize that this option exists. It may prove useful in some situations. There are options available on the IDL-to-Java compiler to instruct it to generate delegation-based server objects (also referred to as *ties*). These compiler options are documented in Chapter 16.

A simple server class

The IDL interface shown in Example 4-1 is the IDL equivalent of the Account class we defined in Example 3-1. The interface, named Account, is declared within some nested modules (oreilly, jent, corba), and declares methods similar to the Account example in Chapter 3. Since this is IDL, the various method argument and return value data types are represented using IDL datatypes (e.g., string instead of String, etc.), and method arguments are declared with in, inout, or out modifiers.

Example 4-1: An Account Interface Defined in IDL

```
//
// [IDL] Account interface defined in IDL.
//

module oreilly {
  module jent {
    module corba {
      // Forward-declare the Account interface, for the typedefs below
      interface Account;

      // Declare some useful typedefs: a list of Accounts and of floats
      typedef sequence<Account> AccountList;
      typedef sequence<float> floatList;

      exception InsufficientFundsException {};

      interface Account {
        // Get the name of the account owner
        string getName();
        // The account balance
        float getBalance();
        // Withdraw funds from the account
        void withdraw(in float amt) raises (InsufficientFundsException);
        // Deposit funds to the account
        void deposit(in float amt);
        // Transfer funds from the source account to this account
        void transfer(in float amt, in Account src)
          raises (InsufficientFundsException);
        // Similar to above, but perform transfers from a series of
        // source Accounts
        void transferBatch(in floatList amts, in AccountList srcs)
          raises (InsufficientFundsException);
      };
    };
  };
};
```

We can run the *idlj* compiler on this IDL interface using the following command line (Windows version):

```
C:\>idlj -fall Account.idl
```

This command creates the five Java classes described in the previous sections: a Java version of the interface, a helper class, a holder class, a client stub, and a server skeleton. The -fall option tells the compiler to generate both client-side and server-side mapping interfaces (see Chapter 16 for complete details on the command-line arguments for *idlj*).

The compiler creates the Java interface shown in Example 4-2, in a file named *Account.java*. This interface doesn't have much meat to it, because all of the method declarations are generated in the AccountOperations interface are extended by this interface, which is shown in Example 4-3. The interface declaration in the IDL file is mapped directly to the Account Java interface declaration, with the interface extending the AccountOperations and org.omg.CORBA. Object interfaces. The module declarations in the IDL file have been mapped into an oreilly.jent.corba package statement at the beginning of all the generated Java files. The IDL data types have been converted into the equivalent Java data types, and, since they don't require any special handling in a remote method call, the in method parameters in IDL are mapped into regular Java input arguments.

Example 4-2 : Java Mapping of the Account Interface

```
package oreilly.jent.corba;

/**
* oreilly/jent/corba/Account.java
* Generated by the IDL-to-Java compiler (portable), version "3.1"
* from ../Account.idl
* Friday, July 6, 2001 8:11:50 AM EDT
*/

public interface Account extends AccountOperations,
     org.omg.CORBA.Object, org.omg.CORBA.portable.IDLEntity
{
} // interface Account
```

Example 4-3: AccountOperations Java Interface

```
package oreilly.jent.corba;

/**
* oreilly/jent/corba/AccountOperations.java
* Generated by the IDL-to-Java compiler (portable), version "3.1"
* from ../Account.idl
* Friday, July 6, 2001 8:11:50 AM EDT
*/

public interface AccountOperations
{

  // Get the name of the account owner
  String getName ();

  // The account balance
  float getBalance ();

  // Withdraw funds from the account
  void withdraw (float amt) throws
       oreilly.jent.corba.InsufficientFundsException;

  // Deposit funds to the account
  void deposit (float amt);
```

Example 4-3: AccountOperations Java Interface (continued)

```
// Transfer funds from the source account to this account
void transfer (float amt, oreilly.jent.corba.Account src)
     throws oreilly.jent.corba.InsufficientFundsException;

// source Accounts
void transferBatch (float[] amts, oreilly.jent.corba.Account[] srcs)
     throws oreilly.jent.corba.InsufficientFundsException;
} // interface AccountOperations
```

The helper class and narrowing references

The compiler also generates a helper class, called `AccountHelper`. We won't provide the full code listing for this generated class here, but it can be found in the downloadable source code examples available for this book, along with all of the other Java interfaces generated by the IDL-to-Java compiler from this IDL interface.

The helper class is a standalone utility class that doesn't extend any other interfaces:

```
abstract public class AccountHelper {
```

As mentioned earlier, the helper class has static methods that let you read and write Account objects to and from CORBA I/O streams:

```
public static
   oreilly.jent.corba.Account read (org.omg.CORBA.portable.InputStream
istream)
public static void write (org.omg.CORBA.portable.OutputStream ostream,
                          oreilly.jent.corba.Account value)
```

a type() method that provides the `TypeCode` for the mapped Account class:

```
synchronized public static org.omg.CORBA.TypeCode type ( )
```

and, most importantly, a narrow() method that safely narrows a CORBA `org.omg.CORBA.Object` reference into an Account reference:

```
public static oreilly.jent.corba.Account narrow
   (org.omg.CORBA.Object obj)
```

Object narrowing is CORBA's equivalent to directly casting object references—we discuss why narrowing is necessary later, in the section "Remote Object References and Narrowing." In the implementation of the narrow() method, the helper class converts a CORBA Object reference to a reference to a specific type. If the CORBA object can't be narrowed to the requested type (e.g., the passed object reference is a null reference, the object's `TypeCode` doesn't match the `TypeCode` of the narrowed type, etc.), then the narrow() method throws a BAD_PARAM exception.

The holder class

The compiler generates a holder class for the Account class, which implements the CORBA `Streamable` interface.

Java IDL (CORBA)

```
public final class AccountHolder implements org.omg.CORBA.portable.
                                                              Streamable
```

The holder class is a wrapper used when Account objects are called for as out or inout arguments in an IDL method. All holder classes implement the Streamable interface from the org.omg.CORBA.portable package, which includes implementations of the _read() and _write() methods of the Streamable interface:

```
public void _read (org.omg.CORBA.portable.InputStream i)
public void _write (org.omg.CORBA.portable.OutputStream o)
```

This allows holders to be transmitted in remote method calls using these _read() and _write() methods; these methods handle whatever serialization the object needs. This functionality is similar to that provided by Java serialization, but CORBA needs its own scheme because it is independent of any particular language, and needs to provide this serialization even if the target language doesn't provide this feature natively.

A holder contains a single instance of the corresponding CORBA object (an Account, in this example) as a data member:

```
public oreilly.jent.corba.Account value = null;
```

This instance is initialized in the constructor of the holder:

```
public AccountHolder (oreilly.jent.corba.Account initialValue)
{
  value = initialValue;
}
```

When a holder object is passed into a remote method call as an inout argument, its _write() method is invoked. This method takes the object instance contained by the holder class, serializes it, and streams it through the ORB to the remote object server. When the remote method call returns, the holder's _read() method is invoked to read the (possibly updated) object from the remote object server, and the holder object replaces its internal value with the updated object.

As an example of using the holder class, let's define another IDL interface that includes a method that uses an Account as an inout parameter:

```
// IDL
interface AccountManager {
  boolean updateAccount(inout Account account);
};
```

The AccountManagerOperations Java interface generated from this IDL interface uses the AccountHolder class as the type for the corresponding Java method parameter:

```
// Java
public interface AccountManagerOperations
{
  boolean updateAccount (AccountHolder account);
} // interface AccountManagerOperations
```

The client stub

The *idlj* compiler generates a Java client stub (_AccountStub) for our CORBA interface. The client stub implements the generated Account Java interface and acts as a client-side proxy for a remote Account object:

```
public class _AccountStub
  extends org.omg.CORBA.portable.ObjectImpl
  implements oreilly.jent.corba.Account
```

When a client acquires a reference to a remote Account object (through any of the methods we'll describe later, in the section "Finding and Using Remote Objects"), it actually receives an instance of this client stub class. The stub has implementations of all the methods from the interface, as mapped into the AccountOperations interface that is the parent of the Account interface. The stub class serves as a proxy for a remote server object, and each method implementation in the stub generates a request to the ORB to make a remote method call on the corresponding server-side object. The method arguments are bundled up ("marshalled") and passed along with the request to the ORB. We're not going to go into the details of the stub's method implementations, because you shouldn't have to worry much about them under normal conditions. But it is enlightening to look at an example to see how your remote objects do what they do in detail, using the core CORBA functions. As an example, here is the generated client stub implementation of the getName() method from our Account interface:

```
// Get the name of the account owner
public String getName ()
{
   org.omg.CORBA.portable.InputStream $in = null;
   try {
     org.omg.CORBA.portable.OutputStream $out = _request ("getName",
true);
     $in = _invoke ($out);
     String $result = $in.read_string ();
     return $result;
   } catch (org.omg.CORBA.portable.ApplicationException $ex) {
     $in = $ex.getInputStream ();
     String _id = $ex.getId ();
     throw new org.omg.CORBA.MARSHAL (_id);
   } catch (org.omg.CORBA.portable.RemarshalException $rm) {
     return getName ();
   } finally {
     _releaseReply ($in);
   }
} // getName
```

As mentioned, when a Java client gets a reference to a remote Account object, it is given one of these stub objects. The client can make method calls on the stub object, and the stub converts these calls into corresponding requests to the ORB to invoke the methods on the remote object and send back the results.

Pre-POA server skeletons

In pre-POA versions of Java IDL (JDK 1.2 and 1.3), the IDL-to-Java compiler generates a server implementation base class that follows the ImplBase scheme. An _AccountImplBase base class for the server implementation is generated:

```
public abstract class _AccountImplBase
    extends org.omg.CORBA.portable.ObjectImpl
    implements oreilly.jent.corba.Account,
                            org.omg.CORBA.portable.InvokeHandler
```

This base class provides the basic "plumbing" for our server implementation. As mentioned earlier in this section, it's principle purpose is to receive requests from remote clients through the ORB and directs them to the proper method on the server implementation class. In the ImplBase version, all this work is done by the server skeleton's _invoke() method, which is called by the ORB:

```
public org.omg.CORBA.portable.OutputStream _invoke (String method,
    org.omg.CORBA.portable.InputStream in,
    org.omg.CORBA.portable.ResponseHandler rh)
```

The _invoke() method figures out which method is being called, unpacks the method arguments (if any) from the request, and calls the method directly on itself.

Note that the server skeleton doesn't have implementations of the remote methods declared in the Account interface (also note that it's declared as an abstract class for this reason). The *idlj* compiler doesn't do everything for you; you still need to create a server implementation for your interface by extending this base class, and provide the logic behind the remotely accessible operations on your CORBA object.

POA server skeletons

In JDK 1.4 and later, the *idlj* compiler generates server implementation skeleton classes that follow the POA specification. In this model, the base class for the server implementation of our Account interface is called AccountPOA:

```
public abstract class AccountPOA
    extends org.omg.PortableServer.Servant
    implements oreilly.jent.corba.AccountOperations,
        org.omg.CORBA.portable.InvokeHandler
```

The structure of the class is very similar to the old ImplBase format (method requests are passed by the ORB to the _invoke() method, where they are delegated to the proper method on the implementation class), but the particulars of the ORB interface follow the POA specification. This helps to guarantee that your CORBA object implementations will migrate easily between different CORBA ORB implementations.

Writing the Implementation

So, we've written an IDL interface and generated the Java interface and support classes for it, including the client stub and the server skeleton. Now we need to create concrete server-side implementations of all of the methods on our interface.

We do this by subclassing from the server-side skeleton class generated by the *idlj* compiler. For our example, we need to subclass either _AccountImplBase or AccountPOA (depending on whether we're using the POA or pre-POA versions of Java IDL). We also need to implement the various methods defined on the Account IDL interface and mapped through the *idlj* compiler into the AccountOperations Java interface. The AccountImplPOA class in Example 4-4 shows the implementation for the POA-compliant case (the pre-POA implementation is virtually identical, with a few minor differences that we'll mention at the end of this section). The pre-POA version won't be shown here, but it is included in the source code examples for this book, downloadable from the O'Reilly web site.

As you look through the implementation class, you'll notice that the method implementations are similar to the RMI version of the Account server implementation example in Chapter 3. The only real difference is that this AccountImpl class extends the generated AccountPOA class (and through it, the generated AccountOperations interface and the CORBA Servant class), while the RMI server implementation implements the RMI Account interface and extends java.rmi. server.UnicastRemoteObject. So in the same way that the two remote object schemes are analogous to each other in terms of functionality, the particulars of the server implementations in each case are analogous as well.

Example 4-4: Server Implementation of the Account CORBA Object

```
/**
 * AccountImplPOA: Implementation of the Account remote interface
 */
public class AccountImplPOA extends AccountPOA {
  // Our current balance
  private float mBalance = 0;
  // Name on account
  private String mName = "";
  // Create a new account with the given name
  public AccountImplPOA(String name) {
    mName = name;
  }

  public String getName() {
    return mName;
  }
  public float getBalance() {
    return mBalance;
  }
  // Withdraw some funds
  public void withdraw(float amt) throws InsufficientFundsException {
    if (mBalance >= amt) {
      mBalance -= amt;
      // Log transaction...
      System.out.println("--> Withdrew " + amt
                                  + " from account " + getName());
      System.out.println("    New balance: " + getBalance());
```

```
      }
      else {
        throw new InsufficientFundsException("Withdrawal request of " + amt +
                                    " exceeds balance of " + mBalance);
      }
    }
    // Deposit some funds
    public void deposit(float amt) {
      mBalance += amt;
      // Log transaction...
      System.out.println("--> Deposited " + amt +
                                    " into account " + getName());
      System.out.println("    New balance: " + getBalance());
    }
    // Move some funds from another (remote) account into this one
    public void transfer(float amt, Account src)
      throws InsufficientFundsException {
      if (checkTransfer(src, amt)) {
        src.withdraw(amt);
        this.deposit(amt);
        // Log transaction...
        System.out.println("--> Transferred " + amt +
                                    " from account " + getName());
        System.out.println("    New balance: " + getBalance());
      }
      else {
        throw new InsufficientFundsException("Source account balance is less
                                    " + "than the requested transfer.");
      }
    }
    // Make several transfers from other (remote) accounts into this one
    public void transferBatch(float[] amts, Account[] srcs)
      throws InsufficientFundsException {
      // Iterate through the accounts and the amounts to be
      // transferred from each
      for (int i = 0; i < amts.length; i++) {
        float amt = amts[i];
        Account src = srcs[i];
        // Make the transaction
        this.transfer(amt, src);
      }
    }
    // Check to see if the transfer is possible, given the source account
    private boolean checkTransfer(Account src, float amt) {
      boolean approved = false;
      if (src.getBalance() >= amt) {
        approved = true;
      }
      return approved;
    }
  }
}
```

Putting It in the Public Eye

We still need to do some work to make the Java implementation of our IDL interface available to remote clients. We must instantiate one or more instances of our CORBA server implementation and connect them to an ORB on the server so that they can receive remote method requests. Then clients need to somehow obtain remote references to our server objects. There are two fundamental ways that a client obtains a remote reference: it can get an initial object reference (usually to a CORBA service of some kind, like a Naming Service) using the ORB.resolve_ initial_references() method and somehow find a reference to the remote object through method calls on the initial object, or it can get a "stringified" reference to the remote object (either an Interoperable Object Reference or an Interoperable Naming Service URL) and use the local ORB to convert it to a live object reference.

For the first case, a remote object needs to be registered in some way with a server-side ORB, and probably with a CORBA service of some kind. Connecting your CORBA object to an ORB enables it to accept remote method requests from clients. Registering your object with a CORBA service makes it easier for remote clients to find your object in the first place.

In order for you to register a remote object, you first have to get a reference to an ORB. We'll look at how to do this, then look at registering the remote object with a Naming Service (the most common way to "publish" remote objects in a CORBA context). Finally, we'll look at two ways that clients can use stringified references to access your CORBA object.

Initializing the ORB

Since the ORB is so central to everything in a CORBA environment, the first thing any CORBA process needs to do (whether it's a CORBA server or client process) is get a reference to an ORB that it can use to find other objects, access CORBA services, and handle remote method calls. A CORBA participant initializes its ORB reference by calling one of the static init() methods on the ORB interface. Each of these methods returns an ORB object that can find CORBA objects and services, among other things. The standard init() methods provided on an ORB are as follows (Sun's Java IDL supports all of these standard initialization methods):

public static ORB ORB.init()
> Returns a shared (static) ORB instance, called the "singleton ORB." Each call within the same runtime environment of this version of init() returns the same ORB reference. If used within an applet context, the ORB has limited abilities. The singleton ORB is used mainly by IDL-generated classes to perform actions like create TypeCode objects that identify the types of CORBA objects.

public static ORB ORB.init(String[] args, Properties props)
> Creates a new ORB using the given arguments and properties, as discussed in the following paragraphs.

```
public static ORB ORB.init(Applet applet, Properties props)
```
Creates a new ORB within an applet context. The applet's codebase and host are used by the ORB as the source of various services, such as the Naming Service.

There are two standard properties defined for an ORB that can be set in the call to init(), using either the String arguments array or a Properties object. These are:

```
org.omg.CORBA.ORBSingletonClass
```
Specifies the class to use for the singleton ORB instance returned by the no-argument version of init().

```
org.omg.CORBA.ORBClass
```
Creates ORB instances when the other versions of init() are called.

In both cases, the class name you provide has to implement the org.omg.CORBA. ORB interface. You can use these two properties to specify a custom ORB implementation, if needed. You may want to override the default ORB implementation (com.sun.CORBA.iiop.ORB in Java IDL) with one of your own that has particular performance characteristics, for example. Or you may be running your CORBA code within an applet and want to ensure that a valid ORB is available no matter what browser version your applet encounters.

Sun's Java IDL also adds two nonstandard properties: ORBInitialHost and ORBInitialPort. By default, each ORB.init() method initializes an ORB that looks for its services (naming service, for example) locally. Java IDL adds these two nonstandard properties to allow your local ORB to defer its services (naming, trading, etc.) to a remote ORB running on a given host and listening on a given port. Be careful before you decide to depend on these properties in your application or applet. They are only honored within Sun's Java IDL implementation of the CORBA standard. If you want your CORBA application to be portable to any implementation of the standard IDL-to-Java binding, and you want to use a remote Naming Service, you should stick to using a stringified reference to the remote object, obtained through a secondary communication channel (as we'll discuss shortly).

Any of these properties can be specified within a Properties object, as a command-line option to a Java application, or in a system properties file. As an example, if you want to specify a different host to use for finding services like the Naming Service, one way to do this is to specify the host explicitly in the code that initializes the ORB, using a Properties object:

```
Properties orbProps = new Properties();
orbProps.put("org.omg.CORBA.ORBInitialHost", "remote.orb.com");
ORB myOrb = ORB.init((String[])null, orbProps);
```

Alternately, you can take command-line arguments passed into your Java code and pass them to the ORB.init() method to be parsed. Say we have a class named InitRemote with a main method implemented as follows:

```
public class InitRemote {
  public static void main(String[] argv) {
    try {
```

```
       ORB myOrb = ORB.init(argv, null);
          ...
   }
  }
 }
```

In this case, we can specify any ORB properties on the command line using specific argument names. Notice that when specifying these, you should omit the org.omg.CORBA package prefix on the property names:

```
orbhost% java InitRemote -ORBInitialHost remote.orb.com
```

Note that you can use the second ORB.init() method with both a String arguments array and a Properties list specified, even though the examples here haven't shown that.

Registering with a Naming Service

One way to make a server object available to remote clients is to register it with a local CORBA Naming Service under a specific name. A remote client can then get a reference to the root NamingContext for the Naming Service, and look up the server object by name.

Java IDL (CORBA)

Regardless of whether you're using a POA-compliant CORBA environment, here are the basic steps that create and register a CORBA object with the ORB:

- Initialize an ORB reference.

- Create an instance of your CORBA server implementation, and get a reference from it that can be registered with the naming service.

- Get a reference to the root NamingContext for the Naming Service from the ORB.

- Construct a name for the object that reflects where you want it to sit in the Naming Service hierarchy.

- Bind your object to that name in the Naming Service, using the root NamingContext.

The mechanics of carrying out each step are slightly different in the POA-compliant and pre-POA versions of Java IDL. We'll start by looking at the pre-POA version, shown in Example 4-5. This code listing shows a utility class named AccountInitPrePOA, whose main() method creates an instance of our AccountImplPrePOA implementation and then registers the object with the Naming Service. The program starts by getting a reference to the local ORB, as discussed in the previous section. Then it asks the ORB for a reference to its registered Naming Service by calling the resolve_initial_references() method on the ORB, using the standard name "NameService." This object reference is the root NamingContext of the Naming Service, so we narrow the object reference using NamingContextHelper. Next, we build the name to use to register the object with the Naming Service. The name of an object in the basic CORBA Naming Service is represented by an array of NameComponent objects, one for each branch in the hierarchy. Here, we're assuming that the user has passed in a simple string as a command-line argument, and we use it to construct a NameComponent array with a single element (representing a simple one-level path for the object in the naming hierarchy). If we wanted to register our object using a multilevel path, we first must create the subcontexts, then register the object (we'll see how that works in a later section). Once the NameComponent array is constructed, we call the rebind() method on the NamingContext to register our Account object with that name. With the object registered, we send this thread into a perpetual wait state (by creating a dummy String variable and doing a synchronized wait() on it). This keeps the thread alive so the Account object can service client requests.

Example 4-5: Creating/Registering an Account Server Object (pre-POA)

```
//
// Initialize a remote Account object and register it with the Naming Service
//

import org.omg.CORBA.*;
import org.omg.CosNaming.*;

public class AccountInitPrePOA {
  public static void main(String[] args) {
    try {
      // Initialize an ORB reference
      ORB myORB = ORB.init(args, null);

      // Create an instance of an Account server implementation
      Account impl = new AccountImplPrePOA(args[0]);

      // Register the local object with the ORB
      myORB.connect(impl);

      // Get the root name context
      org.omg.CORBA.Object objRef =
        myORB.resolve_initial_references("NameService");
      NamingContext nc = NamingContextHelper.narrow(objRef);

      // Register the local object with the Name Service
      NameComponent ncomp = new NameComponent(args[0], "");
      NameComponent[] name = {ncomp};
      nc.rebind(name, impl);

      System.out.println("Registered account under name " + args[0]);

      // Go into a wait state, waiting for clients to connect
      java.lang.Object dummy = new String("I wait...");
      synchronized (dummy) {
        dummy.wait();
      }
    }
    catch (Exception e) {
      System.out.println(
```

```
                    "An error occurred while initializing server object:");
        e.printStackTrace();
      }
    }
}
```

Before running this utility object to create and register our CORBA object, we need to start a Naming Service someplace. A Naming Service daemon listens for Naming Service requests on a specific port and provides access to the named object directory it manages. In Java IDL, the Naming Service is started using the *tnameserv* command:

```
objhost% tnameserv &
```

With that done, we can run our initialization method to register our server object with the ORB:

```
objhost% java oreilly.jent.corba.AccountInitPrePOA JimF
Registered account under name JimF
```

Performing these same tasks under the POA-compliant version of Java IDL (JDK 1.4 and later) is fairly similar, except that using the Portable Object Adaptor adds some new twists in the creation of the server object and its reference. Example 4-6 shows the code listing for AccountInitPOA, which performs the same task as AccountInitPrePOA, but within the POA-compliant version of Java IDL. One key difference in this version is the additional POA operations immediately following the creation of the Account server object. Since we're dealing with an ORB using the POA, and the POA is acting as the mediator between our server object and the ORB, we need to use the POA to obtain a reference to our server object that can be used for registration with the Naming Service (among other things). So we get a reference to the POA from the ORB using the resolve_initial_references() method (this time using the standard name for the POA, "RootPOA"). We then make sure that the POA is active by getting its POA manager and calling its activate() method—every POA has a POAManager that maintains the runtime state of the POA. Finally, we ask the POA for a usable reference to our server object by calling its servant_to_reference() method and converting the resulting Object to an Account reference. For more details on the various POA interfaces and their methods, refer to Chapter 14.

Example 4-6: AccountInitPOA.java

```
//
// CORBA example 9: Initialize a remote object, register it with a naming
// service, and generate a stringified IOR.
//

import org.omg.CORBA.*;
import org.omg.CosNaming.*;
import org.omg.PortableServer.POA;

public class AccountInitPOA {
  public static void main(String[] args) {
```

Example 4-6: AccountInitPOA.java (continued)

```
try {
    // Initialize an ORB reference
    ORB myORB = ORB.init(args, null);

    // Create an instance of an Account server implementation
    AccountImplPOA acct = new AccountImplPOA(args[0]);

    // Get the root Portable Object Adapter (POA)
    POA rootPOA = (POA)myORB.resolve_initial_references("RootPOA");
    // Activate the POA manager
    rootPOA.the_POAManager().activate();

    // Get an object reference from the implementation
    org.omg.CORBA.Object obj = rootPOA.servant_to_reference(acct);
    Account acctRef = (Account)AccountHelper.narrow(obj);

    // Get the root name context (use the INS interface, so that we can use
    // the simpler name construction process)
    org.omg.CORBA.Object objRef =
        myORB.resolve_initial_references("NameService");
    NamingContextExt nc = NamingContextExtHelper.narrow(objRef);

    // Register the local object with the Name Service
    // Use the Interoperable Naming Service interface to simplify matters,
    // and to support URL-formatted names (e.g. "JohnS",
    // "corbaname://orbhost.com#/JohnS", etc.)
    NameComponent[] name = nc.to_name(args[0]);
    nc.rebind(name, acctRef);

    System.out.println("Registered account under name " + args[0]);

    // Go into a wait state, waiting for clients to connect
    myORB.run();
    }
    catch (Exception e) {
        System.out.println(
                    "An error occurred while initializing server object:");
        e.printStackTrace();
    }
  }
}
```

Another difference in this version of our object initialization utility is the actual registration of the server object with the Naming Service. Here, since JDK 1.4 also introduced Java support for the Interoperable Naming Service (INS) interface, we can use the NamingContextExt interface to make binding objects a bit easier. We'll get into the details of the different Naming Service interfaces in the next section.

The last difference in this version of our initialization utility is in how we cause the thread to wait for client requests. The CORBA 2.3 (and higher) versions of the ORB interface include a run() method. Calling this method causes the current thread to wait until the ORB shuts down. This is a clean way to accomplish the same task as our `dummy.wait()` approach in the previous version of this utility class.

Now that we've seen the basic steps involved in creating and registering an object with a CORBA Naming Service, let's look in more detail at binding objects and new contexts within the Naming Service.

Adding Objects to a Naming Context

As was discussed earlier, a CORBA naming service maintains a hierarchy of named objects that can be looked up by remote clients. Initially, a CORBA naming directory is empty, with only its root `NamingContext` and no objects. The `bind()` method on a `NamingContext` object binds a server object to a name within the context. The `bind_new_context()` method creates new subcontexts within a given `NamingContext`. Using a file directory analogy, calling `bind_new_context()` on a `NamingContext` object is like making a new subdirectory from the current directory, while calling `bind()` puts a new file into the current directory.

The Java IDL mapping uses arrays of `NameComponent` objects to represent the names of subcontexts within a naming directory. Each `NameComponent` represents a component of the path to the named object. A `NameComponent` contains `id` and `kind` string fields that serve to label the component in the path. Only the `id` field is significant in determining name uniqueness. So a `NameComponent` with an `id` set to "student" and `kind` set to an empty string conflicts with a `NameComponent` with an `id` of "student" and a `kind` of "doctoral," if both `NameComponent` objects are relative to the same subcontext. The `NameComponent` class has a constructor that takes the `id` and `kind` values as arguments. Here's how to create a single `NameComponent`:

```
NameComponent comp1 = new NameComponent("student", "doctoral");
```

A complete name path can be composed as an array of these objects:

```
NameComponent path[] = { comp1, comp2, ... };
```

The `bind()` method takes two arguments: an array of `NameComponent` objects as the relative name for the object you're putting into the Naming Service and the server object itself. If you're binding a server object using the root context of the Naming Service, the name is also the absolute name of the object in the overall naming directory. If an object is already bound to the name, you can use the `rebind()` method with the same arguments, causing the existing object bound to that name to be replaced by the new object. Note that since the Naming Service is a CORBA service that can be accessed remotely by other CORBA clients, the objects it contains need to be exportable to these remote clients. This means that only `org.omg.CORBA.Object` references can be bound to names within a `NamingContext`.

The following code snippet binds a few of our `Account` objects to names within the root context of a Naming Service:

```
// Get the root naming context
ORB myORB = ORB.init(...);
org.omg.CORBA.Object ref =
                    myORB.resolve_initial_references("NameService");
NamingContext rootNC = NamingContextHelper.narrow(ref);
```

```
// Create a few Accounts
Account acct1 = new AccountImplPOA("JohnSmith");
Account acct2 = new AccountImplPOA("MaryJones");

// Bind them to names in the Naming Service
NameComponent name1 = new NameComponent("Smith,J", "");
NameComponent path1[] = { name1 };
NameComponent name2 = new NameComponent("Jones,M", "");
NameComponent path2[] = { name2 };
rootNC.bind(path1, ref1);
rootNC.bind(path2, ref2);
```

Before you can bind an object to a name with multiple components, all the subcontexts (subdirectories) have to be created using the bind_new_context() method on a NamingContext. The bind_new_context() method takes an array of NameComponent objects as the relative path of the new context and a reference to the NamingContext object to bind to that location in the overall directory. A new NamingContext object can be created from an existing one by calling its new_context() method. If a context already exists at the target name, you can use the rebind_context() method to replace the existing context with a new one. This is useful for emptying out an entire subcontext without removing each object individually.

Here is an example that binds some Account objects within various subcontexts representing different branches of a bank, using the standard Naming Service interfaces; NameComponent and NamingContext (both from the org.omg.CosNaming package). This example shows how to do this with a POA-compliant ORB—the code is very similar for the pre-POA versions of Java IDL:

```
// Initialize the ORB and get the POA and root naming context, as before
ORB myORB = ORB.init(...);
POA rootPOA = ...;
NamingContext rootNC = ...;

// Create the components to the sub-context paths
NameComponent branchComp = new NameComponent("bankBranches", "");
NameComponent cambridgeComp = new NameComponent("Cambridge", "");
NameComponent bostonComp= new NameComponent("Boston", "");

// Create a new context, bind it to the path "bankBranches"
NamingContext ctx = rootNC.new_context();
NameComponent path[] = { branchComp };
rootNC.bind_context(path, ctx)

// Create another context, bind it to the path "bankBranches, Cambridge"
NamingContext cambridgeCtx = rootNC.new_context();
path = { branchComp, cambridgeComp };
rootNC.bind_context(path, cambridgeCtx)

// Create another context, bind it to the path "bankBranches, Boston"
NamingContext bostonCtx = rootNC.new_context();
path = { branchComp, bostonComp };
rootNC.bind_context(path, bostonCtx);
```

```
// Now we can bind Accounts to a name within any of the new sub-contexts
// Create a few Account server objects, and get usable client references
// from the POA
Account johnAcct = new AccountImplPOA("JohnSmith");
Account johnRef =
    AccountHelper.narrow(rootPOA.servant_to_reference(johnAcct));
Account maryAcct = new AccountImplPOA("MarkJonés");
Account maryRef =
    AccountHelper.narrow(rootPOA.servant_to_reference(maryAcct));


// Bind each Account to a name in the appropriate branch path. Assume
// that John has his account out of the Cambridge branch, Mary has hers
// out of the Boston branch.
NameComponent johnComp = new NameComponent("Smith,J", "");
NameComponent johnPath[] = { branchComp, cambridgeComp, johnComp };
rootNC.bind(johnPath, johnRef);
NameComponent maryComp = new NameComponent("Jones,M", "");
NameComponent maryPath[] = { branchComp, bostonComp, maryComp };
rootNC.bind(maryPath, maryRef);
```

If you try to bind an object or a subcontext to a name within a context that hasn't been created yet, an org.omg.CosNaming.NamingContextPackage.NotFound exception is thrown.

Note that names used in the bind() or rebind() methods are relative to the NamingContext object that they're called on. This means we can bind Mary's Account object in the previous example to the same absolute name within the directory by replacing the last two lines of the example with the following:

```
NameComponent maryRelativePath[] = { maryComp };
bostonCtx.bind(maryRelativePath, maryRef);
```

The bostonCtx context is bound to the {"bankBranches", "Boston" } subdirectory, so binding an object to the name { "Jones,M" } within this context is equivalent to binding it to the full path { "bankBranches", "Boston", "Jones,M" } from the root context. You can use similar shorthand when binding new contexts within a directory. In other words, you can bind a context to a relative name within a subcontext, instead of an absolute name within the root context.

A slightly simpler approach: The Interoperable Naming Service

The Interoperable Naming Service (INS) interfaces make both the binding and lookup of objects in a Naming Service a bit easier. In our previous examples, we bound objects to specific locations in the naming hierarchy by first creating the subcontexts (subdirectories) we needed, then binding the remote objects to names within those contexts. In each step, we needed to construct fully qualified names for both the contexts and the objects we were binding. Prior to the introduction of the INS, the only way to do this is the way shown earlier examples: manually construct an array of NameComponents representing the intended path to the object. Using the INS interfaces, and their support for new types of stringified object references and URLs, it's possible to create new contexts and bind objects in a slightly simpler way. We can convert stringified object references directly to

NameComponent arrays using the to_name() method on the org.omg.CosNaming. NamingContextExt interface. For example, assuming that we've created the necessary subcontexts already, we could bind John Smith's account to the same path as before by specifying the full path as a string and converting it using to_name():

```
NamingContextExt rootNC = ...;
String johnURL = "bankBranches/Cambridge/Smith,J";
NameComponent johnPath[] = rootNC.to_name(johnURL);
rootNC.rebind(johnPath, johnRef);
```

Finding and Using Remote Objects

Now that we've seen how to implement a CORBA remote object and register it with an ORB, we can turn our attention to the heart of the matter: client applications that want to use the object. As we said earlier, every CORBA process needs a reference to an ORB. Once a client application has access to an ORB, next it must find remote objects to interact with. But before we can discuss finding remote objects, we need to talk a bit about what remote object references look like in the CORBA environment.

The whole point of CORBA is to be able to distribute objects across the network and use them from any point. In order for a local process to make requests of a remote object, it needs to have some kind of reference to that remote object. This object reference needs to contain enough information for the local ORB to find the ORB serving the target object and send the request to the remote ORB using an agreed-upon protocol.

Remote Object References and Narrowing

In most situations, a CORBA client has a reference to a remote object in the form of an object stub. The stub encapsulates the actual object reference, providing what seems like a direct interface to the remote object within the local environment. If the client is implemented in C++, Java, or some other object-oriented language, the object stub is a native object in that language. Other nonobject languages represent remote object references in whatever way is dictated in the CORBA language binding for that language.

CORBA includes its own root object class, because some object-programming languages may have different inheritance structures. In the Java binding for CORBA, all CORBA object references (local or remote) implement the org.omg.CORBA. Object interface. So, when a client of a remote CORBA object receives a stub for the object, it actually gets an org.omg.CORBA.Object that serves as a proxy for the remote object. The org.omg.CORBA.portable.ObjectImpl class provides default client-side implementations for the methods defined on org.omg.CORBA.Object. Java stubs (generated from the IDL-to-Java compiler, as discussed earlier) for CORBA objects are actually subclassed from the ObjectImpl class. Internally, ObjectImpl deals with delegating client requests on the object stub to the proper target object, whether it's a local or remote object. `ObjectImpl` implements the `org.omg.CORBA.Object` interface and inherently extends the `java.lang.Object` class, so it provides a joining point between the CORBA and Java object environments.[*]

A reference to an `org.omg.CORBA.Object` instance that is connected to a remote object is actually all a client needs to invoke methods on a remote object. Using the Dynamic Invocation Interface defined by the CORBA standard, you can create method requests and send them to the remote object directly through the generic `Object` interface, as we'll discuss later in this chapter. If your client has the actual Java interface for the remote object available at compile time, however, you probably want to convert the `Object` reference into a reference of that type, so you can use the interface to call remote methods directly.

Converting an `org.omg.COBRA.Object` to a specific remote interface is done by narrowing the object reference to the corresponding interface type, using type-specific helper classes. We've already seen how the Java IDL compiler, *idlj*, creates a helper class from an IDL interface (e.g., `AccountHelper`). The helper class includes a `narrow()` method that safely converts an `org.omg.CORBA.Object` reference to a reference of the given type. If the object reference you pass into the `narrow()` method is not the type the helper expects, an `org.omg.CORBA.BAD_PARAM` exception is thrown. This is a `RuntimeException`, so it doesn't have to be caught by your code, unless you're trying to test the type of a CORBA reference for some reason.

This `narrow()` operation highlights one of the key differences between RMI and CORBA. In the Java environment, class bytecodes are portable, and all remote object types are objects that can be specified by their full class names. An RMI client can automatically download the bytecodes for a remote stub from the object server, if the class for the stub can't be found locally (see Chapter 3 for more details on the mechanics of remote class loading). CORBA is a language-independent remote object scheme, so there is no portable way to specify a remote object's native type when a client obtains a stub reference. In Java you could do this using the same remote classloading scheme as RMI, but there isn't a similar scheme available in C or C++, for example. As a result, the stub reference is initially represented by a basic object type that knows how to forward method requests to its server object, but doesn't necessarily satisfy the mapped interface for the remote object type the client is expecting. The client application is forced to "cast" this stub to the correct local type, using the appropriate `narrow()` method. In the Java mapping of IDL, this means calling the `narrow()` method on the corresponding helper class. The `narrow()` method converts the reference, making a type-specific stub interface that also includes the remote object reference information needed to forward method requests to the actual object implementation.

[*] In pre-POA versions of Java IDL (JDK 1.2 and 1.3), the server skeletons generated for CORBA interfaces were also subclassed from `ObjectImpl`. In POA-compliant versions, the skeletons are subclassed from `org.omg.PortableServer.Servant`, which provides an alternative implementation of the `org.omg.CORBA.Object` interface, as well as a number of methods specific to servant objects.

Accessing Remote Objects

With that background material out of the way, let's discuss actually finding remote object references. There are many ways that an object reference can find its way through the ORB into a client application, but they all boil down to one of these methods:

- Getting an initial reference directly from the ORB

- Getting an object reference through a method call on another remote object reference

- Using a stringified object reference obtained through a secondary channel and converting it to a live object reference

ORB Initial Object References

In addition to providing core object communication services, an ORB can also provide additional services, such as a Naming Service, a Trading Service, a Security Service, etc. These services are represented as CORBA objects and are typically available through the ORB directly, based on how it is configured. The ORB interface provides the resolve_initial_references() method for obtaining references to the objects that represent these services. Each CORBA service is represented by one or more object interfaces, and these objects can be asked for using standard names. As we saw earlier when we registered CORBA objects, the standard name for the Naming Service is "NameService," and the object representing access to the Naming Service is a NamingContext or NamingContextExt object. These represent the root of the naming hierarchy.

Once you've initialized your ORB reference (as described earlier in the section "Initializing the ORB"), you can ask the ORB for a list of the names of the initial objects it has available, using the list_initial_references() method:

```
String names[] = myORB.list_initial_references();
```

This method returns an array of String objects that contain the names of all initial objects in the ORB. These names can then be used to get references to the objects through the resolve_initial_references() method.

Here's how we used resolve_initial_references() to obtain a reference to the Naming Service in our earlier examples:

```
ORB myORB = ORB.init(...);
org.omg.CORBA.Object nameRef =
myORB.resolve_initial_references("NameService");
```

Although the list_initial_references() and resolve_initial_references() methods are a standard element of the ORB interface, how a particular ORB implements these initial object references is not standardized. Sun's Java IDL implementation, for example, stores an ORB's initial object references as root objects in its internal Naming Service.

Getting Objects from Other Remote Objects

In addition to getting remote objects directly from an ORB reference, a client can obtain remote objects from other remote objects. The most common variation on this approach is to get a reference to a Naming Service object and then look up objects in the naming directory by name. Another variation (that we won't cover in detail in this section) is to obtain an application-specific object reference, either directly from the ORB or through the Naming Service, and use this initial reference to request other objects. An object used in this way in a distributed application is sometimes called a *factory* object.

Naming service lookups

Once you have a `NamingContext` reference that points to a position (either the root or a subdirectory) in a Naming Service, you can look up objects within the context by passing names to its `resolve()` method. As before, when we were binding objects, a name is represented by an ordered array of `NameComponent` objects. Each `NameComponent` (both the `id` field and the `kind` field) must exactly match the path to an object within the context in order to successfully find the object. If an object is not found at a specified name, an `org.omg.CosNaming.NamingContextPackage.NotFound` exception is thrown.

So, if a client wants to find the account for Mary Jones, we stored in the last binding example, which needs to do the following:

```
// Set up the full path to the account
NameComponent comp1 = new NameComponent("bankBranches", "");
NameComponent comp2 = new NameComponent("Cambridge", "");
NameComponent acctName = new NameComponent("Jones,M", "");
NameComponent acctPath[] = { comp1, comp2, acctName };

// Find the object in the directory
org.omg.CORBA.Object acctRef = rootNC.resolve(acctPath);
Account acct = AccountHelper.narrow(acctRef);
```

We're assuming that `rootNC` is a reference to the root context of the Naming Service holding the `Account` object references. Note the use of the `narrow()` method on `AccountHelper` to "cast" the generic object reference to an `Account` object.

In addition to finding references to objects (leaf nodes) in the Naming Service, you can also use the `resolve()` method on a `NamingContext` to get a reference to a subcontext (a subdirectory). Just use the path to the context itself and `narrow()` it to a `NamingContext` reference:

```
NameComponent cambridgePath[] = { comp1, comp2 };
org.omg.CORBA.Object ncRef = rootNC.resolve(cambridgePath);
NamingContext cambridgeContext = NamingContextHelper.narrow(ncRef);
```

Object URLs

As we've seen, Sun's implementation of Java IDL provides a nonstandard way to initialize an ORB to reference a remote Naming Service, so that one of the ORB's initial references is to the root context of the remote Naming Service. But what do you do if you want an object from a remote Naming Service and your Java IDL implementation doesn't provide a way to directly initialize a reference to the remote service? Or, worse yet, what if the object that you want isn't stored in a Naming Service or available through any other CORBA service? How can your client get a reference to the object?

The CORBA standard comes to the rescue again. CORBA defines several ways to represent *stringified object references*, or remote object URLs. In other words, you can fully specify a specific CORBA server object using a URL syntax, which is very similar to the URL syntax used to specify Java RMI objects in an RMI registry (see Chapter 3 for more details on RMI registry URLs). These object URLs are called "stringified object references" in the CORBA specifications, because that's exactly what they are: strings that can be sent around the network (in email, in configuration files, etc.), and used by clients to obtain a living reference to the object that the URL specifies. So these object URLs are called "stringified object references" in the same way that you could call HTML document URLs "stringified document references."

In these URL schemes, the objects being referenced need to be hosted behind an ORB someplace on the network, and they must have a server process running that is listening for remote method requests for that object. In some cases; the objects and their request servers can just be connected directly to the ORB, in other cases they have to be bound to a name in a Naming Service, with the Naming Service acting as the method request mediator.

There are three basic forms of object URLs defined in the CORBA standards:

Interoperable Object References (IORs)

These URLs are based on a syntax for representing a remote object reference in the form of a printable, but not human-readable, string of characters. This stringified object reference includes enough information for a remote CORBA client to locate the object's home ORB and convert the string to a runtime stub reference to the object. Two methods on the ORB interface, object_to_ string() and string_to_object(), let you convert a CORBA object reference to an IOR and back into an object reference. An object doesn't need to be bound to a name in a Naming Service in order to have an IOR; it simply needs to be exported through an ORB using an object adaptor, like the POA.

corbaloc URLs

These URLs are a human-readable URL format for object references. They are similar in purpose to IORs: an object needs to be exported through an ORB for remote access in order to have a corbaloc URL associated with it. So corbaloc URLs point to a single object accessible directly through an ORB, without the help of a service of some kind. The same restrictions apply for making servants accessible through corbaloc URLs as for IORs—the servant object needs to be connected to an ORB through some kind of object adaptor, like the POA.

corbaname URLs

These URLs are extensions to the corbaloc syntax to allow for references to objects that are registered with a CORBA Naming Service. The URL format includes additional information that specifies the object's location (name) in the Naming Service.

The full syntax for all three of these CORBA object URL schemes is spelled out fully in Chapter 15. But the following examples should demonstrate their basic use.

Example 4-7 shows AccountInit, a server that creates an instance of our AccountImplPOA and makes it available for clients to access. In its main( ) method, it initializes the ORB, then creates an instance of our Account servant. We're assuming that a POA-compliant version of Java IDL is being used, so the next thing to do is get a reference to the root POA (using resolve_initial_ references( )) and activate the POA manager, then ask the POA to activate our servant object. By activating our servant object this way, we're guaranteed that any "direct" IIOP requests (through either an IOR or a corbaloc URL) will be accepted immediately. Note that in order for the generated IOR to be acceptable to another ORB, both your ORB and the remote ORB have to be using the same inter-ORB communication protocol (IIOP, DCE-CIOP, etc.). In this example, we'll assume that our client and object server are both running IIOP.

Example 4-7: Initializing an Account/Getting Stringified References

```
//
// AccountInit: Initialize an Account object, register it with a naming
// service, and generate URLs for the object.
//

import org.omg.CORBA.*;
import org.omg.CosNaming.*;
import org.omg.PortableServer.POA;
import java.net.InetAddress;

public class AccountInit {
  public static void main(String[] args) {
    try {
      // Initialize an ORB reference
      ORB myORB = ORB.init(args, null);

      // Create an instance of an Account server implementation
      AccountImplPOA acct = new AccountImplPOA(args[0]);

      // Get the root Portable Object Adapter (POA)
      POA rootPOA = (POA)myORB.resolve_initial_references("RootPOA");
      // Activate the POA manager
      rootPOA.the_POAManager().activate();
      // Activate our servant, so that corbaloc and IOR requests will work
      // immediately
      rootPOA.activate_object(acct);

      // Get an object reference from the implementation
      org.omg.CORBA.Object obj = rootPOA.servant_to_reference(acct);
      Account acctRef = (Account)AccountHelper.narrow(obj);
```

```
    // Get the root name context (use the INS interface, so that we can use
    // the simpler name construction process)
    org.omg.CORBA.Object objRef =
      myORB.resolve_initial_references("NameService");
    NamingContextExt nc = NamingContextExtHelper.narrow(objRef);

    // Register the local object with the Name Service
    // Use the Interoperable Naming Service interface to simplify matters,
    // and to support URL-formatted names (e.g. "JohnS",
    // "corbaname://orbhost.com#JohnS", etc.)
    NameComponent[] name = nc.to_name(args[0]);
    nc.rebind(name, acctRef);

    System.out.println("Registered account under name " + args[0]);
    System.out.println("New account created and registered.  URLs are: ");
    System.out.println("\nIOR");
    System.out.println("\t" + myORB.object_to_string(acctRef));
    System.out.println("\ncorbaname");
    System.out.println("\tcorbaname:iiop:" +
                        InetAddress.getLocalHost().getHostName() +
                        "#" + args[0]);

    // Go into a wait state, waiting for clients to connect
    myORB.run();
  }
  catch (Exception e) {
    System.out.println(
                "An error occurred while initializing server object:");
    e.printStackTrace();
  }
 }
}
```

Next, we ask the POA to generate an Account reference for us from the servant object; we use this reference to register the Account with the Naming Service. The request to convert the reference to an Account reference is necessary in POA-compliant environments, because the object implementation class doesn't directly extend the mapped object interface (in the section "POA server skeletons" we saw how the generated skeleton extends the AccountOperations interface, not the Account interface).

Now that the server object is both connected to the ORB through the POA and registered with a Naming Service, we can generate various URLs for this object that clients can use to get direct references to the object. First we get the IOR of the object, using the object_to_string() method on the ORB. Then we create the corbaname URL for the object, using the local hostname, the port number of the ORB, and the name the user passed in on the command line and used to register the object with the Naming Service. Each of these is printed to the console, and we can distribute these URLs to the clients that need them. Note that we aren't creating a corbaloc URL for our object. This is because the server-side creation of corbaloc URLs is not standardized; CORBA vendors currently provide nonstandard ways to generate these in their implementations.

Notice we're only showing how to initialize the server object in a POA-compliant environment. In the pre-POA versions of Java IDL, instead of activating the object using the POA interface, you would simply "connect" the object to the local ORB:

```
Account acctRef = new AccountImplPrePOA(...);
myORB.connect(acctRef);
```

You also wouldn't need to perform the conversion into an `Account` reference, since in the `ImplBase` inheritance model, the server skeleton `_AccountImplBase` directly extends the generated `Account` interface, and can be used to register the object with the Naming Service.

To demonstrate using these URLs, Example 4-8 shows a simple client for our `Account` server. This client uses a command-line interface and allows the user to perform transactions on a given `Account`, by specifying the `Account` to use (using its object URL), a transaction type ("deposit", "withdrawal" or "balance"), and an optional amount (for deposits and withdrawals). After doing the standard ORB initialization, the client first checks the name of the `Account` object (the first command-line argument). If the name of the `Account` is an object URL (IOR, corbalo, or corbaname), then the client simply uses the `string_to_object()` method on the ORB to get a reference to the specified `Account` object, and narrows the returned `Object` to an `Account` reference using the `AccountHelper`. If some other string is passed in, the client assumes the string is a name to be used to do a lookup in the Naming Service accessible from the ORB, and performs the lookup using the standard Naming Service operations (described earlier). Once the client has the reference to the remote `Account` object, the rest is easy—just parse the remaining command-line options given by the user, and perform the requested transaction on the account.

Example 4-8: A Client for the Account Servant

```
import org.omg.CORBA.*;
import org.omg.CORBA.ORBPackage.*;
import org.omg.CosNaming.*;
import java.util.*;

/**
 * AccountClient: A client that looks up the account "named" on the
 *    command-line, then performs the requested transaction on the account.
 */

public class AccountClient {
  public static void main(String args[]) {
    // Initialize the ORB
    ORB orb = ORB.init(args, null);
    org.omg.CORBA.Object ref = null;
    // The object name passed in on the command line
    String name = args[0];
    Account acct = null;
    // See if a stringified object reference/URL was provided
```

Example 4-8: A Client for the Account Servant (continued)

```
if (name.startsWith("corbaname") || name.startsWith("corbaloc") ||
    name.startsWith("IOR")) {
  System.out.println("Attempting to lookup " + args[0]);
  ref = orb.string_to_object(args[0]);
  acct = AccountHelper.narrow(ref);
}
// Otherwise, do a traditional Naming Service lookup using the
// services being referenced by our local ORB
else {
  try {
    ref = orb.resolve_initial_references("NameService");
  }
  catch (InvalidName invN) {
    System.out.println("Couldn't locate a Naming Service");
    System.exit(1);
  }
  NamingContext nameContext = NamingContextHelper.narrow(ref);
  NameComponent comp = new NameComponent(args[0], "");
  NameComponent path[] = {comp};
  try {
    ref = nameContext.resolve(path);
    System.out.println("ref = " + ref);
    acct = AccountHelper.narrow(ref);
  }
  catch (Exception e) {
    System.out.println("Error resolving name against Naming Service");
    e.printStackTrace();
  }
}

if (acct != null) {
  // We managed to get a reference to the named account, now check the
  // requested transaction from the command-line
  String action = args[1];
  float amt = 0.0f;
  if (action.equals("deposit") || action.equals("withdrawal")) {
    amt = Float.parseFloat(args[2]);
  }
  System.out.println("Got account, performing transaction...");
  try {
    // Did user ask to do a deposit?
    if (action.equals("deposit")) {
      acct.deposit(amt);
      System.out.println("Deposited " + amt + " to account.");
      System.out.println("New balance = " + acct.getBalance());
    }
    // Did user ask to do a withdrawal?
    else if (action.equals("withdrawal")) {
      acct.withdraw(amt);
      System.out.println("Withdrew " + amt + " from account.");
      System.out.println("New balance = " + acct.getBalance());
    }
```

Example 4-8: A Client for the Account Servant (continued)

```
        // Assume a balance inquiry if no deposit or withdrawal was given
        else {
          System.out.println(
              "Current account balance = " + acct.getBalance());
        }
      }
      catch (InsufficientFundsException ife) {
        System.out.println("Insufficient funds for transaction.");
        System.out.println("Current account balance = " + acct.getBalance());
      }
      catch (Exception e) {
        System.out.println("Error occurred while performing transaction:");
        e.printStackTrace();
      }
    }
    else {
      System.out.println("Null account returned.");
      System.exit(1);
    }
  }
}
}
```

To run this example, we first have to have a Naming Service running somewhere, then initialize an Account object for the client to use:

```
orbhost% tnameserv &
Initial Naming Context:
IOR:000000000000002b49444c3a6f6d672e6f72672f436f734e616d696e672f4e616d696
e67436f6e746578744578743a312e30000000000000010000000000000007c00010200000000
0a3132372e302e302e3100041a00000035afabcb0000000020363e1ad7000000010000000
0000000010000000d544e616d655365727276696963650000000000000004000000003000000
0000000010000001000000200000000000001000100000002050100010001002000010100900
0000010001010101
TransientNameServer: setting port for initial object references to: 900
Ready.
orbhost% java oreilly.jent.corba.AccountInit JimF
Registered account under name JimF
New account created and registered. URLs are:

IOR
IOR:00000000000000234944c3a6f7265696c6c792f6a656e742f636f7262612f4163636
f756e743a312e30000000000000100000000000000068000102000000000a3132372e302e30
2e3100046600000021afabcb0000000020363f810b0000000010000000000000000000000000
40000000000300000000000001000000010000002000000000000010001000000205010001
0001002000101090000000100010100
```

corbaname

```
        corbaname:iiop:orbhost#JimF
```

To perform transactions on this newly created and registered Account object, we run the AccountClient, passing in one of these object URLs as the "name" of the Account. Here we'll use the corbaname URL.

```
myclient% java oreilly.jent.corba.AccountClient
corbaname:iiop:orbhost#JimF
Attempting to lookup corbaname:iiop:orbhost#JimF
Got account, performing transaction...
Deposited 1000.0 to account.
New balance = 1000.0
```

What if I Don't Have the Interface?

In the examples we've seen so far, we've always assumed that the Java interfaces for the remote objects are available at compile time. But what happens if they aren't? You might get a reference to a CORBA Object from a Naming Service, for example, and not know what interface that object implements, or (more likely) not have that Java interface in the client JVM. We mentioned earlier that you can use an org.omg.CORBA.Object reference directly to make requests and exchange data with its remote object—now we'll briefly look at how the Dynamic Invocation Interface (DII) makes that possible.

The CORBA standard actually defines two complementary APIs for this purpose. The DII is used by a CORBA client to make remote method requests of a server object, while the Dynamic Skeleton Interface (DSI) can be used by a server-side skeleton to forward method invocations to its server implementation object in cases where it doesn't have the actual servant interface available. Both of these APIs provide the same essential function: a dynamic interface to an object whose interface is not known at compile time.

The DII and DSI may seem like sidebar topics in the CORBA world, but in reality they are at the heart of CORBA and how it works. When we generate Java stubs and skeletons from IDL interfaces, the generated code uses the DII and DSI to execute remote method calls. The details of how this is done are shielded from you, the developer, by the Java interface you use to interact with the remote object. But it's still worthwhile to understand how CORBA objects implement their distributed nature, especially in situations where the Java interface for the remote object is not there and you need to deal directly with these details.

On a more pragmatic note, there are cases where you might find yourself needing the DII and/or the DSI. In all the examples we've gone through in this chapter so far, we've assumed that both the server and client JVM's had all of the relevant interfaces available locally. For clients, we assumed that somehow they had acquired the IDL-generated Java interface for our objects (Account, etc.). It is safe to assume you have access to the client machines directly, or can provide an easy way for users to download the required classes themselves as part of some installation process. Since the clients will obviously need to acquire your client code in the first place, it's usually possible to provide the other CORBA client classes as well, and the DII isn't needed. But if not (perhaps you want to minimize class downloads for some reason, for example), then it may be useful to use the DII to create a client that operates without the need for the object interfaces themselves.

In this section, we take a look at how the DII works and how you might use it in a client. We won't cover the DSI in this book, since its practical uses are even more limited for the average developer. Note, however, that the API of the DSI is analogous to that of the DII, so you shouldn't have much trouble mapping the following explanation to the DSI as well.

Dynamic Invocation Interface

The Dynamic Invocation Interface provides abstract representations of remote method requests and their arguments. In simple terms, this means it includes objects that represent remote method requests and parameters that are passed with these method requests. Methods on these objects allow you to set the parameters to the request, make the request, and get the results. DII's central classes are:

Request
> A request to invoke a method on a remote object. Created by the client and issued through the ORB to the server object.

NamedValue
> A named parameter to a method request. Conceptually, this is a name tied to an Any value. The name of the value must match the name of the parameter as specified in the IDL interface the remote object satisfies.

NVList
> A list of NamedValue parameters used to represent an argument list passed into a remote method request.

Any
> A general argument value. An Any object can contain the Java equivalent of any basic IDL type or an Object that can be described in IDL.

Context
> A list of NamedValue objects used to specify any details of the client environment that shouldn't be passed as method arguments.

Once you get an org.omg.CORBA.Object reference to a remote object (using any of the approaches we've already covered), you can create and issue a method request to the object by building a parameter list for the method call, making a NamedValue object to hold the result, making a Context object and putting any useful environment values in it, and then using all of these items to create a Request object that corresponds to a particular method on the object. In general, the various create_XXX() methods on the ORB interface are used to construct all of these elements of a DII request, except for the Request itself. That is created by calling _create_request() on the Object that is the target of the remote method call.

Example 4-9 shows a version of our Account client that uses DII calls to invoke the deposit() or getBalance() methods on a remote Account object (the case for the withdraw() method is very similar to the deposit() case, so it's omitted here for the sake of brevity.) The client is structured very much like the client in Example 4-8, except that the actual calls to the remote Account object are constructed as DII calls. For the deposit requests, the method has a single float argument and no return value, so the call to create the Request includes a null NamedValue for the result, and an NVList containing a single NamedValue holding the amount to be deposited. In the case of requests for the Account balance, the getBalance() method has no arguments and a single float return value, so the creation of the Request includes a null NVList for the arguments, and a NamedValue containing an Any object intended to hold a floating-point value.

Example 4-9: Account Client DII.java

```java
import org.omg.CORBA.*;
import org.omg.CosNaming.*;

public class AccountClientDII {
  public static void main(String args[]) {
    ORB myORB = ORB.init(args, null);
    try {
      // The object name passed in on the command line
      String name = args[0];
      org.omg.CORBA.Object acctRef = null;
      if (name.startsWith("corbaname") || name.startsWith("corbaloc") ||
          name.startsWith("IOR")) {
        System.out.println("Attempting to lookup " + args[0]);
        acctRef = myORB.string_to_object(args[0]);
      }
      else {
        System.out.println("Invalid object URL provided: " + args[0]);
        System.exit(1);
      }

      // Make a dynamic call to the doThis method
      if (acctRef != null) {
        // We managed to get a reference to the named account, now check the
        // requested transaction from the command-line
        String action = args[1];
        float amt = 0.0f;
        if (action.equals("deposit")) {
          amt = Float.parseFloat(args[2]);
        }
        System.out.println("Got account, performing transaction...");
        try {
          // Did user ask to do a deposit?
          if (action.equals("deposit")) {
            // The following DII code is equivalent to this:
            //   acct.deposit(amt);

            // First build the argument list.  In this case, there's a single
            // float argument to the method.
            NVList argList = myORB.create_list(1);
            Any arg1 = myORB.create_any();
            // Set the Any to hold a float value, and set the value to the
            // amount to be deposited.
            arg1.insert_float(amt);
            NamedValue nvArg =
              argList.add_value("amt", arg1, org.omg.CORBA.ARG_IN.value);
            // Java IDL doesn't implement the get_default_context() operation
            // on the ORB, so we just set the Context to null
```

Example 4-9: Account Client DII.java (continued)

```
      Context ctx = null;
      // Create the request to call the deposit() method
      Request depositReq =
        acctRef._create_request(ctx, "deposit", argList, null);

      // Invoke the method...
      depositReq.invoke();
      System.out.println("Deposited " + amt + " to account.");
    }
    else {
      // The following DII code is equivalent to this:
      //   acct.balance();

      // No argument list is needed here, since the getBalance() method
      // has no arguments.  But we do need a result value to hold the
      // returned balance
      Any result = myORB.create_any();
      // Set the Any to hold a float value
      result.insert_float(0.0f);
      NamedValue resultVal =
        myORB.create_named_value("result", result,
                                 org.omg.CORBA.ARG_OUT.value);
      // Java IDL doesn't implement the get_default_context() operation
      // on the ORB, so we just set the Context to null
      Context ctx = null;
      // Create the request to call getBalance()
      Request balanceReq =
        acctRef._create_request(ctx, "getBalance", null, resultVal);

      // Invoke the method...
      balanceReq.invoke();
      System.out.println("Current account balance: " +
                         result.extract_float());
    }
  }
  catch (Exception e) {
    System.out.println("Error occurred while performing transaction:");
    e.printStackTrace();
  }
  }
  else {
    System.out.println("Null account returned.");
    System.exit(1);
  }
  }
  catch (Exception e) {
    e.printStackTrace();
  }
  }
}
```

Again, note that in most situations you will actually have the Java interface for the remote object available in your client along with its helper class, so you'll be able to narrow the Object reference to a specific type and call its methods directly. One exception might be if you're building some kind of software development tool, and you want to provide a dynamic execution utility for the CORBA code being developed. The previous example demonstrates how a CORBA method call can be carried out at this lower level, in case you ever find it necessary to do so. And when you're trying to fix a problem with your CORBA application, it's always better to understand what's going on under the hood, so to speak.

CHAPTER 5

Java Servlets

Over the last few years, Java has become the predominant language for server-side programming. This is due in no small part to the Java Servlet API, which provides a standard way to extend web servers to support dynamic content generation. With the introduction of the J2EE specification for enterprise applications, servlets have taken over as the primary interface for thin-client applications. In terms of enterprise computing, servlets are a natural fit if you are using the Web as your deployment platform. You can take advantage of web browsers as universally available thin clients using the web server as middleware for running application logic. Under this model, the user makes a request of the web server, the server invokes a servlet designed to handle the request, the servlet fulfills the request, and the result is returned to the user for display in the web browser.

While this sounds like every other dynamic content technology (such CGI, ISAPI, ASP, PHP, and the like), servlets have some major advantages. For one, servlets are persistent between invocations, which dramatically improves performance relative to CGI-style programs. Servlets are also 100% portable across operating systems and servers, unlike any of the alternatives. Finally, servlets have access to all the APIs of the Java platform, so, for example, it is easy to create a servlet that interacts with a database, using the JDBC API.

The first edition of this book, which covered Versions 2.0 and 2.1 of the Servlets API, focused on servlets as a replacement for other dynamic content technologies. During the following two years, there have been two additional revisions, the latest, Version 2.3, being finalized in September 2001 after a lengthy draft period. The new APIs integrate the Servlet API much more closely with the J2EE environment, introducing an explicit concept of a "web application." This is a collection of static content, servlets, JavaServer pages, and configuration information that can be easily deployed as a single unit (and can easily coexist with other web applications on the same web server). Version 2.3 of the Servlet API is a required component of J2EE Version 1.3.

This chapter demonstrates the basic techniques used to write servlets using Versions 2.2 and 2.3 of the Java Servlet API, including some common web-development tasks such as cookie manipulation and session tracking. This chapter assumes that you have some experience with web development; if you are new to web development, you may want to brush up on web basics by consulting *Webmaster in a Nutshell*, by Stephen Spainhour and Robert Eckstein (O'Reilly). For a more complete treatment of servlets, check out *Java Servlet Programming* by Jason Hunter with William Crawford (O'Reilly).

Getting a Servlet Environment

You need a *servlet container* to run servlets. A servlet container uses a Java Virtual Machine[*] to run servlet code as requested by a web server. The servlet container is also responsible for managing other aspects of the servlet lifecycle: user sessions, class loading, servlet contexts (which we will discuss in the next session), servlet configuration information, servlet persistence, and temporary storage.

There are a few varieties of servlet containers. Some are simply add-ons to existing web servers. The most popular of these is Apache/JServ, a Servlets 2.0 container that adds servlet capability to the Apache Web Server. Since interaction with servlets occurs almost exclusively through a web browser, these servlet engines aren't useful on their own. Other servlet engines include embedded web servers. Mortbay.com's Jetty server and IBM's WebSphere product line fall into this category. Finally, there are servlet engines that can be used either as standalone web servers or connected to other servers, (for example, the Tomcat server from the Apache Jakarta Project).

Because Tomcat is the reference implementation for the Servlet API, and Tomcat 4.0 is the only 2.3-compliant container available at press time, all the examples in this chapter have been tested with it. Since Tomcat falls under the Apache umbrella, distribution is free, and you can download a copy (including, if you like, full source code) from *http://jakarta.apache.org*. Binary installations are available for Windows and several Unix flavors. Other 2.3-compatible containers should be available by press time, but since 2.2 containers (including Tomcat 3.x and all current commercially available J2EE environments) will likely be around for quite some time, the relatively small differences between 2.2 and 2.3 are noted throughout this chapter.

Servlet Basics

The Servlet API consists of two packages, `javax.servlet` and `javax.servlet.http`. The `javax` is there because servlets are a standard extension to Java, rather than a mandatory part of the API. This means that while servlets are official Java, Java virtual machine developers aren't required to include the classes for them in their Java development and execution environments. As mentioned already, however, the Servlet API is required for J2EE 1.3

---

[*] As of Servlets 2.3, a JDK 1.2 or higher JVM is required.

The Servlet Lifecycle

When a client makes a request involving a servlet, the server loads and executes the appropriate Java classes. Those classes generate content, and the server sends the content back to the client. In most cases, the client is a web browser, the server is a web server, and the servlet returns standard HTML. From the web browser's perspective, this isn't any different from requesting a page generated by a CGI script, or, indeed, standard HTML. On the server side, however, there is an important difference: persistence.* Instead of shutting down at the end of each request, the servlet can remain loaded, ready to handle subsequent requests. Figure 5-1 shows how this all fits together.

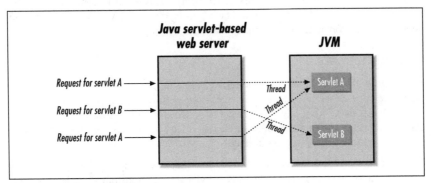

Figure 5-1: The servlet lifecycle

Java Servlets

The request-processing time for a servlet can vary, but it is typically quite fast when compared to a similar CGI program. The real performance advantage of a servlet, however, is that you incur most of the startup overhead only once. When a servlet loads, its init() method is called. You can use init() to create I/O-intensive resources, such as database connections, for use across multiple invocations. If you have a high-traffic site, the performance benefits can be quite dramatic. Instead of putting up and tearing down a hundred thousand database connections, the servlet just needs to create a connection once.

After the init() method runs, the servlet container marks the servlet as available. For each incoming connection directed at a particular servlet, the container calls the service() method on the servlet to process the request. The service() method can have access to all the resources created in the init() method. The servlet's destroy() method is called to clean up resources when the server shuts down.

Because servlets are persistent, you can actually remove a lot of filesystem and/or database accesses altogether. For example, to implement a page counter, you can simply store a number in a static variable, rather than consulting a file (or database) for every request. Using this technique, you need to read and write to the disk only occasionally to preserve state. Since a servlet remains active, it can

---

* Note that we use persistent to mean "enduring between invocations," not "written to permanent storage."

perform other tasks when it is not servicing client requests, such as running a background processing thread (i.e., where clients connect to the servlet to view a result) or even acting as an RMI host, enabling a single servlet to handle connections from multiple types of clients. For example, if you write an order processing servlet, it can accept transactions from both an HTML form and an applet using RMI.

The Servlet API includes numerous methods and classes for making application development easier. Most common CGI tasks require a lot of fiddling on the programmer's part; even decoding HTML form parameters can be a chore, to say nothing of dealing with cookies and session tracking. Libraries exist to help with these tasks, but they are, of course, decidedly nonstandard. You can use the Servlet API to handle most routine tasks, thus cutting development time and keeping things consistent for multiple developers on a project.

Writing Servlets

The three core elements of the Servlet API are the `javax.servlet.Servlet` interface, the `javax.servlet.GenericServlet` class, and the `javax.servlet.http.HttpServlet` class. Normally, you create a servlet by subclassing one of the two classes, although if you are adding servlet capability to an existing object, you may find it easier to implement the interface.

The `GenericServlet` class is used for servlets that don't implement any particular communication protocol. Here's a basic servlet that demonstrates servlet structure by printing a short message:

```
import javax.servlet.*;
import java.io.*;

public class BasicServlet extends GenericServlet {

    public void service(ServletRequest req, ServletResponse resp)
        throws ServletException, IOException {

        resp.setContentType("text/plain");
        PrintWriter out = resp.getWriter();
        // We won't use the ServletRequest object in this example
        out.println("Hello.");
    }
}
```

`BasicServlet` extends the `GenericServlet` class and implements one method: `service()`. Whenever a server wants to use the servlet, it calls the `service()` method, passing `ServletRequest` and `ServletResponse` objects (we'll look at these in more detail shortly). The servlet tells the server what type of response to expect, gets a `PrintWriter` from the response object, and transmits its output.

The `GenericServlet` class can also implement a *filtering servlet* that takes output from an unspecified source and performs some kind of alteration. For example, a filter servlet might be used to prepend a header, scan servlet output or raw HTML files for <DATE> tags and insert the current date, or remove <BLINK> tags. A more advanced filtering servlet might insert content from a database into HTML templates. We'll talk a little more about filtering later in this chapter, as well as discuss additional content filtering support available with 2.3 containers.

Although most servlets today work with web servers, there's no requirement for that in GenericServlet; the class implements just that, a generic servlet. As we'll see in a moment, the HttpServlet class is a subclass of GenericServlet that is designed to work with the HTTP protocol. It is entirely possible to develop other subclasses of GenericServlet that work with other server types. For example, a Java-based FTP server might use servlets to return files and directory listings or perform other tasks, although this capability has in general been underutilized. Later versions of the API have increased the coupling between servlets and HTTP.

HTTP Servlets

The HttpServlet class is an extension of GenericServlet that includes methods for handling HTTP-specific data.* HttpServlet provides a number of methods, such as doGet(), doPost(), and doPut(), to handle particular types of HTTP requests (GET, POST, and so on). These methods are called by the default implementation of the service() method, which figures out what kind of request is being made and then invokes the appropriate method. Here's a simple HttpServlet:

```
import javax.servlet.*;
import javax.servlet.http.*;
import java.io.*;

public class HelloWorldServlet extends HttpServlet {

  public void doGet(HttpServletRequest req, HttpServletResponse resp)
      throws ServletException, IOException {

    resp.setContentType("text/html");
    PrintWriter out = resp.getWriter();

    out.println("<HTML>");
    out.println(
        "<HEAD><TITLE>Have you seen this before?</TITLE></HEAD>");
    out.println(
        "<BODY><H1>Hello, World!</H1><H6>Again.</H6></BODY></HTML>");
  }
}
```

HelloWorldServlet demonstrates many essential servlet concepts. First, HelloWorldServlet extends HttpServlet. This is standard practice for an HTTP servlet. HelloWorldServlet defines one method, doGet(), which is called whenever anyone requests a URL that points to this servlet.† The doGet() method is actually called by the default service() method of HttpServlet. The service()

---

* HttpServlet is an abstract class, implemented by the provider of the servlet container.

† In a standard Java Web Server installation, with the servlet installed in the standard *servlets* directory, this URL is *http://site:8080/servlet/HelloWorldServlet*. Note that the name of the directory (*servlets*) is unrelated to the use of "servlet" in the URL.

method is called by the web server when a request is made of HelloWorldServlet; the method determines what kind of HTTP request is being made and dispatches the request to the appropriate doXXX() method (in this case, doGet()). doGet() is passed two objects, HttpServletRequest and HttpServletResponse, that contain information about the request and provide a mechanism for the servlet to produce output, respectively.

The doGet() method itself does three things. First, it sets the output type to text/html, which indicates that the servlet produces standard HTML as its output. Second, it calls the getWriter() method of the HttpServletResponse parameter to get a java.io.PrintWriter that points to the client. Finally, it uses the stream to send some HTML back to the client. This isn't really a whole lot different from the BasicServlet example, but it gives us all the tools we'll need later on for more complex web applications. We do have to explicitly set the content type, as there is no default setting, even for HTTP servlets where one might reasonably expect text/html.

If you define a doGet() method for a servlet, you may also want to override the getLastModified() method of HttpServlet. The server calls getLastModified() to find out if the content delivered by a servlet has changed. The default implementation of this method returns a negative number, which tells the server that the servlet doesn't know when its content was last updated, so the server is forced to call doGet() and return the servlet's output. If you have a servlet that changes its display data infrequently (such as a servlet that verifies uptime on several server machines once every 15 minutes), you should implement getLastModified() to allow browsers to cache responses. getLastModified() should return a long value that represents the time the content was last modified as the number of milliseconds since midnight, January 1, 1970, GMT. This number can be easily obtained by calling the getTime() method java.util.Date.

A servlet should also implement getServletInfo(), which returns a string that contains information about the servlet, such as name, author, and version (just like getAppletInfo() in applets). This method is called by the web server and generally used for logging purposes.

Web Applications

Now that we've seen a basic servlet, we can step back for a moment and talk about how servlets are integrated into the servlet container. Version 2.2 of the Servlet API popularized the concept of a web application installed within a web server. A web application consists of a set of resources, including servlets, static content, JSP files, and class libraries, installed within a particular path on a web server. This path is called the *servlet context,* and all servlets installed within the context are given an isolated, protected environment to operate in, without interference from (or the ability to interfere with) other software running on the server.

A servlet context directory tree contains several different types of resources. These include class files and JAR files (which aren't exposed to clients connecting via web browsers), JSP files (which are processed by the JSP servlet before being fed back to the client), and static files, such as HTML documents and JPEG images, which are served directly to the browser by the web server.

Finally, there is a virtual component to the context. For each context, the servlet container will instantiate separate copies of servlets (even if those servlets are shared) and will create a private address space that can be accessed via the `ServletContext` class. Servlets can use this class to communicate with other servlets running in the same context. We'll discuss this more later.

The simplest servlet installations will just create a single context, rooted at /, which is the top of the web server path tree. Servlets and static content will be installed within this context. This is the way the Servlet API 2.0 treated the entire server. More modern servlet containers allow the creation of multiple servlet contexts, rooted lower down on the directory tree. A catalog application, for example, could be rooted at */catalog*, with all of the application paths below the context root.

If you write a web application that will be installed on multiple web servers, it isn't safe to assume the context root will be fixed. If the path of a resource within your application is */servlet/CatalogServlet,* and it's installed within the */catalog* context, rather than writing:

```
out.println("<a href=\"/catalog/servlet/CatalogServlet\">");
```

you should write:

```
out.println("<a href=\"" + request.getContextPath() + "/servlet/
                                    CatalogServlet\">");
```

This approach works regardless of the context path installed within the web server.

Structure of Web Applications

On disk, a web application consists of a directory. The directory contains a subdirectory called *WEB-INF*, and whatever other content is required for the application. The *WEB-INF* directory contains a classes directory (containing application code), a lib directory (containing application JAR files), and a file called *web.xml*. The *web.xml* file contains all of the configuration information for the servlets within the context, including names, path mappings and initialization parameters and context-level configuration information. For a detailed explanation of *web.xml*, consult your server documentation or take a look at the well-commented XML DTD itself at *http://java.sun.com/dtd/web-app_2_3.dtd*.

The procedure for installing a web application into a servlet container varies from product to product, but it generally consists of selecting a context root and pointing the server to the directory containing the web application.[*]

Mapping Requests with a Context

Servlets are installed within the servlet container and mapped to URIs. This is done either via global properties that apply to all servlets or by specific, servlet-by-servlet mappings. In the first case, a client invokes a servlet by requesting it by name. Most servers map servlets to a */servlet/* or */servlets/* URL. If a servlet is

---

[*] Web applications can be packaged into JAR file equivalents called WAR files. To do this, simply use the *jar* utility that comes with the JDK to pack up the web application directory (including the *WEB-INF* subdirectory) and give the resulting file a *.war* extension.

installed as `PageServlet`, then a request to */servlet/PageServlet* would invoke it. Servlets can also be individually mapped to other URIs or to file extensions. PageServlet might be mapped to */pages/page1*, or to all files with a *.page* extension (using **.page*).

All of these mappings exist below the context level. If the web application is installed at */app*, then the paths entered into the browser for the examples above would be */app/servlet/PageServlet, /app/pages/page1,* or */app/file.page*.

To illustrate, imagine the following servlet mappings (all are below the context root):

Mapping	Servlet
/store/furniture/*	FurnitureServlet
/store/furniture/tables/*	TableServlet
/store/furniture/chairs	ChairServlet
*.page	PageServlet

The asterisk serves as a wildcard. URIs matching the pattern are mapped to the specified servlet, providing that another mapping hasn't already been used to deal with the URL. This can get a little tricky when building complex mapping relationships, but the servlet API does require servers to deal with mappings consistently. When the servlet container receives a request, it always maps it to the appropriate servlet in the following order:

1. By *exact path matching*. A request to */store/furniture/chairs* is served by ChairServlet.

2. By *prefix mapping*. A request to */store/furniture/sofas* is served by FurnitureServlet. The longest matching prefix is used. A request to */store/furniture/tables/dining* is served by TableServlet.

3. By *extension*. Requests for */info/contact.page* are served by PageServlet. However, requests for */store/furniture/chairs/about.page* is served by FurnitureServlet (since prefix mappings are checked first, and ChairServlet is available only for exact matches).

If no appropriate servlet is found, the server returns an error message or attempts to serve content on its own. If a servlet is mapped to the / path, it becomes the default servlet for the application and is invoked when no other servlet can be found.

Context Methods

Resources within a servlet context (such as HTML files, images, and other data) can be accessed directly via the web server. If a file called *index.html* is stored at the root of the */app* context, then it can be accessed with a request to */app/index.html*. Context resources can also be accessed via the ServletContext object, which is accessed via the getResource() and getResourceAsStream() methods. A full list of available resources can be accessed via the getResourcePaths() method. In this case, an InputStream containing the contents of the *index.html* file can be retrieved by calling getResourceAsStream("/index.html") on the ServletContext object associated with the */app* context.

The `ServletContext` interface provides servlets with access to a range of information about the local environment. The `getInitParameter()` and `getInitParameterNames()` methods allow servlets to retrieve context-wide initialization parameters. `ServletContext` also includes a number of methods that allow servlets to share attributes. The new `setAttribute()` method allows a servlet to set an attribute that can be shared by any other servlets that live in its `ServletContext`, and `removeAttribute()` allows them to be removed. The `getAttribute()` method, which previously allowed servlets to retrieve hardcoded server attributes, provides access to attribute values, while `getAttributeNames()` returns an `Enumeration` of all the shared attributes.

The servlet container is required to maintain a temporary working directory on disk for each servlet context. This directory is accessed by retrieving the `javax.servlet.context.tempdir` attribute, which consists of a `java.io.File` object pointing to the temporary directory. The temporary directory is exclusive to the context. The servlet container is not required to maintain its contents across restarts.

Version 2.1 of the Servlet API deprecated all methods related to accessing other servlets directly, due to the fact that they are inherently insecure. Thus, `getServlet()` and `getServletNames()` join the already deprecated `getServlets()`. The problem was that `getServlet()` incorrectly allowed one servlet to call another servlet's life-cycle methods, including `init()` and `destroy()`.

Servlet Requests

When a servlet is asked to handle a request, it typically needs specific information about the request so that it can process the request appropriately. Most frequently, a servlet will retrieve the value of a form variable and use that value in its output. A servlet may also need access to information about the environment in which it is running. For example, a servlet may need to find out about the actual user who is accessing the servlet, for authentication purposes.

The `ServletRequest` and `HttpServletRequest` interfaces provide access to this kind of information. When a servlet is asked to handle a request, the server passes it a request object that implements one of these interfaces. With this object, the servlet can determine the actual request (e.g., protocol, URL, type), access parts of the raw request (e.g., headers, input stream), and get any client-specific request parameters (e.g., form variables, extra path information). For instance, the `getProtocol()` method returns the protocol used by the request, while `getRemoteHost()` returns the name of the client host. The interfaces also provide methods that let a servlet get information about the server (e.g., `getServername()`, `getServerPort()`). As we saw earlier, the `getParameter()` method provides access to request parameters such as form variables. There is also the `getParameterValues()` method, which returns an array of strings that contains all the values for a particular parameter. This array generally contains only one string, but some HTML form elements (as well as non-HTTP oriented services) do allow multiple selections or options, so the method always returns an array, even if it has a length of one.

HttpServletRequest adds a few more methods for handling HTTP-specific request data. For instance, getHeaderNames() returns an enumeration of the names of all the HTTP headers submitted with a request, while getHeader() returns a particular header value. Other methods exist to handle cookies and sessions, as we'll discuss later.

Example 5-1 shows a servlet that restricts access to users who are connecting via the HTTPS protocol, using Digest style authentication, and coming from a government site (a domain ending in *.gov*).

Example 5-1: Checking Request Information to Restrict Servlet Access

```java
import javax.servlet.*;
import javax.servlet.http.*;
import java.io.*;

public class SecureRequestServlet extends HttpServlet {

  public void doGet(HttpServletRequest req, HttpServletResponse resp)
    throws ServletException, IOException {

    resp.setContentType("text/html");
    PrintWriter out = resp.getWriter();

    out.println("<HTML>");
    out.println("<HEAD><TITLE>Semi-Secure Request</TITLE></HEAD>");
    out.println("<BODY>");

    String remoteHost = req.getRemoteHost();
    String scheme = req.getScheme();
    String authType = req.getAuthType();

    if((remoteHost == null) || (scheme == null) || (authType == null)) {
      out.println("Request Information Was Not Available.");
      return;
    }

    if(scheme.equalsIgnoreCase("https") && remoteHost.endsWith(".gov")
       && authType.equals("Digest")) {
      out.println("Special, secret information.");
    }
    else {
      out.println("You are not authorized to view this data.");
    }

    out.println("</BODY></HTML>");
  }
}
```

Forms and Interaction

The problem with creating a servlet like HelloWorldServlet is that it doesn't do anything we can't already do with HTML. If we are going to bother with a servlet at all, we should do something dynamic and interactive with it. In many cases, this means processing the results of an HTML form. To make our example less impersonal, let's have it greet the user by name. The HTML form that calls the servlet using a GET request might look like this:

```
<HTML>
<HEAD><TITLE>Greetings Form</TITLE></HEAD>
<BODY>
<FORM METHOD=GET ACTION="/servlet/HelloServlet">
What is your name?
<INPUT TYPE=TEXT NAME=username SIZE=20>
<INPUT TYPE=SUBMIT VALUE="Introduce Yourself">
</FORM>
</BODY>
</HTML>
```

This form submits a form variable named username to the URL */servlet/HelloServlet*. The HelloServlet itself does little more than create an output stream, read the username form variable, and print a nice greeting for the user. Here's the code:

```
import javax.servlet.*;
import javax.servlet.http.*;
import java.io.*;

public class HelloServlet extends HttpServlet {

    public void doGet(HttpServletRequest req, HttpServletResponse resp)
        throws ServletException, IOException {

        resp.setContentType("text/html");
        PrintWriter out = resp.getWriter();

        out.println("<HTML>");
        out.println("<HEAD><TITLE>Finally, interaction!</TITLE></HEAD>");
        out.println("<BODY><H1>Hello, " + req.getParameter("username") +
                                                        "!</H1>");
        out.println("</BODY></HTML>");
    }
}
```

All we've done differently is use the getParameter() method of HttpServletRequest to retrieve the value of a form variable.* When a server calls a servlet, it can also pass a set of request parameters. With HTTP servlets, these parameters come from the HTTP request itself—in this case, in the guise of URL-encoded form variables. Note that a GenericServlet running in a web server also has access to these parameters using the simpler ServletRequest object. When the HelloServlet runs, it inserts the value of the username form variable into the HTML output, as shown in Figure 5-2.

---

* In the Java Web Server 1.1, the getParameter() method was deprecated in favor of getParameterValues(), which returns a String array rather than a single string. However, after an extensive write-in campaign, Sun took getParameter() off the deprecated list for Version 2.0 of the Servlet API, so you can safely use this method in your servlets. This is not an issue with later versions of the API.

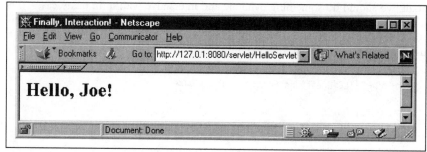

Figure 5-2: Output from HelloServlet

POST, HEAD, and Other Requests

As mentioned earlier, doGet() is just one of a collection of enabling methods for HTTP request types. doPost() is the corresponding method for POST requests. The POST request is designed for posting information to the server, although in practice it is also used for long parameterized requests and larger forms, to get around limitations on the length of URLs.

If your servlet is performing database updates, charging a credit card, or doing anything that takes an explicit client action, you should make sure this activity is happening in a doPost() method. That's because POST requests aren't *idempotent*, which means that they aren't safely repeatable, and web browsers treat them specially. For example, a browser can't bookmark or, in some cases, reload a POST request. On the other hand, GET requests are idempotent, so they can safely be bookmarked, and a browser is free to issue the request repeatedly without necessarily consulting the user. You can see why you don't want to charge a credit card in a GET method!

To create a servlet that can handle POST requests, all you have to do is override the default doPost() method from HttpServlet and implement the necessary functionality in it. If necessary, your application can implement different code in doPost() and doGet(). For instance, the doGet() method might display a post-able data entry form that the doPost() method processes. doPost() can even call doGet() at the end to display the form again.

The less common HTTP request types, such as HEAD, PUT, TRACE, and DELETE, are handled by other doXXX() dispatch methods. A HEAD request returns HTTP headers only, PUT and DELETE allow clients to create and remove resources from the web server, and TRACE returns the request headers to the client. Since most servlet programmers don't need to worry about these requests, the HttpServlet class includes a default implementation of each corresponding doXXX() method that either informs the client that the request is unsupported or provides a minimal implementation. You can provide your own versions of these methods, but the details of implementing PUT or DELETE functionality go rather beyond our scope.

Servlet Responses

In order to do anything useful, a servlet must send a response to each request that is made to it. In the case of an HTTP servlet, the response can include three components: a status code, any number of HTTP headers, and a response body.

The ServletResponse and HttpServletResponse interfaces include all the methods needed to create and manipulate a servlet's output. We've already seen that you specify the MIME type for the data returned by a servlet using the setContentType() method of the response object passed into the servlet. With an HTTP servlet, the MIME type is generally text/html, although some servlets return binary data: a servlet that loads a GIF file from a database and sends it to the web browser should set a content type of image/gif while a servlet that returns an Adobe Acrobat file should set it to application/pdf.

ServletResponse and HttpServletResponse each define two methods for producing output streams, getOutputStream() and getWriter(). The former returns a ServletOutputStream, which can be used for textual or binary data. The latter returns a java.io.PrintWriter object, which is used only for textual output. The getWriter() method examines the content-type to determine which charset to use, so setContentType() should be called before getWriter().

HttpServletResponse also includes a number of methods for handling HTTP responses. Most of these allow you to manipulate the HTTP header fields. For example, setHeader(), setIntHeader(), and setDateHeader() allow you to set the value of a specified HTTP header, while containsHeader() indicates whether a certain header has already been set. You can use either the setStatus() or sendError() method to specify the status code sent back to the server. HttpServletResponse defines a long list of integer constants that represent specific status codes (we'll see some of these shortly). You typically don't need to worry about setting a status code, as the default code is 200 ("OK"), meaning that the servlet sent a normal response. However, a servlet that is part of a complex application structure (such as the file servlet included in the Java Web Server that handles the dispatching of HTML pages) may need to use a variety of status codes. Finally, the sendRedirect() method allows you to issue a page redirect. Calling this method sets the Location header to the specified location and uses the appropriate status code for a redirect.

Request Dispatching

Request dispatching allows a servlet to delegate request handling to other components on the server. A servlet can either forward an entire request to another servlet or include bits of content from other components in its own output. In either case, this is done with a RequestDispatcher object that is obtained from the ServletContext via the getRequestDispatcher() method (also available via the HttpServletRequest object.) When you call this method, you specify the path to the servlet to which you are dispatching the request. The path should be relative to the servlet context. If you want to dispatch a request to the */servlet/TargetServlet* URI within the */app* context (which is accessed from a user's browser by */app/servlet/TargetServlet*), request a dispatcher for */servlet/TargetServlet*.

When you dispatch a request, you can set request attributes using the `setAttribute()` method of `ServletRequest` and read them using the `getAttribute()` method. A list of available attributes is returned by `getAttributeNames()`. All three of these methods were new in Version 2.1. Rather than taking only `String` objects (like parameters), an attribute may be any valid Java object.

`RequestDispatcher` provides two methods for dispatching requests: `forward()` and `include()`. To forward an entire request to another servlet, use the `forward()` method. When using `forward()`, the `ServletRequest` object is updated to include the new target URL. If a `ServletOutputStream` or `PrintWriter` has already been retrieved from the `ServletResponse` object, the `forward()` method throws an `IllegalStateException`.

The `include()` method of `RequestDispatcher` causes the content of the dispatchee to be included in the output of the main servlet, just like a server-side include. To see how this works, let's look at part of a servlet that does a keep-alive check on several different servers. The `ServerMonitorServlet` referenced in this example relies on the `serverurl` attribute to determine which server to display monitoring information for:

```
out.println("Uptime for our servers");

// Get a RequestDispatcher to the ServerMonitorServlet
RequestDispatcher d = getServletContext().
    getRequestDispatcher("/servlet/ServerMonitorServlet");

req.setAttribute("serverurl", new URL("http://www1.company.com"));
d.include(req, res);

req.setAttribute("serverurl", new URL("http://www2.company.com"));
d.include(req, res);
```

Error Handling

Sometimes things just go wrong. When that happens, it's nice to have a clean way out. The Servlet API gives you two ways of to deal with errors: you can manually send an error message back to the client or you can throw a `ServletException`. The easiest way to handle an error is simply to write an error message to the servlet's output stream. This is the appropriate technique to use when the error is part of a servlet's normal operation, such as when a user forgets to fill in a required form field.

Status codes

When an error is a standard HTTP error, you should use the `sendError()` method of `HttpServletResponse` to tell the server to send a standard error status code. `HttpServletResponse` defines integer constants for all the major HTTP status codes. Table 5-1 lists the most common status codes. For example, if a servlet can't find a file the user has requested, it can send a 404 ("File Not Found") error and let the browser display it in its usual manner. In this case, we can replace the typical setContentType() and getWriter() calls with something like this:

```
response.sendError(HttpServletResponse.SC_NOT_FOUND);
```

If you want to specify your own error message (in addition to the web server's default message for a particular error code), you can call sendError() with an extra String parameter:

```
response.sendError(HttpServletResponse.SC_NOT_FOUND,
                   "It's dark. I couldn't find anything.");
```

Table 5-1: Some Common HTTP Error Codes

Mnemonic Content	Code	Default Message	Meaning
SC_OK	200	OK	The client's request succeeded, and the server's response contains the requested data. This is the default status code.
SC_NO_CONTENT	204	No Content	The request succeeded, but there is no new response body to return. A servlet may find this code useful when it accepts data from a form, but wants the browser view to stay at the form. It avoids the "Document contains no data" error message.
SC_MOVED_ PERMANENTLY	301	Moved Permanently	The requested resource has permanently moved to a new location. Any future reference should use the new location given by the Location header. Most browsers automatically access the new location.
SC_MOVED_ TEMPORARILY	302	Moved Temporarily	The requested resource has temporarily moved to another location, but future references should still use the original URL to access the resource. The temporary new location is given by the Location header. Most browsers automatically access the new location.
SC_ UNAUTHORIZED	401	Unauthorized	The request lacked proper authorization. Used in conjunction with the WWW-Authenticate and Authorization headers.
SC_NOT_FOUND	404	Not Found	The requested resource is not available.
SC_INTERNAL_ SERVER_ERROR	500	Internal Server Error	An error occurred inside the server that prevented it from fulfilling the request.
SC_NOT_ IMPLEMENTED	501	Not Implemented	The server doesn't support the functionality needed to fulfill the request.
SC_SERVICE_ UNAVAILABLE	503	Service Unavailable	The server is temporarily unavailable, but service should be restored in the future. If the server knows when it will be available again, a Retry-After header may also be supplied.

Java Servlets

Servlet exceptions

The Servlet API includes two Exception subclasses, ServletException and its derivative, UnavailableException. A servlet throws a ServletException to indicate a general servlet problem. When a server catches this exception, it can handle the exception however it sees fit.

`UnavailableException` is a bit more useful, however. When a servlet throws this exception, it is notifying the server that it is unavailable to service requests. You can throw an `UnavailableException` when some factor beyond your servlet's control prevents it from dealing with requests. To throw an exception that indicates permanent unavailability, use something like this:

```
throw new UnavailableException(this, "This is why you can't use the
servlet.");
```

`UnavailableException` has a second constructor to use if the servlet is going to be temporarily unavailable. With this constructor, you specify how many seconds the servlet is going to be unavailable, as follows:

```
throw new UnavailableException(120, this, "Try back in two minutes");
```

One caveat: the servlet specification doesn't mandate that servers actually try again after the specified interval. If you choose to rely on this capability, you should test it first.

A file serving servlet

Example 5-2 demonstrates both of these error-handling techniques, along with another method for reading data from the server. `FileServlet` reads a pathname from a form parameter and returns the associated file. Note that this servlet is designed only to return HTML files. If the file can't be found, the servlet sends the browser a 404 error. If the servlet lacks sufficient access privileges to load the file, it sends an `UnavailableException` instead. Keep in mind that this servlet exists as a teaching exercise: you should not deploy it on your web server. (For one thing, any security exception renders the servlet permanently unavailable, and for another, it can serve files from the root of your hard drive.)

Example 5-2: Serving Files

```
import javax.servlet.*;
import javax.servlet.http.*;
import java.io.*;

public class FileServlet extends HttpServlet {

  public void doGet(HttpServletRequest req, HttpServletResponse resp)
    throws ServletException, IOException {

    File r;
    FileReader fr;
    BufferedReader br;
    try {
      r = new File(req.getParameter("filename"));
      fr = new FileReader(r);
      br = new BufferedReader(fr);
      if(!r.isFile()) {  // Must be a directory or something else
        resp.sendError(resp.SC_NOT_FOUND);
        return;
      }
    }
```

Example 5-2: Serving Files (continued)

```
    catch (FileNotFoundException e) {
      resp.sendError(resp.SC_NOT_FOUND);
      return;
    }
    catch (SecurityException se) { // Be unavailable permanently
      throw(new UnavailableException(this,
        "Servlet lacks appropriate privileges."));
    }

    resp.setContentType("text/html");
    PrintWriter out = resp.getWriter();
    String text;
    while( (text = br.readLine()) != null )
      out.println(text);

    br.close();
  }
}
```

Custom Servlet Initialization

At the beginning of this chapter, we talked about how a servlet's persistence can be used to build more efficient web applications. This is accomplished via class variables and the init() method. When a server loads a servlet for the first time, it calls the servlet's init() method and doesn't make any service calls until init() has finished. In the default implementation, init() simply handles some basic housekeeping, but a servlet can override the method to perform whatever one-time tasks are required. This often means doing some sort of I/O-intensive resource creation, such as opening a database connection. You can also use the init() method to create threads that perform various ongoing tasks. For instance, a servlet that monitors the status of machines on a network might create a separate thread to periodically ping each machine. When an actual request occurs, the service methods in the servlet can use the resources created in init(). Thus, the status monitor servlet might display an HTML table with the status of the various machines. The default init() implementation is not a do-nothing method, so you should remember to always call the super.init() method as the first action in your own init() routines.[*]

The server passes the init() method a ServletConfig object, which can include specific servlet configuration parameters (for instance, the list of machines to monitor). ServletConfig encapsulates the servlet initialization parameters, which are accessed via the getInitParameter() and getInitParameterNames() methods. GenericServlet and HttpServlet both implement the ServletConfig interface, so these methods are always available in a servlet. (One task the default init() implementation does is store the ServletConfig object for these methods, which is

---

[*] Note that you no longer have to do this with Version 2.1 of the Servlet API. The specification has been changed so that you can simply override a no-argument init() method, which is called by the Generic Servlet init(ServletConfig) implementation.

why it is important you always call `super.init()`.) Different web servers have different ways of setting initialization parameters, so we aren't going to discuss how to set them. Consult your server documentation for details.

Every servlet also has a `destroy()` method that can be overwritten. This method is called when, for whatever reason, a server unloads a servlet. You can use this method to ensure that important resources are freed, or that threads are allowed to finish executing unmolested. Unlike `init()`, the default implementation of `destroy()` is a do-nothing method, so you don't have to worry about invoking the superclass' `destroy()` method.

Example 5-3 shows a counter servlet that saves its state between server shutdowns. It uses the `init()` method to first try to load a default value from a servlet initialization parameter. Next the `init()` method tries to open a file named */data/counter.dat* and read an integer from it. When the servlet is shut down, the `destroy()` method creates a new *counter.dat* file with the current hit-count for the servlet.

Example 5-3: A Persistent Counter Servlet

```
import javax.servlet.*;
import javax.servlet.http.*;
import java.io.*;

public class LifeCycleServlet extends HttpServlet {

  int timesAccessed;

  public void init(ServletConfig conf) throws ServletException {

    super.init(conf);

    // Get initial value
    try {
      timesAccessed = Integer.parseInt(getInitParameter("defaultStart"));
    }
    catch(NullPointerException e) {
     timesAccessed = 0;
    }
    catch(NumberFormatException e) {
      timesAccessed = 0;
    }

    // Try loading from the disk
    try {
      File r = new File("./data/counter.dat");
      DataInputStream ds = new DataInputStream(new FileInputStream(r));
      timesAccessed = ds.readInt();
    }
    catch (FileNotFoundException e) {
      // Handle error
    }
    catch (IOException e) {
      // This should be logged
```

Example 5-3: A Persistent Counter Servlet (continued)

```
    }
    finally {
      ds.close();
    }
  }

  public void doGet(HttpServletRequest req, HttpServletResponse resp)
    throws ServletException, IOException {

    resp.setContentType("text/html");
    PrintWriter out = resp.getWriter();

    timesAccessed++;

    out.println("<HTML>");
    out.println("<HEAD>");
    out.println("<TITLE>Life Cycle Servlet</TITLE>");
    out.println("</HEAD><BODY>");

    out.println("I have been accessed " + timesAccessed + " time[s]");
    out.println("</BODY></HTML>");
  }

  public void destroy() {

    // Write the Integer to a file
    File r = new File("./data/counter.dat");
    try {
      DataOutputStream dout = new DataOutputStream(new FileOutputStream(r));
      dout.writeInt(timesAccessed);
    }
    catch(IOException e) {
      // This should be logged
    }
    finally {
      dout.close();
    }
  }
}
```

Servlet Context Initalization

Version 2.3 of the Servlet API adds support for application-level events via a listener-style interface. Classes that implement the ServletContextListener interface can be associated with a servlet context, and will be notified when the context is unitized or destroyed. This provides programmers with the opportunity to create application-level resources, such as database connection pools, before any servlets are unitized, and to share single resources among multiple servlets using the ServletContext attribute functionality.

ServletContextListener contains two methods, contextInitialized() and contextDestroyed(), which take a ServletContextEvent. Context listeners are associated with their context in the *web.xml* file for the web application. Example 5-4 defines a listener that creates a hashtable of usernames and unencrypted passwords and associates it as a context attribute. We use it in a later example:

Example 5-4: A Servlet Context Listener

```
import javax.servlet.ServletContextListener;
import javax.servlet.ServletContextEvent;

public class ContextResourceLoader implements ServletContextListener {

  public void contextInitialized(ServletContextEvent sce) {
    java.util.Hashtable users = new Hashtable();
    users.put("test", "test");
    users.put("admin", "bob3jk");
    sce.getServletContext().setAttribute("enterprise.users", users);
  }

  public void contextDestroyed(ServletContextEvent sce) {
    // This is where we clean up resources on server shutdown/restart
  }
}
```

Obviously, a real application would retrieve the usernames and passwords in a more efficient manner. In this case, we can count on the JVM to properly garbage-collect the Hashtable object. If we do something more complex (such as maintaining a pool of connections to a relational database), we would use the contextDestroyed() method to make sure those resources were properly freed.

Security

Servlets don't have to handle their own security arrangements. Instead, they can rely on the capabilities of the web server to limit access where required. The security capabilities of most web servers are limited to basic on-or-off access to specific resources, controlled by username and password (or digital certificate), with possible encryption-in-transmission using SSL. Most servers are limited to basic authentication, which transmits passwords more or less in the clear, while some support the more advanced digest authentication protocol, which works by transmitting a hash of the user's password and a server-generated value, rather than the password itself. Both of these approaches look the same to the user; the familiar "Enter username and password" window pops up in the web browser.

Recent versions of the Servlet API take a much less hands-off approach to security. The *web.xml* file can be used to define which servlets and resources are protected, and which users have access. The user access model is the J2EE User-Role model, in which users can be assigned one or more Roles. Users with a particular role are granted access to protected resources. A user named Admin might have both the Administrator role and the User role, while users Bob and Ted might only have the User role.

In addition to basic, digest and SSL authentication, the web application framework allows for HTML form-based logins. This approach allows the developer to specify an HTML or JSP page containing a form like the following:

```
<form method="POST" action="j_security_check">
<input type="text" name="j_username">
<input type=password" name="j_password">
<input type="submit" value="Log In">
</form>
```

Note that forms-based authentication is insecure, and will only work if the client session is being tracked via Cookies or SSL signatures.

In Servlets 2.0, the HttpServletRequest interface included a pair of basic methods for retrieving standard HTTP user authentication information from the web server. If your web server is equipped to limit access, a servlet can retrieve the username with getRemoteUser() and the authentication method (basic, digest, or SSL) with getAuthType(). Version 2.2 of the Servlet API added the isUserInRole() and getUserPrincipal() methods to HttpServletRequest. isUserInRole() allows the program to query whether the current user is member of a particular role (useful for dynamic content decisions that can not be made at the container level). The getUserPrincipal() method returns a java.security.Principal object identifying the current user.

The process used to authenticate users (by validating their usernames and passwords) is up the developer of the servlet container.

Servlet Chains and Filters

So far, we have looked at servlets that take requests directly from the server and return their results directly to the client. Servlets were designed as a generic server extension technology, however, rather than one devoted solely to performing CGI-like functions. A servlet can just as easily take its input from another servlet, and a servlet really doesn't care very much about where its output goes.

Most web servers that implement servlets have also implemented a feature called *servlet chaining*, where the server routes a request through an administrator-defined chain of servlets. At the end of the sequence, the server sends the output to the client. Alternately, some servers can be configured to route certain MIME types through certain servlets. If a filtering servlet is configured to take all of the output with the MIME type "servlet/filterme," another servlet can produce data with that MIME type, and that data will be passed to the filtering servlet. The filtering servlet, after doing its work, can output HTML for the browser. MIME-based filtering also allows servlets to filter objects that don't come from a servlet in the first place, such as HTML files served by the web server.

Example 5-5 demonstrates a basic servlet, derived from HttpServlet, that examines incoming text for a <DATE> tag and replaces the tag with the current date. This servlet is never called on its own, but instead after another servlet (such as an HTML generator) has produced the actual content.

Example 5-5: Date Filtering Servlet

```
import javax.servlet.*;
import javax.servlet.http.*;
import java.io.*;
import java.util.*;

public class DateFilter extends HttpServlet {

    public void doGet(HttpServletRequest req, HttpServletResponse resp)
    throws ServletException, IOException {

        PrintWriter out = resp.getWriter();

        String contentType = req.getContentType();
        if (contentType == null)
            return; // No incoming data

        // Note that if we were using MIME filtering we would have to set this to
        // something different to avoid an infinite loop
        resp.setContentType(contentType);

        BufferedReader br = new BufferedReader(req.getReader());

        String line = null;
        Date d = new Date();
        while ((line = br.readLine()) != null) {
            int index;
            while ((index=line.indexOf("<DATE>")) >= 0)
                line = line.substring(0, index) + d + line.substring(index + 6);
            out.println(line);
        }

        br.close();
    }
}
```

The DateFilter servlet works by reading each line of input, scanning for the text
<DATE>, and replacing it with the current date. This example introduces the
getReader() method of HttpServletRequest, which returns a PrintReader that
points to the original request body. When you call getReader() in an
HttpServlet, you can read the original HTTP form variables, if any. When this
method is used within a filtering servlet, it provides access to the output of the
previous servlet in the chain.

Filters

Version 2.3 of the Servlet API introduced a new method of handling requests, via
the javax.servlet.Filter class. When filters are used, the servlet container
creates a *filter chain*. This consists of zero or more Filter objects and a destination resource, which can be either a servlet or another resources available on the
web server (such as an HTML or JSP file).

Filters are installed in the server and associated with particular request paths (just like servlets). When a filtered resource is requested, the servlet constructs a filter chain and calls the doFilter() method of the first filter in the filter chain, passing a ServletRequest, a ServletResponse, and the FilterChain object. The filter can then perform processing on the request. The processing is sometimes noninterventionary (such as logging characteristics of the request or tracking a clickstream). However, the filter can also wrap the ServletRequest and ServletResponse classes with its own versions, overriding particular methods. For instance, one of the example filters included with the Tomcat server adds support for returning compressed output to browsers that support it.

After the filter has processed the response, it can call the doFilter() method of the FilterChain to invoke the next filter in the sequence. If there are no more filters, the request will be passed on to its ultimate destination. After calling doFilter(), the filter can perform additional processing on the response received from farther down the chain.

In the event of an error, the filter can stop processing, returning to the client whatever response has already been created, or forwarding the request on to a different resource.

Example 5-6 duplicates the form-based authentication feature that already exists in the servlet API, but could be customized to provide additional functionality not available directly from the server (for instance, authenticating users against systems other than those supported by the servlet container). It works by intercepting each request and checking the HttpSession for an attribute called "enterprise.login." If that attribute contains a Boolean.TRUE, access is permitted. If not, the filter checks for request parameters named "login_name" and "login_pass," and searches for a match in a hashtable containing valid username/password pairs. If valid login credentials are found, processing the filter chain is allowed to continue. If not, the user is served a login page located at /login.jsp, retrieved via a RequestDispatcher.*

Astute readers will note that we try to retrieve the users' hashtable from a servlet context attribute. We showed how to set this attribute at server startup in the section "Custom Servlet Initialization." In case you don't have that set up, the Filter's init() method will create its own if it can't find one in the context.

Example 5-6: AuthenticationFilter

```
import javax.servlet.*;
import javax.servlet.http.*;
```

---

* This isn't a highly secure system. Unless the client has connected via SSL, the username/password combination is transmitted unencrypted over the Internet. Also, successful logins leave the login_name and login_pass parameters in the request when processing it, potentially making them available to a malicious JSP file or servlet. This can be an issue when designing a shared security scheme for dynamic content created by a group of different users (such as at an ISP). One way to get around this is to create a custom HttpServletRequest wrapper that filters out the login_name and login_pass parameters for filters and resources further down the chain.

Example 5-6: AuthenticationFilter (continued)

```java
import java.util.Hashtable;

public class AuthenticationFilter implements Filter {

  private Hashtable users = null;

  public void init(FilterConfig config)
    throws javax.servlet.ServletException {

    users = (Hashtable)config.getServletContext().getAttribute(
                            "enterprise.users");
    if(users == null) {
      users = new Hashtable(5);
      users.put("test", "test");
    }
  }

  public void doFilter(
    ServletRequest req, ServletResponse res, FilterChain chain)
    throws java.io.IOException, javax.servlet.ServletException {

    HttpServletRequest request = (HttpServletRequest)req;
    HttpSession sess = request.getSession(true);

    if(sess != null) {
      Boolean loggedIn = (Boolean)sess.getAttribute("enterprise.login");
      if (loggedIn != Boolean.TRUE) {
        String login_name = request.getParameter("login_name");
        String login_pass = request.getParameter("login_pass");
        if((login_name != null) && (login_pass != null))
          if(users.get(login_name).toString().equals(login_pass)) {
            loggedIn = Boolean.TRUE;
            sess.setAttribute("enterprise.login", Boolean.TRUE);
            sess.setAttribute("enterprise.loginname", login_name);
          }
      }

      if (loggedIn == Boolean.TRUE) {
        chain.doFilter(req, res);
      } else {
        request.setAttribute("originaluri", request.getRequestURI());
        request.getRequestDispatcher("/login.jsp").forward(req, res);
      }
    }
  }

  public void destroy() {
    // Code cleanup would be here
  }
}
```

Here's the JSP page used to display the login form. The important thing to note is that the form submits back to the original URI. The filter uses the `setAttribute()` method of `HttpServletRequest` to specify the URI to post the form back to; the filter is then reapplied, and if the user has provided appropriate credentials access to the resource is granted. For more on JSP, see Chapter 6.

```
<html><body bgcolor="white">

<% out.print ("<FORM METHOD=POST ACTION=\""+request.
getAttribute("originaluri").toString() +"\">"); %>
Login Name: <INPUT TYPE=TEXT NAME="login_name"><br>
Password: <INPUT TYPE=PASSWORD NAME="login_pass">
<INPUT TYPE=SUBMIT VALUE="Log In">
</FORM>

</body></html>
```

When configuring the filter, map it to the paths you wish to protect. Mapping it to /* will not work, as that would also protect the *login.jsp* file (which will be run through its own filter chain by the `RequestDispatcher` object). If you did want to protect your whole application, you could build the login form internally to the filter; but this is generally considered bad practice.

Thread Safety

In a typical scenario, only one copy of any particular servlet or filter is loaded at any given time. Each servlet might, however, be called upon to deal with multiple requests at the same time. This means that a servlet needs to be thread-safe. If a servlet doesn't use any class variables (that is, any variables with a scope broader than the service method itself), it is generally already thread-safe. If you are using any third-party libraries or extensions, make sure that those components are also thread-safe. However, a servlet that maintains persistent resources needs to make sure that nothing untoward happens to those resources. Imagine, for example, a servlet that maintains a bank balance using an `int` in memory.* If two servlets try to access the balance at the same time, you might get this sequence of events:

1. User 1 connects to the servlet to make a $100 withdrawal.
2. The servlet checks the balance for User 1, finding $120.
3. User 2 connects to the servlet to make a $50 withdrawal.
4. The servlet checks the balance for User 2, finding $120.
5. The servlet debits $100 for User 1, leaving $20.
6. The servlet debits $50 for User 2, leaving –$30.
7. The programmer is fired.

Obviously, this is incorrect behavior, particularly that last bit. We want the servlet to perform the necessary action for User 1, and then deal with User 2 (in this case, by giving him an insufficient funds message). We can do this by surrounding

---

* Hey, bear with us on this one. This is an example.

sections of code with synchronized blocks. While a particular synchronized block is executing, no other sections of code that are synchronized on the same object (usually the servlet or the resource being protected) can execute. For more information on thread safety and synchronization, see *Java Threads* by Scott Oaks and Henry Wong (O'Reilly).

Example 5-7 implements the ATM display for the First Bank of Java. The doGet() method displays the current account balance and provides a small ATM control panel for making deposits and withdrawals, as shown in Figure 5-3.*

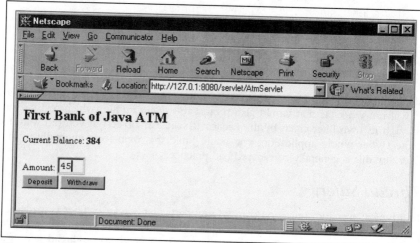

Figure 5-3: The First Bank of Java ATM display

The control panel uses a POST request to send the transaction back to the servlet, which performs the appropriate action and calls doGet() to redisplay the ATM screen with the updated balance.

Example 5-7: An ATM Servlet

```java
import javax.servlet.*;
import javax.servlet.http.*;
import java.util.*;
import java.io.*;

public class AtmServlet extends HttpServlet {

  Account act;

  public void init(ServletConfig conf) throws ServletException {
    super.init(conf);
    act = new Account();
    act.balance = 0;
  }
```

---

* Despite the fact that Java is a very large island, there's still only one account.

Example 5-7: An ATM Servlet (continued)

```
public void doGet(HttpServletRequest req, HttpServletResponse resp)
  throws ServletException, IOException {

  resp.setContentType("text/html");
  PrintWriter out = resp.getWriter();

  out.println("<HTML><BODY>");
  out.println("<H2>First Bank of Java ATM</H2>");
  out.println("Current Balance: <B>" + act.balance + "</B><BR>");
  out.println("<FORM METHOD=POST ACTION=/servlet/AtmServlet>");
  out.println("Amount: <INPUT TYPE=TEXT NAME=AMOUNT SIZE=3><BR>");
  out.println("<INPUT TYPE=SUBMIT NAME=DEPOSIT VALUE=\"Deposit\">");
  out.println("<INPUT TYPE=SUBMIT NAME=WITHDRAW VALUE=\"Withdraw\">");
  out.println("</FORM>");
  out.println("</BODY></HTML>");
}

public void doPost(HttpServletRequest req, HttpServletResponse resp)
  throws ServletException, IOException {

  int amt=0;

  try {
    amt = Integer.parseInt(req.getParameter("AMOUNT"));
  }
  catch (NullPointerException e) {
    // No Amount Parameter passed
  }
  catch (NumberFormatException e) {
    // Amount Parameter was not a number
  }

  synchronized(act) {
    if(req.getParameter("WITHDRAW") != null) && (amt < act.balance)
      act.balance = act.balance - amt;
    if(req.getParameter("DEPOSIT") != null) && (amt > 0)
      act.balance = act.balance + amt;
  } // end synchronized block

  doGet(req, resp);                          // Show ATM screen
}

public void destroy() {
  // This is where we would save the balance to a file
}

class Account {
  public int balance;
}
}
```

The doPost() method alters the account balance contained within an Account object act (since Account is so simple, we've defined it as an inner class). In order to prevent multiple requests from accessing the same account at once, any code that alters act is synchronized on act. This ensures that no other code can alter act while a synchronized section is running.

The destroy() method is defined in the AtmServlet, but it contains no actual code. A real banking servlet would obviously want to write the account balance to disk before being unloaded. And if the servlet were using JDBC to store the balance in a database, it would also want to destroy all its database-related objects.

A more complex servlet than AtmServlet might need to synchronize its entire service method, limiting the servlet to one request at a time. In these situations, it sometimes makes sense to modify the standard servlet lifecycle a little bit. We can do this by implementing the SingleThreadModel interface. This is a tag interface that has no methods; it simply tells the server to create a pool of servlet instances, instead of a single instance of the servlet. To handle an incoming request, the server uses a servlet from the pool and only allows each copy of the servlet to serve one request at a time. Implementing this interface effectively makes a servlet thread-safe, while allowing the server to deal with more than one connection at a time. Of course, using SingleThreadModel does increase resource requirements and make it difficult to share data objects within a servlet.

Another use for SingleThreadModel is to implement simple database connection sharing. Having multiple database connections can improve performance and avoid connection overloading. Of course, for more advanced or high-traffic applications, you generally want to manage connection pooling explicitly, rather than trusting the web server to do it for you.

Cookies

Cookies spent a year or two as a little-known feature of Netscape Navigator before becoming the focus of a raging debate on electronic privacy. Ethical and moral considerations aside, cookies allow a web server to store small amounts of data on client systems. Cookies are generally used to store basic user identification or configuration information. Because a cookie's value can uniquely identify a client, cookies are often used for session tracking (although, as we'll see shortly, the Servlet API provides higher-level support for this).

To create a cookie, the server (or, more precisely, a web application running on the server) includes a Cookie header with a specific value in an HTTP response. The browser then transmits a similar header with that value back to the server with subsequent requests, which are subject to certain rules. The web application can use the cookie value to keep track of a particular user, handle session tracking, etc. Because cookies use a single Cookie header, the syntax for a cookie allows for multiple name/value pairs in the overall cookie value.

More information about the cookies is available from the original Netscape specification document at *http://home.netscape.com/newsref/std/cookie_spec.html*. The Internet Engineering Task Force is currently working on a standard cookie specification, defined in RFC-2109, available at *http://www.internic.net/rfc/rfc2109.txt*.

The Servlet API includes a class, `javax.servlet.http.Cookie`, that abstracts cookie syntax and makes it easy to work with cookies. In addition, `HttpServletResponse` provides an `addCookie()` method and `HttpServletRequest` provides a `getCookies()` method to aid in writing cookies to and reading cookies from the HTTP headers, respectively. To find a particular cookie, a servlet needs to read the entire collection of values and look through it:

```
Cookie[] cookies;
cookies = req.getCookies();
String userid = null;

for (int i = 0; i < cookies.length; i++)
  if (cookies[i].getName().equals("userid"))
    userid = cookies[i].getValue();
```

A cookie can be read at any time, but can be created only before any content is sent to the client. This is because cookies are sent using HTTP headers. These headers can be sent to the client before the regular content. Once any data has been written to the client, the server can flush the output and send the headers at any time, so you can't create any new cookies safely. You must create new cookies before sending any output. Here's an example of creating a cookie:

```
String userid = createUserID();      // Create a unique ID
Cookie c = new Cookie("userid", userid);
resp.addCookie(c);                    // Add the cookie to the HTTP headers
```

Note that a web browser is only required to accept 20 cookies per site and 300 total per user, and the browser can limit each cookie's size to 4096 bytes.

Cookies can be customized to return information only in specific circumstances. In particular, a cookie can specify a particular domain, a particular path, an age after which the cookie should be destroyed, and whether the cookie requires a secure (HTTPS) connection. A cookie is normally returned only to the host that specified it. For example, if a cookie is set by *server1.company.com*, it isn't returned to *server2.company.com*. You can get around this limitation by setting the domain to *.company.com* with the `setDomain()` method of `Cookie`. By the same token, a cookie is generally returned for pages only in the same directory as the servlet that created the cookie, or it's returned under that directory. We can get around this limitation using `setPath()`. Here's a cookie that is returned to all pages on all top-level servers at *company.com*:

```
String userid = createUserID();      // Create a unique ID
Cookie c = new Cookie("userid", userid);
c.setDomain(".company.com");  // *.company.com, but not *.web.company.com
c.setPath("/");               // All pages
resp.addCookie(c);            // Add the cookie to the HTTP headers
```

Session Tracking

Very few web applications are confined to a single page, so having a mechanism for tracking users through a site can often simplify application development. The Web, however, is an inherently stateless environment. A client makes a request, the server fulfills it, and both promptly forget about each other. In the past, applications that needed to deal with a user through multiple pages (for instance, a shopping cart) had to resort to complicated dodges to hold onto state information, such as hidden fields in forms, setting and reading cookies, or rewriting URLs to contain state information.

The Servlet API provides classes and methods specifically designed to handle session tracking. A servlet can use the session-tracking API to delegate most of the user-tracking functions to the server. The first time a user connects to a session-enabled servlet, the servlet simply creates a `javax.servlet.http.HttpSession` object. The servlet can then bind data to this object, so subsequent requests can read the data. After a certain amount of inactive time, the session object is destroyed.

A servlet uses the `getSession()` method of `HttpServletRequest` to retrieve the current session object. This method takes a single `boolean` argument. If you pass `true`, and there is no current session object, the method creates and returns a new `HttpSession` object. If you pass `false`, the method returns `null` if there is no current session object. For example:

```
HttpSession thisUser = req.getSession(true);
```

When a new `HttpSession` is created, the server assigns a unique session ID that must somehow be associated with the client. Since clients differ in what they support, the server has a few options that vary slightly depending on the server implementation. In general, the server's first choice is to try to set a cookie on the client (which means that `getSession()` must be called before you write any other data back to the client). If cookie support is lacking, the API allows servlets to rewrite internal links to include the session ID, using the `encodeURL()` method of `HttpServletResponse`. This is optional, but recommended, particularly if your servlets share a system with other, unknown servlets that may rely on uninterrupted session tracking. However, this on-the-fly URL encoding can become a performance bottleneck because the server needs to perform additional parsing on each incoming request to determine the correct session key from the URL. (The performance hit is so significant that the Java Web Server disables URL encoding by default.)

To use URL encoding run all your internal links through `encodeURL()`. If you have a line of code like this:

```
out.println("<A HREF=\"/servlet/CheckoutServlet\">Check Out</A>");
```

you should replace it with:

```
out.print("<A HREF=\"");
out.print(resp.encodeURL("/servlet/CheckoutServlet"));
out.println("\">Check Out</A>");
```

JWS, in this case, adds an identifier beginning with $ to the end of the URL. Other servers have their own methods. Thus, with JWS, the final output looks like this:

```
<A HREF="/servlet/CheckoutServlet$FASEDAW23798ASD978">Check Out</A>"
```

In addition to encoding your internal links, you need to use encodeRedirectURL( ) to handle redirects properly. This method works in the same manner as encodeURL( ).*

You can access the unique session ID via the getID( ) method of HttpSession. This is enough for most applications, since a servlet can use some other storage mechanism (i.e., a flat file, memory, or a database) to store the unique information (e.g., hit count or shopping cart contents) associated with each session. However, the API makes it even easier to hold onto session-specific information by allowing servlets to bind objects to a session using the putValue( ) method of HttpSession. Once an object is bound to a session, you can use the getValue( ) method.†

Objects bound using putValue( ) are available to all servlets running on the server. The system works by assigning a user-defined name to each object (the String argument); this name is used to identify objects at retrieval time. In order to avoid conflicts, the general practice is to name bound objects with names of the form *applicationname. objectname*. For example:

```
session.putValue("myservlet.hitcount", new Integer(34));
```

Now that object can be retrieved with:

```
Integer hits = (Integer)session.getValue("myservlet.hitcount")
```

Example 5-8 demonstrates a basic session-tracking application that keeps track of the number of visits to the site by a particular user. It works by storing a counter value in an HttpSession object and incrementing it as necessary. When a new session is created (as indicated by isNew( ), which returns true if the session ID has not yet passed through the client and back to the server), or the counter object is not found, a new counter object is created.

Example 5-8: Counting Visits with Sessions

```
import javax.servlet.*;
import javax.servlet.http.*;
import java.io.*;

public class VisitCounterServlet extends HttpServlet {

  public void doGet(HttpServletRequest req, HttpServletResponse resp)
      throws ServletException, IOException {

    PrintWriter out = resp.getWriter();
    resp.setContentType("text/html");
```

---

* These methods were introduced inVersion 2.1 of the Servlet API, replacing two earlier methods named encodeUrl( ) and encodeRedirectUrl( ). This was done to bring the capitalization scheme in line with other Java APIs.

† The putValue( ) and getValue( ) methods should be used only with Servlet 2.0 containers because they have been deprecated in favor of the work-alive setAttribute( ) and getAttribute( ) methods. The naming change was done to create consistency across various attribute-capable elements of the Servlet API.

Example 5-8: Counting Visits with Sessions (continued)

```
    HttpSession thisUser = req.getSession(true);
    Integer visits;

    if(!thisUser.isNew()) {           //Don't check newly created sessions
      visits = (Integer)thisUser.getValue("visitcounter.visits");
      if(visits == null)
        visits = new Integer(1);
      else
        visits = new Integer(visits.intValue() + 1);
    }
    else
      visits = new Integer(1);

    // Put the new count in the session
    thisUser.putValue("visitcounter.visits", visits);

    // Finally, display the results and give them the session ID too
    out.println("<HTML><HEAD><TITLE>Visit Counter</TITLE></HEAD>");
    out.println("<BODY>You have visited this page " + visits + " time[s]");
    out.println("since your last session expired.");
    out.println("Your Session ID is " + thisUser.getId());
    out.println("</BODY></HTML>");
  }
}
```

HttpSessionBindingListener

Sometimes it is useful to know when an object is getting bound or unbound from a session object. For instance, in an application that binds a JDBC java.sql. Connection object to a session (something that, by the way, is ill-advised in all but very low traffic sites), it is important that the Connection be explicitly closed when the session is destroyed.

The javax.servlet.http.HttpSessionBindingListener interface handles this task. It includes two methods, valueBound() and valueUnbound(), that are called whenever the object that implements the interface is bound or unbound from a session, respectively. Each of these methods receives an HttpSessionBindingEvent object that provides the name of the object being bound or unbound and the session involved in the action. Here is an object that implements the HttpSessionBindingListener interface in order to make sure that a database connection is closed properly:

```
  class ConnectionHolder implements HttpSessionBindingListener {

    java.sql.Connection dbCon;

    public ConnectionHolder(java.sql.Connection con) {
      dbCon = con;
    }
```

```
public void valueBound(HttpSessionBindingEvent event) {
  // Do nothing
}

public void valueUnbound(HttpSessionBindingEvent event) {
  dbCon.close();
}
}
```

Session Contexts

Version 2.0 of the Servlet API included the getContext() method of HttpSession, coupled with an interface named HttpSessionContext. Together, these allowed servlets to access other sessions running in the same context. Unfortunately, this functionality also allowed a servlet to accidentally expose all the session IDs in use on the server, meaning that an outsider with knowledge could spoof a session. To eliminate this minor security risk, the session-context functionality was deprecated in Version 2.1 of the Servlet API. Instead, web applications can use the getAttribute() and setAttribute() methods of ServletContext to share information across sessions.

Databases and Non-HTML Content

Most web applications need to communicate with a database, either to generate dynamic content or collect and store data from users, or both. With servlets, this communication is easily handled using the JDBC API described in Chapter 2. Thanks to JDBC and the generally sensible design of the servlet lifecycle, servlets are an excellent intermediary between a database and web clients.

Most of the general JDBC principles discussed in Chapter 2 apply to servlets. However, servlet developers should keep a few things in mind for optimal performance. First, JDBC Connection objects can be created in the servlet's init() method. This allows the servlet to avoid reconnecting to the database (a la CGI) with each request, saving up to a second or more on every single page request.If you anticipate high volume, you may want to create several connections and rotate between them. An excellent freeware connection-pooling system is available at *http://www.javaexchange.com*. Or, if you're using JDBC 2.0, the javax.sql package provides a connection-pooling mechanism. Finally, if you plan on using JDBC's transaction support, you need to create individual connections for each request or obtain exclusive use of a pooled connection.

So far, all our servlets have produced standard HTML content. Of course, this is all most servlets ever do, but it's not all that they can do. Say, for instance, that your company stores a large database of PDF documents within an Oracle database, where they can be easily accessed. Now say you want to distribute these documents on the Web. Luckily, servlets can dish out any form of content that can be defined with a MIME header. All you have to do is set the appropriate content type and use a ServletOuputStream if you need to transmit binary data. Example 5-9 shows how to pull an Adobe Acrobat document from an Oracle database.

Example 5-9: A Servlet That Serves PDF Files from a Database

```java
import java.io.*;
import java.sql.*;
import javax.servlet.*;
import javax.servlet.http.*;

public class DBPDFReader extends HttpServlet {

  Connection con;

  public void init(ServletConfig config) throws ServletException {
    super.init(config);
    try {
      Class.forName("oracle.jdbc.driver.OracleDriver");
      con = DriverManager.getConnection("jdbc:oracle:oci8:@DBHOST",
                                        "user", "passwd");
    }
    catch (ClassNotFoundException e) {
      throw new UnavailableException(this, "Couldn't load OracleDriver");
    }
    catch (SQLException e) {
      throw new UnavailableException(this, "Couldn't get db connection");
    }
  }

  public void doGet(HttpServletRequest req, HttpServletResponse res)
    throws ServletException, IOException {

    try {
      res.setContentType("application/pdf");
      ServletOutputStream out = res.getOutputStream();

      Statement stmt = con.createStatement();
      ResultSet rs = stmt.executeQuery(
        "SELECT PDF FROM PDF WHERE PDFID = " + req.getParameter("PDFID"));

      if (rs.next()) {
        BufferedInputStream pdfData =
          new BufferedInputStream(rs.getBinaryStream("PDF"));
        byte[] buf = new byte[4 * 1024];  // 4K buffer
        int len;
        while ((len = pdfData.read(buf, 0, buf.length)) != -1) {
          out.write(buf, 0, len);
        }
      }
      else {
        res.sendError(res.SC_NOT_FOUND);
      }
```

Example 5-9: A Servlet That Serves PDF Files from a Database (continued)

```
      rs.close();
      stmt.close ();
    }
    catch(SQLException e) {
      // Report it
    }
  }
}
```

CHAPTER 6

JavaServer Pages

In Chapter 5, we looked at Java servlets, J2EE's primary technology for communicating with web browsers. Servlets are a great technology, but they don't solve every problem faced by web developers, and they introduce a few issues of their own. One major problem is that developing complex HTML-based user interfaces with servlets is time-consuming. Embedding strings of `println()` statements is tedious and error-prone, and requires that pages be assembled by a fully qualified programmer who, just perhaps, should be off doing other things. Configuration is also a problem, although it has been simplified a great deal since the original servlet API. Adding a new servlet to a web application involves editing the deployment XML file and, typically reloading the application or restarting the server.* Changes to a servlet create the same issues, turning rapid prototyping into regular prototyping.

On the design side, servlets can also blend application logic with presentation logic, undoing one of the primary benefits of the client-server architectures that they often replace. In a true J2EE environment, where business logic is abstracted into Enterprise JavaBeans or other middleware, this is not much of a concern. But in real life, full J2EE systems aren't always appropriate. Many applications don't need the full weight of an application server, and often developers lack the interest or time to create a full J2EE implementation. And even within a J2EE application, there are substantial benefits to separating flow-control (accomplished by servlets) from actual pages.

One obvious approach is to use static HTML content for most pages, reserving servlets for forms processing with a redirect or forward to another HTML page upon completion. Such an approach breaks down fairly quickly, as most pages in a web application have at least some dynamic element. A better solution,

---

* Dynamic class reloading and change detection solve some of these problems, but not for all servers and not always reliably.

however, is to embed dynamic elements directly into the static content. This is the reverse of the approach servlets use, where static content is embedded within the dynamic framework.* Static web pages with a few dynamic content extensions can be edited using any HTML authoring tool and previewed live in the browser, either with or without the dynamic elements (obviously, the efficacy of this last technique depends on the complexity of the page).

There have been a few different approaches creating dynamic web pages without a full servlet. Generally, these involve inserting either custom tags or control statements within HTML document templates and then running the documents through a server-side processor that replaces tags and directives with dynamically generated content. The resulting pure HTML is delivered to the client. This type of templating system is shown in Figure 6-1. In a servlet environment, the template processor will be implemented as one or more servlets. Examples of templating engines include WebMacro (*http://www.webmacro.org*) and Velocity (*http://jakarta.apache.org*).

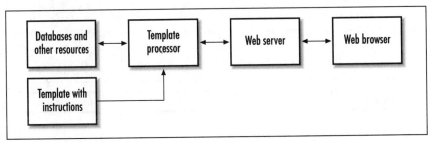

Figure 6-1: Generic templating engines

Sun's templating solution is called JavaServer™ Pages, or JSP, which is currently at Revision 1.2. JSP is a highly integrated dynamic content system that is built on top of the Java Servlet API. In fact, JSP pages are compiled into Java Servlets before being executed by the web server. This allows JSP developers to obtain all the advantages of Java Servlets (efficient lifecycles, integration with Java middleware, and so on) without spending hours integrating HTML into actual Java code. JSP also allows page developers to access properties of JavaBeans without writing code. Finally, custom JSP tags can be created by developers for use by page designers, removing Java code from the JSPs entirely.

In this chapter, we are going to look at JSP from a Java programmer's perspective as opposed to that of a web site designer. Of course, one of the great things about JSPs, and other templating technologies, is that you don't have to be a programmer to use them. However, for a more thorough introduction to JSP, as well as some substantial additional detail for experienced developers, we suggest *JavaServer Pages* by Hans Bergsten (O'Reilly).

---

* Since the dawn of civilization, man has sought to embed code within content. Great, if virtual, wars have been fought over the advisability of actually doing so. At this point, very few people consider it wise to embed all of their presentation HTML directly within a servlet, but there is wide divergence of opinion on how much code is appropriate for a JSP. In truth, the answer depends on your application.

JSP Basics

The JSP specification is part of the full J2EE specification, and JSP engines are included with most major servlet engines. The Tomcat 4.0 server from the Apache project is the reference implementation for both the Servlet 2.3 and JSP 1.2 specifications, and is freely available. For information on downloading and installing Tomcat, see *http://jakarta.apache.org*. The rest of this chapter will assume familiarity with the concept of a web application and servlets. If you haven't read Chapter 5, you should probably do so before continuing.

Since the JSP architecture is based on the servlet architecture, JSP support within a web server provides a translation layer. Individual JSP pages are text files stored on the web server and accessed via their real path. For example, if a JSP named *index.jsp* resides at the root of the *enterprise* web application, it would be accessed by a request to *http://localhost:8080/enterprise/index.jsp*, assuming that the web server is running on port 8080 of localhost. When the JSP is first requested, the JSP engine uses the JSP file to generate the source code for a Java Servlet. The generated source is then compiled, installed into the servlet engine, and used to service the request. Once the JSP has been compiled, the compiled version is saved and used to service additional requests according to the standard servlet lifecycle. Figure 6-2 shows the process in more detail.

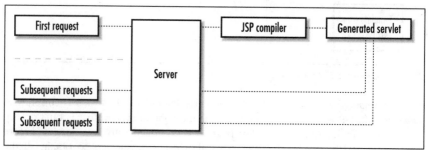

Figure 6-2: JSP lifecycle

When the JSP file is modified, the server detects the change and rebuilds the corresponding servlet. The compilation phase imposes a slight delay the first time the page is retrieved. If necessary, many servers allow precompilation of JSPs to get around this problem.

Now is a good time to look at a simple JSP, so here's an example that displays the current date:

```
<HTML>
<BODY>
Hello, visitor. It is now <%= new java.util.Date().toString() %>
</BODY>
</HTML>
```

This looks easy enough. The only part of the example that is not regular HTML is the % tag. JSP elements come in two forms: the simple <% %> entity, used for directly embedding Java code and issuing JSP specific directives, and XML style "action tags," which we'll see a little later. The <%= %> tag is an *expression* tag, which inserts the value of a single Java expression into the page's output. For space reasons, we're not going to include the Java code produced by the system, but if you want to look at it you can find it in the web server's working areas. For Tomcat 4, the path is */tomcat4/work/servername/webappname*. Here's the output sent to the client browser:

Now, let's try something a little more complicated. The <%...%> element can insert regular Java code, which can control the flow of the page. The following example checks whether it's before or after noon (we'll count nighttime as the afternoon for the purpose of this sample) and displays an appropriate greeting:

```
<HTML>
<BODY>
<%
java.util.Date theDate = new java.util.Date();
%>
<% if (theDate.getHours() < 12) { %>
Good morning,
<% } else { %>
Good afternoon,
<% } %>
 visitor. It is now <%= theDate.toString() %>
</BODY>
</HTML>
```

There are two things that should be noted about this example. The first is the declaration of a local variable in the first pair of <% .. %> tags. Unlike the %= tags, nothing is displayed. The next JSP element includes a Java if statement that operates on the variable. Note that we don't finish the if statement in the JSP tag, but return to template text. This text will be displayed if the if clause evaluates to true. The next JSP element closes the if and begins an else. It is followed by the text to be displayed in the else case, and a final JSP element to close the else. The rest of the file is the same as in the first example, except we use the Date object created earlier rather than instantiating a new one.

When viewed in the afternoon, the JSP-generated servlet produces HTML that looks like this:

```
<HTML>
<BODY>

Good afternoon,

 visitor. It is now Mon Dec 24 14:50:39 EST 2001
</BODY>
</HTML>
```

Note that there is some whitespace where some of the JSP tags were. This is because we placed whitespace around them in the source JSP file. The JSP processor removes the tags themselves, but has no way of determining whether it should also remove the carriage returns that follow them. This is not a problem for HTML, since the web browser compresses all whitespace characters into a single space character, but you should be aware of this behavior when debugging or producing plain-text output.

Directives and Declarations

JSP also allows the insertion of *JSP directives*, which control behavior for the entire page. Directive tags begin with <%@ rather than <%. There are three directives. The first, include, simply includes a static file into the page output. So to include a copyright notice at the bottom of each JSP page, you can just add the tag:

```
<% @include file="copyright.html"%>
```

The second directive, page, is more flexible. It defines parameters that relate to the current JSP page, and will be valid across all invocations of that page. Table 6-1 displays the possible attributes of the page directive.

Table 6-1: JSP Page Directive Values

Name	Description
autoFlush	Set to true or false, identifying whether the page buffer should be flushed when full. The default is true.
buffer	Set the buffer size, in kilobytes. The default is 8kb, and values must be in the format of *number* + kb, or none.
contentType	Set the MIME type or MIME type and charset. The default is text/html.
errorPage	An optional path to a custom error-handling page
extends	An optional fully qualified class name of a class implementing javax.servlet.jsp.JspPage or javax.servlet.jsp.HttpJspPage.
import	A comma-separated list of Java classes or packages to import.
info	Text describing this JSP page. The text entered here can be used by a server administration tool.
isErrorPage	Identifies this page as an error page, making the exception object (see next section) available to script elements.
isThreadSafe	Set to true or false, indicating whether this JSP should implement the servlet SingleThreadModel.
language	The scripting language for this page. The default is java, and the JSP specification doesn't require support for any other language, although some application servers support JavaScript.
session	Set to true or false depending on whether the page should participate in user sessions. The default is true.

The final directive, taglib, is discussed in the last section of this chapter.

JSP supports another tag sequence that globally affects all instances of a page. This is the declaration element, which begins with <%!, and declares a global variable within the JSP. Unlike variables declared in a standard <% %> tag pair, variables declared with <%! will be available for all invocations of the JSP. For example:

```
<%! int globalHitCounts = 0; %>
This page has been accessed <%= ++globalHitCounts %> times.
```

However, use of declarations introduces thread-safety and life-cycle issues. For example, there is no guarantee that the JSP will not be rebuilt and reloaded. If this happens, the hit count will return to 0. Therefore, for most applications you should use other approaches for maintaining global data.

Built-in Objects

In addition to objects declared within a JSP file itself, Java code running within a JSP has access to a set of classes provided by the web server. These classes allow for communication between JSPs, interaction with the JSP container, and support for sessions and elaborate output. In servlets, for instance, request parameters are retrieved from the browser via the getParameter() method of an HttpServletRequest object. JSPs can do the same thing. The following JSP fragment uses the built-in request object (which maps to HttpServletRequest) and the out object (which provides a PrintWriter) to echo the form parameters submitted by the client):

```
<ul>
<%
    java.util.Enumeration e = request.getParameterNames();
    while(e.hasMoreElements()) {
    String name = (String)e.nextElement();
    out.println("<li>" + name + ":" +
    request.getParameter(name));
    }
%>
</li>
```

Table 6-2 lists the objects available to a JSP.

Table 6-2: Objects Available in JSP Pages

Name	Type	Description
application	javax.servlet.ServletContext	The servlet context for this web application
config	javax.servlet.ServletConfig	The ServletConfig object associated with this page
exception	java.lang.Throwable	For error pages only, the exception that triggered the error
out	javax.servlet.jsp.JspWriter	A PrintWriter subclass that writes to the page's output stream
pageContext	javax.servlet.jsp.PageContext	The page context for this JSP
page	java.lang.Object	The implementation class instance currently processing the request. When Java is the scripting language, page is synonymous to this
request	javax.servlet.ServletRequest or javax.servlet.http.HttpServletRequest	The protocol-specific request object for this request
response	javax.servlet.ServletResponse or javax.servlet.http.HttpServletResponse	The protocol-specific response object for this request
session	javax.servlt.http.HttpSession	For pages retrieved over HTTP, the current user's HttpSession object

Sharing Data Between JSPs, Other JSPs, and Servlets

HTTP is a stateless protocol, and by extension, the Web is inherently a stateless environment. If a client makes a series of connections to a web server, there is no built-in fool-proof mechanism for the web server to associate the sequential requests with the same user. Similarly, a JSP or servlet will treat each request individually, regardless of whether the user has made other requests in the recent past.

The simplest form of communication between JSPs is hyperlink. A JSP page produces an HTML-formatted link, which the user can then click on to request another JSP. HTTP allows name=value parameters to be associated with an HTTP request. So, for example, if JSP 1 needs to inform JSP 2 of the user's language, it might use a JSP fragment like this one to produce a link:

```
<a href="page2.jsp?language=<%= userLanguage %>">Go to page 2</a>
```

This HTML fragment includes a JSP expression that passes a variable called userLanguage as a request parameter to *page2.jsp*, which can then retrieve it from the session.

This is a clumsy approach, however, for all but the simplest applications. For one thing, as soon as the user accesses a page that doesn't pass the language parameter on, such as a static HTML page or a link off-site, the information is gone, and must somehow be retrieved again. A better place to store this information is the user's session, accessible via the session object made available to all JSP pages served over HTTP. For more on the session object, see Chapter 5. Information that is global to the entire application can be stored in the ServletContext object, which is accessible via the application object.

All information loaded into the session and application contexts will be available to any JSP that participates in the session or is part of the application. Servlets within the application will also be able to access the data. In the next section, we'll look at some other ways of using these mechanisms to share data across JSPs.

JSP Actions

If you've spent any time working with servlets, our examples up to this point really haven't been anything new. Essentially, we've replaced reams of println() calls with template text in a JSP. This certainly saves time, but we aren't doing anything different. For one thing, at the beginning of this chapter, we promised that JSP allowed nonprogramming web designers and content creators to help create dynamic content. The techniques we've just seen let you do that, but you have to teach them Java first, which pretty much defeats the purpose.

HTML developers may not be confident tackling server-side Java code (and, frankly, they probably shouldn't be), but they're certainly comfortable with markup tags. Web browsers, after all, just treat tags as instructions. If a browser sees a <b> tag, it turns the running text to boldface until it sees another </b> tag. Scriptlets in JSP do the same thing, except in two steps: the server processes the script, possibly producing more HTML, and the browser then views it. This is not a difficult concept, but we haven't gotten around the fact that the first set of instructions are provided as Java code and hence require a Java programmer with some time on her hands.

JSP solves this problem with *action tags*. An action tag looks like a regular HTML tag, and doesn't follow the <% %> syntax conventions we've seen before. JSP actions are divided into two categories: built-in functions, which we'll discuss in this section, and custom tags, which we'll discuss in the last section of the chapter. Built-in JSP actions provide access to many of the features we've already seen with scriptlets—for instance, there is another form of the <%@ include %> directive:

```
<jsp:include page="/headers/header.jsp"/>
```

If you think this looks like an XML tag, you're right: the syntax requirements are the same as for namespace-enabled XML. The *jsp* namespace is reserved for JSP built-in actions (we'll see the real value of this in the next section.) The tag name is specified after the namespace and the action to be performed. Tags can then have zero or more attributes (such as page, as, noted). Tags can be closed with a standard closing tag (such as </jsp:include>) or with a / before the final >, for tags that don't have any elements within them.

The <jsp:include> tag itself includes the contents of the specified relative URL (it must be from the same server) in the output of the current page.[*] Parameters for the included page can be included by nesting a <jsp:param> tag into the include:

```
<jsp:include page="/headers/header.jsp">
  <jsp:param name="company" value="The Company"/>
</jsp:include>
```

The <jsp:forward> tag works similarly, but transfers control to the destination page rather than including its content:

```
<jsp:forward page="/login/access.jsp" />
```

or, with parameters:

```
<jsp:forward page="/login/access.jsp">
  <jsp:param name="redirect" value="<%= request.getRequestURI()%>" />
</jsp:forward>
```

The example above uses a JSP expression to generate the parameter value. One caution on <jsp:forward>: if any output has been written to the client (either because the output buffer was flushed or because buffering was turned off via a page directive), an attempt to use <jsp:forward> will produce an IllegalStateException.

JSP Tags and JavaBeans

JSP actions combine with JavaBeans to provide data to page designers. Programmers can write a JavaBean that handles data access and business logic (including accessing Enterprise JavaBeans) and makes that information available to a JSP page, without embedding all of the necessary JDBC (or whatever) code within the JSP itself.

---

[*] In pure servlets, this is the functionality handled by the RequestDispatcher object.

Since JavaBeans are a Java class, they can be instantiated in scriptlets. If we want to use a bean named `ProductBean` in the `com.company` package, we could write a JSP like this:

```
<% com.company.ProductBean product =
new com.company.ProductBean();
product.setProductId("DH2309-AX");
%>
```

The `ProductBean`, after setting the product ID, retrieves the necessary product information, which is exposed via other properties. So if the JavaBean has a `Price` property, we could retrieve it with:

```
<%= product.getPrice() %>
```

However, JSPs offer another way to access the bean, using the `<jsp:useBean>` tag:

```
<jsp:useBean id="product" class="com.company.ProductBean" />
```

It's that simple. Once the bean is created, properties can be set using the `<jsp:setProperty>` tag:

```
<jsp:setProperty name="product" property="ProductID" value="DH2309-AX"/>
```

The `<jsp:setProperty>` tag can be nested within the `<jsp:useBean>` tag, or used later. Properties are retrieved in the same way, using the `<jsp:getProperty>` tag:

```
<jsp:getProperty name="product" property="Price"/>
```

There's one more trick to the `<jsp:setProperty>` tag. If the value attribute is not included, the JSP will search the incoming request parameters for a name=value pair with the same name as the bean property currently being set, and will use the value from the request. For example, the request *http://shop.company.com/schlock/ product.jsp?ProductId=DH2309-AX* has a `ProductId` parameter containing the ID for the product we want to display. If the *product.jsp* file contains these lines:

```
<jsp:useBean id="product" class="com.company.ProductBean" />
<jsp:setProperty name="product" property="ProductId" />
```

the `ProductId` property is set to DH2309-AX. For further convenience, we can use the special property name (*), which populates every property of the bean from the request parameters.

Scoping Beans

The JavaBean used in the last example existed within the scope of the current page. This means that it was created when the client requested the page and destroyed when the page was destroyed. For some applications this is fine: a Java-Bean that retrieves and displays information about a particular product in an online catalog doesn't need to hang around, although it should use efficient strate-gies to speed its interior execution.* But what about a bean that retrieves information about the current user-display preferences, identity, and so on? This

---

* For instance, if the bean retrieves product information from a SQL database, it should use a connection-pooling strategy, possibly via JDBC 2.0, to avoid the overhead of creating a new connection for each database access.

information is used by every page the user accesses, but doesn't change except in very specific situations. We want to create the bean once and store it in the user's session, where it can remain until the user leaves the site.

One way to accomplish this is to use a scriptlet to add the bean directly to the user's session using the implicit JSP session object, and then to retrieve it manually for each page that uses it. However, the <jsp:useBean> tag offers a way around this, via the scope argument, which will apply to every instance of that particular JavaBean class with the specified ID. By default, beans have a "PAGE" scope, but they also can be set to have a "USER" scope, where the same instance is used whenever a <jsp:useBean> tag is invoked for that class and ID. The *application* scope goes even further, applying to the web application as a whole by inserting the bean instance into the ServletContext object associated with the web application. This allows servlets to access beans created by JSPs, and vice versa.

The other available scope is *request*. Elements scoped to the request level will be available for the duration of the current request. This means they can be accessed by other JSPs referenced via <jsp:include> or <jsp:forward>.

Custom Tags

JSP and JavaBeans provide a nice way to abstract data access away from the page itself, but it still doesn't get code entirely out of the system. Page designers still must use script elements for control functions such as loops or branching logic. In addition, JavaBeans sometimes aren't enough to fully encapsulate a web application's internal logic, leaving large chunks of code embedded in JSPs. And of course, there's the matter of code reuse. While utility methods can be abstracted out into classes and made available to JSPs, scripting code embedded within a particular JSP tends not to lend itself to abstraction.

The JSP specification addresses this by allowing the creation of custom tags. Tags are organized into Tag Libraries, which can be loaded by pages as needed. Each tag library gets its own namespace, and can be shared by as many pages as necessary. Properly designed custom tags can cut most, if not all, of the remaining pure Java code out your JSPs.

Imagine a simple tag that displays the current date and time. Let's call the tag Date. After creating and configuring it, we can access it within a JSP page:

```
<enterprise:Date/>
```

Note that the namespace is no longer *jsp*. Instead, we have a custom specified namespace that identifies a *tag library*, or *taglib*, containing a set of custom tags. We declare the tag library at the beginning of the JSP file with the <%@ taglib %> directive:

```
<%@ taglib uri="http://ora.com/enterprise/
                examples-taglib" prefix="enterprise"%>
```

The taglib containing the Date tag is identified by a specific URI. However, the system doesn't actually retrieve the taglib from the URI provided. Instead, the URI serves as an identifier for a taglib installed in the web application's *web.xml* file, using a <taglib> element like this one:

```
<taglib>
<taglib-uri>http://ora.com/enterprise/examples-taglib</taglib-uri>
<taglib-location>
    /WEB-INF/jsp/enterprise-taglib.tld
   </taglib-location>
</taglib>
```

The <taglib-location> tag points to a *.tld* file, which is an XML-formatted tag library deployment descriptor. Here's the *.tld* file that describes a single tag library:

```
<?xml version="1.0" encoding="ISO-8859-1"?>
<!DOCTYPE taglib PUBLIC "-//Sun Microsystems, Inc.//DTD JSP Tag Library
1.2//EN"
"http://java.sun.com/j2ee/dtd/web-jsptaglibrary_1_2.dtd">
<taglib>
<tlib-version>1.0</tlib-version>
<jsp-version>1.2</jsp-version>
<short-name>enterprise</short-name>
<uri>http://ora.com/enterprise/examples-taglib</uri>
<description>A simple tag library for JEIAN</description>
<tag>
<name>Date</name>
<tag-class>enterprise.DateTag</tag-class>
<description>Display current date</description>
</tag>
</taglib>
```

The key thing here is the <tag> tag with its subtags, <name> and <tag-class> (descriptions are optional). The name tag specifies the name that JSPs will use to refer to the tag itself, and the tag class specifies the Java class that implements the tag functionality. In this case, it's a class named DateTag in the enterprise package. This class file must be available to the web application.

By this point, we've described a tag, put it in a library, associated the library with the web application, retrieved the library from the web application for use in a JSP page, mapped it to the "enterprise" namespace for the page, and invoked the tag itself. The only thing remaining is the actual implementing class.

Implementing Custom Tags

Custom tags come in two basic varieties: basic tags and body tags. Basic tags don't access their bodies (the content between the open and close tags), although they can control whether or not the JSP servlet processes their content. Body tags are just like basic tags, but have access to their body content. Support interfaces and classes for all custom tags are in the javax.servlet.jsp.tagext package.

Basic tags implement the Tag interface, which has two methods of interest to the tag developer: doStartTag() and doEndTag(). The doStartTag() method is called when the page processing reaches the opening of the tag (<enterprise:Date> in the previous example), and the doEndTag() method is called when execution

---

reaches the end tag (</enterprise:Date>). These are called sequentially for empty tags.

The doStartTag() method can return Tag.SKIP_BODY or Tag.EVAL_BODY_INCLUDE. Skipping the body causes execution to jump right to the end of the tag. Evaluating the body will cause the JSP to process the body normally, as if it was outside of the tag. The doEndTag() method can return Tag.EVAL_PAGE or Tag.SKIP_PAGE. If EVAL_PAGE is returned, the rest of the page will be processed; if SKIP_PAGE is returned, processing stops.

Here, finally, is the DateTag class. It extends the TagSupport class, which implements the Tag interface and provides stub versions of both do- methods, as well as the other methods in the interface (which are used by the JSP to provide resources to the tag). It implements the doEndTag() method:

```
package enterprise;

import javax.servlet.jsp.*;
import javax.servlet.jsp.tagext.*;

public class DateTag extends TagSupport {

  public int doEndTag() throws JspException {

    try {
    pageContext.getOut().println((new java.util.Date()).toString());
    } catch (java.io.IOException e) {
      throw new JspException(e);
    }
    return Tag.EVAL_PAGE;
  }
}
```

The pageContext object is an instance of PageContext, and is provided by the TagSupport class. The PageContext object provides access to the current output writer (via getOut()), as well as the ServletRequest and ServletResponse objects for the request, page attributes, ServletConfig and ServletContext objects, and the HttpSession object.

Here's another TagSupport-based tag, which is a little fancier. The <enterprise:Evening> tag encloses content and displays it only if the current server time is not within the work day. Here's how it works in a JSP:

```
<enterprise:Evening dayStart="9" dayEnd="17">
Sorry, we're closed for the day. Please try us tomorrow.
</enterprise:Evening>
```

The code is simple, but this time we extend the doStartTag() method instead, and return SKIP_BODY if the current time is within the working day:

```
package enterprise;

import java.util.*;
import javax.servlet.jsp.*;
```

```
import javax.servlet.jsp.tagext.*;

public class EveningTag extends TagSupport {
  private int i_dayStart = 9;
  private int i_dayEnd = 17; // 24 hour time

  // In production, we should propagate errors with exceptions
  public void setDayStart(String value) {
    i_dayStart = Integer.parseInt(value);
  }
  public void setDayEnd(String value) {
    i_dayEnd = Integer.parseInt(value);
  }

  public int doStartTag() throws JspException {
    int hour = GregorianCalendar.getInstance().get(Calendar.HOUR_OF_DAY);

    if((hour >= i_dayStart) && (hour <= i_dayEnd))
      return Tag.SKIP_BODY;

    return Tag.EVAL_BODY_INCLUDE;
  }
}
```

Note that we also have two optional tag attributes: dayStart and dayEnd, which
accept an hour value, defaulting to 9 AM to 5 PM. These values are communi-
cated to the Tag via JavaBean-style setter objects. The JSP implementation will call
the setters for every supplied attribute before calling any of the doXXX() methods.
Attributes also need to be declared in the tag library descriptor. Here's the extension to the previous tag library for the Evening tag:

```
<tag>
  <name>Evening</name>
  <tag-class>enterprise.EveningTag</tag-class>
  <description>Display text if it's the evening</description>
  <attribute>
    <name>dayStart</name>
    <required>false</required>
  </attribute>
  <attribute>
  <name>dayEnd</name>
  <required>false</required>
  </attribute>
</tag>
```

More Tag Lifecycle

JSP tags are frequently called upon to perform an action more than once. The JSP
specification supports this capability via the IterationTag interface, which adds an
additional lifecycle method, doAfterBody(). The doAfterBody() method is
invoked after the tag body has been processed, and can return IterationTag.
EVAL_BODY_AGAIN to have the tag body reprocessed. The tag body is reprocessed

immediately, and the doAfterBody() method is called again. Returning Tag.SKIP_ BODY stops the loop.

The next example creates a tag named <enterprise:Loop>, which processes its content a given number of times (specified via the times attribute).

```java
package enterprise;

import javax.servlet.jsp.*;
import javax.servlet.jsp.tagext.*;

public class ForTag extends TagSupport {
  private int current = 1;
  private int times = 0;

  public void setTimes(int i) {
    times = i;
  }

  public int doStartTag() throws JspException {
    pageContext.setAttribute("current", new Integer(current));
    if(current < times)
    return Tag.EVAL_BODY_INCLUDE;
  }

  public int doAfterBody() throws JspException {
    if(current >= times)
      return Tag.SKIP_BODY;
    current ++;
    pageContext.setAttribute("current", new Integer(current));
    return IterationTag.EVAL_BODY_AGAIN;
  }
}
```

This tag also uses the setAttribute() method to create a variable in the page context named current. This allows us to see the loop count in our JSP body. Here's an example:

```jsp
<enterprise:Loop times="4">
Loop <%= current %> <br>
</enterprise:Loop>
```

The output in the browser will be:

```
Loop 1
Loop 2
Loop 3
Loop 4
```

We can't just create variables at will, though. At the minimum, they have to be described in the tag library descriptor, so that the JSP compiler can create the appropriate references. Here's the descriptor for the Loop tag:

```xml
<tag>
  <name>Loop</name>
  <tag-class>enterprise.ForTag</tag-class>
```

```
    <description>For Loop</description>
    <variable>
      <name-given>current</name-given>
      <variable-class>java.lang.Integer</variable-class>
      <scope>NESTED</scope>
    </variable>
    <attribute>
      <name>times</name>
      <required>true</required>
      <rtexprvalue>true</rtexprvalue>
    </attribute>
  </tag>
```

The <variable> tag declares the current variable as a java.lang.Integer. Its scope is defined as NESTED, which means it will be available to code inside the tag only. The other legal values are AT_BEGIN and AT_END. If you want to create variables dynamically (for instance, to allow the user to choose the name of the counter variable) you can create a TagExtraInfo class and associate it with the tag using <tei-class>.

Also, note the <rtexprvalue> tag associated with the times attribute. This means that the attribute can accept a JSP expression as its value. So if you have created a variable named count, the Loop tag could be opened with:

```
<enterprise:Loop times="<%= count %>">
```

Body Tags

Tags that need to interact with their body content extend the BodyTag interface instead of the Tag interface. BodyTag introduces a new method, doInitBody(), which runs before the tag body is first processed. It also introduces the BodyContent object, which provides access to the tag body. BodyContent is an extension of JspWriter, with additional methods to retrieve its content in various ways, including as a String object. The BodyTagSupport class fills the same role for BodyTag as TagSupport does for Tag and IterationTag. All BodyTag objects are also IterationTag objects.

The next example shows a simple tag that retrieves the body content, processes it through the java.net.URLEncoder object, and outputs the result:

```
import javax.servlet.jsp.*;
import javax.servlet.jsp.tagext.*;

public class EncodeTag extends BodyTagSupport {

  public int doAfterBody() throws JspException {
    BodyContent c = getBodyContent(); // Get the tag body
    JspWriter out = getPreviousOut(); // get the enclosing Writer
    try {
      out.print(java.net.URLEncoder.encode(c.getString()));
    } catch(java.io.IOException e) {
      throw new JspException(e);
    }
```

```
    return BodyTag.SKIP_BODY; // do not process again
  }
}
```

The `getPreviousOut()` method of `BodyTagSupport` retrieves the `JspWriter` associated with the tag's parent. This might be the main `JspWriter` for the page, or it might be the `BodyContent` object of another JSP tag.

Inter-Tag Communication

As just mentioned, it's possible for JSP custom tags to be nested within other JSP custom tags. The inner tags are executed between the `doStartTag()` and `doEndTag()` methods of the outer tags. Let's imagine an `<enterprise:Email>` tag. In the JSP file, it might be used like this:

```
<enterprise:Email>
<enterprise:EmailAddress addr="from">bob@company.com
                                    </enterprise:EmailAddress>
<enterprise:EmailAddress addr="to">will@company.com
                                    </enterprise:EmailAddress>
<enterprise:EmailText>Where's that JSP Chapter?</enterprise:EmailText>
</enterprise:Email>
```

The `Email` tag is be implemented with either a `Tag` or a `BodyTag`, with JavaBean-style methods to set from and to addresses and email content. The `doEndTag()` method assembles and sends the email. Assuming that the `doStartTag()` method of the email tag class doesn't stop the tag's processing, each of the three interior tags will be processed in turn. These tags can access the parent tag using the `findAncestorWithClass()` method, which takes a `Tag` and a `class` reference and finds the first appearance of the specified class in the tag's hierarchy, working up from the specified tag.

Here's the code for the `EmailAddress` tag, which sets the to and from addresses of the `EmailTag` class (not included):

```
package enterprise;

import javax.servlet.jsp.tagext.*;

public class EmailAddressTag extends BodyTagSupport {
    String addrType = null;
  public void setAddr(String s) {
    addrType = s;
  }
  public int doEndTag() {
    Tag t = findAncestorWithClass(this, enterprise.EmailTag.class);
    if(t != null) {
      EmailTag et = (EmailTag)t;
      if(addrType.equalsIgnoreCase("to"))
        et.setToAddress(getBodyContent().getString());
      else if (addrType.equalsIgnoreCase("from"))
        et.setFromAddress(getBodyContent().getString());
    }
```

```
      return Tag.EVAL_PAGE;
  }
}
```

And that's all there is to it. If the `EmailAddressTag` object doesn't find an `EmailTag` in its parent hierarchy, it exits without taking any action.

Wrapping Up

We've just gone through a great deal of JSP material, and you should now have a pretty good grasp of the range of capabilities provided by JSPs. Obviously, there is more depth and nuance than we can cover in a tutorial chapter, but the material we've discussed covers the full range of capabilities. For more information, there are several good sources. The first is Hans Bergsten's excellent book *JavaServer Pages* (O'Reilly), which provides more detail on some of the features we've flown rather lightly over, and also addresses internationalization, database access from JSPs, and other important approaches to putting all the pieces together.

For tag developers, another necessary stop is the Jakarta Taglibs project, one of several groups working on putting together a standardized, well-tested set of tags, at *http://jakarta.apache.org/taglibs/index.html*. The taglibs project includes tags to handle a wide array of tasks, and can save days or weeks of custom development. Many of these tags will eventually work their way into the JSP Standard Tag Library (JSTL), currently under development as part of the Java Community Process.

Finally, before deploying JSP, take a look at some of the other Java-based content frameworks, such as the Jakarta Velocity project (*http://jakarta.apache.org/ velocity*). Velocity provides a different, less code-focused approach to templating that many nonprogrammers find easier to deal with. Which solution is appropriate for your application depends entirely on your needs. In fact, the Resin servlet container supports Velocity-like syntax as a replacement for Java-based scripting, and a taglib is available to embed Velocity templates in JSP pages, letting you mix and match the various building blocks of your J2EE applications.

CHAPTER 7

JNDI

The Java Naming and Directory Interface (JNDI) is an API that supports accessing naming and directory services in Java programs. The purpose of a naming service is to associate names with objects and provide a way to access objects based on their names. You should be familiar with naming systems; you use them every day when you browse the filesystem on your computer or surf the Web by typing in a URL. Objects in a naming system can range from files in a filesystem and names located in Domain Name System (DNS) records, to Enterprise JavaBeans (EJB) components in an application server and user profiles in an LDAP (Lightweight Directory Access Protocol) directory. If you want to use Java to write an application such as a search utility, a network-enabled desktop, an application launcher, an address book, a network management utility, or a class browser—in short, anything that accesses objects in a naming system—JNDI is a good candidate for writing that application.

As its name implies, JNDI doesn't just deal with naming services. JNDI also encompasses directory services, which are a natural extension of naming services. The primary difference between the two is that a directory service allows the association of attributes with objects, such as an email address attribute for a user object, while a naming service does not. Thus, with a directory service, you can access the attributes of objects and search for objects based on their attributes. You can use JNDI to access directory services like LDAP and Novell Directory Services (NDS) directories.

JNDI is an integral part of the J2EE standard framework; it is used by J2EE components to access deployment information and various runtime resources, such as Enterprise JavaBean references, JDBC data sources, etc. Details on how JNDI plays a role specifically in accessing EJBs can be found in Chapter 8.

JNDI Architecture

The architecture of JNDI is somewhat like the JDBC architecture, in that both provide a standard protocol-independent API built on top of protocol-specific driver or provider implementations. This layer insulates an application from the actual data source it is using, so, for example, it doesn't matter whether the application is accessing an NDS or LDAP directory service.

The JNDI architecture includes both an application programming interface (API) and a service provider interface (SPI), as shown in Figure 7-1. A Java application uses the JNDI API to access naming and directory services, primarily through the Context and DirContext interfaces. The JNDI API is defined in the javax.naming and javax.naming.directory packages. Note that JNDI is a standard extension to the Java 2 platform; it is included in the core APIs in JDK 1.3 and 1.4. If you are using an earlier version of the Java environment, the JNDI API classes and various providers are also available separately at *http://java.sun.com/products/jndi/*. This chapter covers Version 1.2 of JNDI, which is the version included in JDK 1.3 and 1.4, and is a standard component in the J2EE 1.2 and 1.3 specifications.

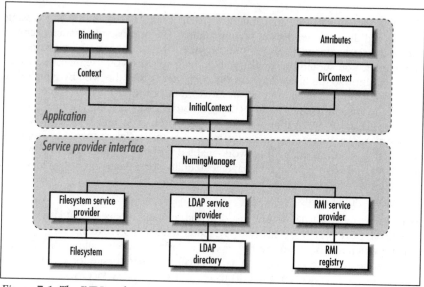

Figure 7-1: The JNDI architecture

In order for an application to actually interact with a particular naming or directory service, there must be a JNDI service provider for that service. This is where the JNDI SPI comes in. A service provider is a set of classes that implements various JNDI interfaces for a specific naming or directory service, much like a JDBC driver implements various JDBC interfaces for a particular database system. The provider can also implement other interfaces that aren't part of JNDI, such as Novell's NdsObject interface.

The classes and interfaces in the javax.naming.spi package are only of interest to developers who are creating service providers. For instance, the NamingManager class defines methods for creating Context objects and otherwise controlling the operation of the underlying service provider. As an application programmer, you don't have to worry about the JNDI SPI. All you have to do is make sure that you have a service provider for each naming or directory service you want to use. Sun maintains a list of available service providers on the JNDI web page listed earlier.

A Simple Example

Before going any further, let's take a look at a simple JNDI example. To access an object in a naming system, we need to create an initial context for the naming system, to give us an entry point into it. Once we have an initial context, we can look up an object by name.

Example 7-1 demonstrates the basic JNDI tasks of getting an initial context to a naming system and looking up an object in that naming system. With slight modification, this code can be used to look up objects with any JNDI provider. So, for example, you could use this Lookup class to look up Enterprise JavaBeans or remote objects in an RMI registry and handle them however you like. All you have to change is the properties that control the naming system being accessed.

Example 7-1: Looking Up an Object in a Naming System

```java
import java.util.Properties;
import javax.naming.*;

public class Lookup {
  public static void main(String[] args) {
    String name = "";
    if (args.length > 0)
      name = args[0];

    try {
      // Create a Properties object and set default properties
      Properties props = new Properties();
      props.put(Context.INITIAL_CONTEXT_FACTORY,
                "com.sun.jndi.fscontext.RefFSContextFactory");
      props.put(Context.PROVIDER_URL, "file:///");

      // Optional command-line args to specify alternate factory and URL
      if (args.length > 1) {
        props.put(Context.INITIAL_CONTEXT_FACTORY, args[1]);
      }
      if (args.length > 2) {
        props.put(Context.PROVIDER_URL, args[2]);
      }

      // Create the initial context from the properties we just created
      Context initialContext = new InitialContext(props);

      // Look up the named object
      Object obj = initialContext.lookup(name);
      if (name.equals(""))
        System.out.println("Looked up the initial context");
```

Example 7-1: Looking Up an Object in a Naming System (continued)

```
        else
            System.out.println(name + " is bound to: " + obj);
      }
      catch (NamingException nnfe) {
        System.out.println("Encountered a naming exception");
        nnfe.printStackTrace();
      }
    }
}
```

The first thing the Lookup application does is create a java.util.Properties object and use it to store some String values. The keys used for these values are constants defined in the javax.naming.Context class. Each constant corresponds to an underlying standard JNDI property name that is meant to communicate specific information about the JNDI service the application is using. Context. INITIAL_CONTEXT_FACTORY specifies the factory class that creates an initial context for the service we want to use. The class com.sun.jndi.fscontext. RefFSContextFactory is a factory class from the filesystem service provider from Sun. It isn't provided by default in the Sun JDK downloads, but it can be downloaded from *http://java.sun.com/products/jndi/*. Context.PROVIDER_URL tells the factory class the protocol, server name, and path to use in creating an initial context. We specify the URL *file:///* to indicate the root of the local filesystem. This works on any Unix or Windows filesystem.

Once we have created the Properties object and set the default values for the context factory and the provider URL, we check the command-line arguments for specific values that the user may have provided. Finally, we pass the Properties to the javax.naming.InitialContext constructor, which returns the initial context object that is our entry point into this particular naming system. Next, we call the lookup() method on initialContext, specifying the name we want to look up. This call returns an object from the naming system, which, in this case, is a file or directory.

You can run Lookup from the command line and specify an optional name to look up. For example, on a typical Windows machine:

```
% java Lookup boot.ini
boot.ini is bound to: C:\boot.ini
```

If the name is actually a directory, the output looks a bit different:

```
% java Lookup winnt
winnt is bound to: com.sun.jndi.fscontext.RefFSContext@803adec0
```

Note that if we wanted to make Lookup more general, we might change it so that it reads its property values from a properties file. Luckily, JNDI takes care of this for you; it automatically loads any of its standard properties from a *jndi.properties* file if it finds the file in your CLASSPATH. Changing the naming system is a simple matter of editing this properties file to specify an appropriate factory object and URL. You can always override the properties loaded from jndi.properties in your code, as we've done in the Lookup example. In the next section we'll discuss the properties that can be set to control how JNDI operates.

JNDI throws naming exceptions when naming operations can't be completed. The root naming exception, javax.naming.NamingException, is a catch all for any JNDI exception. The javax.naming package defines numerous subclasses of NamingException. A common naming exception, NameNotFoundException, is thrown when a name can't be found, either because it doesn't exist or is spelled incorrectly. JNDI throws a NoPermissionException when a program doesn't have sufficient rights or permissions, and throws an OperationNotSupportedException when an application uses a JNDI method on an object that doesn't support that specific naming operation.

Introducing the Context

A naming service associates names with objects. An association between a name and an object is called a *binding*, and a set of such bindings is called a *context*. A name in a context can be bound to another context that uses the same naming conventions; the bound context is called a *subcontext*. Using a filesystem as an analogy, a directory (such as */temp*) is a context that contains bindings between filenames and objects that the system can use to manipulate the files (often called *file handles*). If a directory contains a binding for another directory (e.g., */temp/ javax*), the subdirectory is a subcontext.

JNDI represents a context in a naming system using the javax.naming.Context interface. This is the key interface for interacting with naming services. A Context knows about its set of bindings in the naming system, but little else. While you might be tempted to think of a Context as an exotic java.io.File object, you should resist making that analogy, as it will just confuse you. Unlike a File object, which can tell you its absolute and relative names as well as return a reference to its parent, a Context object can tell you only about its bindings. A Context can't go up a level, tell you its absolute pathname, or even tell you its own name. When you think of a Context, think of an object that encapsulates its children as data and has methods that perform operations on that data, not on the Context itself.

Using the InitialContext Class

The javax.naming.InitialContext class implements the Context interface and serves as our entry point to a naming system. To use JNDI to access objects in a naming system, you must first create an InitialContext object. The InitialContext constructors take a set of properties in the form of a java.util. Hashtable or one of its subclasses, such as a Properties object. Here is how we created an InitialContext in the Lookup example:

```
// Create a Properties object and set default properties
Properties props = new Properties();
props.put(Context.INITIAL_CONTEXT_FACTORY,
        "com.sun.jndi.fscontext.RefFSContextFactory");
props.put(Context.PROVIDER_URL, "file:///");

...

// Create the initial context from the properties we just created
Context initialContext = new InitialContext(props);
```

JNDI

The most fundamental property key is `java.naming.factory.initial`, which corresponds to the `Context.INITIAL_CONTEXT_FACTORY` constant. The value for this property specifies the name of a factory class in a JNDI service provider. It is the job of this factory class to create an `InitialContext` that is appropriate for its service and then hand the object back to us. We have to give the factory class all the information 'it needs to create an `InitialContext` in the form of other property values. For example, the factory class learns the protocol, server name, and path to use from the `java.naming.provider.url` property (`Context.PROVIDER_URL`).

The filesystem factory class (`com.sun.jndi.fscontext.RefFSContxtFactory`) requires a minimal set of properties; it needs only to have its context factory and provider URL specified. Other JNDI providers can be more demanding. For example, the factory class in Sun's LDAP service provider requires the URL of the LDAP server and directory entry you want to access, a username and password, and an authentication type. Here are some properties (shown in the file format used by the `Properties` class) you might use to create an `InitialContext` with the LDAP factory class:

```
java.naming.factory.initial=com.sun.jndi.ldap.LdapCtxFactory
java.naming.provider.url=ldap://192.168.1.20/o=Planetary,c=US
java.naming.security.authentication=simple
java.naming.security.principal=cn=kris
java.naming.security.credentials=secret
```

These properties create an `InitialContext` for an organization called "Planetary" in the global X.500 namespace.

The standard JNDI properties can be specified in several ways. Our `Lookup` example set them explicitly in the source, using some hardwired default values and (optionally) reading alternate values from the command line. Since these are Java properties, they can also be specified using -D arguments to the Java runtime, for example:

```
% java -Djava.naming.factory.initial=org.my.jndi.factory
-Djava.naming.provider.url=file:/// MyJNDIClient
```

JNDI can also read its properties from a *jndi.properties* file located in your `CLASSPATH`. If we put the following into a *jndi.properties* file in the root of one of the directories on our `CLASSPATH`:

```
java.naming.factory.initial=org.my.jndi.factory
java.naming.provider.url=file:///
```

it will have the same effect as the Java runtime arguments just shown.

Other Naming Systems

There are many companies that support JNDI, and therefore many naming system service providers. You can find a reasonably comprehensive list of public JNDI providers from the JNDI page on the Sun web site (currently at *http://java.sun. com/products/jndi/serviceproviders.html*). You should contact the vendor of your enterprise naming system or directory for more details regarding its specialized providers. Table 7-1 lists the factory classes for some common JNDI providers. The first three are provided out-of-the-box with Sun's JDK 1.3 and 1.4 implementations.

JDK 1.4 also includes the DNS provider by default. The others can be downloaded from the URL just specified.

Table 7-1: JNDI Factory Classes

Service	Factory Class
LDAPv3	`com.sun.jndi.ldap.LdapCtxFactory`
COSNaming	`com.sun.jndi.cosnaming.CNCtxFactory`
RMI registry	`com.sun.jndi.rmi.registry.RegistryContextFactory`
DNS	`com.sun.jndi.dns.DnsContextFactory`
Filesystem	`com.sun.jndi.fscontext.FSContextFactory` or `com.sun.jndi.fscontext.RefFSContextFactory`
NDS	`com.novell.naming.service.nds.NdsInitialContextFactory`
NIS	`com.sun.jndi.nis.NISCtxFactory`

Looking Up Objects in a Context

Retrieving an object by name from a naming system or directory is called *looking up the object*. This is the job of the `lookup()` method of `Context`. Performing a lookup is analogous to getting the number of a friend from a telephone book by looking up his name. You can use JNDI to look up and retrieve an EJB home interface from an application server or a remote object from a remote RMI registry.

When you call `lookup()`, you specify the name of the child of the `Context` you want to find. `lookup()` returns a `java.lang.Object` that represents the child. Here's how we did it in the `Lookup` example:

```
Object obj = initialContext.lookup(name);
```

Calling `lookup()` retrieves an object from the underlying naming system. The JNDI service provider determines the Java representation of these objects, and we have no way of affecting the provider's decision. Depending on the naming system and the design of the provider, the object you retrieve may or may not implement `Context`. For example, if you use the Sun filesystem provider, and your current context is a directory, looking up a child that is a file returns an instance of `java.io.File`. Looking up a directory, however, returns an instance of `FSContext` or `RefFSContext`, both of which implement `Context`. As another example, say you use Novell's NDS provider, and the current context is an NDS tree. If you look up an organization, you get back an `OrganizationDirContext` that implements both `Context` and Novell's `NdsObject` interface. The bottom line is that the class you get back from `lookup()` depends on how the service provider is implemented.

JNDI leaves it up to the service provider to choose whether objects should implement `Context`. There are no strict rules about when an object should implement it, but there are some general guidelines. An object with children is a container, and the guideline for containers is that they should implement `Context`. This is because we generally perform naming operations upon these objects. In the filesystem provider, for example, directories can contain other objects (files and other directories), so the object that represents a directory should implement `Context` (which is how Sun's filesystem provider behaves). If directories don't support `Context` methods, we can't use JNDI to look up any children of the directory.

Objects without children are leaves, and leaves may or may not implement Context, depending on how they are used. For example, because files have no children to look up, the methods we perform on them lie outside the naming system. The author of the Sun filesystem provider made a design choice that once we have looked up a file, we're done with JNDI. So, we can read the input stream on a file or write an output stream to it, but we can't use JNDI to perform naming operations on the file.

The NamingShell Application

The rest of the examples in this chapter are going to be based on the NamingShell code shown in Example 7-2. NamingShell is an extensible JNDI shell that enables us to perform naming operations in any JNDI-accessible naming system. The shell provides methods for getting and setting the current object and other shell-related details, and it also keeps track of the name of the current object, something a Context can't do for itself.

Example 7-2: The NamingShell Class

```
import java.io.*;
import java.util.*;
import javax.naming.*;

class NamingShell {

    // Private variables
    private static Hashtable COMMAND_TABLE = new Hashtable();
    private static String  JNDIPROPS_FILENAME  = ".jndienv";
    private static String  PROMPT = "[no initial context]";
    private static String  VERSION = "1.0";
    private static Context CURRENT_CONTEXT, INITIAL_CONTEXT;
    private static String  CURRENT_NAME, INITIAL_NAME;
    private static boolean RUNNING = true;

    // Shell operations
    private static void exit(int status) { System.exit(status); }

    // Accessor methods
    public static Hashtable getCommands() { return COMMAND_TABLE; }
    public static Context getCurrentContext() { return CURRENT_CONTEXT; }
    public static String getCurrentName() { return CURRENT_NAME; }
    public static String getDefaultPropsFilename() {
                        return JNDIPROPS_FILENAME; }
    public static Context getInitialContext() { return INITIAL_CONTEXT; }
    public static String getInitialName() { return INITIAL_NAME; }
    public static String getPrompt() { return PROMPT; }
    public static void setCurrentContext(Context ctx) {
                        CURRENT_CONTEXT = ctx; }
    public static void setInitialContext(Context ctx) {
                        INITIAL_CONTEXT = ctx; }
    public static void setInitialName(String name) { INITIAL_NAME = name; }
    public static void setPrompt(String prompt) { PROMPT = prompt; }
    public static void setCurrentName(String name) {
```

Example 7-2: The NamingShell Class (continued)

```
    CURRENT_NAME = name;
    setPrompt(name);
}

// Executes a preinstantiated command we are sure is already
// present in the table
private static void execute(Command c, Vector v) {
  if (c == null) {
    System.out.println("No command was loaded;
                       cannot execute the command.");
    return;
  }
  try {
    c.execute(CURRENT_CONTEXT, v);
  }
  catch (CommandException ce) {
    System.out.println(ce.getMessage());
  }
}

// Another private method that enables us to specify a command
// by its string name and that loads the command first
private static void execute(String s, Vector v) {
  execute(loadCommand(s), v);
}

// Loads the command specified in commandName; the help command
// relies on this method
public static Command loadCommand(String commandName) {
  // The method returns a null command unless some of its
  // internal logic assigns a new reference to it
  Command theCommand = null;

  // First see if the command is already present in the hashtable
  if (COMMAND_TABLE.containsKey(commandName)) {
    theCommand = (Command)COMMAND_TABLE.get(commandName);
    return theCommand;
  }

  try {
    // Here we use a little introspection to see if a class
    // implements Command before we instantiate it
    Class commandInterface = Class.forName("Command");
    Class commandClass = Class.forName(commandName);

    // Check to see if the class is assignable from Command
    // and if so, put the instance in the command table
    if (!(commandInterface.isAssignableFrom(commandClass)))
      System.out.println("[" + commandName + "]: Not a command");
    else {
      theCommand = (Command)commandClass.newInstance();
      COMMAND_TABLE.put(commandName, theCommand);
```

JNDI

Example 7-2: The NamingShell Class (continued)

```
return theCommand;
      }
   }
   catch (ClassNotFoundException cnfe) {
     System.out.println("[" + commandName + "]: command not found");
   }
   catch (IllegalAccessException iae) {
     System.out.println("[" + commandName + "]: illegal acces");
   }
   catch (InstantiationException ie) {
     System.out.println("["+commandName+"]:
                            command couldn't be instantiated");
   }
   finally {
     return theCommand;         // theCommand is null if we get here
   }
}


// This method reads a line of input, gets the command and arguments
// within the line of input, and then dynamically loads the command
// from the current directory of the running shell
private static void readInput() {
   // Get the input from System.in
   BufferedReader br = new BufferedReader(new InputStreamReader(System.in));

   // Begin reading input
   try {
     while (RUNNING) {
       System.out.print(PROMPT + "% ");

       // Tokenize the line, read each token, and pass the token
       // into a convenient remaining arguments Vector that we
       // pass into the Command
       StringTokenizer tokenizer = new StringTokenizer(br.readLine());
       Vector remainingArgs = new Vector();
       String commandToken = "";
       if (tokenizer.hasMoreTokens()) {
         commandToken = tokenizer.nextToken();
         while (tokenizer.hasMoreTokens())
           remainingArgs.addElement(tokenizer.nextToken());
       }

       // Dynamically load the class for the appropriate command
       // based upon the case-sensitive name of the first token,
       // which is the command token
       if (!(commandToken.equals("")))
         execute(commandToken, remainingArgs);
     }
   }
   catch (java.io.IOException ioe) {
     System.out.println("Caught an IO exception reading a line of input");
```

Example 7-2: The NamingShell Class (continued)

```
    }
  }
  // Constructor
  NamingShell(String[] args) {
  }

  // Main method that reads input until the user exits
  public static void main(String[] args) {
    System.out.println("NamingShell " + VERSION);
    System.out.println("Type help for more information or exit to quit");
    shell.readInput();
    System.out.println("Exiting");
  }
}
```

Once you've loaded NamingShell, you can use the shell to execute JNDI-related commands, just as you would use a regular shell to execute operating-system commands. we encourage you to download the code for NamingShell right now, so that you can experiment with it as we proceed through the rest of the chapter. NamingShell uses the name you type to locate a command dynamically from the filesystem. The shell has no interpreter; however, NamingShell expects a command to implement the Command interface and its execute() method. This means a command really interprets itself. A command throws a CommandException when execution fails.

As you can see, NamingShell itself contains very little real JNDI code. All the JNDI functionality is implemented in the various Command classes we create to handle particular JNDI operations. The shell simply supports the loading of commands and keeps track of various shell-related details.

The Command Interface

The Command interface (shown in Example 7-3) describes a standard interface for a shell command. It has an execute() method that contains the command logic and a help() method for displaying online help for the command. If execute() encounters a naming exception (or some other exception), it throws a CommandException (shown in Example 7-4), which stores the first exception as an instance variable so that the shell can display the exception appropriately.

Example 7-3: The Command Interface

```
import java.util.Vector;
import javax.naming.Context;

public interface Command {
  public void execute(Context c, Vector v)
    throws CommandException;
  public void help();
}
```

Example 7-4: The CommandException Class

```
public class CommandException extends Exception {
  Exception e; // root exception
  CommandException(Exception e, String message) {
    super(message);
    this.e = e;
  }
  public Exception getRootException() {
    return e;
  }
}
```

A Command for Loading an Initial Context

As we said earlier, to use JNDI to look up an object in a naming system (or, in fact, to do anything with the naming system), you first have to create an InitialContext for that naming system. So, the first command we need to implement is *initctx*, for loading an initial context into NamingShell. Example 7-5 shows an implementation of this command.

Example 7-5: The initctx Command

```
import java.io.*;
import java.util.*;
import javax.naming.*;

public class initctx implements Command {

  public void execute(Context c, Vector v) {
    String jndiPropsFilename = null;

    // Check for a properties filename
    if (!v.isEmpty())
      jndiPropsFilename = (String)v.firstElement();

    System.out.println("file = " + jndiPropsFilename);

    try {
      // If no properties file is specified, let JNDI get its properties from
      // the default jndi.properties file on the CLASSPATH. Otherwise, use
      // the specified properties file.
      if (jndiPropsFilename != null) {
        Properties props = new Properties();
        File jndiProps = new File(jndiPropsFilename);
        props.load(new FileInputStream(jndiProps));

        NamingShell.setInitialContext(new InitialContext(props));
      }
      else {
        NamingShell.setInitialContext(new InitialContext());
      }
      NamingShell.setInitialName("/");
      NamingShell.setCurrentContext(NamingShell.getInitialContext());
```

Example 7-5: The initctx Command (continued)

```
      NamingShell.setCurrentName(NamingShell.getInitialName());
      System.out.print("Created initial context using ");
      if (jndiPropsFilename != null) {
        System.out.println(jndiPropsFilename);
      }
      else {
        System.out.println("jndi.properties.");
      }
    }
    catch (NamingException ne) {
      System.out.println("Couldn't create the initial context");
    }
    catch (FileNotFoundException fnfe) {
      System.out.print("Couldn't find properties file: ");
      System.out.println(jndiPropsFilename);
    }
    catch (IOException ioe) {
      System.out.print("Problem loading the properties file: ");
      System.out.println(jndiPropsFilename);
    }
    catch (Exception e) {
      System.out.println("There was a problem starting the shell");
    }
  }

  public void help() { System.out.println("Usage: initctx [filename]"); }
}
```

The *initctx* command accepts an optional argument that specifies the name of a
properties file to use in creating the Properties object that is passed to the
InitialContext constructor. If no filename is specified, *initctx* creates the
InitialContext using the no-argument constructor, which in turn uses the default
jndi.properties file in the CLASSPATH. So, with NamingShell, all you have to do to
use a particular naming service is create an appropriate properties file for that
service and either specify it explicitly when you invoke the *initctx* command, or
put it in your CLASSPATH as jndi.properties.

Running the Shell

With NamingShell and *initctx*, we have enough functionality to actually run the
shell. Before you try this, make sure that the JNDI libraries (in *jndi.jar*) and any
other specialized providers are specified in your CLASSPATH. Here's how we might
start NamingShell and establish an initial context, once the CLASSPATH is set
appropriately:

```
% java NamingShell
[no initial context]% initctx
Created initial context using jndi.properties
/%
```

In this case, since we didn't specify a properties file on the command line, the no-
argument InitialContext constructor is called, and it looks for a *jndi.properties*

file in the CLASSPATH. For the purpose of our next few examples, let's assume that this file contains property settings that allow us to use the filesystem provider from Sun. You can change initial contexts at any time during the shell session by running *initctx* with a new filename. After you create an initial context, you can begin performing naming operations by typing in commands. To exit the shell, simply use the *exit* command.* If you aren't sure how a command works, you can get help for that command by typing:

```
/% help command
```

Listing the Children of a Context

A common JNDI operation is retrieving the list of names of an object's children. For example, an application might get the names of Enterprise JavaBeans in a Java application server, or list the names of user profile information in an LDAP server in order to populate a Swing JTree component in an address-book application. You list the names of an object's children using the list() method of Context:

```
NamingEnumeration children = initialContext.list("");
```

The list() method returns a javax.naming.NamingEnumeration of javax.naming. NameClassPair objects, where each NameClassPair contains the name and class of a single child of the Context. Note that the NameClassPair is not the child itself. Its getName() method, however, enables us to learn the name of the child, while getClassName() lets us access the child's class name. The NamingEnumeration implements the java.util.Enumeration interface, so it allows us to loop through the results of calling list() using the familiar enumeration methods. JNDI actually uses NamingEnumeration as the return type of a number of naming operations; the actual objects in the enumeration vary depending on the operation.

Example 7-6 shows the implementation of a *list* command for our NamingShell. Because executing list() requires a current Context, the execute() method queries the shell to determine whether one exists. If there is no current Context, the method throws an exception.

Example 7-6: The list Command

```
import java.util.Vector;
import javax.naming.*;

public class list implements Command {
    public void execute(Context c, Vector v) throws CommandException {

        String name = "";

        // An empty string is OK for a list operation as it means
        // list children of the current context.
        if (!(v.isEmpty()))
```

---

* The *help* and *exit* commands are implemented as separate classes, just like the JNDI-related commands. We don't examine the code for these commands, because they don't use JNDI. However, the code is provided in the example available online at *http://www.oreilly.com/catalog/jentnut2/.*

Example 7-6: The list Command (continued)

```
    name = (String)v.firstElement();

  // Check for current context; throw an exception if there isn't one
  if (NamingShell.getCurrentContext() == null)
    throw new CommandException(new Exception(),
      "Error: no current context.");

  // Call list() and then loop through the results, printing the names
  // and class names of the children
  try {
    NamingEnumeration enum = c.list(name);
    while (enum.hasMore()) {
      NameClassPair ncPair = (NameClassPair)enum.next();
      System.out.print(ncPair.getName() + " (type ");
      System.out.println(ncPair.getClassName() + ")");
    }
  }
  catch (NamingException e) {
    throw new CommandException(e, "Couldn't list " + name);
  }
}

public void help() { System.out.println("Usage: list [name]"); }
}
```

Let's continue with our example of using NamingShell with the filesystem provider. Say that we are accessing a filesystem where we have unpacked a JAR file that contains, among others, a *javax* directory and a *naming* subdirectory. If the current Context is the *naming* directory (ignoring for a moment how we set the current Context; we'll see how to do that shortly), we can use the *list* command with the following results:

```
naming% list
AuthenticationException.class (type java.io.File)
AuthenticationNotSupportedException.class (type java.io.File)
BinaryRefAddr.class (type java.io.File)
Binding.class (type java.io.File)
CannotProceedException.class (type java.io.File)
CommunicationException.class (type java.io.File)
CompositeName.class (type java.io.File)
CompoundName.class (type java.io.File)
ConfigurationException.class (type java.io.File)
Context.class (type java.io.File)
ContextNotEmptyException.class (type java.io.File)
directory (type javax.naming.Context)
...
```

How Names Work

The list() method on Context allows us to list the names of the children of any arbitrary child of a Context. We just saw that we can list the names of the children of a Context itself (in this case, the *naming* directory) by calling its list()

method using an empty string as a parameter. Again, let's assume we have a `Context` object for the *naming* subdirectory under *javax*. Here's how a call to get the names of the children of this `Context` might look:

```
NamingEnumeration childrenOfNaming = namingContext.list("");
```

The result is a `NamingEnumeration` that contains `NameClassPair` objects representing all the children of *naming* (i.e., the classes and subpackages of `javax.naming`), including the *directory* directory (i.e., the `javax.naming.directory` subpackage).

To list the names of the children of an arbitrary child of a `Context`, we have to pass a name to `list()`. For example, we can list the children of *directory* by specifying the `String` "directory" as a parameter to `list()`:

```
NamingEnumeration childrenOfDirectory = namingContext.list("directory");
```

The result here is a `NamingEnumeration` that contains `NameClassPair` objects representing all the children of *directory* (i.e., the classes of `javax.naming.directory`, such as `DirContext`).

You can also specify a name using something called a compound name. A *compound name* is composed of atomic names, like "naming" and "directory," that are separated by separator characters. In the case of the filesystem provider, these can be either a Unix-style forward slash (/) or a Windows-style backslash (\). Any JNDI method that takes a name as a parameter can accept a compound name.

Say we have a `Context` object for the *javax* directory. We can get a list of the children of *directory* as follows:

```
NamingEnumeration childrenOfDirectory = javaxContext.list(
    "naming/directory");
```

This call returns the same `NamingEnumeration` we got earlier. Now consider the following call:

```
NamingEnumeration childrenOfContext = javaxContext.list(
    "naming/Context");
```

The compound name here specifies an object that is not a `Context`, so it has no children. In this case, the call to `list()` throws a `NamingException`.

The separator character used in JNDI compound names varies across naming and directory services; the separator is analogous to the separator used in `java.io.File`. Although the Sun filesystem provider allows us to use the Unix-style forward slash and the Windows-style backslash interchangeably, most service providers are very picky about the separator character used for that service. Unfortunately, the JNDI API doesn't provide a way to get the separator character programmatically the way `java.io.File` does. Although the `javax.naming.CompoundName` class reads a property called `jndi.syntax.separator` that contains the separator character, this property can't be accessed outside the service provider. So, to find out the separator character for a particular service provider, you have to consult the documentation or some sample code for that provider.

Browsing a Naming System

So far, we know how to look up an object in a Context using lookup() and list the children of that Context with list(). Browsing is a composite operation that involves repeated calls to list() and lookup() to see what objects are available in the naming system and to move around in those objects.

Context objects are the key to browsing. You start with a current Context and list the children of that Context to see which child you (or, more likely, the user) are interested in. Once you have selected an interesting child, look up that child to get the actual child object. If the object implements Context, you can use this new Context object to continue browsing, by calling list() again, selecting a child, and looking up its object. If the object doesn't implement Context, however, you obviously can't continue browsing down that branch of the naming system. Once you have a Context object, it is always possible to list its children and look up objects within it. So, for example, you can always use the InitialContext for a naming system to go back and start browsing at the entry point to the naming system

Example 7-7 shows an implementation of a *cd* command for NamingShell. The *cd* command changes the current context of NamingShell to the specified context; you use it in conjunction with the *list* command to browse the naming system. The name of this command comes from the Unix *cd* command for changing directories, because changing the directory on a Unix system is an analogous operation to changing the current context when NamingShell is used with the filesystem provider. To change the current context back to the initial context, use either *cd /* or *cd *. Note, however, that you can't use *cd..*, because Context objects don't know about their parents, and so you can't go up the Context hierarchy.

Example 7-7: The cd Command

```
import java.util.Vector;
import javax.naming.*;

class cd implements Command {
  public void execute(Context ctx, Vector v) throws CommandException {
    if (NamingShell.getCurrentContext() == null)
      throw new CommandException(new Exception(), "No current context");
    else if (v.isEmpty())
      throw new CommandException(new Exception(), "No name specified");

    // Get args[0] and throw away the other args
    else {
      String name = (String)v.firstElement();
      try {
        if (name.equals("..")) {
          throw new CommandException(new Exception(),
            "Contexts don't know about their parents.");
        }
        else if (((name.equals("/")) || (name.equals("\\")))) {
          NamingShell.setCurrentContext(NamingShell.getInitialContext());
          NamingShell.setCurrentName(NamingShell.getInitialName());
          System.out.println("Current context now " + name);
```

Example 7-7: The cd Command (continued)

```
      }
      else {
        Context c = (Context) (
                             NamingShell.getCurrentContext()).lookup(name);
        NamingShell.setCurrentContext(c);
        NamingShell.setCurrentName(name);
        System.out.println("Current context now " + name);
      }
    }
    catch (NamingException ne) {
      throw new CommandException(ne, "Couldn't change to context " + name);
    }
    catch (ClassCastException cce) {
      throw new CommandException(cce, name + " not a Context");
    }
  }
}

  public void help() { System.out.println("Usage: cd [name]"); }
}
```

Earlier, when demonstrating the *list* command, we asked you to assume that the current Context for NamingShell was the *naming* subdirectory. Now you can see just how to change the current Context to that directory:

```
initctx% cd temp
Current context now temp
temp% cd javax
Current context now javax
javax% cd naming
Current context now naming
```

Of course, these commands assume you are starting from the initial context and that the *naming* directory is available in the filesystem at */temp/javax/naming*.

Listing the Bindings of a Context

The listBindings() method of Context provides an alternative way to access the children of a Context. We've seen that list() returns a NamingEnumeration of NameValuePair objects, where each NameValuePair provides access to the name and class name of a single child of the Context. listBindings() also returns a NamingEnumeration, but, in this case, the enumeration contains Binding objects. Binding is a subclass of NameValuePair that contains the actual child object in addition to its name and class. You can use the getObject() method of Binding to get the child object.

Just as with list(), we can pass an empty string to listBindings() to return the bindings for a Context:

```
NamingEnumeration bindings = initialContext.listBindings("");
```

listBindings() is designed for situations in which you need to perform some sort of operation on all the children of a Context, and you want to save yourself

---

the time and trouble of looking up each child individually. Be aware, however, that listBindings() is potentially a very expensive operation, as it has to get each child object from the underlying naming system. If you don't need all the objects, you are better off using list() to get the names of the children and then just looking up the objects you need.

Creating and Destroying Contexts

With JNDI, you can create a context in a naming system using the createSubcontext() method of an existing Context. All you have to specify in this call is the name of the new subcontext. Note that Context doesn't provide a public constructor; creating a new context requires a parent Context (such as an InitialContext) whose createSubcontext() method we can call.

When you call createSubcontext(), the JNDI service provider you are using looks at the class of the Context whose method you are calling. Based on this class and the provider's own internal logic, the provider creates a new object of a particular class. You don't get to pick the class of this object; the provider has all the control over the class of the object it creates (you do, however, have control over the class of object that is created when using directory services, as we'll see shortly.) The documentation for a service provider should tell you what kinds of objects createSubcontext() can create. Note that whatever object the provider creates, it always implements Context; there is no way to use JNDI to create an object that doesn't implement Context.

For example, if we are using the Sun filesystem provider, and our current Context is a directory, calling createSubcontext() causes the provider to create a directory, not a file. This makes sense, as a directory can have subordinates and thus implements Context. There is actually no way to create a file using the JNDI API and the filesystem provider; you have to drop out of JNDI to do this, as we'll see in the next section.

Example 7-8 shows the implementation of a *create* command for NamingShell command that demonstrates how to use createSubcontext().

Example 7-8: The create Command

```
import java.util.Vector;
import javax.naming.*;

public class create implements Command {

  public void execute(Context c, Vector v) throws CommandException {

    // Check to see if we have the name we need to create a context
    if (v.isEmpty())
      throw new CommandException(new Exception(), "No name specified");

    String name = (String)v.firstElement();
    try {
      c.createSubcontext(name);
      System.out.println("Created " + name);
    }
```

Example 7-8: The create Command (continued)

```
    catch (NoPermissionException npe) {
      throw new CommandException(npe,
        "You don't have permission to create " + name + " at this context");
    }
    catch (NamingException ne) {
      throw new CommandException(ne, "Couldn't create " + name);
    }
  }

  public void help() { System.out.println("Usage: create [name]"); }
}
```

Here is the *create* command, in conjunction with the *cd* and *list* commands we've already seen:

```
/% create test
Created test
/% cd test
Current context now test
test% create another
Created another
test% list
another (type javax.naming.Context)
```

The destroySubcontext() method of Context destroys a context, as you might expect from its name. Again, you have to specify the name of the context to be destroyed; you can't destroy the current object by specifying an empty name. Calling the destroySubcontext() method on a Context from the Sun filesystem provider is analogous to removing a directory in the filesystem.

Example 7-9 shows the implementation of a *destroy* command for NamingShell. Note that it contains several catch statements, to handle such exceptions as insufficient permission to destroy a context, trying to destroy an object that doesn't implement the Context interface, and trying to destroy an object that has children.

Example 7-9: The destroy Command

```
import java.util.Vector;
import javax.naming.*;

public class destroy implements Command {
  public void execute(Context c, Vector v) throws CommandException {

    // Check to see if we have the name we need
    if (v.isEmpty())
      throw new CommandException(new Exception(), "No name specified");

    String name = (String)v.firstElement();

    try {
      c.destroySubcontext(name);
      System.out.println("Destroyed " + name);
    }
```

Example 7-9: The destroy Command (continued)

```
  catch (NameNotFoundException nnfe) {
    throw new CommandException(nnfe, "Couldn't find " + name);
  }
  catch (NotContextException nce) {
    throw new CommandException(nce,
      name + " is not a Context and couldn't be destroyed");
  }
  catch (ContextNotEmptyException cnee) {
    throw new CommandException(cnee,
      name + " is not empty and couldn't be destroyed");
  }
  catch (NamingException ne) {
    throw new CommandException(ne, name + " couldn't be destroyed");
  }
}

  public void help() { System.out.println("Usage: destroy [name]"); }
}
```

Binding Objects

A Context stores its subordinates as a set of Binding objects. A binding is an association between an object and its name. Thus, as we've already seen, a Binding object contains an object, its name, and its class. We can add a new Binding to a Context with the bind() method. For example, here's how to add a binding for a new file object to an existing Context:

```
  java.io.File newfile = java.io.File("c:\temp\newfile");
  tempContext.bind("newfile", newfile);
```

Now, if we call list() on this Context, you see a new child named newfile. Recall in the previous section we said that you have to drop out of JNDI to create a new file when using the Sun filesystem provider. The previous example shows what we meant. To create a file, use the java.io.File constructor, which isn't part of JNDI. To bind the file into the naming system, use the bind() method of Context.

If you try to bind a name to an object, and the name has already been used, the method throws a NameAlreadyBoundException. If you want to bind a new object to an existing name, use the rebind() method instead. Context also has an unbind() method you can use to remove a binding.

Accessing Directory Services

So far, we've only discussed JNDI in the context of naming services. Now it's time to turn to directory services. At its root, a directory is merely a naming service whose objects have attributes as well as names. Programming for a directory service, such as an LDAP directory, is roughly as hard as programming for a relational database.

As we've seen, a binding in JNDI is an association between a name and an object. While this association is sufficient for some naming services, a directory service needs to be able to associate more than just a name with an object. Attributes associate specialized data with an object. In JNDI, an object with attributes as well as a name is called a *directory entry*.

We've been talking about the filesystem as though it were a naming system because that is how Sun's filesystem provider implements it. But if you think about it, a filesystem is really a directory system; files and directories have attributes like permissions, user IDs, and group IDs (we just can't get at these attributes using Sun's filesystem provider).

Most of the directories you'll interact with using JNDI are based on the X.500 directory services standard. For example, both standard LDAP directories and Novell's NDS directories have been influenced by X.500. As such, it is important that you know a little bit about X.500, so that you can understand how these directories work.

X.500 Directories

X.500 is a directory services standard that was developed through a collaboration between ISO and CCITT in the late 1980s. It is the "big daddy" of most directories in use today. Like all such collaborations between standards bodies and treaty organizations, the X.500 specification has the bulk of an earthmover and is about as maneuverable. But, like an earthmover, it can really get the big jobs done.

A large contributor to X.500's bulk is its *schema*, which is the directory type system. A directory schema is a set of rules that govern the layout of the objects in the directory. The schema determines what classes of objects can reside in a directory system, what classes of children and kinds of attributes an object is permitted to have, and what classes of values those attributes can have. If you have worked with databases, be careful not to confuse a directory schema with a database schema. A database schema is the layout of tables in the database, while a directory schema is the set of rules that control the directory layout, not the layout itself.

During the mid 1990s, researchers at the University of Michigan began to examine ways of reducing the complexity of the X.500 Directory Access Protocol (DAP). These researchers came up with the "lightweight" DAP, or LDAP, which significantly slimmed down the protocol's bulk. LDAP has gathered considerable support in the industry, so that it is now considered the standard Internet directory access protocol. Netscape is in part responsible for the acceptance of LDAP, as it declared LDAP the preferred method for accessing address books incorporated into its product line and developed the Netscape Directory Server, which is the most popular general-purpose LDAP-based directory server in use today. Note that while the LDAP protocol is simpler than the X.500 protocol, an LDAP directory still uses a directory schema.

Novell's NDS is another X.500-based directory. In the early 1990s, Novell released NetWare 4.0, which included something called NetWare Directory Services (NDS). this is a directory that was heavily influenced by X.500. NDS provides information about various networking services, such as printing and file services. As Novell ported NDS to other non-NetWare platforms, the name of the directory morphed into Novell Directory Services, and then NDS became its official name. As further proof of the acceptance of the LDAP protocol, even Novell has declared that the LDAP protocol is the preferred directory access protocol for NDS.

JNDI supports the X.500-based notion of a directory schema. But it can just as easily support non-X.500 schema, such as the informal schema of a filesystem. Keep in mind that what we are discussing in this section applies to all directory services, not just X.500, LDAP, or NDS directories. As with naming services, to access a particular directory service, all you need is a service provider for that service.

The DirContext Interface

`javax.naming.directory.DirContext` is JNDI's directory services interface. It extends `Context` and provides modified methods that support operations involving attributes. Like a `Context`, a `DirContext` encapsulates a set of name-to-object bindings. In addition, a `DirContext` contains a `javax.naming.directory.Attributes` object for each bound object that holds the attributes and values for that object.

The names of objects in X.500-based directories look a little different from the names we've seen so far for filesystems. If you've worked with an LDAP directory, you've probably seen names like "cn=Billy Roberts, o=Acme Products". This name is actually a compound name, while something like "o=Acme Products" is an atomic name. By convention, in an LDAP directory, the part of the name before the equals sign (e.g., "cn", "o") is stored as an attribute of the directory entry, and the rest of the name (e.g., "Billy Roberts", "Acme Products") is stored as its value. This attribute is called the *key attribute*. Table 7-2 lists some commonly used key attributes. Note that when a `DirContext` is used with an LDAP directory, it knows its name, unlike a `Context`.

Table 7-2: Common Key X.500 Attributes

Attribute	Meaning
"c"	A country, such as the United States or Lithuania
"o"	An organization or corporation, such as the Humane Society or Omni Consumer Products
"ou"	A division of an organization, such as the Public Relations Department or the Robotic Peace Officer Division
"cn"	The common name of an entity (often a user, where it can be a first name or a full name)
"sn"	The surname (last name) of a user

The key attribute is closely tied to the directory entry's *object class definition*, otherwise known as its type. For example, in an LDAP directory, an entry that has an object class of "user" has a key attribute of "cn", while the an object with a class of "organization" has a key attribute or "o".

The schema for a directory defines the object classes that can be used in the directory, analogous to the way that the schema for a relational database defines the data tables that are available in the database. The object class of a directory entry is stored as an attribute of the entry. Note that the values used for object classes are directory-dependent, so a user entry from one directory might have a different object class than a user entry from another directory.

The Attributes Interface

The Attributes interface represents the set of attributes for a directory entry. It has accessor methods that enable access to the entire set, as well as to specific attributes. In X.500-based directories, the name of an attribute (also called an attribute ID), such as "name", "address", or "telephonenumber", determines the type of the attribute and is called the *attribute type definition.* An attribute type definition is part of a directory's schema; the corresponding *attribute syntax definition* specifies the syntax for the attribute's value and whether it can have multiple values, among other things.

You can retrieve all attributes of a directory entry by calling the getAttributes() method of DirContext, followed by the getAll() method of Attributes. getAttributes() returns an Attributes object. Calling the getAll() method of this object returns a NamingEnumeration of javax.naming.directory.Attribute objects, one for each attribute of the directory entry.

Example 7-10 shows the implementation of a *listattrs* command for NamingShell. This command prints the attributes of a directory entry, as well as string representations of the attribute values.

Example 7-10: The listattrs Command

```
import java.util.Vector;
import javax.naming.*;
import javax.naming.directory.*;

class listattrs implements Command {
  public void execute(Context c, Vector v) throws CommandException {

    String name = "";

    // An empty string is OK for a listattrs operation
    // as it means list attributes of the current context
    if (!(v.isEmpty()))
      name = (String)v.firstElement();

    if (NamingShell.getCurrentContext() == null)
      throw new CommandException(new Exception(), "No current context");

    try {
      // Get the Attributes and then get enumeration of Attribute objects
      Attributes attrs = ((DirContext)c).getAttributes(name);
      NamingEnumeration allAttr = attrs.getAll();
      while (allAttr.hasMore()) {
        Attribute attr = (Attribute)allAttr.next();
        System.out.println("Attribute: " + attr.getID());

        // Note that this can return human-unreadable garbage
        NamingEnumeration values = attr.getAll();
```

Example 7-10: The listattrs Command (continued)

```
        while (values.hasMore())
          System.out.println("Value: " + values.next());
      }
    }
    catch (NamingException e) {
      throw new CommandException(e, "Couldn't list attributes of " + name);
    }
    catch (ClassCastException cce) {
      throw new CommandException(cce, "Not a directory context");
    }
  }

  public void help() { System.out.println("Usage: listattrs [name]"); }
}
```

To use the *listattrs* command, you need access to a live directory server. To experiment with a live LDAP directory server, you might try the University of Michigan's server at *ldap://ldap.itd.umich.edu* or Novell's test server at *ldap://nldap.com*. Another option is to download and compile the OpenLDAP source code from *http://www.openldap.org* and get an LDAP server running on your local network. To use the University of Michigan's LDAP server with NamingShell, you need to create a properties file that contains the following properties:

```
java.naming.factory.initial=com.sun.jndi.ldap.LdapCtxFactory
java.naming.provider.url=ldap://ldap.itd.umich.edu/
```

Make sure that the JAR file for the LDAP service provider is in the CLASSPATH of NamingShell when you use this initial context information. If you are using Sun's JDK 1.3 or 1.4, then this LDAP provider is built into the runtime.

Once you have NamingShell set up to use a directory server, here's how you might use the *listattrs* command:

```
o=NOVELL% listattrs cn=admin
Attribute: groupMembership
Value: cn=DEVNET SYSOP,ou=Groups,o=NOVELL
Attribute: revision
Value: 235
Attribute: uid
Value: admin
Attribute: objectClass
Value: top
Value: person
Value: organizationalPerson
Value: inetOrgPerson
Attribute: sn
Value: admin
Attribute: cn
Value: admin
```

JNDI

The following code in *listattrs* retrieves the `Attributes` object of the named directory context and enumerates the individual `Attribute` objects:

```
Attributes attrs = ((DirContext)c).getAttributes(name);
NamingEnumeration allAttr = attrs.getAll();
```

Calling `getAttributes()` with the name of a directory entry returns an `Attributes` object that contains all the attributes for that entry. Another variation of `getAttributes()` allows you to pass the name of a directory entry and an array of attribute names (as `String` objects). This method returns an `Attributes` object that contains only the specified attributes. For example:

```
String[] attrIDs = {"name", "telephonenumber"};
Attributes partialAttrs = dirContext.getAttributes(name, attrIDs);
```

In *listattrs*, we used the `getAll()` method of `Attributes` to return an enumeration of `Attribute` objects. The `Attributes` interface also provides a `getIDs()` method that returns an enumeration of just the attribute names (or IDs) for the directory entry. If you know the attribute you want, you can specify the attribute name in a call to the `get()` method, which returns a single `Attribute` object. For example:

```
Attribute addr = attrs.get("address");
```

The Attribute Interface

The `Attribute` interface represents a single directory attribute. We've already seen this interface in the *listattrs* command, where we used it to print the names and values of all the attributes of a directory context.

An attribute can have a single value or multiple values, as specified in the schema for the directory. For example, a "name" attribute might have a single value (e.g., "Billy"), while a "telephonenumber" attribute might have multiple values (e.g., "800 555 1212" and "303 444 6633").

JNDI provides several methods for working with values in an attribute. For instance, we can get one or more values, add or remove a single value, remove all values, or determine if a particular value is present.

The `get()` method of `Attribute` returns a single attribute value as a `java.lang.Object`. If the attribute has only a single value, `get()` returns that value. If the attribute has multiple values, the service provider determines the value that is returned. The following code shows how to get a single value from an attribute:

```
DirContext user ... ; // Created somewhere else in the program
Attributes attrs = user.getAttributes("");
Attribute attr = attrs.get("telephonenumber");
Object onePhoneNumber = attr.get();
```

The `getAll()` method returns multiple attribute values as a `NamingEnumeration` of objects, as we saw in *listattrs*. Here's how to print all values stored in an attribute:

```
Attribute attr = attrs.get("telephonenumber");
NamingEnumeration phoneNumbers = attr.getAll();
while (phoneNumbers.hasMore())
  System.out.println(phoneNumbers.next());
```

The add() method of Attribute enables us to add another value to an attribute:

```
Attribute attr = attrs.get("telephonenumber");
attr.add("520 765 4321"); // Add a new number
```

If we try to add a value to an attribute that doesn't support multiple values, the method doesn't throw an exception. The attribute simply doesn't accept the new value. By the same token, you can use the remove() method to remove a value from an attribute.

```
Attribute attr = attrs.get("telephonenumber");
attr.remove("303 444 6633"); // Remove the old number
```

To remove all the values from an attribute, you can call the clear() method. Note that none of these method calls actually affect the directory entry; they simply modify the local Attribute object. To make a permanent change, you have to call the modifyAttributes() method of DirContext and provide it with a modified Attribute object, as discussed in the next section.

The contains() method lets you determine whether an attribute has a certain value, while size() returns the number of values the attribute has:

```
Attribute attr = attrs.get("telephonenumber");
// Check for certain value
boolean itsThere = attr.contains("800 555 1212");
int valuesItHas = attr.size(); // Check how many values it has
```

Modifying Directory Entries

Modifying the attribute values of a directory entry involves using the modifyAttributes() method of DirContext. One variant of this method takes the name of a directory entry, a modification type, and an Attributes object that contains modified Attribute objects; another variant takes a name and an array of javax.naming.directory.ModificationItem objects. A ModificationItem encapsulates a modified Attribute object and a modification type.

The only part of this operation that warrants much explanation is the creation of modified Attribute objects. The javax.naming.directory.BasicAttributes and javax.naming.directory.BasicAttribute classes implement the Attributes and Attribute interfaces, respectively. These are the classes you'll typically use to create modified attribute values.

For example, let's say we want to remove the phone number "303 444 6633" from a user entry's "telephonenumber" attribute and replace it with the new number "520 765 4321." In the following code, we create two BasicAttributes objects, newNumber and oldNumber, and use them in calls to modifyAttributes():

```
DirContext user ... ; // Created somewhere else in the program

BasicAttribute newAttr = new BasicAttribute();
newAttr.add("telephonenumber", "520 765 4321");
BasicAttributes newNumber = new BasicAttributes();
newNumber.put(newAttr);
```

```
BasicAttributes oldNumber =
    new BasicAttributes("telephonenumber", "303 444 6633");

user.modifyAttributes("", DirContext.REMOVE_ATTRIBUTE, oldNumber);
user.modifyAttributes("", DirContext.ADD_ATTRIBUTE, newNumber);
```

In this code, we use two different techniques to create BasicAttributes objects. For newNumber, we first create a new BasicAttribute and add a "telephonenumber" attribute to it. Then we create a new BasicAttributes object and put the BasicAttribute in it. With oldNumber, we use the convenience constructor of BasicAttributes to accomplish the same task in one line of code.

Now we use the two BasicAttributes objects in two calls to modifyAttributes(), one to remove the old number and one to add the new. DirContext defines three constants we can use to specify the type of modification we are doing: ADD_ATTRIBUTES, REMOVE_ATTRIBUTES, and REPLACE_ATTRIBUTES. With any of these types, modifyAttributes() uses the ID of each Attribute object to determine which attribute to modify by adding, removing, or replacing attribute values. The net result of our two calls is the old number is replaced with the new number. Of course, we could have done this with one call to modifyAttributes() if we had used the REPLACE_ATTRIBUTES modification type.

The following code shows how to make the same change using a variant of modifyAttributes() that takes an array of ModificationItem objects:

```
ModificationItem[] mods = new ModificationItem[2];
mods[0] = new ModificationItem(DirContext.REMOVE_ATTRIBUTE,
        new BasicAttribute("telephonenumber", "303 444 6633"));
mods[1] = new ModificationItem(DirContext.ADD_ATTRIBUTE,
        new BasicAttribute("telephonenumber", "520 765 4321"));
user.modifyAttributes("", mods);
```

Again, this change could also have been done with a single ModificationItem, using REPLACE_ATTRIBUTES.

Note that the examples here don't reflect any particular directory. In order to change a directory's "telephonenumber" attribute value, you need to consult the schema of that directory for the appropriate attribute type and syntax definitions.

Note also that we have only discussed modifying existing attribute values, not adding new attributes altogether. The reason is that adding new attribute IDs requires modifying the schema, or type system, of a directory. JNDI supports schema access and modification, but the details on how to do so are beyond the scope of this chapter.

Creating Directory Entries

So far, we have been accessing directory entries that are already present in the directory. Now it's time to learn how to create directory entries of our own, using the createSubcontext() method of DirContext. As we discussed earlier, when you create a subcontext of a Context object, the service provider controls the type of object that is created. With a DirContext, this is not the case; you actually have complete control over the type of object you create with createSubcontext() (within the constraints of the directory schema, of course).

As noted earlier, the object class definition determines the type of a directory entry, and the entry stores its object class as an attribute. So, in order to create a directory entry, we must pass the object class attribute and some other attributes into the parent entry's createSubcontext() method.

Most directories require that you specify attributes for at least the object class definition (e.g., "objectclass=") and key attribute (e.g., common name, "cn=") of a directory entry. Often directories require that you specify more attributes than just these. The minimum set of attributes necessary for creating a directory entry are called the *mandatory attributes*. They are mandatory because if you don't specify them, createSubcontext() throws an InvalidAttributesException. Other attributes that aren't required, but that add more useful data to the entry, are called *extended attributes*.

Say we have a reference to a DirContext called orgUnit (where this directory entry lives in an LDAP v3 directory), and we want to create a user entry that is a child of orgUnit to represent the network user Billy Roberts. Here's how we can create a user entry for Billy:[*]

```
DirContext orgUnit = ... ; // Created somewhere else in the program
BasicAttributes mandatory = new BasicAttributes("cn", "Billy");
BasicAttribute objectclass = new BasicAttribute("objectclass", "user");
BasicAttribute surname = new BasicAttribute("surname", "Roberts");
mandatory.put(objectclass);
mandatory.put(surname);

orgUnit.createSubcontext("cn=Billy", mandatory);
```

Note that the createSubcontext() method of DirContext resembles the createSubcontext() method of Context; the only difference is the addition of an Attributes parameter. In this example, we create a BasicAttributes object and put three attributes in it. While all the attribute values here are String objects (because that's what an LDAP directory requires), the JNDI API allows you to specify any kind of object as an attribute value.

In this example, orgUnit represents an organizational unit, under which Billy Roberts' newly created user entry resides. In an LDAP directory, an organizational unit is an object class definition that represents a division of a company, and a user is an object class definition that represents a person who uses network resources. It is natural that a division of a company can contain a person, but it doesn't necessarily work in the opposite direction; it doesn't make sense that a user can contain an organizational unit. The LDAP schema dictates these rules and also specifies the values we can use for the objectclass attribute (which is where "user" came from in the example code).

When you are creating your own directory entries, be sure to consult the schema for the directory you are using. If you attempt to create a type of entry that can't reside under a particular DirContext, or you specify an incorrect value for the objectclass attribute, createSubcontext() throws an exception.

---

[*] Note that we didn't implement a "create directory entry" command for NamingShell because most public-access LDAP servers don't allow you to create new entries.

Searching a Directory

One of the most useful features a directory service can offer is the ability to search its entries for attribute values that meet certain criteria. JNDI supports this kind of searching in directory systems, which means you can implement search functionality in your JNDI applications. DirContext provides different search() methods that allow you to specify what you are searching for and control how the search operates.

Search Criteria

There are two ways to specify what you are searching for. The simpler technique is to create a set of attributes that serve as the search criteria. In this case, you can set an attribute value, meaning that an entry must have that attribute value to match or leave the value empty, so that all entries that have the attribute match no matter what the value.

The more flexible way to specify search criteria is with a search filter string. A search filter allows you to express search criteria using LDAP search syntax, specified in RFC-2254. Note that this syntax works with all JNDI providers, not just LDAP; it's the JNDI standard for searching all kinds of directories. The search filter is a String that takes the following general form:

```
(attribute operator value)
```

You can use an asterisk (*) to represent a wildcard. For example, here's how to search for all entries in an LDAP directory:

```
(objectclass=*)
```

A search for all users takes the form of:

```
(objectclass=user)
```

You can also use the wildcard character to represent completion, just like in a Unix shell or a DOS prompt. For example, here's a filter for searching for all users whose first names start with "k":

```
(cn=k*)
```

You can use operators other than equals (=), as in:

```
(revision<24)
```

You can also combine search filters with operators such as AND (&) and OR (|). The way to do this is to wrap the entire expression in parentheses:

```
(&(objectclass=computer)(cn=Billy))
```

Finally, you can nest search expressions:

```
(&(|(objectclass=computer)(objectclass=user))(cn=Billy)))
```

Obviously, the attributes you specify in a search depend on the directory service you are searching.

Search Results

Regardless of how you specify the search criteria, the search() method you call returns a NamingEnumeration of SearchResult objects. There is a SearchResult for each directory entry that matches the search criteria. SearchResult is a direct subclass of Binding that stores a set of Attributes along with the usual name, class name, and object. (As we'll see shortly, the object in a SearchResult may be null, depending on the SearchControls you set.) Since a search operation returns a NamingEnumeration, you must cast the object that the enumeration returns from the next() method to a SearchResult object. Once you're done, you can retrieve attributes with the getAttributes() method and use methods inherited from Binding (and NameClassPair) to get other information about the matching entry.

Search Controls

The search() methods that take a SearchControls object allow you to control how a search operates. You can set the scope of a search, whether the search should return objects, and the maximum amount of time the search should take, among other things. The easiest way to create a SearchControls object is to use the default constructor and then call various set() methods to set particular search properties.

For example, the setSearchScope() method controls where the search should look for matching directory entries. Most of the time, you set the scope of a SearchControls object to search an entire subtree, but you can also limit the search to an object or its children. Table 7-3 lists the available search scopes.

Table 7-3: SearchControls Search Scopes

Scope	Meaning
OBJECT_SCOPE	Searches only the object itself
ONELEVEL_SCOPE	Searches only the children of the search target
SUBTREE_SCOPE	Searches the entire subtree

The setReturningObjFlag() method determines whether the results of a search contain references to the actual directory entries or only the names and class names of the entries. The default behavior is not to return the actual entries, meaning that calling getObject() on a SearchResult returns null.

The SearchControls object also allows you to specify other aspects of the behavior of a search:

- The number of milliseconds to wait for the directory to return the search results (by default, a search can take as long as it takes)
- The number of entries that can be returned from the search (by default, as many as are present)
- Whether to follow links to finish the search (no by default)
- What attributes if any to return (all by default)

In general, the default behavior is typically what you want for these parameters.

A Search Command

Now that we've discussed how the various search( ) methods work, let's look at a real example. Example 7-11 shows the implementation of a *search* command for NamingShell. This example uses the search( ) method that takes the name of the context to be searched, a search filter that describes the search criteria, and a SearchControls object.

Example 7-11: The search Command

```java
import java.util.Vector;
import javax.naming.*;
import javax.naming.directory.*;

class search implements Command {
  public void execute(Context c, Vector v) throws CommandException {

    if (NamingShell.getCurrentContext() == null)
      throw new CommandException(new Exception(), "No current context");
    else if (v.isEmpty())
      throw new CommandException(new Exception(), "No filter specified");
    String filter = (String)v.firstElement();
    try {
      SearchControls cons = new SearchControls();
      cons.setSearchScope(SearchControls.SUBTREE_SCOPE);
      NamingEnumeration results = ((DirContext)c).search("", filter, cons);
      while (results.hasMore()) {
        SearchResult result = (SearchResult)results.next();
        System.out.println(result.getName());
      }
    }
    catch (InvalidSearchFilterException isfe) {
      throw new CommandException(isfe,
      "The filter [" + filter + "] is invalid");
    }
    catch (NamingException e) {
      throw new CommandException(e, "The search for " + filter + " failed");
    }
    catch (ClassCastException cce) {
      throw new CommandException(cce, "Not a directory context");
    }
  }

  public void help() { System.out.println("Usage: search filter"); }
}
```

The *search* command always starts searching in the current context, so you need to move to the appropriate location in the directory service using *cd* before you use *search*. *search* requires you to specify a search filter as its first argument. Note that you can't use any spaces in the filter, or the filter will be parsed as multiple arguments and therefore not work. Here's how to use the *search* command:

```
o=Novell% search (&(objectclass=person)(cn=a*))
cn=admin
```

```
cn=admin,ou=cook1,ou=user
cn=admin,ou=fj,ou=user
cn=admin,ou=Stanford,ou=user
cn=admin,ou=Ed Reed,ou=user
cn=admin,ou=antimony,ou=user
cn=admin,ou=keaves,ou=user
cn=admin,ou=acme,ou=user
cn=admin,ou=nld,ou=user
cn=admin,ou=wibble,ou=user
cn=admin,ou=xxx,ou=user
cn=admin,ou=piet,ou=user
cn=admin,ou=adamtest1,ou=user
cn=admin,ou=novell,ou=user
...
```

Event Notification

In addition to finding, browsing, searching, and altering objects stored in a naming or directory service, the JNDI API also supports the concept of event notification. This involves registering listeners for various types of events that may occur in a naming/directory server. This functionality is provided through the `javax.naming.event` package.

Essentially, JNDI event notification is similar to other event models in the Java platform: you obtain a reference to an event source, and then register an event listener with the source. When the specified events fire in the event source, notifications are made by invoking callback methods on the event listeners.

Event Sources

Event sources in JNDI are represented by special subclasses of `Context` and `DirContext`: `EventContext` and `EventDirContext`, both from the `javax.naming.event` package. These interfaces provide the additional functionality required to register event listeners with a naming/directory service. Acquiring a reference to an event source is simply a matter of casting a returned `Context` or `DirContext`. For example, if we wanted to get an event source for the "person" branch of a directory service:

```
Context ctx = new InitialContext(props).lookup("ou=person");
EventDirContext evCtx = (EventDirContext)ctx;
```

In order to take advantage of event notification, the JNDI provider (and the underlying naming or directory service) needs to support event notification, and its `Context` implementations need to implement the `EventContext` and/or `EventDirContext` interfaces. If the provider doesn't support event notification, the cast in the second line of the previous example fails with a `ClassCastException`. There is a more fault-tolerant way to check for event notification support:

```
Context ctx = new InitialContext(props).lookup("ou=People");
if (ctx instanceof EventDirContext) {
```

```
    // Register listeners with directory event source
    ...
}
else if (ctx instanceof EventContext) {
    // Register listeners with naming event source
    ...
}
else {
    // No event notification support
    System.out.println("Sorry, provider doesn't support event
notification");
}
```

The LDAP provider supplied with Sun's JDK 1.3 and 1.4 does support event notification, so the remainder of our examples will assume that we're accessing LDAP services.

Writing Event Listeners

Once you have an event source from your naming/directory service, you can register listeners for various events. Event listeners in JNDI are simply classes that implement the NamingListener interface. This interface acts as the base interface for the other types of listeners supported by JNDI, which we'll discuss next. It also supports handling errors that occur in the naming service. If you register a listener with the naming service and the service then encounters some error that will prevent it from notifying you of events, it makes you aware of the error by calling the namingExceptionThrown() callback on the NamingListener interface.

There are two types of events that can occur in a naming or directory service. The first involves changes relative to the namespace of the service, i.e., when objects are added or removed from a naming service, or an object's name in the service is changed. The second type of event involves changes relative to the actual objects stored in the naming service, i.e., when an object's binding in the naming service has been changed, or its attributes (in a directory service) have been altered.

To match these two types of events, there are two subclasses of NamingListener provided in JNDI: NamespaceChangeListener and ObjectChangeListener. To be notified of changes in the namespace, create an implementation of the NamespaceChangeListener interface and register it with an event source. There are three event notification callbacks on this interface that you can implement. The objectAdded() method is called when a new object is added to the namespace, objectRemoved() is called when any object is removed, and objectRenamed() is called when an object's binding in the namespace is changed. A very simple NamespaceChangeListener implementation is shown in Example 7-12. This listener simply logs events to standard output as they occur.

Example 7-12: Listener for Namespace Changes

```
import javax.naming.*;
import javax.naming.event.*;

public class NamespaceChangeLogger implements NamespaceChangeListener {
    // Default constructor
```

Example 7-12: Listener for Namespace Changes (continued)

```
public NamespaceChangeLogger() {}

// Callback for object addition events
public void objectAdded(NamingEvent ev) {
  Binding b = ev.getNewBinding();
  System.out.println("--> ADD: Object of type " + b.getClassName() +
                     " added at binding \"" + b.toString() + "\"");
}

// Callback for object removal events
public void objectRemoved(NamingEvent ev) {
  Binding b = ev.getOldBinding();
  System.out.println("--> REMOVE: Object of type " + b.getClassName() +
                     " removed from binding \"" + b.toString() + "\"");
}

// Callback for object addition events
public void objectRenamed(NamingEvent ev) {
  Binding bNew = ev.getNewBinding();
  Binding bOld = ev.getOldBinding();
  System.out.println("--> RENAME: Object of type " + bNew.getClassName() +
                     " renamed from binding \"" + bOld.toString() +
                     "\" to binding \"" + bNew.toString() + "\"");
}

// Callback for errors in the naming service
public void namingExceptionThrown(NamingExceptionEvent ev) {
  System.out.println(
                  "--> ERROR: An error occurred in the naming service:");
  ev.getException().printStackTrace();
}
}
```

Each event notification callback takes a single NamingEvent argument. NamingEvent is a subclass of the generic java.util.EventObject class that is the base class for events in the AWT event model and the JavaBeans event model. A NamingEvent, as the name implies, contains information describing an event that occurred in the naming service. The getOldBinding() and getNewBinding() methods return Binding objects that indicate the state of the affected object's binding before and after the event. In the case of add events, the old binding is null; in the case of removal events, the new binding is null. The NamingEvent interface also allows you to access the EventContext that fired the event. In our example listener, we simply log the old and/or new binding when we are notified of add, remove, or change events.

In the case of errors encountered by the naming service, the namingContext-Thrown() callback will be called on our listener and given a NamingExceptionEvent. This is another subclass of EventObject; NamingExceptionEvent wraps a NamingException that has been thrown within the naming service. In our example, when a naming error occurs, we simply log it to standard output, and print out the stack trace for the NamingException enclosed in the NamingExceptionEvent.

Changes to objects in the naming service are tracked using an implementation of the ObjectChangeListener interface. Creating an ObjectChangeListener is similar to the NamespaceChangeListener: create a subclass that includes concrete implementations of the notification callbacks defined in the interface. For ObjectChangeListener, there is only one event callback to implement: objectChanged(). You also need to implement namingExceptionThrown() to handle any errors. Example 7-13 shows an example of an ObjectChangeListener implementation.

Example 7-13: Listener for Object Change Events

```
import javax.naming.*;
import javax.naming.event.*;

public class ObjectChangeLogger implements ObjectChangeListener {
  // Default constructor
  public ObjectChangeLogger() {}

  // Callback for object change events
  public void objectChanged(NamingEvent ev) {
    Binding bNew = ev.getNewBinding();
    Binding bOld = ev.getOldBinding();
    System.out.println("--> CHANGE: Object of type " + bNew.getClassName() +
                       " changed, previous binding = \"" + bOld.toString() +
                       "\" post-change binding = \"" + bNew.toString() + "\"");
  }

  // Callback for errors in the naming service
  public void namingExceptionThrown(NamingExceptionEvent ev) {
    System.out.println(
              "--> ERROR: An error occurred in the naming service:");
    ev.getException().printStackTrace();
  }
}
```

Of course, you could also create a single listener that receives both namespace change events and object change events by simply implementing both listener interfaces with a single class.

Registering Event Listeners

Event listeners are registered with an event source by specifying a target (the subset of objects in the naming service for which you want notifications), along with the listener that should receive the notifications. This is done using the addNamingListener() methods available on the EventContext and EventDir-Context interfaces.

The target objects for a listener can be specified in a few different ways. To define a subset of objects based strictly on their bindings and parent-child relationships in the naming service, you can use the addNamingListener() methods on the

EventContext interface. With these registration methods, the target of a listener is specified by providing the name of an object (in the form of either a string or a Name object) and a scope. The name is simply a valid binding within the naming service being used—in an LDAP directory it is an X.500-style name such as "ou=people,cn=Smith, John". The scope is indicated by one of three static constants defined on the EventContext interface, with the following meanings:

OBJECT_SCOPE

Limit the target to just the named object or context.

ONELEVEL_SCOPE

Limit the target to the children of the named context, excluding the context itself. The name must refer to a context when this scope is used.

SUBTREE_SCOPE

Extend the target to include the entire subtree of the naming hierarchy, starting at (and including) the named object or context.

So, for example, if we wanted to listen for object-change events on the entry for "John Smith" in our LDAP directory, we would register one of our ObjectChangeLogger listeners like so:

```
EventContext ctx = (EventContext)(new InitialContext());
ObjectChangeLogger ocLogger = new ObjectChangeLogger();
ctx.addNamingListener("ou=people,cn=Smith, John",
                      EventContext.OBJECT_SCOPE, ocLogger;
```

If we wanted to be notified for any changes in the namespace in the entire context starting with "John Smith," we might do this:

```
NamespaceChangeLogger ncLogger = new NamespaceChangeLogger();
ctx.addNamingListener("ou=people,cn=Smith, John",
                      EventContext.SUBTREE_SCOPE, ncLogger);
```

It's also possible to use more elaborate filters to specify the target of your listener, using the EventDirContext interface and its overloaded versions of addNamingListener(). In these versions, specify the name of an object or context as before, but instead of a simple scope value, specify a search filter that defines the subset of the naming service that you want to target. Specifying your notification target this way is very similar to performing a search on a directory service using the DirContext.search() method. The search filter takes the form of a filter string, an optional set of filter arguments (in the form of an Object array), and a set of search controls (in the form of a SearchControls object). So if we wanted to listen for object change events on any objects in the "people" branch with a surname of "Jim," we could do the following:

```
EventDirContext dirCtx = (EventDirContext)(new InitialContext());
ObjectChangeLogger ocLogger = new ObjectChangeLogger();
SearchControls sctl = new SearchControls();
sctl.setSearchScope(SearchControl.SUBTREE_SCOPE);
dirCtx.addNamingListener("ou=people", "(sn=Jim)", sctl, ocLogger);
```

Notice that in this case, we specify the scope of the target using the setSearchScope() method on the SearchControls that we provide with the filter.

A listen command

Returning to our `NamingShell` example, we can use the event notification features of JNDI to add a listen command to our shell. We can use this command to register listeners for events in the naming service. First, we'll create a single listener that can be registered for both namespace events and object events, by implementing both the `NamespaceChangeListener` and `ObjectChangeListener` interfaces. This listener, `AnyChangeLogger`, is just a merging of the two listeners we created in the previous section, and is shown in Example 7-14.

Example 7-14: Listener for Any Naming Events

```
import javax.naming.*;
import javax.naming.event.*;

public class AnyChangeLogger
  implements NamespaceChangeListener, ObjectChangeListener {
  // Default constructor
  public AnyChangeLogger() {}

  //
  // NamespaceChangeListener methods
  //

  // Callback for object addition events
  public void objectAdded(NamingEvent ev) {
    Binding b = ev.getNewBinding();
    System.out.println("--> ADD: Object of type " + b.getClassName() +
                    " added at binding \"" + b.toString() + "\"");
  }

  // Callback for object removal events
  public void objectRemoved(NamingEvent ev) {
    Binding b = ev.getOldBinding();
    System.out.println("--> REMOVE: Object of type " + b.getClassName() +
                    " removed from binding \"" + b.toString() + "\"");
  }

  // Callback for object rename events
  public void objectRenamed(NamingEvent ev) {
    Binding bNew = ev..getNewBinding();
    Binding bOld = ev.getOldBinding();
    System.out.println("--> RENAME: Object of type " + bNew.getClassName() +
                    " renamed from binding \"" + bOld.toString() +
                    "\" to binding \"" + bNew.toString() + "\"");
  }

  //
  // ObjectChangeListener methods
  //

  // Callback for object change events
  public void objectChanged(NamingEvent ev) {
```

Example 7-14: Listener for Any Naming Events (continued)

```
    Binding bNew = ev.getNewBinding();
    Binding bOld = ev.getOldBinding();
    System.out.println("--> CHANGE: Object of type " + bNew.getClassName() +
                       " changed, previous binding = \"" + bOld.toString() +
                       "\" post-change binding = \"" + bNew.toString() + "\"");
  }

  // Callback for errors in the naming service
  public void namingExceptionThrown(NamingExceptionEvent ev) {
    System.out.println(
        "--> ERROR: An error occurred in the naming service:");
    ev.getException().printStackTrace();
  }
}
```

Our *listen* command takes one required argument, the name of the target object or context, and an optional search filter argument that can further define the target of the listener. The command class is shown in Example 7-15.

Example 7-15: The listen Command

```
import java.util.Vector;
import javax.naming.*;
import javax.naming.event.*;
import javax.naming.directory.*;

class listen implements Command {
  public void execute(Context c, Vector v) throws CommandException {

    if (NamingShell.getCurrentContext() == null)
      throw new CommandException(new Exception(), "No current context");
    else if (v.isEmpty())
      throw new CommandException(new Exception(), "No target specified");
    String name = (String)v.firstElement();
    String filter = null;
    if (v.size() > 1) {
      filter = (String)v.elementAt(1);
    }

    try {
      // Cast context to an event context
      EventContext evCtx = (EventContext)c;
      // Create our listener
      NamingListener listener = new AnyChangeLogger();
      // If no filter specified, just register a listener using EventContext
      if (filter == null) {
        evCtx.addNamingListener(name, EventContext.OBJECT_SCOPE, listener);
      }
      // If we have a filter, use the EventDirContext to specify the target
      else {
        EventDirContext evDirCtx = (EventDirContext)c;
```

JNDI

Example 7-15: The listen Command (continued)

```
        evDirCtx.addNamingListener(name, filter, null, listener);
      }
      System.out.println("Registered listener for " + name +
                        (filter != null ? (" and filter " + filter) : ""));
    }
    catch (ClassCastException cce) {
      cce.printStackTrace();
      throw new CommandException(cce,
                "The current context does not support event notification.");
    }
    catch (NamingException e) {
      throw new CommandException(e, "The search for " + filter + " failed");
    }
  }

  public void help() { System.out.println("Usage: listen name [filter]"); }
}
```

The execute( ) method checks the incoming command arguments to see what kind of target is being specified. If just a single argument is given, it's assumed to be the name of the object or context target, and we use the EventContext interface to register one of our listeners. If a second argument is provided, it's assumed to be a search filter string, and we user the EventDirContext interface to register the listener using both the name and filter to specify the target. If we are unable to cast the current Context to an EventContext or EventDirContext, then we assume that the naming service doesn't support event notification, and report that to the user by throwing a CommandException.

With this command, we can use the NamingShell to register listeners in our naming service. For example, if we're connected to an LDAP-based person directory and want to listen for any events surrounding a person with a UID of "jsmith":

```
> java oreilly.jent.jndi.NamingShell
Created initial context using jndi.properties
/% cd ou=People
Current context now ou=People
ou=People% listen uid=jsmith
Registered listener for uid=jsmith
ou=People%
```

CHAPTER 8

Enterprise JavaBeans (EJB)

The introduction of RMI and JavaBeans to the core Java APIs brought a standard distributed object framework and a component model to Java. The Enterprise Java-Beans (EJB*) architecture builds on these foundations to provide a standard *distributed component model.*

So, you may ask, how are EJB components different from regular distributed objects built using RMI or local (nondistributed) components defined using the JavaBeans component model? Well, they aren't, in a sense. An EJB component has the remote capabilities of an RMI or CORBA object, in the sense that it can be exported as a remote object using RMI or RMI/IIOP. An EJB component is also a JavaBeans component, since it has properties that can be introspected, and it uses JavaBeans conventions for defining accessor methods for its properties. An EJB is much more than the sum of these parts, however. The EJB architecture provides a framework in which the enterprise bean developer can easily take advantage of transaction processing, security, persistence, and resource-pooling facilities provided by an EJB environment. These facilities don't come for free, of course. You need to understand how they work and what rules your EJB object needs to follow in order to take advantage of these services.

Enterprise JavaBeans are useful in any situation where regular distributed objects are useful. They excel, however, in situations that take advantage of the compo-nent nature of EJB objects and the other services that EJB objects can provide with relative ease, such as transaction processing and persistence. A good example is an online banking application. A user sitting at home wants to connect to all of her financial accounts, no matter where and with whom they may live, and see them tied together into one convenient interface. The EJB component architecture allows the various financial institutions to export user accounts as different

* For the sake of space on the page, strain on your eyes, and our time on the keyboard, we're going to abbreviate "Enterprise JavaBeans" as "EJB" throughout this chapter. We hope you don't mind.

implementations of a common Account interface, just as we would do with other distributed object APIs. But since the Account objects are also EJBs, we can use the EJB server's transaction management capabilities to implement the Accounts as transactional components, which allows the client to perform a number of account operations within a single transaction, and then either commit them all or roll them back. This can be a critical feature in financial applications, especially if you need to ensure that a supporting transfer can be executed before a withdrawal request is submitted. The transactional support in EJB ensures that if an error occurs during the transfer and an exception is raised, the entire transaction can be rolled back, and the client-side application can inform you of the reason. And of course, an application such as this may also take advantage of any of the other EJB-related component services.

The EJB component model insulates applications and beans (for the most part) from the details of the component services included in the specification. A benefit of this separation is the ability to deploy the same enterprise bean under different conditions, as needed by specific applications. The parameters used to control a bean's transactional nature, persistence, resource pooling, and security management are specified in separate *deployment descriptors*, and not embedded in the bean implementation or the client application code. So, when a bean is deployed in a distributed application, the properties of the deployment environment (client load levels, database configuration, etc.) can be accounted for and reflected in the settings of the bean's deployment options.

The EJB API is a standard extension to Java, available in the javax.ejb package and its subpackages. You have to explicitly install this extension API in order to write code against the EJB interfaces. You can find the latest version of the API at *http://java.sun.com/products/ejb/*. You should also note that EJB is just a specification for how distributed components should work within the Java environment. In order to actually create and use EJB objects, you need to install an EJB-enabled server. A J2EE-compliant application server will provide this service, and will be bundled with the standard EJB API classes and interfaces.

Finally, it's important to note that this chapter provides only a basic introduction to Enterprise JavaBeans, which is an extensive specification with many features. For more complete coverage, see *Enterprise JavaBeans,* by Richard Monson-Haefel (O'Reilly).

A Note on Evolving Standards

For the most part, the information and code examples in this chapter are based on Version 2.0 of the Enterprise JavaBeans specification, released in August 2001. The code examples have been tested in two different EJB servers for compatibility: BEA's WebLogic application server (Version 6.1) and the J2EE Reference Implementation provided by Sun (Version 1.3).

Although the current released version of the EJB specification is 2.0, at the time of this writing most application servers still support the earlier EJB 1.1 specification. The EJB 2.0 specification added some significant features (local interfaces for EJBs, a new model for container-managed persistence, message-driven EJBs, etc.), and it has taken the J2EE vendors time to bring their products up to the current spec. Another reason for the delay in supporting EJB 2.0 is due to the larger J2EE specification. J2EE 1.2 specifies that compliant servers implement EJB 1.1, while J2EE 1.3 specifies EJB 2.0. So, in order for a J2EE server vendor to add EJB 2.0 support to their product, he typically needs to bring his entire J2EE support level up to the 1.3 spec, which involves updating implementations for a number of other APIs as well (JSP, Java Servlets, etc.). Since EJB 1.1 support is still fairly prevalent in the industry for these reasons, this chapter also makes mention of the valid EJB features in both versions of the spec, which are 2.0 only, and where code would need to be modified to function in an EJB 1.1 container.

EJB Roles

In Chapter 3, we described two fundamental roles in the RMI environment: the client of the remote object, and the object itself, which acts as a kind of server or service provider. These two roles exist in the EJB environment as well, but EJB adds a third role, called the *container provider*. This is responsible for implementing all the extra services for an EJB object mentioned earlier: transaction processing, security, object persistence, and resource pooling. If you're familiar with CORBA, you can think of the EJB container as being roughly equivalent to the ORB in CORBA, with a few of the CORBA services thrown in as well. In EJB, however, the container is strictly a server-side entity. The client doesn't need its own container to use EJB objects, but an EJB object needs to have a container in order to be exported for client use. Figure 8-1 shows a conceptual diagram of how the three EJB roles interact with each other.

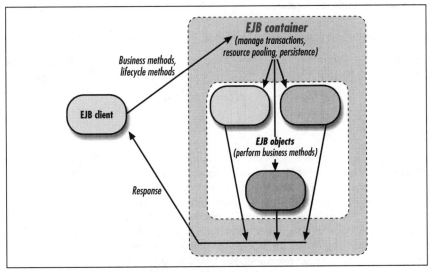

Figure 8-1: The basic roles in an EJB environment

The EJB Client

An EJB client uses remote EJB objects to access data, perform tasks, and generally get things done. In the EJB environment, the first action a client performs is to find the home interface for a type of EJB object that it wants to use. This home interface is a kind of object factory, used to create new instances of the EJB type, look up existing instances (only when using entity EJB objects, discussed later), and delete EJB objects. This is a bit different from RMI, where the client first has to get a direct handle to an existing RMI servant. In many RMI applications, this first RMI object is a kind of object factory that is used to create other RMI object references. So, in a sense, the use of home interfaces in EJB is just formalizing the role of factory objects in distributed component applications.

EJB home interfaces are located by clients using JNDI, the same way that other J2EE resources like JDBC `DataSources` and JMS `ConnectionFactory` resources are accessed. An EJB server publishes the home interface for a particular EJB object under a particular name in a JNDI namespace. The EJB client needs to connect to the JNDI server and look up the EJB home interface under the appropriate name in order to start things off.

We'll see concrete examples of EJB clients a bit later in the chapter, but the following is a summary of the fundamental steps an EJB client performs:

1. Gets a JNDI context from the EJB/J2EE server
2. Uses this context to look up a home interface for the bean you want to use
3. Uses this home interface to create (or find) a reference to an EJB
4. Calls methods on the bean

The Enterprise JavaBeans Object

If you develop your own EJB object, you typically need to provide three Java interfaces/classes in order to fully describe your EJB object to an EJB container:

- A bean interface (remote and/or local versions)
- A home interface (remote and/or local versions)
- An enterprise bean implementation

Depending on the type of EJB you are developing, there may be more or fewer classes and interfaces you'll need to provide (e.g, primary key classes for certain entity EJBs, message-driven beans that don't require home interfaces, etc.), but the items just listed are a typical set for most session and entity EJBs. The bean interface defines the externally callable operations on the EJB. The EJB's remote interface specifies the operations that remote clients can call on the bean, while the local interface specifies the operations that local clients (other EJBs, JavaBeans or servlets running within the same Java VM) can call on the bean. Note that local home and bean interfaces are a feature added in EJB 2.0, in order to provide an efficient means for components running in the same JVM to access EJBs. Prior to that EJB 2.0, EJBs could only have remote interfaces, and could only be accessed using remote interfaces. A client (local or remote) issues method requests through a stub derived from the bean interface and eventually these requests make their way to the corresponding bean instance running within the EJB container. The home interface acts as a bean factory, providing a way for a client to create, locate, and destroy EJB objects that it uses.

The following is a remote client interface for a `Person` bean that has a single name property:

```
import javax.ejb.*;
import java.rmi.Remote;
import java.rmi.RemoteException;

public interface Person extends EJBObject {
    // Access the person's name
    public String getName() throws RemoteException;
    public String setName() throws RemoteException;
}
```

This interface shows the business methods that are available to remote clients. When a client gets a reference to a bean through the remote home interface for this bean, it is given a stub that implements this `Person` interface. In EJB 2.0, it's also possible to provide a local interface for an EJB, which offers an efficient nonremote interface for clients that are located with the EJBs they are trying to access.

Here is an example remote home interface for the `Person` bean just shown:

```
import javax.ejb.*;
import java.rmi.RemoteException;

// The "home" interface for the PersonBean.  This interface provides
// methods used to create beans on the server.  The container provider is
// responsible for implementing this interface, most likely using
// auto-generated Java classes derived from the interface bytecodes.
public interface PersonHome extends EJBHome {
    // Create a new (nameless) person
    public Person create() throws CreateException, RemoteException;
    // Create a named person.
    public Person create(String name)
        throws CreateException, RemoteException;

    // Lookup a Person by name (the primary key)
    public Person findByPrimaryKey(String key)
        throws RemoteException, FinderException;
}
```

This home interface includes methods to create `Person` beans and to find them if they already exist on the server.

The EJB object implementation needs to implement all the business methods exposed in its remote and local interfaces, plus some methods used by the container to tell it about various events in its lifetime. The EJB object doesn't need to directly implement or extend the remote or local interface, which is another new twist compared to RMI, where the server object always implements the remote interface. In EJB, the container arranges for method calls on the bean interface to be transferred to the EJB object. You just need to ensure that the EJB object has methods that match the signatures of the methods in the client interface(s). We'll see an example of EJB object implementations a bit later.

Home and client interfaces to the EJB are provided strictly for the sake of the client, and allow the client to create EJB objects and call methods on them. The bean implementation class, on the other hand, implements functionality not only to support these client-accessible methods, but also for the sake of the EJB container, to allow it to notify the EJB object about transaction- and persistence-related events, for example.

In addition to the interfaces that describe the EJB component type, an EJB component also provides a *deployment descriptor* to its container. The deployment descriptor tells the container the name to use for registering the bean's home interface in JNDI, how to manage transactions for the bean, the access rights that remote identities are given to invoke methods on the EJB, how persistence of the EJB objects should be handled, declares references to resources that the EJB uses in its implementation, and offers a number of other parameters concerning how the EJB should be managed by the container. The container does all the heavy lifting with regard to providing these services, but the EJB object has to tell the container how it would prefer to have these services managed.

Types of EJBs: Session, entity and message-driven

There are three fundamental types of Enterprise JavaBeans: *session*, *entity*, and *message-driven*. The key difference between these component models lies in how they are managed during their lifetime by the EJB container, and what component services are available to them through the container.

A session bean is typically accessed by one single client at a time and is nonpersistent. It lives for a specific period of time (a session), and then gets removed by the server. An entity bean, on the other hand, represents a data entity stored in persistent storage (e.g., a database or filesystem). Entity EJBs that represent the same persistent entity can be accessed by multiple clients concurrently and are persistent beyond a client session or the lifetime of the EJB server. Message-driven beans are a new type of EJB introduced in EJB 2.0. They use the JMS API to support asynchronous interactions between clients and beans, in which a client uses indirect messages to invoke operations on beans rather than synchronous method calls.

To illustrate the differences between session, entity, and message beans, suppose you're building an online banking system using EJB components. An automated bank teller, which reports on account balances and executes deposits and withdrawals on specified accounts, could be implemented as a session bean. A single client uses the teller bean to perform services on bank accounts that are maintained in some separate persistent store (the bank's database). An EJB object that directly represents a bank account, however, should be an entity bean. Multiple clients can access the account to perform transactions, and the state of the account entity should be persistent across the lifetime of the online banking server. If we want to provide wireless access to the banking system from PDAs or mobile phones, we might have these devices communicate with the system using lightweight, asynchronous messaging, since their network connectivity is typically unstable and low bandwidth. This may lead us to use message-driven EJBs, which can respond to these client messages but still take advantage of the lifecycle management capabilities of the EJB container.

The EJB Container

Most readers need to be familiar only with EJB containers from the perspective of an EJB client or an EJB object. For example, a J2EE application server that you might use to deploy an EJB-based application provides an internal EJB container, along with other required aspects of the J2EE framework. EJB-enabled application servers, with their own EJB containers and deployment tools, are available from BEA, IBM, Sun/iPlanet, and many others.

The EJB container implements the value-added features that EJB provides over standard remote objects built using RMI or CORBA. The EJB container manages the lifecycle of your EJBs and the details of transactional processing, security, resource pooling, and data persistence, which reduces the burden on client applications and EJB objects and allows them to deal with just the business at hand.

An EJB container is the heart of an EJB environment, in the same way that an ORB is the heart of a CORBA environment. The container registers EJB objects for client access, manages transactions between clients and EJB objects, provides access control over specific methods on the EJB, and manages the creation, pooling, and destruction of enterprise beans. The container also registers the home interface for each type of bean under a given name in a JNDI namespace, allowing clients to find the home interfaces and use them to create enterprise beans.

Once you provide the EJB container with the home and client interfaces, the implementation class for your bean, and a deployment descriptor, the container is responsible for generating the various classes that connect these components, as shown in Figure 8-2. The home and client interfaces are provided by the developer; the container generates both the client and the server-side implementations for these interfaces, as needed. As the figure shows, EJBs can support both local and remote clients (EJB 1.1 supports only remote clients; EJB 2.0 introduced the concept of local clients and supports local interfaces for them). When a remote client looks up a bean's remote home interface through JNDI, it receives an instance of a remote stub class. All methods invoked on this stub are remotely invoked, via RMI or IIOP, on the corresponding home implementation object on the EJB server. Similarly, if the client creates or finds any beans through the remote home stub, the client receives remote object stubs, and methods invoked on the stubs are passed through RMI to corresponding implementation objects on the server. These remote objects are linked, through the EJB container, to a corresponding enterprise bean object, which is an instance of your bean-implementation class. Local clients interact with EJBs in a simplified, and therefore more efficient, way. Home objects and bean interfaces are obtained the same way as remote ones, but the objects that are obtained are nonremote objects that interact locally with their implementations within the EJB container.

It's important to remember that all client requests to create, look up, delete, or call methods on EJBs are mediated by the EJB container. It either handles them itself or passes the requests to corresponding methods on the EJB object. Once the

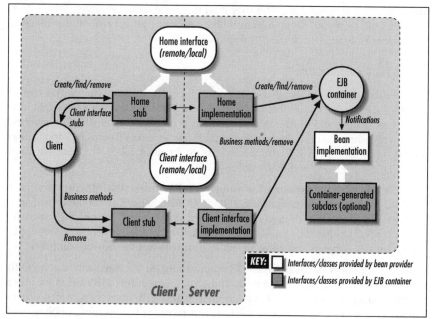

Figure 8-2: Relationship of bean-provider classes and container-generated classes

client obtains a reference to an interface for an EJB object, the container intercedes in all method calls on the bean, to provide the bean with required transaction management and security measures. The container also provides support for persistence of enterprise beans, either by storing/loading the bean state itself or by notifying the bean that it needs to store or reload its state from persistent storage.

A container can maintain multiple EJB objects and object types during its lifetime. The container has some freedom to manage resources on the server for performance or other reasons. For example, a container can choose to temporarily serialize a bean and store it to the server filesystem or some other persistent store; this is called *passivating* a bean. The EJB object is notified of this and given a chance to release any shared resources or transient data that shouldn't be serialized. The bean is also notified after it is activated again, to allow it to restore any transient state or reopen shared resources.

When you deploy an EJB object within an EJB server, you can specify how the container should manage the bean during runtime, in terms of transaction management, resource pooling, access control, and data persistence. This is done using deployment descriptors, which contain parameter settings for these various options. These settings can be customized for each deployment of an EJB object. You might purchase an EJB object from a vendor and deploy it on your EJB server with a particular set of container management options, while someone else who purchased the same bean can deploy it with a different set of deployment options. We discuss the details of the runtime options available in deployment descriptors and how to use them later in this chapter when we talk about deploying EJB components.

Implementing a Basic EJB

Now it's time to discuss actually implementing an Enterprise JavaBeans component. If you are creating either an entity or a session bean, there are three Java interfaces/classes you need to provide:

Home interfaces
> This is accessed directly by clients and used to create and/or find EJB objects of a specific type. An EJB can have both local and remote home interfaces, though in most cases only one or the other is needed, based on the context in which the EJB is being deployed.

Client interfaces
> The interface (local or remote) for the bean is also accessed directly by clients. When a client creates or finds an EJB object through a home interface, it is given a reference to a stub that implements the interface for the bean. The interface defines the methods the EJB object exports to clients. As with home interfaces, an EJB can have both local and remote bean interfaces.

Bean implementation
> The EJB object implementation itself must implement all the methods defined in its remote and local interfaces, provide methods that correspond to the methods on its home interface for creating and/or finding the bean, and also implement the methods used by the EJB container to manage the bean.

Message-driven beans require the bean implementation class only. They don't have home interfaces or client interfaces since the client interface is implemented using JMS message-passing—we'll see more details on creating and using message-driven beans later in the chapter.

To demonstrate the various components that make up an Enterprise JavaBeans object, we'll look at a simple example: a profile server. The *profile server* is a bean that provides profile information for named users. This profile information consists of name/value pairs that might represent preferences in an application, historical usage patterns, etc. You might see a profile server running behind an online information service, allowing users to personalize the content and appearance of the site when they enter. After we've gone through this general example of writing a bean, we'll look more closely at the differences between implementing session and entity beans.

Client Interfaces

You usually start putting together an EJB by defining its client interface(s). Client interfaces contain declarations of the methods that are available to clients, and really point to the heart of the purpose of the EJB object. A remote client interface for our ProfileServer is shown in Example 8-1. A remote EJB client interface must extend the javax.ejb.EJBObject interface. EJBObject in turn extends the java.rmi.Remote interface, which makes the remote client interface an RMI remote interface as well.

Example 8-1: Remote Interface for the Profile Server Bean

```
import javax.ejb.*;
import java.rmi.RemoteException;
import java.rmi.Remote;
import oreilly.jent.ejb.*;

public interface ProfileServer extends EJBObject {
  public ProfileBean getProfile(String acctName)
    throws NoSuchPersonException, RemoteException;
}
```

The ProfileServer interface defines a single method, getProfile(), that accepts an account name as its only argument. It returns a ProfileBean object, containing the profile information for the person named. If the person's profile can't be found on the server, a NoSuchPersonException is thrown. This is an application-specific exception whose implementation isn't discussed in this chapter. Since the ProfileServer interface is an RMI remote interface, its methods must throw RemoteException in case some RMI communication problem occurs during a method call. Also, the arguments and return values for the methods have to be Serializable, and/or they need to be exportable RMI objects themselves. Our getProfile() method returns a ProfileBean object, which we'll implement as a Serializable object, as shown in Example 8-2. The ProfileBean is a fairly straightforward JavaBean: it simply has methods that allow you to get and set the profile entry values.

Example 8-2: A Serializable Profile

```
import java.util.*;
import java.io.Serializable;

public class ProfileBean implements Serializable {
  protected Properties mPEntries = new Properties();

  public ProfileBean() {}

  public ProfileBean(String name) {
  mPEntries.put("Name", name);
  }

  public Hashtable getEntries() {
  return (Hashtable)mPEntries.clone();
  }

  public String getEntry(String name) {
  return mPEntries.getProperty(name);
  }

  public void setEntry(String name, String value) {
  mPEntries.put(name, value);
  }
}
```

A local client interface for an EJB is defined in a similar way, but the rules and usage of the interface are different from its remote counterpart. As we've mentioned, local interfaces are used by clients that reside in the same JVM as the EJB itself, so they follow the same argument-passing and return-value rules as normal, nonremote Java classes: objects are passed by reference, basic data types are passed by value. There aren't any remote operations involved in the use of a local interface, so there's no need to ensure that method arguments and return values are Remote or Serializable object types. And methods in a local interface aren't required to throw RemoteException. Local interfaces extend the EJBLocalObject interface, which is a simplified, nonremote interface. A local interface for our profile server is shown in Example 8-3.

Example 8-3: Local Interface for the Profile Server

```
import javax.ejb.*;
import oreilly.jent.ejb.*;

public interface ProfileServerLocal extends EJBLocalObject {
  public ProfileBean getProfile(String acctName)
  throws NoSuchPersonException;
}
```

An EJB implementation class needs to provide implementations for all the methods exposed in its remote and local interfaces.

Home Interfaces

The client needs a way to create a reference to a profile server, so we have to provide a home interface for our bean, as shown in Example 8-4. This provides a single create() method that takes no arguments and returns the bean's remote interface type, ProfileServer.

Example 8-4: Remote Home Interface for the Profile Server Bean

```
import javax.ejb.*;
import java.rmi.RemoteException;

public interface ProfileServerHome extends EJBHome {
  public ProfileServer create() throws CreateException, RemoteException;
}
```

A remote home interface for an EJB object extends the javax.ejb.EJBHome interface. The remote home interface is also an RMI remote interface, since EJBHome extends java.rmi.Remote. The home interface can contain multiple create() methods that take various initialization arguments to create the bean. A corresponding local home interface is shown in Example 8-5.

Example 8-5: Local Home Interface for the Profile Server Bean

```
import javax.ejb.*;

public interface ProfileServerLocalHome extends EJBLocalHome {
```

```
  public ProfileServerLocal create() throws CreateException;
}
```

For each create() method on a home interface, the EJB object implementation must have a matching ejbCreate() method that takes the same arguments. In either remote or local home interfaces, create() methods are required to throw javax.ejb.CreateException, in case some error occurs during the EJB creation process. Create methods (and all other methods) on remote home interfaces must also throw java.rmi.RemoteException (or one of its parent exceptions), since the home interface is an RMI remote interface, and it's possible for some sort of network/communication error to occur between the client and the home implementation on the server. If the corresponding ejbCreate() method on the bean implementation throws any other exceptions, the create() method has to include these in its throws clause as well. As we'll see in our bean implementation in the next section, the bean's ejbCreate() method doesn't throw any special exceptions, so we don't need to add any additional exceptions in the home interfaces.

Home interfaces for entity beans can also include finder methods, used to find previously created existing persistent entity beans. We'll discuss them a bit later, when we talk about entity beans in detail.

The Bean Implementation

Now that we have a home interface that lets clients create EJB references and interfaces that describe what the EJB can do for the client, we need to actually implement the EJB object itself. Our ProfileServerBean is shown in Example 8-6. There are a number of EJB-related methods here, which aren't represented in either the home or client interfaces for this EJB, that serve as the hooks the EJB container uses to manage the bean as a component. The implementation of the getProfile() method from the remote client interface is at the end of the class. The ejbCreate() method is also included here, to match the create() method on the home interface.

Example 8-6: ProfileServer EJB Implementation

```
import javax.ejb.*;
import java.rmi.RemoteException;
import oreilly.jent.ejb.*;

// A stateless EJB implementation of the ProfileServer interface.

public class ProfileServerBean implements SessionBean {
  // Store session context
  private SessionContext mContext = null;

  public ProfileServerBean() {}

  //----------------------------------------------------
  // Session bean methods
  //----------------------------------------------------
```

Example 8-6: ProfileServer EJB Implementation (continued)

```java
// No need for us to activate anything in this bean, but we need to
// provide an implementation.
public void ejbActivate() {
  System.out.println("ProfileServerBean activated.");
}

// Nothing to do on a remove for this bean.
public void ejbRemove() {
  System.out.println("ProfileServerBean removed.");
}

// No state to store on passivation.
public void ejbPassivate() {
  System.out.println("ProfileServerBean passivated.");
}

// Get context from container, store in a member variable.
public void setSessionContext(SessionContext context) {
  System.out.println("ProfileServerBean context set.");
mContext = context;
}

// No-argument create() -- nothing to initialize in this case.
public void ejbCreate() {
  System.out.println("ProfileServerBean created.");
}

//----------------------------------------------------
// Business methods
//----------------------------------------------------

// Get a profile for a named person. Throws NoSuchPersonException if the
// named person cannot be found in the persistent storage used to store
// profile information.
public ProfileBean getProfile(String name) throws NoSuchPersonException {
// Here, we just create one of our serializable Profile objects and return
// it (i.e., no persistence of profile data is provided).
  ProfileBean profile = new oreilly.jent.ejb.stateless.ProfileBean(name);
  return profile;
}
}
```

The implementation class for any EJB object must implement the `javax.ejb.EnterpriseBean` interface. This is usually done indirectly, through either the `SessionBean`, `EntityBean`, or `MessageDrivenBean` interface. These interfaces include the required callback/notification methods that the EJB container needs in order to effectively manage the lifecycle of the EJB at runtime. In our example, we define a session bean, so the `ProfileServerBean` class implements the `SessionBean` interface.

The EJB class must be declared as `public`, to allow the container to introspect the class when generating the classes that hook the bean to the container and to allow the container to invoke methods on the bean directly where necessary. The bean class doesn't implement the bean's remote and/or local interface. This may seem a bit strange at first, especially if you're familiar with remote object systems like RMI and CORBA, since the purpose of the bean is to provide a concrete implementation of the EJB's interfaces, and in these other contexts this is done through direct inheritance. But in an EJB context, the EJB container always mediates between a client method request and the actual call on the corresponding method on a bean instance. As long as the container is explicitly told the EJB's various interfaces and its implementation class (and we'll see how to do that with deployment descriptors in a later section), then it has all the information it needs to make this connection. When the EJB server generates the classes that bridge the bean to the container, it also provides a class that implements the remote interface and acts as a proxy to the EJB class itself.

In fact, for practical reasons, you probably don't want your EJB implementation to directly inherit the remote or local interface for your bean. The remote interface has to extend the EJBObject interface, which includes a set of abstract methods that clients can use to retrieve the bean's home interface, get the primary key for entity beans, etc. When you deploy your bean, you'll use tools provided by the EJB container to generate stub and skeleton classes for the remote interface that implement these methods from EJBObject. If you implement the remote interface with your bean implementation class, you have to provide implementations for the EJBObject methods as well.

All Enterprise JavaBean objects that are session or entity beans must implement the following methods. Message-driven beans have simpler requirements, as described in the section "Implementing Message-Driven Beans":

`public void ejbActivate()`

Called by the container when the bean has been deserialized from passive storage on the server. Allows the bean to reclaim any resources freed during passivation (e.g., file handles, network connections) or restore any other state not explicitly saved when the bean was serialized.

`public void ejbPassivate()`

Called by the container just before the bean is to be serialized and stored in passive storage (e.g., disk, database) on the server. Allows the bean to release any nonserializable resources (e.g., open files, network connections).

`public void ejbCreate(...)`

Called after the client invokes the corresponding create() method on the bean's home interface. The bean and its home interface usually provide at least one create()/ejbCreate() pair to allow the client to create new beans. Session beans are required to provide at least one create method, but create methods are optional on entity beans, since entity beans can also be acquired using finder methods. The container creates the bean object using one of its standard constructors and might create several beans of the same type at server startup to act as a pool for future client requests. The ejbCreate() method indicates that a client is ready to use the bean; the arguments indicate the identity or starting state of the bean. Note that the return type of ejbCreate() methods depends on the component model being used by the EJB. Session and message-driven beans have ejbCreate() methods with a

return type of void, as shown previously. An entity bean's ejbCreate()
methods may return void or its primary key type, depending on the type of
entity bean. For more details, see the section "Implementing Entity Beans".

`public void ejbRemove()`

Called by the container just before the bean is to be removed from the
container and made eligible for garbage collection. Again, the exact semantics of this method depend on the component model of the EJB. "Removing"
a session or a message-driven bean simply pulls the bean out of its active
state before it is actually destroyed by the container. Removing an entity bean
means to delete the bean's persistent state data from the underlying database.

These methods are used by the bean's container to notify the bean of various
changes in its runtime state. In our example, the ProfileServerBean doesn't need
to perform any actions in these methods, so they are implemented as empty
methods that simply print messages to standard output, indicating that they have
been called.

Deploying EJBs

As with web components (servlets and JavaServer Pages), EJB components in the
J2EE environment are packaged into JAR files, and the components are described
and configured within an application server using deployment descriptors that are
included in these JAR files. These deployment descriptors are based on an XML
DTD that is published as part of the EJB specification.

Once you've written the home and remote interfaces and the implementation of
your enterprise bean, you need to deploy your beans in an EJB container, which
involves the following steps:

1. Specify the deployment information and options for your bean, in the form of
   an XML file called an EJB *deployment descriptor.* The information in this
   deployment descriptor includes the names of classes that serve as the client
   interfaces, the home interfaces, and implementation for your EJB, plus transaction support options, access control settings, etc. In addition to the basic
   deployment information, different types of EJBs (session, entity, message-
   passing) require different sets of additional metadata (e.g., data mappings for
   container-managed entity beans and, session timeouts for session EJBs).

2. Generate the container-provided classes shown in Figure 8-2.

3. Package your EJBs into an *ejb-jar* file.

As shown in Figure 8-2, the EJB container generates a set of classes that deploy
your EJB object. It's up to the EJB container to provide a tool or tools for generating these classes. Some may be command-line tools that read a standard EJB
deployment descriptor and generate the needed classes, while others may be GUI
tools that let you control the deployment options of your bean using a visual
interface.

Deployment descriptors

All EJB deployment descriptors include a listing of the Java classes that serve as
the home, client, and implementation classes for a particular EJB. They also

include various metadata about the bean, such as a description, a display name for the bean (useful in application server management interfaces), etc. The general structure for an EJB deployment descriptor is as follows:

```
<? xml version="1.0" ?>
<!DOCTYPE ejb-jar PUBLIC
    '-//Sun Microsystems, Inc.//DTD Enterprise JavaBeans 2.0//EN'
    'http://java.sun.com/dtd/ejb-jar_2_0.dtd'>
>
<ejb-jar>
  <!-- Metadata about the contents of the ejb-jar file ... -->
  ...
  <!-- Provide an element for each EJB contained in the JAR -->
  <enterprise-beans>
    <!-- Describe a session bean -->
    <session>
    ...
    </session>
    <!-- Describe an entity bean -->
    <entity>
    ...
    </entity>
    <!-- Describe a message-driven bean -->
    <message-driven>
    ...
    </message-driven>
  </enterprise-beans>
<!-- Any additional metadata (EJB relationships, assembly info, etc.) -->
  <relationships>
  ...
  </relationships>
  <assembly-descriptor>
  ...
  </assembly-descriptor>
  <ejb-client-jar>
  ...
  </ejb-client-jar>
  ...
</ejb-jar>
```

The EJB descriptor starts with the usual XML preface and a DOCTYPE tag that references the standard DTD for EJB deployment. The top-level element in the deployment descriptor is always an ejb-jar element, and it contains an enterprise-beans element that lists each EJB in the jar. Each entry within the enterprise-beans element contains the deployment information for a single EJB, including the various classes that make up the EJBs implementation, runtime management parameters, etc.

Example 8-7 shows a complete deployment descriptor that describes our ProfileServer EJB.

Example 8-7: Deployment Descriptor for the Profile Server EJB

```xml
<? xml version="1.0" ?>

<!DOCTYPE ejb-jar PUBLIC
    '-//Sun Microsystems, Inc.//DTD Enterprise JavaBeans 2.0//EN'
    'http://java.sun.com/j2ee/dtds/ejb-jar_2_0.dtd'>

<ejb-jar>
  <!-- Description of contents -->
  <description>Introductory EJB Example:
                    Stateless ProfileServer Bean</description>
  <display-name>ProfileServer Bean Example (stateless)</display-name>
  <enterprise-beans>
    <!-- A stateless session profile server EJB -->
    <session>
      <display-name>ProfileServer Bean</display-name>
      <ejb-name>ProfileServerBean</ejb-name>
      <!-- Remote home interface -->
      <home>ProfileServerHome</home>
      <!-- Remote bean interface -->
      <remote>ProfileServer</remote>
      <!-- Local home interface -->
      <local-home>ProfileServerLocalHome</local-home>
      <!-- Local bean interface -->
      <local>ProfileServerLocal</local>
      <!-- Bean implementation class -->
      <ejb-class>ProfileServerBean</ejb-class>
      <session-type>Stateless</session-type>
      <transaction-type>Container</transaction-type>
    </session>
  </enterprise-beans>
  <ejb-client-jar>profileServerClient.jar</ejb-client-jar>
</ejb-jar>
```

We're using the description and display-name elements to provide some text descriptions of the contents within the top-level ejb-jar element. The information contained in these elements might be used by a management console on an application server or within an EJB-enabled IDE.

The enterprise-beans element contains one element for each EJB contained in an EJB JAR. There are three possible subelements of enterprise-beans, one for each type of EJB: session, entity, and message-driven. Our ProfileServer EJB is a session bean, so we use the session element here. Within the session element, we provide a display name for the bean itself, and an ejb-name element that provides a name that can be used to refer to this bean from other J2EE components. Then we specify all of the classes that make up our EJB: the remote home and client interfaces (home and remote), the local home and client interfaces (local-home and local), and the EJB implementation class itself (ejb-class).

At the end of the session element, there is configuration information that is specific to session EJBs. In this case, we are using the session-type element to specify that this is a stateless session bean, and the transaction-type element to indicate that we want transactions managed by the EJB container for this EJB. This information is used primarily by the EJB container to determine how the EJB should be managed at runtime. The information that is specified in this section of the deployment descriptor depends on the type of EJB being described (session, entity, message-driven). There are examples of the kind of metadata required for the various types of EJBs in later sections of this chapter.

Security-Related Deployment Attributes

Security management is another important service provided by the EJB container for your components. Essentially, the EJB container needs to provide some means for mapping a client identity to a named user or role defined on the EJB server itself. Then you, the bean provider, specify which users and/or roles can access each method on your bean. This approach to specifying security details keeps the access details out of the bean implementation code, and allows the same bean to be deployed in different EJB containers, using different underlying security systems and access settings that suit the local context.

Client security roles

The EJB specification allows you to specify security roles and access control levels for these roles in the EJB deployment descriptor. Suppose that we are deploying our EJB-based profile service, and for our current purposes, we want any client at all to be able to read entries off of profiles, but we only want clients (individual users or client applications) identified as administrators to be able to set entries on profiles. To do this, we first have to define an appropriate security role in our EJB deployment descriptor. This is done in the `assembly-descriptor` element, which follows the `enterprise-beans` and `relationships` elements in the root `ejb-jar` element. Within the `assembly-descriptor`, you define a security role using the `security-role` element:

```
...
<assembly-descriptor>
  <security-role>
    <description>
      Profile administrators, allowed to update entries
    </description>
    <role-name>profile-admin</role-name>
  </security-role>
...
```

In order for these security roles to actually mean anything, they need to be assigned to concrete principals and/or groups defined within the security realms of whatever J2EE application server you are using to deploy your EJBs. The specific details of how this is done depends on the particular vendor you are using. In Sun's J2EE Reference Implementation, you would add new users (with an accompanying certificates or password) to the server using the bundled `realmtool` utility, and then refer to these usernames when defining your security roles in your deployment descriptor. In BEA WebLogic, you would create new realms that refer to existing LDAP, RDBMS, native OS and/or custom authentication services, and then map your security roles to principals defined in these realms. Other application servers will provide other schemes for authenticating users and tying their identities into the EJB context.

Method permissions

So far we've declared some application-specific security roles, but we haven't given these roles any rights to invoke methods on our EJBs. To do this, we have to add one or more method-permission elements to the assembly-descriptor. A method-permission element gives a particular role rights to access one or more methods on an EJB.

Suppose we defined a Profile EJB that represents persistent data about a profile. This is an EJB version of the serializable ProfileBean that we used in our stateless session example earlier (this EJB will be shown in detail in later sections). We might have a setEntry() method on this EJB that's used to alter entry values on the Profile, and we might want to only give the profile-admin role the rights to execute the setEntry() method on our Profile bean. If so, then we would use a method-permission element such as:

```
<method-permission>
  <description>
    Only allow profile administrators to set entries on profiles
  </description>
  <role-name>profile-admin</role-name>
  <method>
    <ejb-name>BMPProfileBean</ejb-name>
    <method-name>setEntry</method-name>
  </method>
</method-permission>
```

This allows any user who has the profile-admin role to invoke the setEntry() method on the Profile, while all other client methods on the bean are accessible to everyone. The role-name indicates which role should have access to this method, and the method element(s) indicates the EJB and method that this role can access. Here, we have a single method specified: any method named setEntry on the CMP20ProfileBean EJB defined in this deployment descriptor. If setEntry() is overloaded on our bean, we can be more specific by including the method parameters of the single method we want made accessible:

```
<method-permission>
  <description>
    Only allow profile administrators to set entries on profiles
  </description>
  <role-name>profile-admin</role-name>
  <method>
    <ejb-name>CMP20ProfileBean</ejb-name>
    <method-name>setEntry</method-name>
    <method-params>
      <method-param>java.lang.String</method-param>
      <method-param>java.lang.String</method-param>
    </method-params>
  </method>
</method-permission>
```

You can also give access to all methods on an EJB by using an asterisk * as the value of the method-name element. By default, all methods on all EJBs are accessible to everyone. Any methods not specified in a method-permission element in the deployment descriptor maintain this global accessibility.

Propagating identities

It's also possible in EJB to specify how identities are propagated from your EJB to other EJBs and resources, by indicating which role your EJB will assume when its methods are executed. The identity used to execute the EJB methods will be passed forward when the EJB makes calls to other EJBs or accesses other J2EE resources. This identity will be used to determine access rights to these resources in the same way that the caller's credentials are used to control access to the EJB itself, and so on down the call chain.

To specify the runtime identity used to execute your EJB methods, use the security-identity element in the session, entity, and message-driven sections of the deployment descriptor. The security-identity element allows you to specify either that the methods on the bean will be invoked using the identity of the calling client, or that a specific named security role will be used to invoke the bean methods.

The first option simply passes on the identity of the calling client when an EJB method invokes other EJBs or resources. To specify this option, include the following in the EJB's deployment descriptor section (a session bean is used as the example here):

```
...
<enterprise-beans>
...
  <session>
    ...
    <security-identity>
      <use-caller-identity />
    </security-identity>
    ...
  </session>
  ...
</enterprise-beans>
...
```

This scheme is most appropriate when the client operates in a context where they can be authenticated against a shared authority (e.g., a servlet is the user entry point, and the user is challenged with an HTTP authentication prompt), and the user's identity can be propagated to the EJB container. Note that the use-caller-identity option can't be used with message-driven beans, since there is no path for a user's credentials to be propagated to the EJB container via message destinations. A message-driven bean has to assume its own role when handling messages.

The other alternative is to specify a role under which all invocations of your EJB will be executed. For this, use the run-as option in the security-identity:

```
...
<session>
```

```
...
<security-identity>
  <run-as>
    <role-name>profile-admin</role-name>
  </run-as>
</security-identity>
  ...
</session>
...
```

Here, we're specifying that all method invocations on our EJB will run under the profile-admin role, and also will assume that role's access rights when invoking other EJBs and resources.

Packaging Enterprise JavaBeans

An *ejb-jar* file is the standard packaging format for Enterprise JavaBeans. It is a normal Java archive (JAR) file, created using the standard *jar* utility, but it contains specific files that provide all the information needed for an EJB container to deploy the beans that are contained in the JAR file. An *ejb-jar* file can contain one or more EJBs.

An *ejb-jar* file contains two types of contents:

- The class files for each bean, including their home and client interfaces, and the bean implementations. An *ejb-jar* file can also include container-generated classes (concrete implementations of home and client interfaces, for example).

- Deployment descriptor files, as described in the previous sections. At a minimum, an *ejb-jar* file must include a standard *ejb-jar.xml* file. Different EJB container vendors may also require additional deployment descriptor files that allow you to control vendor-specific aspects of how your EJBs will be managed at runtime.

An *ejb-jar* file is truly a way to package a set of EJBs for deployment in an EJB container; it contains all the information an EJB container requires to manage your EJBs.

The compiled Java classes that make up your EJBs are included in the *ejb-jar* file in package-specific directories, just as in a regular JAR file. The deployment descriptor that describes and configures the EJBs must be included in the *ejb-jar* file as *META-INF/ejb-jar.xml*. So the *ejb-jar* file for our ProfileServer example is laid out as shown in Figure 8-3. The class files in this example sit in the top of the JAR file directory structure, since all of our classes were defined without packages. If they were packaged (which is more traditional practice), then the classes would sit in subdirectories that match their packages.

Some EJB container vendors include a utility to facilitate the creation of *ejb-jar* files from your bean classes. Sun's J2EE reference implementation, for example, provides a *deploytool* that allows you to specify the elements and configuration parameters of your EJBs and automatically generates a complete *ejb-jar* file. It's a simple matter, however, to create an *ejb-jar* using the *jar* utility provided with nearly every JDK implementation. Assuming that you have created a valid *ejb-jar*

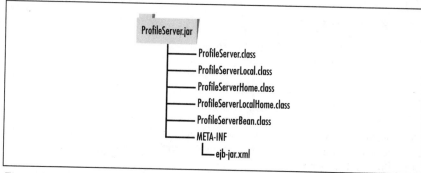

Figure 8-3: *ejb-jar file layout for the ProfileServer EJB*

xml deployment descriptor file, such as the one shown earlier, simply compile all of your relevant classes into a given directory, create a *META-INF* directory in this same area, and put the *ejb-jar.xml* file in it, then use *jar* to create your *ejb-jar* file:

```
% jar cvf ProfileServer.jar *.class META-INF
added manifest
adding: ProfileServer.class(in = 344) (out= 225)(deflated 34%)
adding: ProfileServerBean.class(in = 1254) (out= 598)(deflated 52%)
adding: ProfileServerHome.class(in = 317) (out= 208)(deflated 34%)
adding: ProfileServerLocal.class(in = 327) (out= 214)(deflated 34%)
adding: ProfileServerLocalHome.class(in = 305) (out= 198)(deflated 35%)
ignoring entry META-INF/
adding: META-INF/ejb-jar.xml(in = 0) (out= 0)(stored 0%)
```

This command creates an *ejb-jar* file named *ProfileServer.jar* in the current directory, with the structure shown in Figure 8-3. Note that this *ejb-jar* file doesn't contain any container-generated classes; these need to be created using tools provided by the EJB vendor, as described in the next section.

Generating the Container Classes

So far we've seen the basic elements that make up an EJB (home interface(s), client interface(s), and a bean implementation class), how the configuration parameters for one or more beans are specified in an XML deployment descriptor, and how all of these can be packaged into a standard *ejb-jar* file. In order for an EJB container to deploy your EJBs, it still needs to generate the container-specific classes depicted in Figure 8-2. How this is done depends on the EJB container you are using. Sun's J2EE Reference Implementation, for example, generates the runtime support classes for your EJB(s) when you deploy them to the application server using the graphical *deploytool.* If you are using BEA's WebLogic application server, you can use the ejbc tool that is provided with the server to generate the runtime support classes needed by WebLogic. If we've packaged our EJB classes and deployment descriptor into an *ejb-jar* file named *ProfileServer.jar,* then we could use the ejbc tool like so (for a Unix environment):

```
> java -classpath $WL_HOME/lib/weblogic.jar:$CLASSPATH weblogic.ejbc
ProfileServer.jar wl-ProfileServer.jar
```

If the EJB(s) contained in the specified *ejb-jar* file check out (the interfaces, implementation classes, and deployment descriptor meet the EJB specification requirements), this will generate a new *ejb-jar* file, *wl-ProfileServer.jar*, that contains all the classes need to run your EJB(s) within the WebLogic server. This *ejb-jar* file can be directly deployed to the server.

Each EJB container will have its own scheme for generating support classes for your EJBs. Consult your EJB vendor's documentation for specific details.

Using Enterprise JavaBeans

So far, we've seen the high-level details on implementing and deploying an EJB. Now let's look at how you use an enterprise bean as a client.

It's important to note that a "client" for a given EJB can be many things. In a fairly typical scenario, a client may be a Java servlet or JavaServer Page (JSP), running in the same or different J2EE server as the EJBs being used. A client can also be a standalone GUI client (in J2EE parlance, an "application client") that directly connects to a local or remote EJB container and makes requests of beans. A client can also be another EJB, invoking an EJB on the same or different EJB server in order to satisfy a client request. Regardless of which of these scenarios is the case, the following details apply.

Local Versus Remote Clients

A local client (i.e., a client that resides in the same Java virtual machine as the EJB container) can interact with EJBs using either the local or remote interfaces for the EJB. If the EJB has a local home and client interface, then this provides an efficient way for the client to make requests, since their method calls don't need to be marshalled into a remote method call and transmitted over an RMI or IIOP connection to the EJB container. If the EJB doesn't have a local client and home interface, or if the local interfaces don't expose the functionality that the client needs (remember that local and remote interfaces for the same EJB don't need to be equivalent to each other), then a local client must use its remote home and client interface. Local EJB interfaces were introduced in EJB 2.0, so if you are using EJB 1.1, then your EJBs can only have remote interfaces.

Remote clients (i.e., clients that run in a different Java virtual machine than the EJB container) must use the EJB's remote client and home interfaces. Remote interfaces are RMI client stubs (see Chapter 3 for full details on Java RMI), and the underlying remote method protocol being used can be RMI/JRMP (the "native" RMI protocol), or RMI/IIOP (the CORBA protocol). In order for a client to maintain portability across different EJB implementations, it's important that remote references obtained from the EJB container be cast to their interface types using the narrow() method on javax.rmi.PortableRemoteObject. This ensures that RMI/IIOP remote references will be safely cast to their expected type.

Finding Home Interfaces Through JNDI

Once an enterprise bean is deployed within an EJB container, the home interface(s) for the bean have been exported under a particular name using JNDI according to the settings in the deployment descriptor. As a client, you need to know how to connect to the JNDI context of the EJB/J2EE server and know the name for the bean home interface you're interested in. Full details on using JNDI and the options for creating InitialContexts can be found in Chapter 7, but in general you need to set whatever connection properties are relevant for the JNDI provider you're connecting to, and then create an InitialContext object that points to the root of the naming system:

```
Hashtable props = new Hashtable();
// Specify the necessary properties
...
// Trying looking up the context
javax.naming.Context ctx = null;
try {
  ctx = new javax.naming.InitialContext(props);
}
catch (NamingException ne) {
  System.out.println("Failed to connect to JNDI service for EJB server");
}
```

If you're running within a J2EE environment (e.g, the EJB client is actually a web component running within the same J2EE server), then you typically won't need to specify any connection properties. The J2EE server will be configured so that the default JNDI connection properties point to its internal JNDI service, and you can use the no-argument form of the InitialContext constructor:

```
ctx = new javax.naming.InitialContext();
```

Now that we have a JNDI naming context from the EJB server, we can look up the home interface for the bean we're interested in. Assuming that we deployed our bean and specified to the EJB container that its JNDI name should be "ProfileServerHome", we can obtain a reference to a home interface to the bean with code such as the following:

```
ProfileServerHome pHome = null;
try {
  Object pRef = ctx.lookup("ProfileServerHome");
  pHome =
    (ProfileServerHome)PortableRemoteObject.narrow(pRef,
                                       ProfileServerHome.class);
}
catch (NamingException ne) {
  System.out.println("Failed to lookup home for ProfileServer bean.");
}
```

Notice that we're using the javax.rmi.PortableRemoteObject.narrow() method to safely cast the remote reference obtained from the EJB container to the expected home interface type. This allows our client to work safely with EJB servers that provide RMI/IIOP remote references to their beans.

Creating and Finding Beans

As we saw in the previous sections, home interface(s) for the an EJB contain methods that allow a client to create new beans or find existing beans (for entity beans). Continuing our example client, assuming we're using our `ProfileServer` bean from Example 8-6 and its corresponding home interface, we can create a reference to a `ProfileServer` bean as follows:

```
ProfileServer pServer = null;
try {
  pServer = pHome.create();
}
catch (RemoteException re) {
  System.out.println("Remote exception while creating ProfileServer: " +
                     re.getMessage());
}
catch (CreateException ce) {
  System.out.println("Error occurred during creation:
                     " + ce.getMessage());
}
```

We're using the `create()` method defined on our `ProfileServerHome` interface. Since this is a remote home interface, we need to catch both `RemoteException` and `CreateException` in our client code, in case some error occurs while communicating with the remote EJB container or during the create process itself. Assuming all goes well, we can now use our `ProfileServer` bean, invoking its business methods as needed by our client.

In the sections that follow, we'll examine client usage of each type of EJB (session, entity, and message-driven) in more detail, after we discuss the implementation and deployment details of each EJB component type.

EJB Handles and Home Handles

Every bean's remote client interface (if it has one) extends the `EJBObject` interface. This interface allows the client to obtain a serializable *handle* on the remote enterprise bean. This handle is a persistent reference to the bean that can be serialized and then stored in local storage on the client side, or emailed as an attachment to other users, for example. Later, a client can deserialize the handle object and continue interacting with the bean it references. The handle contains all of the information needed to reestablish a remote reference to the enterprise bean it represents. Since this is only useful for beans that are still valid when the handle is reconstituted, it is usually only applicable to entity beans, since they are persistent. But handles to session beans can also be used this way, as long as the handle is deserialized during the lifetime of the session bean (e.g., the EJB container doesn't shut down in the meantime, or the session bean is not removed from memory by the container).

The handle for a bean can be obtained using the `getHandle()` method on a remote bean object reference:

```
ProfileServer profileServ = ...;
Handle pHandle = pServ.getHandle();
```

The `getHandle()` method returns a `javax.ejb.Handle` object. Typically, the `Handle` implementation for a particular EJB is provided by the EJB container, and is generated automatically from the EJB remote client interface and bean implementation class that you provide. Every `Handle` implementation is a `Serializable` object, in order to allow it to be transmitted to remote clients, and to allow it to be stored in serialized format, if needed:

```
ObjectOutputStream oout = ...;
oout.writeObject(pHandle);
```

Later, you can read the object back from its serialized state and obtain a reference to the same remote EJB, using the getEJBObject() method on the handle:

```
ObjectInputStream oin = ...;
Handle pHandleIn = (Handle)oin.readObject();
EJBObject pRef = pHandleIn.getEJBObject();
ProfileServer pIn =
  (ProfileServer)PortableRemoteObject.narrow(pRef, ProfileServer.class);
ProfileBean prof = pIn.getProfile("JohnSmith");
```

When we call getEJBObject() on the Handle, the Handle communicates with its source EJB container and attempts to construct a remote reference to the bean that the handle came from originally. As with other situations where we receive a remote reference from the EJB container, we use the PortableRemoteObject. narrow() method to safely cast the remote EJB interface to the expected type, and then we can use the EJB.

It's also possible to get a handle for a remote home EJB interface. Calling getHomeHandle() on a remote home interface returns a HomeHandle reference that can be serialized and stored just like a bean Handle:

```
ProfileServerHome pHome = ...
HomeHandle pHomeHandle = pHome.getHomeHandle();
ObjectOutputStream oout = ...;
oout.writeObject(pHomeHandle);
```

We can deserialize the serialized HomeHandle later and use its getEJBHome() method to get a new remote home reference for the same EJB:

```
ObjectInputStream oin = ...;
HomeHandle pHomeHandleIn = (HomeHandle)oin.readObject();
EJBHome pHomeRef = pHomeHandleIn.getEJBHome();
ProfileServerHome profileHomeIn =
  (ProfileServerHome)PortableRemoteObject.narrow(
                          pHomeRef, ProfileHome.class);
ProfileServer pServer = profileHomeIn.create();
```

The EJB specification doesn't dictate the usable lifetime of a home handle. It may become invalid after the source EJB container restarts, it may expire after some timeout period, or it may remain valid for an extended period of time. Consult your EJB vendor documentation for specific details.

Implementing Session Beans

Now that we've seen all the basic elements of implementing, deploying, and using an EJB, let's move on and talk about the specifics of implementing session beans (we'll get to entity beans and message-passing beans after that). A session bean serves as a functional extension of the client that uses it, running within an EJB server. A client acquires a reference to a session bean, and asks it to perform services by calling methods on the bean. These method calls might retrieve or update data in a remote database, interact with an external enterprise system of some kind, filter or otherwise process a set of data, or perform some other useful task.

A session bean doesn't live beyond the lifetime of its server—in other words, it is not *persistent*. If an EJB client has a reference to a session bean and the host EJB server restarts, that session bean reference is no longer valid. You can reacquire a session bean of the same type from the same server after the restart, but it's not guaranteed to be in the same state as the bean you had before the server restart (unless, of course, you explicitly alter its state to exactly match the state of its ancestor). An EJB container also has the option of destroying a session bean after some timeout period if the bean is in an inactive state on the server (e.g., if there are no client references to the session bean for a period that exceeds the session timeout for the bean).

Session beans implement the `javax.ejb.SessionBean` interface. In addition to the standard EJB object methods mentioned in the previous section, a session bean also needs to implement the `setSessionContext()` method specified in the `SessionBean` interface. The container calls this method on the session bean just after the bean has been created, passing in a `javax.ejb.SessionContext` object that represents the runtime context for the bean. This session context is valid for the life of the bean. The session bean can use the `SessionContext` to get a valid remote stub reference to itself, by calling the `getEJBObject()` method on the context object. If the bean doesn't have a remote interface, then an `IllegalStateException` is thrown. Similarly, the bean can access a valid local stub for itself using the `getEJBLocalObject()` method on its `SessionContext`.

The `SessionContext` the container passes to a session bean is also an `EJBContext`, which is a general representation for runtime context information, regardless of whether the bean is an entity or session bean. Among other things, the `EJBContext` has accessors that allow the bean to get a reference to its home interface (`getEJBHome()`), a list of environment properties used to deploy the bean (`getEnvironment()`), and the identity of the client that is currently executing a transaction with the bean (`getCallerPrincipal()`).

Stateless Versus Stateful Session Beans

Session beans can be either stateful or stateless. A *stateless* session bean doesn't maintain client state across method calls. If a client makes a series of remote method calls and/or transactions with the stateless bean, the bean should be in the same effective state at the start of each method call or transaction. Our `ProfileServerBean` is such a bean. Stateless session beans of the same type can be considered identical to each other, and can be pooled and reused by multiple clients. A stateless session bean can be used concurrently by multiple clients without fear of conflicting with each other, since there should be no shared state data that can be corrupted. Stateless beans don't need to be passivated since they have no state that needs to be restored when they're reactivated. The container simply destroys any stateless session beans it feels are no longer needed.

A *stateful* session bean, on the other hand, does maintain state that can be accessed and changed directly by a client. A stateful session bean is not meant to be accessed by more than a single client; the state of the stateful session bean is owned by the client that created the bean.

To illustrate the difference between stateless and stateful session beans, let's take our stateless `ProfileServerBean` and convert it to a stateful session bean. The `ProfileServerBean` is stateless because all it does is accept requests for user profiles and return the profiles directly to the client as `Serializable` objects. The client then interacts with the `ProfileBean` object directly, and the `ProfileBean` state holds the conversational state for the client, in the form of the values of the profile entries. Profile data is only useful if it's recorded persistently someplace. To accomplish this using our stateless `ProfileServer`, we must add a business method that allows us to pass back an altered `ProfileBean` and have it recorded on the server. But if the profile itself is a stateful enterprise bean, we wouldn't need the `ProfileServer` at all; changes the client makes to the profile can be persisted directly by the stateful profile EJB.

Example 8-8 shows the remote interface for a `Profile` EJB (we won't implement a local interface for this example). It's similar to the interface for the `ProfileBean` we used in the stateless `ProfileServerBean` example. It has `setEntry()` and `getEntry()` methods that access entries using their names. The `Profile` EJB also has accessors for the name of its user.

Example 8-8: Remote Interface for Profile EJB

```
import java.rmi.Remote;
import java.rmi.RemoteException;
import javax.ejb.*;

public interface Profile extends EJBObject {
    // Get the name of the user associated with this profile
    public String getName() throws RemoteException;
    // Lookup an entry by name
    public String getEntry(String name) throws RemoteException;
    // Set an entry value
    public void setEntry(String name, String value) throws RemoteException;
}
```

A stateful session implementation of `Profile` EJB is shown in Example 8-9. It has the requisite implementations for the bean methods needed by the container and includes two `ejbCreate()` methods: one with no arguments that creates an unnamed profile, and another that takes the name of the user of the profile. The corresponding `create()` methods on the `ProfileHome` interface are shown in Example 8-10. The state of this stateful session bean is maintained in two member variables: a `String` field that holds the profile user's name, and a `Properties` object that keeps the profile entries. The get/set accessors from the remote `Profile` interface are implemented here as operations on these fields.

Example 8-9: Stateful Session Implementation of a Profile EJB

```
import javax.ejb.*;
import java.rmi.RemoteException;
import oreilly.jent.ejb.*;
import java.util.Properties;
```

Example 8-9: Stateful Session Implementation of a Profile EJB (continued)

```java
// A stateful session Profile, which provides profile information
// for a named person.
public class ProfileBean implements SessionBean {

  // State for this (stateful) bean

  // Name of the person owning the profile
  private String mName = "";
  // Entries in the profile (name/value pairs)
  private Properties mEntries = new Properties();

  // Store session context
  private SessionContext mContext = null;

  //----------------------------------------------------
  // Session bean methods
  //----------------------------------------------------

  // No need for us to activate anything in this bean, but we need to
  // provide an implementation.
  public void ejbActivate() {
    System.out.println("ProfileBean activated.");
  }

  // Nothing to do on a remove.
  public void ejbRemove() {
    System.out.println("ProfileBean removed.");
  }

  // No resources to release on passivation...
  public void ejbPassivate() {
    System.out.println("ProfileBean passivated.");
  }

  // Get context from container.
  public void setSessionContext(SessionContext context) {
    System.out.println("ProfileBean context set.");
    mContext = context;
  }

  // Create method (corresponds to each create() method on the
  // home interface, ProfileHome). Nothing to initialize in this case.
  public void ejbCreate() {
    System.out.println("Nameless ProfileBean created.");
  }

  // Create method with name of profile owner.
  public void ejbCreate(String name) throws NoSuchPersonException {
    mName = name;
    System.out.println("ProfileBean created for " + mName + ".");
  }
```

Example 8-9: Stateful Session Implementation of a Profile EJB (continued)

```
//------------------------------------------------
// Business methods
//------------------------------------------------

  public String getName() {
    return mName;
  }

  public String getEntry(String key) {
    return mEntries.getProperty(key);
  }

  public void setEntry(String key, String value) {
    mEntries.put(key, value);
  }
}
```

Example 8-10: Remote Home Interface for Profile EJB

```
import oreilly.jent.ejb.*;
import javax.ejb.*;
import java.rmi.RemoteException;

public interface ProfileHome extends EJBHome {
  // Create a new (nameless) profile
  public Profile create() throws RemoteException, CreateException;

  // Create a profile for a named person. Throws an exception if the person's
  // profile can't be found.
  public Profile create(String name)
    throws RemoteException, CreateException, NoSuchPersonException;
}
```

To make the state of the profile entries persistent, we can reimplement these methods to store/retrieve this profile data from a database or data files of some sort. Despite the general characterization of session beans as transient and entity beans as persistent, it is legal and often useful to perform database transactions from within a session EJB. The session bean lifecycle, however, doesn't directly support persistence management. The entity bean model is often more appropriate for creating objects that have a definable identity, need to be persistent, and need to be accessed concurrently by multiple clients. An entity bean implementation of our Profile is described in the section "Implementing Entity Beans."

This stateful bean can be used by clients to maintain a set of application-specific profile entries for a named user. Here is an example client-usage scenario:

```
// Get the Profile bean's home interface
ProfileHome pHome = ...
// Create a profile for a person
System.out.println("Creating profile for " + name);
Profile profile = pHome.create(name);
// Get/set some entries in the profile
```

```
System.out.println("Setting profile entries for " + name);
profile.setEntry("favoriteColor", "blue");
profile.setEntry("language", "German");
System.out.println("Getting profile entries for " + name);
System.out.println("\tFavorite color: " +
                   profile.getEntry("favoriteColor"));
System.out.println("\tLanguage: " + profile.getEntry("language"));
```

After getting the home interface for the `Profile`, this client creates a profile for a named user, sets the values for some profile entries, and retrieves them again.

Container Management of Stateless and Stateful Session Beans

An EJB container must be told at deployment time whether a session bean is stateful or stateless. The container uses this information to determine how to handle pooling of the session beans and whether to passivate the bean or not, among other things. The type of a session EJB is specified using the `session-type` element in the deployment descriptor:

```
...
<enterprise-beans>
  ...
  <session>
    ...
    <session-type>Stateful</session-type>
    ...
  </session>
  ...
</enterprise-beans>
...
```

A `session-type` of `Stateful` indicates stateful session management. `Stateless` indicates stateless sessions.

Since stateless beans can be used by any client. The container pools stateless beans and doles them out to clients as needed. If new stateless beans are required, the container creates them; when they aren't (e.g., the rate of client requests decreases), they are simply destroyed. To allow the container to fill its pool, any stateless session bean must provide a single `ejbCreate()` method with no arguments. The container can call this whenever it decides another bean is needed in its ready pool.

Stateful beans are tied to the clients that create them, and they do maintain conversational state with their clients, so the container will necessarily manage them differently. Stateful beans are created on-demand when the container receives client requests for them. The container may still keep a pool of pre-constructed instances of a stateful bean, but they aren't ready to accept method requests until a client calls one of the `create()` methods on the home interface, and the container subsequently calls the corresponding `ejbCreate()` method on one of the beans. At this point, the bean is "owned" by the client, and it's not removed until the client explicitly removes it by calling `remove()` on the client interface for the bean, or if the client's reference to the bean goes away (the client quits or the bean reference goes out of scope on the client).

Stateful session beans can also be passivated and activated by the EJB container. The container may decide to do this in order to free up runtime resources on the server, for example. Passivating a session bean involves serializing its state and saving it to disk or some other storage area. When the container decides to passivate a stateful session bean, it invokes its ejbPassivate() method. The bean can do any cleanup of resources that it deems appropriate before it is serialized (close I/O streams or database connections, release file handles, etc.). When the container decides to re-activate a passivated session bean, it first deserializes the bean, then invokes the bean's ejbActivate() method to give the bean a chance to restore any resources that it may need during runtime.

Stateless session beans aren't passivated or activated by the container, since they aren't intended to maintain client state data. Instead, when the container decides a stateless session bean instance is no longer needed, it simply removes it entirely, and all of the stateless session bean's internal state is lost.

Optional Transaction Support

Stateful session beans can optionally receive notification of transaction boundaries from the EJB container. The container can notify the bean when a new client transaction is beginning and when the client transaction has either been completed or rolled back. For more information on EJB transaction management, see the section "Transaction Management."

Since session beans don't typically represent persistent shared data, and stateful session beans can only be accessed by a single client at a time, user transaction boundaries may not be important in general to session beans. If, however, the session bean is managing database data for the user, it may want to know about the beginning and ending of user transactions, so that it can cache data at the start and commit its database updates at the end. For this reason, the EJB specification allows stateful session beans to optionally implement the javax.ejb. SessionSynchronization interface. By implementing this interface, the session bean indicates that it wants the container to notify it about the beginning and end of transactions.

In this case, the bean must implement the three methods declared on the SessionSynchronization interface: afterBegins(), beforeCompletion(), and afterCompletion(). The container calls the bean's afterBegin() method just after a new transaction begins. This lets the bean allocate any resources it might need during the transaction and cache database data, for example. Just before the transaction completes, the container calls the bean's beforeCompletion() method. In this method, the bean can release any resources or cached data it may have initialized during the transaction. The afterCompletion() method is called just after the transaction has completed. The container passes in a boolean value that is true if the transaction was committed and false if the transaction was rolled back. The bean can use this notification to deal with rollbacks, for example, allowing the bean to undo any changes made during the transaction.

Implementing Entity Beans

An entity bean represents data that is stored in a database or some other persistent storage. Entity beans are persistent across client sessions and the lifetime of the server. No matter when or where you get a reference to an entity bean with a given identity, the bean should reflect the current state of the persistent data it represents. Multiple clients can access entity beans with the same identity at the same time. The EJB container manages these concurrent transactions for the underlying entity, ensuring that client transactions are properly isolated from each other, consistent, persistent, etc.

An entity bean can be passivated by its container, but the meaning of being passivated is slightly different than it is with session beans. A container passivates an entity bean (calling its `ejbPassivate()` method in the process) when it wants to disassociate the bean from the persistent data entity it has been representing. After being passivated, the bean may be put into the container's "wait" pool, to be associated with another client-requested entity at a later time, or it may be removed from the server altogether.

At a fundamental level, entity beans are implemented similarly to session beans. You need to provide a local and/or home interface, a local and/or remote client interface, and a bean implementation. An entity bean, however, requires some additional methods in its home interface and bean implementation, to support the management of its persistent state and to allow clients to look up an entity from persistent storage. Entity beans must also provide a class that serves as its primary key, or index, into its persistent storage.

There are two ways persistent storage for an entity bean can be managed: by the EJB container or by the bean itself. In the first case, called *container-managed persistence*, or CMP, you leave the database calls to the container, and instead you instruct the container about bean properties and references that need to be persisted. The deployment tools provided with the EJB server are responsible for generating the corresponding database calls in the classes it uses to implement and deploy your bean. In the second case, called *bean-managed persistence*, or BMP, you provide the database calls for managing your bean's persistent storage as part of your bean implementation.

If you can rely on the EJB container to handle your entity bean's persistence, this can be a huge benefit, since it saves you from having to add JDBC code to your beans, and potentially makes your bean more portable across different persistent storage schemes (database vendors, schema variations, even other persistence mechanisms like object databases, etc.). But even with the new and expanded CMP support introduced in EJB 2.0, the automated persistence support in EJB is limited, and there are times when you'll need to manage persistence directly in your bean implementation. We discuss the pros and cons of each of these scenarios a bit later in this section.

Primary Keys

If you develop an entity bean, you must tell the EJB container the primary key for your bean. The primary key includes all of the information needed to uniquely identify an item in persistent storage. The primary key for a person's records in a database, for example, might be a first and last name, or a Social Security number (for U.S. citizens), or some other identification number. If you're developing an EJB object that represents a bank account, you might make the primary key an object that holds the account number, which is a unique identifier for an Account object. The primary key used for entity beans is a public unique identifier, in that clients can see the primary key for an entity bean, and the primary key is used directly by the bean implementation to load/update its state from persistent storage.

A primary key can be either a custom class that we write as part of the EJB implementation, or it can be a basic Java object type, like a String, Float, or Integer. Our Profile bean is uniquely identified by the name of the user, so a custom primary key class for an entity bean implementation of our Profile might look something like the following:

```java
public class ProfilePK implements java.io.Serializable {
    public String mName;
    public ProfilePK() {
        mName = null;
    }
    public ProfilePK(String name) {
        mName = name;
    }

    public boolean equals(Object other) {
        if (other instanceof ProfilePK &&
            this.mName.equals(((ProfilePK)other).mName)) {
            return true;
        }
        else {
            return false;
        }
    }

    public int hashCode() {
        return mName.hashCode();
    }
}
```

However, since the unique identifier for a Profile is simply a single String, we can just use java.lang.String as the primary key for our entity Profile bean.

A primary key class needs to satisfy the requirements of being a Value type in RMI-IIOP, because it may need to be transmitted to remote clients. In practical terms, this means that the primary key class has to be Serializable, and must not implement the java.rmi.Remote interface. A primary key class also has to have a valid implementation of the equals() and hashCode() methods, so that the container can manage primary keys internally using collections, etc. In addition, if your entity bean uses container-managed persistence, the primary key class must obey the following rules.

- It must be a public class.

- It must have a default constructor (one with no arguments) that is public.

- All its data members must be public.

- All of the names of the data members on the class must match the names of container-managed data members on the entity bean.

We've satisfied all of these requirements with our `ProfilePK` primary key class (note that the only data member, `mName`, has to have a matching `mName` data member on the entity implementation of the `Profile` bean).

Finder and Select Methods

Since entity beans are persistent and can be accessed by multiple clients, clients have to be able to find them as well as create them. To this end, an entity bean's home interface(s) can provide finder methods, named with a `findXXX()` scheme, that a client can invoke to lookup pre-existing entities in persistent storage and have them returned in the form of an EJB reference. For each finder method, the bean implementation has to have a corresponding `ejbFindXXX()` method that takes the same arguments. The `findXXX()` methods on the home interface can have any name, as long as the method name begins with `find`. A bank account bean, for example, might define a `findByName()` method that accepts a string that is the name of the person whose accounts are desired. The EJB implementation class must then have an `ejbFindByName()` method that implements this lookup function.

In addition to finder methods, EJB 2.0 adds the option of providing *select* methods for entity beans that use CMP. Select methods are utility methods that are only accessible from the bean implementation class itself; they aren't visible to the client. One of the principles behind CMP is to encapsulate the persistence details and not expose them in the EJB implementation. However, it is sometimes necessary to perform lookups against the underlying persistent store from business methods in your EJB implementation. Select methods provide this lookup functionality without forcing you to put database details into your bean code. You can define any number of `ejbSelectXXX()` methods as abstract methods on your bean implementation class. The EJB container is responsible for providing implementations for these methods, based on the persistence logic you provide for these methods in your deployment descriptors.

Each `findXXX()` method on the home interface must return either an instance of the bean's remote interface or a collection of these objects. If a finder method can potentially return multiple beans, then it has to have a return type that is either an `Enumeration` or a `Collection`. In our bank account example, the `findByName()` method can return multiple accounts (e.g., if a person has both checking and savings accounts), so it should be declared as returning a `Collection` or an `Enumeration`.

Every entity bean is required to have a `findByPrimaryKey()` method defined on each of its home interfaces. This finder method takes a single argument (an instance of the primary key for the entity bean) and returns the entity corresponding to that primary key.

A remote home interface for an entity-based `Profile` is shown in Example 8-11. It provides two finder methods. `findByPrimaryKey()` finds a profile by its primary key (which encapsulates the user's name), and `findByEntryValue()` finds profiles that have a particular attribute value set. The first finder method returns a single `Profile` object, since there is only a single `Profile` for each primary key (by definition). The second finder method returns a collection of `Profile` objects (as a `Collection`), since multiple user profiles might have a given attribute value. In our case, we're going to take the simpler route of using `String` as the primary key type for our bean (our `ProfilePK` class simply encapsulates a `String`, so it isn't really necessary).

Example 8-11: Remote Home Interface for the Entity Profile EJB

```
import javax.ejb.*;
import java.rmi.RemoteException;
import java.util.Collection;
import oreilly.jent.ejb.*;

public interface ProfileHome extends EJBHome {
   // Create a new (nameless) profile
   public Profile create() throws CreateException, RemoteException;

   // Create a profile for a named person.
   public Profile create(String name)
      throws CreateException, RemoteException, DuplicateProfileException;

   // Lookup a Profile by name (the primary key)
   public Profile findByPrimaryKey(String key)
      throws RemoteException, FinderException;

   // Lookup a Profile by the value of a particular entry in the profile.
   public Collection findByEntryValue(String key, String value)
      throws RemoteException, FinderException;
}
```

A client can use the `findXXX()` methods on the home interface to determine if an entity (or entities) with a given identity already exists in persistent storage. From the client's point of view, if a `findXXX()` method finds an appropriate entity or entities, entity bean instances are created and associated with these persistent entities and references to the matching beans are returned to the client. If the identified entity can't be found in persistent storage, a `javax.ejb.FinderException` is thrown. All `findXXX()` methods on the bean's home interface must declare that they can throw `FinderException` and, if it's a remote home interface, `RemoteException`.

Within the EJB container, things are a bit more complicated. The EJB container intercepts the client's invocation of the finder method and invokes the corresponding `ejbFindXXX()` method on an instance of the entity bean on the server. An entity bean of the appropriate type is pulled from the container's pool and its `ejbFindXXX()` method is called with the client's arguments. The `ejbFindXXX()` method on the bean should do the necessary queries to persistent storage to determine if the requested data exists there, then create primary key instances and initialize them with the results of the query. The primary key objects are the return value of the `ejbFindXXX()` method. The EJB container is responsible for taking the key(s) returned by the `ejbFindXXX()` method and converting them to remote objects, whose stubs are returned to the client that invoked the finder method.

It's important to note that the entity bean that executes the `ejbFindXXX()` method won't necessarily be asked by the container to represent the entities being looked up by the client. The container just uses a random entity bean from its "wait" pool to call the finder method, takes the returned primary key or keys, and then uses them to either create new beans or associated existing beans with these identities.

An entity bean implementation must at a minimum provide an `ejbFindByPrimaryKey()` method that accepts a primary key object as its argument, to correspond to the required `findByPrimaryKey()` method on the entity bean's home interface(s). The implementation must also provide additional `findXXX()` methods to match any other `ejbfindXXX()` methods on the home interface. Each `ejbFindXXX()` method must have the same arguments and return types as the corresponding `findXXX()` method.

Entity Bean Implementations

We've already mentioned a few additional requirements on entity bean implementations, but here is a list of all the additional methods an entity bean implementation either must implement or has the option to implement:

`public primaryKeyType ejbFindByPrimaryKey(primaryKeyType)`
`throws FinderException`

> The only required finder method on an entity bean. Both the argument and the return type must be the bean's primary key type. The container is responsible for converting the returned primary key into a valid EJB reference for the client.

`public void ejbPostCreate(...)`

> If needed, an entity bean can optionally supply an `ejbPostCreate()` method for each `ejbCreate()` method it provides, taking the same arguments. The container calls the `ejbPostCreate()` method after the bean's `ejbCreate()` method has been called and after the container has initialized the transaction context for the bean.

`public void ejbLoad()`

> This method is called by the container to cause the bean instance to load its state from persistent storage. The container can call this bean method any time after the bean has been created to do an initial load from persistent storage, or to refresh the bean's state from the database (e.g., after a business method on the bean has completed, or after the container has detected an update to the same persistent entity by another bean instance).

`public void ejbStore()`

> This method is called by the container to cause the bean to write its current runtime state to persistent storage. This method can be called any time after a bean is created.

```
public void setEntityContext(EntityContext ctx)
```
The container calls this method after a new instance of the bean has been constructed, but before any of its ejbCreate() methods are called. The bean is responsible for storing the context object. This method takes the place of the corresponding setSessionContext() method on session beans.

```
public void unsetEntityContext(EntityContext ctx)
```
The container calls this method before the entity bean is destroyed, to disassociate the bean from its identity, represented by its primary key.

In addition to these entity-specific methods on bean implementations, the semantics of some of the other standard methods are slightly different for entity beans. Each ejbCreate() method, for example, is actually a request to create a new entity in persistent storage. So the implementations of the create methods should not only assign any state data passed in as arguments, but also create a record in persistent storage for the new entity bean described by the method arguments. In addition to this semantic difference, the signatures of ejbCreate() methods on entity beans can be different from session beans. For an entity bean that manages its own persistence (a bean-managed entity bean), the ejbCreate() methods return the primary key type for the bean. For a container-managed entity bean, the ejbCreate() methods return void, the same as for session beans.

A client calling the remove() method on an entity bean reference or on the home interface for a bean is also interpreted differently: it's a request to remove the entity from persistent storage entirely. The entity bean implementation should therefore remove its state from the persistent storage in its ejbRemove() implementation.

For more details and actual examples of entity bean implementations, please refer to the sections "Bean-Managed Persistence" and "Container-Managed Persistence."

Deployment Options for Entity Beans

When deploying entity EJBs, include an entity element in the enterprise-beans element within the deployment descriptor. A sample entity element for our Profile EJB is shown here:

```
...
<enterprise-beans>

  <entity>
    <display-name>BMP Profile Bean</display-name>
    <ejb-name>BMP Profile Bean</ejb-name>
    <home>oreilly.jent.ejb.beanManaged.ProfileHome</home>
    <remote>oreilly.jent.ejb.Profile</remote>
    <ejb-class>oreilly.jent.ejb.beanManaged.ProfileBean</ejb-class>
    <persistence-type>Bean</persistence-type>
    <prim-key-class>java.lang.String</prim-key-class>
    <reentrant>False</reentrant>
    <resource-ref>
      <res-ref-name>jdbc/ProfileDB</res-ref-name>
      <res-type>javax.sql.DataSource</res-type>
      <res-auth>Container</res-auth>
```

```
        </resource-ref>
      </entity>
      ...
    </enterprise-beans>
    ...
```

The entity element contains many of the same basic required information as a session element (ejb-name, home, remote, local-home, local, ejb-class), but it also contains several elements specific to entity beans. Three of these are required: persistence-type, prim-key-class, and reentrant.

The persistence-type element specifies how the persistence for your entity bean is to be managed. The allowed values for this element are "Bean" or "Container," indicating the two fundamental ways that entity persistence can be handled. Our ProfileBean is written to use bean-managed persistence, so we set the persistence-type to "Bean."

The prim-key-class element specifies which class is being used as the primary key for this bean. We chose to use Strings rather than our custom ProfilePK class, so we specify java.lang.String as our primary key.

The reentrant element indicates whether an EJB can be accessed by multiple clients concurrently. If an EJB is marked reentrant, it's eligible for concurrent access; otherwise it's run in a "single-threaded" manner—only one client request is processed at a time by any given EJB instance within the container. In our example, we haven't written our ProfileBean to be thread-safe (a quick look at the setEntry() implementation in Example 8-12 will confirm that), so we've set the reentrant element to "False." The reentrant property has other implications related to *loopback* calls (method implementations on the bean that result in calls back to the same bean instance). Refer to O'Reilly's *Enterprise JavaBeans* or the EJB specification for full details on loopback calls.

The Entity Context

The EJB container provides context information to an entity bean in the form of an EntityContext object. The container sets this object using the bean's setEntityContext() method and removes it when the bean is being removed by calling the bean's unsetEntityContext() method. Like SessionContext, EntityContext provides the bean with access to its corresponding remotely exported object through the getEJBObject() method. The EntityContext also, gives an entity bean access to its primary key through getPrimaryKey(). The declared return type of this method is Object, but the object returned is of the bean's primary key type. Note that the data accessed through the EntityContext might be changed by the EJB container during the bean's lifetime, as explained in the next section. For this reason, you shouldn't store the EJB remote object reference or primary key in data variables in the bean object, since they might not be valid for the entire lifetime of the bean. Our entity ProfileBean, for example, stores the EntityContext reference in an instance variable, where it can access the context data as needed during its lifetime.

Lifecycle of an Entity Bean

Before the first client asks for an entity bean by calling a create() or findXXX() method on its home interface, an EJB container might decide to create a pool of entity beans to handle client requests for beans. This potentially reduces the amount of time it takes for a client to receive an entity bean remote reference after it makes a request for an entity bean. To add a bean to its pool, the container creates an instance of your bean implementation class and sets its context using the setEntityContext() method. At this point, the entity bean hasn't been associated with a particular data entity, so it doesn't have an identity and therefore isn't eligible for handling client business-method calls on bean references.

When a client calls a create() method on the bean's home interface, the container picks a bean out of this wait pool and calls the corresponding ejbCreate() method on the bean. If the ejbCreate() method is successful, it returns one or more primary key objects to the container. For each primary key, the container picks an entity bean out of its pool to be assigned to the entity represented by the key. Next, the container assigns the bean's identity by setting the properties in its EntityContext object (e.g., its primary key and remote object values). If the bean has an ejbPostCreate() method, that gets called after the bean's entity identity has been set. The ejbCreate() method should create the entity in persistent storage, if the bean is managing its own persistence.

Alternately, the client might call a findXXX() method on the home interface. The container picks one of the pooled entity beans and calls the corresponding ejbFindXXX() method on it. If the finder method finds one or more matching entities in persistent storage, the container uses pooled entity beans to represent these entities. It picks entity beans out of the pool and calls their ejbActivate() methods. Before calling ejbActivate(), the container sets the bean's context by assigning the corresponding primary key and remote object reference in its context.

After an entity bean has been activated (either by being created through one of its ejbCreate() methods or by being found and having its ejbActivate() method called), it is associated with a specific entity in persistent storage and with a specific client stub. At any point after this, the container can call the bean's ejbLoad() or ejbStore() method to force the bean to read or write its state from or to persistent storage. The bean's business methods can also be invoked by clients when it is in this state.

At some point, the container may decide to put the bean back into its internal pool. This might happen after all remote references to the bean have been released or after a certain period of inactivity with the bean. The container might also do this as a reaction to client-loading issues (e.g., time-sharing pooled beans between client requests). When the container wants to remove the association between the entity bean instance and the client stub, but doesn't want the object's state removed from persistent store, it calls the bean's ejbPassivate() method. The bean can release any resources it allocated while in the active state, but it doesn't have to update persistent storage for the entity it represents, as this was done the last time its ejbStore() method was invoked by the container.

The bean can also lose its association with an entity when the client decides to remove the entity. The client does this either by calling a remove() method on the bean's home interface or calling the remove() method directly on an EJB object. When one of these things happens, the container calls the bean's ejbRemove() method, and the bean deletes the data in persistent storage pertaining to the entity it represents. After the ejbRemove() method completes, the container puts the bean back into its internal pool.

Bean-Managed Persistence

Bean-managed persistence is one option for dealing with the persistence of the state of entity EJBs. In BMP, all of the persistence management is done directly in the EJB implementation class, using custom JDBC calls or whatever API is appropriate for the persistent storage being used. The persistence management of an entity bean is handled in the ejbCreate(), ejbRemove(), ejbLoad(), and ejbStore() methods on the bean implementation. The persistent store is also accessed directly in the ejbFindXXX() methods on the implementation of BMP beans.

Going back to our Profile example, the major drawback in our stateful session Profile is that the profile data it represents isn't persistent. A profile is created by a client and updated through client method calls, but once the Profile reference is given up by the client, or if the server crashes or shuts down for some reason, the accumulated profile data is lost. What we really want is a bean whose state is stored in a relational database or some other persistent storage, and that can be reloaded at a later time, when the user re-enters a profiled application. An entity EJB object provides this functionality, and an EJB container provides your bean with facilities that make it easier to manage persistent state. It's also possible to have the container manage the persistence of the bean for you, if that's desired.

Let's look at an implementation of a BMP entity bean version of our Profile EJB, shown in Example 8-12. We've already seen the home interface and remote interface for this entity bean in earlier sections. The purpose of the bean is the same as our stateful session version: it represents a profile for a named application user, maintaining a list of name/value pairs for various attributes and options. The difference is that this ProfileBean represents a profile entity that exists as a set of data in persistent storage (a database, in this case). The most obvious differences in the actual code are the JDBC calls peppered throughout the class, where the bean manages its persistent data. This entity bean is using bean-managed persistence, so it is making the calls to load, store, or update its persistent data itself.

Example 8-12: Bean-Managed Persistence Version of Entity Profile EJB

```
import javax.ejb.*;
import java.util.*;
import java.sql.*;
import javax.sql.*;
import javax.naming.*;
import java.io.*;
import oreilly.jent.ejb.*;

public class ProfileBean implements EntityBean {
```

```java
// Entries in the profile (name/value pairs)
public Properties mEntries;

// Our EJB context (non-persistent)
public EntityContext mContext = null;

//----------------------------------------------------
// Entity bean methods
//----------------------------------------------------

// EJB activation method. During activation, create our entry lookup table.
public void ejbActivate() {
  mEntries = new Properties();
  System.out.println("ProfileBean activated.");
}


// Load bean from persistent store. In this case, we're managing the dbase
// storage, so we store our profile entries as independent records in a
// separate "PROFILE_ENTRY" table.
public void ejbLoad() {
  try {
    String key = (String)mContext.getPrimaryKey();
    loadFromDB(key);
  }
  catch (Exception e) {
    System.out.println("Failed to load ProfileBean: ");
    e.printStackTrace();
    throw new EJBException("ejbLoad failed: ", e);
  }
  System.out.println("ProfileBean load finished.");
}

protected void loadFromDB(String key) throws FinderException {
  boolean found = false;
  try {
    Connection conn = getConnection();
    Statement s = conn.createStatement();
    s.executeQuery("select name from profile where name = '" + key + "'");
    ResultSet rs = s.getResultSet();
    if (rs.next()) {
      found = true;
      s.executeQuery("select key, value from profile_entry
                                  where name = '" + key + "'");
      rs = s.getResultSet();
      while (rs.next()) {
        String pKey = rs.getString(1);
        String pValue = rs.getString(2);
        mEntries.put(pKey, pValue);
      }
    }
  }
```

```
  catch (SQLException e) {
    throw new FinderException("Failed to load profile entries from DB: " +
                                                    e.toString());
  }
  catch (NamingException ne) {
    throw new FinderException("Failed to access DataSource from server: " +
                                                    ne.toString());
  }
  if (!found) {
    throw new FinderException("No profile found for " + key);
  }
}


// Store bean to persistent store. Properties are stored as records in the
// PROFILE_ENTRY table.
public void ejbStore() {
  String key = (String)mContext.getPrimaryKey();
  try {
    Connection conn = getConnection();
    // Clear out old profile entries and replace with the current ones
    Statement s = conn.createStatement();
    s.executeUpdate("delete from profile_entry where name =
                                            '" + key + "'");
    Enumeration pKeys = mEntries.propertyNames();
    while (pKeys.hasMoreElements()) {
      String pKey = (String)pKeys.nextElement();
      String pValue = mEntries.getProperty(pKey);
      s.executeUpdate("insert into profile_entry (name, key, value)
          values " + "('" + key + "', '" + pKey + "', '" + pValue + "')");
    }
    // Close the statement and the connection, just to be tidy...
    s.close();
    conn.close();
  }
  catch (Exception e) {
    System.out.println("Failed to store ProfileBean: ");
    e.printStackTrace();
    throw new EJBException("ejbStore failed: ", e);
  }
  System.out.println("ProfileBean store finished.");
}


// Remove this named profile from the database.
public void ejbRemove() {
  // Get this profile's name
  String key = (String)mContext.getPrimaryKey();
  try {
    Connection conn = getConnection();
    // Clear out any profile entries
    Statement s = conn.createStatement();
    s.executeUpdate("delete from profile_entry where name =
                                            '" + key + "'");
```

```
    // Clear out the profile itself
    s.executeUpdate("delete from profile where name = '" + key + "'");

    s.close();
    conn.close();
    System.out.println("ProfileBean removed.");
  }
  catch (SQLException se) {
    System.out.println("Error removing profile for " + key);
    se.printStackTrace();
  }
  catch (NamingException ne) {
    System.out.println("Error accessing DataSource");
    ne.printStackTrace();
  }
}

// When we're passivated, release our entry table.
public void ejbPassivate() {
  mEntries = null;
  System.out.println("ProfileBean passivated.");
}

// Get context from container.
public void setEntityContext(EntityContext context) {
  mContext = context;
  System.out.println("ProfileBean context set.");
}

// Container is removing our context.
public void unsetEntityContext() {
  mContext = null;
  System.out.println("ProfileBean context unset.");
}

// Since we're managing persistence here in the bean, we need to
// implement the finder methods.
public String ejbFindByPrimaryKey(String key) throws FinderException {
  loadFromDB(key);
  return key;
}

public Collection ejbFindByEntryValue(String key, String value)
  throws FinderException {
  LinkedList userList = new LinkedList();
  // Get a new connection from the EJB server
  try {
    Connection conn = getConnection();
    Statement s = conn.createStatement();
    // Issue a query for matching profile entries, grabbing just the name
    s.executeQuery("select distinct(name) from profile_entry where " +
                   " key = '" + key + "' and value = '" + value + "'");
```

```
      // Convert the results in primary keys and return an enumeration
      ResultSet results = s.getResultSet();
      while (results.next()) {
        String name = results.getString(1);
        userList.add(name);
    }
  }
}
catch (SQLException se) {
  // Failed to do database lookup
  throw new FinderException();
}
catch (NamingException ne) {
  // Failed to access DataSource
  throw new FinderException();
}
return userList;
}

// Create method with name of profile owner.
public String ejbCreate(String name)
  throws DuplicateProfileException, CreateException {
  try {
    Connection conn = getConnection();
    Statement s = conn.createStatement();
    .executeUpdate("insert into profile (name) values ('" + name + "')");
    s.close();
    conn.close();
  }
  catch (SQLException se) {
    System.out.println("Error creating profile, assuming duplicate.");
    try {
      StringWriter strw = new StringWriter();
      PrintWriter prntw = new PrintWriter(strw);
      se.printStackTrace(prntw);
      throw new DuplicateProfileException("SQL error creating profile for " +
                  name + ": " + se.toString() +  "\n" + strw.toString());
    }
    catch (Exception e) {}
  }
catch (NamingException ne) {
  System.out.println("Error accessing DataSource");
  throw new CreateException("Error accessing DataSource.");
}
System.out.println("ProfileBean created for " + name + ".");
return name;
}

// Post-creation notification. Nothing to do here, but we need
// to provide an implementation.
public void ejbPostCreate(String name) {
  System.out.println("ProfileBean post-create called for " + name + ".");
}
```

```
//----------------------------------------------------
// Utility methods
//----------------------------------------------------

// Get a connection from our J2EE data source.
private Connection getConnection() throws SQLException, NamingException {
  Context ctx = new InitialContext();
  DataSource profileDB =
  (DataSource)ctx.lookup("java:comp/env/jdbc/profileDB");
return profileDB.getConnection();
}


//----------------------------------------------------
// Business methods
//----------------------------------------------------

// Returns the name of the owner of this profile.
public String getName() {
  return (String)mContext.getPrimaryKey();
}

// Returns the value of the given entry in this profile, or null
// if the given property isn't present in this profile.
public String getEntry(String key) {
  return mEntries.getProperty(key);
}

// Sets the value of the property to the given value.
public void setEntry(String key, String value) {
  if (mEntries == null) {
    mEntries = new Properties();
  }
  mEntries.put(key, value);
  }
}
```

The structure of the entity `ProfileBean` is similar to the stateful session bean version in Example 8-9. A `Properties` object holds the profile entries for the user, and the `getEntry()` and `setEntry()` remote method implementations access this `Properties` object for the client. The name is found in the primary key object, and the primary key is stored for us in the `EntityContext` the container gives us through the `setEntityContext()` method. The `getName()` remote method on `ProfileBean` shows how we retrieve the username for the profile using the `getPrimaryKey()` method on the `EntityContext`.

We've also removed the `setName()` method from the entity `ProfileBean`, since we don't want to allow the client to change the name of an existing, active entity bean. The `Profile` remote interface for this bean, not shown here, is similar to the `Profile` interface in Example 8-8, but doesn't have a `setName()` method. Since the `Profile` is now a persistent entity bean and the name is the primary key, or identifying attribute, of the bean, the name of the bean should only be set when the bean is created. While the entity bean is active, it is associated with a profile entity for a specific user, and the client should only read the name associated with the profile.

In the `ProfileBean` code, you'll notice all of the EJB-required methods, including `ejbActivate()`, `ejbPassivate()`, `ejbCreate()`, and `ejbRemove()`. The `ejbActivate()` and `ejbPassivate()` methods are called as the container moves the bean in and out of the entity bean "wait" pool. The `ejbCreate()` methods on the `ProfileBean` create a new profile entity in the database. There is a matching `ejbCreate()` method for each `create()` method on our `ProfileHome` interface from Example 8-11. The EJB container is responsible for intercepting the primary key object returned by the `ejbCreate()` method, converting it to a reference to a live `Profile` EJB, and returning a `Profile` stub to the client that originally called the `create()` method on the `ProfileHome` interface. The `ejbRemove()` method on our `ProfileBean` deletes all the records for this profile entity from the database.

The `ProfileBean` also contains methods specific to entity beans. For each `ejbCreate()` method, it has a corresponding `ejbPostCreate()` method, which is called by the container after the `ejbCreate()` method has returned and after the container has initialized the bean's transaction context. In our case, there's nothing that needs to be done in the `ejbPostCreate()` methods, so we simply log that they've been called and return.

There is an `ejbFindXXX()` method in our entity `ProfileBean` that corresponds to each `findXXX()` method in `ProfileHome`. The `ejbFindByPrimaryKey()` method simply takes the primary key passed in as an argument and attempts to load the data for the entity from the database. If successful, it returns the primary key back to the container, where it is converted to a remote `Profile` object to be returned to the client. Note that it's not necessary for us to actually load all the profile data here in the finder method; we need only to verify that the specified entity exists in the database and either return the primary key to signal success or throw an exception. If successful, the container takes the returned primary key and assigns it to one of the beans in its pool (possibly the same one it called the finder method on, but not necessarily). Since we already have the `loadFromDB()` method used in `ejbLoad()`, it is a simple matter to reuse it in the finder method. If the performance hit for loading the profile data twice is too great, we must rewrite the finder method to simply check the `PROFILE` table for a record matching the name in the primary key.

The `ejbFindByEntryValue()` method takes a key and value `String` arguments and attempts to find any and all profile entities with a matching key/value pair in the `PROFILE_ENTRY` table. Each name that has such a record is converted to a primary key object and returned to the container in an `Enumeration`. The container converts each primary key object into a remote `Profile` object and returns the set to the client. If we encounter a database problem along the way, we throw a `FinderException`.

Container-Managed Persistence

In our first entity-based `Profile`, the persistent state of the profile entity is managed by the bean itself. There's custom JDBC code in the `ProfileBean` implementation in Example 8-12 that loads, stores, and removes the entity's database entries. This is called *bean-managed persistence.* The EJB container calls the appropriate methods on your entity bean, but your bean implementation is responsible for connecting to the database and making all of the necessary queries and updates to reflect the lifecycle of the data entity.

Container-managed persistence allows you to define properties on your entity bean implementation that represent the state of the entity, and tell the EJB container how to map these properties to persistent storage. How this mapping is defined is the principle difference between the EJB 1.1 and EJB 2.0 versions of CMP, and is described next. But generally speaking, if the persistent storage is a relational database, tell the container which columns in which tables hold the various data members of your entity. With container-managed persistence, the container is responsible for loading, updating, and removing the entity data from persistent storage, based on the mapping you provide. The container invokes the callbacks on your bean implementation to notify it when it has performed these tasks for you, allowing your bean to do any follow-up work that may be required. The container also implements all the finder methods required by the bean's home interface.

If you want to take advantage of container-managed persistence, you have to indicate this to the EJB container when you deploy the bean, you need to provide a bean implementation that assumes that the container is performing all persistence management, and you need to supply the container with a data mapping at deployment time.

The scheme for container-managed persistence was altered significantly between the 1.1 and 2.0 versions of the EJB specification. Since EJB 1.1 implementations are still prevalent in the market at the time of this writing, but EJB 2.0 implementations are starting to become more broadly available, we're going to cover both CMP models here.

Regardless of whether you are using EJB 1.1 or 2.0, the basic steps for using CMP are the same, even if the particular details are different:

1. In your bean implementation class, declare persistent properties that represent the state of the bean that is to be managed by the container.

2. Declare finder and select methods in the home interface(s) for the EJB.

3. Map the persistent state properties to persistent storage in the EJB deployment descriptor

4. Provide the container with the information needed to implement the finder and select methods.

The EJB container is responsible for generating the relevant code to load, store, and update the state of the EJB to and from persistent storage, and to implement the finder and select methods defined on your home interface(s). The various persistence-related EJB methods on your implementation class (ejbLoad(), ejbStore(), ejbCreate(), and ejbRemove()) are used as callbacks by the EJB container; they're invoked by the container just before and after it performs the corresponding persistence operation.

The manner in which this persistence information is provided to the container is the key advancement in EJB 2.0 CMP. The mapping of persistent properties to database storage is done using *abstract persistence schemas*, and persistence logic for finder methods is provided using a generic query language called *EJB QL*. In EJB 1.1, concrete data members are added to your implementation class; these are flagged as persistent fields in the deployment descriptor, and mapped to persistent storage.

Example 8-13 shows another implementation of our `Profile` EJB, which uses the EJB 2.0 CMP model. We'll refer to this version as we discuss the details of using CMP, and where necessary, highlight areas in which the code needs to change if you're using EJB 1.1 CMP.

Example 8-13: CMP Implementation of the Entity Profile EJB

```
import javax.ejb.*;
import java.util.Properties;
import java.io.*;
import oreilly.jent.ejb.*;

abstract public class ProfileBean implements EntityBean {
  //----------------------------------------------------
  // Persistent data properties
  //----------------------------------------------------

  // EJB 2.0: Just provide abstract accessors for the properties

  // Name of the person owning the profile
  abstract public String getName();
  abstract public void setName(String name);

  // Serialized representation of profile entries, for storage in persistent
  // store, or passivated state
  abstract public byte[] getEntriesBytes();
  abstract public void setEntriesBytes(byte[] entries);

  // EJB 1.1: Define actual data members to hold persistent data

  // Name of the person owning the profile
  //public String mName = "";
  // Serialized representation of profile entries, for storage in persistent
  // store, or passivated state
  //public byte[] mEntriesBytes = null;

  // Entries in the profile (name/value pairs)
  transient private Properties mEntries = new Properties();

  // Our entity context
  private EntityContext mContext = null;

  //----------------------------------------------------
  // Utility methods
  //----------------------------------------------------
```

Example 8-13: CMP Implementation of the Entity Profile EJB (continued)

```java
// Transfer the list of entries from our Properties member to the byte
// array.
private void transferToBytes() throws IOException {
  // Serialize the Properties into a byte array using an ObjectOutputStream
  if (mEntries != null && !mEntries.isEmpty()) {
    ByteArrayOutputStream byteOut = new ByteArrayOutputStream();
    ObjectOutputStream objOut = new ObjectOutputStream(byteOut);
    objOut.writeObject(mEntries);
    SetEntriesBytes(byteOut.toByteArray());
  }
  else {
    setEntriesBytes(null);
  }
}


// Convert the serialized byte array into our Properties entry list.
private void transferToProps() throws IOException {
  // Take the raw byte array and de-serialize it
  // back into a Properties object using an ObjectInputStream
  try {
    if (getEntriesBytes() != null) {
      ByteArrayInputStream byteIn =
        new ByteArrayInputStream(getEntriesBytes());
      ObjectInputStream objIn = new ObjectInputStream(byteIn);
      mEntries = (Properties)objIn.readObject();
    }
    // If no entries in database, set properties to a new, empty collection
    else {
      mEntries = new Properties();
    }
  }
  catch (ClassNotFoundException cnfe) {
    System.out.println(
                    "Properties class not found during de-serialization");
  }
}


//----------------------------------------------------
// Entity bean methods
//----------------------------------------------------


// After the container reloads our byte array from passivated state,
// convert it back into a Properties object.
public void ejbActivate() {
  try {
    transferToProps();
    System.out.println("ProfileBean activated.");
  }
  catch (IOException ioe) {
    System.out.println("Failed to convert entries during activation.");
```

Example 8-13: CMP Implementation of the Entity Profile EJB (continued)

```
      ioe.printStackTrace();
    }
  }

  // Before passivation occurs, copy the entries list from the Properties
  // member into the byte array.
  public void ejbPassivate() {
    try {
      transferToBytes();
      System.out.println("ProfileBean being passivated.");
    }
    catch (IOException ioe) {
      System.out.println("Failed to convert entries during activation.");
      ioe.printStackTrace();
    }
  }

  // Load bean from persistent store. Since the profile entries are stored in
  // a nonprimitive object (Properties), they are stored in the database as a
  // raw byte array (BLOB). In this load method, we convert the serialized
  // bytes loaded by the container into the original Properties object.
  public void ejbLoad() {
    try {
      transferToProps();
    }
    catch (IOException e) {
      System.out.println("Failed to load ProfileBean: ");
      e.printStackTrace();
      throw new EJBException("ejbLoad failed: ", e);
    }
    System.out.println("ProfileBean load finished.");
  }

  // Store bean to persistent store. We store our Properties object in the
  // database as a serialized byte array. Here, we serialize the Properties
  // object so that the container can store it.
  public void ejbStore() {
    try {
      transferToBytes();
    }
    catch (IOException e) {
      System.out.println("Failed to store ProfileBean: ");
      e.printStackTrace();
      throw new EJBException("ejbStore failed: ", e);
    }
    System.out.println("ProfileBean store finished.");
  }

  // Nothing to do on a remove.
  public void ejbRemove() {
    System.out.println("ProfileBean removed.");
  }
```

Example 8-13: CMP Implementation of the Entity Profile EJB (continued)

```java
// Get context from container.
public void setEntityContext(EntityContext context) {
  System.out.println("ProfileBean context set.");
  mContext = context;
}

// Container is removing our context.
public void unsetEntityContext() {
  System.out.println("ProfileBean context unset.");
  mContext = null;
}

// Create method (corresponds to each create() method on the
// home interface, ProfileHome). Here, we initialize our persistent
// properties to sensible starting values.
public String ejbCreate() {
  System.out.println("Nameless ProfileBean created.");
  setName(" ");
  setEntriesBytes(null);
  return null;
}

// Post-creation notification. Nothing to do here, but we need
// to provide an implementation.
public void ejbPostCreate() {
  System.out.println("ProfileBean post-create called.");
}

// Create method with name of profile owner.
public String ejbCreate(String name) throws NoSuchPersonException {
  setName(name);
  setEntriesBytes(null);
  System.out.println("ProfileBean created for " + name + ".");
  return null;
}

// Post-creation notification. Nothing to do here, what we need
// to provide an implementation.
public void ejbPostCreate(String name) {
  System.out.println("ProfileBean post-create called.");
}

//----------------------------------------------------
// Business methods
//----------------------------------------------------

public String getEntry(String key) {
  System.out.println("getEntry(): principle = " +
                              mContext.getCallerPrincipal().getName());
  return mEntries.getProperty(key);
}
```

Example 8-13: CMP Implementation of the Entity Profile EJB (continued)

```
public void setEntry(String key, String value) {
  mEntries.put(key, value);
}

// EJB 2.0: Accessors for the relationship with the corresponding
// Person bean.

// Get local person for this profile
// abstract public PersonLocal getPersonLocal();
// abstract public void setPersonLocal(PersonLocal person);
}
```

In comparison to our BMP-based `ProfileBean` from Example 8-12, this bean is somewhat simpler, since the `ejbRemove()`, `ejbLoad()`, and `ejbStore()` methods don't need to perform database calls. The container is handling the loading and storing of the bean's data and the removal of any entities from the database, so we don't need to do anything about these operations in our bean implementation.

Mapping container-managed fields: Abstract persistence schema

In the CMP model, the persistent state of your entity EJBs is specified in terms of an *abstract persistence schema*. The abstract schema consists of a set of named EJBs (the "tables" of the schema) and the persistent properties declared on your entity EJBs (the "columns" of the schema). Describe the components of this abstract schema in your EJB deployment descriptor, then provide the container with a mapping from this abstract schema to a real persistence store (a relational database schema, an object database, etc.). The container takes all of this information and uses it to generate persistence management code for your EJB.

EJB 2.0. In EJB 2.0, you define abstract persistence fields on your bean by providing accessors (JavaBean-style set and/or get methods) on the EJB implementation class. These accessors are defined as abstract methods on your implementation class. The EJB container provides concrete implementations in its generated classes. In our `ProfileBean` implementation class, we have two sets of accessors for the two abstract persistent fields needed by our bean: `get/setName()` for the `name` property and `get/setEntriesBytes()` for the `entriesBytes` property. Note that, since we need to define persistent field accessors as abstract in our implementation class, the class itself must be declared as abstract as well. As we'll see later in this section, this isn't the case in EJB 1.1 CMP, in which bean implementation classes are nonabstract, concrete classes.

Next, we need to describe our abstract persistence schema in the EJB's deployment descriptor. This essentially amounts to specifying an abstract schema name for each EJB we are creating (thus defining the "tables"), and listing the persistent properties of each EJB (defining the "columns"). A partial listing of the *ejb-jar.xml* file for our `Profile` bean is shown in Example 8-14.

Example 8-14: Section of ejb-jar.xml File for CMP Profile EJB

```xml
<?xml version="1.0"?>

<!DOCTYPE ejb-jar PUBLIC '-//Sun Microsystems, Inc.
    //DTD Enterprise JavaBeans 2.0//EN'
    'http://java.sun.com/dtd/ejb-jar_2_0.dtd'>

<ejb-jar>
 <enterprise-beans>
 <!-- A Profile EJB using container-managed persistence -->
 <entity>
 <ejb-name>CMP20ProfileBean</ejb-name>
 <home>ProfileHome</home>
 <remote>Profile</remote>
 <local-home>ProfileLocalHome</local-home>
 <local>ProfileLocal</local>
 <ejb-class>ProfileBean</ejb-class>
 <persistence-type>Container</persistence-type>
 <prim-key-class>java.lang.String</prim-key-class>
 <reentrant>False</reentrant>
 <cmp-version>2.x</cmp-version>
 <abstract-schema-name>ProfileBean</abstract-schema-name>

 <!-- Indicate which fields need to be managed persistently -->
 <cmp-field>
 <description>Name of the profile owner</description>
 <field-name>name</field-name>
 </cmp-field>
 <cmp-field>
 <description>Binary data containing profile entries.</description>
 <field-name>entriesBytes</field-name>
 </cmp-field>

 <!-- Since our primary key is simple (one-column), we need to specify
 to the container which field maps to the primary key -->
 <primkey-field>name</primkey-field>
      ...
```

Before listing our persistent fields, we provide an abstract-schema-name element, which labels our EJB with an abstract name within the abstract persistence schema we're defining. Think of this abstract name as a sort of virtual table name; it's a way to refer to it in the EJB QL statements that define finder and select methods.

Following this, we list the cmp-field elements that describe the persistent properties on our EJB. We have two persistent properties for our Profile bean: name and entriesBytes, represented by the corresponding accessor methods in the bean implementation. So we have two cmp-field elements that serve to "tag" these bean properties as ones that need to be treated as persistent state.

In addition, the container needs to know how the bean's primary key is mapped. The primary key has to be mapped to one or more of the cmp-field elements listed in the deployment descriptor. If it maps to a single cmp-field, the name of the field has to be provided in the deployment descriptor as a primkey-field element. If the primary key is a complex key that maps to multiple cmp-fields on the EJB, then no primkey-field is provided, and instead the data members on the primary key class must have variable names that match the corresponding persistent fields on the EJB implementation class. The container will automatically make the mapping from primary key fields to persistent bean fields. In our case, the primary key is simply the name property on the bean, so we've included a primkey-field element in our deployment descriptor to that affect.

All we've done so far in the *ejb-jar.xml* file is provide the basic deployment information for our EJB and list the fields on the bean implementation that need to be persisted. But the container doesn't know how to persist these fields yet. Neither the EJB 1.1 nor 2.0 versions of CMP define a standard way to provide this mapping to physical data storage. One reason for not including this in the specification is because it would require assumptions about the type of persistence being used by the container. EJB containers can (ostensibly) use any kind of persistent storage to maintain the state of entity beans: relational databases, object databases, XML databases, even flat files. Undoubtedly, virtually all of the major J2EE vendors provide relational persistence support in their CMP implementations, but the EJB specification team did not want to build this assumption into the specification, so they left the mapping of abstract persistent fields to physical storage up to the container vendors.

When using Sun's J2EE Reference Implementation, for example, we would use the graphical *deploytool* that is bundled with the server to specify all of the CMP deployment information for our bean. The Reference Implementation supports only RDBMS-based persistence, so the *deploytool* allows you to specify persistence mappings in terms of relational tables and columns. As a side note, we can also use *deploytool* to provide all the information we specified in the standard *ejb-jar.xml* file and let the tool construct the XML file for us.

If we're using BEA's WebLogic application server, on the other hand, we would specify the CMP deployment parameters using some additional deployment files that are specific to WebLogic. All EJBs (session, entity, or message-driven) deployed in WebLogic need to have an additional deployment file named *weblogic-ejb-jar.xml*, where things such as the JNDI binding for the EJB home interface can be specified. For container-managed entity beans, this file can also be used to specify another deployment file that contains all the persistence-management information for the bean. Here is a relevant section from a WebLogic deployment descriptor for our Profile EJB:

```
<?xml version="1.0"?>

<!DOCTYPE weblogic-ejb-jar PUBLIC
    '-//BEA Systems, Inc.//DTD WebLogic 6.0.0 EJB//EN'
    'http://www.bea.com/servers/wls600/dtd/weblogic-ejb-jar.dtd'>

<weblogic-ejb-jar>
  <weblogic-enterprise-bean>
    <ejb-name>CMP20ProfileBean</ejb-name>
    <entity-descriptor>
      <persistence>
        <persistence-type>
```

```
        <type-identifier>WebLogic_CMP_RDBMS</type-identifier>
        <type-version>6.0</type-version>
        <type-storage>META-INF/weblogic-cmp-rdbms-jar.xml
                                                    </type-storage>
      </persistence-type>
      <persistence-use>
        <type-identifier>WebLogic_CMP_RDBMS</type-identifier>
        <type-version>6.0</type-version>
      </persistence-use>
    </persistence>
  </entity-descriptor>
    . . .
```

There are several deployment parameters listed here, having to do with the type of CMP management we want WebLogic to use, where in WebLogic's JNDI space we want our EJB home to be published, etc. The type-storage element, which is a child of the entity-descriptor element, specifies an XML file within the enclosing EJB JAR that WebLogic should consult to find the persistent storage parameters for our EJB. Here, we're specifying the file *META-INF/weblogic-cmp-rdbms-jar.xml*. In this file, we tell WebLogic how to map the persistent fields on our EJB to the underlying database. Here's the relevant section from the *weblogic-cmp-rdbms-jar.xml* file for our Profile EJB:

```
  . . .
  <!-- CMP info for Profile bean -->
  <weblogic-rdbms-bean>
    <ejb-name>CMP20ProfileBean</ejb-name>
    <data-source-name>jdbc/ProfileDB</data-source-name>
    <table-name>PROFILE_BIN</table-name>
    <field-map>
      <cmp-field>name</cmp-field>
      <dbms-column>NAME</dbms-column>
    </field-map>
    <field-map>
      <cmp-field>entriesBytes</cmp-field>
      <dbms-column>ENTRIES_BYTES</dbms-column>
    </field-map>
  </weblogic-rdbms-bean>
    . . .
```

The data-source-name element specifies the JNDI binding for a WebLogic JDBC connection pool that should be used to connect to the database (this pool would be configured elsewhere in the WebLogic server), and the table-name element specifies which database table (PROFILE_BIN) holds the persistent data for our EJB. Then there are a series of field-map elements that map cmp-field elements from the *ejb-jar.xml* file to specific columns in the PROFILE_BIN table. Here, we're telling the container that the name field should be mapped to the PROFILE_BIN. NAME column, and entriesBytes should be mapped to the PROFILE_BIN.ENTRIES_ BYTES column.

These two examples (Sun's J2EE Reference Implementation and BEA WebLogic) are just two possible ways to provide CMP field mapping information. Each EJB-enabled server vendor will have its own scheme, but the basic required information will be roughly the same. Regardless of how you specify the CMP field mapping, the EJB container reads the information and generates the necessary code to load and store the bean's persistent data to and from the underlying persistent storage system. It's your responsibility to ensure that the underlying physical persistence schema (whether it's relational, object-oriented, hierarchical, etc.) is compatible with the deployment information provided to the container. In our example, we need to make sure there is a PROFILE_BIN table with NAME and ENTRIES_BYTES columns, and the data types of these columns have to be compatible with the data types of the bean properties we've mapped them to.

EJB 1.1. In EJB 1.1, the persistent properties of an entity EJB are concrete data members defined in the bean implementation. So in an EJB 1.1 version of our CMP Profile bean, rather than providing abstract accessor methods for our persistent properties, we need to provide concrete data members for our persistent state—for example:

```
// Name of the person owning the profile
public String mName = "";
// Serialized representation of profile entries,
                        for storage in persistent
// store, or passivated state
public byte[] mEntriesBytes = null;
```

The entity element in EJB 1.1 deployment descriptors is very similar to the new EJB 2.0 version. We still use cmp-field and primkey-field elements to specify the persistent data fields and the primary key field. But instead of using abstract Java-Bean property names in these elements, we use the physical variable names:

```
<!-- Indicate which fields need to be managed persistently -->
<cmp-field><field-name>mName</field-name></cmp-field>
<cmp-field><field-name>mEntriesBytes</field-name></cmp-field>
<!-- Since our primary key is simple (one-column), we need to specify
                to the container which field maps to the primary key -->
<primkey-field>mName</primkey-field>
```

As in EJB 2.0, we need to somehow map these persistent fields to persistent storage; how this is done is vendor-dependent. In Sun's J2EE Reference Implementation, we would use its graphical *deploytool* to provide this information, in BEA WebLogic we would use a *weblogic-cmp-rdbms-jar.xml* file with a slightly different DTD; in other application servers, other schemes for collecting this information might be used.

Persistence callbacks

If your EJB object is using container-managed persistence, the container is handling the loading and storing of persistent data. You still can provide ejbLoad() and ejbStore() methods on your bean implementation, however. The ejbLoad() method is called just after the container has loaded the specified data fields from persistent storage into your data members, and ejbStore() is called just before the container writes your data members to persistent storage. If there is any conversion or bookkeeping you need to handle, you can do that in these methods.

Container-managed beans also rely on the container to create and remove the entities they represent from persistent storage. However, the bean can still provide ejbCreate() and ejbRemove() methods. The appropriate creation method is called just before the container creates the required records for the new entity in the database. The bean can use these methods to initialize any data members the container accesses while creating the records. The container also invokes the bean's ejbRemove() method just before the container removes the necessary records from persistent storage. This lets you do any cleanup before the entity is removed.

Handling complex data structures

Each EJB container is limited to some degree in the way that data on your bean implementation can be mapped into persistent data fields. There is no standard format defined for the data mapping a particular container supports, so it's possible a particular EJB provider won't support whatever complicated mapping you require for your bean. For the most part, however, you can expect EJB providers to limit the format to a single persistent data field being mapped to a single data member on your bean implementation. If the data structures on your bean are too complicated for you to provide an explicit mapping to persistent data fields, you have to decide how to deal with this.

In our entity Profile example, we've stored the profile entries in a Properties data member on our bean implementation. We don't know at deployment time how many entries there will be, so we can't enumerate a mapping to particular database fields. Ideally, we really want each entry in the Properties object to be stored in separate entry tables in our database, along with the name of the owner of the entry, which is exactly how we implemented our bean-managed implementation in Example 8-12. But since we're using CMP, we can't count on the EJB container supporting this type of persistence mapping (and, in fact, chances are that it won't).

One option is to give up on container-managed persistence and manage it yourself in the bean implementation. Another is to make each entry in the profile its own EJB and store the entries as a list of Entry beans on the profile bean. This would probably turn out to be too expensive in terms of interactions with the container and memory usage, however. Each entry in the profile would need to be managed separately by the container, with all of the relevant lifecycle notifications.

Another option, and the one we used in our bean implementation in Example 8-13, is to serialize your complex data structures into byte arrays on your bean and allow the container to read and write the serialized bytes to database fields as binary data. In our entity Profile example, rather than using the PROFILE and PROFILE_ENTRY tables we used in the bean-managed version, we defined a single PROFILE_BIN table with a NAME column to hold the name of the profile owner, and an ENTRIES_BYTES column to hold the serialized bytecodes for the Properties object. We map the data members on our bean to these database columns, as we did earlier in this section, and the container will generate the necessary JDBC calls to load and store these data members to and from these columns.

This gives us a persistent binary field on our EJB, but we still have to serialize the Properties object into the byte array when it needs to be stored persistently, and deserialize the byte array into the Properties object when the persistent data is loaded. As we mentioned before, when using CMP, the ejbLoad() and ejbStore() methods are used by the container as callbacks. The ejbStore() method is called just before the container performs an automatic store of the bean's persistent fields to the database, and ejbLoad() is called just after the container has loaded the persistent fields from the database. So we can use the ejbStore() method on our bean to copy the Properties object on our ProfileBean to the mEntriesBytes persistent data member. If you look at the ejbStore() method in Example 8-13, you'll see that it simply calls our transferToBytes() method:

```
// Transfer the list of entries from our Properties member to the byte
// array.
private void transferToBytes() throws IOException {
  // Serialize the Properties into a byte array using an
ObjectOutputStream
  if (mEntries != null && !mEntries.isEmpty()) {
    ByteArrayOutputStream byteOut = new ByteArrayOutputStream();
    ObjectOutputStream objOut = new ObjectOutputStream(byteOut);
    objOut.writeObject(mEntries);
    setEntriesBytes(byteOut.toByteArray());
  }
  else {
    setEntriesBytes(null);
  }
}
```

This method uses I/O streams to serialize the mEntries Properties object into the mEntriesBytes byte array. After the container calls our ejbStore() method, it can write the mEntriesBytes data member on our bean to a raw data field in the database (e.g., a LONG BINARY field in a SQL database). On the reading end, the container will load the bytes stored in the database column into the mEntriesBytes byte array, then it will call our ejbLoad() method. We can use the ejbLoad() method to convert the bytes loaded by the container into a Properties object; our ejbLoad() method simply calls transferToProps():

```
// Convert the serialized byte array into our Properties entry list.
private void transferToProps() throws IOException {
  // Take the raw byte array and de-serialize it
  // back into a Properties object using an ObjectInputStream
  try {
    if (getEntriesBytes() != null) {
      ByteArrayInputStream byteIn =
        new ByteArrayInputStream(getEntriesBytes());
      ObjectInputStream objIn = new ObjectInputStream(byteIn);
      mEntries = (Properties)objIn.readObject();
    }
    // If no entries in database, set properties
    // to a new, empty collection
    else {
      mEntries = new Properties();
```

```
        }
      }
      catch (ClassNotFoundException cnfe) {
        System.out.println(
                    "Properties class not found during de-serialization");
      }
    }
```

This workaround is a good example of how the ejbLoad() and ejbStore() methods can be useful for CMP entity beans. It may also seem like an ideal solution for our Profile example, since it allows us to deploy our entity Profile with container-managed persistence and still have a variable-sized list of entries on a profile. But this solution comes with a price tag: it makes our database records unusable for other, non-Java applications. The data stored in the PROFILE_BIN. ENTRIES_BYTES column is a serialized Java object, so there's no way, for example, to check on a user's profile entries using a simple SQL query, or to use a standard RDBMS reporting tool to show categories of users sorted by profile entries. As we'll see in the next section, the limitations of CMP also make it more difficult to implement certain complex finder methods.

Finder and select methods

When using container-managed persistence, the EJB container also generates all of the ejbFindXXX() methods required for the finder methods on the home interface(s). It can automatically generate an ejbFindByPrimaryKey() method, based on the data mapping and primary key information you provide at deployment time (although the EJB specifications are unclear as to whether the container is required to do this). But for any other ejbFindXXX() methods, you need to provide the container with the logic for the methods. The container can't infer the semantics of what you're trying to do based solely on method arguments. The same is true of select methods.

As an example, suppose we want to add a finder method for our Profile EJB, called findEmptyProfiles(), that finds all the profiles in the persistent store that have no entries in them. We would add the finder method to the home interface(s) for Profile bean:

```
    public Collection findEmptyProfiles()
                            throws RemoteException, FinderException;
```

The finder method returns a Collection because it could potentially find more than one empty profile in the database. Now we need to tell the EJB container how to implement this method.

EJB 2.0. The persistence logic for both finder and select methods in EJB 2.0 are provided using *EJB QL*, a standard query language defined as part of the EJB 2.0 specification. EJB QL is similar in syntax to SQL, except that queries are defined using the abstract schema elements defined in the deployment descriptors for your EJBs.

Query logic for finder and select methods is included in the *ejb-jar.xml* deployment descriptor, using query elements within the corresponding entity section. So to provide the query logic for the findEmptyProfiles() finder method on our

---

Profile EJB, we would add the following stanza to our *ejb-jar.xml* file, within the entity element for our Profile bean:

```
<entity>
   ...
   <query>
     <query-method>
       <method-name>findEmptyProfiles</method-name>
       <method-params></method-params>
     </query-method>
     <ejb-ql>
       <![CDATA[SELECT OBJECT(p) FROM ProfileBean AS p
               WHERE p.entriesBytes IS NULL]]>
     </ejb-ql>
   </query>
   ...
</entity>
```

The full syntax for EJB QL is provided in Part III, but it should be fairly obvious in our example what we're doing. The findEmptyProfiles() method takes no arguments, so we specify the query-method using findEmptyProfiles as its method-name, and an empty method-params element. We want this finder to return all Profiles that have no entries in the database, so we specify an EJB QL statement that selects all ProfileBeans (using the abstract "table" name we defined earlier for our Profile EJB) whose entriesBytes persistent fields are null.

Select methods are defined using the same query element in the deployment descriptor. We simply specify the corresponding ejbSelectXXX() method name in the method-name element.

This persistence logic, in combination with the abstract schema information provided earlier in the deployment descriptor, is used by the container to generate the concrete implementations of the finder and select methods for our bean. The EJB QL might be "compiled" in SQL for a relational database, Object Query Language (OQL) for an object-oriented database, or some other native persistence query language.

You may have noticed in our CMP bean implementation that we've removed the ejbFindByEntryValue() finder method that we had in our BMP version in Example 8-12. Because of the way we decided to implement the persistence of the entries of the Profile bean (using a single serialized byte array stored in a single binary database column), there isn't any way to implement the logic of findByEntryValue(). From the perspective of EJB QL, the entriesBytes "column" is simply an array of bytes, with no way to query for the data stored in the Properties object that it came from. Again, we could fix this problem by changing our persistence mapping—for example, we could create a new Entry EJB and have the Profile bean maintain a set of references to Entry beans. But as mentioned in the previous section, this would impose some significant resource needs on our profile service, since each entry in each profile would now be a full-blown EJB object with all of the requisite container management.

EJB 1.1. The EJB 1.1 specification doesn't provide a standard format for specifying the persistence logic for finder methods. Nor does it provide a means for you to specify some of the finder methods in the bean implementation and leave the rest for the EJB container to implement. The details of specifying this information are left entirely to the EJB container vendor. Some EJB 1.1 containers allow you to provide code segments at deployment time for the finder methods, while other vendors define their own descriptive scripting language that allows you to describe the logic of the method implementation to the EJB container.

If we are using BEA's WebLogic server and its EJB 1.1 container, the logic for our finder method is given in the *weblogic-cmp-rdbms-jar.xml* file, along with the CMP field mapping information we just saw. Just after the attribute-map element, we would add a finder-list element and provide the relevant logic for each finder method on the home interface(s) for our EJB. Here is the finder-list for our Profile bean:

```
<finder-list>
  <finder>
    <method-name>findEmptyProfiles</method-name>
    <finder-query><![CDATA[(isNull mEntriesBytes)]]></finder-query>
  </finder>
</finder-list>
```

Here we are using a WebLogic-specific query language, called WLQL, to tell the container what logic to use for our finder method. The finder-query element contains a CDATA section with a logical expression that the WebLogic server will convert to the corresponding SQL queries needed for the finder method. Here, we're telling WebLogic that the findEmptyProfiles() finder method should return any Profiles with a null mEntriesBytes persistent field (e.g., a null PROFILE_BIN. ENTRIES_BYTES column, according to our earlier field mapping).

If you are using EJB 1.1 and implementing an entity bean with many complicated finder methods, or if you are concerned with your bean being easily portable between EJB server providers, you may want to avoid container-managed persistence and stick with managing the persistent data yourself. With some EJB 1.1 providers, you may find that the format they provide for describing finder methods is too limited for your purposes. And deploying the bean in different EJB servers means porting the descriptions of your finder methods from server to server, which defeats the purpose of writing to a distributed component standard. EJB 2.0 and the standard EJB QL format for specifying query logic help quite a bit in this regard.

EJB relationships

EJB 2.0 also introduces the concept of EJB relationships. In keeping with the idea of an abstract persistence schema, EJB relationships can be thought of as abstract foreign-key constraints between our EJB "tables." Suppose, for example, that in addition to our Profile bean, we also defined a Person entity bean that provided access to more general information about a person (name, address, etc.). Within the Profile bean implementation, it might be useful to access the Person bean corresponding to the owner of a particular Profile. In the EJB 2.0 CMP model, we can do this using EJB relationships.

Since EJB relationships are a way to extend the abstract persistence schema of a set of CMP EJBs, they can only be established between EJBs that are using CMP. Session beans, message-driven beans and BMP entity beans can't participate in EJB relationships. EJB relationships are accessible only from the within the bean implementations—they aren't exposed directly to clients. EJB relationships can be one-to-one or one-to-many. In our case, we want a single Person to be related to a single Profile, so the relationship will be one-to-one. If we plan to change our Profile bean so that it uses a new Entry EJB to represent its entries, and we want to establish a persistence relationship between the two, we make the relationship one-to-many.

It's important to note that EJB relationships are created using the local interfaces for EJBs. If an EJB doesn't have a local interface, then it can have one-way relationships to other beans, but other EJBs can't have relationships with it.

The process for establishing an EJB relationship is similar to defining persistent fields; you define the accessor method(s) on either end of the relationship, specify the relationship in the EJB deployment descriptor, and then provide the container with the information on how the relationship is mapped to the underlying persistent storage system. In our case, we want to define a one-to-one relationship between our Profile bean and a new Person bean. Let's suppose that the Person bean has a very simple local client interface:

```
import javax.ejb.*;

public interface PersonLocal extends EJBLocalObject {
    // Access the person's first and last name
    public String getFirstName();
    public String getLastName();
}
```

We won't show all of the details of the implementation of this Person EJB, we'll just highlight the details relevant to the EJB relationship.

The first step in creating the relationship is defining abstract accessor methods on the implementations of the beans involved. On our ProfileBean implementation class, we would add the following accessors:

```
// Get local person related to this profile
abstract public PersonLocal getPersonLocal();
abstract public void setPersonLocal(PersonLocal person);
```

If we wanted the relationship to be bidirectional, we would also define accessor methods on the implementation class for our Person bean to read and write the Profile associated with the Person:

```
// Get/set local Profile using CMP relationships
abstract public ProfileLocal getProfileLocal();
abstract public void setProfileLocal(ProfileLocal profile);
```

Notice that these accessors need to be defined in terms of the local interfaces of the beans involved.

Now we need to specify the relationship between these two beans in the EJB deployment descriptor. Assuming that both beans are defined in the same *ejb-jar.xml* file, the relationship is defined like so:

```
...
<ejb-jar>
  <enterprise-beans>
    <!-- A Profile EJB using container-managed persistence -->
    <entity>
      <ejb-name>CMP20ProfileBean</ejb-name>
      ...
    </entity>
    <!-- A Person EJB using container-managed persistence -->
    <entity>
      <ejb-name>CMP20PersonBean</ejb-name>
      ...
    </entity>
  </enterprise-beans>
  <!-- Establish EJB relationships between Person and Profile -->
  <relationships>
    <ejb-relation>
      <ejb-relation-name>Person-Profile</ejb-relation-name>
      <!-- Relation from person to profile -->
      <ejb-relationship-role>
        <ejb-relationship-role-name>
          Person-has-Profile
        </ejb-relationship-role-name>
        <!-- One profile per person -->
        <multiplicity>one</multiplicity>
        <relationship-role-source>
          <ejb-name>CMP20PersonBean</ejb-name>
        </relationship-role-source>
        <cmr-field>
          <cmr-field-name>profileLocal</cmr-field-name>
        </cmr-field>
      </ejb-relationship-role>
      <!-- Relation from profile to person -->
      <ejb-relationship-role>
        <ejb-relationship-role-name>
          Profile-belongs-to-Person
        </ejb-relationship-role-name>
        <!-- One person per profile -->
        <multiplicity>one</multiplicity>
        <relationship-role-source>
          <ejb-name>CMP20ProfileBean</ejb-name>
        </relationship-role-source>
        <cmr-field>
          <cmr-field-name>personLocal</cmr-field-name>
        </cmr-field>
      </ejb-relationship-role>
    </ejb-relation>
  </relationships>
  ...
</ejb-jar>
```

Here we've added a relationships element to our *ejb-jar.xml* file, after the enterprise-beans section that describes the EJBs themselves. Each ejb-relation element in this section defines a relationship between two EJBs. Here we have a single ejb-relation that defines the relationship between the Person and Profile beans described earlier in the deployment descriptor. Each "side" of the relationship is described using an ejb-relationship-role element. The ejb-relationship-role element includes a name to assign to the role, the multiplicity of the role ("one" or "many"), the source EJB of the role (using the ejb-name associated with the EJB), and the a cmr-field element that specifies the property on the bean that the role is associated with. In our case, we use the profileLocal and personLocal properties for the cmr-fields, to correspond to the accessor methods we defined earlier on our beans.

The last thing we need to do is provide the EJB container with the information specifying how this relationship is represented in persistent storage. Again, a format for specifying this information isn't defined in the EJB specification. You need to determine what form of persistence your J2EE server supports and how it requires the persistence mapping to be defined. Using BEA WebLogic as our example, we would add a weblogic-rdbms-relation element to our *weblogic-cmp-rdbms-jar.xml* file:

```
<!-- Bean relations -->
<weblogic-rdbms-relation>
  <relation-name>Person-Profile</relation-name>
  <weblogic-relationship-role>
    <relationship-role-name>
      Person-has-Profile
    </relationship-role-name>
    <column-map>
      <foreign-key-column>NAME</foreign-key-column>
      <key-column>NAME</key-column>
    </column-map>
  </weblogic-relationship-role>
  <weblogic-relationship-role>
    <relationship-role-name>
      Profile-belongs-to-Person
    </relationship-role-name>
    <column-map>
      <foreign-key-column>NAME</foreign-key-column>
      <key-column>NAME</key-column>
    </column-map>
  </weblogic-relationship-role>
</weblogic-rdbms-relation>
```

Each weblogic-relationship-role element corresponds to an ejb-relationship-role element in the *ejb-jar.xml* file, and specifies which RDBMS columns represent the foreign key link between the beans' underlying tables.

Since we defined both read and write accessors for either end of this EJB relationship, we can alter the persistent relationship between a Person and their Profile by simply using the setPersonLocal() or setProfileLocal() methods on the Profile or Person implementations, respectively. The data in persistent storage will be adjusted accordingly by the EJB container to reflect the new relationship.

In the case of RDBMS persistent storage, the foreign-key column(s) will be set to point to the appropriate row in the target table.

Implementing Message-Driven Beans

The EJB 2.0 specification added a new component model for EJBs to the session and entity models already available in EJB 1.1. Message-driven EJBs are components that are managed by an EJB container like other EJBs, but they are invoked asynchronously by clients using JMS messages rather than method calls. In terms of their runtime lifecycle and container management, message-driven beans are closest in nature to stateless session beans. They are invoked indirectly and asynchronously, so they don't maintain conversational state on behalf of clients, and they can be pooled by the container to handle incoming messages.

From the client's perspective, a message-driven bean is seen as simply another JMS destination with which to exchange messages. Clients need not even know that an EJB container is involved—they simply perform the usual steps to establish a session with the JMS queue or topic and exchange messages with it. We'll only touch on these JMS-specific details here—for more details, see Chapter 10.

Message-driven EJBs are the simplest to implement, since they require only a bean implementation class. The only client interaction with them is through JMS messages, so there's no need for client interfaces or home interfaces. A message-driven bean must implement both the MessageDrivenBean interface from the EJB API, as well as the MessageListener interface from JMS. The bean's lifecycle is managed by the EJB container, including its association with a JMS destination. While a simple, standalone JMS MessageListener needs to be manually associated with it message destination, the EJB container associates message-driven beans with their destinations automatically, using the information provided in the bean's deployment descriptor. Once a message-driven bean is activated, it receives messages from its designated JMS destination and responds to them through its onMessage() method, just like any JMS MessageListener.

As an example, suppose we want to expose the profile-management capabilities of our Profile EJB to messaging clients. We may decide to do this if we plan to support clients that can't utilize direct EJB calls, or that have a need for asynchronous calls. We can use a message-driven EJB to do this. Our message-driven EJB can run within our EJB container along with our Profile EJB, and act as a proxy between the Profile EJB and messaging clients.

The message-driven proxy for our Profile EJB is shown in Example 8-15.

Example 8-15: Message-Driven Profile EJB

```
import javax.ejb.*;
import javax.rmi.*;
import java.rmi.*;
import javax.jms.*;
import javax.naming.*;
import java.util.*;
```

Example 8-15: Message-Driven Profile EJB (continued)

```java
public class ProfileProxyBean implements MessageDrivenBean, MessageListener {
  private MessageDrivenContext mContext;
  private ProfileHome mProfileHome;

  // Required create method. Here, we lookup the home interface for the
  // Profile EJB we are acting as a proxy for. We use the Profile's local
  // home interface, assuming that we're running in the same container.
  public void ejbCreate () throws CreateException {
    System.out.println("Create called on ProfileProxyBean.");
    try {
      Context ctx = new InitialContext();
      mProfileHome =
        (ProfileHome)PortableRemoteObject.narrow(
                  ctx.lookup("ejb/CMP20-ProfileHome"), ProfileHome.class);
    }
    catch (NamingException ne) {
      throw new CreateException("
                                Failed to locate Profile home interface: " +
                                ne.getMessage());
    }
  }

  // Receive context from the container.
  public void setMessageDrivenContext(MessageDrivenContext ctx) {
    mContext = ctx;
  }

  // Required remove method - no action needed in our case.
  public void ejbRemove() {
    System.out.println("Remove called on ProfileProxyBean.");
  }

  // Implementation of message listener. Here, we check the type of the
  // incoming message. If it's other than a MapMessage, we ignore it. If it
  // is a MapMessage, we interpret it as a set of new entry values for a
  // profile named by the "OWNER" field in the map. We lookup the
  // corresponding Profile EJB, and set the entries according
  // to the contents of the MapMessage.
  public void onMessage(Message msg) {
    if (msg instanceof MapMessage) {
      MapMessage mMsg = (MapMessage)msg;
      try {
        String name = mMsg.getString("OWNER");
        if (name != null) {
          Profile prof = mProfileHome.findByPrimaryKey(name);
          Enumeration eNames = mMsg.getMapNames();
          while (eNames.hasMoreElements()) {
            String eName = (String)eNames.nextElement();
            String eVal = mMsg.getString(eName);
            if (!eName.equals("OWNER")) {
              prof.setEntry(eName, eVal);
```

Example 8-15: Message-Driven Profile EJB (continued)

```
                }
              }
            }
          }
          catch (JMSException je) {
            System.out.println("JMS error processing message to ProfileProxy: " +
                            je.getMessage());
          }
          catch (RemoteException re) {
            System.out.println("Remote exception while accessing profile: " +
                            re.getMessage());
          }
          catch (FinderException fe) {
            System.out.println("Failed to find Profile named in message: " +
                            fe.getMessage());
          }
        }
        else {
          System.out.println("Non-MapMessage received by ProfileProxy, type = " +
                          msg.getClass().getName());
        }
      }
    }
}
```

The `ProfileProxyBean` contains the EJB callbacks required on message-driven beans:

ejbCreate( )

>   Message-driven beans must have a single, no-argument `ejbCreate( )` method, used by the EJB container to initialize a new instance when it's needed. Here, we initialize our reference to the home interface for our entity `Profile` bean, by performing a JNDI lookup and casting the returned object to a `ProfileHome` reference.

setMessageDrivenContext( )

>   This method is analogous to the `setSessionContext( )` and `setEntityContext( )` methods on session and entity beans, respectively. The `MessageDrivenContext` is used to access the runtime environment of the EJB container. The container calls this method just before it calls the bean's `ejbCreate( )` method.

ejbRemove( )

>   This method is called when the container decides that a message-driven bean is no longer needed in active memory, and wants to destroy the bean to reclaim its resources.

A message-driven bean also implements the `javax.jms.MessageListener` interface, and therefore needs to have an `onMessage( )` method for dealing with incoming messages. In our `ProfileProxyBean`, we expect to receive a `MapMessage` containing name/value pairs representing entries to be set on a particular profile. The name of the profile owner is expected in the `OWNER` property on the `MapMessage`. In the `onMessage( )` method, we get the name of the target profile, then use `findByPrimaryKey()` on the `ProfileHome` to get a reference to the `Profile` to be updated. Next, we get a list of the property names present in the `MapMessage`, and set the corresponding entry on the `Profile` according to the values found in the message.

Deploying our message-driven bean is the same general procedure as session and entity beans. We need to provide a message-driven element in an *ejb-jar.xml* file that describes our bean. In this case, we would use an entry such as the following:

```
<ejb-jar>
  <enterprise-beans>
    <!-- A message-driven proxy for the Profile beans -->
    <message-driven>
      <ejb-name>MessageDrivenProfileProxy</ejb-name>
      <ejb-class>ProfileProxyBean</ejb-class>
      <transaction-type>Container</transaction-type>
      <message-driven-destination>
        <destination-type>javax.jms.Queue</destination-type>
      </message-driven-destination>
    </message-driven>
    ...
  </enterprise-beans>
</ejb-jar>
```

The message-driven element lists the name used to refer to the bean (`ejb-name`), the class of the bean implementation (`ejb-class`), whether we want the transactions managed by the bean or the container (`transaction-type`), and what type of JMS destination the bean should be connected to (`message-driven-destination`).

Client use of message-driven beans

As mentioned earlier, a client of a message-driven EJB simply connects to the JMS destination for the bean and exchanges messages to it: it doesn't need to use any EJB API calls at all. A client that wanted to use our message-driven `Profile` bean would use basic JMS code such as the following to update a user's profile:

```
Context context = new InitialContext(...);

// Look up the JMS queue connection factory, make a connection, start it
QueueConnectionFactory qFactory =
  (QueueConnectionFactory)context.lookup(
                          "java:comp/env/jms/jent-EJB-connFactory");
QueueConnection qConn = qFactory.createQueueConnection();
qConn.start();

// Lookup the JMS message queue for the message-driven bean, and
// create a session with it
Queue profQueue = (Queue)context.lookup("jms/ProfileProxyQueue");
QueueSession qSession =
  qConn.createQueueSession(false, Session.AUTO_ACKNOWLEDGE);

// Create a sender
QueueSender sender = qSession.createSender(profQueue);
```

```
// Create a MapMessage
MapMessage msg = qSession.createMapMessage();
// Set the name for the target profile
msg.setString("OWNER", "Kaitlyn");

// Set an entry value
msg.setString("favoriteColor", "green");

// Send the message
sender.send(msg);
```

The first half of this code segment is simply establishing a session with the message destination. Here, we've assumed that our message-driven bean has been associated with a message queue stored in JNDI under the name *java:comp/env/ jms/jent-EJB-connFactory*. In the last few lines of this client code, we construct a MapMessage, set the OWNER field in the map to be the name of the owner of the target profile, and then set one or more profile entries to be used to update the profile.

Transaction Management

One of the advanced value-added features that Enterprise JavaBeans provides over regular remote objects is transaction management. The EJB container can broker transaction contexts on behalf of your EJBs, making sure to "do the right thing" in terms of handling transaction defers, commits, or rollbacks. This section introduces some basic transaction-management concepts, then goes into specifics about transaction management for EJBs. The information in this section is especially important if you need to correctly manage client-defined transactions with requests that your bean may make of transactional resources, like databases or messaging systems.

Transactions break up a series of interactions into units of work that can be either committed if they are successfully executed or rolled back at any time before the transaction is committed. If a transaction is rolled back, all parties involved in the transaction are responsible for restoring their state to its pretransaction condition. Transaction support is especially important in a distributed environment, since agents may lose network contact with each other or one agent may die while engaged in a series of interactions with another agent.

The EJB container is the principal player in the area of transaction management, since it is responsible for either generating transactions around client interactions with the bean, or detecting client-requested transactions and then notifying the EJB objects about transaction boundaries (start and commit/rollback).

The Enterprise JavaBeans architecture relies on the Java Transaction API (JTA) for transaction support. The JTA represents a transaction with the javax.transaction. UserTransaction interface. Complete coverage of the JTA and the concepts of transaction-based processing are beyond the scope of this chapter, but a few words of overview here should be enough for you to get an understanding of how this can be a valuable feature of Enterprise JavaBeans. In addition, the JTA interfaces and classes are documented in Part III.

A client or a J2EE component like an EJB can declare a new transaction by creating a `UserTransaction` object. The transaction is started by calling the `begin()` method on the transaction object, and ended by calling either the `commit()` method (for a successful completion) or the `rollback()` method (to abort the transaction and revert to the state before the transaction began). Suppose we have a client that is using one of the entity versions of our `Profile` EJB, and it maintains user profiles for multiple distinct applications. Perhaps the client is a web-based portal of some kind, and it maintains separate user profiles for each application accessible through the portal. If the user changes a preference that needs to be updated across multiple application profiles, the portal system will want to ensure that the update is made successfully to all affected `Profile` entities before committing the entire transaction. This code excerpt shows how the portal client might use its own `Transaction` to accomplish this:

```
// Get the name of the user, the entry to be changed and the new value
String userName = ...;
String entry = ...;
String val = ...;
// Get the JNDI context, and use it to get the Profile home interface
Context ctx = new InitialContext(props);
Object pRef = ctx.lookup("CMPProfileHome");
ProfileHome profHome =
   (ProfileHome)PortableRemoteObject.narrow(pRef, ProfileHome.class);

// Get the two affected profiles
Profile calProf = profHome.findByPrimaryKey(userName + "-calendar");
Profile annProf = profHome.findByPrimaryKey(userName + "-announce");

// Get a transaction object, using a JNDI lookup on the EJB context
UserTransaction xaction =
           (UserTransaction)ctx.lookup("java:comp/UserTransaction");

// Perform a transaction to update the
xaction.begin();
try {
  calProf.setEntry(entry, val);
  annProf.setEntry(entry, val);
  // If all is well, commit the entire transaction
  xaction.commit();
}
// If anything goes wrong, roll back the work we've done.
catch (Exception e) {
  xaction.rollback();
}
```

The client is using the transaction to ensure that the changes to both `Profiles` are successful before committing the overall transaction. If either update fails, the `rollback()` method is called on the transaction to ensure that any changes are undone. Note that the client is retrieving the `UserTransaction` from the J2EE server's JNDI context using the name `java:comp/UserTransaction`. This is a standard location where a compliant J2EE server is required to provide a `UserTransaction` object for clients and J2EE components.

An EJB object might use similar procedures if it is managing its own transactions. The only difference is the bean would be able to use its EJBContext to get a transaction directly from its container:

```
xaction = myContext.getUserTransaction();
```

In the context of an Enterprise JavaBeans component, transaction boundaries can be defined by any of the three runtime roles that participate in the EJB architecture: the client of the EJB object, the EJB container, or the EJB object itself. In all cases, the EJB container decides how to handle the transaction context whenever a method is invoked on an EJB object. During a bean's lifetime, the container decides whether to execute the bean's business methods within the client's transaction, or within a transaction that the container defines, or to allow the bean to manage its own transaction boundaries. EJB supports what is called a flat transaction model, meaning that transactions can't be nested within each other. If a client defines its own transaction (as shown previously), and invokes an EJB method, which attempts to define its own, separate transaction context, the EJB container needs to decide how to mitigate these two transaction contexts so that there is only one (or else throw an exception if the situation can't be resolved). What the container does in a particular transactional situation is determined in large part by deployment descriptor elements that indicate how an EJBs transaction is to be managed.

Transaction management: Bean-managed vs. container-managed

First, at a high level, you need to specify to the container whether your EJB will manage its own transactions (by creating its own UserTransaction objects and starting/committing them in its business methods), or it will rely on the container to manage its transactions. This is done in the deployment descriptor using the transaction-type element:

```
...
<enterprise-beans>
  <session>
    ...
    <transaction-type>Container</transaction-type>
    ...
  </session>
  ...
</enterprise-beans>
...
```

A "Container" values indicates container-managed transactions; a "Bean" value indicates bean-management. If you specify bean-managed transactions, the container will automatically suspend any client-defined transactions before calling methods on your EJB, and resume them after the any bean-defined transaction contexts have been committed/rolled back. If you use container-managed transactions, then the container will use the method-level transaction support attributes discussed in the next section to determine how it deals with transactions. Normally you will want to use container-managed transactions, since managing your own transaction boundaries within your bean code isn't usually necessary. One situation where bean-managed transactions may be necessary is a case where you need to define multiple transaction contexts in the span of a single method. But situations like this are rare, and where possible you should avoid the additional complexity in your code and leave the transaction management to the EJB container.

Entity beans aren't allowed to use bean-managed transaction management, because the persistence management services of the EJB container require that entity beans never create their own UserTransactions. So you never specify a transaction-type for entity beans in their deployment descriptor; it's always assumed to be "Container".

Transaction support attributes

If your EJB uses container-managed transaction management, you can further specify how each method on the EJB "supports" transactions, and therefore how the container should deal with different transaction contexts when it invokes these methods on your beans. The following transaction-support values are available when specifying them in your deployment descriptor:

NotSupported
> The method can't support transactions, so it must be called without a transaction context. If the client has initiated a transaction, it is suspended by the container before the bean's method is invoked. After the method completes, the container resumes the client's transaction. The container doesn't define its own transaction context for the method call, so if the EJB calls other EJBs from the method, no transaction context is passed along to these methods.

Supports
> The method supports transactions if requested. If the client calls a method on the bean while within a transaction, the method is invoked within the client's transaction context; this transaction will be passed on to any other EJB methods called within this method. If the client calls the method with no transaction context, the container doesn't create one; it runs the method with no transaction context.

Required
> The method must be executed within a transaction context. If the client is already in a transaction of its own, the transaction context is used to invoke the EJB method. If not, the container creates a new transaction before calling the bean's method and commits/rolls back the transaction when the bean's method finishes, but before the method results are returned to the client.

RequiresNew
> The method must be executed within a new transaction. The container automatically starts a new transaction before calling a remote method on the bean, and commits the transaction when the method finishes, but before the results are returned to the client. If the client calls a remote method while within a transaction, the client's transaction is suspended by the container before executing the bean's method within the new transaction, and resumed after the new transaction is committed.

Enterprise JavaBeans

Mandatory

The method must be run within the context of a client-initiated transaction. If the client calls the method on the bean without starting a transaction first, the container throws a javax.transaction.TransactionRequiredException if the client is remote. It throws a javax.ejb.TransactionRequiredLocalException for local clients.

Never

The method must never be called with a transaction context. If a client calls this method from within its own transaction, the container will throw an exception back to the client (java.rmi.RemoteException if the client is remote, javax.ejb.EJBException if the client is local).

All of these different transaction support attributes can be used by session and entity beans using container-managed transactions. For message-driven beans, only the NotSupported and Required attributes are relevant, since client transactions can't be propagated to the EJB through an asynchronous messaging service.

These attributes are associated with methods on the EJB in the assembly-descriptor section of the deployment descriptor. You provide container-transaction elements that specify one or more methods, and a transaction support attribute to apply to those methods. Using our stateless session ProfileServer EJB as an example, we can specify that its getProfile() method "supports" transactions using this XML stanza:

```
...
<assembly-descriptor>
  <container-transaction>
    <method>
      <ejb-name>ProfileServerBean</ejb-name>
      <method-name>getProfile</method-name>
    </method>
    <trans-attribute>Supports</trans-attribute>
  </container-transaction>
...
```

CHAPTER 9

Java and XML

The Extensible Markup Language (XML) has become an essential technology for Enterprise Applications. The XML specification* allows users to define unique and structured document formats, allowing for easy and flexible data exchange between applications. Since the syntax of an XML document is bound by a public specification, XML documents can be read and manipulated by a wide variety of tools. Also, because XML documents are text-based, they can be easily transmitted between different systems using a number of transportation mechanisms, from JMS to HTTP.

XML documents can be freely structured, although they must abide by a basic set of XML rules that define a *well-formed* document. More commonly, however, the document structure is further defined by a *Document Type Definition* (DTD). With a standardized DTD, enterprise applications can exchange data without knowledge of each other's native formats. Industry working groups have defined DTDs for everything from bank transactions to medical records to electronic books

XML is also an integral part of the emerging concept of web services. XML based messaging systems, such as the Simple Object Access Protocol (SOAP), allow web services to interact with each other across vendors, platforms, and implementations. Another XML-based standard, WSDL (the Web Services Description Language) describes web services and how to integrate with them. XML-based service registries built on Universal Description, Discovery and Integration (UDDI) allow web services to publish information about themselves in the WSDL format. Clearly, XML is not going anywhere in the enterprise world.

The advantages of combining Java and XML are obvious—a cross-platform language and a cross-platform data specification. We don't have space here to

---

* The complete specification, developed by the World Wide Web Consortium, is available from the W3C web site at *http://www.w3.org/XML/*. The site also includes a variety of related specifications and other useful resources.

discuss XML itself in depth—for more information, try *Learning XML*, by Erik Ray (O'Reilly). This book covers the XML specification itself, including topics such as XML namespaces, DTDs, the XLink and XPointer specifications for rich links, and the XSLT transformation specification (which we will touch on later in this chapter). We have tried to include enough information to give newcomers a taste of what can be done.

In this chapter, we're going to take a quick look at Sun's Java API for XML Processing (JAXP) Version 1.1, which provides a standardized approach to processing XML files in Java. JAXP is included in Version 1.3 of the J2EE specification. JAXP includes three other specifications by reference: the Simple API for XML parsing (SAX), Version 2; the W3C's Document Object Model (DOM), Level 2; and the XSLT (XML Stylesheet) specification. We also discuss using JAXP to access DOM and SAX parsers and XSLT processors and offer a quick introduction to using DOM and SAX. If you want to know more about using Java with XML, try Brett McLaughlin's *Java and XML* (O'Reilly).

Using XML Documents

XML allows developers to create tag-based markup structures that are bound by a set of rules defined in a public specification. The actual content of any particular XML file is left undefined by the specification. Here's an example, *orders.xml,* that represents two orders made to a fictional online shopping site. Each order includes identifying information (an order number and a customer number), a shipping address, and one or more items. The shipping address encapsulates both the shipping method and the shipping destination, and each item includes an identifying number and the quantity ordered, as well as an optional handling instruction.

Most elements include an opening and closing tag, with the element attributes set in the opening tag. Some elements are "empty," such as the first example of the `<item>` tag. Empty elements terminate with `/>` instead of simply `>`, and don't need a separate closing tag. The significance of an empty tag is either in its attributes or its mere presence. The data is simple enough that the structure should be clear to the reader. Here's the actual XML:

```xml
<?xml version="1.0" encoding="UTF-8"?>
<!DOCTYPE orders SYSTEM "orders.dtd">
<orders>
  <order idnumber="3123" custno="121312">
    <shippingaddr method="Camel"><![CDATA[One Main St
                              Boston, MA 02112]]></shippingaddr>
    <item idnumber="7231" quantity="13"/>
    <item idnumber="1296" quantity="2">
      <handling>Please embroider in a tasteful manner!</handling>
    </item>
  </order>
  <order idnumber="3124" custno="12">
    <shippingaddr method="FedEx"><![CDATA[285 York St.
                              New Haven, CT 06510]]></shippingaddr>
    <item idnumber="12" quantity="8"/>
  </order>
</orders>
```

At the simplest level, an XML document must merely be well-formed, meaning that the document adheres to all of the syntax rules defined by the XML specification. These rules define the XML declaration on the first line and specify how tags may be formed and nested.* The requirements for a well-formed document don't include any particular XML tags except for the XML version, and specify only structure in the broadest possible terms. So for most applications, simply knowing that a document is well-formed is not particularly helpful. Of course, one can specify that only files of a particular format should be used as input for a particular program, but without a way to define what that format should be and whether documents conform to it, an eXtensible Markup Language doesn't make a great deal of sense.

However, there is a solution. The second line of *orders.xml* specifies that the file should conform to a DTD. The DTD goes a step beyond the well-formed requirement and specifies the allowable XML tags, their formats, and the allowable structure. The DTD for the *orders.xml* file requires that all <order> tags be nested within an <orders> tag, all orders have at least one item and a shipping address, all items include identifier and quantity attributes, and so forth. Here's the DTD *orders.dtd*:

```
<?xml version="1.0" encoding="UTF-8"?>
<!ELEMENT orders (order+)>
<!ELEMENT order (shippingaddr, item+)>
<!ELEMENT shippingaddr (#PCDATA)>
<!ELEMENT item (handling?)>
<!ELEMENT handling (#PCDATA)>
<!ATTLIST order
    idnumber CDATA #REQUIRED
    custno CDATA #REQUIRED
>
<!ATTLIST shippingaddr
    method (FedEx | UPS | USPS | Camel) #REQUIRED
>
<!ATTLIST item
    idnumber CDATA #REQUIRED
    quantity CDATA #REQUIRED
>
```

The XML layer of an application generally consists of one or more DTDs and a set of documents. The DTDs are written ahead of time, either by an individual developer, a working group, Application Server vendor, or other provider. Some documents, particularly those related to configuration and profiling tasks (such as the J2EE deployment descriptors), are edited by hand and read by software.

The previous example is more transaction-oriented. Documents like *orders.xml* would likely be generated by a purchasing front-end (such as a web site) and transmitted over the network to a fulfillment system (such as a corporate order tracking database) via HTTP, JMS, or some other transport layer. The receiving

---

* And quite a bit more, including entity escape sequences, namespaces, valid character sets, and so on. But we don't have room here for a full discussion, so again, we recommend O'Reilly's *Learning XML*.

software reads the document and processes it, often without any human intervention at all. Standardized DTDs mean that the two sides of the exchange can easily be provided by different vendors.

Java API for XML Processing

The JAXP API is an optional package for Java 1.1 and above. It is also a standard component of the J2EE 1.3 platform. The full specification and a reference implementation are available from *http://java.sun.com/xml/*.

The SAX and DOM APIs that are actually used for processing XML files don't include a standard method for creating a parser object; this is one of the voids JAXP fills. The API provides a set of Factory objects that will create parsers or XSLT processors. Additionally, JAXP defines a programmatic interface to XSLT processors.

The actual parser and processor implementations used by JAXP are pluggable. You can use the Crimson parser, the Apache Xerces parser (available from *http://xml.apache.org*), or any other JAXP-compatible parser. Version 1.1 of the reference implementation ships with Sun's Crimson XML parser and the Xalan XSL engine from the Apache XML project (again, see *http://xml.apache.org*). Future JAXP implementations will likely replace Crimson with Xerces. There are still variations in support for different levels of functionality across parser implementations. The examples in this chapter have been tested with the Crimson parser that ships with JAXP and all other Sun products.

JAXP 1.1 is included in the J2EE 1.3 platform. To use JAXP with JDK 1.1 or Java2, you can download the reference implementation from *http://java.sun.com/xml/*. You will need to add the *jaxp.jar* file to your CLASSPATH, as well as the JAR files containing the XML parsers and XSLT processors you wish to use. The reference implementation includes *crimson.jar* (the Crimson parser) and *xalan.jar* (the Apache Xalan XSL processor). If you use different parser and processor implementations you don't need to include crimson.jar and xalan.jar on your CLASSPATH.

Getting a Parser or Processor

To retrieve a parser or processor from inside a Java program, call the newInstance() method of the appropriate factory class, either SAXParserFactory, DocumentBuilderFactory, or TransformerFactory. The actual factory implementation is provided by the parser vendor. For example, to retrieve the platform default SAX parser:

```
SAXParserFactory spf = SAXParserFactory.newInstance();
spf.setValidating(true); //request a validating parser
try {
  SAXParser saxParser = spf.newSAXParser();
  // Processs XML here
} catch (SAXException e) {
  e.printStackTrace();
} catch (ParserConfigurationException pce) {
  pce.printStackTrace();
```

```
    } catch (IOException ioe) {
      ioe.printStackTrace();
    }
```

The next three sections will deal with what you can do once you've actually retrieved a parser. For the time being, let's treat it as an end in itself.

SAXParserFactory includes a static method called newInstance(). When this method is called, the JAXP implementation searches for an implementation of javax.xml.parsers.SAXParserFactory, instantiates, and returns it. The implementation of SAXParserFactory is provided by the parser vendor; it's org.apache.crimson.jaxp.SAXParserFactoryImpl for the Crimson parser.

The system looks for the name of the class to instantiate in the following four locations, in order:

1. One of these system properties:
   - javax.xml.parsers.SAXParserFactory
   - javax.xml.parsers.DocumentBuilderFactory
   - javax.xml.parsers.TransformerFactory

2. The *lib/jaxp.properties* file in the JRE directory. The configuration file is in key=value format, and the key is the name of the corresponding system property. Therefore, to set Crimson as the default parser, *jaxp.properties* would contain the following line:

   ```
   javax.xml.parsers.SAXParserFactory=org.apache.crimson.jaxp.
           SAXParserFactoryImpl
   ```

3. In the application JAR file, via the Services API. The API looks for the classname in a file called *META-INF/services/parserproperty* in which the filename (*parserproperty*) is the property name corresponding to the desired factory. The runtime environment checks every available JAR, so if you have multiple parsers available to your application, specify the desired factory using one of the previous methods to prevent nondeterministic behavior.

4. A platform default factory instance.

Once you have a factory, various parser options can be set using the factory specific set methods. SAXParser and DOMParser, for instance, include setNamespaceAware() and setValidating() methods, which tell the factory whether to produce a parser that is aware of XML namespaces (and will fail if the document being parsed doesn't properly conform to the namespace specification) and whether to validate against the DTD specified by the XML document itself.

Factories are thread-safe, so a single instance can be shared by multiple threads. This allows parser factories to be instantiated in a Java Servlet init() method or other centralized location. Parsers and processors, however, aren't guaranteed to be thread-safe.

SAX

The SAX API provides a procedural approach to parsing an XML file. As a SAX parser iterates through an XML file, it performs callbacks to a user-specified object.

These calls indicate the start or end of an element, the presence of character data, and other significant events during the life of the parser.

SAX doesn't provide random access to the structure of the XML file; each tag must be handled as it is encountered by the browser. This means that SAX provides a relatively fast and efficient method of parsing. Because the SAX parser deals only with one element at a time, implementations can be extremely memory-efficient, making it often the only reasonable choice for dealing with particularly large files.

SAX Handlers

The SAX API allows programs to define three kinds of objects, implementing the org.xml.sax.ContentHandler, org.xml.sax.ErrorHandler, and org.xml.sax. DTDHandler interfaces, respectively. Processing a document with SAX involves passing a handler implementation to the parser and calling the parse() method of SAXParser. The parser will read the contents of the XML file, calling the appropriate method on the handler when significant events (such as the start of a tag) occur. All handler methods may throw a SAXException in the event of an error.

We'll take a closer look at the ContentHandler and ErrorHandler interfaces next.

ContentHandler

Most, if not all, SAX applications implement the ContentHandler interface. The SAX parser will call methods on a ContentHandler when it encounters basic XML elements: chiefly, the start or end of a document, the start or end of an element, and character data within an element.

The startDocument() and endDocument() methods are called at the beginning* and end of the parsing process, and take no parameters. Most applications use startDocument() to create any necessary internal data stores, and use endDocument() to dispose of them (for example, by writing to the database.)

When the parser encounters a new element, it calls the startElement() method of the ContentHandler, passing a namespace URI, the local name of the element, the fully qualified name of the element (the namespace and the local name), and an org.xml.sax.Attributes object containing the element attributes.

The Attributes interface allows the parser to inform the ContentHandler of attributes attached to an XML tag. For instance, the <order> tag in our earlier example contained two attributes, idnumber and custno, specified like this:

```
<order idnumber="321" custno="98173">
```

---

* The first method called by the parser is actually setDocumentLocator(), which provides the handler with an implementation of org.xml.sax.Locator. This object can report the current position of the parser within the XML file via its getColumnNumber(), getLineNumber(), getPublicId(), and getSystemId() methods. However, while parser implementations are strongly encouraged to implement this method, they aren't required to.

To retrieve attributes when processing an element, call the getValue() method of attributes:

```
public void startElement(String namespaceURI, String localName,
                                    String qName, Attributes atts)
            throws SAXException {
    if(localName.equals("order")
        System.out.println("New Order Number " + atts.getValue("idnumber") +
                        " for Customer Number " + atts.getValue("custno"));
}
```

Note that before we can safely run this line, we need to make sure that we are processing an <order> tag; otherwise there is no guarantee that the particular attributes we are querying will be available.*

When the parser encounters the closing tag of an element (</order>, in this case), the parser calls the endElement() method, passing the same namespace URI, local name, and qualified name that were passed to startElement(). Every startElement() call will have a corresponding endElement() call, even when the element is empty.

These four methods all deal with handling information about XML tags but not with the data within a tag (unless that data is another tag). Much XML content consists of textual data outside the confines of tags and attributes. For example, here's the handling instruction from *orders.xml*:

```
<handling>Please embroider in a tasteful manner!</handling>
```

When the SAX parser encounters the text between the tags, it calls the characters() method, passing a character array, a starting index within that array, and the length of the relevant character sequence within the array. This simple implementation of characters() prints the output to the screen:

```
public void characters(char[] ch, int start, int length)
                    throws SAXException {
    System.out.print(new String(ch, start, length));
}
```

Note that there is no guarantee that all of the characters you want will be delivered in the same call. Also, since the characters() method doesn't include any references to the parent element, to perform more complicated tasks (such as treating the characters differently depending on the element that contains them), you will need to store the name of the current element within the handler class itself. Example 9-1 shows how to do this via the startElement() method.

The characters() method might also be called when the parser encounters ignorable whitespace, such as a carriage return separating nested elements that don't otherwise have nested character data. If the parser is validating the document against a DTD, it must instead call the ignoreableWhitespace() method to report these characters.

---

* The parser returns all the attributes specified in the XML document; either explicitly or through a default value specified in the DTD. Attributes without defaults that aren't explicitly specified in the XML document itself aren't included.

ErrorHandler

Since SAX is a language-independent specification, it doesn't handle parsing errors by throwing exceptions. Instead, a SAX parser reports errors by calling methods on a user-supplied object that implements the ErrorHandler interface. The ErrorHandler interface includes three methods: error(), fatalError(), and warning(). Each method takes a org.xml.sax.SAXParseException parameter. The programmer is free to handle the errors in whatever manner she deems appropriate; however, the specification doesn't require parsing to continue after a call to fatalError().

DefaultHandler

The API also provides the org.xml.sax.helpers.DefaultHandler class that implements all three handler interfaces. Since most handlers don't need to override every handler method, or even most, the easiest way to write a custom handler is to extend this object and override methods as necessary

Using a SAX Parser

Once you have a handler or set of handlers, you need a parser. JAXP generates SAX parsers via a SAXParserFactory, as we just saw. The SAXParserFactory has three methods for further specifying parser behavior: setValidating() (which instructs the parser to validate the incoming XML file against its DTD), setNamespaceAware() (which requests support for XML namespaces), and setFeature() (which allows configuration of implementation specific attributes for parsers from particular vendors).

It is possible to parse a document directly from a SAXParser object by passing an object that implements the ContentHandler interface to the parse() method, along with a path, URI, or InputStream containing the XML to be parsed. For more control, call the getXMLReader() method of SAXParser, which returns an org.xml. sax.XMLReader object. This is the underlying parser that actually processes the input XML and calls the three handler objects. Accessing the XMLReader directly allows programs to set specific ErrorHandler and DTDHandler objects, rather than being able to set a ContentHandler only.

All events in the SAX parsing cycle are synchronous. The parse() method will not return until the entire document has been parsed, and the parser will wait for each handler method to return before calling the next one.

A SAX example: Processing orders

Example 9-1 users a SAX DefaultHandler to process an XML document containing a set of incoming orders for a small business. It uses the startElement() method of ContentHandler to process each element, displaying relevant information. Element attributes are processed via the Attributes object passed to the startElement() method. When the parser encounters text within a tag, it calls the characters() method of ContentHandler.

Example 9-1: Parsing XML with SAX

```java
import javax.xml.parsers.*;
import org.xml.sax.*;
import org.xml.sax.helpers.*;

public class OrderHandler extends org.xml.sax.helpers.DefaultHandler {

  public static void main(String[] args) {
    SAXParserFactory spf = SAXParserFactory.newInstance();
    spf.setValidating(true); //request a validating parser

    XMLReader xmlReader = null;
    try {
      SAXParser saxParser = spf.newSAXParser();
      /* We need an XMLReader to use an ErrorHandler
         We could just pass the DataHandler to the parser if we wanted
         to use the default error handler. */

      xmlReader = saxParser.getXMLReader();
      xmlReader.setContentHandler(new OrderHandler());
      xmlReader.setErrorHandler(new OrderErrorHandler());
      xmlReader.parse("orders.xml");
    } catch (Exception e) {
      e.printStackTrace();
    }
  }

  // The startDocument() method is called at the beginning of parsing
  public void startDocument() throws SAXException {
    System.out.println("Incoming Orders:");
  }

  // The startElement() method is called at the start of each element
  public void startElement(String namespaceURI, String localName,
                           String rawName, Attributes atts)
                    throws SAXException {
   if(localName.equals("order")) {
    System.out.print("\nNew Order Number " + atts.getValue("idnumber") +
     " for Customer Number " + atts.getValue("custno"));
   } else if (localName.equals("item")) {
    System.out.print("\nLine Item: " + atts.getValue("idnumber") + " (Qty " +
     atts.getValue("quantity") + ")");
   } else if (localName.equals("shippingaddr")) {
    System.out.println("\nShip by " + atts.getValue("method") + " to:");
   } else if (localName.equals("handling")) {
    System.out.print("\n\tHandling Instructions: ");
   }
  }

  // Print Characters within a tag
  // This will print the contents of the <shippingaddr> and <handling> tags
  // There is no guarantee that all characters will be delivered in a
  // single call
```

Example 9-1: Parsing XML with SAX (continued)

```
public void characters(char[] ch, int start, int length)
                        throws SAXException {
  System.out.print(new String(ch, start, length));
}

/* A custom error handling class, although DefaultHandler implements both
        interfaces. Here we just throw the exception back to the user.*/
private static class OrderErrorHandler implements ErrorHandler {

  public void error(SAXParseException spe) throws SAXException {
    throw new SAXException(spe);
  }

  public void warning(SAXParseException spe) throws SAXException {
    System.out.println("\nParse Warning: " + spe.getMessage());
  }

  public void fatalError(SAXParseException spe) throws SAXException {
    throw new SAXException(spe);
  }
 }
}
```

In a real application, we would want to treat error handling in a more robust fashion, probably by reporting parse errors to a logging utility or EJB. An actual order management utility would populate a database table or an Enterprise Java-Bean object.

DOM

The DOM API, unlike the SAX API, allows programmers to construct an object model representing a document, and then traverse and modify that representation. The DOM API is not Java-specific; it was developed by the W3C XML working group as a cross-platform API for manipulating XML files (see *http://www. w3c.org/XML/*). As a result, it sometimes doesn't take the most direct Java-based path to a particular result. The JAXP 1.1 API incorporates DOM Level 2.

DOM is useful when programs need random access to a complex XML document, or to a document whose format is not known ahead of time. This flexibility does come at a cost, however, as the parser must build a complete in-memory object representation of the document. For larger documents, the resource requirements mount quickly. Consequently, many applications use a combination of SAX and DOM, using SAX to parse longer documents (such as importing large amounts of transactional data from an Enterprise Reporting System), and using DOM to deal with smaller, more complex documents that may require alteration (such as processing configuration files or transforming existing XML documents).

Getting a DOM Parser

The DOM equivalent of a SAXParser is the org.w3c.dom.DocumentBuilder. Many DocumentBuilder implementations actually use SAX to parse the underlying document, so the DocumentBuilder implementation itself can be thought of as a layer that sits on top of SAX to provide a different view of the structure of an XML document. We use the JAXP API to get a DocumentBuilder interface in the first place, via the DocumentBuilderFactory class:

```
DocumentBuilderFactory dbf = DocumentBuilderFactory.newInstance();

// Validation
dbf.setValidating(false);
// Ignore text elements that are completely empty:
dbf.setIgnoringElementContentWhitespace(false);
// Expand XML entities according to the DTD
dbf.setExpandEntityReferences(true);
// Treat CDATA sections the same as text
dbf.setCoalescing(true);

DocumentBuilder db = null;
try {
   db = dbf.newDocumentBuilder();
} catch (ParserConfigurationException pce) {
   pce.printStackTrace();
}
```

The set() methods, as with the SAXParserFactory, provide a simple method for configuring parser options:

setCoalescing()
> Joins XML CDATA nodes with adjoining text nodes. The default is false.

setExpandEntityReferences()
> Expands XML entity reference nodes. The default is true.

setIgnoringComments()
> Ignores XML comments. The default is false.

setIgnorningElementContentWhitespace()
> Ignores whitespace in areas defined as element-only by the DTD. The default is false.

setNamespaceAware()
> Requests a namespace aware parser. The default is false.

setValidating()
> Requests a validating parser. The default is false.

Once the DocumentBuilder is instantiated, call the parse(String URI) method to return a org.w3c.dom.Document object.

Navigating the DOM Tree

The Document object provides the starting point for working with a DOM tree. Once the parser has produced a Document, your program can traverse the document structure and make changes. In addition, Document implements the Node interface, which is the core of DOM's tree structure, and provides methods for traversing the tree and retrieving information about the current node.

All elements, attributes, entities, and text strings (indeed, every distinct component within an XML document) are represented in DOM as a node. To determine what kind of node you are working with, you can call the getNodeType() method. This returns one of the constants specified by the Node interface. All node objects have methods for dealing with child elements, although not all nodes may have children. The DOM API also provides a set of interfaces that map to each node type

The most important DOM node types and their corresponding interfaces are listed in Table 9-1. If you attempt to add child elements to a node that doesn't support children, a DOMException is thrown.

Table 9-1: Important DOM Node Types

Interface	Name Property Contains	Value	Children	Node Constant
Attr	Name of attribute	Yes	No	ATTRIBUTE_NODE
CDATASection	#cdata-section	Yes	No	CDATA_SECTION_ NODE
Comment	#comment	Yes	No	COMMENT_NODE
Document	#document	No	Yes	DOCUMENT_NODE
DocumentFragment	#document-fragment	No	Yes	DOCUMENT_ FRAGMENT_NODE
DocumentType	Document type name	No	No	DOCUMENT_TYPE_ NODE
Element	Tag name	No	Yes	ELEMENT_NODE
Entity	Entity name	No	No	ENTITY_NODE
EntityReferenced	Name of referenced entity	No	No	ENTITY_ REFERENCE_NODE
ProcessingInstruction	PI target	Yes	No	PROCESSING_ INSTRUCTION_ NODE
Text	#text	No	No	TEXT_NODE

For most applications, element nodes, identified by Node.ELEMENT_NODE, and text nodes, identified by Node.TEXT_NODE, are the most important. An element node is created when the parser encounters an XML markup tag. A text node is created when the parser encounters text that is not included within a tag. For example, if the input XML (we're using XHTML in this example) looks like this:

```
<p>
  Here is some <b>boldface</b> text.
</p>
```

The parser creates a top-level node that is an element node with a local name of "p." The top level node contains three child nodes: a text node containing "here is some," an element node named "b," and another text node containing "text." The "b" element node contains a single child text node containing the word "boldface."

The getNodeValue() method returns the contents of a text node, or the value of other node types. It returns null for element nodes.

To iterate through a node's children, use the getFirstChild() method, which will return a Node reference. To retrieve subsequent child nodes, call the getNextSibling() method of the node that was returned by getFirstChild(). To print the names of all the children of a particular Node (assume that the node variable is a valid Node):

```
for (c = node.getFirstChild(); c != null; c = c.getNextSibling()) {
    System.out.println(c.getLocalName());
}
```

Note that there is no getNextChild() method, and you can't iterate through child nodes except via the getNextSibling() method. As a result, if you use the removeChild() method to remove one of a node's children, calls to the child node's getNextSibling() method immediately return null.

Element attributes

Element attributes are accessed via the getAttributes() method, which returns a NamedNodeMap object. The NamedNodeMap contains a set of Node objects of type ATTRIBUTE_NODE. The getNodeValue() method can read the value of a particular attribute.

```
NamedNodeMap atts = elementNode.getAttributes();
if(atts != null) {
  Node sizeNode = atts.getNamedItem("size");
  String size = sizeNode.getValue();
}
```

Alternately, you can case a node to its true type (in this case, an org.w3c.dom. Element) and retrieve attributes or other data more directly:

```
if(myNode.getNodeType() == Node.ELEMENT_NODE) {
        Element myElement = (org.w3c.dom.Element)myNode;
    String attributeValue = myElement.getAttribute("attr");
// attributeValue will be  an empty string if  "attr" does not exist
    }
```

This is often easier than retrieving attribute nodes from a NamedNodeMap.

Manipulating DOM Trees

DOM is particularly useful when you need to manipulate the structure of an XML file. Example 9-2 is an HTML document condenser. It loads an HTML file (which must be well-formed XML, although not necessarily XHTML), iterates through the tree, and preserves only the important content. In this case, it's text within <em>, <th>, <title>, <li>, and <h1> through <h6>. All text nodes that aren't contained within one of these tags are removed. A more sophisticated algorithm is no doubt possible.

Example 9-2: DocumentCondenser

```java
import javax.xml.parsers.*;
import javax.xml.transform.*;
import javax.xml.transform.dom.*;
import javax.xml.transform.stream.*;
import org.w3c.dom.*;
import java.io.*;

public class DocumentCondenser {
  public static void main(String[] args) throws Exception {

    DocumentBuilderFactory dbf = DocumentBuilderFactory.newInstance();

    // For HTML, we don't want to validate without a DTD
    dbf.setValidating(false);
    // Ignore text elements that are completely empty:
    dbf.setIgnoringElementContentWhitespace(false);
    dbf.setExpandEntityReferences(true);
    dbf.setCoalescing(true);

    DocumentBuilder db = null;
    try {
      db = dbf.newDocumentBuilder();
    } catch (ParserConfigurationException pce) {
      pce.printStackTrace();
      return;
    }

    Document html = null;
    try {
      html = db.parse("enterprisexml.html");
      process(html);

      // Use the XSLT Transformer to see the output
      TransformerFactory tf = TransformerFactory.newInstance();
      Transformer output = tf.newTransformer();
      output.transform(new DOMSource(html), new StreamResult(System.out));
    } catch (Exception ex) {
      ex.printStackTrace();
      return;
    }

  }

  /* We want to keep text if the parent is <em>, <title>, <b>, <li>, <th>
     or <h1>..<h6>. We also want to keep text if it is in a <font> tag with
     a size attribute set to a larger than normal size */
  private static boolean keepText(Node parentNode) {
    if(parentNode == null) return true; // top level

    String parentName = parentNode.getLocalName();
    if((parentName.equalsIgnoreCase("em")) ||
       (parentName.equalsIgnoreCase("title")) ||
```

Example 9-2: DocumentCondenser (continued)

```
        (parentName.equalsIgnoreCase("b")) ||
        (parentName.equalsIgnoreCase("li")) ||
        (parentName.equalsIgnoreCase("th")) ||
        ((parentName.toLowerCase().startsWith("h")) &&
         (parentName.length() == 2))
      ) return true;

  if((parentNode.getNodeType() == Node.ELEMENT_NODE) &&
     (parentName.equalsIgnoreCase("font"))) {
       NamedNodeMap atts = parentNode.getAttributes();
       if(atts != null) {
        Node sizeNode = atts.getNamedItem("size"); //get an attribue Node
        if(sizeNode != null)
         if(sizeNode.getNodeValue().startsWith("+"))
           return true;
       }
  }
  return false;
}

private static void process(Node node) {

  Node c = null;
  Node delNode = null;

  for (c = node.getFirstChild(); c != null; c = c.getNextSibling()) {
     if(delNode != null)
      delNode.getParentNode().removeChild(delNode);
     delNode = null;
     if(( c.getNodeType() == Node.TEXT_NODE ) &&
        (!keepText(c.getParentNode()))) {
          delNode = c;
     } else if(c.getNodeType() != Node.TEXT_NODE) {
       process(c);
     }
  } // End For

  if(delNode != null) // Delete, if the last child was text
     delNode.getParentNode().removeChild(delNode);

 }
}
```

After the DOM tree has been processed, use the JAXP XSLT API to output new HTML. We will discuss how to use XSL with JAXP in the next section.

If you want to replace the text with a condensed version, call the setNodeValue() method of Node when processing a text node.

Extending DOM Trees

Manipulating DOM trees falls, broadly, into three categories. We can add, remove, and modify nodes on existing trees; we can create new trees; finally, we can merge trees together.

Back in the last example we saw how to delete nodes from a DOM tree with the removeChild() method. If we want to add new nodes, we have two options. While there is no direct way to instantiate a new Node object, we can copy an existing Node using its cloneNode() method. The cloneNode() method takes a single Boolean parameter, which specifies whether the node's children will be cloned as well.

```
Node newNodeWithChildren = oldElementNode.cloneNode(true);
Node childlessNode = oldElementNode.cloneNode(false);
```

Regardless of whether children are cloned, clones of an element node will include all of the attributes of the parent node. The DOM specification leaves certain cloning behaviors, specifically Document, DocumentType, Entity and Notation nodes, up to the implementation.

New nodes can also be created via the createXXX() methods of the Document object. The createElement() method accepts a String containing the new element name, and returns a new element Node. The createElementNS() method does the same thing, but accepts two parameters, a namespace and an element name. The createAttribute() method also has a namespace-aware version, createAttributeNS().

Once a new Node is created, it can be inserted or appended into the tree using the appendChild(), insertBefore(), and replaceChild() methods. Attribute nodes can be inserted into the NamedNodeMap returned by the getAttributes() method of Node. You can also add attributes to an element by casting the Node to an Element and calling setAttribute().

Creating new trees involves creating a new Document object. The easiest way to do this is via the DOMImplementation interface. An implementation of DOMImplementation can be retrieved from a DocumentBuilder object via the getDOMImplementation() method. Example 9-3 builds a version of the XML from a blank slate.

Example 9-3: TreeBuilder

```
import javax.xml.parsers.*;
import javax.xml.transform.*;
import javax.xml.transform.dom.*;
import javax.xml.transform.stream.*;
import org.w3c.dom.*;
import java.io.*;

public class TreeBuilder {

    public static void main(String[] args) {
        DocumentBuilderFactory dbf = DocumentBuilderFactory.newInstance();
```

Example 9-3: TreeBuilder (continued)

```
        dbf.setValidating(false);

        DocumentBuilder db = null;
        try {
         db = dbf.newDocumentBuilder();
        } catch (ParserConfigurationException pce) {
            pce.printStackTrace();
            return;
        }

        Document doc = db.getDOMImplementation().createDocument(
            null, "orders", null);
        // create the initial document element
        Element orderNode = doc.createElement("order");
        orderNode.setAttribute("orderno", "123433");

        Node item = doc.createElement("item");
        Node subitem = doc.createElement("number");
        subitem.appendChild(doc.createTextNode("3AGM-5"));
        item.appendChild(subitem);

        subitem = doc.createElement("handling");
        subitem.appendChild(doc.createTextNode("With Care"));
        item.appendChild(subitem);

        orderNode.appendChild(item);
        doc.getDocumentElement().appendChild(orderNode);

    }
}
```

The second parameter to createDocument() specifies the name of the base document element—in this case, the <orders> tag. Subsequent tags can be appended to the base tag. If we were to look at the results of this program as regular XML, it would look like this (we've added some whitespace formatting to make it more readable):

```
<?xml version="1.0" encoding="UTF-8"?>
<orders>
    <order orderno="123433">
        <item>
            <number>3AGM-5</number>
            <handling>With Care</handling>
        </item>
    </order>
</orders>
```

You've probably noticed that each Node implementation we've created has been based on a particular instance of the Document object. Since each node is related to its parent document, we can't go around inserting one document's nodes into another document without triggering an exception. The solution is to use the importNode() method of Document, which creates a copy of a node from another document. The original node from the source document is left untouched. Here's an example that takes the <orders> tag from the first document and puts it into a new document under an <ordersummary> tag:

```
Document doc2 = db.getDOMImplementation().createDocument(
                null, "ordersummary", null);

DocumentFragment df = doc.createDocumentFragment();
df.appendChild(doc.getDocumentElement().cloneNode(true));
doc2.getDocumentElement().appendChild(doc2.importNode(df, true));
```

We use a DocumentFragment object to hold the data we're moving. Document fragment nodes provide a lightweight structure for dealing with subsets of a document. Fragments must be valid XML, but don't need to be DTD-conformant, and can have multiple top-level children. When appending a document fragment to a document tree, the DocumentFragment node itself is ignored, and its children are appended directly to the parent node. In the example above we cloned the source element when creating the document fragment, since assigning a node to a fragment releases the node's relationship with its previous parent. The XML in the second document object looks like this:

```
<?xml version="1.0" encoding="UTF-8"?>
<ordersummary>
    <orders>
        <order orderno="123433">
            <item><number>3AGM-5</number>
            <handling>With Care</handling></item>
        </order>
    </orders>
</ordersummary>
```

XSLT

The final specification incorporated into the JAXP API is the XML Stylesheet Transformation (XSLT) system. An XSLT transformation takes an input XML document and transforms it into an output format (not necessarily XML) according to a set of rules specified in an XSL stylesheet. One common application of XSL stylesheets is transforming XML into HTML for presentation in a browser; this is often done in the browser directly, or on the web server via a content management system such as the Apache Project's Cocoon (*http://xml.apache.org/cocoon*).

The following XSL document converts the *orders.xml* file from the SAX example into HTML:

```
<?xml version="1.0" encoding="UTF-8"?>
<xsl:stylesheet version="1.0" xmlns:xsl="http://www.w3.org/1999/XSL/
Transform" xmlns:fo="http://www.w3.org/1999/XSL/Format">
    <xsl:template match="orders">
      <html>
        <head><title>Order Summary</title></head>
        <body>
        <xsl:apply-templates/>
        </body>
      </html>
```

```
    </xsl:template>
    <xsl:template match="order">
      <h1>Order Number  <xsl:value-of select="@idnumber"/></h1>
      Ship To:
      <pre>
      <xsl:value-of select="shippingaddr"/>
      </pre>
      <ul>
      <xsl:apply-templates select="item"/>
      </ul>
    </xsl:template>
    <xsl:template match="item">
          <li><xsl:value-of select="@quantity"/> of item
            <xsl:value-of select="@idnumber"/><xsl:apply-templates/></li>
    </xsl:template>
    <xsl:template match="handling">
     <br/>Special Instructions: <xsl:value-of select="."/>
    </xsl:template>
</xsl:stylesheet>
```

The XSL file consists of a series of *templates*. The XSL processor matches each template to a particular XML tag and replaces the tag with the template contents. For example, when the processor encounters an <orders> and an </orders> tag, it replaces them with:

```
<html>
    <head><title>Order Summary</title></head>
    <body>
    <xsl:apply-templates/>
    </body>
</html>
```

The *<xsl:apply-templates/>* command tells the XSLT processor to recursively apply all of the available templates to the XML content contained within the <orders> tag pair. Other XSL commands allow the processor to display element attributes, limit recursion to specific templates, and so forth. For more examples, please check one of the books recommended at the beginning of this chapter. After running the *orders.xml* file through the stylesheet, we get this HTML:

```
<html xmlns:fo="http://www.w3.org/1999/XSL/Format">
<head>
<META http-equiv="Content-Type" content="text/html; charset=UTF-8">
<title>Order Summary</title>
</head>
<body>

<h1>Order Number  3123</h1>
      Ship To:
    <pre>One Main St
Boston, MA 02112</pre>
<ul>
<li>13 of item 7231</li>
<li>2 of item 1296
      <br/>Special Instructions: Please embroider in a tasteful manner!
        </li>
```

```
</ul>
<!-- Snipped for brevity -->
</body>
</html>
```

The classes in the JAXP `javax.xml.transform` package allow programs to use XSLT Transformer objects, such as Apache Xalan (which ships with the JAXP reference implementation) to transform XML documents.

At this point we should point out that JAXP doesn't require XSLT at all: instead, it is a generic transformations API that theoretically can be used with a variety of transformation systems. However, XSLT is by far the most popular and widely implemented, so the remainder of this section (and most books on the subject) will assume XSLT is a transformation system.

JAXP Data Sources

The DOM example earlier in this chapter briefly introduced the `TransformerFactory` class. `TransformerFactory` works just like the SAX and DOM parser factories, but returns a `Transformer` object instead of a parser. The default behavior of a `Transformer` is to pass the input XML through without modification, which is what will occur if no transformation stylesheet is given.

Input and output from a `Transformer` are handled via the `javax.xml.transform.Source` and `javax.xml.transform.Result` interfaces. Each has three implementing classes, one each for DOM, SAX, and streams (`DOMSource`, `SAXSource`, `StreamSource`, `DOMResult`, `SAXResult`, and `StreamResult`). Note that the JAXP processors will not necessarily support all six. We handled the output in the DOM example by creating a `DOMSource` and outputting to a `StreamResult` that targeted `System.out` (in this example the document variable contains a DOM `Document` object):

```
TransformerFactory tf = TransformerFactory.newInstance();
Transformer output = tf.newTransformer();
output.transform(new DOMSource(document), new StreamResult(System.out));
```

The `Source` objects can also specify the source of the stylesheet used for the conversion. If we want to use a stylesheet located in */home/will/orderdisplay.xsl*:

```
TransformerFactory tf = TransformerFactory.newInstance();
Transformer output = tf.newTransformer(
            new StreamSource("file://home/will/orderdisplay.xsl"));
output.transform(new DOMSource(document), new StreamResult(System.out));
```

The different source and result types can streamline processing. Rather than load an XML file, transform it, write it to disk, reload it, and parse it with a SAX `ContentHandler`, the transformation process can feed its results directly into a `ContentHandler` that can deal with the transformation results.

Example 9-4 shows transformation of a document and its immediate processing by a SAX `ContentHandler`. We'll use the `OrderHandler` program from earlier in the chapter as the content handler, and we'll use the same *orders.xml* file. To keep things simple, we'll do a one-to-one transformation, rather than use an XSLT file to actually alter the structure of the *orders.xml* file.

Example 9-4: Transforming a Document into a SAXResult

```
import javax.xml.transform.*;
import javax.xml.transform.sax.*;
import javax.xml.transform.stream.*;
import org.xml.sax.*;
import org.xml.sax.helpers.*;

public class SAXTransformTarget {

    public static void main(String[] args) {
            try {

                    StreamSource ss = new StreamSource("orders.xml");
                    SAXResult sr = new SAXResult(new OrderHandler());
                    TransformerFactory tf = TransformerFactory.newInstance();
                Transformer t = tf.newTransformer();
                t.transform(ss, sr);
            } catch (TransformerConfigurationException e) {
                e.printStackTrace();
            } catch (TransformerException e) {
                    e.printStackTrace();
        }
    }
}
```

The output from this program should be identical to the output from Example 9-1; we've simply replaced the XMLReader with a transformation stream.

Determining data source support

The TransformerFactory class includes a method named getFeature(), which takes a String and returns true if the feature identified by the string is supported by the processor. Each of the Source and Result implementations includes a String constant named FEATURE. So to determine whether the XSL processor supports a DOM sources:

```
TransformerFactory tf = TransformerFactory.newInstance();
boolean supportsDOMSource = tf.getFeature(DOMSource.FEATURE);
```

Custom URI resolution

When processing XSL files, it is sometimes necessary to resolve relative URIs. Ordinarily, the parser will do the best possible job, but sometimes it is necessary to override this behavior (for instance, in a web content management system where the document tree apparent to the content creator and client might not match the system structure, or when XML output from a servlet is being transformed within the servlet). In these cases, the setURIResolver(URIResolver) method of Transformer allows you to specify resolution behavior by implementing the URIResolver interface. The resolve() method of URIResolver must return a Source or null:

```
class XSLResolver implements URIResolver {
   public Source resolve(String href, String base)
     throws TransformerException {
```

```
    // Check for a null Base URI, and provider it if so
    if((base == null) || (base.equals("/servlet/")))
     base = "http://www.oreilly.com/catalog/jentnut/";
    if(href == null)
     return null;
    return new StreamSource(base + href);
   }
  }
```

Finally, JAXP supports XSLT transformations that can convert between DOM, SAX, and streams, transform an XML document based on an XSL stylesheet, or both.

CHAPTER 10

Java Message Service

The standard Java networking APIs, as well as remote object systems such as RMI and CORBA, operate by default under the assumption of synchronous communications. In other words, if a client makes a request of a remote server (e.g., opens a socket and attempts to read some data from it, or makes a remote method call on a remote object), the thread that made the request will block until the response comes back from the server. In some situations, it might be necessary or useful to engage in asynchronous communications, e.g., a client sends a request to the server and then continues doing other work, while the server possibly invokes some kind of callback on the client when the request is complete. This is where the Java Message Service (JMS) comes in.

JMS is an API for performing asynchronous messaging. JMS is principally a client-focused API, in that it provides a standard, portable interface for Java/J2EE clients to interact with native message-oriented middleware (MOM) systems like IBM MQ Series, Sonic MQ, etc. JMS isn't intended to be a platform for implementing a full messaging system, since it doesn't provide a service-provider interface for all of the internals of a message-service implementation. In a sense, JMS plays a role with native messaging systems that is analogous with the role that JDBC plays with relational database systems, or the role JNDI plays with naming and directory services. Java clients using JMS to interact with messaging systems can (ostensibly) be more easily ported from one native messaging system to another, because they are insulated from the proprietary particulars of the underlying vendor's message system.

The JMS API is provided in the `javax.jms` package. The material in this chapter is based on Version 1.0.2b of the JMS specification, released in August 2001, which is the most current version at the time of this writing. The examples in the chapter have been tested against the JMS services embedded in Sun's J2EE 1.3 Reference Implementation and BEA's WebLogic 6.1 application server.

JMS in the J2EE Environment

The J2EE 1.2 specification requires that compliant J2EE servers support only JMS clients accessing external JMS providers. In other words, a J2EE 1.2 server only needs to provide the JMS API to allow components to interact with external JMS servers, and doesn't need to provide a JMS implementation of its own. J2EE 1.3 extended this requirement to include a full JMS provider, including support for both point-to-point and publish-subscribe message destinations (these are described in detail next). So any compliant J2EE 1.3 server will have its own JMS server capable of hosting its own message destinations.

Given this, the material concerning developing JMS clients is relevant regardless of whether you are using a J2EE 1.2- or 1.3-compliant application server. The material about the setup and configuration of JMS destinations requires a JMS provider, so you'll need a full JMS provider, either as part of a J2EE 1.3 server, an extended J2EE 1.2 server, or as a standalone JMS server.

Elements of Messaging with JMS

The principle players in a JMS system are *messaging clients*, *message destinations*, and a JMS-compatible *messaging provider*.

Messaging clients produce and consume messages. Typically messaging takes place asynchronously; a client produces a message and sends it to a message destination, and some time later another client receives the message. Message clients can be implemented using JMS, or they can use a native messaging API to participate in the messaging system. If a native message client (e.g., a client using the native IBM MQ Series APIs) produces a message to a message destination, a JMS connection to the native message system is responsible for retrieving the message, converting it into the appropriate JMS message representation, and delivering it to any relevant JMS-based clients.

Message destinations are places where JMS clients send and receive messages from. Message destinations are created within a JMS provider that manages all of the administrative and runtime functions of the messaging system. At a minimum, a JMS provider allows you to specify a network address for a destination, allowing clients to find the destination on the network. But providers may also support other administrative options on destinations, such as persistence options, resource limits, etc.

Messaging Styles: Point-to-Point and Publish-Subscribe

Generally speaking, asynchronous messaging usually comes in two flavors: a message can be addressed and sent to a single receiver (*point-to-point*), or a message can be published to particular channel or topic and any receiver that subscribes to that channel will receive the message (*publish-subscribe*). These two messaging styles have analogies at several levels in the distributed computing "stack," all the way from the network level (standard TCP packet delivery versus multicast networking) to the application level (email versus newsgroups). Figure 10-1 depicts the two message models supported by JMS, as well as the key interfaces that come into play in a JMS context. We discuss the specifics of these interfaces later in the chapter.

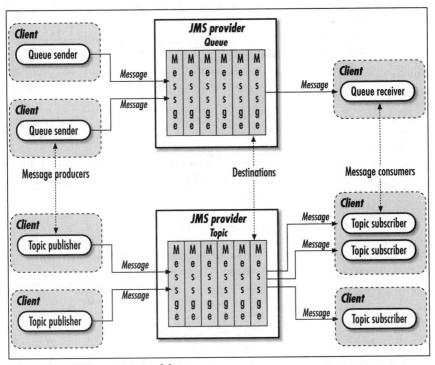

Figure 10-1: JMS message models

Most messaging providers support one or both of these messaging styles, so JMS provides support for them both in its API. JMS includes a set of generic messaging interfaces, described next. Each style of messaging is supported by specialized subclasses of these generic interfaces.

Key JMS Interfaces

The following key interfaces represent the concepts that come into play in any JMS client application, whether it is using point-to-point or publish-subscribe messaging. Information about all of the classes, interfaces, and exceptions in the JMS API can be found in Part III.

Message

Messages are at the heart of JMS, naturally. Messages have accessor methods for their header fields, properties, and body contents. Subtypes of this interface provide implementations for different types of content.

MessageListener

A MessageListener is attached to a MessageConsumer by a client, and receives a callback for each Message received by that consumer. MessageListeners are the key to asynchronous message delivery to clients, since the client attaches a listener to a consumer and then carries on with its thread(s) of control. MessageListeners must implement an onMessage() method, which is the callback used to notify the listener that a message has arrived.

ConnectionFactory

A ConnectionFactory creates connections to a JMS provider. ConnectionFactory references are obtained from a JMS provider through a JNDI lookup. A QueueConnectionFactory creates connections in a point-to-point context; TopicConnectionFactory creates connections in publish-subscribe contexts.

Destination

A Destination represents a network location, managed by a JMS provider, that can be used to exchange messages. A JMS client sends messages to Destinations, and attaches MessageListeners to Destinations to receive messages from other clients. A client obtains references to Destinations using JNDI lookups. Queues and Topics are the Destinations in point-to-point and publish-subscribe contexts, respectively.

Connection

A Connection is a live connection to a JMS provider, and is used for the receipt and delivery of messages. Before a client can exchange any messages with a JMS destination, it must have a live connection that has been started by the client. A Connection is obtained from a ConnectionFactory using its createXXXConnection() methods. The QueueConnectionFactory. createQueueConnection() methods return QueueConnections, and the TopicConnectionFactory.createTopicConnection() methods return TopicConnections.

Session

A Session can be thought of as a single, serialized flow of messages between a client and a JMS provider. A Session is used to create message consumers and producers, and to create Messages that a client wishes to send. A Session is used within a single thread of control on a client. Since a Session is only accessed from within a single thread, the messages sent or received through its consumers and producers are serialized with respect to the client. Sessions also provide a context for defining transactions around message operations; details on transactional messaging can be found in the section Transactional Messaging. Sessions are created from Connections using their createXXXSession() methods. The QueueConnection.createQueueSession() method returns a QueueSession, and the TopicConnection. createTopicSession() method returns a TopicSession.

MessageProducer/MessageConsumer

MessageProducers and MessageConsumers are used to send and receive messages from a destination, respectively. Producers and consumers are created using various createXXX() methods on Sessions, using the target Destination as the argument. In a point-to-point context, QueueSenders are created using the QueueSession.createSender() method, and QueueReceivers are created using the QueueSession.createReceiver() methods. In a publish-subscribe context, TopicPublishers are created using TopicSession. createPublisher(), and TopicSubscribers are created using TopicSession. createSubscriber() and TopicSession.createDurableSubscriber() methods.

A Generic JMS Client

A JMS client follows the same general sequence of operations, regardless of whether it's using point-to-point or publish-subscribe messaging, or both. We'll walk through these steps here, using the point-to-point JMS interfaces to demonstrate. For the most part, the same pseudocode can be used with the publish-subscribe interfaces by just substituting "Topic" for "Queue" in the code samples in this section.

General setup

The very first step for a JMS client is to get a reference to an `InitialContext` for the JNDI service of the JMS provider. Full details on the various options for obtaining a JNDI `Context` can be found in Chapter 7, but in general, the client will create an `InitialContext` using a set of `Properties` that specify the location and type of the JNDI service associated with the JMS provider:

```
Properties props = ...;
Context ctx = new InitialContext(props);
```

Next, the JMS client needs to acquire a `ConnectionFactory` from the JMS provider using a JNDI lookup. The client would have to know what name the JMS provider used to publish the `ConnectionFactory` in JNDI space. Here, we lookup a `QueueConnectionFactory` registered in JNDI under the name "jms/someQFactory":

```
QueueConnectionFactory qFactory =
    (QueueConnectionFactory)ctx.lookup("jms/someQFactory");
```

An administrator would have to set up this `ConnectionFactory` on the JMS provider and associate it with this JNDI name on the server.

The client also uses JNDI to find `Destinations` published by the JMS provider. Here, we look up a `Queue` published under the JNDI name "jms/someQ":

```
Queue queue = (Queue)ctx.lookup("jms/someQ");
```

Once we have a `ConnectionFactory` and one or more `Destinations` to talk to, we need to create a `Connection` with the JMS provider. This `Connection` is the conduit through which messages will be physically sent and received. A `Connection` has to be started before messages can be received through it, but a `Connection` can always be used to send messages, regardless of whether it's started or stopped. Normally, a client won't `start()` a `Connection` until it's ready to receive and process messages. Here, we use our `QueueConnectionFactory` to create a `QueueConnection`, and defer starting it until we create a `MessageConsumer` to receive messages:

```
QueueConnection qConn = qFactory.createQueueConnection(...);
```

Client identifiers

When a client makes a connection to a JMS provider, a client identifier is associated with the client. The client identifier is used to maintain state on the JMS provider on behalf of the client, and the state data can persist beyond the lifetime of a client connection. The server-side state can be retrieved for the client when it reconnects using the same client ID. The only client state information defined by the JMS specification is durable topic subscriptions (described in the section "Durable Subscriptions"), but a JMS provider may support its own state information on behalf of clients as well. Only one client is allowed to be associated with a client ID (and its state information) on the JMS provider, so only a single connection with a given client ID can be made to a JMS provider at any given time.

The JMS client identifier can be set in two ways. A client can set a client ID on any Connections that it makes with the JMS provider, using the Connection.setClientID() method:

```
qConn.setClientID("client-1");
```

Again, only a single connection with a given client ID is allowed at any given time. If a client with this same client ID (even this one) already has a connection with the client ID, then an InvalidClientIDException will be thrown when setClientID() is called. Alternatively, a ConnectionFactory can be configured on the JMS provider with a client ID that is applied to any Connections that are created through it. The ConnectionFactory interface doesn't provide a facility for the client to set the factory's client ID; this is a function that would have to be provided in the JMS provider's administrative interface. A ConnectionFactory with a preset client ID is, by definition, intended to be used by a single client.

Authenticated connections

When a client creates a connection, they have the option to provide a username and password that will be authenticated by the JMS provider. This is done using overloaded versions of the createXXXConnection() methods on a Connection-Factory. We can create an authenticated QueueConnection, for example, with a call like this:

```
QueueConnection authQConn =
    qFactory.createQueueSession("JimFarley", "myJMSPassword");
```

If this is successful, the client will operate under the given principal name and be given the appropriate rights. JMS providers aren't required to support authentication of connections. If a JMS provider does support authenticated connections, the principals and access rights will be administered on the JMS server.

Sessions

Once a connection to the JMS provider is established, we need to create one or more Sessions to be used to send and receive messages. Again, Sessions are a single-threaded context for handling messages, so we need a separate Session for each concurrent thread that we plan to use for messaging. Sessions are created from Connections. Here, we create a QueueSession from our QueueConnection:

```
QueueSession qSess =
    qConn.createQueueSession(false, Session.AUTO_ACKNOWLEDGE);
```

When creating either QueueSessions or TopicSessions, there are two arguments used to create the Session. The first is a boolean flag indicating whether we want the Session to be transacted. (See the section "Transactional Messaging" for details

---

on transactional sessions.) The second argument indicates how we want the Session to acknowledge received messages with the JMS provider. There are three options for the acknowledge mode of a Session, and they are specified using static final values on the Session class:

Session.AUTO_ACKNOWLEDGE

This instructs the Session to acknowledge messages automatically for the client. A message is acknowledged when received by the client. If a MessageListener handles the message, then the acknowledgment is not sent until the listener's onMessage() method returns. If the message is received because of a call to receive() on a MessageConsumer, then the acknowledgement is sent immediately after the call to receive() returns.

Session.DUPS_OK_ACKNOWLEDGE

This option instructs the Session to do "lazy acknowledgment," where acknowledgments can be delayed if the Session decides to do so. This could lead to a message being delivered to a client more than once, if the delay between delivery and acknowledgment is longer than the JMS provider's timeout and it assumed the message was never received.

Session.CLIENT_ACKNOWLEDGE

This option is used when the client wants to manually acknowledge messages, by calling the acknowledge() method on the Message.

Sending messages

Messages are sent to Destinations using MessageProducers, which are created from Sessions. When they are created, producers are associated with a Destination, and any Messages sent using the producer are delivered to that Destination using the Connection from which the Session was generated.

In a point-to-point context, the message producers are QueueSenders, generated from QueueSessions using the Queue the sender should point to:

```
QueueSender qSender = qSess.createSender(queue);
```

Once a producer has been created, the client needs to create and initialize Messages to be sent. Messages are also created from a Session. Here, we create a TextMessage from our QueueSession, and set its text body to be some interesting text we want to send to the Queue:

```
TextMessage tMsg = qSess.createTextMessage();
tMsg.setText("The sky is blue.");
```

To actually send the message, we simply invoke the appropriate method on our MessageProducer. Here, we call send() on our QueueSender:

```
qSender.send(tMsg);
```

Note that it's not necessary to ensure that the underlying Connection (from which we generated our Session) is started in order to send messages. Starting the Connection is only required to commence delivery of messages from the Destination to the client.

Receiving messages

Receiving messages involves creating a MessageConsumer that is associated with a particular Destination. This establishes a consumer with the JMS provider, and the provider is responsible for delivering any appropriate messages that arrive at the Destination to the new consumer. MessageConsumers are also generated from Sessions, in order to associate them with a serialized flow of messages. In a point-to-point context, a QueueReceiver is generated from a QueueSession using its createReceiver() methods. Here, we simply create a new receiver tied to our Queue. Other options for creating QueueReceivers are discussed in "Point-to-Point Messaging."

```
QueueReceiver qReceiver = qSess.createReceiver(queue);
```

By creating a MessageConsumer, all we've done is told the JMS provider that we want to receive messages from a particular Destination. We haven't specified what to do with the Messages on the client side. Since JMS is an asynchronous message delivery system, it uses the same listener pattern that is used in Swing GUI programming or JavaBeans event handling (two other asynchronous event contexts). Messages in JMS are processed using MessageListeners. A client needs to implement a MessageListener with an onMessage() method that does something useful with the Messages coming from the Destination. Example 10-1 shows a basic MessageListener—a TextLogger that simply prints the contents of any TextMessages it encounters.

Example 10-1: Simple MessageListener Implementation

```java
import javax.jms.*;

public class TextLogger implements MessageListener {
  // Default constructor
  public TextLogger() {}

  // Message handler
  public void onMessage(Message msg) {
    // If it's a text message, print it to stdout
    if (msg instanceof TextMessage) {
      TextMessage tMsg = (TextMessage)msg;
      try {
        System.out.println("Received message: " + tMsg.getText());
      }
      catch (JMSException je) {
        System.out.println("Error retrieving message text: " +
                            je.getMessage());
      }
    }
    // For other types of messages, print an error
    else {
      System.out.println("Unsupported message type encountered.");
    }
  }
}
```

Once a `MessageListener` has been defined, the client needs to create one and register it with a `MessageConsumer`. In our running example, we create one of our `TextLoggers` and associate it with our `QueueReceiver` using its `setMessageListener()` method:

```
MessageListener listener = new TextLogger();
qReceiver.setMessageListener(listener);
```

It's important to remember that no messages will be delivered over our underlying `Connection` until it's been started. In our running example, we created our `QueueConnection` but never started it, so we do that now to start delivery of `Messages` to our `QueueReceiver`, and from there to our `TextLogger` listener:

```
qConn.start();
```

Temporary destinations

A client can create its own temporary destinations, which are `Destinations` that are visible only to the `Connection` that created it, and that only live for the duration of the `Connection` used to create them. Although a temporary destination lives only for the life of the `Connection` it was created from, they are created using methods on the `Session`. For example, to create a `TemporaryQueue`:

```
Queue tempQueue = qSession.createTemporaryQueue();
```

Temporary destinations can be used, for example, to receive responses to messages that are sent with a `JMSReplyTo` header;

```
TextMessage request = qSession.createTextMessage();
request.setJMSReplyTo(tempQueue);
```

They can also be used to exchanging asynchronous messages between threads in the same client.

Cleaning up

`Connections` and `Sessions` require resources to be allocated by the JMS provider (similar to how JDBC connections use up resources on a RDBMS), so it's a good idea to free them up explicitly when you are done with them.

Sessions are closed by simply calling `close()` on them:

```
qSess.close();
```

When a `Session` is closed, all `MessageConsumers` and `MessageProducers` associated with it are rendered unusable. If you try to use them to communicate with the JMS provider, they will throw an `IllegalStateException`. A call to `Session.close()` will block until any pending processing of incoming `Messages` (e.g., a `MessageListener`'s onMessage() method) is complete.

Closing a `Session` doesn't close the underlying `Connection` from which it came. You can close one `Session` and open up another one as long as the `Connection` is active. To close a `Connection` and free up its server-side resources, call its `close()` method:

```
qConn.close();
```

All Sessions (and, subsequently, all of their consumers and producers) generated from a Connection become unusable once it is closed. The call to Connection. close() will block until incoming Message processing has completed on all of the Sessions associated with it.

The Anatomy of Messages

Creating a messaging-based application involves more than establishing communication channels between participants. Players in a message-driven system need to understand the content of the messages and know what to do with them.

Native messaging systems, such as IBM MQ Series or Microsoft MQ (MSMQ), define their own proprietary formats for messages. JMS attempts to bridge these native messaging systems by defining its own standard message format. All JMS clients can interact with any messaging system that supports JMS. "Supports" in this case can mean one of two things. The messaging system can be implemented in a native, proprietary architecture, with a JMS bridge that maps the JMS message formats (and other aspects of the JMS specification) to the native scheme and back again. Or, the messaging system can be written to use the JMS message format as its native format.

JMS messages are made up of a set of standard header fields, optional client-defined properties, and a body. JMS also provides a set of subclasses of Message that support various types of message bodies.

Message Header Fields and Properties

Table 10-1 lists the standard header fields that any JMS message can have. The table indicates the name and type of the field, when the field is set in the message delivery process, and a short description of the semantics of the field.

Table 10-1: Standard JMS Message Headers

Field Name	Data Type	When Set	Description
JMSCorrelationID	String	Before send	Correlates multiple messages. This field can be used in addition to the JMSMessageID header as an application-defined message identifier (JMSMessageIDs are assigned by the provider).
JMSDestination	Destination	During send	Indicates to the message receiver which Destination the Message was sent to.
JMSDeliveryMode	int	During send	Indicates which delivery mode to use to deliver this message, DeliveryMode.PERSISTENT or DeliveryMode.NON_PERSISTENT. PERSISTENT delivery indicates that the messaging provider should take measures to ensure that the message is delivered despite failures on the JMS server. NON_PERSISTENT delivery doesn't require the provider to deliver the message if a failure occurs on the JMS server.

Table 10-1: Standard JMS Message Headers (continued)

Field Name	Data Type	When Set	Description
JMSExpiration	long	During send	The time the message will expire on the provider. If no client receives the message by this time, the provider drops the message. It is calculated as the sum of the current time plus the time-to-live of the MessageProducer that sent the message. The value is given in milliseconds since the epoch (January 1, 1970, 00:00:00 GMT). A value of zero indicates no expiration time.
JMSMessageID	String	During send	A unique message ID assigned by the provider. Message Ids always start with the prefix "ID:". These IDs are unique for a given JMS provider. Applications can set their own message identifier using the JMSCorrelationID header.
JMSPriority	int	During send	A provider-assigned value indicating the priority with which the message will be delivered. JMS providers aren't required to implement strict priority ordering of messages. This field is simply a "hint" from the server about how the message will be handled. Message priorities and how they are assigned are determined by the configuration of the JMS provider.
JMSRedelivered	boolean	Before delivery	A provider-provided value that indicates to the receiver that the message may have been delivered in the past with no acknowledgment from the client. On the sender, this header value is always unassigned.
JMSReplyTo	Destination	Before send	A Destination, set by the sending client, indicating where a reply message should be sent.
JMSTimestamp	long	During send	The time at which the message was handed off to the JMS provider to be sent. This value is given in milliseconds since the epoch (January 1, 1970, 00:00:00 GMT).
JMSType	String	Before send	A message type, set by the sending client. Some JMS providers require that this header be set, so it's a good idea to set it even if your application isn't using it. Some JMS providers also allow an administrator to configure a set of message types that will be matched against this header, and used to selectively set handling of the message based on its type.

These standard message headers are read and written using corresponding accessors on the Message interface. The JMSTimestamp field, for example, is set using setJMSTimestamp( ), and read using getJMSTimestamp( ).

A client can also create its own custom properties on a `Message`, using a set of generic property accessors on the `Message` interface. Custom message properties can be `boolean`, `byte`, `short`, `int`, `long`, `float`, `double`, or `String` values, and they are accessed using corresponding `get/setXXXProperty()` methods on `Message`. A `boolean` header can be set using the `setBooleanProperty()` method, for example. Each custom property has to be given a unique name, specified when the value is set. For example, we could set a custom `boolean` property with the name "reviewed" on a message, like so:

```
TextMessage tMsg = ...;
tMsg.setBooleanProperty("reviewed", false);
```

Custom property names have certain restrictions on them. They have to be valid Java identifiers, they can't begin with "JMSX" or "JMS_" (these are reserved for JMS-defined and vendor-defined properties, respectively), and they can't be one of the following reserved words: NULL, TRUE, FALSE, NOT, AND, OR, BETWEEN, LIKE, IN, IS, or ESCAPE. Custom property names are also case-sensitive, so "reviewed" isn't the same property as "Reviewed."

JMS Message Types

To support various application scenarios, JMS provides the following subclasses of `Message`, each providing a different type of message body.

TextMessage

> Arguably the most popular type of `Message`, this has a body that is a simple `String`. The format of the `String` contents is left to the application to interpret. The `String` may contain a simple informational phrase, it may contain conversational text input by a user in a collaboration application, or it may contain formatted text such as XML.

BytesMessage

> This type of message contains an array of bytes as its body. `BytesMessages` can be used to send binary data in a message, and/or it can be used to wrap a native message format with a JMS message.

ObjectMessage

> The body of this message is a serialized Java object.

MapMessage

> The body of this message is a set of name/value pairs. The names are `Strings`, and the values are Java primitive types, like `double`, `int`, `String`, etc. The values of the entries are accessed using `get/setXXX()` methods on `MapMessage`. Note that these entries are stored in the body of the message: they aren't message header properties and can't be used for message selection (see the section "Filtering Messages").

StreamMessage

> A `StreamMessage` contains a stream of Java primitive data types (`double`, `int`, `String`, etc.). Data elements are written sequentially to the body of the message using various `writeXXX()` methods, and they are read sequentially on the receiving end using corresponding `readXXX()` methods. If the receiver

doesn't know the types of data in the message, they can be introspected using the readObject() method:

```
StreamMessage sMsg = ...;
Object item = sMsg.readObject();
if (item instanceof Float) {
  float fData = ((Float)item).floatValue()1
  ...
}
```

Accessing Message Content

When a client receives a Message, its body is read-only. Attempting to change the body of a received Message will cause a MessageNotWriteableException to be thrown.

When a message sender first creates a Message object, the body of the Message is unset. For TextMessages and ObjectMessages, this means that their body starts with a null value, and for MapMessages this means there are no entries in the message body. For BytesMessages and StreamMessages, their bodies start in write-only mode, and they can't be read by the sending client until it calls their reset() method. If you create a BytesMessage or StreamMessage and attempt to read its body content before calling reset() on it, a MessageNotReadableException will be thrown.

A Message's body can be emptied by the sender at any point by calling its clearBody() method. This reverts its body back to its initial state, but doesn't affect any of the header or property values on the Message. Calling clearBody() on a BytesMessage or StreamMessage puts their body back into write-only mode, until a subsequent call to BytesMessage.reset() or StreamMessage.reset() is made. The sender can clear any custom properties on a Message by calling its clearProperties() method. The standard JMS header fields have to be updated using their specific accessors on the Message interface. Receivers of messages can't call clearBody(), clearProperties(), or reset() on a received Message, since the Message is read-only at this point.

Filtering Messages

JMS allows messaging participants to selectively filter what Messages it receives from a JMS provider. This is done using message selectors, which are expressions that filter messages based on the values found in their headers and custom properties. The syntax of message selectors is based on SQL92 conditional expressions.

A message selector is associated with a MessageConsumer when it is created from a Session. Each type of Session (QueueSession and TopicSession) has overloaded versions of their consumer create methods that take a message selector as a String argument. For example, the following creates a QueueReceiver that receives only messages that have a custom property named transaction-type and whose JMSType header field is acknowledge:

```
String selector = "JMSType = 'acknowledge'
                        AND transaction-type IS NOT NULL";
QueueReceiver receiver = qSession.createReceiver(queue, selector);
```

Message filtering is performed by the JMS provider. When the provider determines that a message should be delivered to a particular MessageConsumer, based on the rules of the particular message context (point-to-point or publish-subscribe), it first checks that consumer's message selector, if one exists. If the selector evaluates to true when the message's headers and properties are applied to it, then the message is delivered; otherwise it isn't. Undelivered messages are handled differently, depending on the message context, as described in the following sections.

Point-to-Point Messaging

Point-to-point messaging involves the sending of messages from one or more senders to a single receiver through a message queue. Point-to-point messaging is analogous to email messaging: a client delivers a message to a named mailbox (queue), and the owner of the mailbox (queue) reads them in the order they were received. Queues attempt to maintain the send order of messages generated by the sender(s) attached to them. In other words, if sender A sends messages A1, A2, and A3, in that order, to a queue, then the receiver attached to the queue will receive message 2 after message 1, and message 3 after message 2 (assuming that no message selectors filter out any of these messages). If there are multiple senders attached to a queue, then the relative order of each individual sender is preserved by the queue when it delivers the messages, but the queue doesn't attempt to impose a predefined absolute order on the messages across all senders. So if there is another sender, B, attached to the same queue as A, and it sends messages B1, B2, and B3, in that order, then the receiver will receive B2 after B1, and B3 after B2, but the messages from sender A may be interleaved with the messages from sender B. The receiver may receive the messages in order A1, A2, B1, A3, B2, B3, the messages may be delivered in order B1, B2, B3, A1, A2, A3, or some other order altogether. There is nothing in the JMS specification that dictates how a JMS provider should queue messages from multiple senders.

Point-to-point messaging is performed in JMS using the queue-related interfaces and classes in the javax.jms package. Queues are represented by Queue objects, which are looked up in JNDI from the JMS provider. QueueConnectionFactory objects are looked up in JNDI as well, and used to create QueueConnections. QueueConnections and Queues are used to create QueueSessions, which are in turn used to create QueueSenders and QueueReceivers.

Sample Client

Example 10-2 shows a full point-to-point messaging client. The PTPMessagingClient is capable of sending and receiving a message from a given queue, as well as browsing the current contents of the queue.

Example 10-2: Point-to-Point Messaging Client

```
import java.util.*;
import javax.naming.*;
import javax.jms.*;
import java.io.*;
```

Example 10-2: Point-to-Point Messaging Client (continued)

```java
public class PTPMessagingClient implements Runnable {

  // Our connection to the JMS provider.  Only one is needed for this client.
  private QueueConnection mQueueConn = null;

  // The queue used for message-passing
  private Queue mQueue = null;

  // Our message receiver - only need one.
  private QueueReceiver mReceiver = null;

  // A single session for sending and receiving from all remote peers.
  private QueueSession mSession = null;

  // The message type we tag all our messages with
  private static String MSG_TYPE = "JavaEntMessage";

  // Constructor, with client name, and the JNDI locations of the JMS
  // connection factory and queue that we want to use.
  public PTPMessagingClient(String cFactoryJNDIName, String queueJNDIName) {
    init(cFactoryJNDIName, queueJNDIName);
  }

  // Do all the JMS-setup for this client.  Assumes that the JVM is
  // configured (perhaps using jndi.properties) so that the default JNDI
  // InitialContext points to the JMS provider's JNDI service.
  protected boolean init(String cFactoryJNDIName, String queueJNDIName) {
    boolean success = true;

    Context ctx = null;
    // Attempt to make connection to JNDI service
    try {
      ctx = new InitialContext();
    }
    catch (NamingException ne) {
      System.out.println("Failed to connect to JNDI provider:");
      ne.printStackTrace();
      success = false;
    }

    // If no JNDI context, bail out here
    if (ctx == null) {
      return success;
    }

    // Attempt to lookup JMS connection factory from JNDI service
    QueueConnectionFactory connFactory = null;
    try {
      connFactory = (QueueConnectionFactory)ctx.lookup(cFactoryJNDIName);
      System.out.println("Got JMS connection factory.");
    }
    catch (NamingException ne2) {
```

Example 10-2: Point-to-Point Messaging Client (continued)

```
      System.out.println("Failed to get JMS connection factory: ");
      ne2.printStackTrace();
      success = false;
    }

    try {
      // Make a connection to the JMS provider and keep it.
      // At this point, the connection is not started, so we aren't
      // receiving any messages.
      mQueueConn = connFactory.createQueueConnection();
      // Try to find our designated queue
      mQueue = (Queue)ctx.lookup(queueJNDIName);
      // Make a session for queueing messages: no transactions,
      // auto-acknowledge
      mSession =
        mQueueConn.createQueueSession(false,
                                      javax.jms.Session.AUTO_ACKNOWLEDGE);
    }
    catch (JMSException e) {
      System.out.println("Failed to establish connection/queue:");
      e.printStackTrace();
      success = false;
    }
    catch (NamingException ne) {
      System.out.println("JNDI Error looking up factory or queue:");
      ne.printStackTrace();
      success = false;
    }

    try {
      // Make our receiver, for incoming messages.
      // Set the message selector to only receive our type of messages,
      // in case the same queue is being used for other purposes.
      mReceiver = mSession.createReceiver(mQueue,
                                          "JMSType = '" + MSG_TYPE + "'");
    }
    catch (JMSException je) {
      System.out.println("Error establishing message receiver:");
      je.printStackTrace();
    }

    return success;
  }

  // Send a message to the queue
  public void sendMessage(String msg) {
    try {
      // Create a JMS msg sender connected to the destination queue
      QueueSender sender = mSession.createSender(mQueue);
      // Use the session to create a text message
      TextMessage tMsg = mSession.createTextMessage();
      tMsg.setJMSType(MSG_TYPE);
      // Set the body of the message
```

Example 10-2: Point-to-Point Messaging Client (continued)

```
      tMsg.setText(msg);
      // Send the message using the sender
      sender.send(tMsg);
      System.out.println("Sent the message");
    }
    catch (JMSException je) {
      System.out.println("Error sending message " + msg + " to queue");
      je.printStackTrace();
    }
  }

  // Register a MessageListener with the queue to receive
  // messages asynchronously
  public void registerListener(MessageListener listener) {
    try {
      // Set the listener on the receiver
      mReceiver.setMessageListener(listener);
      // Start the connection, in case it's still stopped
      mQueueConn.start();
    }
    catch (JMSException je) {
      System.out.println("Error registering listener: ");
      je.printStackTrace();
    }
  }

  // Perform an synchronous receive of a message from the queue.  If it's a
  // TextMessage, print the contents.
  public String receiveMessage() {
    String msg = "-- No message --";
    try {
      Message m = mReceiver.receive();
      if (m instanceof TextMessage) {
        msg = ((TextMessage)m).getText();
      }
      else {
        msg = "-- Unsupported message type received --";
      }
    }
    catch (JMSException je) {
    }
    return msg;
  }

  // Print the current contents of the message queue, using a QueueBrowser
  // so that we don't remove any messages from the queue
  public void printQueue() {
    try {
      QueueBrowser browser = mSession.createBrowser(mQueue);
      Enumeration msgEnum = browser.getEnumeration();
      System.out.println("Queue contents:");
      while (msgEnum.hasMoreElements()) {
```

Example 10-2: Point-to-Point Messaging Client (continued)

```
      System.out.println("\t" + (Message)msgEnum.nextElement());
    }
  }
  catch (JMSException je) {
    System.out.println("Error browsing queue: " + je.getMessage());
  }
}


// When run within a thread, just wait for messages to be delivered to us
public void run() {
  while (true) {
    try { this.wait(); } catch (Exception we) {}
  }
}


// Take command-line arguments and send or receive messages from the
// named queue
public static void main(String args[]) {
  if (args.length < 3) {
    System.out.println("Usage: PTPMessagingClient" +
                       " connFactoryName queueName" +
                       " [send|listen|recv_synch] <messageToSend>");
    System.exit(1);
  }

  // Get the JNDI names of the connection factory and
  // queue, from the command-line
  String factoryName = args[0];
  String queueName = args[1];

  // Get the command to execute (send, recv, recv_synch)
  String cmd = args[2];

  // Create and initialize the messaging participant
  PTPMessagingClient msger =
    new PTPMessagingClient(factoryName, queueName);

  // Run the participant in its own thread, so that it can react to
  // incoming messages
  Thread listen = new Thread(msger);
  listen.start();

  // Send a message to the queue
  if (cmd.equals("send")) {
    String msg = args[3];
    msger.sendMessage(msg);
    System.exit(0);
  }
  // Register a listener
  else if (cmd.equals("listen")) {
```

Example 10-2: Point-to-Point Messaging Client (continued)

```
      MessageListener listener = new TextLogger();
      msger.registerListener(listener);
      System.out.println("Client listening to queue " + queueName
                              + "...");
      System.out.flush();
      try { listen.wait(); } catch (Exception we) {}
    }
    // Synchronously receive a message from the queue
    else if (cmd.equals("recv_synch")) {
      String msg = msger.receiveMessage();
      System.out.println("Received message: " + msg);
      System.exit(0);
    }
    else if (cmd.equals("browse")) {
      msger.printQueue();
      System.exit(0);
    }
  }
}
}
```

The `main()` method takes a minimum of three command-line arguments. The first
two are the JNDI names of a target JMS connection factory and queue, in that
order. The third argument is a command indicating what to do:

- *send* sends a message, using the next command-line argument as the text of a
  `TextMessage`.

- *recv* registers a listener with the queue and waits for messages to come in.

- *recv_synch* synchronously polls the queue for the next message that's sent.

- *browse* is a request to print the current contents of the queue without emptying it, using a `QueueBrowser`.

The `main()` method creates a `PTPMessagingClient` using the two JNDI names. The
constructor passes these to the `init()` method, where all of the JMS initialization
we've discussed takes place. The client attempts to connect to its JNDI provider
and get its `InitialContext` first. There are no properties provided to the
`InitialContext` constructor, so the environment would have to have these properties specified in a *jndi.properties* file, or on the command line using `-D` options to
the JVM. Once the `Context` is acquired, the client looks up the
`QueueConnectionFactory` and `Queue` from JNDI. It also creates a `QueueConnection`
and a `QueueSession`, so that it can later create senders and receivers as needed.
Finally, the `init()` method creates a `QueueReceiver` from the session, in case it's
needed later. The connection hasn't been started yet, so the receiver is not
receiving messages from the JMS provider yet.

Back in the `main()` method, once the client is created, it's put into a `Thread` and
run. This is useful for the case where we're going to wait for messages sent to a
listener. Finally, the requested command is checked. If the command is *send*, we
call the client's `sendMessage()` method, which creates a `QueueSender` and a
`TextMessage` (using the last command-line argument, passed in from the `main()`
method). Then the message is sent by passing it to the `send()` method on the

QueueSender. If a "recv" command is given, we create a TextLogger (see Example 10-1) and attach it as a MessageListener to our QueueReceiver, by calling the client's registerListener() method where the call to the receiver's setMessageListener() method is made. If a *recv_synch* command is given, then we call the client's receiveMessage() method, where the receive() method on the QueueReceiver is called. This will block until the next message is sent to the queue. Finally, a *browse* command causes a call to the client's printQueue() method, where a QueueBrowser is created from our session, then asked for an Enumeration of the current messages in the queue. Each message is printed to the console, in the order they would be received.

Browsing Queues

In addition to the conventional use of queues for sending and receiving of messages, a client can also browse the contents of a queue without actually pulling the messages from the queue. This is done using a QueueBrowser, which is generated from a client's QueueSession using its createQueueBrowser() methods:

```
QueueBrowser browser = qSession.createQueueBrowser(queue);
```

Like QueueReceivers, QueueBrowsers can use message selectors to filter what messages they see in the queue:

```
QueueBrowser filterBrowser =
  qSession.createQueueBrowser(queue, "transaction-type = 'update'");
```

This QueueBrowser "sees" only messages in the queue that have a transaction-type property set to update.

To iterate over the messages in the queue, a client asks the browser for an Enumeration of the messages in the queue that match the browser's message selector, if it has one:

```
Enumeration msgEnum = browser.getEnumeration();
while (msgEnum.hasMoreElements()) {
  Message msg = (Message)msgEnum.nextElement();
  System.out.println("Found message, ID = " + msg.getJMSMessageID());
}
```

The Enumeration returns messages in the order that they would be delivered to the client, using the message selector set on the QueueBrowser. So if you had an existing QueueReceiver and wanted to look ahead in the queue to see what messages would be delivered based on the current contents of the queue, you could create a browser using the same message selector as the receiver:

```
QueueReceiver recvr = ...;
QueueBrowser recvrBrowser =
  qSession.createQueueBrowser(queue, recvr.getMessageSelector());
```

Publish-Subscribe Messaging

Publish-subscribe messaging involves one or more MessageProducers "publishing" messages to a particular topic, and one or more MessageConsumers "subscribing" to the topic and receiving any messages published to it. The JMS provider is responsible for delivering a copy of any message sent to a topic to all subscribers of the topic at the time that the message is received. Unlike point-to-point messaging, where messages are kept on the queue until a receiver reads them, any messages received at a topic while a subscriber is not active (e.g., hasn't subscribed to the topic yet, or subscribed and then went out of scope or exited) are lost with respect to that subscriber.

Publish-subscribe messaging is performed in JMS using the topic-related interfaces and classes in the `javax.jms` package. Topics are represented by `Topic` objects, which are looked up in JNDI from the JMS provider. `TopicConnectionFactory` objects are looked up in JNDI as well, and used to create `TopicConnections`. `TopicConnections` and `Topics` are used to create `TopicSessions`, which are in turn used to create `TopicPublishers` and `TopicSubscribers`.

Sample Client

Example 10-3 shows a publish-subscribe client, `PubSubMessagingClient`, that mirrors the `PTPMessagingClient` in Example 10-2. The structure and function of the client is virtually identical to that described for the `PTPMessagingClient`, except that topics, subscribers, and publishers are used instead of queues, receivers, and senders. The only significant difference with this client is it doesn't have a "browse" option, since browsing a topic is not possible. As they arrive, topics deliver their messages to any subscribers currently attached to the topic, otherwise they are dropped, so browsing a topic's contents doesn't make much sense.

Example 10-3: Publish-Subscribe Client

```
import java.util.*;
import javax.naming.*;
import javax.jms.*;
import java.io.*;

public class PubSubMessagingClient implements Runnable {

  // Our connection to the JMS provider.  Only one is needed for this client.
  private TopicConnection mTopicConn = null;

  // The topic used for message-passing
  private Topic mTopic = null;

  // Our message subscriber - only need one.
  private TopicSubscriber mSubscriber = null;

  // A single session for sending and receiving from all remote peers.
  private TopicSession mSession = null;

  // The message type we tag all our messages with
  private static String MSG_TYPE = "JavaEntMessage";

  // Constructor, with client name, and the JNDI location of the JMS
  // connection factory and topic that we want to use.
  public PubSubMessagingClient(String cFactJNDIName, String topicJNDIName) {
    init(cFactJNDIName, topicJNDIName);
  }
```

Example 10-3: Publish-Subscribe Client (continued)

```
// Do all the JMS-setup for this client.  Assumes that the JVM is
// configured (perhaps using jndi.properties) so that the default JNDI
// InitialContext points to the JMS provider's JNDI service.
protected boolean init(String cFactoryJNDIName, String topicJNDIName) {
  boolean success = true;

  Context ctx = null;

  // Attempt to make connection to JNDI service
  try {
    ctx = new InitialContext();
  }
  catch (NamingException ne) {
    System.out.println("Failed to connect to JNDI provider:");
    ne.printStackTrace();
    success = false;
  }

  // If no JNDI context, bail out here
  if (ctx == null) {
    return success;
  }

  // Attempt to lookup JMS connection factory from JNDI service
  TopicConnectionFactory connFactory = null;
  try {
    connFactory = (TopicConnectionFactory)ctx.lookup(cFactoryJNDIName);
    System.out.println("Got JMS connection factory.");
  }
  catch (NamingException ne2) {
    System.out.println("Failed to get JMS connection factory: ");
    ne2.printStackTrace();
    success = false;
  }

  try {
    // Make a connection to the JMS provider and keep it
    // At this point, the connection is not started, so we aren't
    // receiving any messages.
    mTopicConn = connFactory.createTopicConnection();
    // Try to find our designated topic
    mTopic = (Topic)ctx.lookup(topicJNDIName);
    // Make a session for topicing messages
    // no transactions, auto-acknowledge
    mSession =
      mTopicConn.createTopicSession(false,
                                    javax.jms.Session.AUTO_ACKNOWLEDGE);
  }
  catch (JMSException e) {
    System.out.println("Failed to establish connection/topic:");
```

Example 10-3: Publish-Subscribe Client (continued)

```
      e.printStackTrace();
      success = false;
    }
    catch (NamingException ne) {
      System.out.println("JNDI Error looking up factory or topic:");
      ne.printStackTrace();
      success = false;
    }

    try {
      // Make our subscriber, for incoming messages
      // Set the message selector to only receive our type of messages,
      // in case the same topic is being used for other purposes
      // Also indicate we don't want any message sent from this connection
      mSubscriber =
        mSession.createSubscriber(
                          mTopic, "JMSType = '" + MSG_TYPE + "'", true);
    }
    catch (JMSException je) {
      System.out.println("Error establishing message subscriber:");
      je.printStackTrace();
    }

    return success;
  }

  // Send a message to the topic
  public void publishMessage(String msg) {
    try {
      // Create a JMS msg publisher connected to the destination topic
      TopicPublisher publisher = mSession.createPublisher(mTopic);
      // Use the session to create a text message
      TextMessage tMsg = mSession.createTextMessage();
      tMsg.setJMSType(MSG_TYPE);
      // Set the body of the message
      tMsg.setText(msg);
      // Send the message using the publisher
      publisher.publish(tMsg);
      System.out.println("Published the message");
    }
    catch (JMSException je) {
      System.out.println("Error sending message " + msg + " to topic");
      je.printStackTrace();
    }
  }

  // Register a MessageListener with the topic to receive
  // messages asynchronously
  public void registerListener(MessageListener listener) {
    try {
      // Set the listener on the subscriber
```

Example 10-3: Publish-Subscribe Client (continued)

```
      mSubscriber.setMessageListener(listener);
      // Start the connection, in case it's still stopped
      mTopicConn.start();
    }
    catch (JMSException je) {
      System.out.println("Error registering listener: ");
      je.printStackTrace();
    }
  }


  // Perform an synchronous receive of a message from the topic.  If it's a
  // TextMessage, print the contents.
  public String receiveMessage() {
    String msg = "-- No message --";
    try {
      Message m = mSubscriber.receive();
      if (m instanceof TextMessage) {
        msg = ((TextMessage)m).getText();
      }
      else {
        msg = "-- Unsupported message type received --";
      }
    }
    catch (JMSException je) {
    }
    return msg;
  }


  // When run within a thread, just wait for messages to be delivered to us
  public void run() {
    while (true) {
      try { this.wait(); } catch (Exception we) {}
    }
  }


  // Take command-line arguments and send or receive messages from the
  // named topic
  public static void main(String args[]) {
    if (args.length < 3) {
      System.out.println("Usage: PubSubMessagingClient" +
                          " connFactoryName topicName" +
                          " [publish|subscribe|recv_synch] <messageToSend>");
      System.exit(1);
    }

    // Get our client name, and the JNDI name of the connection factory and
    // topic, from the command-line
    String factoryName = args[0];
    String topicName = args[1];

    // Get the command to execute (publish, subscribe, recv_synch)
    String cmd = args[2];
```

Example 10-3: Publish-Subscribe Client (continued)

```
    // Create and initialize the messaging participant
    PubSubMessagingClient msger =
      new PubSubMessagingClient(factoryName, topicName);

    // Run the participant in its own thread, so that it can react to
    // incoming messages
    Thread listen = new Thread(msger);
    listen.start();

    // Send a message to the topic
    if (cmd.equals("publish")) {
      String msg = args[3];
      msger.publishMessage(msg);
      System.exit(0);
    }
    // Register a listener
    else if (cmd.equals("subscribe")) {
      MessageListener listener = new TextLogger();
      msger.registerListener(listener);
      System.out.println("Client listening to topic " + topicName
                         + "...");
      try { listen.wait(); } catch (Exception we) {}
    }
    // Synchronously receive a message from the topic
    else if (cmd.equals("recv_synch")) {
      String msg = msger.receiveMessage();
      System.out.println("Received message: " + msg);
      System.exit(0);
    }
  }
}
```

Durable Subscriptions

If a client needs to guarantee delivery of messages from a Topic beyond the life-time of a single subscriber, it can register a durable subscription with the JMS provider for the target Topic. A durable subscription to a Topic is made using the createDurableSubscriber() methods on a TopicSession. In its simplest form, a durable subscriber is created by specifying a Topic and a subscriber name:

```
    TopicConnection tConn = ...;
    tConn.setClientID("client-1");
    TopicSession tSession =
      tConn.createTopicSession(false, Session.AUTO_ACKNOWLEDGE);
    TopicSubscriber durableSub =
      tSession.createDurableSubscriber(topic, "subscriber-1");
```

This registers a durable subscription to the Topic under the name "subscriber-1." Durable subscriptions and their names are associated by the JMS provider with the client ID of the client that created them (see the earlier section "Client identifiers," for details on client IDs). Here, we're setting our client ID to "client-1" by calling setClientID() on the TopicConnection.

As long as this TopicSubscriber is live, it will receive any messages published to the Topic, as it would if it were a nondurable subscriber. But if the subscriber dies (goes out of scope, or the client dies), the JMS provider will retain messages on behalf of the named subscriber (based on its client identifier), until another durable subscriber attaches to the topic from the same connection using the same client ID and specifying the same subscriber name. Any pending messages will be delivered to the new subscriber when it attaches.

It's important to remember that durable subscriptions can be a costly resource on the JMS provider. The provider will have to create database records, or otherwise allocate server resources, in order to preserve the subscription information and any pending messages for the client. If there are many durable subscriptions, or if the number of pending messages being held on the server for subscribers becomes large, this can eventually have a significant impact on the performance of the JMS provider. So durable subscriptions should be used with discretion.

Transactional Messaging

JMS supports transactional messaging in two ways. In its simplest form, a Session is created with the transactional option (the first argument to QueueConnection. createQueueSession( ) and TopicConnection.createTopicSession( )).

```
QueueSession xactSession =
    qConn.createQueueSession(TRUE, Session.AUTO_ACKNOWLEDGE);
```

When using a transactional Session, the client performs a series of "transactions" with the Session (sends and/or receives messages from consumers and producers associated with the Session). These sends and receives are either committed by calling the Session's commit( ) method, or cancelled by calling rollback( ). If a Session is committed, all of the sends and receives are committed to the JMS provider, which causes the new state of the Destination(s) affected to be committed. If a Session is rolled back, all changes to the resources on the JMS provider are rolled back. In either case, the transaction is closed and a new one is started automatically, for any subsequent messaging actions.

JMS providers can also support transactional messaging through the Java Transaction API (JTA), which allows messaging transactions to be integrated with other resources, like databases. These JTA-based transactions are distributed: the underlying transactional resources can be distributed across the enterprise. The JMS API supports this form of transactional messaging with a set of interfaces that provide access to JTA-aware Connections and Sessions. If a JMS provider supports JTA, it can export an XAConnectionFactory in its JNDI space. An XAConnectionFactory is used to create XAConnections, and XAConnections are used to create XASessions. An XASession is a specialization of Session that overloads the commit( ) and rollback( ) methods to implement them within a JTA context. There are subclasses of these XA interfaces for point-to-point and publish-subscribe messaging. For example, to create a JTA-aware TopicSession:

```
XATopicConnectionFactory xFactory =
    (XATopicConnectionFactory)ctx.lookup("xact-factory");
XATopicConnection xConn = xFactory.createXATopicConnection();
XATopicSession xSession = xConn.createXATopicSession();
```

When a client performs a series of sends/receives with a JTA-aware Session, these actions are performed in the context of the surrounding UserTransaction, if one exists. For example, if we use our XATopicSession to create a TopicPublisher (xPublisher) and a TopicSubscriber (xSubscriber), we can create our own JTA transaction and use it to commit or roll back a series of message operations:

```
javax.transaction.UserTransaction xaction = ...;
xaction.start();
try {
  Message request = ...;
  Message response = ...;
  xPublisher.publish(request);
  response = xSubscriber.receive();
  // Made it here, so commit the topic changes
  xaction.commit();
}
catch (JMSException je) {
  // Something bad happened, so cancel the topic changes caused
  // by our message sends/receives
  xaction.rollback();
}
```

Message Selector Syntax

JMS message selectors are used by JMS clients to filter the messages that a JMS server delivers to a given MessageConsumer. A message selector is provided (optionally) when a MessageConsumer is created, using either the QueueSession. createReceiver() or the TopicSession.createSubscriber() methods.

A message selector is a string that specifies a predicate to be applied to each message the provider wants to deliver to a MessageConsumer. If the predicate evaluates to true, the message is delivered; if false, the message isn't delivered. In point-to-point messaging, when messages are filtered out by a message selector, the message remains in the queue until the client eventually reads it, or the message times out, and the server removes it from the queue. In publish-subscribe messaging, messages that are filtered are never delivered to the subscriber.

Structure of a Selector

A message selector is made up of one or more boolean expressions, joined together by logical operators and grouped using parentheses. For example:

```
(<expression1> OR <expression2> AND <expression3>) OR
(<expression4> AND NOT <expression5>) ...
```

A message selector is evaluated left to right in precedence order. So in this example, expression2 is evaluated followed by expression3 (since AND has higher precedence than OR), and if they evaluate to false, expression1 is evaluated, etc.

Expressions are made up of literal values, identifiers (referring to either message headers or properties), conditional operators, and arithmetic operators.

Identifiers

An identifier refers to either a standard JMS header field name or a custom message property name. Any JMS header field name can be used as an identifier, except for JMSDestination, JMSExpiration, JMSRedelivered, and JMSReplyTo, which can be used as identifiers in a message selector. JMSDestination and JMSReplyTo are Destination values, and message selector operators support only numeric, boolean or string values. The time at which message selectors are applied to messages isn't specified in the JMS specification, so using the value of JMSExpiration doesn't provide a consistent, well-defined result. Using JMSRedelivered in a selector can result in unexpected results. If, for example, a selector checks for JMSRedelivered being true, the first delivery attempt by a provider will fail the selector because the redelivered flag should be false, but the provider can then immediately redeliver the message and pass the selector, making the redelivered part of the predicate ineffective.

Identifier names are case-sensitive and follow the same general rules as Java identifiers. They must start with a valid Java identifier start character as determined by the java.lang.Character.isJavaIdentifierStart() method. For example, a letter, currency symbol, or connecting punctuation character such as an underscore _ contain valid Java identifier characters as determined by the Character.isJavaIdentifierPart() method. You can't use these reserved words for identifiers: NULL, TRUE, FALSE, NOT, AND, OR, BETWEEN, LIKE, IN, IS, or ESCAPE.

The type of an identifier is the type of the header field or property being referenced as its value is set in the message. It's important to remember that the evaluation of an identifier in a message selector doesn't apply type conversion functions according to the context in which it's used. If you attempt to refer to a numeric property value in an expression with a string comparison operator, for example, the expression always evaluates to false. If the named header field or property isn't present in a message, the identifier evaluates to a null value.

Literals

String literals are indicated with single quotes. For example:

```
JMSType = 'updateAck'
```

If you need to use a single quote in a string literal, use two single quotes:

```
JMSCorrelationID = 'Joe''s message'
```

Numeric literals are either integer values or floating-point values. Integer values follow the rules for Java integer literals. They are all numerals, with no decimal point, and can have a value in the same range as a Java long value:

```
42, 149, -273
```

Floating-point literals follow the syntax of Java floating-point literals. They are numerals with a decimal point:

```
3.14, 98.6, -273.0
```

They are also in scientific notation:

```
31.4e-1, 6.022e23, 2.998e8
```

Literals can also be the boolean values `true` or `false`.

Operators

Operators compose identifiers and literals into larger expressions. Operators can be logical operators, arithmetic operators, or comparison operators.

Logical Operators

The logical operators are `NOT`, `AND`, and `OR`. These are in precedence order. These have the usual boolean logic semantics. If a logical operator is applied to header fields or properties whose value is `null`, then the following rules apply:

- `ANDing` a `null` value with a `false` value evaluates to `false`; `ANDing` a `null` with a `true` or `null` value evaluates to a `null` (or unknown) value.

- `ORing` a `null` value with a `true` value evaluates to `true`; `ORing` a `null` with a `false` or a `null` value evaluates to a `null` (or unknown) value.

- Applying `NOT` to a `null` value evaluates to a `null` (or unknown) value.

Arithmetic Operators

The arithmetic operators, in precedence order, are + and - (unary), * and /, + and - (binary). These have the usual arithmetic semantics. Any arithmetic operator that is applied to one or more `null` values evaluates to a `null` value.

Comparison Operators

The comparison operators can be loosely grouped into equality comparisons and range comparisons. The basic equality comparison operators, in precedence order, are =, >, >=, <, <=, and **< >**. These binary operators have to be applied to two values of the same type, else the expression always evaluates to `false`. If either value is `null`, the result of the comparison is `null`. There are also the equality operators `IS NULL` and `IS NOT NULL` to compare a value to `null`. This can also check for the presence of a header or property:

```
timezone IS NOT NULL AND country = 'United Kingdom'
```

There are also set and range comparison operators. The `BETWEEN` operator can check the range of numeric values:

```
userid BETWEEN 00000000 AND 09999999
currRate NOT BETWEEN 0.0 AND 0.9999
```

The `IN` operator can set memberships operations on string values:

```
JMSType IN ('msgAck', 'queryAck', 'updateAck')
JMSType NOT IN ('msgBroadcast', 'synchMessage')
```

There is also a string comparison operator, `LIKE`, that allows for wildcard matching on string values. A pattern is used for the right side of the `LIKE` operator. The pattern consists of a valid string literal in which the underscore character matches against any single character, and the % character matches any sequence of zero or more characters. For example:

```
JMSType like '%Ack'
label not like 'Step _'
```

The _ and % characters can be used in these string comparison operators if they are escaped by a backslash \:

```
slogan LIKE '99 44/100\% pure'
```

Expressions

Expressions are simply literals and identifiers assembled together using the various operators described earlier. A message selector must eventually evaluate to a boolean value, so its combination of expressions must be structured to result in a boolean value. Expressions can be grouped in a message selector using parentheses in order to control the order of evaluation.

Arithmetic expressions are composed of arithmetic operators used with numeric literals and identifier values. Arithmetic expressions can be combined to form compound arithmetic expressions:

```
(userid + 10000) / (callerid - 10000)
```

Conditional expressions are made up of comparison and logical operators used with numeric, string or boolean literals or identifiers, and evaluate to true, false or null (i.e., unknown). Conditional expressions can also be combined to form compound conditional expressions:

```
(JMSType like '%Ack') AND ((userid + 10000) / (callerid - 10000) < 1.0)
```

Notice that, although the last example includes an arithmetic expression fragment:

```
(userid + 10000) / (callerid - 1000)
```

it becomes part of a conditional expression when used with a comparison operator with the numeric literal 1.0.

Every complete message selector must be a conditional expression. A message selector that evaluates to true matches the message; one that evaluates to false or null doesn't match the message.

CHAPTER 11

JavaMail

The JavaMail APIs provide a platform and protocol-independent framework to build Java-based mail and messaging applications with a particular focus on Internet email. JavaMail can be used to build mail user agent (MUA) programs. This includes such applications as mail clients, but, in an enterprise setting, the primary application for JavaMail might be to add electronic mail capability to existing and new applications. For example, a Java servlet can use JavaMail to implement a web-based mail reading system, to send confirmations and notifications, receive commands from users, or even communicate with middleware.

Sun Microsystems, Inc. included a basic SMTP email class in the first version of the JDK. However, because this class could only send email, and was only available with Sun's implementation of the JDK, developers who wished to include more advanced electronic mail capability into their applications generally needed to start from scratch. The JavaMail API, first introduced in early 1998 and now in Version 1.2, fills this niche, giving Java applications a complete mail and messaging framework.

Frankly speaking, the JavaMail API isn't really an email API at all. The JavaMail classes provide an interface to a generic set of messaging functions for creating, storing, and transporting messages. Developers can extend these classes to implement custom transport protocols and develop standardized mail applications. As an add-on, the distribution includes implementations of popular mail related protocols and a set of helper classes specifically designed to work with email on the Internet. Also, since JavaMail includes built-in support for Multipurpose Internet Mail Extensions (MIME)* formatted messages, this communication can be extremely rich, opening up a range of new possibilities for large-scale applications.

---

* MIME was originally defined in RFCs 1521 and 1522. These have been replaced by RFCs 2045 through 2049. The complete set, along with additional information, related RFCs, and helpful links, is available at *http://www.nacs.uci.edu/indiv/ehood/MIME/MIME.html*.

Email and JavaMail

The vast majority of JavaMail applications use the system to interact with Internet email. While it's safe to assume that anyone reading this book has some conceptual familiarity with electronic mail, a quick overview of Internet-based email from a technical perspective is in order. If you would like more details about email services, see *Programming Internet Email* by David Wood (O'Reilly).

The primary mechanism for email transport over the Internet is, the Simple Mail Transfer Protocol (SMTP), as defined in RFC-822. SMTP clients, such as desktop email programs, send messages by connecting to another SMTP server and transmitting a series of headers followed by a message body. Once the SMTP server receives a message, it is either stored for access by local users or forwarded to another SMTP server nearer to its destination. Most ISP and corporate mail servers will only accept messages for delivery to local users, or from local users for delivery elsewhere. In the latter case, the SMTP server is responsible for determining the appropriate destination for the message.

If the SMTP server determines that a message is for local delivery (for instance, *mail.oreilly.com* handles incoming email for O'Reilly & Associates), it handles the message in a number of ways. Early SMTP-based email systems just stored the incoming messages in the Unix mailbox format for retrieval off the local disk by mail reader software. However, as systems grew and mail services became decoupled from other systems, a need arose for a standardized way to access centralized "post office" systems that pooled the incoming mail for an entire domain (or, in the case of many ISPs, multiple domains). At the minimum, this involved providing access to Unix mailboxes over the Internet. POP, which stands for Post Office Protocol, was the first successful attempt to do this. A mail client (such as PINE, Eudora, or Outlook) can use POP to connect to a POP server and download the messages waiting for a particular user. POP has subsequently been replaced with POP3 (which is universally supported) and IMAP, a more flexible successor that has rapidly gained acceptance since Version 4 was introduced in 1994.

Figure 11-1 shows the path of a typical email message from the sender's email client to the recipient's email client. Note that this is a very simple case, with two SMTP servers relaying mail over the long haul (like AT&T long distance), and a POP3 or IMAP server at the receiving end (acting like a Baby Bell). Depending on server and client configurations, there may be only one SMTP server involved, or there may be several as messages are routed from ISP to ISP.

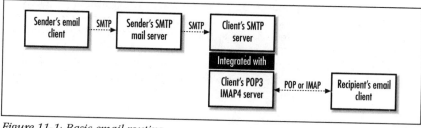

Figure 11-1: Basic email routing

JavaMail Layers

At this point, we'll give you a brief overview of the JavaMail layers. The abstract layer of the JavaMail APIs can be divided into three categories: *sessions, services,* and *messages*. Sessions contain information about the current user, mail hosts, protocols, etc. They serve as factories for various types of objects. Messages are exactly that: text sent through the mail system. Services allow you to do useful things with messages, and are subdivided (as of JavaMail Version 1.2) into two categories: *stores* and *transports*. Stores act as containers for sets of messages, while transports route messages from one site to another.

As we mentioned earlier, most of the JavaMail API consists of abstract classes. Where necessary, however, implementations of those classes are provided by an *implementation layer*. Implementation layers may include SMTP, IMAP, NNTP, or POP3 protocols or a message storage system. The implementation layer handles the actual message processing tasks.

Installing and Configuring JavaMail

Installing JavaMail is quite straightforward, although there are a few options. First, download the JavaMail 1.2 distribution from *http://java.sun.com/products/javamail.* J2EE Version 1.2 comes with a JavaMail implementation, but it only supports Java-Mail 1.1. Because JavaMail 1.2 added a number of bug fixes and few convenience methods, you will probably want to install the newer version. J2EE Version 1.3 does incorporate JavaMail 1.2. In addition, you will also need the JavaBeans Activation Framework, which contains the `javax.activation` classes used to handle certain content formatting tasks. JAF is available from *http://java.sun.com/beans/ glasgow/jaf.html.*

After unpacking the two archives, you can install JavaMail by adding the JAF's *activation.jar* and JavaMail's *mail.jar* to your system CLASSPATH or your JDK's *lib* directory. If you look at the JavaMail archive, you'll notice some additional jars: *mailapi.jar, imap.jar, smtp.jar,* and *pop3.jar.* The *mail.jar* file contains the contents of all four files, but you can use the smaller jars to selectively include service implementations in your environment. This can help reduce download times for applets or gain small performance increases in other applications.

By simply adding these JAR files to the CLASSPATH, most JavaMail programs should compile and execute. However, there are some additional configuration options available. JavaMail allows you to set a number of system properties to provide email-related system defaults. In addition to the eight properties listed in Table 11-1, each service has its own set of specific properties. Note that you don't need to set any of these to use the APIs.

Table 11-1: Core JavaMail Environment Properties

Property	Description	Default
`mail.store.protocol`	Default Message Store Protocol (such as POP or IMAP).	First message store specified in the JavaMail configuration files

Table 11-1: (continued)Core JavaMail Environment Properties (continued)

Property	Description	Default
mail.transport.protocol	Default Message Transport Protocol (such as SMTP).	First transport specified in the JavaMail configuration files
mail.host	Default host. JavaMail providers will attempt to connect to this system if no other host is specified.	The local machine
mail.user	Default username to use when connecting to a provider.	user.name
mail.protocol.host	Default host for a particular protocol. To set the default IMAP host, use mail.imap. host. Overrides mail.host	Value of mail.host
mail.protocol.user	Default user for a particular protocol. To set the default IMAP user, use mail.imap. user.	Value of mail.user
mail.from	Return address of the current user.	*username@host*
mail.debug	Whether JavaMail should operate in debug mode. Debug mode can also be toggled via the setDebug() method of Session.	false

Provider registries

JavaMail is designed to allow third parties to provide service implementations. JavaMail identifies the installed providers via the *javamail.providers* and *javamail. address.map* registry files. When starting up a JavaMail session, the system searches for *javamail.providers* files in the following locations:

* *JAVA_HOME/lib/javamail.providers*

* *META-INF/javamail.providers* (in application JAR files)

* *META-INF/javamail.default.providers* (in application JAR files; generally only found in the JavaMail *mail.jar* file)

Note that under JDK 1.1, only one *META-INF/javamail.providers* file will be found due to classloader limitations. Java 2 addresses this limitation. The first entries found will provide the defaults unless specifically changed by the application; if two POP3 providers are found, the first one identified will become the default.

The *javamail.providers* file is formatted like this:

```
protocol=imap; type=store;
class=com.sun.mail.imap.IMAPStore;
vendor=SunMicrosystems,Inc;
version=1.2;
```

The semicolon is the field delimiter. The *javamail.address.map* file is located in the same fashion as *javamail.providers* (including the *javamail.default.address. map* file in *mail.jar*), and contains mappings of address types to transport services.

For example, messages to RFC 822–formatted addresses are transported via the SMTP protocol, and this relationship is indicated by a line in the *javamail.address. map* file like this one:

```
rfc822=smtp
```

Unless you are developing your own service providers, you probably won't need to alter either of these files.

The Mail Session

As we mentioned earlier, the JavaMail API provides a Session class that fills two roles. First, it stores messaging-related properties, both global and user-specific, and provides this information to most new JavaMail objects via their constructors. Second, it provides factory methods for Store and Transport objects.

The JavaMail API provides two types of Session objects: the default session and local sessions. The default session is created only once using the static Session. getDefaultInstance() method. There are two overloaded versions of the getDefaultInstance() method: one accepts a java.util.Properties object, and one accepts a Properties object and a javax.mail.Authenticator. The Properties object can be use to set JavaMail system properties.* The Authenticator can also be used to limit access to the default session; if the first call to getDefaultInstance() includes an Authenticator, all subsequent calls must pass either the same instance of the Authenticator object, or an instance from the same class loader as the original Authenticator object. Note that no Authenticator implementations are provided with the basic JavaMail distribution—you have to create your own by subclassing the abstract javax.mail. Authenticator class provided by the API.

The Session.getInstance() method behaves the same way that the getDefaultInstance() method does, but also provides a local instance of the Session object that is not shared across the JVM. With this approach, the Authenticator is used only to determine usernames and passwords for services that require them.

The following code sample retrieves a default session, using the JVM system properties to define JavaMail properties, and using an Authenticator implementation called myAuthenticator. It then tries to retrieve a second reference to the default session without using an authenticator. If this fails (which, in this case, it will) the code gets a local instance instead:

```
Session session = Session.getDefaultInstance(System.getProperties(),
    new MyAuthenticator());

// Try again to get it again, without the authenticator; get local
// instance on failure

Session sess2 = null;
```

---

* The Properties-only version of this method was added in the JavaMail 1.2 release, so if you are running against a stock J2EE 1.2 installation or the JavaMail 1.1 release, you won't find it. Everything else in this chapter should apply equally to Versions 1.1 and 1.2.

```
try {
    sess2 = Session.getDefaultInstance(System.getProperties(), null);
} catch(SecurityException se) {
    sess2 = Session.getInstance(System.getProperties(), null);
}
```

Authenticators

Besides controlling access to the default session, `javax.mail.Authenticator` objects
are also used to provide usernames and passwords to messaging services such as
mail servers. This is accomplished by extending the abstract `Authenticator` class
and overriding the `getPasswordAuthentication()` method, which returns a Java-
Mail `PasswordAuthentication` object:

```
class BasicAuthenticator extends Authenticator {
    protected PasswordAuthentication getPasswordAuthentication() {
        return new PasswordAuthentication("scott", "tw7182");
    }
```

The `PasswordAuthentication` object is simple: it just serves as a container for the
two strings. In most applications, these would be entered by the user via a dialog
box or retrieved from some centralized directory service. Since `Authenticator`
objects are global to the session, the base `Authenticator` class contains a number
of final methods, which can be used to provide information about the particular
authentication request—for instance, using `getRequestingProtocol()`,,and
`getRequestingSite()` the `getPasswordAuthentication()` code can determine
whether to provide the IMAP login information for *mailserver.myco.com*, or the
POP3 login information for *pop.prep.edu*.

Providers

A `Session` itself doesn't provide any mail handling capabilities—it simply provides
the means to access other messaging services. Generally, you will know what sort
of messaging protocols and services are available before sitting down to code your
application, and won't need to determine them on the fly. However, the `javax.
mail.Provider` object provides a convenient view of the implementation details for
particular services: the protocol (such as SMTP), the service type (message storage
or message transport), vendor, version, and implementing class name.

For most applications, you don't actually need to worry about the `Provider` object,
because you don't need access to the object itself to access the features it
provides. However, if you do need one, the `getProviders()` method of `Session`
will allow you to interrogate the current session to determine which service
providers are installed. This method returns an array of `Provider` objects
describing the different protocol implementations available to the session. To
retrieve the `Provider` object for a particular protocol, call the `getProvider(String)`
method and pass it the protocol name, as in the following:

```
mySession.getProvider("smtp");
```

By default, provider information is specified in the *javamail.providers* and
javamail.default.providers resource files. This means that if you are using the
providers in the Sun JavaMail distribution, you don't have to do anything to obtain

access to the standard services. If you want to programmatically install your own implementation of a particular protocol, you can pass a vendor supplied Provider object to the setProvider() method of Session.

URL names

JavaMail provides a number of mechanisms for identifying services, including the system properties discussed earlier in this chapter. JavaMail services can also be identified via URLs in the form *protocol://server*. An IMAP URL, for example, might look like *imap://mailserver.cs.edu*. This sort of addressing is seen in Netscape's email client, among other places. The javax.mail.URLName object is used to encapsulate information about a connection to a mail service. This can be quite convenient, since it allows all necessary information about a connection to be assembled in a centralized location. Since service URLs are protocol-specific, this can include an arbitrary *range of precision*—IMAP URLs, for instance, allow the specification of particular messages and folders within the IMAP message store.[*]

A URLName object is only a container for connection information—hence the "Name." It doesn't actually connect to the service it identifies. Instead, it can be passed to various methods of Session, including getFolder(), getStore(), and getTransport().

URLName objects can be retrieved from existing service connections via the getURLName() method of Service (we'll look at specific services later in this chapter). They can also be created directly, via three constructors:

```
URLName(String url)
URLName(java.net.URL url)
URLName(java.lang.String protocol, java.lang.String host, int port,
    java.lang.String file, java.lang.String username,
    java.lang.String password)
```

The first two are fairly straightforward, accepting a raw URL in a String format or encapsulated as a java.net.URL object. The third option—the detailed constructor—allows you to build up the URL from its individual components, including some components (i.e., password) that might not be included in the actual URL at all. Not all options apply to all protocols, so to keep the default value for each field, pass in null. The obvious exception is the port parameter, which accepts -1 as its default value indicator.

The other way to associate login information with a URLName (particularly if the URLName was created by some mechanism other than the detailed constructor) is to associate a PasswordAuthentication object with the URL. This is done at the session level via the Session.setPasswordAuthentication(URLName, Password-Authentication) and Session.getPasswordAuthentication(URLName) methods. Once a PasswordAuthentication object has been associated with a URLName, it will be used to handle authentication for future connections to that URL.

---

[*] RFC-2192 contains full information about the IMAP URL scheme. It can be found online at *http://www.faqs.org/rfcs/rfc2192.html*.

Creating and Sending Messages

JavaMail messages are encapsulated within the abstract Message class. Since Java-Mail is a transport-independent API, the default message class is very generic. A standard Message has three attributes: a subject, a set of headers, and content. The Message class defines get- and set- methods for each of these. In addition, the Message class implements the Part interface, which defines a set of methods for dealing with message headers in an abstract fashion, and for associating content with the message. The actual message content is contained in a javax.activation.DataHandler object, part of the JavaBeans Activation Framework.

Message origins and destinations are set via Address objects. Since Address is abstract, subclasses are provided to handle particular address types. The basic JavaMail implementation includes an InternetAddress class for SMTP mail, and a NewsAddress class for NNTP (Usenet) news. Note that because there is no NNTP service included with the JavaMail distribution, the InternetAddress class will be of the greatest use to most programmers.

The easiest way to create an InternetAddress is to instantiate a new object, passing an RFC-822-formatted (*user@host*) address into the constructor:

```
InternetAddress addr = new InternetAddress("adams@whitehouse.gov");
```

If the address format is invalid, an AddressException is thrown. You can also supply a personal name as a second parameter:

```
InternetAddress addr = new InternetAddress(
                       "adams@whitehouse.gov", "John Adams");
```

If you supply a personal name, no AddressException is thrown, even if the address provided is improperly formatted.

The JavaMail distribution comes with one Message implementation: the MimeMessage class, which handles Internet email. Instantiating a simple MimeMessage is easy:

```
Message msg = new MimeMessage(session);
msg.setFrom(new InternetAddress("tip@house.gov"));
msg.setRecipients(Message.RecipientType.TO,
                  InternetAddress.parse("mike@state.ma.us", false));
msg.setText("We need to discuss a highway project.");
```

Additional set- methods can be called to set other attributes of the message, such as the subject, header fields, and so on. The Part interface also offers ways to set message content. The simplest is to use the setText() method, which sets the message content to a text string, with the content MIME type set to text/plain. The more fine-grained approach is to create a JAF DataHandler object, assign it content and MIME type, and use the setDataHandler() method to associate the DataHandler with the message. The equivalent of the setText() call would be:

```
javax.activation.DataHandler dh = new javax.activation.DataHandler(
            "We need to discuss a highway project.", "text/plain");
msg.setDataHandler(dh);
```

Other content types besides plain text are possible. To send HTML-formatted mail, pass the HTML into a DataHandler with the content type set to text/html.

Sending Messages

Once a message has been created, sending it is simple. The Address object identifies the type of address used (Internet email or Usenet news), so the JavaMail API can determine the appropriate transport mechanism. The simplest way to do this is to call the static send(Message) method of Transport. This approach will use the default session to determine mail servers (via the environment properties) and appropriate protocols (via *javamail.address.map*).

To obtain a little more control, you can retrieve a protocol-specific Transport object from a Session:

```
Transport t = session.getTransport("smtp");
t.send(msg);
```

Example 11-1 puts all the pieces together, retrieving the default session, assembling a simple message, and using the default transport mechanism to send it:

Example 11-1: Sending an SMTP Mail Message

```
import javax.mail.*;
import javax.mail.internet.*;
import java.util.Properties;

public class MailSend {
  public static void main(String[] args) {
    Properties props = System.getProperties();
    props.put("mail.smtp.host", "mail.college.edu");
    Session session = Session.getDefaultInstance(props, null);

    try {
      Message msg = new MimeMessage(session);
      msg.setFrom(new InternetAddress("you@yourhost.com"));
      msg.setRecipients(Message.RecipientType.TO,
                        InternetAddress.parse("me@myhost.com", false));
      msg.setSubject("Test Message");
      msg.setText("This is the sample Message Text");
      msg.setHeader("X-Mailer", "O'Reilly SimpleSender");
      Transport.send(msg);
    } catch (AddressException ae) {
      ae.printStackTrace(System.out);
    } catch (MessagingException me) {
      me.printStackTrace(System.out);
    }
  }
}
```

Retrieving Messages

In addition to allowing programs to create and send messages, the JavaMail API also provides facilities to retrieve incoming messages. This is done via a "message store." For standard Internet mail, the message store is generally held on a mail server and accessed via a mail client protocol.

The JavaMail 1.2 distribution includes message store implementations for POP3 and IMAP mail client protocols. POP3 is an older protocol that is still used by most ISPs and many corporate environments. It allows clients to list all available messages, retrieve them, and delete them. POP, which stands for "Post Office Protocol," was designed to work like a post office, acting as a central clearing-house for incoming messages and providing a mechanism to deliver those messages to the recipient.

POP3 stops at the point of message delivery. IMAP, however, is a newer protocol that allows more complex message handling. IMAP clients can organize messages into different "folders" on the server, based on user commands or built-in server filtering rules. In some implementations, the IMAP server is intended as the final repository for all of a user's messages. The mail client simply accesses the IMAP folders and retrieves message information as required

Message Stores

Message stores are accessed via implementations of the Store object. The getStore() method of Session is used to retrieve a Store implementation. getStore() provides a variety of ways to specify the desired message retrieval method, using the JavaMail system properties to created or lesser degrees. Calling getStore() without any arguments will return a message store based completely on JavaMail system properties. You can also pass getStore() a text string specifying the protocol to use, a Provider object, or a URLName object that completely defines the connection. If the message store provider requested is unavailable, a NoSuchProviderException is thrown:

```
Session session = Session.getDefaultInstance(
                                    System.getProperties(), null);

try {
  // get the default message store
  Store defaultStore = session.getStore();

  // get a store using the default server for IMAP
  Store imapStore = session.getStore("imap");

  // get the default IMAP store based on a Provider
  Store imapStore2 = session.getStore(session.getProvider("imap"));

  // get an IMAP store based on a URLName
  Store namedStore = session.getStore(
  new URLName("imap", "imap.my.com", -1, null, "user", "pw"));

} catch (NoSuchProviderException nsp) {
}
```

Once you have a Store object, you need to connect to it before retrieving messages. Store extends the abstract Service class, which provides generic connection services for both Store and Transport objects, as well as hooks to the

JavaMail event model. To connect to the store, use the connect() method, which comes in three variants. The parameterless version can be used with message stores that don't require authentication, or with authenticated stores that have already had the username and password specified via a URLName or an Authenticator. The other two versions allow you to specify the mail host, username, and password, or the mail host, port, username, and password. To use the default value for any of these parameters, pass null (for object parameters) or -1 (for integer parameters.)

Between the system properties, the getStore() method, and the connect() method, JavaMail provides a variety of ways to specify the attributes of message stores. This is because different protocols require different information to successfully connect to a server. The information that is most directly provided always overrides the system or store defaults.

Handling Incoming Messages

Message stores provide the most general collection of messages possible. However, it is not a good idea to assume that every message in a system will be collected in the same place. JavaMail supports grouping of messages into folders. Every message store contains a default folder, represented by a Folder object. The default folder generally contains one or more subfolders that contain actual messages. The default folder is retrieved via the getDefaultFolder() method of a Store object. Subfolders can then be retrieved by calling the getFolder() method on the default folder:

```
Folder defaultFolder = myStore.getDefaultFolder();
Folder inboxFolder = defaultFolder.getFolder("INBOX");
```

In this example, we first retrieve the default folder from the message store, and "INBOX" folder. This is, by the way, the standard hierarchy for both IMAP and POP3 message stores; actual messages are stored, by default, in the INBOX folder. IMAP message stores allow users to configure a broader range of folders internally, either via a mail client or by configuring settings on the mail server. These folders can be nested indefinitely.

After obtaining a folder, you can open it with the Folder.open() method. Folders can either be opened in read-only or read-write mode, depending on whether the Folder.READ_ONLY or Folder.READ_WRITE constant is passed to the open() method. For example:

```
// open a folder for read-write access:
inboxFolder.open(Folder.READ_WRITE);
```

Example 11-2 connects to a message store located at *mail.college.edu*, via the IMAP and POP3 protocols and using an Authenticator to handle usernames and passwords.

Example 11-2: IMAP and POP Message Retrieval

```
Displaying a Multipart Message
import javax.mail.*;
import javax.mail.internet.*;
```

Example 11-2: IMAP and POP Message Retrieval (continued)

```java
import java.util.Properties;

public class MailCheck {

  static String mailhost = "mail.college.edu";

  public static void main(String[] args) {

    Session session = Session.getDefaultInstance(System.getProperties(),
     new myAuthenticator());

    try {
      Store imapStore = session.getStore(new URLName("imap://" + mailhost));
      imapStore.connect();
      System.out.println(imapStore.getURLName());
      // Get a default folder, and use it to open a real folder
      Folder defaultFolder = imapStore.getDefaultFolder();
      defaultFolder = defaultFolder.getFolder("INBOX");
      defaultFolder.open(Folder.READ_WRITE);

      Message[] msgs = defaultFolder.getMessages();
      if(msgs != null)
        for (int i = 0; i < msgs.length; i++) {
          System.out.println(msgs[i].getSubject());
        }

      // Now, get it with POP3, using authenticator
      Store popStore = session.getStore("pop3");
      popStore.connect(mailhost, null, null);

      // Get a default folder, and use it to open a real folder
      Folder defaultPopFolder = popStore.getDefaultFolder();
      defaultPopFolder = defaultPopFolder.getFolder("INBOX");
      defaultPopFolder.open(Folder.READ_ONLY);

      msgs = defaultPopFolder.getMessages();
      if(msgs != null)
        for (int i = 0; i < msgs.length; i++) {
          System.out.println(msgs[i].getSubject());
        }

    } catch (MessagingException me) {
      me.printStackTrace(System.out);
    }
  } // end main()
}

class myAuthenticator extends Authenticator {
  protected PasswordAuthentication getPasswordAuthentication() {
    return new PasswordAuthentication("mailname", "test");
  }
}
```

Searches and Message Management

JavaMail includes a mechanism for programmatically generating search criteria for finding messages within folders. Searches are built via the SearchTerm object. SearchTerm is an abstract class with a single method, match(Message), which returns true or false depending on whether the message matches the term's criteria. JavaMail provides a number of SearchTerm implementations that allow for searching on various aspects of a message. SubjectTerm, for instance, does substring matching on the Subject header. The following code will search a folder for all messages with "Urgent" in the subject line:

```
SearchTerm t = new SubjectTerm("Urgent");
Message[] msgs = folder.search(t);
```

More complex searches use the AndTerm, OrTerm, and NotTerm objects, which allow chaining and nesting of search criteria. Here's how to tell when we haven't gotten something to our editor on time:

```
SearchTerm t = new AndTerm(new FromStringTerm("oreilly.com"),
  new SubjectTerm("late"));
Message[] msgs = folder.search(t);
```

The search will match messages from *oreilly.com* in which the subject contains the word "late." You can nest AndTerm and OrTerm objects as deeply as you want, although performance will obviously suffer with more complex searches.

The default implementation of the search functionality will rely on the data provided via Message objects to perform searches. This has the advantage of working regardless of whether or not the underlying message store supports search functionality, and allows programmers to easily define their own search terms by extending the SearchTerm class. If the underlying message store does support search functionality, the implementation has the option of translating the search, where possible, into native terms.

Unsolicited commercial email (spam) is of great concern to many readers, so we offer our contribution to cleaner inboxes. Example 11-3 will connect to a mailbox and perform a set of subject searches for strings that generally indicate less than desirable content. Once identified, a copy of the message is sent to a separate address for monitoring purposes, and the original is deleted.

Example 11-3: SpamCleaner.java

```
import javax.mail.*;
import javax.mail.internet.*;
import javax.mail.search.*;

import java.util.Properties;

public class SpamCleaner {

    static String mailhost = "imap.mycompany.com";
    static String smtphost = "mail.mycompany.com";
    static String redirectEmail = "spamlog@mycompany.com";
```

Example 11-3: SpamCleaner.java (continued)

```java
    static String[] badSubjects = {"XXX", "MAKEMONEYFAST", "!!!!"};

    public static void main(String[] args) {

        Properties props = new Properties();
        props.setProperty("mail.smtp.host", smtphost);
        Session session = Session.getDefaultInstance(props, null);

        try {
            Store imapStore = session.getStore("imap");
            imapStore.connect(mailhost, "scott", "yu7xx");

            Folder defaultFolder = imapStore.getDefaultFolder();
            Folder inboxFolder = defaultFolder.getFolder("INBOX");
            inboxFolder.open(Folder.READ_WRITE);

            // Assemble some search Criteria, using nested OrTerm objects
            SearchTerm spamCriteria = null;
            for(int i=0; i<badSubjects.length; i++) {
                SubjectTerm st = new SubjectTerm(badSubjects[i]);
                if(spamCriteria == null)
                    spamCriteria = st;
                else
                    spamCriteria = new OrTerm(spamCriteria, st);
            }

            Message[] msgs = inboxFolder.search(spamCriteria);

            if(msgs != null)
                for (int i = 0; i < msgs.length; i++) {
                    // Redirect the message
                    Message m = new MimeMessage((MimeMessage)msgs[i]);
                    m.setRecipient(Message.RecipientType.TO,
                        new InternetAddress(redirectEmail));
// Clear out the cc: field so we don't loop or anything
                    m.setHeader("CC", "");
                    Transport.send(m);

                    // Now delete the original
                    System.out.println(
                                "Deleting Message "+msgs[i].getMessageNumber()+":"
                        + msgs[i].getSubject());
                    msgs[i].setFlag(Flags.Flag.DELETED, true);
                }

            // Close inbox folder, with "Expunge" flag set to true
            inboxFolder.close(true);

            imapStore.close();
        } catch (MessagingException me) {
            me.printStackTrace(System.out);
```

Example 11-3: SpamCleaner.java (continued)

```
    }
  } // end main()
}
```

Example 11-3 also shows how to delete a message from an IMAP message store. Rather than calling a delete method on a folder or message object, we call the setFlag() method of Message and set the deletion flag (identified by the Flags. Flag.DELETED constant) to true. You can examine all the flags set on a particular message by calling the getFlags() method of Message, which returns a Flags object. However, in most cases the ability to set the DELETED flag is all you need.

Note that marking a message as deleted doesn't actually delete it. Messages aren't removed from the message store until the store is expunged. This can be done either by calling the expunge() method of Folder, or passing a boolean true value to the close() method of Folder. Once a message has been expunged, the message numbers within the folder (returned by the getMessageNumber() method of Message).

Example 11-3 also shows how to clone a message. JavaMail 1.2 added a new constructor to the MimeMessage object, which causes the new MimeMessage to be populated with all the fields and content from the original. The example does something dangerous in assuming that the message retrieved by the search() function will actually be a MimeMessage. This is fine when using the Sun service implementations, but a more general version of this program would have to be more careful, either constructing the new Message object by hand or trying to modify and resend the copy pulled from the message store (which is generally not allowed).

If you are working with a message store that supports modification of message content, the loop in Example 11-3 could be replaced with this instead:

```
    for (int i = 0; i < msgs.length; i++) {
    // Alter the message
      System.out.println("Altering Message "+msgs[i].getMessageNumber()+":"
        + msgs[i].getSubject());
      msgs[i].setSubject("SPAM:" + msgs[i].getSubject());
      msgs[i].saveChanges();
    }
```

Rather than deleting the message, this code alters the subject line and inserts the word "SPAM:" before the original subject. The saveChanges() method writes the changes back to the message stores. However, we can't use this approach with this code because incoming IMAP messages are read-only.

Multipart Messages

Up until now, we haven't discussed viewing or creating messages except at a very simplistic level. Let's close this chapter by taking a look at the MimeMessage class, the standard Message implementation for Internet email, and the Multipart class, which allows MIME-formatted messages that contain multiple parts (for instance, text and HTML versions of content, and file attachments).

Displaying Multipart Messages

MimeMessage objects are either single part or multipart. A single-part message has a content-type attribute matching the content of the message (often "text/plain"); the actual message content is stored in the message's content attribute, accessed via the getContent() method.

Multipart messages of content types begin with "multipart" and contain a Multipart object as their content. The Multipart object contains a series of BodyPart objects (in the case of a MIME-formatted message, these will be MimeBodyPart objects and can be cast as such). Each BodyPart has its own content type and associated content.

The getContent() and getContentType() methods of Message are actually inherited from the Part interface, which is also implemented by BodyPart and MimeBodyPart. Part provides another useful method, isMimeType(), which allows testing for particular content types. The isMimeType() method will compare only the primary and sub-content types (the types immediately before and after the / character). So, isMimeType("text/plain") will return true if the MIME type is "text/plain" or "text/plain; charset=USASCII." You use the wildcard character * in place of the subtype ("text/*") to match all data with a particular primary type.

Example 11-4 is an enhanced version of the mail viewer from Example 11-2 (although it just pulls from a single source). It starts by connecting to a POP server and downloading copies of the messages in the inbox. For each message the program displays subject and senders, and determines whether the message is multipart or not. If it is, the Multipart object is retrieved and each individual part is processed. Textual content is written to the screen. Nontextual content with a filename associated with it, such as a file attachment, is written to disk and the path is displayed.

Example 11-4: Multipart Display

```
import javax.mail.*;
import javax.mail.internet.*;

import java.util.Properties;
import java.io.*;

public class MimeShow {

static String mailhost = "pop.company.com";

public static void main(String[] args) {

  Session session = Session.getDefaultInstance(
                                    System.getProperties(), null);

  try {

    Store popStore = session.getStore("pop3");
      popStore.connect(mailhost, "username", "password");

      // Get a default folder, and use it to open a real folder
```

Example 11-4: Multipart Display (continued)

```
      Folder defaultPopFolder = popStore.getDefaultFolder();
      defaultPopFolder = defaultPopFolder.getFolder("INBOX");
      defaultPopFolder.open(Folder.READ_ONLY);

      Message[] msgs = defaultPopFolder.getMessages();
      if(msgs != null)
        for (int i = 0; i < msgs.length; i++) {
          // Display the message envelope
          System.out.println("\n\r---------------------------------");
          System.out.println("Subject: " + msgs[i].getSubject());
          Address[] from = msgs[i].getFrom();
          if(from != null)
            for(int a = 0; a < from.length; a++)
              System.out.println("From: " + from[a]);

          // Display the content
          if (msgs[i].isMimeType("text/plain")) {
            System.out.println((String)msgs[i].getContent());
          } else if (msgs[i].isMimeType("multipart/*")) {
            Multipart mp = (Multipart)msgs[i].getContent();
            int count = mp.getCount();
            for(int m = 0; m < count; m++) {
              showBodyPart((MimeBodyPart)mp.getBodyPart(m));
            }
          } else if (msgs[i].isMimeType("message/rfc822")) {
            System.out.println("Nested Message");
          } else {
            System.out.println(msgs[i].getContent().toString());
          }
        }// end for

  } catch (MessagingException me) {
    me.printStackTrace(System.out);
  } catch (IOException ie) {
    ie.printStackTrace(System.out);
  }
} // end main()

  // Show or save a MIME Body Part; Very Simple
  public static void showBodyPart(MimeBodyPart p) {
    try {
      String contentType = p.getContentType();
      System.out.println("-- MIME Part: " + contentType);

      if(contentType.startsWith("text/"))
        System.out.println((String)p.getContent());
      else if(p.getFileName() != null) {

        File f = new File(p.getFileName());
        FileOutputStream fos = new FileOutputStream(f);
        byte[] b = new byte[1024];
        InputStream is = p.getInputStream();
        fos.write(b);
```

Example 11-4: Multipart Display (continued)

```
        is.close();
        fos.close();
        System.out.println("Attachment saved as " + f.getAbsolutePath());
      } else {
        System.out.println(
        "Cannot display this content type and no filename supplied.");
      }
    } catch(Exception e) {
      System.out.println("Exception Caught: " + e.getMessage());
    }
  } // End showBodyPart()
} // End class
```

Sending Multipart Messages

Creating a multipart message isn't any more complex than creating a regular MIME message. First, instantiate a `MimeMultipart` object, which will serve as a container for the various parts of the message. For each part, create a `MimeBodyPart`, and set its content via the `setContent()` method. Add each body part to the `MimeMultipart` object using the `addBodyPart()` method. Finally, add the `Multipart` object as the content of a `MimeMessage`, and send that message normally.

There are, of course, a few wrinkles in the process, particularly when dealing with file attachments. To attach a file to a message, you need to specify the filename when creating the `MimeBodyPart` (via the `setFileName()` method), and provide the actual file data. Note that the content is provided via the JavaBeans Activation Framework's `DataHandler` object, which we discussed earlier in this chapter. `DataHandler` objects can be fed via `DataSource` objects. JAF provides two of these: `FileDataSource` and `URLDataSource`, which are more or less as advertised—one retrieves data from a file, the other from a URL. In addition to retrieving raw bytes, the `DataSource` will also provide the `DataHandler` with an appropriate content type. Here's how:

```
File f = new File("foo.jpg");
MimeBodyPart mbp = new MimeBodyPart();
mbp.setFileName(f.getName());
mbp.setDataHandler(new DataHandler(new FileDataSource(f)));
```

Example 11-5 puts the pieces together. It sends an email to *root@company.com* from *logs@company.com*, with a brief text message and a file attachment containing */var/logs/today.log*:

Example 11-5: Sending a Multipart Message

```
import javax.mail.*;
import javax.mail.internet.*;
import javax.activation.*;
import java.io.File;
import java.util.Properties;

public class MimeAttach {
```

Example 11-5: Sending a Multipart Message (continued)

```java
public static void main(String[] args) {
  try {
    Properties props = System.getProperties();
    props.put("mail.smtp.host", "mail.company.com");
    Session session = Session.getDefaultInstance(props, null);

    Message msg = new MimeMessage(session);
    msg.setFrom(new InternetAddress("logs@company.com"));
    msg.setRecipient(Message.RecipientType.TO,
                    new InternetAddress("root@company.com"));
    msg.setSubject("Today's Logs");

    Multipart mp = new MimeMultipart();
    MimeBodyPart mbp1 = new MimeBodyPart();
    mbp1.setContent("Log file for today is attached.", "text/plain");

    mp.addBodyPart(mbp1);

    File f = new File("/var/logs/today.log");
    MimeBodyPart mbp = new MimeBodyPart();
    mbp.setFileName(f.getName());
    mbp.setDataHandler(new DataHandler(new FileDataSource(f)));
    mp.addBodyPart(mbp);

    msg.setContent(mp);
    Transport.send(msg);
  } catch (MessagingException me) {
    me.printStackTrace();
  }
}
}
```

JavaMail's support for multipart messages opens up some interesting possibilities for using email within your enterprise applications. With a few POP or IMAP mailboxes, you can write software that will exchange without any user intervention. This can be used to synchronize configuration files, exchange XML documents, or even handling more mundane tasks such as generating automated status emails.

PART II

Enterprise Reference

Part II contains reference material on two enterprise-related technologies, SQL and IDL, and on the tools provided with Sun's Java Development Kit for RMI and Java IDL.

CHAPTER 12

SQL Reference

There are dozens of different database management systems on the market today, from nearly as many vendors. Developing applications that are more or less database-independent requires a standardized interface to the underlying data. Since the early 1980s, this interface has been SQL, a sophisticated database manipulation language.[*]

Unlike Java, SQL is a declarative language. It allows users to specify particular actions on the database and retrieve the results of those actions. It specifies a set of standardized data types and standard error messages, but it lacks procedural constructs. There are no conditionals or loops standard in SQL.

There are several versions of the SQL standard. SQL-86 and SQL-89 have been superceded by SQL-92, which is supported by most database vendors, although there are a number of platform-specific variations. Many databases also include additional data types, operators, and functions beyond those specified in the SQL-92 standard. In addition, there are three levels of SQL-92 conformance: entry-level, intermediate, and full. Many products support only the entry-level SQL-92 standard, leaving out some advanced features. JDBC drivers are supposed to provide entry-level functionality and, for the most part, they do.

This chapter presents a brief introduction to the structure of a relational database system and a quick reference to the most commonly used SQL commands. The complete set of SQL commands is simply too large to cover here; even a concise SQL reference can run to several hundred pages. we have endeavored to provide the information that most client-side programmers need. For a complete introduc-

---

[*] The acronym expands out to either Structured Query Language (based on the original IBM acronym from the 1970s) or Standard Query Language (which has been more popular in recent years). Perhaps because of this confusion, most people just say SQL, pronounced either see-quell or ess-cue-ell.

tion to most aspects of SQL, we highly recommend *SQL Clearly Explained* by Jan Harrington (AP Professional).

Relational Databases

Data storage and retrieval are two of the biggest tasks facing most enterprise applications. There are lots of ways to store data on a disk, but for large-scale applications, a relational database management system (RDBMS) is far and away the most popular choice.

Data in an RDBMS is organized into tables, which contain rows and columns. You can think of an individual table as a spreadsheet with a little more organization: column data types are fixed, and there may be rules governing the formatting of each column. This alone is enough for a database system (plain DBMS). A relational database system has one other key attribute: individual tables can be *related* based on some common data. Figure 12-1 shows three tables in a relational structure. The CUSTOMERS table is related to the ORDERS table based on the CUSTOMER_ID field, and the ORDERS table is related to the ITEMS table based on the ORDER_ID field. SQL provides a standardized means of accessing the data in tables and working with the relationships between tables.

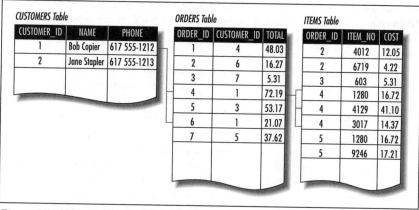

CUSTOMERS Table

CUSTOMER_ID	NAME	PHONE
1	Bob Copier	617 555-1212
2	Jane Stapler	617 555-1213

ORDERS Table

ORDER_ID	CUSTOMER_ID	TOTAL
1	4	48.03
2	6	16.27
3	7	5.31
4	1	72.19
5	3	53.17
6	1	21.07
7	5	37.62

ITEMS Table

ORDER_ID	ITEM_NO	COST
2	4012	12.05
2	6719	4.22
3	603	5.31
4	1280	16.72
4	4129	41.10
4	3017	14.37
5	1280	16.72
5	9246	17.21

Figure 12-1: Three related tables

The highest-level organizational concept in an RDBMS system is a *cluster.** A cluster contains one or more *catalogs*, which are usually the highest-level object a programmer ever has to deal with. A catalog contains a group of schemas. A schema contains a group of tables and other objects and is generally assigned to a particular application or user account. Generally, the database administrator is responsible for dealing with clusters and catalogs. Most users work within a particular schema.

---

* The naming comes from the older SQL standards, where a cluster represented physical storage space. This is no longer the case, but the name persists.

To reference a table within a particular schema, separate the schema name and the table name with a dot:

schema_name.table_name

To reference a particular column within a particular schema:

schema_name.table_name.column_name

To set a particular schema as the default, use the SET SCHEMA SQL statement:

SET SCHEMA *schema_name*

When you log into a database, you are generally assigned a default schema. When accessing tables within the default schema, you may omit the schema name.

When creating new objects, the names you assign to them must be unique within the schema. SQL-92 allows names up to 128 characters, including letters, numbers, and the underscore (_) character.

Data Types

Each column in a table has a particular data type associated with it. SQL-92 defines a fairly broad set of data types. Different RDBMS packages provide extensions to these basic types, for multimedia data, Java objects, and so on. Oracle's NUMBER data type, for instance, allows database designers to specify the exact precision of integer and floating-point data types. The basic SQL-92 types are listed in Figure 12-1. The names in parentheses are SQL-92 specified alternates for the main type names.

Table 12-1: SQL-92 Data Types

SQL Data Type	Description
INTEGER (INT)	A signed integer value. The number of bits represented is implementation-dependent.
SMALLINT	A smaller signed integer value, used when storage or memory is at a premium. Generally 8 bits but implementation-dependent.
NUMERIC	A signed fixed-precision decimal. When creating a NUMERIC, you must specify the total length of the number (including the decimal point) and the number of decimal places. NUMERIC(8, 4) allows three digits, a decimal point, and four more digits.
DECIMAL	Defined the same way as a NUMERIC but may store additional precision (more decimal places).
REAL	A single-precision floating-point value. Range and accuracy are implementation-dependent.
DOUBLE PRECISION (DOUBLE)	A double-precision floating-point value. Range and accuracy are implementation dependent, but are equal to or better than a REAL.
BIT	A fixed number (one or more) of bits. A length specifier (BIT(*n*)) is optional. The default size is 1 bit.
BIT VARYING	Storage for up to *n* bits (BIT VARYING (*n*)). Many databases have alternate implementations of this data type, such as Oracle's VARBINARY.
DATE	A date value (day, month, and year).
TIME	A time value. Precision is implementation-dependent.
TIMESTAMP	A date and time.

Table 12-1: SQL-92 Data Types (continued)

SQL Data Type	Description
CHARACTER (CHAR)	A fixed-length character string. Specified as CHAR(*n*). Unused characters are padded with blanks. The default size is 1.
CHARACTER VARYING (VARCHAR)	A variable length string, up to size *n*. Specified as VARCHAR(*n*).
INTERVAL	A date or time interval. Not directly supported by JDBC.

Note that the data types given here aren't the same as those in Table 2-1 in Chapter 2. When mapping between SQL types and Java types, a JDBC driver matches the physical data type (either SQL-92 or database-specific) and the closest Java type. For example, calling the getType() method of ResultSet on a BIT VARYING field generally returns a Types.LONGVARBINARY value. This translation allows most JDBC programs to switch between different databases without losing functionality. Also, many databases implement additional types: the FLOAT type is so common that many people think it is required by the specification.

Schema Manipulation Commands

SQL includes two broad classes of commands. The first class is schema manipulation commands, which allow the creation, modification, and deletion of high-level database objects such as tables. This section describes these commands. We've provided a syntax summary for each command. In case you aren't familiar with the style, items in square brackets are optional or not always required, while items in curly braces are either always required or required within the context of some optional item. A vertical bar (|) indicates a choice, while an ellipsis indicates that an entry may be repeated any number of times. Items in uppercase constant width are part of the SQL statement, while items in lowercase *constant width italic* represent names and values that you supply when using the statement.

CREATE TABLE

As its name says, the CREATE TABLE command creates a table. Here's the syntax:

```
CREATE [ [ GLOBAL | LOCAL ] TEMPORARY ] TABLE table_name
   ( { column_name { data_type | domain_name } [ column_size ]
       [ column_constraint ... ] ... }
     [ DEFAULT default_value ], ...
     [ table_constraint ], ...
     [ ON COMMIT { DELETE | PRESERVE } ROWS ] )
```

Here's a simple example:

```
CREATE TABLE BOOKS
  (
    TITLE VARCHAR (25) PRIMARY KEY,
    AUTHOR VARCHAR(25) NOT NULL DEFAULT 'Unknown',
    EDITION INTEGER,
    PRICE NUMBER(6,2)
  )
```

The PRIMARY KEY and NOT NULL identifiers are column constraints. The NOT NULL constraint prevents any entry in a column from being set to null. Here, it's combined it with a default value. PRIMARY KEY identifies the column that's used as the primary key (or main unique identifier) for the table. If a table has a primary key column (it doesn't have to), there can be only one such column; no row has a null value in the primary key column, and no two rows have the same primary key.

A table constraint affects every row in the table. UNIQUE is a common example:

```
CREATE TABLE BOOKS
    (
    TITLE VARCHAR (25),
    AUTHOR VARCHAR(25),
    EDITION INTEGER,
    PRICE NUMBER(6,2),
    UNIQUE
    )
```

Used as a table constraint, UNIQUE indicates that each row in the table must have a unique combination of values. You can also specify particular columns that must form a unique combination:

```
UNIQUE(TITLE, AUTHOR, EDITION)
```

This mandates only unique title/author/edition combinations. Note that UNIQUE can also be used as a column constraint.

We can use PRIMARY KEY as a table constraint to specify more than one column as the primary key:

```
CREATE TABLE BOOKS
    (
    TITLE VARCHAR (25) NOT NULL,
    AUTHOR VARCHAR(25) NOT NULL,
    EDITION INTEGER NOT NULL,
    PRICE NUMBER(6,2),
    PRIMARY KEY (TITLE, AUTHOR, EDITION)
    )
```

Since entry-level SQL-92 requires that primary keys remain not null, we use NOT NULL column constraints on the primary key columns in this case.

ALTER TABLE

The ALTER TABLE command allows you to modify the structure of an existing table. Here's the syntax:

```
ALTER TABLE table_name
    { ADD [COLUMN] column_name definition }
    { ALTER [COLUMN] column_name definition
        { SET DEFAULT default_value } | { DROP DEFAULT } }
    { DROP [COLUMN] COLUMN_NAME [ RESTRICT | CASCADE ] }
    { ADD table_constraint_definition }
    { DROP constraint_name [ RESTRICT | CASCADE] }
```

Note that the modifications you can make are somewhat limited. While you can add and remove columns (subject to the requirements of any constraints that may have been placed on the table), you can't reorder columns. To perform major changes, you generally need to create a new table and move the existing data from the old table to the new table.

Here's a statement that adds two columns to a table:

```
ALTER TABLE BOOKS
  ADD PUBLISHED_DATE DATE,
  ADD PUBLISHER CHAR (30) NOT NULL
```

Note that the ability to specify multiple operations in an ALTER TABLE command is not part of the SQL specification, although most databases support this functionality.

Here's how to change the type of a column:*

```
ALTER TABLE BOOKS
  MODIFY PUBLISHER VARCHAR (25)
```

When this statement runs, the database attempts to convert all existing data into the new format. If this is impossible, the modification fails. In the previous example, if any record has a publisher entry of more than 30 characters, the statement might fail (exact behavior depends on the implementation). If you are converting from a character field to, say, an integer field, the whole ALTER TABLE command might fail entirely. At the minimum, such a change requires that all entries contain a valid string representation of an integer.

To allow null values in the PUBLISHER column, use MODIFY:

```
ALTER TABLE BOOKS
  MODIFY PUBLISHER NULL
```

To remove the PUBLISHER column entirely, use DROP:

```
ALTER TABLE BOOKS
  DROP PUBLISHER
```

The ALTER TABLE command is not required for entry-level SQL-92 conformance. Due to its extreme usefulness, however, it is supported by most DBMS packages, although it often varies from the standard. More esoteric features, such as the RENAME command, aren't supported by most packages. In general, it is not safe to count on anything beyond the basic ADD, DROP, and MODIFY (ALTER) commands.

DROP

The DROP command allows you to permanently delete an object within the database. For example, to drop the BOOKS table, execute this statement:

```
DROP TABLE BOOKS
```

DROP also can delete other database objects, such as indexes, views, and domains:

---

* If you look back at the syntax for ALTER TABLE, you'll see that the official syntax for this kind of operation is ALTER, although most databases use MODIFY instead.

```
DROP INDEX index_name
DROP VIEW view_name
DROP DOMAIN domain_name
```

Once something has been dropped, it is usually gone for good—certainly once the current transaction has been committed, but often before.

Data Manipulation Commands

Empty tables aren't very useful, and, even once they've been populated with data, we need some way of getting that data back out. The SQL data manipulation commands allow you to read data from a table and to create, update, and remove existing data.

SELECT

The SELECT statement is the most important statement in SQL and also the most complex. It allows you to retrieve data from a table or a set of tables. Here's the syntax:

```
SELECT [ DISTINCT ]
    { summary_function, ... }
    | { data_manipulation_expression, ... }
    | { column_name, ... }
FROM
    { { table_name [ AS correlation_name ] }
    | { subquery [ AS correlation_name ] }
    | joined_tables}
[ WHERE predicate ]
[ GROUP BY column_name, ... [ HAVING group_selection_predicate ] ]
[ { UNION | INTERSECT | EXCEPT } [ ALL ]
    [ CORRESPONDING [ BY (column_name, ...] ]
      select_statement | { TABLE table_name }
                       | table_value_constructor ]
[ ORDER BY {{output_column [ ASC | DESC ]}, ...}
          | {{positive_integer [ ASC | DESC ]}, ...}]
```

The simplest possible SELECT, which displays all columns of all rows of a single table, looks like this:

```
SELECT * FROM BOOKS
```

If this statement is executed in a command-line SQL interpreter, the output might look like this:

```
TITLE                 | AUTHOR           | EDITION | PRICE
----------------------+------------------+---------+-------
Me                    | Garrison Keillor |     1 | 24.99
Bleak House           | Charles Dickens  |    57 |  8.99
A Tale Of Two Cities  | Charles Dickens  |   312 |  4.99
```

To sort the output by title, we can add an ORDER BY clause to the statement:

```
SELECT * FROM BOOKS ORDER BY TITLE
```

Now the output is:

```
   TITLE                 | AUTHOR            | EDITION | PRICE
---------------------+-------------------+---------+-------
A Tale Of Two Cities | Charles Dickens   |    312  |  4.99
Bleak House          | Charles Dickens   |     57  |  8.99
Me                   | Garrison Keillor  |      1  | 24.99
```

To select just the TITLE and AUTHOR columns:

```
SELECT TITLE, AUTHOR FROM BOOKS
```

To select a subset of records, use the WHERE clause:

```
SELECT * FROM BOOKS WHERE PRICE < 10.0
```

This returns the Charles Dickens bookskm, but not the Garrison Keillor book. You can have multiple criteria:

```
SELECT * FROM BOOKS WHERE PRICE < 10.0 OR EDITION = 1
```

This returns all three books. If we had specified a price less than 10 and an edition equal to 1, we wouldn't have received any records back. The various predicates you can use are listed in Table 12-2. Note that not all of the more esoteric ones (such as LIKE) are supported by all databases.

Table 12-2: SQL Predicates

Operator	Meaning
=	Equals
<	Less than
>	Greater than
<=	Less than or equal to
>=	Greater than or equal to
!= or <>	Not equal to (some implementations may support only one)
LIKE	Wildcard match
IS NULL	Checks for a null value
IN	Checks to see if a value is contained within a set
BETWEEN	Checks to see if a date value is between two other date values

The final four predicates in the table can be used with the NOT modifier (e.g., NOT LIKE, IS NOT NULL, etc.).

String comparisons

The = operator can generally be used for exact string comparisons. The LIKE operator allows wildcard searches using two wildcard characters: % to match any number of characters, and _ to match, at most, one character. Here's a query that selects all records that have a LAST_NAME that contains the letters "for":

```
SELECT LAST_NAME FROM CUSTOMERS WHERE LAST_NAME LIKE'%for%'
```

This matches last names like Buford, Crawford, and Trefor, but may not match Fordham, since most databases implement LIKE in a case-sensitive manner (Microsoft Access is a notable exception to this rule). Case-insensitive searches generally require a single-case version of the column or the use of a case-adjusting function (we'll discuss functions later in this chapter).

Subqueries and joins

The IN predicate allows you to check whether a value appears in another set of values. The simplest way to use this feature is in a SQL statement like this:

```
SELECT * FROM BOOKS WHERE PRICE IN (5.95, 4.95, 7.95)
```

This is simply another form for:

```
SELECT * FROM BOOKS WHERE PRICE = 5.95 OR PRICE = 4.95 OR PRICE = 7.95
```

But we can do something more interesting with IN. Let's assume that we have a table, called PRICES, that holds all the prices we want to search on. In this case, we can generate the set of values using another query, as follows:

```
SELECT * FROM BOOKS WHERE PRICE IN
    SELECT PRICE FROM PRICES
```

Note that we didn't put parentheses around the second SELECT statement; use parentheses only when you are specifying the entire list manually.

Subqueries like this are useful, but they still restrict the output columns to those of a single table.

Rather than using subqueries, two tables are normally connected via a join. A *join* allows a query to include references to multiple tables and to restrict the output based on the relations between those tables. The basic join is an *equi-join* (or inner join): data in two tables is linked based on a shared value. An order-tracking database might include a CUSTOMERS table and an ORDERS table. The CUSTOMERS table has a customer identifier (CUSTOMER_ID) as its primary key. The orders table also has a CUSTOMER_ID column, although not as a primary key, since there may be more than one order per customer (see Figure 12-1 for a graphical representation of these tables). Here's the SQL to combine the two tables based on the CUSTOMER_ID column:

```
SELECT * FROM CUSTOMERS, ORDERS WHERE ORDERS.CUSTOMER_ID =
    CUSTOMERS.CUSTOMER_ID
```

Since it's an equi-join, it works just as well the other way around:

```
SELECT * FROM CUSTOMERS, ORDERS WHERE CUSTOMERS.CUSTOMER_ID =
    ORDERS.CUSTOMER_ID
```

In SQL-92, there is a JOIN operator that performs the same operation with a slightly different syntax:[*]

```
SELECT CUSTOMERS.CUSTOMER_ID, CUSTOMERS.NAME, ORDERS.ORDER_ID, ORDERS.
TOTAL
    FROM CUSTOMERS INNER JOIN ORDERS ON CUSTOMERS.CUSTOMER_ID = ORDERS.
CUSTOMER_ID
```

---

[*] Note that some databases allow you to use JOIN without the ON clause. In this case, the join operates on columns that have the same name.

This example indicates the specific columns to return. Using the data shown in Figure 12-1, the output of this query might look like this:

```
CUSTOMER_ID | NAME       | ORDER_ID | TOTAL
------------+------------+----------+--------
       1 | Bob Copier |      4 | 72.19
       1 | Bob Copier |      6 | 21.07
```

Note that some databases require you to use INNER JOIN instead of JOIN, while others allow just JOIN because inner joins are the default join.

To join on more than one table, use multiple JOIN statements. Here we add an ITEMS table that includes the ORDER_ID from the ORDERS table:

```
SELECT * FROM ITEMS JOIN ORDERS JOIN CUSTOMERS
```

This query joins the CUSTOMERS and ORDERS tables based on CUSTOMER_ID, and the ORDERS and ITEMS tables based on ORDER_ID. The join is performed from left to right, so this three-table join goes from the largest table to the smallest table.

As useful as the JOIN keyword is, it is not required for entry-level SQL-92 implementations, so here's a three-column join using the syntax we started with:

```
SELECT CUSTOMERS.CUSTOMER_ID, CUSTOMERS.NAME, ORDERS.ORDER_ID, ORDER.
TOTAL,
   ITEMS.ITEM_NO, ITEMS.COST FROM CUSTOMERS, ORDERS, ITEMS
   WHERE ORDERS.CUSTOMER_ID = CUSTOMERS.CUSTOMER_ID
   AND ITEMS.ORDER_ID = ORDERS.ORDER_ID
```

Again, using the data shown in Figure 12-1, the output from this query might look as follows:

```
CUSTOMER_ID | NAME       | ORDER_ID | TOTAL | ITEM_NO | COST
------------+------------+----------+-------+---------+-------
       1 | Bob Copier |      4 | 72.19 |    1280 | 16.72
       1 | Bob Copier |      4 | 72.19 |    4129 | 41.10
       1 | Bob Copier |      4 | 72.19 |    3017 | 14.37
```

So far, all we've talked about is equi-joins, (or inner joins). There are also outer joins, which don't require a matching key in both tables. An *outer join* includes all the records from one table and any records from another table that match the primary key of the first table. If there are no corresponding records in the second table, those columns are simply left blank in the result. Outer joins are divided into left outer and right outer joins. In a left join, the primary key table is on the left, and in a right join, it is on the right. Here's the syntax for a LEFT JOIN (or LEFT OUTER JOIN) on CUSTOMERS and ORDERS:

```
SELECT CUSTOMERS.CUSTOMER_ID, CUSTOMERS.NAME, ORDERS.ORDER_ID, ORDERS.
TOTAL
   FROM CUSTOMERS LEFT JOIN ORDERS ON CUSTOMERS.CUSTOMER_ID = ORDERS.
CUSTOMER_ID
```

This includes all the customer records and order records for all the customers that have them. Here's some possible output using the data shown in Figure 12-1.

```
CUSTOMER_ID | NAME       | ORDER_ID | TOTAL
------------+------------+----------+--------
       1 | Bob Copier |      4 | 72.19
```

```
1 | Bob Copier   |      6 | 21.07
2 | John Stapler |        |
```

If we were to do a RIGHT JOIN on CUSTOMERS and ORDERS, the result would be the same as an inner join, since there are no records in ORDERS that don't have a match in CUSTOMERS.

Groups

The GROUP BY clause allows you to collapse multiple records into groups with a common field. For instance, to select all the records in the BOOKS table grouped by AUTHOR:

```
SELECT AUTHOR FROM BOOKS GROUP BY AUTHOR
```

This returns one row for each distinct author in the table. This query is not really that useful though, since we can do the same thing with the DISTINCT keyword (SELECT DISTINCT). However, we can use an aggregate function on each of the groups to do something more useful:

```
SELECT AUTHOR, COUNT(*) FROM BOOKS GROUP BY AUTHOR
```

This query returns two columns: the author and the number of books by that author in the table. Here's the output, based on the BOOKS table we used earlier:

```
AUTHOR            | COUNT(*)
------------------+----------
Charles Dickens   |     2
Garrison Keillor  |     1
```

We'll talk more about aggregate functions later in this chapter.

INSERT

The INSERT statement loads data into a table. Here's the syntax:

```
INSERT INTO table_name
    [ (column_name, ...) ]
    subquery | { VALUES (val1, val2,...) } | DEFAULT VALUES
```

To load static data, simply specify the table and the actual data:

```
INSERT INTO CUSTOMERS VALUES (3, 'Tom Fax', '617 555-1214')
```

This statement inserts the values 3, "Tom Fax", and "617 555-1214" into the first three fields of a new row in the CUSTOMERS table. If there are more than three fields in the CUSTOMERS table, this statement fails. If you don't want to insert into every column, you can specify the columns you want to insert into:

```
INSERT INTO CUSTOMERS (CUSTOMER_ID, NAME) VALUES (3, 'Tom Fax')
```

Note, however, that this kind of statement can fail if we don't provide a value for a field that is specified as NOT NULL.

To add more than one row at a time and to add data from other tables, we can specify a subquery rather than a set of specific values. To fill the JUNKMAIL table with values from the CUSTOMERS and ADDRESSES tables, run this query:

```
INSERT INTO JUNKMAIL (NAME, ADDR, CITY, STATE, ZIP)
```

```
SELECT NAME, ADDR, CITY, STATE, ZIP FROM CUSTOMERS JOIN ADDRESSES
```

The database first performs a join on CUSTOMERS and ADDRESSES. It matches on the CUSTOMER_ID field and outputs the NAME field from CUSTOMERS and the other fields from ADDRESSES. The rows from the join are then inserted into the JUNKMAIL table, which can now be used to fill our mailboxes with catalogs.

UPDATE

The UPDATE statement modifies data in one or more existing rows. It consists of one or more SET statements and an optional WHERE clause. If the WHERE clause is not present, the operation is performed on every row in the table. Here's the syntax:

```
UPDATE table_name
    SET { column_name = { value | NULL | DEFAULT }, ...}
    [ { WHERE predicate }
    | { WHERE CURRENT OF cursor_name } ]
```

Here's an example that updates a few fields:

```
UPDATE ADDRESSES
    SET ADDR = '1282 Country Club Drive', STATE='CA' WHERE CUSTOMER_ID
    = 432
```

This statement sets the ADDR and STATE fields of the ADDRESSES table to particular values on all records where CUSTOMER_ID equals 432. Sometimes we do want to run an UPDATE on all records. Here's an example that makes sure all the STATE fields are in uppercase:

```
UPDATE ADDRESSES SET STATE = UPPER(STATE)
```

Note how we can use a field from the table itself in the SET statement.

The WHERE CURRENT OF clause allows you to update the row at the current cursor location in a multiple-table row. This is not something that JDBC programmers need to concern themselves with, although it can be of interest to an underlying JDBC 2.0 driver.

DELETE

DELETE is very simple: it removes rows from a table. Here's the syntax:

```
DELETE FROM table_name
    [ { WHERE predicate }
    | { WHERE CURRENT OF cursor_name } ]
```

To delete all the rows in ORDERS:

```
DELETE FROM ORDERS
```

To delete a specific record:

```
DELETE FROM ORDERS WHERE ORDER_ID = 32
```

Once a row has been deleted, there is no way to recover it.

Functions

SQL is not a procedural language, but it does provide some data-transformation capabilities. In addition to the string concatenation operator (||), the SQL-92 specification defines two sets of functions: aggregate and value.

Aggregate Functions

In the section on the SELECT statement, we saw an aggregate function used to count the number of records within a group. Mainly aggregate functions act on all the records of query, counting rows, averaging fields, and so forth. For example, here's how to count the number of rows returned by a SELECT statement:

```
SELECT COUNT(*) FROM CUSTOMERS
```

Instead of returning each row of the CUSTOMERS table, this query returns a single-column, single-row result that contains the number of records in CUSTOMERS.

The other aggregate functions are AVG, SUM, MAX, and MIN. Unlike COUNT, which works on either a single column or all columns, the other functions work only on a single column. AVG and SUM can be applied against numerical data types only (integers, reals, etc.), while MAX and MIN work with any data type. Here are some examples:

```
SELECT MIN(AGE) FROM GUESTS
SELECT MAX(NAME) FROM GUESTS
SELECT AVG(AGE), SUM(AGE) FROM GUESTS
```

Value Functions

Value functions work on particular column values and return modified data. Some of them also generate values from system information.

Date/time functions

There are three date and time functions that retrieve the current date, current time, and current timestamp, respectively, from the database:

```
CURRENT_DATE
CURRENT_TIME[(precision)]
CURRENT_TIMESTAMP[(precision)]
```

CURRENT_TIME and CURRENT_TIMESTAMP accept an optional precision level, which specifies the decimal fractions of a second to be included in the time portion of the value. The current time zone is used with all these functions.

Here's how you might use these functions in a query:

```
SELECT * FROM ORDERS WHERE ORDER_DATE = CURRENT_DATE
INSERT INTO VISITORS (VISIT_TS) VALUES (CURRENT_TIMESTAMP)
```

Some databases have platform-specific commands that duplicate this functionality (these commands often predate SQL-92). Oracle's SYSDATE is one example. Note that these functions aren't required for entry-level SQL-92.

String manipulation functions

The concatenation operator, ||, has been around since before the SQL-92 standard. It allows you to concatenate multiple column values and string literals. Say we have a table that contains FIRST_NAME and LAST_NAME fields, and we want to display them in a "last, first" form. Here's a SQL statement that returns a single column that does just that:

```
SELECT LAST_NAME || ', ' || FIRST_NAME FROM CUSTOMERS
```

In addition, the SQL-92 standard defines a number of other functions that can be used in SQL statements. UPPER and LOWER convert a column into uppercase or lowercase, respectively:

```
SELECT UPPER(LAST_NAME) FROM CUSTOMERS
SELECT LOWER(FIRST_NAME) FROM CUSTOMERS
```

These functions can also be used in WHERE predicates, for example, to produce a case-insensitive search:

```
SELECT * FROM CUSTOMERS WHERE UPPER(FIRST_NAME) LIKE 'WILL%'
```

Most databases support UPPER and LOWER, but they are only required for full SQL-92 conformance, not entry-level conformance.

The TRIM function removes characters from one or both ends of a string:

```
TRIM ([ [ LEADING | TRAILING | BOTH ] [ character ] FROM ] string )
```

Calling TRIM on a string trims leading CURRENT_TIME and CURRENT_TIMESTAM-Pand trailing whitespace. Here's how to trim just leading blanks:

```
SELECT TRIM(LEADING ' ' FROM FIRST_NAME) FROM CUSTOMERS
```

And here's how to trim all "-" characters from both sides of a string:

```
SELECT TRIM(BOTH '-' FROM FIRST_NAME) FROM CUSTOMERS
```

Like UPPER and LOWER, TRIM is only required for full SQL-92 conformance, although it is supported by most database implementations.

The SUBSTRING command extracts a given number of characters from a larger string. It is defined as:

```
SUBSTRING (source_string FROM start_pos FOR number_of_characters)
```

For example, to get each customer's initials, we might use the following query:

```
SELECT SUBSTRING (FIRST_NAME FROM 1 FOR 1), SUBSTRING(LAST_NAME FROM 1
FOR 1)
```

SUBSTRING is required only for intermediate level SQL-92 conformance.

Return Codes

The SQL-92 standard defines a set of SQLSTATE return codes. SQLSTATE is defined as a five-character string, where the leftmost two characters define the error class, and the remaining three characters define the error subclass. Some database vendors may extend these return codes; classes beginning with the numbers 5 through 9 and letters I through Z are reserved for such implementation-specific extensions. The SQLSTATE code for a particular JDBC action can be retrieved via the getSQLState() method of SQLException. Table 12-3 lists the SQLSTATE return codes defined in SQL-92.

Table 12-3: SQL-92 SQLSTATE Return Codes

Class	Class Definition	Subclass	Subclass Definition
00	Successful completion	000	None
01	Warning	000	None
		001	Cursor operation conflict
		002	Disconnect error
		003	Null value eliminated in set function
		004	String data, right truncation
		005	Insufficient item descriptor areas
		006	Privilege not revoked
		007	Privilege not granted
		008	Implicit zero-bit padding
		009	Search expression too long for information schema
		00A	Query expression too long for information schema
02	No data	000	None
07	Dynamic SQL error	000	None
		001	Using clause doesn't match dynamic parameters
		002	Using clause doesn't match target specifications
		003	Cursor specification can't be executed
		004	Using clause required for dynamic parameters
		005	Prepared statement not a cursor specification
		006	Restricted data type attribute violation
		007	Using clause required for result fields
		008	Invalid descriptor count
		009	Invalid descriptor index
08	Connection exception	000	None
		001	SQL-client unable to establish SQL-connection
		002	Connection name in use
		003	Connection doesn't exist
		004	SQL-server rejected establishment of SQL-connection
		006	Connection failure
		007	Transaction resolution unknown
0A	Feature not supported	000	None
		001	Multiple server transactions
21	Cardinality violation	000	None

Table 12-3: SQL-92 SQLSTATE Return Codes (continued)

Class	Class Definition	Subclass	Subclass Definition
22	Data exception	000	None
		001	String data, right truncation
		002	Null value, no indicator
		003	Numeric value out of range
		005	Error in assignment
		007	Invalid date-time format
		008	Date-time field overflow
		009	Invalid time zone displacement value
		011	Substring error
		012	Division by zero
		015	Internal field overflow
		018	Invalid character value for cast
		019	Invalid escape character
		021	Character not in repertoire
		022	Indicator overflow
		023	Invalid parameter value
		024	Unterminated C string
		025	Invalid escape sequence
		026	String data, length mismatch
		027	Trim error
23	Integrity constraint violation	000	None
24	Invalid cursor state	000	None
25	Invalid transaction state	000	None
26	Invalid SQL statement name	000	None
27	Triggered data change violation	000	None
28	Invalid authorization specification	000	None
2A	Syntax error or access rule violation in direct SQL statement	000	None
2B	Dependent privilege descriptors still exist	000	None
2C	Invalid character set name	000	None
2D	Invalid transaction termination	000	None
2E	Invalid connection name	000	None
33	Invalid SQL descriptor name	000	None
34	Invalid cursor name	000	None
35	Invalid condition number	000	None

Table 12-3: SQL-92 SQLSTATE Return Codes (continued)

Class	Class Definition	Subclass	Subclass Definition
37	Syntax error or access rule violation in dynamic SQL statement	000	None
3C	Ambiguous cursor name	000	None
3F	Invalid schema name	000	None
40	Transaction rollback	000	None
		001	Serialization failure
		002	Integrity constraint violation
		003	Statement completion unknown
42	Syntax error or access rule violation	000	None
44	With check option violation	000	None

SQL Reference

CHAPTER 13

RMI Tools

In this chapter, the tools documented are the default RMI-related tools shipped with Sun's implementation of the JDK. Other Java/J2EE vendors may ship their own versions of these tools with different behavior and options than those described here, or they may provide their own toolset altogether. Consult your vendor's documentation for details.

---

rmic: The Java RMI Compiler   JDK 1.1 and later

Synopsis

```
rmic [ options ] fully-qualified-classnames
```

Description

The *rmic* compiler generates the stub and skeleton classes for remote objects that you've written. Once you've compiled your remote objects using a standard Java compiler, such as *javac*, you need to run *rmic*, specifying the class names of your remote implementation classes using their full packages.

For example, suppose you define an interface named `utils.remote.TimeServer` that extends `java.rmi.Remote`, and write an implementation of this interface called `utils.remote.TimeServerImpl`. After compiling both with a Java compiler, you can run *rmic*, specifying `utils.remote.TimeServerImpl` as the class-name argument.

The native RMI remote method protocol, JRMP, was updated in Java 2 Version 1.2. The *rmic* compiler in JDK 1.2 and later supports the generation of stubs that are compatible with the Version 1.1 of JRMP or both. A key difference between the two is that 1.1 required the generation of both stub and skeleton classes for a remote interface, while 1.2 requires only the stub class is required (the server-side skeleton operations are implemented dynamically by the RMI runtime). The

`-vcompat`, `-v1.1`, and `-v1.2` options, described in the next section, control what flavor of stubs and skeletons are generated when you run *rmic*.

Running *rmic* with 1.1 compatibility generates a skeleton class for each remote object type, named `xxx_Skel`, where the `xxx` is the name of the remote interface. The skeleton is responsible for receiving client requests on a server object and dispatching these requests to the actual remote object. A stub class, named `xxx_Stub`, is also generated; this is used for client references to the remote object. When a client gets a reference to a remote object, it receives an instance of the stub class, which forwards any method requests to the server object over the network. In our example, the stub and skeleton classes would be called `utils.remote.TimeServer_Stub` and `utils.remote.TimeServer_Skel`, respectively. When using just 1.2 compatibility (e.g., the `-v1.2` option), only the stub classes are generated.

Both the stub class and the skeleton class implement the same remote interface as your remote object implementation, so they can be type-cast to the remote interface.

IIOP-compatible stubs and skeletons can also be generated with *rmic*, using the `-iiop` option. In CORBA parlance, the skeletons are called *ties*. The concepts are the same as JRMP-compatible stubs and skeletons, except that the generated classes speak the IIOP protocol, and the class names are `_rmtinterface_stub` and `_rmiimpl_tie` (where `rmtinterface` is the class name of the RMI remote interface, and `rmiimpl` is the class name of the RMI object implementation). It's also important to note that, when using IIOP-compatible stubs and skeletons, a client has to use the `javax.rmi.PortableRemoteObject.narrow()` method to safely cast remote object references to their expected remote interface type, rather than just using the Java cast operator.

Options

`-always`
`-alwaysgenerate`

> Applicable only when used with the `-idl` or `-iiop` options. They tell *rmic* to regenerate the stub and tie classes, regardless of the timestamps on the classes. These options were added as of JDK 1.3.

`-bootclasspath pathlist`

> Allows you to override the path used by *rmic* to find its bootstrap classes. This is useful if a custom RMI runtime implementation is used. The directories in the list are separated by colons in Unix environments (including MacOS X) and by semicolons in Windows environments. This option was added as of JDK 1.3.

`-classpath pathlist`

> Provides the classpath *rmic* uses to find any required classes (remote object implementation, remote interface, and classes referenced by these). This option overrides the environment `CLASSPATH` and the default classpath. The directories in the list are separated by colons in Unix environments (including MacOS X) and by semicolons in Windows environments.

`-d path`

The destination directory where the compiler should write the class files that are generated. If a `-d` option is given, the package of the generated classes places the stubs and skeletons in their proper subdirectories in the given destination. If the directories don't exist, *rmic* creates them for you. If no `-d` option is given, the stubs and skeletons are still generated to have the same package as the remote implementation, but the class files are placed in the current directory (e.g., the compiler assumes `-d`).

`-depend`

Forces the compiler to attempt to recompile interdependent classes whose class files are out of date with each other. Without this option, the compiler attempts to recompile only class files explicitly referenced in the command-line options.

`-extdirs path`

Overrides the location of runtime extensions. Normally, extensions are found in a standard location in the JRE, such as `lib/ext`. This option allows you to specify a custom directory to find these extension libraries.It was added as of JDK 1.3.

`-factory`

Applicable only if used with the `-idl` option. It tells *rmic* to generate declarations for initializers for value types in the generated IDL, using the IDL factory keyword. This option is relevant only if your RMI-IIOP implementation class uses CORBA Objects-By-Value. It was added as of JDK 1.3.

`-g` Includes debugging information in the generated stub and skeleton classes; for use with Java debuggers.

`-idl`

Uses the *rmic* compiler to generate CORBA IDL interfaces for your RMI remote objects, generating according to the CORBA Java Language to IDL Mapping specification. Note that the implementation class specified needs to be implemented as an RMI-IIOP remote object, as described in Chapter 3. Remote objects that support only JRMP can't use the IIOP protocol and can't have IDL interfaces generated for them. The `-factory`, `-idlModule`, `-noValueMethods`, and `-idlFile` options are allowed only when used with the `-idl` option. The `-d` option can control where the IDL files are generated. This option was added as of JDK 1.3.

`-idlModule javapackage[.class] idlmodule`

Valid only when used with the `-idl` option. It overrides the default package mapping of IDL entity references, allowing you to specify another IDL module to map them to in the generated IDL. For example, if you want the generated IDL to map entities referenced in the Java `jent.corba` package to a custom `corba::custom::mod` module:

```
> rmic -idl -idlModule jent.corba corba::custom::
    mod jent.corba.MyIIOPObjImpl
```

This option was added as of JDK 1.3.

`-idlFile javapackage[.class] idlfile`

Valid only when used with the `-idl` option. It overrides the default mapping of IDL entities in the Java class to an IDL file. For example, to have the IDL from any entities in the `jent.corba` package mapped into a `jententities.idl` file:

```
> rmic -idl -idlFile jent.corba jententities.idl
    jent.corba.MyIIOPObjImpl
```

This option was added as of JDK 1.3.

`-iiop`

Instructs the compiler to generate IIOP-compatible stubs and ties instead of JRMP stubs and skeletons. The implementation class specified needs to be implemented as an RMI-IIOP remote object, as described in Chapter 3. The `-nolocalstubs` and `-poa` options are allowed only when used with the `-iiop` option. The `-d` option can control where the stub and tie classes are generated. This option was added as of JDK 1.3.

`-J[javaoption]`

Passes the option immediately following the `-J` to the Java interpreter. There should be no spaces between the `-J` and the option to be passed to the interpreter.

`-keep`
`-keepgenerated`

Keeps the Java source files for the stub and skeleton classes generated by the compiler. The Java files will be written to the same directory as the class files, with or without a `-d` option specified. Without the `-keep` or `-keepgenerated` option present, the Java source files will be removed after the stub and skeleton classes are generated.

`-nolocalstubs`

Used with the `-iiop` option, to instruct the compiler to avoid generating IIOP stubs that are optimized for local clients. Without this option, the generated stub classes attempts to detect if the client is running in the same process as the servant and optimizes the IIOP operations. With this option, these checks aren't generated, and the stub assumes that the servant is always remote. This option was added as of JDK 1.3.

`-noValueMethods`

Used in conjunction with the `-idl` option, to instruct the compiler to avoid generating `valuetype` methods and initializers in the generated IDL. This option was added as of JDK 1.3.

`-nowarn`

Instructs the *rmic* compiler to eliminate warning messages from its output. Only errors encountered during compilation are reported.

`-poa`

Used with the `-iiop` option, `-poa` tells *rmic* to generate POA-compatible servants. The generated server class inherits from `org.omg.PortableServer.Servant` interface rather than the default `org.omg.CORBA_2_3.portable.ObjectImpl` interface. It was added as of JDK 1.4.

`-vcompat`

Creates stub and skeleton classes that are compatible with both JDK 1.1 and 1.2 (and later) versions of RMI. This option is enabled by default and doesn't need to be specified.

`-verbose`

Prints verbose messages as compilation takes place, including which class is being compiled and class files that are loaded during compilation.

`-v1.1`

Creates stub and skeleton classes that are compatible with the JDK 1.1 version of RMI. These classes may not run in a 1.2 or higher Java runtime environment, unless its RMI runtime supports 1.1 compatibility.

`-v1.2`

Creates stub and skeleton classes that are compatible with the JDK 1.2 and higher RMI runtime. These classes will not run in a 1.1 Java runtime environment.

Environment

CLASSPATH

An ordered list of directories, ZIP files, and/or JAR files the *rmic* compiler uses to look for classes. This list is separated by colons in Unix environments (including MacOS X) and by semicolons in Windows environments. The list is searched, in order, for a given class when it is encountered during compilation. The compiler automatically appends the system classpath to the CLASSPATH, if it is specified. If the CLASSPATH isn't set in the environment, the compiler uses the current directory and the system CLASSPATH as its classpath. The CLASSPATH environment variable is overridden by the `-classpath` option to *rmic*.

---

rmiregistry: The Java RMI Object Registry   JDK 1.1 and later

Synopsis

```
rmiregistry [ port ]
```

Description

The *rmiregistry* command starts a remote object naming registry on the current host. The RMI registry binds remote objects to names, so that remote clients can request object references by name. It uses the object references to invoke methods.

Internally, the *rmiregistry* command uses the `java.rmi.registry.LocateRegistry` class to instantiate a registry object. If no port is provided, the default port for the registry is 1099. Typically, the registry is run in the background on a server and remains running for the lifetime of the objects it contains. If the registry crashes, and the registry is running in a separate Java VM from the actual remote objects, the remote objects is still available over RMI, and any remote references to these objects that existed before the crash are still valid. However, all the name bindings the objects had in the registry are lost and need to be recreated after a new registry is started.

Options

-J[javaoption]

Anything immediately following the -J is passed as an option to the underlying Java interpreter. There should be no spaces between the -J and the option to be passed to the interpreter.

Environment

CLASSPATH

An ordered list of directories, ZIP files, and/or JAR files the *rmiregistry* command uses to look for classes. This list is separated by colons in Unix environments and semicolons in Windows environments. It is searched, in order, for a given class when it is encountered during execution. The registry automatically appends the system CLASSPATH to the classpath, if it is specified. If the CLASSPATH isn't set in the environment, the daemon uses the current directory and the system CLASSPATH as its classpath.

---

rmid: The RMI Activation Daemon   JDK 1.2 and later

Synopsis

rmid [*options*]

Description

The *rmid* command starts an RMI activation daemon on the local host. The activation daemon services all requests to register activatable objects and is responsible for activating objects due to client requests to invoke methods on them.

If no port option is given, the activation daemon runs on a default port of 1098. Internally, the activation daemon creates a java.rmi.activation.Activator and its own RMI naming registry (listening to port 1098). The daemon binds a java.rmi. activation.ActivationSystem object to the name java.rmi.activation. ActivationSystem in its internal registry.

As of JDK 1.3, the *rmid* daemon provided by Sun requires you to specify a security policy file on the command line, using the -J option:

```
> rmid -J-Djava.security.policy=myrmid.policy ...
```

This policy file determines what operations are allowed when launching JVMs for activation groups. For example, a policy file for *rmid* might include permissions such as the following:

```
grant {
  permission com.sun.rmi.rmid.ExecPermission
    "/opt/rmid/bin/*";
  permission com.sun.rmi.rmid.ExecOptionPermission
    "-Djava.security.policy=/usr/rmi-app/act-group.policy";
};
```

This allows *rmid* to execute any commands in the */opt/rmid/bin* directory and to start any activation groups using the command-line option to invoke the security policy file *act-group.policy*. When registering activation groups, you can specify what commands to use to start the group's JVM, what command-line arguments to include, and what Java properties to override using the -D option for the JVM. Permission to run the specified commands has to be given to *rmid* in its policy file using com.sun.rmi.rmid.ExecPermission entries. The ability to add command-line options to the activation startup command is granted using com.sun.rmi.rmid. ExecOptionPermission entries.

You can also control the application of security policies using the sun.rmi. activation.execPolicy JVM option on the *rmid* command:

```
> rmid -J-Dsun.rmi.activation.execPolicy=<default|policyClass|none> ...
```

If this option isn't used or is used with the value default, the *java.security.policy* file determines the ability of the activator to execute commands and add command-line options to the JVM startup commands. If a class name is provided as the value of this option, then instead of using the security policy file, call the checkExecCommand() on this class before activating groups:

```
public void checkExecCommand(ActivationGroupDesc desc, String[] command)
  throws SecurityException {
    if (command or options are not allowed) {
      throw new SecurityException(...);
    }
}
```

If the value of the execPolicy property is none, *rmid* won't do any checking of security policies before running activation commands.

Options

-C<cmdlineOption>

Uses the given option as a command-line option to the Java VM for each activation group started by the daemon. This can pass default properties to the VMs, for example, or set their memory limits to some default value. The Java interpreter option should immediately follow the -C option, with no spaces.

-J[javaoption]

Anything immediately following the -J is passed as an option to the underlying Java interpreter. There should be no spaces between -J and the option to be passed to the interpreter.

-log path

Uses the given directory for any logging or temporary files needed by the activation daemon. If this option isn't specified, the daemon writes its log files to a new directory named *log* in the current directory.

-port portnum

Uses this port for the internal registry started by the activation daemon. If this option isn't given, the daemon's internal naming registry runs by default on port 1098 of the local host. If you want the activation daemon's registry to listen to the default registry port, start the daemon with this command (Unix version):

```
$ rmid -port 1099 &
```

-stop

Stops any activation daemon currently running on the specified port or the default port of 1098 if none is specified.

Environment

CLASSPATH

An ordered list of directories, ZIP files, and/or JAR files the *rmid* daemon uses to look for classes. This list is separated by colons in Unix environments and semicolons in Windows environments. The list is searched, in order, for a given class when it is encountered during execution. The daemon automatically appends the system CLASSPATH to the classpath, if it is specified. If the CLASSPATH isn't set in the environment, the daemon uses the current directory and the system CLASSPATH as its classpath.

---

serialver: The RMI Serial Version Utility

JDK 1.1 and later

Synopsis

serialver [*options*] *fully-qualified-classnames*

Description

The *serialver* utility generates a serial version ID you can use to mark a given class definition to track its versions as it evolves. The utility returns a static int member declaration you can paste into your Java class definition. For example, this command:

% serialver AccountImpl

generates output something like:

AccountImpl: static final long serialVersionUID = 37849129093280989384L;

If versioning of your remote object classes becomes a problem for clients, this utility can tag a class with a version ID that can be checked to see if the proper version is being exported by your server for a given client, or if its local version is out of date. Serial version IDs are used by Java object serialization to uniquely identify class definitions.

Options

-classpath pathlist

Provides the classpath *serialver* uses to find any required classes or resources. This option overrides the environment CLASSPATH and the default classpath. The directories in the list are separated by colons in Unix environments (including MacOS X), and by semicolons in Windows environments.

-J[javaoption]

Anything immediately following the -J is passed as an option to the underlying Java interpreter. There should be no spaces between the -J and the option to be passed to the interpreter.

-show

Uses the graphical version of the tool. The GUI interface allows you to type a fully qualified class name and press a button to see the serial version ID generated.

Environment

CLASSPATH

An ordered list of directories, ZIP files, and/or JAR files the *serialver* utility uses to look for classes. This list is separated by colons in Unix environments and semicolons in Windows environments. The list is searched, in order, for a given class when it is encountered during execution. The utility automatically appends the system CLASSPATH to the classpath, if it's specified. If the CLASSPATH isn't set in the environment, the utility uses the current directory and the system CLASSPATH as its classpath.

CHAPTER 14

IDL Reference

This chapter serves as a quick reference for CORBA's language-independent Interface Definition Language (IDL). It also gives a summary of the Java mapping of IDL, i.e., how IDL interface definitions are mapped by an IDL-to-Java compiler into equivalent Java interfaces. For a complete, definitive reference on IDL and the Java mapping of IDL, consult the IDL specification issued by the OMG.

Since this reference combines an IDL reference with an overview of the Java mapping of IDL, we'll be using a combination of IDL and Java examples throughout. In order to make it clear which language is being used in each example, we've stolen a convention from the CORBA standards documents, where a comment preceding the example code indicates which language is in use.

IDL, as the name implies, is a language for defining object interfaces. IDL is language-neutral, so interfaces defined in IDL can be converted to objects implemented in any language with an IDL mapping. One way to think of the role that IDL plays is to imagine that you already have a set of interacting objects defined, and IDL is a way to export a subset of those interfaces so that they can be accessed by remote entities. Any member variables or operations that you define in the IDL interfaces will be visible and accessible by remote entities, providing they can obtain a reference to instances of these interfaces (refer to Chapter 4 of this book for more details on the use of CORBA objects). If you proceed this way, the definitions of the variables and operations on the IDL interfaces would have to match those on the actual implementations you are exporting, according to the rules of the IDL mapping to the language they are written in.

Of course, this is not the typical way that you use IDL in practice.* You usually want to do an abstract design of a distributed application and its set of objects first, define the IDL interfaces for the objects that need to be used remotely, then

---

* One notable exception is the task of wrapping legacy code with a CORBA front-end, but even here you would normally use middleware objects to interface directly to the legacy code.

compile these IDL interfaces into language-specific interfaces. Then implementations of the interfaces can be written in whatever programming language you are using. You are free to add additional operations and member variables to your language-specific implementations, but these features won't be accessible remotely unless you add them to the corresponding IDL interface.

There are five high-level entities that you can define in an IDL specification:

- Modules, which act as namespaces
- Interfaces to objects (with their operations and data attributes)
- Data types
- Constants
- Exceptions

These high-level entities are listed here in roughly hierarchical order. Modules contain other modules, interfaces, data types, constants, and exceptions. Interfaces contain data types, constants, and exceptions that are specific to that interface, along with the operations and attributes for the interface. We'll look at the IDL syntax used to define each of these, and in each case we'll see how the IDL is mapped into equivalent Java code. Before we do that, let's go over some of the basics of IDL: the keywords, identifiers, comments, and various types of literals.

IDL Keywords

Table 14-1 lists the reserved keywords in the IDL language.

Table 14-1: IDL Reserved Keywords

abstract	float	sequence
any	in	short
attribute	inout	string
boolean	interface	struct
case	local	supports
char	long	switch
const	module	true
context	native	truncatable
custom	Object	typedef
default	octet	unsigned
double	oneway	union
enum	out	ValueBase
exception	private	valuetype
factory	public	void
false	raises	wchar
fixed	readonly	wstring

These keywords are case-sensitive. They can't be used as an identifier in any IDL construct.

Identifiers

Identifiers can name various IDL constructs, such as modules, interfaces, and constants. In IDL, an identifier has to follow these rules:

- It can be any length of alphanumeric characters from the ISO Latin-1* character set (e.g., a–z, A–Z, 0–9, plus various characters with accents, graves, tildes, etc.), and the underscore character (_).

- All characters in an identifier are significant.

- The first character must be an alphabetic character.

- Identifiers are case-insensitive, in the sense that two identifiers that differ only by case are considered a name collision and will cause an IDL compiler error. This rule stems from the fact that IDL needs to be mappable into many implementation languages, some of which are case-insensitive.

- Identifiers must be spelled and capitalized consistently throughout an IDL file.

- All IDL identifiers share the same namespace, so interfaces, modules, user-defined types, etc. within the same scope all must have unique identifiers. An interface named List and a module named List within the same scope will cause a name collision and an IDL compiler error. See the section "Naming Scopes" for more details.

Mapping Identifiers to Java

An IDL-to-Java compiler attempts to map all IDL identifiers unchanged into equivalent Java identifiers.

An exception is the case where a mapped identifier conflicts with an identifier created automatically by the IDL compiler. IDL interfaces, for example, when they are mapped to Java, have two additional Java interfaces created for them, named using the name of the original interface with Helper and Holder appended (see Chapter 4 for details on the purpose of these generated interfaces). So an interface named List will be mapped into a Java interface named List, but will also cause the creation of a Java interface named ListHelper and another named ListHolder. If there is another identifier in the IDL file that you've named ListHelper or ListHolder, its mapped Java identifier will have an underscore prepended to it (e.g., _ListHelper, _ListHolder), to avoid a conflict with the generated interface names. In general, identifiers automatically generated by the IDL compiler have precedence over other identifiers declared explicitly in the IDL file.

The other exception to the general rule of directly mapping IDL identifiers to Java identifiers is with a mapping that conflicts with Java keywords. In these cases, the mapped Java identifier has an underscore prepended to it. If, for example, you declared a constant namedpackage (not a reserved keyword in IDL), it is mapped into a Java variable named _package.

---

* This refers to the ISO standard 8859, "Information Processing—8-bit single-byte coded graphic character sets—Part 1: Latin alphabet No. 1," ISO 8859-1:1987. You can find a listing of the character set in the HTML 4.0 standard at *http://www.w3.org/TR/html4/*.

Comments

Comments in IDL follow the format of C, C++, and Java comments. A block comment starts with the character sequence /*, and ends with the character sequence */. A line comment begins with the character sequence //, and ends at the end of the line on which it begins.

Mapping Comments to Java

There are no rules for mapping IDL comments to Java. Many IDL-to-Java compilers will simply drop comments from IDL files during the conversion to Java, since in many cases the comments refer to the IDL code and may not be totally relevant in the generated Java code.

Basic Data Types

IDL supports the basic data types shown in Table 14-2. The table also shows the Java type that each is mapped to according to the standard IDL Java mapping. Note that there isn't a standard mapping defined for the long double IDL type, because Java doesn't have a basic data type that supports the precision required. Another important thing to note is that Java doesn't support unsigned types, such as unsigned short. So you'll see in the table that IDL short and unsigned short are both mapped to the Java short data type. You should be aware of this when writing implementations of IDL-generated Java interfaces, since it is up to you to either ensure that their values remain positive or deal with the fact that their values may in fact be set to negative values.

Table 14-2: IDL Basic Data Types, Sizes, and Java Mappings

IDL Type Specifier	Required Size	Java Data Type
short	16 bits	short
long	32 bits	int
long long	64 bits	long
unsigned short	16 bits	short
unsigned long	32 bits	int
unsigned long long	64 bits	long
char	8 bits	char
wchar	Implementation-dependent	char
string	Unlimited	java.lang.String
string<size>	size chars	java.lang.String
wstring	unlimited	java.lang.String
wstring<size>	size wchars	java.lang.String
boolean	Implementation-dependent	boolean
octet	8 bits	byte
Any	Implementation-dependent	org.omg.CORBA.Any
float	IEEE single-precision	float
double	IEEE double-precision	double

Table 14-2: IDL Basic Data Types, Sizes, and Java Mappings (continued)

IDL Type Specifier	Required Size	Java Data Type
long double	IEEE double-extended	Not supported
fixed	31 decimal digits	java.math.BigDecimal

Strings and Characters

There are two character types included in IDL: char and wchar. A char represents an 8-bit character from a single-byte character set, such as ASCII. A wchar represents a wide character from any character set, including multibyte character sets like Kanji. The size of a wchar is implementation-specific.

We've included the IDL string and wstring data types in this table as well, although technically they should be considered constructed data types (arrays of a basic data type, characters). Since they're so frequently used, it's useful to have them together with all of the IDL basic data types.

A string is the equivalent of an array of chars, and a wstring is an array of wchars. In both cases, there are two ways to specify a string type: with or without a size specification, or in angle brackets following the type name. If you provide a size specification in your IDL declaration (e.g., string<10> name), the language mapping is responsible for enforcing the bounds limits of the string. If you don't provide a size specification, the string is allowed to grow to any size, limited only by the implementation language.

If support for a multibyte character set is important for your application, then it's best to declare all of your character and string data as wchars and wstrings. This way you'll be sure to get multibyte support in languages that support it.

Mapping strings and characters to Java

In the IDL Java mapping, both char and wchar are mapped to the Java char type, and both string and wstring types are mapped to the java.lang.String class. In Java, the char type represents a two-byte Unicode character, and can therefore support multibyte character sets by default.

When marshalling and unmarshalling data items during remote method calls, the ORB is responsible for performing bounds checks on the data members being set. If a value exceeds the bounds limits declared for the string member in the IDL specification of the interface, then an org.omg.CORBA.BAD_PARAM exception is thrown. If a character in a string falls outside the range supported by IDL, then an org.omg.CORBA.DATA_CONVERSION exception is thrown.

Constants and Literals

Literals are explicit values inserted into IDL code. Sometimes literals are used to specify a default value for interface attributes, or to declare the value for a constant. Literals can be boolean (true or false), numeric (integer, floating point, or fixed point), or character-based (a single character or a string).

Literals are most often used in IDL to initialize the value of constants. Constants are named variables that are restricted from being modified after being initialized. In IDL, a constant is declared using the syntax:

```
// IDL
const <type spec> <identifier> = <value>;
```

where <type spec> is any valid basic data type or declared interface type, <identifier> is any valid IDL identifier, and <value> is any IDL expression that evaluates to a literal value. The initialization expression can be a simple literal or it can be a complex expression combining multiple literals using logical or mathematical operators. You could declare a few useful numeric constants as follows, for example:

```
// IDL
const float half = 1 / 2;
const float quarter = 1 / 4;
```

Most of the operators present in C/C++, such as addition (+), subtraction (-), multiplication (*), and the logical and bitwise operators (|, &, ^, ||, &&, etc.) are supported by IDL.

Mapping Constants to Java

If an IDL constant is declared within an interface definition, then the constant is mapped to a `public static final` static member on the corresponding Java interface.

If the IDL constant is declared outside of an interface definition, then a Java interface is created to hold the constant value as a `public static final` value. The generated interface has the same name as the IDL identifier given to the constant, and the static class member has the name `value`. So this IDL constant declaration:

```
// IDL
const float PI = 3.1416;
interface GeometricOperators {
  const long maxDims = 3;
    ...
```

causes the generation of a Java `GeometricOperators` interface:

```
public interface GeometricOperators extends foobarOperations,
    org.omg.CORBA.Object, org.omg.CORBA.portable.IDLEntity
{
  public static final int maxVals = (int)((int)-3);
    ...
```

as well as a separate interface to hold the IDL constant PI that is declared outside of any interface:

```
// Java
public final class PI {
    public static final float value = (float) (3.1416D);
}
```

In your Java code, you can reference the value of PI using PI.value, and the value of the interface-specific constant using GeometricOperators.maxDims.

Boolean Literals

There are two boolean literals (naturally) in IDL. They are specified using the keywords true and false. Their IDL type is boolean. In Java, they are mapped into the boolean values true and false.

Numeric Literals

Integer literals

An integer value in IDL can be declared in decimal, octal or hexadecimal notation. Any sequence of digits that doesn't start with a zero is considered a decimal integer value. If the sequence is all digits but starts with a zero, it's assumed to be an octal value. If the literal starts with 0X or 0x, it's taken to be a hexadecimal value.

Floating-point literals

A floating-point literal is a decimal integer, optionally followed by a decimal point and a fractional component, and/or by the letter e or E followed by an exponent expressed as a decimal integer. Either the fractional component (with the decimal point), or the exponent (with the e or E) must be present for the literal to be interpreted as a floating-point value and not an integer. Similarly, either the initial integer component or the decimal point must be present. So, for example, these are valid floating-point literals:

```
2.34
0.31416e1
3E19
.0003413
```

Fixed-point literals

A fixed-point literal consists of a decimal integer, optionally followed by a decimal point and fractional component (expressed as a decimal value), followed by the letter d or D. Either the integer component or the fractional component must be present. The decimal point is optional. The trailing d or D must be present in order for the literal to be interpreted as a fixed-point value. The following are all valid fixed-point literals:

```
1.50d
.025d
1.333D
12d
```

Mapping numeric literals to Java

Numeric literals are mapped by taking into account the context in which they are used. Typically a literal initializes a constant, and the declared type of the constant has to be checked to determine whether the literal is valid for the type and how it should be mapped to a Java literal. For example, these two similar IDL constant declarations:

```
// IDL
const short largeVal = 2000;
const float largeFloatVal = 2000;
```

are mapped by Sun's *idlj* compiler to these Java declarations:

```
// Java
public static final short largeVal = (short) (2000);
public static final float largeFloatVal = (float) (2000);
```

Sun's *idlj* compiler does some type and range checking on the IDL literal before converting it to its Java form and inserting it into the cast operation shown previously. For example, if we change the first constant declaration to:

```
// IDL
const short largeVal = 2e5;
```

the *idlj* compiler emits an error saying that the value is too large for a short variable.

Character Literals

A character literal is a character specification enclosed in single quotes, e.g., 'a'. Character literals can only be specified using elements of the ISO 8859-1 character set. Some characters need to be specified with a sequence of more than one character. These include characters that are nonprintable, or the single- and double-quote characters that are used to delimit string and character literals. These characters are specified with escape sequences, which start with a backslash character. Table 14-3 lists the escape sequences supported by IDL and the nonprintable characters they represent.

Table 14-3: IDL Escape Sequences

\a	Alert
\\	Backslash
\b	Backspace
\r	Carriage return
\"	Double quote
\f	Formfeed
\x## (e.g., \x4e)	Hexadecimal number
\n	Newline
\### (e.g., \012)	Octal number
\?	Question mark
\'	Single quote
\t	Tab
\v	Vertical tab

Character literals, including the escape sequences listed in Table 14-3, are converted unchanged into Java literals.

String Literals

A string literal is a sequence of characters delimited by double-quote (") characters. If two string literals are adjacent to each other in an IDL file, then they are concatenated. So in this example:

```
// IDL
const string acctHolder = "Jim " "Farley";
```

the generated Java code is:

```
// Java
public static final String acctHolder = "Jim Farley";
```

If you want to use the double-quote character in a string literal, you have to use its escape sequence (see Table 14-3).

Naming Scopes

Each IDL file that you create defines a namespace or naming scope for identifiers that you declare within that file. This namespace is further subdivided into nested scopes whenever you declare a new module, interface, structure, union, or exception in your IDL file. You can think of the naming scope within an IDL file as a sort of naming directory. By default, you start at the root of the directory, and each time you open a declaration of one of these items, you start a new subdirectory of the naming directory, named after the identifier you use for the item.

You can specify scopes using the :: delimiter, which is analogous to the . delimiters in Java class names, or the / or \ delimiters in file directories. The root scope for the IDL file is represented as :: by itself, and nested scopes are specified by adding their names, such as ::utils::math::MatrixOps. The names in a scope name can refer to any identifiers that might exist in each scope. In this example case, utils and math might refer to modules (the math module is declared within the utils module), and MatrixOps might refer to an interface declared within the math module. The intermediate elements of a scoped name must refer to one of the IDL elements that define their own scopes (listed previously), but the final element of a scoped name can refer to any item with its own identifier, including constants, data members on interfaces, etc.

Within any particular scope in the naming scope of an IDL file (including the root scope), all identifiers within that scope must be unique. Separate nested scopes off of one parent scope can have identical identifiers declared within them, and can share identifiers with their parent scope as well, but two identifiers at the same level within a scope can't be the same. So you can legally declare the following in an IDL file:

```
// IDL
module utils {
    interface math {
        const float PI = 3.1416;
    };
```

```
    interface baking {
        const string PI = "apple";
    };
};
```

The two definitions of PI (::utils::math::PI, and ::utils::baking::PI) don't conflict, since they each have distinct absolute scoped names within the IDL file. You can't, however, declare a constant named math within the utils module, since it's fully scoped name is also ::utils::math, and conflicts with the name of the math interface.

Scoped names that begin with :: are absolute names and are relative to the root file scope of the IDL file. Names that don't start with :: are relative to the local scope in which they appear. So in our previous example, we could add two new constants to our math interface that use scoped names to reference our versions of PI:

```
// IDL
module utils {
    interface math {
        const float PI = 3.1416;
        const float PIsquared = PI * PI;
        const string PIOfTheDay = ::utils::baking::PI;
    };
    interface baking {
        const string PI = "apple";
    };
};
```

The reference to PI in the definition of the PIsquared constant is relative to the ::utils::math scope, so it refers to the float constant. The reference to PI in the PIOfTheDay definition is absolute, and references the string definition of PI in the baking interface.

User-Defined Data Types

In addition to the basic data types already described, IDL supports user-defined data types, which are aggregations of these basic types. These complex data types include arrays, sequences, enumerations, and constructed data types that you define yourself using structs and unions. We'll go over each of these in detail in this section.

Complex data types are used in IDL by first giving them a type name, then using the type name wherever you would use a basic data type name, or an interface type name (e.g., declaring attributes, method arguments, etc.). There are a few ways that a name is assigned to a complex data type:

- With structures, unions, and enumerations, the name is included in the declaration of the data type.

- A typedef can be used to assign a name to a specific type (basic or complex).

Before we go on to see how complex data types are declared in IDL, let's take a look at how typedefs are used to assign type names to these complex data types.

Typedefs

A `typedef` is used to associate a name with another data type. The syntax of an IDL `typedef` is:

```
typedef <type_spec> <identifier>
```

The `<type_spec>` can be any basic IDL data type, a user-defined data structure (structure, union, or enumeration), an IDL interface type, or a sequence. The `<identifier>` can be a simple IDL identifier, or it can include dimension specifications for an array. So the following are all valid `typedef` statements:

```
// IDL
typedef short myShort;
typedef long longArray[2][2];
typedef PrintServer pserver;
```

After declaring these `typedef`s in your IDL file, you can use `myShort`, `longArray`, and `pserver` as type names when declaring method arguments, return values, or interface attributes.

Mapping typedefs to Java

If an IDL `typedef` refers to a basic IDL type, then the Java equivalent to that type is used wherever the `typedef` identifier is used. So our `myShort` typedef shown in the previous section is replaced by the Java type `short` wherever it's used.

Any `typedef`s that refer to user-defined types are replaced by the mapped Java class or interface for the target IDL type. If the type used in an IDL `typedef` is itself a `typedef`, then its target type is found, and so on until a final user-defined type or basic IDL type is found. So in this example:

```
// IDL
struct LinkedList {
    any item;
    any next;
};

typedef LinkedList DefList;
typedef DefList MyList;
```

wherever either `DefList` or `MyList` appear in the IDL file, it is mapped to the Java class generated for the `LinkedList` type, since they both refer (directly or indirectly) to that type.

A helper class is also generated for each `typedef`, providing the usual helper methods in terms of the underlying mapped type. So a `myShortHelper` class is generated from our example, but its methods are declared in terms of the underlying `short` type (e.g., its `read()` method returns a `short`). If the underlying type is a sequence or array, then a holder class is also generated for the `typedef`.

Arrays

Arrays can only be declared within the context of a `typedef`. Once you've assigned the array type to a type name using the `typedef`, you can use the new type name to declare array members on interfaces. Since IDL doesn't provide a way to initialize array values, you can't declare array constants in IDL, since constants have to be initialized in their declaration.

To declare an array, simply add dimensions in brackets to a variable identifier. For example, to define a two-dimensional array of short values:

```
// IDL
typedef short short2x2Array[2][2];
```

IDL requires that you specify explicitly each dimension of the array, in order to support mappings to languages that have a similar requirement.

Mapping arrays to Java

Arrays are mapped into Java as arrays (naturally). So if we used our short2x2Array type defined above in an IDL interface:

```
// IDL
interface MatrixOps {
    attribute short2x2Array identity2D;
    ...
```

the corresponding Java code would look like so:

```
// Java
public interface MatrixOps {
    short[][] identity2D();
    void identity2D(short[][] arg);
    ...
```

We'll look more at how interface attributes are mapped to Java later, but you can infer from this that the short IDL array is mapped into a short array in Java. The attribute is mapped into a *get* and *set* method for that attribute, and since Java doesn't allow array type specifiers to include dimensions, our declaration that the identity2D attribute be a 2 × 2 array has been lost in the mapping. It's up to you to provide an implementation of this interface that enforces the intended dimensions of the array within the Java interface.

In addition to the mapping of the array type to equivalent type specifiers, each array typedef in IDL causes the generation of corresponding helper and holder classes in Java. The type name specified in the IDL typedef is used as the prefix for the xxxHelper and xxxHolder class names. So our short2x2Array type has a short2x2ArrayHelper class and a short2x2ArrayHolder class generated for it. The helper class provides the static methods that read and write the array type over CORBA I/O streams, when the array type is used as a method argument or return type. These methods enforce the array dimensions that you dictate in your IDL typedef; if the array is not of the correct type when being marshalled, then the write() method throws an org.omg.CORBA.MARSHAL exception. The holder class is used whenever you use your array type as an inout or out method argument. For more details on the purposes on helper and holder classes, see Chapter 4.

Sequences

An IDL sequence is a one-dimensional array. To declare a sequence, you need to declare the type of the elements in the sequence and optionally, the maximum size of the sequence:

```
// IDL
typedef sequence<long, 2> longVector;
typedef sequence<short> unboundedShortVector;
typedef sequence<sequence<float, 2> > coordVector;
```

Like arrays, sequences have to be declared within a `typedef`, and then the new type name can be used for typing attributes, method arguments and return values. Notice in our last example that the elements in a sequence can themselves be a sequence. Also notice that, if you don't provide a bound for a sequence of sequences, you need to put a space between the two > brackets, so that they aren't parsed as a >> operator.

Mapping sequences to Java

Sequences are mapped to Java almost identically to arrays. A sequence of a given IDL type becomes a Java array of the equivalent Java type. Sequences of sequences become two-dimensional arrays, etc. A holder and helper class are generated for each sequence `typedef` as well, using the type name specified in the `typedef`. The `write()` method on the helper class enforces any size bounds that you specify on the sequence, throwing an `org.omg.CORBA.MARSHAL` exception if they don't match.

Structs

A fixed data structure is declared using the `struct` construct in IDL. A `struct` is declared using the following syntax:

```
// IDL
struct <type name> {
    <data member>;
    <data member>;
    ...
};
```

The type name is any valid identifier in IDL. Each data member is specified using a type spec and an identifier used to reference the member (similar to attributes on an interface, described later). You can use basic data types, arrays, sequences, and any other `typedef`s as types for members of a `struct`. You can declare a recursive structure (a structure that includes members of its own type) by using a sequence declaration:

```
// IDL
struct LispStringList {
    string car;
    sequence<LispStringList> cdr;
};
```

Mapping structs to Java

An IDL struct is mapped into a `public final` Java class with the same name as the struct. Each member of the struct is mapped to a public instance member on the Java class. The Java class includes a default constructor that leaves the member variables uninitialized, and a constructor that accepts a value for each member. Our previous example struct is mapped to the following Java class:

```
// Java
public final class LispStringList {
    //     instance variables
    public String car;
    public LispStringList[] cdr;
    //     constructors
    public LispStringList() { }
    public LispStringList(String __car, LispStringList[] __cdr) {
        car = __car;
        cdr = __cdr;
    }
}
```

Each struct also has a Java holder class generated for it, which is used to marshall the data type when it's used as an `inout` or `out` method argument or as a method return value.

Enumerations

An enumeration in IDL declares an ordered list of identifiers, whose values are assigned in ascending order according to their order in the enumeration. An enumerator is given a type name so that the elements of the enumeration can be referenced. The syntax for declaring an IDL enumeration is:

```
// IDL
enum <type name> { <element name>, <element name>, ... };
```

The elements in the enumeration are guaranteed to be assigned actual values so that the comparison operators in the implementation language will recognize the order of the elements as specified in the `enum` declaration. So the first element is less than the second, the second is less than the third, etc. An example enum declaration follows:

```
// IDL
enum ErrorCode { BadValue, DimensionError, Overflow, Underflow };
```

Mapping enumerations to Java

Each enumerated type that you declare in IDL is mapped to a public final Java class of the same name as the enumeration. The class holds a single `private int` instance member. A single private constructor is generated for the class, which takes an `int` argument used to initialize the `value` member.

For each element of the enumeration, two components are added to the Java class: a `static final int` data member, and a `static` instance of the generated Java class. The static data member generated for each element is given a value that enforces the order of the elements in the enumeration, and the static class instance generated for each element is initialized with this same value. The static class instance is given the same name as the element in the enumeration, and the static data member is given the element's name prepended with an underscore. These two representations for each element of the enumeration let you reference the element value using either a corresponding int value or the generated Java class type. If the enumerated type is used as a method argument or return value in an IDL interface, your Java implementation will have to use the object versions of the elements.

Our example enumeration generates a Java class like the following:

```java
// Java
public class ErrorCode implements org.omg.CORBA.portable.IDLEntity
{
  private        int __value;
  private static int __size = 4;
  private static ErrorCode[] __array = new ErrorCode [__size];

  public static final int _BadValue = 0;
  public static final ErrorCode BadValue = new ErrorCode(_BadValue);
  public static final int _DimensionError = 1;
  public static final ErrorCode DimensionError =
    new ErrorCode(_DimensionError);
  public static final int _Overflow = 2;
  public static final ErrorCode Overflow = new ErrorCode(_Overflow);
  public static final int _Underflow = 3;
  public static final ErrorCode Underflow = new ErrorCode(_Underflow);

  public int value ()
  {
    return __value;
  }

  public static ErrorCode from_int (int value)
  {
    if (value >= 0 && value < __size)
      return __array[value];
    else
      throw new org.omg.CORBA.BAD_PARAM ();
  }

  protected ErrorCode (int value)
  {
    __value = value;
    __array[__value] = this;
  }
}
```

So we can refer to the elements in the enumeration in our Java code using any of the following forms:

```java
// Java
int error1 = ErrorCode._BadValue;
ErrorCode error2 = ErrorCode.Overflow;
int error2Val = error2.value();
```

Each enumerated type also has a holder class generated for it, which is used whenever the enumerated type is used in IDL as an out or inout method argument. Although not strictly required by the IDL Java mapping as defined by the OMG, an enumerated type might also have a helper class generated for it.

Unions

IDL unions are similar in nature to discriminated unions in C and C++. A single tag field, or *discriminator*, is used to determine the data element held by the union. Depending on the value of the discriminator field, a particular instance of the union type may hold a different data member. The union is declared using a switch statement to declare the various possible formats, or branches, of the union structure:

```
// IDL
union <type name> switch (<discriminator type>) {
    case <tag value>:
        [<data element>;]
    case <tag value>:
        [<data element>;]
    ...
    [default:]
        <data element>;
};
```

The discriminator for the union is declared using only the type for the discriminator (no identifier is given to the discriminator, since there is only a single discriminator per union type). The type for the discriminator must be an integer, character, boolean, or enumerated type (no strings, structs, unions, arrays, or sequences allowed).

Each branch in the switch defines a data element that represents the value of the union if its discriminator is a given value. Each data member identifier in a union switch has to be unique. Multiple cases can be mapped to the same data element by listing them sequentially within the switch. A single optional default case can be given for any values not given their own cases. So for example, the following union:

```
// IDL
typedef sequence<long, 2> Coord2d;
typedef sequence<long, 3> Coord3d;
union MultiCoord switch (short) {
    case 1:
        long pos;
    case 2:
        Coord2d val2d;
    case 3:
    default:
        Coord3d val3d;
};
```

declares a type named MultiCoord, which represents a one-, two- or three-dimensional coordinate, depending on the value of its discriminator value. The default is for the coordinate to be 3D, so the case for a discriminator value of 3 is the same as the default case. Since a union can only have a single data member per case, you have to use `typedef` types for the coordinate values. Depending on the discriminator value, the union contains either a simple integer position, a `Coord2D` type that is declared as a `sequence` of two integer values, or a `Coord3D` type that is a `sequence` of three integer values.

If the discriminator value is given a value not listed in a case, the union consists of the data member in the default case, if present. If there is no default case, the union has only its discriminator value, and no data members.

Mapping unions to Java

Each IDL union is mapped to a `public final` Java class of the same name as the union identifier. The class contains a single, default constructor. The class has some kind of data member for maintaining the value of the union discriminator (the details of which aren't dictated by the IDL-to-Java mapping), and a `discriminator()` method for accessing it as a `short` value. The standard also doesn't specify how data members for the union are implemented in the Java class. Each branch that you specify in the IDL union is mapped to an accessor method and modifier method for that branch; these methods are named after the identifier given to the data member in the branch. If you use one of the modifier methods to set that branch of the union type, then the discriminator is automatically set to the corresponding value. If you attempt to access the value from a branch and the union is not set to that branch, then a `CORBA::BAD_OPERATION` exception (`org.omg.CORBA.BAD_OPERATION` in Java) is thrown. The return value types and method arguments for the `discriminator()` method and the case accessor/modifier methods are determined based on the standard type conversion rules for mapping IDL to Java.

Our `MultiCoord` union example is mapped to the following Java class by Sun's *idltojava* compiler:

```java
// Java
public final class MultiCoord implements org.omg.CORBA.portable.IDLEntity
{
  private int ___pos;
  private int[] ___val2d;
  private int[] ___val3d;
  private short __discriminator;
  private boolean __uninitialized = true;

  public MultiCoord ()
  {
  }

  public short discriminator ()
  {
    if (__uninitialized)
      throw new org.omg.CORBA.BAD_OPERATION ();
    return __discriminator;
  }
```

```java
public int pos ()
{
  if (__uninitialized)
    throw new org.omg.CORBA.BAD_OPERATION ();
  verifypos (__discriminator);
  return ___pos;
}

public void pos (int value)
{
  __discriminator = 1;
  ___pos = value;
  __uninitialized = false;
}

private void verifypos (short discriminator)
{
  if (discriminator != 1)
    throw new org.omg.CORBA.BAD_OPERATION ();
}

public int[] val2d ()
{
  if (__uninitialized)
    throw new org.omg.CORBA.BAD_OPERATION ();
  verifyval2d (__discriminator);
  return ___val2d;
}

public void val2d (int[] value)
{
  __discriminator = 2;
  ___val2d = value;
  __uninitialized = false;
}

private void verifyval2d (short discriminator)
{
  if (discriminator != 2)
    throw new org.omg.CORBA.BAD_OPERATION ();
}

public int[] val3d ()
{
  if (__uninitialized)
    throw new org.omg.CORBA.BAD_OPERATION ();
  verifyval3d (__discriminator);
  return ___val3d;
}

public void val3d (int[] value)
{
```

```
      __discriminator = 3;
      ___val3d = value;
      __uninitialized = false;
    }

    public void val3d (short discriminator, int[] value)
    {
      verifyval3d (discriminator);
      __discriminator = discriminator;
      ___val3d = value;
      __uninitialized = false;
    }

    private void verifyval3d (short discriminator)
    {
      if (discriminator == 1 || discriminator == 2)
        throw new org.omg.CORBA.BAD_OPERATION ();
    }

}
```

Notice that Sun's *idlj* compiler implements the data branches in the union using a set of data members, one for each branch of the union. Other IDL-to-Java compilers can choose to implement the union differently.

In this example, the default case and the third case share the same branch, so no accessor or modifier method is generated for the default case. If we have a default case that is separate from all other explicit cases in the union (i.e., has its own branch), then an accessor and modifier method is generated for its branch as well. If two explicit cases are mapped to the same branch in the switch, then the Java modifier method generated for that branch sets the discriminator value to the value of the first case included for that branch. In these cases, another modifier method, which takes a second argument that is the value for the discriminator, is also generated. As an example, if we want to use a Coord2D for both 1D and 2D coordinates, we can modify our IDL union to have both case 1 and 2 use the same branch:

```
typedef sequence<long, 2> Coord2d;
typedef sequence<long, 3> Coord3d;
union MultiCoord switch (short) {
  case 1:
  case 2:
    Coord2d val2d;
  case 3:
    Coord3d val3d;
  default:
    Coord3d valDef;
};
```

In this situation, the generated Java has an additional method included for the val2d branch:

```
public void val2d (short discriminator, int[] value) { ... }
```

This allows you to set the union to that branch and also specify which discriminator is intended. This can be useful in some cases, such as our modified MultiCoord example, where the value of the discriminator determines the usage for the object.

If no explicit default case is given in the union, and if the listed cases don't completely cover the possible values for the discriminator, then the generated Java class includes a single method named default() that takes no arguments and returns a void. This serves as the modifier for the default case, setting the union discriminator to some unused value.

The union also has a holder and helper class generated for it in the mapped Java.

Exceptions

You can define exceptions in IDL, which are used to signal errors or other unusual circumstances that may occur during a remote method call. Exceptions are declared with a unique name, and an optional set of data attributes:

```
// IDL
exception identifier { <data member>; <data member>; ...};
```

Each data member on the exception type is simply a type specification followed by a unique identifier for the data member. The data is used to provide the caller with additional information about what went wrong during the remote method call.

Using our geometric examples from earlier, we might define an exception that is thrown when a MultiCoord with unexpected dimensions is passed into a method:

```
// IDL
exception BadDimension {
    short expected;
    short passed;
};
```

The server object raising one of these exceptions can set these data values, and the client making the request can read these values to interpret what went wrong.

Exceptions can be declared within any module or interface scope in your IDL file.

Standard Exceptions

In addition to user-defined exceptions, there are a set of standard exceptions defined within the CORBA module. These standard exceptions can be raised by any method, even though they aren't listed explicitly in the method definition. These exceptions can be referenced in IDL using the CORBA:: scope (e.g., CORBA::BAD_PARAM). The standard CORBA exceptions are listed in Table 14-4. Every standard CORBA exception includes two data members: an unsigned long minor error code, which can further specify the type of error that occurred, and a completion_status enum that can be one of COMPLETED_YES, COMPLETED_NO, and COMPLETED_MAYBE. These status values indicate that before the exception was raised, the method was either completed, never initiated, or in an unknown state, respectively. A more complete description of the standard exceptions (in their Java form) can be found in Part III.

Table 14-4: Standard CORBA Exceptions

Exception Name	Meaning
BAD_CONTEXT	Failure while accessing the context object.
BAD_INV_ORDER	Some methods were called out of their expected order.
BAD_OPERATION	An invalid method was called.
BAD_PARAM	An invalid argument was passed into a method.
BAD_TYPECODE	A bad typecode was used.
CODESET_INCOMPATIBLE	The underlying protocol codesets between the client and the server are incompatible.
COMM_FAILURE	A communication failure occurred.
DATA_CONVERSION	Error while converting data.
FREE_MEM	Failed to free some memory.
IMP_LIMIT	Some implementation limit was exceeded.
INITIALIZE	The ORB initialization failed.
INTERNAL	An internal ORB error occurred.
INTF_REPOS	Error attempting to access interface repository.
INV_FLAG	An invalid flag was given.
INV_IDENT	Invalid identifier syntax was encountered.
INV_OBJREF	An invalid object reference was encountered.
INV_POLICY	An operation couldn't be performed because of incompatible security policy settings.
INVALID_TRANSACTION	An invalid transaction was used.
MARSHAL	An error occurred while marshalling method arguments or results.
NO_IMPLEMENT	The implementation for the method is not available.
NO_MEMORY	Failed to allocate dynamic memory needed to execute the request.
NO_PERMISSION	Not allowed to execute the method.
NO_RESOURCES	There were insufficient resources for the request.
NO_RESPONSE	No response received for request.
OBJ_ADAPTER	The object adapter encountered an error.
OBJECT_NOT_EXIST	The referenced object doesn't exist on the server.
PERSIST_STORE	An error occurred while accessing persistent storage.
TRANSACTION_REQUIRED	An operation requiring a transaction was called without one.
TRANSACTION_ROLLEDBACK	A transactional operation didn't complete because its transaction was rolled back.
TRANSIENT	A transient error occurred, but the method can be tried again.
UNKNOWN	An error occurred that the ORB couldn't interpret.

Mapping Exceptions to Java

User-defined exceptions are mapped to public final Java classes that extend org.omg.CORBA.UserException, which is derived directly from java.lang. Exception. Otherwise, the exception is mapped to Java in the same way as struct, as described previously. Each data member is mapped to a `public` data member of the corresponding type, and a set of constructors are defined for the exception class.

Module Declarations

A module is a name-scoping construct in IDL. It's similar to packages in Java or LISP, or to namespaces in C++. A module is declared with the `module` keyword, followed by an identifier for the module, and then the body of the module, enclosed in braces:

```
// IDL
module identifier { ... };
```

Modules can contain IDL interface definitions, constants, or user-defined types, such as `typedefs`, `structs`, unions, and enumerations.

Mapping Modules to Java

Modules in IDL are mapped to packages in Java, and nested modules are mapped to subpackages, with the innermost module being mapped to the rightmost subpackage. If we have the following interfaces and modules defined in IDL:

```
// IDL
module util{
    interface MatrixOps { ... };

    module dbase {
        interface Query { ... };
    };
};
```

the generated Java code includes an interface named `MatrixOps`, starting with this `package` statement:

```
// Java
package util;
```

and another interface named `Query`, with this `package` statement:

```
// Java
package util.dbase;
```

Interface Declarations

An IDL interface is just a collection of data attributes and methods that define the semantics of the interface. Declaring an interface is another way to create a new data type in IDL, but unlike `structs` and unions, an interface can have both data members and methods that can be called on objects of its type. An interface is also a name-scoping construct, similar to a module. You can declare an IDL interface, and simply include a set of constants that you want associated with that interface name. In this case, you have to specify the interface scope in order to refer to the constants from within other scopes.

An interface consists of the following elements:

```
// IDL
interface identifier [: inheritance spec] {
    interface body
};
```

The interface identifier can be any valid IDL identifier. The body of the interface can contain any of the following constructs:

- A user-defined type (struct, union, typedef, enum)

- A constant declaration

- An interface-specific exception declaration

- Data attributes

- Methods, or operations

We've already seen the syntax for the first three of these items in earlier sections of this IDL overview. They become part of an interface simply by being declared within the braces of the body of the interface. In the next few sections, we'll see how to define interface attributes and methods, and then we'll look at how inheritance of IDL interfaces works.

Attributes

Attributes are data members that belong to interfaces. To readers familiar with JavaBeans, declaring an attribute on an interface is roughly analogous to adding a property to a JavaBean. An attribute in an IDL interface indicates that the interface provides some way to read and (in most cases) write the attribute value.

The syntax for declaring an attribute within an interface body is:

```
// IDL
[readonly] attribute <type spec> <identifier> [, <identifier>, ...];
```

The attribute is signified by the attribute keyword, following by a type specification for the attribute and an identifier name. You can declare multiple attributes of the same type by providing their identifiers in a comma-delimited list after the type specifier:

```
// IDL
attribute short coord_x, coord_y, coord_z;
```

The type specifier can be any valid type, including IDL basic types, other interfaces, and user-defined types previously defined or declared in a typedef. For example:

```
// IDL
enum ErrorCode { BadValue, DimensionError, Overflow, Underflow };

interface AttrTest {
  struct coord {
    short x;
    short y;
  };
  attribute ErrorCode lastError;
```

```
readonly attribute coord COG;
attribute string name;
};
```

The optional `readonly` keyword can precede the attribute declaration. This indicates that the attribute can only be read externally, and not directly written. This typically means that the value of this attribute is only set as a side effect of some other method(s). In our example, the `COG` attribute may represent the center-of-gravity of some geometric object, and we'll only want that to be recomputed as the result of other methods that change the geometry of the object.

Methods

Methods (or *operations*, to use the IDL vernacular) provide a way for remote clients to interact with the objects defined by an interface. A method declaration in IDL is composed of an identifier for the method, the type of data returned by the method, and a list of data arguments or parameters that the method accepts. An IDL method can also (optionally) be declared to use specific call semantics, to possibly raise certain exceptions during its execution, and to accept certain context variables from the client environment.

The syntax of a method declaration within an IDL interface is:

```
// IDL
[<call semantics>] <return type> <identifier> ([<param>, <param>, ...])
[<exception clause>] [<context clause>];
```

The only required elements in a method declaration are the method identifier and the return type, so an example of the simplest form of method declaration is:

```
// IDL
boolean doSomething();
```

This method simply returns a `boolean` flag when it is complete. It doesn't accept any arguments, uses the default call semantics, doesn't raise a nonstandard exception, and accepts no context variables from the client environment.

The return type for an IDL method can be any valid type, including user-defined types such as structs and other interfaces. If a method doesn't return any data, then the return type should be declared as `void`.

The identifier for a method is a valid IDL identifier. In IDL, two methods in the same interface can't have the same identifier (i.e., there is no method overloading, as there is in C++ and Java).

Arguments

The arguments to a method on an interface are declared within the parentheses following the method identifier, and are separated by commas. The syntax for an individual method argument is:

```
<arg direction> <arg type> <identifier>
```

The identifier is any valid IDL identifier, and the argument type is any valid IDL type, including user-defined types.

The "direction" specification indicates whether the argument is passed into the server, returned from the server, or both. The direction specification can have one of three values: in, out, or inout. An argument tagged as in is only passed from the client to the server object. An argument tagged as out is not taken from the client, but its value is set by the server and returned if the method returns successfully. An inout argument is passed in both directions; the object/data from the client is passed to the server, and the server may modify the data and have the updates returned back to the client if the method returns successfully.

For example, suppose we want to change the doSomething() method that we just declared, have it pass a directive to the server object in the form of a string, telling it what to do, and have another string passed in as the thing to act on. In this case, we want the first argument (the string directive) to be input-only, and we want the modified object to be passed in and returned in its changed state. So we declare the method as follows:

```
boolean doSomething(in string whatToDo, inout string whatToDoItTo);
```

If a method raises an exception during its execution, then the values of any out or inout arguments to the method are undefined. They may or may not have been modified by the method before the exception was raised and execution was halted.

Exceptions

If a method on an interface can raise any exceptions during its execution, then you have to declare this in IDL by adding a clause to the method declaration that lists all of the exceptions that can be raised by the method. This is similar to the throws clause on Java methods. The syntax for the raises clause looks like:

```
// IDL
raises (<exception type>, <exception type>, ...)
```

Every exception that you list in this clause has to be defined earlier.

Every method that you declare on an IDL interface can potentially throw one of the standard ORB exceptions that we mentioned earlier (see Table 14-4). You can't list these standard exceptions in the *raises* clause for your methods.

For example, suppose we define our own BadDirective exception for our doSomething() method, which is raised if the client passes in a string directive that the server object doesn't understand. We modify the method declaration to look like the following:

```
// IDL
boolean doSomething(in string whatToDo, inout string whatToDoItTo)
    raises (BadDirective);
```

Again, we have to declare the BadDirective exception, and any data it contains, earlier in the IDL file.

Context values

IDL supports the concept of a client context, which can contain name/value pairs that describe the client's environment is some way. You might have an authenticated username stored in the client's context, for example. The name of a value is a string, and its value is an Any object. The interface to the context is provided by the IDL Context interface, and a mapping of this interface must be provided in any language-specific binding of the CORBA standard.

You can add a context clause to your method declarations, which indicates which client context variables should be propagated to the server when the method is invoked. The server object can then query these context variables during the execution of the method. The syntax for adding a context clause to your method declaration is:

```
// IDL
context (<var name>, <var name>, ...)
```

Each <var name> is a string literal that names the context variable to be propagated to the server when the method is called.

Suppose that when we invoke our doSomething() method we want to be able to log who is making the request. We'll look for a username variable in the client context, and assume that it is the authenticated identity of the client. We can specify that this context variable should be included in the method call by adding a context clause to our method declaration:

```
// IDL
boolean doSomething(in string whatToDo, inout string whatToDoItTo)
    raises (BadDirective) context ("username");
```

A Java client might use this method like so:

```
// Java
// Get our context
Context ctx = ORB.get_default_context();
// Add our username to the context
Any username = new Any();
username.insert_string("JimF");
ctx.set_one_value("username", username);
// Call the remote method
obj.doSomething("anything", "entity");
```

Since we declared the doSomething() method to include the username context variable in its invocations, this variable appears in the server's context and can be queried during execution of the method.*

You might ask when this context feature can be used as opposed to adding a method argument to the method declaration. We could have just as easily added another string argument to our declaration for the doSomething() method:

```
boolean doSomething(in string whatToDo, inout string whatToDoItTo,
    in string username) raises BadDirective;
```

---

* Sun's implementation of the Java IDL binding (including its *idltojava* compiler) doesn't support context variables. The Context interface is available in the Java IDL API, but context clauses on IDL methods aren't represented in the generated Java code, and no context data is transferred to the server.

One argument for using context variables is to make things easier on the client when certain data for a method is optional. Rather than including an explicit argument and forcing the user to add a `nil` value of some kind to the method call (null in Java, for example), you can make the optional data a context variable and the user can choose to set it or not. In most cases, you'll find the context variables used rarely, if at all.

Call semantics

If you don't specify any call semantics at the start of your method declaration, then the default semantics are "at-most-once." This means that if a method call returns with no exceptions, then the method was called a single time on the server object. If an exception is raised, then the method is called at most once (the exception occurred either before the method was invoked, or during execution of the method).

You can choose to use alternate call semantics for your method by including a call attribute at the start of your method declaration. In the current CORBA standard, only a single alternative is available, which is called "best-effort" semantics. In this case, whether the method call returns successfully or not, there's no guarantee that the method was actually invoked on the server object. The difference between the default semantics and best-effort semantics is roughly equivalent to the difference between TCP and UDP IP network connections and their handling of data packets.

Specify best-effort call semantics by adding the keyword `oneway` to the start of your method declaration:

```
// IDL
oneway void tryToDoSomething(in whatToDo);
```

If you specify that a method is `oneway`, then the return type of the method has to be `void`, and it can't have any `out` or `inout` arguments. The method is effectively called asynchronously, so the client can't synchronously receive return data from the server object.

Interface Inheritance

You can inherit attributes and methods from other IDL interfaces by deriving your interface from them. The syntax for declaring the inheritance of an interface in its header is:

```
interface identifier : <parent interface>, <parent interface>, ... {
```

The parent interfaces can be any predefined interfaces, in the same module as this interface or in different modules. If the parent interfaces are from other modules, you need to use the `::` scope specifier to identify them.

Method and attribute inheritance

A derived interface inherits all of the attributes and methods from its parent interfaces. Although IDL allows for multiple inheritance, it's illegal to have two inherited attributes or methods with the same identifier. You also can't declare an attribute or method within your interface with the same name as an inherited attribute or method (i.e., *overload* a method or attribute). So if you have two interfaces declared as follows:

```
// IDL
interface A {
    boolean f(int float x);
};

interface B {
    void f();
};
```

you can't define a new interface that derives from both of these interfaces, since the definition of the method f() is ambiguous. Notice that, unlike C++ and Java, IDL uses only the name for the method as its unique identifier, and not the entire method signature. This rule is a result of IDL's multilanguage support, since some languages may be similarly limited.

Constant, type, and exception inheritance

A derived interface also inherits any constants, user-defined types, or exceptions defined in its parent interfaces. They can be referred to in the derived interface as if they had been defined within the interface. If we define the following base interface, for example:

```
// IDL
interface Server {
    exception ServiceInterrupted {};
    boolean doSomething(in string what) raises (ServiceInterrupted);
};
```

we can use the ServiceInterrupted exception that we defined within the Server interface in another interface by naming its scope:

```
// IDL
interface PrintServer {
    boolean printSomething(in string what)
        raises (Server::ServiceInterrupted);
};
```

Alternatively, we could derive the PrintServer from the Server interface, and then the exception can be used as if it existed in the PrintServer scope:

```
// IDL
interface PrintServer : Server {
  boolean printSomething(in string what) raises (ServiceInterrupted);
};
```

It is legal to define constants, types, and exceptions in a derived interface using the same names as those in its parent interfaces. If you do this, though, you need to refer to them unambiguously in your interface declaration, using fully scoped names if necessary. If you declare your own ServiceInterrupted exception in the PrintServer interface, for example, you need to provide a scope for the exception in the raises clause, in order for the IDL compiler to know which version you're referring to:

```
// IDL
interface PrintServer : Server {
    exception ServiceInterrupted { string printerName; };
    boolean printSomething(in string what)
        raises (PrintServer::ServiceInterrupted);
```

If you don't provide a scope, the IDL compiler throws back an error about
ServiceInterrupted being ambiguous.

IDL early binding

It's important to realize that IDL does "early binding" of constants, user-defined
types, and exceptions as it compiles your IDL. This means that the definition of a
constant, type, or exception is bound to a particular reference within an interface
as it's encountered in your IDL file—not after all definitions have been examined.
If we have the following IDL definitions, for example:

```
// IDL
struct Coord {
    short x;
    short y;
};

interface GeometricObj {
    attribute Coord cog;
};

interface GeometricObj3D : GeometricObj {
    struct Coord {
        short x;
        short y;
        short z;
    };
    attribute Coord cog3D;
};
```

then the cog attribute in the GeometricObj interface is the global Coord type (with
x and y members only), since at the time that the cog attribute is encountered in
the IDL file, this is the binding definition for Coord. The GeometricObj3D interface
inherits this attribute with this type, but the cog3D attribute declared in the
GeometricObj3D interface is the GeometricObj3D::Coord type (with x, y, and z
members), since at that point, the Coord struct within the GeometricObj3D scope
is defined and is the default reference of the relative Coord type used in the cog3D
declaration.

Mapping Interfaces to Java

As you might expect, each interface that you define in IDL is mapped to a public
interface in Java. There is also a helper and holder class generated for each interface—the names of these interfaces are generated using the identifier of the IDL
interface, with Helper and Holder appended to it.

The Java interface extends the org.omg.CORBA.Object interface. Any inheritance
specification that you provide in your IDL interface is mapped directly to interface

inheritance in Java, using extends clauses. So our earlier PrintServer example, inheriting from Server, is mapped into a Java interface that begins with the following:

```
// Java
public interface GeometricObj3D
    extends org.omg.CORBA.Object, GeometricObj { ...
```

Helper and holder classes

The helper class generated for an interface includes a static narrow() method that allows you to safely downcast a CORBA Object reference to a reference of the interface type. If the Object isn't of the expected type, then a org.omg.CORBA.BAD_PARAM exception is thrown. The helper class also includes other static methods that let you read or write objects of the interface type over I/O streams or insert/extract an object of this type from an Any value.

The holder class is used whenever the interface is used as the type for an out or inout method argument. The holder class is responsible for marshaling the contents of the object to the server object for the method call (for inout arguments), and then unmarshalling the (possibly updated) return value. The holder class has a constructor defined that lets you wrap the holder around an existing instance of the original interface, and it has a public value member that let's you access the object argument both before and after the method call. You can see more details on using holder classes in Chapter 4.

Attributes

Each attribute that you declare on the IDL interface is mapped into two accessor methods, each with the same name as the attribute. So an attribute declared within an IDL interface as follows:

```
// IDL
attribute string name;
```

is mapped into these two methods on the corresponding Java interface:

```
// Java
String name();
void name(String n);
```

If you include the readonly tag on your IDL attribute declaration, the Java interface has only the read accessor method and not the update accessor.

Methods

Methods declared on your IDL interface are mapped one-to-one to methods on the Java interface. The return values and any in arguments are mapped directly to their corresponding types in Java. Any out or inout arguments in the IDL method are mapped to their holder classes in the Java method. This includes basic IDL types, which have their own holder classes defined for them in the standard Java mapping. So this IDL method:

```
// IDL
boolean setPrintServer(in PrintServer server,
    out PrintServer previousServer,
    out long requestsHandled);
```

is be mapped into the following Java method on the corresponding interface:

```
// Java
boolean setPrintServer(PrintServer server,
    PrintServerHolder previousServer,
    IntHolder requestsHandled);
```

Notice that the last argument is declared a long in IDL, which is mapped to int in Java. The IntHolder class is therefore used in the mapped Java method.

To use this method, we have to create holder objects for the output parameters, then check their values after the method call.

```
// Java
PrintServer newServer = ...;
PrintServerHolder prevHolder = new PrintServerHolder();
IntHolder numReqHolder = new IntHolder();
xxx.setPrintServer(newServer, prevHolder, numReqHolder);
int numReq = numReqHolder.value;
PrintServer prevServer = prevHolder.value;
```

We don't need to initialize the contents of the holders, since they are being used for out parameters. If they are used for inout parameters, we have to initialize their contents at construction time or set their value members directly.

If there is a raises clause on your IDL method declaration, then it is mapped to an equivalent throws clause on the Java method. The context clause and call semantics (oneway) on an IDL method declaration affect only the implementation of the generated Java method, not its signature.

Value Type Declarations

Value types are a new IDL construct introduced when Objects-By-Value was adopted in the CORBA specification, for Version 2.3. Prior to the adoption of Objects-By-Value, there were two argument passing semantics available in IDL. Interface types were passed by reference, and basic data types were passed by value. But there wasn't any way to pass an object by value between remote agents, in the way that Java serialization provides when using Java RMI. The CORBA Objects-By-Value specification extends IDL to include a new entity, called a *value type*, that is similar in syntax to an interface or a struct.

Value types are declared using the valuetype IDL keyword:

```
valuetype Coord3DVal { ... };
```

Any entity declared as a valuetype is passed by value when used as the argument to an operation. In other words, the servant of the operation receives a copy of the entity, not a remote reference to the entity residing on the caller, as is the normal case for IDL interfaces.

Value types can be declared with a custom modifier, which indicates that it will use custom marshalling code provided by the developer in an implementation class:

```
custom valuetype Coord3DValCustom { ... };
```

This modifier alters the nature of the generated "native" code, as described in the next section.

Value types can also inherit other value types, which have similar semantics as interface inheritance: the value type inherits all of the attributes, operations, state members, and initializers of its parent(s). The syntax of value type inheritance is the same as interface inheritance:

```
valuetype childVal : parentVal { ... };
```

Value type definitions can contain everything an interface can, as well as state members and initializers. Any members declared as state members are considered part of the state of the value type, which needs to be marshalled and transmitted over the network when this valuetype is used in a remote operation call. Any attributes declared in a valuetype aren't considered part of the state that is passed by value—instead, they're considered part of the local state of the entity. State members are declared using either a public or private modifier, followed by a type specification and the declaration of the member identifier itself. Public state members are publicly available to the application code, private members are accessible only in the implementation code and during marshal operations. It's the responsibility of the language mapping to determine how this is implemented in a particular language.

An initializer is a declaration of a constructor for this valuetype. Initializer declarations are identical to operation declarations, except that they start with a special factory modifier. An initializer should have arguments that are sufficient for the entity's state to be initialized fully.

For example, suppose we want to declare an object-like version of our Coord3d typedef, in that we want our Coord3d to be able to have operations of its own. But we still want to be able to pass these coordinates by value in remote operations. We can declare a new valuetype:

```
valuetype Coord3DVal {
    // The state that should be passed by value
    private Coord3d coord;
    // A local short attribute, not passed in remote operations
    attribute short localShort;
    // Initializer for this type
    factory makeCoord(in long x, in long y, in long z);
    // Operations to access state, etc.
    long getX();
    long getY();
    long getZ();
};
```

The Coord3DVal valuetype has a single state member, coord, that holds the coordinate value as a Coord3D (our earlier typedef). This state data is marshalled and passed by value when a Coord3DVal is used as an argument in a remote operation.

The coord member is declared as private, so it is not directly accessible to the application code. The Coord3DVal also has a local attribute, localShort, that is not considered part of the state, and is not transferred in remote operation calls. We declare a single initializer, makeCoord(), for our valuetype, which takes the three coordinate values for the Coord3d state member. Finally, our valuetype has some operations that provide access to the individual coordinate values of the Coord3d state member.

Mapping Valuetypes to Java

For the most part, valuetypes are mapped to Java along the same lines as interfaces, but with some key differences. A valuetype is mapped into an abstract Java class of the same name, rather than a Java interface. Each attribute is mapped to instance variables in the same manner as interface attributes are mapped, using accessors that suit the modifiers on the attribute. State members, however, are mapped directly to instance variables. Public state members are mapped to public instance variables, and private state members become protected instance variables. Regular IDL operations are mapped to methods on the Java class in the same way as interface operations. Initializers, however, are mapped into a separate Java interface, named xxxValueFactory, where "xxx" is the name of the valuetype. Each initializer declared in the IDL valuetype is mapped to an equivalent method on the xxxValueFactory interface. To complete the mapping of the valuetype, you need to provide concrete implementations of both the mapped abstract class and the xxxValueFactory interface.

Our Coord3dVal valuetype is mapped by *idlj* to the following Java abstract class:

```
public abstract class Coord3DVal implements org.omg.CORBA.portable.
StreamableValue
{

  // The state that should be passed by value
  protected int coord[] = null;

  private static String[] _truncatable_ids = {
    test.Coord3DValHelper.id ()
  };

  public String[] _truncatable_ids() {
    return _truncatable_ids;
  }

  // A local short attribute, not passed in remote operations
  public abstract short localShort ();

  // A local short attribute, not passed in remote operations
  public abstract void localShort (short newLocalShort);

  // Operations to access state, etc.
  public abstract int getX ();

  public abstract int getY ();
```

```
public abstract int getZ ();

public void _read (org.omg.CORBA.portable.InputStream istream)
{
   this.coord = test.Coord3dHelper.read (istream);
}

public void _write (org.omg.CORBA.portable.OutputStream ostream)
{
   test.Coord3dHelper.write (ostream, this.coord);
}

public org.omg.CORBA.TypeCode _type ()
{
   return test.Coord3DValHelper.type ();
}
}
```

The generated class inherits from org.omg.CORBA.portable.StreamableValue, which ensures that it is streamable over an I/O stream. The generated _write() and _read() methods provide the code to marshal and unmarshal this value type when it is passed in a remote CORBA method call.

In addition, a Coord3DValValueFactory interface is generated to hold our single initializer method:

```
public interface Coord3DValValueFactory extends
   org.omg.CORBA.portable.ValueFactory
{
   // Initializer for this type
   Coord3DVal makeCoord (int x, int y, int z);
}
```

Once you provide the concrete implementations of these interfaces, an application creates one of these value types by constructing a concrete subclass of the Coord3DValValueFactory interface and calling its makeCoord() method to obtain a Coord3DVal. This object can then be passed by value into any CORBA remote method.

CHAPTER 15

CORBA Services Reference

The overall CORBA standard includes a rich set of object services. These services can be optionally offered by CORBA providers as part of their CORBA-compliant environments. Most vendors include a Naming Service, because it is the principal way to find CORBA objects, but the others, such as Security and Event Services, aren't required by everyone developing CORBA-based enterprise systems, so they are often available as optional add-ons.

This quick reference for the CORBA services is just that: a quick reference, not a comprehensive one. While it's important to understand what the CORBA services can offer, it's beyond the scope of this book to provide a complete reference for all 17 of them. So in this reference, we've provided a short overview of each service, along with a few of the particulars on each, such as their principle interfaces and other services that they depend upon. If any of the services seem like a viable solution for your needs in a CORBA environment, then you can get full details on the specification for the services from the OMG. Each CORBA Service is documented as a separate specification; the current versions of these specifications are available at *http://www.omg.org*.

Generally speaking, each of the CORBA services defines a standard, ordered, explicit way of doing things that you may be able to do otherwise, but in a non-standard, ad hoc, implicit way, using the core CORBA interfaces only. For example, you can construct a means whereby your object is automatically notified of a change in another, possibly remote, object, just using standard CORBA constructs. But the Event Service provides a standardized set of interfaces for defining these notification channels so that outside agents can participate as well. The level to which you need to depend on this service, your need for interoperability with other agents in this area, and the costs involved all have to be considered when deciding between a custom build approach or turning to one of these CORBA services.

Collection Service

The Collection Service supports the grouping of objects into various types of collections, such as sets, queues, and sequences. The service also includes representations for iterators of these collections, and for operations to be performed to elements of a collection.

The Collection interface is the root of a large family of subclasses that define specific types of collections, such as Set, Heap, Stack, Queue, SortedSet, etc. There are also factory classes for these type of collections that allow you to create collections of each type. Similarly, the Iterator interface is the root of the hierarchy of iterator types, like EqualityIterator and SequentialIterator. The Operations interface is provided as a base class for any operation that a user may want to perform on a collection.

Concurrency Service

The Concurrency Service defines a framework for managing concurrent access to remote objects from multiple clients. It is analogous to the multithreading support present in some programming languages, such as C++ and Java, but in a distributed context. The Concurrency Service provides facilities for interfacing with the Transaction Service to allow transactional clients to participate in concurrent access to resources from within transaction contexts.

The model used by the Concurrency Service is that of locks acquired by clients on defined resources. Locks can be of different types (read, write, etc.), and different locking models can be specified, such as multiple-possession, two-phase locks, and so on. Clients that attempt to acquire a lock on a resource and are refused because of conflicts with existing locks are queued in a first-come, first-serve basis.

Resources are implicitly represented by the LockSet interface, which can be used to request and relinquish locks on resources. The TransactionalLockSet is an equivalent interface for transactional clients. Lock sets are created using the LockSetFactory interface.

The transaction-related interfaces in this service depend on the Transaction Service interfaces.

Enhanced View of Time Service

This strangely named service provides extended support for alternative "clocks" not provided by the Time Service.

Event Service

The Event Service provides a flexible framework for asynchronous interaction between distributed objects. The asynchronous method invocation facility provided by the Dynamic Invocation Interface is a very basic form of the services that the Event Service provides. These kinds of asynchronous communications can be useful in situations where *notification*, rather than *interaction*, is needed. You may want your client to be notified when data in a dynamically updated database is updated, for example. The Event Service provides a framework for setting up these communications channels.

Agents engaged in Event Services are distinguished as event consumers or event suppliers—in both cases they can either engage in push or pull event communications. These four cases are represented by the PushConsumer, PullConsumer, PushSupplier and PullSupplier interfaces. Event communications take place over EventChannels, to which consumers and suppliers of events are connected.

Externalization Service

This service defines the means for converting objects into a form suitable for export over general media, such as network streams or disk storage, and then reconstituting this data back into object references, potentially in a different ORB and/or process. The service allows for "pluggable" data formats for externalized objects, but a standard serialized format for objects is provided, to ensure that a baseline protocol can be shared amongst users of the service.

The Externalization Service uses a streaming model for externalizing and internalizing objects, where objects that support the function can be read or written using a stream.

A Stream object externalizes and internalizes objects. A StreamFactory creates Streams. Specific sources or destinations for streams can be supported by subclasses of the StreamFactory (e.g., FileStreamFactory). Object's that are to be externalized must extend the Streamable interface.

The Life Cycle Service is used by this service to create and destroy Stream and StreamFactory objects. The Relationship Service is used to manage the externalization of graphs of related objects.

Licensing Service

The Licensing Service is a protocol for the controlled access to objects and services under a licensing model. Conceptually, you can think of it as an extension of the Security Service, with some additional access semantics having to do with consumable access and expirable access. A license gives a user certain limited rights to use a particular remote object or set of objects.

In the License Service model, a client makes a request for a licensed service from a service provider, giving the provider some proof of ownership of a license. The provider then turns to a license manager to acquire a license service, which it uses to verify the existence of a license and check its policy against the proposed usage. The producer can then ask to be notified of license expiration during its use, or it can poll the license service for changes in the license state.

The LicenseServiceManager provides access to license services specific to certain producers. The ProducerSpecificLicenseService provides a producer with the methods needed to check on license validity and start and end license usage sessions.

The License Service depends on the Security Service for license verification and secure communications, and it depends on the Event Service for asynchonous notification of license events to producers. Some implementations may also use the Relationship, Property, and Query Services.

Life Cycle Service

This service defines a standard protocol by which clients of distributed objects can cause the creation, copying, movement, and deletion of remote objects. The service is defined around the concept of object *factories*, which are responsible for creating objects of specific types.

All objects participating in the Life Cycle Service implement the LifeCycleObject interface. There is no specific interface defined for object factories, but they can be located using the FactoryFinder interface.

Some of the interfaces in this service reference the Naming Service interfaces. Also, when dealing with connected graphs of objects, the Relationship Service structures are referenced.

Naming Service

The Naming Service is the most commonly used service in CORBA, since it provides the principle way for clients to find objects on the network. Remote object references can be bound to names within the Naming Service, and clients can access these object references over the network by asking for them by name from the Naming Service. There are more details on the Naming Service available in Chapter 4.

A NamingContext represents a directory or subdirectory of named objects. This interface can be used to bind, lookup, and unbind objects and subcontexts within the naming directory. The names of objects within a NamingContext are composed of NameComponent arrays. Browsing through the contents of a NamingContext can be done with a BindingIterator.

Notification Service

The OMG Notification Service extends the asynchronous message exchange of the Event Service and allows multiple event suppliers to send events to multiple event consumers. Similar in many respects to JMS, the Notification Service supports both the push and pull models and allows event channels to be federated without the use of intermediators. In addition, the Notification Service allows clients to specify exactly which events they are interested in receiving by attaching filters to each proxy in an event channel. Finally, the Notification Service provides mechanisms to configure various QoS properties on a per-channel, per-proxy, or per-event basis.

The CORBA Notification service uses the StructuredEvent class to represent its messages. In addition, it contains the EventChannel and EventType classes, which are analogous to the Queue and Topic classes of JMS. It also uses the StructuredPushConsumer and StructuredPushSupplier classes for its message consumer and producer objects, respectively.

Persistent Object Service

This service provides a common framework for CORBA objects to interact with various underlying persistence engines (relational databases, object databases, etc.), for the purpose of either accessing the persistent state of other objects or storing their own state persistently. In a sense, the Persistent Object Service can be thought of as middleware between CORBA objects and database protocols such as ODMG.

Persistence is managed at either the object level or at the data member level. The typical usage of the Persistent Object Service is to allow an object to control its own persistent state, but if necessary, a client of an object can control particular elements of the object's persistent state.

The definers of the Persistent Object Service seemed to have a penchant for acronyms. A persistent object is represented by the PO interface. Each PO has a PID, which is a unique identifier for its persistent data. Methods on the PO allow you to load and store its state to persistent storage. Internally, PO's use the persistent object manager interface, POM. Interfaces to specific data storage services are provided by persistent data services, represented as PDS objects.

This service depends on both the Externalization Service (for converting objects into a format suitable for persistent storage media) and on the Life Cycle Service (for creating, moving, and deleting objects).

Property Service

This service defines name/value pairs that can be assigned to objects, without being explicitly defined or required by their IDL interfaces. Properties can represent any application-specific attributes that can be used to tag objects for various purposes.

The Property Service provides interfaces for defining, initializing, and iterating through sets of properties, but it doesn't specify how properties are associated with objects, believing this to be an implementation detail.

A set of properties is represented by the PropertySet interface, which allows you to create, modify, or delete properties in the set. A property is represented as a string name and an Any value. A subclass of PropertySet, PropertySetDef, allows you to query for metadata about the properties (e.g., whether each is read/write or read-only). A PropertiesIterator can be used to iterate through the contents of a set, and a PropertySetFactory allows you to create new PropertySet objects.

Query Service

This service provides a general object query mechanism for distributed objects. With this service, collections of objects can be searched to generate subcollections, or subsets of objects within a collection can be deleted or updated through a query. The facilities defined in the query service can be mapped to, but aren't limited to, persistent storage facilities, such as relational or object databases.

Collections of objects are represented by Collection objects, which are created using a CollectionFactory. Iterate through a Collection of objects using an

Iterator. QueryEvaluator objects are used to issue a Query against a given Collection. The result of evaluating a Query can be any type, but typically it is a Collection of some kind. A QueryManager is a type of QueryEvaluator that allows you to create queries.

Relationship Service

This service allows for the explicit definition of relationships among objects. Relationships are defined in terms of type, roles within the relationship, and the cardinality of each role. Objects fulfill a role when they participate in a relationship. You can define an agent/proxy relationship, for example, in which a single object fulfills the agent role, and multiple objects serve as proxies for that agent.

The Relationship and Role interfaces are at the heart of the service. A RelationshipFactory is used to create Relationships, and similarly for the RoleFactory. A RelationshipIterator can iterate through the relationships a given object plays roles in. In addition to these generic relationship interfaces, the service also provides several specific relationship types in their own modules. Object graphs can be created using the interfaces in the CosGraphs module, containment relationships can be created using the CosContainment module, and reference relationships are defined using the CosReference module.

Security Service

The CORBA Security Service provides the tools you need to secure your distributed application. It provides the means to authenticate remote users of your object services, define access control for users to key objects and services in the system, audit functions, as well as the ability to establish secure communications channels between clients and object services and nonrepudiated events. Note that encryption functions (i.e., algorithms for encrypting data and generating digital signatures) aren't included in the Security Service specification. The Security Service is a higher-level security framework, which needs to use cryptography in its implementation, but this use is not spelled out in the specification. Implementors are free to use whatever lower-level cryptographic APIs suit their needs, as long as their use supports the higher-level specifications of the Security Service specification.

The framework dictated by the Security Service for secure CORBA interactions, layers security measures on top of the basic ORB object-to-object model defined in the core CORBA architecture. Security measures are made on either end of a secure communication (provide identifying information within the inter-ORB messages, authenticate identities, check access, perform auditing, etc.). Access control is defined down to the level of individual methods on objects, and access rights can be delegated by one authenticated object to another.

The PrincipleAuthenticator is used to authenticate identities. A Credentials object is assigned to each user and describes their access rights, authenticated identities, etc. The Current object tells you about the security features in effect in the current execution context. There are also extensions to the org.omg.CORBA. Object interface to allow you to query for an Object's Credentials, and so on.

Time Service

This service gives program the ability to acquire an accurate value for the current time, and an estimate of the error of the value provided. The Time Service uses Universal Time Coordinated time representation to report time values. This representation uses time intervals of 100 nanoseconds, starting on midnight, October 15, 1582. The time reported is always relative to the Greenwich Time Zone.

The Time Service also provides facilities for generating time-based events, using timers and alarms, and for the ordering and linear positioning of events in time.

An implementation of the Time Service is responsible for communicating with an accurate time source, such as a Cesium clock or radio time broadcasts, for determining its time estimates and error estimates.

Time is reported from a TimeService object in the form of UTO objects, which stand for "universal time objects." Time intervals are given in the form of TIO objects, or time interval objects. A timer event is represented by a TimerEventT structure that includes the time that the event triggered and any data that was specified to be delivered with the event. A timer event is indirectly created through the TimerEventService by registering a consumer for the event, which returns a TimerEventHandler object that can be used to set the trigger time for the event, set the data to be delivered with the event, or cancel the event.

The timer event portion of the Time Service depends on an Event Service being available.

Trading Object Service

The Trading Service is analogous with a market trading context, in which agents make buy offers for items they want (bids), and sell offers for items that they have (asks), and the trading system is responsible for matching the bids and asks to execute trades. In the Trading Service, objects describe the services that they can offer to the system, and clients issue a description of the desired properties of an object. The Trading Service then matches object services with the clients seeking these services.

Buyers, or importers, of services use a Lookup interface to advertise their needs, while sellers, or exporters, of services use a Register interface to advertise the properties of their services. If an importer receives multiple hits on a query issued through the Lookup interface, they are given an OfferIterator to iterate through the offers for any that they want to accept. An Admin interface is used to query for all outstanding offers and queries, and to control parameters related to how the two are matched.

Transaction Service

Transactions are best defined using the tried-and-true ACID characteristics, which are familiar to researchers in databases. ACID refers to units of work that are:

Atomic
> Any and all actions carried out as part of the transaction are committed when the transaction is committed, or undone/cancelled if the transaction is cancelled (rolled back).

Consistent
> The actions within a transaction produce results that are consistent.

Isolated
> Transactions don't see each other's effects until they are committed. If they are rolled back, their effects aren't seen by other contexts.

Durable
> If a transaction completes successfully, its effects are made permanent.

The Transaction Service defines interfaces that allow distributed objects to create and engage in transactional interactions. A transactional interaction can involve a series of remote method calls, and if a significant error is encountered along the way, the transaction can be rolled back and the effects of all previous method calls are to be undone, as if the transaction never started in the first place. When a transactional client starts a transaction and then makes remote method calls, its transaction context is propagated along with the requests. Only transactional objects (i.e., objects whose internal actions and side effects should be undone by a rollback of the transaction, and who participate in the Transaction Service protocol) will heed the transaction context information.

An important item to note about the Transaction Service, and about transaction APIs in general, is that they principally provide a framework for the notification and management of transaction boundaries but no facilities to ease the rollback of transactions. The application objects still need to do the hard work of undoing any work that was done during a transaction if it gets rolled back. The Transaction Service will tell you when to do it, but not how.

Transactions are usually managed using the Current interface, which is used to start and end transactions. Transactions can be directly manipulated using the Control interface, which contains a Terminator that ends the transaction with either a commit or rollback, and a Coordinator, which checks for relationships between transactions. Resource objects can be registered as participating in transactions, which allows them to be notified of transaction boundaries (commit, rollback).

The Transaction Service depends on both the Concurrency Service, for its locking services, and the Persistent Object Service, to support the durability (persistence) of transaction effects on objects.

CHAPTER 16

Java IDL Tools

This chapter offers details on the IDL-related tools provided with Sun's JDK implementation. Other JDK implementations or J2EE environments may supply their own versions of these tools, or other tools altogether. Consult your vendor's documentation for details on their tools.

---

idlj: The Java IDL Compiler   JDK 1.3 and later[*]

Synopsis

```
idlj [ options ] IDLfile
```

Description

The *idlj* compiler generates Java source files from interfaces, modules, and type descriptions defined in IDL. The compiler implements the standard IDL-to-Java mapping defined by the OMG.

The *idlj* compiler accepts the standard IDL preprocessor directives, such as #include, which includes declarations from another IDL file, and #define, which defines symbols to be used for conditional compilation with #ifdef directives.

Run with no arguments at all, *idlj* generates all the client-side Java classes mapped from the specified IDL file. To generate both client and server-side Java bindings, you need to use the -fall option described later.

As of JDK 1.4, *idlj* generates POA-compliant server-side classes. The server skeletons inherit from org.omg.PortableServer.Servant and use the POA operations to implement the skeleton. In JDK 1.3, *idlj* generates server classes based on the

Java IDL Tools

---

[*] In JDK 1.2, the *idltojava* tool was provided as a separate download for Sun's JDK. The *idltojava* tool was replaced by *idlj* as of JDK 1.3.

nonstandard `ImplBase` inheritance scheme. The `ImplBase` scheme can also be used in JDK 1.4, by using the `-oldImplBase` option described later.

Options

`-d symbol`

Defines the named symbol during preprocessing of the IDL file. Invoking *idlj*:

```
% idlj -d foobar Account.idl
```

is equivalent to placing the following preprocessing directive at the top of the *Account.idl* file:

```
#define foobar
```

`-emitAll`

By default, *idlj* emits Java mappings only for entities found directly in the specified IDL file. This options causes *idlj* to emit Java mappings for all entities found in this file and in any files #include'd in the file.

`-f<side>`

Controls whether to generate client- and/or server-side mappings and which flavor of mappings to generate. The following values are supported:

`client`	Default value. Emits only the client-side mappings for the IDL entities.
`server`	Emits only the server-side mappings. In JDK 1.3, it generates `ImplBase`-style skeletons by default; in JDK 1.4, it generates POA-compliant skeletons by default.
`serverTIE`	Emits server-side mappings based on the `TIE` delegation model. See Chapter 4 for more details on the `TIE` model.
`all`	Generates both client and server mappings. This is equivalent to specifying `-fclient -fserver` on the command line.
`allTIE`	Generates both client and server mappings, but the server mappings follow the `TIE` delegation model. This is equivalent to specifying `-fclient -fserverTIE` on the command line.

`-i <path>`

The given path should be used to search for files specified in #include directives found in the IDL file. You can include multiple paths using multiple `-i` options on the command line.

`-keep`

Don't overwrite a generated file if it already exists. By default, the compiler overwrites existing Java files. This is handy if you've customized generated Java files and only want to regenerate other files emitted from the IDL.

`-nowarn`

Don't print warning messages if encountered when compiling the IDL.

`-oldImplBase`

Added as of JDK 1.4. This version of *idlj* generates POA-compliant server classes by default. This option instructs the compiler to generate the `ImplBase`-style server skeletons used in older versions of Java IDL (1.3 and 1.2).

`-pkgPrefix <entity> <prefix>`

Overrides the normal package prefix given to the named entity. Normally entities such as an IDL module, interface, value type, and so on, are placed into a package based on the modules it falls within. This option lets you override this procedure for a given entity using a specific package name.

-pkgTranslate <moduleName> <newName>

Added as of JDK 1.4. Wherever the string specified by <moduleName> is found in an IDL identifier, it's replaced with the <newName> in the generated Java files. For example, if you have an IDL file containing a module Servers with an interface PrintServer, this invocation of *idlj*:

> idlj -pkgTranslate Servers com.myorg.Servers servers.idl

causes the PrintServer interface to map to the package com.myorg.Servers. You can use multiple -pkgTranslate options on the command line.

-skeletonName <prefix>%<postfix>

Added as of JDK 1.4. It allows you to customize the name of generated server skeletons, where % represents the name of the IDL interface being mapped. If you have an IDL file containing an interface PrintServer, the following:

> idlj -skeletonName foo%bar servers.idl

generates a server skeleton class named fooPrintServerbar, in a file of the same name. By default, skeletons are named <interfaceName>POA if POA-compliant server classes are generated; they are named _<interfaceName>ImplBase if ImplBase-style server classes are generated. This custom naming scheme is applied only to the skeleton files, it doesn't affect any TIE delegates (use the -tieName option to customize these).

-td <path>

The given path should be used as the destination for the generated Java source files. If a Java class is mapped to a Java package, the compiler automatically creates subdirectories in the given destination to store the Java files. If this option isn't used, the compiler generates the Java files in the current directory.

-tieName <prefix>%<postfix>

Added as of JDK 1.4. It allows you to customize the name of generated TIE delegates, where % represents the name of the IDL interface being mapped. If you have an IDL file containing an interface named PrintServer, the following:

> idlj -fallTIE -tieName foo%bar servers.idl

generates a TIE delegate class named fooPrintServerbar, in a file of the same name. By default, TIE delegate classes are named <interfaceName>POATie if POA-compliant server classes are generated; they are named <interfaceName>_Tie if ImplBase-style server classes are generated. This naming scheme is applied only to the TIE files; it doesn't affect any skeletons. Use the -skeletonName option to customize these.

-verbose

Runs the compiler in verbose mode, printing out progress messages as the IDL is parsed.

-version

Prints the version information for *idlj*. The compiler doesn't compile any files when this option is specified; it simply prints the version and exits.

```
-J<javaoption>
```
Passes the specified option directly to the underlying Java virtual machine. There is no space between the -J and the option. For example, use the following to run the JVM in verbose mode:

```
> idlj -J-verbose ...
```

orbd: Naming Service Daemon   JDK 1.4

Synopsis
```
orbd -ORBInitialPort <ns-port> [ options ]
```

Description

The *orbd* tool is a server daemon that runs a CORBA Naming Service. It's a replacement for the *tnameserv* tool, which is still provided as part of Sun's JDK (described later). *orbd* supports both transient and persistent CORBA servants running within its Naming Service. For transient naming services, *orbd* can be used in a similar fashion to *tnameserv*. The Naming Service is started and told to listen on a particular port using the -ORBInitialPort option, and CORBA servants are registered directly to this Naming Service on the given port. These servants are transient, in the sense that their references in the Naming Service last only for the lifetime of the *orbd* process.

To access the persistent services of *orbd*, you must use *servertool* (described later in the chapter). The *orbd* daemon has a persistent reference manager internally and a database of persistent references. The daemon can use these to reinitialize a servant if it dies or to reinitialize a servant reference if the *orbd* daemon dies and is restarted. On their own, CORBA servants can access the default transient services of *orbd*, but *servertool* can invoke *orbd*'s persistent reference services using an internal protocol between itself and *orbd*. To make a CORBA servant persistent, register it with *orbd* using the *servertool* command interface.

To start the *orbd* daemon, run it from the command line with (at a minimum) an initial port specified:

```
> orbd -ORBInitialPort 1050
```

If you want to register persistent CORBA server objects with *orbd*, start *servertool* using the same port so that it connects to the running *orbd* process:

```
> servertool -ORBInitialPort 1050
```

This presents the *servertool* command-line interface, which allows you to register CORBA servers with *orbd*, as described later.

Options
```
-defaultdb <path>
```
Specifies the directory where *orbd* should maintain its persistent information in a file called *orbd.db*. By default, the current directory is used for this file.

`-J<javaoption>`

Passes the given option directly to the underlying Java virtual machine. There is no space between the -J and the option. For example, to run the JVM in verbose mode, use:

```
> orbd -J-verbose ...
```

`-ORBInitialPort <portnum>`

Required. The standard CORBA property controls the initial port used for services, such as the Naming Service. Normally it's optional for CORBA servants and tools, but the *orbd* daemon requires this option be specified on the command line. The default port for the Naming Service is port 900, but on some Unix variants, ports less than 1024 are restricted to root access, so you need to specify a higher port number, such as 1050.

`-port <port>`

Customizes the port number used by *orbd* for requests to reactivate persistent servers. This option is useful when the default port of 1049 is isn't available.

`-serverPollingTime <time>`

Sets the frequency (in milliseconds) the daemon checks on its persistent servers. If not specified, the default time is 1000 ms.

`-serverStartupDelay <time>`

Sets the delay *orbd* inserts between the time it restarts a persistent server and the time it forwards the next request targeted for that server. This gives the server a chance to initialize itself. If not specified, the default time is 1000 ms.

---

servertool JDK 1.4

Synopsis

```
servertool -ORBInitialPort <ns-port> [ options ] [ commands ]
```

Description

The *servertool* is used with the *orbd* Naming Service to provide persistent CORBA server objects. A CORBA server registered with an *orbd* daemon using *servertool* is managed as a persistent named server. If the server object dies, the next request made of that server through *orbd* causes *orbd* to reactivate the server object using information in *orbd*'s persistent store. This information is registered with *orbd* using *servertool*'s command interface.

Options

`-J<javaoption>`

The given option is passed directly to the underlying Java virtual machine. There is no space between the -J and the option. For example, to run the JVM in verbose mode, use:

```
> servertool -J-verbose ...
```

`-ORBInitialPort <ns-port>`

Required. This is the standard CORBA property that controls the initial port used for services such as the Naming Service. Normally it's optional for CORBA servants and tools, but the *servertool* requires it be specified on the command line. The default port for the Naming Service is port 900, but on some Unix variants, ports less than 1024 are restricted to root access, so you need to specify a higher port number, such as 1050. The port number specified when starting *servertool* should match the ORBInitialPort used to start the *orbd* daemon.

Commands

The following commands are executed using the *servertool* command line or prompt. You can specify a single command from the list on the command line when you invoke *servertool servertool* executes the command and exits. If you don't provide a command on startup, *servertool* presents a prompt, allowing you to execute the command.

getserverid -applicationName <appName>
> Prints the server identifier for a server object, given its application name.

help
> Prints a list of the available commands.

list
> Lists details about all the persistent servers registered with the *orbd* daemon.

listappnames
> Lists the application names for all the persistent servers registered with the *orbd* daemon.

listactive
> Lists details about all currently active server objects (i.e., all servers that are registered and running, not awaiting activation or reactivation).

locate -serverid <serverID> [-endpointType <type>]
locate -applicationName <appName> [-endpointType <type>]
> Prints details of the ports used by the ORB(s) created for a particular server object. The server object can be specified using either its server identifier (obtained using the *getserverid, list,* or *listactive* commands) or using its application name (obtained using the *list, listappnames,* or *listactive* commands). If an endpoint type is specified, only ports of that type are listed. At the time of this writing, the only port type that seems to be supported is IIOP_CLEAR_TEXT.
>
> If the specified server object isn't running when this command is invoked, it is activated.

locateperorb -serverid <serverID> [-orbid <orbID>]
locateperorb -applicationName <appName> [-orbid <orbID>]
> The same as *locate,* except that it allows you to specify a specific ORB started by the server object and prints ports only for that ORB. If no -orbid option is used, an empty ORB name (i.e., "") is used. The names given to ORBs that are started by a given server object are obtained using the *orblist* command.

orblist -serverid <serverID>
orblist -applicationName <appName>
> Lists the identifiers for the ORBs created by a server object. If the specified server object isn't running, it is activated.

---

quit

Quits the *servertool* process but doesn't stop the *orbd* daemon.

register -server <serverClass> -classpath <pathlist> [-applicationName <name>]
[-args <serverArgs>] [-vmargs <javaoptions>]

Registers a new CORBA server object with the persistent naming services of *orbd*. The -server option specifies the fully qualified name of a server object that registers CORBA objects with the Naming Service. The specified class must have a main() method, which is executed by the daemon to activate and reactivate the CORBA server. The server object is activated automatically when this *register* command is invoked. If the server object also has an install() method with the following signature:

```
public static void install(org.omg.CORBA.ORB orb)
```

then this method is also invoked once when this command is invoked in servertool. This provides a way for the server object to have a one-time setup of persistent resources.

The -classpath option specifies where to search for the classes required by the server object.

The -applicationName option specifies a name to associate with the server object. This name is used in the information printed by the *list, listappnames,* and *listactive* commands, and can also unregister a server object using the *unregister* command.

The -args option specifies arguments to give to the server object when its main() method is invoked.

The -vmargs option specifies arguments to pass to the JVM when the server object is activated.

shutdown -serverid <serverID>
shutdown -applicationName <appName>

Shuts down (deactivates) a server object registered with the ORB. If the server class has a shutdown() method, it's called when this method is invoked.

startup -serverid <serverID>
startup -applicationName <appName>

Manually reactivates a server object. If the specified server is already running, the command returns an error and does nothing.

unregister -serverid <serverID>
unregister -applicationName <appName>

Removes a server object from the Naming Service's persistence services. The server object can be referenced using either its server identifier (which can be obtained using the *getserverid, list,* or *listactive* commands) or using its application name (which can be obtained using the *list, listappnames,* or *listactive* commands).

If the server object has a static uninstall() method with the signature:

```
public static void uninstall(org.omg.CORBA.ORB orb)
```

then this method is invoked when *unregister* is called on the server object. This lets the server object clean up any persistent resources.

tnameserv: Transient Naming Service Daemon   JDK 1.2 and later

Synopsis

```
tnameserv [ options ]
```

Description

The *tnameserv* daemon is a transient implementation of the CORBA Naming Service and is provided with Java IDL. *tnameserv* allows remote CORBA objects to bind to names with the naming directory of the service. Remote clients can connect to *tnameserv* through standard CORBA APIs and ask for references to these objects by name or browse through the objects bound to names in the directory. This daemon runs a Naming Service implementation whose object bindings persist only for the lifetime of the daemon process. The *orbd* tool, described earlier, provides both persistent and transient naming services.

Options

`-J<javaoption>`

Passes the given option directly to the underlying Java virtual machine. There is no space between the `-J` and the option. For example, use the following to run the JVM in verbose mode:

```
> tnameserv -J-verbose ...
```

`-ORBInitialPort <portnum>`

Listens to the specified port for client requests on the Naming Service. The default port is 900. This option corresponds to the Java property `org.omg.CORBA.ORBInitialPort`.

CHAPTER 17

Enterprise JavaBeans Query Language Syntax

EJB Query Language (EJB QL) was introduced in the EJB 2.0 specification as a scheme for specifying the logic for finder and select methods on EJBs using container-managed persistence (CMP). As described in detail in Chapter 8, the CMP model in EJB 2.0 includes an abstract schema defined around your entity beans and their relationships, where beans become abstract tables, the CMP fields on the beans become abstract columns of sorts, and the relationships between beans act as abstract foreign-key constraints. EJB QL allows you to specify queries based on this abstract schema, to be used by the container in the implementation of finder and select methods for your entity beans.

EJB QL is similar in syntax (naturally) to SQL, but is much simpler since EJB QL needs only to deal with selecting beans and CMP fields from the abstract schema. EJB QL can't be used to update or delete entity beans (the bean client interfaces are used for that), and it can't be used to adjust the structure of the abstract schema. "Schema changes" are accomplished using the *ejb-jar* deployment descriptor: new entity beans are defined, or unneeded ones are removed, and the deployment descriptor is adjusted to include/exclude these beans and define relationships between them. Full details on EJB deployment descriptors can be found in Chapter 10 and examples of their use are shown in Chapter 8.

Basic Structure of EJB QL Queries

EJB QL queries contain three clauses:

SELECT *clause (required)*
    Indicates what beans or CMP fields are being returned

FROM *clause (required)*
    Indicates what subset of the abstract schema is being queried

WHERE *clause (optional)*
    Indicates optional conditional logic to use in selecting the results

So an EJB QL query takes the following high-level form:

```
SELECT <select clause> FROM <from clause> [WHERE <where clause>]
```

Queries are declared in an EJB deployment descriptor using the following format:

```
...
<entity>
  ...
  <query>
    ...
    <ejb-ql>
      <![CDATA[SELECT p FROM Person p WHERE p.name IS NOT NULL]]>
    </ejb-ql>
    ...
  </query>
  ...
</entity>
...
```

The complete syntax for EJB deployment descriptors can be found in Chapter 10.

In a query, the FROM clause specifies the domain of the abstract schema that is being queried. This is done by declaring variables that are bound to different elements of the abstract schema. The SELECT clause is used to specify what elements of the schema you want returned as the result set. The SELECT clause specifies which element from the FROM clause elements is returned by the query. The optional WHERE clause is used to specify the conditions used to match the elements to return.

Since the FROM clause defines the variables involved in the query, we'll start there, then describe the SELECT clause, and leave the WHERE clause and its conditional expressions for last.

FROM Clause

The FROM clause in an EJB QL query declares the subset of elements from the abstract schema that are the target of the query. Any elements referenced in the conditional expressions in the WHERE clause, as well as the element that is specified as the return type in the SELECT clause, must be included in the FROM clause declarations.

The FROM clause is made up of a list of variable declarations. Each variable is declared with a type and a unique variable name. Variable names can be any valid Java identifier. The types of the variables are taken from the abstract schema elements defined by the entity EJBs. These variables are declared as either *range variables* or *collection member variables*.

Range Variables

Range variables are query variables that take the type of one of the entity EJBs in your abstract schema. They are called range variables because their actual value can range over any of the actual entities present in the persistent store at the time that the query is executed (limited by the conditions in the WHERE clause, if present). For example, we used the following EJB QL query for one of the finder methods on our `Profile` EJB in Chapter 8.

```
SELECT OBJECT(p) FROM ProfileBean p WHERE p.entriesBytes IS NULL
```

In this query, the `FROM` clause declares a single range variable, p, and it's declared to range over the EJB type `ProfileBean`. `ProfileBean` is the abstract schema type that we declared for our `Profile` EJB. This is analogous to declaring a query variable in SQL that ranges over the rows in a particular table. In the case of EJB QL, rather than being satisfied by any of the rows in a table, the variable can take the value of any instance of the EJB present in the persistent store.

You can also optionally use the AS operator when declaring range variables:

```
SELECT OBJECT(p) FROM ProfileBean AS p WHERE p.entriesBytes IS NULL
```

The AS operator is simply an optional syntactic element and doesn't have any affect on the query itself.

You can declare multiple range variables of the same type in the `FROM` clause, of course:

```
SELECT OBJECT(p1) FROM ProfileBean p1, ProfileBean p2 WHERE ...
```

Collection Member Variables

A collection member variable is declared to range over the values obtained from an entity bean's container-managed relationship fields (cmr-fields). These variables are declared using a path expression (prefixed by the IN operator) that specifies the particular cmr-field on the bean. For example, suppose we extend our `Profile` EJB example to include a `Person` entity bean that contains a one-to-many cmr-field that refers to all the `Profiles` owned by the `Person`. We made a similar extension in Chapter 8, but in that case, we defined the relationship as one-to-one. Here, to demonstrate the collection member variable, we assume it's one-to-many. We can declare a collection member variable that ranges over all `Profiles` owned by a `Person` with an EJB QL query, such as:

```
SELECT DISTINCT OBJECT(prof) FROM Person p, IN(p.profiles) prof WHERE ...
```

In the `FROM` clause, we declare a range variable p that ranges over all `Person` beans, then declare a collection member variable prof that ranges over the members of the `profiles` cmr-field on the matching `Person` beans. This type of the collection member variable is the abstract schema type of the collection members. In this case, the profiles cmr-field contains `ProfileBean` EJBs, so that is the type of the prof variable.

SELECT Clause

As with standard SQL queries, the `SELECT` clause in EJB QL can specify what you want returned from the persistent store. The `SELECT` clause takes the form:

```
SELECT [DISTINCT] <schema type>
```

The clause contains a single variable reference to indicate the type of result returned by the query. The optional `DISTINCT` operator specifies that the return results should be unique. The variable reference can either be to a specific variable declared in the FROM clause, or it can be a path expression that refers to a single-valued cmr-field on an abstract schema type. In our previous example, we used a specific variable reference:

```
SELECT OBJECT(p) FROM ProfileBean AS p WHERE p.entriesBytes IS NULL
```

The SELECT clause specifies OBJECT(p) as the return value of the query. If a single query variable is being used in the SELECT clause, then it has to be qualified with the OBJECT operator. The p variable is declared in the FROM clause as a range variable with type ProfileBean, so the query results are one or more ProfileBeans that match the conditions in the WHERE clause. In our other query example:

```
SELECT DISTINCT OBJECT(prof) FROM Person p, IN(p.profiles) prof WHERE ...
```

the SELECT clause specifies OBJECT(prof) as the return value of the query. The prof variable is declared in the FROM clause as a collection member variable that refers to the profiles cmr-field in the Person bean. This cmr-field contains EJBs with the abstract schema type of ProfileBean, so the query results again are ProfileBean objects.

You can also use path expressions to specify the return type of the query. Suppose, for example, that our Person abstract schema type has a one-to-one relationship named "employer" with an Organization bean that represents the organization that employs the person. We can use a path expression in our SELECT clause to have the query return the Organizations of the selected Person beans:

```
SELECT DISTINCT p.employer FROM Person p WHERE ...
```

Note that the path expression has to be single-valued. If a cmr-field is many-valued, then you need to declare a collection member variable in the FROM clause and refer to that variable in the SELECT clause. We did this in the previous example when we used the prof variable to refer to the ProfileBeans associated with the Person beans selected by the query.

If the EJB QL query is for a finder method, then the type specified in the SELECT clause has to be the abstract schema type of an EJB, since finder methods can only return EJB references. If the query is for a select method, then the SELECT clause can also specify CMP fields on abstract schema types, using a path expression. If, for example, our Person bean has a name CMP field, we could use the following query for a select method on the Person bean:

```
SELECT p.name FROM Person p WHERE ...
```

In this case, the return type of the select method needs to match the type of the name CMP field.

DISTINCT Queries

The DISTINCT option is used in the SELECT clause to specify that any duplicate values in the result set should be eliminated. It only makes sense when used in EJB QL queries for methods that return a Collection of some kind. If a finder or select method returns a single value, then the result set needs to be unique by definition. If a select method is declared as returned a java.util.Set, then the results set has to be distinct, so the EJB container has to assume the DISTINCT keyword in these cases even if it's not specified in the EJB QL for the method. For example, if we have a select method, such as the following, defined in an EJB implementation class:

```
public abstract java.util.Set ejbSelectPreferredClients(...)
  throws FinderException;
```

and we put this entry in our *ejb-jar* deployment descriptor to specify the EJB QL for this method:

```
<ejb-ql>
  <?[CDATA[SELECT OBJECT(c) FROM Customers c WHERE c.preferred IS NOT
NULL]]>
</ejb-ql>
```

the EJB container still executes the query as if the DISTINCT clause had been included in the EJB QL.

WHERE Clause

The WHERE clause of an EJB QL query is used to specify conditional logic that is used to select a subset of the beans references in the FROM clause. Any beans that you want to refer to in your conditional query logic must be declared in the FROM clause of the query.

The syntax of the WHERE clause mirrors the syntax of SQL WHERE clauses. The WHERE clause is made up of literals and variables composed into various conditional expressions. The variables used in a WHERE clause can be query variables declared in the FROM clause, path expressions derived from the query variables, or input parameters provided in the arguments to the corresponding finder or select method. The conditional expressions in the WHERE clause can be composed using arithmetic operators, comparison operators, or logical operators.

Literals

Literals are either strings, numeric values, or boolean values. String literals are enclosed in single quotes:

```
SELECT OBJECT(p) FROM ProfileBean p WHERE p.name = 'Fred'
```

If you want to include a single quote in a literal, use two single quotes:

```
SELECT OBJECT(p) FROM ProfileBean p WHERE p.name = 'Fred''s profile'
```

Numeric literals can be either exact integer values or approximate floating-point values. Integer values are specified using a sequence of digits with no decimal point:

```
SELECT OBJECT(prof) FROM ProfileBean prof WHERE prof.id < 1000
```

Floating-point values are specified using either scientific notation or a numeric value with a decimal point:

```
SELECT OBJECT(p) FROM Person p WHERE p.salary >
  +5e4 AND p.overhead < 1.32
```

Floating-point values can be in the range supported by the Java double type.

Boolean literals are specified using true or false. These values are case-insensitive.

Variables

Variables used in expressions in a WHERE clause can be query variables declared in the FROM clause, input parameter variables that refer to arguments to the finder or select method, or path expressions based on query variables or input parameter variables.

Simple query variables

Query variables can be used directly in conditional expressions where it is necessary to directly compare abstract schema types. This makes sense only in comparison expressions where the equality of two entity beans is being compared. For example:

```
SELECT OBJECT(p) FROM Person p1, Person p2, Organization o1, Organization
o2 WHERE o1 = p1.employer AND o2 = p2.employer AND o1 = o2 AND ...
```

In this case we're comparing the two Organization beans for equality. Equality between entity beans is based on the equality of their primary keys, e.g., if the two primary keys are equal, then the two entities are considered equal.

Input parameter variables

Input variables refer to the arguments of the query's finder or select method. They are specified using a ? followed by the integer index (starting with 1) of the method argument. For example, if we are defining a query for a finder method declared with the following signature:

```
abstract public Collection findEmployees(String companyName);
```

We can refer to the string argument in the query using an input parameter variable:

```
SELECT OBJECT(e) FROM Person e, Organization o
    WHERE o.name = $1 AND e.employer = o
```

If the input variable is an entity bean object with an abstract schema type, you can also use the input parameter variable in path expressions. For example, if we have a finder method on our Person bean:

```
abstract public Collection findCoWorkers(Person p);
```

a corresponding query might be:

```
SELECT OBJECT(w) FROM Person w, Organization o
    WHERE $1.employer = o AND w.employer = o
```

Input parameter variables can only be used in comparison expressions that use the basic comparison operators and the MEMBER OF comparison operator, as described later in the section "Comparison operators."

Path expression variables

Path expressions are specified using either query variables or input parameter variables. A path expression is a variable followed by one or more "dot-delimited" cmp-field or cmr-field references. In one of our earlier examples, we used a path expression to refer to the name cmp-field on the Organization bean:

```
SELECT OBJECT(e) FROM Person e, Organization o
    WHERE o.name = $1 AND e.employer = o
```

Here, the path expression o.name uses the query variable Organization o declared in the FROM clause, and then refers to the cmp-field name on the variable.

References to cmr-fields on variables can be referenced further in multilevel path expressions. For example, a simplified version of the previous query is:

```
SELECT OBJECT(e) FROM Person e WHERE p.employer.name = $1
```

Here, we're referencing the cmr-field employer on the Person bean, then further referencing the cmp-field name on the resulting Organization. Referencing cmr-fields in path expressions is only possible if the relationship is navigable from the bean at the root of the reference. So in this case, we're assuming that the employer cmr-field is navigable from the Person bean, which allows us to reference it as an Organization and then further reference the name cmp-field on the Organization.

Path expressions can evaluate to either single values or collection values. If, for example, a cmr-field is one-to-many or many-to-many, a reference to it in a path expression is collection-valued. Path expressions that are collection-valued can only be used in comparison expressions using the IS EMPTY operator or the MEMBER OF operator (described in the section "Comparison operators").

Functions

EJB QL also includes several built-in functions that can be applied to literals, variables, or values derived from other expressions. They are listed in Table 17-1.

Table 17-1: EJB QL Built-in Functions

Function	Description
CONCAT(<string1>,<string2>)	Concatenates the two strings and returns a string value.
SUBSTRING(<string>,<start>, <length>)	Extracts the specified substring from the first argument, and returns a string value, or null if the specified substring can't be extracted (e.g., the start position is greater than the length of the string). The <start> argument is indexed from 1.
LOCATE(<string1>,<string2> [,<start>])	Finds the index of the location of <string1> in <string2>, optionally starting at the specified location in <string2>. The return value is an integer index, indexed from 1. If <string1> is not found in <string2>, a value of 0 is returned.
LENGTH(<string val>)	Returns the number of characters in the string value as an integer value.

EJB QL
Syntax

Table 17-1: EJB QL Built-in Functions (continued)

Function	Description
ABS(<numeric val>)	Returns the absolute value of the given numeric value. The return type is the same as the type of the numeric expression used as the argument.
SQRT(<floating-point val>)	Returns the square root of the given floating-point value as a double.

Conditional Expressions

Conditional expressions are composed of a sequence of one or more other expressions, joined together by logical AND or OR operators. A single expression is made up of literals and/or variables joined by operators to result in a boolean value. Conditional expressions follow the usual evaluation/precedence rules: they are evaluated left-to-right, taking into account operator precedence rules (as discussed next), and grouping of expressions using parentheses.

The operators available in EJB QL for creating conditional expressions fall into three categories: logical operators, arithmetic operators and comparison operators.

Logical operators

The logical operators in EJB QL are NOT, AND, and OR, in precedence order, with the usual semantics: NOT is the unary negation operator, AND is the binary intersection operator, and OR is the binary union operator. These can be applied to any expressions that evaluate to a boolean value.

Arithmetic operators

Arithmetic operators are applied to numeric variables and literals. They are listed in Table 17-2.

Table 17-2: Arithmetic Operators

Operator	Description
+<numeric expression>	Unary positive operator. Specifies a positive literal value or a variable with an unchanged sign.
-<numeric expression>	Unary negation operator. Specifies a negative literal or a variable whose sign is negated.
<numeric exp> * <numeric exp>	Binary multiplication.
<numeric exp> / <numeric exp>	Binary division.
<numeric exp> + <numeric exp>	Binary addition.
<numeric exp> - <numeric exp>	Binary subtraction.

Comparison operators

The comparison operators are used to perform various value and range comparisons on variables, and are listed in Table 17-3. Some comparison operators can only be applied to variables of a certain type—these restrictions are mentioned in the description where applicable.

Table 17-3: Comparison Operators

Operators	Description	Examples
<exp> = <exp> <exp> <> <exp>	Equality and inequality operators, respectively. The two operands to these operators must be of compatible types: two Strings, two entity beans with the same abstract schema type, or two compatible numeric values.	```...FROM Person p WHERE p.age = 65``` ```...FROM Employee p WHERE p.dept <> 'Finance'``` ```...FROM Employee p WHERE p.title = 'Director'``` ```...FROM Person p1, Person p2 WHERE p1 <> p2 AND...``` ```...FROM Organization a, Person p, IN(p.affiliations) b WHERE a = b...```
<exp> > <exp> <exp> >= <exp> <exp> < <exp> <exp> <= <exp>	Greater-than, greater-than-or-equal, less-than, less-than-or-equal operators, respectively. These operators can be applied only to numeric and String values, not to entity beans.	```...FROM Item b WHERE b.size > 4``` ```...FROM Item a, Item b WHERE b.name > a.name``` ```...FROM Item b WHERE b.size <= 4``` ```...FROM Item a, Item b WHERE b.name >= a.name```
<arith exp1> [NOT] BETWEEN <arith-exp2> AND <arith-exp3>	Checks whether a given numeric value is between two other numeric values. The NOT operator checks that the first numeric value is not within the range. If any arithmetic expression used in a BETWEEN operator is null, the entire expression evaluates to NULL (boolean "unknown").	```...FROM Person p WHERE p.age BETWEEN 18 AND 65``` ```...FROM Person p, Rate r WHERE p.salary NOT BETWEEN r.base AND 1.05 * r.base```
<string-exp> [NOT] IN (str-literal [,str-literal]*)	Checks whether a given string value is contained (or not contained) in a list of string literals. The string values are matched exactly. If the string value to compare to the set is null, the expression evaluates to NULL (boolean "unknown").	```...WHERE p.name IN ('John','Mary')``` ```...WHERE p.dept NOT IN ('Finance', 'Human Resource', 'Corporate')```
<string-exp> [NOT] LIKE <pattern> [ESCAPE<esc-char>]	Compares a string value to a pattern. The pattern consists of a sequence of characters, where _ is a wildcard that stands for any single character, and % stands for any sequence of characters. If you want to use the literal _ and % characters in the pattern, escape them with a character and specify the escape character with the optional ESCAPE clause. If the string to compare is null, the value of the LIKE expression is NULL (boolean "unknown").	```...WHERE o.title LIKE '%Professor%'``` ```...WHERE p.state_prov NOT LIKE '%Province'``` ```...WHERE p.version LIKE 'v_1._' ESCAPE '\'```

Table 17-3: Comparison Operators (continued)

Operators	Description	Examples

`<exp> IS [NOT] NULL`	Checks if the value of the expression is null. The expression must be single-valued and not evaluate to a collection.	`...FROM Person o`
		`    WHERE o.employer`
		`    IS NOT NULL`
		`...FROM Publication p`
		`    WHERE p.title`
		`    IS NULL`

`<collection-exp> IS [NOT] EMPTY`	Checks whether a given collection-valued expression is empty. The collection expression must evaluate to a collection of entity beans.	`...FROM Person p`
		`    WHERE p.profiles`
		`    IS NOT EMPTY`
		`...FROM Order o`
		`    WHERE o.items`
		`    IS EMPTY`

`<exp> [NOT] MEMBER OF <collection-exp>`	Checks whether a given single value is contained within a given collection. The value being checked for membership must be a singular value (not a collection), and the collection expression must evaluate to a collection of entity beans.	`...FROM Person p,`
		`    Organization o`
		`    WHERE p MEMBER OF`
		`    o.employees`
		`...FROM Item i,`
		`    Warehouse w WHERE`
		`    i NOT MEMBER OF`
		`    w.backorders`

PART III

API Quick Reference

Part III is the real heart of this book: quick-reference material for the Java Enterprise APIs. Please read the following section, "How To Use This Quick Reference," to learn how to get the most out of this material.

How to Use This Quick Reference

The section that follows packs a lot of information into a small space. This introduction explains how to get the most out of it. It describes how the quick reference is organized and how to read the individual entries.

Finding a Quick-Reference Entry

The quick reference is organized into chapters, one per package. Each chapter begins with an overview of the package and includes a hierarchy diagram for the classes and interfaces in the package. Following this overview are quick-reference entries for all the classes and interfaces in the package.

Entries are organized alphabetically by class and package name, so that related classes are grouped near each other. Thus, in order to find an entry for a particular class, you must also know the name of the package that contains that class. Usually, the package name is obvious from the context, and you should have no trouble looking up the quick-reference entry you want. Use the chapter tabs and the "dictionary-style" headers, which are located at the upper outside corner of each page, to help you find packages and classes.

Occasionally, you may need to look up a class for which you don't already know the package. In this case, refer to the *Class, Method, and Field Index*. This index allows you to look up a class by name and find the package it is part of. (The index also allows you to look up a method or field name and find the class or classes define it.)

Reading a Quick-Reference Entry

Each quick-reference entry contains quite a bit of information. The sections that follow describe the structure of a quick-reference entry, explaining what information is available, where it is found, and what it means. While reading the following descriptions, you will find it helpful to flip through the reference section itself to find examples of the features being described.

Class Name, Package Name, Availability, and Flags

Each quick-reference entry begins with a four-part title that specifies the name, package, and availability of the class, and may also specify various additional flags that describe the class. The class name appears in bold at the upper left of the title. The package name appears, in smaller print, in the lower left, below the class name.

The upper-right portion of the title indicates the availability of the class; it specifies the earliest release that contained the class. If a class was introduced in Java 1. 1, for example, this portion of the title reads "Java 1.1." If the class was introduced in Version 1.2 of the Java 2 platform, the availability reads "Java 1.2," for simplicity's sake. If the class is part of a standard extension, this portion of the title specifies the name (or acronym) of the standard extension and the earliest version in which the class appeared. For example, the availability might read "Servlets 2.0" or "JNDI 1.1." The availability section of the title also indicates whether a class has been deprecated, and, if so, in what release. For example, it might read "Java 1.1; Deprecated in Java 1.2."

In the lower-right corner of the title, you may find a list of flags that describe the class. The possible flags and their meanings are as follows:

checked
> The class is a checked exception, which means that it extends java.lang. Exception, but not java.lang.RuntimeException. In other words, it must be declared in the throws clause of any method that may throw it.

cloneable
> The class, or a superclass, implements java.lang.Cloneable.

collection
> The class, or a superclass, implements java.util.Collection or java.util. Map.

comparable
> The class, or a superclass, implements java.lang.Comparable.

error
> The class extends java.lang.Error.

event
> The class extends java.util.EventObject.

event adapter
> The class, or a superclass, implements java.util.EventListener, and the class name ends with "Adapter."

event listener
> The class, or a superclass, implements java.util.EventListener.

layout manager
> The class, or a superclass, implements java.awt.LayoutManager.

PJ1.1

The class or interface is part of the Personal Java 1.1 platform.

PJ1.1(mod)

The class or interface is supported, in modified form, by the Personal Java 1.1 platform.

PJ1.1(opt)

The class or interface is an optional part of the Personal Java 1.1 platform. Support for the class is implementation-dependent.

remote

The class, or a superclass, implements java.rmi.Remote.

runnable

The class, or a superclass, implements java.lang.Runnable.

serializable

The class, or a superclass, implements java.io.Serializable and may be serialized.

unchecked

The class is an unchecked exception, which means it extends java.lang. RuntimeException and, therefore, doesn't need to be declared in the throws clause of a method that may throw it.

Description

The title of each quick-reference entry is followed by a short description of the most important features of the class or interface. This description may be anywhere from a couple of sentences to several paragraphs long.

Synopsis

The most important part of every quick-reference entry is the *class synopsis*, which follows the title and description. The synopsis for a class looks a lot like the source code for the class, except that the method bodies are omitted, and some additional annotations are added. If you know Java syntax, you can read the class synopsis.

The first line of the synopsis contains information about the class itself. It begins with a list of class modifiers, such as public, abstract, and final. These modifiers are followed by the class or interface keyword and then by the name of the class. The class name may be followed by an extends clause that specifies the superclass and an implements clause that specifies any interfaces the class implements.

The class definition line is followed by a list of the fields and methods the class defines. Once again, if you understand basic Java syntax, you should have no trouble making sense of these lines. The listing for each member includes the modifiers, type, and name of the member. For methods, the synopsis also includes the type and name of each method parameter and an optional throws clause that lists the exceptions the method can throw. The member names are in boldface, so that it is easy to scan the list of members looking for the one you want. The names of method parameters are in italics to indicate that they aren't to be used literally. The member listings are printed on alternating gray and white backgrounds to keep them visually separate.

Member availability and flags

Each member listing is a single line that defines the API for that member. These listings use Java syntax, so their meaning is immediately clear to any Java programmer. There is some auxiliary information associated with each member synopsis, however, that requires explanation.

Recall that each quick-reference entry begins with a title section that includes the release in which the class was first defined. When a member is introduced into a class after the initial release of the class, the version in which the member was introduced appears, in small print, to the left of the member synopsis. For example, if a class was first introduced in Java 1.1, but had a new method added in Version 1.2 of Java 2, the title contains the string "Java 1.1," and the listing for the new member is preceded by the number "1.2." Furthermore, if a member has been deprecated, that fact is indicated with a hash mark (#) to the left of the member synopsis.

The area to the right of the member synopsis displays a variety of flags that provide additional information about the member. Some of these flags indicate additional specification details that don't appear in the member API itself. Other flags contain implementation-specific information. This information can be quite useful in understanding the class and in debugging your code, but be aware that it may differ between implementations. The implementation-specific flags displayed in this book are based on Sun's implementation of Java for Microsoft Windows.

The following flags may be displayed to the right of a member synopsis:

native

An implementation-specific flag that indicates that a method is implemented in native code. Although `native` is a Java keyword and can appear in method signatures, it is part of the method implementation, not part of its specification. Therefore, this information is included with the member flags, rather than as part of the member listing. This flag is useful as a hint about the expected performance of a method.

synchronized

An implementation-specific flag that indicates a method implementation is declared `synchronized`, meaning that it obtains a lock on the object or class before executing. Like the `native` keyword, the `synchronized` keyword is part of the method implementation, not part of the specification, so it appears as a flag, not in the method synopsis itself. This flag is a useful hint that the method is probably implemented in a thread-safe manner.

Whether or not a method is thread-safe is part of the method specification, and this information *should* appear (although it often doesn't) in the method documentation. There are a number of different ways to make a method thread-safe, however, and declaring the method with the `synchronized` keyword is only one possible implementation. In other words, a method that doesn't bear the `synchronized` flag can still be thread-safe.

Overrides:

Indicates that a method overrides a method in one of its superclasses. The flag is followed by the name of the superclass that the method overrides. This is a specification detail, not an implementation detail. As we'll see in the next section, overriding methods are usually grouped together in their own section of the class synopsis. The Overrides: flag is used only when an overriding method is not grouped in that way.

Implements:

Indicates that a method implements a method in an interface. The flag is followed by the name of the interface that is implemented. This is a specification detail, not an implementation detail. As we'll see in the next section, methods that implement an interface are usually grouped into a special section of the class synopsis. The Implements: flag is used only for methods that aren't grouped in this way.

empty

Indicates that the implementation of the method has an empty body. This can be a hint to the programmer that the method may need to be overridden in a subclass.

constant

An implementation flag that indicates a method has a trivial implementation. Only methods with a void return type can be truly empty. Any method declared to return a value must have at least a return statement. The "constant" flag indicates the method implementation is empty except for a return statement that returns a constant value. Such a method might have a body like return null; or return false;. Like the "empty" flag, this indicates that a method may need to be overridden.

default:

This flag is used with property accessor methods that read the value of a property (i.e., methods whose names begins with "get" and take no arguments). The flag is followed by the default value of the property. Strictly speaking, default property values are a specification detail. In practice, however, these defaults aren't always documented, and care should be taken, because the default values may change between implementations.

Not all property accessors have a *default:* flag. A default value is determined by dynamically loading the class in question, instantiating it using a no-argument constructor, and then calling the method to find what it returns. This technique can be used only on classes that can be dynamically loaded and instantiated and that have no-argument constructors, so default values are shown for those classes only. Furthermore, note that when a class is instantiated using a different constructor, the default values for its properties may be different.

bound

This flag is used with property accessor methods for bound properties of JavaBeans components. The presence of this flag means that calling the method generates a java.beans.PropertyChangeEvent. This is a specification detail, but it is sometimes not documented. Information about bound properties is obtained from the BeanInfo object for the class.

constrained

Indicates that a JavaBeans component property is constrained. In other words, the method may throw a `java.beans.PropertyVetoException`. This is a specification detail, not an implementation detail.

expert

Indicates that the `BeanInfo` object for this class specifies this method is intended for use by experts only. This hint is intended for visual programming tools, but users of this book may find the hint useful as well.

hidden

Indicates that the `BeanInfo` object for this class specifies this method is for internal use only. This is a hint that visual programming tools should hide the property or event from the programmer. This book doesn't hide these methods, of course, but this flag indicates you should probably avoid using the method.

preferred

Indicates that the `BeanInfo` object for this class specifies that this method is an accessor for a default or preferred property or event. This is a hint to visual programming tools to display the property or event in a prominent way, and it may also be a useful hint to readers of this book.

= For `static final` fields, this flag is followed by the constant value of the field. Only constants of primitive and `String` types and constants with the value `null` are displayed. Some constant values are specification details, while others are implementation details. The reason that symbolic constants are defined, however, is so you can write code that doesn't rely directly upon the constant value. Use this flag to help you understand the class, but don't rely upon the constant values in your own programs.

Functional grouping of members

Within a class synopsis, the members aren't listed in strict alphabetical order. Instead, they are broken into functional groups and listed alphabetically within each group. Constructors, methods, fields, and inner classes are listed separately. Instance methods are kept separate from static (class) methods. Constants are separated from nonconstant fields; public members are listed separately from protected members. Grouping members by category breaks a class down into smaller, more comprehensible segments, making the class easier to understand. This grouping also makes it easier for you to find a desired member.

Functional groups are separated from each other in a class synopsis with Java comments, such as "// Public Constructors," "// Inner Classes," and "// Methods Implementing Servlet." The various functional categories are as follows (in the order in which they appear in a class synopsis):

Constructors

Displays the constructors for the class. Public constructors and protected constructors are displayed separately in subgroupings. If a class defines no constructor at all, the Java compiler adds a default no-argument constructor that is displayed here. If a class defines only private constructors, it can't be instantiated, and a special, empty grouping entitled "No Constructor" indicates this fact. Constructors are listed first because the first thing you do with most classes is instantiate them by calling a constructor.

Constants

Displays all constants (i.e., fields that are declared static and final) defined by the class. Public and protected constants are displayed in separate subgroups. Constants are listed here, near the top of the class synopsis, because constant values are often used throughout the class as legal values for method parameters and return values.

Inner classes

Groups all inner classes and interfaces defined by the class or interface. For each inner class, there is a single-line synopsis. Each inner class also has its own quick-reference entry that includes a full class synopsis for the inner class. Like constants, inner classes are listed near the top of the class synopsis because they are often used by other members of the class.

Static methods

Lists the static methods (class methods) of the class, broken down into subgroups for public static methods and protected static methods.

Event Listener Registration methods

Lists the public instance methods that register and deregister event listener objects with the class. The names of these methods begin with the words "add" and "remove" and end in "Listener." These methods are always passed a java.util.EventListener object, and are typically defined in pairs, so the pairs are listed together. The methods are listed alphabetically by event name, rather than by method name.

Public Instance methods

Contains all public instance methods that aren't grouped elsewhere.

Implementing methods

Groups the methods that implement the same interface. There is one subgroup for each interface implemented by the class. Methods defined by the same interface are almost always related to each other, so this is a useful functional grouping of methods.

Overriding methods

Groups the methods that override methods of a superclass broken into subgroups by superclass. This is typically a useful grouping, because it helps to make it clear how a class modifies the default behavior of its superclasses. In practice, it is also often true that methods that override the same superclass are functionally related to each other.

Protected Instance methods

Contains all protected instance methods that aren't grouped elsewhere.

Fields

Lists all nonconstant fields of the class, breaking them down into subgroups for public and protected static fields and public and protected instance fields. Many classes don't define any publicly accessible fields. For those that do, many object-oriented programmers prefer not to use those fields directly, but instead to use accessor methods when such methods are available.

Deprecated members

Deprecated methods and deprecated fields are grouped at the very bottom of the class synopsis. Use of these members is strongly discouraged.

Class Hierarchy

For any class or interface that has a nontrivial class hierarchy, the class synopsis is followed by a "Hierarchy" section. This section lists all superclasses of the class, as well as any interfaces implemented by those superclasses. It may also list any interfaces extended by an interface. In the hierarchy listing, arrows indicate super-class to subclass relationships, while the interfaces implemented by a class follow the class name in parentheses. For example, the following hierarchy indicates that javax.servlet.ServletException extends Exception, which extends Throwable (which implements Serializable), which extends Object:

If a class has subclasses, the "Hierarchy" section is followed by a "Subclasses" section that lists those subclasses. If an interface has implementations, the "Hier-archy" section is followed by an "Implementations" section that lists those implementations. While the "Hierarchy" section shows ancestors of the class, the "Subclasses" or "Implementations" section shows descendants.

Cross References

The class hierarchy section of a quick-reference entry is followed by a number of optional "cross reference" sections that indicate other, related classes and methods that may be of interest. These sections are:

Passed To

This section lists all methods and constructors that are passed an object of this type as an argument. This is useful when you have an object of a given type and want to figure out what you can do with it.

Returned By

This section lists all methods (but not constructors) that return an object of this type. This is useful when you know that you want to work with an object of this type, but don't know how to obtain one.

Thrown By

For checked exception classes, this section lists all methods and constructors that throw exceptions of this type. This material helps you figure out when a given exception or error may be thrown. Note, however, that this section is based on the exception types listed in the throws clauses of methods and constructors. Subclasses of RuntimeException and Error don't have to be listed in throws clauses, so it is not possible to generate a complete cross reference of methods that throw these types of unchecked exceptions.

Type Of

This section lists all of the fields and constants that are of this type, which can help you figure out how to obtain an object of this type.

A Note About Class Names

Throughout the quick reference, you'll notice that classes are sometimes referred to by class name alone and at other times referred to by class name and package name. If package names were always used, the class synopses would become long and hard to read. On the other hand, if package names were never used, it would sometimes be difficult to know what class was being referred to. The rules for including or omitting the package name are complex. They can be summarized approximately as follows, however:

- If the class name alone is ambiguous, the package name is always used.

- If the class is part of java.lang or java.io, the package name is omitted.

- If the class being referred to is part of the current package (and has a quick-ref entry in the current chapter), the package name is omitted. The package name is also omitted if the class being referred to is part of a package that contains the current package. And it is sometimes omitted if the class being referred to is part of a subpackage of the current package.

CHAPTER 18

java.rmi

The main package in RMI contains the principle objects used in RMI clients and servers. The Remote interface and the Naming class are used to define and locate RMI objects over the network. The RMISecurityManager class provides additional security semantics required for RMI interactions. The MarshalledObject class is used during remote method calls for certain method arguments. In addition, this core package contains a number of basic RMI exception types used during remote object lookups and remote method calls.

Interfaces:

public interface **Remote**;

Classes:

public final class **MarshalledObject** implements Serializable;
public final class **Naming**;
public class **RMISecurityManager** extends SecurityManager;

Exceptions:

public class **AlreadyBoundException** extends Exception;
public class **NotBoundException** extends Exception;
public class **RemoteException** extends java.io.IOException;
    └ public class **AccessException** extends RemoteException;
    └ public class **ConnectException** extends RemoteException;
    └ public class **ConnectIOException** extends RemoteException;
    └ public class **MarshalException** extends RemoteException;
    └ public class **NoSuchObjectException** extends RemoteException;
    └ public class **ServerError** extends RemoteException;
    └ public class **ServerException** extends RemoteException;
    └ public class **ServerRuntimeException** extends RemoteException;
    └ public class **StubNotFoundException** extends RemoteException;
    └ public class **UnexpectedException** extends RemoteException;

└ public class **UnknownHostException** extends RemoteException;
└ public class **UnmarshalException** extends RemoteException;
public class **RMISecurityException** extends SecurityException;

AccessException   Java 1.1

java.rmi   *serializable checked*

This subclass of RemoteException is thrown when you attempt to perform an improper operation on a Naming or Registry object. A registry will only allow local requests to bind, rebind or unbind objects, so an attempt to call these methods on a remote registry will result in an AccessException being thrown.

```
Object ─ Throwable ─ Exception ─ IOException ─ RemoteException ─ AccessException
          ┊ Serializable
```

```
public class AccessException extends RemoteException {
// Public Constructors
    public AccessException(String s);
    public AccessException(String s, Exception ex);
}
```

Thrown By: java.rmi.registry.Registry.{bind(), list(), lookup(), rebind(), unbind()}

AlreadyBoundException   Java 1.1

java.rmi   *serializable checked*

An exception that is thrown when an attempt is made to bind an object to a name that is already bound.

```
Object ─ Throwable ─ Exception ─ AlreadyBoundException
          ┊ Serializable
```

```
public class AlreadyBoundException extends Exception {
// Public Constructors
    public AlreadyBoundException();
    public AlreadyBoundException(String s);
}
```

Thrown By: Naming.bind(), java.rmi.registry.Registry.bind()

ConnectException   Java 1.1

java.rmi   *serializable checked*

A RemoteException that's thrown when a remote host refuses to connect during a remote method call.

```
Object ─ Throwable ─ Exception ─ IOException ─ RemoteException ─ ConnectException
          ┊ Serializable
```

```
public class ConnectException extends RemoteException {
// Public Constructors
    public ConnectException(String s);
    public ConnectException(String s, Exception ex);
}
```

ConnectIOException

java.rmi   *serializable checked*

A RemoteException, thrown if there is an I/O error while attempting to make a remote method call.

```
Object ─ Throwable ─ Exception ─ IOException ─ RemoteException ─ ConnectIOException
         Serializable
```

```
public class ConnectIOException extends RemoteException {
// Public Constructors
    public ConnectIOException(String s);
    public ConnectIOException(String s, Exception ex);
}
```

MarshalException

java.rmi   *serializable checked*

A RemoteException, thrown if an I/O error occurs while attempting to marshal any part of a remote method call (header data or method arguments).

```
Object ─ Throwable ─ Exception ─ IOException ─ RemoteException ─ MarshalException
         Serializable
```

```
public class MarshalException extends RemoteException {
// Public Constructors
    public MarshalException(String s);
    public MarshalException(String s, Exception ex);
}
```

MarshalledObject

java.rmi   *serializable*

A MarshalledObject represents an object that has been serialized and marshalled according to the RMI specifications. If the original object was a remote object reference, then the MarshalledObject contains a serialized stub for the object. Otherwise, the object is serialized, and tagged with a codebase URL that can be used on the receiving end to find the class definition for the object, if needed.

The MarshalledObject constructor allows you to serialize an existing object into marshalled form. Methods on the MarshalledObject allow you to get() a copy of the serialized object it contains, and compare the equality of the serialized objects of two MarshalledObjects.

MarshalledObjects are used primarily by the RMI activation API, to allow for the passing of initialization parameters for activated objects in a standard way, for example.

```
Object ─ MarshalledObject ┈ Serializable
```

```
public final class MarshalledObject implements Serializable {
// Public Constructors
    public MarshalledObject(Object obj) throws IOException;
// Public Instance Methods
    public Object get() throws IOException, ClassNotFoundException;
// Public Methods Overriding Object
```

```
    public boolean equals(Object obj);
    public int hashCode();
}
```

Passed To: java.rmi.activation.Activatable.{Activatable(), exportObject()},
java.rmi.activation.ActivationDesc.ActivationDesc(), java.rmi.activation.ActivationGroup.activeObject(),
java.rmi.activation.ActivationGroupDesc.ActivationGroupDesc(),
java.rmi.activation.ActivationMonitor.activeObject()

Returned By: java.rmi.activation.ActivationDesc.getData(),
java.rmi.activation.ActivationGroup_Stub.newInstance(),
java.rmi.activation.ActivationGroupDesc.getData(),
java.rmi.activation.ActivationInstantiator.newInstance(), java.rmi.activation.Activator.activate()

Naming
java.rmi

Java 1.1

This is the primary application interface to the naming service within the RMI registry. References to remote objects are obtained with the lookup() method. Local object implementations can be bound to names within the local registry using the bind() and rebind() methods. Locally bound objects can be removed from the name registry using unbind(). All of the names for objects currently stored in the registry can be obtained using the list() method.

Each name argument to the methods on the Naming interface takes the form of a URL, e.g., rmi://remoteHost:port/objName. If a local object is being referenced, and the object is exported to the default registry port, then the URL can simply take the form of the object's name in the local registry, e.g., objName. This is possible because the rmi: protocol is assumed if it isn't present in the URL, and the default host is the local host.

Note that, while the lookup() method can reference any remote RMI registry, the bind(), rebind() and unbind() methods can only be called on the local registry. Attempting to call these methods against a remote registry will result in an AccessException being thrown.

```
public final class Naming {
// No Constructor
// Public Class Methods
    public static void bind(String name, Remote obj) throws AlreadyBoundException, java.net.MalformedURLException,
        RemoteException;
    public static String[ ] list(String name) throws RemoteException, java.net.MalformedURLException;
    public static Remote lookup(String name) throws NotBoundException, java.net.MalformedURLException,
        RemoteException;
    public static void rebind(String name, Remote obj) throws RemoteException, java.net.MalformedURLException;
    public static void unbind(String name) throws RemoteException, NotBoundException,
        java.net.MalformedURLException;
}
```

NoSuchObjectException
java.rmi

Java 1.1

serializable checked

This subclass of RemoteException is thrown when you attempt to invoke a method on a remote object that is no longer available.

| Object | Throwable | Exception | IOException | RemoteException | NoSuchObjectException |
| Serializable |

```
public class NoSuchObjectException extends RemoteException {
// Public Constructors
    public NoSuchObjectException(String s);
}
```

Thrown By: java.rmi.activation.Activatable.unexportObject(), java.rmi.server.RemoteObject.toStub(),
java.rmi.server.UnicastRemoteObject.unexportObject(), javax.rmi.PortableRemoteObject.{toStub(),
unexportObject()}, javax.rmi.CORBA.PortableRemoteObjectDelegate.{toStub(), unexportObject()},
javax.rmi.CORBA.Tie.deactivate(), javax.rmi.CORBA.Util.unexportObject(),
javax.rmi.CORBA.UtilDelegate.unexportObject()

NotBoundException   Java 1.1

java.rmi   *serializable checked*

An exception that is thrown by a Naming instance when a lookup is attempted using a
name with no object bound to it.

| Object | Throwable | Exception | NotBoundException |
| Serializable |

```
public class NotBoundException extends Exception {
// Public Constructors
    public NotBoundException();
    public NotBoundException(String s);
}
```

Thrown By: Naming.{lookup(), unbind()}, java.rmi.registry.Registry.{lookup(), unbind()}

Remote   Java 1.1

java.rmi   *remote*

Every remote object implements the Remote interface, and any methods intended to be
remotely callable have to be defined within an interface that extends Remote interface.
This is a place-holder interface that identifies all remote objects, but doesn't define any
methods of its own.

```
public interface Remote {
}
```

Implementations: java.rmi.activation.ActivationGroup_Stub,
java.rmi.activation.ActivationInstantiator, java.rmi.activation.ActivationMonitor,
java.rmi.activation.ActivationSystem, java.rmi.activation.Activator, java.rmi.dgc.DGC,
java.rmi.registry.Registry, java.rmi.server.RemoteObject, javax.ejb.EJBHome, javax.ejb.EJBObject,
org.omg.stub.java.rmi._Remote_Stub

Passed To: Too many methods to list.

Returned By: Naming.lookup(), java.rmi.activation.Activatable.{exportObject(), register()},
java.rmi.activation.ActivationID.activate(), java.rmi.registry.Registry.lookup(),
java.rmi.server.RemoteObject.toStub(), java.rmi.server.UnicastRemoteObject.exportObject(),
javax.rmi.PortableRemoteObject.toStub(), javax.rmi.CORBA.PortableRemoteObjectDelegate.toStub(),
javax.rmi.CORBA.Tie.getTarget()

RemoteException

java.rmi   *serializable checked*

This subclass of IOException is thrown when an error occurs during any remote object
operation. The RemoteException includes a Throwable data member that represents the
nested exception that caused the RemoteException to be thrown. For example, if an
exception occurs on the server while executing a remote method, then the client
receives a RemoteException (in the form of a ServerException, one of its sub-classes) with its
Throwable data member initialized to the server-side exception that caused the client-side
RemoteException to be delivered.

```
Object ─┬─ Throwable ─┬─ Exception ─┬─ IOException ─┬─ RemoteException
        └─ Serializable
```

```
public class RemoteException extends IOException {
// Public Constructors
    public RemoteException();
    public RemoteException(String s);
    public RemoteException(String s, Throwable ex);
// Public Methods Overriding Throwable
1.4 public Throwable getCause();                                              default:null
    public String getMessage();                                              default:null
// Public Instance Fields
    public Throwable detail;
}
```

Subclasses: AccessException, java.rmi.ConnectException, ConnectIOException, MarshalException,
NoSuchObjectException, ServerError, ServerException, ServerRuntimeException,
StubNotFoundException, UnexpectedException, java.rmi.UnknownHostException, UnmarshalException,
java.rmi.activation.ActivateFailedException, java.rmi.server.ExportException,
java.rmi.server.SkeletonMismatchException, java.rmi.server.SkeletonNotFoundException,
javax.transaction.InvalidTransactionException, javax.transaction.TransactionRequiredException,
javax.transaction.TransactionRolledbackException

Returned By: javax.rmi.CORBA.Util.{mapSystemException(), wrapException()},
javax.rmi.CORBA.UtilDelegate.{mapSystemException(), wrapException()}

Thrown By: Too many methods to list.

RMISecurityException

java.rmi   *serializable unchecked*

A SecurityException thrown by the RMISecurityManager when a security violation is detected
during a remote operation.

```
Object ─┬─ Throwable ─┬─ Exception ─── RuntimeException ─── SecurityException ─── RMISecurityException
        └─ Serializable
```

```
public class RMISecurityException extends java.lang.SecurityException {
// Public Constructors
#   public RMISecurityException(String name);
#   public RMISecurityException(String name, String arg);
}
```

RMISecurityManager

Java 1.1

java.rmi

The RMISecurityManager enforces the security policy for classes that are loaded as stubs for remote objects, by overriding all of the relevant access-check methods from the SecurityManager. By default, stub objects are only allowed to perform class definition and class access operations. If you don't set the local security manager to be an RMISecurity-Manager (using the System.setSecurityManager() method), then stub classes will only be loadable from the local file system. Applets engaging in RMI calls do not need to use the RMISecurityManager, since the security manager provided by the browser will do the necessary access control on loading remote classes, etc.

You normally won't need to interact with the RMISecurityManager directly within your application code, except to set it as the system security manager before starting your RMI code.

Object — SecurityManager — RMISecurityManager

```
public class RMISecurityManager extends SecurityManager {
// Public Constructors
   public RMISecurityManager();
}
```

ServerError

Java 1.1

java.rmi

serializable checked

A (non-recoverable) error that occurs while a server is executing a remote method. The nested Throwable data member (inherited from RemoteException) contains the server-side exception that generated the error.

Object — Throwable — Exception — IOException — RemoteException — ServerError
Serializable

```
public class ServerError extends RemoteException {
// Public Constructors
   public ServerError(String s, Error err);
}
```

ServerException

Java 1.1

java.rmi

serializable checked

This exception is thrown if a RemoteException is thrown while the server object is executing a remote method.

Object — Throwable — Exception — IOException — RemoteException — ServerException
Serializable

```
public class ServerException extends RemoteException {
// Public Constructors
   public ServerException(String s);
   public ServerException(String s, Exception ex);
}
```

ServerRuntimeException

Java 1.1; Deprecated in Java 1.2
serializable checked

java.rmi

An exception that occurs if a RuntimeException is thrown while a server object is executing a remote method. The nested Throwable data member (inherited from RemoteException) contains the server-side runtime exception that generated the exception.

Object — Throwable — Exception — IOException — RemoteException — ServerRuntimeException
       Serializable

```
public class ServerRuntimeException extends RemoteException {
// Public Constructors
#    public ServerRuntimeException(String s, Exception ex);
}
```

StubNotFoundException

Java 1.1
serializable checked

java.rmi

This exception can occur either when an object is being exported to participate in remote RMI calls, or during a remote method call. During export on the server, this exception is thrown if the stub class for the object can't be found or used for some reason (e.g., the stub class isn't in the CLASSPATH of the server process, or the stub class can't be instantiated). During a remote method call, the client can receive this exception if the remote object hasn't been exported completely or correctly.

Object — Throwable — Exception — IOException — RemoteException — StubNotFoundException
       Serializable

```
public class StubNotFoundException extends RemoteException {
// Public Constructors
    public StubNotFoundException(String s);
    public StubNotFoundException(String s, Exception ex);
}
```

UnexpectedException

Java 1.1
serializable checked

java.rmi

An UnexpectedException is thrown if an exception that isn't specified on a remote method's signature is encountered during the return from a remote method call. The unexpected exception can occur on the server or on the client. The nested Throwable object inherited from RemoteException contains the actual exception that occurred.

Object — Throwable — Exception — IOException — RemoteException — UnexpectedException
       Serializable

```
public class UnexpectedException extends RemoteException {
// Public Constructors
    public UnexpectedException(String s);
    public UnexpectedException(String s, Exception ex);
}
```

UnknownHostException

Java 1.1

java.rmi

serializable checked

This RemoteException is thrown if the host specified during a Naming lookup can't be found.

```
Object ─ Throwable ─ Exception ─ IOException ─ RemoteException ─ UnknownHostException
         Serializable
```

```
public class UnknownHostException extends RemoteException {
// Public Constructors
    public UnknownHostException(String s);
    public UnknownHostException(String s, Exception ex);
}
```

Thrown By: java.rmi.registry.RegistryHandler.registryStub()

UnmarshalException

Java 1.1

java.rmi

serializable checked

This RemoteException is thrown if an error occurs while unmarshalling the return value from a remote method call. The source of the error could be an I/O error while sending the header or the value of the return from the server to the client, or the fact that the class of the return object is not found.

```
Object ─ Throwable ─ Exception ─ IOException ─ RemoteException ─ UnmarshalException
         Serializable
```

```
public class UnmarshalException extends RemoteException {
// Public Constructors
    public UnmarshalException(String s);
    public UnmarshalException(String s, Exception ex);
}
```

CHAPTER 19

java.rmi.activation

This package contains the interfaces, classes and exceptions that represent the RMI activation system, introduced in JDK 1.2. This RMI service allows you to define remote objects that are not instantiated on the server until a client request triggers their activation. The activation system provides the means to specify how a remote object is activated and how activated objects are grouped into Java VMs.

Interfaces:

public interface **ActivationInstantiator** extends java.rmi.Remote;
public interface **ActivationMonitor** extends java.rmi.Remote;
public interface **ActivationSystem** extends java.rmi.Remote;
public interface **Activator** extends java.rmi.Remote;

Classes:

public abstract class **Activatable** extends java.rmi.server.RemoteServer;
public final class **ActivationDesc** implements Serializable;
public abstract class **ActivationGroup** extends java.rmi.server.UnicastRemoteObject
                                        implements ActivationInstantiator;
public final class **ActivationGroup_Stub** extends java.rmi.server.RemoteStub
                                        implements ActivationInstantiator, java.rmi.Remote;
public final class **ActivationGroupDesc** implements Serializable;
public static class **ActivationGroupDesc.CommandEnvironment** implements Serializable;
public class **ActivationGroupID** implements Serializable;
public class **ActivationID** implements Serializable;

Exceptions:

public class **ActivateFailedException** extends java.rmi.RemoteException;
public class **ActivationException** extends Exception;
    └ public class **UnknownGroupException** extends ActivationException;
    └ public class **UnknownObjectException** extends ActivationException;

Activatable

java.rmi.activation

This abstract subclass of java.rmi.server.RemoteServer represents a server object that is persistent and activatable, as opposed to a UnicastRemoteObject which represents a server object that is only available during the lifetime of the server process. Both UnicastRemoteObjects and Activatables only support point-to-point communications.

The Activatable class provides a set of constructors and a corresponding set of static exportObject() methods that can be used to register and export a server object, either pre-instantiated or not. The exportObject() methods are provided for server objects that choose not to extend the Activatable class. The getID() method on the class allows you to get the server object's ActivationID. Other static methods on the class are the register() method, which can be used to register an activatable object without instantiating it, unexportObject(), which removes the specified object from the RMI runtime, unregister(), which removes the activation registration for the given ActivationID, and inactive(), which specifies that the activatable object specified by the given ActivationID is currently not active.

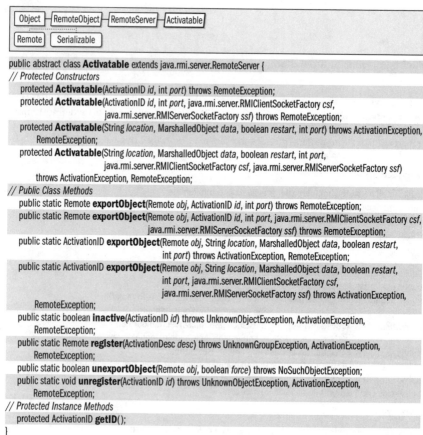

```
public abstract class Activatable extends java.rmi.server.RemoteServer {
// Protected Constructors
    protected Activatable(ActivationID id, int port) throws RemoteException;
    protected Activatable(ActivationID id, int port, java.rmi.server.RMIClientSocketFactory csf,
                java.rmi.server.RMIServerSocketFactory ssf) throws RemoteException;
    protected Activatable(String location, MarshalledObject data, boolean restart, int port) throws ActivationException,
        RemoteException;
    protected Activatable(String location, MarshalledObject data, boolean restart, int port,
                java.rmi.server.RMIClientSocketFactory csf, java.rmi.server.RMIServerSocketFactory ssf)
        throws ActivationException, RemoteException;
// Public Class Methods
    public static Remote exportObject(Remote obj, ActivationID id, int port) throws RemoteException;
    public static Remote exportObject(Remote obj, ActivationID id, int port, java.rmi.server.RMIClientSocketFactory csf,
                java.rmi.server.RMIServerSocketFactory ssf) throws RemoteException;
    public static ActivationID exportObject(Remote obj, String location, MarshalledObject data, boolean restart,
                int port) throws ActivationException, RemoteException;
    public static ActivationID exportObject(Remote obj, String location, MarshalledObject data, boolean restart,
                int port, java.rmi.server.RMIClientSocketFactory csf,
                java.rmi.server.RMIServerSocketFactory ssf) throws ActivationException,
        RemoteException;
    public static boolean inactive(ActivationID id) throws UnknownObjectException, ActivationException,
        RemoteException;
    public static Remote register(ActivationDesc desc) throws UnknownGroupException, ActivationException,
        RemoteException;
    public static boolean unexportObject(Remote obj, boolean force) throws NoSuchObjectException;
    public static void unregister(ActivationID id) throws UnknownObjectException, ActivationException,
        RemoteException;
// Protected Instance Methods
    protected ActivationID getID();
}
```

ActivateFailedException

Java 1.2

java.rmi.activation   *serializable checked*

This subclass of RemoteException is thrown to a client when a remote method call fails because the object could not be activated.

```
Object—Throwable—Exception—IOException—RemoteException—ActivateFailedException
     Serializable
```

```
public class ActivateFailedException extends RemoteException {
// Public Constructors
    public ActivateFailedException(String s);
    public ActivateFailedException(String s, Exception ex);
}
```

ActivationDesc

Java 1.2

java.rmi.activation   *serializable*

An ActivationDesc represents a description for how a remote object should be activated. It contains an activation group ID for the object, the class name for the object to be instantiated, a codebase that can be used to load the class description if necessary, and a MarshalledObject that contains object-specific initialization data. Once an ActivationDesc has been created, it can be used to register an object for activation using the Activatable.register() method.

```
Object—ActivationDesc···Serializable
```

```
public final class ActivationDesc implements Serializable {
// Public Constructors
    public ActivationDesc(String className, String location, MarshalledObject data) throws ActivationException;
    public ActivationDesc(ActivationGroupID groupID, String className, String location, MarshalledObject data);
    public ActivationDesc(String className, String location, MarshalledObject data, boolean restart)
        throws ActivationException;
    public ActivationDesc(ActivationGroupID groupID, String className, String location, MarshalledObject data,
                    boolean restart);
// Property Accessor Methods (by property name)
    public String getClassName();
    public MarshalledObject getData();
    public ActivationGroupID getGroupID();
    public String getLocation();
    public boolean getRestartMode();
// Public Methods Overriding Object
    public boolean equals(Object obj);
    public int hashCode();
}
```

Passed To: Activatable.register(), ActivationGroup_Stub.newInstance(), ActivationInstantiator.newInstance(), ActivationSystem.{registerObject(), setActivationDesc()}

Returned By: ActivationSystem.{getActivationDesc(), setActivationDesc()}

ActivationException

Java 1.2

java.rmi.activation   *serializable checked*

This is a base class used for all non-remote activation-related exceptions (i.e., exceptions thrown between components of the activation system, or by the local activation system to clients invoking its methods).

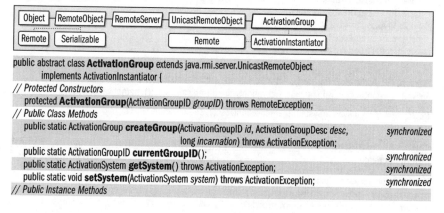

```
public class ActivationException extends Exception {
// Public Constructors
    public ActivationException();
    public ActivationException(String s);
    public ActivationException(String s, Throwable ex);
// Public Methods Overriding Throwable
1.4 public Throwable getCause();                                                    default:null
    public String getMessage();                                                     default:null
// Public Instance Fields
    public Throwable detail;
}
```

Subclasses: UnknownGroupException, UnknownObjectException

Thrown By: Too many methods to list.

ActivationGroup

Java 1.2

java.rmi.activation

serializable remote

An ActivationGroup represents a group of activatable objects that are to run within the same Java VM. The ActivationGroup serves as a go-between for the ActivationMonitor and the activatable objects, forwarding messages about the active state of objects in its group. The activeObject() methods are used to forward a message to the activation system about a newly activated object in the group, and the inactiveObject() method does the same for deactivated objects.

You can explicitly create your own ActivationGroups using the createGroup() method. If you don't specify a group id when you create an ActivationDesc for your activatable object, then it will be assigned to a default group. When you create an ActivationGroup, you provide an ActivationGroupDesc object that describes how the group is to be created (e.g, from what class the group object should be constructed, what Properties should be set for the group, etc.).

The ActivationGroup class is abstract, so concrete implementations must be provided in order to create groups. In addition to satisfying the interface defined in ActivationGroup, the subclass must also provide a constructor that takes an ActivationGroupID and a MarshalledObject as arguments. This constructor will be invoked by the createGroup() method. In addition, a concrete subclass of ActivationGroup must implement the newInstance() method inherited from ActivationInstantiator.

```
public abstract class ActivationGroup extends java.rmi.server.UnicastRemoteObject
        implements ActivationInstantiator {
// Protected Constructors
    protected ActivationGroup(ActivationGroupID groupID) throws RemoteException;
// Public Class Methods
    public static ActivationGroup createGroup(ActivationGroupID id, ActivationGroupDesc desc,   synchronized
                                    long incarnation) throws ActivationException;
    public static ActivationGroupID currentGroupID();                                           synchronized
    public static ActivationSystem getSystem() throws ActivationException;                      synchronized
    public static void setSystem(ActivationSystem system) throws ActivationException;           synchronized
// Public Instance Methods
```

public abstract void **activeObject**(ActivationID *id*, Remote *obj*) throws ActivationException,
　　UnknownObjectException, RemoteException;
public boolean **inactiveObject**(ActivationID *id*) throws ActivationException, UnknownObjectException,
　　RemoteException;
// Protected Instance Methods
protected void **activeObject**(ActivationID *id*, MarshalledObject *mobj*) throws ActivationException,
　　UnknownObjectException, RemoteException;
protected void **inactiveGroup**() throws UnknownGroupException, RemoteException;
}

Returned By: ActivationGroup.createGroup()

ActivationGroup_Stub

java.rmi.activation

serializable remote

The *rmic*-generated stub class for the ActivationGroup remote interface.

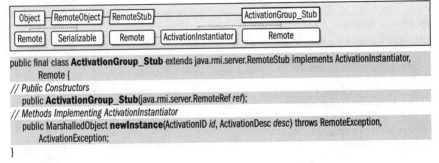

public final class **ActivationGroup_Stub** extends java.rmi.server.RemoteStub implements ActivationInstantiator,
　　Remote {
// Public Constructors
public **ActivationGroup_Stub**(java.rmi.server.RemoteRef *ref*);
// Methods Implementing ActivationInstantiator
public MarshalledObject **newInstance**(ActivationID *id*, ActivationDesc *desc*) throws RemoteException,
　　ActivationException;
}

ActivationGroupDesc

java.rmi.activation

serializable

An ActivationGroupDesc contains the information needed to create a new activation group.
It includes the class that should be used to construct the group object, a codebase that
can be used to find the class description, if necessary, and a MarshalledObject containing
any additional initialization information required by your group. In addition, the constructors allow you to specify a Properties list that will override any default runtime
properties in the Java VM for the group, and a CommandEnvironment object which allows
you to customize the Java executable that is executed to start the group's VM, and its
command-line arguments.

public final class **ActivationGroupDesc** implements Serializable {
// Public Constructors
public **ActivationGroupDesc**(java.util.Properties *overrides*, ActivationGroupDesc.CommandEnvironment *cmd*);
public **ActivationGroupDesc**(String *className*, String *location*, MarshalledObject *data*,
　　　　　　java.util.Properties *overrides*, ActivationGroupDesc.CommandEnvironment *cmd*);
// Inner Classes
public static class **CommandEnvironment** implements Serializable;
// Property Accessor Methods (by property name)
public String **getClassName**();
public ActivationGroupDesc.CommandEnvironment **getCommandEnvironment**();
public MarshalledObject **getData**();

```
    public String getLocation();
    public java.util.Properties getPropertyOverrides();
// Public Methods Overriding Object
    public boolean equals(Object obj);
    public int hashCode();
}
```

Passed To: ActivationGroup.createGroup(), ActivationSystem.{registerGroup(), setActivationGroupDesc()}

Returned By: ActivationSystem.{getActivationGroupDesc(), setActivationGroupDesc()}

ActivationGroupDesc.CommandEnvironment

Java 1.2

java.rmi.activation

serializable

This inner class of ActivationGroupDesc provides a means for specifying customized startup parameters for the Java VM for an activation group. It contains a command path, which specified where to find the Java executable to be run, and an array of command-line arguments for the Java executable.

```
public static class ActivationGroupDesc.CommandEnvironment implements Serializable {
// Public Constructors
    public CommandEnvironment(String cmdpath, String[ ] argv);
// Public Instance Methods
    public String[ ] getCommandOptions();
    public String getCommandPath();
// Public Methods Overriding Object
    public boolean equals(Object obj);
    public int hashCode();
}
```

Passed To: ActivationGroupDesc.ActivationGroupDesc()

Returned By: ActivationGroupDesc.getCommandEnvironment()

ActivationGroupID

Java 1.2

java.rmi.activation

serializable

An ActivationGroupID uniquely identifies a group within the activation system. The ActivationGroup can also use its ActivationGroupID to query for its ActivationSystem, if needed. An ActivationGroupID is generated for a new group by the ActivationSystem.registerGroup() method.

```
Object ─ ActivationGroupID ┈ Serializable
```

```
public class ActivationGroupID implements Serializable {
// Public Constructors
    public ActivationGroupID(ActivationSystem system);
// Public Instance Methods
    public ActivationSystem getSystem();
// Public Methods Overriding Object
    public boolean equals(Object obj);
    public int hashCode();
}
```

Passed To: ActivationDesc.ActivationDesc(), ActivationGroup.{ActivationGroup(), createGroup()}, ActivationMonitor.inactiveGroup(), ActivationSystem.{activeGroup(), getActivationGroupDesc(), setActivationGroupDesc(), unregisterGroup()}

Returned By: ActivationDesc.getGroupID(), ActivationGroup.currentGroupID(), ActivationSystem.registerGroup()

ActivationID

java.rmi.activation

Java 1.2

serializable

An ActivationID uniquely identifies an activatable object within the activation system. It also contains an opaque reference to the Activator responsible for activating the object, which it uses when its activate() method is invoked. An ActivationID is generated for an activatable object by registering it using the Activatable.register() method (the stub returned by this method is initialized with the ActivationID), or by using one of the appropriate Activatable.exportObject() methods.

Object — ActivationID ·· Serializable

```
public class ActivationID implements Serializable {
// Public Constructors
    public ActivationID(Activator activator);
// Public Instance Methods
    public Remote activate(boolean force) throws ActivationException, UnknownObjectException, RemoteException;
// Public Methods Overriding Object
    public boolean equals(Object obj);
    public int hashCode();
}
```

Passed To: Activatable.{Activatable(), exportObject(), inactive(), unregister()}, ActivationGroup.{activeObject(), inactiveObject()}, ActivationGroup_Stub.newInstance(), ActivationInstantiator.newInstance(), ActivationMonitor.{activeObject(), inactiveObject()}, ActivationSystem.{getActivationDesc(), setActivationDesc(), unregisterObject()}, Activator.activate()

Returned By: Activatable.{exportObject(), getID()}, ActivationSystem.registerObject()

ActivationInstantiator

java.rmi.activation

Java 1.2

remote

This interface represents an object that is responsible for activating objects, using its newInstance() method. The arguments to the method provide the ActivationID for the object within the activation system, and the ActivationDesc provided for the object when it was registered, which includes the information needed to activate the object. The ActivationGroup class implements this interface, and concrete subclasses of ActivationGroup must provide an implementation of the newInstance() method.

Remote ·· ActivationInstantiator

```
public interface ActivationInstantiator extends Remote {
// Public Instance Methods
    public abstract MarshalledObject newInstance(ActivationID id, ActivationDesc desc) throws ActivationException,
        RemoteException;
}
```

Implementations: ActivationGroup, ActivationGroup_Stub

Passed To: ActivationSystem.activeGroup()

ActivationMonitor

Java 1.2

java.rmi.activation

remote

An ActivationMonitor monitors a single activation group. It must be notified by the group when objects within the group become active or inactive, or when the group as a whole becomes inactive. This lets the ActivationMonitor know when an object needs to be (re)activated, for example.

Remote ⊢ ActivationMonitor

```
public interface ActivationMonitor extends Remote {
// Public Instance Methods
    public abstract void activeObject(ActivationID id, MarshalledObject obj) throws UnknownObjectException,
        RemoteException;
    public abstract void inactiveGroup(ActivationGroupID id, long incarnation) throws UnknownGroupException,
        RemoteException;
    public abstract void inactiveObject(ActivationID id) throws UnknownObjectException, RemoteException;
}
```

Returned By: ActivationSystem.activeGroup()

ActivationSystem

Java 1.2

java.rmi.activation

remote

The ActivationSystem is the backbone of the activation runtime, and interacts with Activators for activating objects and groups, and ActivationMonitors for determining when such activations are necessary. The ActivationSystem handling a particular Java VM can be obtained using the static ActivationGroup.getSystem() method.

The methods on the ActivationSystem are largely used by other classes in the activation package to implement various functions. The Activatable.register() method, for example, registers the activatable object by calling the registerObject() on the ActivationSystem.

Remote ⊢ ActivationSystem

```
public interface ActivationSystem extends Remote {
// Public Constants
    public static final int SYSTEM_PORT;                                            =1098
// Public Instance Methods
    public abstract ActivationMonitor activeGroup(ActivationGroupID id, ActivationInstantiator group, long incarnation)
        throws UnknownGroupException, ActivationException, RemoteException;
    public abstract ActivationDesc getActivationDesc(ActivationID id) throws ActivationException,
        UnknownObjectException, RemoteException;
    public abstract ActivationGroupDesc getActivationGroupDesc(ActivationGroupID id) throws ActivationException,
        UnknownGroupException, RemoteException;
    public abstract ActivationGroupID registerGroup(ActivationGroupDesc desc) throws ActivationException,
        RemoteException;
    public abstract ActivationID registerObject(ActivationDesc desc) throws ActivationException,
        UnknownGroupException, RemoteException;
    public abstract ActivationDesc setActivationDesc(ActivationID id, ActivationDesc desc) throws ActivationException,
        UnknownObjectException, UnknownGroupException, RemoteException;
    public abstract ActivationGroupDesc setActivationGroupDesc(ActivationGroupID id, ActivationGroupDesc desc)
        throws ActivationException, UnknownGroupException, RemoteException;
    public abstract void shutdown() throws RemoteException;
    public abstract void unregisterGroup(ActivationGroupID id) throws ActivationException, UnknownGroupException,
        RemoteException;
```

```
public abstract void unregisterObject(ActivationID id) throws ActivationException, UnknownObjectException,
    RemoteException;
}
```

Passed To: ActivationGroup.setSystem(), ActivationGroupID.ActivationGroupID()

Returned By: ActivationGroup.getSystem(), ActivationGroupID.getSystem()

Activator   Java 1.2
java.rmi.activation   *remote*

An Activator is responsible for activating remote objects and their groups. Its only
method, activate(), triggers the activation system protocol. The activator first finds the
ActivationDesc matching the given ActivationID, and checks the activation information contained in it. If the target group for the object is not active, then the Activator starts its
Java VM and activates the group object itself. Finally, the Activator tells the group to
(re)create the object by calling the newInstance() method on the group.

```
Remote --- Activator
```

```
public interface Activator extends Remote {
// Public Instance Methods
    public abstract MarshalledObject activate(ActivationID id, boolean force) throws ActivationException,
        UnknownObjectException, RemoteException;
}
```

Passed To: ActivationID.ActivationID()

UnknownGroupException   Java 1.2
java.rmi.activation   *serializable checked*

This exception is thrown if an ActivationGroupID is provided, either directly as a method
argument, or indirectly within an ActivationDesc, that is not registered with the Activation-
System.

```
Object -- Throwable -- Exception -- ActivationException -- UnknownGroupException
       Serializable
```

```
public class UnknownGroupException extends ActivationException {
// Public Constructors
    public UnknownGroupException(String s);
}
```

Thrown By: Activatable.register(), ActivationGroup.inactiveGroup(), ActivationMonitor.inactiveGroup(),
ActivationSystem.{activeGroup(), getActivationGroupDesc(), registerObject(), setActivationDesc(),
setActivationGroupDesc(), unregisterGroup()}

UnknownObjectException   Java 1.2
java.rmi.activation   *serializable checked*

This exception is thrown if an invalid ActivationID is passed as a method argument, e.g.,
the ID was not generated by the current ActivationSystem.

```
Object ─ Throwable ─ Exception ─ ActivationException ─ UnknownObjectException
         Serializable
```

```
public class UnknownObjectException extends ActivationException {
// Public Constructors
   public UnknownObjectException(String s);
}
```

Thrown By: Activatable.{inactive(), unregister()}, ActivationGroup.{activeObject(), inactiveObject()}, ActivationID.activate(), ActivationMonitor.{activeObject(), inactiveObject()}, ActivationSystem.{getActivationDesc(), setActivationDesc(), unregisterObject()}, Activator.activate()

CHAPTER 20

java.rmi.dgc

The java.rmi.dgc package contains an interface and two classes that support distributed garbage collection in RMI. Distributed garbage collection is normally handled automatically by the RMI system, so most applications do not need to use this package.

Interfaces:

public interface **DGC** extends java.rmi.Remote;

Classes:

public final class **Lease** implements Serializable;
public final class **VMID** implements Serializable;

DGC   Java 1.1

java.rmi.dgc   *remote*

The DGC represents the distributed garbage collection system. The dirty method is called whenever a client obtains a reference to a remote object, and the clean method is called when a particular client has no more references to a given remote object.

```
Remote ⋯ DGC
```

```
public interface DGC extends Remote {
// Public Instance Methods
    public abstract void clean(java.rmi.server.ObjID[ ] ids, long sequenceNum, VMID vmid, boolean strong)
        throws RemoteException;
    public abstract Lease dirty(java.rmi.server.ObjID[ ] ids, long sequenceNum, Lease lease) throws RemoteException;
}
```

Lease   Java 1.1

java.rmi.dgc   *serializable*

A **Lease** represents a client's lease on a remote object reference. It contains a unique VM identifier and the duration of the lease granted by the DGC.

```
Object ├─ Lease ┈┈ Serializable
```

```
public final class Lease implements Serializable {
// Public Constructors
    public Lease(VMID id, long duration);
// Public Instance Methods
    public long getValue();
    public VMID getVMID();
}
```

Passed To: DGC.dirty()

Returned By: DGC.dirty()

VMID   Java 1.1

java.rmi.dgc   *serializable*

An identifier used to uniquely identify VMs across a distributed system.

```
Object ├─ VMID ┈┈ Serializable
```

```
public final class VMID implements Serializable {
// Public Constructors
    public VMID();
// Public Methods Overriding Object
    public boolean equals(Object obj);
    public int hashCode();
    public String toString();
// Deprecated Public Methods
#   public static boolean IsUnique();                                  constant
}
```

Passed To: DGC.clean(), Lease.Lease()

Returned By: Lease.getVMID()

CHAPTER 21

java.rmi.registry

This package contains classes that provide an interface and an implementation for the various elements of the RMI object naming registry.

Interfaces:

public interface **Registry** extends java.rmi.Remote;
public interface **RegistryHandler**;

Classes:

public final class **LocateRegistry**;

LocateRegistry   Java 1.1
java.rmi.registry

This is a low-level interface to an RMI registry service, residing either on the local host or on remote servers. On lookups, the Naming service parses the host and port from the remote object URL and uses the LocateRegistry interface to connect to the remote registry. The various getRegistry() methods provide the means to get a reference to the local registry, or a stub to a remote registry running on a given host and port. The createRegistry() methods create a registry running on the local host on the given port number. The second form of the createRegistry() method allows you to specify custom socket factories to be used by the registry when it communicates with clients and server objects.

```
public final class LocateRegistry {
// No Constructor
// Public Class Methods
      public static Registry createRegistry(int port) throws RemoteException;
  1.2 public static Registry createRegistry(int port, java.rmi.server.RMIClientSocketFactory csf,
                                    java.rmi.server.RMIServerSocketFactory ssf) throws RemoteException;
      public static Registry getRegistry() throws RemoteException;
      public static Registry getRegistry(int port) throws RemoteException;
      public static Registry getRegistry(String host) throws RemoteException;
```

```
      public static Registry getRegistry(String host, int port) throws RemoteException;
1.2 public static Registry getRegistry(String host, int port, java.rmi.server.RMIClientSocketFactory csf)
          throws RemoteException;
}
```

Registry   Java 1.1

java.rmi.registry   *remote*

The Registry is an interface to the RMI object registry that runs on every node in a distributed RMI system. While the Naming interface can be used to lookup objects stored in any registry on the network, a Registry operates on a single registry on a single host. URL object names are passed into methods on the Naming service, which finds the right Registry stub using the LocateRegistry interface, and then calls the lookup() method on the remote (or local) Registry to get a stub for the remote object. A similar sequence of calls takes place with the local Registry when bind(), rebind() or unbind() are called on the Naming interface.

The Registry stores objects under unique names. An object is assigned to a name in the Registry using its bind() method. The object assigned to a particular name can be changed using the rebind(0 method. Objects are removed from the Registry using the unbind() method. The lookup() method is used to find objects by name in the Registry, and the list() method is used to get a list of the names of all of the objects currently in the Registry.

```
[ Remote ]---[ Registry ]
```

```
public interface Registry extends Remote {
// Public Constants
    public static final int REGISTRY_PORT;                                        =1099
// Public Instance Methods
    public abstract void bind(String name, Remote obj) throws RemoteException, AlreadyBoundException,
        AccessException;
    public abstract String[ ] list() throws RemoteException, AccessException;
    public abstract Remote lookup(String name) throws RemoteException, NotBoundException, AccessException;
    public abstract void rebind(String name, Remote obj) throws RemoteException, AccessException;
    public abstract void unbind(String name) throws RemoteException, NotBoundException, AccessException;
}
```

Returned By: LocateRegistry.{createRegistry(), getRegistry()}, RegistryHandler.{registryImpl(), registryStub()}

RegistryHandler   Java 1.1; Deprecated in Java 1.2

java.rmi.registry

This interface is mainly of interest to implementors of RMI registry services. It defines the interface to the internal registry-handling implementation.

```
public interface RegistryHandler {
// Deprecated Public Methods
#   public abstract Registry registryImpl(int port) throws RemoteException;
#   public abstract Registry registryStub(String host, int port) throws RemoteException,
        java.rmi.UnknownHostException;
}
```

CHAPTER 22

java.rmi.server

This package contains the classes used to implement server implementations of remote objects. The RemoteServer class in this package acts as the base class for all RMI server objects. A single subclass of RemoteServer, UnicastRemoteObject, is provided in this package. It implements a non-persistent, point-to-point object communication scheme. Other subclasses of RemoteServer could be written to implement multicast object communication, replicated objects, etc. This package also contains several Exception subclasses relevant to the server implementation of a remote object.

Interfaces:

public interface **LoaderHandler**;
public interface **RemoteCall**;
public interface **RemoteRef** extends java.io.Externalizable;
public interface **RMIClientSocketFactory**;
public interface **RMIFailureHandler**;
public interface **RMIServerSocketFactory**;
public interface **ServerRef** extends RemoteRef;
public interface **Skeleton**;
public interface **Unreferenced**;

Classes:

public class **LogStream** extends java.io.PrintStream;
public final class **ObjID** implements Serializable;
public class **Operation**;
public abstract class **RemoteObject** implements java.rmi.Remote, Serializable;
    ∟ public abstract class **RemoteServer** extends RemoteObject;
        ∟ public class **UnicastRemoteObject** extends RemoteServer;
    ∟ public abstract class **RemoteStub** extends RemoteObject;
public class **RMIClassLoader**;
public abstract class **RMIClassLoaderSpi**;

public abstract class **RMISocketFactory** implements RMIClientSocketFactory, RMIServerSocketFactory;
public final class **UID** implements Serializable;

Exceptions:

public class **ExportException** extends java.rmi.RemoteException;
   └ public class **SocketSecurityException** extends ExportException;
public class **ServerCloneException** extends CloneNotSupportedException;
public class **ServerNotActiveException** extends Exception;
public class **SkeletonMismatchException** extends java.rmi.RemoteException;
public class **SkeletonNotFoundException** extends java.rmi.RemoteException;

ExportException

Java 1.1

java.rmi.server

serializable checked

This RemoteException is thrown if an attempt is made to export a remote object on a port that is already in use.

Object ─ Throwable ─ Exception ─ IOException ─ RemoteException ─ ExportException
         └ Serializable

```
public class ExportException extends RemoteException {
// Public Constructors
    public ExportException(String s);
    public ExportException(String s, Exception ex);
}
```

Subclasses: SocketSecurityException

LoaderHandler

Java 1.1; Deprecated in Java 1.2

java.rmi.server

This defines the interface to the internal handler used by the RMIClassLoader to load classes over the network.

```
public interface LoaderHandler {
// Public Constants
    public static final String packagePrefix;                          ="sun.rmi.server"
// Deprecated Public Methods
#   public abstract Object getSecurityContext(ClassLoader loader);
#   public abstract Class loadClass(String name) throws java.net.MalformedURLException, ClassNotFoundException;
#   public abstract Class loadClass(java.net.URL codebase, String name) throws java.net.MalformedURLException,
        ClassNotFoundException;
}
```

LogStream

Java 1.1; Deprecated in Java 1.2

java.rmi.server

This class provides the server with an output stream to an error log. LogStreams can't be created directly by the application. Instead, a handle on a LogStream is obtained by calling the static log() method with the name of the desired log. If the named log doesn't exist, the default log is returned. The default PrintStream used to create new LogStreams can be gotten through the getDefaultStream() method, and set using the setDefaultStream() method.

```
Object ─ OutputStream ─ FilterOutputStream ─ PrintStream ─ LogStream
```

```
public class LogStream extends PrintStream {
// No Constructor
// Public Constants
    public static final int BRIEF;                                              =10
    public static final int SILENT;                                              =0
    public static final int VERBOSE;                                            =20
// Deprecated Public Methods
#   public static PrintStream getDefaultStream();                        synchronized
#   public java.io.OutputStream getOutputStream();                       synchronized
#   public static LogStream log(String name);
#   public static int parseLevel(String s);
#   public static void setDefaultStream(PrintStream newDefault);         synchronized
#   public void setOutputStream(java.io.OutputStream out);               synchronized
#   public String toString();                                        Overrides:Object
#   public void write(int b);                                    Overrides:PrintStream
#   public void write(byte[ ] b, int off, int len);             Overrides:PrintStream
}
```

Returned By: LogStream.log()

ObjID   Java 1.1

java.rmi.server   *serializable*

An ObjID is used on an object server to uniquely identify exported remote objects. Its
primary use in an RMI server is during distributed garbage collection.

The equals() method is overridden from Object to return true only if the objects identified
by the two ObjID's are equal. The ObjID class also has read() and write() methods that
serve to marshal and unmarshal an ObjID from I/O streams.

```
Object ─ ObjID ┈ Serializable
```

```
public final class ObjID implements Serializable {
// Public Constructors
    public ObjID();
    public ObjID(int objNum);
// Public Constants
1.2 public static final int ACTIVATOR_ID;                                        =1
    public static final int DGC_ID;                                              =2
    public static final int REGISTRY_ID;                                         =0
// Public Class Methods
    public static ObjID read(ObjectInput in) throws IOException;
// Public Instance Methods
    public void write(ObjectOutput out) throws IOException;
// Public Methods Overriding Object
    public boolean equals(Object obj);
    public int hashCode();
    public String toString();
}
```

Passed To: java.rmi.dgc.DGC.{clean(), dirty()}

Returned By: ObjID.read()

Operation   Java 1.1; Deprecated in Java 1.2
java.rmi.server

An Operation contains a description of a method on a remote object.

```
public class Operation {
// Public Constructors
#    public Operation(String op);
// Deprecated Public Methods
#    public String getOperation();
#    public String toString();                              Overrides:Object
}
```

Passed To: RemoteRef.newCall()

Returned By: Skeleton.getOperations()

RemoteCall   Java 1.1; Deprecated in Java 1.2
java.rmi.server

A RemoteCall is the interface used by stubs and skeletons to perform remote method calls. The getInputStream() and getOutputStream() methods return streams that can be used to marshal arguments or return values, and unmarshal them on the other end of the method call.

```
public interface RemoteCall {
// Deprecated Public Methods
#    public abstract void done() throws IOException;
#    public abstract void executeCall() throws Exception;
#    public abstract ObjectInput getInputStream() throws IOException;
#    public abstract ObjectOutput getOutputStream() throws IOException;
#    public abstract ObjectOutput getResultStream(boolean success) throws IOException, StreamCorruptedException;
#    public abstract void releaseInputStream() throws IOException;
#    public abstract void releaseOutputStream() throws IOException;
}
```

Passed To: RemoteRef.{done(), invoke()}, Skeleton.dispatch()

Returned By: RemoteRef.newCall()

RemoteObject   Java 1.1
java.rmi.server   *serializable remote*

The RemoteObject class reimplements key Object methods for remote objects and maintains a RemoteRef object that is a handle to the actual remote object. The equals() implementation returns true only if the two referenced remote objects are equal. The hashCode() method is implemented so that every remote stub that refers to the same remote object will have the same hash code.

```
Object ─ RemoteObject
Remote    Serializable
```

```
public abstract class RemoteObject implements Remote, Serializable {
// Protected Constructors
     protected RemoteObject();
     protected RemoteObject(RemoteRef newref);
// Public Class Methods
1.2 public static Remote toStub(Remote obj) throws NoSuchObjectException;
```

```
// Public Instance Methods
1.2 public RemoteRef getRef();
// Public Methods Overriding Object
    public boolean equals(Object obj);
    public int hashCode();
    public String toString();
// Protected Instance Fields
    protected transient RemoteRef ref;
}
```

Subclasses: RemoteServer, RemoteStub

Passed To: RemoteRef.newCall()

RemoteRef

java.rmi.server

A handle on the object implementing a remote object reference. Each RemoteObject contains a RemoteRef which acts as its interface to the actual remote object it represents. Normally, you won't need to interact directly with RemoteRefs from your application code. Rather, application code will interact with RemoteObjects, which use their internal RemoteRefs to perform remote method invocations.

The newCall() method is used to create a call object for invoking a remote method on the referenced object. The invoke() method actually executes a remote method invocation. If a remote method returns successfully, then the done() method is called to clean up the connection to the remote object.

The remoteEquals(), remoteHashCode() and remoteToString() methods on RemoteRef are used by RemoteObjects to implement the remote versions of the equals(), hashCode() and toString() methods.

```
Serializable ·· Externalizable ·· RemoteRef

public interface RemoteRef extends Externalizable {
// Public Constants
    public static final String packagePrefix;                                     ="sun.rmi.server"
1.2 public static final long serialVersionUID;                                =3632638527362204081
// Public Instance Methods
    public abstract String getRefClass(ObjectOutput out);
1.2 public abstract Object invoke(Remote obj, java.lang.reflect.Method method, Object[] params, long opnum)
        throws Exception;
    public abstract boolean remoteEquals(RemoteRef obj);
    public abstract int remoteHashCode();
    public abstract String remoteToString();
// Deprecated Public Methods
#   public abstract void done(RemoteCall call) throws RemoteException;
#   public abstract void invoke(RemoteCall call) throws Exception;
#   public abstract RemoteCall newCall(RemoteObject obj, Operation[] op, int opnum, long hash)
        throws RemoteException;
}
```

Implementations: ServerRef

Passed To: java.rmi.activation.ActivationGroup_Stub.ActivationGroup_Stub(), RemoteObject.RemoteObject(), RemoteRef.remoteEquals(), RemoteServer.RemoteServer(), RemoteStub.{RemoteStub(), setRef()}

Returned By: RemoteObject.getRef()

Type Of: RemoteObject.ref

RemoteServer

java.rmi.server

serializable remote

This class acts as an abstract base class for all remote object server implementations. The intent is for sub-classes to implement the semantics of the remote object (e.g. multicast remote objects, replicated objects). In the current version of RMI, the only concrete sub-class provided is UnicastRemoteServer, which implements a non-replicated remote object.

The getClientHost() method returns the name of the host for the client being served in the current thread. The getLog() and setLog() methods access the call log for this RemoteServer.

```
public abstract class RemoteServer extends RemoteObject {
// Protected Constructors
    protected RemoteServer();
    protected RemoteServer(RemoteRef ref);
// Public Class Methods
    public static String getClientHost() throws ServerNotActiveException;
    public static PrintStream getLog();
    public static void setLog(java.io.OutputStream out);
}
```

Subclasses: java.rmi.activation.Activatable, UnicastRemoteObject

RemoteStub

java.rmi.server

serializable remote

All client stub classes generated by the *rmic* compiler are derived from this abstract class. A client receives a RemoteStub when it successfully looks up a remote object through the RMI registry. A client stub serves as a client interface to the remote object it references, converting method calls on its interface into remote method invocations on the remote object implementation.

```
public abstract class RemoteStub extends RemoteObject {
// Protected Constructors
    protected RemoteStub();
    protected RemoteStub(RemoteRef ref);
// Deprecated Protected Methods
#   protected static void setRef(RemoteStub stub, RemoteRef ref);
}
```

Subclasses: java.rmi.activation.ActivationGroup_Stub

Passed To: RemoteStub.setRef()

Returned By: ServerRef.exportObject(), UnicastRemoteObject.exportObject()

RMIClassLoader

java.rmi.server

This class loads classes over the network using URLs. The class has two loadClass() methods, one for loading a class from a given (absolute) URL, and another for loading a class from a given (relative) URL, starting at a particular codebase.

```
public class RMIClassLoader {
// No Constructor
// Public Class Methods
1.2 public static String getClassAnnotation(Class cl);
1.3 public static ClassLoader getClassLoader(String codebase) throws java.net.MalformedURLException,
        java.lang.SecurityException;
1.4 public static RMIClassLoaderSpi getDefaultProviderInstance();
    public static Class loadClass(java.net.URL codebase, String name) throws java.net.MalformedURLException,
        ClassNotFoundException;
1.2 public static Class loadClass(String codebase, String name) throws java.net.MalformedURLException,
        ClassNotFoundException;
1.4 public static Class loadClass(String codebase, String name, ClassLoader defaultLoader)
        throws java.net.MalformedURLException, ClassNotFoundException;
1.4 public static Class loadProxyClass(String codebase, String[] interfaces, ClassLoader defaultLoader)
        throws ClassNotFoundException, java.net.MalformedURLException;
// Deprecated Public Methods
#   public static Object getSecurityContext(ClassLoader loader);
#   public static Class loadClass(String name) throws java.net.MalformedURLException, ClassNotFoundException;
}
```

RMIClassLoaderSpi

java.rmi.server

The service-provider interface for impelementing custom RMI class loaders. A concrete subclass of this interface can be used to provide a custom backend to the RMIClassLoader interface. Added as of JDK 1.4.

```
public abstract class RMIClassLoaderSpi {
// Public Constructors
    public RMIClassLoaderSpi();
// Public Instance Methods
    public abstract String getClassAnnotation(Class cl);
    public abstract ClassLoader getClassLoader(String codebase) throws java.net.MalformedURLException;
    public abstract Class loadClass(String codebase, String name, ClassLoader defaultLoader)
        throws java.net.MalformedURLException, ClassNotFoundException;
    public abstract Class loadProxyClass(String codebase, String[] interfaces, ClassLoader defaultLoader)
        throws java.net.MalformedURLException, ClassNotFoundException;
}
```

Returned By: RMIClassLoader.getDefaultProviderInstance()

RMIClientSocketFactory

java.rmi.server

This interface represents a source for client sockets that is used by the RMI internals to make client connections during RMI calls. It's possible to provide a custom socket factory to be used with a particular remote object, by using the appropriate constructors on the UnicastRemoteObject or Activatable classes, or with a particular registry, by using the appropriate LocateRegistry.createRegistry() method. This can be useful in situations where a firewall lies between the client and the server object or remote registry, and specialized sockets are needed to negotiate the firewall protocol.

The RMIClientSocketFactory associated with a remote object is used by any remote stub references to establish connections with the server object.

```
public interface RMIClientSocketFactory {
// Public Instance Methods
    public abstract java.net.Socket createSocket(String host, int port) throws IOException;
}
```

Implementations: RMISocketFactory

Passed To: java.rmi.activation.Activatable.{Activatable(), exportObject()},
java.rmi.registry.LocateRegistry.{createRegistry(), getRegistry()}, UnicastRemoteObject.{exportObject(),
UnicastRemoteObject()}

RMIFailureHandler   Java 1.1

java.rmi.server

The failure() method on the current RMIFailureHandler is called when the RMI communications system fails to create a Socket or ServerSocket. The current handler is set using the setFailureHandler() method on RMISocketFactory. The failure() method returns a boolean value that indicates whether the RMI system should retry the socket connection.

```
public interface RMIFailureHandler {
// Public Instance Methods
    public abstract boolean failure(Exception ex);
}
```

Passed To: RMISocketFactory.setFailureHandler()

Returned By: RMISocketFactory.getFailureHandler()

RMIServerSocketFactory   Java 1.2

java.rmi.server

This interface represents a source for server sockets that is used by the RMI internals to make client connections during RMI calls. It's possible to provide a custom socket factory to be used with a particular remote object, by using the appropriate constructors on the UnicastRemoteObject or Activatable classes, or with a particular registry, by using the appropriate LocateRegistry.createRegistry() method. This can be useful in situations where a firewall lies between the client and the server object or the remote registry, and specialized sockets are needed to negotiate the firewall protocol.

The RMIServerSocketFactory is used to create ServerSockets that are used by remote objects to accept client connections.

```
public interface RMIServerSocketFactory {
// Public Instance Methods
    public abstract java.net.ServerSocket createServerSocket(int port) throws IOException;
}
```

Implementations: RMISocketFactory

Passed To: java.rmi.activation.Activatable.{Activatable(), exportObject()},
java.rmi.registry.LocateRegistry.createRegistry(), UnicastRemoteObject.{exportObject(),
UnicastRemoteObject()}

RMISocketFactory   Java 1.1

java.rmi.server

This abstract class provides an interface for the RMI internals to use to create sockets for both client and server communications. It extends both the RMIClientSocketFactory and

---

the RMIServerSocketFactory interfaces, so it can create either Sockets for clients, or Server-Sockets for servers. The factory maintains a RMIFailureHandler that it uses to deal with failures encountered while attempting to create sockets. If an error is encountered while creating a socket, the failure() method on the current RMIFailureHandler is called. If the return value is true, then the RMISocketFactory attempts the socket creation again, otherwise the factory gives up and throws an IOException.

Client sockets are created using the createSocket() method (inherited from RMIClientSocketFactory), while server sockets are created using the createServerSocket() method (inherited from RMIServerSocketFactory). The current RMISocketFactory for the runtime is accessed using the static getSocketFactory() and setSocketFactory() methods. The RMIFailureHandler for the current factory is accessed using the getFailureHandler() and setFailureHandler() methods.

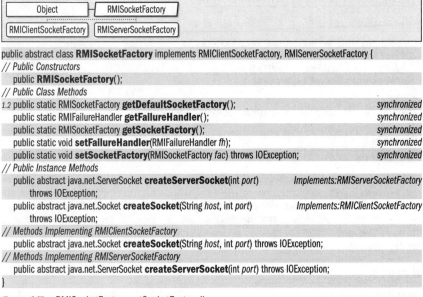

```
public abstract class RMISocketFactory implements RMIClientSocketFactory, RMIServerSocketFactory {
// Public Constructors
    public RMISocketFactory();
// Public Class Methods
1.2 public static RMISocketFactory getDefaultSocketFactory();                              synchronized
    public static RMIFailureHandler getFailureHandler();                                   synchronized
    public static RMISocketFactory getSocketFactory();                                     synchronized
    public static void setFailureHandler(RMIFailureHandler fh);                            synchronized
    public static void setSocketFactory(RMISocketFactory fac) throws IOException;          synchronized
// Public Instance Methods
    public abstract java.net.ServerSocket createServerSocket(int port)            Implements:RMIServerSocketFactory
        throws IOException;
    public abstract java.net.Socket createSocket(String host, int port)           Implements:RMIClientSocketFactory
        throws IOException;
// Methods Implementing RMIClientSocketFactory
    public abstract java.net.Socket createSocket(String host, int port) throws IOException;
// Methods Implementing RMIServerSocketFactory
    public abstract java.net.ServerSocket createServerSocket(int port) throws IOException;
}
```

Passed To: RMISocketFactory.setSocketFactory()

Returned By: RMISocketFactory.{getDefaultSocketFactory(), getSocketFactory()}

ServerCloneException   Java 1.1

java.rmi.server   *serializable checked*

This exception is thrown if an attempt to clone a RemoteServer object fails while the clone is being exported. The nested exception is the RemoteException that was thrown during the cloning operation.

```
public class ServerCloneException extends CloneNotSupportedException {
// Public Constructors
    public ServerCloneException(String s);
    public ServerCloneException(String s, Exception ex);
// Public Methods Overriding Throwable
1.4 public Throwable getCause();
```

```
    public String getMessage();
// Public Instance Fields
    public Exception detail;
}
```

ServerNotActiveException   Java 1.1

java.rmi.server   *serializable checked*

This exception is thrown if the getClientHost() method is called on a RemoteServer when
the server isn't handling a remote method call.

```
Object ─ Throwable ─ Exception ─ ServerNotActiveException
         Serializable
```

```
public class ServerNotActiveException extends Exception {
// Public Constructors
    public ServerNotActiveException();
    public ServerNotActiveException(String s);
}
```

Thrown By: RemoteServer.getClientHost(), ServerRef.getClientHost()

ServerRef   Java 1.1

java.rmi.server   *serializable*

This is an interface to the server-side implementation of a remote object. The getClien-
tHost() method returns the name of the host whose remote method call is currently
being serviced by the object implementation. If the server object is not servicing a
remote method call when getClientHost() is called, then a ServerNotActiveException is
thrown. The exportObject() method is meant to either create or find a client stub for the
given object implementation, using the data provided.

```
Serializable ┈ Externalizable ┈ RemoteRef ┈ ServerRef
```

```
public interface ServerRef extends RemoteRef {
// Public Constants
1.2 public static final long serialVersionUID;                         =-4557750989390278438
// Public Instance Methods
    public abstract RemoteStub exportObject(Remote obj, Object data) throws RemoteException;
    public abstract String getClientHost() throws ServerNotActiveException;
}
```

Skeleton   Java 1.1; Deprecated in Java 1.2

java.rmi.server

A Skeleton object lives with a server-side object implementation, dispatching method
calls to the remote object implementation. Server implementations generated by the
rmic compiler use Skeletons.

The dispatch() method invokes the method specified by the operation number opnum on
the object implementation obj. It unmarshals the method arguments from the input
stream obtained from the RemoteCall argument, passes them to the appropriate method
on the Remote object, marshals the results (if any), and returns them to the caller using
the output stream on the RemoteCall. The getOperations() method returns an array of Operation objects, which represent the methods available on the remote object.

```
public interface Skeleton {
// Deprecated Public Methods
#    public abstract void dispatch(Remote obj, RemoteCall theCall, int opnum, long hash) throws Exception;
#    public abstract Operation[ ] getOperations();
}
```

SkeletonMismatchException

java.rmi.server

serializable checked

This RemoteException is thrown during a remote method call if a mismatch is detected on the server between the hash code of the client stub and the has code of the server implementation. It is usually received by the client wrapped in a ServerException.

Object — Throwable — Exception — IOException — RemoteException — SkeletonMismatchException

Serializable

```
public class SkeletonMismatchException extends RemoteException {
// Public Constructors
#    public SkeletonMismatchException(String s);
}
```

SkeletonNotFoundException

Java 1.1; Deprecated in Java 1.2

java.rmi.server

serializable checked

This RemoteException is thrown during the export of a remote object, if the corresponding skeleton class for the object either can't be found or can't be loaded for some reason.

Object — Throwable — Exception — IOException — RemoteException — SkeletonNotFoundException

Serializable

```
public class SkeletonNotFoundException extends RemoteException {
// Public Constructors
    public SkeletonNotFoundException(String s);
    public SkeletonNotFoundException(String s, Exception ex);
}
```

SocketSecurityException

Java 1.1

java.rmi.server

serializable checked

This exception is a sub-class of ExportException that is thrown if a socket security violation is encountered while attempting to export a remote object. An example would be an attempt to export an object on an illegal port.

Object — Throwable — Exception — IOException — RemoteException — ExportException — SocketSecurityException

Serializable

```
public class SocketSecurityException extends ExportException {
// Public Constructors
    public SocketSecurityException(String s);
    public SocketSecurityException(String s, Exception ex);
}
```

UID

java.rmi.server

A UID is an identifier that is unique with respect to a particular host. UIDs are used internally by RMI's distributed garbage collector and are generally not dealt with directly in application code.

```
Object ├─ UID ┈┈ Serializable

public final class UID implements Serializable {
// Public Constructors
    public UID();
    public UID(short num);
// Public Class Methods
    public static UID read(DataInput in) throws IOException;
// Public Instance Methods
    public void write(DataOutput out) throws IOException;
// Public Methods Overriding Object
    public boolean equals(Object obj);
    public int hashCode();
    public String toString();
}
```

Returned By: UID.read()

UnicastRemoteObject

java.rmi.server

This represents a non-replicated remote object., e.g., one that lives as a singular implementation on a server, with point-to-point connections to each client. through reference stubs. This remote server class does not implement persistence, so client references to the object are only valid during the lifetime of the object.

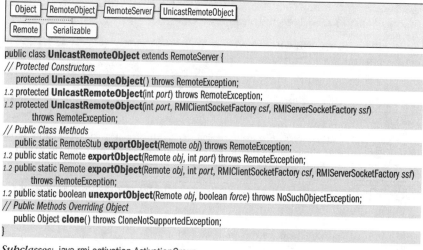

```
Object ─ RemoteObject ─ RemoteServer ─ UnicastRemoteObject
Remote      Serializable

public class UnicastRemoteObject extends RemoteServer {
// Protected Constructors
    protected UnicastRemoteObject() throws RemoteException;
1.2 protected UnicastRemoteObject(int port) throws RemoteException;
1.2 protected UnicastRemoteObject(int port, RMIClientSocketFactory csf, RMIServerSocketFactory ssf)
        throws RemoteException;
// Public Class Methods
    public static RemoteStub exportObject(Remote obj) throws RemoteException;
1.2 public static Remote exportObject(Remote obj, int port) throws RemoteException;
1.2 public static Remote exportObject(Remote obj, int port, RMIClientSocketFactory csf, RMIServerSocketFactory ssf)
        throws RemoteException;
1.2 public static boolean unexportObject(Remote obj, boolean force) throws NoSuchObjectException;
// Public Methods Overriding Object
    public Object clone() throws CloneNotSupportedException;
}
```

Subclasses: java.rmi.activation.ActivationGroup

Unreferenced

java.rmi.server

If a server object implements this interface, then the unreferenced() method is called by the RMI runtime when the last client reference to a remote object is dropped. A remote object shouldn't be garbage collected until all of its remote and local references are gone. So the unreferenced() method isn't a trigger for an object to be finalized, but rather a chance for the remote object to respond appropriately when its client reference count goes to zero. The unreferenced object could, for example, start a timer countdown to move the object to persistent storage after a given idle time with respect to remote clients.

```
public interface Unreferenced {
// Public Instance Methods
    public abstract void unreferenced();
}
```

CHAPTER 23

java.sql

Package java.sql

The java.sql package contains the core JDBC 3.0 API that is used for sending SQL (Structured Query Language) statements to relational databases and for retrieving the results of executing those SQL statements. The JDBC API intially became part of the Java API in Java 1.1. JDBC 3.0 is part of the J2SE version 1.4.

The Driver interface represents a specific JDBC implementation for a particular database system. Connection represents a connection to a database. The Statement, PreparedStatement, and CallableStatement interfaces support the execution of various kinds of SQL statements. ResultSet is a set of results returned by the database in response to a SQL query. The ResultSetMetaData interface provides metadata about a result set, while DatabaseMetaData provides metadata about the database as a whole.

Interfaces:

public interface **Array**;
public interface **Blob**;
public interface **CallableStatement** extends PreparedStatement;
public interface **Clob**;
public interface **Connection**;
public interface **DatabaseMetaData**;
public interface **Driver**;
public interface **ParameterMetaData**;
public interface **PreparedStatement** extends Statement;
public interface **Ref**;
public interface **ResultSet**;
public interface **ResultSetMetaData**;
public interface **Savepoint**;
public interface **SQLData**;
public interface **SQLInput**;
public interface **SQLOutput**;
public interface **Statement**;

public interface **Struct**;

Classes:

public class **Date** extends java.util.Date;
public class **DriverManager**;
public class **DriverPropertyInfo**;
public final class **SQLPermission** extends java.security.BasicPermission;
public class **Time** extends java.util.Date;
public class **Timestamp** extends java.util.Date;
public class **Types**;

Exceptions:

public class **SQLException** extends Exception;
   └ public class **BatchUpdateException** extends SQLException;
   └ public class **SQLWarning** extends SQLException;
      └ public class **DataTruncation** extends SQLWarning;

Array

java.sql

Provides an interface to SQL ARRAY objects. Each getArray() method returns a standard Java array of objects of the type returned by getBaseType(). Two of the getArray() methods support a java.util.Map parameter that can be used to customize the SQL-type-to-Java-object mapping. The contents of the array can also be returned as a ResultSet using the various getResultSet() methods.

```
public interface Array {
// Public Instance Methods
    public abstract Object getArray() throws SQLException;
    public abstract Object getArray(java.util.Map map) throws SQLException;
    public abstract Object getArray(long index, int count) throws SQLException;
    public abstract Object getArray(long index, int count, java.util.Map map) throws SQLException;
    public abstract int getBaseType() throws SQLException;
    public abstract String getBaseTypeName() throws SQLException;
    public abstract java.sql.ResultSet getResultSet() throws SQLException;
    public abstract java.sql.ResultSet getResultSet(java.util.Map map) throws SQLException;
    public abstract java.sql.ResultSet getResultSet(long index, int count) throws SQLException;
    public abstract java.sql.ResultSet getResultSet(long index, int count, java.util.Map map) throws SQLException;
}
```

Passed To: PreparedStatement.setArray(), java.sql.ResultSet.updateArray(), SQLOutput.writeArray(), javax.sql.RowSet.setArray()

Returned By: CallableStatement.getArray(), java.sql.ResultSet.getArray(), SQLInput.readArray()

BatchUpdateException

java.sql   *serializable checked*

This exception, which is a subclass of SQLException, is thrown when a batch update operation fails. The exception includes a method, getUpdateCounts(), that returns an array of int values, where the values correspond to the update counts for the successful update operations in the batch.

Object — Throwable — Exception — SQLException — BatchUpdateException

Serializable

```
public class BatchUpdateException extends SQLException {
// Public Constructors
    public BatchUpdateException();
    public BatchUpdateException(int[ ] updateCounts);
    public BatchUpdateException(String reason, int[ ] updateCounts);
    public BatchUpdateException(String reason, String SQLState, int[ ] updateCounts);
    public BatchUpdateException(String reason, String SQLState, int vendorCode, int[ ] updateCounts);
// Public Instance Methods
    public int[ ] getUpdateCounts();                                                    default:null
}
```

Blob   Java 1.2

java.sql

The Blob interface encapsulates a SQL BLOB (binary large object) field. The interface actually contains a pointer to the BLOB within the database, rather than the complete (and potentially very large) object. Data can be retrieved via a java.io.InputStreamreturned by getInputStream() or as an array of bytes returned by getBytes(). The length() method returns the number of bytes in the BLOB. The position() methods scan the contents of the Blob for a particular content sequence, represented by either another Blobobject or a byte array. (The position() methods do not provide the current read-index within the BLOB). JDBC 3.0 adds the setBinaryStream() and setBytes() methods, which allow JDBC applications to create and edit BLOB data as well as reading it.

```
public interface Blob {
// Public Instance Methods
    public abstract java.io.InputStream getBinaryStream() throws SQLException;
    public abstract byte[ ] getBytes(long pos, int length) throws SQLException;
    public abstract long length() throws SQLException;
    public abstract long position(Blob pattern, long start) throws SQLException;
    public abstract long position(byte[ ] pattern, long start) throws SQLException;
1.4 public abstract java.io.OutputStream setBinaryStream(long pos) throws SQLException;
1.4 public abstract int setBytes(long pos, byte[ ] bytes) throws SQLException;
1.4 public abstract int setBytes(long pos, byte[ ] bytes, int offset, int len) throws SQLException;
1.4 public abstract void truncate(long len) throws SQLException;
}
```

Passed To: Blob.position(), PreparedStatement.setBlob(), java.sql.ResultSet.updateBlob(), SQLOutput.writeBlob(), javax.sql.RowSet.setBlob()

Returned By: CallableStatement.getBlob(), java.sql.ResultSet.getBlob(), SQLInput.readBlob()

CallableStatement   Java 1.1

java.sql

The CallableStatement interface allows programs to access SQL stored procedures within the database. You create a CallableStatement with the prepareCall() method of Connection. Question mark characters (?) are used as placeholders for input and output values in the syntax used to call stored procedures:

```
{? = call procedure_name[(?[,?...])]}{call procedure_name[(?[,?...])]}
```

Parameters are numbered sequentially starting from 1. Input parameters are set with the same setXXX() methods as in a PreparedStatement. Output parameters must be registered using the registerOutParameter() methods, and may be retrieved after the statement executes using the getXXX() methods, which are identical to those in ResultSet. To execute a statement, you call execute(), which is inherited from PreparedStatement.

```
┌─────────────┐   ┌──────────────────┐   ┌────────────────────┐
│ Statement   │┈┈┤ PreparedStatement │┈┈┤ CallableStatement  │
└─────────────┘   └──────────────────┘   └────────────────────┘
```

public interface **CallableStatement** extends PreparedStatement {
// *Public Instance Methods*
1.2 public abstract java.sql.Array **getArray**(int *i*) throws SQLException;
1.4 public abstract java.sql.Array **getArray**(String *parameterName*) throws SQLException;
1.2 public abstract java.math.BigDecimal **getBigDecimal**(int *parameterIndex*) throws SQLException;
1.4 public abstract java.math.BigDecimal **getBigDecimal**(String *parameterName*) throws SQLException;
1.4 public abstract Blob **getBlob**(String *parameterName*) throws SQLException;
1.2 public abstract Blob **getBlob**(int *i*) throws SQLException;
1.4 public abstract boolean **getBoolean**(String *parameterName*) throws SQLException;
    public abstract boolean **getBoolean**(int *parameterIndex*) throws SQLException;
1.4 public abstract byte **getByte**(String *parameterName*) throws SQLException;
    public abstract byte **getByte**(int *parameterIndex*) throws SQLException;
    public abstract byte[ ] **getBytes**(int *parameterIndex*) throws SQLException;
1.4 public abstract byte[ ] **getBytes**(String *parameterName*) throws SQLException;
1.2 public abstract Clob **getClob**(int *i*) throws SQLException;
1.4 public abstract Clob **getClob**(String *parameterName*) throws SQLException;
1.4 public abstract java.sql.Date **getDate**(String *parameterName*) throws SQLException;
    public abstract java.sql.Date **getDate**(int *parameterIndex*) throws SQLException;
1.2 public abstract java.sql.Date **getDate**(int *parameterIndex*, java.util.Calendar *cal*) throws SQLException;
1.4 public abstract java.sql.Date **getDate**(String *parameterName*, java.util.Calendar *cal*) throws SQLException;
    public abstract double **getDouble**(int *parameterIndex*) throws SQLException;
1.4 public abstract double **getDouble**(String *parameterName*) throws SQLException;
    public abstract float **getFloat**(int *parameterIndex*) throws SQLException;
1.4 public abstract float **getFloat**(String *parameterName*) throws SQLException;
    public abstract int **getInt**(int *parameterIndex*) throws SQLException;
1.4 public abstract int **getInt**(String *parameterName*) throws SQLException;
1.4 public abstract long **getLong**(String *parameterName*) throws SQLException;
    public abstract long **getLong**(int *parameterIndex*) throws SQLException;
1.4 public abstract Object **getObject**(String *parameterName*) throws SQLException;
    public abstract Object **getObject**(int *parameterIndex*) throws SQLException;
1.4 public abstract Object **getObject**(String *parameterName*, java.util.Map *map*) throws SQLException;
1.2 public abstract Object **getObject**(int *i*, java.util.Map *map*) throws SQLException;
1.4 public abstract Ref **getRef**(String *parameterName*) throws SQLException;
1.2 public abstract Ref **getRef**(int *i*) throws SQLException;
    public abstract short **getShort**(int *parameterIndex*) throws SQLException;
1.4 public abstract short **getShort**(String *parameterName*) throws SQLException;
1.4 public abstract String **getString**(String *parameterName*) throws SQLException;
    public abstract String **getString**(int *parameterIndex*) throws SQLException;
1.4 public abstract Time **getTime**(String *parameterName*) throws SQLException;
    public abstract Time **getTime**(int *parameterIndex*) throws SQLException;
1.4 public abstract Time **getTime**(String *parameterName*, java.util.Calendar *cal*) throws SQLException;
1.2 public abstract Time **getTime**(int *parameterIndex*, java.util.Calendar *cal*) throws SQLException;
1.4 public abstract Timestamp **getTimestamp**(String *parameterName*) throws SQLException;
    public abstract Timestamp **getTimestamp**(int *parameterIndex*) throws SQLException;
1.2 public abstract Timestamp **getTimestamp**(int *parameterIndex*, java.util.Calendar *cal*) throws SQLException;
1.4 public abstract Timestamp **getTimestamp**(String *parameterName*, java.util.Calendar *cal*) throws SQLException;
1.4 public abstract java.net.URL **getURL**(String *parameterName*) throws SQLException;
1.4 public abstract java.net.URL **getURL**(int *parameterIndex*) throws SQLException;
1.4 public abstract void **registerOutParameter**(String *parameterName*, int *sqlType*) throws SQLException;
    public abstract void **registerOutParameter**(int *parameterIndex*, int *sqlType*) throws SQLException;
1.4 public abstract void **registerOutParameter**(String *parameterName*, int *sqlType*, String *typeName*)
    throws SQLException;

1.4 public abstract void **registerOutParameter**(String *parameterName*, int *sqlType*, int *scale*) throws SQLException;
1.2 public abstract void **registerOutParameter**(int *paramIndex*, int *sqlType*, String *typeName*) throws SQLException;
　　public abstract void **registerOutParameter**(int *parameterIndex*, int *sqlType*, int *scale*) throws SQLException;
1.4 public abstract void **setAsciiStream**(String *parameterName*, java.io.InputStream *x*, int *length*)
　　　　throws SQLException;
1.4 public abstract void **setBigDecimal**(String *parameterName*, java.math.BigDecimal *x*) throws SQLException;
1.4 public abstract void **setBinaryStream**(String *parameterName*, java.io.InputStream *x*, int *length*)
　　　　throws SQLException;
1.4 public abstract void **setBoolean**(String *parameterName*, boolean *x*) throws SQLException;
1.4 public abstract void **setByte**(String *parameterName*, byte *x*) throws SQLException;
1.4 public abstract void **setBytes**(String *parameterName*, byte[ ] *x*) throws SQLException;
1.4 public abstract void **setCharacterStream**(String *parameterName*, Reader *reader*, int *length*) throws SQLException;
1.4 public abstract void **setDate**(String *parameterName*, java.sql.Date *x*) throws SQLException;
1.4 public abstract void **setDate**(String *parameterName*, java.sql.Date *x*, java.util.Calendar *cal*) throws SQLException;
1.4 public abstract void **setDouble**(String *parameterName*, double *x*) throws SQLException;
1.4 public abstract void **setFloat**(String *parameterName*, float *x*) throws SQLException;
1.4 public abstract void **setInt**(String *parameterName*, int *x*) throws SQLException;
1.4 public abstract void **setLong**(String *parameterName*, long *x*) throws SQLException;
1.4 public abstract void **setNull**(String *parameterName*, int *sqlType*) throws SQLException;
1.4 public abstract void **setNull**(String *parameterName*, int *sqlType*, String *typeName*) throws SQLException;
1.4 public abstract void **setObject**(String *parameterName*, Object *x*) throws SQLException;
1.4 public abstract void **setObject**(String *parameterName*, Object *x*, int *targetSqlType*) throws SQLException;
1.4 public abstract void **setObject**(String *parameterName*, Object *x*, int *targetSqlType*, int *scale*) throws SQLException;
1.4 public abstract void **setShort**(String *parameterName*, short *x*) throws SQLException;
1.4 public abstract void **setString**(String *parameterName*, String *x*) throws SQLException;
1.4 public abstract void **setTime**(String *parameterName*, Time *x*) throws SQLException;
1.4 public abstract void **setTime**(String *parameterName*, Time *x*, java.util.Calendar *cal*) throws SQLException;
1.4 public abstract void **setTimestamp**(String *parameterName*, Timestamp *x*) throws SQLException;
1.4 public abstract void **setTimestamp**(String *parameterName*, Timestamp *x*, java.util.Calendar *cal*)
　　　　throws SQLException;
1.4 public abstract void **setURL**(String *parameterName*, java.net.URL *val*) throws SQLException;
　　public abstract boolean **wasNull**( ) throws SQLException;
// *Deprecated Public Methods*
# 　public abstract java.math.BigDecimal **getBigDecimal**(int *parameterIndex*, int *scale*) throws SQLException;
}

Returned By: java.sql.Connection.prepareCall()

Clob

java.sql

The Clob interface encapsulates a SQL CLOB (character large object) field. The interface actually contains a pointer to the CLOB within the database, rather than the complete character string. Data is retrieved via getAsciiStream(), which returns an InputStream, or via getCharacterStream(), which returns a Reader. The getSubString()method returns a specific substring within the CLOB, while the position()methods search the CLOB for a pattern and return the index of the pattern's first appearance. JDBC 3.0 adds the setString(), setAsciiStream(), and setCharacterStream() methods, which allow JDBC applications to create and edit CLOB data in addition to reading it.

public interface **Clob** {
// *Public Instance Methods*
　public abstract java.io.InputStream **getAsciiStream**( ) throws SQLException;
　public abstract Reader **getCharacterStream**( ) throws SQLException;
　public abstract String **getSubString**(long *pos*, int *length*) throws SQLException;
　public abstract long **length**( ) throws SQLException;

```
    public abstract long position(Clob searchstr, long start) throws SQLException;
    public abstract long position(String searchstr, long start) throws SQLException;
1.4 public abstract java.io.OutputStream setAsciiStream(long pos) throws SQLException;
1.4 public abstract Writer setCharacterStream(long pos) throws SQLException;
1.4 public abstract int setString(long pos, String str) throws SQLException;
1.4 public abstract int setString(long pos, String str, int offset, int len) throws SQLException;
1.4 public abstract void truncate(long len) throws SQLException;
}
```

Passed To: Clob.position(), PreparedStatement.setClob(), java.sql.ResultSet.updateClob(), SQLOutput.writeClob(), javax.sql.RowSet.setClob()

Returned By: CallableStatement.getClob(), java.sql.ResultSet.getClob(), SQLInput.readClob()

Connection   Java 1.1

java.sql

The Connection interface represents an individual database connection. The object includes factory methods for Statement, PreparedStatement and CallableStatement objects and a number of transaction control methods (setAutoCommit(), commit(), rollback(), getAutoCommit(), setTransactionIsolation(), getTransactionIsolation()). Other methods provide information about the database. The most important of these is getMetaData(), which returns a DatabaseMetaData object. The getWarnings() method returns any warnings pending for this connection.

Connection objects are created with the static DriverManager.getConnection() method. Newly created connections are in auto-commit mode by default, and use the default type map for mapping database entities to Java objects. The setTypeMap() method can be used to create a new type mapping for custom data types. JDBC 3.0 introduces support for savepoints through the Connection and Savepoint interfaces.

```
public interface Connection {
// Public Constants
    public static final int TRANSACTION_NONE;                                    =0
    public static final int TRANSACTION_READ_COMMITTED;                          =2
    public static final int TRANSACTION_READ_UNCOMMITTED;                        =1
    public static final int TRANSACTION_REPEATABLE_READ;                         =4
    public static final int TRANSACTION_SERIALIZABLE;                            =8
// Property Accessor Methods (by property name)
    public abstract boolean getAutoCommit() throws SQLException;
    public abstract void setAutoCommit(boolean autoCommit) throws SQLException;
    public abstract String getCatalog() throws SQLException;
    public abstract void setCatalog(String catalog) throws SQLException;
    public abstract boolean isClosed() throws SQLException;
1.4 public abstract int getHoldability() throws SQLException;
1.4 public abstract void setHoldability(int holdability) throws SQLException;
    public abstract DatabaseMetaData getMetaData() throws SQLException;
    public abstract boolean isReadOnly() throws SQLException;
    public abstract void setReadOnly(boolean readOnly) throws SQLException;
    public abstract int getTransactionIsolation() throws SQLException;
    public abstract void setTransactionIsolation(int level) throws SQLException;
1.2 public abstract java.util.Map getTypeMap() throws SQLException;
1.2 public abstract void setTypeMap(java.util.Map map) throws SQLException;
    public abstract SQLWarning getWarnings() throws SQLException;
// Public Instance Methods
    public abstract void clearWarnings() throws SQLException;
    public abstract void close() throws SQLException;
```

```
        public abstract void commit() throws SQLException;
        public abstract java.sql.Statement createStatement() throws SQLException;
1.2 public abstract java.sql.Statement createStatement(int resultSetType, int resultSetConcurrency)
            throws SQLException;
1.4 public abstract java.sql.Statement createStatement(int resultSetType, int resultSetConcurrency,
                                                int resultSetHoldability) throws SQLException;
        public abstract String nativeSQL(String sql) throws SQLException;
        public abstract CallableStatement prepareCall(String sql) throws SQLException;
1.2 public abstract CallableStatement prepareCall(String sql, int resultSetType, int resultSetConcurrency)
            throws SQLException;
1.4 public abstract CallableStatement prepareCall(String sql, int resultSetType, int resultSetConcurrency,
                                                int resultSetHoldability) throws SQLException;
        public abstract PreparedStatement prepareStatement(String sql) throws SQLException;
1.4 public abstract PreparedStatement prepareStatement(String sql, String[ ] columnNames) throws SQLException;
1.4 public abstract PreparedStatement prepareStatement(String sql, int autoGeneratedKeys) throws SQLException;
1.4 public abstract PreparedStatement prepareStatement(String sql, int[ ] columnIndexes) throws SQLException;
1.2 public abstract PreparedStatement prepareStatement(String sql, int resultSetType, int resultSetConcurrency)
            throws SQLException;
1.4 public abstract PreparedStatement prepareStatement(String sql, int resultSetType, int resultSetConcurrency,
                                                int resultSetHoldability) throws SQLException;
1.4 public abstract void releaseSavepoint(Savepoint savepoint) throws SQLException;
        public abstract void rollback() throws SQLException;
1.4 public abstract void rollback(Savepoint savepoint) throws SQLException;
1.4 public abstract Savepoint setSavepoint() throws SQLException;
1.4 public abstract Savepoint setSavepoint(String name) throws SQLException;
}
```

Returned By: DatabaseMetaData.getConnection(), Driver.connect(), DriverManager.getConnection(), java.sql.Statement.getConnection(), javax.sql.DataSource.getConnection(), javax.sql.PooledConnection.getConnection(), javax.sql.RowSetInternal.getConnection()

DatabaseMetaData   Java 1.1

java.sql

The getMetaData() method of the Connection interface returns a DatabaseMetaData object that encapsulates non-connection-dependent information about the underlying database. A number of methods return ResultSet objects that should be treated like any other ResultSet.

DatabaseMetaData methods that accept String parameters with names ending in Pattern allow for simple wildcard searching. These methods treat the % character as matching any number of characters and the _ character as matching any single character. If these parameters are set to null, pattern matching is not performed.

```
public interface DatabaseMetaData {
// Public Constants
1.4 public static final short attributeNoNulls;                                    =0
1.4 public static final short attributeNullable;                                   =1
1.4 public static final short attributeNullableUnknown;                            =2
        public static final int bestRowNotPseudo;                                  =1
        public static final int bestRowPseudo;                                     =2
        public static final int bestRowSession;                                    =2
        public static final int bestRowTemporary;                                  =0
        public static final int bestRowTransaction;                                =1
        public static final int bestRowUnknown;                                    =0
        public static final int columnNoNulls;                                     =0
```

```
      public static final int columnNullable;                              =1
      public static final int columnNullableUnknown;                       =2
      public static final int importedKeyCascade;                          =0
      public static final int importedKeyInitiallyDeferred;                =5
      public static final int importedKeyInitiallyImmediate;               =6
      public static final int importedKeyNoAction;                         =3
      public static final int importedKeyNotDeferrable;                    =7
      public static final int importedKeyRestrict;                         =1
      public static final int importedKeySetDefault;                       =4
      public static final int importedKeySetNull;                          =2
      public static final int procedureColumnIn;                           =1
      public static final int procedureColumnInOut;                        =2
      public static final int procedureColumnOut;                          =4
      public static final int procedureColumnResult;                       =3
      public static final int procedureColumnReturn;                       =5
      public static final int procedureColumnUnknown;                      =0
      public static final int procedureNoNulls;                            =0
      public static final int procedureNoResult;                           =1
      public static final int procedureNullable;                           =1
      public static final int procedureNullableUnknown;                    =2
      public static final int procedureResultUnknown;                      =0
      public static final int procedureReturnsResult;                      =2
1.4   public static final int sqlStateSQL99;                               =2
1.4   public static final int sqlStateXOpen;                               =1
      public static final short tableIndexClustered;                       =1
      public static final short tableIndexHashed;                          =2
      public static final short tableIndexOther;                           =3
      public static final short tableIndexStatistic;                       =0
      public static final int typeNoNulls;                                 =0
      public static final int typeNullable;                                =1
      public static final int typeNullableUnknown;                         =2
      public static final int typePredBasic;                               =2
      public static final int typePredChar;                                =1
      public static final int typePredNone;                                =0
      public static final int typeSearchable;                              =3
      public static final int versionColumnNotPseudo;                      =1
      public static final int versionColumnPseudo;                         =2
      public static final int versionColumnUnknown;                        =0
// Property Accessor Methods (by property name)
      public abstract boolean isCatalogAtStart() throws SQLException;
      public abstract java.sql.ResultSet getCatalogs() throws SQLException;
      public abstract String getCatalogSeparator() throws SQLException;
      public abstract String getCatalogTerm() throws SQLException;
1.2   public abstract java.sql.Connection getConnection() throws SQLException;
1.4   public abstract int getDatabaseMajorVersion() throws SQLException;
1.4   public abstract int getDatabaseMinorVersion() throws SQLException;
      public abstract String getDatabaseProductName() throws SQLException;
      public abstract String getDatabaseProductVersion() throws SQLException;
      public abstract int getDefaultTransactionIsolation() throws SQLException;
      public abstract int getDriverMajorVersion();
      public abstract int getDriverMinorVersion();
      public abstract String getDriverName() throws SQLException;
      public abstract String getDriverVersion() throws SQLException;
      public abstract String getExtraNameCharacters() throws SQLException;
      public abstract String getIdentifierQuoteString() throws SQLException;
```

1.4 public abstract int **getJDBCMajorVersion**() throws SQLException;
1.4 public abstract int **getJDBCMinorVersion**() throws SQLException;
public abstract int **getMaxBinaryLiteralLength**() throws SQLException;
public abstract int **getMaxCatalogNameLength**() throws SQLException;
public abstract int **getMaxCharLiteralLength**() throws SQLException;
public abstract int **getMaxColumnNameLength**() throws SQLException;
public abstract int **getMaxColumnsInGroupBy**() throws SQLException;
public abstract int **getMaxColumnsInIndex**() throws SQLException;
public abstract int **getMaxColumnsInOrderBy**() throws SQLException;
public abstract int **getMaxColumnsInSelect**() throws SQLException;
public abstract int **getMaxColumnsInTable**() throws SQLException;
public abstract int **getMaxConnections**() throws SQLException;
public abstract int **getMaxCursorNameLength**() throws SQLException;
public abstract int **getMaxIndexLength**() throws SQLException;
public abstract int **getMaxProcedureNameLength**() throws SQLException;
public abstract int **getMaxRowSize**() throws SQLException;
public abstract int **getMaxSchemaNameLength**() throws SQLException;
public abstract int **getMaxStatementLength**() throws SQLException;
public abstract int **getMaxStatements**() throws SQLException;
public abstract int **getMaxTableNameLength**() throws SQLException;
public abstract int **getMaxTablesInSelect**() throws SQLException;
public abstract int **getMaxUserNameLength**() throws SQLException;
public abstract String **getNumericFunctions**() throws SQLException;
public abstract String **getProcedureTerm**() throws SQLException;
public abstract boolean **isReadOnly**() throws SQLException;
1.4 public abstract int **getResultSetHoldability**() throws SQLException;
public abstract java.sql.ResultSet **getSchemas**() throws SQLException;
public abstract String **getSchemaTerm**() throws SQLException;
public abstract String **getSearchStringEscape**() throws SQLException;
public abstract String **getSQLKeywords**() throws SQLException;
1.4 public abstract int **getSQLStateType**() throws SQLException;
public abstract String **getStringFunctions**() throws SQLException;
public abstract String **getSystemFunctions**() throws SQLException;
public abstract java.sql.ResultSet **getTableTypes**() throws SQLException;
public abstract String **getTimeDateFunctions**() throws SQLException;
public abstract java.sql.ResultSet **getTypeInfo**() throws SQLException;
public abstract String **getURL**() throws SQLException;
public abstract String **getUserName**() throws SQLException;
// Public Instance Methods
public abstract boolean **allProceduresAreCallable**() throws SQLException;
public abstract boolean **allTablesAreSelectable**() throws SQLException;
public abstract boolean **dataDefinitionCausesTransactionCommit**() throws SQLException;
public abstract boolean **dataDefinitionIgnoredInTransactions**() throws SQLException;
1.2 public abstract boolean **deletesAreDetected**(int *type*) throws SQLException;
public abstract boolean **doesMaxRowSizeIncludeBlobs**() throws SQLException;
1.4 public abstract java.sql.ResultSet **getAttributes**(String *catalog*, String *schemaPattern*, String *typeNamePattern*,
                                    String *attributeNamePattern*) throws SQLException;
public abstract java.sql.ResultSet **getBestRowIdentifier**(String *catalog*, String *schema*, String *table*, int *scope*,
                                    boolean *nullable*) throws SQLException;
public abstract java.sql.ResultSet **getColumnPrivileges**(String *catalog*, String *schema*, String *table*,
                                    String *columnNamePattern*) throws SQLException;
public abstract java.sql.ResultSet **getColumns**(String *catalog*, String *schemaPattern*, String *tableNamePattern*,
                                    String *columnNamePattern*) throws SQLException;

```
    public abstract java.sql.ResultSet getCrossReference(String primaryCatalog, String primarySchema,
                                        String primaryTable, String foreignCatalog,
                                        String foreignSchema, String foreignTable)
        throws SQLException;
    public abstract java.sql.ResultSet getExportedKeys(String catalog, String schema, String table)
        throws SQLException;
    public abstract java.sql.ResultSet getImportedKeys(String catalog, String schema, String table)
        throws SQLException;
    public abstract java.sql.ResultSet getIndexInfo(String catalog, String schema, String table, boolean unique,
                                        boolean approximate) throws SQLException;
    public abstract java.sql.ResultSet getPrimaryKeys(String catalog, String schema, String table)
        throws SQLException;
    public abstract java.sql.ResultSet getProcedureColumns(String catalog, String schemaPattern,
                                        String procedureNamePattern,
                                        String columnNamePattern) throws SQLException;
    public abstract java.sql.ResultSet getProcedures(String catalog, String schemaPattern,
                                        String procedureNamePattern) throws SQLException;
1.4 public abstract java.sql.ResultSet getSuperTables(String catalog, String schemaPattern, String tableNamePattern)
        throws SQLException;
1.4 public abstract java.sql.ResultSet getSuperTypes(String catalog, String schemaPattern, String typeNamePattern)
        throws SQLException;
    public abstract java.sql.ResultSet getTablePrivileges(String catalog, String schemaPattern,
                                        String tableNamePattern) throws SQLException;
    public abstract java.sql.ResultSet getTables(String catalog, String schemaPattern, String tableNamePattern,
                                        String[] types) throws SQLException;
1.2 public abstract java.sql.ResultSet getUDTs(String catalog, String schemaPattern, String typeNamePattern,
                                        int[] types) throws SQLException;
    public abstract java.sql.ResultSet getVersionColumns(String catalog, String schema, String table)
        throws SQLException;
1.2 public abstract boolean insertsAreDetected(int type) throws SQLException;
1.4 public abstract boolean locatorsUpdateCopy() throws SQLException;
    public abstract boolean nullPlusNonNullIsNull() throws SQLException;
    public abstract boolean nullsAreSortedAtEnd() throws SQLException;
    public abstract boolean nullsAreSortedAtStart() throws SQLException;
    public abstract boolean nullsAreSortedHigh() throws SQLException;
    public abstract boolean nullsAreSortedLow() throws SQLException;
1.2 public abstract boolean othersDeletesAreVisible(int type) throws SQLException;
1.2 public abstract boolean othersInsertsAreVisible(int type) throws SQLException;
1.2 public abstract boolean othersUpdatesAreVisible(int type) throws SQLException;
1.2 public abstract boolean ownDeletesAreVisible(int type) throws SQLException;
1.2 public abstract boolean ownInsertsAreVisible(int type) throws SQLException;
1.2 public abstract boolean ownUpdatesAreVisible(int type) throws SQLException;
    public abstract boolean storesLowerCaseIdentifiers() throws SQLException;
    public abstract boolean storesLowerCaseQuotedIdentifiers() throws SQLException;
    public abstract boolean storesMixedCaseIdentifiers() throws SQLException;
    public abstract boolean storesMixedCaseQuotedIdentifiers() throws SQLException;
    public abstract boolean storesUpperCaseIdentifiers() throws SQLException;
    public abstract boolean storesUpperCaseQuotedIdentifiers() throws SQLException;
    public abstract boolean supportsAlterTableWithAddColumn() throws SQLException;
    public abstract boolean supportsAlterTableWithDropColumn() throws SQLException;
    public abstract boolean supportsANSI92EntryLevelSQL() throws SQLException;
    public abstract boolean supportsANSI92FullSQL() throws SQLException;
    public abstract boolean supportsANSI92IntermediateSQL() throws SQLException;
1.2 public abstract boolean supportsBatchUpdates() throws SQLException;
    public abstract boolean supportsCatalogsInDataManipulation() throws SQLException;
```

```
     public abstract boolean supportsCatalogsInIndexDefinitions() throws SQLException;
     public abstract boolean supportsCatalogsInPrivilegeDefinitions() throws SQLException;
     public abstract boolean supportsCatalogsInProcedureCalls() throws SQLException;
     public abstract boolean supportsCatalogsInTableDefinitions() throws SQLException;
     public abstract boolean supportsColumnAliasing() throws SQLException;
     public abstract boolean supportsConvert() throws SQLException;
     public abstract boolean supportsConvert(int fromType, int toType) throws SQLException;
     public abstract boolean supportsCoreSQLGrammar() throws SQLException;
     public abstract boolean supportsCorrelatedSubqueries() throws SQLException;
     public abstract boolean supportsDataDefinitionAndDataManipulationTransactions() throws
        SQLException;
     public abstract boolean supportsDataManipulationTransactionsOnly() throws SQLException;
     public abstract boolean supportsDifferentTableCorrelationNames() throws SQLException;
     public abstract boolean supportsExpressionsInOrderBy() throws SQLException;
     public abstract boolean supportsExtendedSQLGrammar() throws SQLException;
     public abstract boolean supportsFullOuterJoins() throws SQLException;
1.4  public abstract boolean supportsGetGeneratedKeys() throws SQLException;
     public abstract boolean supportsGroupBy() throws SQLException;
     public abstract boolean supportsGroupByBeyondSelect() throws SQLException;
     public abstract boolean supportsGroupByUnrelated() throws SQLException;
     public abstract boolean supportsIntegrityEnhancementFacility() throws SQLException;
     public abstract boolean supportsLikeEscapeClause() throws SQLException;
     public abstract boolean supportsLimitedOuterJoins() throws SQLException;
     public abstract boolean supportsMinimumSQLGrammar() throws SQLException;
     public abstract boolean supportsMixedCaseIdentifiers() throws SQLException;
     public abstract boolean supportsMixedCaseQuotedIdentifiers() throws SQLException;
1.4  public abstract boolean supportsMultipleOpenResults() throws SQLException;
     public abstract boolean supportsMultipleResultSets() throws SQLException;
     public abstract boolean supportsMultipleTransactions() throws SQLException;
1.4  public abstract boolean supportsNamedParameters() throws SQLException;
     public abstract boolean supportsNonNullableColumns() throws SQLException;
     public abstract boolean supportsOpenCursorsAcrossCommit() throws SQLException;
     public abstract boolean supportsOpenCursorsAcrossRollback() throws SQLException;
     public abstract boolean supportsOpenStatementsAcrossCommit() throws SQLException;
     public abstract boolean supportsOpenStatementsAcrossRollback() throws SQLException;
     public abstract boolean supportsOrderByUnrelated() throws SQLException;
     public abstract boolean supportsOuterJoins() throws SQLException;
     public abstract boolean supportsPositionedDelete() throws SQLException;
     public abstract boolean supportsPositionedUpdate() throws SQLException;
1.2  public abstract boolean supportsResultSetConcurrency(int type, int concurrency) throws SQLException;
1.4  public abstract boolean supportsResultSetHoldability(int holdability) throws SQLException;
1.2  public abstract boolean supportsResultSetType(int type) throws SQLException;
1.4  public abstract boolean supportsSavepoints() throws SQLException;
     public abstract boolean supportsSchemasInDataManipulation() throws SQLException;
     public abstract boolean supportsSchemasInIndexDefinitions() throws SQLException;
     public abstract boolean supportsSchemasInPrivilegeDefinitions() throws SQLException;
     public abstract boolean supportsSchemasInProcedureCalls() throws SQLException;
     public abstract boolean supportsSchemasInTableDefinitions() throws SQLException;
     public abstract boolean supportsSelectForUpdate() throws SQLException;
1.4  public abstract boolean supportsStatementPooling() throws SQLException;
     public abstract boolean supportsStoredProcedures() throws SQLException;
     public abstract boolean supportsSubqueriesInComparisons() throws SQLException;
     public abstract boolean supportsSubqueriesInExists() throws SQLException;
     public abstract boolean supportsSubqueriesInIns() throws SQLException;
     public abstract boolean supportsSubqueriesInQuantifieds() throws SQLException;
```

```
    public abstract boolean supportsTableCorrelationNames() throws SQLException;
    public abstract boolean supportsTransactionIsolationLevel(int level) throws SQLException;
    public abstract boolean supportsTransactions() throws SQLException;
    public abstract boolean supportsUnion() throws SQLException;
    public abstract boolean supportsUnionAll() throws SQLException;
1.2 public abstract boolean updatesAreDetected(int type) throws SQLException;
    public abstract boolean usesLocalFilePerTable() throws SQLException;
    public abstract boolean usesLocalFiles() throws SQLException;
}
```

Returned By: java.sql.Connection.getMetaData()

DataTruncation
java.sql

Java 1.1

serializable checked

This subclass of SQLWarning is a special warning used when JDBC unexpectedly truncates a data value. It is chained as a warning on read operations and thrown as an exception on write operations.

```
Object — Throwable — Exception — SQLException — SQLWarning — DataTruncation
       Serializable
```

```
public class DataTruncation extends SQLWarning {
// Public Constructors
    public DataTruncation(int index, boolean parameter, boolean read, int dataSize, int transferSize);
// Property Accessor Methods (by property name)
    public int getDataSize();
    public int getIndex();
    public boolean getParameter();
    public boolean getRead();
    public int getTransferSize();
}
```

Date
java.sql

Java 1.1

cloneable serializable comparable

A wrapper around the java.util.Date class that adjusts the time value (milliseconds since January 1, 1970 0:00:00 GMT) to conform to the SQL DATE specification. The DATE type only deals with the day, month, and year, so the hours, minutes, seconds, and milliseconds are set to 00:00:00.00 in the current time zone. The Date class also includes a static valueOf() method that decodes the JDBC Date escape syntax *yyyy-mm-dd* into a Date value.

```
Object                    Date — Date
Cloneable  Comparable  Serializable
```

```
public class Date extends java.util.Date {
// Public Constructors
    public Date(long date);
#   public Date(int year, int month, int day);
// Public Class Methods
    public static java.sql.Date valueOf(String s);
// Public Methods Overriding Date
    public void setTime(long date);
    public String toString();
```

```
// Deprecated Public Methods
#   public int getHours();                                          Overrides:Date
#   public int getMinutes();                                        Overrides:Date
#   public int getSeconds();                                        Overrides:Date
#   public void setHours(int i);                                    Overrides:Date
#   public void setMinutes(int i);                                  Overrides:Date
#   public void setSeconds(int i);                                  Overrides:Date
}
```

Passed To: CallableStatement.setDate(), PreparedStatement.setDate(), java.sql.ResultSet.updateDate(), SQLOutput.writeDate(), javax.sql.RowSet.setDate()

Returned By: CallableStatement.getDate(), java.sql.Date.valueOf(), java.sql.ResultSet.getDate(), SQLInput.readDate()

Driver   Java 1.1

java.sql

Every JDBC driver must implement the Driver interface. Most programmers never need to deal with this interface, except when using the DriverManager.registerDriver() method, which is generally not recommended. The better way to register a driver is to load the driver by calling Class.forName() on the driver class, which automatically register the driver as well. Older JDBC drivers can be used to with newer versions of the API, although some functionality will not be supported.

```
public interface Driver {
// Public Instance Methods
    public abstract boolean acceptsURL(String url) throws SQLException;
    public abstract java.sql.Connection connect(String url, java.util.Properties info) throws SQLException;
    public abstract int getMajorVersion();
    public abstract int getMinorVersion();
    public abstract DriverPropertyInfo[ ] getPropertyInfo(String url, java.util.Properties info) throws SQLException;
    public abstract boolean jdbcCompliant();
}
```

Passed To: DriverManager.{deregisterDriver(), registerDriver()}

Returned By: DriverManager.getDriver()

DriverManager   Java 1.1

java.sql

The DriverManager class is responsible for loading JDBC drivers and creating Connection objects. It starts by loading all of the drivers specified in the jdbc.drivers system property. Individual drivers can also be loaded by calling Class.forName() with the driver class name.

Programs use the static DriverManager.getConnection() method to create individual database connections. The driver manager creates the Connection using the appropriate driver, based on the JDBC URL specified in the call to getConnection().

```
public class DriverManager {
// No Constructor
// Public Class Methods
    public static void deregisterDriver(Driver driver) throws SQLException;              synchronized
    public static java.sql.Connection getConnection(String url) throws SQLException;     synchronized
    public static java.sql.Connection getConnection(String url, java.util.Properties info)  synchronized
        throws SQLException;
```

```
   public static java.sql.Connection getConnection(String url, String user, String password)          synchronized
      throws SQLException;
   public static Driver getDriver(String url) throws SQLException;                                     synchronized
   public static java.util.Enumeration getDrivers();                                                   synchronized
   public static int getLoginTimeout();
1.2 public static PrintWriter getLogWriter();
   public static void println(String message);
   public static void registerDriver(Driver driver) throws SQLException;                               synchronized
   public static void setLoginTimeout(int seconds);
1.2 public static void setLogWriter(PrintWriter out);
// Deprecated Public Methods
#  public static PrintStream getLogStream();
#  public static void setLogStream(PrintStream out);                                                    synchronized
}
```

DriverPropertyInfo   Java 1.1

java.sql

The DriverPropertyInfo class contains the properties required to create a new database connection using a particular driver. It is returned by the getDriverProperties() method of Driver. This class is only useful for programmers who need to interact directly with the driver in a dynamic manner.

```
public class DriverPropertyInfo {
// Public Constructors
   public DriverPropertyInfo(String name, String value);
// Public Instance Fields
   public String[ ] choices;
   public String description;
   public String name;
   public boolean required;
   public String value;
}
```

Returned By: Driver.getPropertyInfo()

ParameterMetaData   Java 1.4

java.sql

This interface provides information about the parameters required by a PreparedStatement object.

```
public interface ParameterMetaData {
// Public Constants
   public static final int parameterModeIn;                                                          =1
   public static final int parameterModeInOut;                                                       =2
   public static final int parameterModeOut;                                                         =4
   public static final int parameterModeUnknown;                                                     =0
   public static final int parameterNoNulls;                                                         =0
   public static final int parameterNullable;                                                        =1
   public static final int parameterNullableUnknown;                                                 =2
// Public Instance Methods
   public abstract String getParameterClassName(int param) throws SQLException;
   public abstract int getParameterCount() throws SQLException;
   public abstract int getParameterMode(int param) throws SQLException;
   public abstract int getParameterType(int param) throws SQLException;
```

```
    public abstract String getParameterTypeName(int param) throws SQLException;
    public abstract int getPrecision(int param) throws SQLException;
    public abstract int getScale(int param) throws SQLException;
    public abstract int isNullable(int param) throws SQLException;
    public abstract boolean isSigned(int param) throws SQLException;
}
```

Returned By: PreparedStatement.getParameterMetaData()

PreparedStatement   Java 1.1

java.sql

The PreparedStatement interface allows programs to precompile SQL statements for increased performance. You obtain a PreparedStatement object with the prepareStatement() method of Connection. Parameters in the statement are denoted by ? characters in the SQL string and indexed from 1 to n. Individual parameter values are set using the setXXX() methods, while the clearParameters() method clears all the parameters. Note that some JDBC drivers do not implement setObject() properly when dealing with null field types. Once all parameters have been set, the statement is executed using execute(), executeQuery(), or executeUpdate(). Unlike with the Statement object, the execution methods take no parameters.

Statement ⊢ PreparedStatement

```
public interface PreparedStatement extends java.sql.Statement {
// Public Instance Methods
1.2 public abstract void addBatch() throws SQLException;
    public abstract void clearParameters() throws SQLException;
    public abstract boolean execute() throws SQLException;
    public abstract java.sql.ResultSet executeQuery() throws SQLException;
    public abstract int executeUpdate() throws SQLException;
1.2 public abstract ResultSetMetaData getMetaData() throws SQLException;
1.4 public abstract ParameterMetaData getParameterMetaData() throws SQLException;
1.2 public abstract void setArray(int i, java.sql.Array x) throws SQLException;
    public abstract void setAsciiStream(int parameterIndex, java.io.InputStream x, int length) throws SQLException;
    public abstract void setBigDecimal(int parameterIndex, java.math.BigDecimal x) throws SQLException;
    public abstract void setBinaryStream(int parameterIndex, java.io.InputStream x, int length) throws SQLException;
1.2 public abstract void setBlob(int i, Blob x) throws SQLException;
    public abstract void setBoolean(int parameterIndex, boolean x) throws SQLException;
    public abstract void setByte(int parameterIndex, byte x) throws SQLException;
    public abstract void setBytes(int parameterIndex, byte[ ] x) throws SQLException;
1.2 public abstract void setCharacterStream(int parameterIndex, Reader reader, int length) throws SQLException;
1.2 public abstract void setClob(int i, Clob x) throws SQLException;
    public abstract void setDate(int parameterIndex, java.sql.Date x) throws SQLException;
1.2 public abstract void setDate(int parameterIndex, java.sql.Date x, java.util.Calendar cal) throws SQLException;
    public abstract void setDouble(int parameterIndex, double x) throws SQLException;
    public abstract void setFloat(int parameterIndex, float x) throws SQLException;
    public abstract void setInt(int parameterIndex, int x) throws SQLException;
    public abstract void setLong(int parameterIndex, long x) throws SQLException;
    public abstract void setNull(int parameterIndex, int sqlType) throws SQLException;
1.2 public abstract void setNull(int paramIndex, int sqlType, String typeName) throws SQLException;
    public abstract void setObject(int parameterIndex, Object x) throws SQLException;
    public abstract void setObject(int parameterIndex, Object x, int targetSqlType) throws SQLException;
    public abstract void setObject(int parameterIndex, Object x, int targetSqlType, int scale) throws SQLException;
1.2 public abstract void setRef(int i, Ref x) throws SQLException;
```

```
    public abstract void setShort(int parameterIndex, short x) throws SQLException;
    public abstract void setString(int parameterIndex, String x) throws SQLException;
    public abstract void setTime(int parameterIndex, Time x) throws SQLException;
1.2 public abstract void setTime(int parameterIndex, Time x, java.util.Calendar cal) throws SQLException;
    public abstract void setTimestamp(int parameterIndex, Timestamp x) throws SQLException;
1.2 public abstract void setTimestamp(int parameterIndex, Timestamp x, java.util.Calendar cal) throws SQLException;
1.4 public abstract void setURL(int parameterIndex, java.net.URL x) throws SQLException;
    // Deprecated Public Methods
#   public abstract void setUnicodeStream(int parameterIndex, java.io.InputStream x, int length)
        throws SQLException;
}
```

Implementations: CallableStatement

Returned By: java.sql.Connection.prepareStatement()

Ref   Java 1.2

java.sql

The Ref interface provides a pointer to a structured data type within the database. The getBaseType() method returns the name of the underlying type. Since a Ref object implementation maps back to a particular row instance of a particular column, the object can be used as a proxy for that value in PreparedStatement objects. With the introduction of structured type support to JDBC, the Ref object now supports retrieval of the underlying referenced object via the getObject() and setObject() methods.

```
public interface Ref {
    // Public Instance Methods
    public abstract String getBaseTypeName() throws SQLException;
1.4 public abstract Object getObject() throws SQLException;
1.4 public abstract Object getObject(java.util.Map map) throws SQLException;
1.4 public abstract void setObject(Object value) throws SQLException;
}
```

Passed To: PreparedStatement.setRef(), java.sql.ResultSet.updateRef(), SQLOutput.writeRef(), javax.sql.RowSet.setRef()

Returned By: CallableStatement.getRef(), java.sql.ResultSet.getRef(), SQLInput.readRef()

ResultSet   Java 1.1

java.sql

The ResultSet interface represents a database result set, allowing programs to access the data in the result set. ResultSet objects are usually generated by the execute(), executeUpdate(), and executeQuery() methods of Statementand PreparedStatement. They are also returned by certain metadata methods.

The JDBC 1.0 ResultSet allows you to scroll navigate through the data once from beginning to end, iterating through rows using the next() method and retrieving individual fields using the getXXX() methods. The getMetaData() method returns a ResultSetMetaData object that describes the structure of the underlying data.

JDBC 2.0 introduces a number of new features: including complete scrolling capabilities (the previous(), first(), last(), and related methods), direct updating of data via the updateXXX() methods, and insertion of new data rows using the insertRow() method. JDBC 3.0 adds updater methods for BLOBs, CLOBs, Refs, and URLs.

```
public interface ResultSet {
// Public Constants
1.4 public static final int CLOSE_CURSORS_AT_COMMIT;                                =2
1.2 public static final int CONCUR_READ_ONLY;                                    =1007
1.2 public static final int CONCUR_UPDATABLE;                                    =1008
1.2 public static final int FETCH_FORWARD;                                       =1000
1.2 public static final int FETCH_REVERSE;                                       =1001
1.2 public static final int FETCH_UNKNOWN;                                       =1002
1.4 public static final int HOLD_CURSORS_OVER_COMMIT;                              =1
1.2 public static final int TYPE_FORWARD_ONLY;                                   =1003
1.2 public static final int TYPE_SCROLL_INSENSITIVE;                             =1004
1.2 public static final int TYPE_SCROLL_SENSITIVE;                              =1005
// Property Accessor Methods (by property name)
1.2 public abstract boolean isAfterLast() throws SQLException;
1.2 public abstract boolean isBeforeFirst() throws SQLException;
1.2 public abstract int getConcurrency() throws SQLException;
    public abstract String getCursorName() throws SQLException;
1.2 public abstract int getFetchDirection() throws SQLException;
1.2 public abstract void setFetchDirection(int direction) throws SQLException;
1.2 public abstract int getFetchSize() throws SQLException;
1.2 public abstract void setFetchSize(int rows) throws SQLException;
1.2 public abstract boolean isFirst() throws SQLException;
1.2 public abstract boolean isLast() throws SQLException;
    public abstract ResultSetMetaData getMetaData() throws SQLException;
1.2 public abstract int getRow() throws SQLException;
1.2 public abstract java.sql.Statement getStatement() throws SQLException;
1.2 public abstract int getType() throws SQLException;
    public abstract SQLWarning getWarnings() throws SQLException;
// Public Instance Methods
1.2 public abstract boolean absolute(int row) throws SQLException;
1.2 public abstract void afterLast() throws SQLException;
1.2 public abstract void beforeFirst() throws SQLException;
1.2 public abstract void cancelRowUpdates() throws SQLException;
    public abstract void clearWarnings() throws SQLException;
    public abstract void close() throws SQLException;
1.2 public abstract void deleteRow() throws SQLException;
    public abstract int findColumn(String columnName) throws SQLException;
1.2 public abstract boolean first() throws SQLException;
1.2 public abstract java.sql.Array getArray(int i) throws SQLException;
1.2 public abstract java.sql.Array getArray(String colName) throws SQLException;
    public abstract java.io.InputStream getAsciiStream(String columnName) throws SQLException;
    public abstract java.io.InputStream getAsciiStream(int columnIndex) throws SQLException;
1.2 public abstract java.math.BigDecimal getBigDecimal(String columnName) throws SQLException;
1.2 public abstract java.math.BigDecimal getBigDecimal(int columnIndex) throws SQLException;
    public abstract java.io.InputStream getBinaryStream(String columnName) throws SQLException;
    public abstract java.io.InputStream getBinaryStream(int columnIndex) throws SQLException;
1.2 public abstract Blob getBlob(int i) throws SQLException;
1.2 public abstract Blob getBlob(String colName) throws SQLException;
    public abstract boolean getBoolean(int columnIndex) throws SQLException;
    public abstract boolean getBoolean(String columnName) throws SQLException;
    public abstract byte getByte(int columnIndex) throws SQLException;
    public abstract byte getByte(String columnName) throws SQLException;
    public abstract byte[ ] getBytes(String columnName) throws SQLException;
    public abstract byte[ ] getBytes(int columnIndex) throws SQLException;
1.2 public abstract Reader getCharacterStream(int columnIndex) throws SQLException;
```

ResultSet

1.2 public abstract Reader **getCharacterStream**(String *columnName*) throws SQLException;
1.2 public abstract Clob **getClob**(int *i*) throws SQLException;
1.2 public abstract Clob **getClob**(String *colName*) throws SQLException;
   public abstract java.sql.Date **getDate**(String *columnName*) throws SQLException;
   public abstract java.sql.Date **getDate**(int *columnIndex*) throws SQLException;
1.2 public abstract java.sql.Date **getDate**(String *columnName*, java.util.Calendar *cal*) throws SQLException;
1.2 public abstract java.sql.Date **getDate**(int *columnIndex*, java.util.Calendar *cal*) throws SQLException;
   public abstract double **getDouble**(int *columnIndex*) throws SQLException;
   public abstract double **getDouble**(String *columnName*) throws SQLException;
   public abstract float **getFloat**(String *columnName*) throws SQLException;
   public abstract float **getFloat**(int *columnIndex*) throws SQLException;
   public abstract int **getInt**(String *columnName*) throws SQLException;
   public abstract int **getInt**(int *columnIndex*) throws SQLException;
   public abstract long **getLong**(int *columnIndex*) throws SQLException;
   public abstract long **getLong**(String *columnName*) throws SQLException;
   public abstract Object **getObject**(int *columnIndex*) throws SQLException;
   public abstract Object **getObject**(String *columnName*) throws SQLException;
1.2 public abstract Object **getObject**(String *colName*, java.util.Map *map*) throws SQLException;
1.2 public abstract Object **getObject**(int *i*, java.util.Map *map*) throws SQLException;
1.2 public abstract Ref **getRef**(String *colName*) throws SQLException;
1.2 public abstract Ref **getRef**(int *i*) throws SQLException;
   public abstract short **getShort**(String *columnName*) throws SQLException;
   public abstract short **getShort**(int *columnIndex*) throws SQLException;
   public abstract String **getString**(int *columnIndex*) throws SQLException;
   public abstract String **getString**(String *columnName*) throws SQLException;
   public abstract Time **getTime**(String *columnName*) throws SQLException;
   public abstract Time **getTime**(int *columnIndex*) throws SQLException;
1.2 public abstract Time **getTime**(String *columnName*, java.util.Calendar *cal*) throws SQLException;
1.2 public abstract Time **getTime**(int *columnIndex*, java.util.Calendar *cal*) throws SQLException;
   public abstract Timestamp **getTimestamp**(String *columnName*) throws SQLException;
   public abstract Timestamp **getTimestamp**(int *columnIndex*) throws SQLException;
1.2 public abstract Timestamp **getTimestamp**(String *columnName*, java.util.Calendar *cal*) throws SQLException;
1.2 public abstract Timestamp **getTimestamp**(int *columnIndex*, java.util.Calendar *cal*) throws SQLException;
1.4 public abstract java.net.URL **getURL**(int *columnIndex*) throws SQLException;
1.4 public abstract java.net.URL **getURL**(String *columnName*) throws SQLException;
1.2 public abstract void **insertRow**() throws SQLException;
1.2 public abstract boolean **last**() throws SQLException;
1.2 public abstract void **moveToCurrentRow**() throws SQLException;
1.2 public abstract void **moveToInsertRow**() throws SQLException;
   public abstract boolean **next**() throws SQLException;
1.2 public abstract boolean **previous**() throws SQLException;
1.2 public abstract void **refreshRow**() throws SQLException;
1.2 public abstract boolean **relative**(int *rows*) throws SQLException;
1.2 public abstract boolean **rowDeleted**() throws SQLException;
1.2 public abstract boolean **rowInserted**() throws SQLException;
1.2 public abstract boolean **rowUpdated**() throws SQLException;
1.4 public abstract void **updateArray**(String *columnName*, java.sql.Array *x*) throws SQLException;
1.4 public abstract void **updateArray**(int *columnIndex*, java.sql.Array *x*) throws SQLException;
1.2 public abstract void **updateAsciiStream**(int *columnIndex*, java.io.InputStream *x*, int *length*) throws SQLException;
1.2 public abstract void **updateAsciiStream**(String *columnName*, java.io.InputStream *x*, int *length*)
       throws SQLException;
1.2 public abstract void **updateBigDecimal**(int *columnIndex*, java.math.BigDecimal *x*) throws SQLException;
1.2 public abstract void **updateBigDecimal**(String *columnName*, java.math.BigDecimal *x*) throws SQLException;
1.2 public abstract void **updateBinaryStream**(int *columnIndex*, java.io.InputStream *x*, int *length*)
       throws SQLException;

1.2 public abstract void **updateBinaryStream**(String *columnName*, java.io.InputStream *x*, int *length*)
        throws SQLException;
1.4 public abstract void **updateBlob**(String *columnName*, Blob *x*) throws SQLException;
1.4 public abstract void **updateBlob**(int *columnIndex*, Blob *x*) throws SQLException;
1.2 public abstract void **updateBoolean**(int *columnIndex*, boolean *x*) throws SQLException;
1.2 public abstract void **updateBoolean**(String *columnName*, boolean *x*) throws SQLException;
1.2 public abstract void **updateByte**(int *columnIndex*, byte *x*) throws SQLException;
1.2 public abstract void **updateByte**(String *columnName*, byte *x*) throws SQLException;
1.2 public abstract void **updateBytes**(String *columnName*, byte[ ] *x*) throws SQLException;
1.2 public abstract void **updateBytes**(int *columnIndex*, byte[ ] *x*) throws SQLException;
1.2 public abstract void **updateCharacterStream**(int *columnIndex*, Reader *x*, int *length*) throws SQLException;
1.2 public abstract void **updateCharacterStream**(String *columnName*, Reader *reader*, int *length*)
        throws SQLException;
1.4 public abstract void **updateClob**(String *columnName*, Clob *x*) throws SQLException;
1.4 public abstract void **updateClob**(int *columnIndex*, Clob *x*) throws SQLException;
1.2 public abstract void **updateDate**(String *columnName*, java.sql.Date *x*) throws SQLException;
1.2 public abstract void **updateDate**(int *columnIndex*, java.sql.Date *x*) throws SQLException;
1.2 public abstract void **updateDouble**(int *columnIndex*, double *x*) throws SQLException;
1.2 public abstract void **updateDouble**(String *columnName*, double *x*) throws SQLException;
1.2 public abstract void **updateFloat**(int *columnIndex*, float *x*) throws SQLException;
1.2 public abstract void **updateFloat**(String *columnName*, float *x*) throws SQLException;
1.2 public abstract void **updateInt**(String *columnName*, int *x*) throws SQLException;
1.2 public abstract void **updateInt**(int *columnIndex*, int *x*) throws SQLException;
1.2 public abstract void **updateLong**(String *columnName*, long *x*) throws SQLException;
1.2 public abstract void **updateLong**(int *columnIndex*, long *x*) throws SQLException;
1.2 public abstract void **updateNull**(int *columnIndex*) throws SQLException;
1.2 public abstract void **updateNull**(String *columnName*) throws SQLException;
1.2 public abstract void **updateObject**(String *columnName*, Object *x*) throws SQLException;
1.2 public abstract void **updateObject**(int *columnIndex*, Object *x*) throws SQLException;
1.2 public abstract void **updateObject**(int *columnIndex*, Object *x*, int *scale*) throws SQLException;
1.2 public abstract void **updateObject**(String *columnName*, Object *x*, int *scale*) throws SQLException;
1.4 public abstract void **updateRef**(int *columnIndex*, Ref *x*) throws SQLException;
1.4 public abstract void **updateRef**(String *columnName*, Ref *x*) throws SQLException;
1.2 public abstract void **updateRow**( ) throws SQLException;
1.2 public abstract void **updateShort**(int *columnIndex*, short *x*) throws SQLException;
1.2 public abstract void **updateShort**(String *columnName*, short *x*) throws SQLException;
1.2 public abstract void **updateString**(String *columnName*, String *x*) throws SQLException;
1.2 public abstract void **updateString**(int *columnIndex*, String *x*) throws SQLException;
1.2 public abstract void **updateTime**(int *columnIndex*, Time *x*) throws SQLException;
1.2 public abstract void **updateTime**(String *columnName*, Time *x*) throws SQLException;
1.2 public abstract void **updateTimestamp**(int *columnIndex*, Timestamp *x*) throws SQLException;
1.2 public abstract void **updateTimestamp**(String *columnName*, Timestamp *x*) throws SQLException;
    public abstract boolean **wasNull**( ) throws SQLException;
// Deprecated Public Methods
\#   public abstract java.math.BigDecimal **getBigDecimal**(String *columnName*, int *scale*) throws SQLException;
\#   public abstract java.math.BigDecimal **getBigDecimal**(int *columnIndex*, int *scale*) throws SQLException;
\#   public abstract java.io.InputStream **getUnicodeStream**(String *columnName*) throws SQLException;
\#   public abstract java.io.InputStream **getUnicodeStream**(int *columnIndex*) throws SQLException;
}

Implementations: javax.resource.cci.ResultSet, javax.sql.RowSet

Returned By: Too many methods to list.

ResultSetMetaData
Java 1.1

java.sql

This interface provides metainformation about the data underlying a particular ResultSet. In particular, you can get information about the columns of the ResultSet with getColumn-Count(), getColumnLabel(), and getColumnTypeName().

```
public interface ResultSetMetaData {
// Public Constants
    public static final int columnNoNulls;                                          =0
    public static final int columnNullable;                                         =1
    public static final int columnNullableUnknown;                                  =2
// Public Instance Methods
    public abstract String getCatalogName(int column) throws SQLException;
1.2 public abstract String getColumnClassName(int column) throws SQLException;
    public abstract int getColumnCount() throws SQLException;
    public abstract int getColumnDisplaySize(int column) throws SQLException;
    public abstract String getColumnLabel(int column) throws SQLException;
    public abstract String getColumnName(int column) throws SQLException;
    public abstract int getColumnType(int column) throws SQLException;
    public abstract String getColumnTypeName(int column) throws SQLException;
    public abstract int getPrecision(int column) throws SQLException;
    public abstract int getScale(int column) throws SQLException;
    public abstract String getSchemaName(int column) throws SQLException;
    public abstract String getTableName(int column) throws SQLException;
    public abstract boolean isAutoIncrement(int column) throws SQLException;
    public abstract boolean isCaseSensitive(int column) throws SQLException;
    public abstract boolean isCurrency(int column) throws SQLException;
    public abstract boolean isDefinitelyWritable(int column) throws SQLException;
    public abstract int isNullable(int column) throws SQLException;
    public abstract boolean isReadOnly(int column) throws SQLException;
    public abstract boolean isSearchable(int column) throws SQLException;
    public abstract boolean isSigned(int column) throws SQLException;
    public abstract boolean isWritable(int column) throws SQLException;
}
```

Implementations: javax.sql.RowSetMetaData

Returned By: PreparedStatement.getMetaData(), java.sql.ResultSet.getMetaData()

Savepoint
Java 1.4

java.sql

This interface represents a transaction savepoint. Savepoint objects are used in conjunction with the savepoint methods of Connection to rollback transactions to specific points.

```
public interface Savepoint {
// Public Instance Methods
    public abstract int getSavepointId() throws SQLException;
    public abstract String getSavepointName() throws SQLException;
}
```

Passed To: java.sql.Connection.{releaseSavepoint(), rollback()}

Returned By: java.sql.Connection.setSavepoint()

SQLData

Java 1.2

java.sql

Allows custom mapping of user-defined SQL types. This interface is generally implemented by a development tool or driver vendor and is never called by the programmer directly.

```
public interface SQLData {
// Public Instance Methods
    public abstract String getSQLTypeName( ) throws SQLException;
    public abstract void readSQL(SQLInput stream, String typeName) throws SQLException;
    public abstract void writeSQL(SQLOutput stream) throws SQLException;
}
```

Passed To: SQLOutput.writeObject()

SQLException

Java 1.1

java.sql

serializable checked

A SQLException object is thrown by any JDBC method that encounters an error. SQLException extends the java.lang.Exception class and adds a vendor-specific error code and an XOPEN SQL state code. SQLException objects can be chained together. The next exception in the chain is retrieved via getNextException(), which returns null if there are no more exceptions available. The setNextException() method adds an exception to the end of the chain.

```
Object ─ Throwable ─ Exception ─ SQLException
          Serializable
```

```
public class SQLException extends Exception {
// Public Constructors
    public SQLException( );
    public SQLException(String reason);
    public SQLException(String reason, String SQLState);
    public SQLException(String reason, String SQLState, int vendorCode);
// Property Accessor Methods (by property name)
    public int getErrorCode( );                                          default:0
    public SQLException getNextException( );                          default:null
    public void setNextException(SQLException ex);                    synchronized
    public String getSQLState( );                                     default:null
}
```

Subclasses: BatchUpdateException, SQLWarning

Passed To: SQLException.setNextException(), javax.sql.ConnectionEvent.ConnectionEvent()

Returned By: SQLException.getNextException(), javax.sql.ConnectionEvent.getSQLException()

Thrown By: Too many methods to list.

SQLInput

Java 1.2

java.sql

Represents an input stream for a user-defined SQL type. SQLInput is used by the driver and is never called by the programmer directly.

```
public interface SQLInput {
// Public Instance Methods
```

```
    public abstract java.sql.Array readArray() throws SQLException;
    public abstract java.io.InputStream readAsciiStream() throws SQLException;
    public abstract java.math.BigDecimal readBigDecimal() throws SQLException;
    public abstract java.io.InputStream readBinaryStream() throws SQLException;
    public abstract Blob readBlob() throws SQLException;
    public abstract boolean readBoolean() throws SQLException;
    public abstract byte readByte() throws SQLException;
    public abstract byte[ ] readBytes() throws SQLException;
    public abstract Reader readCharacterStream() throws SQLException;
    public abstract Clob readClob() throws SQLException;
    public abstract java.sql.Date readDate() throws SQLException;
    public abstract double readDouble() throws SQLException;
    public abstract float readFloat() throws SQLException;
    public abstract int readInt() throws SQLException;
    public abstract long readLong() throws SQLException;
    public abstract Object readObject() throws SQLException;
    public abstract Ref readRef() throws SQLException;
    public abstract short readShort() throws SQLException;
    public abstract String readString() throws SQLException;
    public abstract Time readTime() throws SQLException;
    public abstract Timestamp readTimestamp() throws SQLException;
1.4 public abstract java.net.URL readURL() throws SQLException;
    public abstract boolean wasNull() throws SQLException;
}
```

Passed To: SQLData.readSQL()

SQLOutput Java 1.2

java.sql

Represents an output stream for a user-defined SQL type. SQLOutput is used by the driver and is never called by the programmer directly.

```
public interface SQLOutput {
// Public Instance Methods
    public abstract void writeArray(java.sql.Array x) throws SQLException;
    public abstract void writeAsciiStream(java.io.InputStream x) throws SQLException;
    public abstract void writeBigDecimal(java.math.BigDecimal x) throws SQLException;
    public abstract void writeBinaryStream(java.io.InputStream x) throws SQLException;
    public abstract void writeBlob(Blob x) throws SQLException;
    public abstract void writeBoolean(boolean x) throws SQLException;
    public abstract void writeByte(byte x) throws SQLException;
    public abstract void writeBytes(byte[ ] x) throws SQLException;
    public abstract void writeCharacterStream(Reader x) throws SQLException;
    public abstract void writeClob(Clob x) throws SQLException;
    public abstract void writeDate(java.sql.Date x) throws SQLException;
    public abstract void writeDouble(double x) throws SQLException;
    public abstract void writeFloat(float x) throws SQLException;
    public abstract void writeInt(int x) throws SQLException;
    public abstract void writeLong(long x) throws SQLException;
    public abstract void writeObject(SQLData x) throws SQLException;
    public abstract void writeRef(Ref x) throws SQLException;
    public abstract void writeShort(short x) throws SQLException;
    public abstract void writeString(String x) throws SQLException;
    public abstract void writeStruct(Struct x) throws SQLException;
    public abstract void writeTime(Time x) throws SQLException;
```

```
      public abstract void writeTimestamp(Timestamp x) throws SQLException;
1.4 public abstract void writeURL(java.net.URL x) throws SQLException;
   }
```

Passed To: SQLData.writeSQL()

SQLPermission
Java 1.3

java.sql
serializable permission

This class allows a SecurityManager to identify whether or not an applet may set the location of the SQL logging stream using the "setLog" permission target (currently the only one supported). Note that this is a dangerous permission to grant as the log may contain security sensitive information.

```
public final class SQLPermission extends java.security.BasicPermission {
// Public Constructors
   public SQLPermission(String name);
   public SQLPermission(String name, String actions);
}
```

SQLWarning
Java 1.1

java.sql
serializable checked

Represents a non-fatal warning condition. Warnings are silently chained to the object whose method produced them. You can retrieve warnings with the getWarnings() method implemented by most JDBC classes.

```
public class SQLWarning extends SQLException {
// Public Constructors
   public SQLWarning();
   public SQLWarning(String reason);
   public SQLWarning(String reason, String SQLstate);
   public SQLWarning(String reason, String SQLstate, int vendorCode);
// Public Instance Methods
   public SQLWarning getNextWarning();                                        default:null
   public void setNextWarning(SQLWarning w);
}
```

Subclasses: DataTruncation

Passed To: SQLWarning.setNextWarning()

Returned By: java.sql.Connection.getWarnings(), java.sql.ResultSet.getWarnings(), SQLWarning.getNextWarning(), java.sql.Statement.getWarnings()

Statement
Java 1.1

java.sql

The Statement interface is used to execute SQL statements. Statement objects are returned by the createStatement() method of Connection. The execute(), executeUpdate(), and executeQuery() methods each take a Stringparameter that contains a SQL statement. execute() returns a boolean value that indicates whether there is a ResultSetavailable. The ResultSet can then be retrieved with getResultSet(). executeUpdate() returns an update count and is used for INSERT, UPDATE, DELETE and other data manipulation statements. executeQuery() is used for SELECTstatements, so it returns a ResultSet. JDBC 3.0 provides additional methods to retrieve generated keys and to provide better handling of multiple result sets. The getMoreResults() method (which takes an int), in conjunction with the new constants defined in the class, can be used to keep multiple ResultSet objects open per connection

```
public interface Statement {
// Public Constants
1.4 public static final int CLOSE_ALL_RESULTS;                                          =3
1.4 public static final int CLOSE_CURRENT_RESULT;                                       =1
1.4 public static final int EXECUTE_FAILED;                                             =-3
1.4 public static final int KEEP_CURRENT_RESULT;                                        =2
1.4 public static final int NO_GENERATED_KEYS;                                          =2
1.4 public static final int RETURN_GENERATED_KEYS;                                      =1
1.4 public static final int SUCCESS_NO_INFO;                                            =-2
// Property Accessor Methods (by property name)
1.2 public abstract java.sql.Connection getConnection() throws SQLException;
    public abstract void setCursorName(String name) throws SQLException;
    public abstract void setEscapeProcessing(boolean enable) throws SQLException;
1.2 public abstract int getFetchDirection() throws SQLException;
1.2 public abstract void setFetchDirection(int direction) throws SQLException;
1.2 public abstract int getFetchSize() throws SQLException;
1.2 public abstract void setFetchSize(int rows) throws SQLException;
1.4 public abstract java.sql.ResultSet getGeneratedKeys() throws SQLException;
    public abstract int getMaxFieldSize() throws SQLException;
    public abstract void setMaxFieldSize(int max) throws SQLException;
    public abstract int getMaxRows() throws SQLException;
    public abstract void setMaxRows(int max) throws SQLException;
    public abstract boolean getMoreResults() throws SQLException;
1.4 public abstract boolean getMoreResults(int current) throws SQLException;
    public abstract int getQueryTimeout() throws SQLException;
    public abstract void setQueryTimeout(int seconds) throws SQLException;
    public abstract java.sql.ResultSet getResultSet() throws SQLException;
1.2 public abstract int getResultSetConcurrency() throws SQLException;
1.4 public abstract int getResultSetHoldability() throws SQLException;
1.2 public abstract int getResultSetType() throws SQLException;
    public abstract int getUpdateCount() throws SQLException;
    public abstract SQLWarning getWarnings() throws SQLException;
// Public Instance Methods
1.2 public abstract void addBatch(String sql) throws SQLException;
    public abstract void cancel() throws SQLException;
1.2 public abstract void clearBatch() throws SQLException;
    public abstract void clearWarnings() throws SQLException;
    public abstract void close() throws SQLException;
    public abstract boolean execute(String sql) throws SQLException;
1.4 public abstract boolean execute(String sql, int autoGeneratedKeys) throws SQLException;
1.4 public abstract boolean execute(String sql, int[] columnIndexes) throws SQLException;
1.4 public abstract boolean execute(String sql, String[] columnNames) throws SQLException;
1.2 public abstract int[] executeBatch() throws SQLException;
    public abstract java.sql.ResultSet executeQuery(String sql) throws SQLException;
    public abstract int executeUpdate(String sql) throws SQLException;
1.4 public abstract int executeUpdate(String sql, int[] columnIndexes) throws SQLException;
```

1.4 public abstract int **executeUpdate**(String *sql*, int *autoGeneratedKeys*) throws SQLException;
1.4 public abstract int **executeUpdate**(String *sql*, String[ ] *columnNames*) throws SQLException;
}

Implementations: PreparedStatement

Returned By: java.sql.Connection.createStatement(), java.sql.ResultSet.getStatement()

Struct

Java 1.2

java.sql

The Struct interface provides a mapping for an SQL structured type. The getAttributes() method returns an array of objects representing each attribute in the structured type. Custom type maps can be specified by including a java.util.Map attribute.

```
public interface Struct {
// Public Instance Methods
    public abstract Object[ ] getAttributes() throws SQLException;
    public abstract Object[ ] getAttributes(java.util.Map map) throws SQLException;
    public abstract String getSQLTypeName() throws SQLException;
}
```

Passed To: SQLOutput.writeStruct()

Time

Java 1.1

java.sql

cloneable serializable comparable

A wrapper around the java.util.Date class that adjusts the time value (milliseconds since January 1, 1970 0:00:00 GMT) to conform to the SQL TIME specification. The TIME type only deals with the time of day, so the date components are set to January 1, 1970 and should not be altered. The Time class also includes a static valueOf() method that decodes the JDBC Time escape syntax *hh:mm:ss* into a Time value.

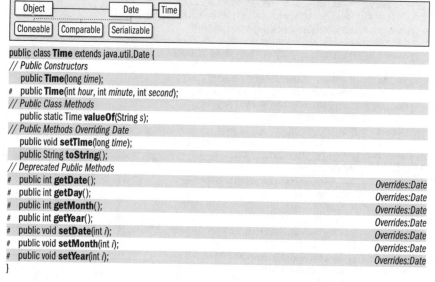

```
public class Time extends java.util.Date {
// Public Constructors
    public Time(long time);
#   public Time(int hour, int minute, int second);
// Public Class Methods
    public static Time valueOf(String s);
// Public Methods Overriding Date
    public void setTime(long time);
    public String toString();
// Deprecated Public Methods
#   public int getDate();                                    Overrides:Date
#   public int getDay();                                     Overrides:Date
#   public int getMonth();                                   Overrides:Date
#   public int getYear();                                    Overrides:Date
#   public void setDate(int i);                              Overrides:Date
#   public void setMonth(int i);                             Overrides:Date
#   public void setYear(int i);                              Overrides:Date
}
```

Passed To: CallableStatement.setTime(), PreparedStatement.setTime(), java.sql.ResultSet.updateTime(), SQLOutput.writeTime(), javax.sql.RowSet.setTime()

Returned By: CallableStatement.getTime(), java.sql.ResultSet.getTime(), SQLInput.readTime(),
Time.valueOf()

Timestamp   Java 1.1

java.sql   *cloneable serializable comparable*

Extends the java.util.Date class to function as an SQL TIMESTAMP value by adding a
nanoseconds component. The getTime() method returns the time in milliseconds since
January 1, 1970 00:00:00 GMT to the latest integral second. To include fractional seconds, divide the value returned by getNanos() by 1000000 and add this to the result
returned by getTime(). This allows accurate comparisons with java.util.Date objects. The
valueOf() method parses a String in the format *yyyy-mm-dd hh:mm:ss.fffffffff* into a Timestamp.

```
Object ─────────── Date ─┤ Timestamp

Cloneable   Comparable   Serializable
```

```
public class Timestamp extends java.util.Date {
// Public Constructors
    public Timestamp(long time);
#   public Timestamp(int year, int month, int date, int hour, int minute, int second, int nano);
// Public Class Methods
    public static Timestamp valueOf(String s);
// Public Instance Methods
    public boolean after(Timestamp ts);
    public boolean before(Timestamp ts);
1.4 public int compareTo(Timestamp ts);
    public boolean equals(Timestamp ts);
    public int getNanos();
    public void setNanos(int n);
// Public Methods Overriding Date
1.4 public int compareTo(Object o);
1.2 public boolean equals(Object ts);
1.4 public long getTime();
1.4 public void setTime(long time);
    public String toString();
}
```

Passed To: CallableStatement.setTimestamp(), PreparedStatement.setTimestamp(),
java.sql.ResultSet.updateTimestamp(), SQLOutput.writeTimestamp(), Timestamp.{after(), before(),
compareTo(), equals()}, javax.sql.RowSet.setTimestamp()

Returned By: CallableStatement.getTimestamp(), java.sql.ResultSet.getTimestamp(),
SQLInput.readTimestamp(), Timestamp.valueOf()

Types   Java 1.1

java.sql

The Types class defines a set of integer constants that represent SQL data types. The type
names and constant values are the ones specified in the XOPEN specification.

```
public class Types {
// No Constructor
// Public Constants
1.2 public static final int ARRAY;                                            =2003
    public static final int BIGINT;                                             =-5
    public static final int BINARY;                                             =-2
```

```
    public static final int BIT;                          =-7
1.2 public static final int BLOB;                         =2004
1.4 public static final int BOOLEAN;                       =16
    public static final int CHAR;                          =1
1.2 public static final int CLOB;                          =2005
1.4 public static final int DATALINK;                      =70
    public static final int DATE;                          =91
    public static final int DECIMAL;                       =3
1.2 public static final int DISTINCT;                      =2001
    public static final int DOUBLE;                        =8
    public static final int FLOAT;                         =6
    public static final int INTEGER;                       =4
1.2 public static final int JAVA_OBJECT;                   =2000
    public static final int LONGVARBINARY;                 =-4
    public static final int LONGVARCHAR;                   =-1
    public static final int NULL;                          =0
    public static final int NUMERIC;                       =2
    public static final int OTHER;                         =1111
    public static final int REAL;                          =7
1.2 public static final int REF;                           =2006
    public static final int SMALLINT;                      =5
1.2 public static final int STRUCT;                        =2002
    public static final int TIME;                          =92
    public static final int TIMESTAMP;                     =93
    public static final int TINYINT;                       =-6
    public static final int VARBINARY;                     =-3
    public static final int VARCHAR;                       =12
}
```

CHAPTER 24

javax.ejb and javax.ejb.spi

This is the primary package in the Enterprise JavaBeans API. It contains interfaces for all of the key entities you need to create and use EJB objects. It also contains a number of EJB-specific exceptions.

There are no concrete implementations provided for any of the interfaces in the javax.ejb package. EJB providers build their own implementations based on the EJB specification, and provide them in their EJB-enabled servers. You should, however, build EJB server objects and clients strictly using the standard interfaces defined in this package, in order to keep your code compatible with any standard EJB server.

Interfaces:

public interface **EJBContext**;
public interface **EJBHome** extends java.rmi.Remote;
public interface **EJBLocalHome**;
public interface **EJBLocalObject**;
public interface **EJBMetaData**;
public interface **EJBObject** extends java.rmi.Remote;
public interface **EnterpriseBean** extends Serializable;
public interface **EntityBean** extends EnterpriseBean;
public interface **EntityContext** extends EJBContext;
public interface **Handle** extends Serializable;
public interface **HomeHandle** extends Serializable;
public interface **MessageDrivenBean** extends EnterpriseBean;
public interface **MessageDrivenContext** extends EJBContext;
public interface **SessionBean** extends EnterpriseBean;
public interface **SessionContext** extends EJBContext;
public interface **SessionSynchronization**;

Exceptions:

public class **CreateException** extends Exception;
   └ public class **DuplicateKeyException** extends CreateException;
public class **EJBException** extends RuntimeException;
   └ public class **AccessLocalException** extends EJBException;
   └ public class **NoSuchEntityException** extends EJBException;
   └ public class **NoSuchObjectLocalException** extends EJBException;
   └ public class **TransactionRequiredLocalException** extends EJBException;
   └ public class **TransactionRolledbackLocalException** extends EJBException;
public class **FinderException** extends Exception;
   └ public class **ObjectNotFoundException** extends FinderException;
public class **RemoveException** extends Exception;

AccessLocalException
                                                                   EJB 2.0

javax.ejb   *serializable unchecked*

This exception is thrown to local clients of an EJB that attempt to call a method and they don't have permission to call the method. Added as of EJB 2.0.

```
Object ─ Throwable ─ Exception ─ RuntimeException ─ EJBException ─ AccessLocalException
         Serializable
```

```
public class AccessLocalException extends EJBException {
// Public Constructors
   public AccessLocalException();
   public AccessLocalException(String message);
   public AccessLocalException(String message, Exception ex);
}
```

CreateException
                                                                   EJB 1.0

javax.ejb   *serializable checked*

This exception must be thrown by all create() methods declared in an enterprise JavaBean's home interface. It is thrown if an error occurs during the process of creating the bean, as opposed to a communications error with the server before or after the bean is created.

```
Object ─ Throwable ─ Exception ─ CreateException
         Serializable
```

```
public class CreateException extends Exception {
// Public Constructors
   public CreateException();
   public CreateException(String message);
}
```

Subclasses: DuplicateKeyException

DuplicateKeyException
                                                            EJB 1.0

javax.ejb   *serializable checked*

This extension of the CreateException is thrown is a client attempts to create an entity bean using a primary key which matches the key of an existing entity bean of the same type.

```
Object ─ Throwable ─ Exception ─ CreateException ─ DuplicateKeyException
        Serializable
```

```
public class DuplicateKeyException extends CreateException {
// Public Constructors
    public DuplicateKeyException();
    public DuplicateKeyException(String message);
}
```

EJBContext

javax.ejb

The EJBContext interface is the base interface for context objects provided to EJB objects by their containers. The EJBContext represents runtime context information that the EJB object can use during method calls to check on environment variables, query the identity of the caller, etc.

The getCallerIdentity() and isCallerInRole() methods are provided to allow the EJB object to check on the identity of the caller, if it is known. The getEnvironment() method provides a Properties list with any environment variables that the EJB container exports to its EJB objects. The getEJBHome() method returns an instance of the EJB object's home interface, which allows the EJB object to query about its own type, implementing classes, etc. The rest of the EJBContext methods are related to transaction support. The getUserTransaction() method is the EJB object's access to the container-provided implementation of the javax.transaction.UserTransaction interface. The getRollbackOnly() method tells the EJB object if it is operating within a transaction that has been rolled back, and the setRollbackOnly() method sets the current enclosing transaction, if any, to be rolled back.

```
public interface EJBContext {
// Property Accessor Methods (by property name)
1.1 public abstract java.security.Principal getCallerPrincipal();
    public abstract EJBHome getEJBHome();
2.0 public abstract EJBLocalHome getEJBLocalHome();
    public abstract boolean getRollbackOnly() throws java.lang.IllegalStateException;
1.1 public abstract javax.transaction.UserTransaction getUserTransaction() throws java.lang.IllegalStateException;
// Public Instance Methods
1.1 public abstract boolean isCallerInRole(String roleName);
    public abstract void setRollbackOnly() throws java.lang.IllegalStateException;
// Deprecated Public Methods
#   public abstract java.security.Identity getCallerIdentity();
#   public abstract java.util.Properties getEnvironment();
#   public abstract boolean isCallerInRole(java.security.Identity role);
}
```

Implementations: EntityContext, MessageDrivenContext, SessionContext

EJBException

javax.ejb

serializable unchecked

The EJBException is thrown by an enterprise JavaBean implementation when it encounters an error during the execution of a client-invoked business method, or a container-invoked notification method. The container receives the exception (since it serves as a proxy for all client interactions with the bean), and is responsible for converting the EJBException to an appropriate subclass of java.rmi.RemoteException to be returned to the client.

If the EJB object was operating within a container-defined transaction context when the exception was thrown, then the container does a rollback on the transaction before throwing the RemoteException to the client. If the bean was operating within a client-defined transaction context, then the container marks the transaction for rollback, and throws a javax.transaction.TransactionRolledbackException (a subclass of RemoteException) to the client, to indicate that it should give up on its transaction.

```
Object ─┤ Throwable ├── Exception ├── RuntimeException ├── EJBException
        └ Serializable
```

```
public class EJBException extends RuntimeException {
// Public Constructors
    public EJBException();
    public EJBException(Exception ex);
    public EJBException(String message);
2.0 public EJBException(String message, Exception ex);
// Public Instance Methods
    public Exception getCausedByException();                                    default:null
// Public Methods Overriding Throwable
2.0 public String getMessage();                                                 default:null
2.0 public void printStackTrace();
2.0 public void printStackTrace(PrintWriter pw);
2.0 public void printStackTrace(PrintStream ps);
}
```

Subclasses: AccessLocalException, NoSuchEntityException, NoSuchObjectLocalException, TransactionRequiredLocalException, TransactionRolledbackLocalException

Thrown By: EJBLocalHome.remove(), EJBLocalObject.{getEJBLocalHome(), getPrimaryKey(), isIdentical(), remove()}, EntityBean.{ejbActivate(), ejbLoad(), ejbPassivate(), ejbRemove(), ejbStore(), setEntityContext(), unsetEntityContext()}, MessageDrivenBean.{ejbRemove(), setMessageDrivenContext()}, SessionBean.{ejbActivate(), ejbPassivate(), ejbRemove(), setSessionContext()}, SessionSynchronization.{afterBegin(), afterCompletion(), beforeCompletion()}

EJBHome   EJB 1.0

javax.ejb   *remote*

The EJBHome interface is the base interface for all home interfaces for enterprise JavaBeans. If you develop an enterprise JavaBean, you have to provide a home interface for it that extends this interface. The home interface allows clients to create beans of the corresponding type, and to find them, if it is an entity bean. When you extend the EJBHome interface to create a home interface for your EJB object type, you must specify any create or finder methods for the bean that you intend to provide for the client. The EJBHome interface provides two remove() methods that let a client remove its reference to a bean from the container, and a getEJBMetaData() method, which returns an EJBMetaData instance for the EJB object's type.

```
Remote ┄┤ EJBHome
```

```
public interface EJBHome extends java.rmi.Remote {
// Public Instance Methods
    public abstract EJBMetaData getEJBMetaData() throws java.rmi.RemoteException;
1.1 public abstract HomeHandle getHomeHandle() throws java.rmi.RemoteException;
    public abstract void remove(Handle handle) throws java.rmi.RemoteException, RemoveException;
    public abstract void remove(Object primaryKey) throws java.rmi.RemoteException, RemoveException;
}
```

Passed To: javax.ejb.spi.HandleDelegate.writeEJBHome()

Returned By: EJBContext.getEJBHome(), EJBMetaData.getEJBHome(), EJBObject.getEJBHome(), HomeHandle.getEJBHome(), javax.ejb.spi.HandleDelegate.readEJBHome()

EJBLocalHome   EJB 2.0

javax.ejb

The base class for all local home interfaces for EJBs. Added as of EJB 2.0.

```
public interface EJBLocalHome {
// Public Instance Methods
    public abstract void remove(Object primaryKey) throws RemoveException, EJBException;
}
```

Returned By: EJBContext.getEJBLocalHome(), EJBLocalObject.getEJBLocalHome()

EJBLocalObject   EJB 2.0

javax.ejb

The base class for local client interfaces for EJBs. Added as of EJB 2.0.

```
public interface EJBLocalObject {
// Public Instance Methods
    public abstract EJBLocalHome getEJBLocalHome() throws EJBException;
    public abstract Object getPrimaryKey() throws EJBException;
    public abstract boolean isIdentical(EJBLocalObject obj) throws EJBException;
    public abstract void remove() throws RemoveException, EJBException;
}
```

Passed To: EJBLocalObject.isIdentical()

Returned By: EntityContext.getEJBLocalObject(), SessionContext.getEJBLocalObject()

EJBMetaData   EJB 1.0

javax.ejb

This interface provides meta-data object a particular type of enterprise JavaBean. It allows you to query for the bean type's home interface, the Class for its home interface, the Class of its primary key (for entity beans only), the Class for its remote interface, and whether the bean is a session bean.

This meta-data might be used by EJB development tools to introspect on additional aspects of EJB classes that can't be obtained from the Object introspection methods.

Any implementations of this interface are required to be serializable, and must be valid for use over RMI.

```
public interface EJBMetaData {
// Property Accessor Methods (by property name)
    public abstract EJBHome getEJBHome();
    public abstract Class getHomeInterfaceClass();
    public abstract Class getPrimaryKeyClass();
    public abstract Class getRemoteInterfaceClass();
    public abstract boolean isSession();
1.1 public abstract boolean isStatelessSession();
}
```

Returned By: EJBHome.getEJBMetaData()

EJBObject

javax.ejb

This interface is the base interface for all remote interfaces for enterprise JavaBeans. When clients acquire a remote reference to an EJB object, they are given an instance of the EJBObject interface as a stub. If you develop an enterprise JavaBean, you must provide a remote interface for it by extending the EJBObject interface. In the remote interface for your EJB object type, you specify the business methods on your bean that will be accessible by remote clients.

The EJBObject interface provides methods that allow a client to query the bean's home interface, get a portable handle for the remote bean, get the primary key for the bean (if it is an entity bean), compare the bean for equality with another bean, and remove the client's reference to the bean.

```
Remote ---- EJBObject
```

```
public interface EJBObject extends java.rmi.Remote {
// Public Instance Methods
    public abstract EJBHome getEJBHome() throws java.rmi.RemoteException;
    public abstract Handle getHandle() throws java.rmi.RemoteException;
    public abstract Object getPrimaryKey() throws java.rmi.RemoteException;
    public abstract boolean isIdentical(EJBObject obj) throws java.rmi.RemoteException;
    public abstract void remove() throws java.rmi.RemoteException, RemoveException;
}
```

Passed To: EJBObject.isIdentical(), javax.ejb.spi.HandleDelegate.writeEJBObject()

Returned By: EntityContext.getEJBObject(), Handle.getEJBObject(), SessionContext.getEJBObject(), javax.ejb.spi.HandleDelegate.readEJBObject()

EnterpriseBean

javax.ejb

This interface is the base interface for all enterprise JavaBean implementations. If you develop an enterprise JavaBean, your bean implementation must extend this interface, usually by extending the derived interfaces SessionBean, MessageDrivenBean or EntityBean. The EnterpriseBean interface is a marker interface only, and doesn't define any methods.

```
Serializable ---- EnterpriseBean
```

```
public interface EnterpriseBean extends Serializable {
}
```

Implementations: EntityBean, MessageDrivenBean, SessionBean

EntityBean

javax.ejb

This interface is the base interface for all entity EJB objects. The methods defined on the EntityBean interface are used by EJB containers to notify the entity bean about entity-specific events, such as the need to (re)load its state from persistent storage.

The ejbActivate() and ejbPassivate() methods are called on the bean by the container when the bean is associated and disassociated with a specific entity, respectively. The ejbLoad() and ejbStore() methods are called when the entity bean needs to read and write its persistent state, respectively. The ejbRemove() method is called when the entity associated with this bean should be removed from persistent storage. When the container sets the entity bean's context, it calls the setEntityContext() method, and it removes the association with a given context by calling the unsetEntityContext() method.

```
Serializable ---- EnterpriseBean ---- EntityBean

public interface EntityBean extends EnterpriseBean {
// Public Instance Methods
    public abstract void ejbActivate() throws EJBException, java.rmi.RemoteException;
    public abstract void ejbLoad() throws EJBException, java.rmi.RemoteException;
    public abstract void ejbPassivate() throws EJBException, java.rmi.RemoteException;
    public abstract void ejbRemove() throws RemoveException, EJBException, java.rmi.RemoteException;
    public abstract void ejbStore() throws EJBException, java.rmi.RemoteException;
    public abstract void setEntityContext(EntityContext ctx) throws EJBException, java.rmi.RemoteException;
    public abstract void unsetEntityContext() throws EJBException, java.rmi.RemoteException;
}
```

EntityContext   EJB 1.0

javax.ejb

This extension of the EJBContext interface represents runtime context information for an entity bean. In addition to the context provided by the EJBContex methods, the EntityContext allows the entity bean to query for its primary key, and query for a remote reference to itself.

```
EJBContext ---- EntityContext

public interface EntityContext extends EJBContext {
// Public Instance Methods
2.0 public abstract EJBLocalObject getEJBLocalObject() throws java.lang.IllegalStateException;
    public abstract EJBObject getEJBObject() throws java.lang.IllegalStateException;
    public abstract Object getPrimaryKey() throws java.lang.IllegalStateException;
}
```

Passed To: EntityBean.setEntityContext()

FinderException   EJB 1.0

javax.ejb   *serializable checked*

This exception must be thrown by any finder methods declared on an entity bean's home interface. It is thrown if an error occurred while the server attempted to find the requested entity or entities.

```
Object -- Throwable -- Exception -- FinderException
              Serializable

public class FinderException extends Exception {
// Public Constructors
    public FinderException();
    public FinderException(String message);
}
```

Subclasses: ObjectNotFoundException

Handle

EJB 1.0

javax.ejb

serializable

A Handle represents a portable reference to a remote EJB object, in that it can be serialized, passed across Java VM boundaries, and then used to reconstitute a remote reference to the same EJB object from which it was acquired. You acquire a handle for an EJB object using the getHandle() method on its remote EJBObject.

The Handle interface acts as a base interface for EJB type-specific handle classes, which are typically generated for you by the container deployment tools. Its only method is getEJBObject(), which returns a remote reference to the EJB object that it represents.

Serializable ⋯ Handle

```
public interface Handle extends Serializable {
// Public Instance Methods
    public abstract EJBObject getEJBObject() throws java.rmi.RemoteException;
}
```

Passed To: EJBHome.remove()

Returned By: EJBObject.getHandle()

HomeHandle

EJB 1.1

javax.ejb

serializable

All home handle objects implement this interface. A home handle represents a persistent reference to an EJB home interface, obtained by calling getHomeHandle() on the EJB home. The handle can be serialized/deserialized and used to obtain a reference to its corresponding EJB home. Home handles are only supported for remote EJB home interfaces.

Serializable ⋯ HomeHandle

```
public interface HomeHandle extends Serializable {
// Public Instance Methods
    public abstract EJBHome getEJBHome() throws java.rmi.RemoteException;
}
```

Returned By: EJBHome.getHomeHandle()

MessageDrivenBean

EJB 2.0

javax.ejb

serializable

The base interface for all message-driven EJBs. Message-driven beans must implement this interface so that the EJB container can invoke the necessary callbacks during the bean's lifetime.

Serializable ⋯ EnterpriseBean ⋯ MessageDrivenBean

```
public interface MessageDrivenBean extends EnterpriseBean {
// Public Instance Methods
    public abstract void ejbRemove() throws EJBException;
    public abstract void setMessageDrivenContext(MessageDrivenContext ctx) throws EJBException;
}
```

MessageDrivenContext

javax.ejb

This interface represents the runtime context information that the EJB container provides to message-driven beans. It is provided to the bean after it has been created, and remains valid until the bean is removed.

```
EJBContext ┈┈ MessageDrivenContext
```

```
public interface MessageDrivenContext extends EJBContext {
}
```

Passed To: MessageDrivenBean.setMessageDrivenContext()

NoSuchEntityException

javax.ejb

serializable unchecked

This exception is thrown if a method is called on an entity bean that has been removed from the underlying persistent storage. Any of the bean's business methods can throw this exception, as well as the ejbLoad() and ejbStore() methods on the bean implementation class.

```
Object ─ Throwable ─ Exception ─ RuntimeException ─ EJBException ─ NoSuchEntityException
         Serializable
```

```
public class NoSuchEntityException extends EJBException {
// Public Constructors
    public NoSuchEntityException();
    public NoSuchEntityException(Exception ex);
    public NoSuchEntityException(String message);
}
```

NoSuchObjectLocalException

javax.ejb

serializable unchecked

This exception is thrown to local clients that attempt to invoke methods on a bean or object that no longer exists within the container.

```
Object ─ Throwable ─ Exception ─ RuntimeException ─ EJBException ─ NoSuchObjectLocalException
         Serializable
```

```
public class NoSuchObjectLocalException extends EJBException {
// Public Constructors
    public NoSuchObjectLocalException();
    public NoSuchObjectLocalException(String message);
    public NoSuchObjectLocalException(String message, Exception ex);
}
```

ObjectNotFoundException

javax.ejb

serializable checked

This subclass of FinderException is thrown by finder methods that are declared to return a single entity bean, when the requested entity could not be found in the server's persistent storage.

```
Object ─ Throwable ─ Exception ─ FinderException ─ ObjectNotFoundException
         Serializable
```

```
public class ObjectNotFoundException extends FinderException {
// Public Constructors
    public ObjectNotFoundException();
    public ObjectNotFoundException(String message);
}
```

RemoveException

javax.ejb

EJB 1.0

serializable checked

This exception is thrown by the remove methods on an EJB home interface, when an attempt to remove a bean from its container was rejected or failed, at either the container or the EJB object level.

```
Object ─ Throwable ─ Exception ─ RemoveException
         Serializable
```

```
public class RemoveException extends Exception {
// Public Constructors
    public RemoveException();
    public RemoveException(String message);
}
```

Thrown By: EJBHome.remove(), EJBLocalHome.remove(), EJBLocalObject.remove(), EJBObject.remove(), EntityBean.ejbRemove()

SessionBean

javax.ejb

EJB 1.0

serializable

This is the base interface for all session enterprise JavaBean implementations. The methods on this interface are used by the EJB container to notify the bean about certain events.

The ejbActivate() and ejbPassivate() methods are invoked by the container when the bean leaves/enters a passive state in the container, respectively. After the ejbPassivate() method completes, the container should be able to serialize the bean object to be stored to disk or some other persistent storage, if the container chooses. During the ejbActivate() method, the bean can restore any data or resources that it released when it was passivated. The container calls ejbRemove() on the bean just before the bean is to be destroyed. The container sets the bean's context by calling its setSessionContext() method. The session bean keeps the same context throughout its lifetime, so there is no corresponding unset method, as there is for EntityBeans.

```
Serializable ┈ EnterpriseBean ┈ SessionBean
```

```
public interface SessionBean extends EnterpriseBean {
// Public Instance Methods
    public abstract void ejbActivate() throws EJBException, java.rmi.RemoteException;
    public abstract void ejbPassivate() throws EJBException, java.rmi.RemoteException;
    public abstract void ejbRemove() throws EJBException, java.rmi.RemoteException;
    public abstract void setSessionContext(SessionContext ctx) throws EJBException, java.rmi.RemoteException;
}
```

SessionContext
EJB 1.0

javax.ejb

The SessionContext represents the runtime context information that the EJB container provides to session beans. The context is given to the bean after it is created, and it remains valid until the session bean is removed.

```
EJBContext ┈ SessionContext
```

```
public interface SessionContext extends EJBContext {
// Public Instance Methods
2.0  public abstract EJBLocalObject getEJBLocalObject() throws java.lang.IllegalStateException;
     public abstract EJBObject getEJBObject() throws java.lang.IllegalStateException;
}
```

Passed To: SessionBean.setSessionContext()

SessionSynchronization
EJB 1.0

javax.ejb

Session beans are not required to be transactional, but if you want your session bean to be notified of transaction boundaries, you can have your bean implementation class extend the SessionSynchronization interface. The EJB container will invoke the methods on this interface to notify your bean about the start and end of transactions.

The afterBegin() is called when a new transaction has started. Any business methods invoked on the bean between this point and a subsequent call to its beforeCompletion() method, will execute within the context of this transaction. The beforeCompletion() method is called on the bean when a transaction is about to end. The afterCompletion() method is called after the transaction has ended, and the boolean argument tells the bean whether the transaction was committed successfully (true), or rolled back (false).

```
public interface SessionSynchronization {
// Public Instance Methods
    public abstract void afterBegin() throws EJBException, java.rmi.RemoteException;
    public abstract void afterCompletion(boolean committed) throws EJBException, java.rmi.RemoteException;
    public abstract void beforeCompletion() throws EJBException, java.rmi.RemoteException;
}
```

TransactionRequiredLocalException
EJB 2.0

javax.ejb
serializable unchecked

This exception is thrown if a local client attempts to call a bean method that requires a transaction context, but fails to provide one.

```
Object ─ Throwable ─ Exception ─ RuntimeException ─ EJBException ─ TransactionRequiredLocalException
         Serializable
```

```
public class TransactionRequiredLocalException extends EJBException {
// Public Constructors
    public TransactionRequiredLocalException();
    public TransactionRequiredLocalException(String message);
}
```

TransactionRolledbackLocalException

javax.ejb

EJB 2.0

serializable unchecked

This exception is thrown if a local client's method call cannot be completed because the associated transaction context had to be rolled back.

```
Object ─ Throwable ─ Exception ─ RuntimeException ─ EJBException ─ TransactionRolledbackLocalException
         Serializable
```

```
public class TransactionRolledbackLocalException extends EJBException {
// Public Constructors
     public TransactionRolledbackLocalException();
     public TransactionRolledbackLocalException(String message);
     public TransactionRolledbackLocalException(String message, Exception ex);
}
```

Package javax.ejb.spi

EJB 2.0

This package defines interfaces (currently only one) that are implemented by an Enterprise JavaBeans container.

Interfaces:

```
public interface HandleDelegate;
```

HandleDelegate

javax.ejb.spi

EJB 2.0

The HandleDelegate is used internally by implementations of Handles and HomeHandles. It is used to read and write EJB home and object references to I/O streams. An implementation of the HandleDelegate is provided to Handle and HomeHandles through its JNDI namespace, using the name "java:comp/HandleDelegate"

```
public interface HandleDelegate {
// Public Instance Methods
     public abstract EJBHome readEJBHome(ObjectInputStream istream) throws IOException, ClassNotFoundException;
     public abstract EJBObject readEJBObject(ObjectInputStream istream) throws IOException,
         ClassNotFoundException;
     public abstract void writeEJBHome(EJBHome ejbHome, ObjectOutputStream ostream) throws IOException;
     public abstract void writeEJBObject(EJBObject ejbObject, ObjectOutputStream ostream) throws IOException;
}
```

CHAPTER 25

javax.jms

The Java Message Service provides an API for message-based communications between separate Java processes. Message-based communication is asynchronous in nature: a message is sent out addressed to a recipient or group of recipients, and the recipient receives and acts on the message some unspecified time after that. This is different from other network-based communications between clients, like RMI, where the sender of a message waits for a response from the receiver before continuing.

In the JMS model, clients of a message service send and receive messages through a provider that is responsible for delivering messages. JMS 1.0 provides two models for messaging among clients: point-to-point and publish/subscribe. In point-to-point messaging, a message is created by one client and addressed for a single remote client. The provider is handed the message and delivers it to the one client targeted by the message. This model revolves around message queues; a message sender will queue outgoing messages for delivery, a message recipient will queue incoming messages for handling. The interfaces provided in the javax.jms package for point-to-point messaging have "Queue" as their prefix (QueueConnection, QueueSession, etc.). In publish/subscribe messaging, a hierarchical content tree is established, and clients publish messages to specific nodes or topics in the tree, to be delivered to any clients that have subscribed to these nodes. Interfaces related to publish/subscribe messaging have "Topic" as their prefix (TopicConnection, TopicSession, etc.). Point-to-point messaging is analogous to typical email messaging, while publish/subscribe messaging is analogous to newsgroups.

In a typical usage scenario, JMS clients will get a reference to a ConnectionFactory from the JMS provider (usually through a JNDI lookup). The ConnectionFactory is used to create a Connection to the provider. The Connection is used to create Sessions that the client can use to send and receive messages. Within a single Session, messages are sent and received in a serial order. Once the client has a Session, it can send and receive Messages, which are composed of a header, optional properties, and a body. Different types of Messages can hold different contents in their body (text, binary data, name/value pairs, etc.).

For more details on programming with JMS, refer to Chapter 10.

Interfaces:

```
public interface BytesMessage extends Message;
public interface Connection;
public interface ConnectionConsumer;
public interface ConnectionFactory;
public interface ConnectionMetaData;
public interface DeliveryMode;
public interface Destination;
public interface ExceptionListener;
public interface MapMessage extends Message;
public interface Message;
public interface MessageConsumer;
public interface MessageListener;
public interface MessageProducer;
public interface ObjectMessage extends Message;
public interface Queue extends Destination;
public interface QueueBrowser;
public interface QueueConnection extends Connection;
public interface QueueConnectionFactory extends ConnectionFactory;
public interface QueueReceiver extends MessageConsumer;
public interface QueueSender extends MessageProducer;
public interface QueueSession extends Session;
public interface ServerSession;
public interface ServerSessionPool;
public interface Session extends Runnable;
public interface StreamMessage extends Message;
public interface TemporaryQueue extends Queue;
public interface TemporaryTopic extends Topic;
public interface TextMessage extends Message;
public interface Topic extends Destination;
public interface TopicConnection extends Connection;
public interface TopicConnectionFactory extends ConnectionFactory;
public interface TopicPublisher extends MessageProducer;
public interface TopicSession extends Session;
public interface TopicSubscriber extends MessageConsumer;
public interface XAConnection;
public interface XAConnectionFactory;
public interface XAQueueConnection extends XAConnection, QueueConnection;
public interface XAQueueConnectionFactory extends XAConnectionFactory, QueueConnectionFactory;
public interface XAQueueSession extends XASession;
public interface XASession extends Session;
public interface XATopicConnection extends XAConnection, TopicConnection;
public interface XATopicConnectionFactory extends XAConnectionFactory, TopicConnectionFactory;
public interface XATopicSession extends XASession;
```

Classes:

```
public class QueueRequestor;
public class TopicRequestor;
```

Exceptions:

```
public class JMSException extends Exception;
    └ public class IllegalStateException extends JMSException;
```

L public class **InvalidClientIDException** extends JMSException;
L public class **InvalidDestinationException** extends JMSException;
L public class **InvalidSelectorException** extends JMSException;
L public class **JMSSecurityException** extends JMSException;
L public class **MessageEOFException** extends JMSException;
L public class **MessageFormatException** extends JMSException;
L public class **MessageNotReadableException** extends JMSException;
L public class **MessageNotWriteableException** extends JMSException;
L public class **ResourceAllocationException** extends JMSException;
L public class **TransactionInProgressException** extends JMSException;
L public class **TransactionRolledBackException** extends JMSException;

BytesMessage   JMS 1.0

javax.jms

A BytesMessage is a Message that contains an uninterpreted stream of bytes as its body. This would typically be used to wrap an existing (non-JMS) message format so that it could be delivered over JMS. Data is written to the message's binary body using its write methods, and read using its read methods. Once a BytesMessage has been created (using a series of write calls), the reset() method can be used to put the message into read-only mode. Until this is done, the message is in write-only mode, and the contents cannot be read back.

Message ┈ BytesMessage

```
public interface BytesMessage extends javax.jms.Message {
// Public Instance Methods
    public abstract boolean readBoolean() throws JMSException;
    public abstract byte readByte() throws JMSException;
    public abstract int readBytes(byte[ ] value) throws JMSException;
    public abstract int readBytes(byte[ ] value, int length) throws JMSException;
    public abstract char readChar() throws JMSException;
    public abstract double readDouble() throws JMSException;
    public abstract float readFloat() throws JMSException;
    public abstract int readInt() throws JMSException;
    public abstract long readLong() throws JMSException;
    public abstract short readShort() throws JMSException;
    public abstract int readUnsignedByte() throws JMSException;
    public abstract int readUnsignedShort() throws JMSException;
    public abstract String readUTF() throws JMSException;
    public abstract void reset() throws JMSException;
    public abstract void writeBoolean(boolean value) throws JMSException;
    public abstract void writeByte(byte value) throws JMSException;
    public abstract void writeBytes(byte[ ] value) throws JMSException;
    public abstract void writeBytes(byte[ ] value, int offset, int length) throws JMSException;
    public abstract void writeChar(char value) throws JMSException;
    public abstract void writeDouble(double value) throws JMSException;
    public abstract void writeFloat(float value) throws JMSException;
    public abstract void writeInt(int value) throws JMSException;
    public abstract void writeLong(long value) throws JMSException;
    public abstract void writeObject(Object value) throws JMSException;
```

```
    public abstract void writeShort(short value) throws JMSException;
    public abstract void writeUTF(String value) throws JMSException;
}
```

Returned By: javax.jms.Session.createBytesMessage()

Connection   JMS 1.0

javax.jms

A JMS client needs to have a Connection to the JMS provider in order to send or receive messages. The javax.jms.Connection interface for messaging is roughly analogous to the java.sql.Connection interface in JDBC — one connects a client to a messaging service, the other connects a client to a persistent data service. Another analogous property is that JMS Connections are generally expensive to create, because setup requires networks communications with the provider. A client will normally want to have only one, or very few, Connections to their JMS provider.

A Connection can be in either running mode (messages are being sent and received through the connection), or it can be stopped. When a Connection is in stopped mode, it can send messages, but it can't receive messages. A newly-created Connection is in stopped mode, to allow you to finish setting up your client (create Session(s), create MessageConsumers and/or MessageProducers, etc.). A Connection can be started and stopped (using the stop() and start() methods) multiple times, if necessary. When you're done with a Connection, you should free up its resources by calling its close() method.

Connections are used to create sessions for message exchanges. The methods for creating sessions are defined on extensions of the Connection interface (QueueConnection and Topic-Connection).

```
public interface Connection {
// Public Instance Methods
    public abstract void close() throws JMSException;
    public abstract String getClientID() throws JMSException;
    public abstract javax.jms.ExceptionListener getExceptionListener() throws JMSException;
    public abstract javax.jms.ConnectionMetaData getMetaData() throws JMSException;
    public abstract void setClientID(String clientID) throws JMSException;
    public abstract void setExceptionListener(javax.jms.ExceptionListener listener) throws JMSException;
    public abstract void start() throws JMSException;
    public abstract void stop() throws JMSException;
}
```

Implementations: QueueConnection, TopicConnection

ConnectionConsumer   JMS 1.0

javax.jms

A ConnectionConsumer is used in situations where messages need to be read concurrently by multiple agents within the same process (e.g., within an application server running multiple message-based applications). The ConnectionConsumer delivers messages to one or more Sessions that are associated with MessageListeners for individual clients. It contains a reference to a ServerSessionPool which is uses to access the Sessions that are concurrently reading messages. Applications normally don't need to use the ConnectionConsumer interface directly. It would be used by an application server to provide a message-handling service for client applications.

```
public interface ConnectionConsumer {
// Public Instance Methods
```

```
    public abstract void close() throws JMSException;
    public abstract ServerSessionPool getServerSessionPool() throws JMSException;
}
```

Returned By: QueueConnection.createConnectionConsumer(),
TopicConnection.{createConnectionConsumer(), createDurableConnectionConsumer()}

ConnectionFactory   JMS 1.0

javax.jms

Messaging clients use a ConnectionFactory to get Connections to the message provider. A
ConnectionFactory is usually acquired through a JNDI lookup, and then creates a Connection with the factory. The ConnectionFactory interface doesn't define methods for creating
Connections; they are provided by extensions to this interface (e.g., QueueConnectionFactory, TopicConnectionFactory).

```
public interface ConnectionFactory {
}
```

Implementations: QueueConnectionFactory, TopicConnectionFactory

ConnectionMetaData   JMS 1.0

javax.jms

The Connection.getMetaData() method returns a ConnectionMetaData object that holds information about the JMS connection, including the version of JMS in use by the provider,
and version information about the provider itself.

```
public interface ConnectionMetaData {
// Property Accessor Methods (by property name)
    public abstract int getJMSMajorVersion() throws JMSException;
    public abstract int getJMSMinorVersion() throws JMSException;
    public abstract String getJMSProviderName() throws JMSException;
    public abstract String getJMSVersion() throws JMSException;
    public abstract java.util.Enumeration getJMSXPropertyNames() throws JMSException;
    public abstract int getProviderMajorVersion() throws JMSException;
    public abstract int getProviderMinorVersion() throws JMSException;
    public abstract String getProviderVersion() throws JMSException;
}
```

Returned By: javax.jms.Connection.getMetaData()

DeliveryMode   JMS 1.0

javax.jms

This interface defines constants that represent delivery modes that a JMS provider can
support. NON_PERSISTENT delivery implies that a significant failure by the provider
before a message can be delivered will cause the message to be lost. PERSISTENT delivery mode implies that the provider will store message to persistent storage, and that the
messages will survive a crash by the provider. Message senders specify the delivery
mode for a message in its header, using the Message.setJMSDeliveryMode() method, and
the provider is responsible for honoring it.

```
public interface DeliveryMode {
// Public Constants
    public static final int NON_PERSISTENT;                                    =1
```

```
    public static final int PERSISTENT;                                    =2
}
```

Destination   JMS 1.0

javax.jms

A Destination represents a delivery address for a message. This interface is simply a
marker interface, without any methods or members, since JMS doesn't attempt to define
an addressing syntax. Implementors of JMS providers will need to provide implementations of this interface that also define their message addressing syntax. Destinations
might be published by a JMS provider using JNDI. In this case, the JMS client would
need to assemble the name of the queue in the syntax expected by the provider, and
then do a JNDI lookup to get a reference to the Destination.

```
public interface Destination {
}
```

Implementations: Queue, Topic

Passed To: javax.jms.Message.{setJMSDestination(), setJMSReplyTo()}

Returned By: javax.jms.Message.{getJMSDestination(), getJMSReplyTo()}

ExceptionListener   JMS 1.0

javax.jms

An ExceptionListener is used to get asynchronous notification of errors that occur with a
Connection to a JMS provider. If a client registers an ExceptionListener with a Connection
using the Connection.setExceptionListener() method, then on any error the provider will call
the onException() method on the ExceptionListener, passing it the exception describing the
error.

```
public interface ExceptionListener {
// Public Instance Methods
    public abstract void onException(JMSException exception);
}
```

Passed To: javax.jms.Connection.setExceptionListener()

Returned By: javax.jms.Connection.getExceptionListener()

IllegalStateException   JMS 1.0

javax.jms   *serializable checked*

This exception is thrown if a request is made of a provider at a time when the request
can't be satisfied.

```
public class IllegalStateException extends JMSException {
// Public Constructors
    public IllegalStateException(String reason);
    public IllegalStateException(String reason, String errorCode);
}
```

InvalidClientIDException   JMS 1.0

javax.jms   *serializable checked*

This exception is thrown by the Connection.setClientID() method when an invalid client ID
is given.

Object — Throwable — Exception — JMSException — InvalidClientIDException
Serializable

```
public class InvalidClientIDException extends JMSException {
// Public Constructors
    public InvalidClientIDException(String reason);
    public InvalidClientIDException(String reason, String errorCode);
}
```

InvalidDestinationException   JMS 1.0

javax.jms   *serializable checked*

This exception is thrown when the provider encounters a destination that it can't
understand, or that is no longer accessible by the provider (e.g., a topic has been
removed from a publish/subscribe context, or a queue associated with a user account
has been removed because the account has been closed).

Object — Throwable — Exception — JMSException — InvalidDestinationException
Serializable

```
public class InvalidDestinationException extends JMSException {
// Public Constructors
    public InvalidDestinationException(String reason);
    public InvalidDestinationException(String reason, String errorCode);
}
```

InvalidSelectorException   JMS 1.0

javax.jms   *serializable checked*

This exception is thrown when a malformed selector is given to a provider, e.g., as part
of a MessageSelector.

Object — Throwable — Exception — JMSException — InvalidSelectorException
Serializable

```
public class InvalidSelectorException extends JMSException {
// Public Constructors
    public InvalidSelectorException(String reason);
    public InvalidSelectorException(String reason, String errorCode);
}
```

JMSException   JMS 1.0

javax.jms   *serializable checked*

This is the base class for all JMS-related exceptions. It provides a provider-specific error
code and a nested exception that is the source of the error.

```
public class JMSException extends Exception {
// Public Constructors
    public JMSException(String reason);
    public JMSException(String reason, String errorCode);
// Public Instance Methods
    public String getErrorCode();
    public Exception getLinkedException();
    public void setLinkedException(Exception ex);                    synchronized
}
```

Subclasses: javax.jms.IllegalStateException, InvalidClientIDException, InvalidDestinationException, InvalidSelectorException, JMSSecurityException, MessageEOFException, MessageFormatException, MessageNotReadableException, MessageNotWriteableException, javax.jms.ResourceAllocationException, TransactionInProgressException, TransactionRolledBackException

Passed To: javax.jms.ExceptionListener.onException()

Thrown By: Too many methods to list.

JMSSecurityException   JMS 1.0

javax.jms   *serializable checked*

This exception is thrown by a provider when a request can't be satisfied for security reasons, e.g., a client-provided name/password fails authentication.

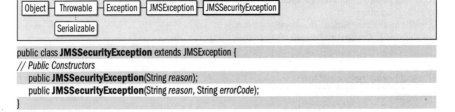

```
public class JMSSecurityException extends JMSException {
// Public Constructors
    public JMSSecurityException(String reason);
    public JMSSecurityException(String reason, String errorCode);
}
```

MapMessage   JMS 1.0

javax.jms

A MapMessage has a set of name/value pairs as its message body. The names of the properties are Strings, and the values are Java primitive types. There are getXXX() and setXXX() methods for each primitive type, plus getObject() and setObject() methods for situations where the type of the value isn't known until runtime. If a property is set to a value of a certain type, it has to be read back using a get method appropriate for that type, according to the following table:

if written as:	boolean	byte	char	short	int	long	float	double	String	byte[]
can be read as:										
boolean		X								X
byte			X		X	X	X			X
char				X						X

if writ-ten as:	boolean	byte	char	short	int	long	float	double	String	byte[]
short					X	X	X			X
int						X	X			X
long							X			X
float								X	X	X
double									X	X
String		X	X	X	X	X	X	X	X	X
byte[]										X

If a value is read using an inappropriate get method, then a MessageFormatException is thrown. The getMapNames() methods returns an Enumeration of names for the values in the MapMessage.

Clients that receive a MapMessage can only read the contents of the message, until they call clearBody() on the message. If a client tries to write values to the message before this, a MessageNotWriteableException will be thrown.

Message ─ MapMessage

```
public interface MapMessage extends javax.jms.Message {
// Public Instance Methods
    public abstract boolean getBoolean(String name) throws JMSException;
    public abstract byte getByte(String name) throws JMSException;
    public abstract byte[ ] getBytes(String name) throws JMSException;
    public abstract char getChar(String name) throws JMSException;
    public abstract double getDouble(String name) throws JMSException;
    public abstract float getFloat(String name) throws JMSException;
    public abstract int getInt(String name) throws JMSException;
    public abstract long getLong(String name) throws JMSException;
    public abstract java.util.Enumeration getMapNames() throws JMSException;
    public abstract Object getObject(String name) throws JMSException;
    public abstract short getShort(String name) throws JMSException;
    public abstract String getString(String name) throws JMSException;
    public abstract boolean itemExists(String name) throws JMSException;
    public abstract void setBoolean(String name, boolean value) throws JMSException;
    public abstract void setByte(String name, byte value) throws JMSException;
    public abstract void setBytes(String name, byte[ ] value) throws JMSException;
    public abstract void setBytes(String name, byte[ ] value, int offset, int length) throws JMSException;
    public abstract void setChar(String name, char value) throws JMSException;
    public abstract void setDouble(String name, double value) throws JMSException;
    public abstract void setFloat(String name, float value) throws JMSException;
    public abstract void setInt(String name, int value) throws JMSException;
    public abstract void setLong(String name, long value) throws JMSException;
    public abstract void setObject(String name, Object value) throws JMSException;
    public abstract void setShort(String name, short value) throws JMSException;
    public abstract void setString(String name, String value) throws JMSException;
}
```

Returned By: javax.jms.Session.createMapMessage()

Message   JMS 1.0

javax.jms

The Message interface is the base interface for all messages in JMS. A Message is composed of a set of predefined header fields, an optional set of application-specific properties, and a body containing the content of the message. A set and get method are
provided for each header field supported by a JMS message.

Properties can be added to a message using the setXXXProperty() methods, and they can
be read using the getXXXProperty() methods. If a property is written with a value of a
given type, it needs to be read from the message according to the following table. If in
invalid get method is used for a property, then a MessageFormatException is thrown:

if writ- ten as: can be read as:	boolean	byte	short	int	long	float	double	String
boolean	X							X
byte		X	X	X	X			X
short			X	X	X			X
int				X	X			X
long					X			X
float						X	X	X
double							X	X
String	X	X	X	X	X	X	X	X

Properties with names prefixed by "JMSX" are reserved for use by the JMS standard.

```
public interface Message {
// Public Constants
    public static final int DEFAULT_DELIVERY_MODE;                                =2
    public static final int DEFAULT_PRIORITY;                                     =4
    public static final long DEFAULT_TIME_TO_LIVE;                                =0
// Property Accessor Methods (by property name)
    public abstract String getJMSCorrelationID() throws JMSException;
    public abstract void setJMSCorrelationID(String correlationID) throws JMSException;
    public abstract byte[ ] getJMSCorrelationIDAsBytes() throws JMSException;
    public abstract void setJMSCorrelationIDAsBytes(byte[ ] correlationID) throws JMSException;
    public abstract int getJMSDeliveryMode() throws JMSException;
    public abstract void setJMSDeliveryMode(int deliveryMode) throws JMSException;
    public abstract javax.jms.Destination getJMSDestination() throws JMSException;
    public abstract void setJMSDestination(javax.jms.Destination destination) throws JMSException;
    public abstract long getJMSExpiration() throws JMSException;
    public abstract void setJMSExpiration(long expiration) throws JMSException;
    public abstract String getJMSMessageID() throws JMSException;
    public abstract void setJMSMessageID(String id) throws JMSException;
    public abstract int getJMSPriority() throws JMSException;
    public abstract void setJMSPriority(int priority) throws JMSException;
    public abstract boolean getJMSRedelivered() throws JMSException;
    public abstract void setJMSRedelivered(boolean redelivered) throws JMSException;
    public abstract javax.jms.Destination getJMSReplyTo() throws JMSException;
    public abstract void setJMSReplyTo(javax.jms.Destination replyTo) throws JMSException;
    public abstract long getJMSTimestamp() throws JMSException;
    public abstract void setJMSTimestamp(long timestamp) throws JMSException;
```

```
    public abstract String getJMSType() throws JMSException;
    public abstract void setJMSType(String type) throws JMSException;
    public abstract java.util.Enumeration getPropertyNames() throws JMSException;
// Public Instance Methods
    public abstract void acknowledge() throws JMSException;
    public abstract void clearBody() throws JMSException;
    public abstract void clearProperties() throws JMSException;
    public abstract boolean getBooleanProperty(String name) throws JMSException;
    public abstract byte getByteProperty(String name) throws JMSException;
    public abstract double getDoubleProperty(String name) throws JMSException;
    public abstract float getFloatProperty(String name) throws JMSException;
    public abstract int getIntProperty(String name) throws JMSException;
    public abstract long getLongProperty(String name) throws JMSException;
    public abstract Object getObjectProperty(String name) throws JMSException;
    public abstract short getShortProperty(String name) throws JMSException;
    public abstract String getStringProperty(String name) throws JMSException;
    public abstract boolean propertyExists(String name) throws JMSException;
    public abstract void setBooleanProperty(String name, boolean value) throws JMSException;
    public abstract void setByteProperty(String name, byte value) throws JMSException;
    public abstract void setDoubleProperty(String name, double value) throws JMSException;
    public abstract void setFloatProperty(String name, float value) throws JMSException;
    public abstract void setIntProperty(String name, int value) throws JMSException;
    public abstract void setLongProperty(String name, long value) throws JMSException;
    public abstract void setObjectProperty(String name, Object value) throws JMSException;
    public abstract void setShortProperty(String name, short value) throws JMSException;
    public abstract void setStringProperty(String name, String value) throws JMSException;
}
```

Implementations: BytesMessage, MapMessage, ObjectMessage, StreamMessage, TextMessage

Passed To: MessageListener.onMessage(), QueueRequestor.request(), QueueSender.send(), TopicPublisher.publish(), TopicRequestor.request()

Returned By: MessageConsumer.{receive(), receiveNoWait()}, QueueRequestor.request(), javax.jms.Session.createMessage(), TopicRequestor.request()

MessageConsumer   JMS 1.0

javax.jms

A message consumer is used by JMS clients to receive messages. A message consumer is created by a client by specifying a Destination from which to receive messages, and an optional message selector that filters messages according to their header fields and property values. The methods for creating MessageConsumers are defined in subclasses of the Connection interface.

A message selector is a filter string whose syntax is based on the SQL92 conditional expression syntax. More details on the syntax of message selectors can be found in chapter X, "Java Message Service".

A client can use a MessageConsumer synchronously, by polling it using its receive methods, or asynchronously, by registering a MessageListener with the consumer. When a message arrives that matches the sending Destination and the message selector, then the onMessage() method on the registered listener is called.

MessageConsumers should be freed by calling their close() method, to free up any resources allocated for them by the provider.

```
public interface MessageConsumer {
// Public Instance Methods
    public abstract void close() throws JMSException;
    public abstract MessageListener getMessageListener() throws JMSException;
    public abstract String getMessageSelector() throws JMSException;
    public abstract javax.jms.Message receive() throws JMSException;
    public abstract javax.jms.Message receive(long timeout) throws JMSException;
    public abstract javax.jms.Message receiveNoWait() throws JMSException;
    public abstract void setMessageListener(MessageListener listener) throws JMSException;
}
```

Implementations: QueueReceiver, TopicSubscriber

MessageEOFException   JMS 1.0

javax.jms   *serializable checked*

This exception is thrown if the end of a StreamMessage or BytesMessage is reached before
it is expected.

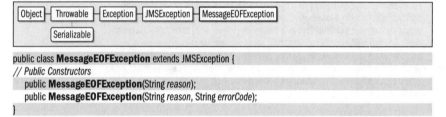

```
public class MessageEOFException extends JMSException {
// Public Constructors
    public MessageEOFException(String reason);
    public MessageEOFException(String reason, String errorCode);
}
```

MessageFormatException   JMS 1.0

javax.jms   *serializable checked*

This exception is thrown when an attempt is made to read data from a message as the
wrong data type, or to write data to a message in a type that it doesn't support.

```
Object — Throwable — Exception — JMSException — MessageFormatException
        Serializable
```

```
public class MessageFormatException extends JMSException {
// Public Constructors
    public MessageFormatException(String reason);
    public MessageFormatException(String reason, String errorCode);
}
```

MessageListener   JMS 1.0

javax.jms

A MessageListener is registered by a client with a MessageConsumer, to allow it to asynchronously receive messages. When the consumer receives a message, the listener's
onMessage() method is invoked. The consumer will wait until the onMessage() method is
complete before delivering the next message.

```
public interface MessageListener {
// Public Instance Methods
    public abstract void onMessage(javax.jms.Message message);
}
```

Passed To: MessageConsumer.setMessageListener(), javax.jms.Session.setMessageListener()

Returned By: MessageConsumer.getMessageListener(), javax.jms.Session.getMessageListener()

MessageNotReadableException

JMS 1.0

serializable checked

javax.jms

This exception is thrown if a client attempts to read data from a write-only message (e.g., a StreamMessage whose contents have not yet been reset).

```
Object ─ Throwable ─ Exception ─ JMSException ─ MessageNotReadableException
           Serializable
```

```
public class MessageNotReadableException extends JMSException {
// Public Constructors
    public MessageNotReadableException(String reason);
    public MessageNotReadableException(String reason, String errorCode);
}
```

MessageNotWriteableException

JMS 1.0

serializable checked

javax.jms

This exception is thrown when an attempt is made to write date to a read-only message (e.g., a received MapMessage that has not had its clearBody() method called yet).

```
Object ─ Throwable ─ Exception ─ JMSException ─ MessageNotWriteableException
           Serializable
```

```
public class MessageNotWriteableException extends JMSException {
// Public Constructors
    public MessageNotWriteableException(String reason);
    public MessageNotWriteableException(String reason, String errorCode);
}
```

MessageProducer

JMS 1.0

javax.jms

Clients use MessageProducers to send messages. MessageProducers can be tied to a specific Destination, and any messages sent through the producer are addressed to the Destination specified when it was created. If a Destination is not specified when a MessageProducer is created, then a Destination has to provided for each message sent. Methods to create MessageProducers are provided by subclasses of the Session interface (e.g., TopicSession, QueueSession).

The MessageProducer has a default delivery mode, priority and time-to-live for messages that it sends. There are get and set methods for these default properties. If these properties are specified on a message, they override the defaults of the MessageProducer.

```
public interface MessageProducer {
// Property Accessor Methods (by property name)
```

```
    public abstract int getDeliveryMode() throws JMSException;
    public abstract void setDeliveryMode(int deliveryMode) throws JMSException;
    public abstract boolean getDisableMessageID() throws JMSException;
    public abstract void setDisableMessageID(boolean value) throws JMSException;
    public abstract boolean getDisableMessageTimestamp() throws JMSException;
    public abstract void setDisableMessageTimestamp(boolean value) throws JMSException;
    public abstract int getPriority() throws JMSException;
    public abstract void setPriority(int defaultPriority) throws JMSException;
    public abstract long getTimeToLive() throws JMSException;
    public abstract void setTimeToLive(long timeToLive) throws JMSException;
// Public Instance Methods
    public abstract void close() throws JMSException;
}
```

Implementations: QueueSender, TopicPublisher

ObjectMessage
JMS 1.0

javax.jms

This is a message that contains a single serialized Java object as its body. Only Serializable objects can be used as the body of an ObjectMessage. When an ObjectMessage is received, it is read-only until the clearBody() method is called on it.

```
Message ‑‑ ObjectMessage
```

```
public interface ObjectMessage extends javax.jms.Message {
// Public Instance Methods
    public abstract Serializable getObject() throws JMSException;
    public abstract void setObject(Serializable object) throws JMSException;
}
```

Returned By: javax.jms.Session.createObjectMessage()

Queue
JMS 1.0

javax.jms

A Queue is a Destination specific to point-to-point messaging. The Queue has a String name, whose syntax is dictated by the provider. Queues are created using the createQueue() method on a QueueSession.

```
Destination ‑‑ Queue
```

```
public interface Queue extends javax.jms.Destination {
// Public Instance Methods
    public abstract String getQueueName() throws JMSException;
    public abstract String toString();
}
```

Implementations: TemporaryQueue

Passed To: QueueConnection.createConnectionConsumer(), QueueRequestor.QueueRequestor(), QueueSender.send(), QueueSession.{createBrowser(), createReceiver(), createSender()}

Returned By: QueueBrowser.getQueue(), QueueReceiver.getQueue(), QueueSender.getQueue(), QueueSession.createQueue()

QueueBrowser

javax.jms

A QueueBrowser is used to "peek" at the contents of a message queue without actually removing the messages. A QueueBrowser has an optional message selector that can be used to filter the messages checked for on the queue. QueueBrowsers are created using the createBrowser() methods on QueueSession.

```
public interface QueueBrowser {
// Public Instance Methods
    public abstract void close() throws JMSException;
    public abstract java.util.Enumeration getEnumeration() throws JMSException;
    public abstract String getMessageSelector() throws JMSException;
    public abstract Queue getQueue() throws JMSException;
}
```

Returned By: QueueSession.createBrowser()

QueueConnection

javax.jms

A QueueConnection is a Connection specific to a point-to-point messaging provider. The QueueConnection allows clients to create QueueSessions using the createQueueSession() method.

Connection ┈ QueueConnection

```
public interface QueueConnection extends javax.jms.Connection {
// Public Instance Methods
    public abstract ConnectionConsumer createConnectionConsumer(Queue queue, String messageSelector,
                                            ServerSessionPool sessionPool, int maxMessages)
        throws JMSException;
    public abstract QueueSession createQueueSession(boolean transacted, int acknowledgeMode)
        throws JMSException;
}
```

Implementations: XAQueueConnection

Returned By: QueueConnectionFactory.createQueueConnection()

QueueConnectionFactory

javax.jms

A QueueConnectionFactory is exported by point-to-point providers to allow clients to create QueueConnections to the provider. The default createQueueConnection() method is used to create a connection under the default user identity of the client JVM, and the other accepts a name and password that is used to authenticate the connection request.

ConnectionFactory ┈ QueueConnectionFactory

```
public interface QueueConnectionFactory extends javax.jms.ConnectionFactory {
// Public Instance Methods
    public abstract QueueConnection createQueueConnection() throws JMSException;
```

```
    public abstract QueueConnection createQueueConnection(String userName, String password)
        throws JMSException;
}
```

Implementations: XAQueueConnectionFactory

QueueReceiver   JMS 1.0
javax.jms

A QueueReceiver is a MessageConsumer specific to point-to-point messaging. The getQueue()
method returns the Queue associated with the receiver. QueueReceivers are created using
the createReceiver() methods on QueueSession.

```
MessageConsumer ┄ QueueReceiver
```

```
public interface QueueReceiver extends MessageConsumer {
// Public Instance Methods
    public abstract Queue getQueue() throws JMSException;
}
```

Returned By: QueueSession.createReceiver()

QueueRequestor   JMS 1.0
javax.jms

The QueueRequestor is a utility class provided for situations where a client wants to send
a message to a specific destination and wait for a response. The QueueRequestor is constructed with a QueueSession and a destination Queue, and then its request() method is
called with the Message to be sent. The QueueRequestor sets the reply-to destination on
the message to a temporary Queue that it creates. It sends the message and waits for a
response. The response Message is the return value of the request() method.

```
public class QueueRequestor {
// Public Constructors
    public QueueRequestor(QueueSession session, Queue queue) throws JMSException;
// Public Instance Methods
    public void close() throws JMSException;
    public javax.jms.Message request(javax.jms.Message message) throws JMSException;
}
```

QueueSender   JMS 1.0
javax.jms

A QueueSender is a MessageProducer used to send messages in a point-to-point context.
QueueSenders are created using the createQueue() method on QueueSession, specifying a
default Queue as the target of messages. Clients can override the default message target
by using one of the send() methods on the QueueSender that accepts a target Queue. If a
send() method is called without a target Queue, and the QueueSender does not have a
default target Queue defined (e.g., it was created with a null target Queue), then an
InvalidDestinationException is thrown.

```
MessageProducer ┄ QueueSender
```

```
public interface QueueSender extends MessageProducer {
// Public Instance Methods
    public abstract Queue getQueue() throws JMSException;
```

```
    public abstract void send(javax.jms.Message message) throws JMSException;
    public abstract void send(Queue queue, javax.jms.Message message) throws JMSException;
    public abstract void send(javax.jms.Message message, int deliveryMode, int priority, long timeToLive)
        throws JMSException;
    public abstract void send(Queue queue, javax.jms.Message message, int deliveryMode, int priority, long timeToLive)
        throws JMSException;
}
```

Returned By: QueueSession.createSender()

QueueSession

JMS 1.0

runnable

javax.jms

The QueueSession is a Session specific to a point-to-point messaging context. It provides methods for creating point-to-point message consumers (QueueReceivers), producers (QueueSenders) and destinations (Queues), as well as utilities objects like QueueBrowsers and TemporaryQueues.

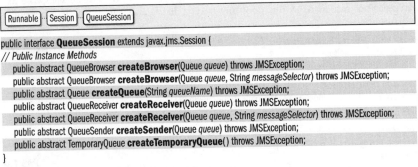

```
public interface QueueSession extends javax.jms.Session {
// Public Instance Methods
    public abstract QueueBrowser createBrowser(Queue queue) throws JMSException;
    public abstract QueueBrowser createBrowser(Queue queue, String messageSelector) throws JMSException;
    public abstract Queue createQueue(String queueName) throws JMSException;
    public abstract QueueReceiver createReceiver(Queue queue) throws JMSException;
    public abstract QueueReceiver createReceiver(Queue queue, String messageSelector) throws JMSException;
    public abstract QueueSender createSender(Queue queue) throws JMSException;
    public abstract TemporaryQueue createTemporaryQueue() throws JMSException;
}
```

Passed To: QueueRequestor.QueueRequestor()

Returned By: QueueConnection.createQueueSession(), XAQueueConnection.createQueueSession(), XAQueueSession.getQueueSession()

ResourceAllocationException

JMS 1.0

serializable checked

javax.jms

This exception is thrown when a request is made of a provider, and it can't be completed due to resource issues.

```
public class ResourceAllocationException extends JMSException {
// Public Constructors
    public ResourceAllocationException(String reason);
    public ResourceAllocationException(String reason, String errorCode);
}
```

ServerSession

JMS 1.0

javax.jms

A ServerSession is used by application servers when there is a need to separate Sessions into individual threads, for concurrent access to and handling of flows of messages.

The ServerSession represents a JMS Session tied to a thread. A ConnectionConsumer keeps a pool of ServerSession objects, which it uses to handle messages as they arrive. The ConnectionConsumer will assign one or more messages to the Session contained in the ServerSession, and then call the ServerSession's start() method. The ServerSession will start() the Thread for the Session, which will eventually call the Session's run() method (Session implements the java.lang.Runnable interface).

```
public interface ServerSession {
// Public Instance Methods
    public abstract javax.jms.Session getSession() throws JMSException;
    public abstract void start() throws JMSException;
}
```

Returned By: ServerSessionPool.getServerSession()

ServerSessionPool   JMS 1.0
javax.jms

A ConnectionConsumer uses a ServerSessionPool to manage a pool of ServerSessions. The ServerSessionPool can manage the pool any way it likes, and can block if the pool is exhausted.

```
public interface ServerSessionPool {
// Public Instance Methods
    public abstract ServerSession getServerSession() throws JMSException;
}
```

Passed To: QueueConnection.createConnectionConsumer(),
TopicConnection.{createConnectionConsumer(), createDurableConnectionConsumer()}

Returned By: ConnectionConsumer.getServerSessionPool()

Session   JMS 1.0
javax.jms   *runnable*

A Session provides a client with the means for creating messages, message producers and message consumers. Subclasses of Session create type-specific versions of these objects (e.g., QueueSenders and TopicPublishers).

Within a Session, messages are sent and received in a serial order. The Session interface also provides facilities for JMS providers that chose to provide transactional support in their Session implementations. A transaction is started when the Session is created. In a messaging context, a transaction consists of a series of message transmissions and receipts. Committing a messaging transaction (by calling commit() on the corresponding Session) causes all of the pending transmissions to be sent and all of the pending receipts to be finalized and acknowledged. If a transaction is aborted (by calling the rollback() method on the Session), then the outgoing messages are destroyed and incoming messages are cancelled. A new transaction is started as soon as the current one is committed or rolled back.

```
Runnable ┄ Session
```

```
public interface Session extends Runnable {
// Public Constants
    public static final int AUTO_ACKNOWLEDGE;                              =1
    public static final int CLIENT_ACKNOWLEDGE;                            =2
    public static final int DUPS_OK_ACKNOWLEDGE;                           =3
// Public Instance Methods
```

```
    public abstract void close() throws JMSException;
    public abstract void commit() throws JMSException;
    public abstract BytesMessage createBytesMessage() throws JMSException;
    public abstract MapMessage createMapMessage() throws JMSException;
    public abstract javax.jms.Message createMessage() throws JMSException;
    public abstract ObjectMessage createObjectMessage() throws JMSException;
    public abstract ObjectMessage createObjectMessage(Serializable object) throws JMSException;
    public abstract StreamMessage createStreamMessage() throws JMSException;
    public abstract TextMessage createTextMessage() throws JMSException;
    public abstract TextMessage createTextMessage(String text) throws JMSException;
    public abstract MessageListener getMessageListener() throws JMSException;
    public abstract boolean getTransacted() throws JMSException;
    public abstract void recover() throws JMSException;
    public abstract void rollback() throws JMSException;
    public abstract void run();
    public abstract void setMessageListener(MessageListener listener) throws JMSException;
}
```

Implementations: QueueSession, TopicSession, XASession

Returned By: ServerSession.getSession()

StreamMessage   JMS 1.0

javax.jms

A StreamMessage is a Message whose body consists of a stream of serialized Java primitive data items. It is similar in many ways to a BytesMessage, except that the contents of a StreamMessage are read in the same order that they are written by the sender. Otherwise, the StreamMessage has a similar set of read/write methods, and similar rules about how certain data types are read from the message, as the BytesMessage.

```
Message -- StreamMessage
```

```
public interface StreamMessage extends javax.jms.Message {
// Public Instance Methods
    public abstract boolean readBoolean() throws JMSException;
    public abstract byte readByte() throws JMSException;
    public abstract int readBytes(byte[ ] value) throws JMSException;
    public abstract char readChar() throws JMSException;
    public abstract double readDouble() throws JMSException;
    public abstract float readFloat() throws JMSException;
    public abstract int readInt() throws JMSException;
    public abstract long readLong() throws JMSException;
    public abstract Object readObject() throws JMSException;
    public abstract short readShort() throws JMSException;
    public abstract String readString() throws JMSException;
    public abstract void reset() throws JMSException;
    public abstract void writeBoolean(boolean value) throws JMSException;
    public abstract void writeByte(byte value) throws JMSException;
    public abstract void writeBytes(byte[ ] value) throws JMSException;
    public abstract void writeBytes(byte[ ] value, int offset, int length) throws JMSException;
    public abstract void writeChar(char value) throws JMSException;
    public abstract void writeDouble(double value) throws JMSException;
    public abstract void writeFloat(float value) throws JMSException;
    public abstract void writeInt(int value) throws JMSException;
    public abstract void writeLong(long value) throws JMSException;
```

```
    public abstract void writeObject(Object value) throws JMSException;
    public abstract void writeShort(short value) throws JMSException;
    public abstract void writeString(String value) throws JMSException;
}
```

Returned By: javax.jms.Session.createStreamMessage()

TemporaryQueue   JMS 1.0
javax.jms

A TemporaryQueue is a Queue that is created and used via a particular connection, and only that connection can consume messages from a TemporaryQueue that it creates. TemporaryQueues are typically used when issuing messages with a JMSReplyTo header — a TemporaryQueue can be used as the value of the JMSReplyTo, avoiding the need for a predefined Queue to be created on the JMS server.

Destination ┈ Queue ┈ TemporaryQueue

```
public interface TemporaryQueue extends Queue {
// Public Instance Methods
    public abstract void delete() throws JMSException;
}
```

Returned By: QueueSession.createTemporaryQueue()

TemporaryTopic   JMS 1.0
javax.jms

A TemporaryTopic is a Topic that is created and used via a particular connection, and only that connection can consume messages from a TemporaryTopic that it creates. TemporaryTopics are typically used when issuing messages with a JMSReplyTo header — a TemporaryTopic can be used as the value of the JMSReplyTo, avoiding the need for a pre-defined Topic to be created on the JMS server.

Destination ┈ Topic ┈ TemporaryTopic

```
public interface TemporaryTopic extends Topic {
// Public Instance Methods
    public abstract void delete() throws JMSException;
}
```

Returned By: TopicSession.createTemporaryTopic()

TextMessage   JMS 1.0
javax.jms

A TextMessage is a Message whose body is a String. The contents of the message can be retrieved using the getText() method. The text of the message might be simple ASCII, or it could be structured according to a syntax like HTML or XML.

Message ┈ TextMessage

```
public interface TextMessage extends javax.jms.Message {
// Public Instance Methods
```

```
    public abstract String getText() throws JMSException;
    public abstract void setText(String string) throws JMSException;
}
```

Returned By: javax.jms.Session.createTextMessage()

Topic   JMS 1.0

javax.jms

A Topic is an address for a message in a publish/subscribe context. The Topic interface simply defines a String name for the topic. Providers define how topics are defined and grouped into a hierarchy.

```
Destination — Topic
```

```
public interface Topic extends javax.jms.Destination {
// Public Instance Methods
    public abstract String getTopicName() throws JMSException;
    public abstract String toString();
}
```

Implementations: TemporaryTopic

Passed To: TopicConnection.{createConnectionConsumer(), createDurableConnectionConsumer()}, TopicPublisher.publish(), TopicRequestor.TopicRequestor(), TopicSession.{createDurableSubscriber(), createPublisher(), createSubscriber()}

Returned By: TopicPublisher.getTopic(), TopicSession.createTopic(), TopicSubscriber.getTopic()

TopicConnection   JMS 1.0

javax.jms

A TopicConnection is a Connection to a publish/subscribe-based JMS provider. It provides methods for creating TopicSessions, as well as ConnectionConsumers.

```
Connection — TopicConnection
```

```
public interface TopicConnection extends javax.jms.Connection {
// Public Instance Methods
    public abstract ConnectionConsumer createConnectionConsumer(Topic topic, String messageSelector,
                                          ServerSessionPool sessionPool, int maxMessages)
        throws JMSException;
    public abstract ConnectionConsumer createDurableConnectionConsumer(Topic topic,
                                          String subscriptionName, String messageSelector,
                                          ServerSessionPool sessionPool, int maxMessages)
        throws JMSException;
    public abstract TopicSession createTopicSession(boolean transacted, int acknowledgeMode)
        throws JMSException;
}
```

Implementations: XATopicConnection

Returned By: TopicConnectionFactory.createTopicConnection()

TopicConnectionFactory   JMS 1.0

javax.jms

A TopicConnectionFactory is exported by publish/subscribe providers to allow clients to create TopicConnections to the provider. The default createTopicConnection() method is used to create a connection under the default user identity of the client JVM, and the other accepts a name and password that is used to authenticate the connection request.

```
ConnectionFactory ┄┈ TopicConnectionFactory
```

```
public interface TopicConnectionFactory extends javax.jms.ConnectionFactory {
// Public Instance Methods
    public abstract TopicConnection createTopicConnection() throws JMSException;
    public abstract TopicConnection createTopicConnection(String userName, String password)
        throws JMSException;
}
```

Implementations: XATopicConnectionFactory

TopicPublisher

JMS 1.0

javax.jms

A TopicPublisher is a MessageProducer specific to a publish/subscribe context. TopicPublishers are created using the createPublisher() method on a TopicSession. A TopicPublisher is created with a Topic under which it publishes messages. A client can override the default Topic using one of the publish() methods that accepts a Topic as an argument along with the Message to be sent. Sending a Message without a Topic (i.e., the TopicPublisher was created with a null Topic and the Message was sent without specifying a Topic), causes an Invalid-DestinationException to be thrown.

```
MessageProducer ┄┈ TopicPublisher
```

```
public interface TopicPublisher extends MessageProducer {
// Public Instance Methods
    public abstract Topic getTopic() throws JMSException;
    public abstract void publish(javax.jms.Message message) throws JMSException;
    public abstract void publish(Topic topic, javax.jms.Message message) throws JMSException;
    public abstract void publish(javax.jms.Message message, int deliveryMode, int priority, long timeToLive)
        throws JMSException;
    public abstract void publish(Topic topic, javax.jms.Message message, int deliveryMode, int priority, long timeToLive)
        throws JMSException;
}
```

Returned By: TopicSession.createPublisher()

TopicRequestor

JMS 1.0

javax.jms

The TopicRequestor is a utility class provided for situations where a client wants to send a message to a specific Topic and wait for a response. The TopicRequestor is constructed with a TopicSession and a destination Topic, and then its request() method is called with the Message to be sent. The TopicRequestor sets the reply-to destination on the message to a temporary Topic that it creates. It sends the message and waits for a response. The response Message is the return value of the request() method.

```
public class TopicRequestor {
// Public Constructors
    public TopicRequestor(TopicSession session, Topic topic) throws JMSException;
// Public Instance Methods
    public void close() throws JMSException;
    public javax.jms.Message request(javax.jms.Message message) throws JMSException;
}
```

TopicSession
JMS 1.0

javax.jms
runnable

A TopicSession is a Session specific to a publish/subscribe context. It provides methods for creating publish/subscribe message consumers (TopicSubscribers), message producers (TopicPublishers) and message destinations (Topics). It also has methods for creating utilities objects like TemporaryTopics.

```
Runnable ┄ Session ┄ TopicSession
```

```
public interface TopicSession extends javax.jms.Session {
// Public Instance Methods
    public abstract TopicSubscriber createDurableSubscriber(Topic topic, String name) throws JMSException;
    public abstract TopicSubscriber createDurableSubscriber(Topic topic, String name, String messageSelector,
                                            boolean noLocal) throws JMSException;
    public abstract TopicPublisher createPublisher(Topic topic) throws JMSException;
    public abstract TopicSubscriber createSubscriber(Topic topic) throws JMSException;
    public abstract TopicSubscriber createSubscriber(Topic topic, String messageSelector, boolean noLocal)
        throws JMSException;
    public abstract TemporaryTopic createTemporaryTopic() throws JMSException;
    public abstract Topic createTopic(String topicName) throws JMSException;
    public abstract void unsubscribe(String name) throws JMSException;
}
```

Passed To: TopicRequestor.TopicRequestor()

Returned By: TopicConnection.createTopicSession(), XATopicConnection.createTopicSession(), XATopicSession.getTopicSession()

TopicSubscriber
JMS 1.0

javax.jms

A TopicSubscriber is a MessageConsumer specific to a publish/subscribe context. TopicSubscribers are created using the createSubscriber() and createDurableSubscriber() methods on the TopicSession. TopicSubscribers are created with a Topic to subscribe to, and can optionally be created with a message selector, which filters the messages received by the subscriber. If a client is both publishing and subscribing to the same Topic, then the no-local attribute on the TopicSubscriber specifiescan be used to filter out messages published by the same connection.

If a TopicSubscriber is created as durable (using the createDurableSubscriber() on the TopicSession), then the provider collects messages for this subscriber even when the subscriber is inactive. The provider will keep these messages until the subscriber receives them, or until they expire according to the sender's time-to-live header attribute. In order for the client to retrieve the messages collected under a durable TopicSubscriber after it has reactivated itself, it has to create a new TopicSubscriber under the same Topic with the same client ID.

```
MessageConsumer ┄ TopicSubscriber
```

```
public interface TopicSubscriber extends MessageConsumer {
// Public Instance Methods
    public abstract boolean getNoLocal() throws JMSException;
    public abstract Topic getTopic() throws JMSException;
}
```

Returned By: TopicSession.{createDurableSubscriber(), createSubscriber()}

TransactionInProgressException   JMS 1.0
javax.jms   *serializable checked*

This exception is thrown if an invalid request is made during a transactional session, e.g., attempting to commit() a session while a message is still being sent.

```
Object ├─ Throwable ├─ Exception ├─ JMSException ├─ TransactionInProgressException
         └ Serializable
```

```
public class TransactionInProgressException extends JMSException {
// Public Constructors
    public TransactionInProgressException(String reason);
    public TransactionInProgressException(String reason, String errorCode);
}
```

TransactionRolledBackException   JMS 1.0
javax.jms   *serializable checked*

This exception is thrown by the Session.commit() method if the transaction needs to be rolled back because of some internal error.

```
Object ├─ Throwable ├─ Exception ├─ JMSException ├─ TransactionRolledBackException
         └ Serializable
```

```
public class TransactionRolledBackException extends JMSException {
// Public Constructors
    public TransactionRolledBackException(String reason);
    public TransactionRolledBackException(String reason, String errorCode);
}
```

XAConnection   JMS 1.0
javax.jms

This abstract interface represents a Connection to a provider that supports transactional messaging, according to the X/Open XA protocol for transactional processing. Subclasses of XAConnection generate transactional sessions, in the form of XASessions.

```
public interface XAConnection {
}
```

Implementations: XAQueueConnection, XATopicConnection

XAConnectionFactory   JMS 1.0
javax.jms

A transactional JMS provider exports an XAConnectionFactory for clients to use to create XAConnections. Clients will typically find a provider's XAConnectionFactory using a JNDI lookup.

```
public interface XAConnectionFactory {
}
```

Implementations: XAQueueConnectionFactory, XATopicConnectionFactory

XAQueueConnection

javax.jms

An XAQueueConnection is a Connection to a transactional provider of point-to-point messaging. It extends the QueueConnection interface with a createXAQueueSession() method, which creates a transactional XAQueueSession.

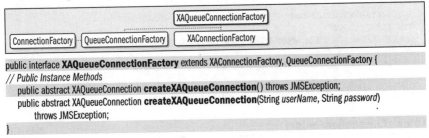

```
public interface XAQueueConnection extends javax.jms.XAConnection, QueueConnection {
// Public Instance Methods
    public abstract QueueSession createQueueSession(boolean transacted, int acknowledgeMode)
        throws JMSException;
    public abstract XAQueueSession createXAQueueSession() throws JMSException;
}
```

Returned By: XAQueueConnectionFactory.createXAQueueConnection()

XAQueueConnectionFactory

javax.jms

A XAQueueConnectionFactory is a QueueConnectionFactory that creates XAQueueConnections to a transactional point-to-point JMS provider.

```
public interface XAQueueConnectionFactory extends XAConnectionFactory, QueueConnectionFactory {
// Public Instance Methods
    public abstract XAQueueConnection createXAQueueConnection() throws JMSException;
    public abstract XAQueueConnection createXAQueueConnection(String userName, String password)
        throws JMSException;
}
```

XAQueueSession

javax.jms

An XAQueueSession is a wrapper around a QueueSession, and represents a transactional session with a JMS point-to-point provider.

```
public interface XAQueueSession extends XASession {
// Public Instance Methods
    public abstract QueueSession getQueueSession() throws JMSException;
}
```

Returned By: XAQueueConnection.createXAQueueSession()

XASession

javax.jms

An XASession is a Session with a provider that support transactional messaging according to the X/Open XA protocol for transactional processing. The XASession contains a javax.transaction.xa.XAResource object that represents the association of the Session with a transaction context.

```
Runnable  Session  XASession
```

```
public interface XASession extends javax.jms.Session {
// Public Instance Methods
    public abstract void commit() throws JMSException;
    public abstract boolean getTransacted() throws JMSException;
    public abstract javax.transaction.xa.XAResource getXAResource();
    public abstract void rollback() throws JMSException;
}
```

Implementations: XAQueueSession, XATopicSession

XATopicConnection   JMS 1.0
javax.jms

An XATopicConnection represents a Connection to a transactional provider of publish/subscribe messaging. It extends the TopicConnection interface with a createXATopicSession() method, which creates a transactional XATopicSession.

```
                              XATopicConnection
Connection  TopicConnection      XAConnection
```

```
public interface XATopicConnection extends javax.jms.XAConnection, TopicConnection {
// Public Instance Methods
    public abstract TopicSession createTopicSession(boolean transacted, int acknowledgeMode)
        throws JMSException;
    public abstract XATopicSession createXATopicSession() throws JMSException;
}
```

Returned By: XATopicConnectionFactory.createXATopicConnection()

XATopicConnectionFactory   JMS 1.0
javax.jms

A XATopicConnectionFactory is a TopicConnectionFactory that creates XATopicConnections to a transactional publish/subscribe JMS provider.

```
                                    XATopicConnectionFactory
ConnectionFactory  TopicConnectionFactory      XAConnectionFactory
```

```
public interface XATopicConnectionFactory extends XAConnectionFactory, TopicConnectionFactory {
// Public Instance Methods
    public abstract XATopicConnection createXATopicConnection() throws JMSException;
    public abstract XATopicConnection createXATopicConnection(String userName, String password)
        throws JMSException;
}
```

XATopicSession   JMS 1.0
javax.jms   *runnable*

An XATopicSession is a wrapper around a TopicSession, and represents a transactional session with a JMS publish/subscribe provider.

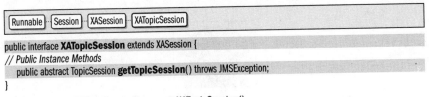

```
public interface XATopicSession extends XASession {
// Public Instance Methods
    public abstract TopicSession getTopicSession() throws JMSException;
}
```

Returned By: XATopicConnection.createXATopicSession()

CHAPTER 26

javax.mail and Subpackages

The javax.mail package contains the core functionality of the JavaMail API. The package provides the basic messaging environment (the JavaMail session, abstract classes for JavaMail services and providers), service naming, and classes for storing and manipulating messages. The package also includes two interfaces extending interfaces from the javax.activation package.

Interfaces:

public interface **MessageAware**;
public interface **MultipartDataSource** extends javax.activation.DataSource;
public interface **Part**;
public interface **UIDFolder**;

Classes:

public abstract class **Address** implements Serializable;
public abstract class **Authenticator**;
public abstract class **BodyPart** implements Part;
public class **FetchProfile**;
public static class **FetchProfile.Item**;
    └ public static class **UIDFolder.FetchProfileItem** extends FetchProfile.Item;
public class **Flags** implements Cloneable, Serializable;
public static final class **Flags.Flag**;
public abstract class **Folder**;
public class **Header**;
public abstract class **Message** implements Part;
public static class **Message.RecipientType** implements Serializable;
public class **MessageContext**;
public abstract class **Multipart**;
public final class **PasswordAuthentication**;
public class **Provider**;

```
public static class Provider.Type;
public abstract class Service;
   └ public abstract class Store extends Service;
   └ public abstract class Transport extends Service;
public final class Session;
public class URLName;
```

Exceptions:

```
public class MessagingException extends Exception;
   └ public class AuthenticationFailedException extends MessagingException;
   └ public class FolderClosedException extends MessagingException;
   └ public class FolderNotFoundException extends MessagingException;
   └ public class IllegalWriteException extends MessagingException;
   └ public class MessageRemovedException extends MessagingException;
   └ public class MethodNotSupportedException extends MessagingException;
   └ public class NoSuchProviderException extends MessagingException;
   └ public class ReadOnlyFolderException extends MessagingException;
   └ public class SendFailedException extends MessagingException;
   └ public class StoreClosedException extends MessagingException;
```

Address   JavaMail 1.1
javax.mail   *serializable*

This is an abstract class that models a Message address. Subclasses provide the actual implementations.

```
Object ─┤Address│···│Serializable│
```

```
public abstract class Address implements Serializable {
// Public Constructors
   public Address();
// Public Instance Methods
   public abstract String getType();
// Public Methods Overriding Object
   public abstract boolean equals(Object address);
   public abstract String toString();
}
```

Subclasses: javax.mail.internet.InternetAddress, javax.mail.internet.NewsAddress

Passed To: Too many methods to list.

Returned By: javax.mail.Message.{getAllRecipients(), getFrom(), getRecipients(), getReplyTo()}, SendFailedException.{getInvalidAddresses(), getValidSentAddresses(), getValidUnsentAddresses()}, javax.mail.event.TransportEvent.{getInvalidAddresses(), getValidSentAddresses(), getValidUnsentAddresses()}, javax.mail.internet.MimeMessage.{getAllRecipients(), getFrom(), getRecipients(), getReplyTo()}, javax.mail.search.AddressTerm.getAddress()

Type Of: SendFailedException.{invalid, validSent, validUnsent}, javax.mail.event.TransportEvent.{invalid, validSent, validUnsent}, javax.mail.search.AddressTerm.address

AuthenticationFailedException   JavaMail 1.1
javax.mail   *serializable checked*

This exception is thrown when the connect() method on a Service fails as a result of an authentication failure.

```
Object ├ Throwable ├ Exception ├ MessagingException ├ AuthenticationFailedException
        └ Serializable
```

```
public class AuthenticationFailedException extends MessagingException {
// Public Constructors
    public AuthenticationFailedException();
    public AuthenticationFailedException(String message);
}
```

Authenticator   JavaMail 1.1

javax.mail

This class retrieves authentication information for a network resource. Subclasses of Authenticator are registered with the JavaMail session at startup, and the Session object will call the getPasswordAuthentication() method when user authentication must be performed. The getRequestingXXX() methods are implemented by the system, and can be used by implementations to retrieve information about the requesting user.

```
public abstract class Authenticator {
// Public Constructors
    public Authenticator();
// Protected Instance Methods
    protected final String getDefaultUserName();
    protected javax.mail.PasswordAuthentication getPasswordAuthentication();          constant
    protected final int getRequestingPort();
    protected final String getRequestingPrompt();
    protected final String getRequestingProtocol();
    protected final java.net.InetAddress getRequestingSite();
}
```

Passed To: javax.mail.Session.{getDefaultInstance(), getInstance()}

BodyPart   JavaMail 1.1

javax.mail

The abstract BodyPart class allows manipulation of a Part contained within a Multipart object. Like a Part, it contains attributes and content. BodyPart also provides a reference to the Multipart object that contains it.

```
Object ├ BodyPart ┈ Part
```

```
public abstract class BodyPart implements Part {
// Public Constructors
    public BodyPart();
// Public Instance Methods
    public Multipart getParent();
// Methods Implementing Part
    public abstract void addHeader(String header_name, String header_value) throws MessagingException;
    public abstract java.util.Enumeration getAllHeaders() throws MessagingException;
    public abstract Object getContent() throws IOException, MessagingException;
    public abstract String getContentType() throws MessagingException;
    public abstract javax.activation.DataHandler getDataHandler() throws MessagingException;
    public abstract String getDescription() throws MessagingException;
    public abstract String getDisposition() throws MessagingException;
    public abstract String getFileName() throws MessagingException;
    public abstract String[ ] getHeader(String header_name) throws MessagingException;
    public abstract java.io.InputStream getInputStream() throws IOException, MessagingException;
```

```
    public abstract int getLineCount() throws MessagingException;
    public abstract java.util.Enumeration getMatchingHeaders(String[ ] header_names) throws MessagingException;
    public abstract java.util.Enumeration getNonMatchingHeaders(String[ ] header_names)
        throws MessagingException;
    public abstract int getSize() throws MessagingException;
    public abstract boolean isMimeType(String mimeType) throws MessagingException;
    public abstract void removeHeader(String header_name) throws MessagingException;
    public abstract void setContent(Multipart mp) throws MessagingException;
    public abstract void setContent(Object obj, String type) throws MessagingException;
    public abstract void setDataHandler(javax.activation.DataHandler dh) throws MessagingException;
    public abstract void setDescription(String description) throws MessagingException;
    public abstract void setDisposition(String disposition) throws MessagingException;
    public abstract void setFileName(String filename) throws MessagingException;
    public abstract void setHeader(String header_name, String header_value) throws MessagingException;
    public abstract void setText(String text) throws MessagingException;
    public abstract void writeTo(java.io.OutputStream os) throws IOException, MessagingException;
// Protected Instance Fields
    protected Multipart parent;
}
```

Subclasses: javax.mail.internet.MimeBodyPart

Passed To: Multipart.{addBodyPart(), removeBodyPart()}

Returned By: Multipart.getBodyPart(), MultipartDataSource.getBodyPart(),
javax.mail.internet.MimeMultipart.getBodyPart()

FetchProfile   JavaMail 1.1

javax.mail

FetchProfile objects allows programs to prefetch certain attributes for sets of messages
(using the fetch() method of Folder). This allows optimized retrieval of particular message
data, such as recipients, senders and subjects. Content that is not included in the Fetch-
Profile will still be accessible, but will be retrieved as it is requested by the user via the
various get methods of the message object.

The add() method accepts a header name, or a FetchProfile.Item object, which defines a
set of headers to retrieve.

```
public class FetchProfile {
// Public Constructors
    public FetchProfile();
// Inner Classes
    public static class Item;
// Public Instance Methods
    public void add(String headerName);
    public void add(FetchProfile.Item item);
    public boolean contains(String headerName);
    public boolean contains(FetchProfile.Item item);
    public String[ ] getHeaderNames();
    public FetchProfile.Item[ ] getItems();
}
```

Passed To: Folder.fetch()

FetchProfile.Item

javax.mail

The static FetchProfile.Item class defines three sets of data that can be requested via a FetchProfile. The CONTENT_INFO item returns information about message content, including ContentType, ContentDisposition, ContentDescription and size. The ENVELOPE item includes Subject, Date, From, To, Cc, Bcc and ReplyTo. The FLAGS item retrieves message flags. Implementations may retrieve additional data for any of these items.

```
public static class FetchProfile.Item {
// Protected Constructors
    protected Item(String name);
// Public Constants
    public static final FetchProfile.Item CONTENT_INFO;
    public static final FetchProfile.Item ENVELOPE;
    public static final FetchProfile.Item FLAGS;
}
```

Subclasses: UIDFolder.FetchProfileItem

Passed To: FetchProfile.{add(), contains()}

Returned By: FetchProfile.getItems()

Type Of: FetchProfile.Item.{CONTENT_INFO, ENVELOPE, FLAGS}

Flags

javax.mail

cloneable serializable

The Flags object defines the message flags set for a particular message. System defined flags are specified in the Flags.Flag inner class. User defined flags may be specified as String objects, and are not case-sensitive.

```
public class Flags implements Cloneable, Serializable {
// Public Constructors
    public Flags();
    public Flags(String flag);
    public Flags(Flags.Flag flag);
    public Flags(Flags flags);
// Inner Classes
    public static final class Flag;
// Public Instance Methods
    public void add(String flag);
    public void add(Flags.Flag flag);
    public void add(Flags f);
    public boolean contains(Flags f);
    public boolean contains(Flags.Flag flag);
    public boolean contains(String flag);
    public Flags.Flag[ ] getSystemFlags();
    public String[ ] getUserFlags();
    public void remove(Flags.Flag flag);
    public void remove(String flag);
    public void remove(Flags f);
// Public Methods Overriding Object
    public Object clone();
```

```
    public boolean equals(Object obj);
    public int hashCode();
}
```

Passed To: Flags.{add(), contains(), Flags(), remove()}, Folder.setFlags(), javax.mail.Message.setFlags(), javax.mail.internet.MimeMessage.setFlags(), javax.mail.search.FlagTerm.FlagTerm()

Returned By: Folder.getPermanentFlags(), javax.mail.Message.getFlags(), javax.mail.internet.MimeMessage.getFlags(), javax.mail.search.FlagTerm.getFlags()

Type Of: javax.mail.internet.MimeMessage.flags, javax.mail.search.FlagTerm.flags

Flags.Flag   JavaMail 1.1
javax.mail

The Flags.Flag class defines a set of message flags that can be used by the Flags object. Messaging implementations are generally expected to support these flags. The USER flag indicates that the folder that returned these flags supports user defined flags.

```
public static final class Flags.Flag {
// No Constructor
// Public Constants
    public static final Flags.Flag ANSWERED;
    public static final Flags.Flag DELETED;
    public static final Flags.Flag DRAFT;
    public static final Flags.Flag FLAGGED;
    public static final Flags.Flag RECENT;
    public static final Flags.Flag SEEN;
    public static final Flags.Flag USER;
}
```

Passed To: Flags.{add(), contains(), Flags(), remove()}, javax.mail.Message.{isSet(), setFlag()}, javax.mail.internet.MimeMessage.isSet()

Returned By: Flags.getSystemFlags()

Type Of: Flags.Flag.{ANSWERED, DELETED, DRAFT, FLAGGED, RECENT, SEEN, USER}

Folder   JavaMail 1.1
javax.mail

The Folder class represents a folder containing mail messages. All messages are retrieved from a message store (represented by a Store object) via a Folder object. Depending on the protocol in use, folders might contain additional folders as well as messages. In these cases, naming and hierarchy are entirely implementation dependent. The folder name INBOX is reserved for the primary folder for the current user.

Folder objects can be retrieved via the getFolder() method of Store or Folder, or via the list() and listSubscribed() methods. Each call to these methods will return a distinct Folder object. Once a Folder has been retrieved, it must be opened (via the open() method) to retrieve messages. Message objects are cached at the level of the Folder object.

Certain Folder methods are not valid across all protocols. For instance, the subscription methods (which allow applications to register interest in a particular folder) are not supported by POP3 email but might be supported by an NNTP news implementation that uses Folders to represent newsgroups. Similarly, POP3 does not support the create(), renameTo() and delete() methods, as POP3 doesn't support nested folders.

```
public abstract class Folder {
// Protected Constructors
    protected Folder(Store store);
// Public Constants
    public static final int HOLDS_FOLDERS;                                                    =2
    public static final int HOLDS_MESSAGES;                                                   =1
    public static final int READ_ONLY;                                                        =1
    public static final int READ_WRITE;                                                       =2
// Event Registration Methods (by event name)
    public void addConnectionListener(javax.mail.event.ConnectionListener l);        synchronized
    public void removeConnectionListener(javax.mail.event.ConnectionListener l);     synchronized
    public void addFolderListener(javax.mail.event.FolderListener l);                synchronized
    public void removeFolderListener(javax.mail.event.FolderListener l);             synchronized
    public void addMessageChangedListener(javax.mail.event.MessageChangedListener l); synchronized
    public void removeMessageChangedListener(javax.mail.event.MessageChangedListener l); synchronized
    public void addMessageCountListener(javax.mail.event.MessageCountListener l);    synchronized
    public void removeMessageCountListener(javax.mail.event.MessageCountListener l); synchronized
// Property Accessor Methods (by property name)
    public abstract String getFullName();
    public abstract int getMessageCount() throws MessagingException;
    public javax.mail.Message[ ] getMessages() throws MessagingException;            synchronized
    public javax.mail.Message[ ] getMessages(int[ ] msgnums) throws MessagingException; synchronized
    public javax.mail.Message[ ] getMessages(int start, int end) throws MessagingException; synchronized
    public int getMode();
    public abstract String getName();
    public int getNewMessageCount() throws MessagingException;                       synchronized
    public abstract boolean isOpen();
    public abstract Folder getParent() throws MessagingException;
    public abstract Flags getPermanentFlags();
    public abstract char getSeparator() throws MessagingException;
    public Store getStore();
    public boolean isSubscribed();
    public void setSubscribed(boolean subscribe) throws MessagingException;              constant
    public abstract int getType() throws MessagingException;
    public int getUnreadMessageCount() throws MessagingException;                    synchronized
    public URLName getURLName() throws MessagingException;
// Public Instance Methods
    public abstract void appendMessages(javax.mail.Message[ ] msgs) throws MessagingException;
    public abstract void close(boolean expunge) throws MessagingException;
    public void copyMessages(javax.mail.Message[ ] msgs, Folder folder) throws MessagingException;
    public abstract boolean create(int type) throws MessagingException;
    public abstract boolean delete(boolean recurse) throws MessagingException;
    public abstract boolean exists() throws MessagingException;
    public abstract javax.mail.Message[ ] expunge() throws MessagingException;
    public void fetch(javax.mail.Message[ ] msgs, FetchProfile fp) throws MessagingException;   empty
    public abstract Folder getFolder(String name) throws MessagingException;
    public abstract javax.mail.Message getMessage(int msgnum) throws MessagingException;
    public abstract boolean hasNewMessages() throws MessagingException;
    public Folder[ ] list() throws MessagingException;
    public abstract Folder[ ] list(String pattern) throws MessagingException;
    public Folder[ ] listSubscribed() throws MessagingException;
    public Folder[ ] listSubscribed(String pattern) throws MessagingException;
    public abstract void open(int mode) throws MessagingException;
    public abstract boolean renameTo(Folder f) throws MessagingException;
    public javax.mail.Message[ ] search(javax.mail.search.SearchTerm term) throws MessagingException;
```

```
    public javax.mail.Message[ ] search(javax.mail.search.SearchTerm term, javax.mail.Message[ ] msgs)
        throws MessagingException;
    public void setFlags(javax.mail.Message[ ] msgs, Flags flag, boolean value)                    synchronized
        throws MessagingException;
    public void setFlags(int[ ] msgnums, Flags flag, boolean value) throws MessagingException;      synchronized
    public void setFlags(int start, int end, Flags flag, boolean value) throws MessagingException;  synchronized
// Public Methods Overriding Object
    public String toString();
// Protected Methods Overriding Object
    protected void finalize() throws Throwable;
// Protected Instance Methods
    protected void notifyConnectionListeners(int type);
    protected void notifyFolderListeners(int type);
    protected void notifyFolderRenamedListeners(Folder folder);
    protected void notifyMessageAddedListeners(javax.mail.Message[ ] msgs);
    protected void notifyMessageChangedListeners(int type, javax.mail.Message msg);
    protected void notifyMessageRemovedListeners(boolean removed, javax.mail.Message[ ] msgs);
// Protected Instance Fields
    protected int mode;
    protected Store store;
}
```

Passed To: Folder.{copyMessages(), notifyFolderRenamedListeners(), renameTo()},
FolderClosedException.FolderClosedException(), FolderNotFoundException.FolderNotFoundException(),
javax.mail.Message.Message(), ReadOnlyFolderException.ReadOnlyFolderException(),
Store.{notifyFolderListeners(), notifyFolderRenamedListeners()},
javax.mail.event.FolderEvent.FolderEvent(), javax.mail.event.MessageCountEvent.MessageCountEvent(),
javax.mail.internet.MimeMessage.MimeMessage()

Returned By: Folder.{getFolder(), getParent(), list(), listSubscribed()},
FolderClosedException.getFolder(), FolderNotFoundException.getFolder(),
javax.mail.Message.getFolder(), ReadOnlyFolderException.getFolder(), javax.mail.Session.getFolder(),
Store.{getDefaultFolder(), getFolder(), getPersonalNamespaces(), getSharedNamespaces(),
getUserNamespaces()}, javax.mail.event.FolderEvent.{getFolder(), getNewFolder()}

Type Of: javax.mail.Message.folder, javax.mail.event.FolderEvent.{folder, newFolder}

FolderClosedException

JavaMail 1.1

javax.mail

serializable checked

This exception is thrown when a Folder method has failed due to a folder having been
prematurely closed. After this exception is thrown the Folder in question can be
regarded as closed, and dependent objects may become invalid.

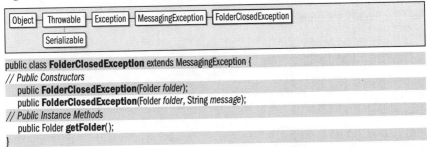

```
public class FolderClosedException extends MessagingException {
// Public Constructors
    public FolderClosedException(Folder folder);
    public FolderClosedException(Folder folder, String message);
// Public Instance Methods
    public Folder getFolder();
}
```

FolderNotFoundException

javax.mail   *serializable checked*

This exception is thrown when methods of the Folder class are invoked on a folder that does not exist within the message store.

```
Object ⊢ Throwable ⊢ Exception ⊢ MessagingException ⊢ FolderNotFoundException
         Serializable
```

```
public class FolderNotFoundException extends MessagingException {
// Public Constructors
    public FolderNotFoundException();
1.2 public FolderNotFoundException(Folder folder);
    public FolderNotFoundException(String s, Folder folder);
1.2 public FolderNotFoundException(Folder folder, String s);
// Public Instance Methods
    public Folder getFolder();                                          default:null
}
```

Header

javax.mail

A holder class for a name/value pair representing a message header.

```
public class Header {
// Public Constructors
    public Header(String name, String value);
// Public Instance Methods
    public String getName();
    public String getValue();
}
```

IllegalWriteException

javax.mail   *serializable checked*

This exception is thrown when there is an attempt to write to a read-only attribute of a JavaMail object. Since different protocols support different sets of functionality, programs that need to interact with a variety of different messaging servers and implementations should be prepared to handle this exception.

```
Object ⊢ Throwable ⊢ Exception ⊢ MessagingException ⊢ IllegalWriteException
         Serializable
```

```
public class IllegalWriteException extends MessagingException {
// Public Constructors
    public IllegalWriteException();
    public IllegalWriteException(String s);
}
```

Message

javax.mail

This is a class that models an email message. Protocol specific subclasses provide the actual implementations. Note that this class defines additional attributes beyond those included in the Part interface, including message recipients, senders, flags and subject.

Where supported by the underlying protocol, data will be read into the Message object as requested by the get methods, rather than when the Message is retrieved from the folder that contains it.

```
Object — Message — Part
```

```
public abstract class Message implements Part {
// Protected Constructors
    protected Message();
    protected Message(javax.mail.Session session);
    protected Message(Folder folder, int msgnum);
// Inner Classes
    public static class RecipientType implements Serializable;
// Property Accessor Methods (by property name)
    public abstract java.util.Enumeration getAllHeaders() throws MessagingException;        Implements:Part
    public Address[ ] getAllRecipients() throws MessagingException;
    public abstract Object getContent() throws IOException, MessagingException;              Implements:Part
    public abstract void setContent(Multipart mp) throws MessagingException;                 Implements:Part
    public abstract void setContent(Object obj, String type) throws MessagingException;      Implements:Part
    public abstract String getContentType() throws MessagingException;                       Implements:Part
    public abstract javax.activation.DataHandler getDataHandler() throws MessagingException; Implements:Part
    public abstract void setDataHandler(javax.activation.DataHandler dh)                     Implements:Part
        throws MessagingException;
    public abstract String getDescription() throws MessagingException;                       Implements:Part
    public abstract void setDescription(String description) throws MessagingException;       Implements:Part
    public abstract String getDisposition() throws MessagingException;                       Implements:Part
    public abstract void setDisposition(String disposition) throws MessagingException;       Implements:Part
    public boolean isExpunged();
    public abstract String getFileName() throws MessagingException;                          Implements:Part
    public abstract void setFileName(String filename) throws MessagingException;             Implements:Part
    public abstract Flags getFlags() throws MessagingException;
    public Folder getFolder();
    public abstract Address[ ] getFrom() throws MessagingException;
    public abstract void setFrom(Address address) throws MessagingException;
    public abstract java.io.InputStream getInputStream() throws IOException, MessagingException;  Implements:Part
    public abstract int getLineCount() throws MessagingException;                            Implements:Part
    public int getMessageNumber();
    public abstract java.util.Date getReceivedDate() throws MessagingException;
    public Address[ ] getReplyTo() throws MessagingException;
    public void setReplyTo(Address[ ] addresses) throws MessagingException;
    public abstract java.util.Date getSentDate() throws MessagingException;
    public abstract void setSentDate(java.util.Date date) throws MessagingException;
    public abstract int getSize() throws MessagingException;                                 Implements:Part
    public abstract String getSubject() throws MessagingException;
    public abstract void setSubject(String subject) throws MessagingException;
    public abstract void setText(String text) throws MessagingException;                     Implements:Part
// Public Instance Methods
    public abstract void addFrom(Address[ ] addresses) throws MessagingException;
    public void addRecipient(Message.RecipientType type, Address address) throws MessagingException;
    public abstract void addRecipients(Message.RecipientType type, Address[ ] addresses)
        throws MessagingException;
    public abstract Address[ ] getRecipients(Message.RecipientType type) throws MessagingException;
    public boolean isSet(Flags.Flag flag) throws MessagingException;
    public boolean match(javax.mail.search.SearchTerm term) throws MessagingException;
    public abstract javax.mail.Message reply(boolean replyToAll) throws MessagingException;
    public abstract void saveChanges() throws MessagingException;
```

```
       public void setFlag(Flags.Flag flag, boolean set) throws MessagingException;
       public abstract void setFlags(Flags flag, boolean set) throws MessagingException;
       public abstract void setFrom() throws MessagingException;
       public void setRecipient(Message.RecipientType type, Address address) throws MessagingException;
       public abstract void setRecipients(Message.RecipientType type, Address[] addresses) throws MessagingException;
// Methods Implementing Part
       public abstract void addHeader(String header_name, String header_value) throws MessagingException;
       public abstract java.util.Enumeration getAllHeaders() throws MessagingException;
       public abstract Object getContent() throws IOException, MessagingException;
       public abstract String getContentType() throws MessagingException;
       public abstract javax.activation.DataHandler getDataHandler() throws MessagingException;
       public abstract String getDescription() throws MessagingException;
       public abstract String getDisposition() throws MessagingException;
       public abstract String getFileName() throws MessagingException;
       public abstract String[] getHeader(String header_name) throws MessagingException;
       public abstract java.io.InputStream getInputStream() throws IOException, MessagingException;
       public abstract int getLineCount() throws MessagingException;
       public abstract java.util.Enumeration getMatchingHeaders(String[] header_names) throws MessagingException;
       public abstract java.util.Enumeration getNonMatchingHeaders(String[] header_names)
           throws MessagingException;
       public abstract int getSize() throws MessagingException;
       public abstract boolean isMimeType(String mimeType) throws MessagingException;
       public abstract void removeHeader(String header_name) throws MessagingException;
       public abstract void setContent(Multipart mp) throws MessagingException;
       public abstract void setContent(Object obj, String type) throws MessagingException;
       public abstract void setDataHandler(javax.activation.DataHandler dh) throws MessagingException;
       public abstract void setDescription(String description) throws MessagingException;
       public abstract void setDisposition(String disposition) throws MessagingException;
       public abstract void setFileName(String filename) throws MessagingException;
       public abstract void setHeader(String header_name, String header_value) throws MessagingException;
       public abstract void setText(String text) throws MessagingException;
       public abstract void writeTo(java.io.OutputStream os) throws IOException, MessagingException;
// Protected Instance Methods
       protected void setExpunged(boolean expunged);
       protected void setMessageNumber(int msgnum);
// Protected Instance Fields
       protected boolean expunged;
       protected Folder folder;
       protected int msgnum;
       protected javax.mail.Session session;
}
```

Subclasses: javax.mail.internet.MimeMessage

Passed To: Too many methods to list.

Returned By: Folder.{expunge(), getMessage(), getMessages(), search()}, javax.mail.Message.reply(),
MessageContext.getMessage(), UIDFolder.{getMessageByUID(), getMessagesByUID()},
javax.mail.event.MessageChangedEvent.getMessage(),
javax.mail.event.MessageCountEvent.getMessages(), javax.mail.event.TransportEvent.getMessage(),
javax.mail.internet.MimeMessage.reply()

Type Of: javax.mail.event.MessageChangedEvent.msg, javax.mail.event.MessageCountEvent.msgs,
javax.mail.event.TransportEvent.msg

Message.RecipientType

javax.mail   *serializable*

This is an inner class that defines the kinds of recipients supported by the Message class. Currently TO, CC and BCC are supported.

```
public static class Message.RecipientType implements Serializable {
// Protected Constructors
    protected RecipientType(String type);
// Public Constants
    public static final Message.RecipientType BCC;
    public static final Message.RecipientType CC;
    public static final Message.RecipientType TO;
// Protected Instance Methods
1.2 protected Object readResolve() throws ObjectStreamException;
// Protected Instance Fields
    protected String type;
}
```

Subclasses: javax.mail.internet.MimeMessage.RecipientType

Passed To: javax.mail.Message.{addRecipient(), addRecipients(), getRecipients(), setRecipient(), setRecipients()}, javax.mail.internet.MimeMessage.{addRecipients(), getRecipients(), setRecipients()}, javax.mail.search.RecipientStringTerm.RecipientStringTerm(), javax.mail.search.RecipientTerm.RecipientTerm()

Returned By: javax.mail.search.RecipientStringTerm.getRecipientType(), javax.mail.search.RecipientTerm.getRecipientType()

Type Of: Message.RecipientType.{BCC, CC, TO}, javax.mail.search.RecipientTerm.type

MessageAware

javax.mail

A javax.activation.DataSource object can implement the MessageAware interface to provide a MessageContext object to a DataContentHandler. See MessageContext for more details.

```
public interface MessageAware {
// Public Instance Methods
    public abstract MessageContext getMessageContext();
}
```

Implementations: javax.mail.internet.MimePartDataSource

MessageContext

javax.mail

The MessageContext object allows javax.activation.DataSource objects implementing the MessageAware interface to retrieve information about the message containing a particular piece of content.

```
public class MessageContext {
// Public Constructors
    public MessageContext(Part part);
// Public Instance Methods
    public javax.mail.Message getMessage();
    public Part getPart();
    public javax.mail.Session getSession();
}
```

Returned By: MessageAware.getMessageContext(),
javax.mail.internet.MimePartDataSource.getMessageContext()

MessageRemovedException   JavaMail 1.1

javax.mail   *serializable checked*

This exception is thrown when any method (except isExpunged() and getMessageNumber()
is called on a Message object that has been expunged from a Folder.

```
Object ─ Throwable ─ Exception ─ MessagingException ─ MessageRemovedException
             Serializable
```

```
public class MessageRemovedException extends MessagingException {
// Public Constructors
    public MessageRemovedException();
    public MessageRemovedException(String s);
}
```

MessagingException   JavaMail 1.1

javax.mail   *serializable checked*

This is the base class for all JavaMail exceptions.

```
Object ─ Throwable ─ Exception ─ MessagingException
             Serializable
```

```
public class MessagingException extends Exception {
// Public Constructors
    public MessagingException();
    public MessagingException(String s);
    public MessagingException(String s, Exception e);
// Public Instance Methods
    public Exception getNextException();                          default:null
    public boolean setNextException(Exception ex);              synchronized
// Public Methods Overriding Throwable
    public String getMessage();                                  default:null
}
```

Subclasses: AuthenticationFailedException, FolderClosedException, FolderNotFoundException,
IllegalWriteException, MessageRemovedException, MethodNotSupportedException,
javax.mail.NoSuchProviderException, ReadOnlyFolderException, SendFailedException,
StoreClosedException, javax.mail.internet.ParseException, javax.mail.search.SearchException

Thrown By: Too many methods to list.

MethodNotSupportedException   JavaMail 1.1

javax.mail   *serializable checked*

This exception is thrown when a service implementation does not support a JavaMail
method.

```
Object ─ Throwable ─ Exception ─ MessagingException ─ MethodNotSupportedException
             Serializable
```

```
public class MethodNotSupportedException extends MessagingException {
// Public Constructors
    public MethodNotSupportedException();
    public MethodNotSupportedException(String s);
}
```

Multipart

javax.mail

This is a container object for multiple body parts within a Message. The Multipart class allows mail programs to access and manipulate the individual subparts of a message.

```
public abstract class Multipart {
// Protected Constructors
    protected Multipart();
// Property Accessor Methods (by property name)
    public String getContentType();
    public int getCount() throws MessagingException;
    public Part getParent();
    public void setParent(Part parent);
// Public Instance Methods
    public void addBodyPart(BodyPart part) throws MessagingException;                    synchronized
    public void addBodyPart(BodyPart part, int index) throws MessagingException;          synchronized
    public BodyPart getBodyPart(int index) throws MessagingException;
    public boolean removeBodyPart(BodyPart part) throws MessagingException;
    public void removeBodyPart(int index) throws MessagingException;
    public abstract void writeTo(java.io.OutputStream os) throws IOException, MessagingException;
// Protected Instance Methods
    protected void setMultipartDataSource(MultipartDataSource mp) throws MessagingException;
// Protected Instance Fields
    protected String contentType;
    protected Part parent;
    protected java.util.Vector parts;
}
```

Subclasses: javax.mail.internet.MimeMultipart

Passed To: BodyPart.setContent(), javax.mail.Message.setContent(), Part.setContent(), javax.mail.internet.MimeBodyPart.setContent(), javax.mail.internet.MimeMessage.setContent()

Returned By: BodyPart.getParent()

Type Of: BodyPart.parent

MultipartDataSource

javax.mail

This is a subinterface of javax.activation.DataSource that can contain multiple body parts. Objects implementing this interface preparse incoming multipart messages (such as from an IMAP mail server). Note that this interface is optional; if a provider does not support it, a regular DataSource object will be used instead. In that case, all data must be read via the InputStream object provided by the DataSource.

```
DataSource --- MultipartDataSource
```

```
public interface MultipartDataSource extends javax.activation.DataSource {
// Public Instance Methods
```

```
    public abstract BodyPart getBodyPart(int index) throws MessagingException;
    public abstract int getCount();
}
```

Passed To: Multipart.setMultipartDataSource()

NoSuchProviderException

JavaMail 1.1

javax.mail

serializable checked

This exception is thrown when a session attempts to use a provider that has not been installed on the system.

```
Object — Throwable — Exception — MessagingException — NoSuchProviderException
         Serializable
```

```
public class NoSuchProviderException extends MessagingException {
// Public Constructors
    public NoSuchProviderException();
    public NoSuchProviderException(String message);
}
```

Thrown By: javax.mail.Session.{getProvider(), getStore(), getTransport(), setProvider()}

Part

JavaMail 1.1

javax.mail

The Part interface provides the core functionality for JavaMail messages. It is used by both Message objects and BodyPart objects to manipulate message attributes and content. When implemented by a Message object, Part provides overall information about the entire message, including content type and message headers. In this case, the content of the Part can be of one type (such as text) or a Multipart object containing a set of BodyPart objects. Each BodyPart also implements Part, and contains a component of a multipart message (body text, HTML text, file attachments and so on). The attributes of each BodyPart object define the nature and disposition of that particular part. Part models a MIME Entity (see RFC-2045 for more information).

The Part interface provides set and get methods for commonly used message attributes: content, filename, size, and disposition. Arbitrary message headers can be set using the setHeader() and addHeader() methods, or by using the additional set and get methods provided by the various Part subclasses.

The content of a Part can be set in a variety of ways. The simplest is to call setText(), which allows String content with a MIME type of "text/plain." Content can also be set via the various setContent() methods, which accept Java objects and MIME types, as well as DataHandler objects from the JavaMail Activation Framework.

```
public interface Part {
// Public Constants
    public static final String ATTACHMENT;                                       ="attachment"
    public static final String INLINE;                                               ="inline"
// Property Accessor Methods (by property name)
    public abstract java.util.Enumeration getAllHeaders() throws MessagingException;
    public abstract Object getContent() throws IOException, MessagingException;
    public abstract void setContent(Multipart mp) throws MessagingException;
    public abstract void setContent(Object obj, String type) throws MessagingException;
    public abstract String getContentType() throws MessagingException;
```

```
    public abstract javax.activation.DataHandler getDataHandler() throws MessagingException;
    public abstract void setDataHandler(javax.activation.DataHandler dh) throws MessagingException;
    public abstract String getDescription() throws MessagingException;
    public abstract void setDescription(String description) throws MessagingException;
    public abstract String getDisposition() throws MessagingException;
    public abstract void setDisposition(String disposition) throws MessagingException;
    public abstract String getFileName() throws MessagingException;
    public abstract void setFileName(String filename) throws MessagingException;
    public abstract java.io.InputStream getInputStream() throws IOException, MessagingException;
    public abstract int getLineCount() throws MessagingException;
    public abstract int getSize() throws MessagingException;
    public abstract void setText(String text) throws MessagingException;
// Public Instance Methods
    public abstract void addHeader(String header_name, String header_value) throws MessagingException;
    public abstract String[ ] getHeader(String header_name) throws MessagingException;
    public abstract java.util.Enumeration getMatchingHeaders(String[ ] header_names) throws MessagingException;
    public abstract java.util.Enumeration getNonMatchingHeaders(String[ ] header_names)
        throws MessagingException;
    public abstract boolean isMimeType(String mimeType) throws MessagingException;
    public abstract void removeHeader(String header_name) throws MessagingException;
    public abstract void setHeader(String header_name, String header_value) throws MessagingException;
    public abstract void writeTo(java.io.OutputStream os) throws IOException, MessagingException;
}
```

Implementations: BodyPart, javax.mail.Message, javax.mail.internet.MimePart

Passed To: MessageContext.MessageContext(), Multipart.setParent()

Returned By: MessageContext.getPart(), Multipart.getParent()

Type Of: Multipart.parent

PasswordAuthentication   JavaMail 1.1

javax.mail

A holder object for a username/password pair, used along with an Authenticator object to log in to a protected messaging resource.

```
public final class PasswordAuthentication {
// Public Constructors
    public PasswordAuthentication(String userName, String password);
// Public Instance Methods
    public String getPassword();
    public String getUserName();
}
```

Passed To: javax.mail.Session.setPasswordAuthentication()

Returned By: javax.mail.Authenticator.getPasswordAuthentication(),
javax.mail.Session.{getPasswordAuthentication(), requestPasswordAuthentication()}

Provider   JavaMail 1.1

javax.mail

This is an abstract class that describes a particular protocol implementation, such as POP3, SMTP, or IMAP.

```
public class Provider {
// No Constructor
```

```
// Inner Classes
    public static class Type;
// Property Accessor Methods (by property name)
    public String getClassName();
    public String getProtocol();
    public Provider.Type getType();
    public String getVendor();
    public String getVersion();
// Public Methods Overriding Object
    public String toString();
}
```

Passed To: javax.mail.Session.{getStore(), getTransport(), setProvider()}

Returned By: javax.mail.Session.{getProvider(), getProviders()}

Provider.Type

JavaMail 1.1

javax.mail

An inner class of Provider, identifying whether the Provider in question is a message store or a message transport.

```
public static class Provider.Type {
// No Constructor
// Public Constants
    public static final Provider.Type STORE;
    public static final Provider.Type TRANSPORT;
}
```

Returned By: javax.mail.Provider.getType()

Type Of: Provider.Type.{STORE, TRANSPORT}

ReadOnlyFolderException

JavaMail 1.2

javax.mail

serializable checked

This exception is thrown when a read/write method is called on a read-only folder, or on a folder retrieved from a read-only message store.

```
Object ├ Throwable ├ Exception ├ MessagingException ├ ReadOnlyFolderException
       Serializable
```

```
public class ReadOnlyFolderException extends MessagingException {
// Public Constructors
    public ReadOnlyFolderException(Folder folder);
    public ReadOnlyFolderException(Folder folder, String message);
// Public Instance Methods
    public Folder getFolder();
}
```

SendFailedException

JavaMail 1.1

javax.mail

serializable checked

This exception is thrown when a message could not be sent to one or more of its recipients. The getValidSentAddresses() will return the addresses to which the message was sent successfully, the getInvalidAddresses() method returns the addresses that could not be sent to, and the getValidUnsentAddresses() method returns the addresses to which the message could have been sent, but wasn't.

```
Object ─ Throwable ─ Exception ─ MessagingException ─ SendFailedException
         Serializable
```

```
public class SendFailedException extends MessagingException {
// Public Constructors
    public SendFailedException();
    public SendFailedException(String s);
    public SendFailedException(String s, Exception e);
    public SendFailedException(String msg, Exception ex, Address[ ] validSent, Address[ ] validUnsent,
                                                     Address[ ] invalid);
// Property Accessor Methods (by property name)
    public Address[ ] getInvalidAddresses();                                              default:null
    public Address[ ] getValidSentAddresses();                                            default:null
    public Address[ ] getValidUnsentAddresses();                                          default:null
// Protected Instance Fields
    protected transient Address[ ] invalid;
    protected transient Address[ ] validSent;
    protected transient Address[ ] validUnsent;
}
```

Service   JavaMail 1.1

javax.mail

An abstract class that defines functionality common to all messaging services, including message stores and message transports. Service objects are retrieved, when necessary, from the Session object.

```
public abstract class Service {
// Protected Constructors
    protected Service(javax.mail.Session session, URLName urlname);
// Event Registration Methods (by event name)
    public void addConnectionListener(javax.mail.event.ConnectionListener l);            synchronized
    public void removeConnectionListener(javax.mail.event.ConnectionListener l);         synchronized
// Public Instance Methods
    public void close() throws MessagingException;                                        synchronized
    public void connect() throws MessagingException;
    public void connect(String host, String user, String password) throws MessagingException;
    public void connect(String host, int port, String user, String password) throws MessagingException;
    public URLName getURLName();
    public boolean isConnected();
// Public Methods Overriding Object
    public String toString();
// Protected Methods Overriding Object
    protected void finalize() throws Throwable;
// Protected Instance Methods
    protected void notifyConnectionListeners(int type);
    protected boolean protocolConnect(String host, int port, String user, String password)   constant
        throws MessagingException;
    protected void queueEvent(javax.mail.event.MailEvent event, java.util.Vector vector);
    protected void setConnected(boolean connected);
    protected void setURLName(URLName url);
// Protected Instance Fields
    protected boolean debug;
```

```
    protected javax.mail.Session session;
    protected URLName url;
}
```

Subclasses: Store, Transport

Session

javax.mail

The Session object provides access to the current JavaMail session and, therefore, to most JavaMail functionality. Instances of Session are retrieved via the static getSession() method, which allows creation of unshared mail sessions, and getDefaultInstance(), which returns a default session for the current JVM.

The various get methods of Session can be used to retrieve message stores and transports. The set methods can be used to specify default service providers, or to set a PasswordAuthentication object for a particular mail URL.

```
public final class Session {
// No Constructor
// Public Class Methods
1.2 public static javax.mail.Session getDefaultInstance(java.util.Properties props);
    public static javax.mail.Session getDefaultInstance(java.util.Properties props,
                                            javax.mail.Authenticator authenticator);
1.2 public static javax.mail.Session getInstance(java.util.Properties props);
    public static javax.mail.Session getInstance(java.util.Properties props, javax.mail.Authenticator authenticator);
// Property Accessor Methods (by property name)
    public boolean getDebug();
    public void setDebug(boolean debug);
    public java.util.Properties getProperties();
    public void setProvider(javax.mail.Provider provider) throws javax.mail.NoSuchProviderException;
    public javax.mail.Provider[ ] getProviders();
    public Store getStore() throws javax.mail.NoSuchProviderException;
    public Store getStore(URLName url) throws javax.mail.NoSuchProviderException;
    public Store getStore(String protocol) throws javax.mail.NoSuchProviderException;
    public Store getStore(javax.mail.Provider provider) throws javax.mail.NoSuchProviderException;
    public Transport getTransport() throws javax.mail.NoSuchProviderException;
    public Transport getTransport(URLName url) throws javax.mail.NoSuchProviderException;
    public Transport getTransport(Address address) throws javax.mail.NoSuchProviderException;
    public Transport getTransport(javax.mail.Provider provider) throws javax.mail.NoSuchProviderException;
    public Transport getTransport(String protocol) throws javax.mail.NoSuchProviderException;
// Public Instance Methods
    public Folder getFolder(URLName url) throws MessagingException;
    public javax.mail.PasswordAuthentication getPasswordAuthentication(URLName url);
    public String getProperty(String name);
    public javax.mail.Provider getProvider(String protocol) throws javax.mail.NoSuchProviderException;
    public javax.mail.PasswordAuthentication requestPasswordAuthentication(java.net.InetAddress addr, int port,
                                            String protocol, String prompt,
                                            String defaultUserName);
    public void setPasswordAuthentication(URLName url, javax.mail.PasswordAuthentication pw);
}
```

Passed To: javax.mail.Message.Message(), Service.Service(), Store.Store(), Transport.Transport(), javax.mail.internet.InternetAddress.getLocalAddress(), javax.mail.internet.MimeMessage.MimeMessage()

Returned By: MessageContext.getSession(), javax.mail.Session.{getDefaultInstance(), getInstance()}

Type Of: javax.mail.Message.session, Service.session

Store

javax.mail

This is an abstract class modeling a message store service, such as an IMAP or POP3 client. Basic service related methods are provided via the parent Service class.

```
Object — Service — Store
```

```
public abstract class Store extends Service {
// Protected Constructors
    protected Store(javax.mail.Session session, URLName urlname);
// Event Registration Methods (by event name)
    public void addFolderListener(javax.mail.event.FolderListener l);              synchronized
    public void removeFolderListener(javax.mail.event.FolderListener l);           synchronized
    public void addStoreListener(javax.mail.event.StoreListener l);                synchronized
    public void removeStoreListener(javax.mail.event.StoreListener l);             synchronized
// Public Instance Methods
    public abstract Folder getDefaultFolder() throws MessagingException;
    public abstract Folder getFolder(URLName url) throws MessagingException;
    public abstract Folder getFolder(String name) throws MessagingException;
1.2 public Folder[] getPersonalNamespaces() throws MessagingException;
1.2 public Folder[] getSharedNamespaces() throws MessagingException;
1.2 public Folder[] getUserNamespaces(String user) throws MessagingException;
// Protected Instance Methods
    protected void notifyFolderListeners(int type, Folder folder);
    protected void notifyFolderRenamedListeners(Folder oldF, Folder newF);
    protected void notifyStoreListeners(int type, String message);
}
```

Passed To: Folder.Folder(), StoreClosedException.StoreClosedException(), javax.mail.event.StoreEvent.StoreEvent()

Returned By: Folder.getStore(), javax.mail.Session.getStore(), StoreClosedException.getStore()

Type Of: Folder.store

StoreClosedException

serializable checked

javax.mail

This exception is thrown when a JavaMail method attempts to access a message store that has been closed. If this exception is thrown the message store and all dependent objects should be considered invalid.

```
Object — Throwable — Exception — MessagingException — StoreClosedException
       Serializable
```

```
public class StoreClosedException extends MessagingException {
// Public Constructors
    public StoreClosedException(Store store);
    public StoreClosedException(Store store, String message);
// Public Instance Methods
    public Store getStore();
}
```

Transport   JavaMail 1.1

javax.mail

An abstract class modeling a message transport service, such as SMTP. Basic service
related methods are provided via the parent Service class.

```
Object ─ Service ─ Transport
```

```
public abstract class Transport extends Service {
// Public Constructors
     public Transport(javax.mail.Session session, URLName urlname);
// Public Class Methods
     public static void send(javax.mail.Message msg) throws MessagingException;
     public static void send(javax.mail.Message msg, Address[ ] addresses) throws MessagingException;
// Event Registration Methods (by event name)
     public void addTransportListener(javax.mail.event.TransportListener l);                    synchronized
     public void removeTransportListener(javax.mail.event.TransportListener l);                 synchronized
// Public Instance Methods
     public abstract void sendMessage(javax.mail.Message msg, Address[ ] addresses) throws MessagingException;
// Protected Instance Methods
     protected void notifyTransportListeners(int type, Address[ ] validSent, Address[ ] validUnsent, Address[ ] invalid,
                                 javax.mail.Message msg);
}
```

Passed To: javax.mail.event.TransportEvent.TransportEvent()

Returned By: javax.mail.Session.getTransport()

UIDFolder   JavaMail 1.1

javax.mail

Identifies a JavaMail Folder that supports disconnected (off-net) operation by assigning
specific unique identifiers to messages, such as with an IMAP mail server. This allows
client programs to save the unique identifier for a particular message and use it to re-
retrieve that message during a later session. Unique identifiers are strictly ascending,
but not necessarily contiguous.

The getUIDValidity() method is returns a number that can be used to assure that UIDs
from earlier sessions are valid. If unique identifiers from an earlier session have not
persisted into the current session, this method must return a higher value in the subsequent session.

```
public interface UIDFolder {
// Public Constants
     public static final long LASTUID;                                                         =-1
// Inner Classes
     public static class FetchProfileItem extends FetchProfile.Item;
// Public Instance Methods
     public abstract javax.mail.Message getMessageByUID(long uid) throws MessagingException;
     public abstract javax.mail.Message[ ] getMessagesByUID(long[ ] uids) throws MessagingException;
     public abstract javax.mail.Message[ ] getMessagesByUID(long start, long end) throws MessagingException;
     public abstract long getUID(javax.mail.Message message) throws MessagingException;
     public abstract long getUIDValidity( ) throws MessagingException;
}
```

UIDFolder.FetchProfileItem

javax.mail

A fetch profile item for fetching UID for messages contained in UIDFolders.

```
public static class UIDFolder.FetchProfileItem extends FetchProfile.Item {
// Protected Constructors
    protected FetchProfileItem(String name);
// Public Constants
    public static final UIDFolder.FetchProfileItem UID;
}
```

Type Of: UIDFolder.FetchProfileItem.UID

URLName

javax.mail

The URLName class stores the name of a URL, and provides helper methods to retrieve certain standardized information from the URL itself. This information includes host, password, port, protocol, and filename, although availability of particular information depends on the URL scheme in use. Unlike java.net.URL, URLName does not include any support for actually connecting to the identified resource.

```
public class URLName {
// Public Constructors
    public URLName(java.net.URL url);
    public URLName(String url);
    public URLName(String protocol, String host, int port, String file, String username, String password);
// Property Accessor Methods (by property name)
    public String getFile();
    public String getHost();
    public String getPassword();
    public int getPort();
    public String getProtocol();
    public String getRef();
    public java.net.URL getURL() throws java.net.MalformedURLException;
    public String getUsername();
// Public Methods Overriding Object
    public boolean equals(Object obj);
    public int hashCode();
    public String toString();
// Protected Instance Methods
    protected void parseString(String url);
// Protected Instance Fields
    protected String fullURL;
}
```

Passed To: Service.{Service(), setURLName()}, javax.mail.Session.{getFolder(), getPasswordAuthentication(), getStore(), getTransport(), setPasswordAuthentication()}, Store.{getFolder(), Store()}, Transport.Transport()

Returned By: Folder.getURLName(), Service.getURLName()

Type Of: Service.url

Package javax.mail.event

The javax.mail.event package contains event listeners and event objects for the JavaMail event model. Different protocols, as well as different implementations of those protocols, will support this model to varying extents. In particular, changes to structures on a message store (such as an IMAP server) by administrators and other clients will generally not trigger events.

Events:

public abstract class **MailEvent** extends java.util.EventObject;
  └ public class **ConnectionEvent** extends MailEvent;
  └ public class **FolderEvent** extends MailEvent;
  └ public class **MessageChangedEvent** extends MailEvent;
  └ public class **MessageCountEvent** extends MailEvent;
  └ public class **StoreEvent** extends MailEvent;
  └ public class **TransportEvent** extends MailEvent;

Event Listeners:

public abstract class **ConnectionAdapter** implements ConnectionListener;
public interface **ConnectionListener** extends java.util.EventListener;
public abstract class **FolderAdapter** implements FolderListener;
public interface **FolderListener** extends java.util.EventListener;
public interface **MessageChangedListener** extends java.util.EventListener;
public abstract class **MessageCountAdapter** implements MessageCountListener;
public interface **MessageCountListener** extends java.util.EventListener;
public interface **StoreListener** extends java.util.EventListener;
public abstract class **TransportAdapter** implements TransportListener;
public interface **TransportListener** extends java.util.EventListener;

ConnectionAdapter

JavaMail 1.1

javax.mail.event

event adapter

This is a convenience class for implementing a ConnectionListener. The methods in the class are all empty.

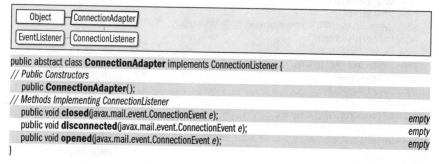

```
public abstract class ConnectionAdapter implements ConnectionListener {
// Public Constructors
    public ConnectionAdapter();
// Methods Implementing ConnectionListener
    public void closed(javax.mail.event.ConnectionEvent e);                          empty
    public void disconnected(javax.mail.event.ConnectionEvent e);                    empty
    public void opened(javax.mail.event.ConnectionEvent e);                          empty
}
```

ConnectionEvent

JavaMail 1.1

javax.mail.event

serializable event

The ConnectionEvent object defines OPENED, CLOSED, and DISCONNECTED events on a mail service.

```
public class ConnectionEvent extends MailEvent {
// Public Constructors
    public ConnectionEvent(Object source, int type);
// Public Constants
    public static final int CLOSED;                                              =3
    public static final int DISCONNECTED;                                        =2
    public static final int OPENED;                                              =1
// Public Instance Methods
    public int getType();
// Public Methods Overriding MailEvent
    public void dispatch(Object listener);
// Protected Instance Fields
    protected int type;
}
```

Passed To: ConnectionAdapter.{closed(), disconnected(), opened()}, ConnectionListener.{closed(), disconnected(), opened()}

ConnectionListener   JavaMail 1.1

javax.mail.event   *event listener*

This is a listener interface for Connection events. This interface allows an object to be notified when a Message Store, Folder, or Transport is opened, closed, or disconnected.

```
EventListener |--- ConnectionListener
```

```
public interface ConnectionListener extends java.util.EventListener {
// Public Instance Methods
    public abstract void closed(javax.mail.event.ConnectionEvent e);
    public abstract void disconnected(javax.mail.event.ConnectionEvent e);
    public abstract void opened(javax.mail.event.ConnectionEvent e);
}
```

Implementations: ConnectionAdapter

Passed To: Folder.{addConnectionListener(), removeConnectionListener()},
Service.{addConnectionListener(), removeConnectionListener()}

FolderAdapter   JavaMail 1.1

javax.mail.event   *event adapter*

This is a convenience class for implementing a FolderListener.

```
Object |-- FolderAdapter

EventListener |--- FolderListener
```

```
public abstract class FolderAdapter implements FolderListener {
// Public Constructors
    public FolderAdapter();
// Methods Implementing FolderListener
    public void folderCreated(FolderEvent e);                                  empty
    public void folderDeleted(FolderEvent e);                                  empty
    public void folderRenamed(FolderEvent e);                                  empty
}
```

FolderEvent

javax.mail.event

The FolderEvent class defines events related to a folder's lifecycle. The getFolder() method returns a Folder object representing the folder that the event occurred on, and the get-NewFolder() will return the new Folder object representing the results of a folder rename.

```
Object ─ EventObject ─ MailEvent ─ FolderEvent
          Serializable
```

```
public class FolderEvent extends MailEvent {
// Public Constructors
    public FolderEvent(Object source, Folder folder, int type);
    public FolderEvent(Object source, Folder oldFolder, Folder newFolder, int type);
// Public Constants
    public static final int CREATED;                                          =1
    public static final int DELETED;                                          =2
    public static final int RENAMED;                                          =3
// Public Instance Methods
    public Folder getFolder();
    public Folder getNewFolder();
    public int getType();
// Public Methods Overriding MailEvent
    public void dispatch(Object listener);
// Protected Instance Fields
    protected transient Folder folder;
    protected transient Folder newFolder;
    protected int type;
}
```

Passed To: FolderAdapter.{folderCreated(), folderDeleted(), folderRenamed()}, FolderListener.{folderCreated(), folderDeleted(), folderRenamed()}

FolderListener

javax.mail.event

This is a listener that allows an object to be notified if a folder is created, deleted, or renamed.

```
EventListener ┈ FolderListener
```

```
public interface FolderListener extends java.util.EventListener {
// Public Instance Methods
    public abstract void folderCreated(FolderEvent e);
    public abstract void folderDeleted(FolderEvent e);
    public abstract void folderRenamed(FolderEvent e);
}
```

Implementations: FolderAdapter

Passed To: Folder.{addFolderListener(), removeFolderListener()}, Store.{addFolderListener(), removeFolderListener()}

MailEvent

javax.mail.event

The MailEvent class provides a basis for all mail-related events. This class defines the dispatch() method, which calls the appropriate listener objects.

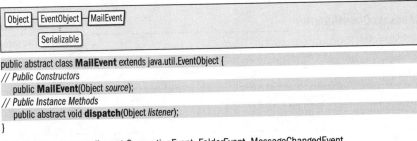

```
public abstract class MailEvent extends java.util.EventObject {
// Public Constructors
    public MailEvent(Object source);
// Public Instance Methods
    public abstract void dispatch(Object listener);
}
```

Subclasses: javax.mail.event.ConnectionEvent, FolderEvent, MessageChangedEvent, MessageCountEvent, StoreEvent, TransportEvent

Passed To: Service.queueEvent()

MessageChangedEvent

javax.mail.event

serializable event

The MessageChangedEvent class describes changes to a message envelope or message flags.

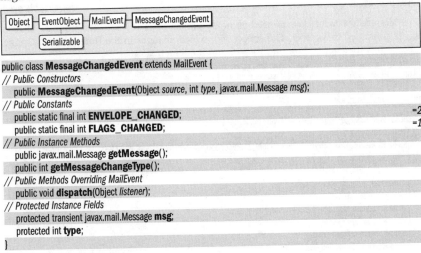

```
public class MessageChangedEvent extends MailEvent {
// Public Constructors
    public MessageChangedEvent(Object source, int type, javax.mail.Message msg);
// Public Constants
    public static final int ENVELOPE_CHANGED;                              =2
    public static final int FLAGS_CHANGED;                                 =1
// Public Instance Methods
    public javax.mail.Message getMessage();
    public int getMessageChangeType();
// Public Methods Overriding MailEvent
    public void dispatch(Object listener);
// Protected Instance Fields
    protected transient javax.mail.Message msg;
    protected int type;
}
```

Passed To: MessageChangedListener.messageChanged()

MessageChangedListener

javax.mail.event

event listener

This is a listener that allows an object to be notified of change to the envelope or flags of a Message object.

```
EventListener  MessageChangedListener
```

```
public interface MessageChangedListener extends java.util.EventListener {
// Public Instance Methods
    public abstract void messageChanged(MessageChangedEvent e);
}
```

Passed To: Folder.{addMessageChangedListener(), removeMessageChangedListener()}

MessageCountAdapter

javax.mail.event   *event adapter*

A convenience class for implementing a MessageCountListener. The methods are all empty.

```
public abstract class MessageCountAdapter implements MessageCountListener {
// Public Constructors
    public MessageCountAdapter();
// Methods Implementing MessageCountListener
    public void messagesAdded(MessageCountEvent e);                    empty
    public void messagesRemoved(MessageCountEvent e);                  empty
}
```

MessageCountEvent

javax.mail.event   *serializable event*

The MessageCountEvent class is used to notify clients of changes to the number of messages contained in a folder. The speed with which changes in the Folder contents trigger this event varies depending on protocol and implementation.

```
public class MessageCountEvent extends MailEvent {
// Public Constructors
    public MessageCountEvent(Folder folder, int type, boolean removed, javax.mail.Message[ ] msgs);
// Public Constants
    public static final int ADDED;                                       =1
    public static final int REMOVED;                                     =2
// Public Instance Methods
    public javax.mail.Message[ ] getMessages();
    public int getType();
    public boolean isRemoved();
// Public Methods Overriding MailEvent
    public void dispatch(Object listener);
// Protected Instance Fields
    protected transient javax.mail.Message[ ] msgs;
    protected boolean removed;
    protected int type;
}
```

Passed To: MessageCountAdapter.{messagesAdded(), messagesRemoved()}, MessageCountListener.{messagesAdded(), messagesRemoved()}

MessageCountListener

javax.mail.event   *event listener*

A listener that allows an object to be notified when messages are added or removed to from a folder.

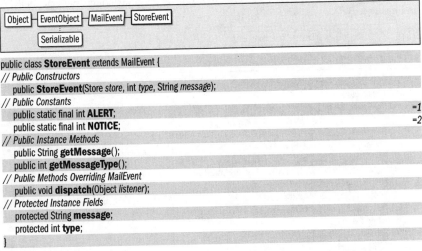

public interface **MessageCountListener** extends java.util.EventListener {
// *Public Instance Methods*
    public abstract void **messagesAdded**(MessageCountEvent e);
    public abstract void **messagesRemoved**(MessageCountEvent e);
}

Implementations: MessageCountAdapter

Passed To: Folder.{addMessageCountListener(), removeMessageCountListener()}

StoreEvent

JavaMail 1.1

serializable event

javax.mail.event

The StoreEvent class models notifications from a message store. Notifications consist of ALERTs and NOTICEs. ALERT notifications are likely critical notifications.

public class **StoreEvent** extends MailEvent {
// *Public Constructors*
    public **StoreEvent**(Store *store*, int *type*, String *message*);
// *Public Constants*
    public static final int **ALERT**;   =1
    public static final int **NOTICE**;   =2
// *Public Instance Methods*
    public String **getMessage**();
    public int **getMessageType**();
// *Public Methods Overriding MailEvent*
    public void **dispatch**(Object *listener*);
// *Protected Instance Fields*
    protected String **message**;
    protected int **type**;
}

Passed To: StoreListener.notification()

StoreListener

JavaMail 1.1

event listener

javax.mail.event

This is a listener that allows an object to be notified of message store events.

public interface **StoreListener** extends java.util.EventListener {
// *Public Instance Methods*
    public abstract void **notification**(StoreEvent e);
}

Passed To: Store.{addStoreListener(), removeStoreListener()}

TransportAdapter

JavaMail 1.1

event adapter

javax.mail.event

This is a convenience class for implementing a TransportListener.

TransportAdapter

```
    Object     ── TransportAdapter
  EventListener ┈┈ TransportListener
```

```
public abstract class TransportAdapter implements TransportListener {
// Public Constructors
     public TransportAdapter();
// Methods Implementing TransportListener
     public void messageDelivered(TransportEvent e);                                    empty
     public void messageNotDelivered(TransportEvent e);                                 empty
     public void messagePartiallyDelivered(TransportEvent e);                           empty
}
```

TransportEvent   JavaMail 1.1

javax.mail.event   *serializable event*

The TransportEvent class models message transport events, including message delivery
and message delivery failure.

```
  Object ─ EventObject ─ MailEvent ─ TransportEvent
             Serializable
```

```
public class TransportEvent extends MailEvent {
// Public Constructors
     public TransportEvent(Transport transport, int type, Address[ ] validSent, Address[ ] validUnsent, Address[ ] invalid,
                          javax.mail.Message msg);
// Public Constants
     public static final int MESSAGE_DELIVERED;                                            =1
     public static final int MESSAGE_NOT_DELIVERED;                                        =2
     public static final int MESSAGE_PARTIALLY_DELIVERED;                                  =3
// Property Accessor Methods (by property name)
     public Address[ ] getInvalidAddresses();
1.2  public javax.mail.Message getMessage();
     public int getType();
     public Address[ ] getValidSentAddresses();
     public Address[ ] getValidUnsentAddresses();
// Public Methods Overriding MailEvent
     public void dispatch(Object listener);
// Protected Instance Fields
     protected transient Address[ ] invalid;
     protected transient javax.mail.Message msg;
     protected int type;
     protected transient Address[ ] validSent;
     protected transient Address[ ] validUnsent;
}
```

Passed To: TransportAdapter.{messageDelivered(), messageNotDelivered(),
messagePartiallyDelivered()}, TransportListener.{messageDelivered(), messageNotDelivered(),
messagePartiallyDelivered()}

TransportListener   JavaMail 1.1

javax.mail.event   *event listener*

This interface is a listener that allows an object to notified when a message has been
delivered, unsuccessfully delivered, or partially delivered. Note that like most JavaMail
APIs, this listener is more meaningful for some mail APIs than others.

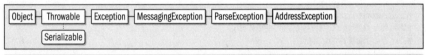

```
public interface TransportListener extends java.util.EventListener {
// Public Instance Methods
    public abstract void messageDelivered(TransportEvent e);
    public abstract void messageNotDelivered(TransportEvent e);
    public abstract void messagePartiallyDelivered(TransportEvent e);
}
```

Implementations: TransportAdapter

Passed To: Transport.{addTransportListener(), removeTransportListener()}

Package javax.mail.internet   JavaMail 1.1

The javax.mail.internet package provides a set of classes that provide support for Internet email based on RFC-822 (SMTP) and RFC-2045 (MIME).

Interfaces:

```
public interface MimePart extends javax.mail.Part;
public interface SharedInputStream;
```

Classes:

```
public class ContentDisposition;
public class ContentType;
public class HeaderTokenizer;
public static class HeaderTokenizer.Token;
public class InternetAddress extends javax.mail.Address implements Cloneable;
public class InternetHeaders;
public class MailDateFormat extends java.text.SimpleDateFormat;
public class MimeBodyPart extends javax.mail.BodyPart implements MimePart;
public class MimeMessage extends javax.mail.Message implements MimePart;
public static class MimeMessage.RecipientType extends javax.mail.Message.RecipientType;
public class MimeMultipart extends javax.mail.Multipart;
public class MimePartDataSource implements javax.activation.DataSource, javax.mail.MessageAware;
public class MimeUtility;
public class NewsAddress extends javax.mail.Address;
public class ParameterList;
```

Exceptions:

```
public class ParseException extends javax.mail.MessagingException;
    └ public class AddressException extends ParseException;
```

AddressException   JavaMail 1.1

javax.mail.internet   *serializable checked*

This exception is thrown when an InternetAddress is badly formatted.

```
Object ─ Throwable ─ Exception ─ MessagingException ─ ParseException ─ AddressException
            Serializable
```

```
public class AddressException extends javax.mail.internet.ParseException {
// Public Constructors
    public AddressException();
```

```
   public AddressException(String s);
   public AddressException(String s, String ref);
   public AddressException(String s, String ref, int pos);
// Public Instance Methods
   public int getPos();                                                        default:-1
   public String getRef();                                                     default:null
// Public Methods Overriding Throwable
   public String toString();
// Protected Instance Fields
   protected int pos;
   protected String ref;
}
```

Thrown By: InternetAddress.{InternetAddress(), parse()}, NewsAddress.parse()

ContentDisposition   JavaMail 1.2

javax.mail.internet

This class can be used to represent a MIME ContentDisposition value, or to create one from scratch.

```
public class ContentDisposition {
// Public Constructors
   public ContentDisposition();
   public ContentDisposition(String s) throws javax.mail.internet.ParseException;
   public ContentDisposition(String disposition, ParameterList list);
// Public Instance Methods
   public String getDisposition();                                            default:null
   public String getParameter(String name);
   public ParameterList getParameterList();                                   default:null
   public void setDisposition(String disposition);
   public void setParameter(String name, String value);
   public void setParameterList(ParameterList list);
// Public Methods Overriding Object
   public String toString();
}
```

ContentType   JavaMail 1.1

javax.mail.internet

This class represents a MIME ContentType, including a primary type (such as "text") and a subtype (such as "html").

```
public class ContentType {
// Public Constructors
   public ContentType();
   public ContentType(String s) throws javax.mail.internet.ParseException;
   public ContentType(String primaryType, String subType, ParameterList list);
// Property Accessor Methods (by property name)
   public String getBaseType();                                          default:"null/null"
   public ParameterList getParameterList();                                   default:null
   public void setParameterList(ParameterList list);
   public String getPrimaryType();                                            default:null
   public void setPrimaryType(String primaryType);
   public String getSubType();                                                default:null
   public void setSubType(String subType);
```

```
// Public Instance Methods
    public String getParameter(String name);
    public boolean match(ContentType cType);
    public boolean match(String s);
    public void setParameter(String name, String value);
// Public Methods Overriding Object
    public String toString();
}
```

Passed To: ContentType.match()

HeaderTokenizer   JavaMail 1.1

javax.mail.internet

This is a utility class that breaks down RFC-822 and MIME headers into the component parts defined by their specifications. The parts are returned as HeaderTokenizer.Token objects.

```
public class HeaderTokenizer {
// Public Constructors
    public HeaderTokenizer(String header);
    public HeaderTokenizer(String header, String delimiters);
    public HeaderTokenizer(String header, String delimiters, boolean skipComments);
// Public Constants
    public static final String MIME;                                =")()<>@,;:
    public static final String RFC822;                              =")()<>@,;:
// Inner Classes
    public static class Token;
// Public Instance Methods
    public String getRemainder();
    public HeaderTokenizer.Token next() throws javax.mail.internet.ParseException;
    public HeaderTokenizer.Token peek() throws javax.mail.internet.ParseException;
}
```

HeaderTokenizer.Token   JavaMail 1.1

javax.mail.internet

This class represents the components of an RFC-822 or MIME header broken down by a HeaderTokenizer object.

```
public static class HeaderTokenizer.Token {
// Public Constructors
    public Token(int type, String value);
// Public Constants
    public static final int ATOM;                                   =-1
    public static final int COMMENT;                                =-3
    public static final int EOF;                                    =-4
    public static final int QUOTEDSTRING;                           =-2
// Public Instance Methods
    public int getType();
    public String getValue();
}
```

Returned By: HeaderTokenizer.{next(), peek()}

InternetAddress

javax.mail.internet

cloneable serializable

This is a subclass of javax.mail.Address that handles an Internet-style (RFC-822) address. Examples of a valid Internet address are: *postmaster@general.com* and "L. Lincoln Penn" *<postmaster@general.com>*.

```
Object ─┤ Address ├─ InternetAddress
        │ Serializable │ │ Cloneable │
```

```
public class InternetAddress extends Address implements Cloneable {
// Public Constructors
    public InternetAddress();
    public InternetAddress(String address) throws AddressException;
    public InternetAddress(String address, String personal) throws UnsupportedEncodingException;
    public InternetAddress(String address, String personal, String charset) throws UnsupportedEncodingException;
// Public Class Methods
    public static InternetAddress getLocalAddress(javax.mail.Session session);
    public static InternetAddress[ ] parse(String addresslist) throws AddressException;
    public static InternetAddress[ ] parse(String s, boolean strict) throws AddressException;
    public static String toString(Address[ ] addresses);
    public static String toString(Address[ ] addresses, int used);
// Public Instance Methods
    public String getAddress();                                                    default:null
    public String getPersonal();                                                   default:null
    public void setAddress(String address);
    public void setPersonal(String name) throws UnsupportedEncodingException;
    public void setPersonal(String name, String charset) throws UnsupportedEncodingException;
1.2 public String toUnicodeString();
// Public Methods Overriding Address
    public boolean equals(Object a);
    public String getType();                                                       default:"rfc822"
    public String toString();
// Public Methods Overriding Object
1.2 public Object clone();
    public int hashCode();
// Protected Instance Fields
    protected String address;
    protected String encodedPersonal;
    protected String personal;
}
```

Returned By: InternetAddress.{getLocalAddress(), parse()}

InternetHeaders

javax.mail.internet

A utility class that decodes RFC-822 headers from a message stream.

```
public class InternetHeaders {
// Public Constructors
    public InternetHeaders();
    public InternetHeaders(java.io.InputStream is) throws MessagingException;
// Public Instance Methods
    public void addHeader(String name, String value);
    public void addHeaderLine(String line);
```

```
    public java.util.Enumeration getAllHeaderLines();
    public java.util.Enumeration getAllHeaders();
    public String[ ] getHeader(String name);
    public String getHeader(String name, String delimiter);
    public java.util.Enumeration getMatchingHeaderLines(String[ ] names);
    public java.util.Enumeration getMatchingHeaders(String[ ] names);
    public java.util.Enumeration getNonMatchingHeaderLines(String[ ] names);
    public java.util.Enumeration getNonMatchingHeaders(String[ ] names);
    public void load(java.io.InputStream is) throws MessagingException;
    public void removeHeader(String name);
    public void setHeader(String name, String value);
}
```

Passed To: MimeBodyPart.MimeBodyPart(), MimeMessage.MimeMessage(), MimeMultipart.createMimeBodyPart()

Returned By: MimeMessage.createInternetHeaders(), MimeMultipart.createInternetHeaders()

Type Of: MimeBodyPart.headers, MimeMessage.headers

MailDateFormat

JavaMail 1.2

javax.mail.internet

cloneable serializable

This is an extension of java.text.SimpleDateFormat, used to format dates based upon the IETF's draft specification from January 26, 2000, which is a followup to RFC-822. Date format patterning strings are ignored by this class.

```
public class MailDateFormat extends java.text.SimpleDateFormat {
// Public Constructors
    public MailDateFormat();
// Public Methods Overriding SimpleDateFormat
    public StringBuffer format(java.util.Date date, StringBuffer dateStrBuf, java.text.FieldPosition fieldPosition);
    public java.util.Date parse(String text, java.text.ParsePosition pos);
// Public Methods Overriding DateFormat
    public void setCalendar(java.util.Calendar newCalendar);
    public void setNumberFormat(java.text.NumberFormat newNumberFormat);
}
```

MimeBodyPart

JavaMail 1.1

javax.mail.internet

This is an extension of the BodyPart class to add MIME-related methods.

```
public class MimeBodyPart extends BodyPart implements MimePart {
// Public Constructors
    public MimeBodyPart();
    public MimeBodyPart(java.io.InputStream is) throws MessagingException;
    public MimeBodyPart(InternetHeaders headers, byte[ ] content) throws MessagingException;
// Public Instance Methods
```

1.2 public java.io.InputStream **getRawInputStream**() throws MessagingException;
    public void **setDescription**(String *description*, String *charset*) throws MessagingException;
// *Methods Implementing MimePart*
    public void **addHeaderLine**(String *line*) throws MessagingException;
    public java.util.Enumeration **getAllHeaderLines**() throws MessagingException;
    public String **getContentID**() throws MessagingException;   *default:null*
    public String[ ] **getContentLanguage**() throws MessagingException;   *default:null*
    public String **getContentMD5**() throws MessagingException;   *default:null*
    public String **getEncoding**() throws MessagingException;   *default:null*
    public String **getHeader**(String *name*, String *delimiter*) throws MessagingException;
    public java.util.Enumeration **getMatchingHeaderLines**(String[ ] *names*) throws MessagingException;
    public java.util.Enumeration **getNonMatchingHeaderLines**(String[ ] *names*) throws MessagingException;
    public void **setContentLanguage**(String[ ] *languages*) throws MessagingException;
    public void **setContentMD5**(String *md5*) throws MessagingException;
    public void **setText**(String *text*) throws MessagingException;
    public void **setText**(String *text*, String *charset*) throws MessagingException;
// *Methods Implementing Part*
    public void **addHeader**(String *name*, String *value*) throws MessagingException;
    public java.util.Enumeration **getAllHeaders**() throws MessagingException;
    public Object **getContent**() throws IOException, MessagingException;
    public String **getContentType**() throws MessagingException;   *default:"text/plain"*
    public javax.activation.DataHandler **getDataHandler**() throws MessagingException;
    public String **getDescription**() throws MessagingException;   *default:null*
    public String **getDisposition**() throws MessagingException;   *default:null*
    public String **getFileName**() throws MessagingException;   *default:null*
    public String[ ] **getHeader**(String *name*) throws MessagingException;
    public java.io.InputStream **getInputStream**() throws IOException, MessagingException;
    public int **getLineCount**() throws MessagingException;   *constant default:-1*
    public java.util.Enumeration **getMatchingHeaders**(String[ ] *names*) throws MessagingException;
    public java.util.Enumeration **getNonMatchingHeaders**(String[ ] *names*) throws MessagingException;
    public int **getSize**() throws MessagingException;   *default:-1*
    public boolean **isMimeType**(String *mimeType*) throws MessagingException;
    public void **removeHeader**(String *name*) throws MessagingException;
    public void **setContent**(Multipart *mp*) throws MessagingException;
    public void **setContent**(Object *o*, String *type*) throws MessagingException;
    public void **setDataHandler**(javax.activation.DataHandler *dh*) throws MessagingException;
    public void **setDescription**(String *description*) throws MessagingException;
    public void **setDisposition**(String *disposition*) throws MessagingException;
    public void **setFileName**(String *filename*) throws MessagingException;
    public void **setHeader**(String *name*, String *value*) throws MessagingException;
    public void **writeTo**(java.io.OutputStream *os*) throws IOException, MessagingException;
// *Protected Instance Methods*
    protected java.io.InputStream **getContentStream**() throws MessagingException;
    protected void **updateHeaders**() throws MessagingException;
// *Protected Instance Fields*
    protected byte[ ] **content**;
1.2 protected java.io.InputStream **contentStream**;
    protected javax.activation.DataHandler **dh**;
    protected InternetHeaders **headers**;
}

Returned By: MimeMultipart.createMimeBodyPart()

MimeMessage

javax.mail.internet

This class is an extension of the Message class to represent a MIME formatted message. MimeMessage is the main Message implementation provided with the standard JavaMail distribution.

```
public class MimeMessage extends javax.mail.Message implements MimePart {
// Public Constructors
1.2  public MimeMessage(MimeMessage source) throws MessagingException;
     public MimeMessage(javax.mail.Session session);
     public MimeMessage(javax.mail.Session session, java.io.InputStream is) throws MessagingException;
// Protected Constructors
     protected MimeMessage(Folder folder, int msgnum);
     protected MimeMessage(Folder folder, java.io.InputStream is, int msgnum) throws MessagingException;
     protected MimeMessage(Folder folder, InternetHeaders headers, byte[] content, int msgnum)
          throws MessagingException;
// Inner Classes
     public static class RecipientType extends Message.RecipientType;
// Property Accessor Methods (by property name)
     public java.util.Enumeration getAllHeaderLines() throws MessagingException;              Implements:MimePart
     public java.util.Enumeration getAllHeaders() throws MessagingException;                      Implements:Part
     public Address[] getAllRecipients() throws MessagingException;                            Overrides:Message
     public Object getContent() throws IOException, MessagingException;                         Implements:Part
     public void setContent(Multipart mp) throws MessagingException;                           Implements:Part
     public void setContent(Object o, String type) throws MessagingException;                  Implements:Part
     public String getContentID() throws MessagingException;                                Implements:MimePart
     public void setContentID(String cid) throws MessagingException;
     public String[] getContentLanguage() throws MessagingException;                        Implements:MimePart
     public void setContentLanguage(String[] languages) throws MessagingException;          Implements:MimePart
     public String getContentMD5() throws MessagingException;                               Implements:MimePart
     public void setContentMD5(String md5) throws MessagingException;                       Implements:MimePart
     public String getContentType() throws MessagingException;                                 Implements:Part
     public javax.activation.DataHandler getDataHandler() throws            Implements:Part synchronized
          MessagingException;
     public void setDataHandler(javax.activation.DataHandler dh) throws MessagingException;    Implements:Part
     public String getDescription() throws MessagingException;                                 Implements:Part
     public void setDescription(String description) throws MessagingException;                 Implements:Part
     public void setDescription(String description, String charset) throws MessagingException;
     public String getDisposition() throws MessagingException;                                 Implements:Part
     public void setDisposition(String disposition) throws MessagingException;                 Implements:Part
     public String getEncoding() throws MessagingException;                                 Implements:MimePart
     public String getFileName() throws MessagingException;                                    Implements:Part
     public void setFileName(String filename) throws MessagingException;                       Implements:Part
     public Flags getFlags() throws MessagingException;                            Overrides:Message synchronized
     public Address[] getFrom() throws MessagingException;                                    Overrides:Message
     public void setFrom(Address address) throws MessagingException;                          Overrides:Message
     public java.io.InputStream getInputStream() throws IOException, MessagingException;        Implements:Part
     public int getLineCount() throws MessagingException;                             Implements:Part constant
     public String getMessageID() throws MessagingException;
1.2  public java.io.InputStream getRawInputStream() throws MessagingException;
     public java.util.Date getReceivedDate() throws MessagingException;               Overrides:Message constant
     public Address[] getReplyTo() throws MessagingException;                                 Overrides:Message
```

public void **setReplyTo**(Address[ ] *addresses*) throws MessagingException;	*Overrides:Message*
public java.util.Date **getSentDate**( ) throws MessagingException;	*Overrides:Message*
public void **setSentDate**(java.util.Date *d*) throws MessagingException;	*Overrides:Message*
public int **getSize**( ) throws MessagingException;	*Implements:Part*
public String **getSubject**( ) throws MessagingException;	*Overrides:Message*
public void **setSubject**(String *subject*) throws MessagingException;	*Overrides:Message*
public void **setSubject**(String *subject*, String *charset*) throws MessagingException;	
public void **setText**(String *text*) throws MessagingException;	*Implements:MimePart*
public void **setText**(String *text*, String *charset*) throws MessagingException;	*Implements:MimePart*

// *Public Instance Methods*
1.2 public void **addRecipients**(Message.RecipientType *type*, String *addresses*) throws MessagingException;
1.2 public void **setRecipients**(Message.RecipientType *type*, String *addresses*) throws MessagingException;
    public void **writeTo**(java.io.OutputStream *os*, String[ ] *ignoreList*) throws IOException, MessagingException;
// *Methods Implementing MimePart*
    public void **addHeaderLine**(String *line*) throws MessagingException;
    public java.util.Enumeration **getAllHeaderLines**( ) throws MessagingException;
    public String **getContentID**( ) throws MessagingException;
    public String[ ] **getContentLanguage**( ) throws MessagingException;
    public String **getContentMD5**( ) throws MessagingException;
    public String **getEncoding**( ) throws MessagingException;
    public String **getHeader**(String *name*, String *delimiter*) throws MessagingException;
    public java.util.Enumeration **getMatchingHeaderLines**(String[ ] *names*) throws MessagingException;
    public java.util.Enumeration **getNonMatchingHeaderLines**(String[ ] *names*) throws MessagingException;
    public void **setContentLanguage**(String[ ] *languages*) throws MessagingException;
    public void **setContentMD5**(String *md5*) throws MessagingException;
    public void **setText**(String *text*) throws MessagingException;
    public void **setText**(String *text*, String *charset*) throws MessagingException;
// *Methods Implementing Part*
    public void **addHeader**(String *name*, String *value*) throws MessagingException;
    public java.util.Enumeration **getAllHeaders**( ) throws MessagingException;
    public Object **getContent**( ) throws IOException, MessagingException;
    public String **getContentType**( ) throws MessagingException;

public javax.activation.DataHandler **getDataHandler**( ) throws MessagingException;	*synchronized*

    public String **getDescription**( ) throws MessagingException;
    public String **getDisposition**( ) throws MessagingException;
    public String **getFileName**( ) throws MessagingException;
    public String[ ] **getHeader**(String *name*) throws MessagingException;
    public java.io.InputStream **getInputStream**( ) throws IOException, MessagingException;

public int **getLineCount**( ) throws MessagingException;	*constant*

    public java.util.Enumeration **getMatchingHeaders**(String[ ] *names*) throws MessagingException;
    public java.util.Enumeration **getNonMatchingHeaders**(String[ ] *names*) throws MessagingException;
    public int **getSize**( ) throws MessagingException;
    public boolean **isMimeType**(String *mimeType*) throws MessagingException;
    public void **removeHeader**(String *name*) throws MessagingException;
    public void **setContent**(Multipart *mp*) throws MessagingException;
    public void **setContent**(Object *o*, String *type*) throws MessagingException;
    public void **setDataHandler**(javax.activation.DataHandler *dh*) throws MessagingException;
    public void **setDescription**(String *description*) throws MessagingException;
    public void **setDisposition**(String *disposition*) throws MessagingException;
    public void **setFileName**(String *filename*) throws MessagingException;
    public void **setHeader**(String *name*, String *value*) throws MessagingException;
    public void **writeTo**(java.io.OutputStream *os*) throws IOException, MessagingException;
// *Public Methods Overriding Message*
    public void **addFrom**(Address[ ] *addresses*) throws MessagingException;
    public void **addRecipients**(Message.RecipientType *type*, Address[ ] *addresses*) throws MessagingException;

```
   public Address[ ] getRecipients(Message.RecipientType type) throws MessagingException;
   public boolean isSet(Flags.Flag flag) throws MessagingException;                                    synchronized
   public javax.mail.Message reply(boolean replyToAll) throws MessagingException;
   public void saveChanges() throws MessagingException;
   public void setFlags(Flags flag, boolean set) throws MessagingException;                             synchronized
   public void setFrom() throws MessagingException;
   public void setRecipients(Message.RecipientType type, Address[ ] addresses) throws MessagingException;
// Protected Instance Methods
1.2 protected InternetHeaders createInternetHeaders(java.io.InputStream is) throws MessagingException;
   protected java.io.InputStream getContentStream() throws MessagingException;
1.2 protected void parse(java.io.InputStream is) throws MessagingException;
   protected void updateHeaders() throws MessagingException;
// Protected Instance Fields
   protected byte[ ] content;
1.2 protected java.io.InputStream contentStream;
   protected javax.activation.DataHandler dh;
   protected Flags flags;
   protected InternetHeaders headers;
1.2 protected boolean modified;
1.2 protected boolean saved;
}
```

Passed To: MimeMessage.MimeMessage()

MimeMessage.RecipientType

JavaMail 1.1

javax.mail.internet   *serializable*

This class extends Message.RecipientType to include a NEWSGROUPS recipient, allowing messages to be directed to Usenet newsgroups when an appropriate JavaMail service is installed.

```
public static class MimeMessage.RecipientType extends Message.RecipientType {
// Protected Constructors
   protected RecipientType(String type);
// Public Constants
   public static final MimeMessage.RecipientType NEWSGROUPS;
// Protected Methods Overriding Message.RecipientType
1.2 protected Object readResolve() throws ObjectStreamException;
}
```

Type Of: MimeMessage.RecipientType.NEWSGROUPS

MimeMultipart

JavaMail 1.1

javax.mail.internet

This is an implementation of the Multipart class used for multipart MIME messages. A MimeMultipart object can be filled with multiple MimePart objects and attached to a MimeMessage. All Multipart objects have a primary content type of "multipart."

Object — Multipart — MimeMultipart

```
public class MimeMultipart extends Multipart {
// Public Constructors
   public MimeMultipart();
   public MimeMultipart(javax.activation.DataSource ds) throws MessagingException;
   public MimeMultipart(String subtype);
```

```
// Public Instance Methods
    public BodyPart getBodyPart(String CID) throws MessagingException;                    synchronized
    public void setSubType(String subtype) throws MessagingException;                     synchronized
// Public Methods Overriding Multipart
    public BodyPart getBodyPart(int index) throws MessagingException;                     synchronized
    public int getCount() throws MessagingException;                            synchronized default:0
    public void writeTo(java.io.OutputStream os) throws IOException, MessagingException;
// Protected Instance Methods
1.2 protected InternetHeaders createInternetHeaders(java.io.InputStream is) throws MessagingException;
1.2 protected MimeBodyPart createMimeBodyPart(java.io.InputStream is) throws MessagingException;
1.2 protected MimeBodyPart createMimeBodyPart(InternetHeaders headers, byte[ ] content)
        throws MessagingException;
1.2 protected void parse() throws MessagingException;                                     synchronized
    protected void updateHeaders() throws MessagingException;
// Protected Instance Fields
    protected javax.activation.DataSource ds;
    protected boolean parsed;
}
```

MimePart
JavaMail 1.1

javax.mail.internet

This interface is a subinterface of Part, modeling a MIME entity. It adds support for MIME and RFC-822 (Internet email) headers.

```
Part ┈ MimePart
```

```
public interface MimePart extends Part {
// Property Accessor Methods (by property name)
    public abstract java.util.Enumeration getAllHeaderLines() throws MessagingException;
    public abstract String getContentID() throws MessagingException;
    public abstract String[ ] getContentLanguage() throws MessagingException;
    public abstract void setContentLanguage(String[ ] languages) throws MessagingException;
    public abstract String getContentMD5() throws MessagingException;
    public abstract void setContentMD5(String md5) throws MessagingException;
    public abstract String getEncoding() throws MessagingException;
    public abstract void setText(String text) throws MessagingException;
    public abstract void setText(String text, String charset) throws MessagingException;
// Public Instance Methods
    public abstract void addHeaderLine(String line) throws MessagingException;
    public abstract String getHeader(String header_name, String delimiter) throws MessagingException;
    public abstract java.util.Enumeration getMatchingHeaderLines(String[ ] names) throws MessagingException;
    public abstract java.util.Enumeration getNonMatchingHeaderLines(String[ ] names)
        throws MessagingException;
}
```

Implementations: MimeBodyPart, MimeMessage

Passed To: MimePartDataSource.MimePartDataSource()

MimePartDataSource
JavaMail 1.1

javax.mail.internet

A utility class that implements the javax.activation.DataSource using the contents of a MimePart object.

```
┌────────┬───────────────────────┐
│ Object │─│ MimePartDataSource  │
├────────┤ ┌───────────────────┐ │
│DataSource│ │  MessageAware    │ │
└────────┘ └───────────────────┘
```

public class **MimePartDataSource** implements javax.activation.DataSource, MessageAware {
// Public Constructors
    public **MimePartDataSource**(MimePart *part*);
// Public Instance Methods
    public String **getContentType**( );
    public java.io.InputStream **getInputStream**( ) throws IOException;
    public String **getName**( );
    public java.io.OutputStream **getOutputStream**( ) throws IOException;
// Methods Implementing MessageAware
    public MessageContext **getMessageContext**( );   *synchronized*
}

MimeUtility   JavaMail 1.1

javax.mail.internet

A utility class for various MIME-related activities, including encoding text into mail-safe forms and converting between Java character set (charset) names and MIME charsets. Most programmers use this class to meet the RFC-822 requirement that mail headers be pure ASCII.

public class **MimeUtility** {
// No Constructor
// Public Constants
    public static final int **ALL**;   *=-1*
// Public Class Methods
    public static java.io.InputStream **decode**(java.io.InputStream *is*, String *encoding*) throws MessagingException;
    public static String **decodeText**(String *etext*) throws UnsupportedEncodingException;
    public static String **decodeWord**(String *eword*) throws javax.mail.internet.ParseException,
        UnsupportedEncodingException;
    public static java.io.OutputStream **encode**(java.io.OutputStream *os*, String *encoding*) throws MessagingException;
1.2 public static java.io.OutputStream **encode**(java.io.OutputStream *os*, String *encoding*, String *filename*)
        throws MessagingException;
    public static String **encodeText**(String *text*) throws UnsupportedEncodingException;
    public static String **encodeText**(String *text*, String *charset*, String *encoding*) throws UnsupportedEncodingException;
    public static String **encodeWord**(String *word*) throws UnsupportedEncodingException;
    public static String **encodeWord**(String *word*, String *charset*, String *encoding*)
        throws UnsupportedEncodingException;
    public static String **getDefaultJavaCharset**( );
1.2 public static String **getEncoding**(javax.activation.DataHandler *dh*);
    public static String **getEncoding**(javax.activation.DataSource *ds*);
    public static String **javaCharset**(String *charset*);
    public static String **mimeCharset**(String *charset*);
    public static String **quote**(String *word*, String *specials*);
}

NewsAddress

javax.mail.internet

serializable

This class models an NNTP URL, such as *news://newserver/news.group.name.*

```
Object ─┤ Address ├─ NewsAddress
        Serializable
```

```
public class NewsAddress extends Address {
// Public Constructors
   public NewsAddress();
   public NewsAddress(String newsgroup);
   public NewsAddress(String newsgroup, String host);
// Public Class Methods
   public static NewsAddress[ ] parse(String newsgroups) throws AddressException;
   public static String toString(Address[ ] addresses);
// Public Instance Methods
   public String getHost();                                              default:null
   public String getNewsgroup();                                         default:null
   public void setHost(String host);
   public void setNewsgroup(String newsgroup);
// Public Methods Overriding Address
   public boolean equals(Object a);
   public String getType();                                             default:"news"
   public String toString();
// Public Methods Overriding Object
   public int hashCode();
// Protected Instance Fields
   protected String host;
   protected String newsgroup;
}
```

Returned By: NewsAddress.parse()

ParameterList

javax.mail.internet

This is a holder class for MIME parameters, which are simply name/value pairs.

```
public class ParameterList {
// Public Constructors
   public ParameterList();
   public ParameterList(String s) throws javax.mail.internet.ParseException;
// Public Instance Methods
   public String get(String name);
   public java.util.Enumeration getNames();
   public void remove(String name);
   public void set(String name, String value);
   public int size();
1.2 public String toString(int used);
// Public Methods Overriding Object
   public String toString();
}
```

Passed To: ContentDisposition.{ContentDisposition(), setParameterList()}, ContentType.{ContentType(), setParameterList()}

Returned By: ContentDisposition.getParameterList(), ContentType.getParameterList()

ParseException   JavaMail 1.1

javax.mail.internet   *serializable checked*

This exception is thrown when an error occurs while parsing message headers.

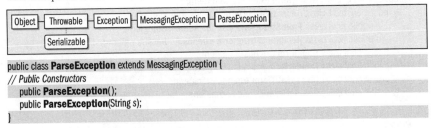

```
public class ParseException extends MessagingException {
// Public Constructors
    public ParseException();
    public ParseException(String s);
}
```

Subclasses: AddressException

Thrown By: ContentDisposition.ContentDisposition(), ContentType.ContentType(), HeaderTokenizer.{next(), peek()}, MimeUtility.decodeWord(), ParameterList.ParameterList()

SharedInputStream   JavaMail 1.2

javax.mail.internet

This interface represents an input stream that backs up to data that can be shared by multiple users. Streams created via the newStream() method access the same data as the main stream, rather than a copy.

```
public interface SharedInputStream {
// Public Instance Methods
    public abstract long getPosition();
    public abstract java.io.InputStream newStream(long start, long end);
}
```

Package javax.mail.search   JavaMail 1.1

The JavaMail Folder class includes a search() method that can return an array of messages matching a specified set of search criteria. The search criteria are defined by a SearchTerm object, which implements a method named match() that returns true or false, depending on whether the message matches the search criteria. There are a number of SearchTerm objects as well, including terms that aggregate other terms, all of which are defined in the javax.mail.search package.

Classes:

```
public abstract class SearchTerm implements Serializable;
    └ public abstract class AddressTerm extends SearchTerm;
        └ public final class FromTerm extends AddressTerm;
        └ public final class RecipientTerm extends AddressTerm;
    └ public final class AndTerm extends SearchTerm;
    └ public abstract class ComparisonTerm extends SearchTerm;
        └ public abstract class DateTerm extends ComparisonTerm;
```

      L public final class **ReceivedDateTerm** extends DateTerm;
      L public final class **SentDateTerm** extends DateTerm;
    L public abstract class **IntegerComparisonTerm** extends ComparisonTerm;
      L public final class **MessageNumberTerm** extends IntegerComparisonTerm;
      L public final class **SizeTerm** extends IntegerComparisonTerm;
  L public final class **FlagTerm** extends SearchTerm;
  L public final class **NotTerm** extends SearchTerm;
  L public final class **OrTerm** extends SearchTerm;
  L public abstract class **StringTerm** extends SearchTerm;
    L public abstract class **AddressStringTerm** extends StringTerm;
      L public final class **FromStringTerm** extends AddressStringTerm;
      L public final class **RecipientStringTerm** extends AddressStringTerm;
  L public final class **BodyTerm** extends StringTerm;
  L public final class **HeaderTerm** extends StringTerm;
  L public final class **MessageIDTerm** extends StringTerm;
  L public final class **SubjectTerm** extends StringTerm;

Exceptions:

public class **SearchException** extends javax.mail.MessagingException;

AddressStringTerm

JavaMail 1.1

javax.mail.search

serializable

An abstract class implementing comparisons against addresses based on string comparisons. The pattern specified in the constructor is used by the match() method, which returns true if the pattern is a substring of the string representation of the Address object passed to the match() method. Character set encoding differences should be accounted for.

```
Object — SearchTerm — StringTerm — AddressStringTerm
        Serializable
```

```
public abstract class AddressStringTerm extends StringTerm {
// Protected Constructors
    protected AddressStringTerm(String pattern);
// Public Methods Overriding StringTerm
1.2 public boolean equals(Object obj);
// Protected Instance Methods
    protected boolean match(Address a);
}
```

Subclasses: FromStringTerm, RecipientStringTerm

AddressTerm

JavaMail 1.1

javax.mail.search

serializable

An abstract class implementing Message Address comparisons based on Address objects.

```
Object — SearchTerm — AddressTerm
        Serializable
```

```
public abstract class AddressTerm extends SearchTerm {
// Protected Constructors
```

```
    protected AddressTerm(Address address);
// Public Instance Methods
    public Address getAddress();
// Public Methods Overriding Object
1.2 public boolean equals(Object obj);
1.2 public int hashCode();
// Protected Instance Methods
    protected boolean match(Address a);
// Protected Instance Fields
    protected Address address;
}
```

Subclasses: FromTerm, RecipientTerm

AndTerm

javax.mail.search

serializable

The AndTerm class provides a match() method that returns true only if the two SearchTerms also evaluate to true.

```
public final class AndTerm extends SearchTerm {
// Public Constructors
    public AndTerm(SearchTerm[ ] t);
    public AndTerm(SearchTerm t1, SearchTerm t2);
// Public Instance Methods
    public SearchTerm[ ] getTerms();
// Public Methods Overriding SearchTerm
    public boolean match(javax.mail.Message msg);
// Public Methods Overriding Object
1.2 public boolean equals(Object obj);
1.2 public int hashCode();
// Protected Instance Fields
    protected SearchTerm[ ] terms;
}
```

BodyTerm

javax.mail.search

serializable

This class implements substring searches on message bodies. The search occurs only if the message is a single-part text message or a multipart message whose first part is text.

```
public final class BodyTerm extends StringTerm {
// Public Constructors
    public BodyTerm(String pattern);
// Public Methods Overriding StringTerm
1.2 public boolean equals(Object obj);
```

```
// Public Methods Overriding SearchTerm
    public boolean match(javax.mail.Message msg);
}
```

ComparisonTerm

javax.mail.search

serializable

This is an abstract class that defines a set of comparison operators. Terms that extend ComparisonTerm support the equals, greater-than-or-equals, less-than-or-equals, greater-than, less-than, and not-equals operators.

```
Object ├ SearchTerm ├ ComparisonTerm
              ┊
          Serializable
```

```
public abstract class ComparisonTerm extends SearchTerm {
// Public Constructors
    public ComparisonTerm();
// Public Constants
    public static final int EQ;                                        =3
    public static final int GE;                                        =6
    public static final int GT;                                        =5
    public static final int LE;                                        =1
    public static final int LT;                                        =2
    public static final int NE;                                        =4
// Public Methods Overriding Object
1.2 public boolean equals(Object obj);
1.2 public int hashCode();
// Protected Instance Fields
    protected int comparison;
}
```

Subclasses: DateTerm, IntegerComparisonTerm

DateTerm

javax.mail.search

serializable

This is the base class for a date comparison.

```
Object ├ SearchTerm ├ ComparisonTerm ├ DateTerm
              ┊
          Serializable
```

```
public abstract class DateTerm extends ComparisonTerm {
// Protected Constructors
    protected DateTerm(int comparison, java.util.Date date);
// Public Instance Methods
    public int getComparison();
    public java.util.Date getDate();
// Public Methods Overriding ComparisonTerm
1.2 public boolean equals(Object obj);
1.2 public int hashCode();
// Protected Instance Methods
    protected boolean match(java.util.Date d);
```

```
// Protected Instance Fields
    protected java.util.Date date;
}
```

Subclasses: ReceivedDateTerm, SentDateTerm

FlagTerm
JavaMail 1.1

javax.mail.search   *serializable*

The FlagTerm class tests for the presence or absence of particular message flags.

```
public final class FlagTerm extends SearchTerm {
// Public Constructors
    public FlagTerm(Flags flags, boolean set);
// Public Instance Methods
    public Flags getFlags();
    public boolean getTestSet();
// Public Methods Overriding SearchTerm
    public boolean match(javax.mail.Message msg);
// Public Methods Overriding Object
1.2 public boolean equals(Object obj);
1.2 public int hashCode();
// Protected Instance Fields
    protected Flags flags;
    protected boolean set;
}
```

FromStringTerm
JavaMail 1.1

javax.mail.search   *serializable*

A subclass of AddressStringTerm that implements a string comparison on the FROM message field.

```
public final class FromStringTerm extends AddressStringTerm {
// Public Constructors
    public FromStringTerm(String pattern);
// Public Methods Overriding AddressStringTerm
1.2 public boolean equals(Object obj);
// Public Methods Overriding SearchTerm
    public boolean match(javax.mail.Message msg);
}
```

FromTerm
JavaMail 1.1

javax.mail.search   *serializable*

This is a subclass of AddressTerm that matches sender addresses based on an Address object.

```
Object — SearchTerm — AddressTerm — FromTerm
         Serializable
```

```
public final class FromTerm extends AddressTerm {
// Public Constructors
   public FromTerm(Address address);
// Public Methods Overriding AddressTerm
1.2 public boolean equals(Object obj);
// Public Methods Overriding SearchTerm
   public boolean match(javax.mail.Message msg);
}
```

HeaderTerm   JavaMail 1.1

javax.mail.search   *serializable*

This class is a term that allows case-insensitive comparisons on message headers.

```
Object — SearchTerm — StringTerm — HeaderTerm
         Serializable
```

```
public final class HeaderTerm extends StringTerm {
// Public Constructors
   public HeaderTerm(String headerName, String pattern);
// Public Instance Methods
   public String getHeaderName();
// Public Methods Overriding StringTerm
1.2 public boolean equals(Object obj);
1.2 public int hashCode();
// Public Methods Overriding SearchTerm
   public boolean match(javax.mail.Message msg);
// Protected Instance Fields
   protected String headerName;
}
```

IntegerComparisonTerm   JavaMail 1.1

javax.mail.search   *serializable*

This is the base class for integer comparisons.

```
Object — SearchTerm — ComparisonTerm — IntegerComparisonTerm
         Serializable
```

```
public abstract class IntegerComparisonTerm extends ComparisonTerm {
// Protected Constructors
   protected IntegerComparisonTerm(int comparison, int number);
// Public Instance Methods
   public int getComparison();
   public int getNumber();
// Public Methods Overriding ComparisonTerm
1.2 public boolean equals(Object obj);
1.2 public int hashCode();
// Protected Instance Methods
   protected boolean match(int i);
```

```
// Protected Instance Fields
   protected int number;
}
```

Subclasses: MessageNumberTerm, SizeTerm

MessageIDTerm

javax.mail.search

This class performs string searches based on the RFC-822 MessageId field.

```
Object ─ SearchTerm ─ StringTerm ─ MessageIDTerm
         : Serializable
```

```
public final class MessageIDTerm extends StringTerm {
// Public Constructors
   public MessageIDTerm(String msgid);
// Public Methods Overriding StringTerm
1.2 public boolean equals(Object obj);
// Public Methods Overriding SearchTerm
   public boolean match(javax.mail.Message msg);
}
```

MessageNumberTerm

javax.mail.search

This class performs comparisons based on message numbers. This term can be used retrieve an individual message, or an arbitary number of first or last messages.

```
Object ─ SearchTerm ─ ComparisonTerm ─ IntegerComparisonTerm ─ MessageNumberTerm
         : Serializable
```

```
public final class MessageNumberTerm extends IntegerComparisonTerm {
// Public Constructors
   public MessageNumberTerm(int number);
// Public Methods Overriding IntegerComparisonTerm
1.2 public boolean equals(Object obj);
// Public Methods Overriding SearchTerm
   public boolean match(javax.mail.Message msg);
}
```

NotTerm

javax.mail.search

This class is a term that can be used to negate another term. Wrapping a Term in a NotTerm will reverse its result.

```
Object ─ SearchTerm ─ NotTerm
         : Serializable
```

```
public final class NotTerm extends SearchTerm {
// Public Constructors
   public NotTerm(SearchTerm t);
```

```
// Public Instance Methods
    public SearchTerm getTerm();
// Public Methods Overriding SearchTerm
    public boolean match(javax.mail.Message msg);
// Public Methods Overriding Object
1.2 public boolean equals(Object obj);
1.2 public int hashCode();
// Protected Instance Fields
    protected SearchTerm term;
}
```

OrTerm
javax.mail.search

JavaMail 1.1
serializable

This class combines two terms, returning true if one of the constituent terms returns true.

```
Object ─┤SearchTerm ├─ OrTerm
          Serializable
```

```
public final class OrTerm extends SearchTerm {
// Public Constructors
    public OrTerm(SearchTerm[ ] t);
    public OrTerm(SearchTerm t1, SearchTerm t2);
// Public Instance Methods
    public SearchTerm[ ] getTerms();
// Public Methods Overriding SearchTerm
    public boolean match(javax.mail.Message msg);
// Public Methods Overriding Object
1.2 public boolean equals(Object obj);
1.2 public int hashCode();
// Protected Instance Fields
    protected SearchTerm[ ] terms;
}
```

ReceivedDateTerm
javax.mail.search

JavaMail 1.1
serializable

Implements a date comparison based on the message receipt date.

```
Object ─┤SearchTerm ├─ ComparisonTerm ├─ DateTerm ├─ ReceivedDateTerm
          Serializable
```

```
public final class ReceivedDateTerm extends DateTerm {
// Public Constructors
    public ReceivedDateTerm(int comparison, java.util.Date date);
// Public Methods Overriding DateTerm
1.2 public boolean equals(Object obj);
// Public Methods Overriding SearchTerm
    public boolean match(javax.mail.Message msg);
}
```

RecipientStringTerm

javax.mail.search   *serializable*

This is a subclass of AddressStringTerm that implements a string comparison on the recipient headers (i.e., TO, CC and BCC, where available).

```
Object ─ SearchTerm ─ StringTerm ─ AddressStringTerm ─ RecipientStringTerm
       Serializable
```

```
public final class RecipientStringTerm extends AddressStringTerm {
// Public Constructors
    public RecipientStringTerm(Message.RecipientType type, String pattern);
// Public Instance Methods
    public Message.RecipientType getRecipientType();
// Public Methods Overriding AddressStringTerm
1.2 public boolean equals(Object obj);
// Public Methods Overriding StringTerm
1.2 public int hashCode();
// Public Methods Overriding SearchTerm
    public boolean match(javax.mail.Message msg);
}
```

RecipientTerm

javax.mail.search   *serializable*

This is a subclass of AddressTerm that matches recipient addresses based on an Address object.

```
Object ─ SearchTerm ─ AddressTerm ─ RecipientTerm
       Serializable
```

```
public final class RecipientTerm extends AddressTerm {
// Public Constructors
    public RecipientTerm(Message.RecipientType type, Address address);
// Public Instance Methods
    public Message.RecipientType getRecipientType();
// Public Methods Overriding AddressTerm
1.2 public boolean equals(Object obj);
1.2 public int hashCode();
// Public Methods Overriding SearchTerm
    public boolean match(javax.mail.Message msg);
// Protected Instance Fields
    protected Message.RecipientType type;
}
```

SearchException

javax.mail.search   *serializable checked*

A SearchException is thrown when a search expression is invalid or can't be processed.

```
Object ─ Throwable ─ Exception ─ MessagingException ─ SearchException
       Serializable
```

```
public class SearchException extends MessagingException {
// Public Constructors
    public SearchException();
    public SearchException(String s);
}
```

SearchTerm

JavaMail 1.1

javax.mail.search   *serializable*

This is the base SearchTerm object. SearchTerm defines the match() method, which will be called once for each candidate message in the search.

```
Object ─ SearchTerm ┈ Serializable
```

```
public abstract class SearchTerm implements Serializable {
// Public Constructors
    public SearchTerm();
// Public Instance Methods
    public abstract boolean match(javax.mail.Message msg);
}
```

Subclasses: AddressTerm, AndTerm, ComparisonTerm, FlagTerm, NotTerm, OrTerm, StringTerm

Passed To: Folder.search(), javax.mail.Message.match(), AndTerm.AndTerm(), NotTerm.NotTerm(), OrTerm.OrTerm()

Returned By: AndTerm.getTerms(), NotTerm.getTerm(), OrTerm.getTerms()

Type Of: AndTerm.terms, NotTerm.term, OrTerm.terms

SentDateTerm

JavaMail 1.1

javax.mail.search   *serializable*

This class implements a date comparison based on the message sent date.

```
Object ─ SearchTerm ─ ComparisonTerm ─ DateTerm ─ SentDateTerm
              Serializable
```

```
public final class SentDateTerm extends DateTerm {
// Public Constructors
    public SentDateTerm(int comparison, java.util.Date date);
// Public Methods Overriding DateTerm
1.2 public boolean equals(Object obj);
// Public Methods Overriding SearchTerm
    public boolean match(javax.mail.Message msg);
}
```

SizeTerm

JavaMail 1.1

javax.mail.search   *serializable*

This class implements an integer comparison on message size.

```
Object ─ SearchTerm ─ ComparisonTerm ─ IntegerComparisonTerm ─ SizeTerm
              Serializable
```

```
public final class SizeTerm extends IntegerComparisonTerm {
// Public Constructors
    public SizeTerm(int comparison, int size);
// Public Methods Overriding IntegerComparisonTerm
1.2 public boolean equals(Object obj);
// Public Methods Overriding SearchTerm
    public boolean match(javax.mail.Message msg);
}
```

StringTerm

javax.mail.search

serializable

This is the base class for a string comparison. Classes that descend from StringTerm will return true if the search pattern specified in the constructor is a substring of the data that the term is comparing against.

```
Object — SearchTerm — StringTerm
        Serializable
```

```
public abstract class StringTerm extends SearchTerm {
// Protected Constructors
    protected StringTerm(String pattern);
    protected StringTerm(String pattern, boolean ignoreCase);
// Public Instance Methods
    public boolean getIgnoreCase();
    public String getPattern();
// Public Methods Overriding Object
1.2 public boolean equals(Object obj);
1.2 public int hashCode();
// Protected Instance Methods
    protected boolean match(String s);
// Protected Instance Fields
    protected boolean ignoreCase;
    protected String pattern;
}
```

Subclasses: AddressStringTerm, BodyTerm, HeaderTerm, MessageIDTerm, SubjectTerm

SubjectTerm

javax.mail.search

serializable

This clss implements a substring comparison on the Subject header of one or more messages.

```
Object — SearchTerm — StringTerm — SubjectTerm
        Serializable
```

```
public final class SubjectTerm extends StringTerm {
// Public Constructors
    public SubjectTerm(String pattern);
// Public Methods Overriding StringTerm
1.2 public boolean equals(Object obj);
// Public Methods Overriding SearchTerm
    public boolean match(javax.mail.Message msg);
}
```

CHAPTER 27

javax.naming

The javax.naming package contains the core interfaces, classes, and exceptions for performing naming operations with JNDI. Context represents named objects in a naming system, while InitialContext provides an entry point into a naming system. Binding is the association between a name and an object in a naming system. NamingException is the root of a large collection of naming exceptions defined by JNDI.

Interfaces:

public interface **Context**;
public interface **Name** extends Cloneable, Serializable;
public interface **NameParser**;
public interface **NamingEnumeration** extends java.util.Enumeration;
public interface **Referenceable**;

Classes:

public class **CompositeName** implements Name;
public class **CompoundName** implements Name;
public class **InitialContext** implements Context;
public class **NameClassPair** implements Serializable;
   └ public class **Binding** extends NameClassPair;
public abstract class **RefAddr** implements Serializable;
   └ public class **BinaryRefAddr** extends RefAddr;
   └ public class **StringRefAddr** extends RefAddr;
public class **Reference** implements Cloneable, Serializable;
   └ public class **LinkRef** extends Reference;

Exceptions:

public class **NamingException** extends Exception;
   └ public class **CannotProceedException** extends NamingException;

└ public class **CommunicationException** extends NamingException;
└ public class **ConfigurationException** extends NamingException;
└ public class **ContextNotEmptyException** extends NamingException;
└ public class **InsufficientResourcesException** extends NamingException;
└ public class **InterruptedNamingException** extends NamingException;
└ public class **InvalidNameException** extends NamingException;
└ public class **LimitExceededException** extends NamingException;
    └ public class **SizeLimitExceededException** extends LimitExceededException;
    └ public class **TimeLimitExceededException** extends LimitExceededException;
└ public class **LinkException** extends NamingException;
    └ public class **LinkLoopException** extends LinkException;
    └ public class **MalformedLinkException** extends LinkException;
└ public class **NameAlreadyBoundException** extends NamingException;
└ public class **NameNotFoundException** extends NamingException;
└ public abstract class **NamingSecurityException** extends NamingException;
    └ public class **AuthenticationException** extends NamingSecurityException;
    └ public class **AuthenticationNotSupportedException** extends NamingSecurityException;
    └ public class **NoPermissionException** extends NamingSecurityException;
└ public class **NoInitialContextException** extends NamingException;
└ public class **NotContextException** extends NamingException;
└ public class **OperationNotSupportedException** extends NamingException;
└ public class **PartialResultException** extends NamingException;
└ public abstract class **ReferralException** extends NamingException;
└ public class **ServiceUnavailableException** extends NamingException;

AuthenticationException

Java 1.3

javax.naming
serializable checked

Thrown when JNDI encounters an error authenticating to the naming system, such as when a bad username or password is used.

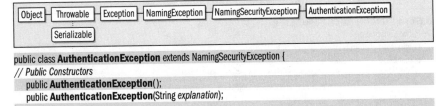

```
public class AuthenticationException extends NamingSecurityException {
// Public Constructors
    public AuthenticationException();
    public AuthenticationException(String explanation);
}
```

AuthenticationNotSupportedException

Java 1.3

javax.naming
serializable checked

Thrown when the requested type of authentication is not supported.

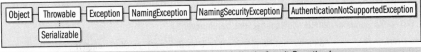

```
public class AuthenticationNotSupportedException extends NamingSecurityException {
// Public Constructors
    public AuthenticationNotSupportedException();
```

```
    public AuthenticationNotSupportedException(String explanation);
}
```

BinaryRefAddr   Java 1.3

javax.naming   *serializable*

A concrete subclass of RefAddr that provides a binary representation of a communications endpoint, such as an IP address.

```
public class BinaryRefAddr extends RefAddr {
// Public Constructors
    public BinaryRefAddr(String addrType, byte[ ] src);
    public BinaryRefAddr(String addrType, byte[ ] src, int offset, int count);
// Public Methods Overriding RefAddr
    public boolean equals(Object obj);
    public Object getContent();
    public int hashCode();
    public String toString();
}
```

Binding   Java 1.3

javax.naming   *serializable*

This class represents the association between a name and an object. The listBindings() method of Context returns a NamingEnumeration of Binding objects.

```
public class Binding extends NameClassPair {
// Public Constructors
    public Binding(String name, Object obj);
    public Binding(String name, String className, Object obj);
    public Binding(String name, Object obj, boolean isRelative);
    public Binding(String name, String className, Object obj, boolean isRelative);
// Public Instance Methods
    public Object getObject();
    public void setObject(Object obj);
// Public Methods Overriding NameClassPair
    public String getClassName();
    public String toString();
}
```

Subclasses: javax.naming.directory.SearchResult

Passed To: javax.naming.event.NamingEvent.NamingEvent()

Returned By: javax.naming.event.NamingEvent.{getNewBinding(), getOldBinding()}

Type Of: javax.naming.event.NamingEvent.{newBinding, oldBinding}

CannotProceedException

Java 1.3

javax.naming   *serializable checked*

Thrown when a service provider cannot further resolve a name, such as when a component of a name resides in another service provider.

```
Object — Throwable — Exception — NamingException — CannotProceedException
         Serializable
```

```
public class CannotProceedException extends NamingException {
// Public Constructors
    public CannotProceedException();
    public CannotProceedException(String explanation);
// Property Accessor Methods (by property name)
    public javax.naming.Name getAltName();                              default:null
    public void setAltName(javax.naming.Name altName);
    public javax.naming.Context getAltNameCtx();                        default:null
    public void setAltNameCtx(javax.naming.Context altNameCtx);
    public java.util.Hashtable getEnvironment();                        default:null
    public void setEnvironment(java.util.Hashtable environment);
    public javax.naming.Name getRemainingNewName();                     default:null
    public void setRemainingNewName(javax.naming.Name newName);
// Protected Instance Fields
    protected javax.naming.Name altName;
    protected javax.naming.Context altNameCtx;
    protected java.util.Hashtable environment;
    protected javax.naming.Name remainingNewName;
}
```

Passed To: javax.naming.spi.DirectoryManager.getContinuationDirContext(),
javax.naming.spi.NamingManager.getContinuationContext()

CommunicationException

Java 1.3

javax.naming   *serializable checked*

Thrown when a JNDI method is unable to communicate with the naming service for some reason.

```
Object — Throwable — Exception — NamingException — CommunicationException
         Serializable
```

```
public class CommunicationException extends NamingException {
// Public Constructors
    public CommunicationException();
    public CommunicationException(String explanation);
}
```

CompositeName

Java 1.3

javax.naming   *cloneable serializable*

This class represents a sequence of names that span multiple namespaces. Each component of a CompositeName is a String name. The CompositeName does not know to which naming system each name component belongs. JNDI uses the forward slash character ("/") to separate constituent name components.

```
public class CompositeName implements javax.naming.Name {
// Public Constructors
    public CompositeName();
    public CompositeName(String n) throws InvalidNameException;
// Protected Constructors
    protected CompositeName(java.util.Enumeration comps);
// Methods Implementing Name
    public javax.naming.Name add(String comp) throws InvalidNameException;
    public javax.naming.Name add(int posn, String comp) throws InvalidNameException;
    public javax.naming.Name addAll(javax.naming.Name suffix) throws InvalidNameException;
    public javax.naming.Name addAll(int posn, javax.naming.Name n) throws InvalidNameException;
    public Object clone();
    public int compareTo(Object obj);
    public boolean endsWith(javax.naming.Name n);
    public String get(int posn);
    public java.util.Enumeration getAll();
    public javax.naming.Name getPrefix(int posn);
    public javax.naming.Name getSuffix(int posn);
    public boolean isEmpty();                                          default:true
    public Object remove(int posn) throws InvalidNameException;
    public int size();
    public boolean startsWith(javax.naming.Name n);
// Public Methods Overriding Object
    public boolean equals(Object obj);
    public int hashCode();
    public String toString();
}
```

CompoundName

Java 1.3

javax.naming
cloneable serializable

This class represents a name that is made up of atomic names from a single name space.

```
public class CompoundName implements javax.naming.Name {
// Public Constructors
    public CompoundName(String n, java.util.Properties syntax) throws InvalidNameException;
// Protected Constructors
    protected CompoundName(java.util.Enumeration comps, java.util.Properties syntax);
// Methods Implementing Name
    public javax.naming.Name add(String comp) throws InvalidNameException;
    public javax.naming.Name add(int posn, String comp) throws InvalidNameException;
    public javax.naming.Name addAll(javax.naming.Name suffix) throws InvalidNameException;
    public javax.naming.Name addAll(int posn, javax.naming.Name n) throws InvalidNameException;
    public Object clone();
    public int compareTo(Object obj);
```

```
    public boolean endsWith(javax.naming.Name n);
    public String get(int posn);
    public java.util.Enumeration getAll();
    public javax.naming.Name getPrefix(int posn);
    public javax.naming.Name getSuffix(int posn);
    public boolean isEmpty();
    public Object remove(int posn) throws InvalidNameException;
    public int size();
    public boolean startsWith(javax.naming.Name n);
// Public Methods Overriding Object
    public boolean equals(Object obj);
    public int hashCode();
    public String toString();
// Protected Instance Fields
    protected transient NameImpl impl;
    protected transient java.util.Properties mySyntax;
}
```

ConfigurationException   Java 1.3

javax.naming   *serializable checked*

Thrown when JNDI has experienced a configuration problem, such as a missing environment property or a misconfigured security protocol.

```
Object ─┤ Throwable ├─ Exception ├─ NamingException ├─ ConfigurationException
         │ Serializable │
```

```
public class ConfigurationException extends NamingException {
// Public Constructors
    public ConfigurationException();
    public ConfigurationException(String explanation);
}
```

Context   Java 1.3

javax.naming

This interface represents an object in a naming system. A Context keeps track of a set of name-to-object bindings for its subordinates in the naming system, so it defines methods to examine and update these bindings. The lookup() method looks up a subordinate object, while list() and listBindings() provide access to all of the subordinates.

A Context only knows about its subordinates, not about itself or what is above it in the naming system. Thus, there are no methods to get the name of a Context or move up in the naming hierarchy.

```
public interface Context {
// Public Constants
    public static final String APPLET;                    ="java.naming.applet"
    public static final String AUTHORITATIVE;             ="java.naming.authoritative"
    public static final String BATCHSIZE;                 ="java.naming.batchsize"
    public static final String DNS_URL;                   ="java.naming.dns.url"
    public static final String INITIAL_CONTEXT_FACTORY;   ="java.naming.factory.initial"
    public static final String LANGUAGE;                  ="java.naming.language"
    public static final String OBJECT_FACTORIES;          ="java.naming.factory.object"
    public static final String PROVIDER_URL;              ="java.naming.provider.url"
```

```
    public static final String REFERRAL;                                        ="java.naming.referral"
    public static final String SECURITY_AUTHENTICATION;              ="java.naming.security.authentication"
    public static final String SECURITY_CREDENTIALS;                    ="java.naming.security.credentials"
    public static final String SECURITY_PRINCIPAL;                          ="java.naming.security.principal"
    public static final String SECURITY_PROTOCOL;                          ="java.naming.security.protocol"
    public static final String STATE_FACTORIES;                              ="java.naming.factory.state"
    public static final String URL_PKG_PREFIXES;                          ="java.naming.factory.url.pkgs"
// Public Instance Methods
    public abstract Object addToEnvironment(String propName, Object propVal) throws NamingException;
    public abstract void bind(String name, Object obj) throws NamingException;
    public abstract void bind(javax.naming.Name name, Object obj) throws NamingException;
    public abstract void close() throws NamingException;
    public abstract javax.naming.Name composeName(javax.naming.Name name, javax.naming.Name prefix)
          throws NamingException;
    public abstract String composeName(String name, String prefix) throws NamingException;
    public abstract javax.naming.Context createSubcontext(javax.naming.Name name) throws NamingException;
    public abstract javax.naming.Context createSubcontext(String name) throws NamingException;
    public abstract void destroySubcontext(javax.naming.Name name) throws NamingException;
    public abstract void destroySubcontext(String name) throws NamingException;
    public abstract java.util.Hashtable getEnvironment() throws NamingException;
    public abstract String getNameInNamespace() throws NamingException;
    public abstract NameParser getNameParser(javax.naming.Name name) throws NamingException;
    public abstract NameParser getNameParser(String name) throws NamingException;
    public abstract NamingEnumeration list(javax.naming.Name name) throws NamingException;
    public abstract NamingEnumeration list(String name) throws NamingException;
    public abstract NamingEnumeration listBindings(javax.naming.Name name) throws NamingException;
    public abstract NamingEnumeration listBindings(String name) throws NamingException;
    public abstract Object lookup(javax.naming.Name name) throws NamingException;
    public abstract Object lookup(String name) throws NamingException;
    public abstract Object lookupLink(javax.naming.Name name) throws NamingException;
    public abstract Object lookupLink(String name) throws NamingException;
    public abstract void rebind(javax.naming.Name name, Object obj) throws NamingException;
    public abstract void rebind(String name, Object obj) throws NamingException;
    public abstract Object removeFromEnvironment(String propName) throws NamingException;
    public abstract void rename(javax.naming.Name oldName, javax.naming.Name newName)
          throws NamingException;
    public abstract void rename(String oldName, String newName) throws NamingException;
    public abstract void unbind(javax.naming.Name name) throws NamingException;
    public abstract void unbind(String name) throws NamingException;
}
```

Implementations: InitialContext, javax.naming.directory.DirContext, javax.naming.event.EventContext

Passed To: CannotProceedException.setAltNameCtx(),
javax.naming.ldap.ControlFactory.getControlInstance(),
javax.naming.spi.DirectoryManager.{getObjectInstance(), getStateToBind()},
javax.naming.spi.DirObjectFactory.getObjectInstance(),
javax.naming.spi.DirStateFactory.getStateToBind(),
javax.naming.spi.NamingManager.{getObjectInstance(), getStateToBind()},
javax.naming.spi.ObjectFactory.getObjectInstance(), javax.naming.spi.StateFactory.getStateToBind()

Returned By: CannotProceedException.getAltNameCtx(), javax.naming.Context.createSubcontext(),
InitialContext.{createSubcontext(), getDefaultInitCtx(), getURLOrDefaultInitCtx()},

ReferralException.getReferralContext(), javax.naming.ldap.LdapReferralException.getReferralContext(),
javax.naming.spi.InitialContextFactory.getInitialContext(),
javax.naming.spi.NamingManager.{getContinuationContext(), getInitialContext(), getURLContext()}

Type Of: CannotProceedException.altNameCtx, InitialContext.defaultInitCtx

ContextNotEmptyException
Java 1.3

javax.naming
serializable checked

Thrown when the destroySubcontext() method is called to destroy a Context that is not empty.

```
Object ├ Throwable ├ Exception ├ NamingException ├ ContextNotEmptyException
       └ Serializable
```

```
public class ContextNotEmptyException extends NamingException {
// Public Constructors
    public ContextNotEmptyException();
    public ContextNotEmptyException(String explanation);
}
```

InitialContext
Java 1.3

javax.naming

This class represents the starting point for accessing a naming system. Typically, you set the value of the java.naming.factory.initial property (represented by the constant Context.INITIAL_CONTEXT_FACTORY) to the fully qualified package name of a factory class in a JNDI service provider. This factory class creates an InitialContext that is appropriate for the naming system you are using.

```
Object ├ InitialContext ┈ Context
```

```
public class InitialContext implements javax.naming.Context {
// Public Constructors
    public InitialContext() throws NamingException;
    public InitialContext(java.util.Hashtable environment) throws NamingException;
// Protected Constructors
    protected InitialContext(boolean lazy) throws NamingException;
// Methods Implementing Context
    public Object addToEnvironment(String propName, Object propVal) throws NamingException;
    public void bind(String name, Object obj) throws NamingException;
    public void bind(javax.naming.Name name, Object obj) throws NamingException;
    public void close() throws NamingException;
    public String composeName(String name, String prefix) throws NamingException;
    public javax.naming.Name composeName(javax.naming.Name name, javax.naming.Name prefix)
        throws NamingException;
    public javax.naming.Context createSubcontext(javax.naming.Name name) throws NamingException;
    public javax.naming.Context createSubcontext(String name) throws NamingException;
    public void destroySubcontext(String name) throws NamingException;
    public void destroySubcontext(javax.naming.Name name) throws NamingException;
    public java.util.Hashtable getEnvironment() throws NamingException;
    public String getNameInNamespace() throws NamingException;
    public NameParser getNameParser(javax.naming.Name name) throws NamingException;
    public NameParser getNameParser(String name) throws NamingException;
    public NamingEnumeration list(javax.naming.Name name) throws NamingException;
```

```
      public NamingEnumeration list(String name) throws NamingException;
      public NamingEnumeration listBindings(javax.naming.Name name) throws NamingException;
      public NamingEnumeration listBindings(String name) throws NamingException;
      public Object lookup(String name) throws NamingException;
      public Object lookup(javax.naming.Name name) throws NamingException;
      public Object lookupLink(String name) throws NamingException;
      public Object lookupLink(javax.naming.Name name) throws NamingException;
      public void rebind(javax.naming.Name name, Object obj) throws NamingException;
      public void rebind(String name, Object obj) throws NamingException;
      public Object removeFromEnvironment(String propName) throws NamingException;
      public void rename(String oldName, String newName) throws NamingException;
      public void rename(javax.naming.Name oldName, javax.naming.Name newName) throws NamingException;
      public void unbind(String name) throws NamingException;
      public void unbind(javax.naming.Name name) throws NamingException;
// Protected Instance Methods
      protected javax.naming.Context getDefaultInitCtx() throws NamingException;
      protected javax.naming.Context getURLOrDefaultInitCtx(String name) throws NamingException;
      protected javax.naming.Context getURLOrDefaultInitCtx(javax.naming.Name name) throws NamingException;
      protected void init(java.util.Hashtable environment) throws NamingException;
// Protected Instance Fields
      protected javax.naming.Context defaultInitCtx;
      protected boolean gotDefault;
      protected java.util.Hashtable myProps;
}
```

Subclasses: javax.naming.directory.InitialDirContext

InsufficientResourcesException   Java 1.3
javax.naming   *serializable checked*

Thrown when there are insufficient system resources, such as memory or disk space, to perform an operation. The resource issue can occur on the client or on the server.

```
Object ─ Throwable ─ Exception ─ NamingException ─ InsufficientResourcesException
         Serializable
```

```
public class InsufficientResourcesException extends NamingException {
// Public Constructors
    public InsufficientResourcesException();
    public InsufficientResourcesException(String explanation);
}
```

InterruptedNamingException   Java 1.3
javax.naming   *serializable checked*

Thrown when a naming operation has been interrupted.

```
Object ─ Throwable ─ Exception ─ NamingException ─ InterruptedNamingException
         Serializable
```

```
public class InterruptedNamingException extends NamingException {
// Public Constructors
    public InterruptedNamingException();
```

```
    public InterruptedNamingException(String explanation);
}
```

InvalidNameException

javax.naming   *serializable checked*

Thrown when a specified name violates the syntax of a particular naming system.

```
Object ├─ Throwable ├─ Exception ├─ NamingException ├─ InvalidNameException
        └ Serializable
```

```
public class InvalidNameException extends NamingException {
// Public Constructors
    public InvalidNameException();
    public InvalidNameException(String explanation);
}
```

Thrown By: CompositeName.{add(), addAll(), CompositeName(), remove()},
CompoundName.{add(), addAll(), CompoundName(), remove()}, javax.naming.Name.{add(), addAll(),
remove()}

LimitExceededException

javax.naming   *serializable checked*

Thrown when a method fails because it has exceeded a user- or system-specified limit.

```
Object ├─ Throwable ├─ Exception ├─ NamingException ├─ LimitExceededException
        └ Serializable
```

```
public class LimitExceededException extends NamingException {
// Public Constructors
    public LimitExceededException();
    public LimitExceededException(String explanation);
}
```

Subclasses: SizeLimitExceededException, TimeLimitExceededException

LinkException

javax.naming   *serializable checked*

Thrown when a method cannot resolve a link.

```
Object ├─ Throwable ├─ Exception ├─ NamingException ├─ LinkException
        └ Serializable
```

```
public class LinkException extends NamingException {
// Public Constructors
    public LinkException();
    public LinkException(String explanation);
// Property Accessor Methods (by property name)
    public String getLinkExplanation();                                default:null
    public void setLinkExplanation(String msg);
    public javax.naming.Name getLinkRemainingName();                   default:null
    public void setLinkRemainingName(javax.naming.Name name);
```

```
      public javax.naming.Name getLinkResolvedName();                          default:null
      public void setLinkResolvedName(javax.naming.Name name);
      public Object getLinkResolvedObj();                                        default:null
      public void setLinkResolvedObj(Object obj);
// Public Methods Overriding NamingException
      public String toString();
      public String toString(boolean detail);
// Protected Instance Fields
      protected String linkExplanation;
      protected javax.naming.Name linkRemainingName;
      protected javax.naming.Name linkResolvedName;
      protected Object linkResolvedObj;
}
```

Subclasses: LinkLoopException, MalformedLinkException

LinkLoopException   Java 1.3

javax.naming   *serializable checked*

Thrown when a loop is detected when resolving a link or when JNDI has reached a
limit on link counts.

```
Object ─ Throwable ─ Exception ─ NamingException ─ LinkException ─ LinkLoopException
         Serializable
```

```
public class LinkLoopException extends LinkException {
// Public Constructors
      public LinkLoopException();
      public LinkLoopException(String explanation);
}
```

LinkRef   Java 1.3

javax.naming   *cloneable serializable*

LinkRef is a subclass of Reference that contains a name, called the link name, that is
bound to an atomic name in a context.

```
Object ─ Reference ─ LinkRef
Cloneable  Serializable
```

```
public class LinkRef extends javax.naming.Reference {
// Public Constructors
      public LinkRef(String linkName);
      public LinkRef(javax.naming.Name linkName);
// Public Instance Methods
      public String getLinkName() throws NamingException;
}
```

MalformedLinkException   Java 1.3

javax.naming   *serializable checked*

Thrown when a link name is improperly constructed.

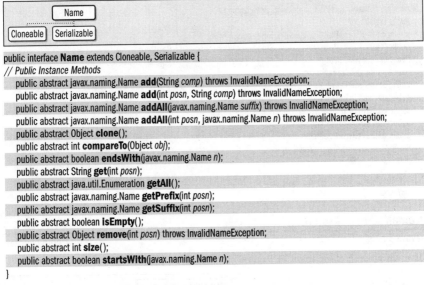

```
Object ─ Throwable ─ Exception ─ NamingException ─ LinkException ─ MalformedLinkException
         └ Serializable
```

```
public class MalformedLinkException extends LinkException {
// Public Constructors
    public MalformedLinkException();
    public MalformedLinkException(String explanation);
}
```

Name   Java 1.3

javax.naming   *cloneable serializable*

This interface represents the name of an object in a naming system. A Name can be either a compound name or a composite name. This interface is used primarily by developers who are writing JNDI service providers, not by JNDI application developers. As an application developer, you can use String objects instead of Name objects to specify names in Context and javax.naming.directory.DirContext method calls.

```
                    Name
    ┌──────────┐  ┌──────────┐
    │Cloneable │  │Serializable│
    └──────────┘  └──────────┘
```

```
public interface Name extends Cloneable, Serializable {
// Public Instance Methods
    public abstract javax.naming.Name add(String comp) throws InvalidNameException;
    public abstract javax.naming.Name add(int posn, String comp) throws InvalidNameException;
    public abstract javax.naming.Name addAll(javax.naming.Name suffix) throws InvalidNameException;
    public abstract javax.naming.Name addAll(int posn, javax.naming.Name n) throws InvalidNameException;
    public abstract Object clone();
    public abstract int compareTo(Object obj);
    public abstract boolean endsWith(javax.naming.Name n);
    public abstract String get(int posn);
    public abstract java.util.Enumeration getAll();
    public abstract javax.naming.Name getPrefix(int posn);
    public abstract javax.naming.Name getSuffix(int posn);
    public abstract boolean isEmpty();
    public abstract Object remove(int posn) throws InvalidNameException;
    public abstract int size();
    public abstract boolean startsWith(javax.naming.Name n);
}
```

Implementations: CompositeName, CompoundName

Passed To: Too many methods to list.

Returned By: Too many methods to list.

Type Of: CannotProceedException.{altName, remainingNewName},
LinkException.{linkRemainingName, linkResolvedName}, NamingException.{remainingName,
resolvedName}, javax.naming.spi.ResolveResult.remainingName

NameAlreadyBoundException   Java 1.3

javax.naming   *serializable checked*

Thrown when a binding operation fails because the name is already bound.

```
Object ─ Throwable ─ Exception ─ NamingException ─ NameAlreadyBoundException
         Serializable
```

```
public class NameAlreadyBoundException extends NamingException {
// Public Constructors
    public NameAlreadyBoundException();
    public NameAlreadyBoundException(String explanation);
}
```

NameClassPair

javax.naming

serializable

This class represents the name and class of an object bound to a Context. The list() method of Context returns an NamingEnumeration of NameClassPair objects. Note that Name-ClassPair does not represent the object itself; that is the job of its subclass Binding.

```
Object ─ NameClassPair ┈ Serializable
```

```
public class NameClassPair implements Serializable {
// Public Constructors
    public NameClassPair(String name, String className);
    public NameClassPair(String name, String className, boolean isRelative);
// Public Instance Methods
    public String getClassName();
    public String getName();
    public boolean isRelative();
    public void setClassName(String name);
    public void setName(String name);
    public void setRelative(boolean r);
// Public Methods Overriding Object
    public String toString();
}
```

Subclasses: javax.naming.Binding

NameNotFoundException

javax.naming

serializable checked

Thrown when a component of a name cannot be resolved because it is not bound.

```
Object ─ Throwable ─ Exception ─ NamingException ─ NameNotFoundException
         Serializable
```

```
public class NameNotFoundException extends NamingException {
// Public Constructors
    public NameNotFoundException();
    public NameNotFoundException(String explanation);
}
```

NameParser

javax.naming

This interface is for parsing names from a hierarchical namespace. A NameParser knows the syntactic information, such as left-to-right orientation and the name separator, needed to parse names.

```
public interface NameParser {
// Public Instance Methods
    public abstract javax.naming.Name parse(String name) throws NamingException;
}
```

Returned By: javax.naming.Context.getNameParser(), InitialContext.getNameParser()

NamingEnumeration

javax.naming

This interface represents a list of items returned from a JNDI operation. It extends java.util.Enumeration, so a NamingEnumeration can be treated as a normal enumeration.

Enumeration — NamingEnumeration

```
public interface NamingEnumeration extends java.util.Enumeration {
// Public Instance Methods
    public abstract void close() throws NamingException;
    public abstract boolean hasMore() throws NamingException;
    public abstract Object next() throws NamingException;
}
```

Returned By: Too many methods to list.

NamingException

javax.naming

The base class of all exceptions thrown by Context and javax.naming.directory.DirContext methods. NamingException can include information about where the operation failed, such as the portion of a name that has been resolved and the portion that remains to be resolved. A NamingException can also include a root cause exception, which is the exception object that caused the naming exception to be thrown.

Object — Throwable — Exception — NamingException
Serializable

```
public class NamingException extends Exception {
// Public Constructors
    public NamingException();
    public NamingException(String explanation);
// Property Accessor Methods (by property name)
    public String getExplanation();                                 default:null
    public javax.naming.Name getRemainingName();                    default:null
    public void setRemainingName(javax.naming.Name name);
    public javax.naming.Name getResolvedName();
    public void setResolvedName(javax.naming.Name name);
    public Object getResolvedObj();                                 default:null
    public void setResolvedObj(Object obj);
    public Throwable getRootCause();                                default:null
    public void setRootCause(Throwable e);
// Public Instance Methods
    public void appendRemainingComponent(String name);
    public void appendRemainingName(javax.naming.Name name);
    public String toString(boolean detail);
// Public Methods Overriding Throwable
```

```
    public void printStackTrace();
    public void printStackTrace(PrintStream ps);
    public void printStackTrace(PrintWriter pw);
    public String toString();
// Protected Instance Fields
    protected javax.naming.Name remainingName;
    protected javax.naming.Name resolvedName;
    protected Object resolvedObj;
    protected Throwable rootException;
}
```

Subclasses: Too many classes to list.

Passed To: javax.naming.event.NamingExceptionEvent.NamingExceptionEvent()

Returned By: javax.naming.event.NamingExceptionEvent.getException(),
javax.naming.ldap.UnsolicitedNotification.getException()

Thrown By: Too many methods to list.

NamingSecurityException   Java 1.3

javax.naming   *serializable checked*

The abstract superclass of all security-related naming exceptions.

```
Object ├─ Throwable ├─ Exception ├─ NamingException ├─ NamingSecurityException
       │
       └ Serializable
```

```
public abstract class NamingSecurityException extends NamingException {
// Public Constructors
    public NamingSecurityException();
    public NamingSecurityException(String explanation);
}
```

Subclasses: AuthenticationException, AuthenticationNotSupportedException, NoPermissionException

NoInitialContextException   Java 1.3

javax.naming   *serializable checked*

Thrown when JNDI cannot create an initial context.

```
Object ├─ Throwable ├─ Exception ├─ NamingException ├─ NoInitialContextException
       │
       └ Serializable
```

```
public class NoInitialContextException extends NamingException {
// Public Constructors
    public NoInitialContextException();
    public NoInitialContextException(String explanation);
}
```

NoPermissionException   Java 1.3

javax.naming   *serializable checked*

Thrown when there is an attempt to perform an operation that is forbidden by the
underlying naming system due to insufficient privileges.

```
Object ─ Throwable ─ Exception ─ NamingException ─ NamingSecurityException ─ NoPermissionException
          Serializable
```

public class **NoPermissionException** extends NamingSecurityException {
// *Public Constructors*
    public **NoPermissionException**();
    public **NoPermissionException**(String *explanation*);
}

NotContextException   Java 1.3

javax.naming   *serializable checked*

Thrown when there is an attempt to perform a Context-related operation on an object that is not a Context.

```
Object ─ Throwable ─ Exception ─ NamingException ─ NotContextException
          Serializable
```

public class **NotContextException** extends NamingException {
// *Public Constructors*
    public **NotContextException**();
    public **NotContextException**(String *explanation*);
}

OperationNotSupportedException   Java 1.3

javax.naming   *serializable checked*

Thrown when the provider's implementation of Context does not support a method that has been invoked (e.g., trying to list the subordinates of a leaf object like a print job that by definition cannot have any children).

```
Object ─ Throwable ─ Exception ─ NamingException ─ OperationNotSupportedException
          Serializable
```

public class **OperationNotSupportedException** extends NamingException {
// *Public Constructors*
    public **OperationNotSupportedException**();
    public **OperationNotSupportedException**(String *explanation*);
}

PartialResultException   Java 1.3

javax.naming   *serializable checked*

Thrown when an operation cannot be completed and has returned only a partial result (e.g., returning only a partial list of subordinates).

```
Object ─ Throwable ─ Exception ─ NamingException ─ PartialResultException
          Serializable
```

public class **PartialResultException** extends NamingException {
// *Public Constructors*
    public **PartialResultException**();
    public **PartialResultException**(String *explanation*);
}

RefAddr

javax.naming

This abstract class represents the address of a communications end point. It is used by Reference to represent the communication mechanism and address of a reference. Concrete implementations support addresses such as URLs, DNS names, and IP addresses.

Object — RefAddr — Serializable

```
public abstract class RefAddr implements Serializable {
// Protected Constructors
    protected RefAddr(String addrType);
// Public Instance Methods
    public abstract Object getContent();
    public String getType();
// Public Methods Overriding Object
    public boolean equals(Object obj);
    public int hashCode();
    public String toString();
// Protected Instance Fields
    protected String addrType;
}
```

Subclasses: BinaryRefAddr, StringRefAddr

Passed To: javax.naming.Reference.{add(), Reference()}

Returned By: javax.naming.Reference.get()

Reference

javax.naming

This class represents an object external to a naming system that is referred to by an object in the naming system. A Reference contains an address for retrieving the object from its naming system. The address is a communications end point that enables JNDI to contact the object. The address can be any concrete subclass of RefAddr, such as a StringRefAddr for representing a URL or DNS name. A Reference also contains the class name of the referenced object.

Object — Reference
Cloneable   Serializable

```
public class Reference implements Cloneable, Serializable {
// Public Constructors
    public Reference(String className);
    public Reference(String className, RefAddr addr);
    public Reference(String className, String factory, String factoryLocation);
    public Reference(String className, RefAddr addr, String factory, String factoryLocation);
// Public Instance Methods
    public void add(RefAddr addr);
    public void add(int posn, RefAddr addr);
    public void clear();
    public RefAddr get(int posn);
    public RefAddr get(String addrType);
    public java.util.Enumeration getAll();
    public String getClassName();
    public String getFactoryClassLocation();
```

```
     public String getFactoryClassName();
     public Object remove(int posn);
     public int size();
// Public Methods Overriding Object
     public Object clone();
     public boolean equals(Object obj);
     public int hashCode();
     public String toString();
// Protected Instance Fields
     protected java.util.Vector addrs;
     protected String classFactory;
     protected String classFactoryLocation;
     protected String className;
}
```

Subclasses: LinkRef

Passed To: javax.resource.Referenceable.setReference()

Returned By: javax.naming.Referenceable.getReference()

Referenceable   Java 1.3

javax.naming

This interface is implemented by an object that can provide a reference to itself in the form of a Reference object.

```
public interface Referenceable {
// Public Instance Methods
     public abstract javax.naming.Reference getReference() throws NamingException;
}
```

Implementations: javax.resource.Referenceable

ReferralException   Java 1.3

javax.naming   *serializable checked*

Thrown when a referral cannot be continued, such as when more information is required. Note that this is an abstract class.

```
Object ├ Throwable ├ Exception ├ NamingException ├ ReferralException
         Serializable
```

```
public abstract class ReferralException extends NamingException {
// Protected Constructors
     protected ReferralException();
     protected ReferralException(String explanation);
// Public Instance Methods
     public abstract javax.naming.Context getReferralContext() throws NamingException;
     public abstract javax.naming.Context getReferralContext(java.util.Hashtable env) throws NamingException;
     public abstract Object getReferralInfo();
     public abstract void retryReferral();
     public abstract boolean skipReferral();
}
```

Subclasses: javax.naming.ldap.LdapReferralException

ServiceUnavailableException   Java 1.3

javax.naming   *serializable checked*

Thrown when the name service is not available for some reason.

```
Object ⊢ Throwable ⊢ Exception ⊢ NamingException ⊢ ServiceUnavailableException
         Serializable
```

```
public class ServiceUnavailableException extends NamingException {
// Public Constructors
    public ServiceUnavailableException();
    public ServiceUnavailableException(String explanation);
}
```

SizeLimitExceededException   Java 1.3

javax.naming   *serializable checked*

Thrown when a method produces a result that exceeds a size limit.

```
Object ⊢ Throwable ⊢ Exception ⊢ NamingException ⊢ LimitExceededException ⊢ SizeLimitExceededException
         Serializable
```

```
public class SizeLimitExceededException extends LimitExceededException {
// Public Constructors
    public SizeLimitExceededException();
    public SizeLimitExceededException(String explanation);
}
```

StringRefAddr   Java 1.3

javax.naming   *serializable*

A concrete subclass of RefAddr that provides a string form of the address of a communications end point.

```
Object ⊢ RefAddr ⊢ StringRefAddr
         Serializable
```

```
public class StringRefAddr extends RefAddr {
// Public Constructors
    public StringRefAddr(String addrType, String addr);
// Public Methods Overriding RefAddr
    public Object getContent();
}
```

TimeLimitExceededException   Java 1.3

javax.naming   *serializable checked*

Thrown when a method does not finish within a certain time limit.

```
Object ⊢ Throwable ⊢ Exception ⊢ NamingException ⊢ LimitExceededException ⊢ TimeLimitExceededException
         Serializable
```

```
public class TimeLimitExceededException extends LimitExceededException {
// Public Constructors
```

```
public TimeLimitExceededException();
public TimeLimitExceededException(String explanation);
}
```

CHAPTER 28

javax.naming.directory

Package javax.naming.directory

Java 1.3

The javax.naming.directory package contains the core interfaces, classes, and exceptions for performing directory operations with JNDI. DirContext defines the interface to directory services, while Attribute represents an attribute that is associated with a directory entry.

Interfaces:

public interface **Attribute** extends Cloneable, Serializable;
public interface **Attributes** extends Cloneable, Serializable;
public interface **DirContext** extends javax.naming.Context;

Classes:

public class **BasicAttribute** implements Attribute;
public class **BasicAttributes** implements Attributes;
public class **InitialDirContext** extends javax.naming.InitialContext implements DirContext;
public class **ModificationItem** implements Serializable;
public class **SearchControls** implements Serializable;
public class **SearchResult** extends javax.naming.Binding;

Exceptions:

public class **AttributeInUseException** extends javax.naming.NamingException;
public class **AttributeModificationException** extends javax.naming.NamingException;
public class **InvalidAttributeIdentifierException** extends javax.naming.NamingException;
public class **InvalidAttributesException** extends javax.naming.NamingException;
public class **InvalidAttributeValueException** extends javax.naming.NamingException;
public class **InvalidSearchControlsException** extends javax.naming.NamingException;
public class **InvalidSearchFilterException** extends javax.naming.NamingException;
public class **NoSuchAttributeException** extends javax.naming.NamingException;
public class **SchemaViolationException** extends javax.naming.NamingException;

Attribute

javax.naming.directory

This interface represents an attribute associated with a directory entry. The directory schema determines the classes of attributes that a directory entry with a certain object class definition is permitted to have. The class of a particular attribute is called the attribute type definition. The name of an attribute, called the *attribute ID*, is determined by the attribute type definition and has a String representation that refers to that particular attribute. Each attribute can have zero or more values of a particular class. The class of values an attribute is permitted to have is called the *attribute syntax definition*.

The directory schema, and therefore the attribute type and syntax definitions, depend on the underlying directory your JNDI application is using. You can use getAttributeDefinition() to determine the type definition for a particular attribute and getAttributeSyntaxDefinition() to determine the attribute syntax definition.

The get() method returns a single attribute value as a java.lang.Object, while getAll() returns multiple attribute values as a javax.naming.NamingEnumeration of objects. If the attribute has only a single value, get() returns that value. If the attribute has multiple values, the service provider determines the value that is returned.

Updates performed on Attribute do not affect the directory entry. To modify the directory entry, you must call the modifyAttributes() method of DirContext with an Attributes object that contains a modified Attribute.

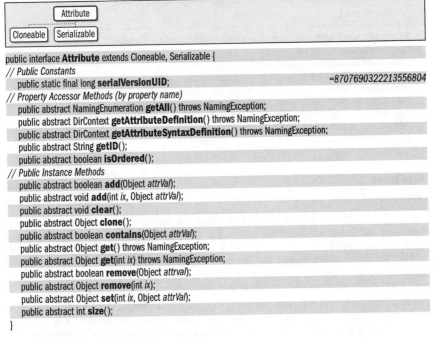

```
public interface Attribute extends Cloneable, Serializable {
// Public Constants
    public static final long serialVersionUID;                              =8707690322213556804
// Property Accessor Methods (by property name)
    public abstract NamingEnumeration getAll() throws NamingException;
    public abstract DirContext getAttributeDefinition() throws NamingException;
    public abstract DirContext getAttributeSyntaxDefinition() throws NamingException;
    public abstract String getID();
    public abstract boolean isOrdered();
// Public Instance Methods
    public abstract boolean add(Object attrVal);
    public abstract void add(int ix, Object attrVal);
    public abstract void clear();
    public abstract Object clone();
    public abstract boolean contains(Object attrVal);
    public abstract Object get() throws NamingException;
    public abstract Object get(int ix) throws NamingException;
    public abstract boolean remove(Object attrval);
    public abstract Object remove(int ix);
    public abstract Object set(int ix, Object attrVal);
    public abstract int size();
}
```

Implementations: BasicAttribute

Passed To: Attributes.put(), BasicAttributes.put(), ModificationItem.ModificationItem()

Returned By: Attributes.{get(), put(), remove()}, BasicAttributes.{get(), put(), remove()}, ModificationItem.getAttribute()

AttributeInUseException

Java 1.3

javax.naming.directory

serializable checked

Thrown when there is an attempt to add an attribute already present in the directory entry.

```
Object ── Throwable ── Exception ── NamingException ── AttributeInUseException
              Serializable
```

```
public class AttributeInUseException extends NamingException {
// Public Constructors
    public AttributeInUseException();
    public AttributeInUseException(String explanation);
}
```

AttributeModificationException

Java 1.3

javax.naming.directory

serializable checked

Thrown when modifyAttributes() method of DirContext cannot be executed because the operation contradicts the directory schema. You can retrieve an array of modification items JNDI could not perform using getUnexecutedModifications().

```
Object ── Throwable ── Exception ── NamingException ── AttributeModificationException
              Serializable
```

```
public class AttributeModificationException extends NamingException {
// Public Constructors
    public AttributeModificationException();
    public AttributeModificationException(String explanation);
// Public Instance Methods
    public ModificationItem[ ] getUnexecutedModifications();                    default:null
    public void setUnexecutedModifications(ModificationItem[ ] e);
// Public Methods Overriding NamingException
    public String toString();
}
```

Attributes

Java 1.3

javax.naming.directory

cloneable serializable

This interface represents a collection of attributes associated with a directory entry. Individual attributes are unordered, and the Attributes object can have zero or more attributes. The getAll() method returns an enumeration of Attribute objects, while getIDs() returns an enumeration of just the attribute names (or IDs) for the directory entry. If you know the attribute you want, you can specify the attribute name in a call to the get() method, which returns a single Attribute object.

An Attributes object can be case-sensitive or insensitive. In an LDAP or NDS directory, a case-insensitive attribute corresponds to "case ignore string." This means when searching for a particular attribute or comparing two attributes, case sensitivity can affect the results.

Updates performed on an Attributes object do not affect the directory entry. To modify the directory entry, you must call the modifyAttributes() method of DirContext using the updated Attributes object.

When creating a set of attributes for use in an application, you typically use a BasicAttributes object.

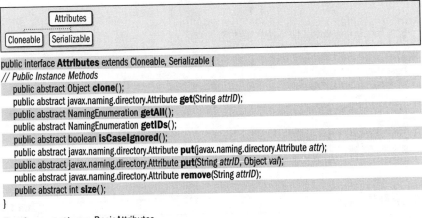

```
public interface Attributes extends Cloneable, Serializable {
// Public Instance Methods
    public abstract Object clone();
    public abstract javax.naming.directory.Attribute get(String attrID);
    public abstract NamingEnumeration getAll();
    public abstract NamingEnumeration getIDs();
    public abstract boolean isCaseIgnored();
    public abstract javax.naming.directory.Attribute put(javax.naming.directory.Attribute attr);
    public abstract javax.naming.directory.Attribute put(String attrID, Object val);
    public abstract javax.naming.directory.Attribute remove(String attrID);
    public abstract int size();
}
```

Implementations: BasicAttributes

Passed To: Too many methods to list.

Returned By: DirContext.getAttributes(), InitialDirContext.getAttributes(), SearchResult.getAttributes(), javax.naming.spi.DirStateFactory.Result.getAttributes()

BasicAttribute

Java 1.3

javax.naming.directory

cloneable serializable

This class is a basic implementation of the Attribute interface. BasicAttribute has a convenience constructor that enables you to create the object with attribute data by using a string that represents the attribute ID and a java.lang.Object that represents the attribute value. This constructor is equivalent to creating a BasicAttribute object with the attribute ID as a parameter and then calling the add() method.

```
public class BasicAttribute implements javax.naming.directory.Attribute {
// Public Constructors
    public BasicAttribute(String id);
    public BasicAttribute(String id, boolean ordered);
    public BasicAttribute(String id, Object value);
    public BasicAttribute(String id, Object value, boolean ordered);
// Methods Implementing Attribute
    public boolean add(Object attrVal);
    public void add(int ix, Object attrVal);
    public void clear();
    public Object clone();
    public boolean contains(Object attrVal);
    public Object get() throws NamingException;
    public Object get(int ix) throws NamingException;
    public NamingEnumeration getAll() throws NamingException;
    public DirContext getAttributeDefinition() throws NamingException;
    public DirContext getAttributeSyntaxDefinition() throws NamingException;
    public String getID();
    public boolean isOrdered();
    public Object remove(int ix);
```

```
    public boolean remove(Object attrval);
    public Object set(int ix, Object attrVal);
    public int size();
// Public Methods Overriding Object
    public boolean equals(Object obj);
    public int hashCode();
    public String toString();
// Protected Instance Fields
    protected String attrID;
    protected boolean ordered;
    protected transient java.util.Vector values;
}
```

BasicAttributes
Java 1.3

javax.naming.directory
cloneable serializable

This class is a basic implementation of the Attributes interface. BasicAttributes has a convenience constructor that enables you to create the set of attributes with attribute data by using a string that represents an attribute ID, and a java.lang.Object that represents an attribute value. This constructor is equivalent to creating a BasicAttributes object with an empty constructor and then calling the two-argument put() method.

You can construct a BasicAttributes object as case-sensitive or insensitive. In an LDAP or NDS directory, a case-insensitive attribute corresponds to "case ignore string."

```
Object ──┤ BasicAttributes │
             ┊
           │ Attributes │
   ┌────────────┊
│ Cloneable │─│ Serializable │
```

```
public class BasicAttributes implements Attributes {
// Public Constructors
    public BasicAttributes();
    public BasicAttributes(boolean ignoreCase);
    public BasicAttributes(String attrID, Object val);
    public BasicAttributes(String attrID, Object val, boolean ignoreCase);
// Methods Implementing Attributes
    public Object clone();
    public javax.naming.directory.Attribute get(String attrID);
    public NamingEnumeration getAll();
    public NamingEnumeration getIDs();
    public boolean isCaseIgnored();                                        default:false
    public javax.naming.directory.Attribute put(javax.naming.directory.Attribute attr);
    public javax.naming.directory.Attribute put(String attrID, Object val);
    public javax.naming.directory.Attribute remove(String attrID);
    public int size();
// Public Methods Overriding Object
    public boolean equals(Object obj);
    public int hashCode();
    public String toString();
}
```

DirContext

javax.naming.directory

This interface provides a Java representation of a directory entry and is a subclass of javax.naming.Context. The practical difference between a Context and a DirContext is the association of attributes with a DirContext and the consequent methods for retrieving and modifying attribute data.

The directory schema determines the classes of directory entries that can be present in a directory. You can access the directory schema using getSchema(). The class of a directory entry is its object class definition. You can access the object class definition using the getSchemaClassDefinition() method. Most directory providers distribute documents that describe their directory schemae. Consult your directory service provider for a schema definition.

The getAttributes() method returns an Attributes object that contains either all the attributes of an entry or just those attributes specified in a String array. createSubcontext() creates a new directory entry, while modifyAttributes() changes attributes values. The various search() methods allow you to search directory entries, using optional search filters and SearchControls objects.

```
Context ┈┤DirContext

public interface DirContext extends javax.naming.Context {
// Public Constants
    public static final int ADD_ATTRIBUTE;                                              =1
    public static final int REMOVE_ATTRIBUTE;                                           =3
    public static final int REPLACE_ATTRIBUTE;                                          =2
// Public Instance Methods
    public abstract void bind(String name, Object obj, Attributes attrs) throws NamingException;
    public abstract void bind(javax.naming.Name name, Object obj, Attributes attrs) throws NamingException;
    public abstract DirContext createSubcontext(String name, Attributes attrs) throws NamingException;
    public abstract DirContext createSubcontext(javax.naming.Name name, Attributes attrs)
        throws NamingException;
    public abstract Attributes getAttributes(javax.naming.Name name) throws NamingException;
    public abstract Attributes getAttributes(String name) throws NamingException;
    public abstract Attributes getAttributes(String name, String[ ] attrIds) throws NamingException;
    public abstract Attributes getAttributes(javax.naming.Name name, String[ ] attrIds) throws NamingException;
    public abstract DirContext getSchema(javax.naming.Name name) throws NamingException;
    public abstract DirContext getSchema(String name) throws NamingException;
    public abstract DirContext getSchemaClassDefinition(javax.naming.Name name) throws NamingException;
    public abstract DirContext getSchemaClassDefinition(String name) throws NamingException;
    public abstract void modifyAttributes(javax.naming.Name name, ModificationItem[ ] mods)
        throws NamingException;
    public abstract void modifyAttributes(String name, ModificationItem[ ] mods) throws NamingException;
    public abstract void modifyAttributes(javax.naming.Name name, int mod_op, Attributes attrs)
        throws NamingException;
    public abstract void modifyAttributes(String name, int mod_op, Attributes attrs) throws NamingException;
    public abstract void rebind(javax.naming.Name name, Object obj, Attributes attrs) throws NamingException;
    public abstract void rebind(String name, Object obj, Attributes attrs) throws NamingException;
    public abstract NamingEnumeration search(javax.naming.Name name, Attributes matchingAttributes)
        throws NamingException;
    public abstract NamingEnumeration search(String name, Attributes matchingAttributes) throws NamingException;
    public abstract NamingEnumeration search(String name, String filter, SearchControls cons)
        throws NamingException;
    public abstract NamingEnumeration search(javax.naming.Name name, String filter, SearchControls cons)
        throws NamingException;
```

```
    public abstract NamingEnumeration search(javax.naming.Name name, Attributes matchingAttributes,
                                    String[ ] attributesToReturn) throws NamingException;
    public abstract NamingEnumeration search(String name, Attributes matchingAttributes, String[ ] attributesToReturn)
       throws NamingException;
    public abstract NamingEnumeration search(String name, String filterExpr, Object[ ] filterArgs, SearchControls cons)
       throws NamingException;
    public abstract NamingEnumeration search(javax.naming.Name name, String filterExpr, Object[ ] filterArgs,
                                    SearchControls cons) throws NamingException;
}
```

Implementations: InitialDirContext, javax.naming.event.EventDirContext,
javax.naming.ldap.LdapContext

Returned By: javax.naming.directory.Attribute.{getAttributeDefinition(),
getAttributeSyntaxDefinition()}, BasicAttribute.{getAttributeDefinition(), getAttributeSyntaxDefinition()},
DirContext.{createSubcontext(), getSchema(), getSchemaClassDefinition()},
InitialDirContext.{createSubcontext(), getSchema(), getSchemaClassDefinition()},
javax.naming.spi.DirectoryManager.getContinuationDirContext()

InitialDirContext   Java 1.3

javax.naming.directory

This class represents the starting context for performing directory operations and is a
subclass of javax.naming.InitialContext. Use this class when your application must perform
directory operations on an initial context.

```
public class InitialDirContext extends InitialContext implements DirContext {
// Public Constructors
    public InitialDirContext() throws NamingException;
    public InitialDirContext(java.util.Hashtable environment) throws NamingException;
// Protected Constructors
    protected InitialDirContext(boolean lazy) throws NamingException;
// Methods Implementing DirContext
    public void bind(String name, Object obj, Attributes attrs) throws NamingException;
    public void bind(javax.naming.Name name, Object obj, Attributes attrs) throws NamingException;
    public DirContext createSubcontext(javax.naming.Name name, Attributes attrs) throws NamingException;
    public DirContext createSubcontext(String name, Attributes attrs) throws NamingException;
    public Attributes getAttributes(javax.naming.Name name) throws NamingException;
    public Attributes getAttributes(String name) throws NamingException;
    public Attributes getAttributes(javax.naming.Name name, String[ ] attrIds) throws NamingException;
    public Attributes getAttributes(String name, String[ ] attrIds) throws NamingException;
    public DirContext getSchema(String name) throws NamingException;
    public DirContext getSchema(javax.naming.Name name) throws NamingException;
    public DirContext getSchemaClassDefinition(javax.naming.Name name) throws NamingException;
    public DirContext getSchemaClassDefinition(String name) throws NamingException;
    public void modifyAttributes(String name, ModificationItem[ ] mods) throws NamingException;
    public void modifyAttributes(javax.naming.Name name, ModificationItem[ ] mods) throws NamingException;
    public void modifyAttributes(String name, int mod_op, Attributes attrs) throws NamingException;
    public void modifyAttributes(javax.naming.Name name, int mod_op, Attributes attrs) throws NamingException;
    public void rebind(String name, Object obj, Attributes attrs) throws NamingException;
    public void rebind(javax.naming.Name name, Object obj, Attributes attrs) throws NamingException;
    public NamingEnumeration search(javax.naming.Name name, Attributes matchingAttributes)
       throws NamingException;
```

```
   public NamingEnumeration search(String name, Attributes matchingAttributes) throws NamingException;
   public NamingEnumeration search(String name, String filter, SearchControls cons) throws NamingException;
   public NamingEnumeration search(javax.naming.Name name, String filter, SearchControls cons)
        throws NamingException;
   public NamingEnumeration search(String name, Attributes matchingAttributes, String[ ] attributesToReturn)
        throws NamingException;
   public NamingEnumeration search(javax.naming.Name name, Attributes matchingAttributes,
                          String[ ] attributesToReturn) throws NamingException;
   public NamingEnumeration search(javax.naming.Name name, String filterExpr, Object[ ] filterArgs,
                          SearchControls cons) throws NamingException;
   public NamingEnumeration search(String name, String filterExpr, Object[ ] filterArgs, SearchControls cons)
        throws NamingException;
}
```

Subclasses: javax.naming.ldap.InitialLdapContext

InvalidAttributeIdentifierException

javax.naming.directory

Java 1.3

serializable checked

Thrown when there is an attempt to create an attribute with an attribute ID that doesn't exist in the directory's schema.

```
public class InvalidAttributeIdentifierException extends NamingException {
// Public Constructors
   public InvalidAttributeIdentifierException();
   public InvalidAttributeIdentifierException(String explanation);
}
```

InvalidAttributesException

javax.naming.directory

Java 1.3

serializable checked

Thrown when an add or modification operation has specified an inappropriate attribute type for the object class specified by the directory's schema.

```
public class InvalidAttributesException extends NamingException {
// Public Constructors
   public InvalidAttributesException();
   public InvalidAttributesException(String explanation);
}
```

InvalidAttributeValueException

javax.naming.directory

Java 1.3

serializable checked

Thrown when an add or modification operation has specified an inappropriate value for the attribute type specified by the directory's schema.

```
Object ─ Throwable ─ Exception ─ NamingException ─ InvalidAttributeValueException
         Serializable
```

```
public class InvalidAttributeValueException extends NamingException {
// Public Constructors
    public InvalidAttributeValueException();
    public InvalidAttributeValueException(String explanation);
}
```

InvalidSearchControlsException

javax.naming.directory

Java 1.3

serializable checked

Thrown when a SearchControls object is invalid.

```
Object ─ Throwable ─ Exception ─ NamingException ─ InvalidSearchControlsException
         Serializable
```

```
public class InvalidSearchControlsException extends NamingException {
// Public Constructors
    public InvalidSearchControlsException();
    public InvalidSearchControlsException(String msg);
}
```

InvalidSearchFilterException

javax.naming.directory

Java 1.3

serializable checked

Thrown when a search filter is invalid.

```
Object ─ Throwable ─ Exception ─ NamingException ─ InvalidSearchFilterException
         Serializable
```

```
public class InvalidSearchFilterException extends NamingException {
// Public Constructors
    public InvalidSearchFilterException();
    public InvalidSearchFilterException(String msg);
}
```

ModificationItem

javax.naming.directory

Java 1.3

serializable

This class encapsulates an attribute that is to be modified and a code that determines the type of modification being performed.

```
Object ─ ModificationItem ┈ Serializable
```

```
public class ModificationItem implements Serializable {
// Public Constructors
    public ModificationItem(int mod_op, javax.naming.directory.Attribute attr);
// Public Instance Methods
    public javax.naming.directory.Attribute getAttribute();
    public int getModificationOp();
// Public Methods Overriding Object
    public String toString();
}
```

Passed To: AttributeModificationException.setUnexecutedModifications(),
DirContext.modifyAttributes(), InitialDirContext.modifyAttributes()

Returned By: AttributeModificationException.getUnexecutedModifications()

NoSuchAttributeException

Java 1.3

javax.naming.directory

serializable checked

Thrown when a method attempts to access a nonexistent attribute.

```
public class NoSuchAttributeException extends NamingException {
// Public Constructors
    public NoSuchAttributeException();
    public NoSuchAttributeException(String explanation);
}
```

SchemaViolationException

Java 1.3

javax.naming.directory

serializable checked

Thrown when a method violates schema rules.

```
public class SchemaViolationException extends NamingException {
// Public Constructors
    public SchemaViolationException();
    public SchemaViolationException(String explanation);
}
```

SearchControls

Java 1.3

javax.naming.directory

serializable

This class represents the information needed to control the behavior of the search() method of DirContext. Contains information that determines the scope of search, the maximum number of results returned by a search, the maximum amount of time permitted to return search results, and other data you can use to fine-tune the behavior of search operations.

```
public class SearchControls implements Serializable {
// Public Constructors
    public SearchControls();
    public SearchControls(int scope, long countlim, int timelim, String[ ] attrs, boolean retobj, boolean deref);
// Public Constants
    public static final int OBJECT_SCOPE;                                              =0
    public static final int ONELEVEL_SCOPE;                                            =1
    public static final int SUBTREE_SCOPE;                                             =2
// Property Accessor Methods (by property name)
    public long getCountLimit();                                                default:0
    public void setCountLimit(long limit);
```

```
    public boolean getDerefLinkFlag();                                    default:false
    public void setDerefLinkFlag(boolean on);
    public String[ ] getReturningAttributes();                            default:null
    public void setReturningAttributes(String[ ] attrs);
    public boolean getReturningObjFlag();                                 default:false
    public void setReturningObjFlag(boolean on);
    public int getSearchScope();                                          default:1
    public void setSearchScope(int scope);
    public int getTimeLimit();                                            default:0
    public void setTimeLimit(int ms);
}
```

Passed To: DirContext.search(), InitialDirContext.search(),
javax.naming.event.EventDirContext.addNamingListener()

SearchResult   Java 1.3

javax.naming.directory   *serializable*

This class represents a result of performing a search() method on a DirContext. It is a subclass of javax.naming.Binding. You can perform directory operations on a SearchResult without first having to look up the object in the directory. Each search() method actually returns an NamingEnumeration of SearchResults objects.

```
Object ─┤NameClassPair├─ Binding ─┤SearchResult│
        └ Serializable ┘
```

```
public class SearchResult extends javax.naming.Binding {
// Public Constructors
    public SearchResult(String name, Object obj, Attributes attrs);
    public SearchResult(String name, String className, Object obj, Attributes attrs);
    public SearchResult(String name, Object obj, Attributes attrs, boolean isRelative);
    public SearchResult(String name, String className, Object obj, Attributes attrs, boolean isRelative);
// Public Instance Methods
    public Attributes getAttributes();
    public void setAttributes(Attributes attrs);
// Public Methods Overriding Binding
    public String toString();
}
```

CHAPTER 29

javax.naming.event

Package javax.naming.event Java 1.3

This package contains classes and interfaces used for event notification with JNDI.

Interfaces:

public interface **EventContext** extends javax.naming.Context;
public interface **EventDirContext** extends EventContext, javax.naming.directory.DirContext;

Events:

public class **NamingEvent** extends java.util.EventObject;
public class **NamingExceptionEvent** extends java.util.EventObject;

Event Listeners:

public interface **NamespaceChangeListener** extends NamingListener;
public interface **NamingListener** extends java.util.EventListener;
public interface **ObjectChangeListener** extends NamingListener;

EventContext Java 1.3
javax.naming.event

The EventContext interface is implemented by NamingContexts that support event notification. It provides methods for adding and removing NamingListeners associated with specific named targets in the namespace.

Context ┈ EventContext

```
public interface EventContext extends javax.naming.Context {
// Public Constants
    public static final int OBJECT_SCOPE;                                              =0
    public static final int ONELEVEL_SCOPE;                                            =1
    public static final int SUBTREE_SCOPE;                                             =2
// Event Registration Methods (by event name)
    public abstract void removeNamingListener(NamingListener l) throws NamingException;
```

```
// Public Instance Methods
    public abstract void addNamingListener(String target, int scope, NamingListener l) throws NamingException;
    public abstract void addNamingListener(javax.naming.Name target, int scope, NamingListener l)
        throws NamingException;
    public abstract boolean targetMustExist() throws NamingException;
}
```

Implementations: EventDirContext

Passed To: NamingEvent.NamingEvent(), NamingExceptionEvent.NamingExceptionEvent()

Returned By: NamingEvent.getEventContext(), NamingExceptionEvent.getEventContext()

EventDirContext   Java 1.3

javax.naming.event

The EventDirContext interface is implemented by DirContexts that support event notification.
It contains methods for adding NamingListeners associated with named targets in the
directory.

```
                              ┌─────────────────┐
                              │ EventDirContext │
                              └─────────────────┘
┌─────────┐  ┌────────────┐  ┌─────────┐  ┌──────────────┐
│ Context │--│ DirContext │  │ Context │--│ EventContext │
└─────────┘  └────────────┘  └─────────┘  └──────────────┘
```

```
public interface EventDirContext extends EventContext, javax.naming.directory.DirContext {
// Public Instance Methods
    public abstract void addNamingListener(String target, String filter, javax.naming.directory.SearchControls ctls,
                            NamingListener l) throws NamingException;
    public abstract void addNamingListener(javax.naming.Name target, String filter,
                            javax.naming.directory.SearchControls ctls, NamingListener l)
        throws NamingException;
    public abstract void addNamingListener(String target, String filter, Object[ ] filterArgs,
                            javax.naming.directory.SearchControls ctls, NamingListener l)
        throws NamingException;
    public abstract void addNamingListener(javax.naming.Name target, String filter, Object[ ] filterArgs,
                            javax.naming.directory.SearchControls ctls, NamingListener l)
        throws NamingException;
}
```

NamespaceChangeListener   Java 1.3

javax.naming.event   *event listener*

A NamespaceChangeListener is used to listen for changes in the namespace (objects being
added, removed or renamed). To implement this listener, you must implement the
objectAdded(), objectRemove() and objectRenamed() callbacks, as well as the namingException-
Thrown() method inherited from NamingListener.

```
┌───────────────┐  ┌─────────────────┐  ┌─────────────────────────┐
│ EventListener │--│ NamingListener  │--│ NamespaceChangeListener │
└───────────────┘  └─────────────────┘  └─────────────────────────┘
```

```
public interface NamespaceChangeListener extends NamingListener {
// Public Instance Methods
    public abstract void objectAdded(NamingEvent evt);
    public abstract void objectRemoved(NamingEvent evt);
    public abstract void objectRenamed(NamingEvent evt);
}
```

NamingEvent

javax.naming.event

A NamingEvent represents any kind of event generated from a naming/directory service. It's state includes the EventContext that fired the event, the type of event, and the new and old binding information for its associated object (in case the event involves a change in this binding).

```
Object ─ EventObject ─ NamingEvent
          Serializable
```

```
public class NamingEvent extends java.util.EventObject {
// Public Constructors
    public NamingEvent(EventContext source, int type, javax.naming.Binding newBd, javax.naming.Binding oldBd,
                        Object changeInfo);
// Public Constants
    public static final int OBJECT_ADDED;                                                        =0
    public static final int OBJECT_CHANGED;                                                      =3
    public static final int OBJECT_REMOVED;                                                      =1
    public static final int OBJECT_RENAMED;                                                      =2
// Property Accessor Methods (by property name)
    public Object getChangeInfo();
    public EventContext getEventContext();
    public javax.naming.Binding getNewBinding();
    public javax.naming.Binding getOldBinding();
    public int getType();
// Public Instance Methods
    public void dispatch(NamingListener listener);
// Protected Instance Fields
    protected Object changeInfo;
    protected javax.naming.Binding newBinding;
    protected javax.naming.Binding oldBinding;
    protected int type;
}
```

Passed To: NamespaceChangeListener.{objectAdded(), objectRemoved(), objectRenamed()}, ObjectChangeListener.objectChanged()

NamingExceptionEvent

javax.naming.event

This event is fired when an exception is encountered while attempting to collect information for a listener. It will be passed to the listener through its namingExceptionThrown() callback.

```
Object ─ EventObject ─ NamingExceptionEvent
          Serializable
```

```
public class NamingExceptionEvent extends java.util.EventObject {
// Public Constructors
    public NamingExceptionEvent(EventContext source, NamingException exc);
// Public Instance Methods
    public void dispatch(NamingListener listener);
```

```
    public EventContext getEventContext();
    public NamingException getException();
}
```

Passed To: NamingListener.namingExceptionThrown()

NamingListener   Java 1.3

javax.naming.event   *event listener*

This is the base interface for all naming listeners. The namingExceptionThrown() callback is used to notify the listener that an exception was encountered while collecting information for the listener. If this callback is invoked, the listener has already been removed from its corresponding EventContext.

```
┌─────────────┐   ┌───────────────┐
│EventListener │···│ NamingListener │
└─────────────┘   └───────────────┘
```

```
public interface NamingListener extends java.util.EventListener {
// Public Instance Methods
    public abstract void namingExceptionThrown(NamingExceptionEvent evt);
}
```

Implementations: NamespaceChangeListener, ObjectChangeListener, javax.naming.ldap.UnsolicitedNotificationListener

Passed To: EventContext.{addNamingListener(), removeNamingListener()}, EventDirContext.addNamingListener(), NamingEvent.dispatch(), NamingExceptionEvent.dispatch()

ObjectChangeListener   Java 1.3

javax.naming.event   *event listener*

This listener is used to listen for changes to the content of objects stored in a name/directory service. This listener is fired when the object's attributes are modified in any way, if the object itself is replaced with a different reference, etc. To implement an ObjectChangeListener you must provide an implementation of the objectChanged() callback, as well as the namingExceptionThrown() callback inherited from NamingListener.

```
┌─────────────┐   ┌───────────────┐   ┌────────────────────┐
│EventListener │···│ NamingListener │···│ ObjectChangeListener │
└─────────────┘   └───────────────┘   └────────────────────┘
```

```
public interface ObjectChangeListener extends NamingListener {
// Public Instance Methods
    public abstract void objectChanged(NamingEvent evt);
}
```

CHAPTER 30

javax.naming.ldap

Package javax.naming.ldap   Java 1.3

The javax.naming.ldap package represents support for LDAP-specific functionality that is accessible through the JNDI interface. The interfaces listed here must be supported by the underlying JNDI provider.

Interfaces:

public interface **Control** extends Serializable;
public interface **ExtendedRequest** extends Serializable;
public interface **ExtendedResponse** extends Serializable;
public interface **HasControls**;
public interface **LdapContext** extends javax.naming.directory.DirContext;
public interface **UnsolicitedNotification** extends ExtendedResponse, HasControls;

Events:

public class **UnsolicitedNotificationEvent** extends java.util.EventObject;

Event Listeners:

public interface **UnsolicitedNotificationListener** extends javax.naming.event.NamingListener;

Other Classes:

public abstract class **ControlFactory**;
public class **InitialLdapContext** extends javax.naming.directory.InitialDirContext implements LdapContext;
public class **StartTlsRequest** implements ExtendedRequest;
public abstract class **StartTlsResponse** implements ExtendedResponse;

Exceptions:

public abstract class **LdapReferralException** extends javax.naming.ReferralException;

Control
Java 1.3

javax.naming.ldap
serializable

A Control is used as a modifier to alter the way in which an LDAP server satisfies requests, and to mark responses back from the LDAP server. Controls can be created using the ControlFactory interface, but more typically an LDAP provider will provide concrete subclasses of Control that provide specific modifiers. Sun's LDAP JNDI provider, for example, includes the com.sun.jndi.ldap.ctl.SortControl, which allows you to request that the LDAP server sort the results of searches according to a set of criteria. There is not a standard set of Controls that all LDAP servers must support, so you'll need to consult the documentation for your particular LDAP JNDI provider and LDAP server to see what options you have.

There are two kinds of Controls that can be set on LdapContexts. Connection request controls affect how LDAP connections are made, and are set when an LdapContext is first created. They can also be changed by calling the LdapContext.reconnect() method, and retrieved by calling LdapContext.getConnectControls(). Context request controls affect the behavior of context-related methods, and are set using the LdapRequestControls.setRequestControls() method.

```
Serializable ┈ Control
```

```
public interface Control extends Serializable {
// Public Constants
    public static final boolean CRITICAL;                                          =true
    public static final boolean NONCRITICAL;                                       =false
// Public Instance Methods
    public abstract byte[ ] getEncodedValue();
    public abstract String getID();
    public abstract boolean isCritical();
}
```

Passed To: ControlFactory.getControlInstance(), InitialLdapContext.{InitialLdapContext(), newInstance(), reconnect(), setRequestControls()}, LdapContext.{newInstance(), reconnect(), setRequestControls()}, LdapReferralException.getReferralContext()

Returned By: ControlFactory.getControlInstance(), HasControls.getControls(), InitialLdapContext.{getConnectControls(), getRequestControls(), getResponseControls()}, LdapContext.{getConnectControls(), getRequestControls(), getResponseControls()}

ControlFactory
Java 1.3

javax.naming.ldap

A ControlFactory can be used to create LDAP Controls. LDAP providers will typically provide specializations of ControlFactory that generate specific types of Controls.

```
public abstract class ControlFactory {
// Protected Constructors
    protected ControlFactory();
// Public Class Methods
    public static javax.naming.ldap.Control getControlInstance(javax.naming.ldap.Control ctl,
                                              javax.naming.Context ctx, java.util.Hashtable env)
        throws NamingException;
// Public Instance Methods
    public abstract javax.naming.ldap.Control getControlInstance(javax.naming.ldap.Control ctl)
        throws NamingException;
}
```

ExtendedRequest

javax.naming.ldap

This interface is the base interface for extended requests, which are used to invoke extended operations supported by an LDAP server. An LDAP server/provider will provide specializations of ExtendedRequest that invoke the extended operation on the server. Extended requests are issued to an LDAP server using the LdapContext.extendedOperation() method.

Serializable ── ExtendedRequest

```
public interface ExtendedRequest extends Serializable {
// Public Instance Methods
    public abstract ExtendedResponse createExtendedResponse(String id, byte[ ] berValue, int offset, int length)
        throws NamingException;
    public abstract byte[ ] getEncodedValue();
    public abstract String getID();
}
```

Implementations: StartTlsRequest

Passed To: InitialLdapContext.extendedOperation(), LdapContext.extendedOperation()

ExtendedResponse

javax.naming.ldap

This is the base interface for responses to extended operations invoked on an LDAP server. An ExtendedResponse is returned by the LdapContext.extendedOperation() method. An LDAP server/provider will typically provide specializations of ExtendedResponse specific to the type of ExtendedRequest that was issued.

Serializable ── ExtendedResponse

```
public interface ExtendedResponse extends Serializable {
// Public Instance Methods
    public abstract byte[ ] getEncodedValue();
    public abstract String getID();
}
```

Implementations: StartTlsResponse, UnsolicitedNotification

Returned By: ExtendedRequest.createExtendedResponse(), InitialLdapContext.extendedOperation(), LdapContext.extendedOperation(), StartTlsRequest.createExtendedResponse()

HasControls

javax.naming.ldap

The HasEntry interface is used to represent Controls in LDAP search results. If a given SearchResult has Controls associated with it, the SearchResult in the NamingEnumeration will also implement the HasControls interface, and the object's Controls can be retrieved using the getControls() method.

```
public interface HasControls {
// Public Instance Methods
    public abstract javax.naming.ldap.Control[ ] getControls() throws NamingException;
}
```

Implementations: UnsolicitedNotification

InitialLdapContext

javax.naming.ldap

An InitialLdapContext is a specialization of InitialDirContext and LdapContext that allows for creating the initial connection to an LDAP server. The InitialLdapContext can be constructed with no arguments, using the default environment and system properties for the connection parameters (e.g., in a J2EE server environment), or it can be constructed with a list of properties and connection Controls.

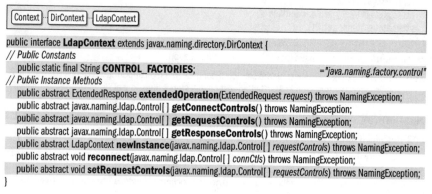

```
public class InitialLdapContext extends javax.naming.directory.InitialDirContext implements LdapContext {
// Public Constructors
    public InitialLdapContext() throws NamingException;
    public InitialLdapContext(java.util.Hashtable environment, javax.naming.ldap.Control[ ] connCtls)
        throws NamingException;
// Methods Implementing LdapContext
    public ExtendedResponse extendedOperation(ExtendedRequest request) throws NamingException;
    public javax.naming.ldap.Control[ ] getConnectControls() throws NamingException;
    public javax.naming.ldap.Control[ ] getRequestControls() throws NamingException;
    public javax.naming.ldap.Control[ ] getResponseControls() throws NamingException;
    public LdapContext newInstance(javax.naming.ldap.Control[ ] reqCtls) throws NamingException;
    public void reconnect(javax.naming.ldap.Control[ ] connCtls) throws NamingException;
    public void setRequestControls(javax.naming.ldap.Control[ ] requestControls) throws NamingException;
}
```

LdapContext

javax.naming.ldap

LdapContext is a specialization of javax.naming.directory.DirContext that provides access to LDAP-specific functionality on Contexts, such as setting/retrieving Controls and invoking extended operations.

```
public interface LdapContext extends javax.naming.directory.DirContext {
// Public Constants
    public static final String CONTROL_FACTORIES;                    ="java.naming.factory.control"
// Public Instance Methods
    public abstract ExtendedResponse extendedOperation(ExtendedRequest request) throws NamingException;
    public abstract javax.naming.ldap.Control[ ] getConnectControls() throws NamingException;
    public abstract javax.naming.ldap.Control[ ] getRequestControls() throws NamingException;
    public abstract javax.naming.ldap.Control[ ] getResponseControls() throws NamingException;
    public abstract LdapContext newInstance(javax.naming.ldap.Control[ ] requestControls) throws NamingException;
    public abstract void reconnect(javax.naming.ldap.Control[ ] connCtls) throws NamingException;
    public abstract void setRequestControls(javax.naming.ldap.Control[ ] requestControls) throws NamingException;
}
```

Implementations: InitialLdapContext

Returned By: InitialLdapContext.newInstance(), LdapContext.newInstance()

LdapReferralException

Java 1.3

javax.naming.ldap   *serializable checked*

This exception is thrown when a referral from an LDAP server fails.

```
Object ├─ Throwable ├─ Exception ├─ NamingException ├─ ReferralException ├─ LdapReferralException
         Serializable
```

```
public abstract class LdapReferralException extends ReferralException {
// Protected Constructors
    protected LdapReferralException();
    protected LdapReferralException(String explanation);
// Public Instance Methods
    public abstract javax.naming.Context getReferralContext(java.util.Hashtable env,
                                        javax.naming.ldap.Control[ ] reqCtls)
        throws NamingException;
// Public Methods Overriding ReferralException
    public abstract javax.naming.Context getReferralContext() throws NamingException;
    public abstract javax.naming.Context getReferralContext(java.util.Hashtable env) throws NamingException;
}
```

StartTlsRequest

Java 1.4

javax.naming.ldap   *serializable*

This class is used with LDAPv3 to establish a TLS connection request over an existing
LDAP connection. Pass an instance of this object to the extendedOperation() method of an
LdapContext object to initiate a TLS connection.

```
Object ├─ StartTlsRequest
Serializable ┈ ExtendedRequest
```

```
public class StartTlsRequest implements ExtendedRequest {
// Public Constructors
    public StartTlsRequest();
// Public Constants
    public static final String OID;                                     ="1.3.6.1.4.1.1466.20037"
// Methods Implementing ExtendedRequest
    public ExtendedResponse createExtendedResponse(String id, byte[ ] berValue, int offset, int length)
        throws NamingException;
    public byte[ ] getEncodedValue();                                          constant default:null
    public String getID();
}
```

StartTlsResponse

Java 1.4

javax.naming.ldap   *serializable*

This class is used with LDAPv3 to estabish a TLS connection response over an existing
LDAP connection. An instance of this class is returned by the extendedOperation() method
of an LdapContext object when initiating a TLS connection.

```
Object ├─ StartTlsResponse
Serializable ┈ ExtendedResponse
```

```
public abstract class StartTlsResponse implements ExtendedResponse {
// Protected Constructors
    protected StartTlsResponse();
// Public Constants
    public static final String OID;                                                    ="1.3.6.1.4.1.1466.20037"
// Public Instance Methods
    public abstract void close() throws IOException;
    public abstract javax.net.ssl.SSLSession negotiate() throws IOException;
    public abstract javax.net.ssl.SSLSession negotiate(javax.net.ssl.SSLSocketFactory factory) throws IOException;
    public abstract void setEnabledCipherSuites(String[ ] suites);
    public abstract void setHostnameVerifier(javax.net.ssl.HostnameVerifier verifier);
// Methods Implementing ExtendedResponse
    public byte[ ] getEncodedValue();                                                                          constant
    public String getID();
}
```

UnsolicitedNotification

Java 1.3

javax.naming.ldap

serializable

An UnsolicitedNotification is an ExtendedResponse that is sent by an LDAP server to a connected client without the client requesting it explicitly. UnsolicitedNotifications are delivered to the client within UnsolicitedNotificationEvents, which a client can listen for using an UnsolicitedNotificationListener.

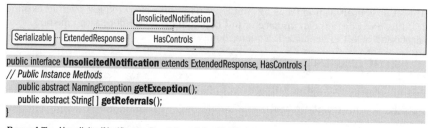

```
public interface UnsolicitedNotification extends ExtendedResponse, HasControls {
// Public Instance Methods
    public abstract NamingException getException();
    public abstract String[ ] getReferrals();
}
```

Passed To: UnsolicitedNotificationEvent.UnsolicitedNotificationEvent()

Returned By: UnsolicitedNotificationEvent.getNotification()

UnsolicitedNotificationEvent

Java 1.3

javax.naming.ldap

serializable event

An UnsolicitedNotificationEvent is a specialization of NamingEvent that delivers an Unsolicited-Notification from the LDAP server to the client. Clients can listen for these events by registering an UnsolicitedNotificationListener with an EventContext, using the EventContext.addNamingListener() method. An LdapContext implementation from a provider needs to support the EventContext interface in order for a client to use event notification with it.

```
public class UnsolicitedNotificationEvent extends java.util.EventObject {
// Public Constructors
    public UnsolicitedNotificationEvent(Object src, UnsolicitedNotification notice);
// Public Instance Methods
```

```
    public void dispatch(UnsolicitedNotificationListener listener);
    public UnsolicitedNotification getNotification();
}
```

Passed To: UnsolicitedNotificationListener.notificationReceived()

UnsolicitedNotificationListener

Java 1.3

javax.naming.ldap

event listener

This specialization of javax.naming.NamingListener is used by clients to listen for Unsolicited-NotificationEvents. An UnsolicitedNotificationListener can be attached to an LDAP context using its addNamingListener() method.

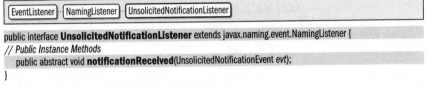

```
public interface UnsolicitedNotificationListener extends javax.naming.event.NamingListener {
// Public Instance Methods
    public abstract void notificationReceived(UnsolicitedNotificationEvent evt);
}
```

Passed To: UnsolicitedNotificationEvent.dispatch()

CHAPTER 31

javax.naming.spi

The javax.naming.spi package defines the service provider interface (SPI) for JNDI. Only system programmers who are developing JNDI providers need to use this package; JNDI application programmers can ignore it. The classes and interfaces in this package allow JNDI service providers to be plugged in underneath the JNDI API.

Interfaces:

public interface **DirObjectFactory** extends ObjectFactory;
public interface **DirStateFactory** extends StateFactory;
public interface **InitialContextFactory**;
public interface **InitialContextFactoryBuilder**;
public interface **ObjectFactory**;
public interface **ObjectFactoryBuilder**;   .
public interface **Resolver**;
public interface **StateFactory**;

Classes:

public static class **DirStateFactory.Result**;
public class **NamingManager**;
   └ public class **DirectoryManager** extends NamingManager;
public class **ResolveResult** implements Serializable;

DirectoryManager   Java 1.3

javax.naming.spi

DirectoryManager is a subclass of NamingManager that contains a method for creating javax.naming.directory.DirContext objects.

```
public class DirectoryManager extends NamingManager {
// No Constructor
// Public Class Methods
    public static javax.naming.directory.DirContext getContinuationDirContext(CannotProceedException cpe)
        throws NamingException;
    public static Object getObjectInstance(Object reflnfo, javax.naming.Name name, javax.naming.Context nameCtx,
                                java.util.Hashtable environment, Attributes attrs) throws Exception;
    public static DirStateFactory.Result getStateToBind(Object obj, javax.naming.Name name,
                                        javax.naming.Context nameCtx,
                                        java.util.Hashtable environment, Attributes attrs)
        throws NamingException;
}
```

DirObjectFactory   Java 1.3

javax.naming.spi

A DirObjectFactory is a specialization of ObjectFactory that supports the use of Attributes
while dynamically loading objects found in the directory. An overloaded version of
getObjectInstance() with an additional Atributes argument is declared in the interface.

```
[ ObjectFactory ]---[ DirObjectFactory ]
```

```
public interface DirObjectFactory extends ObjectFactory {
// Public Instance Methods
    public abstract Object getObjectInstance(Object obj, javax.naming.Name name, javax.naming.Context nameCtx,
                                java.util.Hashtable environment, Attributes attrs) throws Exception;
}
```

DirStateFactory   Java 1.3

javax.naming.spi

A DirStateFactory is a specialization of StateFactory that allows the use of Attributes when
creating state for bound objects. Object states created using this factory are represented
as DirStateFactory.Result objects.

```
[ StateFactory ]---[ DirStateFactory ]
```

```
public interface DirStateFactory extends StateFactory {
// Inner Classes
    public static class Result;
// Public Instance Methods
    public abstract DirStateFactory.Result getStateToBind(Object obj, javax.naming.Name name,
                                        javax.naming.Context nameCtx,
                                        java.util.Hashtable environment, Attributes inAttrs)
        throws NamingException;
}
```

DirStateFactory.Result   Java 1.3

javax.naming.spi

This inner class of DirStateFactory provides access to both the object and the Attributes of
an object that is to be bound in the directory.

```
public static class DirStateFactory.Result {
// Public Constructors
```

```
    public Result(Object obj, Attributes outAttrs);
// Public Instance Methods
    public Attributes getAttributes();
    public Object getObject();
}
```

Returned By: DirectoryManager.getStateToBind(), DirStateFactory.getStateToBind()

InitialContextFactory   Java 1.3

javax.naming.spi

This interface represents a factory that creates an initial context for a naming or directory service. The initial context serves as the entry point into the service. A JNDI service provider always includes an InitialContextFactory that can be used as the value of the java.naming.factory.initial property

```
public interface InitialContextFactory {
// Public Instance Methods
    public abstract javax.naming.Context getInitialContext(java.util.Hashtable environment) throws NamingException;
}
```

Returned By: InitialContextFactoryBuilder.createInitialContextFactory()

InitialContextFactoryBuilder   Java 1.3

javax.naming.spi

This interface represents a builder that creates initial context factories. A program can override the default initial context factory builder by calling NamingManager.setInitialContextFactoryBuilder() and specifying a new builder. Such a builder must implement this interface.

```
public interface InitialContextFactoryBuilder {
// Public Instance Methods
    public abstract InitialContextFactory createInitialContextFactory(java.util.Hashtable environment)
        throws NamingException;
}
```

Passed To: NamingManager.setInitialContextFactoryBuilder()

NamingManager   Java 1.3

javax.naming.spi

The NamingManager class contains methods for creating javax.naming.Context objects and otherwise controlling the operation of the underlying service provider.

```
public class NamingManager {
// No Constructor
// Public Constants
    public static final String CPE;                        ="java.naming.spi.CannotProceedException"
// Public Class Methods
    public static javax.naming.Context getContinuationContext(CannotProceedException cpe)
        throws NamingException;
    public static javax.naming.Context getInitialContext(java.util.Hashtable env) throws NamingException;
    public static Object getObjectInstance(Object refInfo, javax.naming.Name name, javax.naming.Context nameCtx,
                        java.util.Hashtable environment) throws Exception;
    public static Object getStateToBind(Object obj, javax.naming.Name name, javax.naming.Context nameCtx,
                        java.util.Hashtable environment) throws NamingException;
```

```
    public static javax.naming.Context getURLContext(String scheme, java.util.Hashtable environment)
        throws NamingException;
    public static boolean hasInitialContextFactoryBuilder();
    public static void setInitialContextFactoryBuilder(InitialContextFactoryBuilder builder)          synchronized
        throws NamingException;
    public static void setObjectFactoryBuilder(ObjectFactoryBuilder builder)                          synchronized
        throws NamingException;
}
```

Subclasses: DirectoryManager

ObjectFactory   Java 1.3

javax.naming.spi

This interface represents a factory for creating objects. JNDI supports the dynamic loading of object implementations with object factories. For example, say you have a naming system that binds file objects to names in the namespace. If the filesystem service provider binds filenames to Reference objects, a Reference object can create a file object through an object factory. This means that a call to lookup() a filename (in the appropriate Context) returns an actual file object the programmer can manipulate as necessary. An ObjectFactory is responsible for creating objects of a specific type.

```
public interface ObjectFactory {
// Public Instance Methods
    public abstract Object getObjectInstance(Object obj, javax.naming.Name name, javax.naming.Context nameCtx,
                            java.util.Hashtable environment) throws Exception;
}
```

Implementations: DirObjectFactory

Returned By: ObjectFactoryBuilder.createObjectFactory()

ObjectFactoryBuilder   Java 1.3

javax.naming.spi

This interface represents a builder that creates object factories. A program can override the default object factory builder by calling NamingManager.setObjectFactoryBuilder() and specifying a new builder. Such a builder must implement this interface.

```
public interface ObjectFactoryBuilder {
// Public Instance Methods
    public abstract ObjectFactory createObjectFactory(Object obj, java.util.Hashtable environment)
        throws NamingException;
}
```

Passed To: NamingManager.setObjectFactoryBuilder()

Resolver   Java 1.3

javax.naming.spi

The Resolver interface contains methods that are implemented by objects that can act as intermediate contexts for naming resolution purposes.

```
public interface Resolver {
// Public Instance Methods
    public abstract ResolveResult resolveToClass(String name, Class contextType) throws NamingException;
```

```
    public abstract ResolveResult resolveToClass(javax.naming.Name name, Class contextType)
        throws NamingException;
}
```

ResolveResult

javax.naming.spi

This class represents the result of resolving a name.

```
Object ┤ ResolveResult ├┈ Serializable
```

```
public class ResolveResult implements Serializable {
// Public Constructors
    public ResolveResult(Object robj, String rcomp);
    public ResolveResult(Object robj, javax.naming.Name rname);
// Protected Constructors
    protected ResolveResult();
// Public Instance Methods
    public void appendRemainingComponent(String name);
    public void appendRemainingName(javax.naming.Name name);
    public javax.naming.Name getRemainingName();
    public Object getResolvedObj();
    public void setRemainingName(javax.naming.Name name);
    public void setResolvedObj(Object obj);
// Protected Instance Fields
    protected javax.naming.Name remainingName;
    protected Object resolvedObj;
}
```

Returned By: Resolver.resolveToClass()

StateFactory

javax.naming.spi

A StateFactory is used to obtain/create the state information for objects that are bound to names in the naming context. When a JNDI provider is asked to bind an object in the namespace, its implementation of the StateFactory will have its getStateToBind() method invoked to generate the object state that should be stored in the namespace.

```
public interface StateFactory {
// Public Instance Methods
    public abstract Object getStateToBind(Object obj, javax.naming.Name name, javax.naming.Context nameCtx,
                            java.util.Hashtable environment) throws NamingException;
}
```

Implementations: DirStateFactory

CHAPTER 32

javax.resource

The javax.resource package and sub-packages are the Java interfaces for the Java Connector API (JCA). The JCA provides a standard approach to interfacing with enterprise information systems (EISs) such as enterprise resource planning systems, transaction-processing servers, and other systems. Each resource must have a JCA resource adapter associated with it in order for an application to connect to it using JCA.

The JCA includes both a common client interface (CCI), in the javax.resource.cci package, and a service provider interface (SPI) for implementing resource adaptors, etc., in the javax.resource.spi package.

Interfaces:

public interface **Referenceable** extends javax.naming.Referenceable;

Exceptions:

public class **ResourceException** extends Exception;
  └ public class **NotSupportedException** extends ResourceException;

NotSupportedException   J2EE Connector 1.0
javax.resource   *serializable checked*

This exception is thrown if a given resource adapter or resource cannot perform the requested operation because it isn't supported.

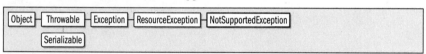

```
public class NotSupportedException extends ResourceException {
// Public Constructors
    public NotSupportedException(String reason);
```

```
    public NotSupportedException(String reason, String errorCode);
}
```

Referenceable   J2EE Connector 1.0

javax.resource

This is a specialization of the javax.naming.Referenceable interface, allowing JCA connection factories to be registered in JNDI namespaces using JNDI references. Every JCA connection factory must implement this interface (as well as Serializable).

```
Referenceable ---- Referenceable
```

```
public interface Referenceable extends javax.naming.Referenceable {
// Public Instance Methods
    public abstract void setReference(javax.naming.Reference reference);
}
```

Implementations: javax.resource.cci.ConnectionFactory

ResourceException   J2EE Connector 1.0

javax.resource   *serializable checked*

This is the base class for all exceptions in the Java Connector API. The ResourceException includes a string message describing the error, a vendor-specific error code, and a reference to a nested exception.

```
Object --- Throwable --- Exception --- ResourceException
        Serializable
```

```
public class ResourceException extends Exception {
// Public Constructors
    public ResourceException(String reason);
    public ResourceException(String reason, String errorCode);
// Public Instance Methods
    public String getErrorCode();
    public Exception getLinkedException();
    public void setLinkedException(Exception ex);
}
```

Subclasses: javax.resource.NotSupportedException, javax.resource.cci.ResourceWarning, javax.resource.spi.ApplicationServerInternalException, javax.resource.spi.CommException, javax.resource.spi.EISSystemException, javax.resource.spi.IllegalStateException, javax.resource.spi.LocalTransactionException, javax.resource.spi.ResourceAdapterInternalException, javax.resource.spi.ResourceAllocationException, javax.resource.spi.SecurityException

Thrown By: Too many methods to list.

CHAPTER 33

javax.resource.cci

The javax.resource.cci package represents the Common Client Interface layer for the JCA. It contains interfaces that a client can exercise for any JCA resource adaptor.

Interfaces:

public interface **Connection**;
public interface **ConnectionFactory** extends Serializable, javax.resource.Referenceable;
public interface **ConnectionMetaData**;
public interface **ConnectionSpec**;
public interface **Interaction**;
public interface **InteractionSpec** extends Serializable;
public interface **LocalTransaction**;
public interface **Record** extends Cloneable, Serializable;
public interface **RecordFactory**;
public interface **ResourceAdapterMetaData**;
public interface **ResultSet** extends Record, java.sql.ResultSet;
public interface **ResultSetInfo**;
public interface **Streamable**;

Collections:

public interface **IndexedRecord** extends Record, java.util.List, Serializable;
public interface **MappedRecord** extends Record, java.util.Map, Serializable;

Exceptions:

public class **ResourceWarning** extends javax.resource.ResourceException;

Connection   J2EE Connector 1.0

javax.resource.cci

A Connection represents a reference to a physical connection to a resource. Connections are obtained using the getConnection() method on a ConnectionFactory, and are used to initiate one or more Interactions with the target resource.

```
public interface Connection {
// Public Instance Methods
    public abstract void close() throws ResourceException;
    public abstract Interaction createInteraction() throws ResourceException;
    public abstract javax.resource.cci.LocalTransaction getLocalTransaction() throws ResourceException;
    public abstract javax.resource.cci.ConnectionMetaData getMetaData() throws ResourceException;
    public abstract ResultSetInfo getResultSetInfo() throws ResourceException;
}
```

Returned By: javax.resource.cci.ConnectionFactory.getConnection(), Interaction.getConnection()

ConnectionFactory

J2EE Connector 1.0

javax.resource.cci

serializable

A ConnectionFactory is obtained by a client through a JNDI namespace lookup, and is used to establish Connections with a resource.

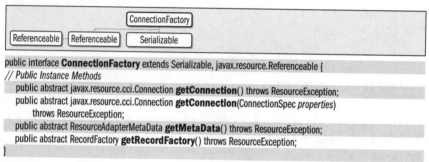

```
public interface ConnectionFactory extends Serializable, javax.resource.Referenceable {
// Public Instance Methods
    public abstract javax.resource.cci.Connection getConnection() throws ResourceException;
    public abstract javax.resource.cci.Connection getConnection(ConnectionSpec properties)
        throws ResourceException;
    public abstract ResourceAdapterMetaData getMetaData() throws ResourceException;
    public abstract RecordFactory getRecordFactory() throws ResourceException;
}
```

ConnectionMetaData

J2EE Connector 1.0

javax.resource.cci

The ConnectionMetaData interface provides information about the resource at the other end of a Connection. The meta-data instance is obtained by calling getMetaData() on a Connection.

```
public interface ConnectionMetaData {
// Public Instance Methods
    public abstract String getEISProductName() throws ResourceException;
    public abstract String getEISProductVersion() throws ResourceException;
    public abstract String getUserName() throws ResourceException;
}
```

Returned By: javax.resource.cci.Connection.getMetaData()

ConnectionSpec

J2EE Connector 1.0

javax.resource.cci

A ConnectionSpec object can be used to pass vendor-specific properties when creating a Connection using the getConnection() method on ConnectionFactory. A vendor may provide its own implementation of this interface containing a set of JavaBeans properties that can be set to control the nature of the connection.

public interface **ConnectionSpec** {
}

Passed To: javax.resource.cci.ConnectionFactory.getConnection()

IndexedRecord

javax.resource.cci

cloneable serializable collection

An IndexedRecord is a specialization of the java.util.List interface that represents an ordered list of record elements obtained from a resource.

public interface **IndexedRecord** extends Record, java.util.List, Serializable {
}

Returned By: RecordFactory.createIndexedRecord()

Interaction

javax.resource.cci

An Interaction is used to invoke specific actions on a resource. An Interaction is obtained from a Connection by calling its createInteraction() method. An interaction with a resource is carried out using the execute() methods, specifying an InteractionSpec object to specify what action is to be taken, and providing either an input and output Record (for actions that require a Record to operate on), or just an output Record (for actions that just produce an output). Interactions may allocate resources on behalf of the client, so they should always be closed when not needed any longer.

public interface **Interaction** {
// Public Instance Methods
    public abstract void **clearWarnings**() throws ResourceException;
    public abstract void **close**() throws ResourceException;
    public abstract Record **execute**(InteractionSpec *ispec*, Record *input*) throws ResourceException;
    public abstract boolean **execute**(InteractionSpec *ispec*, Record *input*, Record *output*) throws ResourceException;
    public abstract javax.resource.cci.Connection **getConnection**();
    public abstract ResourceWarning **getWarnings**() throws ResourceException;
}

Returned By: javax.resource.cci.Connection.createInteraction()

InteractionSpec

javax.resource.cci

serializable

An InteractionSpec is passed into the execute() methods on an Interaction, in order to specify and control the action requested of the resource. Although this interface is simply a base to be implemented by vendors, the JCA does specify a set of standard properties that an InteractionSpec should implement if it is relevant to its underlying resource. They are:

functionName
    The name of the desired function to be executed on the resource.

interactionVerb
> The mode of the interaction, which is one of:

SYNC_SEND
>> (the interaction only sends to the underlying resource),

SYNC_SEND_RECEIVE
>> (the interaction performs a synchronous send/receive sequence with the resource) or

SYNC_RECEIVE
>> (a synchronous receive is performed with the resource, no send is performed).

executionTimeout
> Number of milliseconds to wait for execution of a request.

fetchSize
> A hint about how many records to fetch at a time.

fetchDirection
> A hint about the direction in which to fetch records.

maxFieldSize
> A hint about the maximum field size desired/supported by the client.

resultSetType
> A hint about what type of result set is desired/supported by the client.

resultSetConcurrency
> A hint about the result set concurrency support desired/supported by the client.

```
Serializable ---- InteractionSpec

public interface InteractionSpec extends Serializable {
// Public Constants
    public static final int SYNC_RECEIVE;                          =2
    public static final int SYNC_SEND;                             =0
    public static final int SYNC_SEND_RECEIVE;                     =1
}
```

Passed To: Interaction.execute()

LocalTransaction   J2EE Connector 1.0

javax.resource.cci

A LocalTransaction is used by a client to delimit transaction boundaries. A LocalTransaction can be obtained using the Connection.getLocalTransaction() method. JCA provider support for LocalTransactions is optional.

```
public interface LocalTransaction {
// Public Instance Methods
    public abstract void begin() throws ResourceException;
```

```
    public abstract void commit() throws ResourceException;
    public abstract void rollback() throws ResourceException;
}
```

Returned By: javax.resource.cci.Connection.getLocalTransaction()

MappedRecord

javax.resource.cci

cloneable serializable collection

The MappedRecord interface represents a record from a resource that contains a set of key/value pairs.

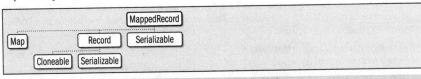

```
public interface MappedRecord extends Record, java.util.Map, Serializable {
}
```

Returned By: RecordFactory.createMappedRecord()

Record

javax.resource.cci

cloneable serializable

A Record represents input and output for the execution of interactions with resources. The CCI provides the MappedRecord, IndexedRecord and ResultSet specializations of this interface, and also supports the use of custom JavaBeans for Records.

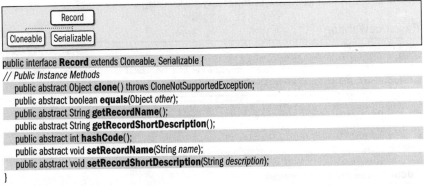

```
public interface Record extends Cloneable, Serializable {
// Public Instance Methods
    public abstract Object clone() throws CloneNotSupportedException;
    public abstract boolean equals(Object other);
    public abstract String getRecordName();
    public abstract String getRecordShortDescription();
    public abstract int hashCode();
    public abstract void setRecordName(String name);
    public abstract void setRecordShortDescription(String description);
}
```

Implementations: IndexedRecord, MappedRecord, javax.resource.cci.ResultSet

Passed To: Interaction.execute()

Returned By: Interaction.execute()

RecordFactory

javax.resource.cci

A RecordFactory is used to create vendor-specific implementations of IndexedRecords and MappedRecords. The vendor implementation of the CCI should provide an implementation of RecordFactory for this purpose.

```
public interface RecordFactory {
// Public Instance Methods
    public abstract IndexedRecord createIndexedRecord(String recordName) throws ResourceException;
    public abstract MappedRecord createMappedRecord(String recordName) throws ResourceException;
}
```

Returned By: javax.resource.cci.ConnectionFactory.getRecordFactory()

ResourceAdapterMetaData   J2EE Connector 1.0

javax.resource.cci

This interface represents metadata about the resource adapter being used to generate and manage connections to a resource. This metadata is obtained by calling the ConnectionFactory.getMetaData() method.

```
public interface ResourceAdapterMetaData {
// Property Accessor Methods (by property name)
    public abstract String getAdapterName();
    public abstract String getAdapterShortDescription();
    public abstract String getAdapterVendorName();
    public abstract String getAdapterVersion();
    public abstract String[] getInteractionSpecsSupported();
    public abstract String getSpecVersion();
// Public Instance Methods
    public abstract boolean supportsExecuteWithInputAndOutputRecord();
    public abstract boolean supportsExecuteWithInputRecordOnly();
    public abstract boolean supportsLocalTransactionDemarcation();
}
```

Returned By: javax.resource.cci.ConnectionFactory.getMetaData()

ResourceWarning   J2EE Connector 1.0

javax.resource.cci   *serializable checked*

This exception is thrown when an anomolous but non-fatal condition is encountered while satisfying a request on a resource.

```
Object — Throwable — Exception — ResourceException — ResourceWarning
         Serializable
```

```
public class ResourceWarning extends ResourceException {
// Public Constructors
    public ResourceWarning(String reason);
    public ResourceWarning(String reason, String errorCode);
// Public Instance Methods
    public ResourceWarning getLinkedWarning();
    public void setLinkedWarning(ResourceWarning warning);
}
```

Passed To: ResourceWarning.setLinkedWarning()

Returned By: Interaction.getWarnings(), ResourceWarning.getLinkedWarning()

ResultSet   J2EE Connector 1.0

javax.resource.cci   *cloneable serializable*

A ResultSet represents a Record that contains tabular data, such as that obtained from a relational database.

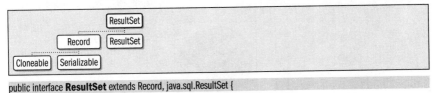

```
public interface ResultSet extends Record, java.sql.ResultSet {
}
```

ResultSetInfo

javax.resource.cci

This interface represents metadata about the support a given connection supports for receiving and generating ResultSet records. It is obtained by calling the Connection.getResultInfo() method.

```
public interface ResultSetInfo {
// Public Instance Methods
    public abstract boolean deletesAreDetected(int type) throws ResourceException;
    public abstract boolean insertsAreDetected(int type) throws ResourceException;
    public abstract boolean othersDeletesAreVisible(int type) throws ResourceException;
    public abstract boolean othersInsertsAreVisible(int type) throws ResourceException;
    public abstract boolean othersUpdatesAreVisible(int type) throws ResourceException;
    public abstract boolean ownDeletesAreVisible(int type) throws ResourceException;
    public abstract boolean ownInsertsAreVisible(int type) throws ResourceException;
    public abstract boolean ownUpdatesAreVisible(int type) throws ResourceException;
    public abstract boolean supportsResultSetType(int type) throws ResourceException;
    public abstract boolean supportsResultTypeConcurrency(int type, int concurrency) throws ResourceException;
    public abstract boolean updatesAreDetected(int type) throws ResourceException;
}
```

Returned By: javax.resource.cci.Connection.getResultSetInfo()

Streamable

javax.resource.cci

A Streamable is used by a resource adapter to read and write data in a Record, in the form of a stream of bytes. This interface is not typically used directly by a client, but is used internally by resource adapters to access data in a Record provided by a client.

```
public interface Streamable {
// Public Instance Methods
    public abstract void read(java.io.InputStream istream) throws IOException;
    public abstract void write(java.io.OutputStream ostream) throws IOException;
}
```

CHAPTER 34

javax.resource.spi and javax.resource.spi.security

The javax.resource.spi package represents a standard API that resource adapter providers must use to implement JCA support for their EIS environments.

Interfaces:

public interface **ConnectionManager** extends Serializable;
public interface **ConnectionRequestInfo**;
public interface **LocalTransaction**;
public interface **ManagedConnection**;
public interface **ManagedConnectionFactory** extends Serializable;
public interface **ManagedConnectionMetaData**;

Events:

public class **ConnectionEvent** extends java.util.EventObject;

Event Listeners:

public interface **ConnectionEventListener** extends java.util.EventListener;

Exceptions:

public class **ApplicationServerInternalException** extends javax.resource.ResourceException;
public class **CommException** extends javax.resource.ResourceException;
public class **EISSystemException** extends javax.resource.ResourceException;
public class **IllegalStateException** extends javax.resource.ResourceException;
public class **LocalTransactionException** extends javax.resource.ResourceException;
public class **ResourceAdapterInternalException** extends javax.resource.ResourceException;
public class **ResourceAllocationException** extends javax.resource.ResourceException;
public class **SecurityException** extends javax.resource.ResourceException;

ApplicationServerInternalException

javax.resource.spi

This exception is thrown when an error specific to an underlying application server is encountered.

```
Object ├ Throwable ├ Exception ├ ResourceException ├ ApplicationServerInternalException
        Serializable
```

```
public class ApplicationServerInternalException extends ResourceException {
// Public Constructors
    public ApplicationServerInternalException(String reason);
    public ApplicationServerInternalException(String reason, String errorCode);
}
```

CommException

javax.resource.spi

This exception is thrown when some sort of communication error is encountered while interacting with a resource.

```
Object ├ Throwable ├ Exception ├ ResourceException ├ CommException
        Serializable
```

```
public class CommException extends ResourceException {
// Public Constructors
    public CommException(String reason);
    public CommException(String reason, String errorCode);
}
```

ConnectionEvent

javax.resource.spi

A ConnectionEvent represents an event related to a ManagedConnection. The types of events supported include the closing of a connection, an error on a connection, and the start, commit or rollback of a LocalTransaction associated with the connection. Resource adapters receive these events by registering a ConnectionEventListener with a ManagedConnection using its addConnectionEventListener() method.

```
Object ├ EventObject ├ ConnectionEvent
        Serializable
```

```
public class ConnectionEvent extends java.util.EventObject {
// Public Constructors
    public ConnectionEvent(ManagedConnection source, int eid);
    public ConnectionEvent(ManagedConnection source, int eid, Exception exception);
// Public Constants
    public static final int CONNECTION_CLOSED;                        =1
    public static final int CONNECTION_ERROR_OCCURRED;                =5
    public static final int LOCAL_TRANSACTION_COMMITTED;              =3
    public static final int LOCAL_TRANSACTION_ROLLEDBACK;             =4
    public static final int LOCAL_TRANSACTION_STARTED;                =2
// Public Instance Methods
    public Object getConnectionHandle();
```

```
    public Exception getException();
    public int getId();
    public void setConnectionHandle(Object connectionHandle);
// Protected Instance Fields
    protected int id;
}
```

Passed To: javax.resource.spi.ConnectionEventListener.{connectionClosed(),
connectionErrorOccurred(), localTransactionCommitted(), localTransactionRolledback(),
localTransactionStarted()}

ConnectionEventListener

javax.resource.spi

event listener

This interface represents a listener that a provider can implement and register with a
ManagedConnection to receive event notifications, using the ManagedConnection.addConnec-
tionEventListener() method.

```
EventListener --- ConnectionEventListener
```

```
public interface ConnectionEventListener extends java.util.EventListener {
// Public Instance Methods
    public abstract void connectionClosed(javax.resource.spi.ConnectionEvent event);
    public abstract void connectionErrorOccurred(javax.resource.spi.ConnectionEvent event);
    public abstract void localTransactionCommitted(javax.resource.spi.ConnectionEvent event);
    public abstract void localTransactionRolledback(javax.resource.spi.ConnectionEvent event);
    public abstract void localTransactionStarted(javax.resource.spi.ConnectionEvent event);
}
```

Passed To: ManagedConnection.{addConnectionEventListener(), removeConnectionEventListener()}

ConnectionManager

javax.resource.spi

serializable

A ConnectionManager is used by a resource adapter to pass a connection request to the
underlying application server.

```
Serializable --- ConnectionManager
```

```
public interface ConnectionManager extends Serializable {
// Public Instance Methods
    public abstract Object allocateConnection(ManagedConnectionFactory mcf,
                            ConnectionRequestInfo cxRequestInfo) throws ResourceException;
}
```

Passed To: ManagedConnectionFactory.createConnectionFactory()

ConnectionRequestInfo

javax.resource.spi

This interface can be used by a resource adapter to pass implementation-specific information along with a connection request to the application server.

```
public interface ConnectionRequestInfo {
// Public Instance Methods
    public abstract boolean equals(Object other);
```

```
    public abstract int hashCode();
}
```

Passed To: ConnectionManager.allocateConnection(), ManagedConnection.getConnection(), ManagedConnectionFactory.{createManagedConnection(), matchManagedConnections()}

EISSystemException

javax.resource.spi   *serializable checked*

This exception is thrown when a system error is encountered with an EIS resource.

```
Object ── Throwable ── Exception ── ResourceException ── EISSystemException
          Serializable
```

```
public class EISSystemException extends ResourceException {
// Public Constructors
    public EISSystemException(String reason);
    public EISSystemException(String reason, String errorCode);
}
```

IllegalStateException

javax.resource.spi   *serializable checked*

This exception is thrown if the resource adapter or underlying EIS application server is in a state which renders it unable to satisfy a request made to it through a connection.

```
Object ── Throwable ── Exception ── ResourceException ── IllegalStateException
          Serializable
```

```
public class IllegalStateException extends ResourceException {
// Public Constructors
    public IllegalStateException(String reason);
    public IllegalStateException(String reason, String errorCode);
}
```

LocalTransaction

javax.resource.spi

A LocalTransaction represents transaction boundaries that are internal to the resource adapter implementation. These transactions are local to the underlying resource, not managed by an external transaction manager. External, distributed transaction management support is provided through the Java Transacation API (JTA). Support for Local-Transactions by resource adapter implementations is optional.

```
public interface LocalTransaction {
// Public Instance Methods
    public abstract void begin() throws ResourceException;
    public abstract void commit() throws ResourceException;
    public abstract void rollback() throws ResourceException;
}
```

Returned By: ManagedConnection.getLocalTransaction()

LocalTransactionException

javax.resource.spi

This exception is thrown when an error occurs in the management of local transactions, such an attempt to start a transaction within an existing transaction context, or attempting to call LocalTransaction.commit() without an existing transaction context.

```
public class LocalTransactionException extends ResourceException {
// Public Constructors
    public LocalTransactionException(String reason);
    public LocalTransactionException(String reason, String errorCode);
}
```

ManagedConnection

javax.resource.spi

A ManagedConnection represents a physical connection to a resource. Every client-side Connection has a corresponding ManagedConnection within the resource adapter implementation.

```
public interface ManagedConnection {
// Event Registration Methods (by event name)
    public abstract void addConnectionEventListener(javax.resource.spi.ConnectionEventListener listener);
    public abstract void removeConnectionEventListener(javax.resource.spi.ConnectionEventListener listener);
// Public Instance Methods
    public abstract void associateConnection(Object connection) throws ResourceException;
    public abstract void cleanup() throws ResourceException;
    public abstract void destroy() throws ResourceException;
    public abstract Object getConnection(javax.security.auth.Subject subject, ConnectionRequestInfo cxRequestInfo)
        throws ResourceException;
    public abstract javax.resource.spi.LocalTransaction getLocalTransaction() throws ResourceException;
    public abstract PrintWriter getLogWriter() throws ResourceException;
    public abstract ManagedConnectionMetaData getMetaData() throws ResourceException;
    public abstract javax.transaction.xa.XAResource getXAResource() throws ResourceException;
    public abstract void setLogWriter(PrintWriter out) throws ResourceException;
}
```

Passed To: javax.resource.spi.ConnectionEvent.ConnectionEvent()

Returned By: ManagedConnectionFactory.{createManagedConnection(), matchManagedConnections()}

ManagedConnectionFactory

javax.resource.spi

A ManagedConnectionFactory is used to create implementation-specific ManagedConnections and ConnectionFactory instances. A vendor-specific resource adapter provides an implementation of a ManagedConnectionFactory, typically as a subclass that can be instantiated directly. The createConnectionFactory() methods are used to create client-accessible ConnectionFactory instances, and the createManagedConnection() methods is used to create ManagedConnections.

Serializable ┈ ManagedConnectionFactory

```
public interface ManagedConnectionFactory extends Serializable {
// Public Instance Methods
    public abstract Object createConnectionFactory() throws ResourceException;
    public abstract Object createConnectionFactory(ConnectionManager cxManager) throws ResourceException;
    public abstract ManagedConnection createManagedConnection(javax.security.auth.Subject subject,
                                                     ConnectionRequestInfo cxRequestInfo)
        throws ResourceException;
    public abstract boolean equals(Object other);
    public abstract PrintWriter getLogWriter() throws ResourceException;
    public abstract int hashCode();
    public abstract ManagedConnection matchManagedConnections(java.util.Set connectionSet,
                                                     javax.security.auth.Subject subject,
                                                     ConnectionRequestInfo cxRequestInfo)
        throws ResourceException;
    public abstract void setLogWriter(PrintWriter out) throws ResourceException;
}
```

Passed To: ConnectionManager.allocateConnection(),
javax.resource.spi.security.PasswordCredential.setManagedConnectionFactory()

Returned By: javax.resource.spi.security.PasswordCredential.getManagedConnectionFactory()

ManagedConnectionMetaData   J2EE Connector 1.0

javax.resource.spi

This interface represents metadata about the resource behind a ManagedConnection. It includes basic information about the name and connection capabilities of the resource. The metadata is obtained using the ManagedConnection.getMetaData() method.

```
public interface ManagedConnectionMetaData {
// Public Instance Methods
    public abstract String getEISProductName() throws ResourceException;
    public abstract String getEISProductVersion() throws ResourceException;
    public abstract int getMaxConnections() throws ResourceException;
    public abstract String getUserName() throws ResourceException;
}
```

Returned By: ManagedConnection.getMetaData()

ResourceAdapterInternalException   J2EE Connector 1.0

javax.resource.spi   *serializable checked*

This exception is thrown when a system-level error is encountered with a resource adapter, such as an internal error encountered while creating a connection to a resource.

Object ─ Throwable ─ Exception ─ ResourceException ─ ResourceAdapterInternalException
        Serializable

```
public class ResourceAdapterInternalException extends ResourceException {
// Public Constructors
    public ResourceAdapterInternalException(String reason);
    public ResourceAdapterInternalException(String reason, String errorCode);
}
```

ResourceAllocationException

J2EE Connector 1.0

javax.resource.spi

serializable checked

This exception is thrown when an attempt to allocate system resources in response to a connection or interaction request fails for some reason.

```
Object ── Throwable ── Exception ── ResourceException ── ResourceAllocationException
           Serializable
```

```
public class ResourceAllocationException extends ResourceException {
// Public Constructors
    public ResourceAllocationException(String reason);
    public ResourceAllocationException(String reason, String errorCode);
}
```

SecurityException

J2EE Connector 1.0

javax.resource.spi

serializable checked

This exception is thrown when a security-related error occurs while satisfying a connection or interaction request, such as failure to authenticate the against the EIS resource, or lack of access to perform an operation under the current credentials.

```
Object ── Throwable ── Exception ── ResourceException ── SecurityException
           Serializable
```

```
public class SecurityException extends ResourceException {
// Public Constructors
    public SecurityException(String reason);
    public SecurityException(String reason, String errorCode);
}
```

Thrown By: javax.resource.spi.security.GenericCredential.getCredentialData()

Package javax.resource.spi.security

J2EE Connector 1.0

This package contains interfaces used in managing security for resource connections and interactions.

Interfaces:

public interface **GenericCredential**;

Classes:

public final class **PasswordCredential** implements Serializable;

GenericCredential

J2EE Connector 1.0

javax.resource.spi.security

This interface represents a general interface for credentials associated with a principal interacting with an EIS resource. This interface is not specific to any particular security mechanism, and a concrete implementation would be provided by the resource adapter provider.

```
public interface GenericCredential {
// Public Instance Methods
```

```
    public abstract boolean equals(Object another);
    public abstract byte[ ] getCredentialData() throws javax.resource.spi.SecurityException;
    public abstract String getMechType();
    public abstract String getName();
    public abstract int hashCode();
}
```

PasswordCredential

javax.resource.spi.security

serializable

This class represents a security credential that consists simply of a username and password.

Object — PasswordCredential ⋯ Serializable

```
public final class PasswordCredential implements Serializable {
// Public Constructors
    public PasswordCredential(String userName, char[ ] password);
// Public Instance Methods
    public ManagedConnectionFactory getManagedConnectionFactory();
    public char[ ] getPassword();
    public String getUserName();
    public void setManagedConnectionFactory(ManagedConnectionFactory mcf);
// Public Methods Overriding Object
    public boolean equals(Object other);
    public int hashCode();
}
```

CHAPTER 35

javax.rmi and javax.rmi.CORBA

This package contains interfaces that support RMI-IIOP, or the interaction of RMI objects with IIOP-enabled CORBA objects, and vice versa.

Classes:

public class **PortableRemoteObject**;

PortableRemoteObject   Java 1.3
javax.rmi

This is the base class for server objects that support RMI-IIOP. The interface supports exporting a remote object to accept client requests, generating client stubs for a server object, and for safely casting references to remote objects (using the narrow() method), among other things. This interface is important in CORBA and EJB contexts when it is desirable to keep your code portable with respect to both RMI and IIOP remote objects.

```
public class PortableRemoteObject {
// Protected Constructors
    protected PortableRemoteObject() throws java.rmi.RemoteException;
// Public Class Methods
    public static void connect(java.rmi.Remote target, java.rmi.Remote source) throws java.rmi.RemoteException;
    public static void exportObject(java.rmi.Remote obj) throws java.rmi.RemoteException;
    public static Object narrow(Object narrowFrom, Class narrowTo) throws ClassCastException;
    public static java.rmi.Remote toStub(java.rmi.Remote obj) throws java.rmi.NoSuchObjectException;
    public static void unexportObject(java.rmi.Remote obj) throws java.rmi.NoSuchObjectException;
}
```

Package javax.rmi.CORBA

This package contains APIs used with RMI-IIOP.

Interfaces:

public interface **PortableRemoteObjectDelegate**;
public interface **StubDelegate**;
public interface **Tie** extends org.omg.CORBA.portable.InvokeHandler;
public interface **UtilDelegate**;
public interface **ValueHandler**;

Classes:

public class **ClassDesc** implements Serializable;
public abstract class **Stub** extends org.omg.CORBA_2_3.portable.ObjectImpl implements Serializable;
public class **Util**;

ClassDesc

javax.rmi.CORBA *serializable*

This class is used while marshalling/unmarshalling Class objects over IIOP.

```
Object — ClassDesc ┄ Serializable
```

```
public class ClassDesc implements Serializable {
// Public Constructors
    public ClassDesc();
}
```

PortableRemoteObjectDelegate

javax.rmi.CORBA

This interface represents a delegate that implements the functionality exported in the javax.rmi.PortableRemoteObject interface. You specify a delegate to be used by your PortableRemoteObject instances by setting the javax.rmi.CORBA.PortableRemoteObjectClass system property.

```
public interface PortableRemoteObjectDelegate {
// Public Instance Methods
    public abstract void connect(java.rmi.Remote target, java.rmi.Remote source) throws java.rmi.RemoteException;
    public abstract void exportObject(java.rmi.Remote obj) throws java.rmi.RemoteException;
    public abstract Object narrow(Object narrowFrom, Class narrowTo) throws ClassCastException;
    public abstract java.rmi.Remote toStub(java.rmi.Remote obj) throws java.rmi.NoSuchObjectException;
    public abstract void unexportObject(java.rmi.Remote obj) throws java.rmi.NoSuchObjectException;
}
```

Stub

javax.rmi.CORBA *serializable*

This is the base class for all RMI-IIOP stubs.

```
Object — ObjectImpl — ObjectImpl — Stub
           Object                 Serializable
```

```
public abstract class Stub extends org.omg.CORBA_2_3.portable.ObjectImpl implements Serializable {
// Public Constructors
    public Stub();
// Public Instance Methods
    public void connect(org.omg.CORBA.ORB orb) throws java.rmi.RemoteException;
// Public Methods Overriding ObjectImpl
    public boolean equals(Object obj);
    public int hashCode();
    public String toString();
}
```

Subclasses: org.omg.stub.java.rmi._Remote_Stub

Passed To: StubDelegate.{connect(), equals(), hashCode(), readObject(), toString(), writeObject()}, Util.isLocal(), UtilDelegate.isLocal()

StubDelegate   Java 1.3

javax.rmi.CORBA

This interface represents a delegate that implements the functionality exported in the javax.rmi.CORBA.Stub class. You specify the delegate for your Stubs by setting the javax.rmi.CORBA.StubClass system property.

```
public interface StubDelegate {
// Public Instance Methods
    public abstract void connect(Stub self, org.omg.CORBA.ORB orb) throws java.rmi.RemoteException;
    public abstract boolean equals(Stub self, Object obj);
    public abstract int hashCode(Stub self);
    public abstract void readObject(Stub self, ObjectInputStream s) throws IOException, ClassNotFoundException;
    public abstract String toString(Stub self);
    public abstract void writeObject(Stub self, ObjectOutputStream s) throws IOException;
}
```

Tie   Java 1.3

javax.rmi.CORBA

This interface is a base class for RMI-IIOP server-side implementations.

```
InvokeHandler --- Tie
```

```
public interface Tie extends org.omg.CORBA.portable.InvokeHandler {
// Public Instance Methods
    public abstract void deactivate() throws java.rmi.NoSuchObjectException;
    public abstract java.rmi.Remote getTarget();
    public abstract org.omg.CORBA.ORB orb();
    public abstract void orb(org.omg.CORBA.ORB orb);
    public abstract void setTarget(java.rmi.Remote target);
    public abstract org.omg.CORBA.Object thisObject();
}
```

Passed To: Util.registerTarget(), UtilDelegate.registerTarget()

Returned By: Util.getTie(), UtilDelegate.getTie()

Util

javax.rmi.CORBA

The Util interface provides a set of static utility methods that can be used by client stubs and server ties.

```
public class Util {
// No Constructor
// Public Class Methods
    public static Object copyObject(Object obj, org.omg.CORBA.ORB orb) throws java.rmi.RemoteException;
    public static Object[ ] copyObjects(Object[ ] obj, org.omg.CORBA.ORB orb) throws java.rmi.RemoteException;
    public static ValueHandler createValueHandler();
    public static String getCodebase(Class clz);
    public static Tie getTie(java.rmi.Remote target);
    public static boolean isLocal(Stub stub) throws java.rmi.RemoteException;
    public static Class loadClass(String className, String remoteCodebase, ClassLoader loader)
        throws ClassNotFoundException;
    public static java.rmi.RemoteException mapSystemException(org.omg.CORBA.SystemException ex);
    public static Object readAny(org.omg.CORBA.portable.InputStream in);
    public static void registerTarget(Tie tie, java.rmi.Remote target);
    public static void unexportObject(java.rmi.Remote target) throws java.rmi.NoSuchObjectException;
    public static java.rmi.RemoteException wrapException(Throwable orig);
    public static void writeAbstractObject(org.omg.CORBA.portable.OutputStream out, Object obj);
    public static void writeAny(org.omg.CORBA.portable.OutputStream out, Object obj);
    public static void writeRemoteObject(org.omg.CORBA.portable.OutputStream out, Object obj);
}
```

UtilDelegate

javax.rmi.CORBA

This interface represents a delegate that implements the functionality exported by the javax.rmi.CORBA.Util class. You specify the delegate your Util instances should use by setting the javax.rmi.CORBA.UtilClass system property.

```
public interface UtilDelegate {
// Public Instance Methods
    public abstract Object copyObject(Object obj, org.omg.CORBA.ORB orb) throws java.rmi.RemoteException;
    public abstract Object[ ] copyObjects(Object[ ] obj, org.omg.CORBA.ORB orb) throws java.rmi.RemoteException;
    public abstract ValueHandler createValueHandler();
    public abstract String getCodebase(Class clz);
    public abstract Tie getTie(java.rmi.Remote target);
    public abstract boolean isLocal(Stub stub) throws java.rmi.RemoteException;
    public abstract Class loadClass(String className, String remoteCodebase, ClassLoader loader)
        throws ClassNotFoundException;
    public abstract java.rmi.RemoteException mapSystemException(org.omg.CORBA.SystemException ex);
    public abstract Object readAny(org.omg.CORBA.portable.InputStream in);
    public abstract void registerTarget(Tie tie, java.rmi.Remote target);
    public abstract void unexportObject(java.rmi.Remote target) throws java.rmi.NoSuchObjectException;
    public abstract java.rmi.RemoteException wrapException(Throwable obj);
    public abstract void writeAbstractObject(org.omg.CORBA.portable.OutputStream out, Object obj);
    public abstract void writeAny(org.omg.CORBA.portable.OutputStream out, Object obj);
    public abstract void writeRemoteObject(org.omg.CORBA.portable.OutputStream out, Object obj);
}
```

ValueHandler

javax.rmi.CORBA

A ValueHandler is responsible for marshalling/unmarshalling objects over CORBA IOP streams.

```
public interface ValueHandler {
// Public Instance Methods
   public abstract String getRMIRepositoryID(Class clz);
   public abstract org.omg.SendingContext.RunTime getRunTimeCodeBase();
   public abstract boolean isCustomMarshaled(Class clz);
   public abstract Serializable readValue(org.omg.CORBA.portable.InputStream in, int offset, Class clz,
                              String repositoryID, org.omg.SendingContext.RunTime sender);
   public abstract Serializable writeReplace(Serializable value);
   public abstract void writeValue(org.omg.CORBA.portable.OutputStream out, Serializable value);
}
```

Returned By: Util.createValueHandler(), UtilDelegate.createValueHandler()

CHAPTER 36

javax.servlet

The javax.servlet package is the core of the Servlet API. It contains the classes necessary for a standard, protocol-independent servlet or filter. In addition, it provides a helper class, GenericServlet, to make it easier to implement the Servlet interface. As of version 2.3 of the Servlet API, this package also includes the interfaces and classes to support filters for request pre- and post-processing.

In Servlet 2.2, the concept of a Web Application was formalized. Hence, the javax.servlet package also includes classes to allow servlets to interact with their parent application via the ServletContext object. Version 2.3 added an event listener to web applications, allowing developers to register classes that participate in the web application's lifecycle.

Interfaces:

public interface **Filter**;
public interface **FilterChain**;
public interface **FilterConfig**;
public interface **RequestDispatcher**;
public interface **Servlet**;
public interface **ServletConfig**;
public interface **ServletContext**;
public interface **ServletRequest**;
public interface **ServletResponse**;
public interface **SingleThreadModel**;

Events:

public class **ServletContextEvent** extends java.util.EventObject;
  └ public class **ServletContextAttributeEvent** extends ServletContextEvent;

Event Listeners:

public interface **ServletContextAttributeListener** extends java.util.EventListener;

public interface **ServletContextListener** extends java.util.EventListener;

Other Classes:

public abstract class **GenericServlet** implements Servlet, ServletConfig, Serializable;
public abstract class **ServletInputStream** extends java.io.InputStream;
public abstract class **ServletOutputStream** extends java.io.OutputStream;
public class **ServletRequestWrapper** implements ServletRequest;
public class **ServletResponseWrapper** implements ServletResponse;

Exceptions:

public class **ServletException** extends Exception;
   └ public class **UnavailableException** extends ServletException;

Filter

javax.servlet

A filter processes a request on either side of the target content. If a web application is configured to filter requests aimed at particular targets (either servlets or paths), the server will instead call the doFilter() method of the first Filter installed for that resource. A FilterChain object passed to the doFilter() method can be used by the filter to call the next filter in the sequence, or to invoke the target resource if all filters have been processed. When the doFilter() method finishes executing, control is ceded back to the web server or the preceding filter.

The Filter interface also provides an init() method which will be called and allowed finish execution before any doFilter() methods are called.

```
public interface Filter {
// Public Instance Methods
    public abstract void destroy();
    public abstract void doFilter(ServletRequest request, ServletResponse response, FilterChain chain)
        throws IOException, ServletException;
    public abstract void init(FilterConfig filterConfig) throws ServletException;
}
```

FilterChain

javax.servlet

A class that implements the FilterChain interface is passed to the doFilter() method of Filter. This allows a filter to pass the request on to the next filter in the chain by invoking the doFilter() method of the next filter configured for that resource or, if all filters have been processed, invoking the target resource.

```
public interface FilterChain {
// Public Instance Methods
    public abstract void doFilter(ServletRequest request, ServletResponse response) throws IOException,
        ServletException;
}
```

Passed To: javax.servlet.Filter.doFilter()

FilterConfig

javax.servlet

The FilterConfig interface is analogous to the ServletConfig interface. It provides the init() method of a Filter with information about the filter's configuration within a web application, as well as a reference to the current ServletContext object.

```
public interface FilterConfig {
// Public Instance Methods
    public abstract String getFilterName();
    public abstract String getInitParameter(String name);
    public abstract java.util.Enumeration getInitParameterNames();
    public abstract ServletContext getServletContext();
}
```

Passed To: javax.servlet.Filter.init()

GenericServlet
javax.servlet

Servlets 2.0

serializable

The GenericServlet class provides a basic implementation of the Servlet and ServletConfig interfaces. If you are creating a protocol-independent servlet, you probably want to subclass this class rather than implement the Servlet interface directly. Note that the service() method is declared as abstract; this is the only method you have to override to implement a generic servlet.

GenericServlet includes basic implementations of the init() and destroy() methods, which perform basic setup and cleanup tasks, respectively. The init() method that takes a ServletConfig object stores that object for later use. This means that if you override the method and fail to call the super.init(ServletConfig) method, you won't be able to use the ServletConfig methods later. In version 2.1 of the Servlet API, you can override a no-argument version of init() that is dispatched by the default init(ServletConfig) method of GenericServlet.

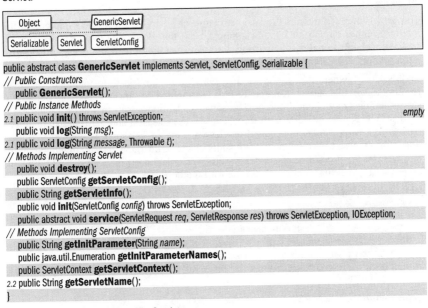

```
public abstract class GenericServlet implements Servlet, ServletConfig, Serializable {
// Public Constructors
    public GenericServlet();
// Public Instance Methods
2.1 public void init() throws ServletException;                                              empty
    public void log(String msg);
2.1 public void log(String message, Throwable t);
// Methods Implementing Servlet
    public void destroy();
    public ServletConfig getServletConfig();
    public String getServletInfo();
    public void init(ServletConfig config) throws ServletException;
    public abstract void service(ServletRequest req, ServletResponse res) throws ServletException, IOException;
// Methods Implementing ServletConfig
    public String getInitParameter(String name);
    public java.util.Enumeration getInitParameterNames();
    public ServletContext getServletContext();
2.2 public String getServletName();
}
```

Subclasses: javax.servlet.http.HttpServlet

RequestDispatcher   Servlets 2.1
javax.servlet

A RequestDispatcher allows a servlet to forward a request to another resource, or to include another resource in its output. The web server is responsible for creating RequestDispatcher objects as well as properly retrieving content for them. The forward() method can be used before a servlet has returned content to the client and will cause the target of the dispatcher to serve the entire request. This is similar issuing a redirect to the client, but since the redirection occurs on the server side, the browser believes it is still at the original URL, which may have consequences for relative paths and related behavior. The include() method enables a server-side include, merging the output of the included resource with the servlet's output stream. If the included resources is a servlet, it cannot change any response codes or headers.

```
public interface RequestDispatcher {
// Public Instance Methods
    public abstract void forward(ServletRequest request, ServletResponse response) throws ServletException,
        IOException;
    public abstract void include(ServletRequest request, ServletResponse response) throws ServletException,
        IOException;
}
```

Returned By: ServletContext.{getNamedDispatcher(), getRequestDispatcher()},
ServletRequest.getRequestDispatcher(), ServletRequestWrapper.getRequestDispatcher()

Servlet   Servlets 2.0
javax.servlet

The Servlet interface defines the basic structure of a servlet. All servlets implement this interface, either directly or by subclassing a class that does. The interface declares the basic servlet functionality—initializing a servlet, handling client requests, and destroying a servlet.

init() is called when the servlet is first initialized. Since init() is intended to create resources that the servlet can reuse, it is guaranteed to finish executing before the servlet handles any client requests. The server calls the service() method for each client request. The servlet interacts with the client via ServletRequest and ServletResponse objects passed to service(). destroy() is called to clean up resources (such as database connections) or save state when the server shuts down. The getServletInfo() method should return a String that describes a servlet, and the getServletConfig() method should return the ServletConfig object that was passed to the init() method.

```
public interface Servlet {
// Public Instance Methods
    public abstract void destroy();
    public abstract ServletConfig getServletConfig();
    public abstract String getServletInfo();
    public abstract void init(ServletConfig config) throws ServletException;
    public abstract void service(ServletRequest req, ServletResponse res) throws ServletException, IOException;
}
```

Implementations: GenericServlet, javax.servlet.jsp.JspPage

Passed To: UnavailableException.UnavailableException(),
javax.servlet.jsp.JspFactory.getPageContext(), javax.servlet.jsp.PageContext.initialize()

Returned By: ServletContext.getServlet(), UnavailableException.getServlet()

ServletConfig   Servlets 2.0

javax.servlet

A ServletConfig object passes configuration information from the server to a servlet. ServletConfig supports initialization parameters (also known simply as init parameters) defined by the server administrator for a particular servlet. These parameters are accessed via the getInitParameter() and getInitParameterNames() methods. ServletConfig also includes a ServletContext object, accessible via getServletContext(), for direct interaction with the server.

```
public interface ServletConfig {
// Public Instance Methods
    public abstract String getInitParameter(String name);
    public abstract java.util.Enumeration getInitParameterNames();
    public abstract ServletContext getServletContext();
2.2 public abstract String getServletName();
}
```

Implementations: GenericServlet

Passed To: GenericServlet.init(), Servlet.init(), javax.xml.messaging.JAXMServlet.init()

Returned By: GenericServlet.getServletConfig(), Servlet.getServletConfig(), javax.servlet.jsp.PageContext.getServletConfig()

ServletContext   Servlets 2.0

javax.servlet

ServletContext defines methods that allow a servlet to interact with the host server. This includes reading server-specific attributes, finding information about particular files located on the server, and writing to the server log files. The ServletContext also allows creation of RequestDispatcher objects. As of the Servlet 2.2 API, which introduced web applications, the ServletContext has been formalized as a programmatic interface to a web application. Each web application has its own ServletContext, which is shared by all of the servlets configured in the web application. The servlets can use the setAttribute() and getAttribute() methods of the ServletContext to share information throughout a web application.

The getServlet(), getServletNames() and getServlets() methods were deprecated in versions 2.0 and 2.1 of the Servlet API, and have not been directly replaced. Instead of accessing each other directly, servlets should share information via the context attributes.

```
public interface ServletContext {
// Property Accessor Methods (by property name)
2.1 public abstract java.util.Enumeration getAttributeNames();
2.2 public abstract java.util.Enumeration getInitParameterNames();
2.1 public abstract int getMajorVersion();
2.1 public abstract int getMinorVersion();
    public abstract String getServerInfo();
2.3 public abstract String getServletContextName();
// Public Instance Methods
    public abstract Object getAttribute(String name);
2.1 public abstract ServletContext getContext(String uripath);
2.2 public abstract String getInitParameter(String name);
    public abstract String getMimeType(String file);
2.2 public abstract RequestDispatcher getNamedDispatcher(String name);
    public abstract String getRealPath(String path);
2.1 public abstract RequestDispatcher getRequestDispatcher(String path);
```

2.1 public abstract java.net.URL **getResource**(String *path*) throws java.net.MalformedURLException;
2.1 public abstract java.io.InputStream **getResourceAsStream**(String *path*);
2.3 public abstract java.util.Set **getResourcePaths**(String *path*);
    public abstract void **log**(String *msg*);
2.1 public abstract void **log**(String *message*, Throwable *throwable*);
2.1 public abstract void **removeAttribute**(String *name*);
2.1 public abstract void **setAttribute**(String *name*, Object *object*);
    // Deprecated Public Methods
  #   public abstract Servlet **getServlet**(String *name*) throws ServletException;
  #   public abstract java.util.Enumeration **getServletNames**();
  #   public abstract java.util.Enumeration **getServlets**();
  #   public abstract void **log**(Exception *exception*, String *msg*);
}

Passed To: ServletContextAttributeEvent.ServletContextAttributeEvent(),
ServletContextEvent.ServletContextEvent()

Returned By: FilterConfig.getServletContext(), GenericServlet.getServletContext(),
ServletConfig.getServletContext(), ServletContext.getContext(), ServletContextEvent.getServletContext(),
javax.servlet.http.HttpSession.getServletContext(), javax.servlet.jsp.PageContext.getServletContext()

ServletContextAttributeEvent

Servlets 2.3

javax.servlet

serializable event

This class is an event notification passed to a ServletContextAttribueListener. The getName()
and getValue() methods return the name and value of the changed attribute. The get-
Value() method returns the old value of the attribute for replacements and deletions.

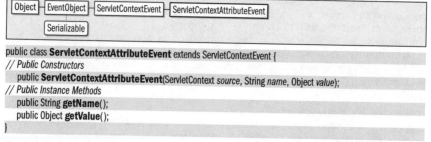

```
public class ServletContextAttributeEvent extends ServletContextEvent {
// Public Constructors
    public ServletContextAttributeEvent(ServletContext source, String name, Object value);
// Public Instance Methods
    public String getName();
    public Object getValue();
}
```

Passed To: ServletContextAttributeListener.{attributeAdded(), attributeRemoved(), attributeReplaced()}

ServletContextAttributeListener

Servlets 2.3

javax.servlet

event listener

Classes that implement this interface can be configured within a web application to
receive a notification when the attribute list in a servlet context has been modified.
Context attribute listeners need to be configured in the *web.xml* file for the web application. They cannot be registered programmatically.

```
public interface ServletContextAttributeListener extends java.util.EventListener {
// Public Instance Methods
    public abstract void attributeAdded(ServletContextAttributeEvent scab);
    public abstract void attributeRemoved(ServletContextAttributeEvent scab);
```

```
    public abstract void attributeReplaced(ServletContextAttributeEvent scab);
}
```

ServletContextEvent

javax.servlet   *serializable event*

An event notification passed to a ServletContextListener; it provides access to the Servlet-
Context that triggered the event.

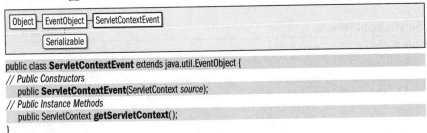

```
public class ServletContextEvent extends java.util.EventObject {
// Public Constructors
    public ServletContextEvent(ServletContext source);
// Public Instance Methods
    public ServletContext getServletContext();
}
```

Subclasses: ServletContextAttributeEvent

Passed To: ServletContextListener.{contextDestroyed(), contextInitialized()}

ServletContextListener

javax.servlet   *event listener*

Classes that implement this interface can be configured within a web application to
receive notifications of servlet context lifecycle events (creation and destruction). Since
the contextInitialized() method will be allowed to complete before the web application
begins to process client requests, ServletContextListener objects can be used to create
application level objects, such as configuration managers or connection pools, for use
by the servlets in the application.

```
public interface ServletContextListener extends java.util.EventListener {
// Public Instance Methods
    public abstract void contextDestroyed(ServletContextEvent sce);
    public abstract void contextInitialized(ServletContextEvent sce);
}
```

ServletException

javax.servlet   *serializable checked*

A generic Exception class used for basic servlet errors. In version 2.1, a servlet can specify a Throwable root cause for this exception (using the constructors that accept Throwable
parameters). The root cause can be retrieved with the getRootCause() method.

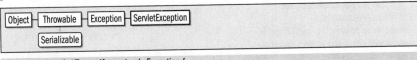

```
public class ServletException extends Exception {
// Public Constructors
    public ServletException();
```

2.1 public **ServletException**(Throwable *rootCause*);
   public **ServletException**(String *message*);
2.1 public **ServletException**(String *message*, Throwable *rootCause*);
// Public Instance Methods
2.1 public Throwable **getRootCause**();   *default:null*
}

Subclasses: UnavailableException

Thrown By: Too many methods to list.

ServletInputStream   Servlets 2.0
javax.servlet

ServletInputStream provides an input stream for reading data from a client request. A servlet can get a ServletInputStream by calling the getInputStream() method of ServletRequest. While ServletInputStream does contain a readLine() method for reading textual data one line at a time, this functionality was taken over by BufferedReader objects and the getReader() method of ServletRequest in version 2.0 of the Servlet API. Thus, ServletInput-Stream should only be used to read binary data, generally in the context of a filtering servlet.

Object — InputStream — ServletInputStream

public abstract class **ServletInputStream** extends java.io.InputStream {
// Protected Constructors
   protected **ServletInputStream**();
// Public Instance Methods
   public int **readLine**(byte[ ] *b*, int *off*, int *len*) throws IOException;
}

Passed To: javax.servlet.http.HttpUtils.parsePostData()

Returned By: ServletRequest.getInputStream(), ServletRequestWrapper.getInputStream()

ServletOutputStream   Servlets 2.0
javax.servlet

ServletOutputStream provides an output stream for sending binary data back to a client. A servlet can get a ServletOutputStream by calling the getOutputStream() method of ServletRe-sponse. ServletOutputStream was the only available output method in version 1.0 of the Servlet API. For text and HTML output, it has been supplanted by PrintWriter objects pro-duced by the getWriter() method of ServletResponse. The various print() and println() meth-ods should therefore be regarded as legacies.

Object — OutputStream — ServletOutputStream

public abstract class **ServletOutputStream** extends java.io.OutputStream {
// Protected Constructors
   protected **ServletOutputStream**();
// Public Instance Methods
   public void **print**(long *l*) throws IOException;
   public void **print**(int *i*) throws IOException;
   public void **print**(double *d*) throws IOException;
   public void **print**(float *f*) throws IOException;
   public void **print**(String *s*) throws IOException;

```
    public void print(boolean b) throws IOException;
    public void print(char c) throws IOException;
    public void println() throws IOException;
    public void println(long l) throws IOException;
    public void println(int i) throws IOException;
    public void println(double d) throws IOException;
    public void println(float f) throws IOException;
    public void println(String s) throws IOException;
    public void println(boolean b) throws IOException;
    public void println(char c) throws IOException;
}
```

Returned By: ServletResponse.getOutputStream(), ServletResponseWrapper.getOutputStream()

ServletRequest

Servlets 2.0

javax.servlet

A ServletRequest object encapsulates information about a client request. The server passes a ServletRequest object to the service() method of a servlet. ServletRequest provides access to request parameters, such as form values or other request-specific parameters. These are accessed using the getParameterNames(), getParameter(), and getParameterValues() methods. Raw request data can be read by the getReader() method (for textual data) and the getInputStream() method (for binary data). The getContentType(), getContentLength(), and getCharacterEncoding() methods can help retrieve this information. Other methods provide information about the client (getRemoteAddr(), getRemoteHost()), the request itself (getScheme(), getProtocol()), and the server (getServerName(), getServerPort()). Version 2.1 also adds the getAttribute() and setAttribute() methods, which are generally used in conjunction with the new RequestDispatcher interface.

```
public interface ServletRequest {
// Property Accessor Methods (by property name)
2.1  public abstract java.util.Enumeration getAttributeNames();
     public abstract String getCharacterEncoding();
2.3  public abstract void setCharacterEncoding(String env) throws UnsupportedEncodingException;
     public abstract int getContentLength();
     public abstract String getContentType();
     public abstract ServletInputStream getInputStream() throws IOException;
2.2  public abstract java.util.Locale getLocale();
2.2  public abstract java.util.Enumeration getLocales();
2.3  public abstract java.util.Map getParameterMap();
     public abstract java.util.Enumeration getParameterNames();
     public abstract String getProtocol();
     public abstract BufferedReader getReader() throws IOException;
     public abstract String getRemoteAddr();
     public abstract String getRemoteHost();
     public abstract String getScheme();
2.2  public abstract boolean isSecure();
     public abstract String getServerName();
     public abstract int getServerPort();
// Public Instance Methods
     public abstract Object getAttribute(String name);
     public abstract String getParameter(String name);
     public abstract String[] getParameterValues(String name);
2.2  public abstract RequestDispatcher getRequestDispatcher(String path);
2.2  public abstract void removeAttribute(String name);
2.1  public abstract void setAttribute(String name, Object o);
```

# public abstract String **getRealPath**(String *path*);
}

Implementations: ServletRequestWrapper, javax.servlet.http.HttpServletRequest

Passed To: javax.servlet.Filter.doFilter(), FilterChain.doFilter(), GenericServlet.service(), RequestDispatcher.{forward(), include()}, Servlet.service(), ServletRequestWrapper.{ServletRequestWrapper(), setRequest()}, javax.servlet.http.HttpServlet.service(), javax.servlet.jsp.JspFactory.getPageContext(), javax.servlet.jsp.PageContext.initialize()

Returned By: ServletRequestWrapper.getRequest(), javax.servlet.jsp.PageContext.getRequest()

ServletRequestWrapper   Servlets 2.3

javax.servlet

A convenience method that can be used by filter developers to modify the behavior of a ServletRequest object. The default implementation of each method calls through to the original ServletRequest object, and methods can be selectively overridden to provide additional functionality. ServletRequestWrapper objects can also be used in calls to the forward() and include() methods of RequestDispatcher.

```
Object ├─ ServletRequestWrapper ┈┈ ServletRequest
```

```
public class ServletRequestWrapper implements ServletRequest {
// Public Constructors
    public ServletRequestWrapper(ServletRequest request);
// Public Instance Methods
    public ServletRequest getRequest();
    public void setRequest(ServletRequest request);
// Methods Implementing ServletRequest
    public Object getAttribute(String name);
    public java.util.Enumeration getAttributeNames();
    public String getCharacterEncoding();
    public int getContentLength();
    public String getContentType();
    public ServletInputStream getInputStream() throws IOException;
    public java.util.Locale getLocale();
    public java.util.Enumeration getLocales();
    public String getParameter(String name);
    public java.util.Map getParameterMap();
    public java.util.Enumeration getParameterNames();
    public String[ ] getParameterValues(String name);
    public String getProtocol();
    public BufferedReader getReader() throws IOException;
    public String getRealPath(String path);
    public String getRemoteAddr();
    public String getRemoteHost();
    public RequestDispatcher getRequestDispatcher(String path);
    public String getScheme();
    public String getServerName();
    public int getServerPort();
    public boolean isSecure();
    public void removeAttribute(String name);
    public void setAttribute(String name, Object o);
```

```
    public void setCharacterEncoding(String enc) throws UnsupportedEncodingException;
}
```

Subclasses: javax.servlet.http.HttpServletRequestWrapper

ServletResponse   Servlets 2.0

javax.servlet

The ServletResponse object sends MIME encoded data back to the client. The interface defines a getOutputStream() method that returns a ServletOutputStream for sending binary data and a getWriter() method that returns a PrintWriter for sending textual data. The setContentType() and setContentLength() methods can be used to explicitly set the content type and content length (often necessary for keep-alive connections and other tasks). If you call setContentType(), you should do so before you call getWriter(), as getWriter() consults the content type to determine which charset to use.

```
public interface ServletResponse {
// Property Accessor Methods (by property name)
2.2 public abstract int getBufferSize();
2.2 public abstract void setBufferSize(int size);
    public abstract String getCharacterEncoding();
2.2 public abstract boolean isCommitted();
    public abstract void setContentLength(int len);
    public abstract void setContentType(String type);
2.2 public abstract java.util.Locale getLocale();
2.2 public abstract void setLocale(java.util.Locale loc);
    public abstract ServletOutputStream getOutputStream() throws IOException;
    public abstract PrintWriter getWriter() throws IOException;
// Public Instance Methods
2.2 public abstract void flushBuffer() throws IOException;
2.2 public abstract void reset();
2.3 public abstract void resetBuffer();
}
```

Implementations: ServletResponseWrapper, javax.servlet.http.HttpServletResponse

Passed To: javax.servlet.Filter.doFilter(), FilterChain.doFilter(), GenericServlet.service(), RequestDispatcher.{forward(), include()}, Servlet.service(), ServletResponseWrapper.{ServletResponseWrapper(), setResponse()}, javax.servlet.http.HttpServlet.service(), javax.servlet.jsp.JspFactory.getPageContext(), javax.servlet.jsp.PageContext.initialize()

Returned By: ServletResponseWrapper.getResponse(), javax.servlet.jsp.PageContext.getResponse()

ServletResponseWrapper   Servlets 2.3

javax.servlet

A convenience method that can be used by filter developers to modify the behavior of a ServletResponse object. The default implementation of each method calls through to the original ServletResponse object, and methods can be selectively overridden to provide additional functionality. ServletResponseWrapper objects can also be used in calls to the forward() and include() methods of RequestDispatcher.

```
Object ├─ ServletResponseWrapper ┄ ServletResponse
```

```
public class ServletResponseWrapper implements ServletResponse {
// Public Constructors
```

```
    public ServletResponseWrapper(ServletResponse response);
// Public Instance Methods
    public ServletResponse getResponse();
    public void setResponse(ServletResponse response);
// Methods Implementing ServletResponse
    public void flushBuffer() throws IOException;
    public int getBufferSize();
    public String getCharacterEncoding();
    public java.util.Locale getLocale();
    public ServletOutputStream getOutputStream() throws IOException;
    public PrintWriter getWriter() throws IOException;
    public boolean isCommitted();
    public void reset();
    public void resetBuffer();
    public void setBufferSize(int size);
    public void setContentLength(int len);
    public void setContentType(String type);
    public void setLocale(java.util.Locale loc);
}
```

Subclasses: javax.servlet.http.HttpServletResponseWrapper

SingleThreadModel

Servlets 2.0

javax.servlet

SingleThreadModel is a tag interface that tells the server to create a pool of servlet instances to serve individual requests. In this case, the server ensures that each instance of the servlet handles only one service request at a time. SingleThreadModel provides easy thread-safety, but imposes performance penalties.

```
public interface SingleThreadModel {
}
```

UnavailableException

Servlets 2.0

javax.servlet

serializable checked

This exception is thrown by a servlet or a filter to indicate it's currently unavailable. The isPermanent() method indicates whether the resource is permanently unavailable or just temporarily unavailable. If the problem is temporary, use the getUnavailableSeconds() method to obtain the expected duration in seconds.

```
public class UnavailableException extends ServletException {
// Public Constructors
2.2 public UnavailableException(String msg);
 #  public UnavailableException(Servlet servlet, String msg);
2.2 public UnavailableException(String msg, int seconds);
 #  public UnavailableException(int seconds, Servlet servlet, String msg);
// Public Instance Methods
    public int getUnavailableSeconds();
    public boolean isPermanent();
// Deprecated Public Methods
 #  public Servlet getServlet();
}
```

CHAPTER 37

javax.servlet.http

Package javax.servlet.http   Servlets 2.0

The javax.servlet.http package supports thedevelopment of servlets that use the HTTP protocol. The classes inthis package extend the basic servlet functionality to support variousHTTP specific features, including request and response headers,different request methods, and cookies. The abstractHttpServlet class extendsjavax.servlet.GenericServlet and serves as the baseclass for HTTP servlets. The HttpServletRequest andHttpServletResponse allow additional interactionwith the client. Finally, since the HTTP protocol is inherentlystateless, the package also includes HttpSessionand some related classes to support session tracking.

Interfaces:

public interface **HttpServletRequest** extends javax.servlet.ServletRequest;
public interface **HttpServletResponse** extends javax.servlet.ServletResponse;
public interface **HttpSession**;
public interface **HttpSessionContext**;

Events:

public class **HttpSessionEvent** extends java.util.EventObject;
    └ public class **HttpSessionBindingEvent** extends HttpSessionEvent;

Event Listeners:

public interface **HttpSessionActivationListener** extends java.util.EventListener;
public interface **HttpSessionAttributeListener** extends java.util.EventListener;
public interface **HttpSessionBindingListener** extends java.util.EventListener;
public interface **HttpSessionListener** extends java.util.EventListener;

Other Classes:

public class **Cookie** implements Cloneable;
public abstract class **HttpServlet** extends javax.servlet.GenericServlet implements Serializable;

```
public class HttpServletRequestWrapper extends javax.servlet.ServletRequestWrapper
                                        implements HttpServletRequest;
public class HttpServletResponseWrapper extends javax.servlet.ServletResponseWrapper
                                        implements HttpServletResponse;
public class HttpUtils;
```

Cookie

Servlets 2.0

javax.servlet.http

cloneable

The Cookie class provides servlets with an easy way to read, create, and manipulate
HTTP-style cookies. Cookies provide a way to store a small amount of information on
the client and are typically used for session tracking or storing user-configuration information. The getCookies() method of HttpServletRequest returns an array of Cookie objects.
To set a new cookie on the client, a servlet creates a new Cookie object and uses the
addCookie() method of HttpServletResponse. This must be done before sending any other
content, since cookies are created within the HTTP header stream. The various methods of the Cookie class allow a servlet to set and get various attributes of a Cookie object,
such as its path and domain.

```
Object — Cookie ┈ Cloneable

public class Cookie implements Cloneable {
// Public Constructors
    public Cookie(String name, String value);
// Property Accessor Methods (by property name)
    public String getComment();
    public void setComment(String purpose);
    public String getDomain();
    public void setDomain(String pattern);
    public int getMaxAge();
    public void setMaxAge(int expiry);
    public String getName();
    public String getPath();
    public void setPath(String uri);
    public boolean getSecure();
    public void setSecure(boolean flag);
    public String getValue();
    public void setValue(String newValue);
    public int getVersion();
    public void setVersion(int v);
// Public Methods Overriding Object
    public Object clone();
}
```

Passed To: HttpServletResponse.addCookie(), HttpServletResponseWrapper.addCookie()

Returned By: HttpServletRequest.getCookies(), HttpServletRequestWrapper.getCookies()

HttpServlet

Servlets 2.0

javax.servlet.http

serializable

The abstract HttpServlet class serves as a framework for servlets that generate content for
the World Wide Web using the HTTP protocol. Rather than overriding the service()
method, you should override one or more of the method-specific request handlers
(doGet(), doPost(), doPut(), etc.). The default service() implementation dispatches incoming
requests to the appropriate methods, and so should not be overridden. The default
implementations of doGet(), doPost(), doDelete(), and doPut() all return an HTTP

BAD_REQUEST error, so if you want to handle one of these kinds of requests, you must override the appropriate method.

A web server calls getLastModified() in response to conditional GET requests. The default implementation returns -1. If you know when the output of your servlet last changed, you can return that time, specified in milliseconds since midnight, January 1, 1970 GMT, instead. This allows web browsers to cache your servlet's response.

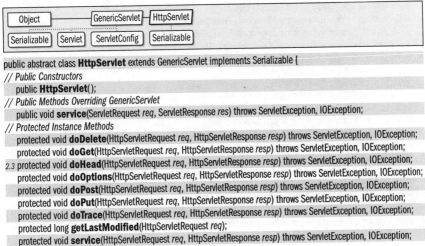

```
public abstract class HttpServlet extends GenericServlet implements Serializable {
// Public Constructors
     public HttpServlet();
// Public Methods Overriding GenericServlet
     public void service(ServletRequest req, ServletResponse res) throws ServletException, IOException;
// Protected Instance Methods
     protected void doDelete(HttpServletRequest req, HttpServletResponse resp) throws ServletException, IOException;
     protected void doGet(HttpServletRequest req, HttpServletResponse resp) throws ServletException, IOException;
2.3  protected void doHead(HttpServletRequest req, HttpServletResponse resp) throws ServletException, IOException;
     protected void doOptions(HttpServletRequest req, HttpServletResponse resp) throws ServletException, IOException;
     protected void doPost(HttpServletRequest req, HttpServletResponse resp) throws ServletException, IOException;
     protected void doPut(HttpServletRequest req, HttpServletResponse resp) throws ServletException, IOException;
     protected void doTrace(HttpServletRequest req, HttpServletResponse resp) throws ServletException, IOException;
     protected long getLastModified(HttpServletRequest req);
     protected void service(HttpServletRequest req, HttpServletResponse resp) throws ServletException, IOException;
}
```

Subclasses: javax.xml.messaging.JAXMServlet

HttpServletRequest   Servlets 2.0

javax.servlet.http

HttpServletRequest extends javax.servlet.ServletRequest and provides a number of methods that make it easy to access specific information related to an HTTP request. This includes methods for directly accessing HTTP headers: getHeader(), getIntHeader(), getDate-Header(), and getHeaderNames(). Other methods return various information about the request, including getMethod(), which returns the request method (GET, POST, etc), get-PathInfo(), which returns any extra path information attached to the request, getPathTrans-lated(), which translates the extra path information into a filesystem path, and getServletPath(), which returns the URI pointing to the current servlet, minus any extra path information. The interface also includes the getCookies() method for retrieving cookie data and getSession() for accessing the current HttpSession object.

```
ServletRequest    HttpServletRequest

public interface HttpServletRequest extends ServletRequest {
// Public Constants
2.3  public static final String BASIC_AUTH;                                    ="BASIC"
2.3  public static final String CLIENT_CERT_AUTH;                        ="CLIENT_CERT"
2.3  public static final String DIGEST_AUTH;                                  ="DIGEST"
2.3  public static final String FORM_AUTH;                                      ="FORM"
// Property Accessor Methods (by property name)
     public abstract String getAuthType();
2.2  public abstract String getContextPath();
     public abstract Cookie[ ] getCookies();
```

```
    public abstract java.util.Enumeration getHeaderNames();
    public abstract String getMethod();
    public abstract String getPathInfo();
    public abstract String getPathTranslated();
    public abstract String getQueryString();
    public abstract String getRemoteUser();
    public abstract String getRequestedSessionId();
    public abstract boolean isRequestedSessionIdFromCookie();
2.1 public abstract boolean isRequestedSessionIdFromURL();
    public abstract boolean isRequestedSessionIdValid();
    public abstract String getRequestURI();
2.3 public abstract StringBuffer getRequestURL();
    public abstract String getServletPath();
2.1 public abstract HttpSession getSession();
    public abstract HttpSession getSession(boolean create);
2.2 public abstract java.security.Principal getUserPrincipal();
// Public Instance Methods
    public abstract long getDateHeader(String name);
    public abstract String getHeader(String name);
2.2 public abstract java.util.Enumeration getHeaders(String name);
    public abstract int getIntHeader(String name);
2.2 public abstract boolean isUserInRole(String role);
// Deprecated Public Methods
#   public abstract boolean isRequestedSessionIdFromUrl();
}
```

Implementations: HttpServletRequestWrapper

Passed To: HttpServlet.{doDelete(), doGet(), doHead(), doOptions(), doPost(), doPut(), doTrace(), getLastModified(), service()}, HttpServletRequestWrapper.HttpServletRequestWrapper(), HttpUtils.getRequestURL(), javax.servlet.jsp.HttpJspPage._jspService(), javax.xml.messaging.JAXMServlet.{doPost(), getHeaders()}

HttpServletRequestWrapper   Servlets 2.3

javax.servlet.http

This is a convenience class that can be used by filter developers to modify the behavior of a HttpServletRequest object. The default implementation of each method calls through to the original HttpServletRequest object, and methods can be selectively overridden to provide additional functionality. HttpServletRequestWrapper objects can also be used in calls to the forward() and include() methods of RequestDispatcher.

```
public class HttpServletRequestWrapper extends ServletRequestWrapper implements HttpServletRequest {
// Public Constructors
    public HttpServletRequestWrapper(HttpServletRequest request);
// Methods Implementing HttpServletRequest
    public String getAuthType();
    public String getContextPath();
    public Cookie[ ] getCookies();
    public long getDateHeader(String name);
    public String getHeader(String name);
    public java.util.Enumeration getHeaderNames();
```

```
    public java.util.Enumeration getHeaders(String name);
    public int getIntHeader(String name);
    public String getMethod();
    public String getPathInfo();
    public String getPathTranslated();
    public String getQueryString();
    public String getRemoteUser();
    public String getRequestedSessionId();
    public String getRequestURI();
    public StringBuffer getRequestURL();
    public String getServletPath();
    public HttpSession getSession();
    public HttpSession getSession(boolean create);
    public java.security.Principal getUserPrincipal();
    public boolean isRequestedSessionIdFromCookie();
    public boolean isRequestedSessionIdFromURL();
    public boolean isRequestedSessionIdFromUrl();
    public boolean isRequestedSessionIdValid();
    public boolean isUserInRole(String role);
}
```

HttpServletResponse

javax.servlet.http

HttpServletResponse extends javax.servlet.ServletResponse and provides additional methods for HTTP-specific actions and a set of HTTP response code constants. The containsHeader(), setHeader(), setDateHeader(), and setIntHeader() methods allow servlets to set and update specific HTTP response headers. The addCookie() method writes a cookie, represented by a Cookie object, to the client. The sendError() and setStatus() methods allow servlets to set specific HTTP result codes, along with an optional customized error message. The encodeUrl() and encodeRedirectUrl() methods (deprecated in 2.1 in favor of encodeURL() and encodeRedirectURL()) methods support session tracking without the use of cookies. The sendRedirect() method handles an HTTP page redirect.

```
ServletResponse ── HttpServletResponse

public interface HttpServletResponse extends ServletResponse {
// Public Constants
    public static final int SC_ACCEPTED;                        =202
    public static final int SC_BAD_GATEWAY;                     =502
    public static final int SC_BAD_REQUEST;                     =400
    public static final int SC_CONFLICT;                        =409
    public static final int SC_CONTINUE;                        =100
    public static final int SC_CREATED;                         =201
2.2 public static final int SC_EXPECTATION_FAILED;              =417
    public static final int SC_FORBIDDEN;                       =403
    public static final int SC_GATEWAY_TIMEOUT;                 =504
    public static final int SC_GONE;                            =410
    public static final int SC_HTTP_VERSION_NOT_SUPPORTED;      =505
    public static final int SC_INTERNAL_SERVER_ERROR;           =500
    public static final int SC_LENGTH_REQUIRED;                 =411
    public static final int SC_METHOD_NOT_ALLOWED;              =405
    public static final int SC_MOVED_PERMANENTLY;               =301
    public static final int SC_MOVED_TEMPORARILY;               =302
    public static final int SC_MULTIPLE_CHOICES;                =300
```

```
    public static final int SC_NO_CONTENT;                                          =204
    public static final int SC_NON_AUTHORITATIVE_INFORMATION;                       =203
    public static final int SC_NOT_ACCEPTABLE;                                      =406
    public static final int SC_NOT_FOUND;                                           =404
    public static final int SC_NOT_IMPLEMENTED;                                     =501
    public static final int SC_NOT_MODIFIED;                                        =304
    public static final int SC_OK;                                                  =200
    public static final int SC_PARTIAL_CONTENT;                                     =206
    public static final int SC_PAYMENT_REQUIRED;                                    =402
    public static final int SC_PRECONDITION_FAILED;                                 =412
    public static final int SC_PROXY_AUTHENTICATION_REQUIRED;                       =407
    public static final int SC_REQUEST_ENTITY_TOO_LARGE;                            =413
    public static final int SC_REQUEST_TIMEOUT;                                     =408
    public static final int SC_REQUEST_URI_TOO_LONG;                                =414
2.2 public static final int SC_REQUESTED_RANGE_NOT_SATISFIABLE;                     =416
    public static final int SC_RESET_CONTENT;                                       =205
    public static final int SC_SEE_OTHER;                                           =303
    public static final int SC_SERVICE_UNAVAILABLE;                                 =503
    public static final int SC_SWITCHING_PROTOCOLS;                                 =101
2.3 public static final int SC_TEMPORARY_REDIRECT;                                  =307
    public static final int SC_UNAUTHORIZED;                                        =401
    public static final int SC_UNSUPPORTED_MEDIA_TYPE;                              =415
    public static final int SC_USE_PROXY;                                           =305
// Public Instance Methods
    public abstract void addCookie(Cookie cookie);
2.2 public abstract void addDateHeader(String name, long date);
2.2 public abstract void addHeader(String name, String value);
2.2 public abstract void addIntHeader(String name, int value);
    public abstract boolean containsHeader(String name);
2.1 public abstract String encodeRedirectURL(String url);
2.1 public abstract String encodeURL(String url);
    public abstract void sendError(int sc) throws IOException;
    public abstract void sendError(int sc, String msg) throws IOException;
    public abstract void sendRedirect(String location) throws IOException;
    public abstract void setDateHeader(String name, long date);
    public abstract void setHeader(String name, String value);
    public abstract void setIntHeader(String name, int value);
    public abstract void setStatus(int sc);
// Deprecated Public Methods
#   public abstract String encodeRedirectUrl(String url);
#   public abstract String encodeUrl(String url);
#   public abstract void setStatus(int sc, String sm);
}
```

Implementations: HttpServletResponseWrapper

Passed To: HttpServlet.{doDelete(), doGet(), doHead(), doOptions(), doPost(), doPut(), doTrace(), service()}, HttpServletResponseWrapper.HttpServletResponseWrapper(), javax.servlet.jsp.HttpJspPage._jspService(), javax.xml.messaging.JAXMServlet.{doPost(), putHeaders()}

HttpServletResponseWrapper   Servlets 2.3

javax.servlet.http

A convenience class that can be used by filter developers to modify the behavior of a HttpServletResponse object. The default implementation of each method calls through to the original HttpServletResponse object, and methods can be selectively overridden to provide additional functionality. HttpServletResponseWrapper objects can also be used in calls to the forward() and include() methods of RequestDispatcher.

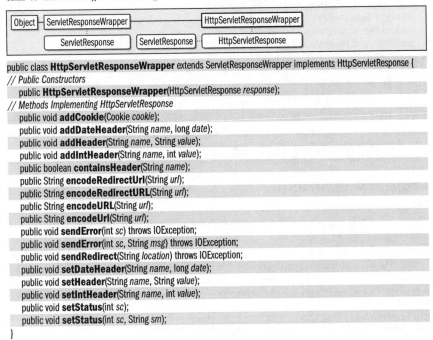

```
public class HttpServletResponseWrapper extends ServletResponseWrapper implements HttpServletResponse {
// Public Constructors
    public HttpServletResponseWrapper(HttpServletResponse response);
// Methods Implementing HttpServletResponse
    public void addCookie(Cookie cookie);
    public void addDateHeader(String name, long date);
    public void addHeader(String name, String value);
    public void addIntHeader(String name, int value);
    public boolean containsHeader(String name);
    public String encodeRedirectUrl(String url);
    public String encodeRedirectURL(String url);
    public String encodeURL(String url);
    public String encodeUrl(String url);
    public void sendError(int sc) throws IOException;
    public void sendError(int sc, String msg) throws IOException;
    public void sendRedirect(String location) throws IOException;
    public void setDateHeader(String name, long date);
    public void setHeader(String name, String value);
    public void setIntHeader(String name, int value);
    public void setStatus(int sc);
    public void setStatus(int sc, String sm);
}
```

HttpSession   Servlets 2.0

javax.servlet.http

The HttpSession interface allows web applications to track individual users across multiple HTTP requests. A session object is associated with each user, either by setting a client cookie or rewriting request URLs using the encodeURL() method of HttpServletResponse. Servlet 2.2 confined the scope of a session object to a particular web application, and replaced the getValue() and putValue() methods with the getAttribute() and setAttribute() methods.

When a session is first created, the isNew() method will return true for the first servlet to process the request. If the session information is lost (e.g., if the client does not support cookies) the container will create a new Session object for each subsequent request.

```
public interface HttpSession {
// Property Accessor Methods (by property name)
2.2 public abstract java.util.Enumeration getAttributeNames();
    public abstract long getCreationTime();
    public abstract String getId();
    public abstract long getLastAccessedTime();
2.1 public abstract int getMaxInactiveInterval();
2.1 public abstract void setMaxInactiveInterval(int interval);
    public abstract boolean isNew();
2.3 public abstract ServletContext getServletContext();
// Public Instance Methods
2.2 public abstract Object getAttribute(String name);
    public abstract void invalidate();
```

```
2.2 public abstract void removeAttribute(String name);
2.2 public abstract void setAttribute(String name, Object value);
// Deprecated Public Methods
#   public abstract HttpSessionContext getSessionContext( );
#   public abstract Object getValue(String name);
#   public abstract String[ ] getValueNames( );
#   public abstract void putValue(String name, Object value);
#   public abstract void removeValue(String name);
}
```

Passed To: HttpSessionBindingEvent.HttpSessionBindingEvent( ), HttpSessionEvent.HttpSessionEvent( )

Returned By: HttpServletRequest.getSession( ), HttpServletRequestWrapper.getSession( ), HttpSessionBindingEvent.getSession( ), HttpSessionContext.getSession( ), HttpSessionEvent.getSession( ), javax.servlet.jsp.PageContext.getSession( )

HttpSessionActivationListener   Servlets 2.3
javax.servlet.http   *event listener*

This is a listener interface that is invoked when a session object is activated or *passivated*. Passivation occurs when a session is persisted to disk or transferred between virtual machines in distributed container environment (in both instances, the session object will be serialized). Sessions should release any non-serializable resources before passivation and reacquire them after activation.

EventListener --- HttpSessionActivationListener

```
public interface HttpSessionActivationListener extends java.util.EventListener {
// Public Instance Methods
    public abstract void sessionDidActivate(HttpSessionEvent se);
    public abstract void sessionWillPassivate(HttpSessionEvent se);
}
```

HttpSessionAttributeListener   Servlets 2.3
javax.servlet.http   *event listener*

This is a listener interface that allows classes to be notified when attributes are bound or unbound from a session. This listener effectively replaces HttpSessionBindingListener, as the getAttribute() and setAttribute() methods have replaced the getValue() and putValue() methods.

EventListener --- HttpSessionAttributeListener

```
public interface HttpSessionAttributeListener extends java.util.EventListener {
// Public Instance Methods
    public abstract void attributeAdded(HttpSessionBindingEvent se);
    public abstract void attributeRemoved(HttpSessionBindingEvent se);
    public abstract void attributeReplaced(HttpSessionBindingEvent se);
}
```

HttpSessionBindingEvent   Servlets 2.0
javax.servlet.http   *serializable event*

An HttpSessionBindingEvent is passed to the appropriate method of an HttpSessionBindingListener when an object is bound to or unbound from an HttpSession. The getName() method returns the name to which the bound object has been assigned, and the getSession() method provides a reference to the session the object is being bound to.

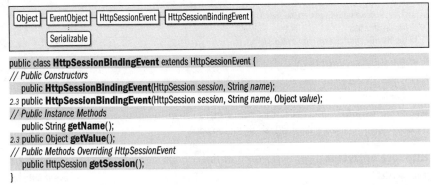

public class **HttpSessionBindingEvent** extends HttpSessionEvent {
// *Public Constructors*
   public **HttpSessionBindingEvent**(HttpSession *session*, String *name*);
2.3 public **HttpSessionBindingEvent**(HttpSession *session*, String *name*, Object *value*);
// *Public Instance Methods*
   public String **getName**();
2.3 public Object **getValue**();
// *Public Methods Overriding HttpSessionEvent*
   public HttpSession **getSession**();
}

Passed To: HttpSessionAttributeListener.{attributeAdded(), attributeRemoved(), attributeReplaced()}, HttpSessionBindingListener.{valueBound(), valueUnbound()}

HttpSessionBindingListener
javax.servlet.http

Servlets 2.0

event listener

A listener interface that allows classes to be notified when attributes are bound or unbound from a session via the getValue() and putValue() methods of HttpSession.

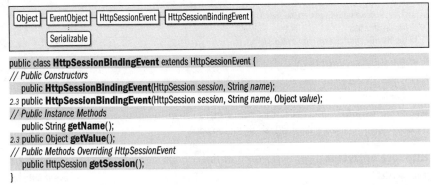

public interface **HttpSessionBindingListener** extends java.util.EventListener {
// *Public Instance Methods*
   public abstract void **valueBound**(HttpSessionBindingEvent *event*);
   public abstract void **valueUnbound**(HttpSessionBindingEvent *event*);
}

HttpSessionContext
javax.servlet.http

Servlets 2.0; Deprecated in Servlets 2.1

This class is deprecated starting with the Java Servlet 2.1 APIs due to security reasons. You should not use this class.

public interface **HttpSessionContext** {
// *Deprecated Public Methods*
 # public abstract java.util.Enumeration **getIds**();
 # public abstract HttpSession **getSession**(String *sessionId*);
}

Returned By: HttpSession.getSessionContext()

HttpSessionEvent
javax.servlet.http

Servlets 2.3

serializable event

This class provides event notifications pertaining to session lifecycle.

```
Object ── EventObject ── HttpSessionEvent
        Serializable
```

```
public class HttpSessionEvent extends java.util.EventObject {
// Public Constructors
   public HttpSessionEvent(HttpSession source);
// Public Instance Methods
   public HttpSession getSession();
}
```

Subclasses: HttpSessionBindingEvent

Passed To: HttpSessionActivationListener.{sessionDidActivate(), sessionWillPassivate()},
HttpSessionListener.{sessionCreated(), sessionDestroyed()}

HttpSessionListener   Servlets 2.3

javax.servlet.http   *event listener*

This is a listener that allows a class to be notified of basic session lifecycle events,
specifically the creation and destruction of a session. This allows for logging and
cleanup of resources.

```
EventListener ┈┈ HttpSessionListener
```

```
public interface HttpSessionListener extends java.util.EventListener {
// Public Instance Methods
   public abstract void sessionCreated(HttpSessionEvent se);
   public abstract void sessionDestroyed(HttpSessionEvent se);
}
```

HttpUtils   Servlets 2.0; Deprecated in Servlets 2.3

javax.servlet.http

The HttpUtils class contains three static methods that perform useful HTTP-related tasks.
getRequestURL() forms a functional approximation of the original request URL, including
scheme, server name, server port, extra path information, and query string, based on an
HttpServletRequest object. The parsePostData() and parseQueryString() methods parse URL-
encoded form variables from an InputStream or a String. In most cases, a servlet should
use the getParameter(), getParameterValues(), and getParameterNames() methods of HttpServletRequest instead.

```
public class HttpUtils {
// Public Constructors
   public HttpUtils();
// Public Class Methods
   public static StringBuffer getRequestURL(HttpServletRequest req);
   public static java.util.Hashtable parsePostData(int len, ServletInputStream in);
   public static java.util.Hashtable parseQueryString(String s);
}
```

CHAPTER 38

javax.servlet.jsp

The javax.servlet.jsp package provides a set of classes, interfaces and exceptions that define a JavaServer page's relationship to both its container and the client.

Interfaces:

public interface **HttpJspPage** extends JspPage;
public interface **JspPage** extends javax.servlet.Servlet;

Classes:

public abstract class **JspEngineInfo**;
public abstract class **JspFactory**;
public abstract class **JspWriter** extends java.io.Writer;
public abstract class **PageContext**;

Exceptions:

public class **JspException** extends Exception;
    └ public class **JspTagException** extends JspException;

HttpJspPage   JSP 1.0
javax.servlet.jsp

This interface is a subclass of the JspPage interface. It defines lifecycle methods for JSP's that are retrieved via the HTTP protocol. This interface adds the _jspService() method, which is generated by the page compiler when a raw .jsp is converted to executable form. Note that this method should never be redefined by a page author.

Servlet ··· JspPage ··· HttpJspPage

public interface **HttpJspPage** extends JspPage {
// Public Instance Methods

```
    public abstract void _jspService(javax.servlet.http.HttpServletRequest request,
                                    javax.servlet.http.HttpServletResponse response) throws ServletException,
        IOException;
}
```

JspEngineInfo

javax.servlet.jsp

An abstract class that provides information on the current version of the JSP specification in use.

```
public abstract class JspEngineInfo {
// Public Constructors
    public JspEngineInfo();
// Public Instance Methods
    public abstract String getSpecificationVersion();
}
```

Returned By: JspFactory.getEngineInfo()

JspException

javax.servlet.jsp   *serializable checked*

A generic JSP exception. This exception supports a root cause that can be used for more complete debugging. A JSP Tag, for instance, can catch an exception internally and bubble up a JspException to the container with the "real" exception attached as the root cause.

```
public class JspException extends Exception {
// Public Constructors
    public JspException();
1.2 public JspException(Throwable rootCause);
    public JspException(String msg);
1.2 public JspException(String message, Throwable rootCause);
// Public Instance Methods
1.2 public Throwable getRootCause();                                    default:null
}
```

Subclasses: JspTagException

Thrown By: javax.servlet.jsp.tagext.BodyTag.doInitBody(),
javax.servlet.jsp.tagext.BodyTagSupport.{doAfterBody(), doEndTag(), doInitBody(), doStartTag()},
javax.servlet.jsp.tagext.IterationTag.doAfterBody(), javax.servlet.jsp.tagext.Tag.{doEndTag(), doStartTag()},
javax.servlet.jsp.tagext.TagSupport.{doAfterBody(), doEndTag(), doStartTag()}

JspFactory

javax.servlet.jsp

JSP containers provide subclasses of this class to create JspInfo and PageContext objects. The methods of the JspFactory class should not be called from within a JSP itself. Instead, the container is responsible for using the factory to create a PageContext object and making it available to the JSP. All JSP pages have a PageContext object available by default.

```
public abstract class JspFactory {
// Public Constructors
    public JspFactory();
// Public Class Methods
    public static JspFactory getDefaultFactory();                                    synchronized
    public static void setDefaultFactory(JspFactory deflt);                          synchronized
// Public Instance Methods
    public abstract JspEngineInfo getEngineInfo();
    public abstract PageContext getPageContext(Servlet servlet, ServletRequest request, ServletResponse response,
                                       String errorPageURL, boolean needsSession, int buffer,
                                       boolean autoflush);
    public abstract void releasePageContext(PageContext pc);
}
```

Passed To: JspFactory.setDefaultFactory()

Returned By: JspFactory.getDefaultFactory()

JspPage   JSP 1.1

javax.servlet.jsp

The JspPage interface defines two methods, jspInit() and jspDestroy(), which are analogous to the init() and destroy() methods of regular servlets. The jspInit() method is called before the JSP serves any page requests and after the rest of the JSP's initialization process. This means that the getServletConfig() method will return a valid javax.servlet.ServletConfig object when called from within the jspInit() method. The jspDestroy() method will be called when the container is shut down or when the JSP instance is unloaded. Both of the methods in this interface can be specified within a JSP page itself by defining the methods within a declaration element.

```
┌─────────┐   ┌─────────┐
│ Servlet │┈┈┤ JspPage │
└─────────┘   └─────────┘
```

```
public interface JspPage extends Servlet {
// Public Instance Methods
    public abstract void jspDestroy();
    public abstract void jspInit();
}
```

Implementations: HttpJspPage

JspTagException   JSP 1.1

javax.servlet.jsp   *serializable checked*

This exception indicates that a JSP Tag Handler has encountered an error. This exception should bubble up to the top page level and produce an error message for the client.

```
┌────────┐  ┌───────────┐  ┌───────────┐  ┌──────────────┐  ┌─────────────────┐
│ Object │──┤ Throwable │──┤ Exception │──┤ JspException │──┤ JspTagException │
└────────┘  └───────────┘  └───────────┘  └──────────────┘  └─────────────────┘
                 ┊
            ┌──────────────┐
            │ Serializable │
            └──────────────┘
```

```
public class JspTagException extends JspException {
// Public Constructors
    public JspTagException();
    public JspTagException(String msg);
}
```

JspWriter

javax.servlet.jsp

This is a Writer subclass that is available to JSP pages as the out variable. JspWriter behaves like a cross between a PrintWriter and a BufferedWriter, providing print() and println() methods and optional buffering. The initial JspWriter associated with a JSP request will be associated with a PrintWriter leading back to the client. JSP custom tags will have JspWriter's that are associated with parent JSP Writers. This means that the page level settings for a JspWriter's behavior will control the overall relationship of the JSP page with the client.

By default, a JspWriter will be buffered in auto-flush mode. The buffer size can be retrieved by getBufferSize() and the number bytes remaining in the buffer can be retrieved via the getRemaining() method. The isAutoFlush() method indicates whether the buffer will flush automatically when it is filled. The autoFlush page directive determines whether or not automatic flushing is enabled. After the buffer has been flushed, either by auto-flushing or by the flush() method, methods that manipulate response headers (such as HttpServletResponse.setContentType()) may not be called.

```
Object ─ Writer ─ JspWriter
```

```
public abstract class JspWriter extends Writer {
// Protected Constructors
     protected JspWriter(int bufferSize, boolean autoFlush);
// Public Constants
     public static final int DEFAULT_BUFFER;                              =-1
     public static final int NO_BUFFER;                                    =0
     public static final int UNBOUNDED_BUFFER;                            =-2
// Public Instance Methods
     public abstract void clear() throws IOException;
     public abstract void clearBuffer() throws IOException;
     public int getBufferSize();
     public abstract int getRemaining();
     public boolean isAutoFlush();
     public abstract void newLine() throws IOException;
     public abstract void print(Object obj) throws IOException;
     public abstract void print(int i) throws IOException;
     public abstract void print(long l) throws IOException;
     public abstract void print(boolean b) throws IOException;
     public abstract void print(char c) throws IOException;
     public abstract void print(float f) throws IOException;
     public abstract void print(String s) throws IOException;
     public abstract void print(char[ ] s) throws IOException;
     public abstract void print(double d) throws IOException;
     public abstract void println() throws IOException;
     public abstract void println(Object x) throws IOException;
     public abstract void println(int x) throws IOException;
     public abstract void println(long x) throws IOException;
     public abstract void println(boolean x) throws IOException;
     public abstract void println(char x) throws IOException;
     public abstract void println(char[ ] x) throws IOException;
     public abstract void println(String x) throws IOException;
     public abstract void println(float x) throws IOException;
     public abstract void println(double x) throws IOException;
// Public Methods Overriding Writer
     public abstract void close() throws IOException;
```

```
    public abstract void flush() throws IOException;
// Protected Instance Fields
    protected boolean autoFlush;
    protected int bufferSize;
}
```

Subclasses: javax.servlet.jsp.tagext.BodyContent

Passed To: javax.servlet.jsp.tagext.BodyContent.BodyContent()

Returned By: PageContext.{getOut(), popBody()},
javax.servlet.jsp.tagext.BodyContent.getEnclosingWriter(),
javax.servlet.jsp.tagext.BodyTagSupport.getPreviousOut()

PageContext   JSP 1.1

javax.servlet.jsp

The PageContext class provides a set of methods for both container implementers and JSP authors. For page authors, this class allows access to the various attributes within the different JSP namespaces (the page, request and session scopes) via the getAttribute() and setAttribute() methods and the scope constants. PageContext also provides convenience methods for retrieving ServletRequest, ServletResponse, ServletConfig and other servlet related objects, forward() and include() methods for request forwarding, and handlePageException() for processing exceptions through the default error page for the JSP or the container.

```
public abstract class PageContext {
// Public Constructors
    public PageContext();
// Public Constants
    public static final String APPLICATION;                    ="javax.servlet.jsp.jspApplication"
    public static final int APPLICATION_SCOPE;                                              =4
    public static final String CONFIG;                             ="javax.servlet.jsp.jspConfig"
    public static final String EXCEPTION;                       ="javax.servlet.jsp.jspException"
    public static final String OUT;                                   ="javax.servlet.jsp.jspOut"
    public static final String PAGE;                                 ="javax.servlet.jsp.jspPage"
    public static final int PAGE_SCOPE;                                                     =1
    public static final String PAGECONTEXT;                    ="javax.servlet.jsp.jspPageContext"
    public static final String REQUEST;                          ="javax.servlet.jsp.jspRequest"
    public static final int REQUEST_SCOPE;                                                  =2
    public static final String RESPONSE;                        ="javax.servlet.jsp.jspResponse"
    public static final String SESSION;                          ="javax.servlet.jsp.jspSession"
    public static final int SESSION_SCOPE;                                                  =3
// Property Accessor Methods (by property name)
    public abstract Exception getException();
    public abstract JspWriter getOut();
    public abstract Object getPage();
    public abstract ServletRequest getRequest();
    public abstract ServletResponse getResponse();
    public abstract ServletConfig getServletConfig();
    public abstract ServletContext getServletContext();
    public abstract javax.servlet.http.HttpSession getSession();
// Public Instance Methods
    public abstract Object findAttribute(String name);
    public abstract void forward(String relativeUrlPath) throws ServletException, IOException;
    public abstract Object getAttribute(String name);
    public abstract Object getAttribute(String name, int scope);
```

```
     public abstract java.util.Enumeration getAttributeNamesInScope(int scope);
     public abstract int getAttributesScope(String name);
     public abstract void handlePageException(Exception e) throws ServletException, IOException;
1.2  public abstract void handlePageException(Throwable t) throws ServletException, IOException;
     public abstract void include(String relativeUrlPath) throws ServletException, IOException;
     public abstract void initialize(Servlet servlet, ServletRequest request, ServletResponse response,
                    String errorPageURL, boolean needsSession, int bufferSize, boolean autoFlush)
        throws IOException, java.lang.IllegalStateException, IllegalArgumentException;
     public JspWriter popBody();                                                          constant
     public javax.servlet.jsp.tagext.BodyContent pushBody();                             constant
     public abstract void release();
     public abstract void removeAttribute(String name);
     public abstract void removeAttribute(String name, int scope);
     public abstract void setAttribute(String name, Object attribute);
     public abstract void setAttribute(String name, Object o, int scope);
}
```

Passed To: JspFactory.releasePageContext(), javax.servlet.jsp.tagext.Tag.setPageContext(), javax.servlet.jsp.tagext.TagSupport.setPageContext()

Returned By: JspFactory.getPageContext()

Type Of: javax.servlet.jsp.tagext.TagSupport.pageContext

CHAPTER 39

javax.sql

Package javax.sql

Java 1.4

The javax.sql package contains what was originally the JDBC 2.0 optional packages; these are now a part of the J2SE 1.4. The classes and interfaces in this package provide new functionality, such as connection pooling, that does not fall under the scope of the original JDBC API and can therefore be safely packaged separately. The DataSource interface serves as a factory for Connection objects; DataSourceobjects can be registered with a JNDI server, making it possible to get the name of a database from a name service. PooledConnection supports connection pooling, which allows an application to handle multiple database connections in a fairly transparent manner. RowSetextends the ResultSet interface into a JavaBeans component that can be manipulated at design-time and used with non-SQL data sources.

Interfaces:

public interface **ConnectionPoolDataSource**;
public interface **DataSource**;
public interface **PooledConnection**;
public interface **RowSet** extends java.sql.ResultSet;
public interface **RowSetInternal**;
public interface **RowSetMetaData** extends java.sql.ResultSetMetaData;
public interface **RowSetReader**;
public interface **RowSetWriter**;
public interface **XAConnection** extends PooledConnection;
public interface **XADataSource**;

Events:

public class **ConnectionEvent** extends java.util.EventObject;
public class **RowSetEvent** extends java.util.EventObject;

Event Listeners:

public interface **ConnectionEventListener** extends java.util.EventListener;
public interface **RowSetListener** extends java.util.EventListener;

ConnectionEvent

javax.sql

serializable event

Provides information about a pooled connection when an event occurs on the connection. If the event is an error event, ConnectionEvent includes the SQLException that is about to be thrown to the application.

```
┌────────┐ ┌───────────┐ ┌────────────────┐
│ Object │─┤ EventObject├─│ ConnectionEvent│
└────────┘ └───────────┘ └────────────────┘
         ┌──────────────┐
         │ Serializable │
         └──────────────┘
```

public class **ConnectionEvent** extends java.util.EventObject {
// Public Constructors
    public **ConnectionEvent**(PooledConnection *con*);
    public **ConnectionEvent**(PooledConnection *con*, java.sql.SQLException *ex*);
// Public Instance Methods
    public java.sql.SQLException **getSQLException**();
}

Passed To: javax.sql.ConnectionEventListener.{connectionClosed(), connectionErrorOccurred()}

ConnectionEventListener

javax.sql

event listener

An object that implements ConnectionEventListener registers to receive event notifications from PooledConnection objects. The connectionClosed() method is called when the close() method of the PooledConnection object is called, while the connectionErrorOccurred() method is called immediately before an SQLException is thrown to indicate a fatal error condition (one that renders the connection unusable in the future).

```
┌───────────────┐ ┌──────────────────────────┐
│ EventListener │┈│ ConnectionEventListener  │
└───────────────┘ └──────────────────────────┘
```

public interface **ConnectionEventListener** extends java.util.EventListener {
// Public Instance Methods
    public abstract void **connectionClosed**(javax.sql.ConnectionEvent *event*);
    public abstract void **connectionErrorOccurred**(javax.sql.ConnectionEvent *event*);
}

Passed To: PooledConnection.{addConnectionEventListener(), removeConnectionEventListener()}

ConnectionPoolDataSource

javax.sql

A factory for PooledConnection objects. Can be registered with a JNDI service or used standalone (for example, in a servlet).

public interface **ConnectionPoolDataSource** {
// Public Instance Methods
    public abstract int **getLoginTimeout**() throws java.sql.SQLException;
    public abstract PrintWriter **getLogWriter**() throws java.sql.SQLException;
    public abstract PooledConnection **getPooledConnection**() throws java.sql.SQLException;
    public abstract PooledConnection **getPooledConnection**(String *user*, String *password*)
        throws java.sql.SQLException;

```
    public abstract void setLoginTimeout(int seconds) throws java.sql.SQLException;
    public abstract void setLogWriter(PrintWriter out) throws java.sql.SQLException;
}
```

DataSource   Java 1.4

javax.sql

A factory for java.sql.Connection objects. Can be registered with a JNDI service, so that an application can get the name of a database from a name service.

```
public interface DataSource {
// Public Instance Methods
    public abstract java.sql.Connection getConnection() throws java.sql.SQLException;
    public abstract java.sql.Connection getConnection(String username, String password)
        throws java.sql.SQLException;
    public abstract int getLoginTimeout() throws java.sql.SQLException;
    public abstract PrintWriter getLogWriter() throws java.sql.SQLException;
    public abstract void setLoginTimeout(int seconds) throws java.sql.SQLException;
    public abstract void setLogWriter(PrintWriter out) throws java.sql.SQLException;
}
```

PooledConnection   Java 1.4

javax.sql

PooledConnection provides an application-level hook into the JDBC Standard Extension's connection pooling functionality. Call getConnection() to retrieve a standard java.sql.Connection object for database access from the connection pool. Use close() to return this connection to the pool.

```
public interface PooledConnection {
// Event Registration Methods (by event name)
    public abstract void addConnectionEventListener(javax.sql.ConnectionEventListener listener);
    public abstract void removeConnectionEventListener(javax.sql.ConnectionEventListener listener);
// Public Instance Methods
    public abstract void close() throws java.sql.SQLException;
    public abstract java.sql.Connection getConnection() throws java.sql.SQLException;
}
```

Implementations: javax.sql.XAConnection

Passed To: javax.sql.ConnectionEvent.ConnectionEvent()

Returned By: ConnectionPoolDataSource.getPooledConnection()

RowSet   Java 1.4

javax.sql

RowSet extends the java.sql.ResultSet interface so that RowSet objects are JavaBeans components and can be manipulated by visual programming tools. A RowSet can be implemented on top of any JDBC-compliant ResultSet. The setCommand() method specifies what data the row set should contain (for a database generated set, this might be an SQL statement). RowSet objects can be either *connected* (in which case they are updated as the underlying data changes and changes to the RowSet object are reflected in the underlying data) or *disconnected* (in which case the RowSet represents a completely self-contained data set). The RowSet interface also allows listener objects to be associated with it, providing notifications of data updates as they occur.

RowSet

public interface **RowSet** extends java.sql.ResultSet {
// Event Registration Methods (by event name)
   public abstract void **addRowSetListener**(RowSetListener *listener*);
   public abstract void **removeRowSetListener**(RowSetListener *listener*);
// Property Accessor Methods (by property name)
   public abstract String **getCommand**();
   public abstract void **setCommand**(String *cmd*) throws java.sql.SQLException;
   public abstract void **setConcurrency**(int *concurrency*) throws java.sql.SQLException;
   public abstract String **getDataSourceName**();
   public abstract void **setDataSourceName**(String *name*) throws java.sql.SQLException;
   public abstract boolean **getEscapeProcessing**() throws java.sql.SQLException;
   public abstract void **setEscapeProcessing**(boolean *enable*) throws java.sql.SQLException;
   public abstract int **getMaxFieldSize**() throws java.sql.SQLException;
   public abstract void **setMaxFieldSize**(int *max*) throws java.sql.SQLException;
   public abstract int **getMaxRows**() throws java.sql.SQLException;
   public abstract void **setMaxRows**(int *max*) throws java.sql.SQLException;
   public abstract String **getPassword**();
   public abstract void **setPassword**(String *password*) throws java.sql.SQLException;
   public abstract int **getQueryTimeout**() throws java.sql.SQLException;
   public abstract void **setQueryTimeout**(int *seconds*) throws java.sql.SQLException;
   public abstract boolean **isReadOnly**();
   public abstract void **setReadOnly**(boolean *value*) throws java.sql.SQLException;
   public abstract int **getTransactionIsolation**();
   public abstract void **setTransactionIsolation**(int *level*) throws java.sql.SQLException;
   public abstract void **setType**(int *type*) throws java.sql.SQLException;
   public abstract java.util.Map **getTypeMap**() throws java.sql.SQLException;
   public abstract void **setTypeMap**(java.util.Map *map*) throws java.sql.SQLException;
   public abstract String **getUrl**() throws java.sql.SQLException;
   public abstract void **setUrl**(String *url*) throws java.sql.SQLException;
   public abstract String **getUsername**();
   public abstract void **setUsername**(String *name*) throws java.sql.SQLException;
// Public Instance Methods
   public abstract void **clearParameters**() throws java.sql.SQLException;
   public abstract void **execute**() throws java.sql.SQLException;
   public abstract void **setArray**(int *i*, java.sql.Array *x*) throws java.sql.SQLException;
   public abstract void **setAsciiStream**(int *parameterIndex*, java.io.InputStream *x*, int *length*)
      throws java.sql.SQLException;
   public abstract void **setBigDecimal**(int *parameterIndex*, java.math.BigDecimal *x*) throws java.sql.SQLException;
   public abstract void **setBinaryStream**(int *parameterIndex*, java.io.InputStream *x*, int *length*)
      throws java.sql.SQLException;
   public abstract void **setBlob**(int *i*, java.sql.Blob *x*) throws java.sql.SQLException;
   public abstract void **setBoolean**(int *parameterIndex*, boolean *x*) throws java.sql.SQLException;
   public abstract void **setByte**(int *parameterIndex*, byte *x*) throws java.sql.SQLException;
   public abstract void **setBytes**(int *parameterIndex*, byte[ ] *x*) throws java.sql.SQLException;
   public abstract void **setCharacterStream**(int *parameterIndex*, Reader *reader*, int *length*)
      throws java.sql.SQLException;
   public abstract void **setClob**(int *i*, java.sql.Clob *x*) throws java.sql.SQLException;
   public abstract void **setDate**(int *parameterIndex*, java.sql.Date *x*) throws java.sql.SQLException;
   public abstract void **setDate**(int *parameterIndex*, java.sql.Date *x*, java.util.Calendar *cal*)
      throws java.sql.SQLException;
   public abstract void **setDouble**(int *parameterIndex*, double *x*) throws java.sql.SQLException;
   public abstract void **setFloat**(int *parameterIndex*, float *x*) throws java.sql.SQLException;
   public abstract void **setInt**(int *parameterIndex*, int *x*) throws java.sql.SQLException;
   public abstract void **setLong**(int *parameterIndex*, long *x*) throws java.sql.SQLException;
   public abstract void **setNull**(int *parameterIndex*, int *sqlType*) throws java.sql.SQLException;

```
    public abstract void setNull(int paramIndex, int sqlType, String typeName) throws java.sql.SQLException;
    public abstract void setObject(int parameterIndex, Object x) throws java.sql.SQLException;
    public abstract void setObject(int parameterIndex, Object x, int targetSqlType) throws java.sql.SQLException;
    public abstract void setObject(int parameterIndex, Object x, int targetSqlType, int scale)
        throws java.sql.SQLException;
    public abstract void setRef(int i, java.sql.Ref x) throws java.sql.SQLException;
    public abstract void setShort(int parameterIndex, short x) throws java.sql.SQLException;
    public abstract void setString(int parameterIndex, String x) throws java.sql.SQLException;
    public abstract void setTime(int parameterIndex, java.sql.Time x) throws java.sql.SQLException;
    public abstract void setTime(int parameterIndex, java.sql.Time x, java.util.Calendar cal)
        throws java.sql.SQLException;
    public abstract void setTimestamp(int parameterIndex, java.sql.Timestamp x) throws java.sql.SQLException;
    public abstract void setTimestamp(int parameterIndex, java.sql.Timestamp x, java.util.Calendar cal)
        throws java.sql.SQLException;
}
```

Passed To: RowSetEvent.RowSetEvent()

RowSetEvent

Java 1.4

javax.sql

serializable event

Generated when an important event, such as a change in a column's value, occurs within a RowSet.

```
Object ─ EventObject ─ RowSetEvent
       Serializable
```

```
public class RowSetEvent extends java.util.EventObject {
// Public Constructors
    public RowSetEvent(RowSet source);
}
```

Passed To: RowSetListener.{cursorMoved(), rowChanged(), rowSetChanged()}

RowSetInternal

Java 1.4

javax.sql

Implemented by a RowSet object that wishes to support the reader/writer row-loading paradigm. Contains additional methods used by RowSetReader and RowSetWriter.

```
public interface RowSetInternal {
// Property Accessor Methods (by property name)
    public abstract java.sql.Connection getConnection() throws java.sql.SQLException;
    public abstract void setMetaData(RowSetMetaData md) throws java.sql.SQLException;
    public abstract java.sql.ResultSet getOriginal() throws java.sql.SQLException;
    public abstract java.sql.ResultSet getOriginalRow() throws java.sql.SQLException;
    public abstract Object[] getParams() throws java.sql.SQLException;
}
```

Passed To: RowSetReader.readData(), RowSetWriter.writeData()

RowSetListener

Java 1.4

javax.sql

event listener

Implemented by an object that wishes to be informed of events generated by a RowSet.

EventListener — RowSetListener

```
public interface RowSetListener extends java.util.EventListener {
// Public Instance Methods
    public abstract void cursorMoved(RowSetEvent event);
    public abstract void rowChanged(RowSetEvent event);
    public abstract void rowSetChanged(RowSetEvent event);
}
```

Passed To: RowSet.{addRowSetListener(), removeRowSetListener()}

RowSetMetaData   Java 1.4

javax.sql

Extends java.sql.ResultSetMetaData to support the functionality of RowSet objects.

ResultSetMetaData — RowSetMetaData

```
public interface RowSetMetaData extends java.sql.ResultSetMetaData {
// Public Instance Methods
    public abstract void setAutoIncrement(int columnIndex, boolean property) throws java.sql.SQLException;
    public abstract void setCaseSensitive(int columnIndex, boolean property) throws java.sql.SQLException;
    public abstract void setCatalogName(int columnIndex, String catalogName) throws java.sql.SQLException;
    public abstract void setColumnCount(int columnCount) throws java.sql.SQLException;
    public abstract void setColumnDisplaySize(int columnIndex, int size) throws java.sql.SQLException;
    public abstract void setColumnLabel(int columnIndex, String label) throws java.sql.SQLException;
    public abstract void setColumnName(int columnIndex, String columnName) throws java.sql.SQLException;
    public abstract void setColumnType(int columnIndex, int SQLType) throws java.sql.SQLException;
    public abstract void setColumnTypeName(int columnIndex, String typeName) throws java.sql.SQLException;
    public abstract void setCurrency(int columnIndex, boolean property) throws java.sql.SQLException;
    public abstract void setNullable(int columnIndex, int property) throws java.sql.SQLException;
    public abstract void setPrecision(int columnIndex, int precision) throws java.sql.SQLException;
    public abstract void setScale(int columnIndex, int scale) throws java.sql.SQLException;
    public abstract void setSchemaName(int columnIndex, String schemaName) throws java.sql.SQLException;
    public abstract void setSearchable(int columnIndex, boolean property) throws java.sql.SQLException;
    public abstract void setSigned(int columnIndex, boolean property) throws java.sql.SQLException;
    public abstract void setTableName(int columnIndex, String tableName) throws java.sql.SQLException;
}
```

Passed To: RowSetInternal.setMetaData()

RowSetReader   Java 1.4

javax.sql

Loads data into a RowSet that implements RowSetInternal. The extensions to ResultSet introduced in JDBC 2.0 are used to insert data.

```
public interface RowSetReader {
// Public Instance Methods
    public abstract void readData(RowSetInternal caller) throws java.sql.SQLException;
}
```

RowSetWriter   Java 1.4

javax.sql

Writes data from a RowSet that implements RowSetInternal. The data from the RowSet can be written back to a data source (not necessarily a database).

```
public interface RowSetWriter {
// Public Instance Methods
    public abstract boolean writeData(RowSetInternal caller) throws java.sql.SQLException;
}
```

XAConnection

javax.sql

An extended version of PooledConnection that can be used in a distributed transaction environment, using the Java Transaction API (in the javax.transaction package).

```
PooledConnection ─ XAConnection
```

```
public interface XAConnection extends PooledConnection {
// Public Instance Methods
    public abstract javax.transaction.xa.XAResource getXAResource() throws java.sql.SQLException;
}
```

Returned By: XADataSource.getXAConnection()

XADataSource

javax.sql

A factory for XAConnection objects.

```
public interface XADataSource {
// Public Instance Methods
    public abstract int getLoginTimeout() throws java.sql.SQLException;
    public abstract PrintWriter getLogWriter() throws java.sql.SQLException;
    public abstract javax.sql.XAConnection getXAConnection() throws java.sql.SQLException;
    public abstract javax.sql.XAConnection getXAConnection(String user, String password)
        throws java.sql.SQLException;
    public abstract void setLoginTimeout(int seconds) throws java.sql.SQLException;
    public abstract void setLogWriter(PrintWriter out) throws java.sql.SQLException;
}
```

CHAPTER 40

javax.transaction and javax.transaction.xa

Package javax.transaction

JTA 1.0

The javax.transaction package is the main package in the Java Transaction API (JTA). The JTA defines the interfaces needed to interact with a transaction manager. A transaction manager sits in between applications and shared resources, like a relational database or a messaging service, and ensures that transactional interactions between the two are handled correctly. An application server interacts directly with the transaction manager on behalf of client applications; application servers use the TransactionManager interface and Transaction objects, and client applications acquire UserTransactions through the application server. See the EJB chapter for an overview of the nature of transactions and how they are used in distributed applications to ensure consistency.

Interfaces:

public interface **Status**;
public interface **Synchronization**;
public interface **Transaction**;
public interface **TransactionManager**;
public interface **UserTransaction**;

Exceptions:

public class **HeuristicCommitException** extends Exception;
public class **HeuristicMixedException** extends Exception;
public class **HeuristicRollbackException** extends Exception;
public class **InvalidTransactionException** extends java.rmi.RemoteException;
public class **NotSupportedException** extends Exception;
public class **RollbackException** extends Exception;
public class **SystemException** extends Exception;
public class **TransactionRequiredException** extends java.rmi.RemoteException;
public class **TransactionRolledbackException** extends java.rmi.RemoteException;

HeuristicCommitException
JTA 1.0

javax.transaction *serializable checked*

The exception is thrown when an attempt is made to rollback a resource whose updates have been committed due to a heuristic decision (e.g., a resource lost contact with the transaction manager and decided to commit after one phase of a two-phase commit).

```
Object ── Throwable ── Exception ── HeuristicCommitException
          Serializable
```

```
public class HeuristicCommitException extends Exception {
// Public Constructors
    public HeuristicCommitException();
    public HeuristicCommitException(String msg);
}
```

HeuristicMixedException
JTA 1.0

javax.transaction *serializable checked*

This exception is thrown by the commit() methods on Transaction and UserTransaction, to indicate that some updates were rolled back due to a heuristic decision (e.g., some resources involved in a transaction lost contact with the transaction manager and decided to rollback, but some others had already committed).

```
Object ── Throwable ── Exception ── HeuristicMixedException
          Serializable
```

```
public class HeuristicMixedException extends Exception {
// Public Constructors
    public HeuristicMixedException();
    public HeuristicMixedException(String msg);
}
```

Thrown By: Transaction.commit(), TransactionManager.commit(), UserTransaction.commit()

HeuristicRollbackException
JTA 1.0

javax.transaction *serializable checked*

This is thrown by the commit() methods on Transaction and UserTransaction, to indicate that the transaction has been rolled back due to a heuristic decision (e.g., the resource(s) lost contact with the transaction manager and decided to abort the transaction).

```
Object ── Throwable ── Exception ── HeuristicRollbackException
          Serializable
```

```
public class HeuristicRollbackException extends Exception {
// Public Constructors
    public HeuristicRollbackException();
    public HeuristicRollbackException(String msg);
}
```

Thrown By: Transaction.commit(), TransactionManager.commit(), UserTransaction.commit()

InvalidTransactionException

javax.transaction   *serializable checked*

This exception is thrown when an attempt is made to operate on a transaction that is in an invalid state.

```
Object ─ Throwable ─ Exception ─ IOException ─ RemoteException ─ InvalidTransactionException
         Serializable
```

```
public class InvalidTransactionException extends java.rmi.RemoteException {
// Public Constructors
    public InvalidTransactionException();
    public InvalidTransactionException(String msg);
}
```

Thrown By: TransactionManager.resume()

NotSupportedException

javax.transaction   *serializable checked*

Thrown when a request is made for an unsupported operation. This is typically thrown by the transaction manager when an attempt is made to create a nested exception and these are not supported by the transaction manager.

```
Object ─ Throwable ─ Exception ─ NotSupportedException
         Serializable
```

```
public class NotSupportedException extends Exception {
// Public Constructors
    public NotSupportedException();
    public NotSupportedException(String msg);
}
```

Thrown By: TransactionManager.begin(), UserTransaction.begin()

RollbackException

javax.transaction   *serializable checked*

This exception is thrown when an invalid operation is requested on a transaction that has either rolled back or been marked for rollback-only. An example is calling TransactionManager.enlistResource() on such a transaction.

```
Object ─ Throwable ─ Exception ─ RollbackException
         Serializable
```

```
public class RollbackException extends Exception {
// Public Constructors
    public RollbackException();
    public RollbackException(String msg);
}
```

Thrown By: Transaction.{commit(), enlistResource(), registerSynchronization()},
TransactionManager.commit(), UserTransaction.commit()

Status JTA 1.0

javax.transaction

This interface simply serves to hold static integer status codes for transactions. The Transaction.getStatus() method can be used to query for the status of a transaction, and these codes indicate the meaning of the returned code value.

```
public interface Status {
// Public Constants
    public static final int STATUS_ACTIVE;                =0
    public static final int STATUS_COMMITTED;             =3
    public static final int STATUS_COMMITTING;            =8
    public static final int STATUS_MARKED_ROLLBACK;       =1
    public static final int STATUS_NO_TRANSACTION;        =6
    public static final int STATUS_PREPARED;              =2
    public static final int STATUS_PREPARING;             =7
    public static final int STATUS_ROLLEDBACK;            =4
    public static final int STATUS_ROLLING_BACK;          =9
    public static final int STATUS_UNKNOWN;               =5
}
```

Synchronization JTA 1.0

javax.transaction

A Synchronization object is used to get notification of the end of transactions. The Synchronization interface must be implemented by a concrete application class, which can then be used to request callbacks from the transaction manager. The Synchronization object is registered with an active transaction by calling the Transaction.registerSynchronization() method, passing in the Synchronization object. An exception is thrown if the transaction isn't active, or has already been marked for rollback. Before the transaction manager starts the commit on the transaction, it calls the beforeCompletion() method on any registered Synchronization objects. After the transaction completes, the transaction manager calls the afterCompletion() method.

```
public interface Synchronization {
// Public Instance Methods
    public abstract void afterCompletion(int status);
    public abstract void beforeCompletion();
}
```

Passed To: Transaction.registerSynchronization()

SystemException JTA 1.0

javax.transaction *serializable checked*

Thrown by the transaction manager when a significant error occurs that effectively disables the manager.

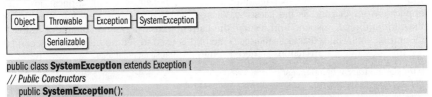

```
public class SystemException extends Exception {
// Public Constructors
    public SystemException();
    public SystemException(int errcode);
    public SystemException(String s);
```

```
// Public Instance Fields
    public int errorCode;
}
```

Thrown By: Transaction.{commit(), delistResource(), enlistResource(), getStatus(),
registerSynchronization(), rollback(), setRollbackOnly()}, TransactionManager.{begin(), commit(),
getStatus(), getTransaction(), resume(), rollback(), setRollbackOnly(), setTransactionTimeout(),
suspend()}, UserTransaction.{begin(), commit(), getStatus(), rollback(), setRollbackOnly(),
setTransactionTimeout()}

Transaction   JTA 1.0

javax.transaction

A Transaction represents a global transaction managed by the transaction manager. When
the TransactionManager interface is used directly (by an application server, for example),
to create and control transactions, Transaction objects represent the transactions created.
The TransactionManager.getTransaction() method is used to get the transaction associated
with the current thread. With the Transaction object, the caller can commit() or rollback()
the Transaction, enlist or remove resources from the transaction, and get the Transaction's
status. The setRollbackOnly() method flags the Transaction so that it can only be rolled
back, not committed. The registerSynchronization() method is used to register a Synchronization callback object with the Transaction.

```
public interface Transaction {
// Public Instance Methods
    public abstract void commit() throws RollbackException, HeuristicMixedException, HeuristicRollbackException,
        java.lang.SecurityException;
    public abstract boolean delistResource(javax.transaction.xa.XAResource xaRes, int flag)
        throws java.lang.IllegalStateException, javax.transaction.SystemException;
    public abstract boolean enlistResource(javax.transaction.xa.XAResource xaRes) throws RollbackException,
        java.lang.IllegalStateException, javax.transaction.SystemException;
    public abstract int getStatus() throws javax.transaction.SystemException;
    public abstract void registerSynchronization(Synchronization sync) throws RollbackException,
        java.lang.IllegalStateException, javax.transaction.SystemException;
    public abstract void rollback() throws java.lang.IllegalStateException, javax.transaction.SystemException;
    public abstract void setRollbackOnly() throws java.lang.IllegalStateException, javax.transaction.SystemException;
}
```

Passed To: TransactionManager.resume()

Returned By: TransactionManager.{getTransaction(), suspend()}

TransactionManager   JTA 1.0

javax.transaction

The TransactionManager interface is used by a transactional application server, such as an
EJB server, to create and manage transactions on behalf of client applications. The
application server can use the TransactionManager interface to create new transactions for
the current thread, suspend and resume the current transaction, and commit or rollback
the transaction. The setTransactionTimeout() method is used to set the timeout (in seconds)
for any subsequent transactions started through the TransactionManager.

```
public interface TransactionManager {
// Public Instance Methods
    public abstract void begin() throws javax.transaction.NotSupportedException, javax.transaction.SystemException;
    public abstract void commit() throws RollbackException, HeuristicMixedException, HeuristicRollbackException,
        java.lang.SecurityException;
```

```
    public abstract int getStatus() throws javax.transaction.SystemException;
    public abstract Transaction getTransaction() throws javax.transaction.SystemException;
    public abstract void resume(Transaction tobj) throws InvalidTransactionException, java.lang.IllegalStateException,
        javax.transaction.SystemException;
    public abstract void rollback() throws java.lang.IllegalStateException, java.lang.SecurityException,
        javax.transaction.SystemException;
    public abstract void setRollbackOnly() throws java.lang.IllegalStateException, javax.transaction.SystemException;
    public abstract void setTransactionTimeout(int seconds) throws javax.transaction.SystemException;
    public abstract Transaction suspend() throws javax.transaction.SystemException;
}
```

TransactionRequiredException

JTA 1.0

javax.transaction

serializable checked

Thrown when a transaction-related operation is requested, but there is no active transaction.

```
Object ─ Throwable ─ Exception ─ IOException ─ RemoteException ─ TransactionRequiredException
           Serializable
```

```
public class TransactionRequiredException extends java.rmi.RemoteException {
// Public Constructors
    public TransactionRequiredException();
    public TransactionRequiredException(String msg);
}
```

TransactionRolledbackException

JTA 1.0

javax.transaction

serializable checked

This exception is thrown when an operation requested on a particular transaction, is irrelevant, because the transaction has been rolled back.

```
Object ─ Throwable ─ Exception ─ IOException ─ RemoteException ─ TransactionRolledbackException
           Serializable
```

```
public class TransactionRolledbackException extends java.rmi.RemoteException {
// Public Constructors
    public TransactionRolledbackException();
    public TransactionRolledbackException(String msg);
}
```

UserTransaction

JTA 1.0

javax.transaction

A UserTransaction is the interface used by client applications to manage transactions. Typically, a transactional application server will publish a UserTransaction through JNDI, and clients will get a reference to the UserTransaction using a lookup on the JNDI Context. The client can use the UserTransaction to begin() a new transaction in the current thread. If there is already an active transaction in the current thread and the transaction manager doesn't support nested transactions, then a NotSupportedException is thrown. The client can either commit() or rollback() the current transaction when it's complete. The setRollbackOnly() method is used to flag the current transaction so that it can only be rolled back. The setTransactionTimeout() method is used to set the timeout, in seconds, of any subsequent transactions started through the transaction manager.

```
public interface UserTransaction {
// Public Instance Methods
    public abstract void begin() throws javax.transaction.NotSupportedException, javax.transaction.SystemException;
    public abstract void commit() throws RollbackException, HeuristicMixedException, HeuristicRollbackException,
        java.lang.SecurityException;
    public abstract int getStatus() throws javax.transaction.SystemException;
    public abstract void rollback() throws java.lang.IllegalStateException, java.lang.SecurityException,
        javax.transaction.SystemException;
    public abstract void setRollbackOnly() throws java.lang.IllegalStateException, javax.transaction.SystemException;
    public abstract void setTransactionTimeout(int seconds) throws javax.transaction.SystemException;
}
```

Returned By: javax.ejb.EJBContext.getUserTransaction()

Package javax.transaction.xa   JTA 1.0

This package represents a Java mapping of certain elements of the X/Open XA interface specification. The XA interface defines a standard two-way communication protocol between a transaction manager and a resource manager, such as a relational database, so that they can engage in distributed transactional processing.

These interfaces are used internally by the JTA to implement its transaction management services. Normally, you shouldn't have to use these interfaces directly in application code.

Interfaces:

public interface **XAResource**;
public interface **Xid**;

Exceptions:

public class **XAException** extends Exception;

XAException   JTA 1.0
javax.transaction.xa   *serializable checked*

This exception is thrown by a resource manager when an error occurs while handling a request from the transaction manager. The static error codes allow the transaction manager to determine the cause of the error.

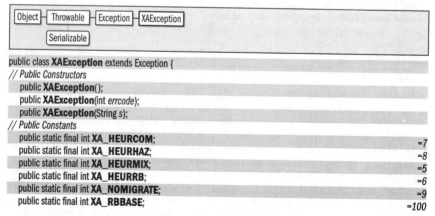

```
public class XAException extends Exception {
// Public Constructors
    public XAException();
    public XAException(int errcode);
    public XAException(String s);
// Public Constants
    public static final int XA_HEURCOM;                                        =7
    public static final int XA_HEURHAZ;                                        =8
    public static final int XA_HEURMIX;                                        =5
    public static final int XA_HEURRB;                                         =6
    public static final int XA_NOMIGRATE;                                      =9
    public static final int XA_RBBASE;                                       =100
```

public static final int **XA_RBCOMMFAIL**;	=101
public static final int **XA_RBDEADLOCK**;	=102
public static final int **XA_RBEND**;	=107
public static final int **XA_RBINTEGRITY**;	=103
public static final int **XA_RBOTHER**;	=104
public static final int **XA_RBPROTO**;	=105
public static final int **XA_RBROLLBACK**;	=100
public static final int **XA_RBTIMEOUT**;	=106
public static final int **XA_RBTRANSIENT**;	=107
public static final int **XA_RDONLY**;	=3
public static final int **XA_RETRY**;	=4
public static final int **XAER_ASYNC**;	=-2
public static final int **XAER_DUPID**;	=-8
public static final int **XAER_INVAL**;	=-5
public static final int **XAER_NOTA**;	=-4
public static final int **XAER_OUTSIDE**;	=-9
public static final int **XAER_PROTO**;	=-6
public static final int **XAER_RMERR**;	=-3
public static final int **XAER_RMFAIL**;	=-7

```
// Public Instance Fields
    public int errorCode;
}
```

Thrown By: XAResource.{commit(), end(), forget(), getTransactionTimeout(), isSameRM(), prepare(), recover(), rollback(), setTransactionTimeout(), start()}

XAResource   JTA 1.0

javax.transaction.xa

The XAResource interface is implemented by shared resources that want to engage in distributed transactions. A single resource manager (e.g., a database server or message service) can export multiple transactional resources (database connections, sessions with a message service), represented as XAResources. The transaction manager uses the XAResource interface to associate a resource with a transaction, using the start() method, to ask the resource to commit() or rollback() any work done while it was associated with a transaction, and finally to end() the association with a transaction. Other methods on XAResource are used to manage the association of the resource with the transaction context.

```
public interface XAResource {
// Public Constants
    public static final int TMENDRSCAN;                        =8388608
    public static final int TMFAIL;                          =536870912
    public static final int TMJOIN;                            =2097152
    public static final int TMNOFLAGS;                               =0
    public static final int TMONEPHASE;                     =1073741824
    public static final int TMRESUME;                        =134217728
    public static final int TMSTARTRSCAN;                     =16777216
    public static final int TMSUCCESS;                        =67108864
    public static final int TMSUSPEND;                        =33554432
    public static final int XA_OK;                                   =0
    public static final int XA_RDONLY;                               =3
// Public Instance Methods
    public abstract void commit(Xid xid, boolean onePhase) throws XAException;
    public abstract void end(Xid xid, int flags) throws XAException;
    public abstract void forget(Xid xid) throws XAException;
```

```
    public abstract int getTransactionTimeout() throws XAException;
    public abstract boolean isSameRM(XAResource xares) throws XAException;
    public abstract int prepare(Xid xid) throws XAException;
    public abstract Xid[] recover(int flag) throws XAException;
    public abstract void rollback(Xid xid) throws XAException;
    public abstract boolean setTransactionTimeout(int seconds) throws XAException;
    public abstract void start(Xid xid, int flags) throws XAException;
}
```

Passed To: Transaction.{delistResource(), enlistResource()}, XAResource.isSameRM()

Returned By: javax.jms.XASession.getXAResource(),
javax.resource.spi.ManagedConnection.getXAResource(), javax.sql.XAConnection.getXAResource()

Xid   JTA 1.0

javax.transaction.xa

An Xid is an identifier for a transaction. This interface is used by transaction managers
and resource managers as the representation for transactions. The methods on the
interface allow these two entities to query for specific components of the transaction
identifier.

```
public interface Xid {
// Public Constants
    public static final int MAXBQUALSIZE;                                    =64
    public static final int MAXGTRIDSIZE;                                    =64
// Public Instance Methods
    public abstract byte[] getBranchQualifier();
    public abstract int getFormatId();
    public abstract byte[] getGlobalTransactionId();
}
```

Passed To: XAResource.{commit(), end(), forget(), prepare(), rollback(), start()}

Returned By: XAResource.recover()

CHAPTER 41

org.omg.CORBA and Subpackages

The org.omg.CORBA package contains the bulk of the Java classes in the Java IDL API, since it represents the mapping of the CORBA module defined in IDL in the CORBA standard, which includes the bulk of the interfaces, constants, etc., that make up CORBA.

Interfaces:

public interface **ARG_IN**;
public interface **ARG_INOUT**;
public interface **ARG_OUT**;
public interface **BAD_POLICY**;
public interface **BAD_POLICY_TYPE**;
public interface **BAD_POLICY_VALUE**;
public interface **CTX_RESTRICT_SCOPE**;
public interface **Current** extends CurrentOperations, Object, org.omg.CORBA.portable.IDLEntity;
public interface **CurrentOperations**;
public interface **CustomMarshal**;
public interface **DataInputStream** extends org.omg.CORBA.portable.ValueBase;
public interface **DataOutputStream** extends org.omg.CORBA.portable.ValueBase;
public interface **DomainManager** extends DomainManagerOperations, Object,
                                    org.omg.CORBA.portable.IDLEntity;
public interface **DomainManagerOperations**;
public interface **DynAny** extends Object;
public interface **DynArray** extends Object, DynAny;
public interface **DynEnum** extends Object, DynAny;
public interface **DynFixed** extends Object, DynAny;
public interface **DynSequence** extends Object, DynAny;
public interface **DynStruct** extends Object, DynAny;
public interface **DynUnion** extends Object, DynAny;
public interface **DynValue** extends Object, DynAny;

public interface **IDLType** extends IDLTypeOperations, IRObject, org.omg.CORBA.portable.IDLEntity;
public interface **IDLTypeOperations** extends IRObjectOperations;
public interface **IRObject** extends IRObjectOperations, Object, org.omg.CORBA.portable.IDLEntity;
public interface **IRObjectOperations**;
public interface **Object**;
public interface **OMGVMCID**;
public interface **Policy** extends PolicyOperations, Object, org.omg.CORBA.portable.IDLEntity;
public interface **PolicyOperations**;
public interface **PRIVATE_MEMBER**;
public interface **PUBLIC_MEMBER**;
public interface **UNSUPPORTED_POLICY**;
public interface **UNSUPPORTED_POLICY_VALUE**;
public interface **VM_ABSTRACT**;
public interface **VM_CUSTOM**;
public interface **VM_NONE**;
public interface **VM_TRUNCATABLE**;

Classes:

public class **_IDLTypeStub** extends org.omg.CORBA.portable.ObjectImpl implements IDLType;
public class **_PolicyStub** extends org.omg.CORBA.portable.ObjectImpl implements Policy;
public abstract class **Any** implements org.omg.CORBA.portable.IDLEntity;
public final class **AnyHolder** implements org.omg.CORBA.portable.Streamable;
public abstract class **AnySeqHelper**;
public final class **AnySeqHolder** implements org.omg.CORBA.portable.Streamable;
public final class **BooleanHolder** implements org.omg.CORBA.portable.Streamable;
public abstract class **BooleanSeqHelper**;
public final class **BooleanSeqHolder** implements org.omg.CORBA.portable.Streamable;
public final class **ByteHolder** implements org.omg.CORBA.portable.Streamable;
public final class **CharHolder** implements org.omg.CORBA.portable.Streamable;
public abstract class **CharSeqHelper**;
public final class **CharSeqHolder** implements org.omg.CORBA.portable.Streamable;
public final class **CompletionStatus** implements org.omg.CORBA.portable.IDLEntity;
public abstract class **CompletionStatusHelper**;
public abstract class **Context**;
public abstract class **ContextList**;
public abstract class **CurrentHelper**;
public final class **CurrentHolder** implements org.omg.CORBA.portable.Streamable;
public class **DefinitionKind** implements org.omg.CORBA.portable.IDLEntity;
public abstract class **DefinitionKindHelper**;
public final class **DoubleHolder** implements org.omg.CORBA.portable.Streamable;
public abstract class **DoubleSeqHelper**;
public final class **DoubleSeqHolder** implements org.omg.CORBA.portable.Streamable;
public class **DynamicImplementation** extends org.omg.CORBA.portable.ObjectImpl;
public abstract class **Environment**;
public abstract class **ExceptionList**;
public abstract class **FieldNameHelper**;
public final class **FixedHolder** implements org.omg.CORBA.portable.Streamable;
public final class **FloatHolder** implements org.omg.CORBA.portable.Streamable;
public abstract class **FloatSeqHelper**;
public final class **FloatSeqHolder** implements org.omg.CORBA.portable.Streamable;
public abstract class **IdentifierHelper**;
public abstract class **IDLTypeHelper**;

public final class **IntHolder** implements org.omg.CORBA.portable.Streamable;
public class **LocalObject** implements Object;
public final class **LongHolder** implements org.omg.CORBA.portable.Streamable;
public abstract class **LongLongSeqHelper**;
public final class **LongLongSeqHolder** implements org.omg.CORBA.portable.Streamable;
public abstract class **LongSeqHelper**;
public final class **LongSeqHolder** implements org.omg.CORBA.portable.Streamable;
public abstract class **NamedValue**;
public final class **NameValuePair** implements org.omg.CORBA.portable.IDLEntity;
public abstract class **NameValuePairHelper**;
public abstract class **NVList**;
public abstract class **ObjectHelper**;
public final class **ObjectHolder** implements org.omg.CORBA.portable.Streamable;
public abstract class **OctetSeqHelper**;
public final class **OctetSeqHolder** implements org.omg.CORBA.portable.Streamable;
public abstract class **ORB**;
public class **ParameterMode** implements org.omg.CORBA.portable.IDLEntity;
public abstract class **ParameterModeHelper**;
public final class **ParameterModeHolder** implements org.omg.CORBA.portable.Streamable;
public abstract class **PolicyErrorCodeHelper**;
public abstract class **PolicyErrorHelper**;
public final class **PolicyErrorHolder** implements org.omg.CORBA.portable.Streamable;
public abstract class **PolicyHelper**;
public final class **PolicyHolder** implements org.omg.CORBA.portable.Streamable;
public abstract class **PolicyListHelper**;
public final class **PolicyListHolder** implements org.omg.CORBA.portable.Streamable;
public abstract class **PolicyTypeHelper**;
public class **Principal**;
public final class **PrincipalHolder** implements org.omg.CORBA.portable.Streamable;
public abstract class **RepositoryIdHelper**;
public abstract class **Request**;
public abstract class **ServerRequest**;
public final class **ServiceDetail** implements org.omg.CORBA.portable.IDLEntity;
public abstract class **ServiceDetailHelper**;
public final class **ServiceInformation** implements org.omg.CORBA.portable.IDLEntity;
public abstract class **ServiceInformationHelper**;
public final class **ServiceInformationHolder** implements org.omg.CORBA.portable.Streamable;
public class **SetOverrideType** implements org.omg.CORBA.portable.IDLEntity;
public abstract class **SetOverrideTypeHelper**;
public final class **ShortHolder** implements org.omg.CORBA.portable.Streamable;
public abstract class **ShortSeqHelper**;
public final class **ShortSeqHolder** implements org.omg.CORBA.portable.Streamable;
public final class **StringHolder** implements org.omg.CORBA.portable.Streamable;
public abstract class **StringSeqHelper**;
public final class **StringSeqHolder** implements org.omg.CORBA.portable.Streamable;
public class **StringValueHelper** implements org.omg.CORBA.portable.BoxedValueHelper;
public final class **StructMember** implements org.omg.CORBA.portable.IDLEntity;
public abstract class **StructMemberHelper**;
public class **TCKind**;
public abstract class **TypeCode** implements org.omg.CORBA.portable.IDLEntity;
public final class **TypeCodeHolder** implements org.omg.CORBA.portable.Streamable;
public abstract class **ULongLongSeqHelper**;

```
public final class ULongLongSeqHolder implements org.omg.CORBA.portable.Streamable;
public abstract class ULongSeqHelper;
public final class ULongSeqHolder implements org.omg.CORBA.portable.Streamable;
public final class UnionMember implements org.omg.CORBA.portable.IDLEntity;
public abstract class UnionMemberHelper;
public abstract class UnknownUserExceptionHelper;
public final class UnknownUserExceptionHolder implements org.omg.CORBA.portable.Streamable;
public abstract class UShortSeqHelper;
public final class UShortSeqHolder implements org.omg.CORBA.portable.Streamable;
public abstract class ValueBaseHelper;
public final class ValueBaseHolder implements org.omg.CORBA.portable.Streamable;
public final class ValueMember implements org.omg.CORBA.portable.IDLEntity;
public abstract class ValueMemberHelper;
public abstract class VersionSpecHelper;
public abstract class VisibilityHelper;
public abstract class WCharSeqHelper;
public final class WCharSeqHolder implements org.omg.CORBA.portable.Streamable;
public abstract class WrongTransactionHelper;
public final class WrongTransactionHolder implements org.omg.CORBA.portable.Streamable;
public abstract class WStringSeqHelper;
public final class WStringSeqHolder implements org.omg.CORBA.portable.Streamable;
public class WStringValueHelper implements org.omg.CORBA.portable.BoxedValueHelper;
```

Exceptions:

```
public abstract class SystemException extends RuntimeException;
  └ public final class BAD_CONTEXT extends SystemException;
  └ public final class BAD_INV_ORDER extends SystemException;
  └ public final class BAD_OPERATION extends SystemException;
  └ public final class BAD_PARAM extends SystemException;
  └ public final class BAD_TYPECODE extends SystemException;
  └ public final class COMM_FAILURE extends SystemException;
  └ public final class DATA_CONVERSION extends SystemException;
  └ public final class FREE_MEM extends SystemException;
  └ public final class IMP_LIMIT extends SystemException;
  └ public final class INITIALIZE extends SystemException;
  └ public final class INTERNAL extends SystemException;
  └ public final class INTF_REPOS extends SystemException;
  └ public final class INV_FLAG extends SystemException;
  └ public final class INV_IDENT extends SystemException;
  └ public final class INV_OBJREF extends SystemException;
  └ public final class INV_POLICY extends SystemException;
  └ public final class INVALID_TRANSACTION extends SystemException;
  └ public final class MARSHAL extends SystemException;
  └ public final class NO_IMPLEMENT extends SystemException;
  └ public final class NO_MEMORY extends SystemException;
  └ public final class NO_PERMISSION extends SystemException;
  └ public final class NO_RESOURCES extends SystemException;
  └ public final class NO_RESPONSE extends SystemException;
  └ public final class OBJ_ADAPTER extends SystemException;
  └ public final class OBJECT_NOT_EXIST extends SystemException;
  └ public final class PERSIST_STORE extends SystemException;
  └ public final class TRANSACTION_REQUIRED extends SystemException;
```

∟ public final class **TRANSACTION_ROLLEDBACK** extends SystemException;
∟ public final class **TRANSIENT** extends SystemException;
∟ public final class **UNKNOWN** extends SystemException;
public abstract class **UserException** extends Exception implements org.omg.CORBA.portable.IDLEntity;
∟ public final class **Bounds** extends UserException;
∟ public final class **PolicyError** extends UserException;
∟ public final class **UnknownUserException** extends UserException;
∟ public final class **WrongTransaction** extends UserException;

_IDLTypeStub

Java 1.3

org.omg.CORBA *serializable*

Generated stub class for the IDLType interface.

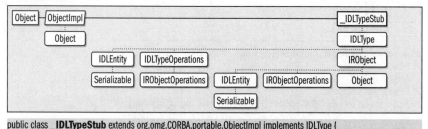

```
public class _IDLTypeStub extends org.omg.CORBA.portable.ObjectImpl implements IDLType {
// Public Constructors
    public _IDLTypeStub();
    public _IDLTypeStub(org.omg.CORBA.portable.Delegate delegate);
// Methods Implementing IDLTypeOperations
    public TypeCode type();
// Methods Implementing IRObjectOperations
    public DefinitionKind def_kind();
    public void destroy();
// Public Methods Overriding ObjectImpl
    public String[] _ids();
}
```

_PolicyStub

Java 1.3

org.omg.CORBA *serializable*

Generated stub class for the Policy interface.

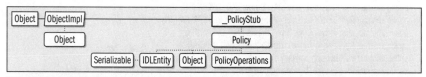

```
public class _PolicyStub extends org.omg.CORBA.portable.ObjectImpl implements org.omg.CORBA.Policy {
// Public Constructors
    public _PolicyStub();
    public _PolicyStub(org.omg.CORBA.portable.Delegate delegate);
// Methods Implementing PolicyOperations
    public org.omg.CORBA.Policy copy();
    public void destroy();
    public int policy_type();
// Public Methods Overriding ObjectImpl
```

```
    public String[ ] _ids();
}
```

Any
org.omg.CORBA

A wrapper for any IDL type, whether user-defined or a basic type. You can access the TypeCode for the contents of the Any object using the type() methods, and you can access the data itself using the extract_XXX() and insert_XXX() methods.

The Any object is the "value" in a NamedValue object. Any objects are used often in the Dynamic Invocation Interface, to compose arguments to method requests. They are also used to retrieve the values in Context objects.

```
┌─────────┐   ┌─────┐
│ Object  ├───┤ Any │
└─────────┘   └─────┘
┌─────────────┐ ┌───────────┐
│ Serializable├─┤ IDLEntity │
└─────────────┘ └───────────┘
```

```
public abstract class Any implements org.omg.CORBA.portable.IDLEntity {
// Public Constructors
    public Any();
// Public Instance Methods
    public abstract org.omg.CORBA.portable.InputStream create_input_stream();
    public abstract org.omg.CORBA.portable.OutputStream create_output_stream();
    public abstract boolean equal(Any a);
    public abstract Any extract_any() throws BAD_OPERATION;
    public abstract boolean extract_boolean() throws BAD_OPERATION;
    public abstract char extract_char() throws BAD_OPERATION;
    public abstract double extract_double() throws BAD_OPERATION;
    public java.math.BigDecimal extract_fixed();
    public abstract float extract_float() throws BAD_OPERATION;
    public abstract int extract_long() throws BAD_OPERATION;
    public abstract long extract_longlong() throws BAD_OPERATION;
    public abstract org.omg.CORBA.Object extract_Object() throws BAD_OPERATION;
    public abstract byte extract_octet() throws BAD_OPERATION;
    public abstract short extract_short() throws BAD_OPERATION;
1.4 public abstract org.omg.CORBA.portable.Streamable extract_Streamable() throws BAD_INV_ORDER;
    public abstract String extract_string() throws BAD_OPERATION;
    public abstract TypeCode extract_TypeCode() throws BAD_OPERATION;
    public abstract int extract_ulong() throws BAD_OPERATION;
    public abstract long extract_ulonglong() throws BAD_OPERATION;
    public abstract short extract_ushort() throws BAD_OPERATION;
    public abstract Serializable extract_Value() throws BAD_OPERATION;
    public abstract char extract_wchar() throws BAD_OPERATION;
    public abstract String extract_wstring() throws BAD_OPERATION;
    public abstract void insert_any(Any a);
    public abstract void insert_boolean(boolean b);
    public abstract void insert_char(char c) throws DATA_CONVERSION;
    public abstract void insert_double(double d);
    public void insert_fixed(java.math.BigDecimal value);
    public void insert_fixed(java.math.BigDecimal value, TypeCode type) throws BAD_INV_ORDER;
    public abstract void insert_float(float f);
    public abstract void insert_long(int l);
    public abstract void insert_longlong(long l);
    public abstract void insert_Object(org.omg.CORBA.Object o);
    public abstract void insert_Object(org.omg.CORBA.Object o, TypeCode t) throws BAD_PARAM;
```

```
    public abstract void insert_octet(byte b);
    public abstract void insert_short(short s);
    public void insert_Streamable(org.omg.CORBA.portable.Streamable s);
    public abstract void insert_string(String s) throws DATA_CONVERSION, MARSHAL;
    public abstract void insert_TypeCode(TypeCode t);
    public abstract void insert_ulong(int l);
    public abstract void insert_ulonglong(long l);
    public abstract void insert_ushort(short s);
    public abstract void insert_Value(Serializable v);
    public abstract void insert_Value(Serializable v, TypeCode t) throws MARSHAL;
    public abstract void insert_wchar(char c);
    public abstract void insert_wstring(String s) throws MARSHAL;
    public abstract void read_value(org.omg.CORBA.portable.InputStream is, TypeCode t) throws MARSHAL;
    public abstract TypeCode type();
    public abstract void type(TypeCode t);
    public abstract void write_value(org.omg.CORBA.portable.OutputStream os);
// Deprecated Public Methods
#   public org.omg.CORBA.Principal extract_Principal() throws BAD_OPERATION;
#   public void insert_Principal(org.omg.CORBA.Principal p);
}
```

Passed To: Too many methods to list.

Returned By: Too many methods to list.

Type Of: AnyHolder.value, AnySeqHolder.value, org.omg.CORBA.NameValuePair.value, UnionMember.label, UnknownUserException.except, org.omg.Dynamic.Parameter.argument, org.omg.DynamicAny.NameValuePair.value

AnyHolder   Java 1.2

org.omg.CORBA

The holder class for Any objects. See Chapter 4 for more information on the uses of holder classes. The AnyHolder class is used primarily to wrap out and inout arguments to methods when composing Dynamic Invocation Interface requests.

```
Object ─ AnyHolder ┈ Streamable
```

```
public final class AnyHolder implements org.omg.CORBA.portable.Streamable {
// Public Constructors
    public AnyHolder();
    public AnyHolder(Any initial);
// Methods Implementing Streamable
    public void _read(org.omg.CORBA.portable.InputStream input);
    public TypeCode _type();
    public void _write(org.omg.CORBA.portable.OutputStream output);
// Public Instance Fields
    public Any value;
}
```

AnySeqHelper   Java 1.3

org.omg.CORBA

The helper class for arrays of Any objects, used to read and write these arrays when they are used as remote method arguments or return values.

```
public abstract class AnySeqHelper {
// Public Constructors
    public AnySeqHelper();
// Public Class Methods
    public static Any[ ] extract(Any a);
    public static String id();
    public static void insert(Any a, Any[ ] that);
    public static Any[ ] read(org.omg.CORBA.portable.InputStream istream);
    public static TypeCode type();                                                    synchronized
    public static void write(org.omg.CORBA.portable.OutputStream ostream, Any[ ] value);
}
```

AnySeqHolder   Java 1.3

org.omg.CORBA

The holder class for the IDL AnySeq typedef, which resolves to an array of Any objects.
This holder class is used wrap out and inout arguments of this type in remote method
calls.

```
Object ├─ AnySeqHolder ┈ Streamable
```

```
public final class AnySeqHolder implements org.omg.CORBA.portable.Streamable {
// Public Constructors
    public AnySeqHolder();
    public AnySeqHolder(Any[ ] initialValue);
// Methods Implementing Streamable
    public void _read(org.omg.CORBA.portable.InputStream i);
    public TypeCode _type();
    public void _write(org.omg.CORBA.portable.OutputStream o);
// Public Instance Fields
    public Any[ ] value;
}
```

Passed To: org.omg.CORBA.DataInputStream.read_any_array()

ARG_IN   Java 1.2

org.omg.CORBA

This abstract interface holds a static value member that is used to specify an input
method argument when creating named values with the ORB.create_named_value()
method. The last argument to this method is a integer flag indicating the argument
mode for the named value, as it will be used in a dynamic method invocation. The
integer flag can be either ARG_IN.value, ARG_OUT.value, or ARG_INOUT.value, to indicate what
type of method argument the named value represents. For example, assuming that you
have a reference to an ORB named myOrb, and an Any object named myAny that holds
the argument value:

```
org.omg.CORBA.NamedValue inArg =
                        myOrb.create_named_value("MethodArg1", myAny,
                        org.omg.CORBA.ARG_IN.value);
```

The inArg named value can now be used in a Dynamic Invocation Interface call to a
method that has an in argument named "MethodArg1".

```
public interface ARG_IN {
// Public Constants
```

```
   public static final int value;                                                    =1
}
```

ARG_INOUT   Java 1.2
org.omg.CORBA

This abstract interface is used to specify inout method arguments, by using its static value member in calls to the ORB.create_named_value() method. See the description for the ARG_IN interface for more details.

```
public interface ARG_INOUT {
// Public Constants
   public static final int value;                                                    =3
}
```

ARG_OUT   Java 1.2
org.omg.CORBA

This abstract interface is used to specify out method arguments, by using its static value member in calls to the ORB.create_named_value() method. See the description for the ARG_IN interface for more details.

```
public interface ARG_OUT {
// Public Constants
   public static final int value;                                                    =2
}
```

BAD_CONTEXT   Java 1.2
org.omg.CORBA   *serializable unchecked*

An standard CORBA exception thrown when a context object cannot be processed.

```
public final class BAD_CONTEXT extends org.omg.CORBA.SystemException {
// Public Constructors
   public BAD_CONTEXT();
   public BAD_CONTEXT(String s);
   public BAD_CONTEXT(int minor, CompletionStatus completed);
   public BAD_CONTEXT(String s, int minor, CompletionStatus completed);
}
```

BAD_INV_ORDER   Java 1.2
org.omg.CORBA   *serializable unchecked*

A standard CORBA exception thrown when methods are called out of order. For example, if you call the arguments() method on a ServerRequest object, then try to set the arguments again by calling the method again, a BAD_INV_ORDER exception will be thrown.

```
public final class BAD_INV_ORDER extends org.omg.CORBA.SystemException {
// Public Constructors
    public BAD_INV_ORDER();
    public BAD_INV_ORDER(String s);
    public BAD_INV_ORDER(int minor, CompletionStatus completed);
    public BAD_INV_ORDER(String s, int minor, CompletionStatus completed);
}
```

Thrown By: Any.{extract_Streamable(), insert_fixed()}

BAD_OPERATION   Java 1.2

org.omg.CORBA   *serializable unchecked*

A standard CORBA exception thrown when an invalid method is invoked. If, for example, you call an extract_XXX() method on an Any object for a type that it does not contain, a BAD_OPERATION will be thrown.

```
Object ─ Throwable ─ Exception ─ RuntimeException ─ SystemException ─ BAD_OPERATION
              Serializable
```

```
public final class BAD_OPERATION extends org.omg.CORBA.SystemException {
// Public Constructors
    public BAD_OPERATION();
    public BAD_OPERATION(String s);
    public BAD_OPERATION(int minor, CompletionStatus completed);
    public BAD_OPERATION(String s, int minor, CompletionStatus completed);
}
```

Thrown By: Any.{extract_any(), extract_boolean(), extract_char(), extract_double(), extract_float(), extract_long(), extract_longlong(), extract_Object(), extract_octet(), extract_Principal(), extract_short(), extract_string(), extract_TypeCode(), extract_ulong(), extract_ulonglong(), extract_ushort(), extract_Value(), extract_wchar(), extract_wstring()}

BAD_PARAM   Java 1.2

org.omg.CORBA   *serializable unchecked*

A standard CORBA exception thrown when an invalid argument is passed into a remote method. This exception defines a single error code value for the SystemException.minor data member:

Minor code	Meaning
1	A null value was passed into a remote method.

```
Object ─ Throwable ─ Exception ─ RuntimeException ─ SystemException ─ BAD_PARAM
              Serializable
```

```
public final class BAD_PARAM extends org.omg.CORBA.SystemException {
// Public Constructors
    public BAD_PARAM();
    public BAD_PARAM(String s);
    public BAD_PARAM(int minor, CompletionStatus completed);
    public BAD_PARAM(String s, int minor, CompletionStatus completed);
}
```

Thrown By: Any.insert_Object(), org.omg.CORBA_2_3.ORB.get_value_def()

BAD_POLICY
Java 1.2

org.omg.CORBA

One of the PolicyErrorCode values that a PolicyError exception carries when it is thrown. Indicates that a Policy was used that the ORB didn't recognize.

```
public interface BAD_POLICY {
// Public Constants
    public static final short value;                                    =0
}
```

BAD_POLICY_TYPE
Java 1.2

org.omg.CORBA

One of the PolicyErrorCode values that a PolicyError exception carries when it is thrown. Indicates that the value requested/given for a Policy was of a type that is incompatible with the corresponding PolicyType.

```
public interface BAD_POLICY_TYPE {
// Public Constants
    public static final short value;                                    =2
}
```

BAD_POLICY_VALUE
Java 1.2

org.omg.CORBA

One of the PolicyErrorCode values that a PolicyError exception carries when it is thrown. Indicates that the value requested/given for a Policy was not within the valid range for the PolicyType.

```
public interface BAD_POLICY_VALUE {
// Public Constants
    public static final short value;                                    =3
}
```

BAD_TYPECODE
Java 1.2

org.omg.CORBA
serializable unchecked

A standard CORBA exception thrown when an invalid TypeCode is specified.

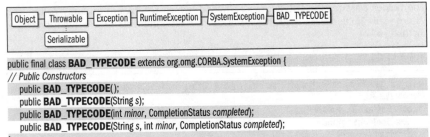

```
public final class BAD_TYPECODE extends org.omg.CORBA.SystemException {
// Public Constructors
    public BAD_TYPECODE();
    public BAD_TYPECODE(String s);
    public BAD_TYPECODE(int minor, CompletionStatus completed);
    public BAD_TYPECODE(String s, int minor, CompletionStatus completed);
}
```

BooleanHolder

org.omg.CORBA

The holder class for out and inout remote method arguments that would be mapped to Java boolean values. See Chapter 4 for more information on the uses of holder classes.

```
Object ├─ BooleanHolder ┈ Streamable
```

```
public final class BooleanHolder implements org.omg.CORBA.portable.Streamable {
// Public Constructors
    public BooleanHolder();
    public BooleanHolder(boolean initial);
// Methods Implementing Streamable
    public void _read(org.omg.CORBA.portable.InputStream input);
    public TypeCode _type();
    public void _write(org.omg.CORBA.portable.OutputStream output);
// Public Instance Fields
    public boolean value;
}
```

BooleanSeqHelper

org.omg.CORBA

The helper class for arrays of Boolean objects, used to read and write these arrays when they are used as remote method arguments or return values.

```
public abstract class BooleanSeqHelper {
// Public Constructors
    public BooleanSeqHelper();
// Public Class Methods
    public static boolean[ ] extract(Any a);
    public static String id();
    public static void insert(Any a, boolean[ ] that);
    public static boolean[ ] read(org.omg.CORBA.portable.InputStream istream);
    public static TypeCode type();                                            synchronized
    public static void write(org.omg.CORBA.portable.OutputStream ostream, boolean[ ] value);
}
```

BooleanSeqHolder

org.omg.CORBA

The holder class for the IDL BooleanSeq typedef, which resolves to an array of boolean values. This holder class is used wrap out and inout arguments of this type in remote method calls.

```
Object ├─ BooleanSeqHolder ┈ Streamable
```

```
public final class BooleanSeqHolder implements org.omg.CORBA.portable.Streamable {
// Public Constructors
    public BooleanSeqHolder();
    public BooleanSeqHolder(boolean[ ] initialValue);
// Methods Implementing Streamable
    public void _read(org.omg.CORBA.portable.InputStream i);
    public TypeCode _type();
    public void _write(org.omg.CORBA.portable.OutputStream o);
// Public Instance Fields
```

```
public boolean[ ] value;
}
```

Passed To: org.omg.CORBA.DataInputStream.read_boolean_array()

Bounds

org.omg.CORBA *serializable checked*

An exception thrown when a value that falls out of the valid bounds is passed into a method, e.g., when an index passed into a list object is greater than the size of the list.

```
Object ─ Throwable ─ Exception ─ UserException ─ Bounds
          Serializable   Serializable      IDLEntity
```

```
public final class Bounds extends UserException {
// Public Constructors
   public Bounds();
   public Bounds(String reason);
}
```

Thrown By: ContextList.{item(), remove()}, ExceptionList.{item(), remove()}, NVList.{item(), remove()}

ByteHolder
Java 1.2

org.omg.CORBA

The holder class for out and inout remote method arguments that would be mapped to Java byte values. See Chapter 4 for more information on the uses of holder classes.

```
Object ─ ByteHolder ─ Streamable
```

```
public final class ByteHolder implements org.omg.CORBA.portable.Streamable {
// Public Constructors
   public ByteHolder();
   public ByteHolder(byte initial);
// Methods Implementing Streamable
   public void _read(org.omg.CORBA.portable.InputStream input);
   public TypeCode _type();
   public void _write(org.omg.CORBA.portable.OutputStream output);
// Public Instance Fields
   public byte value;
}
```

CharHolder
Java 1.2

org.omg.CORBA

The holder class for out and inout remote method arguments that would be mapped to Java char values. See Chapter 4 for more information on the uses of holder classes.

```
Object ─ CharHolder ─ Streamable
```

```
public final class CharHolder implements org.omg.CORBA.portable.Streamable {
// Public Constructors
   public CharHolder();
   public CharHolder(char initial);
// Methods Implementing Streamable
```

```
    public void _read(org.omg.CORBA.portable.InputStream input);
    public TypeCode _type();
    public void _write(org.omg.CORBA.portable.OutputStream output);
// Public Instance Fields
    public char value;
}
```

CharSeqHelper   Java 1.3

org.omg.CORBA

The helper class for arrays of characters, used to read and write these arrays when they are used as remote method arguments or return values.

```
public abstract class CharSeqHelper {
// Public Constructors
    public CharSeqHelper();
// Public Class Methods
    public static char[ ] extract(Any a);
    public static String id();
    public static void insert(Any a, char[ ] that);
    public static char[ ] read(org.omg.CORBA.portable.InputStream istream);
    public static TypeCode type();                                    synchronized
    public static void write(org.omg.CORBA.portable.OutputStream ostream, char[ ] value);
}
```

CharSeqHolder   Java 1.3

org.omg.CORBA

The holder class for the IDL CharSeq typedef, which resolves to an array of character values. This holder class is used wrap out and inout arguments of this type in remote method calls.

```
Object ├─ CharSeqHolder ┈┤ Streamable
```

```
public final class CharSeqHolder implements org.omg.CORBA.portable.Streamable {
// Public Constructors
    public CharSeqHolder();
    public CharSeqHolder(char[ ] initialValue);
// Methods Implementing Streamable
    public void _read(org.omg.CORBA.portable.InputStream i);
    public TypeCode _type();
    public void _write(org.omg.CORBA.portable.OutputStream o);
// Public Instance Fields
    public char[ ] value;
}
```

Passed To: org.omg.CORBA.DataInputStream.read_char_array()

COMM_FAILURE   Java 1.2

org.omg.CORBA   *serializable unchecked*

A standard CORBA exception thrown when a communications failure occurs during a remote operation. Sun's Java IDL defines the following minor error code values for this exception, stored in the minor data member inherited from SystemException:

Minor code	Meaning
1	Unable to connect to the required remote ORB. The location (host and port number) of the ORB can be specified in a caller-provided object reference, or in an object reference acquired while processing the request.
2	A write to a socket failed, either because the socket was closed by the remote peer, or because the socket connection has been aborted.
3	A write to a socket failed because the connection was closed on this side on the socket.
6	Multiple attempts to connect to the remote server have failed.

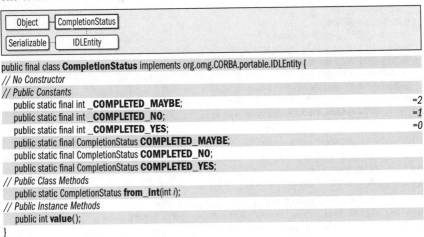

```
public final class COMM_FAILURE extends org.omg.CORBA.SystemException {
// Public Constructors
   public COMM_FAILURE();
   public COMM_FAILURE(String s);
   public COMM_FAILURE(int minor, CompletionStatus completed);
   public COMM_FAILURE(String s, int minor, CompletionStatus completed);
}
```

CompletionStatus   Java 1.2

org.omg.CORBA   *serializable*

When an org.omg.CORBA.SystemException is thrown, it contains a CompletionStatus object that indicates whether the method invoked was completed before the exception was encountered.

The CompletionStatus class has three static instances, COMPLETED_YES, COMPLETED_MAYBE, and COMPLETED_NO, and three static int members, _COMPLETED_YES, _COMPLETED_MAYBE and _COMPLETED_NO. When you receive a CompletionStatus, you can either compare it to one of the static instances, or compare its value (queried using the value() method) to one of the static int values.

```
public final class CompletionStatus implements org.omg.CORBA.portable.IDLEntity {
// No Constructor
// Public Constants
   public static final int _COMPLETED_MAYBE;                        =2
   public static final int _COMPLETED_NO;                           =1
   public static final int _COMPLETED_YES;                          =0
   public static final CompletionStatus COMPLETED_MAYBE;
   public static final CompletionStatus COMPLETED_NO;
   public static final CompletionStatus COMPLETED_YES;
// Public Class Methods
   public static CompletionStatus from_int(int i);
// Public Instance Methods
   public int value();
}
```

Passed To: Too many methods to list.

Returned By: CompletionStatus.from_int(), CompletionStatusHelper.{extract(), read()}

Type Of: CompletionStatus.{COMPLETED_MAYBE, COMPLETED_NO, COMPLETED_YES}, org.omg.CORBA.SystemException.completed

CompletionStatusHelper   Java 1.3

org.omg.CORBA

The helper class for CompletionStatus objects, used to read and write these objects when they are used as remote method arguments or return values.

```
public abstract class CompletionStatusHelper {
// Public Constructors
    public CompletionStatusHelper();
// Public Class Methods
    public static CompletionStatus extract(Any a);
    public static String id();
    public static void insert(Any a, CompletionStatus that);
    public static CompletionStatus read(org.omg.CORBA.portable.InputStream istream);
    public static TypeCode type();                                              synchronized
    public static void write(org.omg.CORBA.portable.OutputStream ostream, CompletionStatus value);
}
```

Context   Java 1.2

org.omg.CORBA

Context objects contain a list of properties, stored as NamedValue objects, that are passed along with method requests to indicate properties of the client context. Every ORB has a default context, accessed using the ORB.get_default_context() method. Contexts can be linked in a hierarchy of contexts. If a search for a property is made on a Context object and the search within the object fails, then the search is continued in the parent Context, and so on until the root context is reached. You can create a new child of a Context using its create_child() method. Other methods on the Context class let you get, set and delete values from the Context.

```
public abstract class Context {
// Public Constructors
    public Context();
// Public Instance Methods
    public abstract String context_name();
    public abstract org.omg.CORBA.Context create_child(String child_ctx_name);
    public abstract void delete_values(String propname);
    public abstract NVList get_values(String start_scope, int op_flags, String pattern);
    public abstract org.omg.CORBA.Context parent();
    public abstract void set_one_value(String propname, Any propvalue);
    public abstract void set_values(NVList values);
}
```

Passed To: LocalObject._create_request(), org.omg.CORBA.Object._create_request(), Request.ctx(), org.omg.CORBA.portable.Delegate.create_request(), org.omg.CORBA.portable.ObjectImpl._create_request(), org.omg.CORBA.portable.OutputStream.write_Context()

Returned By: org.omg.CORBA.Context.{create_child(), parent()}, org.omg.CORBA.ORB.get_default_context(), Request.ctx(), ServerRequest.ctx(), org.omg.CORBA.portable.InputStream.read_Context()

ContextList

org.omg.CORBA

A list of context property names only (i.e., a list of Strings). A ContextList along with an NVList containing NamedValue objects is used to represent the relevant subset of a Context that is passed along with remote method calls.

```
public abstract class ContextList {
// Public Constructors
    public ContextList();
// Public Instance Methods
    public abstract void add(String ctx);
    public abstract int count();
    public abstract String item(int index) throws org.omg.CORBA.Bounds;
    public abstract void remove(int index) throws org.omg.CORBA.Bounds;
}
```

Passed To: LocalObject._create_request(), org.omg.CORBA.Object._create_request(), org.omg.CORBA.portable.Delegate.create_request(), org.omg.CORBA.portable.ObjectImpl._create_request(), org.omg.CORBA.portable.OutputStream.write_Context()

Returned By: org.omg.CORBA.ORB.create_context_list(), Request.contexts()

CTX_RESTRICT_SCOPE

org.omg.CORBA

This abstract interface contains a static value member that can be used as a flag to the search routine accessible through the Context.get_values() method. Using CTX_RESTRICT_SCOPE.value as the flag to this method indicates that the search for context values should be restricted to the scope specified in the first method argument, or to the context object used to invoke the method, if the scope is null. For example, this call to the search method:

```
Context ctx = ... // get context somehow
NVList myVals = ctx.get_values(null,
    org.omg.CORBA.CTX_RESTRICT_SCOPE.value, "username");
```

searches the context represented by the context object for values named "username".

```
public interface CTX_RESTRICT_SCOPE {
// Public Constants
    public static final int value;                                              =15
}
```

Current

org.omg.CORBA

The Current interface represents an optional feature provided by CORBA, which allows the ORB and CORBA services to export information about the thread in which they are running. If an ORB or service provider decides to provide this information, they should create a concrete subclass of this interface, and make it available through the ORB's resolve_initial_references() method.

Sun's Java IDL does not make use of this feature for providing context information.

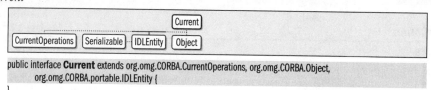

```
public interface Current extends org.omg.CORBA.CurrentOperations, org.omg.CORBA.Object,
        org.omg.CORBA.portable.IDLEntity {
}
```

Implementations: org.omg.PortableInterceptor.Current, org.omg.PortableServer.Current

Passed To: org.omg.CORBA.CurrentHelper.{insert(), write()}, CurrentHolder.CurrentHolder()

Returned By: org.omg.CORBA.CurrentHelper.{extract(), narrow(), read()},
org.omg.CORBA.ORB.get_current()

Type Of: CurrentHolder.value

CurrentHelper   Java 1.3

org.omg.CORBA

The helper class for Current objects, used to safely cast remote references to these
objects, and to read and write these objects when they are used as remote method
arguments or return values.

```
public abstract class CurrentHelper {
// Public Constructors
    public CurrentHelper();
// Public Class Methods
    public static org.omg.CORBA.Current extract(Any a);
    public static String id();
    public static void insert(Any a, org.omg.CORBA.Current that);
    public static org.omg.CORBA.Current narrow(org.omg.CORBA.Object obj);
    public static org.omg.CORBA.Current read(org.omg.CORBA.portable.InputStream istream);
    public static TypeCode type();                                                      synchronized
    public static void write(org.omg.CORBA.portable.OutputStream ostream, org.omg.CORBA.Current value);
}
```

CurrentHolder   Java 1.3

org.omg.CORBA

The holder class for Current objects. This holder class is used wrap out and inout arguments of this type in remote method calls.

```
Object ─ CurrentHolder ┈ Streamable
```

```
public final class CurrentHolder implements org.omg.CORBA.portable.Streamable {
// Public Constructors
    public CurrentHolder();
    public CurrentHolder(org.omg.CORBA.Current initialValue);
// Methods Implementing Streamable
    public void _read(org.omg.CORBA.portable.InputStream i);
    public TypeCode _type();
    public void _write(org.omg.CORBA.portable.OutputStream o);
// Public Instance Fields
    public org.omg.CORBA.Current value;
}
```

CurrentOperations

org.omg.CORBA

The generated Operations interface for the Current interface.

```
public interface CurrentOperations {
}
```

Implementations: org.omg.CORBA.Current, org.omg.PortableInterceptor.CurrentOperations, org.omg.PortableServer.CurrentOperations

CustomMarshal

org.omg.CORBA

An interface that must be implemented (indirectly) by all custom value types, by providing implementations of the marshal and unmarshal methods that will be used by the ORB during remote operations using the custom value type.

```
public interface CustomMarshal {
// Public Instance Methods
    public abstract void marshal(org.omg.CORBA.DataOutputStream os);
    public abstract void unmarshal(org.omg.CORBA.DataInputStream is);
}
```

Implementations: org.omg.CORBA.portable.CustomValue

DATA_CONVERSION

org.omg.CORBA   *serializable unchecked*

A standard CORBA exception thrown when the ORB fails to convert some piece of data, such as during the conversion of a stringified object reference. Sun's Java IDL defines the following minor error code values for this exception, stored in the minor data member inherited from SystemException:

Minor code	Meaning
1	A bad hexadecimal character was found while converting a stringified object reference back to an object reference.
2	The byte length of a stringified object reference is odd, when it must be even.
3	The "IOR:" preface is missing from the stringified object reference passed into string_to_object().
4	The resolve_initial_references() method failed because the location (host and port number) of the remote ORB specified is invalid or unspecified, or the remote server doesn't support the Java IDL bootstrap protocol.

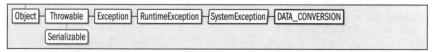

```
public final class DATA_CONVERSION extends org.omg.CORBA.SystemException {
// Public Constructors
    public DATA_CONVERSION();
    public DATA_CONVERSION(String s);
```

```
     public DATA_CONVERSION(int minor, CompletionStatus completed);
     public DATA_CONVERSION(String s, int minor, CompletionStatus completed);
}
```

Thrown By: Any.{insert_char(), insert_string()}

DataInputStream
Java 1.3

org.omg.CORBA
serializable

An interface that declares methods for reading basic data types from input streams.

Serializable ┤ IDLEntity ├ ValueBase ┤ DataInputStream

```
public interface DataInputStream extends org.omg.CORBA.portable.ValueBase {
// Public Instance Methods
   public abstract Object read_Abstract();
   public abstract Any read_any();
   public abstract void read_any_array(AnySeqHolder seq, int offset, int length);
   public abstract boolean read_boolean();
   public abstract void read_boolean_array(BooleanSeqHolder seq, int offset, int length);
   public abstract char read_char();
   public abstract void read_char_array(CharSeqHolder seq, int offset, int length);
   public abstract double read_double();
   public abstract void read_double_array(DoubleSeqHolder seq, int offset, int length);
   public abstract float read_float();
   public abstract void read_float_array(FloatSeqHolder seq, int offset, int length);
   public abstract int read_long();
   public abstract void read_long_array(LongSeqHolder seq, int offset, int length);
   public abstract long read_longlong();
   public abstract void read_longlong_array(LongLongSeqHolder seq, int offset, int length);
   public abstract org.omg.CORBA.Object read_Object();
   public abstract byte read_octet();
   public abstract void read_octet_array(OctetSeqHolder seq, int offset, int length);
   public abstract short read_short();
   public abstract void read_short_array(ShortSeqHolder seq, int offset, int length);
   public abstract String read_string();
   public abstract TypeCode read_TypeCode();
   public abstract int read_ulong();
   public abstract void read_ulong_array(ULongSeqHolder seq, int offset, int length);
   public abstract long read_ulonglong();
   public abstract void read_ulonglong_array(ULongLongSeqHolder seq, int offset, int length);
   public abstract short read_ushort();
   public abstract void read_ushort_array(UShortSeqHolder seq, int offset, int length);
   public abstract Serializable read_Value();
   public abstract char read_wchar();
   public abstract void read_wchar_array(WCharSeqHolder seq, int offset, int length);
   public abstract String read_wstring();
}
```

Passed To: CustomMarshal.unmarshal()

DataOutputStream

org.omg.CORBA

An interface that declares methods for writing basic data types to output streams.

Serializable ┈ IDLEntity ┈ ValueBase ┈ DataOutputStream

```
public interface DataOutputStream extends org.omg.CORBA.portable.ValueBase {
// Public Instance Methods
    public abstract void write_Abstract(Object value);
    public abstract void write_any(Any value);
    public abstract void write_any_array(Any[ ] seq, int offset, int length);
    public abstract void write_boolean(boolean value);
    public abstract void write_boolean_array(boolean[ ] seq, int offset, int length);
    public abstract void write_char(char value);
    public abstract void write_char_array(char[ ] seq, int offset, int length);
    public abstract void write_double(double value);
    public abstract void write_double_array(double[ ] seq, int offset, int length);
    public abstract void write_float(float value);
    public abstract void write_float_array(float[ ] seq, int offset, int length);
    public abstract void write_long(int value);
    public abstract void write_long_array(int[ ] seq, int offset, int length);
    public abstract void write_longlong(long value);
    public abstract void write_longlong_array(long[ ] seq, int offset, int length);
    public abstract void write_Object(org.omg.CORBA.Object value);
    public abstract void write_octet(byte value);
    public abstract void write_octet_array(byte[ ] seq, int offset, int length);
    public abstract void write_short(short value);
    public abstract void write_short_array(short[ ] seq, int offset, int length);
    public abstract void write_string(String value);
    public abstract void write_TypeCode(TypeCode value);
    public abstract void write_ulong(int value);
    public abstract void write_ulong_array(int[ ] seq, int offset, int length);
    public abstract void write_ulonglong(long value);
    public abstract void write_ulonglong_array(long[ ] seq, int offset, int length);
    public abstract void write_ushort(short value);
    public abstract void write_ushort_array(short[ ] seq, int offset, int length);
    public abstract void write_Value(Serializable value);
    public abstract void write_wchar(char value);
    public abstract void write_wchar_array(char[ ] seq, int offset, int length);
    public abstract void write_wstring(String value);
}
```

Passed To: CustomMarshal.marshal()

DefinitionKind

org.omg.CORBA

Used by IRObjects to indicate what type of repository object they represent (e.g., method, attribute). The DefinitionKind object has an integer value that can be compared to the static int members of this class, or the object itself can be compared to the static instances defined in this class, to determine the type of an IRObject.

```
┌─────────────────────────────────────────────────────────┐
│  ┌────────┐   ┌──────────────┐                           │
│  │ Object │───│ DefinitionKind│                          │
│  └────────┘   └──────────────┘                           │
│  ┌────────────┐   ┌──────────┐                           │
│  │Serializable│···│ IDLEntity│                           │
│  └────────────┘   └──────────┘                           │
└─────────────────────────────────────────────────────────┘
```

public class **DefinitionKind** implements org.omg.CORBA.portable.IDLEntity {

// *Protected Constructors*

   protected **DefinitionKind**(int _value);

// *Public Constants*

1.4 public static final int **_dk_AbstractInterface**;	=24
public static final int **_dk_Alias**;	=9
public static final int **_dk_all**;	=1
public static final int **_dk_Array**;	=16
public static final int **_dk_Attribute**;	=2
public static final int **_dk_Constant**;	=3
public static final int **_dk_Enum**;	=12
public static final int **_dk_Exception**;	=4
public static final int **_dk_Fixed**;	=19
public static final int **_dk_Interface**;	=5
public static final int **_dk_Module**;	=6
public static final int **_dk_Native**;	=23
public static final int **_dk_none**;	=0
public static final int **_dk_Operation**;	=7
public static final int **_dk_Primitive**;	=13
public static final int **_dk_Repository**;	=17
public static final int **_dk_Sequence**;	=15
public static final int **_dk_String**;	=14
public static final int **_dk_Struct**;	=10
public static final int **_dk_Typedef**;	=8
public static final int **_dk_Union**;	=11
public static final int **_dk_Value**;	=20
public static final int **_dk_ValueBox**;	=21
public static final int **_dk_ValueMember**;	=22
public static final int **_dk_Wstring**;	=18

1.4 public static final DefinitionKind **dk_AbstractInterface**;

   public static final DefinitionKind **dk_Alias**;

   public static final DefinitionKind **dk_all**;

   public static final DefinitionKind **dk_Array**;

   public static final DefinitionKind **dk_Attribute**;

   public static final DefinitionKind **dk_Constant**;

   public static final DefinitionKind **dk_Enum**;

   public static final DefinitionKind **dk_Exception**;

   public static final DefinitionKind **dk_Fixed**;

   public static final DefinitionKind **dk_Interface**;

   public static final DefinitionKind **dk_Module**;

   public static final DefinitionKind **dk_Native**;

   public static final DefinitionKind **dk_none**;

   public static final DefinitionKind **dk_Operation**;

   public static final DefinitionKind **dk_Primitive**;

   public static final DefinitionKind **dk_Repository**;

   public static final DefinitionKind **dk_Sequence**;

   public static final DefinitionKind **dk_String**;

   public static final DefinitionKind **dk_Struct**;

   public static final DefinitionKind **dk_Typedef**;

   public static final DefinitionKind **dk_Union**;

   public static final DefinitionKind **dk_Value**;

   public static final DefinitionKind **dk_ValueBox**;

   public static final DefinitionKind **dk_ValueMember**;

```
   public static final DefinitionKind dk_Wstring;
// Public Class Methods
   public static DefinitionKind from_int(int i);
// Public Instance Methods
   public int value();
}
```

Passed To: DefinitionKindHelper.{insert(), write()}

Returned By: _IDLTypeStub.def_kind(), DefinitionKind.from_int(), DefinitionKindHelper.{extract(), read()}, IRObjectOperations.def_kind()

Type Of: DefinitionKind.{dk_AbstractInterface, dk_Alias, dk_all, dk_Array, dk_Attribute, dk_Constant, dk_Enum, dk_Exception, dk_Fixed, dk_Interface, dk_Module, dk_Native, dk_none, dk_Operation, dk_Primitive, dk_Repository, dk_Sequence, dk_String, dk_Struct, dk_Typedef, dk_Union, dk_Value, dk_ValueBox, dk_ValueMember, dk_Wstring}

DefinitionKindHelper
Java 1.3

org.omg.CORBA

The helper class for DefinitionKind objects, used to read and write these objects when they are used as remote method arguments or return values.

```
public abstract class DefinitionKindHelper {
// Public Constructors
   public DefinitionKindHelper();
// Public Class Methods
   public static DefinitionKind extract(Any a);
   public static String id();
   public static void insert(Any a, DefinitionKind that);
   public static DefinitionKind read(org.omg.CORBA.portable.InputStream istream);
   public static TypeCode type();                                                    synchronized
   public static void write(org.omg.CORBA.portable.OutputStream ostream, DefinitionKind value);
}
```

DomainManager
Java 1.2

org.omg.CORBA
serializable

As the basis for management facilities to be added to CORBA, the DomainManager interface represents an object that manages a group of objects (a domain) under a common set of access policies. Policies control access to certain operations over the objects in a given domain. You can access the DomainManagers for an org.omg.CORBA.Object by using its _get_domain_managers() method, which returns an array of DomainManagers, one for each domain of the object. DomainManagers can be hierarchical, in that a domain can contain other DomainManagers. Since the DomainManager is an Object, you can use its _get_domain_managers() method to traverse the manager hierarchy.

The DomainManager has a single method, get_domain_policy(), which allows you to get the policy of a given type for the objects in the domain. The policy is represented by a Policy object. The type of policy is indicated with an integer identifier. The possible values for these types of policies are application-specific. The CORBA Security service, for example, defines its own set of policy types. If the policy type you pass into get_domain_policy() is not supported by the ORB, or if the domain doesn't define that type of policy, then an org.omg.CORBA.BAD_PARAM system exception is thrown.

```
public interface DomainManager extends DomainManagerOperations, org.omg.CORBA.Object,
     org.omg.CORBA.portable.IDLEntity {
}
```

Returned By: LocalObject._get_domain_managers(),
org.omg.CORBA.Object._get_domain_managers(),
org.omg.CORBA.portable.Delegate.get_domain_managers(),
org.omg.CORBA.portable.ObjectImpl._get_domain_managers()

DomainManagerOperations   Java 1.3
org.omg.CORBA

The generated operations interface for the DomainManager interface.

```
public interface DomainManagerOperations {
// Public Instance Methods
     public abstract org.omg.CORBA.Policy get_domain_policy(int policy_type);
}
```

Implementations: DomainManager

DoubleHolder   Java 1.2
org.omg.CORBA

The holder class for out and inout remote method arguments that would be mapped to
Java double values. See Chapter 4 for more information on the uses of holder classes.

```
public final class DoubleHolder implements org.omg.CORBA.portable.Streamable {
// Public Constructors
     public DoubleHolder();
     public DoubleHolder(double initial);
// Methods Implementing Streamable
     public void _read(org.omg.CORBA.portable.InputStream input);
     public TypeCode _type();
     public void _write(org.omg.CORBA.portable.OutputStream output);
// Public Instance Fields
     public double value;
}
```

DoubleSeqHelper   Java 1.3
org.omg.CORBA

The helper class for arrays of doubles, used to read and write these arrays when they
are used as remote method arguments or return values.

```
public abstract class DoubleSeqHelper {
// Public Constructors
     public DoubleSeqHelper();
// Public Class Methods
     public static double[] extract(Any a);
     public static String id();
     public static void insert(Any a, double[] that);
```

```
    public static double[ ] read(org.omg.CORBA.portable.InputStream istream);
    public static TypeCode type();                                              synchronized
    public static void write(org.omg.CORBA.portable.OutputStream ostream, double[ ] value);
}
```

DoubleSeqHolder   Java 1.3

org.omg.CORBA

The holder class for the IDL DoubleSeq typedef, which resolves to an array of double values. This holder class is used wrap out and inout arguments of this type in remote method calls.

```
Object ├─ DoubleSeqHolder ┈┈ Streamable
```

```
public final class DoubleSeqHolder implements org.omg.CORBA.portable.Streamable {
// Public Constructors
    public DoubleSeqHolder();
    public DoubleSeqHolder(double[ ] initialValue);
// Methods Implementing Streamable
    public void _read(org.omg.CORBA.portable.InputStream i);
    public TypeCode _type();
    public void _write(org.omg.CORBA.portable.OutputStream o);
// Public Instance Fields
    public double[ ] value;
}
```

Passed To: org.omg.CORBA.DataInputStream.read_double_array()

DynamicImplementation   Java 1.2; Deprecated in Java 1.4

org.omg.CORBA

The abstract base class for servant object implementations in the Dynamic Skeleton Interface. Derived servant classes must implement the invoke() method, which is called by the ORB to handle requests on the object represented by the servant.

```
Object ├─ ObjectImpl ┤─ DynamicImplementation
        └─ Object
```

```
public class DynamicImplementation extends org.omg.CORBA.portable.ObjectImpl {
// Public Constructors
    public DynamicImplementation();
// Public Methods Overriding ObjectImpl
1.4 public String[ ] _ids();
// Deprecated Public Methods
#   public void invoke(ServerRequest request);
}
```

Subclasses: org.omg.CosNaming._BindingIteratorImplBase,
org.omg.CosNaming._NamingContextImplBase

DynAny   Java 1.2

org.omg.CORBA

The DynAny interface provides the core of CORBA's facility for the dynamic introspection of Any values for which the implementation class is not available. This facility has similar goals as Java's built-in introspection facilities, but CORBA provides it as IDL interfaces so that it can be used no matter what implementation language is chosen. The CORBA facility allows services and objects to determine the type and contents of values passed into methods, without having access to their implementation interface. The service or object can wrap an incoming Any value with a DynAny in order to probe its properties and structure.

DynAny objects should not be exported outside of the processes where they are created. If you attempt to create a stringified reference to a DynAny object using the ORB.object_to_string() method, a MARSHAL exception will be thrown.

The DynAny interface provides a series of get_XXX() and insert_XXX() methods that can be used to access or modify the contents of the Any value if it is an IDL basic type. The TypeCode for the contents can also be accessed, using the type() method. If the Any value holds a complex data type, such as a struct, then the next(), seek(), rewind() and current_component() methods on the DynAny interface can be used to iterate through the data members of the contents.

There are various subtypes of DynAny which provide access to the components of specific IDL complex types, such as structs, enums, and unions. These and basic DynAny objects can be created using the create_dyn_XXX() methods available on the ORB interface.

```
Object -- DynAny
```

```
public interface DynAny extends org.omg.CORBA.Object {
// Property Accessor Methods (by property name)
    public abstract Any get_any() throws org.omg.CORBA.DynAnyPackage.TypeMismatch;
    public abstract boolean get_boolean() throws org.omg.CORBA.DynAnyPackage.TypeMismatch;
    public abstract char get_char() throws org.omg.CORBA.DynAnyPackage.TypeMismatch;
    public abstract double get_double() throws org.omg.CORBA.DynAnyPackage.TypeMismatch;
    public abstract float get_float() throws org.omg.CORBA.DynAnyPackage.TypeMismatch;
    public abstract int get_long() throws org.omg.CORBA.DynAnyPackage.TypeMismatch;
    public abstract long get_longlong() throws org.omg.CORBA.DynAnyPackage.TypeMismatch;
    public abstract byte get_octet() throws org.omg.CORBA.DynAnyPackage.TypeMismatch;
    public abstract org.omg.CORBA.Object get_reference() throws org.omg.CORBA.DynAnyPackage.TypeMismatch;
    public abstract short get_short() throws org.omg.CORBA.DynAnyPackage.TypeMismatch;
    public abstract String get_string() throws org.omg.CORBA.DynAnyPackage.TypeMismatch;
    public abstract TypeCode get_typecode() throws org.omg.CORBA.DynAnyPackage.TypeMismatch;
    public abstract int get_ulong() throws org.omg.CORBA.DynAnyPackage.TypeMismatch;
    public abstract long get_ulonglong() throws org.omg.CORBA.DynAnyPackage.TypeMismatch;
    public abstract short get_ushort() throws org.omg.CORBA.DynAnyPackage.TypeMismatch;
    public abstract Serializable get_val() throws org.omg.CORBA.DynAnyPackage.TypeMismatch;
    public abstract char get_wchar() throws org.omg.CORBA.DynAnyPackage.TypeMismatch;
    public abstract String get_wstring() throws org.omg.CORBA.DynAnyPackage.TypeMismatch;
// Public Instance Methods
    public abstract void assign(org.omg.CORBA.DynAny dyn_any) throws org.omg.CORBA.DynAnyPackage.Invalid;
    public abstract org.omg.CORBA.DynAny copy();
    public abstract org.omg.CORBA.DynAny current_component();
    public abstract void destroy();
    public abstract void from_any(Any value) throws org.omg.CORBA.DynAnyPackage.Invalid;
    public abstract void insert_any(Any value) throws org.omg.CORBA.DynAnyPackage.InvalidValue;
    public abstract void insert_boolean(boolean value) throws org.omg.CORBA.DynAnyPackage.InvalidValue;
    public abstract void insert_char(char value) throws org.omg.CORBA.DynAnyPackage.InvalidValue;
    public abstract void insert_double(double value) throws org.omg.CORBA.DynAnyPackage.InvalidValue;
    public abstract void insert_float(float value) throws org.omg.CORBA.DynAnyPackage.InvalidValue;
    public abstract void insert_long(int value) throws org.omg.CORBA.DynAnyPackage.InvalidValue;
    public abstract void insert_longlong(long value) throws org.omg.CORBA.DynAnyPackage.InvalidValue;
    public abstract void insert_octet(byte value) throws org.omg.CORBA.DynAnyPackage.InvalidValue;
```

```
   public abstract void insert_reference(org.omg.CORBA.Object value)
      throws org.omg.CORBA.DynAnyPackage.InvalidValue;
   public abstract void insert_short(short value) throws org.omg.CORBA.DynAnyPackage.InvalidValue;
   public abstract void insert_string(String value) throws org.omg.CORBA.DynAnyPackage.InvalidValue;
   public abstract void insert_typecode(TypeCode value) throws org.omg.CORBA.DynAnyPackage.InvalidValue;
   public abstract void insert_ulong(int value) throws org.omg.CORBA.DynAnyPackage.InvalidValue;
   public abstract void insert_ulonglong(long value) throws org.omg.CORBA.DynAnyPackage.InvalidValue;
   public abstract void insert_ushort(short value) throws org.omg.CORBA.DynAnyPackage.InvalidValue;
   public abstract void insert_val(Serializable value) throws org.omg.CORBA.DynAnyPackage.InvalidValue;
   public abstract void insert_wchar(char value) throws org.omg.CORBA.DynAnyPackage.InvalidValue;
   public abstract void insert_wstring(String value) throws org.omg.CORBA.DynAnyPackage.InvalidValue;
   public abstract boolean next();
   public abstract void rewind();
   public abstract boolean seek(int index);
   public abstract Any to_any() throws org.omg.CORBA.DynAnyPackage.Invalid;
   public abstract TypeCode type();
}
```

Implementations: org.omg.CORBA.DynArray, org.omg.CORBA.DynEnum, org.omg.CORBA.DynFixed, org.omg.CORBA.DynSequence, org.omg.CORBA.DynStruct, org.omg.CORBA.DynUnion, org.omg.CORBA.DynValue

Passed To: org.omg.CORBA.DynAny.assign()

Returned By: org.omg.CORBA.DynAny.{copy(), current_component()}, org.omg.CORBA.DynUnion.{discriminator(), member()}, org.omg.CORBA.ORB.{create_basic_dyn_any(), create_dyn_any()}

DynArray   Java 1.2

org.omg.CORBA

A DynAny object associated with an array. The get and set methods allow for access to the elements of the array, as Any values.

```
public interface DynArray extends org.omg.CORBA.Object, org.omg.CORBA.DynAny {
// Public Instance Methods
   public abstract Any[ ] get_elements();
   public abstract void set_elements(Any[ ] value) throws org.omg.CORBA.DynAnyPackage.InvalidSeq;
}
```

Returned By: org.omg.CORBA.ORB.create_dyn_array()

DynEnum   Java 1.2

org.omg.CORBA

A DynAny object associated with the Java mapping of an IDL enumerated type. The methods on the interface allow you to access the value of the enumerated type as either a String or an int.

```
public interface DynEnum extends org.omg.CORBA.Object, org.omg.CORBA.DynAny {
// Public Instance Methods
    public abstract String value_as_string();
    public abstract void value_as_string(String arg);
    public abstract int value_as_ulong();
    public abstract void value_as_ulong(int arg);
}
```

Returned By: org.omg.CORBA.ORB.create_dyn_enum()

DynFixed   Java 1.2

org.omg.CORBA

A DynAny object associated with the Java mapping of an IDL fixed type.

```
public interface DynFixed extends org.omg.CORBA.Object, org.omg.CORBA.DynAny {
// Public Instance Methods
    public abstract byte[ ] get_value();
    public abstract void set_value(byte[ ] val) throws org.omg.CORBA.DynAnyPackage.InvalidValue;
}
```

DynSequence   Java 1.2

org.omg.CORBA

An extension of DynArray that contains the Java mapping of an IDL sequence type.

```
public interface DynSequence extends org.omg.CORBA.Object, org.omg.CORBA.DynAny {
// Public Instance Methods
    public abstract Any[ ] get_elements();
    public abstract int length();
    public abstract void length(int arg);
    public abstract void set_elements(Any[ ] value) throws org.omg.CORBA.DynAnyPackage.InvalidSeq;
}
```

Returned By: org.omg.CORBA.ORB.create_dyn_sequence()

DynStruct   Java 1.2

org.omg.CORBA

A DynAny object associated with the Java mapping of an IDL struct type. In addition to
the DynAny methods that allow you to traverse the components of the struct, the DynStruct
interface provides methods that allow you to access an array of all the members of the
struct and to access their names within the struct.

```
public interface DynStruct extends org.omg.CORBA.Object, org.omg.CORBA.DynAny {
// Public Instance Methods
    public abstract TCKind current_member_kind();
    public abstract String current_member_name();
    public abstract org.omg.CORBA.NameValuePair[ ] get_members();
    public abstract void set_members(org.omg.CORBA.NameValuePair[ ] value)
        throws org.omg.CORBA.DynAnyPackage.InvalidSeq;
}
```

Returned By: org.omg.CORBA.ORB.create_dyn_struct()

DynUnion   Java 1.2
org.omg.CORBA

A DynAny object associated with the Java mapping of an IDL union type. Methods on the interface allow you to access the discriminator value of the union, and the current member of the union, as a DynAny object.

```
public interface DynUnion extends org.omg.CORBA.Object, org.omg.CORBA.DynAny {
// Public Instance Methods
    public abstract org.omg.CORBA.DynAny discriminator();
    public abstract TCKind discriminator_kind();
    public abstract org.omg.CORBA.DynAny member();
    public abstract TCKind member_kind();
    public abstract String member_name();
    public abstract void member_name(String arg);
    public abstract boolean set_as_default();
    public abstract void set_as_default(boolean arg);
}
```

Returned By: org.omg.CORBA.ORB.create_dyn_union()

DynValue   Java 1.2
org.omg.CORBA

A DynAny object associated with a value being passed using the Objects-by-Value extension to CORBA. This extension to CORBA will allow arguments to be passed by value, rather than strictly be reference, as they are in the core CORBA standard.

```
public interface DynValue extends org.omg.CORBA.Object, org.omg.CORBA.DynAny {
// Public Instance Methods
    public abstract TCKind current_member_kind();
    public abstract String current_member_name();
    public abstract org.omg.CORBA.NameValuePair[ ] get_members();
    public abstract void set_members(org.omg.CORBA.NameValuePair[ ] value)
        throws org.omg.CORBA.DynAnyPackage.InvalidSeq;
}
```

Environment

org.omg.CORBA

After a DII Request has been invoked, any exception that it may have thrown can be accessed by retrieving the Environment from the Request, using its env() method. The exception that was thrown can be retrieved from the Environment using its exception() method.

```
public abstract class Environment {
// Public Constructors
    public Environment();
// Public Instance Methods
    public abstract void clear();
    public abstract Exception exception();
    public abstract void exception(Exception except);
}
```

Returned By: org.omg.CORBA.ORB.create_environment(), Request.env()

ExceptionList

org.omg.CORBA

This class represents a list of exceptions that can be thrown by a remote method, in the form of the TypeCodes for the corresponding Exception classes. An ExceptionList can be created using the ORB.create_exception_list() method, the TypeCodes for each required exception can be created using the ORB.create_exception_tc() method, and the complete ExceptionList can be used to create a DII Request object.

```
public abstract class ExceptionList {
// Public Constructors
    public ExceptionList();
// Public Instance Methods
    public abstract void add(TypeCode exc);
    public abstract int count();
    public abstract TypeCode item(int index) throws org.omg.CORBA.Bounds;
    public abstract void remove(int index) throws org.omg.CORBA.Bounds;
}
```

Passed To: LocalObject._create_request(), org.omg.CORBA.Object._create_request(), org.omg.CORBA.portable.Delegate.create_request(), org.omg.CORBA.portable.ObjectImpl._create_request()

Returned By: org.omg.CORBA.ORB.create_exception_list(), Request.exceptions()

FieldNameHelper

org.omg.CORBA

The helper class for the IDL FieldName typedef for a String. This helper is used to safely cast remote references to these objects, and to read and write these objects when they are used as remote method arguments or return values.

```
public abstract class FieldNameHelper {
// Public Constructors
    public FieldNameHelper();
// Public Class Methods
    public static String extract(Any a);
    public static String id();
    public static void insert(Any a, String that);
```

```
    public static String read(org.omg.CORBA.portable.InputStream istream);
    public static TypeCode type();                                                        synchronized
    public static void write(org.omg.CORBA.portable.OutputStream ostream, String value);
}
```

FixedHolder   Java 1.2

org.omg.CORBA

The holder class for IDL fixed values, which are tentatively mapped to the
java.math.BigDecimal class. A FixedHolder wraps a BigDecimal value. See Chapter 4 for more
information on the uses of holder classes.

```
Object ├─ FixedHolder ┈ Streamable
```

```
public final class FixedHolder implements org.omg.CORBA.portable.Streamable {
// Public Constructors
    public FixedHolder();
    public FixedHolder(java.math.BigDecimal initial);
// Methods Implementing Streamable
    public void _read(org.omg.CORBA.portable.InputStream input);
    public TypeCode _type();
    public void _write(org.omg.CORBA.portable.OutputStream output);
// Public Instance Fields
    public java.math.BigDecimal value;
}
```

FloatHolder   Java 1.2

org.omg.CORBA

The holder class for out and inout remote method arguments that would be mapped to
Java float values. See Chapter 4 for more information on the uses of holder classes.

```
Object ├─ FloatHolder ┈ Streamable
```

```
public final class FloatHolder implements org.omg.CORBA.portable.Streamable {
// Public Constructors
    public FloatHolder();
    public FloatHolder(float initial);
// Methods Implementing Streamable
    public void _read(org.omg.CORBA.portable.InputStream input);
    public TypeCode _type();
    public void _write(org.omg.CORBA.portable.OutputStream output);
// Public Instance Fields
    public float value;
}
```

FloatSeqHelper   Java 1.3

org.omg.CORBA

The helper class for arrays of floats, used to read and write these arrays when they are
used as remote method arguments or return values.

```
public abstract class FloatSeqHelper {
// Public Constructors
    public FloatSeqHelper();
```

```
// Public Class Methods
    public static float[ ] extract(Any a);
    public static String id( );
    public static void insert(Any a, float[ ] that);
    public static float[ ] read(org.omg.CORBA.portable.InputStream istream);
    public static TypeCode type( );                                                    synchronized
    public static void write(org.omg.CORBA.portable.OutputStream ostream, float[ ] value);
}
```

FloatSeqHolder   Java 1.3

org.omg.CORBA

The holder class for the IDL FloatSeq typedef, which resolves to an array of float values. This holder class is used wrap out and inout arguments of this type in remote method calls.

```
Object ├─ FloatSeqHolder ┈┤ Streamable
```

```
public final class FloatSeqHolder implements org.omg.CORBA.portable.Streamable {
// Public Constructors
    public FloatSeqHolder( );
    public FloatSeqHolder(float[ ] initialValue);
// Methods Implementing Streamable
    public void _read(org.omg.CORBA.portable.InputStream i);
    public TypeCode _type( );
    public void _write(org.omg.CORBA.portable.OutputStream o);
// Public Instance Fields
    public float[ ] value;
}
```

Passed To: org.omg.CORBA.DataInputStream.read_float_array()

FREE_MEM   Java 1.2

org.omg.CORBA   *serializable unchecked*

A standard CORBA exception thrown when an attempt to free memory fails.

```
Object ├─ Throwable ├─ Exception ├─ RuntimeException ├─ SystemException ├─ FREE_MEM
       └─ Serializable
```

```
public final class FREE_MEM extends org.omg.CORBA.SystemException {
// Public Constructors
    public FREE_MEM( );
    public FREE_MEM(String s);
    public FREE_MEM(int minor, CompletionStatus completed);
    public FREE_MEM(String s, int minor, CompletionStatus completed);
}
```

IdentifierHelper   Java 1.3

org.omg.CORBA

The helper class for Identifier, which is an IDL typedef for String. This helper is used to read and write these values when they are used as remote method arguments or return values.

```
public abstract class IdentifierHelper {
// Public Constructors
    public IdentifierHelper( );
// Public Class Methods
    public static String extract(Any a);
    public static String id( );
    public static void insert(Any a, String that);
    public static String read(org.omg.CORBA.portable.InputStream istream);
    public static TypeCode type( );                                                    synchronized
    public static void write(org.omg.CORBA.portable.OutputStream ostream, String value);
}
```

IDLType   Java 1.2

org.omg.CORBA   *serializable*

IDLType is an extension of IRObject used to represent IDL basic types in the Interface Repository. It allows you to query the TypeCode of the type it represents. See the IRObject interface for more details on the Interface Repository.

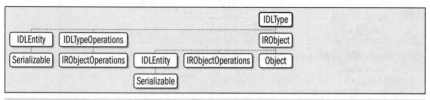

```
public interface IDLType extends IDLTypeOperations, IRObject, org.omg.CORBA.portable.IDLEntity {
}
```

Implementations: _IDLTypeStub

Passed To: IDLTypeHelper.{insert(), write()}, StructMember.StructMember(), UnionMember.UnionMember(), ValueMember.ValueMember()

Returned By: IDLTypeHelper.{extract(), narrow(), read()}

Type Of: StructMember.type_def, UnionMember.type_def, ValueMember.type_def

IDLTypeHelper   Java 1.3

org.omg.CORBA

The helper class for IDLType objects, used to safely cast remote references to these objects, and to read and write these objects when they are used as remote method arguments or return values.

```
public abstract class IDLTypeHelper {
// Public Constructors
    public IDLTypeHelper( );
// Public Class Methods
    public static IDLType extract(Any a);
    public static String id( );
    public static void insert(Any a, IDLType that);
    public static IDLType narrow(org.omg.CORBA.Object obj);
    public static IDLType read(org.omg.CORBA.portable.InputStream istream);
    public static TypeCode type( );                                                    synchronized
    public static void write(org.omg.CORBA.portable.OutputStream ostream, IDLType value);
}
```

IDLTypeOperations

org.omg.CORBA

The generated operations interface for the IDLType interface.

```
[ IRObjectOperations ]--[ IDLTypeOperations ]
```

```
public interface IDLTypeOperations extends IRObjectOperations {
// Public Instance Methods
   public abstract TypeCode type();
}
```

Implementations: IDLType

IMP_LIMIT

org.omg.CORBA   *serializable unchecked*

A standard CORBA exception thrown when some implementation limit has been exceeded.

```
[ Object ]--[ Throwable ]--[ Exception ]--[ RuntimeException ]--[ SystemException ]--[ IMP_LIMIT ]
              [ Serializable ]
```

```
public final class IMP_LIMIT extends org.omg.CORBA.SystemException {
// Public Constructors
   public IMP_LIMIT();
   public IMP_LIMIT(String s);
   public IMP_LIMIT(int minor, CompletionStatus completed);
   public IMP_LIMIT(String s, int minor, CompletionStatus completed);
}
```

INITIALIZE

org.omg.CORBA   *serializable unchecked*

A standard CORBA exception thrown when an error occurs while initializing an ORB.

```
[ Object ]--[ Throwable ]--[ Exception ]--[ RuntimeException ]--[ SystemException ]--[ INITIALIZE ]
              [ Serializable ]
```

```
public final class INITIALIZE extends org.omg.CORBA.SystemException {
// Public Constructors
   public INITIALIZE();
   public INITIALIZE(String s);
   public INITIALIZE(int minor, CompletionStatus completed);
   public INITIALIZE(String s, int minor, CompletionStatus completed);
}
```

INTERNAL

org.omg.CORBA   *serializable unchecked*

A standard CORBA exception thrown when an ORB encounters an internal error. Sun's Java IDL defines the following minor error code values for this exception, stored in the minor data member inherited from SystemException:

Minor code	Meaning
3	An IIOP reply message contained a bad status.
6	The repository ID of a user exception had an incorrect length during an unmarshalling operation.
7	The ORB was failed to get the local hostname through the InetAddress.getLocal-Host().getHostName() method.
8	The ORB was unable to create a listener port on its designated port. This can be caused by the port being in use, the creation of the daemon thread failed, or a security violation occurred.
9	An IIOP locate message contained a bad status.
10	An error was encountered while creating a stringified object reference.
11	An IIOP message contained a bad GIOP v1.0 message type.
14	An error occurred while unmarshalling a user exception.
18	The ORB failed during internal initialization.

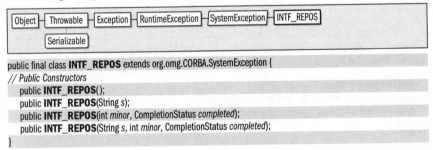

```
public final class INTERNAL extends org.omg.CORBA.SystemException {
// Public Constructors
    public INTERNAL();
    public INTERNAL(String s);
    public INTERNAL(int minor, CompletionStatus completed);
    public INTERNAL(String s, int minor, CompletionStatus completed);
}
```

INTF_REPOS
org.omg.CORBA

Java 1.2

serializable unchecked

A standard CORBA exception thrown when an error occurs while attempting to use the interface repository.

```
Object — Throwable — Exception — RuntimeException — SystemException — INTF_REPOS
         Serializable
```

```
public final class INTF_REPOS extends org.omg.CORBA.SystemException {
// Public Constructors
    public INTF_REPOS();
    public INTF_REPOS(String s);
    public INTF_REPOS(int minor, CompletionStatus completed);
    public INTF_REPOS(String s, int minor, CompletionStatus completed);
}
```

IntHolder
org.omg.CORBA

Java 1.2

The holder class for out and inout remote method arguments that would be mapped to Java int values. See Chapter 4 for more information on the uses of holder classes.

```
Object ─ IntHolder ┈ Streamable
```

```
public final class IntHolder implements org.omg.CORBA.portable.Streamable {
// Public Constructors
   public IntHolder();
   public IntHolder(int initial);
// Methods Implementing Streamable
   public void _read(org.omg.CORBA.portable.InputStream input);
   public TypeCode _type();
   public void _write(org.omg.CORBA.portable.OutputStream output);
// Public Instance Fields
   public int value;
}
```

INV_FLAG

Java 1.2

org.omg.CORBA

serializable unchecked

A standard CORBA exception thrown when an invalid flag is specified in a method call.

```
Object ─ Throwable ─ Exception ─ RuntimeException ─ SystemException ─ INV_FLAG
          ┊
       Serializable
```

```
public final class INV_FLAG extends org.omg.CORBA.SystemException {
// Public Constructors
   public INV_FLAG();
   public INV_FLAG(String s);
   public INV_FLAG(int minor, CompletionStatus completed);
   public INV_FLAG(String s, int minor, CompletionStatus completed);
}
```

INV_IDENT

Java 1.2

org.omg.CORBA

serializable unchecked

A standard CORBA exception thrown when an invalid identifier is specified.

```
Object ─ Throwable ─ Exception ─ RuntimeException ─ SystemException ─ INV_IDENT
          ┊
       Serializable
```

```
public final class INV_IDENT extends org.omg.CORBA.SystemException {
// Public Constructors
   public INV_IDENT();
   public INV_IDENT(String s);
   public INV_IDENT(int minor, CompletionStatus completed);
   public INV_IDENT(String s, int minor, CompletionStatus completed);
}
```

INV_OBJREF

Java 1.2

org.omg.CORBA

serializable unchecked

A standard CORBA exception thrown when an invalid object reference is used. Sun's
Java IDL defines the following minor error code values for this exception, stored in the
minor data member inherited from SystemException:

Minor code	Meaning
1	A stringified object reference had no profile.

```
Object ─ Throwable ─ Exception ─ RuntimeException ─ SystemException ─ INV_OBJREF
         Serializable
```

```
public final class INV_OBJREF extends org.omg.CORBA.SystemException {
// Public Constructors
   public INV_OBJREF();
   public INV_OBJREF(String s);
   public INV_OBJREF(int minor, CompletionStatus completed);
   public INV_OBJREF(String s, int minor, CompletionStatus completed);
}
```

INV_POLICY

Java 1.2

org.omg.CORBA

serializable unchecked

A standard CORBA exception thrown when an incompatibility between Policies is encountered during an remote method call.

```
Object ─ Throwable ─ Exception ─ RuntimeException ─ SystemException ─ INV_POLICY
         Serializable
```

```
public final class INV_POLICY extends org.omg.CORBA.SystemException {
// Public Constructors
   public INV_POLICY();
   public INV_POLICY(String s);
   public INV_POLICY(int minor, CompletionStatus completed);
   public INV_POLICY(String s, int minor, CompletionStatus completed);
}
```

INVALID_TRANSACTION

Java 1.2

org.omg.CORBA

serializable unchecked

A standard CORBA exception thrown when a transaction error occurs during a remote method call.

```
Object ─ Throwable ─ Exception ─ RuntimeException ─ SystemException ─ INVALID_TRANSACTION
         Serializable
```

```
public final class INVALID_TRANSACTION extends org.omg.CORBA.SystemException {
// Public Constructors
   public INVALID_TRANSACTION();
   public INVALID_TRANSACTION(String s);
   public INVALID_TRANSACTION(int minor, CompletionStatus completed);
   public INVALID_TRANSACTION(String s, int minor, CompletionStatus completed);
}
```

IRObject

Java 1.2

org.omg.CORBA

serializable

All the informational interfaces used and exported by the Interface Repository derive from the IRObject interface. The Interface Repository is a component of the ORB that stores definitions of object interfaces. These interface definitions are used by the ORB at runtime to check the correctness of method requests, and to support Dynamic Invocation Interface requests. They can also be used within development tools, to provide information about remote interfaces for browsing and linking them. The Interface Repository is analogous to a table schema in a relational database, in that it describes the type of objects that an ORB is supporting. The Interface Repository uses a set of IDL interfaces (e.g., InterfaceDef, AttributeDef) to represent the modules, interfaces, attributes, methods, etc. that it manages, and all of these interfaces derive from the IRObject interface.

The IRObject has a def_kind() method that provides the type of definition that the object represents (module, attribute, etc.).

```
                                          IRObject
Serializable    IDLEntity    IRObjectOperations    Object
```

```
public interface IRObject extends IRObjectOperations, org.omg.CORBA.Object, org.omg.CORBA.portable.IDLEntity {
}
```

Implementations: IDLType

IRObjectOperations   Java 1.3

org.omg.CORBA

The generated operations interface for the IRObject interface.

```
public interface IRObjectOperations {
// Public Instance Methods
    public abstract DefinitionKind def_kind();
    public abstract void destroy();
}
```

Implementations: IDLTypeOperations, IRObject

LocalObject   Java 1.4

org.omg.CORBA

A LocalObject represents a local interface for an IDL interface, allowing for efficient, local interfaces to objects running in the same VM. Any remote operations that are not relevant for a local object will throw a NO_IMPLEMENT exception. Added as of JDK 1.4.

```
Object    LocalObject    Object
```

```
public class LocalObject implements org.omg.CORBA.Object {
// Public Constructors
    public LocalObject();
// Public Instance Methods
    public org.omg.CORBA.Object _get_interface();
    public org.omg.CORBA.portable.InputStream _invoke(org.omg.CORBA.portable.OutputStream output)
        throws org.omg.CORBA.portable.ApplicationException, org.omg.CORBA.portable.RemarshalException;
    public boolean _is_local();
    public org.omg.CORBA.ORB _orb();
    public void _releaseReply(org.omg.CORBA.portable.InputStream input);
    public org.omg.CORBA.portable.OutputStream _request(String operation, boolean responseExpected);
    public void _servant_postinvoke(org.omg.CORBA.portable.ServantObject servant);
    public org.omg.CORBA.portable.ServantObject _servant_preinvoke(String operation, Class expectedType);
    public boolean validate_connection();
```

```
// Methods Implementing Object
    public Request _create_request(org.omg.CORBA.Context ctx, String operation, NVList arg_list,
                                NamedValue result);
    public Request _create_request(org.omg.CORBA.Context ctx, String operation, NVList arg_list,
                                NamedValue result, ExceptionList exceptions, ContextList contexts);
    public org.omg.CORBA.Object _duplicate();
    public DomainManager[ ] _get_domain_managers();
    public org.omg.CORBA.Object _get_interface_def();
    public org.omg.CORBA.Policy _get_policy(int policy_type);
    public int _hash(int maximum);
    public boolean _is_a(String repository_id);
    public boolean _is_equivalent(org.omg.CORBA.Object that);
    public boolean _non_existent();                                          constant
    public void _release();
    public Request _request(String operation);
    public org.omg.CORBA.Object _set_policy_override(org.omg.CORBA.Policy[ ] policies, SetOverrideType set_add);
}
```

LongHolder   Java 1.2
org.omg.CORBA

The holder class for out and inout remote method arguments that would be mapped to
Java long values. See Chapter 4 for more information on the uses of holder classes.

```
┌─────────┬─────────────┬──────────────┐
│ Object ├─┤ LongHolder ├─┤ Streamable │
└─────────┴─────────────┴──────────────┘
```

```
public final class LongHolder implements org.omg.CORBA.portable.Streamable {
// Public Constructors
    public LongHolder();
    public LongHolder(long initial);
// Methods Implementing Streamable
    public void _read(org.omg.CORBA.portable.InputStream input);
    public TypeCode _type();
    public void _write(org.omg.CORBA.portable.OutputStream output);
// Public Instance Fields
    public long value;
}
```

LongLongSeqHelper   Java 1.3
org.omg.CORBA

The helper class for arrays of longs, used to read and write these arrays when they are
used as remote method arguments or return values.

```
public abstract class LongLongSeqHelper {
// Public Constructors
    public LongLongSeqHelper();
// Public Class Methods
    public static long[ ] extract(Any a);
    public static String Id();
    public static void Insert(Any a, long[ ] that);
    public static long[ ] read(org.omg.CORBA.portable.InputStream istream);
    public static TypeCode type();                                        synchronized
    public static void write(org.omg.CORBA.portable.OutputStream ostream, long[ ] value);
}
```

LongLongSeqHolder   Java 1.3

org.omg.CORBA

The holder class for the IDL LongLongSeq typedef, which maps to an array of long values. This holder class is used wrap out and inout arguments of this type in remote method calls.

```
Object ├─ LongLongSeqHolder ┈┈ Streamable
```

```
public final class LongLongSeqHolder implements org.omg.CORBA.portable.Streamable {
// Public Constructors
    public LongLongSeqHolder();
    public LongLongSeqHolder(long[ ] initialValue);
// Methods Implementing Streamable
    public void _read(org.omg.CORBA.portable.InputStream i);
    public TypeCode _type();
    public void _write(org.omg.CORBA.portable.OutputStream o);
// Public Instance Fields
    public long[ ] value;
}
```

Passed To: org.omg.CORBA.DataInputStream.read_longlong_array()

LongSeqHelper   Java 1.3

org.omg.CORBA

The helper class for arrays of ints, used to read and write these arrays when they are used as remote method arguments or return values.

```
public abstract class LongSeqHelper {
// Public Constructors
    public LongSeqHelper();
// Public Class Methods
    public static int[ ] extract(Any a);
    public static String id();
    public static void insert(Any a, int[ ] that);
    public static int[ ] read(org.omg.CORBA.portable.InputStream istream);
    public static TypeCode type();                                    synchronized
    public static void write(org.omg.CORBA.portable.OutputStream ostream, int[ ] value);
}
```

LongSeqHolder   Java 1.3

org.omg.CORBA

The holder class for the IDL LongSeq typedef, which maps to an array of long values. This holder class is used wrap out and inout arguments of this type in remote method calls.

```
Object ├─ LongSeqHolder ┈┈ Streamable
```

```
public final class LongSeqHolder implements org.omg.CORBA.portable.Streamable {
// Public Constructors
    public LongSeqHolder();
    public LongSeqHolder(int[ ] initialValue);
// Methods Implementing Streamable
    public void _read(org.omg.CORBA.portable.InputStream i);
    public TypeCode _type();
    public void _write(org.omg.CORBA.portable.OutputStream o);
```

```
// Public Instance Fields
    public int[ ] value;
}
```

Passed To: org.omg.CORBA.DataInputStream.read_long_array()

MARSHAL

org.omg.CORBA

A standard CORBA exception thrown when the ORB fails to marshal or unmarshal method arguments, return values or exceptions. Sun's Java IDL defines the following minor error code values for this exception, stored in the minor data member inherited from SystemException:

Minor code	Meaning
4	An error occurred while unmarshalling an object reference.
5	An attempt was made to marshal or unmarshal an IDL type that is not supported in this implementation, such as wchar or wstring.
6	While marshalling or unmarshalling, a character not within the ISO Latin-1 set was encountered.

```
Object ─ Throwable ─ Exception ─ RuntimeException ─ SystemException ─ MARSHAL
        Serializable
```

```
public final class MARSHAL extends org.omg.CORBA.SystemException {
// Public Constructors
    public MARSHAL();
    public MARSHAL(String s);
    public MARSHAL(int minor, CompletionStatus completed);
    public MARSHAL(String s, int minor, CompletionStatus completed);
}
```

Thrown By: Any.{insert_string(), insert_Value(), insert_wstring(), read_value()}

NamedValue

org.omg.CORBA

This class represents a remote method argument or return value. It consists of an argument name (as a String), its value (as an Any object), and an argument mode, which can be one of ARG_IN.value, ARG_OUT.value, ARG_INOUT.value, or zero. If the argument mode is zero, then the NamedValue represents a Context property value. NamedValues are used in DII and DSI operations, e.g., to build the argument list for a client-side method Request object.

```
public abstract class NamedValue {
// Public Constructors
    public NamedValue();
// Public Instance Methods
    public abstract int flags();
    public abstract String name();
    public abstract Any value();
}
```

Passed To: LocalObject._create_request(), org.omg.CORBA.Object._create_request(), org.omg.CORBA.portable.Delegate.create_request(), org.omg.CORBA.portable.ObjectImpl._create_request()

Returned By: NVList.{add(), add_item(), add_value(), item()},
org.omg.CORBA.ORB.create_named_value(), Request.result()

NameValuePair

Java 1.2

org.omg.CORBA

serializable

A DynStruct object uses NameValuePairs to represent its data members. It consists of a
String name and a value represented as an Any object.

```
┌────────┬─────────────────┐
│ Object │─│ NameValuePair  │
├────────┴─────────────────┤
│ Serializable │····│ IDLEntity │
└──────────────────────────┘
```

```
public final class NameValuePair implements org.omg.CORBA.portable.IDLEntity {
// Public Constructors
    public NameValuePair();
    public NameValuePair(String __id, Any __value);
// Public Instance Fields
    public String id;
    public Any value;
}
```

Passed To: org.omg.CORBA.DynStruct.set_members(), org.omg.CORBA.DynValue.set_members(),
org.omg.CORBA.NameValuePairHelper.{insert(), write()}

Returned By: org.omg.CORBA.DynStruct.get_members(), org.omg.CORBA.DynValue.get_members(),
org.omg.CORBA.NameValuePairHelper.{extract(), read()}

NameValuePairHelper

Java 1.3

org.omg.CORBA

The helper class for NameValuePair objects, used to read and write these objects when
they are used as remote method arguments or return values.

```
public abstract class NameValuePairHelper {
// Public Constructors
    public NameValuePairHelper();
// Public Class Methods
    public static org.omg.CORBA.NameValuePair extract(Any a);
    public static String id();
    public static void insert(Any a, org.omg.CORBA.NameValuePair that);
    public static org.omg.CORBA.NameValuePair read(org.omg.CORBA.portable.InputStream istream);
    public static TypeCode type();                                          synchronized
    public static void write(org.omg.CORBA.portable.OutputStream ostream, org.omg.CORBA.NameValuePair value);
}
```

NO_IMPLEMENT

Java 1.2

org.omg.CORBA

serializable unchecked

A standard CORBA exception thrown when a call is made on a method that is not
implemented. Sun's Java IDL defines the following minor error code values for this
exception, stored in the minor data member inherited from SystemException:

Minor code	Meaning
1	An attempt to use the Dynamic Skeleton Interface was made. The DSI is not implemented in Sun's implementation.

```
Object ─ Throwable ─ Exception ─ RuntimeException ─ SystemException ─ NO_IMPLEMENT
       └ Serializable
```

```
public final class NO_IMPLEMENT extends org.omg.CORBA.SystemException {
// Public Constructors
    public NO_IMPLEMENT();
    public NO_IMPLEMENT(String s);
    public NO_IMPLEMENT(int minor, CompletionStatus completed);
    public NO_IMPLEMENT(String s, int minor, CompletionStatus completed);
}
```

NO_MEMORY

Java 1.2

org.omg.CORBA

serializable unchecked

A standard CORBA exception thrown when insufficient dynamic memory is available to carry out a request.

```
Object ─ Throwable ─ Exception ─ RuntimeException ─ SystemException ─ NO_MEMORY
       └ Serializable
```

```
public final class NO_MEMORY extends org.omg.CORBA.SystemException {
// Public Constructors
    public NO_MEMORY();
    public NO_MEMORY(String s);
    public NO_MEMORY(int minor, CompletionStatus completed);
    public NO_MEMORY(String s, int minor, CompletionStatus completed);
}
```

NO_PERMISSION

Java 1.2

org.omg.CORBA

serializable unchecked

A standard CORBA exception thrown when a client does not have sufficient permission to make a request.

```
Object ─ Throwable ─ Exception ─ RuntimeException ─ SystemException ─ NO_PERMISSION
       └ Serializable
```

```
public final class NO_PERMISSION extends org.omg.CORBA.SystemException {
// Public Constructors
    public NO_PERMISSION();
    public NO_PERMISSION(String s);
    public NO_PERMISSION(int minor, CompletionStatus completed);
    public NO_PERMISSION(String s, int minor, CompletionStatus completed);
}
```

NO_RESOURCES

org.omg.CORBA   *serializable unchecked*

A standard CORBA exception thrown when resources cannot be allocated to execute a request, on either the client or the server.

```
Object ├ Throwable ├ Exception ├ RuntimeException ├ SystemException ├ NO_RESOURCES
         Serializable
```

```
public final class NO_RESOURCES extends org.omg.CORBA.SystemException {
// Public Constructors
    public NO_RESOURCES();
    public NO_RESOURCES(String s);
    public NO_RESOURCES(int minor, CompletionStatus completed);
    public NO_RESOURCES(String s, int minor, CompletionStatus completed);
}
```

NO_RESPONSE

org.omg.CORBA   *serializable unchecked*

A standard CORBA exception thrown when a server response to an asynchronous remote method call is not yet available.

```
Object ├ Throwable ├ Exception ├ RuntimeException ├ SystemException ├ NO_RESPONSE
         Serializable
```

```
public final class NO_RESPONSE extends org.omg.CORBA.SystemException {
// Public Constructors
    public NO_RESPONSE();
    public NO_RESPONSE(String s);
    public NO_RESPONSE(int minor, CompletionStatus completed);
    public NO_RESPONSE(String s, int minor, CompletionStatus completed);
}
```

NVList

org.omg.CORBA

A list of NamedValue objects. NVLists can be created using the ORB.create_list() method, or the ORB.create_operation_list() method. The latter method initializes the list with NamedValues that describe the arguments to the method definition that you pass into the create_operation_list() method.

```
public abstract class NVList {
// Public Constructors
    public NVList();
// Public Instance Methods
    public abstract NamedValue add(int flags);
    public abstract NamedValue add_item(String item_name, int flags);
    public abstract NamedValue add_value(String item_name, Any val, int flags);
    public abstract int count();
    public abstract NamedValue item(int index) throws org.omg.CORBA.Bounds;
    public abstract void remove(int index) throws org.omg.CORBA.Bounds;
}
```

Passed To: org.omg.CORBA.Context.set_values(), LocalObject._create_request(), org.omg.CORBA.Object._create_request(), ServerRequest.{arguments(), params()},

org.omg.CORBA.portable.Delegate.create_request(),
org.omg.CORBA.portable.ObjectImpl._create_request()

Returned By: org.omg.CORBA.Context.get_values(), org.omg.CORBA.ORB.{create_list(),
create_operation_list()}, Request.arguments()

OBJ_ADAPTER
Java 1.2

org.omg.CORBA
serializable unchecked

A standard CORBA exception thrown when an error is encountered by an object
adapter in the ORB. Sun's Java IDL defines the following minor error code values for
this exception, stored in the minor data member inherited from SystemException:

Minor code	Meaning
1	On the server, no adapter matching the one referenced in the object reference was found.
2	Same as above, but error occurs during a locate request.
4	An error occurred while attempting to connect a servant to the ORB.

```
Object ─ Throwable ─ Exception ─ RuntimeException ─ SystemException ─ OBJ_ADAPTER
         Serializable
```

```java
public final class OBJ_ADAPTER extends org.omg.CORBA.SystemException {
// Public Constructors
    public OBJ_ADAPTER();
    public OBJ_ADAPTER(String s);
    public OBJ_ADAPTER(int minor, CompletionStatus completed);
    public OBJ_ADAPTER(String s, int minor, CompletionStatus completed);
}
```

Object
Java 1.2

org.omg.CORBA

This is the base interface for all CORBA objects. An Object can be either a reference
(stub) to a remote CORBA object, or it can be a local object implementation. The methods
declared in the Object interface allow you to create DII requests to the object, get its
Interface Repository definition, and check the equivalence of two objects, among other
things. The org.omg.CORBA.portable.ObjectImpl class provides a default concrete implementation
of the Object interface.

```java
public interface Object {
// Public Instance Methods
    public abstract Request _create_request(org.omg.CORBA.Context ctx, String operation, NVList arg_list,
                                            NamedValue result);
    public abstract Request _create_request(org.omg.CORBA.Context ctx, String operation, NVList arg_list,
                                            NamedValue result, ExceptionList exclist, ContextList ctxlist);
    public abstract org.omg.CORBA.Object _duplicate();
    public abstract DomainManager[] _get_domain_managers();
    public abstract org.omg.CORBA.Object _get_interface_def();
    public abstract org.omg.CORBA.Policy _get_policy(int policy_type);
    public abstract int _hash(int maximum);
    public abstract boolean _is_a(String repositoryIdentifier);
    public abstract boolean _is_equivalent(org.omg.CORBA.Object other);
    public abstract boolean _non_existent();
```

```
    public abstract void _release();
    public abstract Request _request(String operation);
    public abstract org.omg.CORBA.Object _set_policy_override(org.omg.CORBA.Policy[ ] policies,
                                                              SetOverrideType set_add);
}
```

Implementations: Too many classes to list.

Passed To: Too many methods to list.

Returned By: Too many methods to list.

Type Of: ObjectHolder.value, org.omg.PortableInterceptor.ForwardRequest.forward, org.omg.PortableServer.ForwardRequest.forward_reference

OBJECT_NOT_EXIST   Java 1.2

org.omg.CORBA   *serializable unchecked*

A standard CORBA exception thrown when a request is made of a server object that no longer exists. Sun's Java IDL defines the following minor error code values for this exception, stored in the minor data member inherited from SystemException:

Minor code	Meaning
1	The target of a locate request sent back a response indicating that it did not know of the object.
2	A method request was received by a server whose ID does not match the server ID referenced in the object reference.
4	The skeleton referenced in the object reference was not found on the server.

```
Object ├─ Throwable ├─ Exception ├─ RuntimeException ├─ SystemException ├─ OBJECT_NOT_EXIST
           Serializable
```

```
public final class OBJECT_NOT_EXIST extends org.omg.CORBA.SystemException {
// Public Constructors
    public OBJECT_NOT_EXIST();
    public OBJECT_NOT_EXIST(String s);
    public OBJECT_NOT_EXIST(int minor, CompletionStatus completed);
    public OBJECT_NOT_EXIST(String s, int minor, CompletionStatus completed);
}
```

ObjectHelper   Java 1.3

org.omg.CORBA

The helper class for Object instances, used to read and write these objects when they are used as remote method arguments or return values.

```
public abstract class ObjectHelper {
// Public Constructors
    public ObjectHelper();
// Public Class Methods
    public static org.omg.CORBA.Object extract(Any a);
    public static String Id();
    public static void Insert(Any a, org.omg.CORBA.Object that);
    public static org.omg.CORBA.Object read(org.omg.CORBA.portable.InputStream istream);
    public static TypeCode type();                                    synchronized
```

public static void **write**(org.omg.CORBA.portable.OutputStream *ostream*, org.omg.CORBA.Object *value*);
}

ObjectHolder

org.omg.CORBA

The holder class for out and inout remote method arguments that would be mapped to
Java org.omg.CORBA.Object values. See Chapter 4 for more information on the uses of
holder classes.

```
Object ─ ObjectHolder ┈ Streamable
```

public final class **ObjectHolder** implements org.omg.CORBA.portable.Streamable {
// *Public Constructors*
  public **ObjectHolder**();
  public **ObjectHolder**(org.omg.CORBA.Object *initial*);
// *Methods Implementing Streamable*
  public void **_read**(org.omg.CORBA.portable.InputStream *input*);
  public TypeCode **_type**();
  public void **_write**(org.omg.CORBA.portable.OutputStream *output*);
// *Public Instance Fields*
  public org.omg.CORBA.Object **value**;
}

OctetSeqHelper

org.omg.CORBA

The helper class for arrays of bytes, used to read and write these arrays when they are
used as remote method arguments or return values.

public abstract class **OctetSeqHelper** {
// *Public Constructors*
  public **OctetSeqHelper**();
// *Public Class Methods*
  public static byte[ ] **extract**(Any *a*);
  public static String **id**();
  public static void **insert**(Any *a*, byte[ ] *that*);
  public static byte[ ] **read**(org.omg.CORBA.portable.InputStream *istream*);
  public static TypeCode **type**();   *synchronized*
  public static void **write**(org.omg.CORBA.portable.OutputStream *ostream*, byte[ ] *value*);
}

OctetSeqHolder

org.omg.CORBA

The holder class for the IDL OctetSeq typedef, which maps to an array of byte values.
This holder class is used to wrap out and inout arguments of this type in remote method
calls.

```
Object ─ OctetSeqHolder ┈ Streamable
```

public final class **OctetSeqHolder** implements org.omg.CORBA.portable.Streamable {
// *Public Constructors*
  public **OctetSeqHolder**();
  public **OctetSeqHolder**(byte[ ] *initialValue*);

```
// Methods Implementing Streamable
    public void _read(org.omg.CORBA.portable.InputStream i);
    public TypeCode _type();
    public void _write(org.omg.CORBA.portable.OutputStream o);
// Public Instance Fields
    public byte[ ] value;
}
```

Passed To: org.omg.CORBA.DataInputStream.read_octet_array()

OMGVMCID   Java 1.3

org.omg.CORBA

This interface is simply a wrapper for the standard OMG minor exception code that is
encoded into all exceptions sent over IOP channels.

```
public interface OMGVMCID {
// Public Constants
    public static final int value;                                    =1330446336
}
```

ORB   Java 1.2

org.omg.CORBA

The ORB is at the heart of the CORBA API. The ORB class provides CORBA clients and
server objects access to the basic CORBA functions needed to engage in remote object
operations. The ORB class provides a set of static init() methods that let you initialize a
reference to an ORB, provides access to initial objects and service through its resolve_ini-
tial_references() method, and provides constructor methods that allow you to create key
objects needed to perform remote method requests, like Any objects and NamedValues.
The ORB also allows you to convert CORBA object references to a portable stringified
form, and back again, using its object_to_string() and string_to_object() methods.

```
public abstract class ORB {
// Public Constructors
    public ORB();
// Public Class Methods
    public static org.omg.CORBA.ORB init();
    public static org.omg.CORBA.ORB init(String[ ] args, java.util.Properties props);
    public static org.omg.CORBA.ORB init(java.applet.Applet app, java.util.Properties props);
// Property Accessor Methods (by property name)
    public abstract org.omg.CORBA.Context get_default_context();
    public abstract Request get_next_response() throws WrongTransaction;
// Public Instance Methods
    public void connect(org.omg.CORBA.Object obj);
    public TypeCode create_abstract_interface_tc(String id, String name);
    public abstract TypeCode create_alias_tc(String id, String name, TypeCode original_type);
    public abstract Any create_any();
    public abstract TypeCode create_array_tc(int length, TypeCode element_type);
    public org.omg.CORBA.DynAny create_basic_dyn_any(TypeCode type)
        throws org.omg.CORBA.ORBPackage.InconsistentTypeCode;
    public abstract ContextList create_context_list();
    public org.omg.CORBA.DynAny create_dyn_any(Any value);
    public org.omg.CORBA.DynArray create_dyn_array(TypeCode type)
        throws org.omg.CORBA.ORBPackage.InconsistentTypeCode;
    public org.omg.CORBA.DynEnum create_dyn_enum(TypeCode type)
        throws org.omg.CORBA.ORBPackage.InconsistentTypeCode;
```

```
    public org.omg.CORBA.DynSequence create_dyn_sequence(TypeCode type)
        throws org.omg.CORBA.ORBPackage.InconsistentTypeCode;
    public org.omg.CORBA.DynStruct create_dyn_struct(TypeCode type)
        throws org.omg.CORBA.ORBPackage.InconsistentTypeCode;
    public org.omg.CORBA.DynUnion create_dyn_union(TypeCode type)
        throws org.omg.CORBA.ORBPackage.InconsistentTypeCode;
    public abstract TypeCode create_enum_tc(String id, String name, String[ ] members);
    public abstract Environment create_environment();
    public abstract ExceptionList create_exception_list();
    public abstract TypeCode create_exception_tc(String id, String name, StructMember[ ] members);
    public TypeCode create_fixed_tc(short digits, short scale);
    public abstract TypeCode create_interface_tc(String id, String name);
    public abstract NVList create_list(int count);
    public abstract NamedValue create_named_value(String s, Any any, int flags);
    public TypeCode create_native_tc(String id, String name);
    public NVList create_operation_list(org.omg.CORBA.Object oper);
    public abstract org.omg.CORBA.portable.OutputStream create_output_stream();
    public org.omg.CORBA.Policy create_policy(int type, Any val) throws PolicyError;
    public TypeCode create_recursive_tc(String id);
    public abstract TypeCode create_sequence_tc(int bound, TypeCode element_type);
    public abstract TypeCode create_string_tc(int bound);
    public abstract TypeCode create_struct_tc(String id, String name, StructMember[ ] members);
    public abstract TypeCode create_union_tc(String id, String name, TypeCode discriminator_type,
                                    UnionMember[ ] members);
    public TypeCode create_value_box_tc(String id, String name, TypeCode boxed_type);
    public TypeCode create_value_tc(String id, String name, short type_modifier, TypeCode concrete_base,
                                    ValueMember[ ] members);
    public abstract TypeCode create_wstring_tc(int bound);
1.3 public void destroy();
    public void disconnect(org.omg.CORBA.Object obj);
    public abstract TypeCode get_primitive_tc(TCKind tcKind);
    public boolean get_service_information(short service_type, ServiceInformationHolder service_info);
    public abstract String[ ] list_initial_services();
    public abstract String object_to_string(org.omg.CORBA.Object obj);
    public void perform_work();
    public abstract boolean poll_next_response();
    public abstract org.omg.CORBA.Object resolve_initial_references(String object_name)
        throws org.omg.CORBA.ORBPackage.InvalidName;
    public void run();
    public abstract void send_multiple_requests_deferred(Request[ ] req);
    public abstract void send_multiple_requests_oneway(Request[ ] req);
    public void shutdown(boolean wait_for_completion);
    public abstract org.omg.CORBA.Object string_to_object(String str);
    public boolean work_pending();
// Protected Instance Methods
    protected abstract void set_parameters(java.applet.Applet app, java.util.Properties props);
    protected abstract void set_parameters(String[ ] args, java.util.Properties props);
// Deprecated Public Methods
#   public abstract TypeCode create_recursive_sequence_tc(int bound, int offset);
#   public org.omg.CORBA.Current get_current();
}
```

Subclasses: org.omg.CORBA_2_3.ORB

Passed To: javax.rmi.CORBA.Stub.connect(), javax.rmi.CORBA.StubDelegate.connect(),
javax.rmi.CORBA.Tie.orb(), javax.rmi.CORBA.Util.{copyObject(), copyObjects()},
javax.rmi.CORBA.UtilDelegate.{copyObject(), copyObjects()},

org.omg.CosNaming.BindingIteratorPOA._this(), org.omg.CosNaming.NamingContextExtPOA._this(),
org.omg.CosNaming.NamingContextPOA._this(), org.omg.PortableServer.Servant._this_object(),
org.omg.PortableServer.ServantActivatorPOA._this(), org.omg.PortableServer.ServantLocatorPOA._this()

Returned By: javax.rmi.CORBA.Tie.orb(), LocalObject._orb(), org.omg.CORBA.ORB.init(),
org.omg.CORBA.portable.Delegate.orb(), org.omg.CORBA.portable.InputStream.orb(),
org.omg.CORBA.portable.ObjectImpl._orb(), org.omg.CORBA.portable.OutputStream.orb(),
org.omg.PortableServer.Servant._orb(), org.omg.PortableServer.portable.Delegate.orb()

ParameterMode   Java 1.4

org.omg.CORBA   *serializable*

This class simply wraps the allowable modes for Parameters. PARAM_IN is used for IDL in
parameters, PARAM_OUT is for out parameters, and PARAM_INOUT is for inout parameters.
Added as of JDK 1.4.

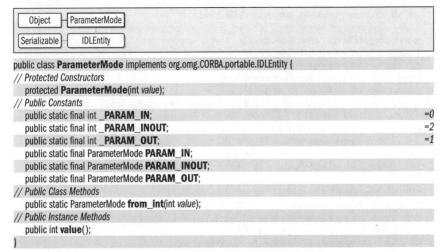

```
public class ParameterMode implements org.omg.CORBA.portable.IDLEntity {
// Protected Constructors
    protected ParameterMode(int value);
// Public Constants
    public static final int _PARAM_IN;                                        =0
    public static final int _PARAM_INOUT;                                     =2
    public static final int _PARAM_OUT;                                       =1
    public static final ParameterMode PARAM_IN;
    public static final ParameterMode PARAM_INOUT;
    public static final ParameterMode PARAM_OUT;
// Public Class Methods
    public static ParameterMode from_int(int value);
// Public Instance Methods
    public int value();
}
```

Passed To: ParameterModeHelper.{insert(), write()}, ParameterModeHolder.ParameterModeHolder(),
org.omg.Dynamic.Parameter.Parameter()

Returned By: ParameterMode.from_int(), ParameterModeHelper.{extract(), read()}

Type Of: ParameterMode.{PARAM_IN, PARAM_INOUT, PARAM_OUT}, ParameterModeHolder.value,
org.omg.Dynamic.Parameter.mode

ParameterModeHelper   Java 1.4

org.omg.CORBA

The helper class for ParameterMode objects, used to read and write these objects when
they are used as remote method arguments or return values. Added as of JDK 1.4.

```
public abstract class ParameterModeHelper {
// Public Constructors
    public ParameterModeHelper();
// Public Class Methods
    public static ParameterMode extract(Any a);
    public static String Id();
    public static void Insert(Any a, ParameterMode that);
    public static ParameterMode read(org.omg.CORBA.portable.InputStream istream);
```

```
    public static TypeCode type();                                                    synchronized
    public static void write(org.omg.CORBA.portable.OutputStream ostream, ParameterMode value);
}
```

ParameterModeHolder

org.omg.CORBA

The holder class for out and inout remote method arguments that would be mapped to
Java org.omg.CORBA.ParameterMode values.

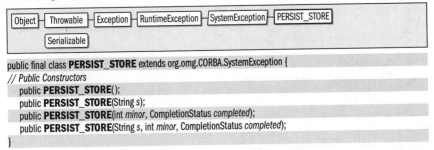

```
public final class ParameterModeHolder implements org.omg.CORBA.portable.Streamable {
// Public Constructors
    public ParameterModeHolder();
    public ParameterModeHolder(ParameterMode initialValue);
// Methods Implementing Streamable
    public void _read(org.omg.CORBA.portable.InputStream i);
    public TypeCode _type();
    public void _write(org.omg.CORBA.portable.OutputStream o);
// Public Instance Fields
    public ParameterMode value;
}
```

PERSIST_STORE
Java 1.2

org.omg.CORBA
serializable unchecked

A standard CORBA exception thrown when a server encounters an error with its persistent storage.

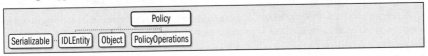

```
public final class PERSIST_STORE extends org.omg.CORBA.SystemException {
// Public Constructors
    public PERSIST_STORE();
    public PERSIST_STORE(String s);
    public PERSIST_STORE(int minor, CompletionStatus completed);
    public PERSIST_STORE(String s, int minor, CompletionStatus completed);
}
```

Policy
Java 1.2

org.omg.CORBA
serializable

This is the base interface for objects that represent usage policies for ORBs and other
CORBA services. Policies for certain objects or domains of objects can be obtained from
a DomainManager, which in turn can be obtained from the Object in question using its
_get_domain_managers() method. The policy_type() method on the Policy provides access to
an integer type indicator. The allowable values are implementation-specific.

```
public interface Policy extends PolicyOperations, org.omg.CORBA.Object, org.omg.CORBA.portable.IDLEntity {
}
```

Implementations: _PolicyStub, org.omg.PortableServer.IdAssignmentPolicy,
org.omg.PortableServer.IdUniquenessPolicy, org.omg.PortableServer.ImplicitActivationPolicy,
org.omg.PortableServer.LifespanPolicy, org.omg.PortableServer.RequestProcessingPolicy,
org.omg.PortableServer.ServantRetentionPolicy, org.omg.PortableServer.ThreadPolicy

Passed To: LocalObject._set_policy_override(), org.omg.CORBA.Object._set_policy_override(),
PolicyHelper.{insert(), write()}, PolicyHolder.PolicyHolder(), PolicyListHelper.{insert(), write()},
PolicyListHolder.PolicyListHolder(), org.omg.CORBA.portable.Delegate.set_policy_override(),
org.omg.CORBA.portable.ObjectImpl._set_policy_override(),
org.omg.PortableServer.POAOperations.create_POA()

Returned By: _PolicyStub.copy(), DomainManagerOperations.get_domain_policy(),
LocalObject._get_policy(), org.omg.CORBA.Object._get_policy(), org.omg.CORBA.ORB.create_policy(),
PolicyHelper.{extract(), narrow(), read()}, PolicyListHelper.{extract(), read()}, PolicyOperations.copy(),
org.omg.CORBA.portable.Delegate.get_policy(), org.omg.CORBA.portable.ObjectImpl._get_policy(),
org.omg.PortableInterceptor.ClientRequestInfoOperations.get_request_policy(),
org.omg.PortableInterceptor.IORInfoOperations.get_effective_policy(),
org.omg.PortableInterceptor.PolicyFactoryOperations.create_policy(),
org.omg.PortableInterceptor.ServerRequestInfoOperations.get_server_policy()

Type Of: PolicyHolder.value, PolicyListHolder.value

PolicyError

Java 1.2

org.omg.CORBA

serializable checked

An exception thrown when an error occurs during creation of a Policy.

```
public final class PolicyError extends UserException {
// Public Constructors
    public PolicyError();
    public PolicyError(short __reason);
    public PolicyError(String reason_string, short __reason);
// Public Instance Fields
    public short reason;
}
```

Passed To: PolicyErrorHelper.{insert(), write()}, PolicyErrorHolder.PolicyErrorHolder()

Returned By: PolicyErrorHelper.{extract(), read()}

Thrown By: org.omg.CORBA.ORB.create_policy(),
org.omg.PortableInterceptor.PolicyFactoryOperations.create_policy()

Type Of: PolicyErrorHolder.value

PolicyErrorCodeHelper

Java 1.4

org.omg.CORBA

The helper class for PolicyCodeError objects, used to read and write these objects when
they are used as remote method arguments or return values. Added as of JDK 1.4.

```
public abstract class PolicyErrorCodeHelper {
// Public Constructors
   public PolicyErrorCodeHelper();
// Public Class Methods
   public static short extract(Any a);
   public static String id();
   public static void insert(Any a, short that);
   public static short read(org.omg.CORBA.portable.InputStream istream);
   public static TypeCode type();                                              synchronized
   public static void write(org.omg.CORBA.portable.OutputStream ostream, short value);
}
```

PolicyErrorHelper   Java 1.4

org.omg.CORBA

The helper class for PolicyError objects, used to read and write these objects when they are used as remote method arguments or return values.

```
public abstract class PolicyErrorHelper {
// Public Constructors
   public PolicyErrorHelper();
// Public Class Methods
   public static PolicyError extract(Any a);
   public static String id();
   public static void insert(Any a, PolicyError that);
   public static PolicyError read(org.omg.CORBA.portable.InputStream istream);
   public static TypeCode type();                                              synchronized
   public static void write(org.omg.CORBA.portable.OutputStream ostream, PolicyError value);
}
```

PolicyErrorHolder   Java 1.4

org.omg.CORBA

The holder class for out and inout remote method arguments that would be mapped to PolicyError values.

```
Object ├ PolicyErrorHolder ┈ Streamable
```

```
public final class PolicyErrorHolder implements org.omg.CORBA.portable.Streamable {
// Public Constructors
   public PolicyErrorHolder();
   public PolicyErrorHolder(PolicyError initialValue);
// Methods Implementing Streamable
   public void _read(org.omg.CORBA.portable.InputStream i);
   public TypeCode _type();
   public void _write(org.omg.CORBA.portable.OutputStream o);
// Public Instance Fields
   public PolicyError value;
}
```

PolicyHelper   Java 1.3

org.omg.CORBA

The helper class for Policy objects, used to safely cast remote references to these objects, and to read and write these objects when they are used as remote method arguments or return values.

```
public abstract class PolicyHelper {
// Public Constructors
    public PolicyHelper();
// Public Class Methods
    public static org.omg.CORBA.Policy extract(Any a);
    public static String id();
    public static void insert(Any a, org.omg.CORBA.Policy that);
    public static org.omg.CORBA.Policy narrow(org.omg.CORBA.Object obj);
    public static org.omg.CORBA.Policy read(org.omg.CORBA.portable.InputStream istream);
    public static TypeCode type();                                              synchronized
    public static void write(org.omg.CORBA.portable.OutputStream ostream, org.omg.CORBA.Policy value);
}
```

PolicyHolder   Java 1.3

org.omg.CORBA

The holder class for out and inout remote method arguments that would be mapped to Policy values.

```
Object ├─ PolicyHolder ┈ Streamable
```

```
public final class PolicyHolder implements org.omg.CORBA.portable.Streamable {
// Public Constructors
    public PolicyHolder();
    public PolicyHolder(org.omg.CORBA.Policy initialValue);
// Methods Implementing Streamable
    public void _read(org.omg.CORBA.portable.InputStream i);
    public TypeCode _type();
    public void _write(org.omg.CORBA.portable.OutputStream o);
// Public Instance Fields
    public org.omg.CORBA.Policy value;
}
```

PolicyListHelper   Java 1.3

org.omg.CORBA

The helper class for Policy arrays, used to safely cast remote references to these arrays, and to read and write these arrays when they are used as remote method arguments or return values.

```
public abstract class PolicyListHelper {
// Public Constructors
    public PolicyListHelper();
// Public Class Methods
    public static org.omg.CORBA.Policy[ ] extract(Any a);
    public static String id();
    public static void insert(Any a, org.omg.CORBA.Policy[ ] that);
    public static org.omg.CORBA.Policy[ ] read(org.omg.CORBA.portable.InputStream istream);
    public static TypeCode type();                                              synchronized
    public static void write(org.omg.CORBA.portable.OutputStream ostream, org.omg.CORBA.Policy[ ] value);
}
```

PolicyListHolder
org.omg.CORBA

The holder class for out and inout remote method arguments that are declared in IDL with type PolicyList.

```
Object ─ PolicyListHolder ┈ Streamable
```

public final class **PolicyListHolder** implements org.omg.CORBA.portable.Streamable {
// *Public Constructors*
   public **PolicyListHolder**();
   public **PolicyListHolder**(org.omg.CORBA.Policy[ ] *initialValue*);
// *Methods Implementing Streamable*
   public void **_read**(org.omg.CORBA.portable.InputStream *i*);
   public TypeCode **_type**();
   public void **_write**(org.omg.CORBA.portable.OutputStream *o*);
// *Public Instance Fields*
   public org.omg.CORBA.Policy[ ] **value**;
}

PolicyOperations
org.omg.CORBA

The generated operations interface for the Policy interface.

public interface **PolicyOperations** {
// *Public Instance Methods*
   public abstract org.omg.CORBA.Policy **copy**();
   public abstract void **destroy**();
   public abstract int **policy_type**();
}

Implementations: org.omg.CORBA.Policy, org.omg.PortableServer.IdAssignmentPolicyOperations,
org.omg.PortableServer.IdUniquenessPolicyOperations,
org.omg.PortableServer.ImplicitActivationPolicyOperations,
org.omg.PortableServer.LifespanPolicyOperations,
org.omg.PortableServer.RequestProcessingPolicyOperations,
org.omg.PortableServer.ServantRetentionPolicyOperations,
org.omg.PortableServer.ThreadPolicyOperations

PolicyTypeHelper
org.omg.CORBA

The helper class for PolicyType, which is an IDL typedef mapped to int. This helper reads and writes these values when they are used as remote method arguments or return values.

public abstract class **PolicyTypeHelper** {
// *Public Constructors*
   public **PolicyTypeHelper**();
// *Public Class Methods*
   public static int **extract**(Any *a*);
   public static String **id**();
   public static void **insert**(Any *a*, int *that*);
   public static int **read**(org.omg.CORBA.portable.InputStream *istream*);

```
    public static TypeCode type();                                                    synchronized
    public static void write(org.omg.CORBA.portable.OutputStream ostream, int value);
}
```

Principal   Java 1.2; Deprecated in Java 1.2

org.omg.CORBA

This deprecated class was used in previous versions of the CORBA standard to hold the identity of a client, in the form of an array of bytes representing the encoded name of the client. This functionality has now been assumed by the Security Service, but the class is still available in the Java IDL API to provide temporary backward compatibility with previous CORBA apps.

```
public class Principal {
// Public Constructors
    public Principal();
// Deprecated Public Methods
#   public byte[ ] name();
#   public void name(byte[ ] value);
}
```

Passed To: Any.insert_Principal(), PrincipalHolder.PrincipalHolder(),
org.omg.CORBA.portable.OutputStream.write_Principal()

Returned By: Any.extract_Principal(), org.omg.CORBA.portable.InputStream.read_Principal()

Type Of: PrincipalHolder.value

PrincipalHolder   Java 1.2; Deprecated in Java 1.2

org.omg.CORBA

This deprecated class is the holder class for out and inout remote method arguments that would be mapped to Java Principal objects. See Chapter 4 for more information on the uses of holder classes.

```
Object ├─ PrincipalHolder ┈ Streamable
```

```
public final class PrincipalHolder implements org.omg.CORBA.portable.Streamable {
// Public Constructors
    public PrincipalHolder();
    public PrincipalHolder(org.omg.CORBA.Principal initial);
// Methods Implementing Streamable
    public void _read(org.omg.CORBA.portable.InputStream input);
    public TypeCode _type();
    public void _write(org.omg.CORBA.portable.OutputStream output);
// Public Instance Fields
    public org.omg.CORBA.Principal value;
}
```

PRIVATE_MEMBER
Java 1.2

org.omg.CORBA

A wrapper for the Visibility value assigned to ValueMembers that are declared private.

```
public interface PRIVATE_MEMBER {
// Public Constants
    public static final short value;                                          =0
}
```

PUBLIC_MEMBER
Java 1.2

org.omg.CORBA

A wrapper for the Visibility value assigned to ValueMembers that are declared public.

```
public interface PUBLIC_MEMBER {
// Public Constants
    public static final short value;                                          =1
}
```

RepositoryIdHelper
Java 1.3

org.omg.CORBA

The helper class for RepositoryId, which is an IDL typedef mapped to String. This helper is used to read and write these values when they are used as remote method arguments or return values.

```
public abstract class RepositoryIdHelper {
// Public Constructors
    public RepositoryIdHelper();
// Public Class Methods
    public static String extract(Any a);
    public static String id();
    public static void insert(Any a, String that);
    public static String read(org.omg.CORBA.portable.InputStream istream);
    public static TypeCode type();                                     synchronized
    public static void write(org.omg.CORBA.portable.OutputStream ostream, String value);
}
```

Request
Java 1.2

org.omg.CORBA

A Request represents a remote method request when using the Dynamic Invocation Interface. Request objects are created by calling the create_request() method on the org.omg.CORBA.Object reference for the remote object that will service the method request. The Request contains the name of the method to be invoked, an NVList containing NamedValue objects that represent the method arguments, and the return value for the method, if appropriate. It can also contain a description of the exceptions that the method can throw, and the client context values that the method accepts.

You add method arguments to a Request by calling one of its add_XXX() methods, which all return an Any object that you can initialize with the value of the argument. Once the Request has been initialized with its arguments and any other information, the method can be invoked synchronously using the invoke() method, asynchronously using the send_deferred() method, or in one-way mode using the send_oneway(). Immediately after the invoke() method returns, any return values or thrown exceptions are available for you to query. After calling the send_deferred() method, you can poll and retrieve the method response by calling the poll_response() and get_response() methods. If the response is ready, then get_response() will initialize the internal return value or exception in the Request object, and it can be retrieved using the return_value() method. After calling send_oneway(), no return value or exception will be returned. You can use send_oneway() on methods even if they weren't declared as one way in the corresponding IDL for the interface.

```
public abstract class Request {
// Public Constructors
    public Request();
// Public Instance Methods
    public abstract Any add_in_arg();
    public abstract Any add_inout_arg();
    public abstract Any add_named_in_arg(String name);
    public abstract Any add_named_inout_arg(String name);
    public abstract Any add_named_out_arg(String name);
    public abstract Any add_out_arg();
    public abstract NVList arguments();
    public abstract ContextList contexts();
    public abstract org.omg.CORBA.Context ctx();
    public abstract void ctx(org.omg.CORBA.Context c);
    public abstract Environment env();
    public abstract ExceptionList exceptions();
    public abstract void get_response() throws WrongTransaction;
    public abstract void invoke();
    public abstract String operation();
    public abstract boolean poll_response();
    public abstract NamedValue result();
    public abstract Any return_value();
    public abstract void send_deferred();
    public abstract void send_oneway();
    public abstract void set_return_type(TypeCode tc);
    public abstract org.omg.CORBA.Object target();
}
```

Passed To: org.omg.CORBA.ORB.{send_multiple_requests_deferred(), send_multiple_requests_oneway()}

Returned By: LocalObject.{_create_request(), _request()}, org.omg.CORBA.Object.{_create_request(), _request()}, org.omg.CORBA.ORB.get_next_response(), org.omg.CORBA.portable.Delegate.{create_request(), request()}, org.omg.CORBA.portable.ObjectImpl.{_create_request(), _request()}

ServerRequest

Java 1.2

org.omg.CORBA

The server-side equivalent of the client-side Request object. A ServerRequest is used in the Dynamic Skeleton Interface to invoke a method on a server object through its DynamicImplementation.

```
public abstract class ServerRequest {
// Public Constructors
    public ServerRequest();
// Public Instance Methods
    public void arguments(NVList args);
    public abstract org.omg.CORBA.Context ctx();
    public String operation();
    public void set_exception(Any any);
    public void set_result(Any any);
```

```
// Deprecated Public Methods
#   public void except(Any any);
#   public String op_name();
#   public void params(NVList params);
#   public void result(Any any);
}
```

Passed To: org.omg.CORBA.DynamicImplementation.invoke(),
org.omg.CosNaming._BindingIteratorImplBase.invoke(),
org.omg.CosNaming._NamingContextImplBase.invoke(),
org.omg.PortableServer.DynamicImplementation.invoke()

ServiceDetail

Java 1.2

org.omg.CORBA

serializable

A component of a ServiceInformation object, which describes a service available through
an ORB. Each ServiceDetail contains an integer type code and an array of bytes containing information about the service. The semantics of the type code and the format of the
byte data is implementation-specific.

```
   Object ─── ServiceDetail

  Serializable ┄ IDLEntity
```

```
public final class ServiceDetail implements org.omg.CORBA.portable.IDLEntity {
// Public Constructors
    public ServiceDetail();
    public ServiceDetail(int service_detail_type, byte[] service_detail);
// Public Instance Fields
    public byte[] service_detail;
    public int service_detail_type;
}
```

Passed To: ServiceDetailHelper.{insert(), write()}, ServiceInformation.ServiceInformation()

Returned By: ServiceDetailHelper.{extract(), read()}

Type Of: ServiceInformation.service_details

ServiceDetailHelper

Java 1.2

org.omg.CORBA

The helper class for the ServiceDetail class, used internally to read and write ServiceDetail
objects when they are used as remote method arguments or return values.

```
public abstract class ServiceDetailHelper {
// Public Constructors
1.4 public ServiceDetailHelper();
// Public Class Methods
    public static ServiceDetail extract(Any a);
    public static String id();
    public static void insert(Any a, ServiceDetail that);
    public static ServiceDetail read(org.omg.CORBA.portable.InputStream in);
    public static TypeCode type();                                                    synchronized
    public static void write(org.omg.CORBA.portable.OutputStream out, ServiceDetail that);
}
```

ServiceInformation

Java 1.2

org.omg.CORBA

serializable

This class represents information about a service available through a CORBA ORB. You query for information about a service using the ORB.get_service_information() method, which returns a ServiceInformation object. The ServiceInformation consists of a set of ServiceDetail objects, each representing a particular piece of information about the service.

```
Object ─ ServiceInformation
Serializable ┈ IDLEntity
```

```
public final class ServiceInformation implements org.omg.CORBA.portable.IDLEntity {
// Public Constructors
   public ServiceInformation();
   public ServiceInformation(int[ ] __service_options, ServiceDetail[ ] __service_details);
// Public Instance Fields
   public ServiceDetail[ ] service_details;
   public int[ ] service_options;
}
```

Passed To: ServiceInformationHelper.{insert(), write()},
ServiceInformationHolder.ServiceInformationHolder()

Returned By: ServiceInformationHelper.{extract(), read()}

Type Of: ServiceInformationHolder.value

ServiceInformationHelper

Java 1.2

org.omg.CORBA

The helper class for ServiceInformation objects, used internally to read and write ServiceInformation objects when they are used as remote method arguments or return values.

```
public abstract class ServiceInformationHelper {
// Public Constructors
1.4 public ServiceInformationHelper();
// Public Class Methods
   public static ServiceInformation extract(Any a);
   public static String id();
   public static void insert(Any a, ServiceInformation that);
   public static ServiceInformation read(org.omg.CORBA.portable.InputStream in);
   public static TypeCode type();                                     synchronized
   public static void write(org.omg.CORBA.portable.OutputStream out, ServiceInformation that);
}
```

ServiceInformationHolder

Java 1.2

org.omg.CORBA

The holder class for out and inout remote method arguments that would be mapped to Java ServiceInformation objects. See Chapter 4 for more information on the uses of holder classes.

```
Object ─ ServiceInformationHolder ┈ Streamable
```

```
public final class ServiceInformationHolder implements org.omg.CORBA.portable.Streamable {
// Public Constructors
   public ServiceInformationHolder();
```

```
  public ServiceInformationHolder(ServiceInformation arg);
// Methods Implementing Streamable
  public void _read(org.omg.CORBA.portable.InputStream in);
  public TypeCode _type();
  public void _write(org.omg.CORBA.portable.OutputStream out);
// Public Instance Fields
  public ServiceInformation value;
}
```

Passed To: org.omg.CORBA.ORB.get_service_information()

SetOverrideType

org.omg.CORBA

Java 1.2

serializable

The mapping of an enumeration containing the indicators for how policies should be
handled for a given Object when using the Object._set_policy_override() method. ADD_OVER-
RIDE indicates that the provided policies should be added to the existing policies of the
Object. SET_OVERRIDE indicates that the given policies should replace any existing policies on the Object.

```
public class SetOverrideType implements org.omg.CORBA.portable.IDLEntity {
// Protected Constructors
  protected SetOverrideType(int _value);
// Public Constants
  public static final int _ADD_OVERRIDE;                                    =1
  public static final int _SET_OVERRIDE;                                    =0
  public static final SetOverrideType ADD_OVERRIDE;
  public static final SetOverrideType SET_OVERRIDE;
// Public Class Methods
  public static SetOverrideType from_int(int i);
// Public Instance Methods
  public int value();
}
```

Passed To: LocalObject._set_policy_override(), org.omg.CORBA.Object._set_policy_override(),
SetOverrideTypeHelper.{insert(), write()}, org.omg.CORBA.portable.Delegate.set_policy_override(),
org.omg.CORBA.portable.ObjectImpl._set_policy_override()

Returned By: SetOverrideType.from_int(), SetOverrideTypeHelper.{extract(), read()}

Type Of: SetOverrideType.{ADD_OVERRIDE, SET_OVERRIDE}

SetOverrideTypeHelper

Java 1.3

org.omg.CORBA

The helper class for SetOverrideType objects, used to read and write these objects when
they are used as remote method arguments or return values.

```
public abstract class SetOverrideTypeHelper {
// Public Constructors
  public SetOverrideTypeHelper();
// Public Class Methods
  public static SetOverrideType extract(Any a);
  public static String id();
```

```
    public static void insert(Any a, SetOverrideType that);
    public static SetOverrideType read(org.omg.CORBA.portable.InputStream istream);
    public static TypeCode type();                                                    synchronized
    public static void write(org.omg.CORBA.portable.OutputStream ostream, SetOverrideType value);
}
```

ShortHolder

Java 1.2

org.omg.CORBA

The holder class for out and inout remote method arguments that are declared in IDL
with type short.

```
Object — ShortHolder ⋯ Streamable
```

```
public final class ShortHolder implements org.omg.CORBA.portable.Streamable {
// Public Constructors
    public ShortHolder();
    public ShortHolder(short initial);
// Methods Implementing Streamable
    public void _read(org.omg.CORBA.portable.InputStream input);
    public TypeCode _type();
    public void _write(org.omg.CORBA.portable.OutputStream output);
// Public Instance Fields
    public short value;
}
```

ShortSeqHelper

Java 1.3

org.omg.CORBA

The helper class for arrays of shorts, used to read and write these arrays when they are
used as remote method arguments or return values.

```
public abstract class ShortSeqHelper {
// Public Constructors
    public ShortSeqHelper();
// Public Class Methods
    public static short[] extract(Any a);
    public static String id();
    public static void insert(Any a, short[] that);
    public static short[] read(org.omg.CORBA.portable.InputStream istream);
    public static TypeCode type();                                                    synchronized
    public static void write(org.omg.CORBA.portable.OutputStream ostream, short[] value);
}
```

ShortSeqHolder

Java 1.3

org.omg.CORBA

The holder class for out and inout remote method arguments that are declared in IDL
with type ShortSeq, mapped in Java to a short array.

```
Object — ShortSeqHolder ⋯ Streamable
```

```
public final class ShortSeqHolder implements org.omg.CORBA.portable.Streamable {
// Public Constructors
    public ShortSeqHolder();
```

```
    public ShortSeqHolder(short[ ] initialValue);
// Methods Implementing Streamable
    public void _read(org.omg.CORBA.portable.InputStream i);
    public TypeCode _type();
    public void _write(org.omg.CORBA.portable.OutputStream o);
// Public Instance Fields
    public short[ ] value;
}
```

Passed To: org.omg.CORBA.DataInputStream.read_short_array()

StringHolder   Java 1.2

org.omg.CORBA

The holder class for out and inout remote method arguments that are declared in IDL with type string.

```
Object ─ StringHolder ┈ Streamable
```

```
public final class StringHolder implements org.omg.CORBA.portable.Streamable {
// Public Constructors
    public StringHolder();
    public StringHolder(String initial);
// Methods Implementing Streamable
    public void _read(org.omg.CORBA.portable.InputStream input);
    public TypeCode _type();
    public void _write(org.omg.CORBA.portable.OutputStream output);
// Public Instance Fields
    public String value;
}
```

StringSeqHelper   Java 1.4

org.omg.CORBA

The helper class for arrays of Strings, used to read and write these arrays when they are used as remote method arguments or return values.

```
public abstract class StringSeqHelper {
// Public Constructors
    public StringSeqHelper();
// Public Class Methods
    public static String[ ] extract(Any a);
    public static String id();
    public static void insert(Any a, String[ ] that);
    public static String[ ] read(org.omg.CORBA.portable.InputStream istream);
    public static TypeCode type();                                          synchronized
    public static void write(org.omg.CORBA.portable.OutputStream ostream, String[ ] value);
}
```

StringSeqHolder   Java 1.4

org.omg.CORBA

The holder class for out and inout remote method arguments that are declared in IDL with type StringSeq, which is mapped in Java to an array of Strings.

```
Object — StringSeqHolder ┈ Streamable
```

```
public final class StringSeqHolder implements org.omg.CORBA.portable.Streamable {
// Public Constructors
   public StringSeqHolder();
   public StringSeqHolder(String[ ] initialValue);
// Methods Implementing Streamable
   public void _read(org.omg.CORBA.portable.InputStream i);
   public TypeCode _type();
   public void _write(org.omg.CORBA.portable.OutputStream o);
// Public Instance Fields
   public String[ ] value;
}
```

StringValueHelper   Java 1.3

org.omg.CORBA

The helper class for StringValue, which is an IDL typedef for Strings. This helper is used to
read and write these values when they are used as remote method arguments or return
values.

```
Object — StringValueHelper ┈ BoxedValueHelper
```

```
public class StringValueHelper implements org.omg.CORBA.portable.BoxedValueHelper {
// Public Constructors
   public StringValueHelper();
// Public Class Methods
   public static String extract(Any a);
   public static String id();
   public static void insert(Any a, String that);
   public static String read(org.omg.CORBA.portable.InputStream istream);
   public static TypeCode type();                                            synchronized
   public static void write(org.omg.CORBA.portable.OutputStream ostream, String value);
// Methods Implementing BoxedValueHelper
   public String get_id();
   public Serializable read_value(org.omg.CORBA.portable.InputStream istream);
   public void write_value(org.omg.CORBA.portable.OutputStream ostream, Serializable value);
}
```

StructMember   Java 1.2

org.omg.CORBA   *serializable*

A class that represents a member of an IDL struct type. StructMembers are used to create
TypeCodes for IDL structs and exceptions with the ORB.create_struct_tc() and ORB.cre-
ate_exception_tc() methods.

```
Object — StructMember
Serializable ┈ IDLEntity
```

```
public final class StructMember implements org.omg.CORBA.portable.IDLEntity {
// Public Constructors
   public StructMember();
   public StructMember(String __name, TypeCode __type, IDLType __type_def);
// Public Instance Fields
   public String name;
   public TypeCode type;
```

```
    public IDLType type_def;
}
```

Passed To: org.omg.CORBA.ORB.{create_exception_tc(), create_struct_tc()},
StructMemberHelper.{insert(), write()}

Returned By: StructMemberHelper.{extract(), read()}

StructMemberHelper   Java 1.3
org.omg.CORBA

The helper class for StructMember objects, used to read and write these objects when
they are used as remote method arguments or return values.

```
public abstract class StructMemberHelper {
// Public Constructors
    public StructMemberHelper();
// Public Class Methods
    public static StructMember extract(Any a);
    public static String id();
    public static void insert(Any a, StructMember that);
    public static StructMember read(org.omg.CORBA.portable.InputStream istream);
    public static TypeCode type();                                       synchronized
    public static void write(org.omg.CORBA.portable.OutputStream ostream, StructMember value);
}
```

SystemException   Java 1.2
org.omg.CORBA   serializable unchecked

This is the base class for all standard CORBA exceptions. A SystemException can be
thrown by any CORBA remote method call, and many CORBA API methods throw Sys-
temExceptions as well. The SystemException class provides an integer minor code that can
be optionally used by subclasses to indicate a more precise reason for the exception.
The class also provides a CompletionStatus that is used to indicate to the caller whether
the method they invoked was completed or not when the exception was encountered.

Subclasses of SystemException represent the many errors that can occur while a remote
method request is be processed by the client's ORB, transferred to the server ORB, executed on the server object, and its response is transferred back to the client. A SystemException can originate on the client or on the server, before, after or during the actual
execution of the method on the remote object.

Since SystemException extends the java.lang.RuntimeException, these exceptions don't need
to be declared in method signatures. But all remote methods declared in IDL interfaces
that are then mapped to Java, can throw any of the subclasses of SystemException during
remote method calls.

```
Object ├ Throwable ┤ Exception ┤ RuntimeException ┤ SystemException

       Serializable
```

```
public abstract class SystemException extends RuntimeException {
// Protected Constructors
    protected SystemException(String reason, int minor, CompletionStatus completed);
// Public Methods Overriding Throwable
    public String toString();
// Public Instance Fields
```

```
    public CompletionStatus completed;
    public int minor;
}
```

Subclasses: Too many classes to list.

Passed To: javax.rmi.CORBA.Util.mapSystemException(),
javax.rmi.CORBA.UtilDelegate.mapSystemException()

Thrown By: org.omg.CORBA.portable.InvokeHandler._invoke()

TCKind

org.omg.CORBA

A class used to represent the type of a TypeCode object. The TCKind class contains a set of
static int values that correspond to the built-in IDL data types. It also contains a set of
static TCKind instances that correspond to each of these IDL types. The TCKind of a Type-
Code can be obtained using its kind() method, and its value can be compared to these
static data members to determine the type of the TypeCode.

```
public class TCKind {
// Protected Constructors
#   protected TCKind(int _value);
// Public Constants
    public static final int _tk_abstract_interface;              =32
    public static final int _tk_alias;                           =21
    public static final int _tk_any;                             =11
    public static final int _tk_array;                           =20
    public static final int _tk_boolean;                          =8
    public static final int _tk_char;                             =9
    public static final int _tk_double;                           =7
    public static final int _tk_enum;                            =17
    public static final int _tk_except;                          =22
    public static final int _tk_fixed;                           =28
    public static final int _tk_float;                            =6
    public static final int _tk_long;                             =3
    public static final int _tk_longdouble;                      =25
    public static final int _tk_longlong;                        =23
    public static final int _tk_native;                          =31
    public static final int _tk_null;                             =0
    public static final int _tk_objref;                          =14
    public static final int _tk_octet;                           =10
    public static final int _tk_Principal;                       =13
    public static final int _tk_sequence;                        =19
    public static final int _tk_short;                            =2
    public static final int _tk_string;                          =18
    public static final int _tk_struct;                          =15
    public static final int _tk_TypeCode;                        =12
    public static final int _tk_ulong;                            =5
    public static final int _tk_ulonglong;                       =24
    public static final int _tk_union;                           =16
    public static final int _tk_ushort;                           =4
    public static final int _tk_value;                           =29
    public static final int _tk_value_box;                       =30
    public static final int _tk_void;                             =1
    public static final int _tk_wchar;                           =26
    public static final int _tk_wstring;                         =27
```

```
    public static final TCKind tk_abstract_interface;
    public static final TCKind tk_alias;
    public static final TCKind tk_any;
    public static final TCKind tk_array;
    public static final TCKind tk_boolean;
    public static final TCKind tk_char;
    public static final TCKind tk_double;
    public static final TCKind tk_enum;
    public static final TCKind tk_except;
    public static final TCKind tk_fixed;
    public static final TCKind tk_float;
    public static final TCKind tk_long;
    public static final TCKind tk_longdouble;
    public static final TCKind tk_longlong;
    public static final TCKind tk_native;
    public static final TCKind tk_null;
    public static final TCKind tk_objref;
    public static final TCKind tk_octet;
    public static final TCKind tk_Principal;
    public static final TCKind tk_sequence;
    public static final TCKind tk_short;
    public static final TCKind tk_string;
    public static final TCKind tk_struct;
    public static final TCKind tk_TypeCode;
    public static final TCKind tk_ulong;
    public static final TCKind tk_ulonglong;
    public static final TCKind tk_union;
    public static final TCKind tk_ushort;
    public static final TCKind tk_value;
    public static final TCKind tk_value_box;
    public static final TCKind tk_void;
    public static final TCKind tk_wchar;
    public static final TCKind tk_wstring;
// Public Class Methods
    public static TCKind from_int(int i);
// Public Instance Methods
    public int value();
}
```

Passed To: org.omg.CORBA.ORB.get_primitive_tc()

Returned By: org.omg.CORBA.DynStruct.current_member_kind(),
org.omg.CORBA.DynUnion.{discriminator_kind(), member_kind()},
org.omg.CORBA.DynValue.current_member_kind(), TCKind.from_int(), TypeCode.kind(),
org.omg.DynamicAny._DynStructStub.current_member_kind(),
org.omg.DynamicAny._DynUnionStub.{discriminator_kind(), member_kind()},
org.omg.DynamicAny._DynValueStub.current_member_kind(),
org.omg.DynamicAny.DynStructOperations.current_member_kind(),
org.omg.DynamicAny.DynUnionOperations.{discriminator_kind(), member_kind()},
org.omg.DynamicAny.DynValueOperations.current_member_kind()

Type Of: Too many fields to list.

TRANSACTION_REQUIRED

Java 1.2

org.omg.CORBA
serializable unchecked

A standard CORBA exception thrown when a remote method that must be run within a transaction is invoked outside of any transaction.

```
Object ─┬─ Throwable ─┤ Exception ─┤ RuntimeException ─┤ SystemException ─┤ TRANSACTION_REQUIRED
        └─ Serializable
```

public final class **TRANSACTION_REQUIRED** extends org.omg.CORBA.SystemException {
// Public Constructors
   public **TRANSACTION_REQUIRED**();
   public **TRANSACTION_REQUIRED**(String s);
   public **TRANSACTION_REQUIRED**(int *minor*, CompletionStatus *completed*);
   public **TRANSACTION_REQUIRED**(String s, int *minor*, CompletionStatus *completed*);
}

TRANSACTION_ROLLEDBACK

Java 1.2

org.omg.CORBA
serializable unchecked

A standard CORBA exception thrown when a remote method that was invoked within a transaction could not be completed because the enclosing transaction was rolled back.

```
Object ─┬─ Throwable ─┤ Exception ─┤ RuntimeException ─┤ SystemException ─┤ TRANSACTION_ROLLEDBACK
        └─ Serializable
```

public final class **TRANSACTION_ROLLEDBACK** extends org.omg.CORBA.SystemException {
// Public Constructors
   public **TRANSACTION_ROLLEDBACK**();
   public **TRANSACTION_ROLLEDBACK**(String s);
   public **TRANSACTION_ROLLEDBACK**(int *minor*, CompletionStatus *completed*);
   public **TRANSACTION_ROLLEDBACK**(String s, int *minor*, CompletionStatus *completed*);
}

TRANSIENT

Java 1.2

org.omg.CORBA
serializable unchecked

A standard CORBA exception thrown when a transient (i.e., not necessarily repeatable) error occurs during a remote method call. Since the error might not occur again, it is possible to try making the same request again.

```
Object ─┬─ Throwable ─┤ Exception ─┤ RuntimeException ─┤ SystemException ─┤ TRANSIENT
        └─ Serializable
```

public final class **TRANSIENT** extends org.omg.CORBA.SystemException {
// Public Constructors
   public **TRANSIENT**();
   public **TRANSIENT**(String s);
   public **TRANSIENT**(int *minor*, CompletionStatus *completed*);
   public **TRANSIENT**(String s, int *minor*, CompletionStatus *completed*);
}

TypeCode

org.omg.CORBA

A TypeCode object describes the IDL type of a CORBA object, analogously to how the Java Class for an object (obtained using the getClass() method on java.lang.Object) describes its Java type. At a minimum, a TypeCode object contains a TCKind element that specifies the IDL data type that it represents. For structured IDL types, such as structs and unions, it also contains additional information about the data type. The member_XXX() methods are used to obtain information about the members of structs, unions, enums, and exceptions, while the length() method gives the length of strings, sequences, and array types, for example.

```
Object ──┤─TypeCode

Serializable ┈┤ IDLEntity
```

```
public abstract class TypeCode implements org.omg.CORBA.portable.IDLEntity {
// Public Constructors
    public TypeCode();
// Public Instance Methods
    public abstract TypeCode concrete_base_type() throws org.omg.CORBA.TypeCodePackage.BadKind;
    public abstract TypeCode content_type() throws org.omg.CORBA.TypeCodePackage.BadKind;
    public abstract int default_index() throws org.omg.CORBA.TypeCodePackage.BadKind;
    public abstract TypeCode discriminator_type() throws org.omg.CORBA.TypeCodePackage.BadKind;
    public abstract boolean equal(TypeCode tc);
    public abstract boolean equivalent(TypeCode tc);
    public abstract short fixed_digits() throws org.omg.CORBA.TypeCodePackage.BadKind;
    public abstract short fixed_scale() throws org.omg.CORBA.TypeCodePackage.BadKind;
    public abstract TypeCode get_compact_typecode();
    public abstract String id() throws org.omg.CORBA.TypeCodePackage.BadKind;
    public abstract TCKind kind();
    public abstract int length() throws org.omg.CORBA.TypeCodePackage.BadKind;
    public abstract int member_count() throws org.omg.CORBA.TypeCodePackage.BadKind;
    public abstract Any member_label(int index) throws org.omg.CORBA.TypeCodePackage.BadKind,
        org.omg.CORBA.TypeCodePackage.Bounds;
    public abstract String member_name(int index) throws org.omg.CORBA.TypeCodePackage.BadKind,
        org.omg.CORBA.TypeCodePackage.Bounds;
    public abstract TypeCode member_type(int index) throws org.omg.CORBA.TypeCodePackage.BadKind,
        org.omg.CORBA.TypeCodePackage.Bounds;
    public abstract short member_visibility(int index) throws org.omg.CORBA.TypeCodePackage.BadKind,
        org.omg.CORBA.TypeCodePackage.Bounds;
    public abstract String name() throws org.omg.CORBA.TypeCodePackage.BadKind;
    public abstract short type_modifier() throws org.omg.CORBA.TypeCodePackage.BadKind;
}
```

Passed To: Too many methods to list.

Returned By: Too many methods to list.

Type Of: StructMember.type, TypeCodeHolder.value, UnionMember.type, ValueMember.type

TypeCodeHolder

org.omg.CORBA

The holder class for out and inout remote method arguments that are declared in IDL with type TypeCode.

```
Object ── TypeCodeHolder ┈ Streamable
```

```
public final class TypeCodeHolder implements org.omg.CORBA.portable.Streamable {
// Public Constructors
    public TypeCodeHolder();
    public TypeCodeHolder(TypeCode initial);
// Methods Implementing Streamable
    public void _read(org.omg.CORBA.portable.InputStream input);
    public TypeCode _type();
    public void _write(org.omg.CORBA.portable.OutputStream output);
// Public Instance Fields
    public TypeCode value;
}
```

ULongLongSeqHelper   Java 1.3

org.omg.CORBA

The helper class for arrays of longs (mapped from the IDL unsigned long long data type),
used to read and write these arrays when they are used as remote method arguments
or return values.

```
public abstract class ULongLongSeqHelper {
// Public Constructors
    public ULongLongSeqHelper();
// Public Class Methods
    public static long[ ] extract(Any a);
    public static String id();
    public static void insert(Any a, long[ ] that);
    public static long[ ] read(org.omg.CORBA.portable.InputStream istream);
    public static TypeCode type();                                    synchronized
    public static void write(org.omg.CORBA.portable.OutputStream ostream, long[ ] value);
}
```

ULongLongSeqHolder   Java 1.3

org.omg.CORBA

The holder class for out and inout remote method arguments that are declared in IDL
with type ULongLongSeq, which is mapped in Java to an array of longs.

```
Object ── ULongLongSeqHolder ┈ Streamable
```

```
public final class ULongLongSeqHolder implements org.omg.CORBA.portable.Streamable {
// Public Constructors
    public ULongLongSeqHolder();
    public ULongLongSeqHolder(long[ ] initialValue);
// Methods Implementing Streamable
    public void _read(org.omg.CORBA.portable.InputStream i);
    public TypeCode _type();
    public void _write(org.omg.CORBA.portable.OutputStream o);
// Public Instance Fields
    public long[ ] value;
}
```

Passed To: org.omg.CORBA.DataInputStream.read_ulonglong_array()

ULongSeqHelper

org.omg.CORBA

The helper class for arrays of longs (mapped from the IDL unsigned long data type), used to read and write these arrays when they are used as remote method arguments or return values.

```
public abstract class ULongSeqHelper {
// Public Constructors
    public ULongSeqHelper();
// Public Class Methods
    public static int[ ] extract(Any a);
    public static String id();
    public static void insert(Any a, int[ ] that);
    public static int[ ] read(org.omg.CORBA.portable.InputStream istream);
    public static TypeCode type();                                        synchronized
    public static void write(org.omg.CORBA.portable.OutputStream ostream, int[ ] value);
}
```

ULongSeqHolder

org.omg.CORBA

The holder class for out and inout remote method arguments that are declared in IDL with type ULongSeq, which is mapped in Java to an array of longs.

```
Object ─ ULongSeqHolder ┈ Streamable
```

```
public final class ULongSeqHolder implements org.omg.CORBA.portable.Streamable {
// Public Constructors
    public ULongSeqHolder();
    public ULongSeqHolder(int[ ] initialValue);
// Methods Implementing Streamable
    public void _read(org.omg.CORBA.portable.InputStream i);
    public TypeCode _type();
    public void _write(org.omg.CORBA.portable.OutputStream o);
// Public Instance Fields
    public int[ ] value;
}
```

Passed To: org.omg.CORBA.DataInputStream.read_ulong_array()

UnionMember

org.omg.CORBA
serializable

A class that represents a member of an IDL union type. UnionMembers are used to create TypeCodes for IDL union types with the ORB.create_union_tc() method.

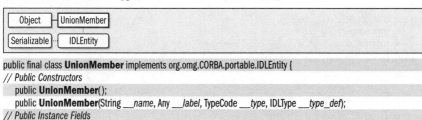

```
Object ─ UnionMember
Serializable ┈ IDLEntity
```

```
public final class UnionMember implements org.omg.CORBA.portable.IDLEntity {
// Public Constructors
    public UnionMember();
    public UnionMember(String __name, Any __label, TypeCode __type, IDLType __type_def);
// Public Instance Fields
    public Any label;
```

```
    public String name;
    public TypeCode type;
    public IDLType type_def;
}
```

Passed To: org.omg.CORBA.ORB.create_union_tc(), UnionMemberHelper.{insert(), write()}

Returned By: UnionMemberHelper.{extract(), read()}

UnionMemberHelper   Java 1.3

org.omg.CORBA

The helper class for UnionMember objects, used to read and write these objects when they are used as remote method arguments or return values.

```
public abstract class UnionMemberHelper {
// Public Constructors
    public UnionMemberHelper();
// Public Class Methods
    public static UnionMember extract(Any a);
    public static String id();
    public static void insert(Any a, UnionMember that);
    public static UnionMember read(org.omg.CORBA.portable.InputStream istream);
    public static TypeCode type();                                          synchronized
    public static void write(org.omg.CORBA.portable.OutputStream ostream, UnionMember value);
}
```

UNKNOWN   Java 1.2

org.omg.CORBA   *serializable unchecked*

A standard CORBA exception thrown when the ORB encounters an error that it can't interpret. Sun's Java IDL defines the following minor error code values for this exception, stored in the minor data member inherited from SystemException:

Minor code	Meaning
1	During unmarshalling of the response to a method request, a user exception was returned by the server implementation that is not in the set of exceptions expected by the client.
3	The server implementation threw an unknown runtime exception.

```
Object ─ Throwable ─ Exception ─ RuntimeException ─ SystemException ─ UNKNOWN
         Serializable
```

```
public final class UNKNOWN extends org.omg.CORBA.SystemException {
// Public Constructors
    public UNKNOWN();
    public UNKNOWN(String s);
    public UNKNOWN(int minor, CompletionStatus completed);
    public UNKNOWN(String s, int minor, CompletionStatus completed);
}
```

UnknownUserException

org.omg.CORBA
serializable checked

This exception class is used to wrap any user exceptions that are thrown during DII remote method calls. If an exception is thrown by the server object during such a call, the client can call the env() method on its Request object to get the requests Environment. The exception contained within the Environment is an UnknownUserException. The actual user exception that the server threw is contained in the except data member of the UnknownUserException, which is an Any object.

```
public final class UnknownUserException extends UserException {
// Public Constructors
    public UnknownUserException();
    public UnknownUserException(Any a);
// Public Instance Fields
    public Any except;
}
```

Passed To: UnknownUserExceptionHelper.{insert(), write()},
UnknownUserExceptionHolder.UnknownUserExceptionHolder()

Returned By: UnknownUserExceptionHelper.{extract(), read()}

Type Of: UnknownUserExceptionHolder.value

UnknownUserExceptionHelper
Java 1.4

org.omg.CORBA

The helper class for UnknownUserException objects, used to read and write these objects when they are used as remote method arguments or return values.

```
public abstract class UnknownUserExceptionHelper {
// Public Constructors
    public UnknownUserExceptionHelper();
// Public Class Methods
    public static UnknownUserException extract(Any a);
    public static String id();
    public static void insert(Any a, UnknownUserException that);
    public static UnknownUserException read(org.omg.CORBA.portable.InputStream istream);
    public static TypeCode type();                                              synchronized
    public static void write(org.omg.CORBA.portable.OutputStream ostream, UnknownUserException value);
}
```

UnknownUserExceptionHolder
Java 1.4

org.omg.CORBA

The holder class for out and inout remote method arguments that are declared in IDL with type UnknownUserException.

```
public final class UnknownUserExceptionHolder implements org.omg.CORBA.portable.Streamable {
// Public Constructors
```

```
    public UnknownUserExceptionHolder();
    public UnknownUserExceptionHolder(UnknownUserException initialValue);
// Methods Implementing Streamable
    public void _read(org.omg.CORBA.portable.InputStream i);
    public TypeCode _type();
    public void _write(org.omg.CORBA.portable.OutputStream o);
// Public Instance Fields
    public UnknownUserException value;
}
```

UNSUPPORTED_POLICY   Java 1.2
org.omg.CORBA

One of the PolicyErrorCode values that a PolicyError exception carries when it is thrown.
Indicates that a Policy was recognized by the ORB, but is not supported.

```
public interface UNSUPPORTED_POLICY {
// Public Constants
    public static final short value;                                     =1
}
```

UNSUPPORTED_POLICY_VALUE   Java 1.2
org.omg.CORBA

One of the PolicyErrorCode values that a PolicyError exception carries when it is thrown.
Indicates that a Policy was recognized by the ORB, and the Policy value is value for the
given type, but the Policy value requested is not supported.

```
public interface UNSUPPORTED_POLICY_VALUE {
// Public Constants
    public static final short value;                                     =4
}
```

UserException   Java 1.2
org.omg.CORBA   *serializable checked*

This is the base class for all user exceptions that are defined in IDL and mapped to
Java. It extends java.lang.Exception directly, so it represents a Java user exception that
must be declared in method signatures and caught in application code that calls these
methods. Unlike the SystemException, the UserException class doesn't declare any data
members for describing the exception to the caller. Subclasses must do this to suit the
type of exception that they represent. It does, however, inherit the message property
from Throwable, which can be used to store a descriptive message on the exception to
describe the reason.

```
public abstract class UserException extends Exception implements org.omg.CORBA.portable.IDLEntity {
// Protected Constructors
    protected UserException();
```

```
        protected UserException(String reason);
}
```

Subclasses: Too many classes to list.

UShortSeqHelper   Java 1.3

org.omg.CORBA

The helper class for arrays of shorts (mapped from the IDL unsigned short data type), used to read and write these arrays when they are used as remote method arguments or return values.

```
public abstract class UShortSeqHelper {
// Public Constructors
    public UShortSeqHelper();
// Public Class Methods
    public static short[ ] extract(Any a);
    public static String id();
    public static void insert(Any a, short[ ] that);
    public static short[ ] read(org.omg.CORBA.portable.InputStream istream);
    public static TypeCode type();                                          synchronized
    public static void write(org.omg.CORBA.portable.OutputStream ostream, short[ ] value);
}
```

UShortSeqHolder   Java 1.3

org.omg.CORBA

The holder class for out and inout remote method arguments that are declared in IDL with type UShortSeq, which is mapped in Java to an array of longs.

```
Object ├─ UShortSeqHolder ┈ Streamable
```

```
public final class UShortSeqHolder implements org.omg.CORBA.portable.Streamable {
// Public Constructors
    public UShortSeqHolder();
    public UShortSeqHolder(short[ ] initialValue);
// Methods Implementing Streamable
    public void _read(org.omg.CORBA.portable.InputStream i);
    public TypeCode _type();
    public void _write(org.omg.CORBA.portable.OutputStream o);
// Public Instance Fields
    public short[ ] value;
}
```

Passed To: org.omg.CORBA.DataInputStream.read_ushort_array()

ValueBaseHelper   Java 1.3

org.omg.CORBA

The helper class for ValueBase objects, which in the IDL-to-Java mapping are mapped to Serializable objects. This helper is used to read and write these values when they are used as remote method arguments or return values.

```
public abstract class ValueBaseHelper {
// Public Constructors
    public ValueBaseHelper();
```

```
// Public Class Methods
    public static Serializable extract(Any a);
    public static String id();
    public static void insert(Any a, Serializable that);
    public static Serializable read(org.omg.CORBA.portable.InputStream istream);
    public static TypeCode type();                                                    synchronized
    public static void write(org.omg.CORBA.portable.OutputStream ostream, Serializable value);
}
```

ValueBaseHolder   Java 1.3

org.omg.CORBA

The holder class for out and inout remote method arguments that are declared in IDL
with type ValueBase, which is mapped in Java to Serializable.

```
Object ─ ValueBaseHolder ┄ Streamable
```

```
public final class ValueBaseHolder implements org.omg.CORBA.portable.Streamable {
// Public Constructors
    public ValueBaseHolder();
    public ValueBaseHolder(Serializable initial);
// Methods Implementing Streamable
    public void _read(org.omg.CORBA.portable.InputStream input);
    public TypeCode _type();
    public void _write(org.omg.CORBA.portable.OutputStream output);
// Public Instance Fields
    public Serializable value;
}
```

ValueMember   Java 1.2

org.omg.CORBA   *serializable*

A class that represents a member of an object passed by value using the Objects-by-
Value extension to CORBA. ValueMembers are used to create TypeCodes for values with the
ORB.create_value_tc() method.

```
Object ─ ValueMember
Serializable ┄ IDLEntity
```

```
public final class ValueMember implements org.omg.CORBA.portable.IDLEntity {
// Public Constructors
    public ValueMember();
    public ValueMember(String __name, String __id, String __defined_in, String __version, TypeCode __type,
                       IDLType __type_def, short __access);
// Public Instance Fields
    public short access;
    public String defined_in;
    public String id;
    public String name;
    public TypeCode type;
    public IDLType type_def;
    public String version;
}
```

Passed To: org.omg.CORBA.ORB.create_value_tc(), ValueMemberHelper.{insert(), write()}

Returned By: ValueMemberHelper.{extract(), read()}

ValueMemberHelper

Java 1.3

org.omg.CORBA

The helper class for ValueMember objects, used to read and write these objects when they are used as remote method arguments or return values.

```
public abstract class ValueMemberHelper {
// Public Constructors
   public ValueMemberHelper();
// Public Class Methods
   public static ValueMember extract(Any a);
   public static String id();
   public static void insert(Any a, ValueMember that);
   public static ValueMember read(org.omg.CORBA.portable.InputStream istream);
   public static TypeCode type();                                                    synchronized
   public static void write(org.omg.CORBA.portable.OutputStream ostream, ValueMember value);
}
```

VersionSpecHelper

Java 1.3

org.omg.CORBA

The helper class for VersionSpec, which is an IDL typedef for String. This helper is used to read and write these values when they are used as remote method arguments or return values.

```
public abstract class VersionSpecHelper {
// Public Constructors
   public VersionSpecHelper();
// Public Class Methods
   public static String extract(Any a);
   public static String id();
   public static void insert(Any a, String that);
   public static String read(org.omg.CORBA.portable.InputStream istream);
   public static TypeCode type();                                                    synchronized
   public static void write(org.omg.CORBA.portable.OutputStream ostream, String value);
}
```

VisibilityHelper

Java 1.3

org.omg.CORBA

The helper class for Visibility, which is an IDL typedef for short. This helper reads and writes these values when they are used as remote method arguments or return values.

```
public abstract class VisibilityHelper {
// Public Constructors
   public VisibilityHelper();
// Public Class Methods
   public static short extract(Any a);
   public static String id();
   public static void insert(Any a, short that);
   public static short read(org.omg.CORBA.portable.InputStream istream);
```

```
    public static TypeCode type();                                                    synchronized
    public static void write(org.omg.CORBA.portable.OutputStream ostream, short value);
}
```

VM_ABSTRACT
Java 1.2

org.omg.CORBA

A wrapper for a value for a TypeCode's value modifier, obtained using its type_modifier() method. VM_ABSTRACT.value indicates that the value type is an abstract type, and cannot be instantiated directly.

```
public interface VM_ABSTRACT {
// Public Constants
    public static final short value;                                                          =2
}
```

VM_CUSTOM
Java 1.2

org.omg.CORBA

A wrapper for a value for a TypeCode's value modifier, obtained using its type_modifier() method. VM_CUSTOM.value indicates that the value type is a custom type.

```
public interface VM_CUSTOM {
// Public Constants
    public static final short value;                                                          =1
}
```

VM_NONE
Java 1.2

org.omg.CORBA

A wrapper for a value for a TypeCode's value modifier, obtained using its type_modifier() method. VM_NONE.value indicates that the value type has no modifiers.

```
public interface VM_NONE {
// Public Constants
    public static final short value;                                                          =0
}
```

VM_TRUNCATABLE
Java 1.2

org.omg.CORBA

A wrapper for a value for a TypeCode's value modifier, obtained using its type_modifier() method. VM_TRUNCATABLE.value indicates that the value type is truncatable.

```
public interface VM_TRUNCATABLE {
// Public Constants
    public static final short value;                                                          =3
}
```

WCharSeqHelper
Java 1.3

org.omg.CORBA

The helper class for arrays of characters (mapped from the IDL wchar data type), used to read and write these arrays when they are used as remote method arguments or return values.

```
public abstract class WCharSeqHelper {
// Public Constructors
    public WCharSeqHelper();
// Public Class Methods
    public static char[ ] extract(Any a);
    public static String id();
    public static void insert(Any a, char[ ] that);
    public static char[ ] read(org.omg.CORBA.portable.InputStream istream);
    public static TypeCode type();                                                    synchronized
    public static void write(org.omg.CORBA.portable.OutputStream ostream, char[ ] value);
}
```

WCharSeqHolder   Java 1.3

org.omg.CORBA

The holder class for out and inout remote method arguments that are declared in IDL
with type WCharSeq, which is mapped in Java to an array of characters.

```
Object ── WCharSeqHolder ┈ Streamable
```

```
public final class WCharSeqHolder implements org.omg.CORBA.portable.Streamable {
// Public Constructors
    public WCharSeqHolder();
    public WCharSeqHolder(char[ ] initialValue);
// Methods Implementing Streamable
    public void _read(org.omg.CORBA.portable.InputStream i);
    public TypeCode _type();
    public void _write(org.omg.CORBA.portable.OutputStream o);
// Public Instance Fields
    public char[ ] value;
}
```

Passed To: org.omg.CORBA.DataInputStream.read_wchar_array()

WrongTransaction   Java 1.2

org.omg.CORBA   *serializable checked*

A user exception thrown when an attempt is made to get the response to a deferred
method request from a different transaction than the original request. If a client makes
an asynchronous DII method request using the Request.send_deferred() method, and this
request is made within a given transaction, and the client later makes a call to the
Request object's get_response() method from within a different transaction, then a Wrong-
Transaction exception is thrown. This exception can also be thrown if the
ORB.get_next_response() method is called from a different transaction than the original
method request.

```
Object ─ Throwable ─ Exception ─ UserException ─ WrongTransaction
         Serializable  Serializable   IDLEntity
```

```
public final class WrongTransaction extends UserException {
// Public Constructors
    public WrongTransaction();
    public WrongTransaction(String reason);
}
```

Passed To: WrongTransactionHelper.{insert(), write()},
WrongTransactionHolder.WrongTransactionHolder()

Returned By: WrongTransactionHelper.{extract(), read()}

Thrown By: org.omg.CORBA.ORB.get_next_response(), Request.get_response()

Type Of: WrongTransactionHolder.value

WrongTransactionHelper   Java 1.4

org.omg.CORBA

The helper class for WrongTransaction objects, used to read and write these objects when
they are used as remote method arguments or return values.

```
public abstract class WrongTransactionHelper {
// Public Constructors
    public WrongTransactionHelper();
// Public Class Methods
    public static WrongTransaction extract(Any a);
    public static String id();
    public static void insert(Any a, WrongTransaction that);
    public static WrongTransaction read(org.omg.CORBA.portable.InputStream istream);
    public static TypeCode type();                                            synchronized
    public static void write(org.omg.CORBA.portable.OutputStream ostream, WrongTransaction value);
}
```

WrongTransactionHolder   Java 1.4

org.omg.CORBA

The holder class for out and inout remote method arguments that are declared in IDL
with type WrongTransaction.

```
Object ─ WrongTransactionHolder ┈ Streamable
```

```
public final class WrongTransactionHolder implements org.omg.CORBA.portable.Streamable {
// Public Constructors
    public WrongTransactionHolder();
    public WrongTransactionHolder(WrongTransaction initialValue);
// Methods Implementing Streamable
    public void _read(org.omg.CORBA.portable.InputStream i);
    public TypeCode _type();
    public void _write(org.omg.CORBA.portable.OutputStream o);
// Public Instance Fields
    public WrongTransaction value;
}
```

WStringSeqHelper   Java 1.4

org.omg.CORBA

The helper class for arrays of Strings (mapped from the IDL wstring data type), used to
read and write these arrays when they are used as remote method arguments or return
values.

```
public abstract class WStringSeqHelper {
// Public Constructors
    public WStringSeqHelper();
```

```
// Public Class Methods
    public static String[ ] extract(Any a);
    public static String id( );
    public static void insert(Any a, String[ ] that);
    public static String[ ] read(org.omg.CORBA.portable.InputStream istream);
    public static TypeCode type( );                                              synchronized
    public static void write(org.omg.CORBA.portable.OutputStream ostream, String[ ] value);
}
```

WStringSeqHolder
Java 1.4

org.omg.CORBA

The holder class for out and inout remote method arguments that are declared in IDL
with type WStringSeq, which is mapped in Java to an array of Strings.

```
Object ├ WStringSeqHolder ┈ Streamable
```

```
public final class WStringSeqHolder implements org.omg.CORBA.portable.Streamable {
// Public Constructors
    public WStringSeqHolder( );
    public WStringSeqHolder(String[ ] initialValue);
// Methods Implementing Streamable
    public void _read(org.omg.CORBA.portable.InputStream i);
    public TypeCode _type( );
    public void _write(org.omg.CORBA.portable.OutputStream o);
// Public Instance Fields
    public String[ ] value;
}
```

WStringValueHelper
Java 1.3

org.omg.CORBA

The helper class for WStringValue, which is an IDL typedef for Strings. This helper is used
to read and write these values when they are used as remote method arguments or
return values.

```
Object ├ WStringValueHelper ┈ BoxedValueHelper
```

```
public class WStringValueHelper implements org.omg.CORBA.portable.BoxedValueHelper {
// Public Constructors
    public WStringValueHelper( );
// Public Class Methods
    public static String extract(Any a);
    public static String id( );
    public static void insert(Any a, String that);
    public static String read(org.omg.CORBA.portable.InputStream istream);
    public static TypeCode type( );                                              synchronized
    public static void write(org.omg.CORBA.portable.OutputStream ostream, String value);
// Methods Implementing BoxedValueHelper
    public String get_id( );
    public Serializable read_value(org.omg.CORBA.portable.InputStream istream);
    public void write_value(org.omg.CORBA.portable.OutputStream ostream, Serializable value);
}
```

Package org.omg.CORBA.DynAnyPackage

Java 1.2

This package contains the exceptions encountered in the dynamic Any classes (DynAny, DynStruct, etc.).

Exceptions:

```
public final class Invalid extends org.omg.CORBA.UserException;
public final class InvalidSeq extends org.omg.CORBA.UserException;
public final class InvalidValue extends org.omg.CORBA.UserException;
public final class TypeMismatch extends org.omg.CORBA.UserException;
```

Invalid

Java 1.2

org.omg.CORBA.DynAnyPackage

serializable checked

This exception is thrown whenever a bad DynAny or Any object is encountered in a dynamic any operation.

```
public final class Invalid extends UserException {
// Public Constructors
    public Invalid();
    public Invalid(String reason);
}
```

Thrown By: org.omg.CORBA.DynAny.{assign(), from_any(), to_any()}

InvalidSeq

Java 1.2

org.omg.CORBA.DynAnyPackage

serializable checked

This exception is thrown whenever an invalid Java array is encountered in a dynamic any operation.

```
public final class InvalidSeq extends UserException {
// Public Constructors
    public InvalidSeq();
    public InvalidSeq(String reason);
}
```

Thrown By: org.omg.CORBA.DynArray.set_elements(),
org.omg.CORBA.DynSequence.set_elements(), org.omg.CORBA.DynStruct.set_members(),
org.omg.CORBA.DynValue.set_members()

InvalidValue

Java 1.2

org.omg.CORBA.DynAnyPackage

serializable checked

An exception thrown when a bad value is inserted into a DynAny object.

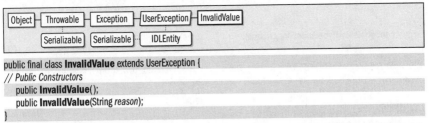

public final class **InvalidValue** extends UserException {
// Public Constructors
    public **InvalidValue**();
    public **InvalidValue**(String *reason*);
}

Thrown By: org.omg.CORBA.DynAny.{insert_any(), insert_boolean(), insert_char(), insert_double(), insert_float(), insert_long(), insert_longlong(), insert_octet(), insert_reference(), insert_short(), insert_string(), insert_typecode(), insert_ulong(), insert_ulonglong(), insert_ushort(), insert_val(), insert_wchar(), insert_wstring()}, org.omg.CORBA.DynFixed.set_value()

TypeMismatch
org.omg.CORBA.DynAnyPackage

Java 1.2

serializable checked

An exception thrown when you ask for a value from a DynAny object that doesn't match the type that it contains.

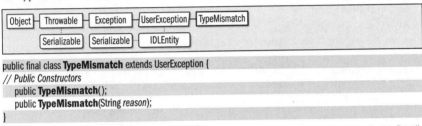

public final class **TypeMismatch** extends UserException {
// Public Constructors
    public **TypeMismatch**();
    public **TypeMismatch**(String *reason*);
}

Thrown By: org.omg.CORBA.DynAny.{get_any(), get_boolean(), get_char(), get_double(), get_float(), get_long(), get_longlong(), get_octet(), get_reference(), get_short(), get_string(), get_typecode(), get_ulong(), get_ulonglong(), get_ushort(), get_val(), get_wchar(), get_wstring()}

Package org.omg.CORBA.ORBPackage

Java 1.2

This package contains miscellaneous exceptions thrown by the ORB interface.

Exceptions:

public final class **InconsistentTypeCode** extends org.omg.CORBA.UserException;
public final class **InvalidName** extends org.omg.CORBA.UserException;

InconsistentTypeCode
org.omg.CORBA.ORBPackage

Java 1.2

serializable checked

An exception thrown by the ORB.create_dyn_XXX() methods when the TypeCode argument does not match the type of DynAny subclass requested.

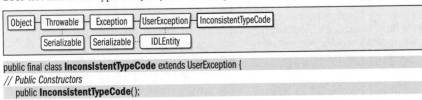

public final class **InconsistentTypeCode** extends UserException {
// Public Constructors
    public **InconsistentTypeCode**();

```
    public InconsistentTypeCode(String reason);
}
```

Thrown By: org.omg.CORBA.ORB.{create_basic_dyn_any(), create_dyn_array(), create_dyn_enum(), create_dyn_sequence(), create_dyn_struct(), create_dyn_union()}

InvalidName   Java 1.2

org.omg.CORBA.ORBPackage   *serializable checked*

An exception thrown by the ORB.resolve_initial_references() method when the name passed in does not have a corresponding object in the ORB's initial reference list.

```
public final class InvalidName extends UserException {
// Public Constructors
    public InvalidName();
    public InvalidName(String reason);
}
```

Thrown By: org.omg.CORBA.ORB.resolve_initial_references()

Package org.omg.CORBA.TypeCodePackage   Java 1.2

This package provides exceptions that are thrown by the TypeCode class.

Exceptions:

public final class **BadKind** extends org.omg.CORBA.UserException;
public final class **Bounds** extends org.omg.CORBA.UserException;

BadKind   Java 1.2

org.omg.CORBA.TypeCodePackage   *serializable checked*

This exception is thrown when a method is called on a TypeCode object that isn't valid for the type that it represents.

```
public final class BadKind extends UserException {
// Public Constructors
    public BadKind();
    public BadKind(String reason);
}
```

Thrown By: TypeCode.{concrete_base_type(), content_type(), default_index(), discriminator_type(), fixed_digits(), fixed_scale(), id(), length(), member_count(), member_label(), member_name(), member_type(), member_visibility(), name(), type_modifier()}

Bounds

org.omg.CORBA.TypeCodePackage

This exception is thrown when you request member information from a TypeCode using an index that is beyond the valid member index of the type.

```
public final class Bounds extends UserException {
// Public Constructors
    public Bounds();
    public Bounds(String reason);
}
```

Thrown By: TypeCode.{member_label(), member_name(), member_type(), member_visibility()}

Package org.omg.CORBA.portable

This package contains interfaces, classes and exceptions used by the portability layer of the CORBA API. The portability layer provides facilities that allow code to be shared between different ORB providers.

Interfaces:

public interface **BoxedValueHelper**;
public interface **CustomValue** extends ValueBase, org.omg.CORBA.CustomMarshal;
public interface **IDLEntity** extends Serializable;
public interface **InvokeHandler**;
public interface **ResponseHandler**;
public interface **Streamable**;
public interface **StreamableValue** extends Streamable, ValueBase;
public interface **ValueBase** extends IDLEntity;
public interface **ValueFactory**;

Classes:

public abstract class **Delegate**;
public abstract class **InputStream** extends java.io.InputStream;
public abstract class **ObjectImpl** implements org.omg.CORBA.Object;
public abstract class **OutputStream** extends java.io.OutputStream;
public class **ServantObject**;

Exceptions:

public class **ApplicationException** extends Exception;
public class **IndirectionException** extends org.omg.CORBA.SystemException;
public final class **RemarshalException** extends Exception;
public class **UnknownException** extends org.omg.CORBA.SystemException;

ApplicationException

org.omg.CORBA.portable

This exception is used by the Delegate and ObjectImpl layer of a stub to indicate that an exception was thrown during a remote method invocation. The ApplicationException provides an org.omg.CORBA.portable.InputStream that is used to read the marshalled exception object.

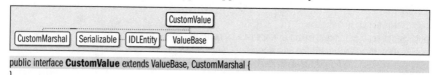

```
public class ApplicationException extends Exception {
// Public Constructors
    public ApplicationException(String id, org.omg.CORBA.portable.InputStream ins);
// Public Instance Methods
    public String getId();
    public org.omg.CORBA.portable.InputStream getInputStream();
}
```

Thrown By: LocalObject._invoke(), org.omg.CORBA.portable.Delegate.invoke(),
org.omg.CORBA.portable.ObjectImpl._invoke()

BoxedValueHelper   Java 1.3
org.omg.CORBA.portable

The helper class for the BoxedValue typedef, mapped in Java to String. This helper interface is used to read and write these objects when they are used as remote method arguments or return values.

```
public interface BoxedValueHelper {
// Public Instance Methods
    public abstract String get_id();
    public abstract Serializable read_value(org.omg.CORBA.portable.InputStream is);
    public abstract void write_value(org.omg.CORBA.portable.OutputStream os, Serializable value);
}
```

Implementations: StringValueHelper, WStringValueHelper

Passed To: org.omg.CORBA_2_3.portable.InputStream.read_value(),
org.omg.CORBA_2_3.portable.OutputStream.write_value()

CustomValue   Java 1.3
org.omg.CORBA.portable   *serializable*

The base class for all custom value types mapped from IDL to Java.

```
public interface CustomValue extends ValueBase, CustomMarshal {
}
```

Delegate   Java 1.2
org.omg.CORBA.portable

A Delegate is responsible for implementing all of the methods on org.omg.CORBA.Object. The Object contains a Delegate and forwards its methods to it. This allows for portability between ORB implementations, since an Object obtained from one ORB can contain a Delegate specific to that ORB, but the Object can still be used within another ORB.

```
public abstract class Delegate {
// Public Constructors
    public Delegate();
// Public Instance Methods
    public abstract Request create_request(org.omg.CORBA.Object obj, org.omg.CORBA.Context ctx, String operation,
                                            NVList arg_list, NamedValue result);
```

```
    public abstract Request create_request(org.omg.CORBA.Object obj, org.omg.CORBA.Context ctx, String operation,
                                    NVList arg_list, NamedValue result, ExceptionList exclist,
                                    ContextList ctxlist);
    public abstract org.omg.CORBA.Object duplicate(org.omg.CORBA.Object obj);
    public boolean equals(org.omg.CORBA.Object self, Object obj);
    public DomainManager[ ] get_domain_managers(org.omg.CORBA.Object self);
    public abstract org.omg.CORBA.Object get_interface_def(org.omg.CORBA.Object self);
    public org.omg.CORBA.Policy get_policy(org.omg.CORBA.Object self, int policy_type);
    public abstract int hash(org.omg.CORBA.Object obj, int max);
    public int hashCode(org.omg.CORBA.Object self);
    public org.omg.CORBA.portable.InputStream invoke(org.omg.CORBA.Object self,
                                    org.omg.CORBA.portable.OutputStream output)
        throws ApplicationException, RemarshalException;
    public abstract boolean is_a(org.omg.CORBA.Object obj, String repository_id);
    public abstract boolean is_equivalent(org.omg.CORBA.Object obj, org.omg.CORBA.Object other);
    public boolean is_local(org.omg.CORBA.Object self);                                          constant
    public abstract boolean non_existent(org.omg.CORBA.Object obj);
    public org.omg.CORBA.ORB orb(org.omg.CORBA.Object obj);
    public abstract void release(org.omg.CORBA.Object obj);
    public void releaseReply(org.omg.CORBA.Object self, org.omg.CORBA.portable.InputStream input);
    public abstract Request request(org.omg.CORBA.Object obj, String operation);
    public org.omg.CORBA.portable.OutputStream request(org.omg.CORBA.Object self, String operation,
                                    boolean responseExpected);
    public void servant_postinvoke(org.omg.CORBA.Object self, ServantObject servant);           empty
    public ServantObject servant_preinvoke(org.omg.CORBA.Object self, String operation,          constant
                                    Class expectedType);
    public org.omg.CORBA.Object set_policy_override(org.omg.CORBA.Object self, org.omg.CORBA.Policy[ ] policies,
                                    SetOverrideType set_add);
    public String toString(org.omg.CORBA.Object self);
}
```

Subclasses: org.omg.CORBA_2_3.portable.Delegate

Passed To: _IDLTypeStub._IDLTypeStub(), _PolicyStub._PolicyStub(),
org.omg.CORBA.portable.ObjectImpl._set_delegate()

Returned By: org.omg.CORBA.portable.ObjectImpl._get_delegate()

IDLEntity   Java 1.2
org.omg.CORBA.portable   *serializable*

This interface is used to mark certain IDL-generated classes. The RMI/IIOP extensions to CORBA look for this marker interface, since it indicates that a Java object being marshalled or unmarshalled has a helper class that can be used to serialize the object.

`Serializable ── IDLEntity`

```
public interface IDLEntity extends Serializable {
}
```

Implementations: Too many classes to list.

IndirectionException   Java 1.3
org.omg.CORBA.portable   *serializable unchecked*

The exception is thrown during an unmarshal operation, usually because a circular reference was encountered in the object being unmarshalled.

```
public class IndirectionException extends org.omg.CORBA.SystemException {
// Public Constructors
   public IndirectionException(int offset);
// Public Instance Fields
   public int offset;
}
```

InputStream   Java 1.2

org.omg.CORBA.portable

An InputStream is used for unmarshalling IDL-generated objects. The InputStream provides
a series of read_XXX() methods for unmarshalling basic IDL types.

```
public abstract class InputStream extends java.io.InputStream {
// Public Constructors
   public InputStream();
// Public Instance Methods
   public org.omg.CORBA.ORB orb();
   public abstract Any read_any();
   public abstract boolean read_boolean();
   public abstract void read_boolean_array(boolean[] value, int offset, int length);
   public abstract char read_char();
   public abstract void read_char_array(char[] value, int offset, int length);
   public org.omg.CORBA.Context read_Context();
   public abstract double read_double();
   public abstract void read_double_array(double[] value, int offset, int length);
   public java.math.BigDecimal read_fixed();
   public abstract float read_float();
   public abstract void read_float_array(float[] value, int offset, int length);
   public abstract int read_long();
   public abstract void read_long_array(int[] value, int offset, int length);
   public abstract long read_longlong();
   public abstract void read_longlong_array(long[] value, int offset, int length);
   public abstract org.omg.CORBA.Object read_Object();
   public org.omg.CORBA.Object read_Object(Class clz);
   public abstract byte read_octet();
   public abstract void read_octet_array(byte[] value, int offset, int length);
   public abstract short read_short();
   public abstract void read_short_array(short[] value, int offset, int length);
   public abstract String read_string();
   public abstract TypeCode read_TypeCode();
   public abstract int read_ulong();
   public abstract void read_ulong_array(int[] value, int offset, int length);
   public abstract long read_ulonglong();
   public abstract void read_ulonglong_array(long[] value, int offset, int length);
   public abstract short read_ushort();
   public abstract void read_ushort_array(short[] value, int offset, int length);
   public abstract char read_wchar();
   public abstract void read_wchar_array(char[] value, int offset, int length);
   public abstract String read_wstring();
// Public Methods Overriding InputStream
```

```
    public int read() throws IOException;
// Deprecated Public Methods
#   public org.omg.CORBA.Principal read_Principal();
}
```

Subclasses: org.omg.CORBA_2_3.portable.InputStream

Passed To: Too many methods to list.

Returned By: Any.create_input_stream(), LocalObject._invoke(),
ApplicationException.getInputStream(), org.omg.CORBA.portable.Delegate.invoke(),
org.omg.CORBA.portable.ObjectImpl._invoke(),
org.omg.CORBA.portable.OutputStream.create_input_stream()

InvokeHandler   Java 1.2
org.omg.CORBA.portable

This interface is used during dynamic method invocations. The InvokeHandler is responsible, through its _invoke() method, for finding a named method, reading marshalled arguments from the given org.omg.CORBA.portable.InputStream, and returning the response in the form of an org.omg.CORBA.portable.OutputStream generated from the given ResponseHandler.

```
public interface InvokeHandler {
// Public Instance Methods
    public abstract org.omg.CORBA.portable.OutputStream _invoke(String method,
                                    org.omg.CORBA.portable.InputStream input,
                                    ResponseHandler handler)
        throws org.omg.CORBA.SystemException;
}
```

Implementations: javax.rmi.CORBA.Tie, org.omg.CosNaming.BindingIteratorPOA,
org.omg.CosNaming.NamingContextExtPOA, org.omg.CosNaming.NamingContextPOA,
org.omg.PortableServer.ServantActivatorPOA, org.omg.PortableServer.ServantLocatorPOA

ObjectImpl   Java 1.2
org.omg.CORBA.portable

The ObjectImpl is the base class for all stub classes, and provides default implementations for the methods declared in the orb.omg.CORBA.Object interface. The ObjectImpl contains a Delegate object that acts as a proxy for the Object methods.

```
Object ─ ObjectImpl ─ Object
```

```
public abstract class ObjectImpl implements org.omg.CORBA.Object {
// Public Constructors
    public ObjectImpl();
// Public Instance Methods
    public org.omg.CORBA.portable.Delegate _get_delegate();
    public abstract String[] _ids();
    public org.omg.CORBA.portable.InputStream _invoke(org.omg.CORBA.portable.OutputStream output)
        throws ApplicationException, RemarshalException;
    public boolean _is_local();
    public org.omg.CORBA.ORB _orb();
    public void _releaseReply(org.omg.CORBA.portable.InputStream input);
    public org.omg.CORBA.portable.OutputStream _request(String operation, boolean responseExpected);
    public void _servant_postinvoke(ServantObject servant);
```

```
    public ServantObject _servant_preinvoke(String operation, Class expectedType);
    public void _set_delegate(org.omg.CORBA.portable.Delegate delegate);
// Methods Implementing Object
    public Request _create_request(org.omg.CORBA.Context ctx, String operation, NVList arg_list,
                                    NamedValue result);
    public Request _create_request(org.omg.CORBA.Context ctx, String operation, NVList arg_list,
                                    NamedValue result, ExceptionList exceptions, ContextList contexts);
    public org.omg.CORBA.Object _duplicate();
    public DomainManager[ ] _get_domain_managers();
    public org.omg.CORBA.Object _get_interface_def();
    public org.omg.CORBA.Policy _get_policy(int policy_type);
    public int _hash(int maximum);
    public boolean _is_a(String repository_id);
    public boolean _is_equivalent(org.omg.CORBA.Object that);
    public boolean _non_existent();
    public void _release();
    public Request _request(String operation);
    public org.omg.CORBA.Object _set_policy_override(org.omg.CORBA.Policy[ ] policies, SetOverrideType set_add);
// Public Methods Overriding Object
    public boolean equals(Object obj);
    public int hashCode();
    public String toString();
}
```

Subclasses: _IDLTypeStub, _PolicyStub, org.omg.CORBA.DynamicImplementation,
org.omg.CORBA_2_3.portable.ObjectImpl, org.omg.CosNaming._BindingIteratorStub,
org.omg.CosNaming._NamingContextExtStub, org.omg.CosNaming._NamingContextStub,
org.omg.DynamicAny._DynAnyFactoryStub, org.omg.DynamicAny._DynAnyStub,
org.omg.DynamicAny._DynArrayStub, org.omg.DynamicAny._DynEnumStub,
org.omg.DynamicAny._DynFixedStub, org.omg.DynamicAny._DynSequenceStub,
org.omg.DynamicAny._DynStructStub, org.omg.DynamicAny._DynUnionStub,
org.omg.DynamicAny._DynValueStub, org.omg.PortableServer._ServantActivatorStub,
org.omg.PortableServer._ServantLocatorStub

OutputStream   Java 1.2

org.omg.CORBA.portable

An OutputStream is used for marshalling IDL-generated objects. The OutputStream provides
a series of write_XXX() methods for marshalling basic IDL types.

```
| Object |—| OutputStream |—| OutputStream |
```

```
public abstract class OutputStream extends java.io.OutputStream {
// Public Constructors
    public OutputStream();
// Public Instance Methods
    public abstract org.omg.CORBA.portable.InputStream create_input_stream();
    public org.omg.CORBA.ORB orb();
    public abstract void write_any(Any value);
    public abstract void write_boolean(boolean value);
    public abstract void write_boolean_array(boolean[ ] value, int offset, int length);
    public abstract void write_char(char value);
    public abstract void write_char_array(char[ ] value, int offset, int length);
    public void write_Context(org.omg.CORBA.Context ctx, ContextList contexts);
    public abstract void write_double(double value);
```

```
    public abstract void write_double_array(double[ ] value, int offset, int length);
    public void write_fixed(java.math.BigDecimal value);
    public abstract void write_float(float value);
    public abstract void write_float_array(float[ ] value, int offset, int length);
    public abstract void write_long(int value);
    public abstract void write_long_array(int[ ] value, int offset, int length);
    public abstract void write_longlong(long value);
    public abstract void write_longlong_array(long[ ] value, int offset, int length);
    public abstract void write_Object(org.omg.CORBA.Object value);
    public abstract void write_octet(byte value);
    public abstract void write_octet_array(byte[ ] value, int offset, int length);
    public abstract void write_short(short value);
    public abstract void write_short_array(short[ ] value, int offset, int length);
    public abstract void write_string(String value);
    public abstract void write_TypeCode(TypeCode value);
    public abstract void write_ulong(int value);
    public abstract void write_ulong_array(int[ ] value, int offset, int length);
    public abstract void write_ulonglong(long value);
    public abstract void write_ulonglong_array(long[ ] value, int offset, int length);
    public abstract void write_ushort(short value);
    public abstract void write_ushort_array(short[ ] value, int offset, int length);
    public abstract void write_wchar(char value);
    public abstract void write_wchar_array(char[ ] value, int offset, int length);
    public abstract void write_wstring(String value);
// Public Methods Overriding OutputStream
    public void write(int b) throws IOException;
// Deprecated Public Methods
#   public void write_Principal(org.omg.CORBA.Principal value);
}
```

Subclasses: org.omg.CORBA_2_3.portable.OutputStream

Passed To: Too many methods to list.

Returned By: Any.create_output_stream(), LocalObject._request(),
org.omg.CORBA.ORB.create_output_stream(), org.omg.CORBA.portable.Delegate.request(),
InvokeHandler._invoke(), org.omg.CORBA.portable.ObjectImpl._request(),
ResponseHandler.{createExceptionReply(), createReply()},
org.omg.CosNaming.BindingIteratorPOA._invoke(),
org.omg.CosNaming.NamingContextExtPOA._invoke(),
org.omg.CosNaming.NamingContextPOA._invoke(),
org.omg.PortableServer.ServantActivatorPOA._invoke(),
org.omg.PortableServer.ServantLocatorPOA._invoke()

RemarshalException   Java 1.2

org.omg.CORBA.portable   *serializable checked*

This exception is thrown by the Delegate._invoke() the ObjectImpl.invoke() methods when a
marshalling error occurs during the method invocation.

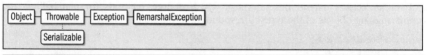

```
public final class RemarshalException extends Exception {
// Public Constructors
```

```
    public RemarshalException();
}
```

Thrown By: LocalObject._invoke(), org.omg.CORBA.portable.Delegate.invoke(),
org.omg.CORBA.portable.ObjectImpl._invoke()

ResponseHandler   Java 1.2

org.omg.CORBA.portable

A ResponseHandler is responsible for generating org.omg.CORBA.portable.OutputStreams that
are used by object servants to write marshalled method responses (return value or
exception).

```
public interface ResponseHandler {
// Public Instance Methods
    public abstract org.omg.CORBA.portable.OutputStream createExceptionReply();
    public abstract org.omg.CORBA.portable.OutputStream createReply();
}
```

Passed To: InvokeHandler._invoke(), org.omg.CosNaming.BindingIteratorPOA._invoke(),
org.omg.CosNaming.NamingContextExtPOA._invoke(),
org.omg.CosNaming.NamingContextPOA._invoke(),
org.omg.PortableServer.ServantActivatorPOA._invoke(),
org.omg.PortableServer.ServantLocatorPOA._invoke()

ServantObject   Java 1.2

org.omg.CORBA.portable

The ServantObject is a wrapper for an object that can handle method requests for a
remote object. The ObjectImpl class defers method requests to a ServantObject acquired
from its internal Delegate.

```
public class ServantObject {
// Public Constructors
    public ServantObject();
// Public Instance Fields
    public Object servant;
}
```

Passed To: LocalObject._servant_postinvoke(),
org.omg.CORBA.portable.Delegate.servant_postinvoke(),
org.omg.CORBA.portable.ObjectImpl._servant_postinvoke()

Returned By: LocalObject._servant_preinvoke(),
org.omg.CORBA.portable.Delegate.servant_preinvoke(),
org.omg.CORBA.portable.ObjectImpl._servant_preinvoke()

Streamable   Java 1.2

org.omg.CORBA.portable

All holder classes extend this interface, which defines methods for marshalling and
unmarshalling objects of the type corresponding to the holder class.

```
public interface Streamable {
// Public Instance Methods
    public abstract void _read(org.omg.CORBA.portable.InputStream istream);
```

```
    public abstract TypeCode _type();
    public abstract void _write(org.omg.CORBA.portable.OutputStream ostream);
}
```

Implementations: Too many classes to list.

Passed To: Any.insert_Streamable()

Returned By: Any.extract_Streamable()

StreamableValue   Java 1.3

org.omg.CORBA.portable   *serializable*

This is a base class for any value types declared in IDL that do not require custom marshalling.

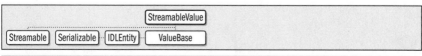

```
public interface StreamableValue extends org.omg.CORBA.portable.Streamable, ValueBase {
}
```

UnknownException   Java 1.3

org.omg.CORBA.portable   *serializable unchecked*

This exception is thrown if an unknown error occurs between a stub and the ORB, or between the ORB and a tie or skeleton. The stub will either convert this exception to an org.omg.CORBA.UNKNOWN exception, convert it to the nested exception of the UnknownException, or pass it on directly to the calling application.

```
Object ┤├ Throwable ├┤ Exception ├┤ RuntimeException ├┤ SystemException ├┤ UnknownException
        └ Serializable
```

```
public class UnknownException extends org.omg.CORBA.SystemException {
// Public Constructors
    public UnknownException(Throwable ex);
// Public Instance Fields
    public Throwable originalEx;
}
```

ValueBase   Java 1.3

org.omg.CORBA.portable   *serializable*

This is the base interface of all mapped IDL value types.

```
Serializable ┈ IDLEntity ┈ ValueBase
```

```
public interface ValueBase extends IDLEntity {
// Public Instance Methods
    public abstract String[] _truncatable_ids();
}
```

Implementations: org.omg.CORBA.DataInputStream, org.omg.CORBA.DataOutputStream, CustomValue, StreamableValue

ValueFactory

org.omg.CORBA.portable

A ValueFactory is used by the ORB to unmarshal value types from an input stream.

```
public interface ValueFactory {
// Public Instance Methods
    public abstract Serializable read_value(org.omg.CORBA_2_3.portable.InputStream is);
}
```

Passed To: org.omg.CORBA_2_3.ORB.register_value_factory()

Returned By: org.omg.CORBA_2_3.ORB.{lookup_value_factory(), register_value_factory()}

CHAPTER 42

org.omg.CORBA_2_3 and org.omg.CORBA_2_3.portable

Package org.omg.CORBA_2_3

This package contains additions to the J2SE CORBA interfaces to account for changes in version 2.3 of the OMG CORBA specification.

Classes:

public abstract class **ORB** extends org.omg.CORBA.ORB;

ORB

org.omg.CORBA_2_3

This is a specialization of the org.omg.CORBA.ORB class, which implements extensions required by the CORBA 2.3 specification, principally related to object-by-value operations.

```
Object ─ ORB ─ ORB
```

```
public abstract class ORB extends org.omg.CORBA.ORB {
// Public Constructors
    public ORB();
// Public Instance Methods
    public org.omg.CORBA.Object get_value_def(String repid) throws org.omg.CORBA.BAD_PARAM;
    public org.omg.CORBA.portable.ValueFactory lookup_value_factory(String id);
    public org.omg.CORBA.portable.ValueFactory register_value_factory(String id,
                                        org.omg.CORBA.portable.ValueFactory factory);
    public void set_delegate(Object wrapper);
    public void unregister_value_factory(String id);
}
```

Package org.omg.CORBA_2_3.portable

This package contains additions to the J2SE CORBA interfaces in the org.omg.CORBA.portable package to account for changes in version 2.3 of the OMG CORBA specification.

Classes:

```
public abstract class Delegate extends org.omg.CORBA.portable.Delegate;
public abstract class InputStream extends org.omg.CORBA.portable.InputStream;
public abstract class ObjectImpl extends org.omg.CORBA.portable.ObjectImpl;
public abstract class OutputStream extends org.omg.CORBA.portable.OutputStream;
```

Delegate

org.omg.CORBA_2_3.portable

Extends the org.omg.CORBA.portable.Delegate class, providing extensions required by the CORBA 2.3 specification.

```
Object ├─ Delegate ├─ Delegate
```

```
public abstract class Delegate extends org.omg.CORBA.portable.Delegate {
// Public Constructors
    public Delegate();
// Public Instance Methods
    public String get_codebase(org.omg.CORBA.Object self);                          constant
}
```

InputStream

org.omg.CORBA_2_3.portable

Extends the org.omg.CORBA.portable.InputStream class to support CORBA 2.3 (e.g., support for value types).

```
Object ├─ InputStream ├─ InputStream ├─ InputStream
```

```
public abstract class InputStream extends org.omg.CORBA.portable.InputStream {
// Public Constructors
    public InputStream();
// Public Instance Methods
    public Object read_abstract_interface();
    public Object read_abstract_interface(Class clz);
    public Serializable read_value();
    public Serializable read_value(Serializable value);
    public Serializable read_value(Class clz);
    public Serializable read_value(org.omg.CORBA.portable.BoxedValueHelper factory);
    public Serializable read_value(String rep_id);
}
```

Passed To: org.omg.CORBA.portable.ValueFactory.read_value()

ObjectImpl

org.omg.CORBA_2_3.portable

Extends org.omg.CORBA.portable.ObjectImpl in order to provide support for CORBA 2.3.

```
Object ┤ObjectImpl├ ObjectImpl
       └ Object
```

public abstract class **ObjectImpl** extends org.omg.CORBA.portable.ObjectImpl {
// *Public Constructors*
  public **ObjectImpl**();
// *Public Instance Methods*
  public String **_get_codebase**();
}

Subclasses: javax.rmi.CORBA.Stub

OutputStream

org.omg.CORBA_2_3.portable

Extends the org.omg.CORBA.portable.OutputStream class to support CORBA 2.3 (e.g., support for value types).

```
Object ┤OutputStream├ OutputStream ┤ OutputStream
```

public abstract class **OutputStream** extends org.omg.CORBA.portable.OutputStream {
// *Public Constructors*
  public **OutputStream**();
// *Public Instance Methods*
  public void **write_abstract_interface**(Object *obj*);
  public void **write_value**(Serializable *value*);
  public void **write_value**(Serializable *value*, org.omg.CORBA.portable.BoxedValueHelper *factory*);
  public void **write_value**(Serializable *value*, Class *clz*);
  public void **write_value**(Serializable *value*, String *repository_id*);
}

CHAPTER 43

org.omg.CosNaming and Subpackages

This package is a Java mapping of the IDL interfaces defined in the CORBA Naming Service. The principal interface in the service is the NamingContext, which represents a directory of named object references, and the various support classes allow you to iterate through the NamingContext and query its contents.

Interfaces:

public interface **BindingIterator** extends BindingIteratorOperations, org.omg.CORBA.Object,
                              org.omg.CORBA.portable.IDLEntity;
public interface **BindingIteratorOperations**;
public interface **NamingContext** extends NamingContextOperations, org.omg.CORBA.Object,
                              org.omg.CORBA.portable.IDLEntity;
public interface **NamingContextExt** extends NamingContextExtOperations, NamingContext,
                              org.omg.CORBA.portable.IDLEntity;
public interface **NamingContextExtOperations** extends NamingContextOperations;
public interface **NamingContextOperations**;

Classes:

public abstract class **_BindingIteratorImplBase** extends org.omg.CORBA.DynamicImplementation
                              implements BindingIterator;
public class **_BindingIteratorStub** extends org.omg.CORBA.portable.ObjectImpl
                              implements BindingIterator;
public class **_NamingContextExtStub** extends org.omg.CORBA.portable.ObjectImpl
                              implements NamingContextExt;
public abstract class **_NamingContextImplBase** extends org.omg.CORBA.DynamicImplementation
                              implements NamingContext;
public class **_NamingContextStub** extends org.omg.CORBA.portable.ObjectImpl
                              implements NamingContext;
public final class **Binding** implements org.omg.CORBA.portable.IDLEntity;
public abstract class **BindingHelper**;

public final class **BindingHolder** implements org.omg.CORBA.portable.Streamable;
public abstract class **BindingIteratorHelper**;
public final class **BindingIteratorHolder** implements org.omg.CORBA.portable.Streamable;
public abstract class **BindingIteratorPOA** extends org.omg.PortableServer.Servant
                          implements BindingIteratorOperations,
                          org.omg.CORBA.portable.InvokeHandler;
public abstract class **BindingListHelper**;
public final class **BindingListHolder** implements org.omg.CORBA.portable.Streamable;
public class **BindingType** implements org.omg.CORBA.portable.IDLEntity;
public abstract class **BindingTypeHelper**;
public final class **BindingTypeHolder** implements org.omg.CORBA.portable.Streamable;
public abstract class **IstringHelper**;
public final class **NameComponent** implements org.omg.CORBA.portable.IDLEntity;
public abstract class **NameComponentHelper**;
public final class **NameComponentHolder** implements org.omg.CORBA.portable.Streamable;
public abstract class **NameHelper**;
public final class **NameHolder** implements org.omg.CORBA.portable.Streamable;
public abstract class **NamingContextExtHelper**;
public final class **NamingContextExtHolder** implements org.omg.CORBA.portable.Streamable;
public abstract class **NamingContextExtPOA** extends org.omg.PortableServer.Servant
                          implements NamingContextExtOperations,
                          org.omg.CORBA.portable.InvokeHandler;
public abstract class **NamingContextHelper**;
public final class **NamingContextHolder** implements org.omg.CORBA.portable.Streamable;
public abstract class **NamingContextPOA** extends org.omg.PortableServer.Servant
                          implements NamingContextOperations,
                          org.omg.CORBA.portable.InvokeHandler;

_BindingIteratorImplBase

Java 1.2

org.omg.CosNaming

serializable

This is the IDL-generated skeleton class for the BindingIterator interface.

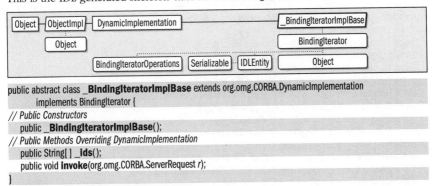

```
public abstract class _BindingIteratorImplBase extends org.omg.CORBA.DynamicImplementation
        implements BindingIterator {
// Public Constructors
    public _BindingIteratorImplBase();
// Public Methods Overriding DynamicImplementation
    public String[] _ids();
    public void invoke(org.omg.CORBA.ServerRequest r);
}
```

_BindingIteratorStub

Java 1.2

org.omg.CosNaming

serializable

This is the IDL-generated stub class for the BindingIterator interface.

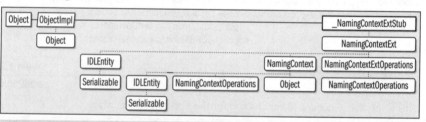

```
public class _BindingIteratorStub extends org.omg.CORBA.portable.ObjectImpl implements BindingIterator {
// Public Constructors
1.4 public _BindingIteratorStub();
// Public Instance Methods
     public void destroy();                                              Implements:BindingIteratorOperations
     public boolean next_n(int how_many, BindingListHolder bl);         Implements:BindingIteratorOperations
     public boolean next_one(BindingHolder b);                          Implements:BindingIteratorOperations
// Methods Implementing BindingIteratorOperations
     public void destroy();
     public boolean next_n(int how_many, BindingListHolder bl);
     public boolean next_one(BindingHolder b);
// Public Methods Overriding ObjectImpl
     public String[ ] _ids();
}
```

_NamingContextExtStub   Java 1.4

org.omg.CosNaming   *serializable*

The generated stub class for NamingContextExt, a NamingContext that supports the Interoperable Naming Service.

```
public class _NamingContextExtStub extends org.omg.CORBA.portable.ObjectImpl implements NamingContextExt {
// Public Constructors
     public _NamingContextExtStub();
// Methods Implementing NamingContextExtOperations
     public org.omg.CORBA.Object resolve_str(String sn) throws NotFound, CannotProceed,
          org.omg.CosNaming.NamingContextPackage.InvalidName;
     public NameComponent[ ] to_name(String sn) throws org.omg.CosNaming.NamingContextPackage.InvalidName;
     public String to_string(NameComponent[ ] n) throws org.omg.CosNaming.NamingContextPackage.InvalidName;
     public String to_url(String addr, String sn) throws org.omg.CosNaming.NamingContextExtPackage.InvalidAddress,
          org.omg.CosNaming.NamingContextPackage.InvalidName;
// Methods Implementing NamingContextOperations
     public void bind(NameComponent[ ] n, org.omg.CORBA.Object obj) throws NotFound, CannotProceed,
          org.omg.CosNaming.NamingContextPackage.InvalidName, AlreadyBound;
     public void bind_context(NameComponent[ ] n, NamingContext nc) throws NotFound, CannotProceed,
          org.omg.CosNaming.NamingContextPackage.InvalidName, AlreadyBound;
     public NamingContext bind_new_context(NameComponent[ ] n) throws NotFound, AlreadyBound, CannotProceed,
          org.omg.CosNaming.NamingContextPackage.InvalidName;
     public void destroy() throws NotEmpty;
     public void list(int how_many, BindingListHolder bl, BindingIteratorHolder bi);
     public NamingContext new_context();
     public void rebind(NameComponent[ ] n, org.omg.CORBA.Object obj) throws NotFound, CannotProceed,
          org.omg.CosNaming.NamingContextPackage.InvalidName;
```

```
    public void rebind_context(NameComponent[ ] n, NamingContext nc) throws NotFound, CannotProceed,
        org.omg.CosNaming.NamingContextPackage.InvalidName;
    public org.omg.CORBA.Object resolve(NameComponent[ ] n) throws NotFound, CannotProceed,
        org.omg.CosNaming.NamingContextPackage.InvalidName;
    public void unbind(NameComponent[ ] n) throws NotFound, CannotProceed,
        org.omg.CosNaming.NamingContextPackage.InvalidName;
// Public Methods Overriding ObjectImpl
    public String[ ] _ids();
}
```

_NamingContextImplBase

Java 1.2

org.omg.CosNaming

serializable

This is the IDL-generated skeleton class for the NamingContext interface.

```
public abstract class _NamingContextImplBase extends org.omg.CORBA.DynamicImplementation
        implements NamingContext {
// Public Constructors
    public _NamingContextImplBase();
// Public Methods Overriding DynamicImplementation
    public String[ ] _ids();
    public void invoke(org.omg.CORBA.ServerRequest r);
}
```

_NamingContextStub

Java 1.2

org.omg.CosNaming

serializable

This is the IDL-generated stub class for the NamingContext interface.

```
public class _NamingContextStub extends org.omg.CORBA.portable.ObjectImpl implements NamingContext {
// Public Constructors
1.4 public _NamingContextStub();
// Public Instance Methods
    public void bind(NameComponent[ ] n, org.omg.CORBA.Object obj)          Implements:NamingContextOperations
        throws NotFound, CannotProceed,
        org.omg.CosNaming.NamingContextPackage.InvalidName,
        AlreadyBound;
    public void bind_context(NameComponent[ ] n, NamingContext nc)          Implements:NamingContextOperations
        throws NotFound, CannotProceed,
        org.omg.CosNaming.NamingContextPackage.InvalidName,
        AlreadyBound;
    public NamingContext bind_new_context(NameComponent[ ] n)               Implements:NamingContextOperations
        throws NotFound, AlreadyBound, CannotProceed,
        org.omg.CosNaming.NamingContextPackage.InvalidName;
```

```
    public void destroy() throws NotEmpty;                                  Implements:NamingContextOperations
    public void list(int how_many, BindingListHolder bl,                    Implements:NamingContextOperations
            BindingIteratorHolder bi);
    public NamingContext new_context();                                     Implements:NamingContextOperations
    public void rebind(NameComponent[ ] n, org.omg.CORBA.Object obj)        Implements:NamingContextOperations
        throws NotFound, CannotProceed,
        org.omg.CosNaming.NamingContextPackage.InvalidName;
    public void rebind_context(NameComponent[ ] n, NamingContext nc)        Implements:NamingContextOperations
        throws NotFound, CannotProceed,
        org.omg.CosNaming.NamingContextPackage.InvalidName;
    public org.omg.CORBA.Object resolve(NameComponent[ ] n)                 Implements:NamingContextOperations
        throws NotFound, CannotProceed,
        org.omg.CosNaming.NamingContextPackage.InvalidName;
    public void unbind(NameComponent[ ] n) throws NotFound, CannotProceed   Implements:NamingContextOperations
        , org.omg.CosNaming.NamingContextPackage.InvalidName;
// Methods Implementing NamingContextOperations
    public void bind(NameComponent[ ] n, org.omg.CORBA.Object obj) throws NotFound, CannotProceed,
        org.omg.CosNaming.NamingContextPackage.InvalidName, AlreadyBound;
    public void bind_context(NameComponent[ ] n, NamingContext nc) throws NotFound, CannotProceed,
        org.omg.CosNaming.NamingContextPackage.InvalidName, AlreadyBound;
    public NamingContext bind_new_context(NameComponent[ ] n) throws NotFound, AlreadyBound, CannotProceed,
        org.omg.CosNaming.NamingContextPackage.InvalidName;
    public void destroy() throws NotEmpty;
    public void list(int how_many, BindingListHolder bl, BindingIteratorHolder bi);
    public NamingContext new_context();
    public void rebind(NameComponent[ ] n, org.omg.CORBA.Object obj) throws NotFound, CannotProceed,
        org.omg.CosNaming.NamingContextPackage.InvalidName;
    public void rebind_context(NameComponent[ ] n, NamingContext nc) throws NotFound, CannotProceed,
        org.omg.CosNaming.NamingContextPackage.InvalidName;
    public org.omg.CORBA.Object resolve(NameComponent[ ] n) throws NotFound, CannotProceed,
        org.omg.CosNaming.NamingContextPackage.InvalidName;
    public void unbind(NameComponent[ ] n) throws NotFound, CannotProceed,
        org.omg.CosNaming.NamingContextPackage.InvalidName;
// Public Methods Overriding ObjectImpl
    public String[ ] _ids();
}
```

Binding   Java 1.2

org.omg.CosNaming   _serializable_

A Binding describes a name binding within a naming context. It contains a NameCompo-nent array, which represents the name associated with the binding, and a BindingType, which indicates whether the bound object is a "regular" object or a NamingContext.

```
┌─────────────────────────────┐
│  ┌────────┐  ┌─────────┐     │
│  │ Object │──┤ Binding │     │
│  └────────┘  └─────────┘     │
│  ┌────────────┐┌──────────┐  │
│  │ Serializable├┤ IDLEntity│  │
│  └────────────┘└──────────┘  │
└─────────────────────────────┘
```

```
public final class Binding implements org.omg.CORBA.portable.IDLEntity {
// Public Constructors
    public Binding();
    public Binding(NameComponent[ ] _binding_name, BindingType _binding_type);
```

```
// Public Instance Fields
    public NameComponent[ ] binding_name;
    public BindingType binding_type;
}
```

Passed To: BindingHelper.{insert(), write()}, BindingHolder.BindingHolder(),
BindingListHelper.{insert(), write()}, BindingListHolder.BindingListHolder()

Returned By: BindingHelper.{extract(), read()}, BindingListHelper.{extract(), read()}

Type Of: BindingHolder.value, BindingListHolder.value

BindingHelper Java 1.2

org.omg.CosNaming

The helper class for Binding objects, used to read and write these objects when they are
used as remote method arguments or return values.

```
public abstract class BindingHelper {
// Public Constructors
1.4 public BindingHelper();
// Public Class Methods
    public static org.omg.CosNaming.Binding extract(org.omg.CORBA.Any a);
    public static String id();
    public static void insert(org.omg.CORBA.Any a, org.omg.CosNaming.Binding that);
    public static org.omg.CosNaming.Binding read(org.omg.CORBA.portable.InputStream istream);
    public static org.omg.CORBA.TypeCode type();                                    synchronized
    public static void write(org.omg.CORBA.portable.OutputStream ostream, org.omg.CosNaming.Binding value);
}
```

BindingHolder Java 1.2

org.omg.CosNaming

The holder class for out and inout IDL method arguments that would be mapped to Java
Binding objects. See the Java IDL chapter of this book for more information on the uses
of holder classes.

```
Object ├ BindingHolder ┈ Streamable
```

```
public final class BindingHolder implements org.omg.CORBA.portable.Streamable {
// Public Constructors
    public BindingHolder();
    public BindingHolder(org.omg.CosNaming.Binding initialValue);
// Methods Implementing Streamable
    public void _read(org.omg.CORBA.portable.InputStream i);
    public org.omg.CORBA.TypeCode _type();
    public void _write(org.omg.CORBA.portable.OutputStream o);
// Public Instance Fields
    public org.omg.CosNaming.Binding value;
}
```

Passed To: _BindingIteratorStub.next_one(), BindingIteratorOperations.next_one()

BindingIterator Java 1.2

org.omg.CosNaming serializable

If you request a set of name/object bindings from a NamingContext using its list() method,
then the BindingListHolder that you pass in will be filled in with any results, up to its

maximum capacity. If the NamingContext contains more bound objects than the binding array you provide can hold, then the BindingIteratorHolder argument is initialized to contain a BindingIterator that will allow you to iterate through the rest of the bindings in the context. You can iterate through the remainder of the bindings one at a time, using the next_one() method, or in sets, using the next_n() method.

```
BindingIteratorOperations   Serializable   IDLEntity   Object   BindingIterator
```

```
public interface BindingIterator extends BindingIteratorOperations, org.omg.CORBA.Object,
        org.omg.CORBA.portable.IDLEntity {
}
```

Implementations: _BindingIteratorImplBase, _BindingIteratorStub

Passed To: BindingIteratorHelper.{insert(), write()}, BindingIteratorHolder.BindingIteratorHolder()

Returned By: BindingIteratorHelper.{extract(), narrow(), read()}, BindingIteratorPOA._this()

Type Of: BindingIteratorHolder.value

BindingIteratorHelper   Java 1.2
org.omg.CosNaming

The helper class for BindingIterator objects, used to safely cast remote references to these objects, and to read and write these objects when they are used as remote method arguments or return values.

```
public abstract class BindingIteratorHelper {
// Public Constructors
1.4 public BindingIteratorHelper();
// Public Class Methods
    public static BindingIterator extract(org.omg.CORBA.Any a);
    public static String id();
    public static void insert(org.omg.CORBA.Any a, BindingIterator that);
    public static BindingIterator narrow(org.omg.CORBA.Object obj);
    public static BindingIterator read(org.omg.CORBA.portable.InputStream istream);
    public static org.omg.CORBA.TypeCode type();                                 synchronized
    public static void write(org.omg.CORBA.portable.OutputStream ostream, BindingIterator value);
}
```

BindingIteratorHolder   Java 1.2
org.omg.CosNaming

The holder class for out and inout IDL method arguments that would be mapped to Java BindingIterator objects. See the Java IDL chapter of this book for more information on the uses of holder classes.

```
Object   BindingIteratorHolder   Streamable
```

```
public final class BindingIteratorHolder implements org.omg.CORBA.portable.Streamable {
// Public Constructors
    public BindingIteratorHolder();
    public BindingIteratorHolder(BindingIterator initialValue);
// Methods Implementing Streamable
    public void _read(org.omg.CORBA.portable.InputStream i);
    public org.omg.CORBA.TypeCode _type();
```

```
    public void _write(org.omg.CORBA.portable.OutputStream o);
// Public Instance Fields
    public BindingIterator value;
}
```

Passed To: _NamingContextExtStub.list(), _NamingContextStub.list(), NamingContextOperations.list()

BindingIteratorOperations

org.omg.CosNaming

The generated operations interface for the BindingIterator interface.

```
public interface BindingIteratorOperations {
// Public Instance Methods
    public abstract void destroy();
    public abstract boolean next_n(int how_many, BindingListHolder bl);
    public abstract boolean next_one(BindingHolder b);
}
```

Implementations: BindingIterator, BindingIteratorPOA

BindingIteratorPOA

org.omg.CosNaming

The generated POA skeleton interface for the BindingIterator interface. Added as of JDK 1.4.

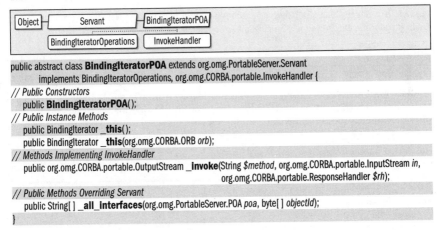

```
public abstract class BindingIteratorPOA extends org.omg.PortableServer.Servant
        implements BindingIteratorOperations, org.omg.CORBA.portable.InvokeHandler {
// Public Constructors
    public BindingIteratorPOA();
// Public Instance Methods
    public BindingIterator _this();
    public BindingIterator _this(org.omg.CORBA.ORB orb);
// Methods Implementing InvokeHandler
    public org.omg.CORBA.portable.OutputStream _invoke(String $method, org.omg.CORBA.portable.InputStream in,
                                org.omg.CORBA.portable.ResponseHandler $rh);

// Public Methods Overriding Servant
    public String[] _all_interfaces(org.omg.PortableServer.POA poa, byte[] objectId);
}
```

BindingListHelper

org.omg.CosNaming

The helper class for Binding arrays, used to read and write these arrays when they are used as remote method arguments or return values.

```
public abstract class BindingListHelper {
// Public Constructors
1.4 public BindingListHelper();
// Public Class Methods
    public static org.omg.CosNaming.Binding[] extract(org.omg.CORBA.Any a);
    public static String Id();
```

```
    public static void insert(org.omg.CORBA.Any a, org.omg.CosNaming.Binding[ ] that);
    public static org.omg.CosNaming.Binding[ ] read(org.omg.CORBA.portable.InputStream istream);
    public static org.omg.CORBA.TypeCode type();                                        synchronized
    public static void write(org.omg.CORBA.portable.OutputStream ostream, org.omg.CosNaming.Binding[ ] value);
}
```

BindingListHolder
Java 1.2

org.omg.CosNaming

The holder class for out and inout IDL method arguments that would be mapped to Java
BindingLists. See the Chapter 4 for more information on the uses of holder classes.

```
Object ├ BindingListHolder ┈ Streamable
```

```
public final class BindingListHolder implements org.omg.CORBA.portable.Streamable {
// Public Constructors
    public BindingListHolder();
    public BindingListHolder(org.omg.CosNaming.Binding[ ] initialValue);
// Methods Implementing Streamable
    public void _read(org.omg.CORBA.portable.InputStream i);
    public org.omg.CORBA.TypeCode _type();
    public void _write(org.omg.CORBA.portable.OutputStream o);
// Public Instance Fields
    public org.omg.CosNaming.Binding[ ] value;
}
```

Passed To: _BindingIteratorStub.next_n(), _NamingContextExtStub.list(), _NamingContextStub.list(),
BindingIteratorOperations.next_n(), NamingContextOperations.list()

BindingType
Java 1.2

org.omg.CosNaming
serializable

A BindingType indicates what type of object is involved in a given binding, a "regular"
object or a NamingContext. Its value() method returns an int value that can be compared to
the two static int values on the class, to differentiate between these two cases.

```
Object ├ BindingType
Serializable ┈ IDLEntity
```

```
public class BindingType implements org.omg.CORBA.portable.IDLEntity {
// Protected Constructors
1.4 protected BindingType(int value);
// Public Constants
    public static final int _ncontext;                                                 =1
    public static final int _nobject;                                                  =0
    public static final BindingType ncontext;
    public static final BindingType nobject;
// Public Class Methods
    public static BindingType from_int(int value);
// Public Instance Methods
    public int value();
}
```

Passed To: org.omg.CosNaming.Binding.Binding(), BindingTypeHelper.{insert(), write()},
BindingTypeHolder.BindingTypeHolder()

Returned By: BindingType.from_int(), BindingTypeHelper.{extract(), read()}

Type Of: org.omg.CosNaming.Binding.binding_type, BindingType.{ncontext, nobject}, BindingTypeHolder.value

BindingTypeHelper Java 1.2

org.omg.CosNaming

The helper class for BindingType objects, used to read and write these objects when they are used as remote method arguments or return values.

```
public abstract class BindingTypeHelper {
// Public Constructors
1.4 public BindingTypeHelper();
// Public Class Methods
    public static BindingType extract(org.omg.CORBA.Any a);
    public static String id();
    public static void insert(org.omg.CORBA.Any a, BindingType that);
    public static BindingType read(org.omg.CORBA.portable.InputStream istream);
    public static org.omg.CORBA.TypeCode type();                                    synchronized
    public static void write(org.omg.CORBA.portable.OutputStream ostream, BindingType value);
}
```

BindingTypeHolder Java 1.2

org.omg.CosNaming

The holder class for out and inout IDL method arguments that would be mapped to Java BindingType objects. See Chapter 4 for more information on the uses of holder classes.

```
Object ├ BindingTypeHolder ┈ Streamable

public final class BindingTypeHolder implements org.omg.CORBA.portable.Streamable {
// Public Constructors
    public BindingTypeHolder();
    public BindingTypeHolder(BindingType initialValue);
// Methods Implementing Streamable
    public void _read(org.omg.CORBA.portable.InputStream i);
    public org.omg.CORBA.TypeCode _type();
    public void _write(org.omg.CORBA.portable.OutputStream o);
// Public Instance Fields
    public BindingType value;
}
```

IstringHelper Java 1.2

org.omg.CosNaming

This is the helper class for the Istring class. The Istring class is used in the Naming Service as a placeholder for an internationalized string type. See the Java IDL chapter for more details on the uses of helper classes.

```
public abstract class IstringHelper {
// Public Constructors
1.4 public IstringHelper();
// Public Class Methods
    public static String extract(org.omg.CORBA.Any a);
    public static String id();
    public static void insert(org.omg.CORBA.Any a, String that);
```

```
    public static String read(org.omg.CORBA.portable.InputStream istream);
    public static org.omg.CORBA.TypeCode type();                                    synchronized
    public static void write(org.omg.CORBA.portable.OutputStream ostream, String value);
}
```

NameComponent   Java 1.2

org.omg.CosNaming   *serializable*

A NameComponent represents one element in a name binding for an object. The name of
an object in a NamingContext is composed of a sequence of NameComponents. Each Name-
Component represents a subcontext the object falls within, and the last NameComponent is
the object's name within its closest context. So an object bound to the name apple-146
within a context bound to the name fruit within a root context, would have two Name-
Components in its fully qualified name within the root context, {'fruit', 'apple-146'}.

A NameComponent contains an ID member, which represents the name associated with
the component, and a kind field, which can optionally be used to further differentiate
branches in a naming directory. The Naming Service does not consider the kind field
on NameComponents when determining the uniqueness of name bindings, so each
ordered list of ID fields extracted from a fully qualified name binding must be unique.

```
    Object ──── NameComponent

  Serializable ···   IDLEntity
```

```
public final class NameComponent implements org.omg.CORBA.portable.IDLEntity {
// Public Constructors
    public NameComponent();
    public NameComponent(String _id, String _kind);
// Public Instance Fields
    public String id;
    public String kind;
}
```

Passed To: Too many methods to list.

Returned By: _NamingContextExtStub.to_name(), NameComponentHelper.{extract(), read()},
NameHelper.{extract(), read()}, NamingContextExtOperations.to_name()

Type Of: org.omg.CosNaming.Binding.binding_name, NameComponentHolder.value,
NameHolder.value, CannotProceed.rest_of_name, NotFound.rest_of_name

NameComponentHelper   Java 1.2

org.omg.CosNaming

The helper class for NameComponent objects, used to read and write these objects when
they are used as remote method arguments or return values.

```
public abstract class NameComponentHelper {
// Public Constructors
1.4 public NameComponentHelper();                                                     ●
// Public Class Methods
    public static NameComponent extract(org.omg.CORBA.Any a);
    public static String id();
    public static void insert(org.omg.CORBA.Any a, NameComponent that);
    public static NameComponent read(org.omg.CORBA.portable.InputStream istream);
    public static org.omg.CORBA.TypeCode type();                                    synchronized
```

```
public static void write(org.omg.CORBA.portable.OutputStream ostream, NameComponent value);
}
```

NameComponentHolder   Java 1.2
org.omg.CosNaming

The holder class for out and inout remote method arguments that are declared in IDL with type NameComponent.

```
Object ├ NameComponentHolder ┈ Streamable
```

```
public final class NameComponentHolder implements org.omg.CORBA.portable.Streamable {
// Public Constructors
    public NameComponentHolder();
    public NameComponentHolder(NameComponent initialValue);
// Methods Implementing Streamable
    public void _read(org.omg.CORBA.portable.InputStream i);
    public org.omg.CORBA.TypeCode _type();
    public void _write(org.omg.CORBA.portable.OutputStream o);
// Public Instance Fields
    public NameComponent value;
}
```

NameHelper   Java 1.2
org.omg.CosNaming

This is the helper class generated for the Name typedef declared in the IDL module for the Naming Service specification. The IDL typedef associates the type Name to a sequence of NameComponents. See Chapter 4 for more details on the uses of helper classes.

```
public abstract class NameHelper {
// Public Constructors
1.4 public NameHelper();
// Public Class Methods
    public static NameComponent[] extract(org.omg.CORBA.Any a);
    public static String id();
    public static void insert(org.omg.CORBA.Any a, NameComponent[] that);
    public static NameComponent[] read(org.omg.CORBA.portable.InputStream istream);
    public static org.omg.CORBA.TypeCode type();                                    synchronized
    public static void write(org.omg.CORBA.portable.OutputStream ostream, NameComponent[] value);
}
```

NameHolder   Java 1.2
org.omg.CosNaming

The holder class for out and inout IDL method arguments that are typed as an IDL Name. An IDL typedef in the Naming Service specification associates the type Name to a sequence of NameComponents, so any in arguments using this type are mapped to NameComponent arrays in Java, and any out or inout arguments are mapped to NameHolders. See Chapter 4 for more information on the uses of holder classes.

```
Object ├ NameHolder ┈ Streamable
```

```
public final class NameHolder implements org.omg.CORBA.portable.Streamable {
// Public Constructors
    public NameHolder();
    public NameHolder(NameComponent[ ] initialValue);
// Methods Implementing Streamable
    public void _read(org.omg.CORBA.portable.InputStream i);
    public org.omg.CORBA.TypeCode _type();
    public void _write(org.omg.CORBA.portable.OutputStream o);
// Public Instance Fields
    public NameComponent[ ] value;
}
```

NamingContext   Java 1.2

org.omg.CosNaming   *serializable*

A NamingContext represents a naming directory structure, where objects are bound to unique branches, or names, in the naming directory. The full name that each object is given in the NamingContext must be unique. New branches in the naming directory are created by binding a NamingContext to a name within another, root NamingContext. The child context represents a sub-directory, or sub-context, within the parent context.

Objects are bound to names in a context by using the bind() and rebind() methods. The rebind() method allows you to reassign a name to another object, if it has already been bound. You can bind contexts using the bind_context(), bind_new_context() and rebind_context() methods. If you want to simply create a new context without binding it to a name, you can use the new_context() method. Bound objects in the context can be found using the resolve() method (for singular objects), and the list() method. The unbind() method lets you remove objects from their bindings in the context.

Objects can be bound to names in multiple NamingContexts at the same time. Their names within each context are independent. The same object can also be bound to multiple, different names in a single context.

```
public interface NamingContext extends NamingContextOperations, org.omg.CORBA.Object,
    org.omg.CORBA.portable.IDLEntity {
}
```

Implementations: _NamingContextImplBase, _NamingContextStub, NamingContextExt

Passed To: _NamingContextExtStub.{bind_context(), rebind_context()},
_NamingContextStub.{bind_context(), rebind_context()}, NamingContextHelper.{insert(), write()},
NamingContextHolder.NamingContextHolder(), NamingContextOperations.{bind_context(),
rebind_context()}, CannotProceed.CannotProceed()

Returned By: _NamingContextExtStub.{bind_new_context(), new_context()},
_NamingContextStub.{bind_new_context(), new_context()}, NamingContextHelper.{extract(), narrow(),
read()}, NamingContextOperations.{bind_new_context(), new_context()}, NamingContextPOA._this()

Type Of: NamingContextHolder.value, CannotProceed.cxt

NamingContextExt   Java 1.4

org.omg.CosNaming   *serializable*

A NamingContext that supports the Interoperable Naming Service, allowing objects to be bound and looked up using URL-based names.

```
public interface NamingContextExt extends NamingContextExtOperations, NamingContext,
      org.omg.CORBA.portable.IDLEntity {
}
```

Implementations: _NamingContextExtStub

Passed To: NamingContextExtHelper.{insert(), write()},
NamingContextExtHolder.NamingContextExtHolder()

Returned By: NamingContextExtHelper.{extract(), narrow(), read()}, NamingContextExtPOA._this()

Type Of: NamingContextExtHolder.value

NamingContextExtHelper   Java 1.4

org.omg.CosNaming

The helper class for NamingContextExt objects, used to safely cast remote references to
these objects, and to read and write these objects when they are used as remote
method arguments or return values. Added as of JDK 1.4.

```
public abstract class NamingContextExtHelper {
// Public Constructors
    public NamingContextExtHelper();
// Public Class Methods
    public static NamingContextExt extract(org.omg.CORBA.Any a);
    public static String id();
    public static void insert(org.omg.CORBA.Any a, NamingContextExt that);
    public static NamingContextExt narrow(org.omg.CORBA.Object obj);
    public static NamingContextExt read(org.omg.CORBA.portable.InputStream istream);
    public static org.omg.CORBA.TypeCode type();                              synchronized
    public static void write(org.omg.CORBA.portable.OutputStream ostream, NamingContextExt value);
}
```

NamingContextExtHolder   Java 1.4

org.omg.CosNaming

The holder class for out and inout IDL method arguments that would be mapped to NamingContextExt objects. Added as of JDK 1.4.

```
public final class NamingContextExtHolder implements org.omg.CORBA.portable.Streamable {
// Public Constructors
    public NamingContextExtHolder();
    public NamingContextExtHolder(NamingContextExt initialValue);
// Methods Implementing Streamable
    public void _read(org.omg.CORBA.portable.InputStream i);
    public org.omg.CORBA.TypeCode _type();
    public void _write(org.omg.CORBA.portable.OutputStream o);
// Public Instance Fields
    public NamingContextExt value;
}
```

NamingContextExtOperations   Java 1.4

org.omg.CosNaming

The generated operations interface for the NamingContextExt interface. Added as of JDK 1.4.

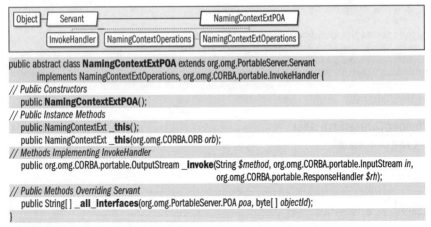

```
public interface NamingContextExtOperations extends NamingContextOperations {
// Public Instance Methods
    public abstract org.omg.CORBA.Object resolve_str(String sn) throws NotFound, CannotProceed,
        org.omg.CosNaming.NamingContextPackage.InvalidName;
    public abstract NameComponent[ ] to_name(String sn)
        throws org.omg.CosNaming.NamingContextPackage.InvalidName;
    public abstract String to_string(NameComponent[ ] n)
        throws org.omg.CosNaming.NamingContextPackage.InvalidName;
    public abstract String to_url(String addr, String sn)
        throws org.omg.CosNaming.NamingContextExtPackage.InvalidAddress,
        org.omg.CosNaming.NamingContextPackage.InvalidName;
}
```

Implementations: NamingContextExt, NamingContextExtPOA

NamingContextExtPOA   Java 1.4

org.omg.CosNaming

The generated POA-compatible skeleton for the NamingContextExt interface. Added as of JDK 1.4.

```
public abstract class NamingContextExtPOA extends org.omg.PortableServer.Servant
        implements NamingContextExtOperations, org.omg.CORBA.portable.InvokeHandler {
// Public Constructors
    public NamingContextExtPOA();
// Public Instance Methods
    public NamingContextExt _this();
    public NamingContextExt _this(org.omg.CORBA.ORB orb);
// Methods Implementing InvokeHandler
    public org.omg.CORBA.portable.OutputStream _invoke(String $method, org.omg.CORBA.portable.InputStream in,
                            org.omg.CORBA.portable.ResponseHandler $rh);
// Public Methods Overriding Servant
    public String[ ] _all_interfaces(org.omg.PortableServer.POA poa, byte[ ] objectId);
}
```

NamingContextHelper   Java 1.2

org.omg.CosNaming

The helper class for NamingContext objects, used to safely cast remote references to these objects, and to read and write these objects when they are used as remote method arguments or return values.

```
public abstract class NamingContextHelper {
// Public Constructors
1.4 public NamingContextHelper();
```

```
// Public Class Methods
    public static NamingContext extract(org.omg.CORBA.Any a);
    public static String id();
    public static void insert(org.omg.CORBA.Any a, NamingContext that);
    public static NamingContext narrow(org.omg.CORBA.Object obj);
    public static NamingContext read(org.omg.CORBA.portable.InputStream istream);
    public static org.omg.CORBA.TypeCode type();                              synchronized
    public static void write(org.omg.CORBA.portable.OutputStream ostream, NamingContext value);
}
```

NamingContextHolder   Java 1.2

org.omg.CosNaming

The holder class for out and inout IDL method arguments that would be mapped to Java NamingContext objects. See Chapter 4 for more information on the uses of holder classes.

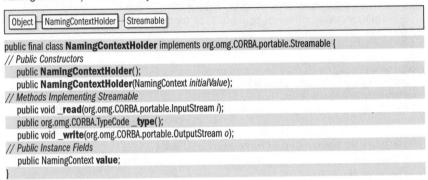

```
public final class NamingContextHolder implements org.omg.CORBA.portable.Streamable {
// Public Constructors
    public NamingContextHolder();
    public NamingContextHolder(NamingContext initialValue);
// Methods Implementing Streamable
    public void _read(org.omg.CORBA.portable.InputStream i);
    public org.omg.CORBA.TypeCode _type();
    public void _write(org.omg.CORBA.portable.OutputStream o);
// Public Instance Fields
    public NamingContext value;
}
```

NamingContextOperations   Java 1.3

org.omg.CosNaming

The generated operations interface for the NamingContext interface. Added as of JDK 1.4.

```
public interface NamingContextOperations {
// Public Instance Methods
    public abstract void bind(NameComponent[ ] n, org.omg.CORBA.Object obj) throws NotFound, CannotProceed,
        org.omg.CosNaming.NamingContextPackage.InvalidName, AlreadyBound;
    public abstract void bind_context(NameComponent[ ] n, NamingContext nc) throws NotFound, CannotProceed,
        org.omg.CosNaming.NamingContextPackage.InvalidName, AlreadyBound;
    public abstract NamingContext bind_new_context(NameComponent[ ] n) throws NotFound, AlreadyBound,
        CannotProceed, org.omg.CosNaming.NamingContextPackage.InvalidName;
    public abstract void destroy() throws NotEmpty;
    public abstract void list(int how_many, BindingListHolder bl, BindingIteratorHolder bi);
    public abstract NamingContext new_context();
    public abstract void rebind(NameComponent[ ] n, org.omg.CORBA.Object obj) throws NotFound, CannotProceed,
        org.omg.CosNaming.NamingContextPackage.InvalidName;
    public abstract void rebind_context(NameComponent[ ] n, NamingContext nc) throws NotFound, CannotProceed,
        org.omg.CosNaming.NamingContextPackage.InvalidName;
    public abstract org.omg.CORBA.Object resolve(NameComponent[ ] n) throws NotFound, CannotProceed,
        org.omg.CosNaming.NamingContextPackage.InvalidName;
```

```
    public abstract void unbind(NameComponent[ ] n) throws NotFound, CannotProceed,
        org.omg.CosNaming.NamingContextPackage.InvalidName;
}
```

Implementations: NamingContext, NamingContextExtOperations, NamingContextPOA

NamingContextPOA
Java 1.4

org.omg.CosNaming

The generated POA-compatible skeleton for the NamingContext interface. Added as of JDK 1.4.

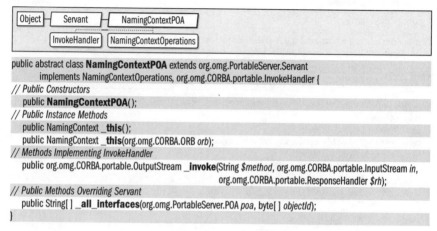

```
public abstract class NamingContextPOA extends org.omg.PortableServer.Servant
        implements NamingContextOperations, org.omg.CORBA.portable.InvokeHandler {
// Public Constructors
    public NamingContextPOA( );
// Public Instance Methods
    public NamingContext _this( );
    public NamingContext _this(org.omg.CORBA.ORB orb);
// Methods Implementing InvokeHandler
    public org.omg.CORBA.portable.OutputStream _invoke(String $method, org.omg.CORBA.portable.InputStream in,
                                            org.omg.CORBA.portable.ResponseHandler $rh);
// Public Methods Overriding Servant
    public String[ ] _all_interfaces(org.omg.PortableServer.POA poa, byte[ ] objectId);
}
```

Package org.omg.CosNaming.NamingContextExtPackage
Java 1.4

This package contains classes which are used by the org.omg.CosNaming.NamingContextExt class.

Classes:

public abstract class **AddressHelper**;
public abstract class **InvalidAddressHelper**;
public final class **InvalidAddressHolder** implements org.omg.CORBA.portable.Streamable;
public abstract class **StringNameHelper**;
public abstract class **URLStringHelper**;

Exceptions:

public final class **InvalidAddress** extends org.omg.CORBA.UserException;

AddressHelper
Java 1.4

org.omg.CosNaming.NamingContextExtPackage

Helper class for the IDL Address typedef, which is mapped in Java to a String.

```
public abstract class AddressHelper {
// Public Constructors
    public AddressHelper( );
// Public Class Methods
    public static String extract(org.omg.CORBA.Any a);
```

```
    public static String id();
    public static void insert(org.omg.CORBA.Any a, String that);
    public static String read(org.omg.CORBA.portable.InputStream istream);
    public static org.omg.CORBA.TypeCode type();                                    synchronized
    public static void write(org.omg.CORBA.portable.OutputStream ostream, String value);
}
```

InvalidAddress   Java 1.4

org.omg.CosNaming.NamingContextExtPackage   *serializable checked*

An exception thrown when an invalid object address is encountered by the naming service.

```
Object ├─ Throwable ├─ Exception ├─ UserException ├─ InvalidAddress
              Serializable    Serializable      IDLEntity
```

```
public final class InvalidAddress extends org.omg.CORBA.UserException {
// Public Constructors
    public InvalidAddress();
    public InvalidAddress(String $reason);
}
```

Passed To: InvalidAddressHelper.{insert(), write()}, InvalidAddressHolder.InvalidAddressHolder()

Returned By: InvalidAddressHelper.{extract(), read()}

Thrown By: _NamingContextExtStub.to_url(), NamingContextExtOperations.to_url()

Type Of: InvalidAddressHolder.value

InvalidAddressHelper   Java 1.4

org.omg.CosNaming.NamingContextExtPackage

The helper class for InvalidAddress objects, used to read and write these objects when they are used as remote method arguments or return values.

```
public abstract class InvalidAddressHelper {
// Public Constructors
    public InvalidAddressHelper();
// Public Class Methods
    public static InvalidAddress extract(org.omg.CORBA.Any a);
    public static String id();
    public static void insert(org.omg.CORBA.Any a, InvalidAddress that);
    public static InvalidAddress read(org.omg.CORBA.portable.InputStream istream);
    public static org.omg.CORBA.TypeCode type();                                    synchronized
    public static void write(org.omg.CORBA.portable.OutputStream ostream, InvalidAddress value);
}
```

InvalidAddressHolder   Java 1.4

org.omg.CosNaming.NamingContextExtPackage

The holder class for out and inout IDL method arguments that would be mapped to InvalidAddress objects.

```
Object ├─ InvalidAddressHolder ┈ Streamable
```

```
public final class InvalidAddressHolder implements org.omg.CORBA.portable.Streamable {
// Public Constructors
    public InvalidAddressHolder();
    public InvalidAddressHolder(InvalidAddress initialValue);
// Methods Implementing Streamable
    public void _read(org.omg.CORBA.portable.InputStream i);
    public org.omg.CORBA.TypeCode _type();
    public void _write(org.omg.CORBA.portable.OutputStream o);
// Public Instance Fields
    public InvalidAddress value;
}
```

StringNameHelper   Java 1.4

org.omg.CosNaming.NamingContextExtPackage

Helper class for the IDL StringName typedef, which is mapped in Java to a String.

```
public abstract class StringNameHelper {
// Public Constructors
    public StringNameHelper();
// Public Class Methods
    public static String extract(org.omg.CORBA.Any a);
    public static String id();
    public static void insert(org.omg.CORBA.Any a, String that);
    public static String read(org.omg.CORBA.portable.InputStream istream);
    public static org.omg.CORBA.TypeCode type();                    synchronized
    public static void write(org.omg.CORBA.portable.OutputStream ostream, String value);
}
```

URLStringHelper   Java 1.4

org.omg.CosNaming.NamingContextExtPackage

Helper class for the IDL URLString typedef, which is mapped in Java to a String.

```
public abstract class URLStringHelper {
// Public Constructors
    public URLStringHelper();
// Public Class Methods
    public static String extract(org.omg.CORBA.Any a);
    public static String id();
    public static void insert(org.omg.CORBA.Any a, String that);
    public static String read(org.omg.CORBA.portable.InputStream istream);
    public static org.omg.CORBA.TypeCode type();                    synchronized
    public static void write(org.omg.CORBA.portable.OutputStream ostream, String value);
}
```

Package org.omg.CosNaming.NamingContextPackage   Java 1.2

This package includes the exceptions thrown by various methods on the NamingContext interface in the org.omg.CORBA.CosNaming package. The package consists of these exceptions, along with their helper and holder interfaces.

Classes:

public abstract class **AlreadyBoundHelper**;
public final class **AlreadyBoundHolder** implements org.omg.CORBA.portable.Streamable;
public abstract class **CannotProceedHelper**;
public final class **CannotProceedHolder** implements org.omg.CORBA.portable.Streamable;
public abstract class **InvalidNameHelper**;
public final class **InvalidNameHolder** implements org.omg.CORBA.portable.Streamable;
public abstract class **NotEmptyHelper**;
public final class **NotEmptyHolder** implements org.omg.CORBA.portable.Streamable;
public abstract class **NotFoundHelper**;
public final class **NotFoundHolder** implements org.omg.CORBA.portable.Streamable;
public class **NotFoundReason** implements org.omg.CORBA.portable.IDLEntity;
public abstract class **NotFoundReasonHelper**;
public final class **NotFoundReasonHolder** implements org.omg.CORBA.portable.Streamable;

Exceptions:

public final class **AlreadyBound** extends org.omg.CORBA.UserException;
public final class **CannotProceed** extends org.omg.CORBA.UserException;
public final class **InvalidName** extends org.omg.CORBA.UserException;
public final class **NotEmpty** extends org.omg.CORBA.UserException;
public final class **NotFound** extends org.omg.CORBA.UserException;

AlreadyBound
Java 1.2

org.omg.CosNaming.NamingContextPackage
serializable checked

This exception is thrown by the bind(), bind_context() and bind_new_context() methods on NamingContext when you attempt to bind an object to a name that already has an object bound to it.

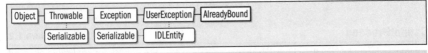

```
public final class AlreadyBound extends org.omg.CORBA.UserException {
// Public Constructors
    public AlreadyBound();
1.4 public AlreadyBound(String $reason);
}
```

Passed To: AlreadyBoundHelper.{insert(), write()}, AlreadyBoundHolder.AlreadyBoundHolder()

Returned By: AlreadyBoundHelper.{extract(), read()}

Thrown By: _NamingContextExtStub.{bind(), bind_context(), bind_new_context()}, _NamingContextStub.{bind(), bind_context(), bind_new_context()}, NamingContextOperations.{bind(), bind_context(), bind_new_context()}

Type Of: AlreadyBoundHolder.value

AlreadyBoundHelper
Java 1.2

org.omg.CosNaming.NamingContextPackage

The helper class for AlreadyBound objects, used to read and write these objects when they are used as remote method arguments or return values.

```
public abstract class AlreadyBoundHelper {
// Public Constructors
```

```
1.4 public AlreadyBoundHelper();
// Public Class Methods
   public static AlreadyBound extract(org.omg.CORBA.Any a);
   public static String id();
   public static void insert(org.omg.CORBA.Any a, AlreadyBound that);
   public static AlreadyBound read(org.omg.CORBA.portable.InputStream istream);
   public static org.omg.CORBA.TypeCode type();                              synchronized
   public static void write(org.omg.CORBA.portable.OutputStream ostream, AlreadyBound value);
}
```

AlreadyBoundHolder   Java 1.2

org.omg.CosNaming.NamingContextPackage

The holder class for out and inout IDL method arguments that would be mapped to
AlreadyBound exceptions. See Chapter 4 for more information on the uses of holder
classes.

```
Object ├ AlreadyBoundHolder ┈ Streamable
```

```
public final class AlreadyBoundHolder implements org.omg.CORBA.portable.Streamable {
// Public Constructors
   public AlreadyBoundHolder();
   public AlreadyBoundHolder(AlreadyBound initialValue);
// Methods Implementing Streamable
   public void _read(org.omg.CORBA.portable.InputStream i);
   public org.omg.CORBA.TypeCode _type();
   public void _write(org.omg.CORBA.portable.OutputStream o);
// Public Instance Fields
   public AlreadyBound value;
}
```

CannotProceed   Java 1.2

org.omg.CosNaming.NamingContextPackage   *serializable checked*

This exceptions is thrown by any of the bind or rebind methods on the NamingContext
interface, when the NamingContext has given up trying to bind the object to the name
specified, for some reason not covered by the other exceptions thrown by these methods. The CannotProceed exception contains a NamingContext that is the last context that it
attempted to traverse, and a NameComponent array, which is the remainder of the name
specified in the method call, relative to the context.

```
Object ├ Throwable ├ Exception ├ UserException ├ CannotProceed
        Serializable   Serializable      IDLEntity
```

```
public final class CannotProceed extends org.omg.CORBA.UserException {
// Public Constructors
   public CannotProceed();
   public CannotProceed(NamingContext _cxt, NameComponent[] _rest_of_name);
1.4 public CannotProceed(String $reason, NamingContext _cxt, NameComponent[] _rest_of_name);
// Public Instance Fields
   public NamingContext cxt;
   public NameComponent[] rest_of_name;
}
```

Passed To: CannotProceedHelper.{insert(), write()}, CannotProceedHolder.CannotProceedHolder()

Returned By: CannotProceedHelper.{extract(), read()}

Thrown By: _NamingContextExtStub.{bind(), bind_context(), bind_new_context(), rebind(), rebind_context(), resolve(), resolve_str(), unbind()}, _NamingContextStub.{bind(), bind_context(), bind_new_context(), rebind(), rebind_context(), resolve(), unbind()}, NamingContextExtOperations.resolve_str(), NamingContextOperations.{bind(), bind_context(), bind_new_context(), rebind(), rebind_context(), resolve(), unbind()}

Type Of: CannotProceedHolder.value

CannotProceedHelper   Java 1.2

org.omg.CosNaming.NamingContextPackage

The helper class for CannotProceed objects, used to read and write these objects when they are used as remote method arguments or return values.

```
public abstract class CannotProceedHelper {
// Public Constructors
1.4 public CannotProceedHelper();
// Public Class Methods
    public static CannotProceed extract(org.omg.CORBA.Any a);
    public static String id();
    public static void insert(org.omg.CORBA.Any a, CannotProceed that);
    public static CannotProceed read(org.omg.CORBA.portable.InputStream istream);
    public static org.omg.CORBA.TypeCode type();                                    synchronized
    public static void write(org.omg.CORBA.portable.OutputStream ostream, CannotProceed value);
}
```

CannotProceedHolder   Java 1.2

org.omg.CosNaming.NamingContextPackage

The holder class for out and inout IDL method arguments that would be mapped to CannotProceed exceptions.

```
Object ├ CannotProceedHolder ┈ Streamable
```

```
public final class CannotProceedHolder implements org.omg.CORBA.portable.Streamable {
// Public Constructors
    public CannotProceedHolder();
    public CannotProceedHolder(CannotProceed initialValue);
// Methods Implementing Streamable
    public void _read(org.omg.CORBA.portable.InputStream i);
    public org.omg.CORBA.TypeCode _type();
    public void _write(org.omg.CORBA.portable.OutputStream o);
// Public Instance Fields
    public CannotProceed value;
}
```

InvalidName   Java 1.2

org.omg.CosNaming.NamingContextPackage   *serializable checked*

This exception is thrown by any of the NamingContext methods for binding, resolving or unbinding objects, when the specified name is invalid, e.g., it contains invalid characters.

```
Object — Throwable — Exception — UserException — InvalidName
        Serializable   Serializable      IDLEntity
```

```
public final class InvalidName extends org.omg.CORBA.UserException {
// Public Constructors
   public InvalidName();
1.4 public InvalidName(String $reason);
}
```

Passed To: org.omg.CosNaming.NamingContextPackage.InvalidNameHelper.{insert(), write()}, InvalidNameHolder.InvalidNameHolder()

Returned By: org.omg.CosNaming.NamingContextPackage.InvalidNameHelper.{extract(), read()}

Thrown By: Too many methods to list.

Type Of: InvalidNameHolder.value

InvalidNameHelper   Java 1.2

org.omg.CosNaming.NamingContextPackage

The helper class for InvalidName objects, used to read and write these objects when they are used as remote method arguments or return values.

```
public abstract class InvalidNameHelper {
// Public Constructors
1.4 public InvalidNameHelper();
// Public Class Methods
   public static org.omg.CosNaming.NamingContextPackage.InvalidName extract(org.omg.CORBA.Any a);
   public static String Id();
   public static void insert(org.omg.CORBA.Any a, org.omg.CosNaming.NamingContextPackage.InvalidName that);
   public static org.omg.CosNaming.NamingContextPackage.InvalidName read(
                                            org.omg.CORBA.portable.InputStream istream);
   public static org.omg.CORBA.TypeCode type();                                    synchronized
   public static void write(org.omg.CORBA.portable.OutputStream ostream,
               org.omg.CosNaming.NamingContextPackage.InvalidName value);
}
```

InvalidNameHolder   Java 1.2

org.omg.CosNaming.NamingContextPackage

The holder class for out and inout IDL method arguments that would be mapped to InvalidName exceptions.

```
Object — InvalidNameHolder — Streamable
```

```
public final class InvalidNameHolder implements org.omg.CORBA.portable.Streamable {
// Public Constructors
   public InvalidNameHolder();
   public InvalidNameHolder(org.omg.CosNaming.NamingContextPackage.InvalidName initialValue);
// Methods Implementing Streamable
   public void _read(org.omg.CORBA.portable.InputStream i);
   public org.omg.CORBA.TypeCode _type();
   public void _write(org.omg.CORBA.portable.OutputStream o);
// Public Instance Fields
   public org.omg.CosNaming.NamingContextPackage.InvalidName value;
}
```

NotEmpty

org.omg.CosNaming.NamingContextPackage

This exception is thrown by the NamingContext.destroy() method, if you attempt to destroy a NamingContext that still has bindings within it.

```
Object ├─ Throwable ├─ Exception ├─ UserException ├─ NotEmpty
         Serializable   Serializable      IDLEntity
```

```
public final class NotEmpty extends org.omg.CORBA.UserException {
// Public Constructors
    public NotEmpty();
1.4 public NotEmpty(String $reason);
}
```

Passed To: NotEmptyHelper.{insert(), write()}, NotEmptyHolder.NotEmptyHolder()

Returned By: NotEmptyHelper.{extract(), read()}

Thrown By: _NamingContextExtStub.destroy(), _NamingContextStub.destroy(), NamingContextOperations.destroy()

Type Of: NotEmptyHolder.value

NotEmptyHelper

org.omg.CosNaming.NamingContextPackage

The helper class for NotEmpty objects, used to read and write these objects when they are used as remote method arguments or return values.

```
public abstract class NotEmptyHelper {
// Public Constructors
1.4 public NotEmptyHelper();
// Public Class Methods
    public static NotEmpty extract(org.omg.CORBA.Any a);
    public static String id();
    public static void insert(org.omg.CORBA.Any a, NotEmpty that);
    public static NotEmpty read(org.omg.CORBA.portable.InputStream istream);
    public static org.omg.CORBA.TypeCode type();                                    synchronized
    public static void write(org.omg.CORBA.portable.OutputStream ostream, NotEmpty value);
}
```

NotEmptyHolder

org.omg.CosNaming.NamingContextPackage

The holder class for out and inout IDL method arguments that would be mapped to NotEmpty exceptions.

```
Object ├─ NotEmptyHolder ┈ Streamable
```

```
public final class NotEmptyHolder implements org.omg.CORBA.portable.Streamable {
// Public Constructors
    public NotEmptyHolder();
    public NotEmptyHolder(NotEmpty initialValue);
// Methods Implementing Streamable
    public void _read(org.omg.CORBA.portable.InputStream i);
    public org.omg.CORBA.TypeCode _type();
    public void _write(org.omg.CORBA.portable.OutputStream o);
```

```
// Public Instance Fields
    public NotEmpty value;
}
```

NotFound

org.omg.CosNaming.NamingContextPackage   *serializable checked*

This exception is thrown by any of the NamingContext methods for binding, resolving or unbinding object names, when a specified name is not found as a binding within the NamingContext. The NotFound exception contains a NameComponent array, which represents the remainder of the name after the first component mismatch was found, and a Not-FoundReason object, that contains an int value that indicates whether the operation failed because one of the components in the name was not found, one of the intermediate components was bound to a regular object instead of a context, or the final component was not bound to an object.

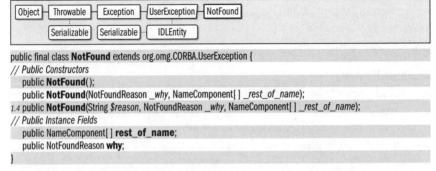

```
public final class NotFound extends org.omg.CORBA.UserException {
// Public Constructors
    public NotFound();
    public NotFound(NotFoundReason _why, NameComponent[ ] _rest_of_name);
1.4 public NotFound(String $reason, NotFoundReason _why, NameComponent[ ] _rest_of_name);
// Public Instance Fields
    public NameComponent[ ] rest_of_name;
    public NotFoundReason why;
}
```

Passed To: NotFoundHelper.{insert(), write()}, NotFoundHolder.NotFoundHolder()

Returned By: NotFoundHelper.{extract(), read()}

Thrown By: _NamingContextExtStub.{bind(), bind_context(), bind_new_context(), rebind(), rebind_context(), resolve(), resolve_str(), unbind()}, _NamingContextStub.{bind(), bind_context(), bind_new_context(), rebind(), rebind_context(), resolve(), unbind()}, NamingContextExtOperations.resolve_str(), NamingContextOperations.{bind(), bind_context(), bind_new_context(), rebind(), rebind_context(), resolve(), unbind()}

Type Of: NotFoundHolder.value

NotFoundHelper

org.omg.CosNaming.NamingContextPackage

The helper class for NotFound objects, used to read and write these objects when they are used as remote method arguments or return values.

```
public abstract class NotFoundHelper {
// Public Constructors
1.4 public NotFoundHelper();
// Public Class Methods
    public static NotFound extract(org.omg.CORBA.Any a);
    public static String id();
    public static void insert(org.omg.CORBA.Any a, NotFound that);
    public static NotFound read(org.omg.CORBA.portable.InputStream istream);
    public static org.omg.CORBA.TypeCode type();                              synchronized
```

```
     public static void write(org.omg.CORBA.portable.OutputStream ostream, NotFound value);
}
```

NotFoundHolder

org.omg.CosNaming.NamingContextPackage

The holder class for out and inout IDL method arguments that would be mapped to Not-
Found exceptions.

```
Object ⊢ NotFoundHolder ⋯ Streamable
```

```
public final class NotFoundHolder implements org.omg.CORBA.portable.Streamable {
// Public Constructors
    public NotFoundHolder();
    public NotFoundHolder(NotFound initialValue);
// Methods Implementing Streamable
    public void _read(org.omg.CORBA.portable.InputStream i);
    public org.omg.CORBA.TypeCode _type();
    public void _write(org.omg.CORBA.portable.OutputStream o);
// Public Instance Fields
    public NotFound value;
}
```

NotFoundReason

org.omg.CosNaming.NamingContextPackage

NotFoundReason objects are used in NotFound exceptions to indicate the reason that an
object binding was not found in a NamingContext. It has a value() method which returns
an int that can be compared to its three static int members to determine the reason for
the failure. A value of _missing_node indicates that an intermediate component of the
name specified was not found in the context, _not_context indicates that an intermediate
component name was not bound to a NamingContext, and _not_object indicates that an
object was not bound to the final component in the name.

```
Object ⊢ NotFoundReason
Serializable ⋯ IDLEntity
```

```
public class NotFoundReason implements org.omg.CORBA.portable.IDLEntity {
// Protected Constructors
1.4 protected NotFoundReason(int value);
// Public Constants
    public static final int _missing_node;                                              =0
    public static final int _not_context;                                               =1
    public static final int _not_object;                                                =2
    public static final NotFoundReason missing_node;
    public static final NotFoundReason not_context;
    public static final NotFoundReason not_object;
// Public Class Methods
    public static NotFoundReason from_int(int value);
// Public Instance Methods
    public int value();
}
```

Passed To: NotFound.NotFound(), NotFoundReasonHelper.{insert(), write()},
NotFoundReasonHolder.NotFoundReasonHolder()

Returned By: NotFoundReason.from_int(), NotFoundReasonHelper.{extract(), read()}

Type Of: NotFound.why, NotFoundReason.{missing_node, not_context, not_object}, NotFoundReasonHolder.value

NotFoundReasonHelper   Java 1.2

org.omg.CosNaming.NamingContextPackage

The helper class for NotFoundReason objects, used to read and write these objects when they are used as remote method arguments or return values.

```
public abstract class NotFoundReasonHelper {
// Public Constructors
1.4 public NotFoundReasonHelper();
// Public Class Methods
   public static NotFoundReason extract(org.omg.CORBA.Any a);
   public static String id();
   public static void insert(org.omg.CORBA.Any a, NotFoundReason that);
   public static NotFoundReason read(org.omg.CORBA.portable.InputStream istream);
   public static org.omg.CORBA.TypeCode type();                                    synchronized
   public static void write(org.omg.CORBA.portable.OutputStream ostream, NotFoundReason value);
}
```

NotFoundReasonHolder   Java 1.2

org.omg.CosNaming.NamingContextPackage

The holder class for out and inout IDL method arguments that would be mapped to Not-FoundReason exceptions.

```
Object ├ NotFoundReasonHolder ┈ Streamable
```

```
public final class NotFoundReasonHolder implements org.omg.CORBA.portable.Streamable {
// Public Constructors
   public NotFoundReasonHolder();
   public NotFoundReasonHolder(NotFoundReason initialValue);
// Methods Implementing Streamable
   public void _read(org.omg.CORBA.portable.InputStream i);
   public org.omg.CORBA.TypeCode _type();
   public void _write(org.omg.CORBA.portable.OutputStream o);
// Public Instance Fields
   public NotFoundReason value;
}
```

CHAPTER 44

org.omg.PortableServer and Subpackages

This package contains the interfaces that define the Portable Object Adaptor (POA) interface that CORBA server-side implementations can use to interface with the core ORB functions in a portable way. Prior to the introduction of the POA (circa CORBA 2.3.1, supported as of JDK 1.4), server-side CORBA skeletons and implementation objects needed to be ported to different CORBA vendor implementations.

Interfaces:

public interface **AdapterActivator** extends AdapterActivatorOperations, org.omg.CORBA.Object,
              org.omg.CORBA.portable.IDLEntity;
public interface **AdapterActivatorOperations**;
public interface **Current** extends CurrentOperations, org.omg.CORBA.Current,
              org.omg.CORBA.portable.IDLEntity;
public interface **CurrentOperations** extends org.omg.CORBA.CurrentOperations;
public interface **ID_ASSIGNMENT_POLICY_ID**;
public interface **ID_UNIQUENESS_POLICY_ID**;
public interface **IdAssignmentPolicy** extends IdAssignmentPolicyOperations, org.omg.CORBA.Policy,
              org.omg.CORBA.portable.IDLEntity;
public interface **IdAssignmentPolicyOperations** extends org.omg.CORBA.PolicyOperations;
public interface **IdUniquenessPolicy** extends IdUniquenessPolicyOperations, org.omg.CORBA.Policy,
              org.omg.CORBA.portable.IDLEntity;
public interface **IdUniquenessPolicyOperations** extends org.omg.CORBA.PolicyOperations;
public interface **IMPLICIT_ACTIVATION_POLICY_ID**;
public interface **ImplicitActivationPolicy** extends ImplicitActivationPolicyOperations,
              org.omg.CORBA.Policy,
              org.omg.CORBA.portable.IDLEntity;
public interface **ImplicitActivationPolicyOperations** extends org.omg.CORBA.PolicyOperations;
public interface **LIFESPAN_POLICY_ID**;
public interface **LifespanPolicy** extends LifespanPolicyOperations, org.omg.CORBA.Policy,
              org.omg.CORBA.portable.IDLEntity;

```
public interface LifespanPolicyOperations extends org.omg.CORBA.PolicyOperations;
public interface POA extends POAOperations, org.omg.CORBA.Object,
                          org.omg.CORBA.portable.IDLEntity;
public interface POAManager extends POAManagerOperations,
                          org.omg.CORBA.Object, org.omg.CORBA.portable.IDLEntity;
public interface POAManagerOperations;
public interface POAOperations;
public interface REQUEST_PROCESSING_POLICY_ID;
public interface RequestProcessingPolicy extends RequestProcessingPolicyOperations,
                          org.omg.CORBA.Policy, org.omg.CORBA.portable.IDLEntity;
public interface RequestProcessingPolicyOperations extends org.omg.CORBA.PolicyOperations;
public interface SERVANT_RETENTION_POLICY_ID;
public interface ServantActivator extends ServantActivatorOperations, ServantManager,
                          org.omg.CORBA.portable.IDLEntity;
public interface ServantActivatorOperations extends ServantManagerOperations;
public interface ServantLocator extends ServantLocatorOperations, ServantManager,
                          org.omg.CORBA.portable.IDLEntity;
public interface ServantLocatorOperations extends ServantManagerOperations;
public interface ServantManager extends ServantManagerOperations, org.omg.CORBA.Object,
                          org.omg.CORBA.portable.IDLEntity;
public interface ServantManagerOperations;
public interface ServantRetentionPolicy extends ServantRetentionPolicyOperations,
                          org.omg.CORBA.Policy,
                          org.omg.CORBA.portable.IDLEntity;
public interface ServantRetentionPolicyOperations extends org.omg.CORBA.PolicyOperations;
public interface THREAD_POLICY_ID;
public interface ThreadPolicy extends ThreadPolicyOperations, org.omg.CORBA.Policy,
                          org.omg.CORBA.portable.IDLEntity;
public interface ThreadPolicyOperations extends org.omg.CORBA.PolicyOperations;
```

Classes:

```
public class _ServantActivatorStub extends org.omg.CORBA.portable.ObjectImpl
                          implements ServantActivator;
public class _ServantLocatorStub extends org.omg.CORBA.portable.ObjectImpl
                          implements ServantLocator;
public abstract class CurrentHelper;
public abstract class ForwardRequestHelper;
public class IdAssignmentPolicyValue implements org.omg.CORBA.portable.IDLEntity;
public class IdUniquenessPolicyValue implements org.omg.CORBA.portable.IDLEntity;
public class ImplicitActivationPolicyValue implements org.omg.CORBA.portable.IDLEntity;
public class LifespanPolicyValue implements org.omg.CORBA.portable.IDLEntity;
public abstract class POAHelper;
public class RequestProcessingPolicyValue implements org.omg.CORBA.portable.IDLEntity;
public abstract class Servant;
    └ public abstract class DynamicImplementation extends Servant;
    └ public abstract class ServantActivatorPOA extends Servant
                          implements ServantActivatorOperations,
                          org.omg.CORBA.portable.InvokeHandler;
    └ public abstract class ServantLocatorPOA extends Servant
                          implements ServantLocatorOperations,
                          org.omg.CORBA.portable.InvokeHandler;
public abstract class ServantActivatorHelper;
```

public abstract class **ServantLocatorHelper**;
public class **ServantRetentionPolicyValue** implements org.omg.CORBA.portable.IDLEntity;
public class **ThreadPolicyValue** implements org.omg.CORBA.portable.IDLEntity;

Exceptions:

public final class **ForwardRequest** extends org.omg.CORBA.UserException;

_ServantActivatorStub

org.omg.PortableServer

Java 1.4
serializable

The stub class generated from the IDL ServantActivator interface.

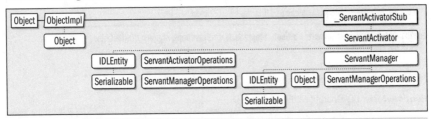

public class **_ServantActivatorStub** extends org.omg.CORBA.portable.ObjectImpl implements ServantActivator {
// *Public Constructors*
  public **_ServantActivatorStub**();
// *Public Constants*
  public static final Class **_opsClass**;
// *Methods Implementing ServantActivatorOperations*
  public void **etherealize**(byte[ ] *oid*, POA *adapter*, Servant *serv*, boolean *cleanup_in_progress*,
                 boolean *remaining_activations*);
  public Servant **incarnate**(byte[ ] *oid*, POA *adapter*) throws org.omg.PortableServer.ForwardRequest;
// *Public Methods Overriding ObjectImpl*
  public String[ ] **_ids**();
}

_ServantLocatorStub

org.omg.PortableServer

Java 1.4
serializable

The stub class generated from the IDL ServantLocator interface.

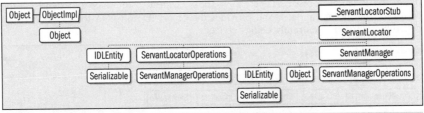

public class **_ServantLocatorStub** extends org.omg.CORBA.portable.ObjectImpl implements ServantLocator {
// *Public Constructors*
  public **_ServantLocatorStub**();
// *Public Constants*
  public static final Class **_opsClass**;
// *Methods Implementing ServantLocatorOperations*
  public void **postinvoke**(byte[ ] *oid*, POA *adapter*, String *operation*, Object *the_cookie*, Servant *the_servant*);
  public Servant **preinvoke**(byte[ ] *oid*, POA *adapter*, String *operation*,
              org.omg.PortableServer.ServantLocatorPackage.CookieHolder *the_cookie*)

```
        throws org.omg.PortableServer.ForwardRequest;
// Public Methods Overriding ObjectImpl
    public String[ ] _ids( );
}
```

AdapterActivator   Java 1.4

org.omg.PortableServer   *serializable*

An AdapterActivator is used to activate POAs as needed to satisfy requests. A servant can register an AdapterActivator if it wants to be activated automatically by the ORB.

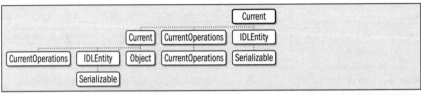

```
public interface AdapterActivator extends AdapterActivatorOperations, org.omg.CORBA.Object,
        org.omg.CORBA.portable.IDLEntity {
}
```

Passed To: POAOperations.the_activator()

Returned By: POAOperations.the_activator()

AdapterActivatorOperations   Java 1.4

org.omg.PortableServer

This is the Operations interface mapped from the IDL for the AdapterActivator interface, and contains the methods inherited by AdapterActivator.

```
public interface AdapterActivatorOperations {
// Public Instance Methods
    public abstract boolean unknown_adapter(POA parent, String name);
}
```

Implementations: AdapterActivator

Current   Java 1.4

org.omg.PortableServer   *serializable*

The Current interface provides access to the identity of the servant that was the target of a method request on an ORB. The ORB provides a Current instance through ORB.resolve_initial_references("POACurrent"). The Current interface extends the org.omg.CORBA.Current interface, and provides the object ID and POA for the servant targetted by the request currently being serviced.

```
public interface Current extends org.omg.PortableServer.CurrentOperations, org.omg.CORBA.Current,
        org.omg.CORBA.portable.IDLEntity {
}
```

Passed To: org.omg.PortableServer.CurrentHelper.{insert(), write()}

Returned By: org.omg.PortableServer.CurrentHelper.{extract(), narrow(), read()}

CurrentHelper
Java 1.4

org.omg.PortableServer

The helper class for the Current object type, used to safely cast Current objects, read/write Current objects using I/O streams, etc.

```
public abstract class CurrentHelper {
// Public Constructors
    public CurrentHelper();
// Public Class Methods
    public static org.omg.PortableServer.Current extract(org.omg.CORBA.Any a);
    public static String id();
    public static void insert(org.omg.CORBA.Any a, org.omg.PortableServer.Current that);
    public static org.omg.PortableServer.Current narrow(org.omg.CORBA.Object obj);
    public static org.omg.PortableServer.Current read(org.omg.CORBA.portable.InputStream istream);
    public static org.omg.CORBA.TypeCode type();                                        synchronized
    public static void write(org.omg.CORBA.portable.OutputStream ostream, org.omg.PortableServer.Current value);
}
```

CurrentOperations
Java 1.4

org.omg.PortableServer

This is the Operations interface mapped from the IDL for the Current interface, and contains the methods inherited by Current.

```
CurrentOperations ├ CurrentOperations
```

```
public interface CurrentOperations extends org.omg.CORBA.CurrentOperations {
// Public Instance Methods
    public abstract byte[ ] get_object_id() throws org.omg.PortableServer.CurrentPackage.NoContext;
    public abstract POA get_POA() throws org.omg.PortableServer.CurrentPackage.NoContext;
}
```

Implementations: org.omg.PortableServer.Current

DynamicImplementation
Java 1.4

org.omg.PortableServer

This is the base class for all Dynamic Skeleton Interfaces that support the POA.

```
Object ├ Servant ├ DynamicImplementation
```

```
public abstract class DynamicImplementation extends Servant {
// Public Constructors
    public DynamicImplementation();
// Public Instance Methods
    public abstract void invoke(org.omg.CORBA.ServerRequest request);
}
```

ForwardRequest
Java 1.4

org.omg.PortableServer
serializable checked

This exception is thrown by a ServantManager when an object request has to be forwarded on to another object.

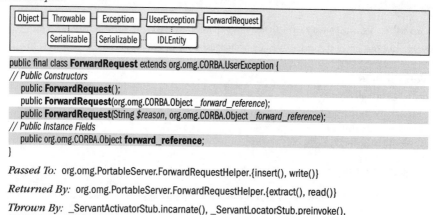

```
public final class ForwardRequest extends org.omg.CORBA.UserException {
// Public Constructors
    public ForwardRequest();
    public ForwardRequest(org.omg.CORBA.Object _forward_reference);
    public ForwardRequest(String $reason, org.omg.CORBA.Object _forward_reference);
// Public Instance Fields
    public org.omg.CORBA.Object forward_reference;
}
```

Passed To: org.omg.PortableServer.ForwardRequestHelper.{insert(), write()}

Returned By: org.omg.PortableServer.ForwardRequestHelper.{extract(), read()}

Thrown By: _ServantActivatorStub.incarnate(), _ServantLocatorStub.preinvoke(), ServantActivatorOperations.incarnate(), ServantLocatorOperations.preinvoke()

ForwardRequestHelper   Java 1.4

org.omg.PortableServer

The helper class for the ForwardRequest object type, used to read/write ForwardRequest objects using I/O streams, etc.

```
public abstract class ForwardRequestHelper {
// Public Constructors
    public ForwardRequestHelper();
// Public Class Methods
    public static org.omg.PortableServer.ForwardRequest extract(org.omg.CORBA.Any a);
    public static String id();
    public static void insert(org.omg.CORBA.Any a, org.omg.PortableServer.ForwardRequest that);
    public static org.omg.PortableServer.ForwardRequest read(org.omg.CORBA.portable.InputStream istream);
    public static org.omg.CORBA.TypeCode type();                                    synchronized
    public static void write(org.omg.CORBA.portable.OutputStream ostream,
                    org.omg.PortableServer.ForwardRequest value);
}
```

ID_ASSIGNMENT_POLICY_ID   Java 1.4

org.omg.PortableServer

An interface mapped from the IDL PolicyType constant ID_ASSIGNMENT_POLICY_ID. The contained value represents the type of IdAssignmentPolicy objects, obtained by calling their policy_type() method. This can be used to distinguish various Policy objects obtained in collections or arrays.

```
public interface ID_ASSIGNMENT_POLICY_ID {
// Public Constants
    public static final int value;                                                       =19
}
```

ID_UNIQUENESS_POLICY_ID   Java 1.4

org.omg.PortableServer

An interface mapped from the IDL PolicyType constant ID_UNIQUENESS_POLICY_ID. The contained value represents the type of IdUniquenessPolicy objects, obtained by calling their policy_type() method. This can be used to distinguish various Policy objects obtained in collections or arrays.

```
public interface ID_UNIQUENESS_POLICY_ID {
// Public Constants
    public static final int value;                                          =18
}
```

IdAssignmentPolicy

org.omg.PortableServer   *serializable*

A Policy used to determine whether object identifiers are generated by the ORB or by
the application. Its value() is an IdAssignmentPolicyValue object, which takes the value IdAs-
signmentPolicyValue.SYSTEM_ID (indicating that object ids are generated by the POA), or
IdAssignmentPolicyValue.USER_ID, indicating ids are assigned by the application. The default
value is SYSTEM_ID.

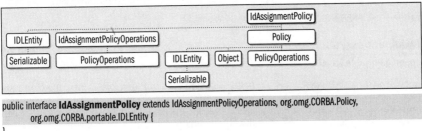

```
public interface IdAssignmentPolicy extends IdAssignmentPolicyOperations, org.omg.CORBA.Policy,
        org.omg.CORBA.portable.IDLEntity {
}
```

Returned By: POAOperations.create_id_assignment_policy()

IdAssignmentPolicyOperations

org.omg.PortableServer

This is the Operations interface mapped from the IDL for the IdAssignmentPolicy interface,
and contains the methods inherited by IdAssignmentPolicy.

```
public interface IdAssignmentPolicyOperations extends org.omg.CORBA.PolicyOperations {
// Public Instance Methods
    public abstract IdAssignmentPolicyValue value();
}
```

Implementations: IdAssignmentPolicy

IdAssignmentPolicyValue

org.omg.PortableServer   *serializable*

This class represents the value of an IdAssignmentPolicy for a POA. A value of IdAssign-
mentPolicyValue.SYSTEM_ID indicates that object ids are generated by the POA, while IdAs-
signmentPolicyValue.USER_ID indicates that ids are assigned by the application. The default
value is SYSTEM_ID.

```
public class IdAssignmentPolicyValue implements org.omg.CORBA.portable.IDLEntity {
// Protected Constructors
```

```
    protected IdAssignmentPolicyValue(int value);
// Public Constants
    public static final int _SYSTEM_ID;                                    =1
    public static final int _USER_ID;                                      =0
    public static final IdAssignmentPolicyValue SYSTEM_ID;
    public static final IdAssignmentPolicyValue USER_ID;
// Public Class Methods
    public static IdAssignmentPolicyValue from_int(int value);
// Public Instance Methods
    public int value();
}
```

Passed To: POAOperations.create_id_assignment_policy()

Returned By: IdAssignmentPolicyOperations.value(), IdAssignmentPolicyValue.from_int()

Type Of: IdAssignmentPolicyValue.{SYSTEM_ID, USER_ID}

IdUniquenessPolicy   Java 1.4

org.omg.PortableServer   *serializable*

A Policy that indicates whether servants activated within the POA must have unique identities or not. A value of IdUniquenessPolicyValue.UNIQUE_ID indicates that ids of servants must be unique, a value of IdUniquenessPolicyValue.MULTIPLE_ID indicates that a servant can have multiple identifiers. The default value is UNIQUE_ID.

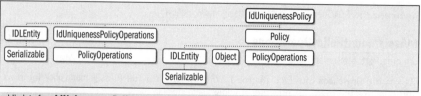

```
public interface IdUniquenessPolicy extends IdUniquenessPolicyOperations, org.omg.CORBA.Policy,
        org.omg.CORBA.portable.IDLEntity {
}
```

Returned By: POAOperations.create_id_uniqueness_policy()

IdUniquenessPolicyOperations   Java 1.4

org.omg.PortableServer

This is the Operations interface mapped from the IDL for the IdUniquenessPolicy interface, and contains the methods inherited by IdUniquenessPolicy.

```
PolicyOperations ... IdUniquenessPolicyOperations
```

```
public interface IdUniquenessPolicyOperations extends org.omg.CORBA.PolicyOperations {
// Public Instance Methods
    public abstract IdUniquenessPolicyValue value();
}
```

Implementations: IdUniquenessPolicy

IdUniquenessPolicyValue

org.omg.PortableServer   *serializable*

This class represents the value of an IdUniquenessPolicy for a POA. A value of IdUniquenessPolicyValue.UNIQUE_ID indicates that ids of servants must be unique, a value of IdUniquenessPolicyValue.MULTIPLE_ID indicates that a servant can have multiple identifiers. The default value is UNIQUE_ID.

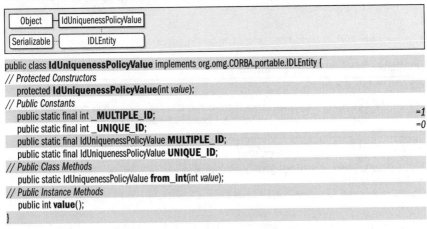

```
public class IdUniquenessPolicyValue implements org.omg.CORBA.portable.IDLEntity {
// Protected Constructors
    protected IdUniquenessPolicyValue(int value);
// Public Constants
    public static final int _MULTIPLE_ID;                                        =1
    public static final int _UNIQUE_ID;                                          =0
    public static final IdUniquenessPolicyValue MULTIPLE_ID;
    public static final IdUniquenessPolicyValue UNIQUE_ID;
// Public Class Methods
    public static IdUniquenessPolicyValue from_int(int value);
// Public Instance Methods
    public int value();
}
```

Passed To: POAOperations.create_id_uniqueness_policy()

Returned By: IdUniquenessPolicyOperations.value(), IdUniquenessPolicyValue.from_int()

Type Of: IdUniquenessPolicyValue.{MULTIPLE_ID, UNIQUE_ID}

IMPLICIT_ACTIVATION_POLICY_ID

org.omg.PortableServer

An interface mapped from the IDL PolicyType constant IMPLICIT_ACTIVATION_POLICY_ID. The contained value represents the type of ImplicitActivationPolicy objects, obtained by calling their policy_type() method. This can be used to distinguish various Policy objects obtained in collections or arrays.

```
public interface IMPLICIT_ACTIVATION_POLICY_ID {
// Public Constants
    public static final int value;                                               =20
}
```

ImplicitActivationPolicy

org.omg.PortableServer   *serializable*

A Policy used to indicate whether a POA supports implicit activation of servants. Its value() is an ImplicitActivationPolicyValue object, which takes the value ImplicitActivationPolicyValue.IMPLICIT_ACTIVATION (indicating that the POA supports implicit activation), or ImplicitActivationPolicyValue.NO_IMPLICIT_ACTIVATION, indicating the POA does not support implicit activation.

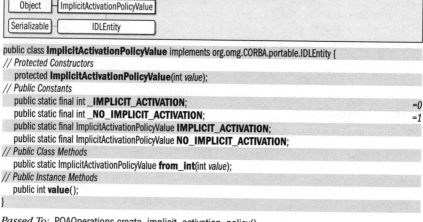

```
public interface ImplicitActivationPolicy extends ImplicitActivationPolicyOperations, org.omg.CORBA.Policy,
       org.omg.CORBA.portable.IDLEntity {
}
```

Returned By: POAOperations.create_implicit_activation_policy()

ImplicitActivationPolicyOperations   Java 1.4

org.omg.PortableServer

This is the Operations interface mapped from the IDL for the ImplicitActivationPolicy interface, and contains the methods inherited by ImplicitActivationPolicy.

```
public interface ImplicitActivationPolicyOperations extends org.omg.CORBA.PolicyOperations {
// Public Instance Methods
    public abstract ImplicitActivationPolicyValue value();
}
```

Implementations: ImplicitActivationPolicy

ImplicitActivationPolicyValue   Java 1.4

org.omg.PortableServer   *serializable*

This class represents the value of an ImplicitActivationPolicy for a POA. A value of Impli-
tActivationPolicyValue.IMPLICIT_ACTIVATION indicates that the POA supports implicit activation,
while ImplicitActivationPolicyValue.NO_IMPLICIT_ACTIVATION indicates that the POA does not
support implicit activation.

```
public class ImplicitActivationPolicyValue implements org.omg.CORBA.portable.IDLEntity {
// Protected Constructors
    protected ImplicitActivationPolicyValue(int value);
// Public Constants
    public static final int _IMPLICIT_ACTIVATION;                                =0
    public static final int _NO_IMPLICIT_ACTIVATION;                             =1
    public static final ImplicitActivationPolicyValue IMPLICIT_ACTIVATION;
    public static final ImplicitActivationPolicyValue NO_IMPLICIT_ACTIVATION;
// Public Class Methods
    public static ImplicitActivationPolicyValue from_int(int value);
// Public Instance Methods
    public int value();
}
```

Passed To: POAOperations.create_implicit_activation_policy()

Returned By: ImplicitActivationPolicyOperations.value(), ImplicitActivationPolicyValue.from_int()

Type Of: ImplicitActivationPolicyValue.{IMPLICIT_ACTIVATION, NO_IMPLICIT_ACTIVATION}

LIFESPAN_POLICY_ID
Java 1.4

org.omg.PortableServer

An interface mapped from the IDL PolicyType constant LIFESPAN_POLICY_ID. The contained value represents the type of LifespanPolicy objects, obtained by calling their policy_type() method. This can be used to distinguish various Policy objects obtained in collections or arrays.

```
public interface LIFESPAN_POLICY_ID {
// Public Constants
    public static final int value;                                              =17
}
```

LifespanPolicy
Java 1.4

org.omg.PortableServer   *serializable*

A Policy that indicates the lifespan of objects served by the POA. A value of LifespanPolicy-Value.TRANSIENT indicates that servants are transient and do not live beyond the life of the POA process. A value of LifespanPolicyValue.PERSISTENT indicates that servants can live beyond the lifetime of the POA process. The default value is TRANSIENT.

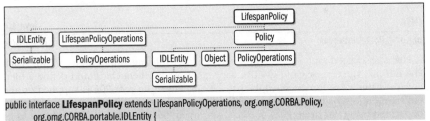

```
public interface LifespanPolicy extends LifespanPolicyOperations, org.omg.CORBA.Policy,
        org.omg.CORBA.portable.IDLEntity {
}
```

Returned By: POAOperations.create_lifespan_policy()

LifespanPolicyOperations
Java 1.4

org.omg.PortableServer

This is the Operations interface mapped from the IDL for the LifespanPolicy interface, and contains the methods inherited by LifespanPolicy.

```
public interface LifespanPolicyOperations extends org.omg.CORBA.PolicyOperations {
// Public Instance Methods
    public abstract LifespanPolicyValue value();
}
```

Implementations: LifespanPolicy

LifespanPolicyValue
Java 1.4

org.omg.PortableServer   *serializable*

This class represents the value of an LifespanPolicy for a POA. A value of LifespanPolicy-Value.TRANSIENT indicates that servants are transient and do not live beyond the life of the POA process. A value of LifespanPolicyValue.PERSISTENT indicates that servants can live beyond the lifetime of the POA process. The default value is TRANSIENT.

```
public class LifespanPolicyValue implements org.omg.CORBA.portable.IDLEntity {
// Protected Constructors
    protected LifespanPolicyValue(int value);
// Public Constants
    public static final int _PERSISTENT;                                    =1
    public static final int _TRANSIENT;                                     =0
    public static final LifespanPolicyValue PERSISTENT;
    public static final LifespanPolicyValue TRANSIENT;
// Public Class Methods
    public static LifespanPolicyValue from_int(int value);
// Public Instance Methods
    public int value();
}
```

Passed To: POAOperations.create_lifespan_policy()

Returned By: LifespanPolicyOperations.value(), LifespanPolicyValue.from_int()

Type Of: LifespanPolicyValue.{PERSISTENT, TRANSIENT}

POA

Java 1.4

org.omg.PortableServer

serializable

A POA is associated with each CORBA server object running within a given ORB. Each POA can manage one or more CORBA servants. POAs are hierarchical and define a hierarchical namespace for the servants that they manage. The root POA is supplied by the ORB itself; it can be accessed using ORB.resolve_initial_references("RootPOA"). Child POAs can be created using the create_POA() method, specifying the name for the POA relative to its parent, the POAManager to be used for the POA, and any Policy objects to be applied to the POA.

```
public interface POA extends POAOperations, org.omg.CORBA.Object, org.omg.CORBA.portable.IDLEntity {
}
```

Passed To: org.omg.CosNaming.BindingIteratorPOA._all_interfaces(),
org.omg.CosNaming.NamingContextExtPOA._all_interfaces(),
org.omg.CosNaming.NamingContextPOA._all_interfaces(), _ServantActivatorStub.{etherealize(),
incarnate()}, _ServantLocatorStub.{postinvoke(), preinvoke()},
AdapterActivatorOperations.unknown_adapter(), POAHelper.{insert(), write()}, Servant._all_interfaces(),
ServantActivatorOperations.{etherealize(), incarnate()}, ServantActivatorPOA._all_interfaces(),
ServantLocatorOperations.{postinvoke(), preinvoke()}, ServantLocatorPOA._all_interfaces()

Returned By: org.omg.PortableServer.CurrentOperations.get_POA(), POAHelper.{extract(), narrow(),
read()}, POAOperations.{create_POA(), find_POA(), the_children(), the_parent()},
Servant.{_default_POA(), _poa()}, org.omg.PortableServer.portable.Delegate.{default_POA(), poa()}

POAHelper

Java 1.4

org.omg.PortableServer

The helper class for the POA object type, used to safely cast POA objects, read/write POA objects using I/O streams, etc.

```
public abstract class POAHelper {
// Public Constructors
    public POAHelper();
// Public Class Methods
    public static POA extract(org.omg.CORBA.Any a);
    public static String id();
    public static void insert(org.omg.CORBA.Any a, POA that);
    public static POA narrow(org.omg.CORBA.Object obj);
    public static POA read(org.omg.CORBA.portable.InputStream istream);
    public static org.omg.CORBA.TypeCode type();                                    synchronized
    public static void write(org.omg.CORBA.portable.OutputStream ostream, POA value);
}
```

POAManager
org.omg.PortableServer

Java 1.4
serializable

A POAManager controls the state of POAs under its control. Each POAManager controls one or more POAs. The POAManager methods (inherited from the POAManagerOperations interface) provide methods for activating and deactivating POAs, and to request that the managed POAs hold or discard incoming requests. A POAManager is automatically created for each new POA created using the POA.create_POA() method, if one is not provided as an argument to the call.

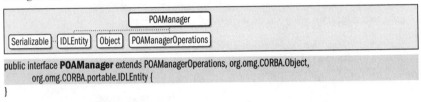

```
public interface POAManager extends POAManagerOperations, org.omg.CORBA.Object,
    org.omg.CORBA.portable.IDLEntity {
}
```

Passed To: POAOperations.create_POA()

Returned By: POAOperations.the_POAManager()

POAManagerOperations
org.omg.PortableServer

Java 1.4

This is the Operations interface mapped from the IDL for the POAManager interface, and contains the methods inherited by POAManager.

```
public interface POAManagerOperations {
// Public Instance Methods
    public abstract void activate() throws org.omg.PortableServer.POAManagerPackage.AdapterInactive;
    public abstract void deactivate(boolean etherealize_objects, boolean wait_for_completion)
        throws org.omg.PortableServer.POAManagerPackage.AdapterInactive;
    public abstract void discard_requests(boolean wait_for_completion)
        throws org.omg.PortableServer.POAManagerPackage.AdapterInactive;
    public abstract org.omg.PortableServer.POAManagerPackage.State get_state();
    public abstract void hold_requests(boolean wait_for_completion)
        throws org.omg.PortableServer.POAManagerPackage.AdapterInactive;
}
```

Implementations: POAManager

POAOperations   Java 1.4

org.omg.PortableServer

This is the Operations interface mapped from the IDL for the POA interface, and contains the methods inherited by POA.

```
public interface POAOperations {
// Public Instance Methods
    public abstract byte[ ] activate_object(Servant p_servant)
        throws org.omg.PortableServer.POAPackage.ServantAlreadyActive,
        org.omg.PortableServer.POAPackage.WrongPolicy;
    public abstract void activate_object_with_id(byte[ ] id, Servant p_servant)
        throws org.omg.PortableServer.POAPackage.ServantAlreadyActive,
        org.omg.PortableServer.POAPackage.ObjectAlreadyActive, org.omg.PortableServer.POAPackage.WrongPolicy;
    public abstract IdAssignmentPolicy create_id_assignment_policy(IdAssignmentPolicyValue value);
    public abstract IdUniquenessPolicy create_id_uniqueness_policy(IdUniquenessPolicyValue value);
    public abstract ImplicitActivationPolicy create_implicit_activation_policy(ImplicitActivationPolicyValue value);
    public abstract LifespanPolicy create_lifespan_policy(LifespanPolicyValue value);
    public abstract POA create_POA(String adapter_name, POAManager a_POAManager,
                                    org.omg.CORBA.Policy[ ] policies)
        throws org.omg.PortableServer.POAPackage.AdapterAlreadyExists,
        org.omg.PortableServer.POAPackage.InvalidPolicy;
    public abstract org.omg.CORBA.Object create_reference(String intf)
        throws org.omg.PortableServer.POAPackage.WrongPolicy;
    public abstract org.omg.CORBA.Object create_reference_with_id(byte[ ] oid, String intf);
    public abstract RequestProcessingPolicy create_request_processing_policy(
                                                RequestProcessingPolicyValue value);
    public abstract ServantRetentionPolicy create_servant_retention_policy(ServantRetentionPolicyValue value);
    public abstract ThreadPolicy create_thread_policy(ThreadPolicyValue value);
    public abstract void deactivate_object(byte[ ] oid) throws org.omg.PortableServer.POAPackage.ObjectNotActive,
        org.omg.PortableServer.POAPackage.WrongPolicy;
    public abstract void destroy(boolean etherealize_objects, boolean wait_for_completion);
    public abstract POA find_POA(String adapter_name, boolean activate_it)
        throws org.omg.PortableServer.POAPackage.AdapterNonExistent;
    public abstract Servant get_servant() throws org.omg.PortableServer.POAPackage.NoServant,
        org.omg.PortableServer.POAPackage.WrongPolicy;
    public abstract ServantManager get_servant_manager() throws
        org.omg.PortableServer.POAPackage.WrongPolicy;
    public abstract byte[ ] id();
    public abstract org.omg.CORBA.Object id_to_reference(byte[ ] oid)
        throws org.omg.PortableServer.POAPackage.ObjectNotActive, org.omg.PortableServer.POAPackage.WrongPolicy;
    public abstract Servant id_to_servant(byte[ ] oid) throws org.omg.PortableServer.POAPackage.ObjectNotActive,
        org.omg.PortableServer.POAPackage.WrongPolicy;
    public abstract byte[ ] reference_to_id(org.omg.CORBA.Object reference)
        throws org.omg.PortableServer.POAPackage.WrongAdapter, org.omg.PortableServer.POAPackage.WrongPolicy;
    public abstract Servant reference_to_servant(org.omg.CORBA.Object reference)
        throws org.omg.PortableServer.POAPackage.ObjectNotActive, org.omg.PortableServer.POAPackage.WrongPolicy,
        org.omg.PortableServer.POAPackage.WrongAdapter;
    public abstract byte[ ] servant_to_id(Servant p_servant)
        throws org.omg.PortableServer.POAPackage.ServantNotActive, org.omg.PortableServer.POAPackage.WrongPolicy;
    public abstract org.omg.CORBA.Object servant_to_reference(Servant p_servant)
        throws org.omg.PortableServer.POAPackage.ServantNotActive, org.omg.PortableServer.POAPackage.WrongPolicy;
    public abstract void set_servant(Servant p_servant) throws org.omg.PortableServer.POAPackage.WrongPolicy;
    public abstract void set_servant_manager(ServantManager imgr)
        throws org.omg.PortableServer.POAPackage.WrongPolicy;
    public abstract AdapterActivator the_activator();
    public abstract void the_activator(AdapterActivator newThe_activator);
```

```
public abstract POA[ ] the_children();
public abstract String the_name();
public abstract POA the_parent();
public abstract POAManager the_POAManager();
}
```

Implementations: POA

REQUEST_PROCESSING_POLICY_ID   Java 1.4
org.omg.PortableServer

An interface mapped from the IDL PolicyType constant REQUEST_PROCESSING_POLICY_ID. The contained value represents the type of RequestProcessingPolicy objects, obtained by calling their policy_type() method. This can be used to distinguish various Policy objects obtained in collections or arrays.

```
public interface REQUEST_PROCESSING_POLICY_ID {
// Public Constants
    public static final int value;                                    =22
}
```

RequestProcessingPolicy   Java 1.4
org.omg.PortableServer   serializable

A Policy that indicates how requests are handled by the POA. A value of RequestProcessingPolicyValue.USE_ACTIVE_OBJECT_MAP_ONLY indicates that requests are checked only against the active object map, and an OBJECT_NOT_EXIST exception is thrown if the object is not found. A value of RequestProcessingPolicyValue.USE_DEFAULT_SERVANT indicates that if the object is not found in the active object map, or if the POA has a ServantRetentionPolicy of NON_RETAIN, and if the POA has a default servant, then the request is passed onto the POA's default servant. A value of RequestProcessingPolicyValue.USE_SERVANT_MANAGER indicates that is the servant isn't found in the active object map, or if the POA has a ServantRetentionPolicy of NON_RETAIN, and if a ServantManager is registed with the POA, then the ServantManager is asked to locate the servant. The default value is USE_ACTIVE_OBJECT_MAP_ONLY.

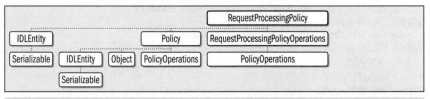

```
public interface RequestProcessingPolicy extends RequestProcessingPolicyOperations, org.omg.CORBA.Policy,
    org.omg.CORBA.portable.IDLEntity {
}
```

Returned By: POAOperations.create_request_processing_policy()

RequestProcessingPolicyOperations   Java 1.4
org.omg.PortableServer

This is the Operations interface mapped from the IDL for the RequestProcessingPolicy interface, and contains the methods inherited by RequestProcessingPolicy.

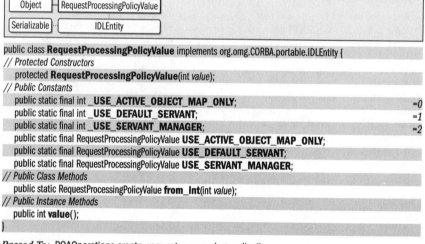

```
public interface RequestProcessingPolicyOperations extends org.omg.CORBA.PolicyOperations {
// Public Instance Methods
    public abstract RequestProcessingPolicyValue value();
}
```

Implementations: RequestProcessingPolicy

RequestProcessingPolicyValue

Java 1.4

org.omg.PortableServer

serializable

This class represents the value of an RequestProcessingPolicy for a POA. A value of Request-ProcessingPolicyValue.USE_ACTIVE_OBJECT_MAP_ONLY indicates that requests are checked only against the active object map, and an OBJECT_NOT_EXIST exception is thrown if the object is not found. A value of RequestProcessingPolicyValue.USE_DEFAULT_SERVANT indicates that if the object is not found in the active object map, or if the POA has a ServantRetentionPolicy of NON_RETAIN, and if the POA has a default servant, then the request is passed onto the POA's default servant. A value of RequestProcessingPolicyValue.USE_SERVANT_MANAGER indicates that is the servant isn't found in the active object map, or if the POA has a ServantRetentionPolicy of NON_RETAIN, and if a ServantManager is registed with the POA, then the ServantManager is asked to locate the servant. The default value is USE_ACTIVE_OBJECT_MAP_ONLY.

```
public class RequestProcessingPolicyValue implements org.omg.CORBA.portable.IDLEntity {
// Protected Constructors
    protected RequestProcessingPolicyValue(int value);
// Public Constants
    public static final int _USE_ACTIVE_OBJECT_MAP_ONLY;                            =0
    public static final int _USE_DEFAULT_SERVANT;                                   =1
    public static final int _USE_SERVANT_MANAGER;                                   =2
    public static final RequestProcessingPolicyValue USE_ACTIVE_OBJECT_MAP_ONLY;
    public static final RequestProcessingPolicyValue USE_DEFAULT_SERVANT;
    public static final RequestProcessingPolicyValue USE_SERVANT_MANAGER;
// Public Class Methods
    public static RequestProcessingPolicyValue from_int(int value);
// Public Instance Methods
    public int value();
}
```

Passed To: POAOperations.create_request_processing_policy()

Returned By: RequestProcessingPolicyOperations.value(), RequestProcessingPolicyValue.from_int()

Type Of: RequestProcessingPolicyValue.{USE_ACTIVE_OBJECT_MAP_ONLY, USE_DEFAULT_SERVANT, USE_SERVANT_MANAGER}

Servant

Java 1.4

org.omg.PortableServer

This is the base class for all POA-compatible server-side CORBA implementations. It contains methods that are invoked by the POA during the lifetime of the servant, and methods that the servant implementation class can invoke to access its runtime CORBA context, such as its ORB, POA, and Delegate.

```
public abstract class Servant {
// Public Constructors
   public Servant();
// Public Instance Methods
   public abstract String[] _all_interfaces(POA poa, byte[] objectId);
   public POA _default_POA();
   public final org.omg.PortableServer.portable.Delegate _get_delegate();
   public org.omg.CORBA.Object _get_interface_def();
   public boolean _is_a(String repository_id);
   public boolean _non_existent();
   public final byte[] _object_id();
   public final org.omg.CORBA.ORB _orb();
   public final POA _poa();
   public final void _set_delegate(org.omg.PortableServer.portable.Delegate delegate);
   public final org.omg.CORBA.Object _this_object();
   public final org.omg.CORBA.Object _this_object(org.omg.CORBA.ORB orb);
}
```

Subclasses: org.omg.CosNaming.BindingIteratorPOA, org.omg.CosNaming.NamingContextExtPOA, org.omg.CosNaming.NamingContextPOA, org.omg.PortableServer.DynamicImplementation, ServantActivatorPOA, ServantLocatorPOA

Passed To: _ServantActivatorStub.etherealize(), _ServantLocatorStub.postinvoke(), POAOperations.{activate_object(), activate_object_with_id(), servant_to_id(), servant_to_reference(), set_servant()}, ServantActivatorOperations.etherealize(), ServantLocatorOperations.postinvoke(), org.omg.PortableServer.portable.Delegate.{default_POA(), get_interface_def(), is_a(), non_existent(), object_id(), orb(), poa(), this_object()}

Returned By: _ServantActivatorStub.incarnate(), _ServantLocatorStub.preinvoke(), POAOperations.{get_servant(), id_to_servant(), reference_to_servant()}, ServantActivatorOperations.incarnate(), ServantLocatorOperations.preinvoke()

SERVANT_RETENTION_POLICY_ID   Java 1.4

org.omg.PortableServer

An interface mapped from the IDL PolicyType constant SERVANT_RETENTION_POLICY_ID. The contained value represents the type of ServentRetentionPolicy objects, obtained by calling their policy_type() method. This can be used to distinguish various Policy objects obtained in collections or arrays.

```
public interface SERVANT_RETENTION_POLICY_ID {
// Public Constants
   public static final int value;                        =21
}
```

ServantActivator   Java 1.4

org.omg.PortableServer   *serializable*

A ServantActivator is a type of ServantManager that is used by POAs to activate servants, if the POA has its RETAIN policy set (in the form of a ServantRetentionPolicy object with a value of ServantRetentionPolicyValue.RETAIN).

```
public interface ServantActivator extends ServantActivatorOperations, ServantManager,
      org.omg.CORBA.portable.IDLEntity {
}
```

Implementations: _ServantActivatorStub

Passed To: ServantActivatorHelper.{insert(), write()}

Returned By: ServantActivatorHelper.{extract(), narrow(), read()}, ServantActivatorPOA._this()

ServantActivatorHelper   Java 1.4

org.omg.PortableServer

The helper class for the ServantActivator object type, used to safely cast ServantActivator objects, read/write ServantActivator objects using I/O streams, etc.

```
public abstract class ServantActivatorHelper {
// Public Constructors
   public ServantActivatorHelper();
// Public Class Methods
   public static ServantActivator extract(org.omg.CORBA.Any a);
   public static String id();
   public static void insert(org.omg.CORBA.Any a, ServantActivator that);
   public static ServantActivator narrow(org.omg.CORBA.Object obj);
   public static ServantActivator read(org.omg.CORBA.portable.InputStream istream);
   public static org.omg.CORBA.TypeCode type();                              synchronized
   public static void write(org.omg.CORBA.portable.OutputStream ostream, ServantActivator value);
}
```

ServantActivatorOperations   Java 1.4

org.omg.PortableServer

This is the Operations interface mapped from the IDL for the ServantActivator interface, and contains the methods inherited by ServantActivator.

```
public interface ServantActivatorOperations extends ServantManagerOperations {
// Public Instance Methods
   public abstract void etherealize(byte[ ] oid, POA adapter, Servant serv, boolean cleanup_in_progress,
                          boolean remaining_activations);
   public abstract Servant incarnate(byte[ ] oid, POA adapter) throws org.omg.PortableServer.ForwardRequest;
}
```

Implementations: ServantActivator, ServantActivatorPOA

ServantActivatorPOA   Java 1.4

org.omg.PortableServer

The servant base class generated from the IDL ServantActivator interface. A CORBA vendor's implementation of ServantActivator must subclass this POA class.

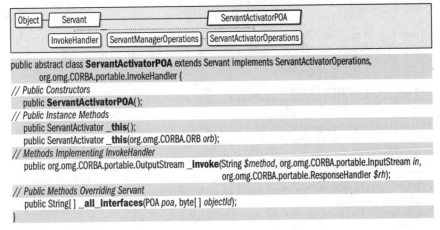

```
public abstract class ServantActivatorPOA extends Servant implements ServantActivatorOperations,
        org.omg.CORBA.portable.InvokeHandler {
// Public Constructors
    public ServantActivatorPOA();
// Public Instance Methods
    public ServantActivator _this();
    public ServantActivator _this(org.omg.CORBA.ORB orb);
// Methods Implementing InvokeHandler
    public org.omg.CORBA.portable.OutputStream _invoke(String $method, org.omg.CORBA.portable.InputStream in,
                                              org.omg.CORBA.portable.ResponseHandler $rh);
// Public Methods Overriding Servant
    public String[ ] _all_interfaces(POA poa, byte[ ] objectId);
}
```

ServantLocator

Java 1.4

org.omg.PortableServer *serializable*

A ServantLocator is a type of ServantManager used by POAs to locate a requested object, if
the POA has its NON_RETAIN policy set (in the form of a ServantRetentionPolicy object with a
value of ServantRetentionPolicyValue.NON_RETAIN).

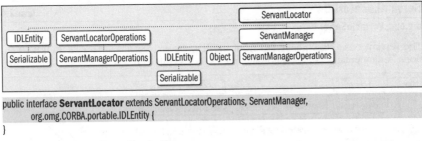

```
public interface ServantLocator extends ServantLocatorOperations, ServantManager,
        org.omg.CORBA.portable.IDLEntity {
}
```

Implementations: _ServantLocatorStub

Passed To: ServantLocatorHelper.{insert(), write()}

Returned By: ServantLocatorHelper.{extract(), narrow(), read()}, ServantLocatorPOA._this()

ServantLocatorHelper

Java 1.4

org.omg.PortableServer

The helper class for the ServantLocator object type, used to safely cast ServantLocator
objects, read/write ServantLocator objects using I/O streams, etc.

```
public abstract class ServantLocatorHelper {
// Public Constructors
    public ServantLocatorHelper();
// Public Class Methods
    public static ServantLocator extract(org.omg.CORBA.Any a);
    public static String id();
    public static void insert(org.omg.CORBA.Any a, ServantLocator that);
    public static ServantLocator narrow(org.omg.CORBA.Object obj);
    public static ServantLocator read(org.omg.CORBA.portable.InputStream istream);
```

```
    public static org.omg.CORBA.TypeCode type();                                    synchronized
    public static void write(org.omg.CORBA.portable.OutputStream ostream, ServantLocator value);
}
```

ServantLocatorOperations   Java 1.4

org.omg.PortableServer

This is the Operations interface mapped from the IDL for the ServantLocator interface, and
contains the methods inherited by ServantLocator.

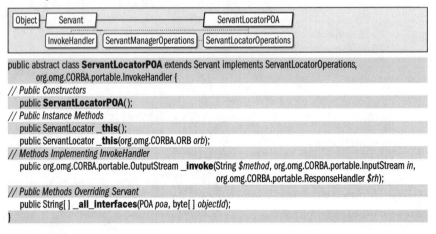

```
public interface ServantLocatorOperations extends ServantManagerOperations {
// Public Instance Methods
    public abstract void postinvoke(byte[ ] oid, POA adapter, String operation, Object the_cookie,
                            Servant the_servant);
    public abstract Servant preinvoke(byte[ ] oid, POA adapter, String operation,
                            org.omg.PortableServer.ServantLocatorPackage.CookieHolder the_cookie)
        throws org.omg.PortableServer.ForwardRequest;
}
```

Implementations: ServantLocator, ServantLocatorPOA

ServantLocatorPOA   Java 1.4

org.omg.PortableServer

The servant base class generated from the IDL ServantLocator interface. A CORBA vendor's implementation of ServantLocator must subclass this POA class.

```
public abstract class ServantLocatorPOA extends Servant implements ServantLocatorOperations,
        org.omg.CORBA.portable.InvokeHandler {
// Public Constructors
    public ServantLocatorPOA();
// Public Instance Methods
    public ServantLocator _this();
    public ServantLocator _this(org.omg.CORBA.ORB orb);
// Methods Implementing InvokeHandler
    public org.omg.CORBA.portable.OutputStream _invoke(String $method, org.omg.CORBA.portable.InputStream in,
                            org.omg.CORBA.portable.ResponseHandler $rh);
// Public Methods Overriding Servant
    public String[ ] _all_interfaces(POA poa, byte[ ] objectId);
}
```

ServantManager   Java 1.4

org.omg.PortableServer   *serializable*

A ServantManager is used by a POA to activate objects when a request is received for an
inactive object.

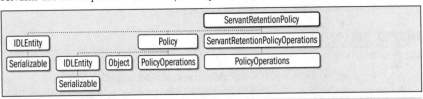

```
public interface ServantManager extends ServantManagerOperations, org.omg.CORBA.Object,
        org.omg.CORBA.portable.IDLEntity {
}
```

Implementations: ServantActivator, ServantLocator

Passed To: POAOperations.set_servant_manager()

Returned By: POAOperations.get_servant_manager()

ServantManagerOperations

org.omg.PortableServer

This is the Operations interface mapped from the IDL for the ServantManager interface.

```
public interface ServantManagerOperations {
}
```

Implementations: ServantActivatorOperations, ServantLocatorOperations, ServantManager

ServantRetentionPolicy
Java 1.4

org.omg.PortableServer   *serializable*

A Policy that indicates whether the POA keeps active servants in an active object map. A value of ServantRetentionPolicyValue.RETAIN indicates that active servants are kept in an active object map. A value of ServantRetentionPolicyValue.NON_RETAIN indicates that active servants are not kept in an active object map. The default value is RETAIN.

```
public interface ServantRetentionPolicy extends ServantRetentionPolicyOperations, org.omg.CORBA.Policy,
        org.omg.CORBA.portable.IDLEntity {
}
```

Returned By: POAOperations.create_servant_retention_policy()

ServantRetentionPolicyOperations
Java 1.4

org.omg.PortableServer

This is the Operations interface mapped from the IDL for the ServantRetentionPolicy interface, and contains the methods inherited by ServantRetentionPolicy.

```
public interface ServantRetentionPolicyOperations extends org.omg.CORBA.PolicyOperations {
// Public Instance Methods
    public abstract ServantRetentionPolicyValue value();
}
```

Implementations: ServantRetentionPolicy

ServantRetentionPolicyValue

Java 1.4

org.omg.PortableServer *serializable*

This class represents the value of an ServantRetentionPolicy for a POA. A value of ServantRetentionPolicyValue.RETAIN indicates that active servants are kept in an active object map. A value of ServantRetentionPolicyValue.NON_RETAIN indicates that active servants are not kept in an active object map. The default value is RETAIN.

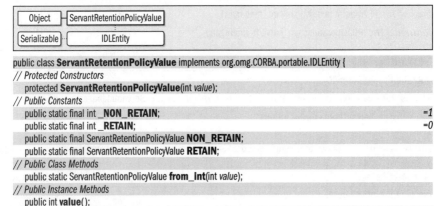

```
public class ServantRetentionPolicyValue implements org.omg.CORBA.portable.IDLEntity {
// Protected Constructors
    protected ServantRetentionPolicyValue(int value);
// Public Constants
    public static final int _NON_RETAIN;                                                =1
    public static final int _RETAIN;                                                    =0
    public static final ServantRetentionPolicyValue NON_RETAIN;
    public static final ServantRetentionPolicyValue RETAIN;
// Public Class Methods
    public static ServantRetentionPolicyValue from_int(int value);
// Public Instance Methods
    public int value();
}
```

Passed To: POAOperations.create_servant_retention_policy()

Returned By: ServantRetentionPolicyOperations.value(), ServantRetentionPolicyValue.from_int()

Type Of: ServantRetentionPolicyValue.{NON_RETAIN, RETAIN}

THREAD_POLICY_ID

Java 1.4

org.omg.PortableServer

An interface mapped from the IDL PolicyType constant THREAD_POLICY_ID. The contained value represents the type of ThreadPolicy objects, obtained by calling their policy_type() method. This can be used to distinguish various Policy objects obtained in collections or arrays.

```
public interface THREAD_POLICY_ID {
// Public Constants
    public static final int value;                                                     =16
}
```


ThreadPolicy

Java 1.4

org.omg.PortableServer *serializable*

A Policy that indicates the threading policy used by the POA. A value of ThreadPolicyValue.ORB_CTRL_MODEL indicates that the ORB allocates POA requests to threads. A value of ThreadPolicyValue.SINGLE_THREAD_MODEL indicates that all requests for the POA are serialized within a single thread. The default value is ORB_CTRL_MODEL.

```
public interface ThreadPolicy extends ThreadPolicyOperations, org.omg.CORBA.Policy,
        org.omg.CORBA.portable.IDLEntity {
}
```

Returned By: POAOperations.create_thread_policy()

ThreadPolicyOperations
Java 1.4

org.omg.PortableServer

This is the Operations interface mapped from the IDL for the ThreadPolicy interface, and contains the methods inherited by ThreadPolicy.

```
public interface ThreadPolicyOperations extends org.omg.CORBA.PolicyOperations {
// Public Instance Methods
    public abstract ThreadPolicyValue value();
}
```

Implementations: ThreadPolicy

ThreadPolicyValue
Java 1.4

org.omg.PortableServer   *serializable*

This class represents the value of an ThreadPolicy for a POA. A value of ThreadPolicy-Value.ORB_CTRL_MODEL indicates that the ORB allocates POA requests to threads. A value of ThreadPolicyValue.SINGLE_THREAD_MODEL indicates that all requests for the POA are serialized within a single thread. The default value is ORB_CTRL_MODEL.

```
public class ThreadPolicyValue implements org.omg.CORBA.portable.IDLEntity {
// Protected Constructors
    protected ThreadPolicyValue(int value);
// Public Constants
    public static final int _ORB_CTRL_MODEL;                                =0
    public static final int _SINGLE_THREAD_MODEL;                           =1
    public static final ThreadPolicyValue ORB_CTRL_MODEL;
    public static final ThreadPolicyValue SINGLE_THREAD_MODEL;
// Public Class Methods
    public static ThreadPolicyValue from_int(int value);
// Public Instance Methods
    public int value();
}
```

Passed To: POAOperations.create_thread_policy()

Returned By: ThreadPolicyOperations.value(), ThreadPolicyValue.from_int()

Type Of: ThreadPolicyValue.{ORB_CTRL_MODEL, SINGLE_THREAD_MODEL}

Package org.omg.PortableServer.CurrentPackage   Java 1.4

This package contains classes that provide method implementations access to the object on which the method was invoked.

Classes:

public abstract class **NoContextHelper**;

Exceptions:

public final class **NoContext** extends org.omg.CORBA.UserException;

NoContext   Java 1.4

org.omg.PortableServer.CurrentPackage   *serializable checked*

This exception is thrown when a POA-related operation is called in a context with no POA.

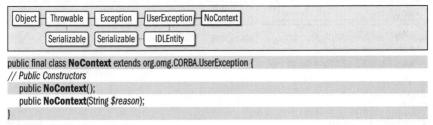

```
public final class NoContext extends org.omg.CORBA.UserException {
// Public Constructors
    public NoContext();
    public NoContext(String $reason);
}
```

Passed To: NoContextHelper.{insert(), write()}

Returned By: NoContextHelper.{extract(), read()}

Thrown By: org.omg.PortableServer.CurrentOperations.{get_object_id(), get_POA()}

NoContextHelper   Java 1.4

org.omg.PortableServer.CurrentPackage

The helper class for the NoContext object type, used to read/write NoContext objects using I/O streams, etc.

```
public abstract class NoContextHelper {
// Public Constructors
    public NoContextHelper();
// Public Class Methods
    public static NoContext extract(org.omg.CORBA.Any a);
    public static String id();
    public static void insert(org.omg.CORBA.Any a, NoContext that);
    public static NoContext read(org.omg.CORBA.portable.InputStream istream);
    public static org.omg.CORBA.TypeCode type();                              synchronized
    public static void write(org.omg.CORBA.portable.OutputStream ostream, NoContext value);
}
```

Package org.omg.PortableServer.POAManagerPackage   Java 1.4

This package contains two classes and one exception that are used to encapsulate the processing state of a POA.

Classes:

public abstract class **AdapterInactiveHelper**;
public class **State** implements org.omg.CORBA.portable.IDLEntity;

Exceptions:

public final class **AdapterInactive** extends org.omg.CORBA.UserException;

AdapterInactive

org.omg.PortableServer.POAManagerPackage   *serializable checked*

This exception is thrown if a request is made of an inactive POAManager.

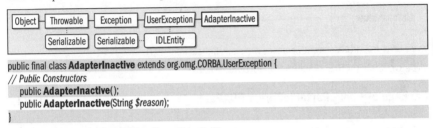

```
public final class AdapterInactive extends org.omg.CORBA.UserException {
// Public Constructors
    public AdapterInactive();
    public AdapterInactive(String $reason);
}
```

Passed To: AdapterInactiveHelper.{insert(), write()}

Returned By: AdapterInactiveHelper.{extract(), read()}

Thrown By: POAManagerOperations.{activate(), deactivate(), discard_requests(), hold_requests()}

AdapterInactiveHelper

org.omg.PortableServer.POAManagerPackage

The helper class for the AdapterInactive object type, used to read/write AdapterInactive objects using I/O streams, etc.

```
public abstract class AdapterInactiveHelper {
// Public Constructors
    public AdapterInactiveHelper();
// Public Class Methods
    public static AdapterInactive extract(org.omg.CORBA.Any a);
    public static String id();
    public static void insert(org.omg.CORBA.Any a, AdapterInactive that);
    public static AdapterInactive read(org.omg.CORBA.portable.InputStream istream);
    public static org.omg.CORBA.TypeCode type();                              synchronized
    public static void write(org.omg.CORBA.portable.OutputStream ostream, AdapterInactive value);
}
```

State

org.omg.PortableServer.POAManagerPackage   *serializable*

This class represents the current state of a POAManager.

```
public class State implements org.omg.CORBA.portable.IDLEntity {
// Protected Constructors
    protected State(int value);
```

```
// Public Constants
    public static final int _ACTIVE;                                          =1
    public static final int _DISCARDING;                                      =2
    public static final int _HOLDING;                                         =0
    public static final int _INACTIVE;                                        =3
    public static final State ACTIVE;
    public static final State DISCARDING;
    public static final State HOLDING;
    public static final State INACTIVE;
// Public Class Methods
    public static State from_int(int value);
// Public Instance Methods
    public int value();
}
```

Returned By: POAManagerOperations.get_state(), State.from_int()

Type Of: State.{ACTIVE, DISCARDING, HOLDING, INACTIVE}

Package org.omg.PortableServer.POAPackage   Java 1.4

This package contains classes and exceptions used to create portable object implementations between ORBs.

Classes:

public abstract class **AdapterAlreadyExistsHelper**;
public abstract class **AdapterNonExistentHelper**;
public abstract class **InvalidPolicyHelper**;
public abstract class **NoServantHelper**;
public abstract class **ObjectAlreadyActiveHelper**;
public abstract class **ObjectNotActiveHelper**;
public abstract class **ServantAlreadyActiveHelper**;
public abstract class **ServantNotActiveHelper**;
public abstract class **WrongAdapterHelper**;
public abstract class **WrongPolicyHelper**;

Exceptions:

public final class **AdapterAlreadyExists** extends org.omg.CORBA.UserException;
public final class **AdapterNonExistent** extends org.omg.CORBA.UserException;
public final class **InvalidPolicy** extends org.omg.CORBA.UserException;
public final class **NoServant** extends org.omg.CORBA.UserException;
public final class **ObjectAlreadyActive** extends org.omg.CORBA.UserException;
public final class **ObjectNotActive** extends org.omg.CORBA.UserException;
public final class **ServantAlreadyActive** extends org.omg.CORBA.UserException;
public final class **ServantNotActive** extends org.omg.CORBA.UserException;
public final class **WrongAdapter** extends org.omg.CORBA.UserException;
public final class **WrongPolicy** extends org.omg.CORBA.UserException;

AdapterAlreadyExists   Java 1.4
org.omg.PortableServer.POAPackage   *serializable checked*

This exception is thrown when an attempt is made to create a POA with the same name as an existing POA.

```
Object ─ Throwable ─ Exception ─ UserException ─ AdapterAlreadyExists
         Serializable   Serializable ┈  IDLEntity
```

```
public final class AdapterAlreadyExists extends org.omg.CORBA.UserException {
// Public Constructors
    public AdapterAlreadyExists();
    public AdapterAlreadyExists(String $reason);
}
```

Passed To: AdapterAlreadyExistsHelper.{insert(), write()}

Returned By: AdapterAlreadyExistsHelper.{extract(), read()}

Thrown By: POAOperations.create_POA()

AdapterAlreadyExistsHelper   Java 1.4

org.omg.PortableServer.POAPackage

The helper class for the AdapterAlreadyExists object type, used to read/write AdapterAlreadyExists objects using I/O streams, etc.

```
public abstract class AdapterAlreadyExistsHelper {
// Public Constructors
    public AdapterAlreadyExistsHelper();
// Public Class Methods
    public static AdapterAlreadyExists extract(org.omg.CORBA.Any a);
    public static String id();
    public static void insert(org.omg.CORBA.Any a, AdapterAlreadyExists that);
    public static AdapterAlreadyExists read(org.omg.CORBA.portable.InputStream istream);
    public static org.omg.CORBA.TypeCode type();                                     synchronized
    public static void write(org.omg.CORBA.portable.OutputStream ostream, AdapterAlreadyExists value);
}
```

AdapterNonExistent   Java 1.4

org.omg.PortableServer.POAPackage   *serializable checked*

This exception is thrown on a POA lookup request when a POA of the given name does not exist.

```
Object ─ Throwable ─ Exception ─ UserException ─ AdapterNonExistent
         Serializable   Serializable ┈  IDLEntity
```

```
public final class AdapterNonExistent extends org.omg.CORBA.UserException {
// Public Constructors
    public AdapterNonExistent();
    public AdapterNonExistent(String $reason);
}
```

Passed To: AdapterNonExistentHelper.{insert(), write()}

Returned By: AdapterNonExistentHelper.{extract(), read()}

Thrown By: POAOperations.find_POA()

AdapterNonExistentHelper   Java 1.4

org.omg.PortableServer.POAPackage

The helper class for the AdapterNonExistent object type, used to read/write AdapterNonExistent objects using I/O streams, etc.

```
public abstract class AdapterNonExistentHelper {
// Public Constructors
    public AdapterNonExistentHelper();
// Public Class Methods
    public static AdapterNonExistent extract(org.omg.CORBA.Any a);
    public static String id();
    public static void insert(org.omg.CORBA.Any a, AdapterNonExistent that);
    public static AdapterNonExistent read(org.omg.CORBA.portable.InputStream istream);
    public static org.omg.CORBA.TypeCode type();                                        synchronized
    public static void write(org.omg.CORBA.portable.OutputStream ostream, AdapterNonExistent value);
}
```

InvalidPolicy   Java 1.4

org.omg.PortableServer.POAPackage   *serializable checked*

This exception is thrown when an attempt is made to create a POA with an invalid set of
Policy objects.

```
Object ─ Throwable ─ Exception ─ UserException ─ InvalidPolicy
          Serializable   Serializable       IDLEntity
```

```
public final class InvalidPolicy extends org.omg.CORBA.UserException {
// Public Constructors
    public InvalidPolicy();
    public InvalidPolicy(short _index);
    public InvalidPolicy(String $reason, short _index);
// Public Instance Fields
    public short index;
}
```

Passed To: InvalidPolicyHelper.{insert(), write()}

Returned By: InvalidPolicyHelper.{extract(), read()}

Thrown By: POAOperations.create_POA()

InvalidPolicyHelper   Java 1.4

org.omg.PortableServer.POAPackage

The helper class for the InvalidPolicy object type, used to read/write InvalidPolicy objects
using I/O streams, etc.

```
public abstract class InvalidPolicyHelper {
// Public Constructors
    public InvalidPolicyHelper();
// Public Class Methods
    public static InvalidPolicy extract(org.omg.CORBA.Any a);
    public static String id();
    public static void insert(org.omg.CORBA.Any a, InvalidPolicy that);
    public static InvalidPolicy read(org.omg.CORBA.portable.InputStream istream);
    public static org.omg.CORBA.TypeCode type();                                        synchronized
    public static void write(org.omg.CORBA.portable.OutputStream ostream, InvalidPolicy value);
}
```

NoServant

org.omg.PortableServer.POAPackage

This exception is thrown when a POA with no servant is asked for its servant.

```
Object ── Throwable ── Exception ── UserException ── NoServant
          Serializable   Serializable      IDLEntity
```

```
public final class NoServant extends org.omg.CORBA.UserException {
// Public Constructors
    public NoServant();
    public NoServant(String $reason);
}
```

Passed To: NoServantHelper.{insert(), write()}

Returned By: NoServantHelper.{extract(), read()}

Thrown By: POAOperations.get_servant()

NoServantHelper

org.omg.PortableServer.POAPackage

The helper class for the NoServant object type, used to read/write NoServant objects using I/O streams, etc.

```
public abstract class NoServantHelper {
// Public Constructors
    public NoServantHelper();
// Public Class Methods
    public static NoServant extract(org.omg.CORBA.Any a);
    public static String id();
    public static void insert(org.omg.CORBA.Any a, NoServant that);
    public static NoServant read(org.omg.CORBA.portable.InputStream istream);
    public static org.omg.CORBA.TypeCode type();                              synchronized
    public static void write(org.omg.CORBA.portable.OutputStream ostream, NoServant value);
}
```

ObjectAlreadyActive

org.omg.PortableServer.POAPackage

This exception is thrown when an attempt is made to activate an object that is already active.

```
Object ── Throwable ── Exception ── UserException ── ObjectAlreadyActive
          Serializable   Serializable      IDLEntity
```

```
public final class ObjectAlreadyActive extends org.omg.CORBA.UserException {
// Public Constructors
    public ObjectAlreadyActive();
    public ObjectAlreadyActive(String $reason);
}
```

Passed To: ObjectAlreadyActiveHelper.{insert(), write()}

Returned By: ObjectAlreadyActiveHelper.{extract(), read()}

Thrown By: POAOperations.activate_object_with_id()

ObjectAlreadyActiveHelper

Java 1.4

org.omg.PortableServer.POAPackage

The helper class for the ObjectAlreadyActive object type, used to read/write ObjectAlreadyActive objects using I/O streams, etc.

```
public abstract class ObjectAlreadyActiveHelper {
// Public Constructors
    public ObjectAlreadyActiveHelper();
// Public Class Methods
    public static ObjectAlreadyActive extract(org.omg.CORBA.Any a);
    public static String id();
    public static void insert(org.omg.CORBA.Any a, ObjectAlreadyActive that);
    public static ObjectAlreadyActive read(org.omg.CORBA.portable.InputStream istream);
    public static org.omg.CORBA.TypeCode type();                            synchronized
    public static void write(org.omg.CORBA.portable.OutputStream ostream, ObjectAlreadyActive value);
}
```

ObjectNotActive

Java 1.4

org.omg.PortableServer.POAPackage

serializable checked

This exception is thrown when an attempt is made to deactivate an object that is not active.

```
┌────────┐  ┌───────────┐  ┌───────────┐  ┌───────────────┐  ┌────────────────┐
│ Object ├──┤ Throwable ├──┤ Exception ├──┤ UserException  ├──┤ ObjectNotActive │
└────────┘  └───────────┘  └───────────┘  └───────────────┘  └────────────────┘
            ┌──────────────┐ ┌──────────────┐  ┌───────────┐
            │ Serializable │ │ Serializable │  │ IDLEntity │
            └──────────────┘ └──────────────┘  └───────────┘
```

```
public final class ObjectNotActive extends org.omg.CORBA.UserException {
// Public Constructors
    public ObjectNotActive();
    public ObjectNotActive(String $reason);
}
```

Passed To: ObjectNotActiveHelper.{insert(), write()}

Returned By: ObjectNotActiveHelper.{extract(), read()}

Thrown By: POAOperations.{deactivate_object(), id_to_reference(), id_to_servant(), reference_to_servant()}

ObjectNotActiveHelper

Java 1.4

org.omg.PortableServer.POAPackage

The helper class for the ObjectNotActive object type, used to read/write ObjectNotActive objects using I/O streams, etc.

```
public abstract class ObjectNotActiveHelper {
// Public Constructors
    public ObjectNotActiveHelper();
// Public Class Methods
    public static ObjectNotActive extract(org.omg.CORBA.Any a);
    public static String id();
    public static void insert(org.omg.CORBA.Any a, ObjectNotActive that);
    public static ObjectNotActive read(org.omg.CORBA.portable.InputStream istream);
    public static org.omg.CORBA.TypeCode type();                            synchronized
    public static void write(org.omg.CORBA.portable.OutputStream ostream, ObjectNotActive value);
}
```

ServantAlreadyActive

org.omg.PortableServer.POAPackage   *serializable checked*

This exception is thrown when an attempt is made to activate an object whose servant is already in the active object map.

```
Object ─ Throwable ─ Exception ─ UserException ─ ServantAlreadyActive
           Serializable   Serializable    IDLEntity
```

```
public final class ServantAlreadyActive extends org.omg.CORBA.UserException {
// Public Constructors
    public ServantAlreadyActive();
    public ServantAlreadyActive(String $reason);
}
```

Passed To: ServantAlreadyActiveHelper.{insert(), write()}

Returned By: ServantAlreadyActiveHelper.{extract(), read()}

Thrown By: POAOperations.{activate_object(), activate_object_with_id()}

ServantAlreadyActiveHelper

org.omg.PortableServer.POAPackage

The helper class for the ServantAlreadyActive object type, used to read/write ServantAlready-Active objects using I/O streams, etc.

```
public abstract class ServantAlreadyActiveHelper {
// Public Constructors
    public ServantAlreadyActiveHelper();
// Public Class Methods
    public static ServantAlreadyActive extract(org.omg.CORBA.Any a);
    public static String id();
    public static void insert(org.omg.CORBA.Any a, ServantAlreadyActive that);
    public static ServantAlreadyActive read(org.omg.CORBA.portable.InputStream istream);
    public static org.omg.CORBA.TypeCode type();                                    synchronized
    public static void write(org.omg.CORBA.portable.OutputStream ostream, ServantAlreadyActive value);
}
```

ServantNotActive

org.omg.PortableServer.POAPackage   *serializable checked*

This exception is thrown when an attempt is made to get a reference or id for a servant that is not active.

```
Object ─ Throwable ─ Exception ─ UserException ─ ServantNotActive
           Serializable   Serializable    IDLEntity
```

```
public final class ServantNotActive extends org.omg.CORBA.UserException {
// Public Constructors
    public ServantNotActive();
    public ServantNotActive(String $reason);
}
```

Passed To: ServantNotActiveHelper.{insert(), write()}

Returned By: ServantNotActiveHelper.{extract(), read()}

Thrown By: POAOperations.{servant_to_id(), servant_to_reference()}

ServantNotActiveHelper   Java 1.4

org.omg.PortableServer.POAPackage

The helper class for the ServantNotActive object type, used to read/write ServantNotActive objects using I/O streams, etc.

```
public abstract class ServantNotActiveHelper {
// Public Constructors
   public ServantNotActiveHelper();
// Public Class Methods
   public static ServantNotActive extract(org.omg.CORBA.Any a);
   public static String id();
   public static void insert(org.omg.CORBA.Any a, ServantNotActive that);
   public static ServantNotActive read(org.omg.CORBA.portable.InputStream istream);
   public static org.omg.CORBA.TypeCode type();                                synchronized
   public static void write(org.omg.CORBA.portable.OutputStream ostream, ServantNotActive value);
}
```

WrongAdapter   Java 1.4

org.omg.PortableServer.POAPackage   *serializable checked*

This exception is raised if an operation is called on a POA referencing an object that is managed by a different POA.

```
Object ─ Throwable ─ Exception ─ UserException ─ WrongAdapter
         Serializable  Serializable    IDLEntity
```

```
public final class WrongAdapter extends org.omg.CORBA.UserException {
// Public Constructors
   public WrongAdapter();
   public WrongAdapter(String $reason);
}
```

Passed To: WrongAdapterHelper.{insert(), write()}

Returned By: WrongAdapterHelper.{extract(), read()}

Thrown By: POAOperations.{reference_to_id(), reference_to_servant()}

WrongAdapterHelper   Java 1.4

org.omg.PortableServer.POAPackage

The helper class for the WrongAdapter object type, used to read/write WrongAdapter objects using I/O streams, etc.

```
public abstract class WrongAdapterHelper {
// Public Constructors
   public WrongAdapterHelper();
// Public Class Methods
   public static WrongAdapter extract(org.omg.CORBA.Any a);
   public static String id();
   public static void insert(org.omg.CORBA.Any a, WrongAdapter that);
   public static WrongAdapter read(org.omg.CORBA.portable.InputStream istream);
   public static org.omg.CORBA.TypeCode type();                                synchronized
```

```
    public static void write(org.omg.CORBA.portable.OutputStream ostream, WrongAdapter value);
}
```

WrongPolicy

org.omg.PortableServer.POAPackage   *serializable checked*

This exception is thrown when a POA operation is called and the POA Policy set is not compatible with the request.

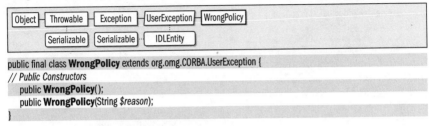

```
public final class WrongPolicy extends org.omg.CORBA.UserException {
// Public Constructors
    public WrongPolicy();
    public WrongPolicy(String $reason);
}
```

Passed To: WrongPolicyHelper.{insert(), write()}

Returned By: WrongPolicyHelper.{extract(), read()}

Thrown By: POAOperations.{activate_object(), activate_object_with_id(), create_reference(), deactivate_object(), get_servant(), get_servant_manager(), id_to_reference(), id_to_servant(), reference_to_id(), reference_to_servant(), servant_to_id(), servant_to_reference(), set_servant(), set_servant_manager()}

WrongPolicyHelper

org.omg.PortableServer.POAPackage

The helper class for the WrongPolicy object type, used to read/write WrongPolicy objects using I/O streams, etc.

```
public abstract class WrongPolicyHelper {
// Public Constructors
    public WrongPolicyHelper();
// Public Class Methods
    public static WrongPolicy extract(org.omg.CORBA.Any a);
    public static String id();
    public static void insert(org.omg.CORBA.Any a, WrongPolicy that);
    public static WrongPolicy read(org.omg.CORBA.portable.InputStream istream);
    public static org.omg.CORBA.TypeCode type();                              synchronized
    public static void write(org.omg.CORBA.portable.OutputStream ostream, WrongPolicy value);
}
```

Package org.omg.PortableServer.ServantLocatorPackage

This package contains classes and interfaces for finding the servant.

Classes:

```
public final class CookieHolder implements org.omg.CORBA.portable.Streamable;
```

CookieHolder

org.omg.PortableServer.ServantLocatorPackage

A holder class generated for the IDL PortableServer::ServantLocator::Cookie type.

Object — CookieHolder — Streamable

```
public final class CookieHolder implements org.omg.CORBA.portable.Streamable {
// Public Constructors
    public CookieHolder();
    public CookieHolder(Object initial);
// Methods Implementing Streamable
    public void _read(org.omg.CORBA.portable.InputStream is);
    public org.omg.CORBA.TypeCode _type();
    public void _write(org.omg.CORBA.portable.OutputStream os);
// Public Instance Fields
    public Object value;
}
```

Passed To: _ServantLocatorStub.preinvoke(), ServantLocatorOperations.preinvoke()

Package org.omg.PortableServer.portable

This package contains classes and interfaces that are used by an ORB implementor. It contains only one interface, Delegate, which exposes the APIs used to connect stubs and skeletons to the ORBs.

Interfaces:

public interface **Delegate**;

Delegate

org.omg.PortableServer.portable

A POA-compliant delegate for a server-side object implementation.

```
public interface Delegate {
// Public Instance Methods
    public abstract POA default_POA(Servant Self);
    public abstract org.omg.CORBA.Object get_interface_def(Servant self);
    public abstract boolean is_a(Servant Self, String Repository_Id);
    public abstract boolean non_existent(Servant Self);
    public abstract byte[ ] object_id(Servant Self);
    public abstract org.omg.CORBA.ORB orb(Servant Self);
    public abstract POA poa(Servant Self);
    public abstract org.omg.CORBA.Object this_object(Servant Self);
}
```

Passed To: Servant._set_delegate()

Returned By: Servant._get_delegate()

CHAPTER 45

Class, Method, and Field Index

The following index allows you to look up a class or interface and find what package it is defined in. It also allows you to look up a method or field and find what class it is defined in. Use it when you want to look up a class but don't know its package, or when you want to look up a method but don't know its class.

_ids(): _BindingIteratorImplBase, _BindingIteratorStub, _IDLTypeStub, _NamingContextExtStub, _NamingContextImplBase, _NamingContextStub, _PolicyStub, _ServantActivatorStub, _ServantLocatorStub, DynamicImplementation, ObjectImpl

_IMPLICIT_ACTIVATION: ImplicitActivationPolicyValue

_INACTIVE: State

_invoke(): BindingIteratorPOA, InvokeHandler, LocalObject, NamingContextExtPOA, NamingContextPOA, ObjectImpl, ServantActivatorPOA, ServantLocatorPOA

_is_a(): LocalObject, Object, ObjectImpl, Servant

_is_equivalent(): LocalObject, Object, ObjectImpl

_is_local(): LocalObject, ObjectImpl

_jspService(): HttpJspPage

_missing_node: NotFoundReason

_MULTIPLE_ID: IdUniquenessPolicyValue

_NamingContextExtStub: org.omg.CosNaming

_NamingContextImplBase: org.omg.CosNaming

_NamingContextStub: org.omg.CosNaming

_ncontext: BindingType

_NO_IMPLICIT_ACTIVATION: ImplicitActivationPolicyValue

_nobject: BindingType

_non_existent(): LocalObject, Object, ObjectImpl, Servant

_NON_RETAIN: ServantRetentionPolicyValue

_not_context: NotFoundReason

_not_object: NotFoundReason

_object_id(): Servant

_opsClass: _ServantActivatorStub, _ServantLocatorStub

_orb(): LocalObject, ObjectImpl, Servant

_ORB_CTRL_MODEL: ThreadPolicyValue

_PARAM_IN: ParameterMode

_PARAM_INOUT: ParameterMode

_PARAM_OUT: ParameterMode

_PERSISTENT: LifespanPolicyValue

_poa(): Servant

_PolicyStub: org.omg.CORBA

_read(): AlreadyBoundHolder, AnyHolder, AnySeqHolder, BindingHolder, BindingIteratorHolder, BindingListHolder, BindingTypeHolder, BooleanHolder, BooleanSeqHolder, ByteHolder, CannotProceedHolder, CharHolder, CharSeqHolder, CookieHolder, CurrentHolder, DoubleHolder, DoubleSeqHolder, FixedHolder, FloatHolder, FloatSeqHolder, IntHolder, InvalidAddressHolder, InvalidNameHolder, LongHolder, LongLongSeqHolder, LongSeqHolder, NameComponentHolder, NameHolder, NamingContextExtHolder, NamingContextHolder, NotEmptyHolder, NotFoundHolder, NotFoundReasonHolder, ObjectHolder, OctetSeqHolder, ParameterModeHolder, PolicyErrorHolder, PolicyHolder, PolicyListHolder, PrincipalHolder, ServiceInformationHolder, ShortHolder,

ShortSeqHolder, Streamable, StringHolder, StringSeqHolder, TypeCodeHolder, ULongLongSeqHolder, ULongSeqHolder, UnknownUserExceptionHolder, UShortSeqHolder, ValueBaseHolder, WCharSeqHolder, WrongTransactionHolder, WStringSeqHolder

_release(): LocalObject, Object, ObjectImpl

_releaseReply(): LocalObject, ObjectImpl

_request(): LocalObject, Object, ObjectImpl

_RETAIN: ServantRetentionPolicyValue

_servant_postinvoke(): LocalObject, ObjectImpl

_servant_preinvoke(): LocalObject, ObjectImpl

_ServantActivatorStub: org.omg.PortableServer

_ServantLocatorStub: org.omg.PortableServer

_set_delegate(): ObjectImpl, Servant

_SET_OVERRIDE: SetOverrideType

_set_policy_override(): LocalObject, Object, ObjectImpl

_SINGLE_THREAD_MODEL: ThreadPolicyValue

_SYSTEM_ID: IdAssignmentPolicyValue

_this(): BindingIteratorPOA, NamingContextExtPOA, NamingContextPOA, ServantActivatorPOA, ServantLocatorPOA

_this_object(): Servant

_tk_abstract_interface: TCKind

_tk_alias: TCKind

_tk_any: TCKind

_tk_array: TCKind

_tk_boolean: TCKind

_tk_char: TCKind

_tk_double: TCKind

_tk_enum: TCKind

_tk_except: TCKind

_tk_fixed: TCKind

_tk_float: TCKind

_tk_long: TCKind

_tk_longdouble: TCKind

_tk_longlong: TCKind

_tk_native: TCKind

_tk_null: TCKind

_tk_objref: TCKind

_tk_octet: TCKind

_tk_Principal: TCKind

_tk_sequence: TCKind

_tk_short: TCKind

_tk_string: TCKind

_tk_struct: TCKind

_tk_TypeCode: TCKind

_tk_ulong: TCKind

_tk_ulonglong: TCKind

_tk_union: TCKind

_tk_ushort: TCKind

_tk_value: TCKind

_tk_value_box: TCKind

_tk_void: TCKind

_tk_wchar: TCKind

_tk_wstring: TCKind
_TRANSIENT: LifespanPolicyValue
_truncatable_ids(): ValueBase
_type(): AlreadyBoundHolder, AnyHolder, AnySeqHolder,
BindingHolder, BindingIteratorHolder, Bind-
ingListHolder, BindingTypeHolder, BooleanHolder,
BooleanSeqHolder, ByteHolder, CannotProceed-
Holder, CharHolder, CharSeqHolder, CookieHolder,
CurrentHolder, DoubleHolder, DoubleSeqHolder,
FixedHolder, FloatHolder, FloatSeqHolder, IntHolder,
InvalidAddressHolder, InvalidNameHolder,
LongHolder, LongLongSeqHolder, LongSeqHolder,
NameComponentHolder, NameHolder, NamingCon-
textExtHolder, NamingContextHolder, NotEmpty-
Holder, NotFoundHolder, NotFoundReasonHolder,
ObjectHolder, OctetSeqHolder, ParameterMode-
Holder, PolicyErrorHolder, PolicyHolder, Poli-
cyListHolder, PrincipalHolder,
ServiceInformationHolder, ShortHolder, ShortSe-
qHolder, Streamable, StringHolder, StringSeqHolder,
TypeCodeHolder, ULongLongSeqHolder, ULongSe-
qHolder, UnknownUserExceptionHolder, UShortSe-
qHolder, ValueBaseHolder, WCharSeqHolder,
WrongTransactionHolder, WStringSeqHolder
_UNIQUE_ID: IdUniquenessPolicyValue
_USE_ACTIVE_OBJECT_MAP_ONLY: RequestProcess-
ingPolicyValue
_USE_DEFAULT_SERVANT: RequestProcessingPolicy-
Value
_USE_SERVANT_MANAGER: RequestProcessingPolicy-
Value
_USER_ID: IdAssignmentPolicyValue
_write(): AlreadyBoundHolder, AnyHolder, AnySeqHolder,
BindingHolder, BindingIteratorHolder, Bind-
ingListHolder, BindingTypeHolder, BooleanHolder,
BooleanSeqHolder, ByteHolder, CannotProceed-
Holder, CharHolder, CharSeqHolder, CookieHolder,
CurrentHolder, DoubleHolder, DoubleSeqHolder,
FixedHolder, FloatHolder, FloatSeqHolder, IntHolder,
InvalidAddressHolder, InvalidNameHolder,
LongHolder, LongLongSeqHolder, LongSeqHolder,
NameComponentHolder, NameHolder, NamingCon-
textExtHolder, NamingContextHolder, NotEmpty-
Holder, NotFoundHolder, NotFoundReasonHolder,
ObjectHolder, OctetSeqHolder, ParameterMode-
Holder, PolicyErrorHolder, PolicyHolder, Poli-
cyListHolder, PrincipalHolder,
ServiceInformationHolder, ShortHolder, ShortSe-
qHolder, Streamable, StringHolder, StringSeqHolder,
TypeCodeHolder, ULongLongSeqHolder, ULongSe-
qHolder, UnknownUserExceptionHolder, UShortSe-
qHolder, ValueBaseHolder, WCharSeqHolder,
WrongTransactionHolder, WStringSeqHolder

A

absolute(): ResultSet
acceptsURL(): Driver
access: ValueMember
AccessException: java.rmi
AccessLocalException: javax.ejb
acknowledge(): Message
Activatable: java.rmi.activation
activate(): ActivationID, Activator, POAManagerOperations
activate_object(): POAOperations
activate_object_with_id(): POAOperations
ActivateFailedException: java.rmi.activation
ActivationDesc: java.rmi.activation
ActivationException: java.rmi.activation
ActivationGroup: java.rmi.activation
ActivationGroup_Stub: java.rmi.activation
ActivationGroupDesc: java.rmi.activation
ActivationGroupDesc.CommandEnvironment:
java.rmi.activation
ActivationGroupID: java.rmi.activation
ActivationID: java.rmi.activation
ActivationInstantiator: java.rmi.activation
ActivationMonitor: java.rmi.activation
ActivationSystem: java.rmi.activation
Activator: java.rmi.activation
ACTIVATOR_ID: ObjID
ACTIVE: State
activeGroup(): ActivationSystem
activeObject(): ActivationGroup, ActivationMonitor
AdapterActivator: org.omg.PortableServer
AdapterActivatorOperations: org.omg.PortableServer
AdapterAlreadyExists: org.omg.PortableServer.POAPack-
age
AdapterAlreadyExistsHelper: org.omg.Portable-
Server.POAPackage
AdapterInactive: org.omg.PortableServer.POAManager-
Package
AdapterInactiveHelper: org.omg.PortableServer.POAMan-
agerPackage
AdapterNonExistent: org.omg.PortableServer.POAPack-
age
AdapterNonExistentHelper: org.omg.PortableServer.POA-
Package
add(): Attribute, BasicAttribute, CompositeName, CompoundName, ContextList, ExceptionList, FetchProfile,
Flags, Name, NVList, Reference
ADD_ATTRIBUTE: DirContext
add_in_arg(): Request
add_inout_arg(): Request
add_item(): NVList
add_named_in_arg(): Request
add_named_inout_arg(): Request
add_named_out_arg(): Request
add_out_arg(): Request

ADD_OVERRIDE: SetOverrideType
add_value(): NVList
addAll(): CompositeName, CompoundName, Name
addBatch(): PreparedStatement, Statement
addBodyPart(): Multipart
addConnectionEventListener(): ManagedConnection,
  PooledConnection
addConnectionListener(): Folder, Service
addCookie(): HttpServletResponse, HttpServletResponseWrapper
addDateHeader(): HttpServletResponse, HttpServletResponseWrapper
ADDED: MessageCountEvent
addFolderListener(): Folder, Store
addFrom(): Message, MimeMessage
addHeader(): BodyPart, HttpServletResponse, HttpServletResponseWrapper, InternetHeaders, Message, MimeBodyPart, MimeMessage, Part
addHeaderLine(): InternetHeaders, MimeBodyPart, MimeMessage, MimePart
addIntHeader(): HttpServletResponse, HttpServletResponseWrapper
addMessageChangedListener(): Folder
addMessageCountListener(): Folder
addNamingListener(): EventContext, EventDirContext
addRecipient(): Message
addRecipients(): Message, MimeMessage
Address: javax.mail
address: AddressTerm, InternetAddress
AddressException: javax.mail.internet
AddressHelper: org.omg.CosNaming.NamingContextExtPackage
AddressStringTerm: javax.mail.search
AddressTerm: javax.mail.search
addRowSetListener(): RowSet
addrs: Reference
addrType: RefAddr
addStoreListener(): Store
addToEnvironment(): Context, InitialContext
addTransportListener(): Transport
after(): Timestamp
afterBegin(): SessionSynchronization
afterCompletion(): SessionSynchronization, Synchronization
afterLast(): ResultSet
ALERT: StoreEvent
ALL: MimeUtility
allocateConnection(): ConnectionManager
allProceduresAreCallable(): DatabaseMetaData
allTablesAreSelectable(): DatabaseMetaData
AlreadyBound: org.omg.CosNaming.NamingContextPackage
AlreadyBoundException: java.rmi
AlreadyBoundHelper:

org.omg.CosNaming.NamingContextPackage
AlreadyBoundHolder: org.omg.CosNaming.NamingContextPackage
altName: CannotProceedException
altNameCtx: CannotProceedException
AndTerm: javax.mail.search
ANSWERED: Flag
Any: org.omg.CORBA
AnyHolder: org.omg.CORBA
AnySeqHelper: org.omg.CORBA
AnySeqHolder: org.omg.CORBA
appendMessages(): Folder
appendRemainingComponent(): NamingException, ResolveResult
appendRemainingName(): NamingException, ResolveResult
APPLET: Context
APPLICATION: PageContext
APPLICATION_SCOPE: PageContext
ApplicationException: org.omg.CORBA.portable
ApplicationServerInternalException: javax.resource.spi
ARG_IN: org.omg.CORBA
ARG_INOUT: org.omg.CORBA
ARG_OUT: org.omg.CORBA
arguments(): Request, ServerRequest
Array: java.sql
ARRAY: Types
assign(): DynAny
associateConnection(): ManagedConnection
ATOM: Token
ATTACHMENT: Part
Attribute: javax.naming.directory
attributeAdded(): HttpSessionAttributeListener, ServletContextAttributeListener
AttributeInUseException: javax.naming.directory
AttributeModificationException: javax.naming.directory
attributeNoNulls: DatabaseMetaData
attributeNullable: DatabaseMetaData
attributeNullableUnknown: DatabaseMetaData
attributeRemoved(): HttpSessionAttributeListener, ServletContextAttributeListener
attributeReplaced(): HttpSessionAttributeListener, ServletContextAttributeListener
Attributes: javax.naming.directory
attrID: BasicAttribute
AuthenticationException: javax.naming
AuthenticationFailedException: javax.mail
AuthenticationNotSupportedException: javax.naming
Authenticator: javax.mail
AUTHORITATIVE: Context
AUTO_ACKNOWLEDGE: Session
autoFlush: JspWriter

B

BAD_CONTEXT: org.omg.CORBA
BAD_INV_ORDER: org.omg.CORBA
BAD_OPERATION: org.omg.CORBA
BAD_PARAM: org.omg.CORBA
BAD_POLICY: org.omg.CORBA
BAD_POLICY_TYPE: org.omg.CORBA
BAD_POLICY_VALUE: org.omg.CORBA
BAD_TYPECODE: org.omg.CORBA
BadKind: org.omg.CORBA.TypeCodePackage
BASIC_AUTH: HttpServletRequest
BasicAttribute: javax.naming.directory
BasicAttributes: javax.naming.directory
BATCHSIZE: Context
BatchUpdateException: java.sql
BCC: RecipientType
before(): Timestamp
beforeCompletion(): SessionSynchronization, Synchronization
beforeFirst(): ResultSet
begin(): LocalTransaction, TransactionManager, UserTransaction
bestRowNotPseudo: DatabaseMetaData
bestRowPseudo: DatabaseMetaData
bestRowSession: DatabaseMetaData
bestRowTemporary: DatabaseMetaData
bestRowTransaction: DatabaseMetaData
bestRowUnknown: DatabaseMetaData
BIGINT: Types
BINARY: Types
BinaryRefAddr: javax.naming
bind(): _NamingContextExtStub, _NamingContextStub, Context, DirContext, InitialContext, InitialDirContext, Naming, NamingContextOperations, Registry
bind_context(): _NamingContextExtStub, _NamingContextStub, NamingContextOperations
bind_new_context(): _NamingContextExtStub, _NamingContextStub, NamingContextOperations
Binding: javax.naming, org.omg.CosNaming
binding_name: Binding
binding_type: Binding
BindingHelper: org.omg.CosNaming
BindingHolder: org.omg.CosNaming
BindingIterator: org.omg.CosNaming
BindingIteratorHelper: org.omg.CosNaming
BindingIteratorHolder: org.omg.CosNaming
BindingIteratorOperations: org.omg.CosNaming
BindingIteratorPOA: org.omg.CosNaming
BindingListHelper: org.omg.CosNaming
BindingListHolder: org.omg.CosNaming
BindingType: org.omg.CosNaming
BindingTypeHelper: org.omg.CosNaming
BindingTypeHolder: org.omg.CosNaming
BIT: Types

BLOB: Types
Blob: java.sql
BodyPart: javax.mail
BodyTerm: javax.mail.search
BOOLEAN: Types
BooleanHolder: org.omg.CORBA
BooleanSeqHelper: org.omg.CORBA
BooleanSeqHolder: org.omg.CORBA
Bounds: org.omg.CORBA, org.omg.CORBA.TypeCodePackage
BoxedValueHelper: org.omg.CORBA.portable
BRIEF: LogStream
bufferSize: JspWriter
ByteHolder: org.omg.CORBA
BytesMessage: javax.jms

C

CallableStatement: java.sql
cancel(): Statement
cancelRowUpdates(): ResultSet
CannotProceed: org.omg.CosNaming.NamingContextPackage
CannotProceedException: javax.naming
CannotProceedHelper: org.omg.CosNaming.NamingContextPackage
CannotProceedHolder: org.omg.CosNaming.NamingContextPackage
CC: RecipientType
changeInfo: NamingEvent
CHAR: Types
CharHolder: org.omg.CORBA
CharSeqHelper: org.omg.CORBA
CharSeqHolder: org.omg.CORBA
choices: DriverPropertyInfo
ClassDesc: javax.rmi.CORBA
classFactory: Reference
classFactoryLocation: Reference
className: Reference
clean(): DGC
cleanup(): ManagedConnection
clear(): Attribute, BasicAttribute, Environment, JspWriter, Reference
clearBatch(): Statement
clearBody(): Message
clearBuffer(): JspWriter
clearParameters(): PreparedStatement, RowSet
clearProperties(): Message
clearWarnings(): Connection, Interaction, ResultSet, Statement
CLIENT_ACKNOWLEDGE: Session
CLIENT_CERT_AUTH: HttpServletRequest
CLOB: Types
Clob: java.sql

clone(): Attribute, Attributes, BasicAttribute, BasicAttributes, CompositeName, CompoundName, Cookie, Flags, InternetAddress, Name, Record, Reference, UnicastRemoteObject

close(): Connection, ConnectionConsumer, Context, Folder, InitialContext, Interaction, JspWriter, MessageConsumer, MessageProducer, NamingEnumeration, PooledConnection, QueueBrowser, QueueRequestor, ResultSet, Service, Session, StartTlsResponse, Statement, TopicRequestor

CLOSE_ALL_RESULTS: Statement

CLOSE_CURRENT_RESULT: Statement

CLOSE_CURSORS_AT_COMMIT: ResultSet

CLOSED: ConnectionEvent

closed(): ConnectionAdapter, ConnectionListener

columnNoNulls: DatabaseMetaData, ResultSetMetaData

columnNullable: DatabaseMetaData, ResultSetMetaData

columnNullableUnknown: DatabaseMetaData, ResultSetMetaData

COMM_FAILURE: org.omg.CORBA

CommandEnvironment: java.rmi.activation.ActivationGroupDesc

COMMENT: Token

CommException: javax.resource.spi

commit(): Connection, LocalTransaction, Session, Transaction, TransactionManager, UserTransaction, XAResource, XASession

CommunicationException: javax.naming

compareTo(): CompositeName, CompoundName, Name, Timestamp

comparison: ComparisonTerm

ComparisonTerm: javax.mail.search

completed: SystemException

COMPLETED_MAYBE: CompletionStatus

COMPLETED_NO: CompletionStatus

COMPLETED_YES: CompletionStatus

CompletionStatus: org.omg.CORBA

CompletionStatusHelper: org.omg.CORBA

composeName(): Context, InitialContext

CompositeName: javax.naming

CompoundName: javax.naming

concrete_base_type(): TypeCode

CONCUR_READ_ONLY: ResultSet

CONCUR_UPDATABLE: ResultSet

CONFIG: PageContext

ConfigurationException: javax.naming

connect(): Driver, ORB, PortableRemoteObject, PortableRemoteObjectDelegate, Service, Stub, StubDelegate

ConnectException: java.rmi

ConnectIOException: java.rmi

Connection: java.sql, javax.jms, javax.resource.cci

CONNECTION_CLOSED: ConnectionEvent

CONNECTION_ERROR_OCCURRED: ConnectionEvent

ConnectionAdapter: javax.mail.event

connectionClosed(): ConnectionEventListener

ConnectionConsumer: javax.jms

connectionErrorOccurred(): ConnectionEventListener

ConnectionEvent: javax.mail.event, javax.resource.spi, javax.sql

ConnectionEventListener: javax.resource.spi, javax.sql

ConnectionFactory: javax.jms, javax.resource.cci

ConnectionListener: javax.mail.event

ConnectionManager: javax.resource.spi

ConnectionMetaData: javax.jms, javax.resource.cci

ConnectionPoolDataSource: javax.sql

ConnectionRequestInfo: javax.resource.spi

ConnectionSpec: javax.resource.cci

contains(): Attribute, BasicAttribute, FetchProfile, Flags

containsHeader(): HttpServletResponse, HttpServletResponseWrapper

content: MimeBodyPart, MimeMessage

CONTENT_INFO: Item

content_type(): TypeCode

ContentDisposition: javax.mail.internet

contentStream: MimeBodyPart, MimeMessage

ContentType: javax.mail.internet

contentType: Multipart

Context: javax.naming, org.omg.CORBA

context_name(): Context

contextDestroyed(): ServletContextListener

contextInitialized(): ServletContextListener

ContextList: org.omg.CORBA

ContextNotEmptyException: javax.naming

contexts(): Request

Control: javax.naming.ldap

CONTROL_FACTORIES: LdapContext

ControlFactory: javax.naming.ldap

Cookie: javax.servlet.http

CookieHolder: org.omg.PortableServer.ServantLocatorPackage

copy(): _PolicyStub, DynAny, PolicyOperations

copyMessages(): Folder

copyObject(): Util, UtilDelegate

copyObjects(): Util, UtilDelegate

count(): ContextList, ExceptionList, NVList

CPE: NamingManager

create(): Folder

create_abstract_interface_tc(): ORB

create_alias_tc(): ORB

create_any(): ORB

create_array_tc(): ORB

create_basic_dyn_any(): ORB

create_child(): Context

create_context_list(): ORB

create_dyn_any(): ORB

create_dyn_array(): ORB

create_dyn_enum(): ORB

create_dyn_sequence(): ORB
create_dyn_struct(): ORB
create_dyn_union(): ORB
create_enum_tc(): ORB
create_environment(): ORB
create_exception_list(): ORB
create_exception_tc(): ORB
create_fixed_tc(): ORB
create_id_assignment_policy(): POAOperations
create_id_uniqueness_policy(): POAOperations
create_implicit_activation_policy(): POAOperations
create_input_stream(): Any, OutputStream
create_interface_tc(): ORB
create_lifespan_policy(): POAOperations
create_list(): ORB
create_named_value(): ORB
create_native_tc(): ORB
create_operation_list(): ORB
create_output_stream(): Any, ORB
create_POA(): POAOperations
create_policy(): ORB
create_recursive_sequence_tc(): ORB
create_recursive_tc(): ORB
create_reference(): POAOperations
create_reference_with_id(): POAOperations
create_request(): Delegate
create_request_processing_policy(): POAOperations
create_sequence_tc(): ORB
create_servant_retention_policy(): POAOperations
create_string_tc(): ORB
create_struct_tc(): ORB
create_thread_policy(): POAOperations
create_union_tc(): ORB
create_value_box_tc(): ORB
create_value_tc(): ORB
create_wstring_tc(): ORB
createBrowser(): QueueSession
createBytesMessage(): Session
createConnectionConsumer(): QueueConnection, Topic-
   Connection
createConnectionFactory(): ManagedConnectionFactory
CREATED: FolderEvent
createDurableConnectionConsumer(): TopicConnection
createDurableSubscriber(): TopicSession
CreateException: javax.ejb
createExceptionReply(): ResponseHandler
createExtendedResponse(): ExtendedRequest, StartTlsRequest
createGroup(): ActivationGroup
createIndexedRecord(): RecordFactory
createInitialContextFactory(): InitialContextFactory-
   Builder
createInteraction(): Connection
createInternetHeaders(): MimeMessage, MimeMultipart

createManagedConnection(): ManagedConnectionFactory
createMapMessage(): Session
createMappedRecord(): RecordFactory
createMessage(): Session
createMimeBodyPart(): MimeMultipart
createObjectFactory(): ObjectFactoryBuilder
createObjectMessage(): Session
createPublisher(): TopicSession
createQueue(): QueueSession
createQueueConnection(): QueueConnectionFactory
createQueueSession(): QueueConnection, XAQueueConnection
createReceiver(): QueueSession
createRegistry(): LocateRegistry
createReply(): ResponseHandler
createSender(): QueueSession
createServerSocket(): RMIServerSocketFactory, RMISocketFactory
createSocket(): RMIClientSocketFactory, RMISocketFactory
createStatement(): Connection
createStreamMessage(): Session
createSubcontext(): Context, DirContext, InitialContext,
   InitialDirContext
createSubscriber(): TopicSession
createTemporaryQueue(): QueueSession
createTemporaryTopic(): TopicSession
createTextMessage(): Session
createTopic(): TopicSession
createTopicConnection(): TopicConnectionFactory
createTopicSession(): TopicConnection, XATopicConnection
createValueHandler(): Util, UtilDelegate
createXAQueueConnection(): XAQueueConnectionFactory
createXAQueueSession(): XAQueueConnection
createXATopicConnection(): XATopicConnectionFactory
createXATopicSession(): XATopicConnection
CRITICAL: Control
ctx(): Request, ServerRequest
CTX_RESTRICT_SCOPE: org.omg.CORBA
Current: org.omg.CORBA, org.omg.PortableServer
current_component(): DynAny
current_member_kind(): DynStruct, DynValue
current_member_name(): DynStruct, DynValue
currentGroupID(): ActivationGroup
CurrentHelper: org.omg.CORBA, org.omg.PortableServer
CurrentHolder: org.omg.CORBA
CurrentOperations: org.omg.CORBA, org.omg.Portable-
   Server
cursorMoved(): RowSetListener
CustomMarshal: org.omg.CORBA
CustomValue: org.omg.CORBA.portable
cxt: CannotProceed

D

DATA_CONVERSION: org.omg.CORBA

DatabaseMetaData: java.sql

dataDefinitionCausesTransactionCommit():
DatabaseMetaData

dataDefinitionIgnoredInTransactions(): DatabaseMeta-Data

DataInputStream: org.omg.CORBA

DATALINK: Types

DataOutputStream: org.omg.CORBA

DataSource: javax.sql

DataTruncation: java.sql

date: DateTerm

Date: java.sql

DATE: Types

DateTerm: javax.mail.search

deactivate(): POAManagerOperations, Tie

deactivate_object(): POAOperations

debug: Service

DECIMAL: Types

decode(): MimeUtility

decodeText(): MimeUtility

decodeWord(): MimeUtility

def_kind(): _IDLTypeStub, IRObjectOperations

DEFAULT_BUFFER: JspWriter

DEFAULT_DELIVERY_MODE: Message

default_index(): TypeCode

default_POA(): Delegate

DEFAULT_PRIORITY: Message

DEFAULT_TIME_TO_LIVE: Message

defaultInitCtx: InitialContext

defined_in: ValueMember

DefinitionKind: org.omg.CORBA

DefinitionKindHelper: org.omg.CORBA

Delegate: org.omg.CORBA.portable,
org.omg.CORBA_2_3.portable, org.omg.Portable-Server.portable

delete(): Folder, TemporaryQueue, TemporaryTopic

delete_values(): Context

DELETED: Flag, FolderEvent

deleteRow(): ResultSet

deletesAreDetected(): DatabaseMetaData, ResultSetInfo

delistResource(): Transaction

DeliveryMode: javax.jms

deregisterDriver(): DriverManager

description: DriverPropertyInfo

Destination: javax.jms

destroy(): _BindingIteratorStub, _IDLTypeStub, _Nam-ingContextExtStub, _NamingContextStub, _PolicyStub, BindingIteratorOperations, DynAny, Filter, GenericServlet, IRObjectOperations, ManagedConnection, NamingContextOperations, ORB, POAOperations, PolicyOperations, Servlet

destroySubcontext(): Context, InitialContext

detail: ActivationException, RemoteException, Server-CloneException

DGC: java.rmi.dgc

DGC_ID: ObjID

dh: MimeBodyPart, MimeMessage

DIGEST_AUTH: HttpServletRequest

DirContext: javax.naming.directory

DirectoryManager: javax.naming.spi

DirObjectFactory: javax.naming.spi

DirStateFactory: javax.naming.spi

DirStateFactory.Result: javax.naming.spi

dirty(): DGC

discard_requests(): POAManagerOperations

DISCARDING: State

disconnect(): ORB

DISCONNECTED: ConnectionEvent

disconnected(): ConnectionAdapter, ConnectionListener

discriminator(): DynUnion

discriminator_kind(): DynUnion

discriminator_type(): TypeCode

dispatch(): ConnectionEvent, FolderEvent, MailEvent, MessageChangedEvent, MessageCountEvent, NamingEvent, NamingExceptionEvent, Skeleton, StoreEvent, TransportEvent, UnsolicitedNotification-Event

DISTINCT: Types

dk_AbstractInterface: DefinitionKind

dk_Alias: DefinitionKind

dk_all: DefinitionKind

dk_Array: DefinitionKind

dk_Attribute: DefinitionKind

dk_Constant: DefinitionKind

dk_Enum: DefinitionKind

dk_Exception: DefinitionKind

dk_Fixed: DefinitionKind

dk_Interface: DefinitionKind

dk_Module: DefinitionKind

dk_Native: DefinitionKind

dk_none: DefinitionKind

dk_Operation: DefinitionKind

dk_Primitive: DefinitionKind

dk_Repository: DefinitionKind

dk_Sequence: DefinitionKind

dk_String: DefinitionKind

dk_Struct: DefinitionKind

dk_Typedef: DefinitionKind

dk_Union: DefinitionKind

dk_Value: DefinitionKind

dk_ValueBox: DefinitionKind

dk_ValueMember: DefinitionKind

dk_Wstring: DefinitionKind

DNS_URL: Context

doDelete(): HttpServlet

doesMaxRowSizeIncludeBlobs(): DatabaseMetaData

doFilter(): Filter, FilterChain
doGet(): HttpServlet
doHead(): HttpServlet
DomainManager: org.omg.CORBA
DomainManagerOperations: org.omg.CORBA
done(): RemoteCall, RemoteRef
doOptions(): HttpServlet
doPost(): HttpServlet
doPut(): HttpServlet
doTrace(): HttpServlet
DOUBLE: Types
DoubleHolder: org.omg.CORBA
DoubleSeqHelper: org.omg.CORBA
DoubleSeqHolder: org.omg.CORBA
DRAFT: Flag
Driver: java.sql
DriverManager: java.sql
DriverPropertyInfo: java.sql
ds: MimeMultipart
duplicate(): Delegate
DuplicateKeyException: javax.ejb
DUPS_OK_ACKNOWLEDGE: Session
DynamicImplementation: org.omg.CORBA,
    org.omg.PortableServer
DynAny: org.omg.CORBA
DynArray: org.omg.CORBA
DynEnum: org.omg.CORBA
DynFixed: org.omg.CORBA
DynSequence: org.omg.CORBA
DynStruct: org.omg.CORBA
DynUnion: org.omg.CORBA
DynValue: org.omg.CORBA

E

EISSystemException: javax.resource.spi
ejbActivate(): EntityBean, SessionBean
EJBContext: javax.ejb
EJBException: javax.ejb
EJBHome: javax.ejb
ejbLoad(): EntityBean
EJBLocalHome: javax.ejb
EJBLocalObject: javax.ejb
EJBMetaData: javax.ejb
EJBObject: javax.ejb
ejbPassivate(): EntityBean, SessionBean
ejbRemove(): EntityBean, MessageDrivenBean, Session-
    Bean
ejbStore(): EntityBean
encode(): MimeUtility
encodedPersonal: InternetAddress
encodeRedirectUrl(): HttpServletResponse, HttpServle-
    tResponseWrapper

encodeRedirectURL(): HttpServletResponse, HttpServle-
    tResponseWrapper
encodeText(): MimeUtility
encodeURL(): HttpServletResponse, HttpServletRespon-
    seWrapper
encodeUrl(): HttpServletResponse, HttpServletRespon-
    seWrapper
encodeWord(): MimeUtility
end(): XAResource
endsWith(): CompositeName, CompoundName, Name
enlistResource(): Transaction
EnterpriseBean: javax.ejb
EntityBean: javax.ejb
EntityContext: javax.ejb
env(): Request
ENVELOPE: Item
ENVELOPE_CHANGED: MessageChangedEvent
Environment: org.omg.CORBA
environment: CannotProceedException
EOF: Token
EQ: ComparisonTerm
equal(): Any, TypeCode
equals(): ActivationDesc, ActivationGroupDesc, Activa-
    tionGroupID, ActivationID, Address,
    AddressStringTerm, AddressTerm, AndTerm, BasicAt-
    tribute, BasicAttributes, BinaryRefAddr, BodyTerm,
    CommandEnvironment, ComparisonTerm, Composite-
    Name, CompoundName, ConnectionRequestInfo,
    DateTerm, Delegate, Flags, FlagTerm, FromStringTerm,
    FromTerm, GenericCredential, HeaderTerm, Inte-
    gerComparisonTerm, InternetAddress, ManagedCon-
    nectionFactory, MarshalledObject, MessageIDTerm,
    MessageNumberTerm, NewsAddress, NotTerm,
    ObjectImpl, ObjID, OrTerm, PasswordCredential,
    ReceivedDateTerm, RecipientStringTerm, Recipient-
    Term, Record, RefAddr, Reference, RemoteObject,
    SentDateTerm, SizeTerm, StringTerm, Stub, StubDele-
    gate, SubjectTerm, Timestamp, UID, URLName, VMID
equivalent(): TypeCode
errorCode: SystemException, XAException
etherealize(): _ServantActivatorStub, ServantActivatorOp-
    erations
EventContext: javax.naming.event
EventDirContext: javax.naming.event
except: UnknownUserException
except(): ServerRequest
EXCEPTION: PageContext
exception(): Environment
ExceptionList: org.omg.CORBA
ExceptionListener: javax.jms
exceptions(): Request
execute(): Interaction, PreparedStatement, RowSet,
    Statement
EXECUTE_FAILED: Statement

executeBatch(): Statement
executeCall(): RemoteCall
executeQuery(): PreparedStatement, Statement
executeUpdate(): PreparedStatement, Statement
exists(): Folder
ExportException: java.rmi.server
exportObject(): Activatable, PortableRemoteObject, PortableRemoteObjectDelegate, ServerRef, UnicastRemoteObject
expunge(): Folder
expunged: Message
extendedOperation(): InitialLdapContext, LdapContext
ExtendedRequest: javax.naming.ldap
ExtendedResponse: javax.naming.ldap
extract(): AdapterAlreadyExistsHelper, AdapterInactiveHelper, AdapterNonExistentHelper, AddressHelper, AlreadyBoundHelper, AnySeqHelper, BindingHelper, BindingIteratorHelper, BindingListHelper, BindingTypeHelper, BooleanSeqHelper, CannotProceedHelper, CharSeqHelper, CompletionStatusHelper, CurrentHelper, DefinitionKindHelper, DoubleSeqHelper, FieldNameHelper, FloatSeqHelper, ForwardRequestHelper, IdentifierHelper, IDLTypeHelper, InvalidAddressHelper, InvalidNameHelper, InvalidPolicyHelper, IstringHelper, LongLongSeqHelper, LongSeqHelper, NameComponentHelper, NameHelper, NameValuePairHelper, NamingContextExtHelper, NamingContextHelper, NoContextHelper, NoServantHelper, NotEmptyHelper, NotFoundHelper, NotFoundReasonHelper, ObjectAlreadyActiveHelper, ObjectHelper, ObjectNotActiveHelper, OctetSeqHelper, ParameterModeHelper, POAHelper, PolicyErrorCodeHelper, PolicyErrorHelper, PolicyHelper, PolicyListHelper, PolicyTypeHelper, RepositoryIdHelper, ServantActivatorHelper, ServantAlreadyActiveHelper, ServantLocatorHelper, ServantNotActiveHelper, ServiceDetailHelper, ServiceInformationHelper, SetOverrideTypeHelper, ShortSeqHelper, StringNameHelper, StringSeqHelper, StringValueHelper, StructMemberHelper, ULongLongSeqHelper, ULongSeqHelper, UnionMemberHelper, UnknownUserExceptionHelper, URLStringHelper, UShortSeqHelper, ValueBaseHelper, ValueMemberHelper, VersionSpecHelper, VisibilityHelper, WCharSeqHelper, WrongAdapterHelper, WrongPolicyHelper, WrongTransactionHelper, WStringSeqHelper, WStringValueHelper
extract_any(): Any
extract_boolean(): Any
extract_char(): Any
extract_double(): Any
extract_fixed(): Any
extract_float(): Any
extract_long(): Any

extract_longlong(): Any
extract_Object(): Any
extract_octet(): Any
extract_Principal(): Any
extract_short(): Any
extract_Streamable(): Any
extract_string(): Any
extract_TypeCode(): Any
extract_ulong(): Any
extract_ulonglong(): Any
extract_ushort(): Any
extract_Value(): Any
extract_wchar(): Any
extract_wstring(): Any

F

failure(): RMIFailureHandler
fetch(): Folder
FETCH_FORWARD: ResultSet
FETCH_REVERSE: ResultSet
FETCH_UNKNOWN: ResultSet
FetchProfile: javax.mail
FetchProfile.Item: javax.mail
FetchProfileItem: javax.mail.UIDFolder
FieldNameHelper: org.omg.CORBA
Filter: javax.servlet
FilterChain: javax.servlet
FilterConfig: javax.servlet
finalize(): Folder, Service
find_POA(): POAOperations
findAttribute(): PageContext
findColumn(): ResultSet
FinderException: javax.ejb
first(): ResultSet
fixed_digits(): TypeCode
fixed_scale(): TypeCode
FixedHolder: org.omg.CORBA
Flag: javax.mail.Flags
FLAGGED: Flag
flags: FlagTerm, MimeMessage
FLAGS: Item
Flags: javax.mail
flags(): NamedValue
Flags.Flag: javax.mail
FLAGS_CHANGED: MessageChangedEvent
FlagTerm: javax.mail.search
FLOAT: Types
FloatHolder: org.omg.CORBA
FloatSeqHelper: org.omg.CORBA
FloatSeqHolder: org.omg.CORBA
flush(): JspWriter
flushBuffer(): ServletResponse, ServletResponseWrapper
Folder: javax.mail

folder: FolderEvent, Message
FolderAdapter: javax.mail.event
FolderClosedException: javax.mail
folderCreated(): FolderAdapter, FolderListener
folderDeleted(): FolderAdapter, FolderListener
FolderEvent: javax.mail.event
FolderListener: javax.mail.event
FolderNotFoundException: javax.mail
folderRenamed(): FolderAdapter, FolderListener
forget(): XAResource
FORM_AUTH: HttpServletRequest
format(): MailDateFormat
forward(): PageContext, RequestDispatcher
forward_reference: ForwardRequest
ForwardRequest: org.omg.PortableServer
ForwardRequestHelper: org.omg.PortableServer
FREE_MEM: org.omg.CORBA
from_any(): DynAny
from_int(): BindingType, CompletionStatus, DefinitionKind, IdAssignmentPolicyValue, IdUniquenessPolicyValue, ImplicitActivationPolicyValue, LifespanPolicyValue, NotFoundReason, ParameterMode, RequestProcessingPolicyValue, ServantRetentionPolicyValue, SetOverrideType, State, TCKind, ThreadPolicyValue
FromStringTerm: javax.mail.search
FromTerm: javax.mail.search
fullURL: URLName

G

GE: ComparisonTerm
GenericCredential: javax.resource.spi.security
GenericServlet: javax.servlet
get(): Attribute, Attributes, BasicAttribute, BasicAttributes, CompositeName, CompoundName, MarshalledObject, Name, ParameterList, Reference
get_any(): DynAny
get_boolean(): DynAny
get_char(): DynAny
get_codebase(): Delegate
get_compact_typecode(): TypeCode
get_current(): ORB
get_default_context(): ORB
get_domain_managers(): Delegate
get_domain_policy(): DomainManagerOperations
get_double(): DynAny
get_elements(): DynArray, DynSequence
get_float(): DynAny
get_id(): BoxedValueHelper, StringValueHelper, WStringValueHelper
get_interface_def(): Delegate
get_long(): DynAny
get_longlong(): DynAny

get_members(): DynStruct, DynValue
get_next_response(): ORB
get_object_id(): CurrentOperations
get_octet(): DynAny
get_POA(): CurrentOperations
get_policy(): Delegate
get_primitive_tc(): ORB
get_reference(): DynAny
get_response(): Request
get_servant(): POAOperations
get_servant_manager(): POAOperations
get_service_information(): ORB
get_short(): DynAny
get_state(): POAManagerOperations
get_string(): DynAny
get_typecode(): DynAny
get_ulong(): DynAny
get_ulonglong(): DynAny
get_ushort(): DynAny
get_val(): DynAny
get_value(): DynFixed
get_value_def(): ORB
get_values(): Context
get_wchar(): DynAny
get_wstring(): DynAny
getActivationDesc(): ActivationSystem
getActivationGroupDesc(): ActivationSystem
getAdapterName(): ResourceAdapterMetaData
getAdapterShortDescription(): ResourceAdapterMetaData
getAdapterVendorName(): ResourceAdapterMetaData
getAdapterVersion(): ResourceAdapterMetaData
getAddress(): AddressTerm, InternetAddress
getAll(): Attribute, Attributes, BasicAttribute, BasicAttributes, CompositeName, CompoundName, Name, Reference
getAllHeaderLines(): InternetHeaders, MimeBodyPart, MimeMessage, MimePart
getAllHeaders(): BodyPart, InternetHeaders, Message, MimeBodyPart, MimeMessage, Part
getAllRecipients(): Message, MimeMessage
getAltName(): CannotProceedException
getAltNameCtx(): CannotProceedException
getArray(): Array, CallableStatement, ResultSet
getAsciiStream(): Clob, ResultSet
getAttribute(): HttpSession, ModificationItem, PageContext, ServletContext, ServletRequest, ServletRequestWrapper
getAttributeDefinition(): Attribute, BasicAttribute
getAttributeNames(): HttpSession, ServletContext, ServletRequest, ServletRequestWrapper
getAttributeNamesInScope(): PageContext
getAttributes(): DatabaseMetaData, DirContext, InitialDirContext, Result, SearchResult, Struct

getAttributesScope(): PageContext
getAttributeSyntaxDefinition(): Attribute, BasicAttribute
getAuthType(): HttpServletRequest, HttpServletRequest-Wrapper
getAutoCommit(): Connection
getBaseType(): Array, ContentType
getBaseTypeName(): Array, Ref
getBestRowIdentifier(): DatabaseMetaData
getBigDecimal(): CallableStatement, ResultSet
getBinaryStream(): Blob, ResultSet
getBlob(): CallableStatement, ResultSet
getBodyPart(): MimeMultipart, Multipart, MultipartData-Source
getBoolean(): CallableStatement, MapMessage, Result-Set
getBooleanProperty(): Message
getBranchQualifier(): Xid
getBufferSize(): JspWriter, ServletResponse, ServletResponseWrapper
getByte(): CallableStatement, MapMessage, ResultSet
getByteProperty(): Message
getBytes(): Blob, CallableStatement, MapMessage, ResultSet
getCallerIdentity(): EJBContext
getCallerPrincipal(): EJBContext
getCatalog(): Connection
getCatalogName(): ResultSetMetaData
getCatalogs(): DatabaseMetaData
getCatalogSeparator(): DatabaseMetaData
getCatalogTerm(): DatabaseMetaData
getCause(): ActivationException, RemoteException, ServerCloneException
getCausedByException(): EJBException
getChangeInfo(): NamingEvent
getChar(): MapMessage
getCharacterEncoding(): ServletRequest, ServletRequestWrapper, ServletResponse, ServletResponseWrapper
getCharacterStream(): Clob, ResultSet
getClassAnnotation(): RMIClassLoader, RMIClassLoaderSpi
getClassLoader(): RMIClassLoader, RMIClassLoaderSpi
getClassName(): ActivationDesc, ActivationGroupDesc, Binding, NameClassPair, Provider, Reference
getClientHost(): RemoteServer, ServerRef
getClientID(): Connection
getClob(): CallableStatement, ResultSet
getCodebase(): Util, UtilDelegate
getColumnClassName(): ResultSetMetaData
getColumnCount(): ResultSetMetaData
getColumnDisplaySize(): ResultSetMetaData
getColumnLabel(): ResultSetMetaData
getColumnName(): ResultSetMetaData
getColumnPrivileges(): DatabaseMetaData

getColumns(): DatabaseMetaData
getColumnType(): ResultSetMetaData
getColumnTypeName(): ResultSetMetaData
getCommand(): RowSet
getCommandEnvironment(): ActivationGroupDesc
getCommandOptions(): CommandEnvironment
getCommandPath(): CommandEnvironment
getComment(): Cookie
getComparison(): DateTerm, IntegerComparisonTerm
getConcurrency(): ResultSet
getConnectControls(): InitialLdapContext, LdapContext
getConnection(): ConnectionFactory, DatabaseMetaData, DataSource, DriverManager, Interaction, Managed-Connection, PooledConnection, RowSetInternal, Statement
getConnectionHandle(): ConnectionEvent
getContent(): BinaryRefAddr, BodyPart, Message, Mime-BodyPart, MimeMessage, Part, RefAddr, StringRefAddr
getContentID(): MimeBodyPart, MimeMessage, MimePart
getContentLanguage(): MimeBodyPart, MimeMessage, MimePart
getContentLength(): ServletRequest, ServletRequest-Wrapper
getContentMD5(): MimeBodyPart, MimeMessage, MimePart
getContentStream(): MimeBodyPart, MimeMessage
getContentType(): BodyPart, Message, MimeBodyPart, MimeMessage, MimePartDataSource, Multipart, Part, ServletRequest, ServletRequestWrapper
getContext(): ServletContext
getContextPath(): HttpServletRequest, HttpServletRequestWrapper
getContinuationContext(): NamingManager
getContinuationDirContext(): DirectoryManager
getControlInstance(): ControlFactory
getControls(): HasControls
getCookies(): HttpServletRequest, HttpServletRequestWrapper
getCount(): MimeMultipart, Multipart, MultipartDataSource
getCountLimit(): SearchControls
getCreationTime(): HttpSession
getCredentialData(): GenericCredential
getCrossReference(): DatabaseMetaData
getCursorName(): ResultSet
getData(): ActivationDesc, ActivationGroupDesc
getDatabaseMajorVersion(): DatabaseMetaData
getDatabaseMinorVersion(): DatabaseMetaData
getDatabaseProductName(): DatabaseMetaData
getDatabaseProductVersion(): DatabaseMetaData
getDataHandler(): BodyPart, Message, MimeBodyPart, MimeMessage, Part
getDataSize(): DataTruncation

getDataSourceName(): RowSet
getDate(): CallableStatement, DateTerm, ResultSet, Time
getDateHeader(): HttpServletRequest, HttpServletRequestWrapper
getDay(): Time
getDebug(): Session
getDefaultFactory(): JspFactory
getDefaultFolder(): Store
getDefaultInitCtx(): InitialContext
getDefaultInstance(): Session
getDefaultJavaCharset(): MimeUtility
getDefaultProviderInstance(): RMIClassLoader
getDefaultSocketFactory(): RMISocketFactory
getDefaultStream(): LogStream
getDefaultTransactionIsolation(): DatabaseMetaData
getDefaultUserName(): Authenticator
getDeliveryMode(): MessageProducer
getDerefLinkFlag(): SearchControls
getDescription(): BodyPart, Message, MimeBodyPart, MimeMessage, Part
getDisableMessageID(): MessageProducer
getDisableMessageTimestamp(): MessageProducer
getDisposition(): BodyPart, ContentDisposition, Message, MimeBodyPart, MimeMessage, Part
getDomain(): Cookie
getDouble(): CallableStatement, MapMessage, ResultSet
getDoubleProperty(): Message
getDriver(): DriverManager
getDriverMajorVersion(): DatabaseMetaData
getDriverMinorVersion(): DatabaseMetaData
getDriverName(): DatabaseMetaData
getDrivers(): DriverManager
getDriverVersion(): DatabaseMetaData
getEISProductName(): ConnectionMetaData, ManagedConnectionMetaData
getEISProductVersion(): ConnectionMetaData, ManagedConnectionMetaData
getEJBHome(): EJBContext, EJBMetaData, EJBObject, HomeHandle
getEJBLocalHome(): EJBContext, EJBLocalObject
getEJBLocalObject(): EntityContext, SessionContext
getEJBMetaData(): EJBHome
getEJBObject(): EntityContext, Handle, SessionContext
getEncodedValue(): Control, ExtendedRequest, ExtendedResponse, StartTlsRequest, StartTlsResponse
getEncoding(): MimeBodyPart, MimeMessage, MimePart, MimeUtility
getEngineInfo(): JspFactory
getEnumeration(): QueueBrowser
getEnvironment(): CannotProceedException, Context, EJBContext, InitialContext
getErrorCode(): JMSException, ResourceException, SQLException
getEscapeProcessing(): RowSet

getEventContext(): NamingEvent, NamingExceptionEvent
getException(): ConnectionEvent, NamingExceptionEvent, PageContext, UnsolicitedNotification
getExceptionListener(): Connection
getExplanation(): NamingException
getExportedKeys(): DatabaseMetaData
getExtraNameCharacters(): DatabaseMetaData
getFactoryClassLocation(): Reference
getFactoryClassName(): Reference
getFailureHandler(): RMISocketFactory
getFetchDirection(): ResultSet, Statement
getFetchSize(): ResultSet, Statement
getFile(): URLName
getFileName(): BodyPart, Message, MimeBodyPart, MimeMessage, Part
getFilterName(): FilterConfig
getFlags(): FlagTerm, Message, MimeMessage
getFloat(): CallableStatement, MapMessage, ResultSet
getFloatProperty(): Message
getFolder(): Folder, FolderClosedException, FolderEvent, FolderNotFoundException, Message, ReadOnlyFolderException, Session, Store
getFormatId(): Xid
getFrom(): Message, MimeMessage
getFullName(): Folder
getGeneratedKeys(): Statement
getGlobalTransactionId(): Xid
getGroupID(): ActivationDesc
getHandle(): EJBObject
getHeader(): BodyPart, HttpServletRequest, HttpServletRequestWrapper, InternetHeaders, Message, MimeBodyPart, MimeMessage, MimePart, Part
getHeaderName(): HeaderTerm
getHeaderNames(): FetchProfile, HttpServletRequest, HttpServletRequestWrapper
getHeaders(): HttpServletRequest, HttpServletRequestWrapper
getHoldability(): Connection
getHomeHandle(): EJBHome
getHomeInterfaceClass(): EJBMetaData
getHost(): NewsAddress, URLName
getHours(): Date
getId(): ApplicationException, ConnectionEvent, HttpSession
getID(): Activatable, Attribute, BasicAttribute, Control, ExtendedRequest, ExtendedResponse, StartTlsRequest, StartTlsResponse
getIdentifierQuoteString(): DatabaseMetaData
getIDs(): Attributes, BasicAttributes
getIds(): HttpSessionContext
getIgnoreCase(): StringTerm
getImportedKeys(): DatabaseMetaData
getIndex(): DataTruncation
getIndexInfo(): DatabaseMetaData

getInitialContext(): InitialContextFactory, NamingManager

getInitParameter(): FilterConfig, GenericServlet, ServletConfig, ServletContext

getInitParameterNames(): FilterConfig, GenericServlet, ServletConfig, ServletContext

getInputStream(): ApplicationException, BodyPart, Message, MimeBodyPart, MimeMessage, MimePartDataSource, Part, RemoteCall, ServletRequest, ServletRequestWrapper

getInstance(): Session

getInt(): CallableStatement, MapMessage, ResultSet

getInteractionSpecsSupported(): ResourceAdapterMetaData

getIntHeader(): HttpServletRequest, HttpServletRequestWrapper

getIntProperty(): Message

getInvalidAddresses(): SendFailedException, TransportEvent

getItems(): FetchProfile

getJDBCMajorVersion(): DatabaseMetaData

getJDBCMinorVersion(): DatabaseMetaData

getJMSCorrelationID(): Message

getJMSCorrelationIDAsBytes(): Message

getJMSDeliveryMode(): Message

getJMSDestination(): Message

getJMSExpiration(): Message

getJMSMajorVersion(): ConnectionMetaData

getJMSMessageID(): Message

getJMSMinorVersion(): ConnectionMetaData

getJMSPriority(): Message

getJMSProviderName(): ConnectionMetaData

getJMSRedelivered(): Message

getJMSReplyTo(): Message

getJMSTimestamp(): Message

getJMSType(): Message

getJMSVersion(): ConnectionMetaData

getJMSXPropertyNames(): ConnectionMetaData

getLastAccessedTime(): HttpSession

getLastModified(): HttpServlet

getLineCount(): BodyPart, Message, MimeBodyPart, MimeMessage, Part

getLinkedException(): JMSException, ResourceException

getLinkedWarning(): ResourceWarning

getLinkExplanation(): LinkException

getLinkName(): LinkRef

getLinkRemainingName(): LinkException

getLinkResolvedName(): LinkException

getLinkResolvedObj(): LinkException

getLocalAddress(): InternetAddress

getLocale(): ServletRequest, ServletRequestWrapper, ServletResponse, ServletResponseWrapper

getLocales(): ServletRequest, ServletRequestWrapper

getLocalTransaction(): Connection, ManagedConnection

getLocation(): ActivationDesc, ActivationGroupDesc

getLog(): RemoteServer

getLoginTimeout(): ConnectionPoolDataSource, DataSource, DriverManager, XADataSource

getLogStream(): DriverManager

getLogWriter(): ConnectionPoolDataSource, DataSource, DriverManager, ManagedConnection, ManagedConnectionFactory, XADataSource

getLong(): CallableStatement, MapMessage, ResultSet

getLongProperty(): Message

getMajorVersion(): Driver, ServletContext

getManagedConnectionFactory(): PasswordCredential

getMapNames(): MapMessage

getMatchingHeaderLines(): InternetHeaders, MimeBodyPart, MimeMessage, MimePart

getMatchingHeaders(): BodyPart, InternetHeaders, Message, MimeBodyPart, MimeMessage, Part

getMaxAge(): Cookie

getMaxBinaryLiteralLength(): DatabaseMetaData

getMaxCatalogNameLength(): DatabaseMetaData

getMaxCharLiteralLength(): DatabaseMetaData

getMaxColumnNameLength(): DatabaseMetaData

getMaxColumnsInGroupBy(): DatabaseMetaData

getMaxColumnsInIndex(): DatabaseMetaData

getMaxColumnsInOrderBy(): DatabaseMetaData

getMaxColumnsInSelect(): DatabaseMetaData

getMaxColumnsInTable(): DatabaseMetaData

getMaxConnections(): DatabaseMetaData, ManagedConnectionMetaData

getMaxCursorNameLength(): DatabaseMetaData

getMaxFieldSize(): RowSet, Statement

getMaxInactiveInterval(): HttpSession

getMaxIndexLength(): DatabaseMetaData

getMaxProcedureNameLength(): DatabaseMetaData

getMaxRows(): RowSet, Statement

getMaxRowSize(): DatabaseMetaData

getMaxSchemaNameLength(): DatabaseMetaData

getMaxStatementLength(): DatabaseMetaData

getMaxStatements(): DatabaseMetaData

getMaxTableNameLength(): DatabaseMetaData

getMaxTablesInSelect(): DatabaseMetaData

getMaxUserNameLength(): DatabaseMetaData

getMechType(): GenericCredential

getMessage(): ActivationException, EJBException, Folder, MessageChangedEvent, MessageContext, MessagingException, RemoteException, ServerCloneException, StoreEvent, TransportEvent

getMessageByUID(): UIDFolder

getMessageChangeType(): MessageChangedEvent

getMessageContext(): MessageAware, MimePartDataSource

getMessageCount(): Folder

getMessageID(): MimeMessage

getMessageListener(): MessageConsumer, Session

getMessageNumber(): Message
getMessages(): Folder, MessageCountEvent
getMessagesByUID(): UIDFolder
getMessageSelector(): MessageConsumer, Queue-
Browser
getMessageType(): StoreEvent
getMetaData(): Connection, ConnectionFactory, ManagedConnection, PreparedStatement, ResultSet
getMethod(): HttpServletRequest, HttpServletRequest-
Wrapper
getMimeType(): ServletContext
getMinorVersion(): Driver, ServletContext
getMinutes(): Date
getMode(): Folder
getModificationOp(): ModificationItem
getMonth(): Time
getMoreResults(): Statement
getName(): Cookie, Folder, GenericCredential, Header,
HttpSessionBindingEvent, MimePartDataSource,
NameClassPair, ServletContextAttributeEvent
getNamedDispatcher(): ServletContext
getNameInNamespace(): Context, InitialContext
getNameParser(): Context, InitialContext
getNames(): ParameterList
getNanos(): Timestamp
getNewBinding(): NamingEvent
getNewFolder(): FolderEvent
getNewMessageCount(): Folder
getNewsgroup(): NewsAddress
getNextException(): MessagingException, SQLException
getNextWarning(): SQLWarning
getNoLocal(): TopicSubscriber
getNonMatchingHeaderLines(): InternetHeaders, Mime-
BodyPart, MimeMessage, MimePart
getNonMatchingHeaders(): BodyPart, InternetHeaders,
Message, MimeBodyPart, MimeMessage, Part
getNotification(): UnsolicitedNotificationEvent
getNumber(): IntegerComparisonTerm
getNumericFunctions(): DatabaseMetaData
getObject(): Binding, CallableStatement, MapMessage,
ObjectMessage, Ref, Result, ResultSet
getObjectInstance(): DirectoryManager, DirObjectFactory,
NamingManager, ObjectFactory
getObjectProperty(): Message
getOldBinding(): NamingEvent
getOperation(): Operation
getOperations(): Skeleton
getOriginal(): RowSetInternal
getOriginalRow(): RowSetInternal
getOut(): PageContext
getOutputStream(): LogStream, MimePartDataSource,
RemoteCall, ServletResponse, ServletResponseWrapper
getPage(): PageContext

getPageContext(): JspFactory
getParameter(): ContentDisposition, ContentType, Data-
Truncation, ServletRequest, ServletRequestWrapper
getParameterClassName(): ParameterMetaData
getParameterCount(): ParameterMetaData
getParameterList(): ContentDisposition, ContentType
getParameterMap(): ServletRequest, ServletRequest-
Wrapper
getParameterMetaData(): PreparedStatement
getParameterMode(): ParameterMetaData
getParameterNames(): ServletRequest, ServletRequest-
Wrapper
getParameterType(): ParameterMetaData
getParameterTypeName(): ParameterMetaData
getParameterValues(): ServletRequest, ServletRequest-
Wrapper
getParams(): RowSetInternal
getParent(): BodyPart, Folder, Multipart
getPart(): MessageContext
getPassword(): PasswordAuthentication, PasswordCredential, RowSet, URLName
getPasswordAuthentication(): Authenticator, Session
getPath(): Cookie
getPathInfo(): HttpServletRequest, HttpServletRequest-
Wrapper
getPathTranslated(): HttpServletRequest, HttpServletRequestWrapper
getPattern(): StringTerm
getPermanentFlags(): Folder
getPersonal(): InternetAddress
getPersonalNamespaces(): Store
getPooledConnection(): ConnectionPoolDataSource
getPort(): URLName
getPos(): AddressException
getPosition(): SharedInputStream
getPrecision(): ParameterMetaData, ResultSetMetaData
getPrefix(): CompositeName, CompoundName, Name
getPrimaryKey(): EJBLocalObject, EJBObject, EntityContext
getPrimaryKeyClass(): EJBMetaData
getPrimaryKeys(): DatabaseMetaData
getPrimaryType(): ContentType
getPriority(): MessageProducer
getProcedureColumns(): DatabaseMetaData
getProcedures(): DatabaseMetaData
getProcedureTerm(): DatabaseMetaData
getProperties(): Session
getProperty(): Session
getPropertyInfo(): Driver
getPropertyNames(): Message
getPropertyOverrides(): ActivationGroupDesc
getProtocol(): Provider, ServletRequest, ServletRequest-
Wrapper, URLName
getProvider(): Session

getProviderMajorVersion(): ConnectionMetaData
getProviderMinorVersion(): ConnectionMetaData
getProviders(): Session
getProviderVersion(): ConnectionMetaData
getQueryString(): HttpServletRequest, HttpServletRequestWrapper
getQueryTimeout(): RowSet, Statement
getQueue(): QueueBrowser, QueueReceiver, QueueSender
getQueueName(): Queue
getQueueSession(): XAQueueSession
getRawInputStream(): MimeBodyPart, MimeMessage
getRead(): DataTruncation
getReader(): ServletRequest, ServletRequestWrapper
getRealPath(): ServletContext, ServletRequest, ServletRequestWrapper
getReceivedDate(): Message, MimeMessage
getRecipients(): Message, MimeMessage
getRecipientType(): RecipientStringTerm, RecipientTerm
getRecordFactory(): ConnectionFactory
getRecordName(): Record
getRecordShortDescription(): Record
getRef(): AddressException, CallableStatement, RemoteObject, ResultSet, URLName
getRefClass(): RemoteRef
getReference(): Referenceable
getReferralContext(): LdapReferralException, ReferralException
getReferralInfo(): ReferralException
getReferrals(): UnsolicitedNotification
getRegistry(): LocateRegistry
getRemainder(): HeaderTokenizer
getRemaining(): JspWriter
getRemainingName(): NamingException, ResolveResult
getRemainingNewName(): CannotProceedException
getRemoteAddr(): ServletRequest, ServletRequestWrapper
getRemoteHost(): ServletRequest, ServletRequestWrapper
getRemoteInterfaceClass(): EJBMetaData
getRemoteUser(): HttpServletRequest, HttpServletRequestWrapper
getReplyTo(): Message, MimeMessage
getRequest(): PageContext, ServletRequestWrapper
getRequestControls(): InitialLdapContext, LdapContext
getRequestDispatcher(): ServletContext, ServletRequest, ServletRequestWrapper
getRequestedSessionId(): HttpServletRequest, HttpServletRequestWrapper
getRequestingPort(): Authenticator
getRequestingPrompt(): Authenticator
getRequestingProtocol(): Authenticator
getRequestingSite(): Authenticator
getRequestURI(): HttpServletRequest, HttpServletRequestWrapper

getRequestURL(): HttpServletRequest, HttpServletRequestWrapper, HttpUtils
getResolvedName(): NamingException
getResolvedObj(): NamingException, ResolveResult
getResource(): ServletContext
getResourceAsStream(): ServletContext
getResourcePaths(): ServletContext
getResponse(): PageContext, ServletResponseWrapper
getResponseControls(): InitialLdapContext, LdapContext
getRestartMode(): ActivationDesc
getResultSet(): Array, Statement
getResultSetConcurrency(): Statement
getResultSetHoldability(): DatabaseMetaData, Statement
getResultSetInfo(): Connection
getResultSetType(): Statement
getResultStream(): RemoteCall
getReturningAttributes(): SearchControls
getReturningObjFlag(): SearchControls
getRMIRepositoryID(): ValueHandler
getRollbackOnly(): EJBContext
getRootCause(): JspException, NamingException, ServletException
getRow(): ResultSet
getRunTimeCodeBase(): ValueHandler
getSavepointId(): Savepoint
getSavepointName(): Savepoint
getScale(): ParameterMetaData, ResultSetMetaData
getSchema(): DirContext, InitialDirContext
getSchemaClassDefinition(): DirContext, InitialDirContext
getSchemaName(): ResultSetMetaData
getSchemas(): DatabaseMetaData
getSchemaTerm(): DatabaseMetaData
getScheme(): ServletRequest, ServletRequestWrapper
getSearchScope(): SearchControls
getSearchStringEscape(): DatabaseMetaData
getSeconds(): Date
getSecure(): Cookie
getSecurityContext(): LoaderHandler, RMIClassLoader
getSentDate(): Message, MimeMessage
getSeparator(): Folder
getServerInfo(): ServletContext
getServerName(): ServletRequest, ServletRequestWrapper
getServerPort(): ServletRequest, ServletRequestWrapper
getServerSession(): ServerSessionPool
getServerSessionPool(): ConnectionConsumer
getServlet(): ServletContext, UnavailableException
getServletConfig(): GenericServlet, PageContext, Servlet
getServletContext(): FilterConfig, GenericServlet, HttpSession, PageContext, ServletConfig, ServletContextEvent
getServletContextName(): ServletContext
getServletInfo(): GenericServlet, Servlet

getServletName(): GenericServlet, ServletConfig
getServletNames(): ServletContext
getServletPath(): HttpServletRequest, HttpServletRequestWrapper
getServlets(): ServletContext
getSession(): HttpServletRequest, HttpServletRequestWrapper, HttpSessionBindingEvent, HttpSessionContext, HttpSessionEvent, MessageContext, PageContext, ServerSession
getSessionContext(): HttpSession
getSharedNamespaces(): Store
getShort(): CallableStatement, MapMessage, ResultSet
getShortProperty(): Message
getSize(): BodyPart, Message, MimeBodyPart, MimeMessage, Part
getSocketFactory(): RMISocketFactory
getSpecificationVersion(): JspEngineInfo
getSpecVersion(): ResourceAdapterMetaData
getSQLException(): ConnectionEvent
getSQLKeywords(): DatabaseMetaData
getSQLState(): SQLException
getSQLStateType(): DatabaseMetaData
getSQLTypeName(): SQLData, Struct
getStatement(): ResultSet
getStateToBind(): DirectoryManager, DirStateFactory, NamingManager, StateFactory
getStatus(): Transaction, TransactionManager, UserTransaction
getStore(): Folder, Session, StoreClosedException
getString(): CallableStatement, MapMessage, ResultSet
getStringFunctions(): DatabaseMetaData
getStringProperty(): Message
getSubject(): Message, MimeMessage
getSubString(): Clob
getSubType(): ContentType
getSuffix(): CompositeName, CompoundName, Name
getSuperTables(): DatabaseMetaData
getSuperTypes(): DatabaseMetaData
getSystem(): ActivationGroup, ActivationGroupID
getSystemFlags(): Flags
getSystemFunctions(): DatabaseMetaData
getTableName(): ResultSetMetaData
getTablePrivileges(): DatabaseMetaData
getTables(): DatabaseMetaData
getTableTypes(): DatabaseMetaData
getTarget(): Tie
getTerm(): NotTerm
getTerms(): AndTerm, OrTerm
getTestSet(): FlagTerm
getText(): TextMessage
getTie(): Util, UtilDelegate
getTime(): CallableStatement, ResultSet, Timestamp
getTimeDateFunctions(): DatabaseMetaData
getTimeLimit(): SearchControls

getTimestamp(): CallableStatement, ResultSet
getTimeToLive(): MessageProducer
getTopic(): TopicPublisher, TopicSubscriber
getTopicName(): Topic
getTopicSession(): XATopicSession
getTransacted(): Session, XASession
getTransaction(): TransactionManager
getTransactionIsolation(): Connection, RowSet
getTransactionTimeout(): XAResource
getTransferSize(): DataTruncation
getTransport(): Session
getType(): Address, ConnectionEvent, Folder, FolderEvent, InternetAddress, MessageCountEvent, NamingEvent, NewsAddress, Provider, RefAddr, ResultSet, Token, TransportEvent
getTypeInfo(): DatabaseMetaData
getTypeMap(): Connection, RowSet
getUDTs(): DatabaseMetaData
getUID(): UIDFolder
getUIDValidity(): UIDFolder
getUnavailableSeconds(): UnavailableException
getUnexecutedModifications(): AttributeModificationException
getUnicodeStream(): ResultSet
getUnreadMessageCount(): Folder
getUpdateCount(): Statement
getUpdateCounts(): BatchUpdateException
getURL(): CallableStatement, DatabaseMetaData, ResultSet, URLName
getUrl(): RowSet
getURLContext(): NamingManager
getURLName(): Folder, Service
getURLOrDefaultInitCtx(): InitialContext
getUserFlags(): Flags
getUsername(): RowSet, URLName
getUserName(): ConnectionMetaData, DatabaseMetaData, ManagedConnectionMetaData, PasswordAuthentication, PasswordCredential
getUserNamespaces(): Store
getUserPrincipal(): HttpServletRequest, HttpServletRequestWrapper
getUserTransaction(): EJBContext
getValidSentAddresses(): SendFailedException, TransportEvent
getValidUnsentAddresses(): SendFailedException, TransportEvent
getValue(): Cookie, Header, HttpSession, HttpSessionBindingEvent, Lease, ServletContextAttributeEvent, Token
getValueNames(): HttpSession
getVendor(): Provider
getVersion(): Cookie, Provider
getVersionColumns(): DatabaseMetaData
getVMID(): Lease

getWarnings(): Connection, Interaction, ResultSet, Statement
getWriter(): ServletResponse, ServletResponseWrapper
getXAConnection(): XADataSource
getXAResource(): ManagedConnection, XAConnection,
XASession
getYear(): Time
gotDefault: InitialContext
GT: ComparisonTerm

HttpSession: javax.servlet.http
HttpSessionActivationListener: javax.servlet.http
HttpSessionAttributeListener: javax.servlet.http
HttpSessionBindingEvent: javax.servlet.http
HttpSessionBindingListener: javax.servlet.http
HttpSessionContext: javax.servlet.http
HttpSessionEvent: javax.servlet.http
HttpSessionListener: javax.servlet.http
HttpUtils: javax.servlet.http

H

Handle: javax.ejb
HandleDelegate: javax.ejb.spi
handlePageException(): PageContext
HasControls: javax.naming.ldap
hash(): Delegate
hashCode(): ActivationDesc, ActivationGroupDesc, Activa-
tionGroupID, ActivationID, AddressTerm, AndTerm,
BasicAttribute, BasicAttributes, BinaryRefAddr, CommandEnvironment, ComparisonTerm, Composite-
Name, CompoundName, ConnectionRequestInfo,
DateTerm, Delegate, Flags, FlagTerm, GenericCredential, HeaderTerm, IntegerComparisonTerm, InternetAddress, ManagedConnectionFactory, MarshalledObject,
NewsAddress, NotTerm, ObjectImpl, ObjID, OrTerm,
PasswordCredential, RecipientStringTerm, Recipient-
Term, Record, RefAddr, Reference, RemoteObject,
StringTerm, Stub, StubDelegate, UID, URLName, VMID
hasInitialContextFactoryBuilder(): NamingManager
hasMore(): NamingEnumeration
hasNewMessages(): Folder
Header: javax.mail
headerName: HeaderTerm
headers: MimeBodyPart, MimeMessage
HeaderTerm: javax.mail.search
HeaderTokenizer: javax.mail.internet
HeaderTokenizer.Token: javax.mail.internet
HeuristicCommitException: javax.transaction
HeuristicMixedException: javax.transaction
HeuristicRollbackException: javax.transaction
HOLD_CURSORS_OVER_COMMIT: ResultSet
hold_requests(): POAManagerOperations
HOLDING: State
HOLDS_FOLDERS: Folder
HOLDS_MESSAGES: Folder
HomeHandle: javax.ejb
host: NewsAddress
HttpJspPage: javax.servlet.jsp
HttpServlet: javax.servlet.http
HttpServletRequest: javax.servlet.http
HttpServletRequestWrapper: javax.servlet.http
HttpServletResponse: javax.servlet.http
HttpServletResponseWrapper: javax.servlet.http

I

id: ConnectionEvent, NameComponent, NameValuePair,
ValueMember
id(): AdapterAlreadyExistsHelper, AdapterInactiveHelper,
AdapterNonExistentHelper, AddressHelper, Already-
BoundHelper, AnySeqHelper, BindingHelper, Bindin-
gIteratorHelper, BindingListHelper, BindingTypeHelper,
BooleanSeqHelper, CannotProceedHelper, CharSe-
qHelper, CompletionStatusHelper, CurrentHelper, Def-
initionKindHelper, DoubleSeqHelper,
FieldNameHelper, FloatSeqHelper, ForwardReques-
tHelper, IdentifierHelper, IDLTypeHelper, InvalidAd-
dressHelper, InvalidNameHelper, InvalidPolicyHelper,
IstringHelper, LongLongSeqHelper, LongSeqHelper,
NameComponentHelper, NameHelper, NameValue-
PairHelper, NamingContextExtHelper, NamingContex-
tHelper, NoContextHelper, NoServantHelper,
NotEmptyHelper, NotFoundHelper, NotFoundReason-
Helper, ObjectAlreadyActiveHelper, ObjectHelper,
ObjectNotActiveHelper, OctetSeqHelper, Parameter-
ModeHelper, POAHelper, POAOperations, PolicyError-
CodeHelper, PolicyErrorHelper, PolicyHelper,
PolicyListHelper, PolicyTypeHelper, RepositoryId-
Helper, ServantActivatorHelper, ServantAlreadyActive-
Helper, ServantLocatorHelper,
ServantNotActiveHelper, ServiceDetailHelper, Service-
InformationHelper, SetOverrideTypeHelper, ShortSe-
qHelper, StringNameHelper, StringSeqHelper,
StringValueHelper, StructMemberHelper, TypeCode,
ULongLongSeqHelper, ULongSeqHelper, UnionMem-
berHelper, UnknownUserExceptionHelper, URL-
StringHelper, UShortSeqHelper, ValueBaseHelper,
ValueMemberHelper, VersionSpecHelper, Visibility-
Helper, WCharSeqHelper, WrongAdapterHelper,
WrongPolicyHelper, WrongTransactionHelper,
WStringSeqHelper, WStringValueHelper
ID_ASSIGNMENT_POLICY_ID: org.omg.PortableServer
id_to_reference(): POAOperations
id_to_servant(): POAOperations
ID_UNIQUENESS_POLICY_ID: org.omg.PortableServer
IdAssignmentPolicy: org.omg.PortableServer
IdAssignmentPolicyOperations: org.omg.PortableServer
IdAssignmentPolicyValue: org.omg.PortableServer

IdentifierHelper: org.omg.CORBA
IDLEntity: org.omg.CORBA.portable
IDLType: org.omg.CORBA
IDLTypeHelper: org.omg.CORBA
IDLTypeOperations: org.omg.CORBA
IdUniquenessPolicy: org.omg.PortableServer
IdUniquenessPolicyOperations: org.omg.PortableServer
IdUniquenessPolicyValue: org.omg.PortableServer
ignoreCase: StringTerm
IllegalStateException: javax.jms, javax.resource.spi
IllegalWriteException: javax.mail
IMP_LIMIT: org.omg.CORBA
impl: CompoundName
IMPLICIT_ACTIVATION: ImplicitActivationPolicyValue
IMPLICIT_ACTIVATION_POLICY_ID: org.omg.Portable-
Server
ImplicitActivationPolicy: org.omg.PortableServer
ImplicitActivationPolicyOperations: org.omg.Portable-
Server
ImplicitActivationPolicyValue: org.omg.PortableServer
importedKeyCascade: DatabaseMetaData
importedKeyInitiallyDeferred: DatabaseMetaData
importedKeyInitiallyImmediate: DatabaseMetaData
importedKeyNoAction: DatabaseMetaData
importedKeyNotDeferrable: DatabaseMetaData
importedKeyRestrict: DatabaseMetaData
importedKeySetDefault: DatabaseMetaData
importedKeySetNull: DatabaseMetaData
INACTIVE: State
inactive(): Activatable
inactiveGroup(): ActivationGroup, ActivationMonitor
inactiveObject(): ActivationGroup, ActivationMonitor
incarnate(): _ServantActivatorStub, ServantActivatorOperations
include(): PageContext, RequestDispatcher
InconsistentTypeCode: org.omg.CORBA.ORBPackage
index: InvalidPolicy
IndexedRecord: javax.resource.cci
IndirectionException: org.omg.CORBA.portable
init(): Filter, GenericServlet, InitialContext, ORB, Servlet
INITIAL_CONTEXT_FACTORY: Context
InitialContext: javax.naming
InitialContextFactory: javax.naming.spi
InitialContextFactoryBuilder: javax.naming.spi
InitialDirContext: javax.naming.directory
INITIALIZE: org.omg.CORBA
initialize(): PageContext
InitialLdapContext: javax.naming.ldap
INLINE: Part
InputStream: org.omg.CORBA.portable,
org.omg.CORBA_2_3.portable
insert(): AdapterAlreadyExistsHelper, AdapterInactive-
Helper, AdapterNonExistentHelper, AddressHelper,
AlreadyBoundHelper, AnySeqHelper, BindingHelper,

BindingIteratorHelper, BindingListHelper, Binding-
TypeHelper, BooleanSeqHelper, CannotProceed-
Helper, CharSeqHelper, CompletionStatusHelper,
CurrentHelper, DefinitionKindHelper, DoubleSe-
qHelper, FieldNameHelper, FloatSeqHelper, For-
wardRequestHelper, IdentifierHelper, IDLTypeHelper,
InvalidAddressHelper, InvalidNameHelper, InvalidPoli-
cyHelper, IstringHelper, LongLongSeqHelper, LongSe-
qHelper, NameComponentHelper, NameHelper,
NameValuePairHelper, NamingContextExtHelper,
NamingContextHelper, NoContextHelper, NoServan-
tHelper, NotEmptyHelper, NotFoundHelper, Not-
FoundReasonHelper, ObjectAlreadyActiveHelper,
ObjectHelper, ObjectNotActiveHelper, OctetSe-
qHelper, ParameterModeHelper, POAHelper, PolicyEr-
rorCodeHelper, PolicyErrorHelper, PolicyHelper,
PolicyListHelper, PolicyTypeHelper, RepositoryId-
Helper, ServantActivatorHelper, ServantAlreadyActive-
Helper, ServantLocatorHelper,
ServantNotActiveHelper, ServiceDetailHelper, Service-
InformationHelper, SetOverrideTypeHelper, ShortSe-
qHelper, StringNameHelper, StringSeqHelper,
StringValueHelper, StructMemberHelper, ULong-
LongSeqHelper, ULongSeqHelper, UnionMember-
Helper, UnknownUserExceptionHelper,
URLStringHelper, UShortSeqHelper, ValueBaseHelper,
ValueMemberHelper, VersionSpecHelper, Visibility-
Helper, WCharSeqHelper, WrongAdapterHelper,
WrongPolicyHelper, WrongTransactionHelper,
WStringSeqHelper, WStringValueHelper
insert_any(): Any, DynAny
insert_boolean(): Any, DynAny
insert_char(): Any, DynAny
insert_double(): Any, DynAny
insert_fixed(): Any
insert_float(): Any, DynAny
insert_long(): Any, DynAny
insert_longlong(): Any, DynAny
insert_Object(): Any
insert_octet(): Any, DynAny
insert_Principal(): Any
insert_reference(): DynAny
insert_short(): Any, DynAny
insert_Streamable(): Any
insert_string(): Any, DynAny
insert_typecode(): DynAny
insert_TypeCode(): Any
insert_ulong(): Any, DynAny
insert_ulonglong(): Any, DynAny
insert_ushort(): Any, DynAny
insert_val(): DynAny
insert_Value(): Any
insert_wchar(): Any, DynAny
insert_wstring(): Any, DynAny

insertRow(): ResultSet
insertsAreDetected(): DatabaseMetaData, ResultSetInfo
InsufficientResourcesException: javax.naming
INTEGER: Types
IntegerComparisonTerm: javax.mail.search
Interaction: javax.resource.cci
InteractionSpec: javax.resource.cci
INTERNAL: org.omg.CORBA
InternetAddress: javax.mail.internet
InternetHeaders: javax.mail.internet
InterruptedNamingException: javax.naming
INTF_REPOS: org.omg.CORBA
IntHolder: org.omg.CORBA
INV_FLAG: org.omg.CORBA
INV_IDENT: org.omg.CORBA
INV_OBJREF: org.omg.CORBA
INV_POLICY: org.omg.CORBA
Invalid: org.omg.CORBA.DynAnyPackage
invalid: SendFailedException, TransportEvent
INVALID_TRANSACTION: org.omg.CORBA
InvalidAddress: org.omg.CosNaming.NamingContextExtPackage
InvalidAddressHelper: org.omg.CosNaming.NamingContextExtPackage
InvalidAddressHolder: org.omg.CosNaming.NamingContextExtPackage
invalidate(): HttpSession
InvalidAttributeIdentifierException: javax.naming.directory
InvalidAttributesException: javax.naming.directory
InvalidAttributeValueException: javax.naming.directory
InvalidClientIDException: javax.jms
InvalidDestinationException: javax.jms
InvalidName: org.omg.CORBA.ORBPackage, org.omg.CosNaming.NamingContextPackage
InvalidNameException: javax.naming
InvalidNameHelper: org.omg.CosNaming.NamingContextPackage
InvalidNameHolder: org.omg.CosNaming.NamingContextPackage
InvalidPolicy: org.omg.PortableServer.POAPackage
InvalidPolicyHelper: org.omg.PortableServer.POAPackage
InvalidSearchControlsException: javax.naming.directory
InvalidSearchFilterException: javax.naming.directory
InvalidSelectorException: javax.jms
InvalidSeq: org.omg.CORBA.DynAnyPackage
InvalidTransactionException: javax.transaction
InvalidValue: org.omg.CORBA.DynAnyPackage
invoke(): _BindingIteratorImplBase, _NamingContextImplBase, Delegate, DynamicImplementation, RemoteRef, Request
InvokeHandler: org.omg.CORBA.portable
IRObject: org.omg.CORBA
IRObjectOperations: org.omg.CORBA

is_a(): Delegate
is_equivalent(): Delegate
is_local(): Delegate
isAfterLast(): ResultSet
isAutoFlush(): JspWriter
isAutoIncrement(): ResultSetMetaData
isBeforeFirst(): ResultSet
isCallerInRole(): EJBContext
isCaseIgnored(): Attributes, BasicAttributes
isCaseSensitive(): ResultSetMetaData
isCatalogAtStart(): DatabaseMetaData
isClosed(): Connection
isCommitted(): ServletResponse, ServletResponseWrapper
isConnected(): Service
isCritical(): Control
isCurrency(): ResultSetMetaData
isCustomMarshaled(): ValueHandler
isDefinitelyWritable(): ResultSetMetaData
isEmpty(): CompositeName, CompoundName, Name
isExpunged(): Message
isFirst(): ResultSet
isIdentical(): EJBLocalObject, EJBObject
isLast(): ResultSet
isLocal(): Util, UtilDelegate
isMimeType(): BodyPart, Message, MimeBodyPart, MimeMessage, Part
isNew(): HttpSession
isNullable(): ParameterMetaData, ResultSetMetaData
isOpen(): Folder
isOrdered(): Attribute, BasicAttribute
isPermanent(): UnavailableException
isReadOnly(): Connection, DatabaseMetaData, ResultSetMetaData, RowSet
isRelative(): NameClassPair
isRemoved(): MessageCountEvent
isRequestedSessionIdFromCookie(): HttpServletRequest, HttpServletRequestWrapper
isRequestedSessionIdFromUrl(): HttpServletRequest, HttpServletRequestWrapper
isRequestedSessionIdFromURL(): HttpServletRequest, HttpServletRequestWrapper
isRequestedSessionIdValid(): HttpServletRequest, HttpServletRequestWrapper
isSameRM(): XAResource
isSearchable(): ResultSetMetaData
isSecure(): ServletRequest, ServletRequestWrapper
isSession(): EJBMetaData
isSet(): Message, MimeMessage
isSigned(): ParameterMetaData, ResultSetMetaData
isStatelessSession(): EJBMetaData
isSubscribed(): Folder
IstringHelper: org.omg.CosNaming
isUnique(): VMID

isUserInRole(): HttpServletRequest, HttpServletRequest-
Wrapper
isWritable(): ResultSetMetaData
Item: javax.mail.FetchProfile
item(): ContextList, ExceptionList, NVList
itemExists(): MapMessage

J

JAVA_OBJECT: Types
javaCharset(): MimeUtility
jdbcCompliant(): Driver
JMSException: javax.jms
JMSSecurityException: javax.jms
jspDestroy(): JspPage
JspEngineInfo: javax.servlet.jsp
JspException: javax.servlet.jsp
JspFactory: javax.servlet.jsp
jspInit(): JspPage
JspPage: javax.servlet.jsp
JspTagException: javax.servlet.jsp
JspWriter: javax.servlet.jsp

K

KEEP_CURRENT_RESULT: Statement
kind: NameComponent
kind(): TypeCode

L

label: UnionMember
LANGUAGE: Context
last(): ResultSet
LASTUID: UIDFolder
LdapContext: javax.naming.ldap
LdapReferralException: javax.naming.ldap
LE: ComparisonTerm
Lease: java.rmi.dgc
length(): Blob, Clob, DynSequence, TypeCode
LIFESPAN_POLICY_ID: org.omg.PortableServer
LifespanPolicy: org.omg.PortableServer
LifespanPolicyOperations: org.omg.PortableServer
LifespanPolicyValue: org.omg.PortableServer
LimitExceededException: javax.naming
LinkException: javax.naming
linkExplanation: LinkException
LinkLoopException: javax.naming
LinkRef: javax.naming
linkRemainingName: LinkException
linkResolvedName: LinkException
linkResolvedObj: LinkException

list(): _NamingContextExtStub, _NamingContextStub,
Context, Folder, InitialContext, Naming, NamingContextOperations, Registry
list_initial_services(): ORB
listBindings(): Context, InitialContext
listSubscribed(): Folder
load(): InternetHeaders
loadClass(): LoaderHandler, RMIClassLoader, RMIClass-
LoaderSpi, Util, UtilDelegate
LoaderHandler: java.rmi.server
loadProxyClass(): RMIClassLoader, RMIClassLoaderSpi
LOCAL_TRANSACTION_COMMITTED: ConnectionEvent
LOCAL_TRANSACTION_ROLLEDBACK: ConnectionEvent
LOCAL_TRANSACTION_STARTED: ConnectionEvent
LocalObject: org.omg.CORBA
LocalTransaction: javax.resource.cci, javax.resource.spi
localTransactionCommitted(): ConnectionEventListener
LocalTransactionException: javax.resource.spi
localTransactionRolledback(): ConnectionEventListener
localTransactionStarted(): ConnectionEventListener
LocateRegistry: java.rmi.registry
locatorsUpdateCopy(): DatabaseMetaData
log(): GenericServlet, LogStream, ServletContext
LogStream: java.rmi.server
LongHolder: org.omg.CORBA
LongLongSeqHelper: org.omg.CORBA
LongLongSeqHolder: org.omg.CORBA
LongSeqHelper: org.omg.CORBA
LongSeqHolder: org.omg.CORBA
LONGVARBINARY: Types
LONGVARCHAR: Types
lookup(): Context, InitialContext, Naming, Registry
lookup_value_factory(): ORB
lookupLink(): Context, InitialContext
LT: ComparisonTerm

M

MailDateFormat: javax.mail.internet
MailEvent: javax.mail.event
MalformedLinkException: javax.naming
ManagedConnection: javax.resource.spi
ManagedConnectionFactory: javax.resource.spi
ManagedConnectionMetaData: javax.resource.spi
MapMessage: javax.jms
MappedRecord: javax.resource.cci
mapSystemException(): Util, UtilDelegate
MARSHAL: org.omg.CORBA
marshal(): CustomMarshal
MarshalException: java.rmi
MarshalledObject: java.rmi
match(): AddressStringTerm, AddressTerm, AndTerm,
BodyTerm, ContentType, DateTerm, FlagTerm, From-
StringTerm, FromTerm, HeaderTerm,

IntegerComparisonTerm, Message, MessageIDTerm, MessageNumberTerm, NotTerm, OrTerm, ReceivedDateTerm, RecipientStringTerm, RecipientTerm, SearchTerm, SentDateTerm, SizeTerm, StringTerm, SubjectTerm

matchManagedConnections(): ManagedConnectionFactory

MAXBQUALSIZE: Xid

MAXGTRIDSIZE: Xid

member(): DynUnion

member_count(): TypeCode

member_kind(): DynUnion

member_label(): TypeCode

member_name(): DynUnion, TypeCode

member_type(): TypeCode

member_visibility(): TypeCode

Message: javax.jms, javax.mail

message: StoreEvent

Message.RecipientType: javax.mail

MESSAGE_DELIVERED: TransportEvent

MESSAGE_NOT_DELIVERED: TransportEvent

MESSAGE_PARTIALLY_DELIVERED: TransportEvent

MessageAware: javax.mail

messageChanged(): MessageChangedListener

MessageChangedEvent: javax.mail.event

MessageChangedListener: javax.mail.event

MessageConsumer: javax.jms

MessageContext: javax.mail

MessageCountAdapter: javax.mail.event

MessageCountEvent: javax.mail.event

MessageCountListener: javax.mail.event

messageDelivered(): TransportAdapter, TransportListener

MessageDrivenBean: javax.ejb

MessageDrivenContext: javax.ejb

MessageEOFException: javax.jms

MessageFormatException: javax.jms

MessageIDTerm: javax.mail.search

MessageListener: javax.jms

messageNotDelivered(): TransportAdapter, TransportListener

MessageNotReadableException: javax.jms

MessageNotWriteableException: javax.jms

MessageNumberTerm: javax.mail.search

messagePartiallyDelivered(): TransportAdapter, TransportListener

MessageProducer: javax.jms

MessageRemovedException: javax.mail

messagesAdded(): MessageCountAdapter, MessageCountListener

messagesRemoved(): MessageCountAdapter, MessageCountListener

MessagingException: javax.mail

MethodNotSupportedException: javax.mail

MIME: HeaderTokenizer

MimeBodyPart: javax.mail.internet

mimeCharset(): MimeUtility

MimeMessage: javax.mail.internet

MimeMessage.RecipientType: javax.mail.internet

MimeMultipart: javax.mail.internet

MimePart: javax.mail.internet

MimePartDataSource: javax.mail.internet

MimeUtility: javax.mail.internet

minor: SystemException

missing_node: NotFoundReason

mode: Folder

ModificationItem: javax.naming.directory

modified: MimeMessage

modifyAttributes(): DirContext, InitialDirContext

moveToCurrentRow(): ResultSet

moveToInsertRow(): ResultSet

msg: MessageChangedEvent, TransportEvent

msgnum: Message

msgs: MessageCountEvent

Multipart: javax.mail

MultipartDataSource: javax.mail

MULTIPLE_ID: IdUniquenessPolicyValue

myProps: InitialContext

mySyntax: CompoundName

N

Name: javax.naming

name: DriverPropertyInfo, StructMember, UnionMember, ValueMember

name(): NamedValue, Principal, TypeCode

NameAlreadyBoundException: javax.naming

NameClassPair: javax.naming

NameComponent: org.omg.CosNaming

NameComponentHelper: org.omg.CosNaming

NameComponentHolder: org.omg.CosNaming

NamedValue: org.omg.CORBA

NameHelper: org.omg.CosNaming

NameHolder: org.omg.CosNaming

NameNotFoundException: javax.naming

NameParser: javax.naming

NamespaceChangeListener: javax.naming.event

NameValuePair: org.omg.CORBA

NameValuePairHelper: org.omg.CORBA

Naming: java.rmi

NamingContext: org.omg.CosNaming

NamingContextExt: org.omg.CosNaming

NamingContextExtHelper: org.omg.CosNaming

NamingContextExtHolder: org.omg.CosNaming

NamingContextExtOperations: org.omg.CosNaming

NamingContextExtPOA: org.omg.CosNaming

NamingContextHelper: org.omg.CosNaming

NamingContextHolder: org.omg.CosNaming

NamingContextOperations: org.omg.CosNaming

NamingContextPOA: org.omg.CosNaming
NamingEnumeration: javax.naming
NamingEvent: javax.naming.event
NamingException: javax.naming
NamingExceptionEvent: javax.naming.event
namingExceptionThrown(): NamingListener
NamingListener: javax.naming.event
NamingManager: javax.naming.spi
NamingSecurityException: javax.naming
narrow(): BindingIteratorHelper, CurrentHelper, IDLType-
    Helper, NamingContextExtHelper, NamingContex-
    tHelper, POAHelper, PolicyHelper,
    PortableRemoteObject, PortableRemoteObjectDele-
    gate, ServantActivatorHelper, ServantLocatorHelper
nativeSQL(): Connection
ncontext: BindingType
NE: ComparisonTerm
negotiate(): StartTlsResponse
new_context(): _NamingContextExtStub, _NamingCon-
    textStub, NamingContextOperations
newBinding: NamingEvent
newCall(): RemoteRef
newFolder: FolderEvent
newInstance(): ActivationGroup_Stub, ActivationInstan-
    tiator, InitialLdapContext, LdapContext
newLine(): JspWriter
NewsAddress: javax.mail.internet
newsgroup: NewsAddress
NEWSGROUPS: RecipientType
newStream(): SharedInputStream
next(): DynAny, HeaderTokenizer, NamingEnumeration,
    ResultSet
next_n(): _BindingIteratorStub, BindingIteratorOpera-
    tions
next_one(): _BindingIteratorStub, BindingIteratorOpera-
    tions
NO_BUFFER: JspWriter
NO_GENERATED_KEYS: Statement
NO_IMPLEMENT: org.omg.CORBA
NO_IMPLICIT_ACTIVATION: ImplicitActivationPolicyValue
NO_MEMORY: org.omg.CORBA
NO_PERMISSION: org.omg.CORBA
NO_RESOURCES: org.omg.CORBA
NO_RESPONSE: org.omg.CORBA
nobject: BindingType
NoContext: org.omg.PortableServer.CurrentPackage
NoContextHelper: org.omg.PortableServer.CurrentPack-
    age
NoInitialContextException: javax.naming
non_existent(): Delegate
NON_PERSISTENT: DeliveryMode
NON_RETAIN: ServantRetentionPolicyValue
NONCRITICAL: Control
NoPermissionException: javax.naming

NoServant: org.omg.PortableServer.POAPackage
NoServantHelper: org.omg.PortableServer.POAPackage
NoSuchAttributeException: javax.naming.directory
NoSuchEntityException: javax.ejb
NoSuchObjectException: java.rmi
NoSuchObjectLocalException: javax.ejb
NoSuchProviderException: javax.mail
not_context: NotFoundReason
not_object: NotFoundReason
NotBoundException: java.rmi
NotContextException: javax.naming
NotEmpty: org.omg.CosNaming.NamingContextPackage
NotEmptyHelper: org.omg.CosNaming.NamingCon-
    textPackage
NotEmptyHolder: org.omg.CosNaming.NamingCon-
    textPackage
NotFound: org.omg.CosNaming.NamingContextPackage
NotFoundHelper: org.omg.CosNaming.NamingCon-
    textPackage
NotFoundHolder: org.omg.CosNaming.NamingCon-
    textPackage
NotFoundReason: org.omg.CosNaming.NamingCon-
    textPackage
NotFoundReasonHelper: org.omg.CosNaming.Naming-
    ContextPackage
NotFoundReasonHolder: org.omg.CosNaming.Naming-
    ContextPackage
NOTICE: StoreEvent
notification(): StoreListener
notificationReceived(): UnsolicitedNotificationListener
notifyConnectionListeners(): Folder, Service
notifyFolderListeners(): Folder, Store
notifyFolderRenamedListeners(): Folder, Store
notifyMessageAddedListeners(): Folder
notifyMessageChangedListeners(): Folder
notifyMessageRemovedListeners(): Folder
notifyStoreListeners(): Store
notifyTransportListeners(): Transport
NotSupportedException: javax.resource, javax.transac-
    tion
NotTerm: javax.mail.search
NULL: Types
nullPlusNonNullIsNull(): DatabaseMetaData
nullsAreSortedAtEnd(): DatabaseMetaData
nullsAreSortedAtStart(): DatabaseMetaData
nullsAreSortedHigh(): DatabaseMetaData
nullsAreSortedLow(): DatabaseMetaData
number: IntegerComparisonTerm
NUMERIC: Types
NVList: org.omg.CORBA

O

OBJ_ADAPTER: org.omg.CORBA
Object: org.omg.CORBA
OBJECT_ADDED: NamingEvent
OBJECT_CHANGED: NamingEvent
OBJECT_FACTORIES: Context
object_id(): Delegate
OBJECT_NOT_EXIST: org.omg.CORBA
OBJECT_REMOVED: NamingEvent
OBJECT_RENAMED: NamingEvent
OBJECT_SCOPE: EventContext, SearchControls
object_to_string(): ORB
objectAdded(): NamespaceChangeListener
ObjectAlreadyActive: org.omg.PortableServer.POAPackage
ObjectAlreadyActiveHelper: org.omg.PortableServer.POA-Package
objectChanged(): ObjectChangeListener
ObjectChangeListener: javax.naming.event
ObjectFactory: javax.naming.spi
ObjectFactoryBuilder: javax.naming.spi
ObjectHelper: org.omg.CORBA
ObjectHolder: org.omg.CORBA
ObjectImpl: org.omg.CORBA.portable,
    org.omg.CORBA_2_3.portable
ObjectMessage: javax.jms
ObjectNotActive: org.omg.PortableServer.POAPackage
ObjectNotActiveHelper: org.omg.PortableServer.POA-Package
ObjectNotFoundException: javax.ejb
objectRemoved(): NamespaceChangeListener
objectRenamed(): NamespaceChangeListener
ObjID: java.rmi.server
OctetSeqHelper: org.omg.CORBA
OctetSeqHolder: org.omg.CORBA
offset: IndirectionException
OID: StartTlsRequest, StartTlsResponse
oldBinding: NamingEvent
OMGVMCID: org.omg.CORBA
ONELEVEL_SCOPE: EventContext, SearchControls
onException(): ExceptionListener
onMessage(): MessageListener
op_name(): ServerRequest
open(): Folder
OPENED: ConnectionEvent
opened(): ConnectionAdapter, ConnectionListener
Operation: java.rmi.server
operation(): Request, ServerRequest
OperationNotSupportedException: javax.naming
ORB: org.omg.CORBA, org.omg.CORBA_2_3
orb(): Delegate, InputStream, OutputStream, Tie
ORB_CTRL_MODEL: ThreadPolicyValue
ordered: BasicAttribute
originalEx: UnknownException

OrTerm: javax.mail.search
OTHER: Types
othersDeletesAreVisible(): DatabaseMetaData, Result-SetInfo
othersInsertsAreVisible(): DatabaseMetaData, Result-SetInfo
othersUpdatesAreVisible(): DatabaseMetaData, Result-SetInfo
OUT: PageContext
OutputStream: org.omg.CORBA.portable,
    org.omg.CORBA_2_3.portable
ownDeletesAreVisible(): DatabaseMetaData, ResultSet-Info
ownInsertsAreVisible(): DatabaseMetaData, ResultSet-Info
ownUpdatesAreVisible(): DatabaseMetaData, ResultSet-Info

P

packagePrefix: LoaderHandler, RemoteRef
PAGE: PageContext
PAGE_SCOPE: PageContext
PAGECONTEXT: PageContext
PageContext: javax.servlet.jsp
PARAM_IN: ParameterMode
PARAM_INOUT: ParameterMode
PARAM_OUT: ParameterMode
ParameterList: javax.mail.internet
ParameterMetaData: java.sql
ParameterMode: org.omg.CORBA
ParameterModeHelper: org.omg.CORBA
ParameterModeHolder: org.omg.CORBA
parameterModeIn: ParameterMetaData
parameterModeInOut: ParameterMetaData
parameterModeOut: ParameterMetaData
parameterModeUnknown: ParameterMetaData
parameterNoNulls: ParameterMetaData
parameterNullable: ParameterMetaData
parameterNullableUnknown: ParameterMetaData
params(): ServerRequest
parent: BodyPart, Multipart
parent(): Context
parse(): InternetAddress, MailDateFormat, MimeMes-sage, MimeMultipart, NameParser, NewsAddress
parsed: MimeMultipart
ParseException: javax.mail.internet
parseLevel(): LogStream
parsePostData(): HttpUtils
parseQueryString(): HttpUtils
parseString(): URLName
Part: javax.mail
PartialResultException: javax.naming
parts: Multipart

PasswordAuthentication: javax.mail
PasswordCredential: javax.resource.spi.security
pattern: StringTerm
peek(): HeaderTokenizer
perform_work(): ORB
PERSIST_STORE: org.omg.CORBA
PERSISTENT: DeliveryMode, LifespanPolicyValue
personal: InternetAddress
POA: org.omg.PortableServer
poa(): Delegate
POAHelper: org.omg.PortableServer
POAManager: org.omg.PortableServer
POAManagerOperations: org.omg.PortableServer
POAOperations: org.omg.PortableServer
Policy: org.omg.CORBA
policy_type(): _PolicyStub, PolicyOperations
PolicyError: org.omg.CORBA
PolicyErrorCodeHelper: org.omg.CORBA
PolicyErrorHelper: org.omg.CORBA
PolicyErrorHolder: org.omg.CORBA
PolicyHelper: org.omg.CORBA
PolicyHolder: org.omg.CORBA
PolicyListHelper: org.omg.CORBA
PolicyListHolder: org.omg.CORBA
PolicyOperations: org.omg.CORBA
PolicyTypeHelper: org.omg.CORBA
poll_next_response(): ORB
poll_response(): Request
PooledConnection: javax.sql
popBody(): PageContext
PortableRemoteObject: javax.rmi
PortableRemoteObjectDelegate: javax.rmi.CORBA
pos: AddressException
position(): Blob, Clob
postinvoke(): _ServantLocatorStub, ServantLocatorOperations
preinvoke(): _ServantLocatorStub, ServantLocatorOperations
prepare(): XAResource
prepareCall(): Connection
PreparedStatement: java.sql
prepareStatement(): Connection
previous(): ResultSet
Principal: org.omg.CORBA
PrincipalHolder: org.omg.CORBA
print(): JspWriter, ServletOutputStream
println(): DriverManager, JspWriter, ServletOutputStream
printStackTrace(): EJBException, NamingException
PRIVATE_MEMBER: org.omg.CORBA
procedureColumnIn: DatabaseMetaData
procedureColumnInOut: DatabaseMetaData
procedureColumnOut: DatabaseMetaData
procedureColumnResult: DatabaseMetaData
procedureColumnReturn: DatabaseMetaData

procedureColumnUnknown: DatabaseMetaData
procedureNoNulls: DatabaseMetaData
procedureNoResult: DatabaseMetaData
procedureNullable: DatabaseMetaData
procedureNullableUnknown: DatabaseMetaData
procedureResultUnknown: DatabaseMetaData
procedureReturnsResult: DatabaseMetaData
propertyExists(): Message
protocolConnect(): Service
Provider: javax.mail
Provider.Type: javax.mail
PROVIDER_URL: Context
PUBLIC_MEMBER: org.omg.CORBA
publish(): TopicPublisher
pushBody(): PageContext
put(): Attributes, BasicAttributes
putValue(): HttpSession

Q

Queue: javax.jms
QueueBrowser: javax.jms
QueueConnection: javax.jms
QueueConnectionFactory: javax.jms
queueEvent(): Service
QueueReceiver: javax.jms
QueueRequestor: javax.jms
QueueSender: javax.jms
QueueSession: javax.jms
quote(): MimeUtility
QUOTEDSTRING: Token

R

read(): AdapterAlreadyExistsHelper, AdapterInactive-Helper, AdapterNonExistentHelper, AddressHelper, AlreadyBoundHelper, AnySeqHelper, BindingHelper, BindingIteratorHelper, BindingListHelper, Binding-TypeHelper, BooleanSeqHelper, CannotProceed-Helper, CharSeqHelper, CompletionStatusHelper, CurrentHelper, DefinitionKindHelper, DoubleSe-qHelper, FieldNameHelper, FloatSeqHelper, For-wardRequestHelper, IdentifierHelper, IDLTypeHelper, InputStream, InvalidAddressHelper, InvalidName-Helper, InvalidPolicyHelper, IstringHelper, Long-LongSeqHelper, LongSeqHelper, NameComponentHelper, NameHelper, NameValue-PairHelper, NamingContextExtHelper, NamingContex-tHelper, NoContextHelper, NoServantHelper, NotEmptyHelper, NotFoundHelper, NotFoundReason-Helper, ObjectAlreadyActiveHelper, ObjectHelper, ObjectNotActiveHelper, ObjID, OctetSeqHelper, ParameterModeHelper, POAHelper,

PolicyErrorCodeHelper, PolicyErrorHelper, Policy-Helper, PolicyListHelper, PolicyTypeHelper, RepositoryIdHelper, ServantActivatorHelper, ServantAlreadyActiveHelper, ServantLocatorHelper, ServantNotActiveHelper, ServiceDetailHelper, ServiceInformationHelper, SetOverrideTypeHelper, ShortSeqHelper, Streamable, StringNameHelper, StringSeqHelper, StringValueHelper, StructMemberHelper, UID, ULongLongSeqHelper, ULongSeqHelper, UnionMemberHelper, UnknownUserExceptionHelper, URLStringHelper, UShortSeqHelper, ValueBaseHelper, ValueMemberHelper, VersionSpecHelper, VisibilityHelper, WCharSeqHelper, WrongAdapterHelper, WrongPolicyHelper, WrongTransactionHelper, WStringSeqHelper, WStringValueHelper

read_Abstract(): DataInputStream

read_abstract_interface(): InputStream

read_any(): DataInputStream, InputStream

read_any_array(): DataInputStream

read_boolean(): DataInputStream, InputStream

read_boolean_array(): DataInputStream, InputStream

read_char(): DataInputStream, InputStream

read_char_array(): DataInputStream, InputStream

read_Context(): InputStream

read_double(): DataInputStream, InputStream

read_double_array(): DataInputStream, InputStream

read_fixed(): InputStream

read_float(): DataInputStream, InputStream

read_float_array(): DataInputStream, InputStream

read_long(): DataInputStream, InputStream

read_long_array(): DataInputStream, InputStream

read_longlong(): DataInputStream, InputStream

read_longlong_array(): DataInputStream, InputStream

read_Object(): DataInputStream, InputStream

read_octet(): DataInputStream, InputStream

read_octet_array(): DataInputStream, InputStream

READ_ONLY: Folder

read_Principal(): InputStream

read_short(): DataInputStream, InputStream

read_short_array(): DataInputStream, InputStream

read_string(): DataInputStream, InputStream

read_TypeCode(): DataInputStream, InputStream

read_ulong(): DataInputStream, InputStream

read_ulong_array(): DataInputStream, InputStream

read_ulonglong(): DataInputStream, InputStream

read_ulonglong_array(): DataInputStream, InputStream

read_ushort(): DataInputStream, InputStream

read_ushort_array(): DataInputStream, InputStream

read_Value(): DataInputStream

read_value(): Any, BoxedValueHelper, InputStream, StringValueHelper, ValueFactory, WStringValueHelper

read_wchar(): DataInputStream, InputStream

read_wchar_array(): DataInputStream, InputStream

READ_WRITE: Folder

read_wstring(): DataInputStream, InputStream

readAny(): Util, UtilDelegate

readArray(): SQLInput

readAsciiStream(): SQLInput

readBigDecimal(): SQLInput

readBinaryStream(): SQLInput

readBlob(): SQLInput

readBoolean(): BytesMessage, SQLInput, StreamMessage

readByte(): BytesMessage, SQLInput, StreamMessage

readBytes(): BytesMessage, SQLInput, StreamMessage

readChar(): BytesMessage, StreamMessage

readCharacterStream(): SQLInput

readClob(): SQLInput

readData(): RowSetReader

readDate(): SQLInput

readDouble(): BytesMessage, SQLInput, StreamMessage

readEJBHome(): HandleDelegate

readEJBObject(): HandleDelegate

readFloat(): BytesMessage, SQLInput, StreamMessage

readInt(): BytesMessage, SQLInput, StreamMessage

readLine(): ServletInputStream

readLong(): BytesMessage, SQLInput, StreamMessage

readObject(): SQLInput, StreamMessage, StubDelegate

ReadOnlyFolderException: javax.mail

readRef(): SQLInput

readResolve(): RecipientType

readShort(): BytesMessage, SQLInput, StreamMessage

readSQL(): SQLData

readString(): SQLInput, StreamMessage

readTime(): SQLInput

readTimestamp(): SQLInput

readUnsignedByte(): BytesMessage

readUnsignedShort(): BytesMessage

readURL(): SQLInput

readUTF(): BytesMessage

readValue(): ValueHandler

REAL: Types

reason: PolicyError

rebind(): _NamingContextExtStub, _NamingContextStub, Context, DirContext, InitialContext, InitialDirContext, Naming, NamingContextOperations, Registry

rebind_context(): _NamingContextExtStub, _NamingContextStub, NamingContextOperations

receive(): MessageConsumer

ReceivedDateTerm: javax.mail.search

receiveNoWait(): MessageConsumer

RECENT: Flag

RecipientStringTerm: javax.mail.search

RecipientTerm: javax.mail.search

RecipientType: javax.mail.internet.MimeMessage, javax.mail.Message

reconnect(): InitialLdapContext, LdapContext

Record: javax.resource.cci

RecordFactory: javax.resource.cci

recover(): Session, XAResource
Ref: java.sql
ref: AddressException, RemoteObject
REF: Types
RefAddr: javax.naming
Reference: javax.naming
reference_to_id(): POAOperations
reference_to_servant(): POAOperations
Referenceable: javax.naming, javax.resource
REFERRAL: Context
ReferralException: javax.naming
refreshRow(): ResultSet
register(): Activatable
register_value_factory(): ORB
registerDriver(): DriverManager
registerGroup(): ActivationSystem
registerObject(): ActivationSystem
registerOutParameter(): CallableStatement
registerSynchronization(): Transaction
registerTarget(): Util, UtilDelegate
Registry: java.rmi.registry
REGISTRY_ID: ObjID
REGISTRY_PORT: Registry
RegistryHandler: java.rmi.registry
registryImpl(): RegistryHandler
registryStub(): RegistryHandler
relative(): ResultSet
release(): Delegate, PageContext
releaseInputStream(): RemoteCall
releaseOutputStream(): RemoteCall
releasePageContext(): JspFactory
releaseReply(): Delegate
releaseSavepoint(): Connection
remainingName: NamingException, ResolveResult
remainingNewName: CannotProceedException
RemarshalException: org.omg.CORBA.portable
Remote: java.rmi
RemoteCall: java.rmi.server
remoteEquals(): RemoteRef
RemoteException: java.rmi
remoteHashCode(): RemoteRef
RemoteObject: java.rmi.server
RemoteRef: java.rmi.server
RemoteServer: java.rmi.server
RemoteStub: java.rmi.server
remoteToString(): RemoteRef
remove(): Attribute, Attributes, BasicAttribute, BasicAt-
    tributes, CompositeName, CompoundName, Con-
    textList, EJBHome, EJBLocalHome, EJBLocalObject,
    EJBObject, ExceptionList, Flags, Name, NVList,
    ParameterList, Reference
REMOVE_ATTRIBUTE: DirContext
removeAttribute(): HttpSession, PageContext, Servlet-
    Context, ServletRequest, ServletRequestWrapper

removeBodyPart(): Multipart
removeConnectionEventListener(): ManagedConnection,
    PooledConnection
removeConnectionListener(): Folder, Service
removed: MessageCountEvent
REMOVED: MessageCountEvent
RemoveException: javax.ejb
removeFolderListener(): Folder, Store
removeFromEnvironment(): Context, InitialContext
removeHeader(): BodyPart, InternetHeaders, Message,
    MimeBodyPart, MimeMessage, Part
removeMessageChangedListener(): Folder
removeMessageCountListener(): Folder
removeNamingListener(): EventContext
removeRowSetListener(): RowSet
removeStoreListener(): Store
removeTransportListener(): Transport
removeValue(): HttpSession
rename(): Context, InitialContext
RENAMED: FolderEvent
renameTo(): Folder
REPLACE_ATTRIBUTE: DirContext
reply(): Message, MimeMessage
RepositoryIdHelper: org.omg.CORBA
REQUEST: PageContext
Request: org.omg.CORBA
request(): Delegate, QueueRequestor, TopicRequestor
REQUEST_PROCESSING_POLICY_ID: org.omg.Portable-
    Server
REQUEST_SCOPE: PageContext
RequestDispatcher: javax.servlet
requestPasswordAuthentication(): Session
RequestProcessingPolicy: org.omg.PortableServer
RequestProcessingPolicyOperations: org.omg.Portable-
    Server
RequestProcessingPolicyValue: org.omg.PortableServer
required: DriverPropertyInfo
reset(): BytesMessage, ServletResponse, ServletRespon-
    seWrapper, StreamMessage
resetBuffer(): ServletResponse, ServletResponseWrapper
resolve(): _NamingContextExtStub, _NamingCon-
    textStub, NamingContextOperations
resolve_initial_references(): ORB
resolve_str(): _NamingContextExtStub, NamingContex-
    tExtOperations
resolvedName: NamingException
resolvedObj: NamingException, ResolveResult
Resolver: javax.naming.spi
ResolveResult: javax.naming.spi
resolveToClass(): Resolver
ResourceAdapterInternalException: javax.resource.spi
ResourceAdapterMetaData: javax.resource.cci
ResourceAllocationException: javax.jms,
    javax.resource.spi

setAltName(): CannotProceedException

setAltNameCtx(): CannotProceedException

setArray(): PreparedStatement, RowSet

setAsciiStream(): CallableStatement, Clob, PreparedStatement, RowSet

setAttribute(): HttpSession, PageContext, ServletContext, ServletRequest, ServletRequestWrapper

setAttributes(): SearchResult

setAutoCommit(): Connection

setAutoIncrement(): RowSetMetaData

setBigDecimal(): CallableStatement, PreparedStatement, RowSet

setBinaryStream(): Blob, CallableStatement, PreparedStatement, RowSet

setBlob(): PreparedStatement, RowSet

setBoolean(): CallableStatement, MapMessage, PreparedStatement, RowSet

setBooleanProperty(): Message

setBufferSize(): ServletResponse, ServletResponseWrapper

setByte(): CallableStatement, MapMessage, PreparedStatement, RowSet

setByteProperty(): Message

setBytes(): Blob, CallableStatement, MapMessage, PreparedStatement, RowSet

setCalendar(): MailDateFormat

setCaseSensitive(): RowSetMetaData

setCatalog(): Connection

setCatalogName(): RowSetMetaData

setChar(): MapMessage

setCharacterEncoding(): ServletRequest, ServletRequestWrapper

setCharacterStream(): CallableStatement, Clob, PreparedStatement, RowSet

setClassName(): NameClassPair

setClientID(): Connection

setClob(): PreparedStatement, RowSet

setColumnCount(): RowSetMetaData

setColumnDisplaySize(): RowSetMetaData

setColumnLabel(): RowSetMetaData

setColumnName(): RowSetMetaData

setColumnType(): RowSetMetaData

setColumnTypeName(): RowSetMetaData

setCommand(): RowSet

setComment(): Cookie

setConcurrency(): RowSet

setConnected(): Service

setConnectionHandle(): ConnectionEvent

setContent(): BodyPart, Message, MimeBodyPart, MimeMessage, Part

setContentID(): MimeMessage

setContentLanguage(): MimeBodyPart, MimeMessage, MimePart

setContentLength(): ServletResponse, ServletResponseWrapper

setContentMD5(): MimeBodyPart, MimeMessage, MimePart

setContentType(): ServletResponse, ServletResponseWrapper

setCountLimit(): SearchControls

setCurrency(): RowSetMetaData

setCursorName(): Statement

setDataHandler(): BodyPart, Message, MimeBodyPart, MimeMessage, Part

setDataSourceName(): RowSet

setDate(): CallableStatement, PreparedStatement, RowSet, Time

setDateHeader(): HttpServletResponse, HttpServletResponseWrapper

setDebug(): Session

setDefaultFactory(): JspFactory

setDefaultStream(): LogStream

setDeliveryMode(): MessageProducer

setDerefLinkFlag(): SearchControls

setDescription(): BodyPart, Message, MimeBodyPart, MimeMessage, Part

setDisableMessageID(): MessageProducer

setDisableMessageTimestamp(): MessageProducer

setDisposition(): BodyPart, ContentDisposition, Message, MimeBodyPart, MimeMessage, Part

setDomain(): Cookie

setDouble(): CallableStatement, MapMessage, PreparedStatement, RowSet

setDoubleProperty(): Message

setEnabledCipherSuites(): StartTlsResponse

setEntityContext(): EntityBean

setEnvironment(): CannotProceedException

setEscapeProcessing(): RowSet, Statement

setExceptionListener(): Connection

setExpunged(): Message

setFailureHandler(): RMISocketFactory

setFetchDirection(): ResultSet, Statement

setFetchSize(): ResultSet, Statement

setFileName(): BodyPart, Message, MimeBodyPart, MimeMessage, Part

setFlag(): Message

setFlags(): Folder, Message, MimeMessage

setFloat(): CallableStatement, MapMessage, PreparedStatement, RowSet

setFloatProperty(): Message

setFrom(): Message, MimeMessage

setHeader(): BodyPart, HttpServletResponse, HttpServletResponseWrapper, InternetHeaders, Message, MimeBodyPart, MimeMessage, Part

setHoldability(): Connection

setHost(): NewsAddress

setHostnameVerifier(): StartTlsResponse

setHours(): Date
setInitialContextFactoryBuilder(): NamingManager
setInt(): CallableStatement, MapMessage, Prepared-
Statement, RowSet
setIntHeader(): HttpServletResponse, HttpServletResponseWrapper
setIntProperty(): Message
setJMSCorrelationID(): Message
setJMSCorrelationIDAsBytes(): Message
setJMSDeliveryMode(): Message
setJMSDestination(): Message
setJMSExpiration(): Message
setJMSMessageID(): Message
setJMSPriority(): Message
setJMSRedelivered(): Message
setJMSReplyTo(): Message
setJMSTimestamp(): Message
setJMSType(): Message
setLinkedException(): JMSException, ResourceException
setLinkedWarning(): ResourceWarning
setLinkExplanation(): LinkException
setLinkRemainingName(): LinkException
setLinkResolvedName(): LinkException
setLinkResolvedObj(): LinkException
setLocale(): ServletResponse, ServletResponseWrapper
setLog(): RemoteServer
setLoginTimeout(): ConnectionPoolDataSource, Data-
Source, DriverManager, XADataSource
setLogStream(): DriverManager
setLogWriter(): ConnectionPoolDataSource, DataSource,
DriverManager, ManagedConnection, ManagedConnectionFactory, XADataSource
setLong(): CallableStatement, MapMessage, Prepared-
Statement, RowSet
setLongProperty(): Message
setManagedConnectionFactory(): PasswordCredential
setMaxAge(): Cookie
setMaxFieldSize(): RowSet, Statement
setMaxInactiveInterval(): HttpSession
setMaxRows(): RowSet, Statement
setMessageDrivenContext(): MessageDrivenBean
setMessageListener(): MessageConsumer, Session
setMessageNumber(): Message
setMetaData(): RowSetInternal
setMinutes(): Date
setMonth(): Time
setMultipartDataSource(): Multipart
setName(): NameClassPair
setNanos(): Timestamp
setNewsgroup(): NewsAddress
setNextException(): MessagingException, SQLException
setNextWarning(): SQLWarning
setNull(): CallableStatement, PreparedStatement,
RowSet

setNullable(): RowSetMetaData
setNumberFormat(): MailDateFormat
setObject(): Binding, CallableStatement, MapMessage,
ObjectMessage, PreparedStatement, Ref, RowSet
setObjectFactoryBuilder(): NamingManager
setObjectProperty(): Message
setOutputStream(): LogStream
SetOverrideType: org.omg.CORBA
SetOverrideTypeHelper: org.omg.CORBA
setParameter(): ContentDisposition, ContentType
setParameterList(): ContentDisposition, ContentType
setParent(): Multipart
setPassword(): RowSet
setPasswordAuthentication(): Session
setPath(): Cookie
setPersonal(): InternetAddress
setPrecision(): RowSetMetaData
setPrimaryType(): ContentType
setPriority(): MessageProducer
setProvider(): Session
setQueryTimeout(): RowSet, Statement
setReadOnly(): Connection, RowSet
setRecipient(): Message
setRecipients(): Message, MimeMessage
setRecordName(): Record
setRecordShortDescription(): Record
setRef(): PreparedStatement, RemoteStub, RowSet
setReference(): Referenceable
setRelative(): NameClassPair
setRemainingName(): NamingException, ResolveResult
setRemainingNewName(): CannotProceedException
setReplyTo(): Message, MimeMessage
setRequest(): ServletRequestWrapper
setRequestControls(): InitialLdapContext, LdapContext
setResolvedName(): NamingException
setResolvedObj(): NamingException, ResolveResult
setResponse(): ServletResponseWrapper
setReturningAttributes(): SearchControls
setReturningObjFlag(): SearchControls
setRollbackOnly(): EJBContext, Transaction, Transaction-
Manager, UserTransaction
setRootCause(): NamingException
setSavepoint(): Connection
setScale(): RowSetMetaData
setSchemaName(): RowSetMetaData
setSearchable(): RowSetMetaData
setSearchScope(): SearchControls
setSeconds(): Date
setSecure(): Cookie
setSentDate(): Message, MimeMessage
setSessionContext(): SessionBean
setShort(): CallableStatement, MapMessage, Prepared-
Statement, RowSet
setShortProperty(): Message

setSigned(): RowSetMetaData
setSocketFactory(): RMISocketFactory
setStatus(): HttpServletResponse, HttpServletRespon-
    seWrapper
setString(): CallableStatement, Clob, MapMessage, Pre-
    paredStatement, RowSet
setStringProperty(): Message
setSubject(): Message, MimeMessage
setSubscribed(): Folder
setSubType(): ContentType, MimeMultipart
setSystem(): ActivationGroup
setTableName(): RowSetMetaData
setTarget(): Tie
setText(): BodyPart, Message, MimeBodyPart, MimeMes-
    sage, MimePart, Part, TextMessage
setTime(): CallableStatement, Date, PreparedStatement,
    RowSet, Time, Timestamp
setTimeLimit(): SearchControls
setTimestamp(): CallableStatement, PreparedStatement,
    RowSet
setTimeToLive(): MessageProducer
setTransactionIsolation(): Connection, RowSet
setTransactionTimeout(): TransactionManager, User-
    Transaction, XAResource
setType(): RowSet
setTypeMap(): Connection, RowSet
setUnexecutedModifications(): AttributeModificationEx-
    ception
setUnicodeStream(): PreparedStatement
setUrl(): RowSet
setURL(): CallableStatement, PreparedStatement
setURLName(): Service
setUsername(): RowSet
setValue(): Cookie
setVersion(): Cookie
setYear(): Time
SharedInputStream: javax.mail.internet
ShortHolder: org.omg.CORBA
ShortSeqHelper: org.omg.CORBA
ShortSeqHolder: org.omg.CORBA
shutdown(): ActivationSystem, ORB
SILENT: LogStream
SINGLE_THREAD_MODEL: ThreadPolicyValue
SingleThreadModel: javax.servlet
size(): Attribute, Attributes, BasicAttribute, BasicAt-
    tributes, CompositeName, CompoundName, Name,
    ParameterList, Reference
SizeLimitExceededException: javax.naming
SizeTerm: javax.mail.search
Skeleton: java.rmi.server
SkeletonMismatchException: java.rmi.server
SkeletonNotFoundException: java.rmi.server
skipReferral(): ReferralException
SMALLINT: Types

SocketSecurityException: java.rmi.server
SQLData: java.sql
SQLException: java.sql
SQLInput: java.sql
SQLOutput: java.sql
SQLPermission: java.sql
sqlStateSQL99: DatabaseMetaData
sqlStateXOpen: DatabaseMetaData
SQLWarning: java.sql
start(): Connection, ServerSession, XAResource
startsWith(): CompositeName, CompoundName, Name
StartTlsRequest: javax.naming.ldap
StartTlsResponse: javax.naming.ldap
State: org.omg.PortableServer.POAManagerPackage
STATE_FACTORIES: Context
StateFactory: javax.naming.spi
Statement: java.sql
Status: javax.transaction
STATUS_ACTIVE: Status
STATUS_COMMITTED: Status
STATUS_COMMITTING: Status
STATUS_MARKED_ROLLBACK: Status
STATUS_NO_TRANSACTION: Status
STATUS_PREPARED: Status
STATUS_PREPARING: Status
STATUS_ROLLEDBACK: Status
STATUS_ROLLING_BACK: Status
STATUS_UNKNOWN: Status
stop(): Connection
STORE: Type
Store: javax.mail
store: Folder
StoreClosedException: javax.mail
StoreEvent: javax.mail.event
StoreListener: javax.mail.event
storesLowerCaseIdentifiers(): DatabaseMetaData
storesLowerCaseQuotedIdentifiers(): DatabaseMeta-
    Data
storesMixedCaseIdentifiers(): DatabaseMetaData
storesMixedCaseQuotedIdentifiers(): DatabaseMeta-
    Data
storesUpperCaseIdentifiers(): DatabaseMetaData
storesUpperCaseQuotedIdentifiers(): DatabaseMeta-
    Data
Streamable: javax.resource.cci, org.omg.CORBA.portable
StreamableValue: org.omg.CORBA.portable
StreamMessage: javax.jms
string_to_object(): ORB
StringHolder: org.omg.CORBA
StringNameHelper: org.omg.CosNaming.NamingContex-
    tExtPackage
StringRefAddr: javax.naming
StringSeqHelper: org.omg.CORBA
StringSeqHolder: org.omg.CORBA

StringTerm: javax.mail.search
StringValueHelper: org.omg.CORBA
STRUCT: Types
Struct: java.sql
StructMember: org.omg.CORBA
StructMemberHelper: org.omg.CORBA
Stub: javax.rmi.CORBA
StubDelegate: javax.rmi.CORBA
StubNotFoundException: java.rmi
SubjectTerm: javax.mail.search
SUBTREE_SCOPE: EventContext, SearchControls
SUCCESS_NO_INFO: Statement
supportsAlterTableWithAddColumn(): DatabaseMeta-Data
supportsAlterTableWithDropColumn(): DatabaseMeta-Data
supportsANSI92EntryLevelSQL(): DatabaseMetaData
supportsANSI92FullSQL(): DatabaseMetaData
supportsANSI92IntermediateSQL(): DatabaseMetaData
supportsBatchUpdates(): DatabaseMetaData
supportsCatalogsInDataManipulation(): DatabaseMeta-Data
supportsCatalogsInIndexDefinitions(): DatabaseMeta-Data
supportsCatalogsInPrivilegeDefinitions():
DatabaseMetaData
supportsCatalogsInProcedureCalls(): DatabaseMeta-Data
supportsCatalogsInTableDefinitions(): DatabaseMeta-Data
supportsColumnAliasing(): DatabaseMetaData
supportsConvert(): DatabaseMetaData
supportsCoreSQLGrammar(): DatabaseMetaData
supportsCorrelatedSubqueries(): DatabaseMetaData
supportsDataDefinitionAndDataManipulationTransac-tions(): DatabaseMetaData
supportsDataManipulationTransactionsOnly():
DatabaseMetaData
supportsDifferentTableCorrelationNames():
DatabaseMetaData
supportsExecuteWithInputAndOutputRecord():
ResourceAdapterMetaData
supportsExecuteWithInputRecordOnly():
ResourceAdapterMetaData
supportsExpressionsInOrderBy(): DatabaseMetaData
supportsExtendedSQLGrammar(): DatabaseMetaData
supportsFullOuterJoins(): DatabaseMetaData
supportsGetGeneratedKeys(): DatabaseMetaData
supportsGroupBy(): DatabaseMetaData
supportsGroupByBeyondSelect(): DatabaseMetaData
supportsGroupByUnrelated(): DatabaseMetaData
supportsIntegrityEnhancementFacility():
DatabaseMetaData
supportsLikeEscapeClause(): DatabaseMetaData

supportsLimitedOuterJoins(): DatabaseMetaData
supportsLocalTransactionDemarcation():
ResourceAdapterMetaData
supportsMinimumSQLGrammar(): DatabaseMetaData
supportsMixedCaseIdentifiers(): DatabaseMetaData
supportsMixedCaseQuotedIdentifiers(): DatabaseMeta-Data
supportsMultipleOpenResults(): DatabaseMetaData
supportsMultipleResultSets(): DatabaseMetaData
supportsMultipleTransactions(): DatabaseMetaData
supportsNamedParameters(): DatabaseMetaData
supportsNonNullableColumns(): DatabaseMetaData
supportsOpenCursorsAcrossCommit(): DatabaseMeta-Data
supportsOpenCursorsAcrossRollback(): DatabaseMeta-Data
supportsOpenStatementsAcrossCommit():
DatabaseMetaData
supportsOpenStatementsAcrossRollback():
DatabaseMetaData
supportsOrderByUnrelated(): DatabaseMetaData
supportsOuterJoins(): DatabaseMetaData
supportsPositionedDelete(): DatabaseMetaData
supportsPositionedUpdate(): DatabaseMetaData
supportsResultSetConcurrency(): DatabaseMetaData
supportsResultSetHoldability(): DatabaseMetaData
supportsResultSetType(): DatabaseMetaData, ResultSet-Info
supportsResultTypeConcurrency(): ResultSetInfo
supportsSavepoints(): DatabaseMetaData
supportsSchemasInDataManipulation(): DatabaseMeta-Data
supportsSchemasInIndexDefinitions(): DatabaseMeta-Data
supportsSchemasInPrivilegeDefinitions():
DatabaseMetaData
supportsSchemasInProcedureCalls(): DatabaseMeta-Data
supportsSchemasInTableDefinitions(): DatabaseMeta-Data
supportsSelectForUpdate(): DatabaseMetaData
supportsStatementPooling(): DatabaseMetaData
supportsStoredProcedures(): DatabaseMetaData
supportsSubqueriesInComparisons(): DatabaseMeta-Data
supportsSubqueriesInExists(): DatabaseMetaData
supportsSubqueriesInIns(): DatabaseMetaData
supportsSubqueriesInQuantifieds(): DatabaseMetaData
supportsTableCorrelationNames(): DatabaseMetaData
supportsTransactionIsolationLevel(): DatabaseMeta-Data
supportsTransactions(): DatabaseMetaData
supportsUnion(): DatabaseMetaData
supportsUnionAll(): DatabaseMetaData

suspend(): TransactionManager
SYNC_RECEIVE: InteractionSpec
SYNC_SEND: InteractionSpec
SYNC_SEND_RECEIVE: InteractionSpec
Synchronization: javax.transaction
SYSTEM_ID: IdAssignmentPolicyValue
SYSTEM_PORT: ActivationSystem
SystemException: javax.transaction, org.omg.CORBA

T

tableIndexClustered: DatabaseMetaData
tableIndexHashed: DatabaseMetaData
tableIndexOther: DatabaseMetaData
tableIndexStatistic: DatabaseMetaData
target(): Request
targetMustExist(): EventContext
TCKind: org.omg.CORBA
TemporaryQueue: javax.jms
TemporaryTopic: javax.jms
term: NotTerm
terms: AndTerm, OrTerm
TextMessage: javax.jms
the_activator(): POAOperations
the_children(): POAOperations
the_name(): POAOperations
the_parent(): POAOperations
the_POAManager(): POAOperations
this_object(): Delegate
thisObject(): Tie
THREAD_POLICY_ID: org.omg.PortableServer
ThreadPolicy: org.omg.PortableServer
ThreadPolicyOperations: org.omg.PortableServer
ThreadPolicyValue: org.omg.PortableServer
Tie: javax.rmi.CORBA
TIME: Types
Time: java.sql
TimeLimitExceededException: javax.naming
Timestamp: java.sql
TIMESTAMP: Types
TINYINT: Types
tk_abstract_interface: TCKind
tk_alias: TCKind
tk_any: TCKind
tk_array: TCKind
tk_boolean: TCKind
tk_char: TCKind
tk_double: TCKind
tk_enum: TCKind
tk_except: TCKind
tk_fixed: TCKind
tk_float: TCKind
tk_long: TCKind
tk_longdouble: TCKind

tk_longlong: TCKind
tk_native: TCKind
tk_null: TCKind
tk_objref: TCKind
tk_octet: TCKind
tk_Principal: TCKind
tk_sequence: TCKind
tk_short: TCKind
tk_string: TCKind
tk_struct: TCKind
tk_TypeCode: TCKind
tk_ulong: TCKind
tk_ulonglong: TCKind
tk_union: TCKind
tk_ushort: TCKind
tk_value: TCKind
tk_value_box: TCKind
tk_void: TCKind
tk_wchar: TCKind
tk_wstring: TCKind
TMENDRSCAN: XAResource
TMFAIL: XAResource
TMJOIN: XAResource
TMNOFLAGS: XAResource
TMONEPHASE: XAResource
TMRESUME: XAResource
TMSTARTRSCAN: XAResource
TMSUCCESS: XAResource
TMSUSPEND: XAResource
TO: RecipientType
to_any(): DynAny
to_name(): _NamingContextExtStub, NamingContextExt-
    Operations
to_string(): _NamingContextExtStub, NamingContextExt-
    Operations
to_url(): _NamingContextExtStub, NamingContextExtOp-
    erations
Token: javax.mail.internet.HeaderTokenizer
Topic: javax.jms
TopicConnection: javax.jms
TopicConnectionFactory: javax.jms
TopicPublisher: javax.jms
TopicRequestor: javax.jms
TopicSession: javax.jms
TopicSubscriber: javax.jms
toString(): Address, AddressException, AttributeModifica-
    tionException, BasicAttribute, BasicAttributes, Bina-
    ryRefAddr, Binding, CompositeName,
    CompoundName, ContentDisposition, ContentType,
    Date, Delegate, Folder, InternetAddress, LinkExcep-
    tion, LogStream, ModificationItem, NameClassPair,
    NamingException, NewsAddress, ObjectImpl, ObjID,
    Operation, ParameterList, Provider, Queue, RefAddr,
    Reference, RemoteObject, SearchResult, Service,

Stub, StubDelegate, SystemException, Time, Timestamp, Topic, UID, URLName, VMID

toStub(): PortableRemoteObject, PortableRemoteObject-Delegate, RemoteObject

toUnicodeString(): InternetAddress

Transaction: javax.transaction

TRANSACTION_NONE: Connection

TRANSACTION_READ_COMMITTED: Connection

TRANSACTION_READ_UNCOMMITTED: Connection

TRANSACTION_REPEATABLE_READ: Connection

TRANSACTION_REQUIRED: org.omg.CORBA

TRANSACTION_ROLLEDBACK: org.omg.CORBA

TRANSACTION_SERIALIZABLE: Connection

TransactionInProgressException: javax.jms

TransactionManager: javax.transaction

TransactionRequiredException: javax.transaction

TransactionRequiredLocalException: javax.ejb

TransactionRolledbackException: javax.transaction

TransactionRolledBackException: javax.jms

TransactionRolledbackLocalException: javax.ejb

TRANSIENT: LifespanPolicyValue, org.omg.CORBA

Transport: javax.mail

TRANSPORT: Type

TransportAdapter: javax.mail.event

TransportEvent: javax.mail.event

TransportListener: javax.mail.event

truncate(): Blob, Clob

Type: javax.mail.Provider

type: ConnectionEvent, FolderEvent, MessageChangedEvent, MessageCountEvent, NamingEvent, RecipientTerm, RecipientType, StoreEvent, StructMember, TransportEvent, UnionMember, ValueMember

type(): _IDLTypeStub, AdapterAlreadyExistsHelper, AdapterInactiveHelper, AdapterNonExistentHelper, AddressHelper, AlreadyBoundHelper, Any, AnySeqHelper, BindingHelper, BindingIteratorHelper, BindingListHelper, BindingTypeHelper, BooleanSeqHelper, CannotProceedHelper, CharSeqHelper, CompletionStatusHelper, CurrentHelper, DefinitionKindHelper, DoubleSeqHelper, DynAny, FieldNameHelper, FloatSeqHelper, ForwardRequestHelper, IdentifierHelper, IDLTypeHelper, IDLTypeOperations, InvalidAddressHelper, InvalidNameHelper, InvalidPolicyHelper, IstringHelper, LongLongSeqHelper, LongSeqHelper, NameComponentHelper, NameHelper, NameValuePairHelper, NamingContextExtHelper, NamingContextHelper, NoContextHelper, NoServantHelper, NotEmptyHelper, NotFoundHelper, NotFoundReasonHelper, ObjectAlreadyActiveHelper, ObjectHelper, ObjectNotActiveHelper, OctetSeqHelper, ParameterModeHelper, POAHelper, PolicyErrorCodeHelper, PolicyErrorHelper, PolicyHelper, PolicyListHelper, PolicyTypeHelper, RepositoryIdHelper, ServantActivatorHelper, ServantAlreadyActiveHelper, ServantLocatorHelper,

ServantNotActiveHelper, ServiceDetailHelper, ServiceInformationHelper, SetOverrideTypeHelper, ShortSeqHelper, StringNameHelper, StringSeqHelper, StringValueHelper, StructMemberHelper, ULongLongSeqHelper, ULongSeqHelper, UnionMemberHelper, UnknownUserExceptionHelper, URLStringHelper, UShortSeqHelper, ValueBaseHelper, ValueMemberHelper, VersionSpecHelper, VisibilityHelper, WCharSeqHelper, WrongAdapterHelper, WrongPolicyHelper, WrongTransactionHelper, WStringSeqHelper, WStringValueHelper

type_def: StructMember, UnionMember, ValueMember

TYPE_FORWARD_ONLY: ResultSet

type_modifier(): TypeCode

TYPE_SCROLL_INSENSITIVE: ResultSet

TYPE_SCROLL_SENSITIVE: ResultSet

TypeCode: org.omg.CORBA

TypeCodeHolder: org.omg.CORBA

TypeMismatch: org.omg.CORBA.DynAnyPackage

typeNoNulls: DatabaseMetaData

typeNullable: DatabaseMetaData

typeNullableUnknown: DatabaseMetaData

typePredBasic: DatabaseMetaData

typePredChar: DatabaseMetaData

typePredNone: DatabaseMetaData

Types: java.sql

typeSearchable: DatabaseMetaData

U

UID: FetchProfileItem, java.rmi.server

UIDFolder: javax.mail

UIDFolder.FetchProfileItem: javax.mail

ULongLongSeqHelper: org.omg.CORBA

ULongLongSeqHolder: org.omg.CORBA

ULongSeqHelper: org.omg.CORBA

ULongSeqHolder: org.omg.CORBA

UnavailableException: javax.servlet

unbind(): _NamingContextExtStub, _NamingContextStub, Context, InitialContext, Naming, NamingContextOperations, Registry

UNBOUNDED_BUFFER: JspWriter

UnexpectedException: java.rmi

unexportObject(): Activatable, PortableRemoteObject, PortableRemoteObjectDelegate, UnicastRemoteObject, Util, UtilDelegate

UnicastRemoteObject: java.rmi.server

UnionMember: org.omg.CORBA

UnionMemberHelper: org.omg.CORBA

UNIQUE_ID: IdUniquenessPolicyValue

UNKNOWN: org.omg.CORBA

unknown_adapter(): AdapterActivatorOperations

UnknownException: org.omg.CORBA.portable

UnknownGroupException: java.rmi.activation

UnknownHostException: java.rmi
UnknownObjectException: java.rmi.activation
UnknownUserException: org.omg.CORBA
UnknownUserExceptionHelper: org.omg.CORBA
UnknownUserExceptionHolder: org.omg.CORBA
unmarshal(): CustomMarshal
UnmarshalException: java.rmi
Unreferenced: java.rmi.server
unreferenced(): Unreferenced
unregister(): Activatable
unregister_value_factory(): ORB
unregisterGroup(): ActivationSystem
unregisterObject(): ActivationSystem
unsetEntityContext(): EntityBean
UnsolicitedNotification: javax.naming.ldap
UnsolicitedNotificationEvent: javax.naming.ldap
UnsolicitedNotificationListener: javax.naming.ldap
unsubscribe(): TopicSession
UNSUPPORTED_POLICY: org.omg.CORBA
UNSUPPORTED_POLICY_VALUE: org.omg.CORBA
updateArray(): ResultSet
updateAsciiStream(): ResultSet
updateBigDecimal(): ResultSet
updateBinaryStream(): ResultSet
updateBlob(): ResultSet
updateBoolean(): ResultSet
updateByte(): ResultSet
updateBytes(): ResultSet
updateCharacterStream(): ResultSet
updateClob(): ResultSet
updateDate(): ResultSet
updateDouble(): ResultSet
updateFloat(): ResultSet
updateHeaders(): MimeBodyPart, MimeMessage, Mime-
  Multipart
updateInt(): ResultSet
updateLong(): ResultSet
updateNull(): ResultSet
updateObject(): ResultSet
updateRef(): ResultSet
updateRow(): ResultSet
updatesAreDetected(): DatabaseMetaData, ResultSet-
  Info
updateShort(): ResultSet
updateString(): ResultSet
updateTime(): ResultSet
updateTimestamp(): ResultSet
url: Service
URL_PKG_PREFIXES: Context
URLName: javax.mail
URLStringHelper: org.omg.CosNaming.NamingContex-
  tExtPackage
USE_ACTIVE_OBJECT_MAP_ONLY: RequestProcessing-
  PolicyValue

USE_DEFAULT_SERVANT: RequestProcessingPolicyValue
USE_SERVANT_MANAGER: RequestProcessingPolicy-
  Value
USER: Flag
USER_ID: IdAssignmentPolicyValue
UserException: org.omg.CORBA
UserTransaction: javax.transaction
usesLocalFilePerTable(): DatabaseMetaData
usesLocalFiles(): DatabaseMetaData
UShortSeqHelper: org.omg.CORBA
UShortSeqHolder: org.omg.CORBA
Util: javax.rmi.CORBA
UtilDelegate: javax.rmi.CORBA

V

validate_connection(): LocalObject
validSent: SendFailedException, TransportEvent
validUnsent: SendFailedException, TransportEvent
value: AlreadyBoundHolder, AnyHolder, AnySeqHolder,
  ARG_IN, ARG_INOUT, ARG_OUT, BAD_POLICY,
  BAD_POLICY_TYPE, BAD_POLICY_VALUE, Bind-
  ingHolder, BindingIteratorHolder, BindingListHolder,
  BindingTypeHolder, BooleanHolder, BooleanSe-
  qHolder, ByteHolder, CannotProceedHolder,
  CharHolder, CharSeqHolder, CookieHolder,
  CTX_RESTRICT_SCOPE, CurrentHolder, DoubleHolder,
  DoubleSeqHolder, DriverPropertyInfo, FixedHolder,
  FloatHolder, FloatSeqHolder, ID_ASSIGNMENT_POL-
  ICY_ID, ID_UNIQUENESS_POLICY_ID, IMPLICIT_ACTI-
  VATION_POLICY_ID, IntHolder, InvalidAddressHolder,
  InvalidNameHolder, LIFESPAN_POLICY_ID,
  LongHolder, LongLongSeqHolder, LongSeqHolder,
  NameComponentHolder, NameHolder, NameValue-
  Pair, NamingContextExtHolder, NamingContextHolder,
  NotEmptyHolder, NotFoundHolder, NotFoundReason-
  Holder, ObjectHolder, OctetSeqHolder, OMGVMCID,
  ParameterModeHolder, PolicyErrorHolder, Policy-
  Holder, PolicyListHolder, PrincipalHolder, PRI-
  VATE_MEMBER, PUBLIC_MEMBER,
  REQUEST_PROCESSING_POLICY_ID, SER-
  VANT_RETENTION_POLICY_ID, ServiceInformation-
  Holder, ShortHolder, ShortSeqHolder, StringHolder,
  StringSeqHolder, THREAD_POLICY_ID, TypeCode-
  Holder, ULongLongSeqHolder, ULongSeqHolder,
  UnknownUserExceptionHolder, UNSUPPORTED_POL-
  ICY, UNSUPPORTED_POLICY_VALUE, UShortSe-
  qHolder, ValueBaseHolder, VM_ABSTRACT,
  VM_CUSTOM, VM_NONE, VM_TRUNCATABLE,
  WCharSeqHolder, WrongTransactionHolder,
  WStringSeqHolder
value(): BindingType, CompletionStatus, DefinitionKind,
  IdAssignmentPolicyOperations, IdAssignmentPolicy-
  Value, IdUniquenessPolicyOperations,

IdUniquenessPolicyValue, ImplicitActivationPolicyOp-
erations, ImplicitActivationPolicyValue, LifespanPoli-
cyOperations, LifespanPolicyValue, NamedValue,
NotFoundReason, ParameterMode, RequestProcess-
ingPolicyOperations, RequestProcessingPolicyValue,
ServantRetentionPolicyOperations, ServantRetention-
PolicyValue, SetOverrideType, State, TCKind, Thread-
PolicyOperations, ThreadPolicyValue

value_as_string(): DynEnum
value_as_ulong(): DynEnum
ValueBase: org.omg.CORBA.portable
ValueBaseHelper: org.omg.CORBA
ValueBaseHolder: org.omg.CORBA
valueBound(): HttpSessionBindingListener
ValueFactory: org.omg.CORBA.portable
ValueHandler: javax.rmi.CORBA
ValueMember: org.omg.CORBA
ValueMemberHelper: org.omg.CORBA
valueOf(): Date, Time, Timestamp
values: BasicAttribute
valueUnbound(): HttpSessionBindingListener
VARBINARY: Types
VARCHAR: Types
VERBOSE: LogStream
version: ValueMember
versionColumnNotPseudo: DatabaseMetaData
versionColumnPseudo: DatabaseMetaData
versionColumnUnknown: DatabaseMetaData
VersionSpecHelper: org.omg.CORBA
VisibilityHelper: org.omg.CORBA
VM_ABSTRACT: org.omg.CORBA
VM_CUSTOM: org.omg.CORBA
VM_NONE: org.omg.CORBA
VM_TRUNCATABLE: org.omg.CORBA
VMID: java.rmi.dgc

W

wasNull(): CallableStatement, ResultSet, SQLInput
WCharSeqHelper: org.omg.CORBA
WCharSeqHolder: org.omg.CORBA
why: NotFound
work_pending(): ORB
wrapException(): Util, UtilDelegate
write(): AdapterAlreadyExistsHelper, AdapterInactive-
Helper, AdapterNonExistentHelper, AddressHelper,
AlreadyBoundHelper, AnySeqHelper, BindingHelper,
BindingIteratorHelper, BindingListHelper, Binding-
TypeHelper, BooleanSeqHelper, CannotProceed-
Helper, CharSeqHelper, CompletionStatusHelper,
CurrentHelper, DefinitionKindHelper, DoubleSe-
qHelper, FieldNameHelper, FloatSeqHelper, For-
wardRequestHelper, IdentifierHelper, IDLTypeHelper,
InvalidAddressHelper, InvalidNameHelper,

InvalidPolicyHelper, IstringHelper, LogStream, Long-
LongSeqHelper, LongSeqHelper, NameComponen-
tHelper, NameHelper, NameValuePairHelper,
NamingContextExtHelper, NamingContextHelper,
NoContextHelper, NoServantHelper, NotEmptyHelper,
NotFoundHelper, NotFoundReasonHelper, ObjectAl-
readyActiveHelper, ObjectHelper, ObjectNotActive-
Helper, ObjID, OctetSeqHelper, OutputStream,
ParameterModeHelper, POAHelper, PolicyErrorCode-
Helper, PolicyErrorHelper, PolicyHelper, PolicyLis-
tHelper, PolicyTypeHelper, RepositoryIdHelper,
ServantActivatorHelper, ServantAlreadyActiveHelper,
ServantLocatorHelper, ServantNotActiveHelper, Ser-
viceDetailHelper, ServiceInformationHelper, SetOver-
rideTypeHelper, ShortSeqHelper, Streamable,
StringNameHelper, StringSeqHelper, StringValue-
Helper, StructMemberHelper, UID, ULongLongSe-
qHelper, ULongSeqHelper, UnionMemberHelper,
UnknownUserExceptionHelper, URLStringHelper,
UShortSeqHelper, ValueBaseHelper, ValueMember-
Helper, VersionSpecHelper, VisibilityHelper, WCharSe-
qHelper, WrongAdapterHelper, WrongPolicyHelper,
WrongTransactionHelper, WStringSeqHelper, WString-
ValueHelper

write_Abstract(): DataOutputStream
write_abstract_interface(): OutputStream
write_any(): DataOutputStream, OutputStream
write_any_array(): DataOutputStream
write_boolean(): DataOutputStream, OutputStream
write_boolean_array(): DataOutputStream, Output-
Stream
write_char(): DataOutputStream, OutputStream
write_char_array(): DataOutputStream, OutputStream
write_Context(): OutputStream
write_double(): DataOutputStream, OutputStream
write_double_array(): DataOutputStream, OutputStream
write_fixed(): OutputStream
write_float(): DataOutputStream, OutputStream
write_float_array(): DataOutputStream, OutputStream
write_long(): DataOutputStream, OutputStream
write_long_array(): DataOutputStream, OutputStream
write_longlong(): DataOutputStream, OutputStream
write_longlong_array(): DataOutputStream, Output-
Stream
write_Object(): DataOutputStream, OutputStream
write_octet(): DataOutputStream, OutputStream
write_octet_array(): DataOutputStream, OutputStream
write_Principal(): OutputStream
write_short(): DataOutputStream, OutputStream
write_short_array(): DataOutputStream, OutputStream
write_string(): DataOutputStream, OutputStream
write_TypeCode(): DataOutputStream, OutputStream
write_ulong(): DataOutputStream, OutputStream
write_ulong_array(): DataOutputStream, OutputStream

write_ulonglong(): DataOutputStream, OutputStream
write_ulonglong_array(): DataOutputStream, Output-
    Stream
write_ushort(): DataOutputStream, OutputStream
write_ushort_array(): DataOutputStream, OutputStream
write_value(): Any, BoxedValueHelper, OutputStream,
    StringValueHelper, WStringValueHelper
write_Value(): DataOutputStream
write_wchar(): DataOutputStream, OutputStream
write_wchar_array(): DataOutputStream, OutputStream
write_wstring(): DataOutputStream, OutputStream
writeAbstractObject(): Util, UtilDelegate
writeAny(): Util, UtilDelegate
writeArray(): SQLOutput
writeAsciiStream(): SQLOutput
writeBigDecimal(): SQLOutput
writeBinaryStream(): SQLOutput
writeBlob(): SQLOutput
writeBoolean(): BytesMessage, SQLOutput, StreamMes-
    sage
writeByte(): BytesMessage, SQLOutput, StreamMessage
writeBytes(): BytesMessage, SQLOutput, StreamMessage
writeChar(): BytesMessage, StreamMessage
writeCharacterStream(): SQLOutput
writeClob(): SQLOutput
writeData(): RowSetWriter
writeDate(): SQLOutput
writeDouble(): BytesMessage, SQLOutput, StreamMes-
    sage
writeEJBHome(): HandleDelegate
writeEJBObject(): HandleDelegate
writeFloat(): BytesMessage, SQLOutput, StreamMessage
writeInt(): BytesMessage, SQLOutput, StreamMessage
writeLong(): BytesMessage, SQLOutput, StreamMessage
writeObject(): BytesMessage, SQLOutput, StreamMes-
    sage, StubDelegate
writeRef(): SQLOutput
writeRemoteObject(): Util, UtilDelegate
writeReplace(): ValueHandler
writeShort(): BytesMessage, SQLOutput, StreamMessage
writeSQL(): SQLData
writeString(): SQLOutput, StreamMessage
writeStruct(): SQLOutput
writeTime(): SQLOutput
writeTimestamp(): SQLOutput
writeTo(): BodyPart, Message, MimeBodyPart, MimeMes-
    sage, MimeMultipart, Multipart, Part
writeURL(): SQLOutput
writeUTF(): BytesMessage
writeValue(): ValueHandler
WrongAdapter: org.omg.PortableServer.POAPackage
WrongAdapterHelper: org.omg.PortableServer.POAPack-
    age
WrongPolicy: org.omg.PortableServer.POAPackage

WrongPolicyHelper: org.omg.PortableServer.POAPackage
WrongTransaction: org.omg.CORBA
WrongTransactionHelper: org.omg.CORBA
WrongTransactionHolder: org.omg.CORBA
WStringSeqHelper: org.omg.CORBA
WStringSeqHolder: org.omg.CORBA
WStringValueHelper: org.omg.CORBA

X

XA_HEURCOM: XAException
XA_HEURHAZ: XAException
XA_HEURMIX: XAException
XA_HEURRB: XAException
XA_NOMIGRATE: XAException
XA_OK: XAResource
XA_RBBASE: XAException
XA_RBCOMMFAIL: XAException
XA_RBDEADLOCK: XAException
XA_RBEND: XAException
XA_RBINTEGRITY: XAException
XA_RBOTHER: XAException
XA_RBPROTO: XAException
XA_RBROLLBACK: XAException
XA_RBTIMEOUT: XAException
XA_RBTRANSIENT: XAException
XA_RDONLY: XAException, XAResource
XA_RETRY: XAException
XAConnection: javax.jms, javax.sql
XAConnectionFactory: javax.jms
XADataSource: javax.sql
XAER_ASYNC: XAException
XAER_DUPID: XAException
XAER_INVAL: XAException
XAER_NOTA: XAException
XAER_OUTSIDE: XAException
XAER_PROTO: XAException
XAER_RMERR: XAException
XAER_RMFAIL: XAException
XAException: javax.transaction.xa
XAQueueConnection: javax.jms
XAQueueConnectionFactory: javax.jms
XAQueueSession: javax.jms
XAResource: javax.transaction.xa
XASession: javax.jms
XATopicConnection: javax.jms
XATopicConnectionFactory: javax.jms
XATopicSession: javax.jms
Xid: javax.transaction.xa

Index

Symbols

& (ampersand), (AND) operator
   combining with search filter, 216
< > (angle brackets), equality comparison
   operator, 351
< (angle bracket, left)
   < (less than) operator, 351
   <= (less than or equal to) operator, 351
> (angle bracket, right)
   > (greater than) operator, 351
   >= (greater than or equal to)
   operator, 351
<%! %> (JSP declaration) tag, 174
<%@ %> (JSP directive) tag, 174
<%= %> (JSP expression) tag, 172
<% %> JSP tags, 172
<%@ taglib %> directive, 179
* (asterisk)
   arithmetic operator, 351
   wildcard character in LDAP
   searches, 216
= (equal sign), (comparison)
   operator, 351
– (minus sign), arithmetic operator, 351
() (parentheses), grouping expressions
   with, 352
% (percent sign), wildcard matching of
   string sequences, 352

+ (plus sign), arithmetic operator, 351
' (single quotes), in string literals, 350
/ (slash), division operator, 351
_ (underscore), wildcard matching of
   string characters, 352
| (vertical bar)
   | (OR) operator, combining with
   search filter, 216
   | | (string concatenation)
   operator, 387, 388

A

abstract foreign-key constraints, 288–292
abstract persistence schema, 279–283
acceptChanges() (CachedRowSet), 47
access control (see authentication)
Access database (Microsoft), metadata, 38
Account interface (example), 51
   defining and implementing, 60
AccountClient class (example), 54
AccountImpl class (example), 51–53
   implementation of Account class, 61
AccountReg class (example), 53
acknowledge() (Message), 329
actions, JSP, 176–179
   combining with JavaBeans, 177–179
Activatable class, 62, 73, 74
   constructors, 74

Enhanced View of Time Service, CORBA, 436
enterprise computing, 3–5
EnterpriseBean interface, 239
<enterprise:Loop> custom JSP tag, 183
entity beans, 232
  container-managed transactions, 300
  EntityBean interface, 239
  implementation interfaces/classes, 235
  implementing, 259–292
    deployment options, 264
    EntityContext, 265
    finder and select methods, 261–263
    life cycle, 266
    methods, additional, 263
    persistence, bean-managed, 267–273
    persistence, container-managed, 273–292
    primary keys, 259
    remote home interface, 262
  methods, 240
entity element in deployment descriptors, 264
entity reference nodes (XML), expanding (DOM parser), 311
EntityContext class, 272
enumerations, IDL, 414–416
equality comparison operators, 351
equals() (RemoteObject), 61
equi-join (or inner join), SQL tables, 383
error handling
  naming services, 220, 221
error() (ErrorHandler), 308
ErrorHandler interface, 306, 308
errors
  binding remote objects to names, 63
  JDBC, handling, 31
  marshaling exception, 56
  remote object URLs, 64
  in remote sessions, 60
  in servlet responses, handling of, 148–151
    status codes, 148
    FileServlet (example), 150
    servlet exceptions, 149
  SQL return codes for, 389–391
  (see also exceptions)
escape sequences, 44
  components (JDBC), 44
  dates (example), 28
  dates (ISO), 28

for IDL character literals, 408
stored procedures, accessing (JDBC), 43
event notification, 8
event notification, JNDI, 219–226
  registering event listeners, 222–226
  listen command, 224–226
  sources of events, 219
  writing event listeners, 220–222
EventContext interface, 219
  addNamingListener(), 222
EventDirContext interface, 219
  addNamingListener(), 222
  filters specifying target of listener, 223
events
  asynchronous, JMS, 330
  CORBA, Notification Service, 438
  Event Service, CORBA, 436
  synchronicity in SAX parsing cycle, 308
exact path matching of servlet requests, 142
examples in this book, downloading, xv
exceptions
  on EJB home interfaces, 238
  IDL, 99, 420–422, 425
    inheritance of, 428
    standard, 420
    user-defined, mapping to Java, 421
  JNDI, 191
  name, object not found at specified, 123
  object references, narrowing (CORBA), 121
  objects, binding to NamingContext, 119
  servlet, 149
  SQL return codes for, 389–391
  (see also errors)
execute() (Statement), 23
executeBatch()
  PreparedStatement interface, 35
  Statement interface, 34
executeQuery() (Statement), 23
executeUpdate()
  PreparedStatement interface, 33
  Statement class, 23
expert flag, 468
expirable leases on remote objects, 58
exportObject() (Activatable), 74
  using instead of initialization constructors, 75

JSPs (JavaServer Pages), 10, 170–186
  actions, 176–179
    combining with JavaBeans, 177–179
  Apache Tomcat server, 172
  built-in objects, 175
  compiling into Java Servlets, 171
  custom tags, 179–186
    body tags, 184
    implementing, 180
    inter-tag communication, 185
    life cycle, 182
    package for, 180
  directives and declarations, 174
  displaying current date (example), 172
  granularity of, 49
  inserting Java code with <%...%>
    element, 173
  sharing data between JSPs and
    servlets, 176
<jsp:setProperty> tags, 178
<jsp:useBean> tag, 178
  scope argument, 179
JspWriter class, 185
JTA (Java Transaction API), 11, 296, 348
  two-phase commit, 44

K

keep-alive checks, servlets performing on
    servers, 148
key attributes, 209
keywords
  escape sequences (JDBC), 44
  IDL, 402
    valuetype, 431
kind field (NameComponent), 123

L

language independence
  CORBA, 94
  inter-ORB communications, 97
large data types, 27
Large Objects (LOBs), 48
LDAP (Lightweight Directory Access
    Protocol), 187
  creating InitialContext with factory
    class, 192
  directory servers, prohibiting new
    entries in, 215
  search filter strings, 216

leaf, CORBA naming directory, 96
leases, expirable (on remote objects), 58
libraries
  native code, wrapping with Java, 20
  native functions, loading, 87
  third-party, thread safety and, 159
Licensing Service, CORBA, 437
Life Cycle Service, CORBA, 438
life cycle, servlets, 137
LIKE operator (SQL), 382
LIKE statement, 44
LIKE (string comparison) operator, 351
links (JSPs), sharing data between, 176
list(), 63, 200
listBindings() (Context), 204
list_initial_references() (ORB), 122
literals
  IDL, 405–409
    character, 408
    numeric, 407
    string literals, 409
  in JMS message selectors, 350
  in WHERE clause, EJB QL, 455
loadFromDB(), 273
loadLibrary() (System), 87
local EJB clients, 237
  remote vs., 249
local EJB home interface, 237
local names of XML elements, 306
LocateRegistry interface, 63
  remote objects, looking up, 65
Locator class, 306
locatorsUpdateCopy()
    (DatabaseMetaData), 48
logical operators, 351
  EJB QL, 458
  in message selectors, 349
login information, associating with
    URLName objects, 359
logins, database, 22
long data type, 350 .
looking up objects in naming
    systems, 189–191
  JNDI context, 193
lookup() (Naming), 57, 63
loopback calls, 265
loops (<enterprise:Loop> custom JSP
    tag), 183
LOWER function, 388

N

<name> tags, JSP, 180
NameAlreadyBoundException class, 207
NameClassPair class, 200
NameComponent class, 117, 123
NamedNodeMap class, 313
NamedValue class, 131
names
    children of Context (JNDI), 201
    fully-qualified, for remote objects, 57
    JMS identifiers, 350
NamespaceChangeListener interface, 220
NamespaceChangeLogger class
    (example), 220–222
namespaces
    IDL, 409
    JSP, 177
        for custom tags, 179
    XML, 306, 316
        DOM parser, awareness of, 311
        support for, requesting, 308
naming and directory services (see
        CORBA; JNDI; RMI)
naming context, obtaining object
        reference from, 123
naming conventions
    bound objects in sessions, 165
    SQL objects (within schemas), 377
    tables and schemas (SQL), 377
Naming interface, 53, 57, 63, 64
    looking up remote objects
        (example), 54
    lookup(), 57
naming scopes, IDL, 409
Naming Service (CORBA), 113, 122
    references, narrowing, 123
naming services, 187
    binding names to objects, 191
    CORBA, 438
        orbd daemon, 446
        registering server object with, 90
        tnamserv daemon, 450
    JNDI, looking up object, 189–191
    non-RMI, using to register RMI remote
        objects, 70
    RMI, 57, 63–65
        converting to JNDI for
            communication with CORBA, 88
naming systems
    browsing, 203
    service providers for JNDI, 192

NamingContext interface, 96
NamingEnumeration interface, 200
NamingEvent interface, 221
NamingException class, 191
namingExceptionThrown(), 220
NamingListener interface, 220
NamingManager class, 188
NamingShell application, 194–200
    cd command, 203
    create command, 205
    destroy command, 206
    help and exit commands, 200
    initctx command, 198
    list command, 200
    listen command, 224–226
    running the shell, 199
    search command, 218
narrow()
    PortableRemoteObject interface, 88
    NamingContextHelper class, 121
    PortableRemoteObject interface, 90,
        250
native code, RMI and, 84–88
Native Interface API, 84
native members, 466
native messaging systems, 324
    proprietary message formats, 332
    wrapping messages with JMS
        format, 334
Native-API Partly-Java Drivers, 20
Native-protocol All-Java Drivers, 21
NDS (Novell Directory Services), 187
nesting search expressions, 216
Net-protocol All-Java Drivers, 21
Netscape, cookie specification, 162
network protocols
    CORBA, defining, 97
networks
    applications, creating with RMI, 6
    architecture (example for hypothetical
        enterprise), 12
    distributed computing over, 3
    heterogeneous nature of, 4
    Jini system for distributed
        computing, 15
    messaging services, 8
newInstance()
    ActivationGroup class, 81
    parser or processor, retrieving from
        Java program, 304
NewsAddress class, 360

World Wide Web Consortium (see W3C)
WSDL (the Web Services Description
Language), 301

X

XAConnectionFactory class, 348
XAConnections class, 348
Xalan XSL engine, 304
XASessions class, 348
Xerces parser (Apache), 304
XML, 301–322
APIs for, 15
combining with Java
advantages of, 301
documents, using, 302
DTDs (orders.xml example), 303
well-formed XML, 303
JAXP and JAXM parsing and messaging
APIs, 7

JAXP (Java API for XML
Processing), 302, 304
parser or processor, getting, 304
parsing with DOM, 310–318
getting a parser, 311
manipulating DOM trees, 313–315
navigating DOM tree, 311
parsing with SAX, 305–310
handlers, 306–308
using a SAX parser, 308–310
specification, web site for, 301
XSLT transformations, 318–322
JAXP data sources, 320–322
XMLReader class, 308
XSL stylesheets, 318
XSLT (XSL for Transformations), 7, 302,
318–322
JAXP data sources, 320–322
JAXP processors for, 304

About the Authors

Jim Farley is a software engineer, computer scientist, and IT manager. His recent activities have included heading up the engineering group at the Harvard Business School and bringing good things to life at GE's Research and Development center. He's dealt with computing (distributed and otherwise) in lots of different ways, from automated image inspection to temporal reasoning systems. Jim has BS and MS degrees in computer systems engineering from Rensselaer Polytechnic Institute.

William Crawford has been developing web-based enterprise applications since 1995, including one of the first web-based electronic medical record systems (at Children's Hospital in Boston) and some of the first enterprise-level uses of Java. He has consulted for a variety of institutional clients, including Boston Children's Hospital, Harvard Medical Center, numerous startups, and several Fortune 500 companies. He received a degree in history and economics from Yale University. He is currently Chief Technology Officer, involved with XML and web services, at Invantage, Inc., a Cambridge, Massachusetts, provider of software and services to the pharmaceutical industry. He can be reached at *http://ww.williamcrawford.info*.

David Flanagan is a computer programmer who spends most of his time writing about Java and JavaScript. His other books with O'Reilly include *Java in a Nutshell, Java Examples in a Nutshell, Java Foundation Classes in a Nutshell*, and *JavaScript: The Definitive Guide*. David has a degree in computer science and engineering from the Massachusetts Institute of Technology. He lives with his wife and son in the U.S. Pacific Northwest between the cities of Seattle, Washington and Vancouver, British Columbia.

Colophon

Our look is the result of reader comments, our own experimentation, and feedback from distribution channels. Distinctive covers complement our distinctive approach to technical topics, breathing personality and life into potentially dry subjects.

The animal appearing on the cover of *Java Enterprise in a Nutshell*, Second Edition, is a sand dollar (*Echinarachnius parma*). The sand dollar is a flattened, rigid, disk-shaped marine invertebrate related to sea urchins and sea stars. It is found in large numbers on the sandy bottoms in the coastal waters of many parts of the world. The sand dollar's shell, or test, is often perforated with petal-shaped slots arranged around a central point. The mouth is located in this central position on the underside of the shell. The shell is covered with spines of varying lengths. These spines aid the sand dollar in locomotion and enable it to burrow just below the surface of the sandy bottom. In this sand, the sand dollar finds the tiny organic material it feeds on, pushing the food towards its mouth with tiny tube feet. Additional tube feet on the upper side of the sand dollar are used for breathing.

The sand dollar's flower-like appearance and its abundance in many parts of the world have made it a favorite of shell collectors. Scientists have also taken an interest in this small invertebrate. The sand dollar is frequently used in the study of mitosis, the process of cell division. It is believed that a better understanding of mitosis may lead to a better understanding of cancer.

Mary Anne Weeks Mayo was the production editor for *Java Enterprise in a Nutshell,* Second Edition. Mary Brady copyedited the book. Jane Ellin and Sheryl Avruch provided quality control. David Chu, Julie Flanagan, and Phil Dangler provided production assistance. Ellen Troutman-Zaig wrote the index. Lenny Muellner provided XML support.

Edie Freedman designed the cover of this book, using a 19th-century engraving from the Dover Pictorial Archive. Emma Colby produced the cover layout with Quark-XPress 4.1 using Adobe's ITC Garamond font.

David Futato designed the interior layout based on a series design by Nancy Priest. The text and heading fonts are ITC Garamond Light and Garamond Book; the code font is Adobe ITC Franklin Gothic.

For Parts I and II, Neil Walls converted the files from SGML to FrameMaker 5.5.6 using tools created by Mike Sierra, as well as tools written in Perl by Erik Ray, Jason McIntosh, and Neil Walls. The print version of Part III was generated from XML using a basic macro set developed by Steve Talbott from the GNU *troff* *-gs* macros and adapted to the book design by Lenny Muellner; Norm Walsh wrote the Perl filter that translates XML source into those macros.

The illustrations that appear in the book were produced by Robert Romano and Jessamyn Read using Macromedia FreeHand 9 and Adobe Photoshop 6. The hierarchy diagrams that appear in Part III were produced in encapsulated PostScript format by a Java program written by David Flanagan.

This colophon was written by Clairemarie Fisher O'Leary.